Ad\

"*Getting By* is an essential, go-t
struggling to understand their soc ... .ccss them. Lucid
and reader-friendly but also precise and comprehensive, this marvelous book will be a
vital resource for claimants negotiating the maze of federal programs and for advocates
seeking to mobilize for much-needed legal reform."

—David Garland,
author of *The Welfare State: A Very Short Introduction*

"This timely, essential book examines the ways that government policies hostile or indifferent to the economically marginalized have resulted in the increasingly, shockingly lop-
sided distribution of economic opportunity and access to even the most basic necessities of
nutrition, health care, education, and housing. Pushing back against the growing divisions
in the country, it calls out the structural forces that harm the unemployed, the underemployed and the underpaid alike. Most importantly, it provides suggestions about what can
and must be done to repair the damage to democracy caused by economic inequality. It is
this rare balance between theory and practical application that makes this volume a necessity to anyone seeking to understand and address fully economic inequality."

—Dennis Parker,
Executive Director, National Center for Law and Economic Justice

"Hershkoff and Loffredo have created a guide to the social safety net that is both comprehensive and easy to read. This is essential reading for students, legislators, legal aid
lawyers, social workers, community organizers, or anyone who cares about our 21st century social safety net."

—Philip Tegeler,
President and Executive Director, Poverty & Race Research Action Council

"Hershkoff and Loffredo's volume is a comprehensive critique of the United States' poverty policies as they manifest in different facets of daily life. From food and housing
to legal protection, and everything in-between, this in-depth account into the vast
ramifications of past and present policy is as startling as it is vital. The authors inform the
reader of the expansive socio-economic plights thrust upon the American working class
and their rights. Moreover, this compelling book succeeds in unifying an often-divided
populace under shared economic disenfranchisement. *Getting By: Economic Rights and
Legal Protections for People with Low Income* is an exceptional chronicle of the United
States' tumultuous political path towards equal economic mobility and security. Most im-
pressively, it empowers the downtrodden and equips them with the necessary knowledge
of their individual and collective power."

—Inimai Chettiar,
former Justice Program Director, Brennan Center for Justice

Getting By

Getting By

*Economic Rights and Legal Protections
for People with Low Income*

HELEN HERSHKOFF & STEPHEN LOFFREDO

OXFORD
UNIVERSITY PRESS

OXFORD
UNIVERSITY PRESS

Oxford University Press is a department of the University of Oxford. It furthers the University's
objective of excellence in research, scholarship, and education by publishing worldwide. Oxford is
a registered trademark of Oxford University Press in the UK and certain other countries.

Published in the United States of America by Oxford University Press
198 Madison Avenue, New York, NY 10016, United States of America.

© Helen Hershkoff & Stephen Loffredo 2020

Library of Congress Cataloging-in-Publication Data
Names: Hershkoff, Helen, 1953– author. | Loffredo, Stephen, 1955– author.
Title: Getting By: Economic rights and legal protections for people with low income/
Helen Hershkoff & Stephen Loffredo.
Other titles: Rights of the poor
Description: New York, New York : Oxford University Press, 2020. | Includes
bibliographical references and index.
Identifiers: LCCN 2019017342 | ISBN 9780190080860 ((hardback) : alk. paper) |
ISBN 9780199938513 ((pbk.) : alk. paper)
Subjects: LCSH: Public welfare—Law and legislation—United States—Miscellanea. |
Poor—Civil rights—United States—Miscellanea. | LCGFT: FAQs.
Classification: LCC KF3720 .H47 2019 | DDC 344.7303/256—dc23
LC record available at https://lccn.loc.gov/2019017342

3 5 7 9 8 6 4 2

Paperback printed by LSC Communications, United States of America
Hardback printed by Bridgeport National Bindery, Inc., United States of America

Note to Readers
This publication is designed to provide accurate and authoritative information in regard to
the subject matter covered. It is based upon sources believed to be accurate and reliable and is
intended to be current as of the time it was written. It is sold with the understanding that the
publisher is not engaged in rendering legal, accounting, or other professional services. If legal
advice or other expert assistance is required, the services of a competent professional person
should be sought. Also, to confirm that the information has not been affected or changed by recent
developments, traditional legal research techniques should be used, including checking primary
sources where appropriate.

*(Based on the Declaration of Principles jointly adopted by a Committee of the
American Bar Association and a Committee of Publishers and Associations.)*

**You may order this or any other Oxford University Press publication
by visiting the Oxford University Press website at www.oup.com.**

Contents

Detailed Contents

Acknowledgments

We are fortunate to be part of a community of lawyers, advocates, organizers, clients, students, teachers, artists, and friends committed to principles of economic justice and social dignity. This book, although we are the listed authors and responsible for all errors, is in a deep sense the product of this community. We hope that the book is useful, and that it supports future activism by and on behalf of the millions of Americans who struggle to get by in the teeth of economic inequality and social injustice.

We owe particular thanks to specific organizations and individuals.

Helen Hershkoff received financial support to undertake this project from the D'Agostino-Greenberg Faculty Research Fund of New York University School of Law.

Stephen Loffredo received support to undertake this project from the City University of New York School of Law.

A number of nonprofit organizations and their current or former staff members and directors generously reviewed earlier drafts of chapters and offered guidance to us. We are grateful to: the American Civil Liberties Union (Steven Shapiro); the Brennan Center for Justice (Myrna Pérez); the Food Research & Action Center (Alexandra Ashbrook, Lauren Badger, Crystal Fitzsimons, Geraldine Henchy, Ellen Teller, and Ellen Vollinger); The Legal Aid Society of New York (Anne Callagy, Steve Godeski, and Susan Welber); the National Education Law Center (Wendy Lecker, Jessica Levin, and David Sciarra); the National Housing Law Project (Kara Brodfuehrer, Jessie Cassella, Karlo Ng, Lisa Sitkin, Deborah Thrope, and Renee Williams); the New Economy Project (Susan Shin); and the Poverty & Race Research Action Council (Philip Tegeler). In addition, we are grateful to Kent Hirozawa and James Reif for comments on employment and labor issues; to David Kamin for insights about tax policy; to Janet Calvo, Lisa Sbrana, and Rebecca Wallace for direction about health policy; to David Super for advice about Temporary Assistance to Needy Families; and to Troy McKenzie for comments about bankruptcy and student loans.

We thank our students at the CUNY, Harvard, and New York University law schools whose research, commitment, and enthusiasm contributed to this book and who, in their practice of law, we hope will carry its work forward: Owen Alexander, Jessica Allen, Torie Atkinson, Ben Atlas, Nicholas Baer, Jeanne Barenholtz, Matthew Barnett, Ansel Bencze, Jeffrey Bengel, Jordan Berger, Alison Bilow, Clark Binkley, Viviana Bonilla-Lopez, Jeremy Brinster, Phillip

Brown, Melissa Byun, Yan Cao, Olivia Carrano, Julia Chen, Andrew Cohen, Shlomit Cohen, Mathews de Carvalho, Peter Devlin, Daniel Dietz, Sarah Dowd, Peter Dubrowski, Amal El Bakhar, Shira Feldman, Carissa Ferrigno, Laura Figueroa, Amelia Frenkel, Miriam Furst, Conor Gaffney, Ryan Gerber, Andrew Gerst, Thomas Gottheil, Ross Guilder, Kristina Harootun, Elizabeth Harrington, Jonathan Harris, Julia Harvey, Cesar Jose Hernandez, Luke Herrine, Charlotte Heyrman, Caila Heyison, Hilary Hoffman, Phil Ingram, Erik Jerrard, Kameron Johnston, Jacob Karr, Dan Liang, Colleen Lee, Frederick Lee, Samantha Lee, Allison Lehrer, Paul Leroux, Daniel Liang, Cerin Lindgrensavage, Hannah Littman, Molly Mangus, Sarah Martin, Janice Pai Martindale, Jennifer Mason (whose work on the 1997 volume deserves special mention), Nathaniel Mattison, James Mayer, William Moran, Shannon Morris, Caitlin Moyles, Oluwadamilola Obaro, Jordan Pate, Sean Petterson, Linnea Pittman, Katie Poor, Julia Popkin, Clara Potter, Julia Quigley, Stefan Rajiyah, Zoe Ridolfi-Starr, Zoni Rockoff, Adam Rosenbloom, Katie Roussos, Aaron Salerno, Richard W. Sawyer, Allyson Scher, Samuel Seham, Max Selver, Rahul Sharma, Melissa Siegel, Sara Silverstein, Maureen Slack, Jonathan Slapp, Krista Staropoli, Vaughn Stewart, David Sydlik, Daniel Treiman, Raquel Villagra, Ruth Vinson, Courtney Weisman, Danielle Whiteman, Lauren Wilfong, Samantha Wilhelm, Megan Wilkie, Angela Wu, Sisi Wu, and Dian Yu.

We are deeply indebted to Ian Brydon and, earlier, to Robert Anselmi, for exemplary administrative support in the preparation of the manuscript.

Superb library support from Gretchen Feltes, Jessica Freeman, and Linda Ramsingh of NYU Law School is gratefully acknowledged.

We thank Southern Illinois University Press for publishing our 1997 book on the rights of the poor, and the ACLU, which for many years sponsored the "know your rights" series.

Finally, we thank our parents, now gone, and our son. The reasons go without saying.

Introduction

Over the last generation, the American dream has become a shameful night-mare for an extraordinary number of people. Inequality in the United States has soared to extremes not seen since before the Great Depression, real wages for working people have stagnated or fallen, and confidence that children will enjoy a better future is at an all-time low. Why do conditions of poverty, oppression, and stunted possibility for so many persist in the wealthiest nation in human his-tory? Social and economic conditions do not just happen. In the United States, these conditions are the product of decades of conscious policy choices and un-conscious indifference—fueled by sharp disparities in political and economic power and deep-seated forms of racism and sexism. We are heartened that, as we write, new waves of activists, students, and workers are swelling the ranks of movements to insist upon universal health care, better public schools, afford-able housing, livable wages, restraints on inequality, and a more just, open, and democratic society. Not everyone shares this vision for America's future. Indeed, the nation has rarely been so divided, and our democracy, so threatened. Yet we are guardedly optimistic that, before long, progressive mobilizations will reor-ient the country toward laws and policies aimed at ensuring dignity and decency for all.

In the meantime, people need to get by. We wrote this book to address that basic imperative. We do not offer legal advice, and we do not provide a compre-hensive or theoretical explanation for current conditions. Nor do we describe an ideal way forward. Instead, the book is designed as an introduction to federal laws and programs that may be beneficial to people who live in poverty or on low in-come. At the same time, the book highlights corporate and governmental abuses that impair economic security and impede upward mobility, and it describes how federal laws may be used to resist and redress these practices. We recognize that social provision in the United States is inadequate, that legal protections for workers and those of modest means are insufficient, and that many legal needs of people with low income go unmet because lawyers are unaffordable and the federal Constitution does not guarantee a right to representation in civil matters. But a patchy safety net and commitment to liberal constitutional rights continue to exist. Although social welfare programs do not go far enough, the benefits they provide may have a profound impact on the people who need them—in some instances, they make the difference between being housed or on the street, having groceries or going hungry, and receiving medical care or facing health crises without it.

In a formal sense, this book has its roots in *The Rights of the Poor*, which we co-authored and published in 1997 as part of the ACLU's "know your rights" series. (We could go back even earlier to a 1973 book with that title by Sylvia Law and Burt Neuborne.) We completed the 1997 book just as the Personal Responsibility and Work Opportunity Reconciliation Act of 1996 ended "welfare as we know it" and the Clinton administration, with a Republican-dominated Congress, began aggressively to press "zero tolerance" drug policies that led, over time, to mass incarceration, the rupturing of poor communities, and inescapable poverty for millions of families, particularly people of color. Then, in 2007, widespread failures to regulate corporate and financial-sector malfeasance resulted in the worst recession since the Great Depression of the 1930s, leaving one in seven Americans below the poverty line, nearly 25 million homes in foreclosure, and almost a third of unemployed people out of work for more than a year. Analysts broadly agree that the economic injuries inflicted on low-income Americans by the Great Recession will carry over for decades, compounding the economic insecurity of groups that traditionally have been marginalized—including African Americans, Latinxs, women, and children—making the need for existing social welfare provision and fair economic policy all the more critical.

But we did not write *Getting By* simply as an update of our earlier volume. That book largely took as its focus the assistance programs associated with the "War on Poverty" declared by President Lyndon Baines Johnson in 1964. The current book extends beyond these poverty programs to encompass the rights of low-wage workers and consumers. It challenges the assumption that working people and people receiving social welfare support comprise distinct groups, and it underlines the deep connections between our systems of wage labor and social welfare. In so doing, the book seeks to emphasize the common interests and possibilities for solidarity among the unemployed, the underemployed, and the underpaid, whether within the home, in the underground economy, or in the regulated wage market. Existing political and programmatic arrangements undermine that solidarity in many ways—by isolating and stigmatizing the poor, by perpetuating negative racial, gender, and class stereotypes, and by falsely framing policy choices as zero sums pitting the interests of those living at the poverty level against the interests of middle-class and working-class people, thereby minimizing the possibility of coalition formation and concerted action.

These possibilities for political solidarity figured prominently at an earlier moment in our nation's history and provide important context for this book. Most of the legislation critical to people living on the economic margins traces back to the New Deal, a wide-ranging program of income supports, financial reforms, labor protections, public works projects, and economic regulations initiated during the administration of President Franklin Delano Roosevelt. Some New Deal programs aimed to alleviate the suffering caused by hunger and unemployment; other programs more broadly recognized the relation among economic security, political power, and democratic governance. FDR gave voice to this broader vision in his call for an "Economic Bill of Rights": "We have come to a clear realization of the fact that true individual freedom cannot exist without security and independence," he wrote.

To be sure, the New Deal was flawed and incomplete; to the nation's shame, it excluded African Americans from many of its programs and contributed to ongoing racial subordination and inequity. This taint, however, should not obscure or undercut a central insight: that poverty and inequality are not facts of nature, but instead are conditions created, supported, and fostered by law. The New Deal openly acknowledged that American law had facilitated concentrations of private economic power that imperiled democracy, and it committed to restrain and counterbalance that power through direct government regulation and laws that promoted and protected the rights of workers to organize and to act collectively.

Since at least the presidency of Ronald Reagan, this core insight of the New Deal has been under assault, illustrated by perennial attacks on "entitlement" programs, efforts to "privatize" Social Security, the elimination of the Aid to Families with Dependent Children program, the extraordinary backlash triggered by the Affordable Care Act, the campaign against labor unions and workers' rights, the return of concentrated wealth and corporate dominance, the "hollowing out" of the middle class, the assaults on people of color, and the persistent decline in upward mobility among those who traditionally have subsisted in the lowest economic stratum. Placing the nation on a different, more equitable, and democratic path is a central challenge of our time. We believe that understanding legal rights, insisting on their enforcement, and pushing against their limits, is a modest but integral piece of both a mobilization strategy and theoretical reorientation of politics.

From this perspective, our goal in writing this book is to offer an integrated, critical account of the programs, rights, and legal protections that most directly affect poor and low-income people in the United States. Everyone in the United States depends in some way on the government for income or social supports (although only poor and low-income people are stigmatized for doing so). Moreover, laws and programs are complex (often unnecessarily so), and it is not always clear how to access protections and benefits. Indeed, even many lawyers, social workers, paralegals, and community organizations that work with low-income communities may lack adequate information about the range of available programs, the legal rights that pertain to those programs, and the processes for accessing complicated bureaucratic systems. We have structured this book in a question-and-answer format, with the intention of making it straightforward and clear. Each chapter refers the reader to online resources that provide additional, more detailed information, links to primary legal sources, and in some instances, links to offices or organizations that provide legal assistance or referrals. We have included extensive endnotes inviting attention to statutes, regulations, case law, and commentary. The book primarily focuses on federal laws and programs, but invites attention in some areas to state programs.

We have organized the book as follows.

Chapters 1 and 2 focus on cash support programs and employment and labor rights. Chapter 1 discusses the public provision of cash support to families and individuals who have insufficient income. The chapter briefly surveys the constitutional and international law status of a right to cash support, and then turns to the three main programs in the United States: the state-federal co-operative Temporary Assistance to Needy Families program, which generally serves very low-income families with minor children; the federal Supplemental Security Income program, which serves low-income elderly, blind, or disabled people; and residual, "general assistance" programs, operated by some states to provide small cash grants to destitute families and individuals who do not qualify for other kinds of cash support. The chapter provides a detailed account of the financial, categorical, and immigration-related eligibility requirements for these programs, the conditions attached to receipt of assistance (such as work requirements), and the processes for application and appeal of agency decisions. Along the way, this chapter calls attention to the history, evolution, and social impacts of cash support programs and offers some critical perspectives on these policies as they have affected racial equality, social mobility, and notions of the family.

Chapter 2 turns to the key federal statutes that protect access to employment opportunities, regulate the terms and conditions of employment, prohibit certain types of employment discrimination, and protect the right of workers to advance their common interests through organizing and collective action. The chapter pays special attention to the wage and hour protections afforded by the federal Fair Labor Standards Act, addresses the rights conferred by the act, offers a critique of the federal minimum wage rate, and notes the emerging nationwide movement to raise the minimum wage to a living wage. The chapter also addresses the most important federal programs that provide economic supports for low-income workers, including unemployment insurance, which replaces a percentage of wages for workers who lose their jobs through no fault of their own; the Earned Income Tax Credit and Child Tax Credit, which effectively can reduce or eliminate payroll taxes for most workers with minor dependents, and can increase family income through refundable tax credits; and the Social Security program, which provides benefits to retired, aged, blind, or disabled workers and their families. The chapter also discusses the importance of collective action to improve wages, working conditions, and social benefits that are of importance to all poor and low-income persons.

As the pair of chapters show, cash support programs set benefits at drastically inadequate, subpoverty levels that structurally reinforce a persistent underclass; the minimum wage is not a living wage and does not boost even many full-time workers out of poverty. The laws and programs described in these chapters are vital sources of protection and support, but they urgently require improvement and expansion.

Chapter 3 focuses on food assistance as a specific type of noncash benefit for poor and low-income persons, including millions of low-wage workers. In 2006, the United States substituted the term "food insecurity" for hunger, but by any measure the United States has too many people without the cash needed to purchase groceries. During the recession of 2008, one in six Americans received federal food assistance. And in 2018, when budget talks failed and the federal government "shut down," it was reported that some unpaid federal employees—like many Americans, living from paycheck to paycheck—were compelled to go to food banks and soup kitchens to have enough to eat. The chapter describes a number of federal programs that are critical to those who need food assistance, and that also boost local economies and support the agricultural sector. The programs include the Supplemental Nutrition Assistance Program (SNAP, known as food stamps); the WIC program, for pregnant women, new mothers, and infant children; the School Lunch and School Breakfast programs; and senior nutrition programs. These programs use different models: some are designed to increase the purchasing power of a poor or low-income recipient of assistance; some provide food assistance together with health and nutritional counseling; some distribute commodities; others give recipients access to organic and other healthy food at regional agricultural markets; and some provide meals in settings that also provide social companionship. These programs are vital to prevent hunger and its harmful effects on health and development, and they are demonstrated to be among the most successful of assistance programs in the country. But they also have arbitrary and harsh rules, for example, time-limiting benefits for single individuals who are unemployed and underemployed, and among the poorest in the country.

Chapter 4 addresses access to health care for poor and low-income people. The United States, virtually alone among developed nations, does not offer universal health care, and the provision of health-related services involves a complex matrix of state and federal programs, employment-based plans, and other health insurance and health care options. The chapter provides a detailed account of Medicaid, the largest provider of health coverage to poor and low-income people in the United States, its eligibility criteria, the scope of its coverage, and the groups that are excluded from its benefits, and Medicare, the federal health insurance program for the aged, blind, and disabled individuals. In 2010, Congress enacted the Patient Protection and Affordable Care Act (ACA), popularly known as Obamacare, to address a health care crisis that left one in six Americans—many with low income—without health insurance or meaningful access to health care. The chapter examines the ACA in detail, including its impact on Medicaid and Medicare, its creation of Health Insurance Exchanges and tax credits to help low-income households obtain private health coverage, and the reform of private health insurance markets through a patient's bill of rights which, among other things, bars insurance companies from refusing coverage for pre-existing medical conditions. Perhaps the most critical aspect of the ACA was its expansion of Medicaid to cover virtually all low-income citizens (and certain immigrants) who do not qualify for other health coverage. The chapter also discusses the Child Health Insurance Program (CHIP), a government-funded program for children in households with too much income to qualify for Medicaid.

Chapter 5 discusses state and federal laws that affect educational opportunity for poor and low-income children. The federal Constitution does not guarantee a right to education. Instead, the provision of public schooling is a state responsibility, and the quality of public education varies considerably based on the wealth of the community in which a public school is located. The result is an educational system characterized by disparities and inequalities—rather than driving children forward, public schools in some disadvantaged neighborhoods serve as a conduit in a school-to-prison pipeline, with highly racialized impacts. The chapter discusses how the education of poor and low-income children is affected by residency requirements, truancy laws, punitive disciplinary policies, school fees, and the absence of state-funded programs for toddlers too young to attend kindergarten. The chapter also discusses some of the federal programs designed to supplement educational opportunities for students who are poor or from low-income households, starting with preschool through to vocational training and loans and grants to attend college. These programs, although important, are largely indifferent to the democratic benefits of racially integrated schools and do not go far enough in ensuring every child a free, quality education. The chapter also discusses the crisis of federal student loans, some of the protections that are available to student borrowers, and the campaign to make public colleges affordable to all.

Chapter 6 turns to banking and credit laws that are designed to help—but in practice may hurt—poor and low-income people in consumer relations. People with low income, people of color, and women face many legal, practical, and structural inequalities in credit markets. Without an adequate cash support system or guarantee of a living wage low-income people are vulnerable to predatory practices that exploit financial instability. The inability to repay a debt can expose a person to punitive consequences that may include imprisonment—even though the indigent has committed no crime. Moreover, the use of consumer reports for employment and housing makes a poor or low-income person hostage to the past; even when the report is accurate (and they often are riddled with error), opportunities are lost because of an earlier bad credit score or contact with the police. Attention in this chapter is given to federal laws that regulate debt collection, consumer reporting, access to credit, and limits on garnishment. These statutes include the Fair Debt Collection Act; the Truth in Lending Act; the Fair Credit Reporting Act; and the Equal Credit Opportunity Act. We also cover antidiscrimination law as it relates to criminal records and credit reporting, In addition, the chapter discusses the fringe economy, including the dangers that payday, auto title, and online lending present, as well as private loans used to finance higher education that have trapped low-income consumers in a lifetime of spiraling debt. The chapter also touches on tax collection by the federal government.

Chapter 7 discusses programs that increase access to affordable, adequate housing. Whether working or unemployed, persons with low income may be housed, under housed, or homeless. Typically, they live in communities that also are in need of support, investment, and development. For many decades the United States has failed to support the public construction of affordable housing; moreover, housing programs are deeply underfunded and leave many income-eligible families without housing assistance. This chapter provides an overview of federal programs dealing with rental assistance, including Public Housing and vouchers, as well as programs for home ownership, community development, and temporary shelter and other services for persons who are homeless.

Chapter 8 turns to public spaces and the laws that regulate or bar the homeless or persons who "look poor" from accessing places such as sidewalks, government buildings, parks, public libraries, and the post office. States and localities regulate public spaces through "quality of life" ordinances that often are punitive in design and aimed at fencing out poor and low-income persons from a community. These restrictions potentially impact not only the individual, but also collective efforts to organize and mobilize. Moreover, by criminalizing acts that are innocent when done in the privacy of one's home, these restrictions reinforce a cycle of poverty be-cause they make it more difficult for poor and homeless people to obtain housing and employment. The chapter addresses such issues as the right to travel to a state and within a state; the right to use streets and parks; begging; street vending; and the requirements for an ID, a post office box, library use, and mobile homes.

Chapter 9 addresses the issue of "access to justice" or the "justice gap"—the question of how people with low incomes can seek legal protection and enforce legal rights. Too many poor and low-income people experience the civil justice system as a source of injustice: subjecting them to meritless default judgments, evictions, fees and fines, imprisonment and forfeiture of property when no crime has been committed, and enforcing harsh collateral consequences of contacts with the criminal justice system. Moreover, many low-income people are blocked from going to court at all, because employment and consumer contracts include boilerplate terms that mandate arbitration, consigning the claimant to a private system of dispute resolution that has been questioned as unfair and in conflict with statutory and constitutional rights. This chapter is designed to help low-income people navigate the civil court system so that it better reflects the ideal of equal justice under law. The chapter focuses on the importance, but insufficiency, of free counsel in civil lawsuits; waivers of filing fees; requests to obtain court-ordered experts and language translators; and the dangers of court-ordered fines and fees. The chapter briefly discusses the rights of the criminally accused; it explains civil forfeiture; it explores how to vacate a default judgment (and why this is important); and it discusses arbitration as a mandatory feature of many consumer and employment contracts (and, again, why this matters).

Chapter 10 concludes with the right to vote. Studies show that people who have low incomes, are members of racial or ethnic minorities, or rent their homes are less likely to register and vote on Election Day than wealthier, white homeowners. Franchise restrictions—when the polls are open, how difficult it is to travel to a polling booth, limitations on early voting, and identification requirements, among others—depress voting participation by low-income people and people of color, and often are intentionally designed to achieve that effect. For its part, the Supreme Court of the United States not only has tolerated voting suppression measures but also has dismantled state and federal campaign finance laws, further magnifying the political power of wealthy corporations and individuals, while marginalizing low-income communities and communities of color. This chapter focuses on the right to vote, including registration and ID requirements, rights under the federal "motor-voter" law (which requires some government assistance offices to offer voter registration to all applicants and recipients), protections for workers who want to exercise the franchise, and voter registration drives.

As these chapters reflect, America's social safety net is flawed and frayed. But laws can be reformed; programs can be expanded; and policies can be changed to reflect principles of fairness and social justice. Existing laws, if understood and properly enforced, can afford important protections from the brutality of economic insecurity. The central goal of this volume is to provide a resource to individuals, groups, and communities that wish to claim existing rights and mobilize for progressive change. We hope that readers find the book to be useful both in their individual and collective actions.

We close with a caveat and disclaimer. This book does not and cannot offer legal advice. It reflects legal developments through March 2019, and includes significant updates as of August 2019. But the laws and programs discussed in this volume are subject to frequent change; federal policy has been particularly fluid during the Trump administration. Of necessity, it falls to the reader to confirm that the information we provide continues to be current. Finally, we add that we are painfully aware of the intersectional nature of the issues we are describing, and it is likely that some readers would have made different choices in their selection and emphasis of topics. We hope, however, that within the boundaries of our project, the book proves to be a helpful resource for advocacy, engagement, and empowerment.

1

Cash Assistance

Introduction

Does the U.S. Constitution guarantee cash assistance to persons unable to maintain a minimum standard of living?

The U.S. Supreme Court has interpreted the federal Constitution to provide no "affirmative right to governmental aid, even where such aid may be necessary to secure life, liberty, or property."[1] Some scholars have argued in support of such a right, especially if the person in need of assistance cannot work, cannot find work, or works but still cannot maintain a minimum standard of living.[2] International law favors a right to basic economic provision;[3] in particular, the United States has signed, although it has not ratified, the United Nations International Covenant on Economic, Social and Cultural Rights, which recognizes "the right of everyone to an adequate standard of living for himself and his family."[4] Moreover, every state in the United States has its own constitution, and some state constitutions authorize assistance for the poor[5] or declare a right to dignity,[6] either of which could provide the legal basis for a right to cash assistance.[7]

Although there is no federal constitutional right to assistance, Congress may enact laws that authorize assistance to poor or low-income persons. A program, once established, must be administered fairly and in ways that comply with the requirements of the Due Process and Equal Protection Clauses of the Fifth and Fourteenth Amendments to the federal Constitution.[8] The programs that the federal government has established form an important but incomplete safety net for indigent persons in need of economic support. This chapter discusses two of the most important of these federally funded programs:

- Temporary Assistance for Needy Families, which is generally limited to families with children; and
- Supplemental Security Income, which is limited to persons with disabilities and the elderly.

In addition, the chapter provides information about General Assistance programs, which are state-based, state-run, state-funded programs, typically

Getting By. Helen Hershkoff and Stephen Loffredo, Oxford University Press (2020). © Helen Hershkoff & Stephen Loffredo.
DOI: 10.1093/oso/9780190080860.001.0001

available to people who do not qualify for federal assistance—but these programs are very narrow in scope. Three other programs that provide cash assistance—Social Security, Unemployment Insurance, and the Earned Income Tax Credit—are discussed in chapter 2.

Temporary Assistance for Needy Families

What is Temporary Assistance for Needy Families?

Temporary Assistance for Needy Families (TANF) is the federally funded assistance program for poor families that Congress created in 1996 to replace the more generous Aid to Families with Dependent Children (AFDC) program. The elimination of AFDC and its replacement with TANF was the centerpiece of regressive "welfare reform" legislation known as the Personal Responsibility and Work Opportunity Reconciliation Act of 1996 (PRA).[9] That legislation, enacted by a Republican Congress as part of its "Contract with America" and signed by President Clinton, imposed new and punitive restrictions on poor families, disqualified millions of immigrants from federally funded benefits, and eliminated the federal guarantee of financial support for needy parents and children.[10] Although the PRA sharply reduced the federal government's commitment to children living in poverty, the TANF program remains a critical, if inadequate, source of support for many families living in poverty.[11]

Through TANF, the U.S. Department of Health and Human Services (HHS) awards block grants to states and territories to operate programs that provide cash or noncash assistance to poor families.[12] State TANF programs must conform to certain federal guidelines, but the PRA gives states broad discretion, so TANF programs vary widely from state to state. Some states have exercised this discretion to provide broader rights and protections than those mandated by the federal laws described in this chapter. However, federal law imposes certain hard constraints on eligibility for TANF. For instance, the PRA sets a lifetime time limit on a family's receipt of TANF-funded benefits. Once a family reaches that limit (60 months, or less at state option) it can no longer receive assistance funded through TANF (though some states continue to provide assistance to such families through state-funded welfare programs). The PRA also imposes strict new work requirements on families receiving TANF, and the statute prohibits use of TANF funds to aid certain kinds of needy people, including many legal immigrants. As a result of such restrictions, and heightened administrative hurdles, many families living in poverty have been excluded or deterred from applying for TANF.[13]

Finally, federal funding for state TANF programs is provided in fixed "block grants" that do not automatically increase during times of economic downturn, when more families are in need and the demand for assistance is greater; nor do federal funds increase to account for rising costs of basic necessities such as food and housing.[14] Rather, TANF block grants remain fixed at the level set in 1996, when the Personal Responsibility Act was first adopted.[15] In real terms, federal funding for state TANF programs has declined by almost 40 percent since 1996.[16] Moreover, Congress has cut supplements that it earlier awarded states for special programs.[17] The impact of these shortcomings on poor families has been severe. In 1996, TANF programs assisted 68 of every 100 needy families. In 2010, that number had dropped to 27 of 100 needy families.[18] By 2016, the number had fallen still further to only 26 out of 100 needy families.[19] In some states, not every eligible family that applies for TANF actually receives assistance; and that assistance may take the form of services (such as counseling) rather than cash. Nevertheless, cash assistance through TANF-funded programs may be critically important to the economically struggling families that receive it.

Did Congress ever guarantee cash assistance to needy families?

Until 1996, Congress authorized a program called Aid to Families with Dependent Children (AFDC).[20] Congress created AFDC—originally called the Aid to Dependent Children program—as part of the Social Security Act of 1935. In legal terms, AFDC was an "entitlement" program; it committed the federal government to fund assistance to every eligible family that applied for benefits. Funding would thus increase in times of economic dislocation and distress, when larger numbers of families had to turn to the government for support. Over the years, AFDC generated a lot of criticism. Some critics wanted to improve the program to increase dignity and opportunities for recipients. Other critics wanted to end the program or at least eliminate cash assistance as an entitlement.

Criticism of AFDC came from different sectors. Some argued that the program was administered in unfair and discriminatory ways. In particular, although AFDC was a federal program, the statute gave the states a great deal of discretion to set eligibility rules and benefit levels, and many states set those levels far below basic subsistence.[21] During the 1950s, some states required female applicants to pass "morality tests" to ensure that they were "good mothers"; other states subjected applicants to different rules, depending on whether they were white or people of color; impoverished black families in those states received smaller cash allotments than white recipients and were far more often denied any assistance at all.[22] During the 1960s, lawyers and activists allied with the Welfare Rights Movement mounted successful legal and political challenges to some of these restrictions, making the administration of the AFDC program less arbitrary, unfair, and discriminatory.[23]

By the 1970s, with the decline of overtly racist state welfare practices, more families of color were able to participate in AFDC.[24] White families continued to account for the largest number of AFDC recipients, but a higher proportion of African American women received AFDC than white women, roughly mirroring the racial disparity in their economic status.[25] At the same time, conservative and neoliberal critics began to argue that AFDC had created a "culture of welfare dependency" and that it discouraged poor families from entering the workforce.[26] Those who defended the program countered that such critiques of AFDC were factually flawed and motivated by racist attitudes, misogyny, and an animus against the poor.[27]

President Clinton, on signing the Personal Responsibility Act of 1996, stated that he intended to "end welfare as we know it."[28] In replacing AFDC with TANF, the statute in fact ended the federal government's 60-year-long commitment to ensuring funding for families in poverty and disclaimed the creation of any federal legal entitlement to TANF-funded assistance.[29] As a result, the number of poor families receiving federal aid—both in absolute terms and as a percentage of families below the poverty line—has fallen far below the numbers that were helped by AFDC. Reduced participation, however, in no way reflects reduced need or hardship; to the contrary, the transition from AFDC to TANF has left larger numbers of needy families without assistance and in deeper poverty.[30] The vast majority of people receiving TANF are economically impoverished women and their minor children.[31]

Does every state have a TANF-funded program?

All states, including the District of Columbia, have established TANF-funded programs.[32] TANF-funded programs go by different names in different states. For instance, New York calls its TANF-funded cash assistance program "Family Assistance"; South Carolina calls its program "Family Independence." The U.S. Department of Health and Human Services, Office of Family Assistance, maintains a website that provides links to state contacts for TANF-funded programs. That website identifies the name of the program, a toll-free phone number to contact for information, and the mailing address of the state office that runs the program.[33] National information is collected each year and made publicly available in a report called the "Welfare Rules Databook."[34]

Must a state TANF program provide cash assistance to eligible families?

No. The Personal Responsibility Act gives states discretion to decide on the form of TANF-funded benefits and to set benefit levels.[35] Currently, all state TANF programs include some provision for cash assistance. However, states generally do not devote a large percentage of their TANF grant to cash assistance. In 2014, cash payments to families accounted for less than one-third of combined federal and state TANF expenditures;[36] by 2016, cash assistance accounted for only 24 percent of TANF funds.[37] Ten states in 2016 (Illinois, Texas, Arkansas, New Jersey, North Carolina, Indiana, North Carolina, Arizona, Mississippi, and Louisiana) used less than 10 percent of their TANF grants for cash assistance.[38]

Federal law permits states to use their TANF grant in "any manner that is reasonably calculated" to accomplish the purposes of the TANF program. In addition to cash payments, states may provide assistance in the form of "vouchers, and other forms of benefits designed to meet a family's ongoing basic needs."[39] "Basic needs" include food, clothing, shelter, and household goods.[40] Assistance also may be given for heating and cooling expenses.[41] States are allowed to "grandfather" in activities supported by their previous assistance programs (such as foster care payments or juvenile justice requirements) even if those activities do not directly advance the stated purposes of the TANF program.[42] TANF funds also may be used to operate employment placement programs,[43] fund individual development accounts,[44] or subsidize certain transportation costs.[45] Finally, states may devote up to 30 percent of their TANF grants to implement programs under the Child Care and Development Block Grant (which provide assistance to low-income families for child care while the parent is at work or in an educational or training program).[46]

How much is a TANF grant?

TANF-funded cash grants to families vary widely in amount, but the grant in every state falls far short of meeting even a family's most essential needs.[47] As of July 2018, most states' TANF-funded cash benefit for a family of three was less than 30 percent of the federal poverty line,[48] a measure that already vastly understates the income required for basic subsistence.[49] The median TANF benefit was $447 a month for a family of three with no other income.[50] Given the glaring inadequacy of this social support, it is not surprising that children in the United States suffer higher rates of poverty than any other age group and that the United States has one of the highest child poverty rates among developed nations.[51]

Is TANF cash assistance actually paid in cash?

No. Assistance payments are generally made through an electronic benefit transfer (EBT) card, which works like a debit card. States must ensure that any fees for accessing benefits electronically be minimal, that households are notified of any charges related to electronic transfer of the funds, and that every household be given the opportunity to elect a method of accessing benefits with no charge.[52] Forty-seven states offer some form of electronic funds transfer for TANF benefits.[53]

What is a diversion payment?

A diversion payment is a one-time, lump-sum grant that a state welfare agency gives to a family instead of providing it a recurring TANF cash grant. The idea of a diversion payment is to enable the family to meet an immediate, short-term need and so "divert" the family from becoming an ongoing TANF recipient.[54] Most states condition the diversion payment upon the recipient's working or actively seeking employment. As of July 2017, 32 states authorized diversion payments as an allowable TANF benefit.[55]

Who is eligible for cash assistance under a TANF-funded program?

Eligibility for TANF cash assistance varies from state to state, but federal law mandates that TANF funds be used only to support needy families with children or families that include a pregnant woman.[56] Each state defines what counts as "needy," setting out how much income and resources a family can have.[57] States must articulate "objective criteria" for the "determination of eligibility" for TANF benefits and must ensure "fair and equitable treatment" of families seeking assistance.[58] In some sense, there are 50 different TANF programs in the United States, with applicants subject to different rules and regulations depending on their state of residence.

Can an otherwise eligible family receive TANF-funded benefits if a child is temporarily living away from home?

It depends. Under federal law, a state ordinarily may not use TANF funds to give a family benefits for a child who has been, or is expected to be, absent from the home for a period of 45 consecutive days. A state has the authority to reduce that period to as little as 30 consecutive days or to increase it to as much as 180 consecutive days, if it specifies this condition in its state plan.[59] States also have discretion to establish good cause exceptions to this rule.[60] A parent may lose benefits if the parent fails to report a child's absence from the home within five days of the "date that it becomes clear to the parent (or relative) that the minor child will be absent for [the number of days that would disqualify the child from receiving TANF at home]."[61]

Can TANF benefits be provided to a child whose parents are ineligible for assistance?

Maybe. The law allows for "child-only" TANF cases when children are not living with their parents or when the parents are ineligible for TANF for a reason other than having too much income.[62] The three most common types of child-only TANF cases are (1) children living in the home of relatives or foster parents who are "nonparent caregivers"; (2) children whose parents are disabled and receiving SSI; and (3) U.S.-citizen children whose parents are ineligible for TANF-funded assistance because of their immigration status. When TANF first became law in 1996, "child-only" cases made up less than 15 percent of the national caseload. By FY 2013, over a third of TANF cases were "child-only."[63]

What are the basic income limits for cash assistance under TANF-funded programs?

Income eligibility limits for TANF vary widely by state. Some states key their income limits to the monthly TANF cash payment amount (meaning a family cannot earn more than the state's TANF cash payment); other states key their income limits to the state or federal poverty index. In some states the income limit varies from county to county.[64] States also differ in how they count a family's income, with most states "disregarding" certain percentages of the family's earned income in determining initial eligibility for TANF and the amount of the grant.[65] As of July 2017, Alabama was the state with the most restrictive income limit; a family of three with countable income over $268 per month is ineligible for TANF-funded cash assistance. Minnesota was the state with the highest maximum income limit, namely, $2,243 for a family of three.[66]

Can a family own anything and still be eligible for cash assistance?

Federal law does not bar families from receiving TANF-funded cash assistance if they own assets. However, as of 2017, 42 states capped the assets that a family could own and still be eligible for benefits. In these states, allowable asset limits range between $1,000 and $10,000. Eight states did not impose an asset limit on eligibility:

States with No Asset Limit for Eligibility, 2017

- Alabama
- Colorado
- Hawaii
- Illinois
- Louisiana
- Maryland
- Ohio
- Virginia

States with asset limits may exclude certain items from consideration, and every state excludes some or all of the value of one vehicle when determining a family's eligibility.[67]

Can a family receive TANF even if it receives child or spousal support from a noncustodial parent or former spouse?

A family may be eligible for TANF-funded cash assistance even if it receives child or spousal support from a noncustodial parent or former spouse, but federal law requires that the family assign the state any rights it may have to such third-party support.[68] The state will then collect the support payments directly from the absent parent or former spouse and use those funds to reimburse itself and the federal government for TANF payments made to the family. If at any point the amount of support payments collected by the state exceeds the amount of the family's TANF grant, the state must close the TANF case and turn the collected support payments over to the family.[69] A state may not ask a family to assign any support payment that becomes due after the family stops receiving TANF benefits.[70]

States have the option to disburse a portion of the child support it collects each month to the family.[71] This is known as a child support "pass-through." Child support payments passed through to a family do not count as income to the family for purposes of determining TANF eligibility, and in many states the payments are disregarded for purposes of calculating grant amount.[72] States may pass through up to $100 per month in child support to families with one child and up to $200 per month to families with two or more children for whom child support is being collected. About half of the states have implemented child support pass-throughs.[73]

Can non-U.S. citizens receive TANF-funded benefits?

It depends. The Personal Responsibility Act imposed new restrictions on the eligibility of noncitizens for federally funded benefits, including TANF.[74] As a result, a state may not use federal TANF funds to provide aid to any immigrant who is not a "qualified alien" as defined by federal law.[75] Currently, the list of "qualified aliens" who may receive TANF-funded assistance includes:[76]

1. Lawful permanent residents ("green card" holders);[77]
2. People who have obtained political asylum;[78]
3. People who have been granted refugee status;[79]
4. People who have been "paroled" into the United States for a period of one year or more;[80]
5. People who have been granted "withholding" of deportation or removal;[81]
6. People who have been granted conditional entry (before April 1, 1980);[82]
7. Cuban and Haitian conditional entrants;[83]
8. Battered spouses and children with a pending or approved petition for relief;[84]
9. Victims of a severe form of trafficking;[85]
10. Active duty or honorably discharged members of the military and their immediate relatives (including certain Hmong and Highland Laotians);[86]
11. Amerasians;[87]
12. Native Americans born in Canada or members of federally recognized tribes;[88] and
13. Iraqi and Afghan citizens who entered the United States with a Special Immigrant Visa.[89]

Not all "qualified aliens" are immediately eligible for TANF. "Specially qualified aliens"—primarily humanitarian entrants, including the categories listed above under numbers 2, 3, 5, 7, and 9–12—immediately qualify for TANF if otherwise eligible, without any waiting period.[90] Most other immigrants must be in a qualified status in the United States for five years before becoming eligible for TANF-funded benefits.[91] This five-year period is known as the "five-year bar." Certain "qualified aliens" are exempt from the five-year bar, even if they are not "specially qualified aliens," including: (1) people under the age of 18 and those 65 or older as of August 22, 1996; (2) people who meet the definition of "disability" applicable to Social Security Administration disability benefits; and (3) people who have 40 qualifying quarters of work in the United States (or can be credited with 40 quarters based on the employment of a spouse or a parent).[92]

Other than these federal restrictions, states have discretion to determine whether or not to provide TANF-funded benefits to "qualified aliens," and as of July 2017, virtually every state and the District of Columbia had elected to do so.[93]

A provision of the TANF statute directs state TANF agencies to report to the Immigration and Naturalization Service the name and address of "any individual who the State knows is not lawfully present in the United States."[94] Under the federal interpretation currently in effect, this provision requires states to report only people the federal government has specifically found to be "not lawfully present in the United States," such as through a finding by the U.S. Citizenship and Immigration Service, Immigration and Customs Enforcement (ICE), or an administrative final order of deportation.[95] However, in light of the Trump administration's anti-immigrant policies, it is highly advisable to consult a legal services office or immigrants' rights advocacy group, such as the National Immigration Law Center (https://www.nilc.org), for the current status of agency practices.

What are the income rules for non-U.S. citizens who apply for TANF-funded cash benefits?

Non-U.S. citizens who apply for TANF-funded cash assistance are subject to the same income rules as U.S. citizens with one important exception: federal law imposes special income rules on noncitizens if they are "sponsored immigrants." A sponsored immigrant is a person for whom a third-party has signed an affidavit of support accepting legal responsibility to ensure that the immigrant has adequate income. (Such affidavits are often required to obtain certain immigrant visas.) If a sponsored immigrant applies for assistance, federal law requires the state to count certain income and resources of the immigrant's sponsor (and the sponsor's spouse) as available to the immigrant in determining eligibility and grant amount.[96] This process, called "sponsor deeming," frequently results in denying TANF to needy families because consideration of the sponsor's income—even when it is not actually available to the immigrant family—often places the family above the TANF income limits.[97] If an immigrant qualifies for and receives TANF, the sponsor is in theory required to reimburse the federal government for the benefits paid to the immigrant.[98]

There are some exceptions to the sponsor deeming requirement.

First, sponsor deeming does not apply to immigrants who have at least 40 quarters of qualifying employment, as long as they were not receiving benefits during those quarters.[99]

Second, sponsor deeming rules may not be used to deny TANF benefits to immigrants who would be unable to afford food and shelter without such benefits.[100]

Third, federal law exempts immigrants or their children who have been battered and/or subjected to "extreme cruelty" in the United States by a spouse or parent (or by a member of the spouse's or parent's family residing in the same household) if the state decides that there is a "substantial connection" between the need for TANF assistance and the battering or cruelty. If the agency that administers TANF determines there was battery or extreme cruelty and a substantial connection, the batterer's income and resources will not be deemed to the immigrant for one year.[101] If the battering or cruelty has been recognized in an administrative or judicial order (for example, an order of protection from family court) or in a determination by the Immigration and Naturalization Services[102] (for example, approval of a battered spouse self-petition under the Violence Against Women Act), the batterer's income will never be deemed to the immigrant (even after 12 months) as long as the batterer is not living with the immigrant.[103]

Can states use state funds to provide "nonqualified aliens" with benefits as part of a TANF program?

Yes. States may use state funds to provide assistance to immigrants who are "nonqualified aliens" under federal law. As of July 2017, eight states funded benefits for some or all nonqualified aliens.[104]

Can children who are U.S. citizens receive TANF-funded assistance even if their parents are not eligible?

Yes. As discussed earlier, otherwise eligible U.S citizen children can receive TANF as "child-only" cases even if their parents are ineligible because of immigration status.[105]

Can parents who are teenagers receive TANF-funded assistance?

It depends. Federal law allows states to provide assistance to teen parents, but if the parent is under age 18 and unmarried, then certain restrictions apply. First, an unmarried parent under age 18 who does not have a high school diploma must attend high school or an equivalent training program unless the parent's child is under 12 weeks old.[106] Second, the parent must live in an "adult supervised setting," which means with a parent, guardian, or adult relative,[107] unless no appropriate adult relative can be located.[108] In that case the teenage parent and child can stay in a "supportive living arrangement," such as a "maternity home" or "second chance home."[109]

Can persons convicted of a crime receive TANF-funded assistance?

It depends on the nature of the crime. The Personal Responsibility Act of 1996 imposes a lifetime ban on those convicted of a drug-related felony, but gives states the option of waiving or modifying the lifetime ban.[110] Forty of the 50 states have either modified the ban or lifted it entirely.[111] However, a state may not provide cash assistance under TANF to any person convicted of fraudulently misrepresenting residence in order to obtain assistance in two or more states at once, unless the conviction is at least 10 years old.[112] In addition, a state may not provide cash assistance to anyone who is fleeing a felony conviction or someone who is in violation of parole or probation terms.[113]

Can a state limit or deny TANF-funded assistance to newly arrived residents?

No. Although a provision of the Personal Responsibility Act of 1996 purported to allow states to treat newcomers less favorably than longer-term residents,[114] the U.S. Supreme Court ruled that state discrimination against newly arrived families in the dispensation of welfare benefits violates the Fourteenth Amendment to the U.S. Constitution.[115] Although the Court did not explicitly declare the PRA provision unconstitutional, it effectively nullified it, holding that "Congress may not authorize the States to violate the Fourteenth Amendment."[116] As for "durational residency requirements" that deny assistance to newcomers altogether, the Supreme Court declared those unconstitutional in 1969 in a case called *Shapiro v. Thompson*.[117]

Are applicants and recipients of TANF-funded benefits tested for drug use?

Federal law gives states the option of requiring applicants for cash assistance to submit to drug tests if they have been convicted of drug-related crimes.[118] States also may require that a recipient's Individual Responsibility Plan, discussed later in this chapter, call for mandatory substance abuse treatment,[119] and can sanction recipients who do not comply with the requirement.[120] As of October 2016, 25 states had drug-testing policies of some kind.[121] Some states require testing only of persons with previous drug convictions, while other states first "screen" for substance abuse, and then conduct a chemical drug test when there is reasonable suspicion of abuse.[122]

Requiring an applicant for a government benefit to undergo drug testing without any reasonable suspicion of wrongdoing has been held to violate the Fourth Amendment to the U.S. Constitution, which protects persons from unreasonable searches.[123] Because drug tests are considered searches under the Fourth Amendment,[124] states may not require them as a condition of receiving TANF-funded benefits unless the requirement meets constitutional standards of reasonableness; indiscriminate or across-the-board drug testing of TANF recipients runs afoul of this constitutional standard.[125] Federal courts in Michigan and Florida have invalidated state laws requiring TANF applicants or recipients to submit to drug tests as a condition of receiving benefits.[126] These courts relied in part upon multiple studies showing that drug use among TANF recipients is lower than the population at large and that drug-testing policies do not save the TANF program money.[127]

Can a state search a person's home before providing or continuing TANF-funded benefits?

Some states and counties require applicants for TANF-funded benefits to submit to searches of their homes as a condition of eligibility and continued receipt of assistance.[128] The search is often referred to as a "home visit." The search could involve having a caseworker inspect the home to confirm that an "absent parent" is not in the residence, that a dependent child actually lives in the home, or that an applicant actually lives in the residence.[129] Home searches raise constitutional privacy concerns, but the U.S. Supreme Court in 1971 upheld the constitutionality of home visits in the context of the earlier AFDC program.[130] Investigation of household conditions is defended as a way to ferret out fraud, but critics of the practice argue that it unconstitutionally singles out poor people—from among all those who receive government funds, taxpayer benefits, or other public largesse—for special, intensely intrusive surveillance, and exposes poor people to the threat of criminal prosecution without any reasonable suspicion that a law has been violated.[131]

How long can an eligible family receive TANF-funded benefits?

The Personal Responsibility Act imposed limits on how long otherwise eligible needy families may receive TANF-funded benefits. States may not use federal

TANF funds to assist any family that includes an adult who has received TANF benefits for 60 months. This marks one of basic changes from the AFDC program and was presented as fulfilling President Clinton's campaign promise to end welfare as "a way of life."[132] TANF time limits do not apply to "child-only" TANF cases described earlier in this chapter. The months need not be consecutive in order to count toward the 60-month limit.[133] However, TANF assistance received while the recipient was a minor child does not count unless the child was the head of the household or married to the head of the household.[134] In addition, the 60-month cap does not include any month in which no adult member of the family received assistance (for example, when a grandparent was caring for a grandchild and assistance was obtained only for the child).[135]

The 60-month limit applies broadly to any TANF-funded benefits the family has received (but does not include benefits underwritten solely with state funds). Benefits include cash payments, vouchers, and other forms of assistance designed to meet a family's ongoing basic needs.[136] It also includes child care and transportation expenses when they are provided to unemployed family members, benefits discussed later in this chapter.[137] States may choose to shorten the 60-month cap, barring families from aid sooner, and about a dozen states have elected to do so.[138] On the other hand, states may make exceptions to the 60-month cap, although within narrow, federally prescribed limits. In particular, states can exempt families experiencing "hardship" and families that include an individual who has been battered or subject to extreme cruelty.[139] Federal law does not define "hardship." "Battery" and "extreme cruelty" are defined as:

- Physical acts that resulted in, or threatened to result in, physical injury to the individual; or
- Sexual abuse; or, sexual activity involving a dependent child; or, being forced as the caretaker relative of a dependent child to engage in nonconsensual sexual acts or activities; or
- Threats of, or attempts at, physical or sexual abuse;
- Mental abuse; or
- Neglect or deprivation of medical care.[140]

A state may not exempt more than 20 percent of the average monthly federally funded TANF caseload under this exception in any fiscal year.[141] This means that some families that qualify for these exceptions may not receive an extension if doing so would increase a state's exempted caseload above the 20 percent cap. Some states recognize additional exceptions to the time limit, and a few states continue to provide TANF benefits to children after the family has reached its time limit.[142]

Lastly, some states operate state-funded cash assistance programs available to families that become ineligible for TANF because of federal time limits.[143] In New York, for instance, families that "time out" from TANF are enrolled in the state's Safety Net Assistance program, which has no time limit.[144]

Are recipients of TANF-funded benefits required to work?

Federal law requires states to engage nonexempt recipients of TANF-funded assistance in "work activities" (including certain types of education and training).[145] More precisely, states must ensure that a certain percentage of the families receiving TANF-funded assistance is "engaged in work activity" as defined by federal law. If a state fails to meet its work participation rate target, the U.S. Department of Health and Human Services (HHS) may impose a penalty in the form of a reduction in the state's TANF block grant for the following year.[146] Federal law sets a standard work participation rate (WPR) requirement at 50 percent of all families receiving TANF in the state, and 90 percent of all such two-parent families,[147] but almost every state has a substantially lower *actual* WPR because of a statutory adjustment called the "caseload reduction credit."[148] As its name implies, the "caseload reduction credit" reduces a state's WPR in proportion to any reduction in the state's TANF caseload. Due to declining TANF enrollment, the adjusted WPR in most states is substantially below 50 percent; in FY 2016, all but nine states had some caseload reduction credit, and 18 states had an adjusted WPR of zero.[149] As a practical matter, states with low adjusted WPRs have broad flexibility to tailor work assignments to the actual needs and best interests of particular families, irrespective of federal work requirements. For instance, the state might increase parents' ability to interact with their children by assigning fewer hours of work activity than prescribed by federal law; or it might enhance parents' ability to secure living wage employment by allowing participation in education and training even if it does not fit the federal definition of work activity. Of course, states are unlikely to adopt such approaches absent pressure from advocates and activists.

Adults receiving assistance, minor heads of household receiving assistance, and parents living with a child who is receiving assistance are all generally subject to TANF work requirements.[150] However, federal law exempts certain individuals from the work requirements, and many states exempt other groups from participating in work activities.[151] The federal exemptions include:

1. Minor parents who are not the head of a household;[152]
2. Immigrant parents who are not "qualified aliens" and so ineligible for TANF benefits;[153]

3. Parents providing care for a disabled family member that requires them to stay at home;[154] and

4. At the state's discretion, disabled recipients receiving SSDI payments.[155]

States have authority to waive the work requirements for domestic violence survivors, single parents of very young children, people receiving federal disability benefits (SSI or SSDI), people who are work limited due to a disability but are not yet receiving federal disability benefits, and people taking care of a severely disabled person in their home. These exceptions are discussed below.

How many hours must a "work-eligible" recipient work?

Federal law specifies how many hours of work-related activities a family receiving TANF-funded benefits must complete in order to count as "engaged in work" for purposes of calculating the state's work participation rate.

Single parents with a preschool-age child (under age six) must participate at least an average of 20 hours per week.[156]

Single parents with children older than age six must participate at least an average of 30 hours per week.[157]

Families with two parents must have both parents participate for a combined total of at least an average of 35 hours,[158] or 55 hours if the family is receiving federally funded child care assistance and no one is disabled or caring for a severely disabled child.[159] As discussed in chapter 2, some courts have held that federal and state minimum wage laws limit the number of hours a state may require TANF recipients to engage in uncompensated work activities.

What activities count toward the work requirement?

Federal law identifies 12 activities that count as work participation.[160] Nine of these activities are referred to as "core" because a family can satisfy all of its required work hours with those activities. Three of the activities are called "noncore," because they can satisfy only a portion of the family's required work hours, leaving the balance of the hours to be met through "core" activities.[161] These work activities are:

1. Unsubsidized employment (core);[162]
2. Subsidized private sector employment (core);[163]
3. Subsidized public sector employment (core);[164]

4. Work experience (including work associated with the refurbishing of publicly assisted housing) if sufficient private sector employment is not available (core);[165]
5. On-the-job training (core);[166]
6. Job search and job readiness assistance (limited to six weeks) (core);[167]
7. Community service programs (core);[168]
8. Vocational educational training (not to exceed 12 months with respect to any individual) (core);[169]
9. Job skills training directly related to employment (non-core);[170]
10. Education directly related to employment, in the case of a recipient who has not received a high school diploma or a certificate of high school equivalency (non-core);[171]
11. Satisfactory attendance at secondary school or in a course of study leading to a certificate of general equivalence, in the case of a recipient who has not completed secondary school or received such a certificate (non-core);[172] and
12. Provision of child care services to an individual who is participating in a community service program (core).[173]

In order to count as "engaged in work activity" under federal law, a recipient subject to TANF work requirements must complete at least 20 of the required 30 hours in "core" activities (those numbered 1 through 8 and 12 above);[174] and a two-parent family must complete 30 of the required 35 hours in core activities (50 of the required 55 hours if the parents are receiving federally funded child care assistance).[175] The balance of the required works hours may be satisfied with any of the approved activities, "core" or "non-core."[176]

Federal "nondisplacement" restrictions prohibit states from assigning TANF recipients to jobs that become vacant due to layoffs or because an employer voluntarily reduced its workforce; nor may an employer terminate an employee in order to fill the position with a TANF recipient.[177] States must provide a grievance process to deal with displacement issues,[178] and state laws protecting against worker displacement remain in force.[179]

Can TANF recipients satisfy the work requirement by attending school or college?

Yes, depending on the state's election of work activities.

First, a TANF recipient who is under age 20, is married or a single-parent head of household, and does not yet have a high school diploma can fulfill the work requirement by attending high school or working toward a high school diploma equivalent full-time.[180]

In addition, federal regulations now give states the option to count a wide array of educational activities as "work activities." TANF recipients can satisfy every hour of their work-participation requirement through "vocational educational activity" for up to a lifetime maximum of 12 months.[181] In 2008, during the administration of George W. Bush, the U.S. Department of Health and Human Services interpreted "vocational educational activity" broadly to encompass not only vocational training, but also postsecondary education, including four-year college and certain postgraduate studies.[182] Hours in class as well as homework time required or recommended by the educational institution can count toward the individual's work requirement.[183]

After 12 months (which may cover nearly four semesters), a TANF recipient's schooling can continue to count as a work activity, but the student must satisfy the first 20 hours[184] of the requirement with a "core activity," as described earlier in this chapter.[185] The student's class hours and homework time may count toward the remaining hours of the work requirement. States may count work-study jobs, internships, and externships as *core* activities that may satisfy any part of the work requirement,[186] and thereby facilitate students' successful completion of school and transition of their families into living wage jobs and out of poverty.[187]

What happens if a work-eligible parent or caretaker fails to meet work requirements?

Federal law generally requires a state TANF program to sanction a family when a work-eligible parent or caretaker refuses without good cause to engage in required work activities.[188] The required sanction is a reduction of the family's assistance by at least the pro rata share of the assistance attributable to the parent or caretaker failing to comply with work requirements.[189] The state may choose to reduce the family's assistance by an even greater amount or to terminate the family's assistance entirely (this latter option is known as "full-family sanctions").[190] A sanction is not required if the family member can show "good cause" for failing to satisfy the work requirement,[191] or if the family meets some other exception that the state recognizes. Rigorous research on the impact of TANF work requirements and sanctions over the past two decades demonstrates that these policies do not reduce child poverty and, to the contrary, have plunged millions of families into dire economic circumstances.[192]

What happens if a work-eligible parent or caretaker cannot find child care and so cannot meet work requirements?

Special rules apply to single parents who care for children younger than age six if appropriate child care is unavailable. Federal law prohibits a state from sanctioning a family if the parent can show an inability to secure suitable child care for one or more of these reasons:[193]

- The parent cannot obtain appropriate child care within a reasonable distance from the individual's home or worksite;[194]
- Informal child care by a relative or other arrangement is either unavailable or unsuitable;[195] or
- Formal child care is unavailable, unaffordable, or inappropriate.[196]

Can states waive out of work-participation rules?

No. On July 2012, the U.S. Department of Health and Human Services announced that it would waive the work-participation rate requirement for states that were willing to develop "alternative and innovative strategies, policies, and procedures that are designed to improve employment outcomes for needy families."[197] The Trump administration rescinded this option in 2017.[198]

Do TANF-funded programs provide any special benefits to survivors of domestic violence?

Federal law allows states to elect a "Family Violence Option" in their TANF-funded programs, which means the state will implement comprehensive strategies for identifying and serving survivors of domestic violence.[199] The Family Violence Option allows the state to waive rules that would make it more difficult for an individual to escape from domestic violence.[200] The rules that may be waived include time limitations on TANF receipt, residence requirements, work requirements, child-support cooperation requirements, and family-cap provisions.[201] Generally, states have broad flexibility in determining which requirements to waive and for how long.[202] As of 2010, all states had adopted a Family Violence Option or a state functional equivalent.[203] Some advocates have criticized the Family Violence Option as inadequate.[204] Part of the problem is the negative effect of other TANF rules on the ability to protect domestic violence survivors from harm. For example, federal law requires states to exempt no more than 20 percent of families from work requirements due to domestic violence,[205] yet research shows that up to 32 percent of current recipients are currently suffering domestic violence and half of recipients have suffered from such violence in the past.[206] Screening procedures for domestic violence, when they occur at all, may occur in public places or with a person's abuser present, which can make identifying domestic violence survivors difficult, though some states have adopted stronger protections and more responsible procedures. TANF-funded programs may require proof of violence, such as documented hospital visits, that individuals may not have. Survivors of domestic violence may not be aware they are entitled to waivers of certain requirements or may be hesitant to apply because of delays in processing applications.[207]

Can a family's cash assistance be terminated or reduced if a child is truant and does not attend school?

Yes. Federal law allows, but does not require, a state to sanction a family that receives cash assistance under TANF if any minor child in the family does not attend school as required by state law.[208] As of July 2017, 37 states had such sanctions in place.[209] Federal law also allows states to provide bonuses to families whose children attend school. Nine states authorize such bonuses.[210]

Relatedly, states may not provide TANF cash assistance to a custodial parent who is under age 18, unmarried, and whose child is at least 12 weeks old, unless the parent has successfully completed or is pursuing a high school diploma or participating in an alternative education or training program approved by the state.[211]

Is an unmarried mother required to identify the child's biological father as a condition of receiving TANF-funded benefits?

Yes. Federal law requires unmarried mothers who seek TANF-funded assistance to cooperate with the state agency in establishing the paternity of a nonmarital child. Federal law also requires the state to impose penalties if a parent refuses without good cause to cooperate in establishing, modifying, or enforcing a child-support order against a noncustodial parent.[212] Good cause for declining to cooperate includes situations in which domestic violence makes pursuing child support unsafe. When a parent does not comply and there is no good cause exception, the state must withhold at least 25 percent of the family's assistance and can eliminate benefits altogether.[213]

What is an Individual Responsibility Plan?

States are required to make initial assessments of the skills, prior work experience, and employability of all TANF recipients who are over age 18 and who do not have, and are not in the process of obtaining, a high school diploma or functional equivalent (like a GED).[214] Once the state has made this required initial assessment, the state may prepare an Individual Responsibility Plan that the TANF recipient must follow. This plan can include employment goals, obligations of the recipient, like immunizing children, and services the state will provide to the recipient.[215] If a recipient fails to comply with the terms and conditions of the Individual Responsibility Plan, the state has authority to sanction the recipient's household by a reduction in benefits.[216]

Can a state penalize a family that does not comply with TANF program rules?

Federal law requires states to penalize families that fail without good cause to comply with certain TANF requirements, even if the noncompliance is by a single family member. Such penalties, known as "sanctions," take the form of a reduction or termination of the family's cash benefits. As described earlier in this chapter, states must sanction willful failure to comply with work requirements and child-support cooperation requirements.[217] States may choose to sanction other behaviors, such as a parent's failure to ensure that minor children maintain adequate school attendance. The set of circumstances that will trigger a sanction varies by state, with some states imposing sanctions for minor violations of a program's administrative rules. A study of the Texas TANF program, for instance, found that the majority of sanctions imposed were for missing a single appointment.[218]

States may waive sanctions if the family has a good reason for its noncompliance, but many case managers, often handling large caseloads, do not give families a chance to explain their actions before imposing the penalty.[219] And while imposition of sanctions may have devastating consequences for vulnerable families (including loss of shelter or worse), multiple studies have revealed a high error rate in state decisions to inflict these penalties.[220] Indeed, although a few commentators have praised the TANF program for reducing caseloads, the U.S. Department of Health and Human Services has acknowledged that error rates in state sanction systems likely played a significant role in reducing participation by eligible—and needy—families during the period under review,[221] and thereby inflicted unnecessary harm on vulnerable families.

How does a family apply for assistance under a TANF-funded program?

Generally speaking, families apply for TANF-funded assistance through their state or county department of human services. Many states also offer an option to apply online. The U.S. Department of Health and Human Services maintains a directory of state TANF offices and contact information at https://www.acf.hhs.gov/ofa/help. The TANF application process differs from state to state. In some states, the application process reflects the policy of encouraging responsible parenting by requiring information about child immunizations and child school attendance. In other states, an emphasis is placed on encouraging applicants to achieve economic self-sufficiency, and so more attention is paid to whether the applicant is employable.[222] And, as discussed earlier in this chapter, some states attempt to divert families from applying for ongoing assistance by offering a one-shot "diversion payment" to meet an immediate short-term need.

Do families applying for or receiving TANF have a right to challenge unfavorable actions?

Yes. The U.S. Supreme Court ruled in a landmark 1970 decision, *Goldberg v. Kelly*, that the Fourteenth Amendment's Due Process Clause gives welfare recipients the right to written notice and an opportunity for a hearing before benefits may be reduced or terminated.[223] Federal regulations codified these due process rights, which extend to applicants for benefits as well as to recipients.[224] Shortly after Congress enacted the Personal Responsibility Act in 1996, at least one state argued that due process guarantees do not apply to TANF benefits because the 1996 law did not create a federal entitlement to those benefits. The courts, however, have rejected such arguments.[225] Moreover, all states have continued to recognize their constitutional obligation to provide due process protections to TANF applicants and recipients.[226] These protections include:

Right to timely and adequate notice: At a minimum, states must provide a TANF recipient with written notice that clearly describes (1) the action the agency intends to take; (2) the reasons for the proposed action, including the facts on which it is based; (3) the specific regulations supporting the action; and (4) the right to request a hearing to challenge the action and, in the case of a proposed reduction of termination of benefits, the right to continue receiving benefits unchanged pending the outcome of the hearing.[227] Notices proposing a reduction or termination of benefits must be issued at least 10 days before the proposed action.[228]

Right to benefits during the appeals process: Families have the right to continue receiving their benefits without change until their appeal is resolved.[229] This is known as "aid-continuing." In order to get "aid-continuing" the family ordinarily must request a hearing within 10 days of the date on the reduction or termination notice.[230] A family may still request a hearing outside of the initial 10-day period, but will not receive aid-continuing. States must provide families a "reasonable time not to exceed 90 days" within which to file an appeal. Many states set deadlines of 60 days or shorter to appeal. The state's notice must provide clear instructions, including time limitations, for how a family can file an appeal.

Right to a "fair hearing": TANF applicants and recipients have a right to an in-person hearing to contest any adverse action taken on their cases. These proceedings, known as "fair hearings," are typically conducted by a state hearing officer. The agency's case is usually presented by a nonlawyer staff person from the welfare agency. Although fair hearings are far less formal than court proceedings, the Constitution and federal regulations afford families important procedural rights,[231] including:

1. The right to examine the contents of their case files at a reasonable time in advance of the hearing (and at the hearing itself) and to examine all evidence that the agency intends to present at the hearing;
2. The right to appear in person at the hearing and present the family's case, or to have a lawyer or other person designated by the family present the case;
3. The right to testify, present testimony of witnesses, and present documents and other evidence;
4. The right to advance any arguments without undue interference;
5. The right to question or refute any testimony or evidence, including an opportunity to confront and cross-examine adverse witnesses; and
6. The right to a hearing conducted by an impartial hearing officer.

Although fair hearings are informal and in theory designed to accommodate claimants who do not have counsel,[232] families should consider consulting with a legal services office to determine whether an appeal is warranted and for help in presenting the challenge.[233]

Supplemental Security Income

What is Supplemental Security Income (SSI)?

Supplemental Security Income is a federal program that makes monthly cash payments to individuals with little or no income and who are disabled or blind or who have reached age 65. The program and its benefits are popularly known as "SSI." Congress created SSI in 1972 to replace a variety of state-administered programs for the aged, blind, and disabled that were jointly funded by the states and the federal government.[234] The federal government funds all but a small part of SSI and sets minimum national benefit levels. SSI grant levels are higher than payments made under state-administered TANF programs or state general assistance programs.

Who runs SSI?

SSI is run by the U.S. Social Security Administration (SSA).[235] The Social Security Administration maintains over 1,000 local offices throughout the United States. These are known as district offices and are the places where individuals can obtain information and forms, submit applications for benefits, and file appeals. The location of the Social Security District Offices can be found in the blue pages (government listings) of a local telephone book under "Social Security Administration," by calling the Social Security Administration's toll-free service and information number, 1-800-772-1213, or by visiting https://www.socialsecurity.gov/locator.

Is SSI the same as Social Security Disability Insurance (SSDI) or Social Security paid after retirement?

No. SSI is not the same as Social Security Disability Insurance (SSDI) or Social Security. The Social Security Administration administers all three programs, but each program provides different benefits for different reasons.

SSDI is a program through which workers who become disabled can receive benefits, regardless of household income, provided the claimant has worked for the required number of years in covered employment and has paid Social Security taxes. In certain circumstances, SSDI also makes payments to disabled spouses and disabled children of workers who have paid Social Security taxes over a sufficient period of time.

Social Security retirement benefits, known simply as "Social Security," are payments made to retired workers based upon the amount of Social Security taxes paid on behalf of the worker during years of employment. (Social Security disability and retirement benefits are discussed in chapter 2 of this book.)

SSI is cash assistance paid to low-income people who are elderly or unable to work because of disabilities, regardless of how many years they worked in employment covered by the Social Security system. It is possible to receive both SSDI or Social Security retirement benefits and SSI.

How many people receive SSI?

As of December 2018, about 8.1 million individuals were receiving SSI. About a quarter of the recipients were age 65 or older, 58 percent were age 18 to 64, and about 15 percent were under age 18.[236]

How large is an SSI payment?

SSI benefits are paid monthly. The grant amount depends upon several factors, including whether the recipient resides in a state that provides a supplement, whether the recipient has other income, and the recipient's living arrangements. In 2019, the basic federal grant was $771 per month for an eligible individual living alone and $1,157 per month for an eligible couple (both spouses eligible for SSI) living together.[237] The actual benefit received by a particular individual may be higher than the basic federal grant if the recipient lives in a state that adds a supplement to the federal grant. Conversely, the benefit may be lower if the recipient has, or is deemed to have, other income.[238]

Do SSI payments increase from year to year?

Yes. Each year the federal government assesses how much it costs to buy regular household goods and services, such as food, clothing, and housing—a measure called the Consumer Price Index (CPI)—and uses that measure to adjust the federal portion of the SSI grant.[239] In theory, this should ensure that SSI payments keep up with the increasing cost of living. However, the CPI does not account fully for a household's reasonable expenses, and in 2015, the basic SSI benefit still left an individual below the federal poverty level. The federal government authorized a 2.8 percent cost-of-living increase to the basic federal grant in 2019.[240]

What is a state supplement?

A "state supplement" is an additional payment that a state may choose to make to an SSI recipient to supplement the basic federal grant.[241] Each state sets the amount of its supplement, and a few states make no supplemental payments at all. In 2018, 46 states and the District of Columbia provided supplemental payments.[242] The amount of a state supplement typically varies depending on the recipient's living arrangements, location within the state, and basis for SSI eligibility.[243]

Who is eligible for SSI?

To qualify for SSI, an individual must:

1. Be blind, disabled, or age 65 or older;[244]
2. Fall within the program's income and resource limits; [245]
3. Be a U.S. citizen or a qualifying immigrant; and
4. Reside in one of the 50 states, the District of Columbia, or the Northern Mariana Islands,[246] though children of personnel in the armed services living overseas and certain international exchange students may qualify.[247]

How does an applicant show age to establish SSI eligibility?

An otherwise eligible person can receive SSI if age 65 or older.[248] The best evidence of age is a birth certificate or religious record of birth recorded before the fifth birthday.[249] If no such document is available, the Social Security Administration will consider other proof of age, including a school record, census record, Bible or other family record, church record of baptism or confirmation made in youth or early adult life, an insurance policy, a marriage record, an employment record, a labor union record, fraternal organization record, military record, voting record, vaccination record, delayed birth certificate, birth certificate of a claimant's child, physician's or midwife's record of birth, immigration record, naturalization record, or passport.[250] If the applicant is age 68 or older, the Social Security Administration will accept any document that is at least three years old and shows the applicant's age, unless there is evidence suggesting that the applicant is younger.[251]

When is a person considered blind for purposes of SSI?

A person is considered blind for purposes of SSI if vision is 20/200 or less in the better eye with the use of glasses.[252] A person may qualify for SSI due to blindness even if the person is able to work and is in fact working,[253] but earnings will be considered as income in determining financial eligibility and the amount of the SSI benefit. A person who is not legally blind may nevertheless qualify for SSI as a disabled person if vision problems, alone or in combination with other medical impairments, prevent employment.[254]

When is an adult considered disabled for purposes of SSI?

An adult is considered disabled for purposes of SSI if there is evidence of a long-term medical condition that makes it impossible for the applicant to work regularly at a paying job. In the language of the Social Security Act, the applicant must be "unable to engage in any substantial gainful activity by reason of any medically determinable physical or mental impairment which can be expected to result in death or which has lasted or can be expected to last for a continuous period of not less than twelve months."[255]

The rules for determining whether an individual is disabled under the SSI program are complicated. Individuals who believe they may qualify for SSI benefits should consider seeking the assistance of a legal aid or legal services lawyer or other experienced advocate who can work with their doctor, medical clinic, and/ or hospital to obtain the medical and other documentation needed to demonstrate disability. This chapter will describe some of the basic rules for deciding whether an individual is disabled under the SSI program. But, because of the volume and complexity of this area of law, a complete presentation of the subject is not practicable.

The Social Security Administration (SSA) has developed a five-part test for determining whether an individual has an impairment or set of impairments that meets the Social Security Act's definition of disability.[256] The SSA sometimes refers to this test as the "sequential evaluation" of disability.[257] The five steps evaluate, in order:

1. Whether the individual currently works.
2. Whether the individual has a "severe" medically determinable physical or mental impairment.
3. Whether the individual's medical condition appears on the Social Security Administration's "Listing" of disabling conditions.
4. Whether the medical condition prevents the individual from performing work done in the past.
5. Whether the individual is capable of doing other work despite the medical condition.[258]

Step 1: Whether the individual is currently working

An applicant who is currently engaged in "substantial gainful activity" will be deemed "not disabled" for purposes of SSI eligibility.[259] "Substantial gainful activity" means work that requires "significant physical or mental activities"[260] and is done "for pay or profit."[261]

Substantial Activity

To decide whether work is substantial activity,[262] the Social Security Administration will consider whether the duties involved require use of the applicant's "experience, skills, supervision and responsibilities, or contribute substantially to the operation of a business";[263] whether the applicant is able to perform the job satisfactorily "without more supervision or assistance than is usually given other people doing similar work";[264] and whether the work is done without "special conditions"—for example, work performed in a sheltered workshop or as a patient in a hospital.[265] Work that involves minimal duties and is of little use to the employer will not be considered substantial gainful activity.[266]

Gainful Activity

To determine whether work is gainful activity, the Social Security Administration will consider how much the applicant is earning from the employment. In making the determination, the Social Security Administration considers only income that is directly related to productivity, will not count as income any portion that is subsidized,[267] and will subtract the cost to the worker of services and items that enable work despite a medical condition.[268] As of 2019, employment that resulted in average earnings of more than $2,040 per month for blind people or $1,220 per month for nonblind people ordinarily was considered to be substantial gainful activity.[269]

   If the individual is not currently engaged in substantial gainful activity, the disability evaluation proceeds to Step 2.

Step 2: Whether the individual has a "severe" medically determinable physical or mental impairment

To be considered disabled, an individual must have a "severe" medically determinable physical or mental impairment.[270] A physical or mental condition, or a combination of such conditions, is "severe" if it significantly limits the individual's ability to do basic work activities.[271] Basic work activities include lifting; carrying; pulling; pushing; reaching; handling; standing; sitting; walking; seeing; hearing; speaking; understanding, carrying out and remembering simple instructions;

using judgment; responding appropriately to supervision, co-workers, and usual work situations; and dealing with changes in a routine work setting.[272] If the medical conditions do not significantly limit the individual's ability to do one or more of these basic work activities, the Social Security Administration will deem the person "not disabled."[273] (The SSA does not consider the applicant's age, education, or work experience in making this determination.)[274]

If the individual's medical condition does significantly limit the applicant's ability to perform basic work activities, the disability evaluation proceeds to Step 3.

Step 3: Whether the individual's medical condition appears on the Social Security Administration's "Listing" of disabling conditions

The Social Security Administration maintains a list of physical and mental conditions that the agency has determined to be disabling, irrespective of the applicant's age, education, or work experience.[275] The list is called the "Listing of Impairments" and is published in Title 20 of the Code of Federal Regulations, Part 404, subpart P, Appendix 1. It is available for viewing at any Social Security office and online.[276] If the individual's medical condition is on this list, or is as severe as a condition on the list, then the Social Security Administration will conclude that the applicant is disabled.[277]

If the individual's medical condition is not on the list or as severe as a condition on the list, the disability evaluation proceeds to Step 4.

Step 4: Whether the medical condition prevents the individual from performing work done in the past

If an individual has a severe medical condition that is not on the Social Security Administration's Listing of Impairments, the Social Security Administration will consider whether the medical condition prevents the person from doing the kind of work the individual performed in the past 15 years.[278] To answer this question, the SSA must first determine which basic work activities the individual can still do, despite the person's medical conditions; this is called the individual's "residual functional capacity."[279] Next, the SSA must compare the individual's residual functional capacity to the physical and mental activities required to undertake the past usual work.[280] If the medical condition does not prevent the individual from performing the activities required by past usual work, the Social Security Administration will deem the individual to be "not disabled."

If the individual's medical condition does prevent performance of past usual work, the disability evaluation continues to Step 5.

Step 5: Whether the individual is capable of doing other work despite the medical condition

If the Social Security Administration finds that an individual's medical condition prevents the performance of past usual work, it will consider whether the person can do any other job that exists in significant numbers in the national economy.[281] If the individual can do other work despite the medical conditions, the SSA will deem the person to be "not disabled"; if, on the other hand, the individual cannot do other work, the SSA will deem the person to be "disabled."[282]

In evaluating whether an individual is able and qualified to do some job other than the person's usual job, the Social Security Administration considers four factors: age, educational background, past work experience, and residual functional capacity (activities that can be done despite the existence of medical conditions).[283]

If an individual's medical condition causes only "exertional limitations" (i.e., limitations on ability to sit, stand, walk, lift, carry, push, or pull), the Social Security Administration will use a series of charts, known as the Medical-Vocational Guidelines or "the grids," to determine whether there are jobs the person can do. The Medical-Vocational Guidelines are published in Title 20 of the Code of Federal Regulations, Part 404, subpart P, Appendix 2 and are available for viewing at any Social Security office or online.[284] For each combination of age, educational background, work skills, and residual functional capacity, there is an entry in the Guidelines that directs a finding of "disabled" or "not disabled."[285]

The Medical-Vocational Guidelines represent the Social Security Administration's findings about the types of jobs that exist in the national economy and the ability of individuals with certain physical restrictions and skill levels to do those jobs. Generally speaking, if an applicant is older, less educated, has a lower skill level, and has a lower residual functional capacity, it is more likely that the Guidelines will direct a finding of disability. On the other hand, if an applicant is younger, more educated, has a higher skill level, and a greater residual functional capacity, it is less likely that the Guidelines will direct a finding of disability.[286]

Here are two illustrations from the numerous permutations covered by the Guidelines:

1. The Guidelines (Rule 202.12) direct a finding of "disabled" for a person who (1) is between ages 50 and 54; (2) has a formal education through at least

high school, but has not "recently completed education which provides a . . . direct entry into skilled sedentary work";[287] (3) has no work skills that are readily transferable to other occupations; and (4) is limited to "sedentary work" by medical conditions. The rule states that a person with these characteristics who cannot do prior customary work is disabled.[288]

2. The Guidelines (Rule 203.23) direct a finding of "not disabled" for a person who (1) is between ages 18 and 49; (2) has completed high school; (3) has some work skills that are transferrable to another occupation; and (4) is limited to "medium work" by medical conditions.[289]

Are there any situations in which the Medical-Vocational Guidelines cannot be used to reject a claim of disability and the payment of SSI?

There are three situations in which the Social Security Administration may not use the Medical-Vocational Guidelines to reject a claim of disability.

Sedentary Work

The Guidelines may not be used to find an applicant "not disabled" if a medical condition prevents the applicant from performing even "sedentary" work on a regular basis.[290] Sedentary work requires the worker to lift and carry no more than 10 pounds at a time, be able to sit at a work station for approximately six hours in an eight-hour workday, and occasionally stand and walk.[291] Extended periods of continuous sitting are required, and workers usually cannot alternate sitting and standing at will.[292] If a medical condition prevents the applicant from doing even this degree of physical exertion, then the Guidelines may not be used to deny SSI.

Nonexertional Limitations

The Guidelines do not apply if the applicant's medical condition causes only "nonexertional" limitations.[293] This is because the Guidelines represent the government's assessment of whether a person of a certain age, educational background, skill level, and *exertional* capacity can perform the tasks required by any job that exists in large numbers in the national economy; the Guidelines do not consider the impact of nonexertional limitations on an individual's employability. A nonexertional limitation is any limitation that "does not directly affect the ability to sit, stand, walk, lift, carry, push or pull."[294] This includes limitations that "affect the mind, vision, hearing, speech, and use of the body to climb, balance, stoop, kneel, crouch, crawl, reach, handle and use of the fingers for fine activities."[295] The Guidelines assume that the individual has no limitation on the ability to see, hear, speak, reach, climb, perform fine manipulations with hands, understand instructions, concentrate, use machinery, and so forth.[296] If an applicant's medical condition causes any such limitations, the Guidelines may not be used to deny SSI. In such cases, the Social Security Administration may consult a vocational specialist to determine whether there are jobs that a particular individual can perform despite specific exertional and nonexertional limitations.[297] When someone has both exertional and nonexertional limitations, the SSA will look at the rules that relate to each limitation and consider the individual's condition as a whole.[298]

For example, the Guidelines may not be used to deny SSI to an individual with a psychological limitation, such as nervousness, anxiety, or depression that results in a "substantial loss of ability to respond appropriately to supervision, coworkers, and usual work settings."[299] Nor may the Guidelines be used to deny SSI where the individual has difficulty maintaining attention or concentration, or understanding or remembering detailed instructions.[300]

If an applicant has exertional and nonexertional limitations, then the Social Security Administration will consult the Guidelines to determine whether the exertional limitations warrant a finding of disability. If not, then the Guidelines may be used as a "framework" for considering whether there are jobs that the applicant can perform.[301]

Unskilled Physical Labor for 35 Years

The Guidelines may not be used to deny a claim for SSI if the applicant has worked for 35 years or more at arduous, unskilled physical labor, is now unable to perform such labor because of a medical condition, and has only a "marginal education" (generally, sixth grade or less).[302] Under such circumstances, the Social Security Administration must find that the applicant is disabled.[303]

Can a person who is disabled due to alcoholism or drug addiction qualify for SSI?

The medical community universally recognizes drug and alcohol addiction as disabling medical conditions,[304] and until 1996 individuals suffering from these conditions could qualify for SSI. Benefits were paid through a responsible third party, and recipients were required to participate in drug or alcohol treatment programs. Congress terminated SSI eligibility for this group of people as part of the "Contract with America Advancement Act of 1996."[305] After March 29, 1996, substance addiction no longer qualified as a disability under the Social Security Act, and effective January 1, 1997, existing SSI recipients who were disabled only by drug addiction or alcoholism were dropped from the program.[306]

At present, an individual with an alcohol or drug addiction can receive SSI disability if the person (1) is disabled because of a medical condition other than alcohol or drug addiction; and (2) would be disabled even if drugs or alcohol were no longer used.[307] If the SSA determines that alcohol or drug addiction is a factor contributing to an individual's disability, the individual may still receive SSI, but only if the person accepts any available, appropriate treatment at an approved facility and makes progress in that treatment.[308] Failure to comply with appropriate treatment can lead to the termination of benefits.[309]

Can a disabled child qualify for SSI?

A child under age 18 can qualify for SSI upon a showing that the applicant "has a medically determinable physical or mental impairment, which results in marked and severe functional limitations, and which can be expected to result in death or which has lasted or can be expected to last for a continuous period of not less than twelve months."[310] Congress tightened the definition of child eligibility as part of the Personal Responsibility Act in 1996, eliminating the individualized functional assessment (IFA) as well as any reference to maladaptive behavior in the children's Listing of Impairments. Congress adopted this restrictive approach to childhood disability explicitly to cut program costs.[311]

As a result, many disabled children who previously qualified for SSI were denied assistance.[312] In the years immediately after 1996, the number of children receiving SSI dropped by roughly 100,000,[313] and by 2001, the childhood SSI caseload was estimated to be 22 percent lower than it would have been under the earlier law.[314] Nevertheless, the number of children receiving SSI has increased since 2001.[315] Researchers associate the upward trend with declining family income after the 2008 recession, cutbacks in cash assistance following the repeal of the AFDC program, and an increase in children's mental health issues.[316]

Are premature and low birthweight infants ever considered disabled?

The Social Security Administration considers two categories of premature and low birthweight babies to be disabled and therefore eligible for SSI. First, infants who weigh less than 1,200 grams at birth are deemed to be disabled at least until age one.[317] In addition, infants who weigh at least 1,200 grams but less than 2,000 grams and who are small for gestational age are deemed to be disabled at least until age one.[318]

What kind of evidence is used to decide whether a person is disabled?

The Social Security Administration must consider any information provided about an individual's medical conditions and how those conditions limit the ability to do work-related activities.[319] Usually the most important kind of evidence is medical, including reports, test results, and other records from doctors, hospitals, or clinics that have treated the individual.[320] It is important that the individual obtain a complete report from the medical professionals who have provided treatment.

The SSA also will consider statements from the individual about how medical conditions, including pain and the side effects of medications, limit daily activities and the ability to work. The individual may provide statements from "nonmedical sources" who have observed the individual's medical conditions and who can comment on how they restrict daily activities and ability to do work-related activities.[321]

Will the Social Security Administration consider the effects of pain and other symptoms in determining whether an individual is able to work?

Yes. When determining disability, the Social Security Administration must consider not only the individual's medical conditions, but also symptoms, such as pain, weakness, fatigue, or nervousness.[322] The weight given to an individual's report of symptoms depends on "the extent to which . . . symptoms can reasonably be accepted as consistent with the objective medical evidence. . . ."[323] Objective medical evidence means test results or physical or psychological abnormalities observed or gathered from laboratory findings by a doctor.[324] If objective medical evidence is shown, the SSA also will consider the individual's statements about the severity and persistence of the symptoms and the effect that the symptoms have on the ability to do ordinary daily and work-related activities. In many cases, pain or other symptoms can be disabling. For instance, severe, persistent back pain that can be relieved only by frequent changes in position and lying down every 30 minutes would likely prevent the individual from holding any job.[325]

How important is it for an SSI applicant to submit a report from a treating physician?

In most cases, complete information from an SSI applicant's treating physician is the most important and convincing evidence of disability. A thorough report from a treating physician is therefore critical. The report should give a medical history and fully describe all of the individual's medical conditions. The report should include a description of all physical and/or psychological abnormalities observed by the doctor, symptoms that the individual has reported to the doctor, the results of any medical tests or laboratory diagnostic techniques (for example, X-rays, CAT scans, electrocardiograms, blood tests, psychological tests, etc.), the treatment prescribed, and the prognosis. In addition, the report should state the degree to which the individual's medical conditions, including symptoms like pain and the impact of medications, limit the ability to do work-related activities.[326]

The treating physician is the health professional most familiar with the individual's medical conditions. For this reason, the Social Security Administration should find a thorough report from the claimant's treating physician persuasive.[327] However, the SSA will give little or no weight to an in-complete report or a brief note stating only that the individual is under treatment and cannot work.[328] Test results and medical observations included in the report can establish that the medical condition meets or equals a condition on the Social Security Administration's "Listing" of disabling conditions. A physician's assessment of the physical and/or mental limitations caused by the individual's medical conditions also can show that the person is no longer able to work. The Social Security Administration provides online guidance for physicians and other health professionals, describing the medical information and documentation required to demonstrate disability.[329] In addition, some legal aid and legal services offices offer written information about SSI that is useful to doctors providing documentation of an applicant's medical conditions.[330] At the least, a doctor preparing a medical report in connection with an SSI application should review the SSA's "Listings" of disabling conditions, because very specific test results and/or clinical findings must be reported to support a finding of disability.[331]

What happens if an individual applying for SSI cannot get a report from a treating doctor or records from a health clinic?

If an applicant is unable to get information from the treating physician or health clinic, federal law requires that the Social Security Administration "make every reasonable effort" to obtain medical records and reports from these sources.[332] If the SSA is unable to do so, it may arrange for the applicant to be examined and/or tested by a doctor or psychologist at the government's expense.[333]

Can the Social Security Administration require an applicant to be examined by a doctor of the government's choosing?

If the information provided by the treating physician, clinic, and/or hospital is not sufficient to determine disability, the Social Security Administration may ask the claimant to submit to physical or psychological tests or examinations, and the government will pay for any such test or examination.[334] If the claimant fails or refuses to submit to the tests or examinations without a good reason, the SSA may make a decision based on the available evidence and conclude that the applicant is not disabled and deny the SSI claim. (If a person already receives benefits, the SSA may find the person not disabled based on the evidence that it has plus the failure to appear for a consultative examination that the SSA has arranged.)[335]

However, an applicant can decline to submit to a particular test or examination if advised not to do so by any medical source.[336] In this situation, the applicant must inform the Social Security Administration immediately about the advice. The person also may object to the government's choice of doctor.[337] Good reasons for such an objection could include:

1. The doctor previously examined the individual in connection with an SSI application that was denied;
2. The doctor assisted an employer in contesting the applicant's workers' compensation claim;
3. The doctor's office is distant from the applicant's residence;
4. The doctor and applicant do not speak the same language and a translator is not available;
5. The doctor "lacks objectivity," which means that the doctor is in some way biased against the SSI claim.[338]

An applicant also may request that the treating physician conduct any additional tests or examinations that are required. The Social Security Administration will choose the treating physician if qualified, willing, and able to perform the test or examination for the fee offered by the government, and generally furnishes complete and timely reports.[339]

Under what circumstances will the Social Security Administration expedite its processing of a disability application?

Applicants suffering from medical conditions so severe that they obviously meet the definition of disability may seek expedited processing under the "Compassionate Allowances" program. Beneficiaries of the program follow the same application process as other claimants, but the SSA usually approves these applications in less than two weeks. As of 2019, the Compassionate Allowances program extended to more than 200 medical conditions.[340]

The Quick Disability Determination (QDD) process is another expedited process for Social Security disability benefits.[341] QDD uses predictive modeling and computer screening to identify cases that are deemed highly likely to result in favorable disability determinations. QDD cases bypass the typical hearings process and are referred to designated QDD examiners.[342]

Does a claimant have to accept and follow prescribed treatment to receive disability benefits?

To receive SSI disability benefits, a claimant must follow any treatment prescribed by medical sources if the treatment is expected to restore the claimant's ability to work.[343] If the claimant refuses such treatment without a good reason, the Social Security Administration may deny or terminate SSI.[344] The SSA has identified the following grounds as illustrative of good reasons for refusing prescribed treatment:

1. The treatment is contrary to the claimant's religious beliefs;
2. The treatment is cataract surgery for one eye when there is a severe, untreatable loss of vision in the other eye;
3. The prescribed treatment is surgery that was previously performed for the same medical condition with unsuccessful results;
4. The treatment is "very risky" because of its "enormity" (for example, open heart surgery), unusual nature (for example, organ transplant), or other reason; and
5. The treatment involves amputation of a limb or major part of a limb.[345]

Does a claimant have to do vocational
rehabilitation to receive disability benefits?

The Social Security Administration may refer an SSI recipient between the ages of 16 and 64 to a state agency that provides vocational rehabilitation services if such services may restore the recipient's ability to work.[346] The SSA cannot, however, suspend a recipient for refusing to accept such services, even if good cause for the refusal does not exist.[347] However, as earlier discussed, the SSA will suspend and then terminate SSI if a recipient fails to comply with drug or alcohol treatment referrals.[348]

How long does a person remain eligible for disability benefits?

By statute, the Social Security Administration must review a recipient's condition at least once every three years to determine whether the person remains disabled, unless there has been a determination of permanent disability.[349] The SSA calls this process "continuing disability review."[350] In conducting this review, the SSA will reassess the original determination of disability and will gather new medical information as necessary. Generally, the SSA will conclude that an individual is no longer eligible for disability benefits if it finds that: (1) the individual's medical condition has improved to such an extent that it no longer prevents the individual from working (though benefits may continue if the individual is participating in vocational rehabilitation or other employment or supportive services); (2) a prior disability determination was incorrect; (3) the individual is refusing medical treatment without good reason; (4) the individual provided false or misleading information for a prior disability determination; or (5) the individual is not cooperating with the SSA and lacks a good reason.[351]

Can an SSI disability recipient work
and continue to receive benefits?

It depends. If an SSI recipient takes a job that does *not* constitute "substantial gainful activity" (described earlier in this chapter), the recipient may still be considered disabled and receive benefits, though any income would be taken into account in calculating the amount of the SSI grant.[352] In addition, a recipient who begins to work at a job that pays more than the amount ordinarily deemed to constitute "substantial gainful activity" may qualify for "special SSI cash benefits" as long as the person continues to have a disabling impairment.[353]

People who qualify for this benefit are generally those whose medical conditions have not significantly improved since they were determined to be disabled, but who manage to work despite their ongoing disability.[354] As noted earlier, an SSI recipient who becomes able to work because of an improvement in the recipient's medical condition may be found not disabled and no longer eligible for SSI.

What is the Ticket to Work program?

The Ticket to Work program, administered by the Social Security Administration, is designed to help recipients of SSI and Social Security disability benefits find and take advantage of employment opportunities.[355] Private organizations and government agencies that participate in the program provide free training and employment support services to beneficiaries. Participation is entirely voluntary and deciding not to participate will not affect an individual's benefits.[356]

Can a person who lives in a public institution receive SSI?

It depends. Generally, a claimant who resides in a "public institution" in a given month cannot receive SSI for that month.[357] A "public institution" for these purposes is a government-operated or government-controlled establishment that provides food, shelter, and some treatment or other services to four or more persons.[358] There are several important exceptions to this rule.

Public Emergency Shelters for the Homeless
A claimant who is residing in a public emergency shelter for the homeless may receive SSI for up to six months in any nine-month period.[359] A public emergency shelter for the homeless is defined as any public institution that provides temporary shelter to homeless people. It does not include institutions that have custody over their occupants, such as foster care facilities and detox centers, or transitional living arrangements, such as halfway houses.[360] Thus, if a claimant lived in a public emergency shelter for an entire year, SSI could be received for the first six months; could not be received for months seven, eight, and nine, but benefits could resume in month 10 for another six months. If a claimant does not live in a public emergency shelter throughout an entire month, the SSI payment for that month does not count toward the six-month limit.[361] There is no limit on receiving SSI by a person who resides in a shelter for the homeless that is not operated or controlled by the government.

Medical Confinement in a Public Institution

A claimant who resides in a public medical or psychiatric institution, or a public or private facility where Medicaid pays more than 50 percent of the cost of care, may receive SSI for up to two months after entering the institution if (1) in the month before admission, the claimant was deemed eligible for SSI pursuant to Social Security Act Section 1619(a) or (b) (which authorize special SSI eligibility for certain individuals who work despite a disabling impairment); and (2) the institution agrees that the SSI will not be used to pay for the cost of institutional care.[362] In addition, if a physician certifies that the stay in the facility is not likely to last over three months, and the claimant needs SSI to pay rent or otherwise maintain a home, then SSI will continue for the first three months the claimant is in the medical facility, whether or not the claimant was working during the month prior to admission.[363] A claimant who does not qualify for a full SSI payment may still receive a reduced payment, sometimes referred to as a "personal needs allowance."[364] The personal needs allowance for an individual is $30 per month, an amount that has not been increased since 1988.[365] (About half of the states provide a state supplement to the federal allowance.)[366]

Educational or Vocational Facilities

A claimant who lives in a public educational institution and receives training, knowledge, or skills to prepare for gainful employment may receive SSI.[367]

Community Residence Serving No More Than 16 People

A claimant who lives in a publicly operated community residence that is designed for and serves no more than 16 individuals may receive SSI.[368]

Can a person who lives outside of the United States receive SSI?

In general, SSI is available only to persons who live in the 50 states, the District of Columbia, or the Northern Mariana Islands, though children of personnel in the U.S. armed services and certain international exchange students may qualify, even if living abroad.[369] This means SSI generally is not available to persons who live in Puerto Rico, Guam, the U.S. Virgin Islands, any other U.S. territory, or any foreign country. A home address within the 50 states, the District of Columbia, or the Northern Mariana Islands will be sufficient proof of residency for SSI eligibility. If the Social Security Administration suspects that a claimant does not live in the United States, it may require proof, such as utility bills, lease, rent receipts, tax forms, or documents showing participation in a U.S.-based social service or educational program.[370]

Can a claimant travel outside of the
United States and still receive SSI?

A claimant may travel outside of the 50 states, the District of Columbia, and the Northern Mariana Islands for up to 29 consecutive days without any loss of SSI. However, if a claimant remains outside of these locations for 30 consecutive days or more, the Social Security Administration will suspend SSI.[371] SSI will resume after the individual has returned and remained for 30 consecutive days in the 50 states, the District of Columbia, or the Northern Mariana Islands.[372]

Are all U.S. citizens eligible for SSI?

A claimant who has proof of birth in one of the 50 states, the District of Columbia, Puerto Rico, Guam, the U.S. Virgin Islands, American Samoa, Swain's Island, or the Northern Mariana Islands, or of naturalization, or U.S. citizenship by virtue of a parent's U.S. citizenship qualifies for SSI if otherwise eligible.[373]

Is SSI limited to U.S. citizens?

No, but only certain immigrants may receive SSI. The Personal Responsibility Act of 1996 (discussed earlier in this chapter) disqualified most elderly and disabled immigrants from receiving SSI, even if they were legal permanent residents. A year later, the Balanced Budget Act of 1997 lifted that exclusion for certain immigrants who had entered the United States before August 22, 1996 and were lawfully in the country.[374] Nevertheless, the number of noncitizens receiving SSI dropped from more than 785,000 in 1995 to less than 500,000 in 2017, reducing the overall percentage of SSI recipients who are noncitizens from 12 percent to 7 percent.[375] The 1996 act maintained SSI eligibility for American Indians born in Canada who were admitted to the United States under Section 289 of the Immigration and Nationality Act, and for noncitizen members of a federally recognized tribe under Section 4(e) of the Indian Self-Determination Act.[376]

Certain other categories of immigrants still qualify for SSI, including the following:

1. Lawful permanent residents ("green card" holders) who were lawfully residing in the United States on August 22, 1996, if blind or disabled;[377]
2. Persons who were lawfully residing in the United States on August 22, 1996 (including persons who are "permanently residing under color of law") and were receiving SSI on that date;[378]

3. Lawful permanent residents who have accumulated 40 calendar quarters of work covered by the Social Security system or can be credited with 40 quarters based on the work of a spouse or parent;[379]
4. Noncitizens lawfully residing in the United States who are active duty members of the U.S. armed forces or honorably discharged veterans, or the spouse or unmarried dependent children of such individuals;[380] and
5. Certain immigrant spouses or children who suffered domestic violence in the United States.[381]

In addition, certain noncitizens may receive SSI, but only for seven years following the granting of their immigration status:[382]

1. Refugees under Section 207 of the Immigration and Nationality Act;
2. Asylees under Section 208 of the Immigration and Nationality Act;
3. Persons granted withholding of deportation or removal under Section 241(b)(3) of the Immigration and Nationality Act;
4. Cuban or Haitian entrants pursuant to Section 501(e) of the Refugee Education Assistance Act of 1980; and
5. "Amerasian entrants" pursuant to P.L. 100-202, with a class of admission of AM-1 through AM-8.[383]

Further, certain victims of human trafficking, admitted to the United States under the Victims of Trafficking and Violence Protection Act of 2000, are not considered "qualified aliens," but may be eligible for SSI upon certification of such status by the U.S. Department of Health and Human Services and in possession of a valid "T" nonimmigrant visa.[384]

In addition, any Iraqi or Afghan national admitted to the United States as a special immigrant may qualify for seven years of SSI benefits if the person served as a translator or interpreter for the U.S. Armed Forces in Iraq or Afghanistan or worked for the U.S. government in Iraq.[385]

How much income can an individual have and still be eligible for SSI?

SSI is a needs-based program. To be eligible for SSI, the applicant's "countable income" cannot exceed the maximum SSI grant level for a person in the applicant's category. "Countable income" means total income minus any allowable exclusions and deductions.[386] As discussed later, an SSI grant is calculated by subtracting the applicant's "countable income" from the maximum applicable SSI grant.[387]

What is income for purposes of SSI?

Federal regulations state that "income" means "anything you receive in cash or in kind that you can use to meet your needs for food and shelter."[388] The Social Security Administration considers three kinds of income when determining the applicant's eligibility and the amount of SSI payable:

1. Cash income, whether earned or unearned. "Earned income" refers to cash or goods received in exchange for work, and includes gross income from wages, certain royalties and honoraria, net earnings from self-employment, and payments for services performed in a sheltered workshop.[389] "Unearned income" refers to other cash or goods that are received (for example, interest on a savings account).[390]
2. "In-kind" income, which means noncash food, clothing, or shelter given to the applicant, or some other noncash benefit that can be used to obtain food, clothing, or shelter.[391]
3. Income received by another person but that the Social Security Administration "deems" available to the applicant; for example, the income of a relative who is legally responsible for the applicant.[392]

Are any cash payments or goods not treated as income for SSI?

Cash payments or goods that are not food or shelter and cannot be used to obtain food or shelter are not "income" for purposes of SSI.[393] In addition, cash or goods received from the sale or exchange of property are not income, although they may be considered "resources"[394] (as discussed later in this chapter). Federal law specifically excludes a wide variety of payments from the definition of income,[395] including the following:

Medical care and services: (1) medical care and services received for free or at a reduced rate, including room and board during any medical confinement; (2) cash received under a medical program or health insurance policy to reimburse the claimant for health services already purchased; (3) medical program or health insurance payments that can be used only for medical services; (4) direct payments of health insurance premiums by a third party on behalf of the claimant; (5) assistance in cash or in kind received from a government program designed to provide medical or vocational care or services; (6) in-kind assistance, other than food or shelter, received from a nongovernmental program designed to provide medical or vocational care or services;[396] and (7) payments from the U.S. Department of Veterans Affairs for unusual medical expenses;[397]

Social services: (1) assistance in cash or in kind received from a governmental program designed to provide social services; (2) in-kind assistance, other than food or shelter, received from a nongovernmental program designed to provide social services; (3) cash assistance received from a nongovernmental social services program to pay for services (for example, homemaker services) other than food or shelter;[398]

Income tax refunds and certain tax credits: refunds of taxes already paid, earned income tax credits, and child tax credits;[399]

Payments by credit life or credit disability insurance: payments made by a credit life or disability policy after the claimant has become disabled for, as an example, a home mortgage, are excluded from income, as is the increased equity in the home;[400]

Proceeds of a loan;[401]

Bills paid for the claimant: if a friend, relative, or other person pays a bill for the claimant, the payment is not income for purposes of SSI, with a few exceptions. If the paid bill was for food or shelter, those goods will be considered in-kind income and may affect the amount of the SSI grant. If the paid bill was for something other than food or shelter, the payment does not count as income at all and does not affect the SSI grant amount;[402]

Educational grants or loans to undergraduate students made or insured under programs administered by the U.S. Secretary of Education and any portion of a grant, scholarship, fellowship, or gift used or set aside for paying tuition, fees, or other necessary educational expenses;[403]

Certain income earned by a student under age 22: in 2018, the first $1,850 per month, up to an annual maximum of $7,350, was not counted as income for determining SSI eligibility or grant amount. The exclusion amount is recalculated annually;[404]

Interest or other earnings from past-due SSI payments made to a child under age 18: earnings from past-due SSI payments made to a child under age 18 do not count as income if the payments are placed in a dedicated account to be used only for the child's educational and training expenses, medical expenses, and certain expenses related to the child's disability, including personal needs assistance, special equipment, housing modification, and therapy or rehabilitation;[405]

Payments from a crime victim's compensation fund;[406]

Certain payments to members of Native American tribes;[407] and

Assistance or benefits from other federal programs: many federal laws explicitly specify that the assistance or benefits that they provide are not counted as income for SSI; the SSA maintains a list of these benefits.[408]

How is the amount of an SSI grant calculated?

The amount of an SSI grant is determined by comparing the claimant's countable income (total income minus exclusions and deductions) to the maximum SSI grant for a person in that income category. One set of exclusions and deductions applies to earned income and a different set of exclusions and deductions applies to unearned income.[409]

Important Earned Income Exclusions

- First $65 of earned income plus one-half of the remainder.
- First $30 of irregularly received earned income in a quarter.
- Earned income set aside to pursue a plan for achieving self-support by a person who is blind or disabled.
- Impairment-related work expenses.

Important Unearned Income Exclusions

- First $20 per month of unearned income.
- First $60 of infrequent or irregularly received unearned income in a quarter.
- Unearned income set aside to pursue a plan for achieving self-support by a person who is blind or disabled.
- Value of SNAP, WIC, and HUD rent subsidies, and any state assistance payments based on need.

What is an approved plan for achieving self-support?

An SSI claimant who is blind or disabled may request that the Social Security Administration help design a "plan to achieve self-support," also known as a PASS plan.[410] PASS plans allow blind or disabled claimants to accumulate income and savings while receiving SSI. The goal of a PASS plan is to enable the claimant to re-enter the workforce. For example, it might be possible that additional education, training, therapy, or resources would enable the claimant to work and achieve self-support. If the Social Security Administration approves a PASS plan, it will allow the claimant to set aside income or resources to carry out the plan, which can include such goals as paying tuition or setting up a business. Income or resources set aside and used to fulfill an approved PASS plan are not counted in determining SSI eligibility or grant amount.[411]

A PASS plan will be approved if certain conditions are met. Among those conditions, the plan must be in writing; it must be specifically designed for the claimant; the plan must be for an initial period of no more than 18 months (although the Social Security Administration may provide an extension of up to 48 months); the plan must state the claimant's specific occupational goal (for example, what job the claimant hopes to do); the plan must state the claimant's income and resources and how they will be used to fulfill the plan; and the plan must show how moneys used for this purpose will be kept separate from the claimant's other funds.[412]

If an individual receives food or shelter from a friend or relative, does that affect SSI eligibility and grant levels?

If a claimant receives food or shelter paid for by another person, the Social Security Administration will count the value of the items as "in-kind income" for purposes of determining SSI eligibility and grant levels.[413] "Shelter" includes room, rent, mortgage payments, property taxes, water, energy costs, sewerage, and garbage collection fees.[414] The SSA uses two rules to determine the dollar value of food, clothing, or shelter that is given to an SSI claimant: the "one-third reduction rule" and the "presumed value rule."

What is the one-third reduction rule?

The one-third reduction rule is used to determine the value of food or shelter if the claimant lives in the household of a person who pays for the claimant's food and shelter (subject to an exception described below).[415] Under this rule, the Social Security Administration does not calculate the actual dollar value of the food and shelter given to the claimant, but rather deems those items to be worth one-third of the federal SSI benefit rate and reduces the grant by that amount.[416] If the SSA applies the one-third reduction rule, it will not count any other in-kind support in determining SSI eligibility or calculating benefit level. However, cash that the claimant receives still counts as income, subject to the regular exclusions and deductions.[417]

Exceptions:

The one-third reduction rule does *not* apply if the person who pays for the claimant's food and shelter is the claimant's spouse, minor child, or parent or other person who is ineligible for SSI and whose income under law is deemed to be available to the claimant (for example, the sponsor of an immigrant or an essential person who lives with an SSI recipient).[418]

The one-third rule also does not apply if (1) all members of the household in which the claimant resides receive some form of cash public assistance;[419] (2) the claimant resides in a "noninstitutional care situation," which includes foster care and family care;[420] (3) the claimant pays at least a pro rata share of household operating expenses;[421] or (4) the claimant, a spouse who lives with the claimant, or any person whose income is deemed to be available to the claimant has an ownership interest in the home or is liable to the landlord for any part of the rent.[422]

What is the presumed value rule?

The Social Security Administration uses the "presumed value rule" to determine the value of in-kind support or maintenance for food or shelter whenever the "one-third reduction rule" does not apply.[423] Under this rule, the presumed value of such in-kind support is deemed to be one-third of the federal SSI benefit rate plus $20.[424] However, the SSA must give the claimant a chance to show that the actual value of the in-kind shelter or food is less than the presumed value, and in such circumstances, only the actual value may be counted as income in determining the claimant's eligibility and grant level.[425]

Does the income of a claimant's family or an immigrant claimant's sponsor count in determining SSI eligibility and grant levels?

It depends. Under certain circumstances, the Social Security Administration will assume that some portion of a relative's or sponsor's income is available to support an SSI claimant. When this assumption is made, the SSA will "deem" that income to the claimant and count it when determining eligibility and benefit levels.[426] Federal law provides for the "deeming of income" to an SSI claimant in the following situations.

The Claimant Lives with a Spouse
Certain income of a spouse who lives with the claimant is deemed available to the claimant and counted as income for eligibility and grant levels provided that the spouse is not eligible for SSI and the spouse's income comes from sources other than public assistance.[427] Two people are considered spouses for SSI purposes if (1) they are legally married under the laws of their state of residence (all states must recognize same-sex marriages); or (2) one person is entitled to Title II (Social Security) benefits as the spouse of the other; or (3) the two people live together and hold themselves out to the community as a married couple.[428] Attributing the income of a spouse to the claimant may reduce the amount of the SSI grant or even make a disabled spouse financially ineligible for SSI.

A Parent Lives with a Claimant Who Is under Age 18

Certain income of a parent who lives with a claimant who is under age 18 may be deemed available to the claimant if the parent is not eligible for SSI, depending on the amount and source of the parent's income.[429] There are exceptions to this rule, including the following.

Child subject to personal needs allowance. If a child becomes a resident of a medical treatment facility and the federal benefit rate of $30 applies, the SSA will not deem the income of ineligible parents to determine the child's SSI eligibility beginning with the first month in which the $30 benefit rate applies.[430]

Ineligible parent becomes eligible. If a parent becomes eligible for SSI, the parent's income will not be deemed available to the child, beginning with the parent's first month of SSI eligibility.[431]

A Sponsored Immigrant

Certain income of the sponsor of a lawful permanent resident ("green card" holder) may be deemed to the immigrant for three years after admission to the United States for permanent residence,[432] whether or not the sponsor lives with the immigrant.[433] However, none of the sponsor's income will be deemed if any of the following exceptions applies:

1. The claimant became blind or disabled after admission to the United States;[434]
2. The claimant was granted political asylum or refugee status;[435]
3. The sponsor is an organization, not an individual;[436] or
4. The claimant worked in the United States for the equivalent of 40 qualifying quarters in the Social Security system, or can be credited with 40 quarters of coverage based on the claimant's work plus the work of the claimant's spouse and/or parents.[437]

In addition, sponsor income will not be deemed for a period of 12 months if the claimant or the claimant's child has been battered or subjected to "extreme cruelty" in the United States by the claimant's spouse or parent (or their family while residing with the claimant), and the Social Security Administration decides that there is a "substantial connection" between the claimant's need for assistance and the battering or cruelty. Under the battery exception, the deeming rule "can be suspended for 12 months," and after 12 months, the exception can be continued if the immigrant shows that the battery or abuse has been recognized by an administrative or judicial order (such as an order of protection from family court, or in a determination by the Immigration and Naturalization Service, for example, an approval of a "battered spouse waiver" or self-petition authorized under the Violence Against Women Act (VAWA)).[438] Lastly, if the claimant will not be able to afford food and shelter without SSI, the SSA will not deem the sponsor's income for 12 months, and then will deem only those amounts that the sponsor actually gives to the claimant.[439]

Can a claimant have savings or other assets and still be eligible for SSI?

To qualify for SSI, a claimant may not have savings or other "resources" that exceed federal limits. In 2019, the resource cap was $2,000 for an individual and $3,000 for a couple.[440] These resource limits have been the same since January 1, 1989, despite increases in the cost of living during the intervening decades. Because retirement plans count toward asset limits, it is very difficult for an SSI recipient to save for retirement (or maintain a retirement plan) and continue to receive benefits.

What is a "resource" for purposes of SSI and how is it different from a "countable resource"?

Federal law defines "resource" as cash, other liquid assets, and any property that the claimant or spouse owns and can convert to cash.[441] Only "countable" resources are considered for SSI eligibility purposes. As discussed later, many items, including a home, a car, child tax credits and earned income tax credits in the month received, certain housing assistance, educational loans and grants, and a burial fund of up to $1,500, are excluded.[442]

Do the resources of persons other than the claimant count in determining the claimant's SSI eligibility?

It depends. As with the deeming of income, certain resources of third parties may be deemed available to the claimant and considered when determining the claimant's eligibility for SSI.[443] Resources of a third party, unless they are "excluded" resources under the Social Security Act or other federal law, will be deemed available to a claimant in these circumstances:

The Claimant Lives with a Spouse
The countable resources of a spouse who lives with the claimant and who is not eligible for SSI will be deemed available to the claimant, except for the spouse's pension or retirement funds.[444] The rules for who is considered a spouse of an

SSI claimant are the same as the rules that apply to deeming of spousal income, as discussed earlier.[445]

A Parent Lives with a Claimant Who Is under Age 18

The countable resources of a parent who is not eligible for SSI and who lives with a claimant under the age of 18 may be deemed available to the claimant,[446] except for the parent's pension or retirement funds.[447] If the claimant lives with one parent, the amount by which the parent's countable resources exceed the SSI annual resource limit for an individual will be deemed available to the child. If the claimant lives with two parents, the amount by which the parents' combined countable resources exceed the SSI limit for couples will be deemed available to the child.[448] The SSA will not deem resources available to a disabled child if: (1) the child previously received an SSI "personal needs allowance" while residing in a medical facility; (2) Medicaid paid more than 50 percent of the cost of the child's care in the facility; (3) the child is now eligible for Medicaid for home care; and (4) deeming of the parent's would render the child ineligible for SSI.[449]

A Sponsored Immigrant

The countable resources of the sponsor of an immigrant who is a lawful permanent resident generally may be deemed for purposes of SSI eligibility for three years after the claimant has been admitted to the United States,[450] but resources are not deemed if:

1. The claimant became blind or disabled after admission to the United States;[451]
2. The claimant was granted political asylum or refugee status;[452]
3. The sponsor is an organization, not an individual;[453]
4. The claimant worked in the United States for the equivalent of 40 qualifying quarters in the Social Security system, or can be credited with 40 quarters of coverage based on the claimant's work plus the work of the claimant's spouse and/or parents.[454]

Moreover, even if none of these exceptions apply, the SSA may decide not to deem resources available upon a showing of indigence or extreme abuse:

1. *Indigence*: If the claimant will not be able to afford food and shelter without SSI, the SSA will not deem the third party's resources for 12 months, and then will deem only those amounts that the third party actually gives to the claimant. After 12 months, the resources will be deemed to the immigrant.[455]

2. *Extreme abuse*: If the claimant and/or claimant's child has been battered or subjected to "extreme cruelty" in the United States by the claimant's spouse or parent or family members while residing with them, and the SSA finds a "substantial connection" between the need for assistance and the battering or cruelty,[456] then resources will not be deemed for 12 months. In addition, the batterer's resources will never be deemed to the claimant if the battering or cruelty has been recognized in an administrative or judicial order, such as an order of protection from family court, or in a determination by the Immigration and Naturalization Service (for example, approval of a "battered spouse" waiver or self-petition), provided the claimant does not live with the batterer.[457]

What resources are not counted in determining SSI eligibility?

Federal law excludes many items from the definition of countable resources for purposes of determining SSI eligibility, including:

The claimant's home. The claimant's home is not counted as a resource, regardless of how much it is worth.[458] A home includes the house, co-op, or condominium that is the claimant's principal place of residence.[459] To be excluded, the claimant need not be living in the home, as long as there is intent to return. Moreover, if the claimant is living in a nursing home or other institution, the home does not count, whatever the claimant's intention, if the claimant's spouse or other dependent lives in the home.

The claimant's household goods and personal effects. Household goods are items found in or near the home that are used on a regular basis and items needed by the householder for maintenance, use, and occupancy of the premises. Personal effects are items of personal property ordinarily worn or carried by the individual and articles otherwise having an intimate relation to the individual. None of these are counted as resources.[460]

The claimant's car or other motor vehicle. An automobile does not count as a resource, regardless of its value, if the claimant or a member of the claimant's household uses the vehicle for transportation.[461] An automobile not used for transportation is counted as a nonliquid resource[462] to the extent that its current market value exceeds $4,500.[463]

Property used for self-support. Property used to produce income, such as land, equipment, or tools, is excluded up to $6,000 if it produces income equal to at least 6 percent of the equity excluded;[464] and property used to produce goods or services necessary for the daily activities of the claimant's household, such as livestock or land, is excluded up to $6,000.[465]

Resources used for a plan to achieve self-support. Resources of a claimant who is blind or disabled used to carry out an approved plan to achieve self-support are not counted.[466]

Life insurance. Life insurance policies with a face value that does not exceed $1,500 for any insured person do not count as resources. If the life insurance exceeds this limit, the cash surrender value (the amount the insurance company will pay upon cancellation of the policy) will be counted as a resource. Term insurance and burial insurance are not considered in determining face value.[467]

Burial plots and funds. Burial spaces, crypts, headstones, containers, and similar items and services for the claimant, claimant's spouse, and members of the immediate family do not count as a resource. In addition, burial funds of up to $1,500 each for the claimant and the claimant's spouse, if clearly designated for this purpose, are not counted. In addition, the interest that accrues for the burial fund will not count as a resource, provided it is retained in the burial fund, even if it pushes the value of the fund above the $1,500 per person limit.[468]

Retroactive Social Security or SSI payments. Retroactive Social Security or SSI payments are not counted as resources for nine months from the date of receipt.[469] At the end of nine months, any part of the retroactive payments that have not been spent will count as a resource.[470] However, retroactive payments made to a claimant under age 18 and placed in a dedicated account used solely for the child's educational and training expenses, medical expenses, and certain expenses related to the child's disability (including special equipment, housing modification, and therapy) are not counted as resources and continue to be excluded until depleted or eligibility is terminated.[471]

Certain benefits from other programs. Federal law excludes some government benefits from resources for SSI eligibility and grant levels, including:[472]

1. SNAP benefits ("food stamps");[473]
2. WIC coupons;[474]
3. Federally donated foods;[475]
4. Meals provided under the National School Lunch and Breakfast Programs;[476]
5. Home Energy Assistance payments;[477]
6. Federal housing assistance;[478]
7. Certain grants or loans to undergraduates made or insured through a program administered by the U.S. Secretary of Education;[479]
8. Distributions made to Native Americans from certain claim funds, judgments, and land trusts;[480]
9. Payments from the Agent Orange Settlement Fund;[481]

10. Payments made under Section 6 of the Radiation Exposure Compensation Act;[482]
11. Assistance received on account of a major disaster;[483]
12. Land allotted to a member of a federally recognized Indian tribe that cannot be sold without permission of other individuals, the tribe, or the federal government;[484] and
13. Cash or goods received to replace lost, damaged, or stolen goods that otherwise are excluded as resources.[485]

Can an individual reduce countable resources to qualify for SSI?

It depends. Generally, a claimant may not give or transfer excess countable resources to another person in order to become eligible for SSI. However, there are a few legal steps that can be taken to meet eligibility requirements.

Transfer Assets to a Third Party
If a claimant sells or transfers countable resources to another person at a price that is below market value, an amount equal to the difference between the fair market value and the compensation received will be counted as a resource for 24 months from the date of transfer (this amount is called the uncompensated value).[486] If the resource was partially excludable, then only the portion of the uncompensated value that is greater than the value of the noncountable resource will be treated as a countable resource at the time of transfer.[487] In addition, the uncompensated value of a transferred resource will not be counted for a given month when doing so would cause undue hardship to the claimant.[488] Keep in mind that a spouse's transfer of assets to another spouse, or a child's transfer of assets to a parent, will not affect eligibility because the resources of a spouse or parent are deemed available to the claimant.[489] In addition, transferring resources may result in the claimant's temporary disqualification from the Medicaid program and prevent assistance for nursing home or other long-term care. In any event, it is important to maintain records of all resources that are transferred.

Spend the Resources on Basic Expenses
A claimant can spend excess countable resources to pay for basic expenses, such as everyday living expenses, to pay tuition for schooling, or to repay debts. Once the resources are "spent down," they no longer count for SSI purposes.[490]

Use the Excess Resource to Acquire Noncountable Resources
A claimant can use countable resources to acquire assets that do not count as resources for SSI purposes. For instance, cash in a bank account counts as a resource for SSI, but if spent to buy a car used by a claimant for transportation, or to purchase

a home, or to pay a mortgage on an existing home, the resulting equity interest will not count as a resource (subject to some caps for particular items as discussed earlier in this chapter). It is important to keep receipts and to track the funds that are spent, because the Social Security Administration may ask for such proof.

Establish a Supplemental Needs Trust

A claimant can establish a "Supplemental Needs Trust," which is a discretionary trust established solely for the benefit of the claimant and usually designed to pay for goods and services not covered by government benefits. Funds placed in a qualifying trust—even if they are countable resources—do not count as a resource for purposes of SSI eligibility.[491] The trust funds may even be used to pay for daily needs, other than food and shelter (covered by SSI) or medical care (covered by Medicaid). The resource transfer may enable the claimant to qualify not only for SSI but also for Medicaid.[492]

A claimant considering the establishment of a Supplemental Needs Trust will need to consult a lawyer. A trust document must be drafted, and a trustee will be needed to manage the trust property and will be responsible for purchasing the goods and services that the claimant needs. Moreover, if the claimant qualifies for Medicaid, any funds that remain in the trust at the time of the claimant's death will be used to repay the Medicaid program for medical assistance received during the claimant's lifetime.

Sell Nonliquid Resources

Nonliquid resources include real estate, machinery, and buildings.[493] Excess nonliquid assets will bar eligibility, even though the claimant may not have enough money to live on. To deal with this problem, the Social Security Administration allows "conditional benefits": SSI is paid while the claimant attempts to sell excess nonliquid resources.[494] A claimant electing this option must agree in writing to sell property within a prescribed period.[495] (Keep in mind that real estate used as the claimant's primary residence is not a countable resource, regardless of its value.)[496] A claimant who is not able to sell real estate within nine months despite reasonable efforts can continue receiving SSI, and the Social Security Administration will only require repayment of nine months of benefits when the real estate ultimately is sold.[497]

What is the process for applying to SSI?

An applicant for SSI must complete and sign an application form.[498] Application forms can be obtained at any Social Security office. If the person applying for SSI is under age 18, mentally incompetent, or physically unable to sign the application, the Social Security Administration will accept an application signed by a responsible relative or other responsible person. A toll-free phone number is available to locate the nearest office or to arrange for an appointment: 1-800-772-1213. In most circumstances, adult disability claimants may file an application online by visiting https://www.ssa.gov/disabilityssi/.

Does the date of the application affect the SSI grant amount?

Yes. If a claimant is eligible for SSI, benefits will be paid starting the first day of the month after the date the application is filed.[499] If the claimant did not meet all conditions of eligibility on that date, benefits will be paid beginning the first day of the month after the claimant becomes eligible. Usually, the date used to determine the start month is the date the application is filed at the Social Security office or filed online.[500] However, there are some important exceptions:

Mailed applications. The postmark counts as the application date if using the date of receipt would result in a loss of benefits.[501]

Oral or written inquiries. If the claimant, the claimant's spouse, or a responsible relative or representative calls or writes to the Social Security Administration to ask about the claimant's eligibility for SSI, the Social Security Administration will send a notice explaining the need to file an application form. If the claimant files the application within 60 days of this notice, the date of the initial inquiry—whether a phone call or letter—counts as the filing date of the application.[502]

Deemed application date based on misinformation. If the claimant was unable to file an application because an employee of the Social Security Administration provided incomplete, misleading, or inaccurate information, the date of application will be the date that the misinformation was provided to the claimant.[503] To get the benefit of this date, the claimant must make a claim in writing to the Social Security Office explaining that misinformation provided by an agency employee caused a delay in the filing of the application.[504]

How long does it take the Social Security Administration to make a decision on an SSI application?

Federal law sets no limit on how long the Social Security Administration can take to determine whether a claimant is eligible for SSI. A wait of two to four months, or more, from application to initial decision is not unusual. The SSA has set a goal of holding pending initial SSI claims to 525,000, but a larger backlog continues to exist.[505]

Can an applicant receive SSI while
the application is being processed?

In some cases, if it is readily apparent that a claimant is disabled or blind the Social Security Administration may make a finding that the applicant is "presumptively disabled" and pay SSI for up to six months while the application is being processed and before there has been a formal finding of disability or blindness.[506] Federal regulations list "specific impairment categories" in which presumptive findings may be made without obtaining any medical evidence.[507]

How does an SSI applicant know when a decision
about eligibility or grant levels has been made?

The Social Security Administration must give the applicant written notice of any action it takes about eligibility or payment levels.[508] If the SSA decides to deny the application, it must give a written notice stating the reasons for the denial, including the facts and the legal basis, and explaining that the applicant has a right to appeal the negative decision within 60 days.[509] If the SSA decides that SSI should be reduced or terminated, it must give the claimant advance written notice and provide the claimant an opportunity to appeal the decision before any reduction or termination of benefits takes place; and if the claimant files an appeal within 10 days of receiving this notice, benefit payments must continue unchanged pending the appeal.[510] If the claimant appeals the decision after 10 days but within 60 days of the notice, the claimant will be required to show good cause to secure continuation or reinstatement of payment.[511]

What is an appeal?

An appeal is a legal opportunity to challenge a negative decision that the Social Security Administration has taken with respect to eligibility or grant levels.[512] Any person who has applied for SSI, or any person currently receiving benefits, who has received a negative "initial determination" may file an appeal.[513] An "initial determination" is any decision made by the Social Security Administration that has an effect on eligibility or coverage, including decisions made about continuing eligibility for benefits, whether the claimant is disabled, whether an overpayment of benefits must be repaid, or whether penalties shall be imposed for failure to report important information. In most cases it is worthwhile to file an appeal. The Social Security Administration is a large bureaucracy and mistakes happen. The SSI appeals process is detailed and goes through different levels of review within the agency.[514] Appeals may be filed in writing at a Social Security office or at https://www.ssa.gov/benefits/disability/appeal.html.

First, if the application is denied, or benefits are reduced, suspended, or terminated, the claimant may ask the agency to reconsider its decision.[515]

Second, if the claimant is dissatisfied with the decision after reconsideration, the claimant may request a hearing before an administrative law judge (ALJ).[516]

Third, if the ALJ does not decide in the claimant's favor, the claimant may appeal that negative decision to the Social Security Administration's Appeals Council.[517]

If a claimant wins at any level of the appeal process, the process usually is over, and the claimant will receive benefits as requested.[518] If the claimant loses at all three levels, the claimant may appeal the agency's decision by filing a lawsuit in federal court.[519]

How long does the appeals process generally take?

Too long. In FY 2018, the average time to process a reconsideration request—the first and usually unsuccessful stage in the appeals process—was 103 days.[520] The delay at the administrative law judge hearing stage was far worse, an average of 595 days in FY 2018, marking a 40 percent increase in processing time from FY 2010.[521] The pending hearings backlog also increased from 705,367 cases to 858,383 cases during this same time period. In practical terms, the average disability claimant must endure nearly two years before receiving a decision through the ALJ appeal stage, leading in many cases to great hardship.[522]

Will the claimant receive benefits during the appeals process?

It depends. In appeals challenging a denial of an application for SSI, the claimant will not receive benefits during the appeals process. However, in appeals challenging a reduction, suspension, or termination of SSI, the claimant can request that benefits continue to be paid pending the outcome of the appeal. As discussed earlier, the claimant must make a request to the SSA within 10 days of receipt of the notice of the change in benefits to continue receiving benefits. If the appeal is ultimately denied, and the claimant is found not eligible, the overpayment of benefits may have to be paid back to the government.[523]

Can a lawyer or other representative help with an appeal?

Yes, the claimant can have a lawyer or other representative help at all points of the appeals process.[524] Representatives are often attorneys, but need not be.[525] If the claimant decides to have a representative, the claimant must sign and submit a written notice to the Social Security Administration appointing the representative and providing authority.[526] Representatives must abide by standards of conduct that the SSA has published.[527] A representative cannot charge for services unless and until the SSA has approved the fee.[528] Legal services organizations do not take a fee for handling appeals.

What steps must be taken to appeal an "initial determination"?

To appeal an "initial determination," the claimant or the claimant's representative must first request reconsideration within 60 days of receiving the initial determination notification.[529] A request for reconsideration may be filed in one of three ways: (1) by submitting a completed form SSA-561 (Request for Reconsideration) at the Social Security Office; (2) by submitting a completed i561 (Request for Reconsideration) online; or (3) by submitting any writing (for example, a letter, facsimile, or additional evidence) to the Social Security Administration indicating disagreement with the initial determination.[530]

When must a request for reconsideration be filed?

As noted earlier, the request for reconsideration must be filed within 60 days from the date the unfavorable determination is received.[531] It is assumed that a claimant receives a written notice from the Social Security Administration five days after the date on the notice.[532] Therefore, it is critical to file the request no later than 65 days from the date printed on the notice of the initial determination. It makes good sense to file the request earlier to avoid any disputes about whether the request is timely.[533] If the claimant does not file on time, the opportunity to appeal may be lost unless good cause for the delay can be shown.[534] Examples of good cause include serious illness of the claimant, a death in the claimant's family, the Social Security Administration providing wrong information, and mental incapacity that prevented the claimant from understanding the review process. A request for additional time to appeal must be made in writing and must describe why an appeal was not filed within the 60-day period.[535]

What is "reconsideration"?

Reconsideration is the first level of the appeal process.[536] Reconsideration of decisions concerning disability are conducted by a disability examiner and a medical or psychological consultant, or a disability hearing officer, different than the officials who made the initial determination.[537] The Social Security Administration must consider all the evidence in the record, including any newly submitted evidence, in deciding a reconsideration.

The SSA has established four procedures for deciding reconsideration requests: case review, informal conference, formal conference, and disability hearing.[538]

Case review. In a case review, the claimant is given the opportunity to present oral and written evidence. The claimant also has the right to examine the agency's files and to discuss the case with the SSA official who conducts the reconsideration. That official then makes a decision based on any information that is already in the file or newly provided.[539]

Informal conference. At an informal conference, the claimant is given a chance to examine the file, to present any additional oral or written evidence, and to bring witnesses to testify. The official conducting the informal conference must make a written record of the proceeding and include that record in the file. The official who conducts the conference makes a decision based on the evidence presented and any information already on file.[540]

Formal conference. A formal conference works the same way as an informal conference, except that the claimant may ask the Social Security Administration to subpoena (that is, to order the appearance of) witnesses and documents that help prove the claimant's case, and the claimant is given a chance to cross-examine any witnesses whose testimony is unfavorable.[541]

Disability hearing. At a disability hearing, the Social Security Administration must review the file and make sure that the medical evidence is complete and up to date.[542] The claimant may request that the Social Security Administration assist in obtaining any relevant medical information and also may submit additional evidence.[543] A hearing is conducted by a "disability hearing officer," a government employee trained to examine and evaluate medical evidence.[544] At the hearing, the claimant has the right to have the Social Security Administration subpoena documents and witnesses.[545]

The procedure used depends upon the type of decision that is being appealed. If an application is denied on medical grounds—for instance, the applicant was found not disabled—the appeal receives a case review.[546] If the application is denied on a nonmedical issue—for example, that countable income is above the SSI limit—the claimant may choose either a case review or an informal conference.[547] If the claimant already receives SSI and is appealing a decision to suspend, reduce, or terminate benefits, the claimant may choose a case review, an informal conference, or a formal conference.[548] If the reason given for stopping or reducing benefits is that the claimant is no longer blind or disabled for medical reasons, the claimant may choose to have a disability hearing.[549]

How long will the reconsideration process take?

Federal law imposes no time limits on the Social Security Administration to decide at the reconsideration stage.

How can a reconsideration decision be appealed?

A claimant who is dissatisfied with a reconsideration decision may request a hearing before an administrative law judge.[550] The request must be made in writing (including an online request) within 60 days of receipt of the adverse reconsideration decision. If the reconsideration decision upheld a reduction, suspension, or termination of SSI, the claimant can continue to receive SSI payments during the appeals process by requesting the hearing within 10 days of receiving the decision.[551]

Who is the administrative law judge?

The administrative law judge (ALJ) is an employee of the federal executive branch who is authorized to conduct hearings and render decisions on appeals concerning Social Security and SSI benefits. ALJs are legally trained, licensed attorneys, but they are not judicial officers; that is, they do not belong to the independent, judicial branch of the federal government. Rather, as officers of the executive branch who review decisions of an executive agency, ALJs act as "quasi-independent" decision makers.[552]

How are claimants notified of the time and place of the hearing?

After a request is made for a hearing before an ALJ, the Social Security Administration mails the claimant a notice announcing the time and place of the hearing. The notice is mailed at least 75 days before the hearing is scheduled.[553] Hearings are usually scheduled two to four months after a request for a hearing has been filed. After the hearing has been scheduled, the claimant may request that the time and/or place of the hearing be changed, and the request will be granted if the claimant has good cause; good cause might include the need for more time to find a representative, or if a witness with important evidence is unable to attend the hearing at the scheduled time.[554]

Are hearings held in a courthouse?

No. Hearings before the administrative law judge typically take place in small hearing rooms at a Social Security Administration office.[555] The rooms are equipped with microphones to record the proceedings. Sometimes the SSA will schedule a hearing to be conducted via video conference. This arrangement generally is not advantageous for the claimant. The claimant has 30 days from the hearing notice to object to a video hearing and demand an in-person hearing.[556] Typically, the only people present at the hearing are the ALJ, the claimant, the claimant's representative, and any witnesses. In some cases, the ALJ may arrange for a medical examiner or a vocational expert to testify. An interpreter will be present if requested by the claimant.

What rights does a claimant have at a hearing before an administrative law judge?

The ALJ has a duty to fully develop the hearing record so that it includes all evidence necessary to arrive at a fair and accurate decision. At the hearing itself, the ALJ will take the lead, asking the claimant and any witnesses questions needed to elicit testimony relevant to the issues on appeal. But the claimant also has a right to participate actively at the hearing and has other procedural rights designed to ensure the fairness of the proceedings. These procedural rights include:

- The right to request copies of the case file and examine any evidence that the Social Security Administration relied upon in making the determination;[557]
- The right to submit additional evidence and to have that evidence included in the file and considered by the ALJ;[558] but the claimant must inform the SSA of any such evidence at least five business days before the hearing, unless there is good cause for not doing so;[559]
- The right to bring witnesses to the hearing and to have them testify on the claimant's behalf;
- The right to cross-examine any witness who gives unfavorable testimony;

- The right to make a statement at the hearing or to submit a written statement explaining the claimant's position;[560]
- The right to notice if the Social Security Administration plans to have a medical expert or vocational expert testify at the hearing;
- The right to have the Social Security Administration issue subpoenas ordering witnesses to testify (for example, a treating physician) and to bring relevant documents to the hearing. The request for the subpoena must be made at least 10 days before the hearing;[561]
- The right to bring an attorney or other representative to advocate for the claimant at the hearing;[562]
- The right to have an audio recording made of the hearing so there is a complete and accurate record of the testimony and statements made;[563] and
- The right, at the conclusion of the hearing, to ask the ALJ for time to obtain and submit additional evidence.

The rules of evidence do not strictly apply at a Social Security hearing, and so the ALJ may accept evidence that would not be admissible in a court of law.[564] In addition, some courts have held that certain procedural protections, such as the right to confront and cross-examine every adverse witness, do not apply as rigidly in the Social Security context.[565] Regulations governing the hearing require the ALJ to "look[] fully into the issues, question[] [the claimant] and the other witnesses, and . . . [a]ccept[] as evidence any documents that are material to the issues."[566] "The administrative law judge may decide when the evidence will be presented and when the issues will be discussed."[567]

How should a claimant prepare for a hearing before an administrative law judge?

As a first step to preparing for a hearing, a claimant should attempt to find legal counsel or an experienced advocate to serve as a representative. Most legal aid and legal services offices have attorneys and paralegals who are experts at representing SSI claimants.[568] If assistance is not available from a legal aid or legal services office, those offices should be able to provide a referral list of other agencies or individuals who may be able to help. Because the process of finding a lawyer or representative may take time, efforts should be started early in the process. Requests to postpone a hearing may be made if there is a serious problem in finding a lawyer or representative despite good efforts.[569]

While looking for representation, a claimant can take steps to be prepared if self-representation becomes necessary. Above all, this involves gathering evidence to support the claim. For instance, if the question to be decided at the hearing is whether or not a disability exists, reports should be requested from treating physicians, as discussed earlier in this chapter. A claimant should review the file that the Social Security Administration has compiled for use at the hearing as soon as that file is available. The file contains the evidence that the Social Security Administration relied on to deny the claimant's claim. If the file is missing important evidence (for example, hospital records), the claimant should immediately request in writing that the ALJ issue a subpoena requiring whomever has the missing evidence to provide copies.[570] In addition, it may be necessary to obtain other evidence or to locate witnesses for the hearing to contest any unfavorable evidence in the file. The claimant should meet with witnesses before the hearing, both to discuss their testimony and to determine if they will come to the hearing voluntarily. If the witness will not appear voluntarily, then it is important to make a written request to the ALJ to issue a subpoena ordering the witness to appear.[571] When a subpoena is issued, the Social Security Administration pays the witness the same fees and transportation expenses that would be paid by a federal court, and will pay the claimant the cost of issuing the subpoena.[572]

Finally, the claimant should think carefully about the claimant's own testimony. The ALJ will ask a series of questions at the hearing, and the claimant's answers may provide some of the most important evidence in the case. For instance, if the issue to be decided is whether or not the claimant is disabled, the ALJ will ask questions about medical conditions and how they limit the ability to function. The claimant likely will be asked to describe daily activities, including the ability to do household chores, to shop for groceries, to take public transportation, and so forth. It is important to describe in detail the symptoms of all medical conditions, including pain and side effects of medication. The claimant should be prepared to describe how medical conditions impact the ability to do activities such as lifting, carrying, pulling, pushing, reaching, handling, sitting, standing, walking, seeing, hearing, speaking, understanding, carrying out and remembering instructions, and working with others in a regular job setting or in doing jobs that the claimant previously had.

How does the administrative law judge evaluate evidence from the claimant's treating physicians?

Different rules apply to claims filed before and after March 27, 2017.

For claims filed on or before March 27, 2017, the administrative law judge will apply the "treating source" rule, which requires that "controlling weight" be given to the opinion of the claimant's own medical source "of the nature and severity" of the claimant's impairment if the opinion "is well-supported by medically acceptable clinical and laboratory diagnostic techniques and is not inconsistent with the other substantial evidence in [the] case record."[573] The length of the treatment relationship is significant.

For claims filed after March 27, 2017, a different regulation applies.[574] The administrative law judge "will not defer or give any specific evidentiary weight, including controlling weight, to any medical opinion(s) or prior administrative medical finding(s), including those from [the claimant's] . . . medical sources." Instead, the weight given to the opinion of the claimant's treating physician will depend upon a number of factors, including:

- The length of the treatment relationship;
- Extent and purpose of treatment relationship, and frequency of examinations;
- The extent to which the physician's opinion is supported by "objective medical evidence";
- The extent to which the physician's opinion is consistent with "evidence from other medical sources and nonmedical sources"; and
- The physician's expertise in the relevant area and familiarity with other evidence in the claimant's case.

Claimants should consider these factors when gathering medical evidence for a hearing.

How does the claimant learn what the administrative law judge has decided?

The ALJ prepares a written decision and mails a copy of the decision to all the parties.[575] The ALJ must issue the decision within 90 days of the claimant's request for a hearing unless a postponement of the hearing was requested or the question to be decided was whether the claimant is disabled.[576]

Can an unfavorable administrative law judge decision be appealed?

Yes. If the claimant disagrees with the ALJ's decision, the claimant has 60 days from receipt of the decision to request review by the Appeals Council.[577] The form to request such review is available online and at a local Social Security office. The completed form is to be signed and mailed to the Appeals Council.[578] Any additional evidence may be submitted with the request for review.[579] The Appeals Council is headquartered in Falls Church, Virginia, and is composed of administrative law judges employed by the Social Security Administration.[580] Upon reviewing the record, the Appeals Council may affirm, modify, or reverse the decision of the administrative law judge.[581] In FY 2010, the Appeals Council remanded 21.77 percent of the cases reviewed; in FY 2018, the Appeals Council remanded 11.83 percent. ("Remand" means that the Appeals Council disagreed with some or all of the ALJ's decision and sent the case back to the ALJ to be reconsidered or corrected.) As these statistics show, the Appeals Council affirms a large majority of the decisions made by administrative law judges.[582] Even though the chances of succeeding at the Appeals Council are small, a claimant must go through this step in order to have the right to file an appeal in federal court.

How can a claimant challenge an unfavorable Appeals Council's review?

If a claimant is dissatisfied with the Appeals Council review, the claimant may request judicial review by filing an action in federal district court.[583] The court will uphold a decision denying benefits only "if the record as a whole is supported by substantial evidence," a standard that the federal courts treat as "less demanding than the preponderance of the evidence standard in ordinary civil lawsuits," and if the ALJ conducted the hearing in a manner that accords with the claimant's procedural rights.[584] If the court determines that a matter must be returned to the Social Security Administration for correction, it may remand for further proceedings or remand for the limited purpose of calculating benefits.

An appeal to federal court must be filed within 60 days of receiving an unfavorable decision from the Appeals Council.[585] Although some claimants file their lawsuits without the benefit of legal representation, it is best to have legal assistance. In some federal courts, a "pro se" office will provide information about how to file the suit, but will not provide legal advice. (For more information on filing an action in federal court, see chapter 9: Access to Justice: Enforcing Rights and Securing Protection.)

Generally, a federal action cannot be filed until after the claimant has received an initial decision and gone through all three levels of administrative appeal (reconsideration, ALJ hearing, and Appeals Council review). However, an exception to this rule may be available if the claimant is arguing that a regulation, policy, or procedure of the Social Security Administration is illegal or unconstitutional, or that a provision of the Social Security Act violates the U.S. Constitution. In these circumstances, it may be possible to file an action directly in federal court without first going through the administrative appeals process.[586]

Other Cash Assistance Programs
for Persons with Disabilities

Do agencies other than the federal Social Security Administration run assistance programs for persons with disabilities?

On the federal side, the U.S. Department of Veterans Affairs administers special programs for veterans who are disabled.[587]

On the state side, all 50 states require employers to participate in a workers' compensation program, which provides payments to workers who receive injuries, including disabling injuries, on the job.[588]

Some states operate Interim Assistance Programs that provide cash assistance to applicants for SSI who are waiting for approval.[589] In some states, the payments are like a loan that must be repaid or will be withheld from a retroactive payment of SSI by the federal government before making an initial SSI payment.[590]

State General Assistance

What is General Assistance?

General Assistance (GA) refers to state-run, state-funded programs that provide cash assistance to destitute people who do not qualify for federally supported assistance, such as TANF or SSI. The groups generally ineligible for federal cash benefits—and thus in need of GA—consist mostly of non-elderly adults who do not have a disability severe enough to meet the federal SSI disability standard, and who have no minor children in their care. At one time, almost every state administered a GA program of some kind. But by 2015, only 26 states and the District of Columbia funded such programs, down from 38 in 1989.[591] A number of states cut back their GA programs after enactment of the Personal Responsibility Act in 1996, when Congress replaced AFDC—which had provided a statutory entitlement to cash assistance for poor families with children— with TANF-funded discretionary programs.[592] Five states closed their programs entirely between 1998 and 2010.

Who is eligible for General Assistance?

General Assistance is a "residual program" or program of last resort; only people who are ineligible for federal cash assistance can qualify for GA. Specific eligibility criteria vary from state to state, as do benefit levels and program requirements. In every state that operates a GA program, people who do not receive SSI but who nevertheless suffer from a disability that prevents them from maintaining employment may qualify for assistance. Applicants must provide some medical documentation of their disability. The severity of the impairment needed to qualify for GA varies by state. Thirteen states require that the disability be expected to last for a specified time period.[593]

In six states, individuals who cannot work for reasons other than disability are eligible for assistance. These reasons may include limited literacy; need to care for a disabled household member; or being above age 55.[594]

In 11 states, all destitute individuals—even those who are employable—may qualify for state General Assistance.[595]

How much assistance do General Assistance programs provide?

General Assistance levels are extremely low—lower than SSI or even TANF benefits, and below the level that could support even basic subsistence needs. In all states the benefits are less than half of the poverty level, and in half of the states GA benefits are less than one-fourth of the poverty line. Many states have not increased their GA benefit grants in decades, or have enacted only small increases, leaving the real value of the grants to erode dramatically. Some programs differentiate by individual characteristics, providing lower grants to people who are not elderly or disabled.

Do states limit how long a person can receive General Assistance?

Some states set time limits on how long a person can receive benefits under the state's General Assistance program, and the limits vary from state to state. (See Table 1.1.)

- California sets a nine-month limit if the recipient is employable, but is unlimited if unemployable.
- Colorado sets a one-year lifetime limit on benefits.
- Delaware sets a two-year lifetime limit on benefits.
- New Jersey sets a five-year lifetime limit on benefits.
- Maryland sets a limit of 12 out of every 36 months on benefits unless the recipient is applying SSI.
- Utah sets a limit of 12 out of every 60 months on benefits.
- Nevada sets a limit of one, three, or six months in any year, depending on the recipient's employability.

Table 1.1 State General Assistance Programs—Monthly Cash Benefit Levels in 2015

State	Benefit Level—Maximum for one person
Alaska	$120 (need only) $280 (aged or disabled)
California	$221
Colorado	$189
Connecticut	$212
Delaware	$90
District of Columbia	$274 (aged or disabled, awaiting SSI) $418 (disabled, not SSI eligible)
Hawaii	$418 (aged or disabled)
Indiana	No maximum (need only)
Iowa	No maximum (need only)
Maine	Varies by locality (need only)
Maryland	$185
Massachusetts	$303.70
Michigan	$200
Minnesota	$203
Nebraska	Varies by locality (need only)
Nevada	$400 (employable or unemployable)
New Hampshire	Varies by county (need only) $735 (disabled terminally or for 48 months)
New Jersey	$140 (employable) $210 (unemployable)
New Mexico	$245 (unemployable, or children ineligible for TANF)
New York	Varies by county $398 (New York City)
Ohio	$115 (unemployable)
Rhode Island	$200 (awaiting SSI)
South Dakota	$350 (housing only)
Utah	$261
Vermont	Varies by county
Washington	$197

Notes

1. DeShaney v. Winnebago County Dept. of Soc. Servs., 489 U.S. 189, 196 (1989).
2. *See* Mark A. Graber, The Clintonification of American Law: Abortion, Welfare, and Liberal Constitutional Theory, 58 Ohio St. L.J. 731 (1997); Erwin Chemerinsky,

Making the Case for a Constitutional Right to Minimum Entitlements, 44 Mercer L. Rev. 525 (1993); Peter B. Edelman, The Next Century of Our Constitution: Rethinking Our Duty to the Poor, 39 Hastings L.J. 1 (1987); Charles Black, Further Reflections on the Constitutional Justice of Livelihood, 86 Colum. L. Rev. 1103 (1986); Laurence H. Tribe, Unraveling National League of Cities: The New Federalism and Affirmative Rights to Essential Government Services, 90 Harv. L. Rev. 1065, 1079 (1977); Frank I. Michelman, Foreword: On Protecting the Poor Through the Fourteenth Amendment, 83 Harv. L. Rev. 7 (1969).

3. Martha F. Davis, International Human Rights and United States Law: Predictions of a Courtwatcher, 64 Albany L. Rev. 417, 428–429 (2001).

4. International Covenant on Economic, Social and Cultural Rights, Adopted and opened for signature, ratification and accession by General Assembly Resolution 2200A (XXI) of Dec. 16, 1966, http://www.ohchr.org/EN/ProfessionalInterest/Pages/CESCR.aspx. The covenant is a multilateral treaty adopted by the United Nations General Assembly. The United States is a signatory, but has not ratified the Covenant.

5. State constitutional provisions are discussed in Elizabeth Pascal, Welfare Rights in State Constitutions, 39 Rutgers L.J. 863 (2008); Helen Hershkoff, Positive Rights and State Constitutions: The Limits of Federal Rationality Review, 112 Harv. L. Rev. 1131 (1999); Burt Neuborne, Foreword: State Constitutions and the Evolution of Positive Rights, 20 Rutgers L.J. 881, 893–895, nn.60–82 (1989). As an example, the Constitution of the Commonwealth of Puerto Rico recognizes the existence of "human rights" that include "[t]he right of every person to [a] standard of living adequate for the health and well-being of himself and his family, and especially to food, clothing, housing and medical care and necessary social services." Puerto Rico Const. Art. II, § 20. This section was excepted from the approval of the Puerto Rico Constitution by a Joint Resolution of Congress of July 3, 1952, c. 567, 66 Stat. 327. The New York State Constitution, through a provision adopted in 1938, explicitly directs the state to provide for "the aid, care, and support of the needy." New York Const. Art. XVII, §1.

6. See Heinz Klug, The Dignity Clause of the Montana Constitution: May Foreign Jurisprudence Lead the Way to an Expanded Interpretation?, 64 Mont. L. Rev. 133 (2003).

7. See Helen Hershkoff & Stephen Loffredo, State Courts and Constitutional Socioeconomic Rights: Exploring the Underutilization Thesis, 115 Penn. St. L. Rev. 923 (2011).

8. In practice, the U.S. Supreme Court has given the government a great deal of leeway in how it carries out assistance programs—leading some critics to argue that these programs sidestep important constitutional protections. See Stephen Loffredo, Poverty, Democracy and Constitutional Law, 141 U. Pa. L. Rev. 1277 (1993). See also Julie A. Nice, Whither the Canaries: On the Exclusion of Poor People from Equal Constitutional Protection, 60 Drake L. Rev. 1023 (2012); Julie A. Nice, No Scrutiny Whatsoever: Deconstitutionalization of Poverty Law, Dual Rules of Law, & Dialogic Default, 35 Fordham Urb. L.J. 629 (2008).

9. Pub. L. No. 104-193, 110 Stat. 2105 (1996).

10. For a description and critique of federal welfare reform and the Personal Responsibility Act, *see, for example*, Gwendolyn Mink, Welfare's End (Cornell 1998).

11. *See* Center on Budget and Policy Priorities, Policy Basics: An Introduction to TANF (Aug. 15, 2018), https://www.cbpp.org/research/policy-basics-an-introduction-to-tanf.

12. Subject to some federal supervision every two years, a participating state submits a "State Plan" to the federal government. The plan describes how the state has chosen to design and administer its TANF program, the policies that it is seeking to implement, and how it intends to meet federal program requirements. 42 U.S.C. § 602. States are required to report annually and quarterly on how much they spend and for what purposes. 45 C.F.R. §§ 265.1–10.

13. *See* Ife Flod, Ladonna Pavetti, Ashley Burnside, & Liz Schott, TANF Reaching Few Poor Families, Center on Budget & Policy Priorities (Nov. 2018), https://www.cbpp.org/research/family-income-support/tanf-reaching-few-poor-families; Robert Moffitt, The Role of Non-Financial Factors in Exit and Entry in the TANF Program, RAND (2003), https://www.researchgate.net/publication/5141376_The_Role_of_Nonfinancial_Factors_in_Exit_and_Entry_in_the_TANF_Program.

14. 42 U.S.C. § 603.

15. The federal TANF appropriation is $16.5 billion. *See* 42 U.S.C. § 603(a)(1)(C); *see also* Consolidated and Further Continuing Appropriations Act, Pub. L. No. 113-235, § 228, 128 Stat. 2130, 2491 (2015). For more information about how the block grant structure affects TANF benefits, *see* Congressional Research Service, Gene Falk, The Temporary Assistance for Needy Families (TANF) Block Grant: Responses to Frequently Asked Questions (Jan. 28, 2019), https://fas.org/sgp/crs/misc/RL32760.pdf.

16. *See* Center on Budget and Policy Priorities, Policy Basics: An Introduction to TANF (Aug. 15, 2018), http://www.cbpp.org/sites/default/files/atoms/files/7-22-10tanf2.pdf. Moreover, Congress has failed to reauthorize the TANF program on a permanent basis, and instead has extended it year-to-year through annual omnibus appropriations bills. *Id.*

As a condition of receiving federal TANF funds, states must contribute their own funds to support their TANF program. The required state contribution is calculated with reference to the amount the state historically spent on AFDC prior to the enactment of TANF in 1996. *See* 42 U.S.C. § 609(a)(7). This provision, known as the maintenance-of-effort requirement, adds about $10.4 billion per year in state funds to TANF programs. *See* Congressional Research Service, Gene Falk, The Temporary Assistance for Needy Families (TANF) Block Grant: Responses to Frequently Asked Questions (Jan. 28, 2019), https://fas.org/sgp/crs/misc/RL32760.pdf. However, accounting for inflation, this funding equals only about half of what states spent on assistance programs for needy families prior to the 1996 Personal Responsibility Act.

17. The Personal Responsibility Act initially provided for high-performance bonuses and made additional funding available to the states, but Congress defunded these provisions in 2005. *See* Deficit Reduction Act of 2005, Pub. L. No. 109-171, § 7101(a), 120 Stat. 4, 135 (2006). Instead, states now may apply for competitive grants of

$150 million a year to fund initiatives for specific goals—to strengthen family formation, promote healthy marriages, and support responsible fatherhood. *See id.* at § 7103, 120 Stat. at 138–140. Congress did create a $2 billion Emergency Contingency Fund for states to use for assistance programs in times of economic recession, but the fund has run out of money early in each budget year since 2010. *See* Center on Budget and Policy Priorities, Policy Basics: An Introduction to TANF, 2 (Aug. 15, 2018), http://www.cbpp.org/sites/default/files/atoms/files/7-22-10tanf2.pdf.

In 2009, during the height of the Great Recession, Congress passed a stimulus bill that appropriated $5 billion for an Emergency Fund; those funds also were exhausted by the time the appropriation expired in September 2010. *See id.* at 3. There also is a federal contingency fund that can be used if a state is deemed a "needy state." Congress appropriated $608 million in federal contingency funds for the 2016 fiscal year. Consolidated and Further Continuing Appropriations Act, Pub. L. No. 113-235, 128 Stat. 2130, 2491, § 228(b)(1) (2009). Federal law allows states to apply for and receive monthly payments from the Contingency Fund for State Welfare Programs if they are deemed a "needy state" for a month. The law defines a needy state as a state where the seasonally adjusted unemployment rate for the most recent three months is 6.5% or more, and the total unemployment rate for the three months is 110% or more than the state unemployment rate for the equivalent three months in either of the last two years in that state. Alternatively, a state may be needy if the number of individuals receiving Supplemental Nutrition Assistance Program benefits exceeds certain parameters as determined by the Secretary of Agriculture. 42 U.S.C. § 603(b)(5)(A)–(B).

18. Danilo Trisi & LaDonna Pavetti, TANF Weakening as a Safety Net for Poor Families, Center on Budget and Policy Priorities (Mar. 2012), http://www.cbpp.org/research/tanf-weakening-as-a-safety-net-for-poor-families.

19. Ife Flod, Ladonna Pavetti, Ashley Burnside, & Liz Schott, TANF Reaching Few Poor Families, Center on Budget and Policy Priorities (Nov. 2018), https://www.cbpp.org/research/family-income-support/tanf-reaching-few-poor-families. The number of families receiving federal assistance dropped from 4.43 million in 1996 (the year Congress passed the Personal Responsibility Act) to 1.48 million in 2016. *See* Congressional Research Service, Gene Falk, The Temporary Assistance for Needy Families (TANF) Block Grant: Responses to Frequently Asked Questions (Jan. 28, 2019), at 16, https://fas.org/sgp/crs/misc/RL32760.pdf.

20. For a comprehensive analysis of the AFDC program across many dimensions, *see* Winifred Bell, Aid to Dependent Children (Columbia 1965). *See also* Congressional Research Service, Gene Falk, Temporary Assistance for Needy Families (TANF): Size and Characteristics of the Cash Assistance Caseload (Jan. 29, 2016), https://www.fas.org/sgp/crs/misc/R43187.pdf.

21. *See* Frances Fox Piven & Richard A. Cloward, Regulating the Poor: The Functions of Public Welfare (Vintage 1993).

22. *See id.* at 130–145; Tonya L. Brito, From Madonna to Proletariat: Constructing a New Ideology of Motherhood in Welfare Discourse, 44 Vill. L. Rev. 415, 422–423 (1999); Gwendolyn Mink, The Lady and the Tramp: Gender, Race, and the Origins of the American Welfare State, in Women, the State, and Welfare 92 (Linda Gordon,

ed.) (Wisconsin 1990), https://muse.jhu.edu/chapter/648458; Charles A. Reich, Individual Rights and Social Welfare: The Emerging Legal Issues, 74 Yale L.J. 1245 (1965).

23. *See* Matthew Diller, Poverty Lawyering in the Golden Age, 93 Mich. L. Rev. 1401 (1995); Frances Fox Piven & Richard A. Cloward, Poor People's Movements (Vintage 1979); *see also* Martha F. Davis, Brutal Need: Lawyers and the Welfare Rights Movement, 1960–1973 (Yale 1995).

24. *See* Jill Quadagno, The Color of Welfare: How Racism Undermined the War on Poverty (Oxford 1994); Michael B. Katz, In the Shadow of the Poorhouse: A Social History of Welfare in America (Basic 1986); Congressional Research Service, Gene Falk, Temporary Assistance for Needy Families (TANF): Size and Characteristics of the Cash Assistance Caseload (2016), https://www.fas.org/sgp/crs/misc/R43187.pdf. Many recent studies have shown that racial bias persists in the administration of TANF programs across the country. *See, for example*, Ladonna Pavetti, TANF Studies Show Work Requirement Proposals for Other Programs Would Harm Millions, Do Little to Increase Work, Center on Budget and Policy Priorities (Nov. 13, 2018), https://www.cbpp.org/sites/default/files/atoms/files/11-13-18tanf.pdf.

25. *See* U.S. House of Rep., House Committee on Ways and Means, 2011 Green Book, Table 7-18: AFDC and TANF Cash Assistance Recipient Adults, By Race/Ethnicity, Selected Years, FY 1988–FY 2009, https://greenbook-waysandmeans.house.gov/sites/greenbook.waysandmeans.house.gov/files/2011/documents/Table%207-18.%20AFDC%20and%20TANF%20Cash%20Assistance%20Recipient%20Adults%2C%20by%20Race%20and%20Ethnicity%2C%20Selected%20Years%2C%20FY1988-FY2009.pdf; U.S. Census Bureau, Econ. & Statistics Admin., U.S. Department of Commerce, Statistical Brief, Mothers Who Receive AFDC Payments: Fertility and Socioeconomic Characteristics (Mar. 1995), https://www.census.gov/population/socdemo/statbriefs/sb2-95.html.

26. *See* Joe Soss, Richard C. Fording, & Sanford F. Schram, Disciplining the Poor: Neoliberal Paternalism and the Persistent Power of Race (Chicago 2011); Gene Falk, Maggie McCarty, & Randy Alison Aussenberg, Work Requirements, Time Limits, and Work Incentives in TANF, SNAP, and Housing Assistance 2–4 (Feb. 12, 2014), https://greenbook-waysandmeans.house.gov/sites/greenbook.waysandmeans.house.gov/files/R43400_gb.pdf.

27. *See* Jill Quadagno, The Color of Welfare: How Racism Undermined the War on Poverty (Oxford 1994); Loic Wacquant, Punishing the Poor: The Neoliberal Government of Social Insecurity (Duke 2009).

28. *See* Barbara Vobejda, Clinton Signs Welfare Bill Amid Division, Washington Post A01 (Aug. 23, 1996), http://www.washingtonpost.com/wp-srv/politics/special/welfare/stories/wf082396.htm; *see also* Alana Semuels, The End of Welfare as We Know It: America's Once-Robust Safety Net Is No More, The Atlantic (Apr. 1, 2016), http://www.theatlantic.com/business/archive/2016/04/the-end-of-welfare-as-we-know-it/476322/.

29. 42 U.S.C. § 601(b) ("This part shall not be interpreted to entitle any individual or family to assistance under any State program funded under this part.").

30. *See* Ife Floyd, Ashley Burnside & Liz Schott, TANF Reaching Fewer Poor Families, Center on Budget and Policy Priorities (Nov. 28, 2018), https://www.cbpp.org/research/family-income-support/tanf-reaching-few-poor-families; Congressional Research Service, Gene Falk, Temporary Assistance for Needy Families (TANF): Size of the Population Eligible for and Receiving Cash Assistance (Jan. 3, 2017), https://fas.org/sgp/crs/misc/R44724.pdf; U.S. Government Accountability Office, Temporary Assistance for Needy Families: Fewer Eligible Families Have Received Cash Assistance Since the 1990s and the Recession's Impact on Caseloads Varies by State (2010), http://www.gao.gov/new.items/d10164.pdf.

31. *See* Congressional Research Service, Gene Falk, Temporary Assistance for Needy Families (TANF): Size and Characteristics of the Cash Assistance Caseload (Jan. 26, 2016), at 5, https://www.fas.org/sgp/crs/misc/R43187.pdf.

32. Separate grants are provided to the territories and tribal organizations that choose to establish TANF programs. *See* 45 C.F.R. Part 286.

33. U.S. Department of Health and Human Services, Office of Family Assistance, Help for Families, http://www.acf.hhs.gov/programs/ofa/help.

34. Christine Heffernan, Benjamin Goehring, Ian Hecker, Linda Giannarelli, & Sarah Minton (Linda Giannerelli & Sarah Minton, Project Directors), Welfare Rules Databook: State TANF Policies as of July 2017, OPRE Report 2018-109, Washington, DC: Office of Planning, Research, and Evaluation, Administration for Children and Families, U.S. Department of Health & Human Servs., https://www.acf.hhs.gov/opre/resource/welfare-rules-databook-state-tanf-policies-as-of-july-2017 (hereinafter "2017 Welfare Rules Databook").

35. 42 U.S.C. § 604(a)(1).

36. Congressional Research Service, Gene Falk, The Temporary Assistance for Needy Families (TANF) Block Grant: Responses to Frequently Asked Questions (Jan. 28, 2019), at 5, https://fas.org/sgp/crs/misc/RL32760.pdf.

37. *See* Center on Budget and Policy Priorities, Policy Basics: An Introduction to TANF (Aug. 15, 2018), http://www.cbpp.org/sites/default/files/atoms/files/7-22-10tanf2.pdf.

38. *See* Ashley Burnside & Ife Floyd, TANF Benefits Remain Low Despite Recent Increases in Some States, Center on Budget and Policy Priorities 1, 5 (Jan. 22, 2019), http://www.cbpp.org/sites/default/files/atoms/files/10-30-14tanf.pdf.

39. 45 C.F.R. § 260.31(a)(1).

40. 45 C.F.R. § 260.31.

41. 45 C.F.R. § 604(a)(1).

42. 42 U.S.C. § 604(a)(2).

43. 42 U.S.C. § 604(f).

44. 42 U.S.C. 604(h). Individual development accounts are intended to allow individuals to accumulate funds for postsecondary educational expenses, first home purchase, or business capital. *See* 45 C.F.R. § 604(h)(2)(b).

45. 42 U.S.C. § 604(k).

46. 42 U.S.C. § 604(d). In recent years, Child Care and Development Block Grant programs reached only about 15% of eligible families, though funding increases in 2018 may improve coverage. *See* Gina Adams, A historic boost to child care funding means states can start to realize the potential of the Child Care and Development Block Grant, Urban Inst. (Feb. 15, 2018), https://www.urban.org/urban-wire/historic-boost-child-care-funding-means-states-can-start-realize-potential-child-care-and-development-block-grant.

47. Center on Budget and Policy Priorities, Chart Book: Temporary Assistance for Needy Families (Aug. 21, 2018), https://www.cbpp.org/research/family-income-support/chart-book-temporary-assistance-for-needy-families. *See* Congressional Research Service, Gene Falk, The Temporary Assistance for Needy Families (TANF) Block Grant: Responses to Frequently Asked Questions (Jan. 28, 2019), https://fas.org/sgp/crs/misc/RL32760.pdf.

48. Center on Budget and Policy Priorities, Chart Book: Temporary Assistance for Needy Families 6 (Aug. 21, 2018), https://www.cbpp.org/research/family-income-support/chart-book-temporary-assistance-for-needy-families.

49. *See* Center for Women's Welfare, Self-Sufficiency Standard, http://www.selfsufficiencystandard.org (providing state specific calculations of income required to meet basic needs at a minimally adequate level).

50. Center on Budget and Policy Priorities, Chart Book: Temporary Assistance for Needy Families 6 (Aug. 21, 2018), https://www.cbpp.org/research/family-income-support/chart-book-temporary-assistance-for-needy-families.

51. Timothy Smeeding & Celine Thevenot, Addressing Child Poverty: How Does the United States Compare with Other Nations?, 16 Academic Pediatrics S67 (2016), https://www.ncbi.nlm.nih.gov/pmc/articles/PMC6087662/.

52. 42 U.S.C. § 602(a)(1)(A)(viii).

53. For a chart of state issuance practices, *see* 2017 Welfare Rules Databook, Table II.A.6. Benefit Issuance Policies, July 2017.

54. *See* 2017 Welfare Rules Databook, at 11.

55. 2017 Welfare Rules Databook, Table I.A.1. Formal Diversion Payments, July 2017.

56. 42 U.S.C. § 608(a)(1). This does not mean that all needy families with children qualify. For instance, some states do not permit two-parent households to receive cash benefits under their TANF programs. *See* 2017 Welfare Rules Databook, Table I.B.2. Eligibility Rules for Two-Parent Nondisabled Applicant Units, July 2017. *See also* Elizabeth Lower-Basch, TANF 101: Cash Assistance, Center for Law & Social Policy (Apr. 2019), https://www.clasp.org/sites/default/files/publications/2019/04/2019_tanf101_cashassistance.pdf.

57. 2017 Welfare Rules Databook, at 25–34.

58. 42 U.S.C. § 602(a)(1)(B)(iii).

59. 42 U.S.C. § 608(a)(10)(A).

60. 42 U.S.C. § 608(a)(10)(B).

61. 42 U.S.C. § 608(a)(10)(C).

62. *See* Olivia Golden & Amelia Hawkins, TANF Child-Only Cases, Urban Institute (Jan. 2012), https://www.acf.hhs.gov/sites/default/files/opre/child_only.pdf. The rules for considering parental income in determining eligibility and grant amount

for child-only cases vary by state. *See, for example,* 2017 Welfare Rules Databook, Table I.D.4. Treatment of Income of Parents Excluded from the Assistance Unit Due to Immigrant Status, July 2017.

63. *See* Congressional Research Service, Gene Falk, Temporary Assistance for Needy Families (TANF): Size and Characteristics of the Case Assistance Caseload (Jan. 29, 2016), https://fas.org/sgp/crs/misc/R43187.pdf (reporting that 38% of the TANF caseload nationally was "child only" in FY 2013).

64. 2017 Welfare Rules Databook, Table L3. Maximum Income for Initial Eligibility for a Family of Three, 1996–2017. For example, in California the eligibility amount differs depending on whether the applicant lives in an urban county (Region I) or a rural county (Region II). Cal. Department of Soc. Servs., Family Engagement & Empowerment Div., California Families on the Road to Self-Sufficiency: Annual Summary 26 (Feb. 2018), http://www.cdss.ca.gov/Portals/9/CalWORKs/CW%20Annual%20Summary_January%202018%20Final%203.28.18.pdf?ver=2018-04-02-093852-433.

65. 2017 Welfare Rules Databook, Table I.E.2. Earned Income Disregards for Initial Eligibility Purpose, July 2017; Table II.A.1 Earned Income Disregards for Benefit Computation, July 2017.

66. 2017 Welfare Rules Databook, Table L3. Maximum Income for Initial Eligibility for a Family of Three, 1996–2017 (July).

67. 2017 Welfare Rules Databook, Table I.C.1. Asset Limits for Applicants, July 2017. Asset limits for TANF have been criticized for depriving needy families of the resources necessary to achieve and maintain economic self-sufficiency. *See, for example,* Jessica Gehr, Eliminating Asset Limits: Creating Savings for Families and State Governments, Center for Law & Social Policy (Apr. 2018), https://www.clasp.org/sites/default/files/publications/2018/04/2018_eliminatingassetlimits.pdf .

68. 42 U.S.C. § 608(a)(3).

69. 42 U.S.C. § 657(a)(1). For a criticism of the support-recovery rules, *see* Daniel L. Hatcher, Child Support Harming Children: Subordinating the Best Interests of Children to the Fiscal Interests of the State, 42 Wake Forest L. Rev. 1029 (2007).

70. 42 U.S.C. § 608(a)(3).

71. 42 U.S.C. § 657(a)(6).

72. *See* Nat'l Conference of State Legislatures, Child Support Pass-Through and Disregard Policies for Public Assistance Recipients (July 18, 2017), http://www.ncsl.org/research/human-services/state-policy-pass-through-disregard-child-support.aspx.

73. *Id.* For an explanation of the child support pass-through and a call for it to be expanded, *see* Center for Law & Social Policy, Child Support Pass-Through Amounts Must Be Increased (Sept. 16, 2016), https://www.clasp.org/blog/child-support-pass-through-amounts-must-be-increased.

74. Section 431 of the PRA set forth the immigration status related restrictions, which were amended by the Illegal Immigration Reform and Immigrant Responsibility Act, Pub. L. No. 104-208, Tit. V, 110 Stat. 3009-546 (1996). The current rules are codified at 8 U.S.C. §§ 1611–15 (restricting federal public benefits to "qualified

aliens") and 8 U.S.C. § 1641 (defining who is a "qualified alien"). Noncitizens who entered the United States prior to August 22, 1996, the day the PRA was signed into law, are generally not subject to these restrictions.

75. 8 U.S.C. § 1611.
76. For more information about what makes an immigrant "qualified" for government benefits, *see* U.S. Citizenship and Immigration Services Glossary, https://www.uscis.gov/tools/glossary?topic_id=a#alpha-listing.
77. 8 U.S.C. § 1641(b)(1).
78. 8 U.S.C. § 1641(b)(2).
79. 8 U.S.C. § 1641(b)(3).
80. 8 U.S.C. § 1641(b)(4).
81. 8 U.S.C. § 1641(b)(5).
82. 8 U.S.C. § 1641(b)(6).
83. 8 U.S.C. § 1641(b)(7).
84. 8 U.S.C. § 1641(c).
85. 8 U.S.C. § 1641(c)(4).
86. 8 U.S.C. §§ 1612(a)(2)(K) & (b)(2)(C); 1613(b)(2). To qualify, the person must be: (1) a veteran with an honorable discharge who fulfills minimum active-duty service requirements; (2) on active duty (other than active duty for training) in the armed forces of the United States; or (3) the spouse or unmarried dependent child of an individual described in (1) or (2) or the remarried surviving spouse of a deceased service person under certain conditions.
87. 8 U.S.C. §§ 1612(a)(2)(A)(i)(v); 1613(b)(1)(E).
88. 8 U.S.C. § 1612(a)(2)(G).
89. Section 8120, Pub. L. No. 111-118, Department of Defense Appropriations Act, 2010 (providing that Iraqi and Afghan citizens entering the United States with a Special Immigrant Visa are to be treated the same as refugees for the purposes of TANF eligibility).
90. 8 U.S.C. § 1612(b)(2)(A)(ii) & (B)-(C).
91. 8 U.S.C. § 1613.
92. 8 U.S.C. § 1612(a)(2)(I), (J), (F), & (B).
93. *See* 2017 Welfare Rules Databook, Table I.B.5. Eligibility of Non-exempt, Pre-PRWORA, Qualified Aliens, July 2017; Table I.B.7. Eligibility of Post-PRWORA Qualified Aliens after Five Years, July 2017. The U.S. Supreme Court has previously ruled that *state* (as distinct from federal) discrimination against legal immigrants in the administration of welfare programs violates the Equal Protection Clause of the Fourteenth Amendment. Graham v. Richardson, 403 U.S. 365 (1971). State TANF rules that discriminate against legal immigrants beyond what federal law *requires* are therefore constitutionally suspect. *See, for example*, Aliessa v. Novello, 96 N.Y.2d 418 (N.Y. 2001); *see also* Helen Hershkoff & Stephen Loffredo, Tough Times and Weak Review: The 2008 Economic Meltdown and Enforcement of Socio-Economic Rights in U.S. State Courts, in Economic and Social Rights After the Global Financial Crisis 234, 250 (Aoife Nolan, ed.) (Cambridge 2014).
94. 42 U.S.C. § 608(g).

95. 65 Fed. Reg. 58301-01 (Sept. 28, 2000).

96. 8 U.S.C. § 1631(a).

97. *See* Tanya Broder, Avideh Moussavian, & Jonathan Blazer, Overview of Immigrant Eligibility for Federal Programs, National Immigration Law Center (2015), at 5–8, https://www.nilc.org/issues/economic-support/overview-immeligfedprograms/.

98. 8 U.S.C. § 1183a(b)(1)(A). Federal law also grants states the authority to do the same with their own programs. *See* 8 U.S.C. § 1632.

99. 8 U.S.C. § 1631(b)(2).

100. 8 U.S.C. § 1631(e). In the case of an immigrant unable to afford necessities without TANF, the state may only consider the income the sponsor actually provides to the immigrant in determining TANF eligibility and grant amount. This exception to the sponsor deeming rule lasts for a period of 12 months. *Id.*

101. 8 U.S.C. § 1631(f)(1)(A).

102. 8 U.S.C. § 1631(f)(1)(B). The Immigration and Naturalization Service was replaced in 2003 by three new federal entities. *See* Homeland Security Act of 2002, Pub. L. No. 107-296, 116 Stat. 2135 §§ 451–460. The agency that now makes such determinations is the U.S. Citizenship and Immigration Services (USCIS).

103. 8 U.S.C. § 1631(f)(1)(B) & (f)(2).

104. 2017 Welfare Rules Databook, Table I.B.6. State Practices Regarding Eligibility of Noncitizens Who Entered after Enactment and Are Ineligible for Federal TANF Assistance, July 2017.

105. U.S. Department of Health and Human Services, Administration for Children & Families, Office of Planning, Research & Evaluation, TANF Child-Only Cases (Jan. 15, 2012), http://www.acf.hhs.gov/opre/resource/tanf-child-only-cases.

106. 42 U.S.C. § 608(a)(4).

107. 42 U.S.C. § 608(a)(5)(A).

108. 42 U.S.C. § 608(a)(5)(B). A home may not be appropriate if the teen parent will be subjected to any kind of abuse (physical, sexual, emotional, etc.), the parent will be in imminent harm, or the agency determines it is not in the best interest of the teen parent or child to be in the home. *Id.*

109. 42 U.S.C. § 608(a)(5)(B).

110. 21 U.S.C. § 862a.

111. Lavanya Mohan, Victoria Palacio, & Elizabeth Lower-Basch, No More Double Punishments: Lifting the Lifetime Ban on Basic Human Needs Help for Poor People with a Prior Drug Conviction, Center for Law & Social Policy (Mar. 2017), at 5–6, https://www.clasp.org/sites/default/files/public/resources-and-publications/publication-1/Safety-Net-Felony-Ban-FINAL.pdf.

112. 42 U.S.C. § 608(a)(8).

113. 42 U.S.C. § 608(a)(9).

114. 42 U.S.C. § 604(c). Specifically, the PRA authorized states to apply the rules of the newcomer's prior state of residence to determine eligibility and benefit level if the applicant has lived in the new state for less than 12 months.

115. Saenz v. Roe, 526 U.S. 489, 506–508 (1999).

116. *Id.*
117. Shapiro v. Thompson, 394 U.S. 618 (1969). *See* Stephen Loffredo, "If You Ain't Got the Do, Re, Mi": The Commerce Clause and State Residence Restrictions on Welfare, 11 Yale L. & Pol'y Rev. 147 (1993).
118. 21 U.S.C. § 862(b).
119. 42 U.S.C. § 608(b)(2)(A)(v).
120. 42 U.S.C. § 608(b)(3).
121. Congressional Research Service, Maggie McCarty, Gene Falk, Randy Alison Aussenberg, & David H. Carpenter, Drug Testing and Crime-Related Restrictions in TANF, SNAP, and Housing Assistance (Nov. 28, 2016), at 8, 29–36, https://www.fas.org/sgp/crs/misc/R42394.pdf.
122. *Id.* at 7, 18.
123. *See* Congressional Research Service, David H. Carpenter, Constitutional Analysis of Suspicionless Drug Testing Requirements for the Receipt of Governmental Benefits (Mar. 6, 2015), https://fas.org/sgp/crs/misc/R42326.pdf.
124. *See, for example,* Bd. of Educ. of Indep. Sch. Dist. No. 92 of Pottawatomie Cty. v. Earls, 536 U.S. 822 (2002); Chandler v. Miller, 520 U.S. 305 (1997).
125. *See* Jordan C. Budd, Pledge Your Body for Your Bread: Welfare, Drug Testing, and the Inferior Fourth Amendment, 19 Wm. & Mary Bill Rts. J. 751 (2011).
126. *See* Marchwinski v. Howard, 113 F. Supp. 2d 1134 (E.D. Mich. 2000), rev'd, 309 F.3d 330 (6th Cir. 2002), reh'g en banc granted, judgment vacated, 319 F.3d 258 (6th Cir. 2003), and on reh'g en banc, 60 Fed. Appx. 601 (6th Cir. 2003) (upholding a district court injunction against the Michigan drug testing law); Lebron v. Sec'y, Fla. Department of Children & Families, 772 F.3d 1352, (11th Cir. 2014) (striking down Florida drug testing law as violation the Fourth Amendment).
127. *Id. See* Lizette Alvarez, No Savings Are Found from Welfare Drug Tests, N.Y. Times (Apr. 17, 2012), http://www.nytimes.com/2012/04/18/us/no-savings-found-in-florida-welfare-drug-tests.html?ref=us&_r=0.
128. *See, for example,* Sanchez v. County of San Diego, 464 F.3d 916, 918–919 (9th Cir. 2006); Smith v. L.A. Cty. Bd. of Supervisors, 128 Cal. Rptr. 2d 700, 703–705 (Ct. App. 2002); Roberson v. Giuliani, No. 99 Civ. 10900 (DLC), 2000 WL 760300, at *2–3 (S.D.N.Y. June 12, 2000).
129. Allison I. L. Brown, Privacy Issues Affecting Welfare Applicants, 35 Clearinghouse Rev. J. Poverty L. & Pol'y 421, 422 (2001).
130. *See* Wyman v. James, 400 U.S. 309, 318–347 (1971) (upholding as constitutional under the Fourteenth Amendment a requirement that AFDC recipients submit to "home visits" if the official visits during working hours and does not snoop or forcibly enter). The Supreme Court has not addressed whether these on-site investigations are constitutional in the context of TANF eligibility, but some lower courts have found the practice to be constitutional. *See, for example,* Sanchez v. Cnty. of San Diego, 464 F.3d 916, 920–928 (9th Cir. 2006) (stating that home visits are not searches under Fourth Amendment, and even if they are, they do not violate the Fourth Amendment); S.L. v. Whitburn, 67 F.3d 1299, 1301 (7th Cir. 1995) (holding

that a state is allowed to conduct home visits when necessary for eligibility if it notifies the person of the date of the intended visit).

131. *See* Jordan C. Budd: A Fourth Amendment for the Poor Alone: Subconstitutional Status and the Myth of the Inviolate Home, 85 Ind. L.J. 355 (2010); Kaaryn Gustafson, The Criminalization of Poverty, 99 J. of Crim. L. & Criminology 643 (2009).

132. 42 U.S.C. § 608(a)(7)(A). *See* Archives: Text of President Clinton's Announcement on Welfare Legislation, N.Y. Times (Aug. 1, 1996), https://www.nytimes.com/ 1996/08/01/us/text-of-president-clinton-s-announcement-on-welfare-legislation. html. For an analysis of the harm inflicted by limiting TANF, *see, for example*, Ife Floyd, Ashley Burnside, & Liz Schott, TANF Reaching Fewer Poor Families, Center on Budget and Policy Priorities (Nov. 28, 2018), https://www.cbpp.org/research/ family-income-support/tanf-reaching-few-poor-families ("Evidence shows that the drop in direct financial assistance receipt under TANF is a main driver of rising 'extreme poverty,' a measure the World Bank uses of the number of households surviving on $2 or less per person per day.").

133. 42 U.S.C. § 608(a)(7)(A). TANF assistance received on an Indian reservation or Alaskan native village does not count toward the 60-month cap if the reservation or village has an unemployment rate of at least 50%. *See* 42 U.S.C. § 608(a)(7)(D).

134. 42 U.S.C. § 608(a)(7)(B).

135. 42 U.S.C. § 608(a)(7)(A).

136. 45 C.F.R. § 260.31(a)(1).

137. 45 C.F.R. § 260.31(b)(3).

138. 2017 Welfare Rules Databook, Table IV.C.1. Time Limit Policies, July 2017.

139. 42 U.S.C. § 608(a)(7)(C)(i).

140. 42 U.S.C. § 608(a)(7)(C)(iii).

141. 42 U.S.C. § 608(a)(7)(C)(ii).

142. *See* 2017 Welfare Rules Databook, Table IV.C.1. Time Limit Policies, July 2017.

143. *See id.*, at Table IV.C.2(b).

144. *See* N.Y. Soc. Servs. L. § 158.

145. 42 U.S.C. § 602(a)(1)(A).

146. *See* 42 U.S.C. § 609.

147. 42 U.S.C. § 607(a)(1)–(2).

148. 42 U.S.C. § 607(b)(3). In any given year, a state's caseload reduction credit (if any) is the number of percentage points by which the state's current TANF caseload falls below its TANF caseload in 2005. That number is subtracted from the statutory 50% to arrive at the state's effective work participation rate requirement for the year. *Id.*

149. *See* Elizabeth Lower-Basch, Work Participation Rate—Temporary Assistance for Needy Families, Center for Law & Social Policy (Jan. 2018), https://www.clasp.org/ sites/default/files/publications/2017/04/TANF-101-Work-Participation-Rate.pdf.

150. 45 C.F.R. § 261.2(n)(1).

151. *See* Heather Hahn, David Kassabian, & Sheila Zedlewski, TANF Work Requirements and State Strategies to Fulfill Them, Urban Institute (Mar. 2012), at 2, https://www. acf.hhs.gov/sites/default/files/opre/work_requirements_0.pdf (noting that many

states exempt ill or incapacitated individuals, people caring for such individuals, parents of very young children, and pregnant women); *See* 2017 Welfare Rules Databook, Table III.B.1. Work-Related Activity Exemptions for Single-Parent Head of Unit, July 2017.

152. 45 C.F.R. § 261.2(n)(1)(i).
153. 45 C.F.R. § 261.2 (n)(1)(ii).
154. 45 C.F.R. § 261.2(n)(2)(i).
155. 45 C.F.R. § 261.2(n)(2)(ii).
156. 42 U.S.C. § 607(c)(2)(B).
157. 42 U.S.C. § 607(c)(1)(A).
158. 42 U.S.C. § 607(c)(1)(B)(i).
159. 42 U.S.C. § 607(c)(1)(B)(ii).
160. 42 U.S.C. § 607(d)(1)–(12).
161. *See* U.S. Department of Health & Human Services, Office of Family Assistance, Q & A: Work Participation Rate, TANF Reporting Questions (July 1, 2012), http://www.acf.hhs.gov/ofa/resource/wpr (referring to core and non-core activities).
162. 45 C.F.R. § 261.2(b).
163. 45 C.F.R. § 261.2(c).
164. 45 C.F.R. § 261.2(d).
165. 45 C.F.R. § 261.2(e).
166. 45 C.F.R. § 261.2(f).
167. 45 C.F.R. § 261.2(g). Participation in job search and readiness activities is limited to four consecutive weeks and six weeks total in a year but may be increased to 12 weeks in certain circumstances of high state unemployment. 42 U.S.C. § 607(c)(2)(A)(i).
168. 45 C.F.R. § 261.2(h).
169. 45 C.F.R. § 261.2(i).
170. 45 C.F.R. § 261.2(j).
171. 45 C.F.R. § 261.2(k).
172. 45 C.F.R. § 261.2(l).
173. 45 C.F.R. § 261.2(m).
174. 42 U.S.C. § 607(c)(1)(A).
175. 42 U.S.C. § 607(c)(1)(B).
176. 42 U.S.C. § 607(c).
177. 42 U.S.C. § 607(f)(2).
178. 42 U.S.C. § 607(f)(3).
179. 42 U.S.C. § 607(f)(4).
180. 45 C.F.R. § 261.33(b)(1).
181. 45 C.F.R. § 261.2(i).
182. 73 Fed. Reg. 6772, 6792 (Feb. 5, 2008). These regulatory amendments expanded the definition of "vocational educational training" and "job skills training" to encompass baccalaureate and advance degree programs, agreeing with advocates that higher educational attainment would increase family earnings. One of the senselessly punitive aspects of the PRA was that it sharply curtailed the ability of welfare recipients to obtain the education and training that could provide the skills and

credentials needed to secure living wage employment and lift their families out of poverty. *See, for example*, Center for Women's Policy Studies, From Poverty to Self-Sufficiency: The Role of Postsecondary Education in Welfare Reform (2002), http://www.ncdsv.org/images/CWPS_From-poverty-to-self-sufficiency_2002.pdf.

183. 45 C.F.R. § 261.60(e). One hour of unsupervised homework per class credit automatically counts toward the work requirement. Additional hours of recommended or required homework time supervised by the educational institution (for example, in a supervised study hall or lab) also count toward the work requirement. *Id.*

184. Two-parent households must engage in core activity for the first 30 hours of their requirement; two-parent households receiving federally funded child care must engage in core activity for the first 50 hours. 42 U.S.C. § 607(c)(1)(B).

185. *See* 45 C.F.R. § 261.33(a); 73 Fed. Reg. at 6792 (college attendance may count as "vocational educational training" (a core activity) for 12 months and as "job skills training" (a non-core activity) thereafter).

186. *See, for example*, N.Y. Soc. Servs. Law § 336(8).

187. *See* Gayle Hamilton & Susan Scrivener, Facilitating Postsecondary Education and Training for TANF Recipients, Urban Institute (Mar. 15, 2012), https://www.acf.hhs.gov/opre/resource/facilitating-postsecondary-education-and-training-for-tanf-recipients. *See also* Stephen Loffredo, Poverty Law and Community Activism: Notes from a Law School Clinic, 150 U. Pa. L. Rev. 173 (2001), https://scholarship.law.upenn.edu/penn_law_review/vol150/iss1/5/ (describing activists' efforts to secure broader access to education for welfare recipients as an anti-poverty strategy).

188. 42 U.S.C. § 607(e)(1).

189. 42 U.S.C. § 607(e)(1)(A).

190. 42 U.S.C. § 607(e)(1)(A)–(B).

191. 42 U.S.C. § 607(e)(1).

192. *See, for example*, LaDonna Pavetti, Work Requirements Don't Cut Poverty, Evidence Shows, Center on Budget and Policy Priorities (June 7, 2016), https://www.cbpp.org/research/poverty-and-inequality/work-requirements-dont-cut-poverty-evidence-shows.

193. 45 C.F.R. § 261.15.

194. 45 C.F.R. § 261.56(a)(1)(i).

195. 45 C.F.R. § 261.56(a)(1)(ii).

196. 45 C.F.R. § 261.56(a)(1)(iii).

197. U.S. Department of Health & Human Services, Off. Family Assistance, TANF-ACF-IM 2012-03 (Guidance Concerning Waiver and Expenditure Authority Under Section 1115) (July 12, 2012), http://www.acf.hhs.gov/programs/ofa/resource/policy/im-ofa/2012/im201203/im201203.

198. LaDonna Pavetti, Ohio TANF Waiver Denial Continues Trump Administration's Attack on Work Programs, Center on Budget and Policy Priorities (Aug. 13, 2017), https://www.cbpp.org/blog/ohio-tanf-waiver-denial-continues-trump-administrations-attack-on-work-programs.

199. 45 C.F.R. § 260.51.

200. 45 C.F.R. § 260.52(c).

201. 42 U.S.C. § 602(a)(7)(A)(iii).
202. 45 C.F.R. § 260.54(a) & (b).
203. Timothy Casey, Jill Davies, Annika Gifford, & Anne Menard, Not Enough: What TANF Offers Family Violence Victims, Legal Momentum & National Resource Center on Domestic Violence (2010), http://www.legalmomentum.org/sites/default/files/reports/not-enough-what-tanf-offers.pdf (hereinafter Casey et al.).
204. See Rachel J. Gallagher, Welfare Reform's Inadequate Implementation of the Family Violence Option: Exploring the Dual Oppression of Poor Domestic Violence Victims, 19 Am. U. J. Gender, Soc. Pol'y & L. 987 (2011).
205. 42 U.S.C. § 608(a)(7)(c)(ii).
206. Rachel J. Gallagher, Welfare Reform's Inadequate Implementation of the Family Violence Option: Exploring the Dual Oppression of Poor Domestic Violence Victims, 19 Am. U. J. Gender, Soc. Pol'y & L. 987, 1001 (2011).
207. Casey et al., at 2–11.
208. 42 U.S.C. § 604(i).
209. 2017 Welfare Rules Databook, Table III.A.1. Behavioral Requirements and Bonuses, July 2017.
210. 2017 Welfare Rules Databook, Table III.A.1. Behavioral Requirements and Bonuses, July 2017.
211. 42 U.S.C. § 608(a)(4).
212. 42 U.S.C. § 608(a)(2).
213. Id.
214. 42 U.S.C. § 608(b)(1).
215. 42 U.S.C. § 608(b)(2).
216. 42 U.S.C. § 608(b)(3).
217. 42 U.S.C. §§ 607(e), 608(a)(2).
218. Vicki Lens, Work Sanctions Under Welfare Reform: Are They Helping Women Achieve Self-Sufficiency?, 13 Duke J. Gender L. & Pol'y 255, 269 (2006).
219. Timothy Casey, The Sanction Epidemic in the Temporary Assistance for Needy Families Program 9–10, Legal Momentum (2012), http://www.legalmomentum.org/sites/default/files/reports/sanction-epidemic-in-tanf.pdf.
220. Id.; Federation of Protestant Welfare Agencies, Guilty Until Proven Innocent: Sanctions, Agency Error, and Financial Punishment within New York State's Welfare System (2012).
221. U.S. Government Accountability Office, Temporary Assistance For Needy Families: Fewer Eligible Families Have Received Cash Assistance Since the 1990s, and the Recession's Impact on Caseloads Varies by State 22 (2010), http://www.gao.gov/new.items/d10164.pdf.
222. See 2017 Welfare Rules Databook, Table I.A.2 Mandatory Job Search at Application, July 2017; Abt Assocs. Inc., Study of the TANF Application Process, Final Report: Volume 1, prepared for U.S. Department of Health and Human Services, Administration for Children & Families E-2 (Apr. 2003), https://www.abtassociates.com/sites/default/files/2018-09/2003159970226_82211.pdf.
223. Goldberg v. Kelly, 397 U.S. 254 (1970).

224. *See* 42 U.S.C. § 602(a)(1)(B)(iii) (state plan must explain how the state intends to "provide opportunities for recipients who have been adversely affected to be heard in a state administrative or appeal process"); 45 C.F.R. § 205.10 (detailed notice and hearing requirements, including hearing rights for applicants).

225. *See* Weston v. Cassata, 37 P.3d 469, 77 (Colo. App. 2001) (holding that once someone has begun receiving TANF benefits, the benefits become a property interest that that cannot be compromised without procedural due process protections); Perdue v. Gargano, 964 N.E. 2d 825, 832 (Ind. 2012) (finding that TANF benefits are property interests protected by the Due Process Clause); State ex rel. K.M. v. West Virginia Department of Health & Human Res., 575 S.E.2d 393, 409 (W. Va. 2002) (declining to find that TANF benefits are property rights, but holding that "once the State has established a scheme for making [cash assistance] payments the State's scheme must provide the program participants with adequate due process protections.").

226. Although the PRA claimed to create no federal entitlement to TANF benefits, the statute requires that states operate their TANF programs in accordance with "fair" and "objective" written eligibility standards, 42 U.S.C. § 602(a)(1)(B)(iii), and many states retain entitlement language in their state laws. In either event, the legal interest created by these federal and state laws should be found sufficient to trigger constitutional due process protections; and impoverished families' critical interest in receiving subsistence benefits should be held to require full notice and hearing rights for TANF applicants and recipients. *See* Cynthia Farina, On Misusing "Revolution" and "Reform": Procedural Due Process and the New Welfare Act, 50 Admin. L. Rev. 591 (1998); Vicki Lens, Bureaucratic Disentitlement After Welfare Reform: Are Fair Hearings the Cure?, 12 Geo. J. Poverty L. & Pol'y 13, 31–32 (2005).

227. Goldberg v. Kelly, 397 U.S. 254 (1970); 45 C.F.R. § 205.10(a)(4).

228. 45 C.F.R. § 205.10(a)(4)(i)(A).

229. *Goldberg*, 397 U.S. at 263–267; 45 C.F.R. § 205.10(a)(4).

230. 45 C.F.R. § 205.10(a)(6).

231. *Goldberg*, 397 U.S. at 268–271; 45 C.F.R. § 205.10(a)(13).

232. *See* Stephen Loffredo & Don Friedman, *Gideon* Meets *Goldberg*: The Case for a Qualified Right to Counsel in Welfare Hearings, 25 Touro L. Rev. 273 (2009) (describing legal structure and reality of welfare hearing process and difficulties confronted by pro se claimants).

233. *Id.* A list of legal services organizations is available through an interactive website, https://www.lawhelp.org.

234. Social Security Amendments of 1972, Pub. L. No. 92-603 (codified as amended at 42 U.S.C. §§ 1381, 1383).

235. The federal law governing the Supplemental Security Income program can be found in Title 42 of the United States Code at Sections 1381 through 1383. Social Security Administration regulations for SSI are published in Title 20 of the Code of Federal Regulations at Part 416. The Social Security Administration publishes several manuals that contain the rules and procedures for programs administered by the agency. These include the Program Operations Manual System (POMS), the Social Security Handbook, and the Supplemental Security Income Handbook. The SSA

also issues "Social Security Rulings" that explain its interpretation of laws governing SSI. Federal law allows anyone to review these materials at any Social Security District Office or Branch Office, *see* 20 C.F.R. § 402.55, and the materials are accessible online at https://www.ssa.gov.

236. U.S. Social Security Administration, Monthly Statistical Snapshot (Dec. 2018), https://www.ssa.gov/policy/docs/quickfacts/stat_snapshot/.

237. U.S. Social Security Administration, Cost-of-Living Increase and Other Determinations for 2019, 83 Fed. Reg. 53702 (Oct. 24, 2018), https://www.govinfo.gov/content/pkg/FR-2018-10-24/pdf/2018-23193.pdf; U.S. Social Security Administration, SSI Federal Payment Amounts for 2019, https://www.ssa.gov/oact/cola/SSI.html.

238. *See* 20 C.F.R. §§ 416.1100–1324.

239. 20 C.F.R. § 416.405.

240. Social Security Administration, Cost-of-Living Adjustment (COLA) Information for 2019, https://www.ssa.gov/cola/.

241. 20 C.F.R. § 416.2001.

242. U.S. Social Security Administration, Understanding Supplemental Security Income SSI Benefits—2018 Edition, https://www.ssa.gov/ssi/text-benefits-ussi.htm.

243. 20 C.F.R. § 416.2030.

244. 20 C.F.R. § 416.202(a).

245. 20 C.F.R. § 416.202(c); 20 C.F.R. § 416.202(d).

246. 20 C.F.R. § 416.202(b); 20 C.F.R. § 416.1603(c).

247. 20 C.F.R. § 416.202(b)(4); 20 C.F.R. § 416.216; U.S. Social Security Administration, Program Operations Manual System (POMS), TN 39 (06-96), Effective Dates: 06/14/1996–Present, SI 00501.411, SSI Eligibility for Students Temporarily Working Abroad, https://secure.ssa.gov/apps10/poms.nsf/lnx/0500501411.

248. 20 C.F.R. § 416.202(a)(1).

249. 20 C.F.R. § 416.802.

250. 20 C.F.R. § 416.803.

251. 20 C.F.R. § 416.801.

252. 20 C.F.R § 416.981. Social Security Administration regulations additionally state: "An eye which has a limitation in the field of vision so that the widest diameter of the visual field subtends an angle no greater than 20 degrees is considered to have a central visual acuity of 20/200 or less." SSI can be received as a blind person if (1) the person is found to be blind as defined under a state plan approved under Title X or Title XVI of the Social Security Act, as in effect for October 1972; (2) the person received aid under that state plan in December 1973; and (3) the person remains blind as defined by the state program. *See* 20 C.F.R. § 416.982.

253. 20 C.F.R. § 416.984.

254. 20 C.F.R. § 416.985. To determine whether a visual impairment makes an individual eligible for SSI, refer to the definition of disability provided in §§ 416.905–907.

255. 42 U.S.C. § 1382c(a)(3)(A); *see also* 20 C.F.R. § 416.905 (using the same language).

256. 20 C.F.R. § 416.920(a)(4)(i)–(v).

257. *See, for example,* 20 C.F.R. § 416.920(a)(1).

258. 20 C.F.R. § 416.920(a)(4)(i)–(v).
259. 20 C.F R. § 416.920(a)(4)(i).
260. 20 C.F.R. § 416.972(a).
261. 20 C.F.R. § 416.972(b).
262. 20 C.F.R. § 416.972 refers to "substantial gainful activity," without disaggregating the terms.
263. 20 C.F.R. § 416.973(a).
264. 20 C.F.R. § 416.973(b).
265. 20 C.F.R. § 416.973(c).
266. 20 C.F.R. § 416.973(b).
267. 20 C.F.R. § 416.974(a)(2).
268. 20 C.F.R. § 416.976(a). These costs are deductible even if the individual also needs or uses the items and services to carry out daily living functions unrelated to the work. *Id.*
269. The monthly earnings average that is sufficient to show substantial gainful employment is the larger of (1) the amount for the previous year, or (2) an amount adjusted for national wage growth, calculated by a statutory formula. *See* 20 C.F.R. § 416.974(b)(2)(ii)(A)–(B). The latter amount is currently $1,950 for blind people and $1,170 for nonblind people. *See* U.S. Social Security Administration., Substantial Gainful Activity, http://www.ssa.gov/OACT/COLA/sga.html.
270. 20 C.F.R. § 416.920(a)(4)(ii).
271. 20 C.F.R. § 416.920(c).
272. 20 C.F.R. § 416.922(b)(1)–(6).
273. 20 C.F.R. § 416.922(a). The Social Security Administration has stated that a physical or mental impairment "can be considered as not severe only if it is a slight abnormality which has such a minimal effect on the individual that it would not be expected to interfere with the [individual's] ability to work irrespective of age, education, or work experience." Social Security Ruling 85-28: Titles II and XVI—Medical Impairments That Are Not Severe, https://www.ssa.gov/OP_Home/rulings/di/01/SSR85-28-di-01.html (internal quotation marks omitted) (quoting Stone v. Heckler, 752 F.2d 1099, 1101 (5th Cir. 1985)).
274. 20 C.F.R. § 416.920(c).
275. 20 C.F.R. § 416.925.
276. The "Listing of Impairments" may be accessed at https://www.ssa.gov/OP_Home/cfr20/404/404-app-p01.htm.
277. 20 C.F.R. § 416.926(a). The Social Security Administration will conclude that a medical condition is as severe as a condition on the list if it is "at least of equal medical significance" to the most similar medical condition that appears on the list. 20 C.F.R. § 416.926(b)(2).
278. 20 C.F.R. §§ 416.920(e)–(f), 416.960(b).
279. 20 C.F.R. § 416.920(e).
280. 20 C.F.R. § 416.920(f).
281. 20 C.F.R. § 416.960(c)(1).
282. 20 C.F.R. § 416.920(g).
283. 20 C.F.R. § 416.920(g)(1).

284. *See* 20 C.F.R. § 416.969a(a) (exertional and nonexertional limitations); 20 C.F.R. § 404, subpart P, App'x 2 §§ 200.00 et seq. (the Medical-Vocational Guidelines), http://www.ssa.gov/OP_Home/cfr20/404/404-app-p02.htm (hereinafter the "Guidelines").

285. The Guidelines divide age into three categories: "advanced" (55 and older), "closely approaching advanced" (50–54), and "younger" (18–49), but recognize that individuals ages 45–49 may be less able to adapt to a new kind of work than younger individuals. Guidelines at § 201.00(h)(1); 20 C.F.R. § 416.963. Education is divided into four categories: "illiterate or unable to communicate in English," "limited or less," "high school graduate or more—does not provide for direct entry into skilled work," and "high school graduate or more—provides for direct entry into skilled work." 20 C.F.R. § 416.964. Skill level is also divided into four categories: "none," "unskilled," "skilled or semi-skilled—skills not transferrable," and "skilled or semi-skilled—skills transferrable." 20 C.F.R. § 416.968. Lastly, the Guidelines set forth five categories of residual capacity: "very heavy work," "heavy work," "medium work," "light work," and "sedentary work." 20 C.F.R. § 416.967. A residual functional capacity for very heavy work means that the individual can lift up to 100 pounds at a time and frequently lift and carry up to 50 pounds. 20 C.F.R. § 416.967(e). At the other end of the spectrum, a residual function capacity for sedentary work means the individual can lift up to 10 pounds at a time, can sit for most of the workday, and occasionally can walk or stand. 20 C.F.R. § 416.967(a).

286. The one exception to this rule is that someone between ages 45 and 49, though considered a "younger" individual, will nevertheless be deemed "disabled" if the person is (1) restricted to sedentary work; (2) has no transferable work skills; (3) is unable to perform prior work; and (4) is illiterate or unable to communicate in English. *See* Guidelines, Rule 201.00(h)(1)(i)–(iv).

287. Guidelines, § 201.00(d).

288. Guidelines, Table 1, Rule 201.12.

289. Guidelines, Table 3, Rule 203.23.

290. *See* Social Security Ruling 83-12: Titles II and XVI: Capability to Do Other Work— The Medical-Vocational Rules as a Framework for Evaluating Exertional Limitations Within a Range of Work or Between Ranges of Work (hereinafter "SSR 83-12"), https://www.ssa.gov/OP_Home/rulings/di/02/SSR83-12-di-02.html (stating that if the full range of sedentary work is "significantly compromised," the Guidelines cannot preclude a finding of disabled).

291. 20 C.F.R. § 416.967(a). *See* Social Security Ruling 83-10: Titles II and XVI— Determining Capability to Do Other Work—The Medical-Vocational Rules of Appendix 2 (hereinafter "SSR 83-10"), https://www.ssa.gov/OP_Home/rulings/di/02/SSR83-10-di-02.html.

292. *See* SSR 83-12 at 4.

293. 20 C.F.R. § 416.969a(c); Guidelines § 200.00(e)(1).

294. SSR 83-10 at 6. *See* 20 C.F.R. § 416.969a(c) (where impairments "affect only [the] ability to meet the demands of jobs other than the strength demands," the impairments present "only nonexertional limitations or restrictions").

295. SSR 83-10 at 6. *See* 20 C.F.R. § 416.969a(c)(1)(vi).

296. *See* 20 C.F.R. § 416.969a(d) (stating that where someone has both exertional and nonexertional limitations, the Guidelines "will not directly apply," but will "provide a framework to guide" the disability determination, unless the guidelines would declare the person disabled based on exertional factors alone).

297. SSR 83-12 at 2. For a recent explanation of vocational expert testimony, and a troubling example of its use to deny a disability claim, *see* Biestek v. Berryhill, 139 S. Ct. 1148 (2019).

298. Guidelines § 200.00(e). If an individual presents solely nonexertional impairments, the disability determination is based on the relevant regulatory sections for those impairments. *See* Guidelines § 200.00(e)(1). If an individual presents exertional and nonexertional impairments, the SSA must consult the Guidelines to see if the individual qualifies as disabled based on exertional limitations alone. If the Guidelines do not direct a finding of disabled based on exertional limitations alone, the SSA may use them as "a framework" to measure diminution of work capacity in light of all facts and relevant regulatory sections. *See* Guidelines § 200.00(e)(2).

299. *See* Social Security Ruling 85-15: Titles II and XVI—The Medical-Vocational Rules as a Framework for Evaluating Solely Nonexertional Impairments, https://www. socialsecurity.gov/OP_Home/rulings/di/02/SSR85-15-di-02.html ("The basic mental demands of competitive, remunerative, unskilled work include the abilities (on a sustained basis) to understand, carry out, and remember simple instructions; to respond appropriately to supervision, coworkers and usual work situations; and to deal with changes in a routine work setting. A substantial loss of ability to meet any of these basic work-related activities . . . would justify a finding of disability [even for young, well-educated, and highly skilled individuals]."). *See* 20 C.F.R. § 416.969a(c)(1)(i).

300. 20 C.F.R. § 416.969a(c)(1)(ii)–(iii).

301. § 416.969a(d); Guidelines § 200.00(e)(2). *See* Social Security Ruling 83-14: Titles II and XVI: Capability to Do Other Work—The Medical Vocational Rules as a Framework for Evaluating a Combination of Exertional and Nonexertional Impairments, https://www.ssa.gov/OP_Home/rulings/di/02/SSR83-14-di-02.html.

302. 20 C.F.R. § 416.964(b)(2).

303. 20 C.F.R. § 416.962(a).

304. *See* American Psychiatric Association, Diagnostic and Statistical Manual (5th ed. 2013) (devoting Chapter 17 to "Substance-Related and Addictive Disorders").

305. Pub. L. No. 104-121, 110 Stat. 847 § 105 (1997) (codified at 42 U.S.C. §§ 423(d)(2), 1382(c)).

306. 42 U.S.C. §§ 105(a)(1)(C), (a)(5), & (b)(5).

307. 20 C.F.R. §§ 416.935(b)(1)–(2); 416.214(a) (conditioning benefits for disabled persons whose alcohol or drug addictions are material to determination of disability on successful participation in a treatment program). To determine whether drug addiction or alcoholism is a contributing factor material to the determination of disability, the SSA will ask whether it would still find an individual disabled if use of drugs or alcohol stopped. *See* 20 C.F.R. § 404.1535(b)(1).

308. 20 C.F.R. § 416.936.

309. *See* 20 C.F.R. § 416.940 (evaluating compliance with treatment).

310. 42 U.S.C. § 1382c(a)(3)(C)(i).

311. Personal Responsibility and Work Opportunity Reconciliation Act of 1996, Pub. L. No. 104-193, 110 Stat. 2105 § 211 (1996), https://www.congress.gov/bill/104th-congress/house-bill/3734/text?overview=closed. Before 1996, a disabled child could qualify for SSI by showing a medical condition comparable to one that would prevent an adult from working. The Social Security Administration would assess the severity of the child's medical condition, and, if necessary, perform an individualized functional assessment to determine whether the child's condition was comparable to one that would be considered disabling in an adult. *See* 82 Fed. Reg. 5879 (Jan. 18, 2017); 20 C.F.R. § 416.924a.

312. *See* Text of President Clinton's Announcement on Welfare Legislation, N.Y. Times (Aug. 1, 1996), http://www.nytimes.com/1996/08/01/us/text-of-president-clinton-s-announcement-on-welfare-legislation.html.

313. *See* U.S. Social Security Administration, Fast Facts & Figures About Social Security 31 (2018), https://www.ssa.gov/policy/docs/chartbooks/fast_facts/2018/fast_facts18.pdf.

314. *See* Lucie Schmidt, Effects of Welfare Reform on Supplemental Security Income (SSI) Program, National Poverty Center (2004), http://www.npc.umich.edu/publications/policy_briefs/brief4/brief4.pdf.

315. *See* U.S. Social Security Administration, Fast Facts & Figures About Social Security 31 (2018), https://www.ssa.gov/policy/docs/chartbooks/fast_facts/2018/fast_facts18.pdf. The number of children receiving SSI decreased each year from 1996 to 2000. However, from 2000 the number once again began to increase.

316. Lucie Schmidt, The New Safety Net?, Supplemental Security Income after Welfare Reform (2013), http://web.williams.edu/Economics/wp/schmidt_ssi_sept_2013_final.pdf.

317. 20 C.F.R. § 416.934(j).

318. 20 C.F.R. § 416.934(k) (small for gestational age means a birthweight at or more than two standard deviations below the mean or that is less than the third growth percentile for the infant's gestational age).

319. *See* 20 C.F.R. § 416.912.

320. For an explanation of how the SSA evaluates medical opinions from a claimant's treating physician, *see* 20 C.F.R. § 416.920c; U.S. Social Security Administration, Revisions to Rules Regarding the Evaluation of Medical Evidence, 82 Fed. Reg. 5844 (Jan. 18, 2017).

321. For an explanation of acceptable medical and nonmedical sources of evidence, *see* 20 C.F.R. §§ 416.912, 416.913(a)(4).

322. 20 C.F.R. § 416.912.

323. 20 C.F.R. § 416.929(a).

324. 20 C.F.R. § 416.913(a)(1).

325. SSR 96-9p: Policy Interpretation Ruling: Titles II and XVI: Determining Capability to Do Other Work—Implications of a Residual Functional Capacity for Less Than

a Full Range of Sedentary Work, https://www.ssa.gov/OP_Home/rulings/di/01/SSR96-09-di-01.html.

326. *See* 20 C.F.R. § 416.913(a)(2) (reviewing the consideration of statements about what an applicant can do despite the person's impairments).

327. *See* 20 C.F.R. § 416.920c(c)(3). Before March 2017, the SSA was required to give controlling weight to adequately supported medical opinions of a claimant's treating physician, but the SSA issued new regulations purporting to eliminate that rule. U.S. Social Security Administration, Revisions to Rules Regarding the Evaluation of Medical Evidence, 82 Fed. Reg. 5844-01 (Jan. 18, 2017).

328. 20 C.F.R. § 416.920c. ("The more relevant the objective medical evidence and supporting explanations presented by a medical source are to support his or her medical opinion(s) or prior administrative medical finding(s), the more persuasive the medical opinions or prior administrative medical finding(s) will be.").

329. The SSA publishes a Frequently Asked Questions page for doctors and other health professionals at https://www.ssa.gov/disability/professionals/answers-pub042.htm.

330. Mobilization for Justice (formerly MFY Legal Services), a New York based non-profit organization that provides free civil legal services, has published a fact sheet for doctors filling out SSI applications. Mobilization for Justice, Tips for Doctors Filling Out Applications for SSI and SSD (2016), http://mobilizationforjustice.org/wp-content/uploads/Tips-for-Doctors-SSI-and-SSD-March-2016-1.pdf.

331. The "Listings" appear at 20 C.F.R. Part 404, subpart P, App. 1, http://www.ssa.gov/OP_Home/cfr20/404/404-app-p01.htm. An easier-to-navigate electronic version is available at: http://www.ssa.gov/disability/professionals/bluebook/AdultListings.htm.

332. 20 C.F.R. § 416. 912(b)(1).

333. 20 C.F.R. § 416.917.

334. 20 C.F.R. § 416.919a.

335. 20 C.F.R. § 416.918(a).

336. 20 C.F.R. § 416.918(c).

337. 20 C.F.R. § 416.919j.

338. 20 C.F.R. § 416.919s.

339. 20 C.F.R. § 416.919h.

340. *See* U.S. Social Security Administration, Compassionate Allowances, https://www.ssa.gov/compassionateallowances/.

341. *See* U.S Social Security Administration, Quick Disability Determinations (QDD), https://www.ssa.gov/disabilityresearch/qdd.htm.

342. *See* 20 C.F.R. § 404.1619.

343. 20 C.F.R. § 416.930(a).

344. 20 C.F.R. § 416.930(b).

345. 20 C.F.R. § 416.930(c)(1)–(5).

346. 20 C.F.R. § 416.1710(a).

347. *See* 45 Fed. Reg. 70,859 (Oct. 27, 1980), amended by 48 Fed. Reg. 6,297 (Feb. 23, 1983) (repealing 20 C.F.R. § 416.1715, which had directed suspension of benefits to recipients who refused without cause to accept vocational rehabilitation services).

348. 20 C.F.R. § 416.1725.

349. 42 U.S.C. § 421(i)(1); 20 C.F.R. § 416.990. For individuals with disabilities deemed to be "permanent," the SSA will conduct a continuing disability review at least once every seven years, but not more frequently than once every five years. *Id.*

350. 20 C.F.R. § 416.989. *See* U.S. Social Security Administration, Understanding Supplemental Security Income Continuing Disability Reviews—2018 Edition, https://www.ssa.gov/ssi/text-cdrs-ussi.htm.

351. 42 U.S.C. § 1382(a)(6); 20 C.F.R. § 416.994. In some very limited circumstances, the SSA may find that an individual whose medical conditions have *not* significantly improved is nevertheless no longer disabled if "advances in medical or vocational therapy or technology" now enable the individual to engage in "substantial gainful activity." 20 C.F.R. § 416.994(b)(3). *See* U.S. Social Security Administration, How We Decide if You Still Have a Qualifying Disability, Pub. 05-10053 (July 2017), https://www.ssa.gov/pubs/EN-05-10053.pdf.

352. *See* 20 C.F.R. §§ 416.972–976, 416.1101–1104.

353. 20 C.F.R. §§ 416.260–265. Income earned by recipients of special SSI cash benefits is considered in calculating benefit amounts in the same manner as the calculation of regular SSI. 20 C.F.R. § 416.261. Recipients of special SSI cash benefits are considered disabled persons receiving SSI for purposes of Medicaid eligibility. *Id.* Individuals who would be eligible for special SSI cash benefits except that their earnings are too high, may still qualify for "special SSI eligibility status," which continues their eligibility for Medicaid. 20 C.F.R. §§ 416.264–269.

354. *See* U.S. Social Security Administration, 2018 Red Book: A Summary Guide to Employment Supports for Persons with Disabilities under the Social Security Disability Insurance (SSDI) and Supplemental Security Income (SSI) Programs, https://www.ssa.gov/redbook/documents/TheRedBook2018.pdf.

355. 20 C.F.R. § 411.105.

356. 20 C.F.R. § 411.115. *See* U.S. Social Security Administration, What Is the Ticket to Work Program, https://www.ssa.gov/work/overview.html.

357. 20 C.F.R. § 416.211(a)(1).

358. 20 C.F.R. § 416.201.

359. 20 C.F.R. § 416.211(d) (the six months need not be consecutive).

360. 20 C.F.R § 416.201.

361. 20 C.F.R. § 416.211(a)(2); *see also* 20 C.F.R. § 416.211(d) (any prior months spent in the shelter without receiving SSI benefits do not count toward the six month limit).

362. 20 C.F.R. § 416.212(a). Social Security Act sections 1619(a) and (b) authorize special SSI payments and continued Medicaid eligibility for individuals who work in spite of a disabling impairment and whose gross income exceeds the amount that the SSA would ordinarily consider to constitute "substantial gainful activity." *See* 20 C.F.R. §§ 416.260–269.

363. 20 C.F.R. § 416.212(b)(1)(i)–(iv).

364. 20 C.F.R. § 416.211(b).

365. 20 C.F.R. § 416.414(b)(1).

366. For the amount of state supplementation for each state in 2011, *see* U.S. Social Security Administration, State Assistance Programs for SSI Recipients, January

2011, http://www.ssa.gov/policy/docs/progdesc/ssi_st_asst/2011/ssi_st_asst2011.
pdf. Current information is available only on individual state websites.
367. 20 C.F.R. § 416.211(c)(5)(ii).
368. 20 C.F.R. § 416.211(c).
369. *See* 20 C.F.R. §§ 416.1600, 416.1603(c); U.S. Social Security Administration,
Program Operations Manual System (POMS), TN 39 (06-96), Effective Dates: 06/
14/1996–Present, SI 00501.411, SSI Eligibility for Students Temporarily Working
Abroad, https://secure.ssa.gov/apps10/poms.nsf/lnx/0500501411.
370. 20 C.F.R. § 416.1603(a).
371. 20 C.F.R. § 416.1327(a).
372. 20 C.F.R. § 416.1327(b).
373. 20 C.F.R. § 416.1610.
374. Balanced Budget Act of 1997, Pub. L. No. 105-33, 111 Stat. 251 (1997). *See* Lucy
Schmidt, Effects of Welfare Reform on Supplemental Security Income, National
Poverty Center, Policy Brief (Oct. 2004), http://www.npc.umich.edu/publications/
policy_briefs/brief4/brief4.pdf.
375. U.S. Social Security Administration, Annual Statistical Supplement, Table 7.E6 (2018),
https://www.ssa.gov/policy/docs/statcomps/supplement/2018/7e.pdf; Michael Fix
& Jeffrey Passel, The Scope and Impact of Welfare Reform's Immigrant Provisions,
Urban Institute (Jan. 15, 2002), http://www.urban.org/uploadedpdf/410412_discussion
02-03.pdf.
376. U.S. Social Security Administration, Spotlight on SSI Benefits for Aliens—2018
Edition, https://www.ssa.gov/ssi/spotlights/spot-non-citizens.htm.
377. 8 U.S.C. § 1612(a)(2)(F).
378. 8 U.S.C. § 1612(a)(2)(E).
379. 8 U.S.C. §§ 1612(a)(2)(B), 1613(a).
380. 8 U.S.C. § 1612(a)(2)(C).
381. U.S. Social Security Administration, Spotlight on SSI Benefits for Aliens—2018
Edition, https://www.ssa.gov/ssi/spotlights/spot-non-citizens.htm.
382. 8 U.S.C. § 1612(a)(2)(A). The seven-year time limit had been temporarily extended
to nine years, effective for the period October 1, 2008 to October 1, 2011, as part of
the SSI Extension for Elderly and Disabled Refugees Act, Pub. L. No. 110-328, 122
Stat. 3567 (2008).
383. Pursuant to § 584 of the Foreign Operations, Export Financing, and Related
Programs Appropriations Act, 1988, as contained in § 101(e) of Pub. L. No. 100-202
and amended by the 9th proviso under Migration and Refugee Assistance in Title II
of the Foreign Operations, Export Financing, and Related Programs Appropriations
Act, 1989, Pub. L. No. 100-461, as amended.
384. U.S. Social Security Administration, Spotlight on SSI Benefits for Aliens—2018
Edition, https://www.ssa.gov/ssi/spotlights/spot-non-citizens.htm.
385. *Id.*
386. 20 C.F.R. § 416.1104.
387. 20 C.F.R. § 416.1100.
388. 20 C.F.R. § 416.1102.

389. 20 C.F.R. § 416.1110.
390. 20 C.F.R. §§ 416.1120–1121.
391. 20 C.F.R. § 416.1110(a)(3).
392. 20 C.F.R. § 416.1110(a)(3).
393. 20 C.F.R. § 416.1103.
394. 20 C.F.R. § 416.1103(c).
395. *See* 20 C.F.R. §§ 416.1112, 416.1124; 20 C.F.R. Part 416, subpart K, App., https://www.ssa.gov/OP_Home/cfr20/416/416-app-k.htm.
396. 20 C.F.R. § 416.1103(a).
397. 20 C.F.R. § 416.1103(a)(7).
398. 20 C.F.R. § 416.1103(b).
399. 20 C.F.R. §§ 416.1103(d); 416.1112(c)(1).
400. 20 C.F.R. § 416.1103(e).
401. 20 C.F.R. § 416.1103(f).
402. 20 C.F.R. § 416.1103(g).
403. *See* 20 C.F.R. Part 416, subpart K, III; 20 C.F.R. § 416.1124(c)(3).
404. 20 C.F.R. § 1112(c)(3).
405. U.S. Social Security Administration, A Guide for Representative Payees (Jan. 2018), at 5, https://www.ssa.gov/pubs/EN-05-10076.pdf.
406. 20 C.F.R. § 416.1124(c)(17).
407. For a current list of payments to Native Americans that do not count as income for SSI purposes, *see* C.F.R. Part 416, subpart K, App., https://www.ssa.gov/OP_Home/cfr20/416/416-app-k.htm.
408. For a list of such programs, *see* C.F.R. Part 416, subpart K, App. A, https://www.ssa.gov/OP_Home/cfr20/416/416-app-k.htm.
409. 20 C.F.R. §§ 416.1110–1112 (earned income); §§ 416.1120–1124 (unearned income); U.S. Social Security Administration, Income Exclusions for SSI Program (2019), https://www.ssa.gov/oact/cola/incomexcluded.html.
410. 20 C.F.R. §§ 416.1180–1182. For a comprehensive list of special programs and resources intended to help disability recipients return to work, *see* U.S. Social Security Administration, 2018 Red Book: A Summary Guide to Employment Supports for Persons with Disabilities under the Social Security Disability Insurance (SSDI) and Supplemental Security Income (SSI) Programs, https://www.ssa.gov/redbook/documents/TheRedBook2018.pdf.
411. 20 C.F.R. §§ 416.1180, 416.1112(c)(9), 1124(c)(13).
412. 20 C.F.R. §§ 416.1181, 416.1226.
413. 20 C.F.R. § 416.1130.
414. 20 C.F.R. § 416.1130(b).
415. 20 C.F.R. § 416.1131(a).
416. 20 C.F.R. § 416.1131(b).
417. 20 C.F.R. § 416.1131(b).
418. 20 C.F.R. § 416.1132(b).
419. 20 C.F.R. § 416.1132(c)(5). If every member of the household receives some form of public assistance payments, the SSA does not consider the claimant to be receiving

in-kind support and maintenance from anyone in the household. *See* 20 C.F.R. §
416.1142. In this situation, the claimant is considered to be living in a "public assistance household," and the one-third reduction rule does not apply. The "presumed
value rule" might still apply, but only if the claimant receives food or shelter from
someone outside the household. *See* 20 C.F.R. § 416.1142(b).

420. 20 C.F.R. § 416.1132(c)(3). A person is living in a "noninstitutional care situation"
if an agency responsible for the person's care places the person in a private household licensed or approved by the agency to provide care under a specific program
(like foster care) and the person, the agency, or a third party pays for the care. *See* 20
C.F.R. § 416.1143(a).

421. 20 C.F.R. § 416.1132(c)(4). The "pro rata share of household operating expenses"
is equal to the average monthly operating expenses paid for by members of the
household divided by the number of persons living in the household. Household
operating expenses are the expenditures made by household members for food,
rent, mortgage, property taxes, home energy, water, sewerage, and garbage collection. (Expenses paid for by persons outside the household are not counted for
these purposes.) 20 C.F.R. § 416.1133. The one-third reduction rule does not apply
if the person is paying a pro rata share of household operating expenses. 20 C.F.R.
§ 416.1133(a). The "presumed value rule" might still apply, but only if the person
receives food or shelter from someone outside the household.

422. 20 C.F.R. § 416.1132(c)(1)–(2).

423. 20 C.F.R. § 416.1141.

424. 20 C.F.R. §§ 416.1140(a)(1), 416.1124(c)(12).

425. 20 C.F.R. § 416.1140(a)(2) & (b)(2).

426. 20 C.F.R. § 416.1160(b). For the rules on income deeming, *see* 20 C.F.R. §§
416.1160–1169.

427. *See* 20 C.F.R. §§ 416.1160–1163. In determining a spouse's countable income for
deeming purposes, the SSA uses the same definition of income and exclusions that
apply to determining the income of a claimant. *See* 20 C.F.R. § 416.1163(a). The SSA
then subtracts from the spouse's countable income certain "allocations" for support
of children not eligible for SSI. If the amount remaining is less than the difference
between the federal benefit rate for an eligible couple and the federal benefit rate for
an individual, none of the spouse's income is deemed. 20 C.F.R. § 416.1163(d)(1). If
the spouse's countable income minus applicable allocations is larger than the difference between the federal benefit rate for an eligible couple and the federal benefit
rate for an individual, the SSA treats the claimant and the ineligible spouse as an eligible couple for purposes of determining financial eligibility and grant amount. 20
C.F.R. § 416.1163(d)(2).

428. U.S. Social Security Administration, Program Operations Manual System (POMS),
TN 34 (01-19), Effective Dates: 07/14/2017–Present, GN 00210.800, Recognition
of Same-Sex Marriages For SSI Purposes, https://secure.ssa.gov/poms.nsf/lnx/
0200210800.

429. 20 C.F.R. §§ 416.1160(a)(2), 416.1161, 416.1165. In determining a parent's income
for deeming purposes, the SSA uses the same definition of income and exclusions

that apply to determining the income of a claimant. *See* 20 C.F.R. § 416.1165(a). The
SSA then subtracts from this amount certain "allocations" for support of the parent
and any other children not eligible for SSI; in most cases, the amount remaining
after the subtraction of these allocations is deemed available to the child claimant.
See 20 C.F.R. § 416.1165(b)–(g).

430. 20 C.F.R. § 416.1165(g)(6).
431. 20 C.F.R. § 416.1165(g)(2).
432. 20 C.F.R. § 416.1166a. The SSA calculates the sponsor's income in accordance with
the same rules and subject to the same exclusions and deductions that apply to the
calculation of a claimant's income. However, not all of the sponsor's countable income is deemed available to the claimant: The SSA first deducts an allocation for the
sponsor (equal to the federal benefit rate for an individual) plus an allocation (equal
to one-half of that federal benefit rate) for each of the sponsor's dependents. The remaining income is deemed to the claimant. *Id.*
433. 20 C.F.R. § 416.1160(a)(3). If the sponsor is also a spouse or parent who is ineligible
for SSI and lives with the claimant, then the spouse-to-spouse or parent-to-child
deeming rules apply instead of the sponsor-to-alien rules. If the sponsor and an ineligible parent or spouse whose income can be deemed to the claimant both live
with the claimant, then both the relational and the immigrant deeming rules apply.
Sponsor-to-immigrant deeming does not apply to persons "permanently residing
in the U.S. under color of law" (PRUCOL). *See* U.S. Social Security Administration,
Program Operations Manual System (POMS), SI 01320.910 (2014), https://secure.
ssa.gov/poms.nsf/lnx/0501320910.
434. 20 C.F.R. § 416.1166a(d)(3).
435. 20 C.F.R. § 416.1166a(d)(1)–(2).
436. 20 C.F.R. § 416.1160.
437. 8 U.S.C. § 1631(b)(2)(A).
438. 8 U.S.C. § 1631(f)(1)(B).
439. 8 U.S.C. § 1631(e).
440. 20 C.F.R. § 416.1205. *See also* U.S. Social Security Administration, 2019 Social
Security Changes, https://www.ssa.gov/news/press/factsheets/colafacts2019.pdf.
441. 20 C.F.R. § 416.1201(a).
442. *See* 20 C.F.R. §§ 416.1210–1239.
443. *See* 20 C.F.R. § 416.1202.
444. 20 C.F.R. § 416.1202(a).
445. *Id.*; 20 C.F.R. §§ 416.1801–1826; *see also* U.S. Social Security Administration,
Program Operations Manual System (POMS), TN 34 (01-19), Effective Dates: 07/
14/2017–Present, GN 00210.800, Recognition of Same-Sex Marriages For SSI
Purposes, https://secure.ssa.gov/poms.nsf/lnx/0200210800.
446. 20 C.F.R. § 416.1202(b)(1).
447. 20 C.F.R. § 416.1202(b)(1)(i).
448. 20 C.F.R. § 416.1202(b)(1).
449. 20 C.F.R. § 416.1202(b)(2).
450. 20 C.F.R. § 416.1204.

451. 20 C.F.R. §§ 416.1204, 416.1166a(d)(3).

452. 20 C.F.R. §§ 416.1204, 416.1166a(d)(1)–(2).

453. 20 C.F.R. §§ 416.1204, 416.1160.

454. 8 U.S.C. § 1631(b)(2)(A).

455. 8 U.S.C. § 1631(e).

456. 8 U.S.C. § 1631(f)(1)(A).

457. 8 U.S.C. § 1631(f)(1)(B).

458. 20 C.F.R. § 416.1212(b).

459. 20 C.F.R. § 416.1212(c).

460. 20 C.F.R. § 416.1216. Examples of household goods include furniture, appliances, electronic equipment (such as personal computers and television sets), utensils, and dishes. Examples of personal effects include wedding and engagement rings, books, musical instruments, and objects of cultural or religious significance.

461. 20 C.F.R. § 416.1218(b)(1).

462. 20 C.F.R. § 416.1218(b)(2); *see also* 20 C.F.R. § 416.1201(c) (deeming of nonliquid resources).

463. U.S. Social Security Administration, Program Operations Manual System (POMS) TN 71 (01-15), SI 01130.200, Effective Dates: 05/31/2018–Present, Automobiles and Other Vehicles Used for Transportation, https://secure.ssa.gov/poms.nsf/lnx/0501130200.

464. 20 C.F.R. § 416.1222(a).

465. 20 C.F.R. § 416.1224.

466. 20 C.F.R. § 416.1225.

467. 20 C.F.R. § 416.1230(a).

468. 20 C.F.R. § 416.1231.

469. 20 C.F.R. § 416.1233.

470. 20 C.F.R. § 416.1233.

471. U.S. Social Security Administration, Program Operations Manual System (POMS), TN 10 (03-12), Effective Dates: 03/29/2013–Present, GN 00602.140 Permitted Expenditures from Dedicated Accounts, https://secure.ssa.gov/poms.nsf/lnx/0200602140.

472. *See* 20 C.F.R §§ 416.1236–1238.

473. 20 C.F.R. § 416.1236(a)(4).

474. 20 C.F.R. § 416.1236(a)(6).

475. 20 C.F.R. § 416.1236(a)(11).

476. 20 C.F.R. § 416.1236(a)(5).

477. 20 C.F.R. § 416.1236(a)(13).

478. This includes assistance paid under the U.S. Housing Act of 1937, the National Housing Act, Section 101 of the Housing and Urban Development Act of 1965, Title V of the Housing Act of 1949, or Section 202(h) of the Housing Act of 1959. 20 C.F.R. §§ 416.1238, 416.1124(c)(14).

479. 20 C.F.R. § 416.1236(a)(7).

480. 20 C.F.R. § 416.1236(a)(2)–(3).

481. 20 C.F.R. § 416.1236(a)(16).

482. 20 C.F.R. § 416.1236(a)(17).

483. 20 C.F.R. § 416.1237.

484. 20 C.F.R. § 416.1234.

485. 20 C.F.R. § 416.1232(a).

486. 20 C.F.R. § 416.1246(a).

487. 20 C.F.R. § 416.1246(d)(1).

488. 20 C.F.R. § 416.1246(d)(2).

489. 20 C.F.R. § 416.1202.

490. 20 C.F.R. § 1207(c).

491. U.S. Social Security Administration, Program Operations Manual System (POMS), TN 47 (02-13), Effective Dates: 06/07/2018–Present, SI 01120.200—Information on Trusts, Including Trusts Established Prior to January 01, 2000, Trusts Established with the Assets of Third Parties, and Trusts Not Subject to Section 1613(e) of the Social Security Act, https://secure.ssa.gov/poms.nsf/lnx/0501120200.

492. *See* 42 U.S.C. § 1396p(d)(4)(A).

493. 20 C.F.R. § 416.1201(c).

494. 20 C.F.R. § 416.1240(a)(1)–(2).

495. 20 C.F.R. §§ 416.1242, 416.1245. *See* U.S. Social Security Administration, Program Operations Manual System TN 14 (02-10), Effective Dates: 03/06/2012–Present, SI 01150.200—Conditional Benefits, https://secure.ssa.gov/poms.nsf/lnx/0501150200.

496. 20 C.F.R. § 416.1245(a).

497. 20 C.F.R. § 416.1245(b).

498. 20 C.F.R. §§ 416.301–360.

499. 20 C.F.R. § 416.330(a).

500. 20 C.F.R. § 416.325(a).

501. 20 C.F.R. § 416.325(b)(1).

502. 20 C.F.R. §§ 416.340, 416.345.

503. 20 C.F.R. § 416.351.

504. 20 C.F.R. § 416.351(f).

505. U.S. Social Security Administration, Office of the Inspector General, Audits and Investigations, Reduce Disability Backlogs and Improve Decisional Quality, https://oig.ssa.gov/audits-and-investigations/top-ssa-management-issues/reduce-disability-backlogs-and-improve-decisional-quality (reporting a backlog of over 568,000 initial disability claims pending at the end of FY 2016).

506. 20 C.F.R. §§ 416.931–932. *See also* 20 C.F.R. § 416.933.

507. 20 C.F.R. § 416.934. The specific impairment categories are listed as:

   (a) Amputation of a leg at the hip;
   (b) Allegation of total deafness;
   (c) Allegation of total blindness;
   (d) Allegation of bed confinement or immobility without a wheelchair, walker, or crutches, due to a long-standing condition, excluding recent accident and recent surgery;
   (e) Allegation of a stroke (cerebral vascular accident) more than three months in the past and continued marked difficulty in walking or using a hand or arm;

(f)   Allegation of cerebral palsy, muscular dystrophy, or muscle atrophy and marked difficulty in walking (for example, use of braces), speaking, or coordination of the hands or arms;

(g)   Allegation of Downs syndrome;

(h)   Allegation of severe mental deficiency made by another individual filing on behalf of a claimant who is at least seven years of age. For example, a mother filing for benefits for her child states that the child attends (or attended) a special school, or special classes in school because of mental deficiency or is unable to attend any type of school (or if beyond school age, was unable to attend), and requires care and supervision of routine daily activities;

(i)   Allegation of amyotrophic lateral sclerosis (ALS, Lou Gehrig's disease);

(j)   Infants weighing less than 1,200 grams at birth, until attainment of one year of age;

(k)   Infants weighing at least 1,200 but less than 2,000 grams at birth, and who are small for gestational age, until attainment of one year of age. (Small for gestational age means a birthweight that is at or more than two standard deviations below the mean or that is less than the third growth percentile for the gestational age of the infant.)

508.   20 C.F.R. § 416.1404(a).

509.   42 U.S.C. § 405. *See* 20 C.F.R. §§ 416.1402, 416.1404, 416.1409.

510.   20 C.F.R. § 416.1336.

511.   *Id. See* 20 C.F.R. § 416.1411 (listing factors that the Social Security Administration considers in determining good cause).

512.   20 C.F.R. § 416.1402.

513.   *Id.*

514.   20 C.F.R. § 416.1400. *See* Harold J. Krent & Scott Morris, Inconsistency and Angst in District Court Resolution of Social Security Disability Appeals, 67 Hastings L.J. 367, 373–377 (2016).

515.   *See* 20 C.F.R. § 416.1407.

516.   20 C.F.R. § 416.1429.

517.   20 C.F.R. § 416.1467.

518.   As a legal matter, the Social Security Administration may reopen and revise "final" decisions, but this is unusual. *See* 20 C.F.R. §§ 416.1487–1494.

519.   20 C.F.R. § 416.1400(a)(5).

520.   U.S. Social Security Administration, Social Security Administration (SSA) Annual Data for Disability Reconsideration Average Processing Time (Dec. 14, 2018), https://www.ssa.gov/open/data/disability_reconsideration_average_processing_time.html.

521.   U.S. Social Security Administration, Office of Inspector General, Fiscal Year 2018 Inspector General's Statement on the Social Security Administration's Major Management and Performance Challenges, A-02-18-50307 (Nov. 9, 2018), at 1, https://oig.ssa.gov/sites/default/files/audit/full/pdf/A-02-18-50307.pdf.

522.   *See* Jeffrey S. Wolfe, Civil Justice Reform in Social Security Adjudications, 64 Admin. L. Rev. 379, 383 (2012). Budget disputes and hiring freezes have impeded efforts to improve the decision-making process. *See* Josh Eidelson,

Trump's Hiring Freeze May Worsen 526-Day Disability Case Backlog, Bloomberg (Jan. 27, 2017), https://www.bloomberg.com/news/articles/2017-01-27/trump-freeze-seen-worsening-526-day-disability-case-backlog.

523. 20 C.F.R. § 416.1336. *See* U.S. Social Security Administration, The Appeals Process (2018), http://www.ssa.gov/pubs/EN-05-10041.pdf.

524. 20 C.F.R. § 416.1500.

525. 20 C.F.R. § 416.1505.

526. 20 C.F.R. § 416.1507. The Social Security Administration makes available Form SSA-1696 to appoint a representative, https://www.ssa.gov/forms/ssa-1696.pdf.

527. 20 C.F.R. § 416.1540.

528. 20 C.F.R. § 416.1520. *See* U.S. Social Security Administration, SSA's Fee Authorization Process, https://www.ssa.gov/representation/overview.htm; Social Security Administration, Fee Agreements, https://www.ssa.gov/representation/fee_agreements.htm.

529. 20 C.F.R. § 416.1409(a).

530. For the Social Security Request for Reconsideration form (SSA-561-U2), *see* https://www.ssa.gov/forms/ssa-561.pdf. A request for reconsideration may be filed online at https://www.ssa.gov/benefits/disability/appeal.html.

531. 20 C.F.R. § 416.1409(a).

532. 20 C.F.R. § 416.1401.

533. 20 C.F.R. § 416.1409(b).

534. 20 C.F.R. § 416.1411.

535. 20 C.F.R. § 416.1409(b).

536. 20 C.F.R. § 416.1407.

537. 20 C.F.R. § 416.1415.

538. 20 C.F.R. § 416.1413.

539. 20 C.F.R. § 416.1413(a).

540. 20 C.F.R. § 416.1413(b).

541. 20 C.F.R. § 416.1413(c).

542. 20 C.F.R. § 416.1416(c).

543. 20 C.F.R. § 416.1416(b).

544. 20 C.F.R. § 416.1415.

545. *See* 20 C.F.R. § 416.1416. *See generally* 20 C.F.R. §§ 416.1414–1418.

546. 20 C.F.R. § 416.1413a(b).

547. 20 C.F.R. § 416.1413a(a).

548. 20 C.F.R. § 416.1413b.

549. 20 C.F.R. § 416.1413b.

550. 20 C.F.R. § 416.1429.

551. 20 C.F.R. §§ 416.1336; 416.1433. As noted earlier, the SSA will assume that a claimant receives a mailed notice no later than five days after the date on the notice. *See* 20 C.F.R. § 416.140. To file an appeal online, go to https://www.ssa.gov/benefits/disability/appeal.html.

552. In 1971, the U.S. Supreme Court rejected a due process challenge arguing that ALJs affiliated with the executive branch and the Social Security Administration

itself were not sufficiently independent and unbiased to provide a fair hearing to claimants challenging decisions of that agency. *See* Richardson v. Perales, 402 U.S. 389 (1971). In 1989, the U.S. Court of Appeals for the Second Circuit expressed concern that SSA's alleged policy of "coerc[ing] ALJs into lowering reversal rates—that is, into deciding more cases against claimants—would, if shown, constitute in the district court's words 'a clear infringement of decisional independence.'" Nash v. Bowen, 869 F.2d 675, 681 (2d Cir. 1989). Nevertheless, the Second Circuit upheld the district court's finding that ALJs had sufficient decisional independence, and that quotas imposed by the SSA did not impede that independence. The Trump administration recently changed the manner in which Social Security ALJs are appointed, citing the U.S. Supreme Court's decision in Lucia v. Securities and Exchange Commission, 138 S. Ct. 2044 (2018), which held that administrative law judges at the Securities and Exchange Commission are "officers of the United States" subject to the Constitution's appointments clause. *See* Excepting Administrative Law Judges from the Competitive Service, Presidential Executive Order 13843 (July 10, 2018). The American Bar Association, along with a number of commentators, oppose this change, expressing concern that it will further erode the independence of Social Security ALJs. *See* Debra Cassens Weis, ABA president says Trump order could politicize the process of hiring administrative law judges, ABA Journal (July 16, 2018), http://www.abajournal.com/news/article/aba_president_says_trump_order_could_politicize_the_process_of_hiring_admin.

553. 20 C.F.R. § 416.1438.
554. 20 C.F.R. § 416.1436(e)–(g).
555. 20 C.F.R. § 416.1436(b).
556. 20 C.F.R. § 416.1436(c)–(d).
557. U.S. Social Security Administration, Program Operations Manual System (POMS), TN 21 (01-12) FN 03103.200 Hearing Disclosure, https://secure.ssa.gov/poms.nsf/lnx/0203103200.
558. 20 C.F.R. § 416.1450(a).
559. 20 C.F.R. §§ 416.912, 416.1435.
560. 20 C.F.R. § 416.1449.
561. 20 C.F.R. § 416.1450(d).
562. 20 C.F.R. § 416.1450(a).
563. 20 C.F.R. § 416.1451.
564. 20 C.F.R. § 416.1450(c) ("[T]he administrative law judge may receive any evidence at the hearing that he or she believes is material to the issues, even though the evidence would not be admissible in court under the rules of evidence used by the court.").
565. *See, for example*, Yancey v. Apfel, 145 F.3d 106, 113 (2d Cir.1998) ("[T]he requirements of due process are satisfied by providing a claimant with the opportunity to cross-examine a reporting physician where reasonably necessary to a full development of the evidence in the case.").
566. 20 C.F.R. § 416.1444.
567. *Id.*

568. A list of legal services organizations is available through an interactive website, https://www.lawhelp.org.

569. 20 C.F.R. § 416.1436(f)–(g).

570. 20 C.F.R. § 416.1450(d).

571. 20 C.F.R. § 416.1450(d)(2), (3).

572. 20 C.F.R. § 416.1450(d)(3)–(4). The witness attendance fee in 2018 is $40 per day plus the actual cost of transportation by common carrier at the most economical rate reasonably available. *See* 28 U.S.C. § 1821(b), (c)(1). If the witness uses an automobile, mileage plus the actual cost of tolls and parking will be paid. *See* 28 U.S.C. § 1821(c)(2)–(3).

573. 20 C.F.R. § 404.1527. *See, for example*, Tonapetyan v. Halter, 242 F.3d 1144, 1150 (9th Cir. 2001) (ALJ rejection of treating physician's diagnosis supported by substantial evidence).

574. 20 C.F.R. § 416.920c. *See* U.S. Social Security Administration, Revisions to Rules Regarding the Evaluation of Medical Evidence, 82 Fed. Reg. 5844 (Jan. 18, 2017).

575. 20 C.F.R. § 416.1453(a).

576. 20 C.F.R. § 416.1453(c).

577. 20 C.F.R. § 416.1466–67.

578. The form entitled "Request for Review of Hearing Decision/Order," OMB No. 0960-0277, is available at https://www.ssa.gov/forms/ha-520.pdf. Instructions are available at https://www.ssa.gov/forms/ha-520.html. However, always follow the instructions on your notice.

579. 20 C.F.R. § 416.1468(a).

580. *See* U.S. Social Security Administration, Hearings and Appeals, Information About Requesting Review of an Administrative Law Judge's Hearing Decision, https://www.ssa.gov/appeals/appeals_process.html.

581. 20 C.F.R. §§ 416.1479, 416.1481.

582. U.S. Social Security Administration, Hearings and Appeals, AC Remands as a Percentage of all AC Dispositions, https://www.ssa.gov/appeals/DataSets/AC03_AC_Remands_All_Dispositions.html.

583. 42 U.S.C. 405(g).

584. *See, for example*, Hepp v. Astrue, 511 F.3d 798, 806 (8th Cir. 2008); Nelms v. Astrue, 553 F.3d 1093 (7th Cir. 2009).

585. 20 C.F.R. § 416.1481.

586. *See, for example*, Mathews v. Eldridge, 424 U.S. 319, 326–332 (1976).

587. *See* U.S. Department of Veterans Affairs, Compensation, http://www.benefits.va.gov/compensation/.

588. *See* U.S. Department of Labor, Office of Workers' Compensation Programs, http://www.dol.gov/owcp/owcpcomp.htm. Additional information about state workers' compensation is available at https://www.dol.gov/owcp/dfec/regs/compliance/wc.htm.

589. *See* U.S. Social Security Administration, Research, Statistics, & Policy Analysis, State Assistance Programs for SSI Recipients, January 2011, https://www.ssa.gov/policy/docs/progdesc/ssi_st_asst/. The last edition of this report is 2011. Additional

information when available is reported in the annual SSI Recipients by State and County, https://www.ssa.gov/policy/docs/statcomps/ssi_sc/index.html.

590. U.S. Social Security Administration, Social Security Handbook: Interim Assistance Reimbursement,https://www.ssa.gov/OP_Home/handbook/handbook.21/handbook-2186.html.

591. Information in this section, including Table 1.1, is drawn from Liz Schott & Misha Hill, State General Assistance Programs Are Weakening Despite Increased Need, Center on Budget and Policy Priorities (July 9, 2015), http://www.cbpp.org/sites/default/files/atoms/files/7-9-15pov.pdf. States with GA programs in 2015 are Alaska, California, Colorado, Connecticut, Delaware, District of Columbia, Hawaii, Indiana, Iowa, Maine, Maryland, Massachusetts, Michigan, Minnesota, Nebraska, Nevada, New Hampshire, New Jersey, New Mexico, New York, Ohio, Rhode Island, South Dakota, Utah, Vermont, and Washington.

592. L. Gerome Gallagher, Cori E. Uccello, Alicia B. Pierce, and Erin B. Reidy, State General Assistance Programs 1998, Urban Institute, Discussion Paper 99-01, at 114, 117–118 (Apr. 1999), https://www.urban.org/sites/default/files/publication/69786/409066-State-General-Assistance-Programs--.PDF.

593. The states are: Alaska, California, Colorado, Connecticut, Delaware, District of Columbia, Hawaii, Indiana, Iowa, Maine, Maryland, Massachusetts, Michigan, Minnesota, Nebraska, Nevada, New Hampshire, New Jersey, New Mexico, New York, Ohio, Rhode Island, South Dakota, Utah, Vermont, and Washington.

594. The states are: Delaware, Massachusetts, Michigan, Minnesota, New York, and Vermont.

595. The states are: Alaska, California, Indiana, Iowa, Maine, Nebraska, Nevada, New Hampshire, New Jersey, New York, and South Dakota.

2

Work-Related Benefits and Employment Protections

Introduction

Does the federal Constitution guarantee a job to everyone who wants to work?

No. The federal Constitution does not guarantee employment to persons who wish to work. Some scholars have advanced arguments in support of such a right, emphasizing the importance of work to self-worth, political participation, and financial independence—indeed, many critically important social goods, such as health insurance and pensions, are linked to a person's employment.[1] Although there is no right to a job, the Constitution bans forced work—the institutions of human slavery and involuntary servitude were formally outlawed by the Thirteenth Amendment.[2] Moreover, the Equal Protection Clause bars the government from refusing to hire a person on the basis of race, ethnicity, or gender.[3] International law more broadly recognizes a right to work, expressed as "the opportunity" to gain a living through employment that is freely chosen.[4]

In addition, Congress constitutionally may enact laws that regulate private employment. Some of these laws protect low-income workers and, if enforced, have the potential to expand economic opportunity.[5] This chapter addresses federal statutes that regulate the terms and conditions of employment and protect the right of workers to engage in collective action.

Access to Employment Opportunities

Can an employer refuse to hire or employ someone because of race, ethnicity, gender, age, or disability?

Congress has enacted statutes that prohibit public and private employers from discriminating against job applicants and workers on the basis of race, ethnicity, religion, gender,[6] age,[7] or disability.[8]

Getting By. Helen Hershkoff and Stephen Loffredo, Oxford University Press (2020). © Helen Hershkoff & Stephen Loffredo.
DOI: 10.1093/oso/9780190080860.001.0001

These federal statutes have a common aim: "eradicating discrimination throughout the economy and making persons whole for injuries suffered through past discrimination."[9] A person who believes that an employer has taken impermissible factors into account in making a hiring decision, or providing different working conditions, should promptly seek legal advice, since the time limit for filing a discrimination claim may be as short as 180 days from the date of the discriminatory act. Individuals may lodge a complaint with the federal or state agency charged with enforcement of the statutes.[10] Some states and localities have enacted laws that provide greater protection than federal law against workplace discrimination.[11]

Can a private employer refuse to hire or employ persons who are not U.S. citizens?

A private employer may not discriminate against job applicants or employees on the basis of citizenship status.[12] However, federal law requires that employers hire only those noncitizens who can document that they are lawfully present and authorized to work in the United States, and the law imposes sanctions on employers who violate these requirements.[13] An employer may not prescreen an applicant for citizenship status or only check employment authorization of certain applicants (for example, because of their skin color or surname).[14] Rather, employers must complete an I-9 Employment Verification Eligibility Form for every new hire. This process requires the worker to show documentation of identity and eligibility to work.[15] Some employers also submit their workers' information to the government through an online system called "E-Verify," which checks whether the information provided on the I-9 (such as a Social Security number) matches the information in the government's databases. If the information the employer submits through E-Verify does not match the government's records, the government will issue a notice of "Tentative Nonconfirmation." An employee who wishes to contest the nonconfirmation decision must do so within eight federal workdays. During that period, an employer is not permitted to fire the worker or take any other adverse action.[16]

What information can an employer use to make hiring decisions?

Employers frequently screen job applicants based on information obtained from companies that are in the business of preparing consumer or investigative reports. These reports are more than just a credit check. Rather, they also include information about character, reputation, and personal characteristics, as well as the kind of information that would be assembled for insurance or to get a credit card. These reports also may include information about an applicant's criminal history or arrest record (though some states and localities restrict use of such information, as discussed below). When a report contains outdated and erroneous information, its use by an employer in the hiring process can seriously harm affected applicants who, as a result, are shut out of jobs.[17]

The Fair Credit Reporting Act (FCRA) regulates an employer's use of information contained in consumer and investigative reports purchased from data-providing companies.[18] It also applies to companies that compile and sell criminal record reports.[19] (The FCRA is discussed in more detail in chapter 6.)

A consumer report is "any written, oral, or other communication of any information by a consumer reporting agency bearing on a consumer's credit worthiness, credit standing, credit capacity, character, general reputation, personal characteristics, or mode of living."[20]

An investigative report is a consumer report, or any part of a consumer report, that contains information about a consumer obtained through "personal interviews with neighbors, friends, or associates of the consumer reported on or with others with whom he is acquainted or who may have knowledge concerning any such items of information,"[21] and covers:

- Character;
- General reputation;
- Personal characteristics; or
- Mode of living.

The FCRA imposes a number of procedural requirements on employers and on consumer reporting agencies before a consumer or investigatory report can be used to make hiring decisions.[22]

Notice of background check. First, an employer must inform an applicant that it plans to conduct a background check. Specifically, the employer must give the applicant written notice that a background check will be done in connection with the hiring decision.[23] The notice must be separate from any other document or form that the employer gives to the applicant.[24]

Written consent to use report. Second, the employer must get the applicant's written consent to use a consumer report or an investigative report as part of the background check.[25]

The applicant's written consent can be affixed to the same form that the employer uses to disclose that it is undertaking a background check, but nothing else can be on the document.[26]

Employer certification. Third, the employer cannot obtain a report from a consumer reporting company unless it has certified that it gave the applicant notice of the background check and the applicant gave written consent to get a report, and that the report will not be used for discriminatory purposes or in violation of applicable federal laws.[27]

Copy of report for adverse actions. Fourth, if the employer does not hire the applicant—or, after hiring the applicant, wants to fire the employee or take any other adverse action[28]—the employer first must give the applicant or worker a copy of the consumer or investigative report, as well as a copy of "A Summary of Your Rights Under the Fair Credit Reporting Act," which is available on the Federal Trade Commission's website.[29] The employer then must give the applicant or worker some time to review and, if necessary, ask to correct the report on which the planned adverse decision will be based. Case law has held that the employer must give "sufficient" notice before the adverse action is taken.[30]

Notice of adverse action. Fifth, then the employer must give the affected person notice of the adverse action taken. Unlike the initial disclosure form, notice of an adverse action can be given in writing, orally, or electronically. The notice must state that the action was based on information provided in a report obtained from a consumer reporting company and must give the name and contact information of that company. The notice also must state that the consumer reporting company did not make the adverse decision and cannot provide specific reasons for it. Finally, the notice must tell the applicant or employee of the rights to get a free copy of the report within a 60-day period and to dispute information in the report.[31]

A job applicant or worker who has good reason to suspect that an employer misused personal information as the basis for a negative employment decision may file a complaint with the Consumer Financial Protection Bureau.[32] Consumer and investigative reports also are discussed in chapter 6.

Can an employer refuse to hire someone who has an arrest or criminal record?

No federal statute specifically bars an employer from considering an applicant's criminal history when making a job decision. The vast majority of employers— 93 percent, according to a study conducted in 2010—screen applicants for criminal histories and arrest records and make hiring decisions based on that information.[33] This practice significantly affects earning and mobility of persons who have had contact with the criminal system.[34] Twenty-five percent of the U.S. population has a criminal record.[35] The United States also has an exceptionally high prison rate; in 2010, more than 2.3 million individuals were in federal and state prisons, up from less than a million in 1980.[36] Arrest rates among men who are African American or Hispanic are two to three times more than their proportion of the general population.[37]

Nevertheless, job applicants have some protection because the hiring process must comply with the Fair Credit Reporting Act, which regulates an employer's using information about an applicant's criminal record when making an employment decision. The Fair Credit Reporting Act generally bars reporting companies from reporting information that is considered too old to be useful, and prohibits the reporting of "records of arrest that, from date of entry, antedate the report by more than seven years."[38] An exception to this prohibition exists if the applicant is expected to earn more than $75,000 a year.[39] Some state laws prohibit employers from seeking information about, or asking job applicants to disclose, arrests that did not result in a conviction.[40] Some of these state laws go further and prohibit consumer reporting agencies from disclosing arrest or conviction records that are more than seven years old for any purpose. [41]

Perhaps more importantly, a majority of states and a large number of localities have adopted "fair chance" or "ban-the-box" laws that prohibit public and/or private employers from screening out job applicants on the basis of past criminal records. Under these laws, employers must first consider a job applicant on the merits of skill and qualifications, and may not inquire about a criminal record or conduct a criminal background check until after a conditional offer of employment has been made.[42] As of 2018, 33 states and over 100 local jurisdictions had adopted fair chance policies for public employment; 11 states and 17 cities had extended these fair chance laws to private employers as well.[43]

Although no federal law bars an employer from considering criminal records in hiring decisions, federal civil rights and federal consumer-protection laws affect the legality of the practice.[44]

In 2012, the Equal Employment Opportunity Commission (EEOC), which enforces federal antidiscrimination rules in the workplace, issued an Enforcement Guidance on the use of arrest records in the hiring process. The EEOC advised that a company may not rely on arrest records as a complete bar to employment because such records lack probative value as to whether the applicant actually engaged in criminal misconduct, and their use could impermissibly screen out disproportionate numbers of persons in violation of federal laws that bar discrimination on the basis of race, ethnicity, and gender. Instead, the Enforcement Guidance advises an employer to make an individualized assessment of the applicant, which may consider factors related to criminal history such as: "1) the nature and gravity of the offense or conduct; 2) the time that has passed since the offense or conduct and/or completion of the sentence; and 3) the nature of the job held or sought."[45] The Restoration of Rights Project maintains a website with a state-by-state analysis of the laws pertaining to restoration of rights and status following arrest and conviction.[46]

Can an employer refuse to hire an applicant who has filed for bankruptcy?

Federal bankruptcy law is designed to give the debtor a "fresh start." Federal law bars a public employer from discriminating against a person who is a debtor or has declared bankruptcy, and the protection extends to hiring, firing, and the terms and conditions of employment.[47] A separate provision of the bankruptcy code bars private employers from terminating and discriminating in the terms and conditions of employment because of a person's indebtedness or bankruptcy.[48] The federal courts are divided on whether the bankruptcy code's antidiscrimination provisions for private employers apply only while a person is employed, or also during the hiring process.[49] If screening for bankruptcy status is a pretext for not hiring persons on the basis of race, ethnicity, or gender, then the practice may be impermissible as a violation of Title VII unless the employer can show that the person's bankruptcy status is related to bona fide job qualifications.[50]

Can an employer refuse to hire an applicant because of an unfavorable credit history?

Federal law does not directly bar an employer from screening an applicant's credit history or from basing hiring decisions upon such information—unless use of this factor is a pretext for decisions impermissibly based on race, ethnicity, or gender, or has a disparate impact upon such persons. With respect to applicants who are disabled within the meaning of federal law, the Equal Employment Opportunity Commission also has stated that an employer's use of financial information as a basis for hiring could trigger the applicant's right to a reasonable accommodation.[51] Finally, as discussed earlier in this chapter, the employer's use of a consumer report must comply with the disclosure requirements of the Fair Credit Reporting Act.

Can an employer refuse to hire persons who are unemployed at the time they apply for the job?

Screening out the unemployed from an employer's applicant pool became a common practice with the rise of "long-term unemployment"—officially defined as being out of work for 27 weeks or longer[52]—beginning with the recession of 2008.[53] In the years following 2008, the average unemployed job applicant had been out of work for over 30 weeks. By 2018, the average spell of unemployment was still nearly 23 weeks, a figure that does not include people "discouraged" from seeking employment.[54] No federal law explicitly bars an employer from screening out job applicants who are currently employed, although using a consumer report to determine an applicant's job history is subject to the Fair Credit Reporting Act.[55] As with credit history and bankruptcy status, an employer cannot use job history as a pretext for impermissible discrimination on the basis of race, ethnicity, or gender.[56] A few states and localities, including Chicago, Madison (Wisconsin), New York City and State, New Jersey, Oregon, and the District of Columbia, have enacted laws prohibiting employers from screening out unemployed job applicants.[57]

Can an employer refuse to hire or employ a person who is pregnant or a parent?

The federal Pregnancy Discrimination Act bars employment discrimination against women on the basis of pregnancy, childbirth, or related medical conditions, and requires that the employer treat women with this status or condition "the same for all employment-related purposes . . . as other persons not so affected but similar in their ability or inability to work."[58] The statute bars outright discrimination—a refusal to hire a woman because she is pregnant or a parent—and also employment practices that result in "disparate treatment" of such women—the legal term for practices that by effect treat an applicant or employee less favorably than others similarly situated but who are not pregnant or parenting.[59] The U.S. Supreme Court has held that the statute is presumptively violated when the applicant or worker can show that an employer's policies impose a significant burden on pregnant women by refusing to provide them with a kind of accommodation that is given to a large percentage of workers who are not pregnant or parenting.[60] For example, the EEOC considers pregnancy a temporary disability, and if the employer accommodates comparable nonpregnancy medical disabilities, it ordinarily must do the same for women in similar positions.[61]

Fair Labor Standards Act—Minimum Wage and Overtime Protections

What is the Fair Labor Standards Act?

The Fair Labor Standards Act (FLSA) is a federal statute setting minimum standards for the wages certain employers must pay their workers. For workers covered by the FLSA, the statute guarantees a minimum wage rate and "overtime" wages for work that goes beyond the usual 40-hour workweek. The FLSA also regulates—and in many instances bans—child labor.[62] Congress enacted the FLSA in 1938 to eliminate "labor conditions detrimental to the maintenance of the minimum standard of living necessary for health, efficiency, and general well-being of workers."[63] The central purpose was "to aid the unprotected, unorganized and lowest paid of the nation's working population; that is, those employees who lacked sufficient bargaining power to secure for themselves a minimum wage."[64] President Franklin D. Roosevelt, who signed the bill into law, said that the purpose of the FLSA was to give "all our able-bodied working men and women a fair day's pay for a fair day's work."[65] However, at the insistence of southern senators, the 1938 statute excluded from its protections domestic workers and farmworkers—employment that accounted for the majority of jobs held by African Americans and other people of color.[66] Over the years, federal and state legislation has gradually extended some labor protection to some these workers, as discussed later in this chapter.

How much is the federal minimum wage?

As of 2019, the federal minimum wage rate was a mere $7.25 per hour, far below a poverty wage for many families, though most states and many localities have adopted higher standards.[67]

Is the minimum wage the same as a living wage?

No. A "living wage" refers to the amount a working household needs to meet basic needs—not merely subsistence needs—of food, housing, clothing, and so forth. The "living wage" movement has its roots in the 1891 Encyclical of Pope Leo XII on capital and labor, which called upon government to ensure that "a workman's wages be sufficient to enable him comfortably to support himself, his wife, and his children."[68] President Franklin D. Roosevelt, in proposing the National Industrial Recovery Act, which preceded the Fair Labor Standards Act

(FLSA), stated, "No business which depends for existence on paying less than living wages to its workers has any right to continue in this country . . . [B]y living wages I mean more than a bare subsistence level—I mean the wages of a decent living."[69]

The wage rates guaranteed by the FLSA fall far short of a living wage, in part because Congress has failed to set the statutory minimum at a level reflective of families' actual needs, and in part because Congress has refused to index the federal minimum wage to inflation.[70] Full-time work at the federal minimum wage has not been sufficient to bring a family of three up to the poverty level since 1968.[71] Congress last raised the federal minimum wage in 2009, entitling covered workers to compensation of at least $7.25 per hour for a 40-hour work-week, and time and a half of their regular wage rate for overtime.[72] Between 2009 and 2018, inflation reduced the minimum wage's effective purchasing power by over 15 percent.[73] A married couple with two children and one wage earner who works full time at the minimum wage rate, even supplemented by tax credits (discussed later this chapter), subsists on a salary that is 17 percent below the federal poverty level.[74]

As noted below, over half of the states and many localities have set minimum wage rates higher than the federal standard,[75] driven in part by the "Fight for 15" movement and other organized efforts to achieve living wages.[76] Increases in the minimum wage have been shown to improve nutrition and health outcomes for the wage earner and the worker's children (for example, decreasing the incidence of low birthweight babies and premature deaths), and to improve the quality of life for people at the bottom of the economic ladder.[77]

How many workers have jobs that pay the federal minimum wage or less?

In 1979, 13.4 percent of all wage and salary workers in the United States received the then-existing federal minimum wage rate or less. In 2017, 2.3 percent, about 3.1 million workers, received that wage or less.[78] Much of the decline is attributable to the growth of state minimum wage laws that require compensation above the federal minimum.[79] Workers under age 25 made up half of workers paid the minimum wage or less.[80] The states with the highest percentages of hourly paid workers earning at or below the federal minimum wage rate were in the South: Alabama, Kentucky, Louisiana, Mississippi, North Carolina, South Carolina, Tennessee, and Virginia.[81] These states also have low numbers of unionized workers.[82] As of the 2019, 29 states and the District of Columbia had established higher minimum wage rates than the federal minimum; at the other end of the spectrum, five states—Alabama, Louisiana,

Mississippi, South Carolina, and Tennessee—still do not provide a minimum wage rate or an overtime compensation guarantee.[83] (State minimum wage rates may be found on the U.S. Department of Labor website at https://www.dol.gov/whd/minwage/america.htm.) Overall, compared to other industrialized nations, the United States consistently has the highest percentage of low-wage workers, linked in part to other legal rules that depress earnings—for example, by requiring workers to pay for health care expenses that elsewhere in the world are government-subsidized.[84]

Is an employer required to tell its workers about the minimum wage and overtime?

Yes. Employers are required to display an official poster from the U.S. Department of Labor that tells workers their basic rights under the Fair Labor Standards Act.[85] A copy of the poster can be downloaded electronically.[86] Requiring posters of this sort recognizes the importance of telling workers about legal protections to make sure their rights are enforced. By knowing what the act requires, workers can monitor their employers and insist that they are properly classified as employees and not as independent contractors; that they receive overtime pay when appropriate; and that breaks are provided when required.[87]

Is an employer required to tell its workers how much its chief executive officer earns?

The Fair Labor Standards Act does not require an employer to tell its workers about executive or managerial compensation. However, the Dodd-Frank Wall Street Reform and Consumer Protection Act, enacted in 2010 in the wake of the 2008 recession, requires "publicly traded" companies (those with shares traded through a stock exchange) to disclose to shareholders—but not to workers—how much their chief executive officers earn relative to the median pay of their workers. During the Obama administration, the Securities and Exchange Commission adopted regulations to enforce the statutory reporting requirement. The first reporting period was to be the first full fiscal year after January 1, 2017,[88] but in February 2017, the Trump administration announced reconsideration of the rule's implementation.[89] The average CEO-to-worker pay ratio in the United States—which was about 20 to 1 in 1950 and 42 to 1 in 1980—has skyrocketed to nearly 400 to 1 in 2018, with the highest disparities close to 5,000 to 1. The United States has long led the developed world in CEO-to-worker pay inequality.[90]

Are all workers protected by the Fair Labor Standards Act?

No. Federal minimum wage protections apply to workers employed by certain kinds of entities ("enterprise coverage"), to workers regularly engaged in work that involves interstate commerce ("individual coverage"),[91] and to domestic service workers (such as housekeepers.).[92] Included are the employees of entities that have annual sales or business of at least $500,000 and the employees of hospitals, businesses providing medical or nursing care for residents, schools and preschools, and state or federal government agencies. In addition, any employee who regularly produces goods or provides services for sale out of state, assists in transactions or engages in communications with people or entities in another state or country, travels out of state on the job, or is otherwise regularly involved interstate commerce, is covered by the act.[93]

Who is an "employee" under the Fair Labor Standards Act?

The Fair Labor Standards Act intentionally defines "employee" very broadly as "any individual employed by an employer."[94] Under the FLSA " '[e]mploy' includes to suffer or permit to work,"[95] meaning that any person an employer requires or allows to work for the enterprise, or has reason to believe is doing work for the enterprise, is an "employee" entitled to minimum wage protections, whether or not the employer requested or contracted for the work.[96] However, the term "employee" is subject to certain statutory exemptions. The major exemptions discussed in this chapter are certain agricultural workers, salespeople who work on commission, domestic companions, so-called "white collar" (administrative, executive, and professional) employees, and "independent contractors."[97] Misclassifying a worker as exempt from the minimum wage and/or overtime protections of the FLSA is illegal, but nevertheless a pervasive problem. One study of New York alone estimated that 10 percent of workers were misclassified as exempt; a study of the construction industry in Maine found that 14 percent of the workers likewise were misclassified.[98] In addition to exempt workers who do not receive the minimum wage or overtime, the FLSA permits employers to pay subminimum wages to three categories of workers (training wages to youth, disabled workers in special programs, and tipped workers) discussed later in this chapter.

Are "independent contractors" covered
by the Fair Labor Standards Act?

No. A worker who is an "independent contractor" as defined by federal law is not protected by the Fair Labor Standards Act.[99] Independent contractors make up a substantial percentage of the workforce—contingent, temporary employees "working" on contract who do not get the benefit of FLSA's protections.[100] Employers have an incentive to misclassify workers as independent contractors, an illegal practice that the U.S. Department of Labor, during the Obama administration, called "one of the most serious problems facing affected workers, employers and the entire economy."[101] In 2015 alone, enforcement activity by the Department of Labor recovered $74 million in back wages for misclassified low-income workers in industries ranging from food service to temporary help.[102]

To decide whether a worker is an independent contractor, the U.S. Department of Labor uses a "economic realities" test, which focuses on the worker's dependence upon the employer and considers such factors as whether the work is an integral part of the employer's business, the employer's degree of control over the worker, and the length of the worker's relation with the employer.[103] Courts likewise use this multifactor test to determine whether the employer has violated the FLSA.[104]

A related issue concerns the status of workers in the "on-demand market" (also known as the "gig economy" or "platform economy") who make use of apps and other electronic technology to provide services whenever requested by the user.[105] On-demand service is becoming increasingly common in the food delivery and private transportation industries (such as Uber or Lyft). Companies that use on-demand workers tend to classify them as independent contractors, thus avoiding the minimum wage and overtime provisions of the FLSA (as well as Social Security and unemployment insurance tax obligations). Under the Department of Labor's "economic realities" test, it seems questionable to classify on-demand workers as independent contractors given their dependence on the company that hired them. Moreover, the labor of an "on-demand" worker is integral to the hiring company's business.[106] At least one local jurisdiction—New York City—has made this legal question academic by mandating minimum wage protections for ride-hail company drivers.[107]

Do administrative, executive, or professional workers
receive the minimum wage or overtime?

The Fair Labor Standards Act exempts administrative, executive, and professional employees from the overtime provisions.[108] However, these employees are exempt only if they meet both a "salary test" and a "duties test." To meet the salary test, employees must earn at least $455 per week ($23,660 per year), and the wage cannot be subject to reduction based on the quality or quantity of work.[109] To meet the "duties test," the nature of the employee's duties must be found to justify an exemption from minimum wage and overtime requirements, an analysis that has been called "not a simple task."[110] A worker who exercises supervisory authority over at least two other workers, including authority to hire and fire, would be treated as an executive under this test.[111] A worker who engages in nonmanual work related to management of business operations and exercises discretion and independent judgment would be treated as an administrative employee.[112] A worker whose job requires "knowledge of an advanced type in a field of science or learning customarily acquired by a prolonged course of specialized intellectual instruction" or "invention, imagination, originality or talent in a recognized field of artistic or creative endeavor" would be treated as a professional.[113]

Do agricultural workers receive the minimum wage and overtime?

There are nearly two million farmworkers in the United States, over 80 percent of whom are Latinx.[114] Generally, these workers are entitled to the minimum wage for hours worked, but do not receive overtime pay for labor in excess of 40 hours a week. In addition, employers that did not use more than 500 "man days" of agricultural labor in any calendar quarter in the previous year are exempt from both the minimum wage and overtime provisions of the Fair Labor Standards Act. A "man day" is any day in which an agricultural employee does at least one hour of agricultural work.[115]

Do sales people who work on commission receive the minimum wage and overtime?

Special rules apply to commissioned sales workers in retail and service companies. The employer may elect to be exempt from overtime provisions if the worker's regular hourly wage exceeds 1.5 times the minimum wage and more than half of the worker's earnings consist of commissions.[116] Different rules apply to "outside sales" employees.[117] These workers are not entitled to either the minimum wage or overtime, but two conditions must be met: the workers' "primary duty" must be making sales, and the workers must be "customarily and regularly engaged away from the employer's place of business."[118]

Do domestic workers and home health care workers receive the minimum wage and overtime?

Since 1974, the Fair Labor Standards Act has provided protection to domestic service workers.[119] This type of work includes nurses, certified nurse aides, and home health care aides, as well as cooks, gardeners, and housekeepers.[120] The FLSA does not cover a worker who is a casual babysitter or predominantly provides "companionship services" in the private home of the person by whom the companion is employed (but FLSA protections do apply if the worker is employed by an agency or other third party, as described later).[121] "Companionship services" means services for the care, fellowship, and protection of persons who cannot care for themselves because of age or infirmity. Such services include "tasks that enable a person to live independently at home," including light housework, meal preparation, bed making, clothes washing, and other similar personal services.[122] General household work may be included only if it does not exceed 20 percent of the total weekly hours worked by the companion; if general household work does exceed the 20 percent limitation, the worker is considered to be engaged in covered domestic service and must be paid at the minimum wage and overtime for all hours worked.[123] Likewise, the exemption is lost for any workweek in which the services include medical tasks that typically require training, even if the provider is not trained or does not have a medically related title. Although the FLSA provides minimum wage protection to workers employed by a household in covered domestic service, the act does not guarantee overtime compensation if worker resides in the employer's household.[124]

Third-party employers of workers who provide companionship services in an individual home (for example, home health agencies) are not entitled to the FLSA exemption regarding the minimum wage or overtime; nor are third-party employers of workers who provide live-in domestic services entitled to those exemptions. Any domestic worker employed by such an agency (or other third party) is entitled to FLSA minimum wage and overtime compensation.[125]

Do participants in state-run workfare programs receive the minimum wage and overtime?

The Fair Labor Standards Act does not specifically exempt workfare or public assistance recipients from its coverage. Courts have applied an "economic reality" test to determine whether an employment relation exists; if it does, then the FLSA requires the payment of the minimum wage.[126] The federal courts are divided on this question.[127]

Do interns receive the minimum wage and overtime?

A decrease in the number of entry-level jobs, employer cost-cutting, and the need to acquire on-the-job skills have made internships a gateway for persons seeking to join the workforce. Internships generally are unpaid, and the practice may be illegal in some contexts.[128] The U.S. Department of Labor has developed a six-part test to determine whether an intern is an employee for purposes of the minimum wage and overtime provisions of the Fair Labor Standards Act. Under this test, an intern in a for-profit company is an employee unless all of the following factors exist:

1. The internship provides training similar to that provided by a vocational school;
2. The internship is for the benefit of the intern;
3. The intern does not displace regular employees and works under close supervision of existing staff;
4. The employer derives no immediate advantage from the activities of the intern, and on occasion, its regular operations are impeded;
5. The intern is not necessarily entitled to a job at the end of the internship; and
6. The employer and the intern understand the intern is not entitled to wages for time spent in the internship.[129]

However, the federal courts generally do not apply the Department of Labor's test, although they are divided as to what test to use. Some courts apply a "primary beneficiary" test that balances seven nonexhaustive factors, including training provided to the intern, the length of the internship, and the extent to which the internship is tied to the intern's formal education. Other courts look to the "totality of the circumstances," which typically applies the factors identified by the Department of Labor but uses a balancing approach. A third group of courts applies an "economic realities" test.[130]

Can a person work as a volunteer and waive the minimum wage and overtime?

The Fair Labor Standards Act applies even to those who would decline its protections.[131] Put another way, workers cannot "waive" their right to a minimum wage. The U.S. Supreme Court has emphasized that the FLSA cannot be abridged by contract,[132] explaining that waiver would "nullify" the purposes of the statute (which recognizes the unequal bargaining power of workers and employers) and thwart the policies the statute is designed to effectuate.[133]

However, both the Supreme Court[134] and the U.S. Department of Labor[135] have acknowledged the public benefit of volunteer work, and the FLSA's minimum wage and overtime provisions do not apply to volunteer activities done for charitable or public purposes, provided they are performed on a part-time basis and do not displace regular employed workers. In addition, some courts have held that a person who performs community service work as a condition of an "adjournment in contemplation of dismissal" of criminal charges is not an employee within the meaning of the FLSA.[136]

Do workers who are not U.S. citizens receive the minimum wage and overtime?

The Fair Labor Standards Act protects every individual who works for an employer covered by the statute, even if the worker is not a U.S. citizen and lacks work authorization. An employer who employs an undocumented immigrant must pay wages as set by the FLSA for work actually performed, is liable to the worker for unpaid wages and the "liquidated damages" prescribed by the FLSA, and may not retaliate (for example, by referring the claimant to the U.S. Citizenship and Immigration Services for investigation) if the immigrant worker seeks to enforce FLSA rights.[137] However, undocumented workers are vulnerable to FLSA violations, and many fear deportation if they report illegal practices.[138] During the Obama administration, the Departments of Homeland Security and Labor issued a joint memorandum to coordinate their enforcement activities and, among other things, "to foster enforcement against abusive employment practices directed against workers regardless of status." In this way, the departments sought to ensure that threats of immigration enforcement would not deter undocumented workers from reporting labor law violations.[139] Although the Trump administration did not as of 2019 formally rescind the memorandum, heightened immigration enforcement has increased, with negative effects on employment enforcement.[140] Several immigrants' rights organizations publish useful manuals with practical advice for undocumented workers.[141]

Do all workers covered by the Fair Labor Standards Act receive the minimum wage for all the time they work?

No. The Fair Labor Standards Act permits employers to pay subminimum wages to three categories of workers. These exceptions are in addition to exemptions already discussed.

Training Wage for Workers under Age 20

Workers under age 20 may be paid a "training wage" of $4.25 per hour for their first 90 consecutive calendar days of employment. Employers are prohibited from displacing other workers in order to hire youth employees at the lower rate.[142]

Certain Workers with Disabilities

Workers whose earning or productive capacity is impaired by a physical or mental disability, including age or injury, may be paid a subminimum wage for certain hours worked. Employers must obtain a certificate from the U.S. Department of Labor Wage and Hour Division for each employee they wish to pay at a subminimum wage due to disability, and any such employee may contest the amount of the wage by petitioning the Department of Labor.[143]

Tipped Employees

Employers of individuals in occupations in which tips of at least $30 per month are customarily and regularly received are entitled to count tips as part of the employees' wages, but must pay such employees at least $2.13 per hour, an amount that has not been increased since 1991. In order to claim a tip credit, an employer must inform the employee in advance of its intent to do so, and all tips received by the employee must be retained by that employee (unless the employees who customarily and regularly receive tips voluntarily pool those tips). If the employer fails to follow these requirements, it may not take the tip credit and must pay the full minimum wage (regardless of the amount the workers earn in tips). Under no circumstances may an employer keep tips received by its employees.[144] An employer that claims the tip credit also must be able to show that each worker's total earnings, when direct wages and tips are combined, equal at least $7.25 per hour. If the worker's tips and direct wages do not add up to $7.25 per hour, the employer must make up the difference. The FLSA prohibits any arrangement between the employer and the employee where the employer keeps a percentage of the tips. Employers may deduct the credit card service charge from an employee's tip, as long as doing so does not reduce the employee's total hourly compensation below $7.25.[145]

Keep in mind that employers cannot take a tip credit for any time attributable to work that is "unrelated" to tipped duties, such as cleaning bathrooms or washing floors in a restaurant.[146] If a tipped employee works more than 40 hours per week, overtime is calculated based on the full minimum wage ($7.25), not the lower $2.13 minimum wage for straight time for tipped employees. The employer is prohibited from taking a larger tip credit for overtime hours than is taken for straight-time hours.[147]

Are workers guaranteed full-time employment?

The Fair Labor Standards Act does not guarantee a worker a minimum number of hours in a workday or workweek, and employers have incentives to cap hours to avoid paying overtime or providing required insurance under the Affordable Care Act. As a result, many employers require their employees to work on a temporary basis, on an irregular schedule, or on an on-call basis—a practice known as "just-in-time" scheduling. The practice can endanger a worker's ability to obtain TANF-related work benefits (described in this chapter) and is disruptive of family life.[148]

Are there limits on how many hours an employee can work a week?

Other than workers who are under age 16, the Fair Labor Standards Act does not limit the number of hours that an employee can work.

Do employers have to keep time records of hours worked by employees?

The Fair Labor Standards Act requires employers to maintain payroll records for at least three years for every worker who is covered by the act.[149] Records pertaining to time worked must be maintained for at least two years.[150] The U.S. Department of Labor does not require that the information be kept on an official form, but lists the following as the information that must be kept:

1. Employee's full name and social security number;
2. Address, including zip code;
3. Birth date, if younger than age 19;
4. Sex and occupation;
5. Time and day of week when employee's workweek begins;
6. Hours worked each day;
7. Total hours worked each workweek;
8. Basis on which employee's wages are paid (for example, "$9 per hour," "$440 a week," "piecework");
9. Regular hourly pay rate;
10. Total daily or weekly straight-time earnings;
11. Total overtime earnings for the workweek;

12. All additions to or deductions from the employee's wages;
13. Total wages paid each pay period; and
14. Date of payment and the pay period covered by the payment.[151]

In addition, employers must keep a record of hours worked by employees, but may use any timekeeping method they want, including having workers write their hours on the firm's records.[152] Courts have held that wages and overtime are owed even when an employee works "off the clock" and does not report hours worked if the employer "knew or had reason to know" that hours were underreported.[153]

Do workers have to keep time records of hours worked?

The Fair Labor Standards Act does not require an employee to maintain records of hours worked. However, it is a good idea for workers to keep their own contemporaneous time records given the widespread problem of "wage theft"—employers' willful failure to pay workers what they have earned.[154] If a worker sues to recover wages owed, the employer must show time records. However, an employer may intentionally fail to record all of a worker's hours, or even fail to maintain records at all, in which case contemporaneous records kept by the worker—though not legally required to win a court case—would provide strong proof.[155] The records can be kept in a note pad or on a calendar and should be written down every day if possible. The U.S. Department of Labor makes available a mobile application that workers who have smartphones can use to track hours worked.[156]

Can employers pay workers on a piece rate, rather than an hourly rate?

The Fair Labor Standards Act does not prohibit employers from paying employees on a piece-rate basis, but paying employees by the number of pieces produced rather than by the number of hours worked does not exempt employers from minimum wage and overtime obligations.[157] Thus, an employer must pay a piece-rate employee at least $7.25 per hour worked even if the employee's piece-rate earnings add up to less than that. Similarly, if a piece worker works more than 40 hours per week, the employer must pay the higher of time and a half of the employee's regular per-piece rate or of the minimum wage rate for any pieces produced during hours worked in excess of 40 hours.[158]

Can employers deduct the cost of employer-required uniforms or tools from a worker's minimum wage or overtime?

An employer is not permitted to deduct the cost of employer-required uniforms or tools from a worker's paycheck (nor amounts to cover merchandise or cash shortages) if doing so would reduce the employee's pay to a rate lower than $7.25 per hour worked or reduce the amount of overtime pay that is owed.[159]

What is overtime?

"Overtime" is the informal way to refer to time that an employee works that must be compensated at a rate higher than the minimum wage. The general rule is that overtime pay is required for hours worked in excess of 40 hours per week, and federal regulations require that covered employees be compensated for overtime at 1.5 times their regular rate of pay.[160] The Fair Labor Standards Act does not require overtime payment for working more than eight hours per day if the total number of hours worked in a week does not exceed 40.[161]

How are "hours worked" counted for calculating overtime?

The Fair Labor Standards Act does not define the term workweek. The U.S. Supreme Court has given the term a "broad" meaning,[162] holding that "the statutory workweek includes all time during which an employee is necessarily required to be on the employer's premises, on duty, or at a prescribed work-place."[163] Applying this standard, federal courts have held that in determining a workweek for purposes of overtime, the employer can use a seven-day week even if it does not coincide with the worker's actual workweek.[164] Regulations issued by the U.S. Department of Labor clarify what kinds of activities count or do not count as "hours worked" for calculating overtime. Many of the categories are straightforward, but there are some gray areas. In addition, some courts have issued decisions defining "hours worked" differently from the U.S. Department of Labor. This section addresses some recurring issues.

Does sleep ever count as "hours worked"?

Short rest periods, between five and 20 minutes, count as hours worked.[165] Similarly, if a shift is shorter than 24 hours, then sleep time while on duty at the employer's premises counts as hours worked.

EXAMPLE: A telephone operator who is required to be on duty during a fixed time period is treated as "working" even if provided a bed and allowed to sleep when not taking calls.[166]

Moreover, under federal regulations, if an employee is required to be on duty for 24 hours or more, all hours are compensable unless the employer and employee "agree to exclude bona fide meal periods and a bona fide regularly scheduled sleeping period of not more than 8 hours from hours worked, provided adequate sleeping facilities are furnished by the employer and the employee can usually enjoy an uninterrupted night's sleep."[167] If the employee's sleep is interrupted by a call to duty, the period of the interruption must be counted as working time; likewise, if the employee's sleep is interrupted to the extent that it forecloses a reasonable night's sleep, the entire eight-hour "sleeping period" will count as work time.[168]

Does travel time to and from work ever count as "working"?

Time spent commuting to work is not work time and does not count for calculating overtime.[169] However, travel time between job sites during the employee's regular workday does count toward hours worked.[170]

Do absences for sickness ever count as "hours worked"?

Hours an employee is out sick do not count as hours worked under federal law.[171] However, time spent waiting for and receiving medical attention at the employer's direction or on the employer's premises is compensable.[172] A growing number of states and localities, including Connecticut, California, Massachusetts, Oregon, Vermont, Washington, Rhode Island, Maryland, New Jersey, and Michigan, have adopted paid sick leave laws.[173]

Does time spent changing clothes or washing up, at the beginning or end of the workday, ever count as "hours worked"?

It depends. Changing clothes or washing up at the beginning or end of the work day does not count as hours worked, unless these activities are indispensable to the employee's work or required by law or by the rules of the employer, or unless compensated by contract or custom.[174] The Supreme Court of the United States has held that time spent by employees waiting for and going through security screenings at the end of the day is not compensable, finding that this activity was not an "integral and indispensable" part of the worker's "principal work performed."[175]

Are meal periods ever counted as "hours worked"?

"Bona fide meal periods" do not count as hours worked. The general rule is that the meal period must be 30 minutes or longer to be noncompensable. Under U.S. Department of Labor interpretive regulations, meal periods are not excludable from hours worked unless the employee is fully relieved of all work duties during the period.[176] Nevertheless, some federal courts have held that a meal period used "predominately for the employee's benefit" and not "predominantly for the benefit of [the] employer" may be noncompensable.[177] The question of "predominant benefit" typically is "a fact question on which the employer bears the burden."[178]

Do breaks taken by nursing mothers ever count as "hours worked"?

The Affordable Care Act generally requires employers to allow a reasonable break time for a worker to express breast milk for a nursing child, and also requires that the employer furnish a reasonable location, other than a bathroom, for this activity. If an employer already provides for paid breaks, then a break taken to express milk by workers who are nursing mothers likewise would count as compensable time. However, if the employer does not provide for paid breaks, then the time expended to express milk does not count as compensable time.[179]

Is time spent "on call" ever counted as "hours worked"?

Time spent "on call" may be compensable depending on whether the worker is required to stay on the employer's premises, at some other workplace, or so close to the workplace that the time cannot be used effectively for personal purposes.[180] However, the employee is not treated as working if only required to be reachable at all times while on call.[181] "On-call" time is distinguished from "waiting time." Whether waiting time is compensable turns on the worker's particular circumstances; if the worker was "engaged to wait," and not "waiting to be engaged,"[182] the time is compensable.[183] The U.S. Supreme Court has held that time spent by workers waiting for required security screenings before leaving the worksite is not compensable.[184]

Is time spent in apprenticeship training ever counted as "hours worked"?

Time spent in an organized, bona fide apprenticeship program of instruction may be excludable from compensable time if (1) the apprentice is employed under a "written apprenticeship agreement or program which substantially meets the fundamental standards of the Bureau of Apprenticeship and Training of the U.S. Department of Labor"; and (2) such time "does not involve productive work or performance of the apprentice's regular duties."[185]

Are workers guaranteed time off or compensation for vacation or sick time?

The Fair Labor Standard Act does not require an employer to provide time off, paid or unpaid, for vacation, holiday, severance, or sick time. The only exception, already discussed, is that an unpaid break must be provided to nursing mothers. However, the Family Medical Leave Act, discussed later in this chapter, does provide some employees with unpaid leave for family and medical emergencies.

What should a worker do if the employer pays a subminimum wage, withholds wages, or retaliates against the worker for asserting rights?

Violation of the Fair Labor Standards Act can take many forms. An employer might misclassify a worker as not covered by the minimum wage and overtime protection, might compel workers to work "off the clock," might withhold lunch or other breaks, or might threaten to fire a worker who complains. The FLSA authorizes both public and private enforcement of the statute's protections,[186] and provides remedies not only when its minimum wage and overtime guarantees are violated,[187] but also when an employer retaliates against a worker who asserts legal rights.[188] FLSA violations may be remedied by the payment of back pay, recognizing that the work has already been performed and therefore is entitled to compensation.

The U.S. Department of Labor, through its Wages and Hour Division, has the authority to bring public enforcement actions in court. In FY 2018, the Division recovered $304 million in unpaid wages for more than 265,000 employees.[189] This is believed to account for only a small percentage of FLSA violations that occurred.[190] Under 29 U.S.C. § 216(c), the Department of Labor, on behalf of an employee, can seek to recover unpaid overtime or minimum wages, plus an equal amount as liquidated damages. Under 29 U.S.C. § 217, the Department of Labor can seek injunctive relief to prevent continued violations by employers, such as unlawful withholding of minimum wage and overtime pay and against the withholding of previously unpaid minimum or overtime wages, but may not recover liquidated damages under that section.[191]

Workers can file a wage and hour complaint with the U.S. Department of Labor through its website at https://www.dol.gov/whd/howtofilecomplaint.htm. State labor departments also handle minimum wage complaints, and should be contacted as an alternative, especially in states that provide broader worker protections.[192]

Workers also can bring individual lawsuits to recover unpaid wages and liquidated damages (in effect awarding the worker double the amount of illegally withheld wages), or collective lawsuits on behalf of groups of workers. The worker must show an employment relationship with the employer, eligibility for the FLSA-mandated wage, and actual hours worked that were not compensated.[193] The statute allows a successful plaintiff to recover attorney's fees and costs in addition to back pay and damages.[194]

Federal law makes it illegal for an employer to take any adverse action against a worker in retaliation for the worker's assertion of rights under the FLSA.[195] An employer that commits such retaliation is liable for damages, including lost wages, liquidated damages, and damages for mental or emotional distress.[196] The U.S. Supreme Court has held that the anti-retaliation provision protects a worker who makes an oral, as well as a written, complaint about a violation of the FLSA, so long as the complaint is "sufficiently clear and detailed for a reasonable employer to understand it."[197] Moreover, at least some courts have held that a complaint need not be filed with a government agency; rather, the statute protects workers who make an oral complaint to an employer.[198] FLSA's anti-retaliation provision also protects workers who agree to testify in a minimum wage suit, or who cooperate in an investigation of minimum violations.[199]

Family and Medical Leave Act

What is the Family and Medical Leave Act?

The Family and Medical Leave Act (FMLA), enacted in 1993, requires employers with 50 or more employees to allow eligible employees a total of 12 weeks of unpaid leave during any 12-month period for any of the following reasons:

- The birth, adoption, or foster care placement of a child;
- The care of a child, spouse, or parent with a serious medical condition;

- A serious health condition that makes the employee unable to perform the job; and
- Any exigency that arises out of the fact that the employee's spouse, son, daughter, or parent is a covered military member on active duty (or has been notified of an impending call or order to active duty) in support of a contingency operation.

Amendments adopted in 2008 further permit eligible employees to take up to 26 weeks of unpaid leave to care for a covered servicemember with a serious illness or injury if the servicemember is the spouse, son, daughter, next of kin, or parent of the employee. Employers may require employees to use as much vacation, annual leave, or sick leave as they have accrued to cover part or all of the 12-week period. Employees also may elect to use paid sick, annual leave, or vacation leave for part or all of the 12-week period rather than unpaid FMLA leave.[200]

Why did the federal government adopt the Family and Medical Leave Act?

Congress enacted the Family and Medical Leave Act to align employment practices with the realities of family life, which assume that workers will care for family members when medical problems arise. Most industrialized nations have laws granting workers time off—without negative consequences—to attend to an important family need or emergency. However, prior to enactment of the FMLA, the majority of U.S. firms were not "family friendly" in this sense: 63 percent of firms with at least 100 employees did not provide maternity leave to female employees, 86 percent of such firms did not provide leave to care for sick children, and 82 percent did not provide leave for elder care.[201] The FMLA recognizes that sensible employment practices need to consider the needs of single and two-parent households; it applies equally to men and women, in part to overcome "the pervasive presumption that women are mothers first and workers second," a stereotype Congress found had fostered subtle yet significant workplace discrimination against women.[202] Overall, the FMLA offers important but incomplete protection for working families. The FMLA is limited to firms that employ 50 or more workers, and so effectively exempts 95 percent of American businesses and leaves 60 percent of workers without its protections.[203] Additionally, because the FMLA authorizes unpaid leave, only those workers who can afford time away from paid employment are in a position to invoke the statute when important family matters arise.[204]

Does the Family and Medical Leave Act apply to all private employers?

The Family and Medical Leave Act applies to private employers who are engaged in commerce or in any industry or activity affecting commerce,[205] who employ at least 50 workers for 20 or more weeks during the current or previous calendar year.[206] The 50-employee count is based on the number of workers employed by the employer within 75 miles of a worksite.[207] The requirement of 20 weeks need not be consecutive.[208] Special questions arise when a corporation is organized into separate divisions; generally such a corporation is considered to be a single employer.[209] However, when one corporation owns another corporation, the two companies are considered to be separate employers unless they meet the regulatory test for joint or integrated employers.[210]

Does the Family and Medical Leave Act apply to all public employers?

The Family and Medical Leave Act applies to all public employers, including public elementary and secondary schools, regardless of how many workers they employ.[211]

Which employees are eligible for leave?

To be eligible for leave under the Family and Medical Leave Act, an employee (1) must work for an employer who is subject to the statute; (2) must have worked for that employer for a total of at least 12 months; and (3) must have worked 1,250 hours in the previous 12 months. The 12 months worked for the employer need not be consecutive.[212] The calculation of hours worked is based on the principle of what constitutes a compensable hour.[213] Time spent on paid or unpaid leave, such as workers' compensation leave, sick leave, or vacation, does not count toward the 12-month minimum or the 1,250 hours worked requirement.[214] However, if the employee is on the payroll for any part of a week, the whole week must be included in the 12-month minimum.[215]

What reasons qualify for a leave under the Family and Medical Leave Act?

A number of reasons qualify for leave under the Family and Medical Leave Act:

Birth, Adoption, or Foster Care Placement of a Child

Covered employees may take leave after the birth of a child or the placement of a child with the employee for foster care or adoption.[216] Child care leave must conclude within 12 months of the birth or placement of the child.[217] The statute states that leave to care for a new child should not be taken "intermittently or on a reduced leave schedule," unless agreed upon by the employer and employee.[218]

Self-Care

Covered employees may take leave "because of a serious health condition that makes the employee unable to perform the functions of the position of such employee."[219] Self-care leave may be taken intermittently when medically necessary. Only days actually taken on FMLA leave may count toward the 12-week maximum, and the employer cannot require the employee to take intermittent leave in longer blocks than necessary to address the employee's medical condition.

Qualifying for self-care leave is subject to a standard less stringent than that for disability leave under the Americans with Disabilities Act of 1990.[220] For self-care leave, federal regulations define "serious health condition" as "an illness, injury, impairment or physical or mental condition that involves inpatient care . . . or continuing treatment by a health care provider."[221] Continuing treatment includes examinations to determine if a serious condition exists, but does not include routine screenings or preventative care.[222] The regulations state that absent complications, a "serious health condition" does not include the common cold, upset stomachs, minor ulcers, earaches, and headaches other than migraines.[223] Mental health conditions and allergies can be serious health conditions if they involve inpatient care or continuing treatment by a health care provider and meet the other conditions of this section.[224] The regulations define incapacity as the "inability to work, attend school, or perform other regular daily activities due to the serious health condition, treatment therefor, or recovery therefrom,"[225] and specifically includes incapacity due to pregnancy or to receive prenatal care.[226] Absences due to incapacity qualify for leave even if the absence does not last more than three consecutive days and medical treatment is not received during the period.[227]

Care for a Covered Family Member with a Serious Health Condition

Covered employees may take leave to "care" for a parent, child, or spouse with a serious health condition. FMLA leave is available to care for the family members identified in the statute: parents, children, and spouses. Employees generally may not take leave to care for other family members, such as parents-in-law, grandparents, or siblings, unless, in some circumstances, a loco parentis relationship is shown.[228] Courts disagree whether "care" requires ongoing medical treatment. The better view is that leave is available to a worker to care for a family member who has a "serious health condition,"[229] even if the family member does not receive ongoing medical treatment.[230]

Which children count as a "son" or "daughter" to qualify for a leave?

The Family and Medical Leave Act defines "son or daughter"—for purposes of determining whether an employee is entitled to take leave to tend to a family's member's serious medical condition—to include a "biological, adopted, or foster child, a stepchild, a legal ward, or a child of a person standing in loco parentis" who is either under age 18, or age 18 or older and "incapable of self-care because of a mental or physical disability."[231] Parents are eligible to take covered leave to care when the child suffers "an impairment that substantially limits one or more major life activities,"[232] and may do so irrespective of the age of the child at the onset of the disability, even if the child is now an adult.[233]

Which life partners count as a "spouse" under the Family and Medical Leave Act?

The U.S. Department of Labor has adopted regulations that define "spouse" as a "husband or wife . . . as defined or recognized under State law for purposes of marriage in the state where the employee resides, including common law marriage in States where it is recognized."[234] The U.S. Supreme Court has held that for purposes of federal statutes the definition of marriage cannot be limited to heterosexual couples.[235] Department of Labor regulations recognize that same-sex spouses are covered by the FMLA.[236]

Does the Family and Medical Leave Act authorize leave to care for a sibling?

The Family and Medical Leave Act does not explicitly refer to siblings as among the relatives for whom leave is authorized. However, during the Obama administration, the U.S. Department of Labor clarified that leaves for the care of siblings is protected when the caregiver functions in the place of a parent (in loco parentis). Factors to consider are the age of the person in need of care, the degree of such person's dependence upon the caregiver, and the extent to which the caregiver carries out duties that typically are associated with parenting.[237]

Can leave to take care of a sick family member be taken intermittently or on a reduced work schedule?

Unlike leave for the birth or adoption of a new child, leave to care for a sick family member may be taken intermittently or on a reduced schedule when medically necessary.[238]

Can leave be taken when a family member is in the armed services?

Under amendments to the Family and Medical Leave Act adopted in 2008 and 2010, covered employees may take leave to attend to "qualifying exigencies" when a family member is in the armed services or to care for the servicemember. The 2008 amendment responded to findings of the 2007 President's Commission on Care for America's Returning Wounded Warriors that servicemembers and their families required more extensive leave coverage than the FMLA then authorized. The National Defense Authorization Act (NDAA) of 2008 amended the FMLA to address these gaps, creating two servicemember-related categories for qualifying leave.[239] The NDAA of 2010 further amended the FMLA to broaden coverage under these two leave categories.[240]

Qualifying Exigency Leave
Covered workers who are the immediate family members of servicemembers may take leave for qualifying exigencies, which include:

- Short notice deployment, meaning, deployment within seven days of notice;
- Attending military events and related activities;
- Certain child care and school activities;
- Certain care of military member's parent who is incapable of self-care;
- Making financial and legal arrangements;
- Attending counseling;
- Servicemember's rest and recuperation (leave may be up to 15 calendar days);
- Certain post deployment activities; and
- Additional activities.

The servicemember must be on covered active duty, meaning deployment abroad, including in international waters, or on call or on notice of an impending call to such duty.[241]

Caregiver Leave
A covered worker who is the immediate family member of a servicemember may take leave to care for the servicemember if the servicemember encountered a "serious injury or illness" while on active duty that rendered the person unable to perform duties, or suffered aggravation of a preexisting condition while in the line of duty. Caregiver leave also is available for certain veterans within five years of their non-dishonorable discharge.[242]

How does the Family and Medical Leave Act protect a worker who takes unpaid leave?

A worker should give the employer at least 30 days' notice of taking FMLA leave when the need for the leave is foreseeable; if the need for the leave was not foreseeable, the worker should notify the employer as soon as practicable. A worker who gives notice and takes unpaid leave is entitled under the Family and Medical Leave Act to be restored to the same or an equivalent position with equivalent pay, benefits, and working conditions after returning from leave.[243] An employer must maintain health benefits for the worker while on leave at the same level as if the worker had continued working.[244]

Can an employer ask a worker to waive claims under the Family and Medical Leave Act?

No. An employer cannot require an employer to waive "prospective" claims under the Family and Medical Leave Act.[245] One federal appeals court has held that "prospective" means "at some unspecified time in the future," so that the bar on waiving prospective claims does not prevent an agreement that the employee will not seek leave based on events that happened before the waiver is signed. Under this reasoning, the appeals court permitted the employer to condition a severance agreement on the worker's waiver of claims for leave based on events that occurred before the severance agreement was signed.[246]

What should a worker do if the employer resists complying with the Family and Medical Leave Act?

The Family and Medical Leave Act can be enforced through litigation, and the act authorizes money damages and injunctive relief both for the employer's violation of the statute and if the employer retaliates against the worker for seeking to enforce statutory rights.[247] "Damages" mean an award of money to compensate the worker for losses, including lost wages; injunctive relief is available, for example, to restore the worker to the prior job if terminated. Lawsuits must be filed within a two-year period "after the date of the last event constituting the alleged violation for which the action is brought," and within a three-year period if the violation is willful.[248]

National Labor Relations Act

What is the National Labor Relations Act?

The National Labor Relations Act (NLRA) was enacted in 1935 and protects the rights of workers to organize and support labor unions, and to work together in other ways to defend and advance their interests in the workplace. According to the NLRA's declaration of policy, the law was intended to address "[t]he denial by employers of the right of employees to organize and the refusal by employers to accept the procedure of collective bargaining."[249] President Franklin D. Roosevelt called the NLRA "necessary as an act of both common justice and economic advance," to protect "the independence of labor" and to ensure that employment contracts rest on "a sound and equitable basis."[250]

What is a labor union?

A labor union is a membership organization through which workers bargain collectively with their employer concerning their wages, benefits, and other employment terms and working conditions.[251] The right to engage in collective bargaining is intended to empower workers and to enable them to demand and obtain higher wages, better working conditions, and greater benefits than any individual worker could negotiate alone. The NLRA also gives workers the right to strike. A strike is a work stoppage intended to exert economic pressure on an employer to bargain with the union or to agree to the workers' demands.[252] Unions also give workers a greater voice in the organization of their work and workplace than they would have as individuals.[253]

Unionized workers earn higher wages and better benefits—sick leave, health insurance, pension plans—than nonunionized workers in comparable jobs, although differences are industry specific.[254] Unionization also improves social conditions overall.[255] In many industries, the wage and benefit gains of union workers have had the effect of improving the wages and benefits of nonunion employees.[256] More broadly, social and economic reforms advocated by unions, such as affordable health care, have benefited nonunion workers who enjoy the same statutory protections and rights.[257]

How many workers belong to unions in the United States?

Union membership (measured as the percentage of workers in the United States who belonged to a union) peaked in 1954, just about 20 years after the NLRA was enacted. In absolute numbers, union membership in the United States topped out at 21 million workers in 1979. [258] However, by 2018, that number had declined to 14.6 million workers, or 10.5 percent of the workforce.[259] Among private sector workers, the unionization rate was even lower—just 6.4 percent. Utilities, transportation, and warehousing workers were among the most likely to be unionized; agricultural and financial workers were among the least likely. The size and strength of unionized labor varies by region. Hawaii and New York have the greatest population density of unionized workers. By contrast, nine states had unionization rates of less than 5 percent, with South Carolina having only 1.6 percent.[260]

Although the number of unionized workers in the United States has declined, public sentiment in favor of unions remains strong, with the Pew Research Center in 2018 reporting that 55 percent of Americans had a favorable view of unions.[261] Historically, unions helped raise wages and benefits for their members, and in the process, raised standards for nonunion workers as well, encouraging all workers to have a greater voice in democratic life—a role that unions also can play today.[262]

How does the National Labor Relations Act protect workers' rights concerning union activity?

The National Labor Relations Act establishes "the right to self-organization." Specifically, the statute gives employees the right:

- "to form, join, or assist labor organizations";
- "to bargain collectively through representatives of their own choosing"; and
- "to engage in other concerted activities for the purpose of collective bargaining or other mutual aid or protection."

Workers also have the right to refrain from union activity.[263]

The NLRA enforces workers' rights to self-organization and union activity by prohibiting certain kinds of employer conduct, which are referred to as "unfair labor practices." Unlawful employer conduct includes discouraging organizing or union activity through adverse action, threats, or promises; discriminating against union members or supporters in hiring, promotion or terms or conditions of employment; retaliating against employees who file charges under the NLRA or give testimony in relation to such charges; and refusing to bargain in good faith with employees' collective-bargaining representatives.[264]

The NLRA also limits what unions can do. Unlawful union conduct includes coercing employees to join a union or participate in union activity; coercing employers in the selection of their representatives for collective bargaining; refusing to bargain collectively with an employer; and coercing a neutral employer to cease doing business with an employer in a labor dispute.[265] Even after a union is recognized, individual workers have the right to present grievances to an employer, although a union representative has the right to be present at any meeting between the employer and the employee, and to make sure that the resolution of the grievance is not at odds with the collective bargaining agreement.[266]

What is the National Labor Relations Board?

The National Labor Relations Board (NLRB) is the federal agency created by Congress to administer and enforce the NLRA. The five members of the Board and the General Counsel are appointed by the President with the advice and consent of the Senate.[267] Most of the work of the agency is done in its field offices, which are responsible for investigating and prosecuting unfair labor practice cases and for conducting elections to determine employee representatives.[268]

Which workers are protected by the National Labor Relations Act?

The National Labor Relations Act protects most private-sector employees.[269] However, it does not cover agricultural workers, domestic workers, individuals employed by a parent or spouse, independent contractors, individuals who work for employers subject to the Railway Labor Act, and supervisors.[270]

With respect to supervisors: the NLRA does not bar supervisory employees from becoming union members. However, it does not give supervisory employees either the right to organize or any of the other rights of employees.[271] Supervisors are defined as individuals:

> having authority, in the interest of the employer, to hire, transfer, suspend, lay off, recall, promote, discharge, assign, reward, or discipline other employees,

or responsibly to direct them, or to adjust their grievances, or effectively to recommend such action, if in connection with the foregoing the exercise of such authority is not of a merely routine or clerical nature, but requires the use of independent judgment.[272]

With respect to independent contractors: the fact that an employer tells workers that they are independent contractors or requires them to sign an agreement to that effect does not necessarily make them independent contractors. Whether a worker is an employee or an independent contractor is a legal question. If the employer exercises sufficient control over the terms and conditions of the work and its terms, the worker is an employee under the National Labor Relations Act notwithstanding any agreement to the contrary.[273]

Does the National Labor Relations Act protect "contingent" workers?

Leased employees, temporary employees, and contract workers are often referred to as "contingent workers."[274] As long as they are employees, not independent contractors, contingent workers are covered by the National Labor Relations Act and are protected from being fired and from other forms of retaliation if they join a union or engage in other protected activity.[275] For contingent workers who are employed through a staffing agency or contractor, there may be a question whether their employer is the supplier employer (the staffing agency or contractor), the user employer (the company in whose operation they are working), or both. The answer as to each entity depends on whether it exercises sufficient control over the terms and conditions of the work.[276] If both the supplier and the user exercise sufficient control to be deemed the contingent worker's employer, then they are joint employers and both are required to bargain with the collective-bargaining representative.[277]

Does the National Labor Relations Act protect public-sector workers?

The National Labor Relations Act does not cover public-sector workers. However, state and local public employees in 22 states have collective bargaining and other rights under the laws of their respective states, and federal personnel have limited collective bargaining rights under the Civil Service Reform Act of 1978.[278]

How do workers obtain union representation?

Many workers obtain union representation by finding a job in a union-represented workplace. Workers in a nonunion workplace may seek the assistance of a union or form their own union, and seek recognition of the union by the employer or certification of the union by the National Labor Relations Board as the representative of the employees. Whether representation is achieved by voluntary employer recognition or through the NLRB process, it requires the support of a majority of the employees.[279] Unless there is already a substantial committed majority ready to take action, the employees seeking union representation will need to undertake an organizing campaign to persuade a majority of their coworkers to join them.[280]

How is majority support for union representation determined?

The first step in determining whether majority support for union representation exists is to identify the group of employees from which majority support is required. In the first instance, the employees or the union seeking to represent them define the group, subject to the requirements of the National Labor Relations Act. It must be a "unit appropriate for the purposes of collective bargaining," following the contours of the employing enterprise, the craft, if any, to which the employees belong, the work location, or a subdivision thereof.[281] In order for a proposed unit to be considered appropriate, the workers in the unit must share enough in common for it to make sense to group them together for purposes of collective bargaining. In the words of the Board's case law, they must share a "community of interest."[282]

Is an employer required to recognize and bargain with a union if a majority of its employees in an appropriate unit have signed a petition or authorization cards stating that they want the union to represent them?

As a general matter, the National Labor Relations Act does not require an employer to recognize the union as its employees' representative based on authorization cards, although the employer may voluntarily recognize the union. However, if the employer has engaged in unfair labor practices that tend to "undermine majority strength and impede the [Board's] election processes," the Board may require the employer to recognize a union that has authorization cards from a majority of the workers in the bargaining unit.[283] In some states as a matter of state law, a public employer is required to recognize a union upon presentation of evidence that there is majority support for a collective bargaining representative.[284]

The Employee Free Choice Act is a legislative proposal that would allow a union to be recognized once a majority of workers within a bargaining unit have signed cards indicating their support. Proponents say the "card check" procedures would reduce employer intimidation and promote organizational efforts.[285]

How does a union obtain bargaining rights if the employer declines to recognize it as the workers' representative?

If the employer declines to recognize the union, the union may petition the National Labor Relations Board to conduct a secret-ballot election. After it receives a petition, the NLRB's regional office investigates:[286]

1. Whether the NLRB is authorized to conduct an election.
2. Whether a sufficient number of employees have shown interest in an election.
3. Whether the employees make up an appropriate bargaining unit.
4. Whether a question affecting commerce exists.

If the NLRB finds that the answer is yes to all of these questions, then it will conduct a secret-ballot election and, if a majority of the valid votes are cast for the union, the NLRB certifies the union as the representative of the employees in the voting unit.[287]

During the election process, the employer is not required to give pro-union workers or union representatives access to the worksite for the purpose of making the case for unionization. By contrast, the employer may require the workers to attend meetings about why they should vote against the union. It is illegal for an employer to threaten to fire workers for supporting unionization or to induce them to reject unionization with tangible benefits, but reports of such unlawful coercion are common.[288]

In 2014, the NLRB amended its procedural rules to streamline the election process. The amendments simplified procedures, eliminated unnecessary litigation and delay, and modernized requirements for filing, service, and communications in light of technological advances. In particular, among other changes, parties and the Board can transmit election petitions, notices, and other documents electronically; before an election, employers are required to provide voter lists with contact information including available e-mail addresses; and parties are required to wait until after an election to mount certain legal challenges.[289]

Does the National Labor Relations Act protect worker action other than union activity?

Yes. The National Labor Relations Act gives workers the right to act together to try to improve their pay or working conditions, with or without a union.[290] This kind of worker action is known as "protected concerted activity." It is unlawful for an employer to discharge or take other adverse action against employees for engaging in such activity, which can include the employees' walking off the job in protest of working conditions,[291] raising employee complaints about policy changes[292] or scheduling,[293] or demanding improvements in wages or benefits,[294] even if no union is involved and the workers are not seeking union representation. In order to constitute protected concerted activity, a worker's action must meet two requirements: First, it must be "concerted,"[295] that is, the activity must be engaged in "with or on the authority of" other workers, or in an effort "to initiate or to induce or to prepare for group action."[296] Second, it must be "for the purpose of . . . mutual aid and protection."[297] Activity engaged in by workers to "improve terms and conditions of employment or otherwise improve their lot as employees," such as advocating for legislative action[298] or asserting a statutory right,[299] in addition to action directly addressing their wages, hours, or other employment terms, meets this second requirement. For example, even an employee's unsuccessful effort to enlist the assistance of coworkers in pursuing a discrimination claim against their employer constitutes protected concerted activity.[300]

What happens if an employer or union violates the National Labor Relations Act?

A violation of the National Labor Relations Act (specifically, Section 8) is called an "unfair labor practice." Any person may file a charge alleging a violation of the act with the regional office of the National Relations Labor Board covering the location where the unlawful conduct took place and the regional office will investigate the charge.[301] If the regional director determines that the charge has merit, a formal complaint usually issues, and a hearing is held before an administrative law judge.[302] The hearing is a formal adversary proceeding in which the

NLRB General Counsel, represented by an NLRB attorney from the regional office, prosecutes the complaint against the respondent, which is the employer or the union, depending on the charge. After the close of the hearing, the judge issues a decision and, if a violation is found, a recommended order directing the respondent to cease and desist from the unlawful conduct and requiring it to take affirmative action to remedy the violation. If the respondent is the employer, relief might include reinstatement of unlawfully discharged employees and payment of back pay and benefits.[303] Exceptions to the judge's decision may be filed with the five-member NLRB in Washington, D.C.[304] If no exceptions are filed, the judge's decision and recommended order become final.[305] The respondent or the charging party may seek review of a final decision and order of the NLRB by a federal court of appeals.[306]

Tax Benefits for the Low-Wage Worker

What are the major tax benefits for low-wage workers?

Over the last four decades, the federal government and many states have adopted tax programs to assist low- and moderate-income families.[307] These programs now account for a much larger share of public anti-poverty expenditures than traditional cash transfer programs, and differentially impact people with low incomes.[308] This section focuses on the two most important tax programs for low-wage workers—the Earned Income Tax Credit and the Child Tax Credit.[309]

Who is considered a low-income taxpayer?

There is no official definition of "low-income" under the federal tax codes. Although many public assistance programs base their eligibility requirements on the federal poverty guidelines, there is no such link between taxes and poverty measures.[310] For purposes of this section, the phrase "low-income taxpayers" generally refers to individuals who are in the lower income tax brackets,[311] particularly those who have incomes low enough to qualify for the Earned Income Tax Credit—approximately $53,000.[312] As a point of comparison, in 2017 the official poverty threshold was $29,986 for a family of five, with two children, two parents, and a great aunt.[313] A person working full-time for 40 hours a week at the existing federal minimum wage of $7.25 earned $15,080 a year, which is less than the official poverty threshold.[314]

How does the federal tax system affect low-income workers?

Most wage earners are required to file a federal income tax return, even if no tax is due.[315] Moreover, low-income workers actually may benefit from the federal tax system if they file a tax return. Currently, the federal tax system is structured to provide low-income working households with certain tax benefits that either lower or eliminate their tax burden, increase their after-tax wages, or provide additional economic assistance for families with children.[316] As a result of these tax benefits, which come in the form of "tax credits" or "tax deductions,"[317] most low-income workers do not pay any federal income tax—though they all pay Social Security and Medicare taxes.[318] Nevertheless, federal tax benefits have the net effect of boosting working families' incomes and ability to obtain child care, education, health care, and housing.[319] The Internal Revenue Service (IRS) is considered not only the collector of revenue but also the "gatekeeper of benefits" to these families.[320] In addition, the federal tax system does not consider any needs-based public assistance, such as food stamps, cash "welfare" benefits, and housing aid, as taxable income.[321]

Deploying the tax system as an income-support tool for low-wage households has been criticized from multiple directions: some argue the tax system should not be used to effectuate "welfare" policies;[322] others argue it would be fairer or more efficient to require employers to pay higher wages,[323] or for the government to establish universal programs to meet essential needs, including providing a guaranteed "living" income to persons who are not able to engage in wage labor.[324] For now, knowing how a low-income worker can obtain benefits through the tax system can provide an important source of assistance.

Does the Tax Cuts and Jobs Act of 2017 affect low-income workers?

The Tax Cuts and Jobs Act (TCJA or the 2017 Act), Republican tax legislation enacted in December 2017, made sweeping changes to federal tax law, providing nearly $2 trillion in tax cuts over 10 years. These tax cuts disproportionately go to corporations and wealthy individuals, exacerbating economic inequality and endangering the government's ability to maintain funding for social programs relied upon by low-income families and individuals.[325] The most significant changes that immediately impact low-income households include: reducing income tax rates, expanding the tax brackets, and repealing personal exemptions in favor of increasing the standard deduction and Child Tax Credit, as well as creating a new dependent tax credit.[326] While each of these major provisions has its own impact on individuals, the projected net impact of the TCJA is that approximately 80 percent of filers would see a lower tax bill, 15 percent would see no material change, and only 5 percent would see a higher tax bill in 2018, as compared to in 2017.[327]

Tax cuts do not necessarily mean bigger tax refunds for more families, however.[328] In fact, the IRS estimated that it would issue about 2 percent fewer refunds for the 2018 tax year than it did for 2017—down from 108.3 million to 105.8 million refunds.[329] Most working taxpayers received a tax cut in the form of larger paychecks throughout 2018, since less money was being withheld due to the IRS's modifications of the withholding tables for employers and the worksheets used to calculate paycheck deductions.[330] If their employers or payroll service providers withheld too little, however, these taxpayers would receive smaller refunds than in the past, or none at all; others might even receive a tax bill from the government.[331] Indeed, a 2018 study by the Government Accountability Office reported that more than 30 million working taxpayers did not have enough withheld from their paychecks and so would owe the government when they file their returns—an increase from 18 percent in 2017 to 21 percent of taxpayers in 2018.[332] As an example, a family of four in Colorado, that received a refund of $3,600 in 2017, owed $8,000 in taxes in 2018 because its withholding amounts were not corrected after the TCJA came into effect.[333]

Tax cuts also do not benefit families equally. Although taxes have declined on average across all income groups, one study has shown that over 70 percent of the tax cuts is geared toward the top 20 percent of households.[334] As a point of comparison, according to the study, the richest 1 percent of taxpayers—with an average income of $1.8 million—get a larger tax cut in a single day than the poorest families—with an average income of $13,000—receive in an entire year. Thus, for most low-income workers, the 2017 tax act did not result in any material change in terms of their tax liability or tax benefits. The TCJA still kept the lowest income tax rate of 10 percent, and to the extent that any reduced tax rates applied, the average tax cut for taxpayers with less than $25,000 of income is estimated to be about $40, or 0.3 percent of after-tax income for the 2018 tax year.[335] The impact of the various tax credits and deductions for low-income workers is discussed below.

What is the difference between a tax credit and a tax deduction?

Both tax credits and tax deductions can reduce the amount of taxes a taxpayer owes, but they function in different ways. A tax credit is a dollar-for-dollar reduction in tax liability—a "straight dollar transfer from the government to the taxpayer."[336] Tax credits can be "nonrefundable" or "refundable" (and sometimes "partially refundable"). A nonrefundable credit can only reduce the amount of taxes owed, but it does not generate a tax refund if the credit amount exceeds the taxes owed. In contrast, a refundable credit (or the refundable percentage of a partially refundable credit) can be fully claimed if the credit amount exceeds the taxes owed, and it may result in a tax refund in the amount of the difference. Even if a taxpayer does not owe any taxes, the taxpayer may still qualify for a refundable tax credit and receive the entire amount as a cash refund.

EXAMPLE:

A taxpayer owes $200 in taxes and is eligible to claim a tax credit of $500. Depending on the type of credit, the taxpayer may receive cash benefits.

A nonrefundable credit eliminates the entire $200 of tax, but the taxpayer does not receive a tax refund for the excess $300.

A refundable credit eliminates the entire $200 of tax, and the taxpayer also receives a tax refund of $300 from the IRS.

A partially refundable credit, up to 40 percent of the credit amount for instance, provides $200 of the credit (40 percent of $500) as refundable and the remaining $300 as nonrefundable. The nonrefundable part of the credit first reduces the tax owed to zero ($200 tax owed minus $300 nonrefundable credit). All of the $200 refundable portion of the credit is then available for distribution to the taxpayer as a refund. Thus, a partially refundable tax credit can eliminate the tax otherwise owed and may provide a tax refund.

Most tax credits are nonrefundable. Examples of nonrefundable credits include the credit for household and dependent care expenses,[337] the credit for the elderly and totally disabled,[338] the Child Tax Credit,[339] credits for higher education,[340] and the credit for contributions to retirement savings.[341] Examples of refundable credits include the credit for withheld taxes,[342] the earned income tax credit,[343] credits for certain health insurance costs or plans,[344] and the homebuyer credit.[345] Several of the key tax credits for low-income workers are discussed later.

A tax deduction, on the other hand, can reduce the amount of income subject to tax, known as "taxable income." Unlike tax credits, deductions *indirectly* reduce tax liability. The value of the deduction is tied to a taxpayer's marginal tax rate, which is the tax rate applied on the last dollar earned by the taxpayer (i.e., at the margin). For instance, if an unmarried taxpayer is in the 12 percent tax bracket (which in 2018 meant a taxable income between $9,701 and $39,475), a $1,000 deduction saves a taxpayer $120 ($1,000 x 12 percent).[346]

How does a low-income worker claim a tax deduction?

There are two ways to claim tax deductions: a taxpayer can use the standard deduction or can itemize deductions.[347] The standard deduction is a flat-dollar reduction of a taxpayer's pretax income, and the specified amount depends on the taxpayer's filing status and income.[348] On the other hand, itemizing deductions permits a taxpayer to take any of the hundreds of available deductions for which the taxpayer may qualify, including the amounts paid for state and local income taxes or sales taxes, real estate taxes, personal property taxes, mortgage interests, gifts to charity, and parts of medical and dental expenses, using a special tax form, Form 1040.[349]

Certain taxpayers are ineligible to use the standard deduction and must therefore itemize, namely: (1) married individuals filing a separate return when either spouse itemizes deductions; (2) nonresident aliens; and (3) individuals filing a return for a period of less than 12 months because of a change in the annual accounting period.[350] In most cases, however, the choice between using the standard deduction and itemizing deductions is simple: whichever results in a larger reduction of tax liability. If the standard deduction is less than the sum of itemized deductions, the taxpayer ought to itemize deductions; otherwise, the taxpayer ought to take the standard deduction. Families who are in the initial stages of home ownership, for instance, tend to choose to itemize their deductions due to the substantial mortgage interest and property taxes involved. Older taxpayers, on the other hand, tend to take the standard deduction, which is accompanied by an additional standard deduction for people age 65 or over.

In some cases, the difference between the standard deduction and itemizing may not be that much. Itemizing deductions generally takes more time, and a taxpayer may have to provide proof to show eligibility to claim the itemized deduction. Nonetheless, in such close cases, a taxpayer may alternate between the two options when filing every year. Moreover, if a taxpayer wants to change the method of deduction—from itemized to the standard deduction, or vice versa—the taxpayer can amend the return by filing Form 1040.

Table 2.1 Standard Deduction

Filing Status	2019 Tax Year	2018 Tax Year	2017 Tax Year
Single	$12,200	$12,000	$6,350
Married, Filing Jointly	$24,400	$24,000	$12,700
Married, Filing Separately	$12,200	$12,000	$6,350
Head of Household	$18,350	$18,000	$9,350

Do low-income taxpayers benefit more from tax credits or tax deductions?

Low-income taxpayers benefit more from tax credits than tax deductions because for many such taxpayers, the total amount of their tax deductions equals or exceeds their income, which means they have no taxable income and receive no tax benefit from any additional deductions, such as the case with itemized deductions.[351] Between the two types of tax credits, refundable credits are more valuable than nonrefundable credits, because they deliver the full amount of the benefit and do not depend on a taxpayer's tax liability or bracket.[352]

To illustrate with a few simple numbers, Table 2.2 compares the value of $2,000 in deductions, nonrefundable credits, and refundable credits for three different low-income taxpayers: (1) a taxpayer with no taxable income; (2) a taxpayer in the lowest marginal tax bracket; and (3) a taxpayer in the second lowest marginal tax bracket. Assume all three taxpayers are married and filed their taxes jointly.

Taxpayer with no taxable income. A taxpayer is in the 0 percent tax bracket when the taxpayer's taxable income is $0. This does not necessarily mean that the taxpayer has no earned income. For instance, a taxpayer may have earned $24,400 of income but took the standard deduction of $24,400 for married, jointly filed taxpayers, reducing their taxable income to zero.

- Deduction: The $2,000 deduction does not provide any benefit because this taxpayer has $0 taxable income.

Table 2.2 Value of Deductions, Nonrefundable Credits, and Refundable Credits[1]

	Marginal Tax Bracket	Value of $2,000 Deduction	Value of $2,000 Nonrefundable Credit	Value of $2,000 Refundable Credit
Taxpayer with No Taxable Income	0 percent	$0	$0	$2,000
Taxpayer in the Lowest Tax Bracket	10 percent	Up to $200	Up to $1,940	$2,000
Taxpayer in the Second Lowest Tax Bracket	12 percent	Up to $240	Up to $2,000	$2,000

[1] The chart is largely based on reports of the Center on Budget and Policy Priorities, but uses the 2019 tax brackets. *See* Center on Budget and Policy Priorities, Policy Basics: Tax Exemptions, Deductions, and Credits, https://www.cbpp.org/research/federal-tax/policy-basics-tax-exemptions-deductions-and-credits.

- Nonrefundable Credit: The $2,000 nonrefundable credit does not provide any benefit because this taxpayer has $0 taxable income.
- Refundable Credit: The $2,000 refundable credit is worth the full amount, even though this taxpayer does not have any taxable liability. This taxpayer will receive the entire $2,000 amount as a refund from the IRS, assuming that the taxpayer had earnings from work of at least $2,000.

Taxpayer in the lowest tax bracket. A taxpayer is in the 10 percent tax bracket when the taxpayer's taxable income is between $1 and $19,400. The first $19,400 of taxable income is subject to a tax rate of 10 percent.

- Deduction: The $2,000 deduction gives this taxpayer up to $200 in tax benefits ($2,000 x 10 percent), which is a product of the amount of the deduction and the marginal tax rate of 10 percent.
- Nonrefundable Credit: The maximum taxable income in the 10 percent bracket is $19,400, and the maximum amount of taxes owed is $1,940. A $2,000 nonrefundable credit eliminates the entire tax liability; but since the credit is nonrefundable, the $60 difference between the credit ($2,000) and tax owed ($1,940) is not issued to the taxpayer as a cash refund.
- Refundable Credit: The $2,000 refundable credit is worth the full amount. The taxpayer's $1,940 tax bill is eliminated, and the taxpayer receives a $60 refund.

Taxpayer in the second lowest tax bracket. A taxpayer is in the 12 percent tax bracket when the taxpayer's taxable income is between $19,401 and $78,950.

- Deduction: The $2,000 deduction gives this taxpayer up to $240 in tax benefits ($2,000 x 12 percent), which is a product of the amount of the deduction and the marginal tax rate of 12 percent.
- Nonrefundable Credit: The maximum taxable income in the 12 percent bracket is $78,950, and the maximum amount of taxes owed is $9,086. A $2,000 nonrefundable credit is worth the full amount because it reduces the taxpayer's bill by $2,000.
- Refundable Credit: The $2,000 refundable credit is worth the full amount, for the same reason as above.

Are there tax deductions specifically available for low-income taxpayers?

Few tax deductions (if any) are specifically designed for low-income taxpayers.[353] In most cases, low-income workers do not have enough taxable income against which they can claim deductions, and they generally do not itemize their deductions. According to a 2016 IRS Statistical Report, only 21 percent of taxpayers with income under $49,999 chose to itemize their deductions, and an even lower 7 percent of taxpayers with income under $30,000 chose to do so.[354] After the 2017 tax act, which doubled the standard deduction amount and eliminated or restricted many itemized deductions, it is expected that even fewer low-income workers will itemize their deductions.[355] The Individual Retirement Account (IRA) deduction, however, may be one tax deduction that tends to be geared more toward the lower-income worker, and it can be claimed even if the worker also claimed the standard deduction.[356] The IRA deduction was enacted to encourage retirement savings by taxpayers who do not participate in employer-provided plans, and it can reduce a taxpayer's taxable income by the amount of the taxpayer's annual contribution to an IRA, depending on several factors, including the type of IRA, the amount of the contribution, and the taxpayer's age, filing status, and income.[357] The maximum IRA contribution in 2019 was $6,000.[358] Taxpayers who qualify for the full annual IRA deduction generally include workers with an income of $64,000 or less if single, or an income of $103,000 or less if married, filing jointly.[359] The amount that a worker saves making the IRA contribution will vary. For instance, for a fully deductible IRA contribution of $5,500, a taxpayer in the 25 percent tax bracket saves $1,375 in taxes the first year; whereas a taxpayer in the 10 percent tax bracket saves $500. In addition to tax savings from deductions, IRA contributions can potentially save low-income workers thousands of dollars over time for low-income workers, depending on their contribution amount, income tax bracket, and the number of years of investment.

Are there tax credits specifically available for low-income taxpayers?

Unlike tax deductions, there are a number of different tax credits specially designed for low-income taxpayers and their families. Tax credits may be granted for certain types of activities, such as working, raising children, paying for child care or dependent care, and pursuing a secondary education. To claim these credits, the low-income worker must file a tax return; however, each of these credits imposes additional filing requirements relating to the worker's earned income, filing status, marital status, and number of children the worker supports.[360] Among all of the credits for low-income workers, the most successful has been the Earned Income Tax Credit.

Earned Income Tax Credit

What is the Earned Income Tax Credit?

The Earned Income Tax Credit (EITC) is a refundable tax credit for eligible low- and moderate-income workers.[361] Congress enacted the EITC to provide economic assistance to low-income workers, and its specific objectives included: (1) offsetting Social Security and Medicare taxes paid by low-income workers; (2) providing a work incentive for individuals who receive cash public assistance or other assistance benefits; (3) providing low-income families with a measure of income security; and (4) attempting to "redress the effects of regressive federal tax proposals."[362] The EITC is now considered one of the federal government's largest and most effective anti-poverty programs, as it has one of the highest take-up rates, with a national participation rate of nearly 80 percent.[363] It differs from other federal programs, however, because it is available only to taxpayers with earnings.[364] Workers who qualify for the EITC will receive a cash payment from the IRS after filing a tax return if the EITC amount exceeds the amount of tax they owe.

> EXAMPLES:
> A family has $1,500 in tax liabilities and receives a $1,000 Earned Income Tax Credit. Their tax bill would be reduced to $500.
> A family has $1,500 in tax liabilities and receives a $2,500 Earned Income Tax Credit. Their tax bill would be reduced to zero, and the taxpayer would receive $1,000 cash refund from IRS.

However, a person who is in extreme poverty but lacks earned income cannot claim the credit, and some analyses report a racial disparity in the distribution of EITC and Child Tax Credit benefits.[365]

In addition to the earned income requirement, a taxpayer's eligibility for the EITC and the range of benefit turn on family size and investment income.[366]

How does the EITC help low-income working families?

The EITC provides an important income boost for eligible families that claim the credit. In 2017, more than 27 million workers and their families received approximately $65 billion in EITC, and the average EITC amount per filer was $2,455.[367] However, in 2018, only 25 million workers and their families received approximately $63 billion in EITC, although the average EITC amount per filer rose slightly to $2,488.[368] Almost all of EITC benefits accrue to workers in the lowest 30 to 40 percent of earners.[369] However, filing for the EITC can be complicated, and an estimated 20 percent of eligible workers do not claim the credit.[370]

By and large, the EITC supports work effort, increases consumer spending, and indirectly improves neighborhood conditions by lifting local economies.[371] In 2016, the EITC brought 5.8 million people out of poverty, including about 3 million children, and reduced the severity of poverty for another 18.7 million people, including 6.9 million children.[372] Moreover, research suggests that the EITC reduces poverty in the long term, especially for single mothers, by facilitating the transition from public assistance to wage labor.[373] One study found that a $1,000 increase in the EITC benefit led to a 7.3 percentage point increase in employment and a 9.4 percentage point reduction in the share of families with after-tax and transfer income in poverty.[374] Receipt of the EITC is associated with improved health status; for example, one study showed that children in families that received the EITC had decreased rates of low birthweight.[375]

Nevertheless, the EITC is an incomplete response to problems of low-wage employment, poverty, and inequality. One commentator has argued that the EITC "does not, and cannot 'make work pay,' because it operates in a legal context that creates deep disadvantage for low-wage workers and children"— underscoring the fact that the EITC does not ensure a socially decent living standard even for persons who can and want to work.[376] Social psychologists posit that the EITC, even if it improves financial stability for some low-income taxpayers, fails to address environmental factors that impede mobility and reduce wellbeing of low income households overall.[377] Other commentators have argued that the EITC discourages savings, especially savings for retirement, and so reinforces cyclical poverty and the likelihood that low-income workers "will live below the poverty level at retirement."[378] An additional criticism is that the EITC, by effectively boosting a low-wage worker's earnings, diminishes market pressure for employers to raise wages; some commentators have suggested that a better approach would be to combine the EITC with an increased minimum wage.[379] Moreover, the EITC not only privatizes the nation's response to social assistance, but also reinforces a distinction between those who are said to deserve assistance because they work and those who do not, and subjects EITC claimants to regulatory surveillance not imposed on other taxpayers.[380]

Did the Tax Cuts and Jobs Act of 2017 affect the EITC rules?

While the 2017 tax act did not make any *direct* changes to the EITC, it indirectly affected the credit's value by permanently establishing a method of measuring inflation that reduces the effective value of earnings.[381] The amount of credit will now increase at a slower rate, and as a result, eligible low-income workers and their families will likely lose out on an estimated $19 billion of the EITC over the next decade.[382]

Who is eligible to claim the EITC?

The EITC divides eligible claimants into eight groups that vary by the taxpayer's filing status and the number of qualifying children the taxpayer has.[383] A taxpayer is eligible to claim the EITC if the following requirements are met:

1. The individual must file a federal income tax return, or a joint tax return if married, even if no taxes are owed.[384]
2. The individual must have earned income for the taxable year.[385]
3. The individual's adjusted gross income (AGI)[386] must be less than a certain threshold amount, which varies depending on the individual's marital status and the number of qualifying children the individual has.[387]
4. The individual must have no more than a threshold amount of investment income, which includes interests, dividends, or income from rentals, royalties, or stock and other asset sales.[388]
5. The individual must be a U.S. citizen or resident alien for the entire taxable year.[389]
6. The individual must provide the Social Security numbers for themselves, their spouse if married, and any children for whom the credit is claimed.[390]
7. The individual cannot file Form 2555 or Form 2555-EZ to exclude income earned in a foreign country or a foreign housing amount.[391]
8. The individual must not be disallowed the credit due to prior fraud or reckless disregard of the rules when a taxpayer previously claimed the EITC.[392]

In addition, the taxpayer must also meet requirements that turn on the number of qualifying children the individual claims for purposes of the EITC. If a taxpayer has at least one qualifying child for EITC purposes, the following three requirements must be met:

1. The child must meet relationship, age, and residency tests.[393]
2. The qualifying child may not be claimed by another taxpayer for EITC purposes.[394]
3. The individual may not claim the EITC for the qualifying child of another person.

If a taxpayer does not claim any children (a "childless taxpayer"), the following four requirements must be met:

1. The individual must have lived in the United States for more than half of the taxable year.[395]
2. The individual must be at least age 25 but under age 65 at the close of the taxable year (if married, either spouse may meet this condition).[396]
3. The individual cannot be claimed as a dependent of another taxpayer.[397]
4. The individual must not be a qualifying child of another individual.[398]

What is a "qualifying child" under the EITC?

A child is considered a "qualifying child" for purposes of the EITC if the child meets the following residency, relationship, and age tests:[399]

1. Residency. The child must principally live with the worker in a home located in the United States for more than half of the taxable year.[400]
2. Relationship. The child can be the worker's biological child or descendant (for example, a grandchild), adoptive child, foster child,[401] or stepchild. The child may also be a sibling, a stepsibling, or the descendent of a sibling or stepsibling. A married child can be a qualifying child only under limited circumstances.[402]
3. Age and/or Disability. The child must be under age 19 at the end of the tax year; or a student under age 24 at the end of the tax year; or of any age if permanently and totally disabled at any time during the tax year.[403]

EXAMPLE:
A taxpayer, who is 30 years old, lives with his sister, who is 15 years old. When their parents passed away two years ago, the taxpayer took over the care of his sister but did not adopt her. The taxpayer's sister is considered a "qualifying child" because she lived with the taxpayer for more than half of the year and meets the age requirement.

In addition, a child claimed as a qualifying child must have a valid Tax Identification Number (TIN). Generally a TIN is a Social Security number issued by the Social Security Administration, on or before the due date for filing the return,[404] and is considered valid for EITC purposes if is issued to a U.S. citizen, or if the card indicates "Valid for Work with INS Authorization" or "Valid for Work only with DHS Authorization." A Social Security card is not valid for the EITC if it states "Not Valid for Employment," and the number was issued solely for use in applying for federally funded benefits, such as Medicaid.[405] To apply for a Social Security number, file Form SS-5 with the local Social Security

Administration.[406] In claiming the EITC, the taxpayer must list the qualifying child's name, age, and Social Security number on the tax return.[407]

Can two taxpayers claim the same qualifying child and "split" the EITC?

Unless taxpayers are married and filing jointly, only one taxpayer may claim a qualifying child, even if the child satisfies all three tests for more than one taxpayer. Nor may two taxpayers "split" the EITC benefit between them. If two or more taxpayers who are not spouses filing a joint return cannot agree on who will claim the qualifying child, then the "tiebreaker" rules apply.[408] Under the tiebreaker rules, if one of the eligible taxpayers is the child's parent, the parent claims the child. If both of the eligible taxpayers are the child's parents (and did not file a joint return), the parent with whom the child lived for the longest period during the year (the custodial parent) claims the child; if the periods of custody are the same, the parent with the highest income claims the child. If neither eligible taxpayer is the child's parent, the taxpayer with the highest income claims the child.[409] These tiebreaker rules also govern other child-related tax benefits, including the child tax credit, the dependent child tax credit, the dependent care credit, the exclusion for dependent care benefits, and head of household filing status, discussed later in this chapter.[410]
If the parents of the child are divorced or separated, only the parent who has custody of the child for more than six months may claim the EITC, even if the noncustodial parent pays child support and may claim the Child Tax Credit.[411]

Keep in mind that if a taxpayer cannot claim a qualifying child, the taxpayer nevertheless still may be eligible to take the EITC as a taxpayer who lacks a qualifying child. The amount of the credit, however, is small: according to an analysis by the Center for Budget and Policy Priorities, a childless taxpayer earning poverty-level wages of $13,340 would receive a credit of $172.[412]

What is "earned income" under the EITC?

The amount of an EITC is calculated as a percentage of the taxpayer's "earned income," up to an inflation-adjusted threshold.[413] "Earned income" for purposes of the EITC has a rather expansive scope and includes: (1) "wages, salaries, tips, and other employee compensation, but only if such amounts are includible in gross income for the taxable year"; (2) net earnings from self-employment less the deduction for one-half of self-employment taxes imposed on such income; (3) long-term disability benefits received under an employer's disability plan before minimum retirement age; (4) strike benefits a labor union pays to its members;[414] and (5) the rental value of a home or housing allowance provided to a minister as part of the minister's pay.[415] The earned income of each individual is computed without regard to any community property law.[416]

"Earned income" does not include: (1) earnings while an inmate;[417] (2) amounts received as a pension or annuity;[418] (3) unemployment compensation;[419] (4) workers' compensation;[420] (5) amounts received as workfare payments by participants in a TANF-funded state public assistance program, but only to the extent such amounts are subsidized under that program; (6) Social Security benefits (including Supplemental Security Income and disability benefits);[421] (7) amounts received from a disability insurance policy on which the taxpayer paid the premiums; (8) nontaxable foster care payments; and (9) alimony and child support.[422]

What are the income limits for the EITC?

A taxpayer's adjusted gross income must be no more than what is shown in Tables 2.3 and 2.4. In addition, investment income must be $3,500 or less (in 2018), but investment income is not a condition for claiming the EITC.

Table 2.3 2018 EITC Income Limits

Filing Status	Number of Qualifying Children Claims			
	Zero	One	Two	Three or more
Single, Head of Household or Surviving Spouse	$15,270	$40,320	$45,802	$49,194
Married, Filing Jointly	$20,950	$46,010	$51,492	$54,884

Table 2.4 2019 EITC Income Limits

Filing Status	Number of Qualifying Children Claims			
	Zero	One	Two	Three or more
Single, Head of Household or Surviving Spouse	$15,570	$41,094	$46,703	$50,162
Married, Filing Jointly	$21,370	$46,884	$52,493	$55,952

What is the amount of EITC that an eligible low-income worker may claim?

The amount of the EITC depends on the taxpayer's marital status and the number of qualifying children. The EITC is calculated as a percentage of the household's total wages, meaning the credit increases as household income increases, up to a maximum dollar amount. After that point, the credit declines as adjusted gross income (including income sources other than wages) moves higher—a process known as the phaseout. The relevant amounts are adjusted annually for changes in the cost of living. For the years 2018 and 2019, the maximum credit amounts are as shown in Tables 2.5 and 2.6.

Table 2.5 2018 Maximum EITC Amounts

Category of Taxpayer	Maximum Credit for Tax Year 2018
No qualifying children	$519
One qualifying child	$3,461
Two qualifying children	$5,716
Three or more qualifying children	$6,431

Table 2.6 2019 Maximum EITC Amounts

Category of Taxpayer	Maximum Credit for Tax Year 2019[431]
No qualifying children	$529
One qualifying child	$3,526
Two qualifying children	$5,828
Three or more qualifying children	$6,557

Source: Internal Revenue Service, 2019 EITC Income Limits, Maximum Credit Amounts and Tax Law Updates (Feb. 15, 2019), https://www.irs.gov/credits-deductions/individuals/earned-income-tax-credit/eitc-income-limits-maximum-credit-amounts-next-year.

The EITC phaseout begins at a lower income for taxpayers who are unmarried, as compared to taxpayers who are married, filing jointly.[423]

Does receiving an EITC bar a household from receiving benefits under a government assistance program?

No. Receiving an EITC does not bar the taxpayer's household from receiving benefits under a government assistance program.[424] The amount of the EITC refund does not count as income for the taxpayer or anyone else in the household when calculating eligibility or benefits for Medicaid, SSI, SNAP (food stamps), Temporary Assistance for Needy Families (TANF), or housing assistance.[425] If the taxpayer saves the EITC, the refund does not count as a resource for at least 12 months after receipt of the credit under these programs.

What documents are needed to prepare taxes and to claim the EITC?

The following documents may be needed to prepare the tax and claim the EITC:[426]

- Social Security cards, a Social Security number verification letter, or other U.S. government document verification for persons listed on the return.
- Birthdates for all persons listed on the return.
- Copies of last year's federal and state returns.
- All income statements: Forms W-2 and 1099, Social Security, unemployment, and other statements, such as pensions, stocks, interest, and any documents showing taxes withheld.
- All records of expenses, such as tuition, mortgage interest, or real estate taxes.
- All information-reporting forms such as the 1095-A, 1095-B, or 1095-C.
- Bank routing numbers and account numbers to directly deposit any refund.
- Dependent child care information: name and address of paid caretakers and either their Social Security number or other tax identification number.

Is it too late to claim an EITC for prior tax years?

A taxpayer can claim an EITC as far back as three years.[427] The taxpayer does not have to be currently eligible for an EITC as long as the taxpayer received earned income during the years for which a refund is claimed. To apply, the individual needs to file a number of different forms with the Internal Revenue Service: an Amended U.S. Individual Tax Return, Form 1040X for the year for which an

EITC is claimed, a copy of that year's income tax form, and Schedule EIC if the taxpayer is claiming a qualifying child.

Where can a taxpayer get help in claiming the Earned Income Tax Credit?

The provisions of the EITC are complex and it is useful to seek professional guidance when filing a tax form.[428] The Internal Revenue Service offers a free online resource called the EITC Assistant to help filers determine whether they qualify and if they should claim the EITC.[429] Also, taxpayers can get free tax preparation help through a federal program called Volunteer Income Tax Assistance (VITA). VITA is administered by the Internal Revenue Service, which sponsors local tax clinics at community centers, churches, shopping malls, libraries, and other public places. The clinics are open from late January or early February through April 15. In addition, the IRS's Tax Counseling for the Elderly program helps those who are age 60 and older. To find out where a provider for these programs is located in your community, call 1-800-906-9887 or visit http://irs.treasury. gov/freetaxprep/. The Internal Revenue Service also provides a toll-free phone line to ask questions and get advice.[430] Keep in mind that informal advice from the IRS hotline has been called "unreliable"; answers provided through this resource are not always accurate, and the taxpayer's reliance on informal guidance from the IRS is not protection against later liability or penalties.[431]

Studies show that the majority of EITC filers use paid tax preparers to help them in filing the tax form and claiming the credit.[432] The use of paid tax preparers comes with unfortunate costs, with reports of inflated fees[433] and high error rates.[434] The Internal Revenue Service is very clear that the taxpayer is responsible for errors in the tax return even if a third party prepared the form.[435]

What are the consequences of a taxpayer's erroneously claiming the EITC?

Errors in claiming the EITC—other than for mathematical or clerical errors— can result in the government's delaying payment of the refund, the taxpayer's having to return a wrongly claimed refund plus interest, or the taxpayer's being barred from claiming the EITC in future. The three most common errors in claiming the EITC are qualifying children errors, income misreporting, and filing status errors.[436] The Internal Revenue Service has estimated that the EITC error rate is between 22 and 26 percent,[437] but commentators have questioned those numbers as overstated.[438] In 2015, Congress enacted the Protecting Americans from Tax Hikes Act, which mandates a delay in payment of refunds to taxpayers claiming the EITC (or the Additional Child Tax Credit, discussed later in the chapter).[439] The delay is intended to give the Internal Revenue Service time to verify the taxpayer's income based on information received from the taxpayer's employers. As of 2017, if a taxpayer claims the EITC (or the Additional Child Tax Credit), no refund payment will be made to the taxpayer before February 15—the Internal Revenue Service will withhold the entire refund, and not just the portion attributed to the EITC (or the child credit).[440]

Erroneously claiming the EITC is not the same thing as fraud; the complexity of the rules and the largely unregulated nature of tax preparation are important sources of the error rate.[441] However, the Internal Revenue Service is more likely to audit a taxpayer who claims the EITC than it does a taxpayer who reports exponentially more income.[442]

How does an audit by the Internal Revenue Service affect a taxpayer who has claimed the EITC?

In practice, auditing the taxpayer's return will likely cause a delay in payment of the refund for several months. If the Internal Revenue Service denies a taxpayer's EITC after an audit, and the refund already has been paid, the taxpayer must pay back the refund plus interest. If the credit is disallowed for any reason other than a mathematical or clerical error, the taxpayer cannot in future claim the credit without filing a completed Form 8862, Information to Claim Refundable Credits After Disallowance, or Form 8862-SP. Failure to attach Form 8862 to the return will result in denial of the EITC. If the error is found to have been due to "reckless or intentional disregard of the rules," the IRS may prohibit the taxpayer from claiming the EITC for the following two years; if the error is found to have been the result of fraud, the ban may be up to 10 years.[443] Tax scholars have called these sanctions "draconian," emphasizing that "[t]here are no analogous sanctions" for other "improper positions taken on federal income tax returns" by wealthier taxpayers.[444]

Do states or localities also give tax credits to low-income workers?

Twenty-nine states, the District of Columbia, and Puerto Rico have their own tax credit programs that supplement the federal EITC. These state EITCs are calculated as a percentage of the federal EITC claimed for the same benefit year. For example, in New York State, the state EITC can be 30 percent of the federal credit. Because of this arrangement, state EITCs are relatively easy to administer and claim; state revenue departments add one line to a state's income tax form, and low-income taxpayers multiply their federal EITC by their state's specified rate. Currently, 23 states, the District of Columbia, and Puerto Rico offer a fully refundable state EITC, which at least partially offsets other substantial state and local taxes that low-income families pay, including sales tax, property tax, excise tax, gas tax, and others.

In recent years, a number of states have expanded their EITCs. For instance, in 2018, Puerto Rico enacted a new local EITC; Louisiana, Massachusetts, New Jersey, and Vermont increased the size of their credits by 3 to 7 percent; and California and Maryland expanded access to the credits to workers who were previously ineligible. Even states without a broad-based income tax have begun to offer a similar type of assistance; for instance, Washington State now provides a "Working Families Tax Rebate," based on federal EITC data that the Internal Revenue Service shares with state revenue departments. Some researchers argue that more states without income tax, such as Florida, Alaska, Nevada, New Hampshire, South Dakota, Tennessee, Texas, and Wyoming, should follow Washington State.[445]

Can the United States seize an EITC for past-due child support?

The U.S. Supreme Court has held that the Internal Revenue Service can intercept the refundable portion of an EITC—just as it can intercept a tax refund—to pay past-due child support payments.[446]

What happens to the EITC if an individual declares bankruptcy?

When a person declares bankruptcy, certain assets are excluded from the bankruptcy estate and are available to be used for essential living expenses. To be excluded from the bankruptcy estate and so retained by the debtor, moneys must be a "social welfare" payment. Bankruptcy courts through the 1990s treated the EITC as the functional equivalent of an assistance payment and so considered the EITC to be an exempt asset. However, some more recent court decisions have treated the EITC as not exempt.[447]

Is the EITC available to taxpayers who are not U.S. citizens?

The EITC is available to otherwise eligible, non-U.S. citizen taxpayers if the taxpayer (1) was a "resident alien"[448] for the entire tax year; or (2) was married to a

U.S. citizen or resident alien, filed a joint return, and reported their foreign income on the return.[449] The taxpayer and qualifying children must have a Social Security number that is valid for employment in the United States.[450] Qualifying children must live with the worker in the United States for more than six months out of the year.[451]

Tax Benefits for Families with Children and Other Dependents

What child-related tax benefits are available for low-income workers?

Tax benefits for families with children take two forms: one specifically for child care, under the Child and Dependent Care Credit ("Child Care Credit"); and the other for children generally, under the Child Tax Credit. Although the two are often confused in policy discussions, the Child Care Credit and the Child Tax Credit serve distinct purposes and operate in different ways for low-income families.

What is the Child and Dependent Care Credit?

The Child and Dependent Care Credit is a nonrefundable tax credit for low-income working parents to help defray the costs associated with child care.[452] The credit can be claimed for dependent care expenses for up to two "qualifying individuals," generally dependents of the taxpayer below the age of 13.[453] To qualify for the credit, the child or dependent care expenses must be needed to allow the taxpayer to work or to look for work.[454]

Who is a "qualifying individual" for purposes of the Child and Dependent Care Credit?

Generally a qualifying individual for the Child and Dependent Care Credit is a child or other dependent, including:

1. A child under age 13 at the time care is provided;
2. A spouse incapable of self-care who lived with the taxpayer for more than half of the year; or
3. A person who was not physically or mentally capable of self-care,[455] lived with the taxpayer for more than half the year, and (a) was the taxpayer's

dependent; or (b) would have been the taxpayer's dependent except that the person's income was too high, or the person filed a joint return, or the taxpayer or the taxpayer's spouse (if filing jointly) could have been claimed as a dependent on another taxpayer's income tax return.[456]

How large is the Child and Dependent Care Tax Credit?

For a family with income of less than $15,000, the credit equals 35 percent of care costs, capped at $3,000 for one qualifying individual or $6,000 for two or more qualifying individuals. The amount of the tax credit is usually much lower than the amount of money that most families actually spend on child care. The annual cost of child care exceeds $10,000 in most states.[457] The credit drops by 1 percent for every $2,000 of income above $15,000 (for example, the credit rate is 31 percent if income is between $21,000 and $23,000).[458] Keep in mind that if the head of the household is single, the credit cannot exceed that person's income for the year. If the head of household is married, both spouses must work or attend school, and the amount of the child care expense cannot exceed the earned income of the lower-earning spouse.[459]

What is the Child Tax Credit?

The Child Tax Credit is a partially refundable tax credit of $2,000 for each of the taxpayer's qualifying dependents under the age of 17.[460] The Child Tax Credit is available to households with an annual income below $200,000 as of 2018. Up to $1,400 of the credit is refundable for each qualifying child, depending on the household's income.[461]

Who counts as a "qualifying child" for purposes of the Child Tax Credit?

To claim a child for purposes of the Child Tax Credit, the child must (1) be under the age of 17; (2) be claimed as a dependent on the taxpayer's return; (3) be the taxpayer's child, stepchild, foster child, adopted child, brother, sister, stepbrother, stepsister, or a descendant of any of these individuals; (4) have resided with the taxpayer for at least half the year (with some exceptions); (5) not have provided for more than 50 percent of the child's own support; and (6) be a U.S citizen, U.S. national, or "resident alien."[462] As with the Earned Income Tax Credit, two taxpayers may not claim the same qualifying child for purposes of the Child Tax Credit. The same "tiebreaker" rules that govern the EITC also govern the Child Tax Credit, with the exception that special rules apply to the Child Tax Credit for taxpayers who are divorced or separated parents, or parents who live apart at all times during the last six months of the calendar year. Under the exception, a child will be treated as the qualifying child of the noncustodial parent for purposes of a Child Tax Credit if: (1) the parents are divorced or legally separated under a decree of divorce or separate maintenance, or are separated under a written separation agreement, or lived apart at all times during the last six months of the year, whether or not they are or were married; (2) the child received over half of the support for the year from the parents; (3) the child is in the custody of one or both parents for more than half of the year; and (4) the custodial parent signed Form 8332 or a substantially similar statement that the custodial parent will not claim the child as a dependent.[463]

How did the Tax Cuts and Jobs Act of 2017 affect the Child Tax Credit?

The TCJA made three major changes to the Child Tax Credit.[464] First, it doubled the maximum Child Tax Credit from $1,000 to $2,000, and it increased the refundable portion to $1,400—but this refund is limited an amount equal to 15 percent of the household's earnings above $2,500 (in effect, reducing its usefulness to very low-income families). Second, the TCJA increased the phaseout income limit from $75,000 ($110,000 if married) to $200,000 ($400,000 if married). Third, dependents who do not qualify for the $2,000 credit can now qualify for a Child Tax Credit of up to $500. This portion of the credit, however, cannot be received as a refund. [465]

Does the Child Tax Credit help low-income families?

In combination with the EITC, the Child Tax Credit has helped lift millions out of poverty. However, it is estimated that approximately 29 million children under age 17 with at least one working parent will not benefit from the full increase because their families earn too little or owe too little in taxes.[466]

TANF-Funded Employment Benefits

What is TANF and does it fund work-related benefits?

TANF refers to the Temporary Assistance for Needy Families block grant, which is how the federal government funds programs administered by the states for poor and low-income persons. (The program is discussed in depth in chapter 1.) States can choose to use TANF funds for work supports to benefit low-income workers. These benefits can include child care, education and job training, tax credits, and transportation, but the availability of such benefits differs from state to state.[467] For information about the benefits that are available in a specific state, contact the state office that administers the TANF-funded program in your state. The U.S. Department of Health and Human Services, Office of Family Assistance, maintains a website that provides links to state contacts for TANF-funded programs.[468]

What is an "Individual Development Account"?

States may offer participants in a TANF-funded program the opportunity to set up an "Individual Development Account" for designated purposes. Individuals deposit money into the account from their earnings that are then matched by the state or a nonprofit.[469] Contributions can come from any source (for example, earnings or Earned Income Tax credits), but may not be more than the person's earned income.[470] Funds in the account do not count as assets for purposes of other benefit programs, so the individual will not lose eligibility or have benefits reduced.[471] The individual can withdraw funds from the account only for the following qualified purposes: to pay for postsecondary educational expenses;[472] to purchase a first home;[473] and to capitalize a business.[474] A state may choose to offer Independent Development Accounts that can be used for other purposes (for example, to purchase a car), but funds in the account would count as assets for purposes of other benefit programs.[475]

Unemployment Benefits

What is unemployment insurance?

Unemployment insurance (UI), also known as unemployment compensation or unemployment benefits, helps people who have lost their jobs for reasons other than misconduct by providing partial wage replacement for a fixed period of time. UI is a federal-state cooperative program funded by a payroll tax on employers and administered by the states, meaning that procedures, rules, and benefits will vary by state.[476] Congress enacted UI as a national program during the Great Depression as part of the Social Security Act of 1935.[477]

Who is eligible to claim unemployment insurance benefits?

Full-time workers who become unemployed typically will be eligible for up to 26 weeks of unemployment insurance benefits. UI covers both public and private employees. All states require workers to have earned a specified amount of wages or to have worked a specified number of weeks in eligible employment during a one-year base period in order to qualify for benefits. Persons who are paid "under the table," who are part-time and fail to earn the minimum amount of wages in the base period, or who are self-employed, generally are not eligible for benefits. State eligibility requirements may vary in certain respects, but federal law sets a minimum requirement that a claimant for UI "must be able to work, available to work, and actively seeking work."[478] The primary reasons for ineligibility are: voluntarily leaving a job without good cause; being terminated from a job for misconduct; or for refusing suitable work.

How large are unemployment insurance benefits?

Unemployment insurance benefits vary from state to state. The average weekly benefit is about $300.[479] Benefits are calculated as a percentage of the claimant's prior wages (usually between one-third and one-half) subject to caps set by state law. After the 2007 recession, when unemployment was high, 36 states exhausted their UI trust funds and had to take loans from the federal government to continue operating their programs. Instead of raising the UI payroll tax to replenish these funds, some states slashed weekly benefits and reduced the maximum number of weeks an unemployed worker could receive UI. North Carolina, for example, cut its maximum weekly benefit by about a third.[480]

What's the process for applying
for unemployment insurance benefits?

The general procedure for claiming benefits involves contacting the state's unemployment agency or department of labor as soon as possible after a job has ended.[481] Time between the job loss and when a worker files the necessary paperwork is not compensable. Additionally, there often is a waiting period of one week or additional processing time before benefits will begin. Each state has its own application and registration requirements, but usually the claimant must submit a written application, including the name and address of the former employer, the worker's job title and duties, and the reason the employment ended.

The last question is critical because a worker who quit without good cause or was fired for misconduct is not eligible for UI. A claimant also may be interviewed in person or by telephone in connection with the UI application. An increasing number of states use (or require) online filing for UI.[482]

In most states, once the claim has been filed, the unemployment agency will contact the employer to verify eligibility and discuss the circumstances surrounding the termination. Benefits will not be paid if the worker left without good cause or committed misconduct. Employers have an incentive to contest eligibility, because their insurance rate is tied to the number of UI claims that must be paid to their former employees each year. If the employer does contest eligibility, the agency representative should contact the claimant to discuss the discrepancy. At this point, the state agency administering the UI program (usually the department of labor) will issue a decision about whether the claimant is entitled to benefits.

What counts as "good cause" for leaving a job?

A worker who quits a job will not receive unemployment insurance benefits unless the worker had good cause for leaving. "Good cause" typically includes situations such as unsafe working conditions, repeated and severe verbal or physical harassment, employer failure to pay lawful wages on time or at all, employer demand to engage in illegal activity, lack of transportation, or family emergency. The precise definition of good cause will vary from state to state.

What counts as "misconduct" that disqualifies a claimant from unemployment insurance benefits?

If an employer contests a worker's eligibility for unemployment insurance benefits on the basis of the worker's misconduct, the employer must show that misconduct in fact occurred. Misconduct refers to willful or wanton behavior, and usually requires intent or substantial disregard of the employer's interests, duties, or obligations. Mere inefficiency, incompetency, unsatisfactory conduct, inadvertencies, ordinary negligence in isolated instances, or good-faith errors in judgment or discretion may be good reasons for an employer to discharge an employee, but they do not count as disqualifying misconduct. Examples of misconduct include insubordination, refusal to do work, or a willful violation of employer policy. In these cases, the employer must usually have warned the employee that their behavior violates policy and jeopardizes their position before the behavior can be deemed disqualifying misconduct. [483]

What can a worker do if a claim for unemployment insurance benefits is denied?

Workers whose UI claims are denied will receive notice of the denial that includes information on how to appeal. The dispute procedures differ from state to state, but an appeal request generally must be filed in writing or online. Federal law requires states to provide an "opportunity for a fair hearing, before an impartial tribunal, for all individuals whose claims for unemployment compensation are denied."[484] In accordance with the statutory mandate, states provide for hearings conducted by an administrative law judge or hearing officer. The claimant and the employer both have the opportunity to appear and present their cases at these hearings. Guidance issued to the states by the U.S. Department of Labor calls for adherence to basic due process standards in UI appeals, including affording claimants the right to testify and present witnesses and documents and the right to confront and cross-examine adverse witnesses.[485]

How long can unemployment insurance benefits be received?

Each state has a different limit on the length of time a claimant can receive benefits, but as of 2019, the majority provided the federal maximum of 26 weeks of coverage. Two states provide more than 26 weeks of benefits, and eight states provide for less (Florida and North Carolina, at the bottom, offer only 12 weeks).[486]

What are the conditions for continuing to receive unemployment insurance benefits?

Because one of the basic eligibility criteria for UI is that the individual be actively seeking work, most states require claimants to file weekly or biweekly statements about continued job search efforts, and to report any earnings, job offers, or job refusals. Many states provide free employment services, such as resume preparation and job listings. Some states may refer workers to training programs or offer testing and counseling to assist transition to new careers. In many states, meetings with representatives from these offices are mandatory for continued receipt of UI. States may require attendance at information sessions, presentations, or job skill training events.[487]

If a claimant refuses a job offer, even one that pays substantially below the previous rate of pay or in another industry, a state may decide to terminate benefits.

Additionally, for each day a claimant works while receiving UI, the benefits are reduced by 25 percent; working four days in a week results in loss of all benefits for that week. In that scenario, however, the duration of the claimant's maximum coverage is extended one day for each day worked.

Does the federal government offer other programs to help unemployed or underemployed persons re-enter the workforce?

The federal government funds more than 40 job-training programs. The Workforce Innovation and Opportunity Act (WIOA) is the primary federal program supporting workforce development to assist unemployed and under-employed individuals enter the labor market.[488] The programs are primarily run by the U.S. Department of Labor through its Employment and Training Administration. A "One-Stop" delivery system coordinates state, local, and partner programs' training and employment activities.[489]

WIOA establishes a tiered system of services. All adults, regardless of their current employment status, can access "core services," which include initial assessments, job search assistance, information about access to sup-portive services, and employment counseling. "Intensive services" are avail-able to adults and dislocated workers who are not able to obtain employment or who remain underemployed after utilizing core services. An individual must have received at least one core service such as an initial assessment that determines that individual's need for these services. Intensive services include comprehensive assessments of skill levels and in-depth evaluation of em-ployment barriers, development of individual employment plans, short-term prevocational services, work experience activities, and case management. Finally, "training services" are available for adults and dislocated workers who are unable to obtain or retain employment through intensive services and unable to obtain grant assistance from other sources such as PELL grants. Training services include occupational skills training, on-the-job training, combination workplace and related instruction training, skills upgrading and retraining, job-readiness training, adult education, and literacy activities combined with other authorized services.[490] There are One-Stop Centers in major population areas in every state, but may have different names. The eas-iest way to find a One-Stop Center is to visit the One-Stop Career website at http://www.careeronestop.org/ or America's Service Locator at https://www.servicelocator.org.

Protections against Mass Layoffs

What is the Worker Adjustment and Retraining Notification (WARN) Act?

The Worker Adjustment and Retraining Notification (WARN) Act requires certain employers to give 60 days' advance notice to affected employees, union representatives, and states and localities of a plant closing or mass layoffs.[491] WARN applies to employers of 100 or more workers, excluding part-time workers.[492] Congress enacted the WARN Act in 1988 to address some of the financial, psychological, and community consequences of job loss and plant closings, with the goal of giving workers, their families, and community leaders time to consider relocation and retraining opportunities before, not after, the employer fires its workforce.[493] In this way, WARN responded to the severe economic dislocation that had begun in the last quarter of the twentieth century, as companies, seeking cost savings through "downsizing," reorganized and made dramatic changes in the way they run their businesses. Although the economic factors for mass layoffs are complex, many companies chose to fire their long-term workers and then replace them through automating,[494] outsourcing to third-party contractors, or hiring nonunionized, contingent, or foreign labor.[495] The legal system's response to the displacement of U.S. workers throughout the country during the 1980s[496]—described as "widespread"[497]—was limited and contributed to many of today's ongoing problems of poverty, immobility, and inequality.[498]

The WARN Act provides an important exception to the American rule that employers generally have no duty to give workers notice before terminating them; but, as described later, the act's protections apply only to certain kinds of layoffs.[499] Moreover, as with much of U.S. employment and labor law, the WARN Act assumes that workplace decisions generally are the sole prerogative of the employer and does not require consultation with workers themselves.[500]

The WARN Act became law only after more than a decade's worth of legislative investigations, economic studies, alternative bills, and a congressional override of President Reagan's veto.[501] Support for the WARN Act's key feature—mandatory notification—gathered steam after 1982, when Congress passed the Job Training Partnership Act (JTPA).[502] The JTPA authorized federal funding to the states for worker retraining and job search assistance to address problems of unemployment due to displacement. Measured even by modest standards, the JTPA was not a success; only 7 percent of laid-off workers had signed up to receive available aid. Also, in 1987, a federal survey of employers that had closed plants or laid off workers indicated that a majority had given little or no advance notice to soon-to-be displaced workers. The WARN Act, it was thought, could help to close the gap, ensuring that displaced workers had the knowledge, time, and resources to plan for new employment even as the ground was shifting under them.

Which employers are covered by the WARN Act?

Businesses that employ 100 or more full-time workers are required to comply with the WARN Act. So, too, are businesses that employ at least 100 full- or part-time workers (including managers and supervisors) who together work at least 4,000 hours per week, not counting overtime.[503] Workers who have been temporarily laid off or who are on leave and who may reasonably expect to be recalled are counted toward a business's total number of employees.[504] Temporary workers also are counted toward a business's total number of employees.[505] The number of employees is measured on the date when notice would be required.[506] If the number of workers on that date is not representative of a business's typical level of employment, then the number of employees on a more representative date or the average number of employees during a recent time period may be used to determine whether the employer is legally required to provide WARN notification to workers.

Whether the workforce of an independent contractor or of a subsidiary is counted for WARN purposes depends on the relative autonomy of the contractor or subsidiary from the parent company.[507] The answer to the question holds important consequences for workers who are laid off. For one thing, as the Third Circuit Court of Appeals explained, "[b]ecause employee layoffs are a necessary condition to WARN Act liability, and layoffs frequently presage a corporation's demise, plaintiffs frequently attempt to gain recovery from parent entities."[508] Federal courts use a number of different tests, but many rely upon regulations of the U.S. Department of Labor, setting out five factors to assess the level of control by the parent company, looking at common ownership; common directors or officers; de facto exercise of control; unity of personnel policies; and dependency of operations.[509] Under this test, a private equity company was held liable for failure to give WARN notice when it was shown that it exerted direct control over the layoff decision.[510] U.S. Department of Labor regulations define "employer" to include companies that were engaged in business at the time of a plant closing or mass layoff, and the agency refused to exclude fiduciaries for companies in bankruptcy proceedings from that definition or from the reach of the statute.[511] Some courts, however, have recognized a "liquidating fiduciary" exception to the WARN Act, exempting entities in bankruptcy proceedings from the statute's requirements.[512] Relatedly, a Delaware bankruptcy court held that the sole manager and president of an insolvent corporation in fact could be held liable for failure to provide notice under the Wisconsin WARN Act.[513] Other courts have held that the federal WARN Act does not provide for the personal liability of corporate officers, only of the employer.[514]

Which job losses trigger rights to notification under the WARN Act?

The WARN Act requires businesses to give advance notice of plant closings or mass layoffs.[515] "Plant closing" means the temporary or permanent shutdown of a single site of employment, or one or more facilities within a single site, causing 50 or more employees, not including part-time employees, to lose their jobs at the site during any 30-day period.[516] "Mass layoff" means a "reduction in force" not caused by a plant closing that results in an employment loss at the single site of employment during any 30-day period for (1) at least 33 percent of the employees (excluding any part-time employees) and involving at least 50 employees (excluding any part-time employees); or (2) at least 500 employees (excluding any part-time employees) irrespective of the percentage of the workforce.[517]

What information must the WARN notice provide?

The notification must communicate specific information, including the date of the expected closing or layoff and the identities of affected workers.[518] It also may communicate supplementary information, such as information regarding assistance for dislocated workers. As the federal court for the Southern District of New York has put it, the notice must contain:

(1) A statement as to whether the planned action is expected to be permanent or temporary and, if the entire plant is to be closed, a statement to that effect;
(2) The expected date when the plant closing or mass layoff will commence and the expected date when the individual employee will be separated;
(3) An indication whether or not bumping rights exist; and
(4) The name and telephone number of a company official to contact for further information.[519]

Are there any exceptions to the notice requirement prior to a plant closing or mass layoff?

The WARN Act contains three exceptions. Two of the exceptions allow companies to reduce the notice period "to as much as practicable."[520] One of the exceptions relieves the employer of any obligation to provide notice. In addition to these exceptions, the WARN Act also does not apply to certain kinds of job loss.

The "faltering company" exception allows an employer to reduce the notice period (or adapt the notice in other ways) if the employer is actively seeking capital to prevent or delay the shutdown, that financing would avoid or postpone the shutdown, "and the employer in good faith believed that the giving the notice required would have precluded the employer from obtaining the needed capital or business."[521] To determine whether the exception applies, courts look to the employer's business judgment; regulations explain that the test is objective and looks to the "economic reasonableness" of the employer's actions.[522]

Similarly, a company that faces unforeseeable business circumstances at the time notice otherwise would have been mandated may reduce or adapt the notice period.[523] A number of courts of appeals have adopted a "probability" standard for determining whether this exception applies, holding that notice is excused if it was merely possible, but not probable, that an event outside the employer's would take place and necessitate layoffs.[524] Under this exception, a company may also reduce the advance notice period otherwise required to extend a mass layoff beyond the duration initially announced, but must give such notice as soon as practicable.[525]

The WARN Act relieves an employer from the notice requirement if the layoffs are a "direct result of a natural disaster."[526] The exception does not apply if the layoffs are only indirectly caused by the disaster.

Certain plant closings and mass layoffs are exempt from the notice requirements. The WARN Act does not apply:

- To a plant closing if the facility to be closed was temporary.
- To a mass layoff if the workers who were let go were hired with the understanding that their tenure was limited to the length of a particular project and that project has concluded.
- When the closing or mass layoff is the result of a strike or a lockout.[527]

In addition, if the closing or layoff is the result of a relocation or consolidation, the employer may sidestep the WARN notice requirement by offering employees jobs at the new site if the offer involves no more than a six-month break in employment and the alternative site is within a reasonable commuting distance, or if the employee accepts the employer's offer regardless of distance within 30 days of the offer or of the closing or layoff, whichever is later.[528] (New York's WARN law requires 90-day notice prior to relocations.)[529]

Do collective bargaining agreements affect notice rights under the WARN Act?

Collective bargaining agreements cannot sign away the employees' WARN rights. However, collective bargaining agreements can include provisions calling for a longer notice period or increased rights and remedies.[530]

Who enforces the WARN Act if an employer fails to give the required notice prior to a plant closing or mass layoff?

The WARN Act authorizes civil lawsuits by affected workers and others to enforce the notice requirement. Litigation is very important; one federal study found that employers were twice as likely to violate the WARN Act as they were to provide the required notice.[531] Workers who are affected by the employer's failure may sue.[532] In addition, a union representing the workers may bring an enforcement suit,[533] as may representatives and units of local government.[534] At least one federal appeals court has held, as a matter of first impression, that an ERISA fund may not enforce the WARN Act.[535] The U.S. Department of Labor, which develops rules and regulations to implement the WARN Act, is not given any role in enforcing the law through court action. The Department of Labor does not issue advisory opinions in specific cases and it does not assist workers in commencing suit.[536] The WARN Act's enforcement scheme thus differs from that of other federal laws which assign important enforcement activity to federal agencies. Commentators have underscored that the law shoulders workers with the burden and expense of enforcing the statute, and that this arrangement has encouraged employer noncompliance and judicial underenforcement of the act's requirements.[537] Five years after the WARN Act took effect, the General Accounting Office reported that only 60 lawsuits had been filed under the law.[538] Predictably, the number of WARN Act suits increased during severe economic dislocation that accompanied the 2008 recession.[539] Regrettably, at least one federal appeals court held that the statute was not triggered because the downturn was an "unforeseeable circumstance."[540] In one notable display of worker solidarity, employees successfully resorted to direct action—occupying a factory that was to be closed—to secure their WARN rights against an employer that had announced a factory closing and mass firings with only three days' notice.[541]

What kind of relief may the court order
to remedy a violation of the WARN Act?

If the plaintiffs are successful, the employer may be held liable for civil penalties payable to the employees, including back pay, accrued vacation days, and benefits.[542] Workers are permitted to recover back pay as a form of "equitable restitutionary relief." The idea is that the amounts awarded by the court are not "compensation" for the workers' discharge, but rather reimbursement of salaries and benefits owed—salaries and benefits that should have been paid, but were wrongfully withheld because the advance warnings were not provided.[543] Tips, overtime, and holiday pay are included in the back pay that may be awarded.[544] Courts are split on the issue of how to count the number of days for which payment must be made. There are two approaches: counting all calendar days during the period of the violation and counting only regular workdays during that period.[545] In addition, a majority of courts take the view that damages should be computed with an eye toward making employees whole. The statute authorizes the amounts owed to the workers to be reduced by "any voluntary and unconditional payment by the employer to the employee that is not required by any legal obligation."[546] Further, the employer may be ordered to pay a civil fine of up to $500 a day of violation if it fails to notify the local government, unless the employer "pays to each aggrieved employee the amount for which the employer is liable to that employee within 3 weeks from the date the employer orders the shutdown or layoff."[547]

A provision of the act provides for a good faith exception: if the employer shows that the failure to provide notice was in "good faith" and that the employer had "reasonable grounds" for believing the act or omission was not a violation of the law, the court in its discretion may reduce the amount of liability.[548]

A successful suit to enforce the WARN Act will not stop a plant closing or mass layoff; statutory remedies do not include an injunction against the employer to halt its employment action, even if the employer is in violation of the WARN Act's notice requirement. Nor may the court award punitive damages.[549] The WARN Act does not specify how long workers have to file their suit after notice has been withheld from them. The U.S. Supreme Court has held that the time period in any lawsuit brought under the act should be borrowed from the most similar statute of limitations in the state where the claim is filed, but the federal court must ensure that the state limitations period is not so short as to frustrate the purposes of the act.[550] The court may award attorney's fees to the prevailing party as a part of costs.[551] There is a division as to whether plaintiffs have a right to a jury trial in an action to enforce rights under the WARN Act.[552]

What role can the U.S. Department of Labor play when workers face mass layoffs?

As already discussed, the U.S. Department of Labor plays no role in enforcing the WARN Act. However, the agency is important because it will assist workers in looking for new employment or obtaining job training.[553] When an employer serves notice on its workers, it also must serve notice on the state's dislocated worker unit, which in turn triggers the U.S. Department of Labor's Rapid Response program, which may include a visit to the affected job site by employment specialists who will apprise workers of the services and benefits available to them.[554] Services and benefits available to workers may include career counseling and job search assistance, resume preparation and interview skills workshops, unemployment insurance, and job training and education. In addition, affected workers have access to One-Stop Career Centers, which provide ongoing services akin to those made available by Rapid Response specialists. Because the Rapid Response program is carried out in partnership with state and local workforce development agencies, services and resources may vary from state to state. A directory of state Rapid Response coordinators is available on the Department of Labor's website at http://www.doleta.gov/layoff/rapid_coord.cfm. Labor experts have documented the positive effects of WARN Act notice, but also noted that for some workers job placement assistance, retraining, and other services, including cash benefits, will be essential.[555]

What other federal laws may provide redress during a period of mass layoff or reduction in labor force?

A mass layoff or reduction in labor force could implicate laws that bar discrimination if the employment action disproportionately and negatively affects persons because of race, national origin, gender, disability, or age without the employer having a valid justification for the decision.[556] Moreover, an employer cannot require a worker to waive rights under these statutes in a severance agreement unless the waiver is knowing and voluntary, and something of value is given in exchange for the waiver.[557] Relatedly, federal law prohibits an employer from forcing a worker to waive the right to file charges with the Equal Employment Opportunity Commission or with the National Labor Relations Board (NLRB) as a condition of receiving severance benefits, and a purported "waiver" of such rights in return for nothing more than the employer providing wages, benefits, and accrued rights already earned is illegal and unenforceable.[558]

The NLRA can help workers affected by mass layoffs because it requires employers to provide information about the company's financial health during the bargaining process.[559] The U.S. Supreme Court held in 1956 that an employer's duty to bargain in good faith includes the obligation to provide financial information substantiating its inability to raise wages.[560] Later, the Supreme Court held that it was an unfair labor practice for a company to refuse to negotiate with a union about a decision to subcontract maintenance work.[561] Although the Court also has held that management may unilaterally decide whether or not to stay in business, the decision did not include a situation in which the employer planned to replace fired workers.[562] Moreover, the National Labor Relations Board has recognized that a company's decision to relocate may be a mandatory subject of collective bargaining.[563]

Old Age, Survivors, and Disability Insurance Program

What is the Old Age, Survivors, and Disability Insurance Program?

The Old Age, Survivors, and Disability Insurance Program (OASDI), also known as Social Security, was established during the Great Depression as the cornerstone of the Social Security Act of 1935.[564] Though initially criticized as a move toward socialism, Social Security has for decades enjoyed overwhelming public support, has survived political efforts to undermine it through privatization, and has played a critical role in the nation's social safety net.[565] In 2018, Social Security payments kept over 22 million Americans out of poverty, including more than 15 million elderly Americans and 1.1 million children.[566] The program provides retirement benefits, survivor benefits, and disability payments. Social Security is funded by taxes deducted from wages and paid into trust funds administered by the U.S. Social Security Administration.[567] The program operates like an insurance fund—"premiums" are paid in the form of payroll deductions from a worker's wages matched by taxes charged to the employer, and when enough premiums are paid, the worker is entitled to benefits if nonfinancial requirements are met. In 2019, nearly 60 million people received Social Security benefits.

To qualify for most types of Social Security benefits, an individual must be "fully insured,"[568] though for certain benefits—such as a lump-sum death payment to a survivor—an individual need only be "currently insured."[569] An individual achieves insured status by accumulating a sufficient number of "quarters of coverage" (sometimes referred to as "QCs" or "credits").[570] Credits are earned for working in a job while also paying Social Security taxes. In 2019, a worker earned one credit for every $1,360 of earnings,[571] up to a maximum of four credits per year. It does not matter in which calendar quarters the income is earned.[572]

Generally, to be "fully insured," people born in or after 1929 must have earned at least 40 credits, the equivalent of working for at least 10 years,[573] but a disabled individual may acquire fully insured status with fewer credits, depending on the person's age at the onset of disability.[574]

To be "currently insured," an individual must have earned at least six credits during the 13-quarter period ending with the quarter in which the individual (1) died; (2) became entitled to retirement benefits; or (3) most recently became entitled to disability benefits.[575]

Who administers Social Security?

The U.S. Social Security Administration (SSA) administers Social Security. The SSA is an independent federal agency, headquartered in Baltimore, Maryland, with over 1,500 offices across the country. The SSA handles all aspects of Social Security, from initial application to payment of benefits to termination of benefits. Additionally, the SSA promulgates regulations governing the program, issues rulings applying and interpreting these regulations,[576] and conducts research and policy analysis useful to the implementation of the program.[577]

Who is entitled to Social Security retirement benefits?

Every individual who is at least 62 years old and "fully insured" qualifies for Social Security retirement benefits with the Social Security Administration.[578] A potential beneficiary must file an application for retirement benefits.[579] No benefits will be paid for any month prior to the month in which the application is filed.[580] An exception to the application requirement applies to individuals who are already receiving disability benefits, in which case those disability benefits automatically convert to retirement benefits upon the individual's entitlement to retirement benefits.[581] The SSA requires documentation and proof prior to issuing retirement benefits, such as proof of age and proof of wages.[582]

How is the amount of Social Security retirement benefits calculated?

The amount of Social Security retirement benefits depends on the individual's earnings record and the age at which the individual initially claims benefits. An individual first becomes eligible for retirement benefits, at a reduced monthly rate, at age 62. An individual qualifies for full retirement benefits on reaching full retirement age. Full retirement age is 66 for individuals born from 1943 to 1954 and then increases in bimonthly increments for each birth year thereafter (for example, full retirement is 66 years and two months for people born in 1955), with the maximum full retirement age set at 67 for individuals born in or after 1960.[583] Claiming benefits before reaching full retirement age results in a permanently reduced monthly retirement benefit.[584] Moreover, if a person claims benefits before reaching full retirement age and earns income over a certain amount, monthly benefits will be further reduced.[585] Waiting until full retirement age to claim benefits results in a higher monthly benefit.[586] Individuals may delay claiming benefits even beyond full retirement age, and the later benefits are claimed, the higher the monthly benefit amount will be, up to the month before the individual turns 70; after that, the benefit rate no longer increases.[587] Of course, delaying a claim for benefits means that the individual will collect Social Security for fewer years.

The amount of retirement benefits an individual would receive at full retirement age is known as the "primary insurance amount" (PIA) and is calculated based on the person's lifetime earnings.[588] (The Social Security Administration keeps a record of all earnings received during an individual's work history and gives the record to each person every year; a person also can check the work record on the SSA's website.[589]) For the "average" worker, Social Security benefits typically replace about 40 percent of pre-retirement income.[590] To determine the "primary insurance amount," the SSA calculates the worker's Average Indexed Monthly Earnings (AIME) and adjusts that number in accordance with a statutory formula.[591] The AIME equals the worker's earnings for the highest 35 years of employment, subject to a statutory cap, multiplied by an index factor that estimates the value of the earnings in current dollars, divided by 420 (the number of months in 35 years).[592] The SSA also provides an online calculator that individuals may use to estimate their retirement benefits.[593]

Upon death, an individual's retirement benefits cease, and benefits are not paid for the month of death.[594] However, members of the individual's family may be entitled to survivor benefits (discussed later in this chapter).

Does a person's gender or race affect the amount of Social Security retirement benefits?

The Social Security Administration pays retirement benefits on gender and race neutral formulas. However, in practice women receive lower benefits than men,[595] and racial minorities receive lower benefits than nonminorities,[596] in part reflecting the earnings gaps between the groups.

Who is entitled to Social Security disability benefits?

Individuals who become unable to work because of a medical condition may be entitled to receive Social Security disability benefits. To qualify, an individual must (1) have disability insured status; (2) be under a disability; (3) not be of retirement age; and (4) file an application for benefits.[597] Social Security disability benefits are not payable to workers with only temporary disabilities,[598] and claimants are subject to a five-month waiting period after the onset of the disability before becoming eligible for disability benefits.[599] However, the waiting period is waived for a former recipient of disability benefits whose benefits were discontinued sometime during the 60 months immediately preceding the onset of the person's current disability.[600] Claimants should apply for disability benefits as soon as they become disabled, as applications can take three to five months to process.[601]

How does an individual acquire the necessary disability insured status?

To obtain disability insured status, claimants must be "fully insured" (as discussed earlier), *and* must meet one of four tests set out by the Social Security Administration.[602] The most commonly applicable test is known as the "20/40 requirement," and requires that the claimant have earned at least 20 quarters of coverage in the 40-quarter (10-year) period immediately preceding the quarter for which the individual is claiming disability.[603] Individuals who become disabled or have periods of disability before the age of 31 can establish "disability insured status" with fewer quarters of coverage.[604] Individuals who are statutorily blind need only be fully insured to obtain disability insured status.[605]

How does an individual establish disability for Social Security disability benefits?

To receive Social Security disability benefits, an individual must be unable to "engage in any substantial gainful activity by reason of any medically determinable physical or mental impairment which can be expected to result in death or which has lasted or can be expected to last for a continuous period of not less than twelve months."[606] A disability must be established by "medical and other evidence" as required by the Social Security Administration.[607] Substantial activity means work that "involves doing significant[608] and productive physical or mental duties"; gainful means work that "is done (or intended) for pay or profit."[609] An individual's impairment must be "of a sufficient medical severity" as determined by the SSA.[610]

The standards and procedures for determining whether an individual has a qualifying "disability" for purposes of Social Security Disability Insurance are the same as those that apply to the Supplemental Security Income (SSI) program, discussed in chapter 1 in the section on Supplemental Security Income.[611]

Who is eligible for Social Security survivors' benefits?

Social Security survivors' benefits are paid to certain surviving family members at the death of a fully insured individual. Potential beneficiaries include surviving spouses, divorced spouses, parents, and children.[612] These surviving family members may receive benefits based on the earnings record of a fully insured or currently insured deceased worker.[613] The Social Security Administration requires documentation and proof of eligibility prior to issuing benefits, such as proof of age, marriage, family relationship, child in care, and proof of death.[614]

Widows and Widowers
A person who was married to a fully insured deceased individual ("the insured") is entitled to survivors' benefits if:

1. The person was married to the insured for at least nine months immediately prior to death, or meets an exception to that requirement;[615] or, for a surviving divorced spouse, was married to the insured for at least 10 years before the divorce became final;[616]
2. The person is unmarried, remarried after reaching age 60, or remarried between age 50 and 60 and meets certain requirements;[617]
3. The person is at least 60 years old, or is disabled and between the ages of 50 and 60;[618]
4. The person files an application for benefits;[619] and
5. The person is not entitled to retirement benefits that are equal to or greater than the deceased spouse's primary insurance amount.[620]

In general, the amount of survivor benefits payable to a surviving spouse or surviving divorced spouse is equal to the deceased insured's primary insurance amount, subject to reduction or increase if the insured claimed early or late retirement benefits.[621] If the survivor already was receiving spousal benefits, those spousal benefits will be converted to survivor benefits once the Social Security Administration is notified of the insured's death. Survivor benefits end in the month before the month in which the surviving spouse dies or becomes entitled to retirement benefits that are equal to or greater than the deceased's primary insurance amount.[622]

Mothers and Fathers of a Deceased Worker's Child

A surviving spouse or surviving divorced spouse who is not entitled to widow(er)'s benefits may receive mother's and father's survivor benefits, based on the primary insurance amount of a fully or currently insured deceased individual, if:

1. The survivor is not married;
2. The survivor is not entitled to retirement benefits that are equal to or greater than the deceased's primary insure amount;
3. The survivor either files an application for mother's or father's benefits or was entitled to spousal benefits on the deceased's Social Security record in the month before the month of death; and
4. The survivor is caring for a child of the deceased who is entitled to child's benefits[623] and is under age 16 or disabled.[624]

In general, the amount of survivor benefits payable to mothers and fathers is equal to 75 percent of the deceased's primary insurance amount.[625] Survivors' benefits end in the month before the month in which the beneficiary dies or in which any of the requirements above is no longer met.[626]

Parents of a Deceased Worker

A parent of a deceased fully insured individual is entitled to survivors' benefits if:

1. The parent is at least age 62;
2. The parent was receiving at least one-half support from the deceased and files proof of such support within two years of the death;[627]
3. The parent has not married since the death;
4. The parent is not entitled to retirement benefits equal to or greater than the amount that the parent would receive in the form of survivor benefits; and
5. The parent files an application for parent's survivor benefits.[628]

The Social Security Administration generally looks to state law to determine whether an individual is a "parent" for Social Security purposes.[629] When only one parent is entitled to parent's benefits, the amount payable is 82.5 percent of the deceased's primary insurance amount.[630] When more than one parent is entitled, the amount is 75 percent.[631] A parent may receive benefits on the basis of only one child's Social Security earnings record, and the SSA will base benefits on the record that will yield the highest payment.[632] Parent's benefits end in the month before the month in which the parent dies, marries, or becomes entitled to retirement benefits in an amount equal to or greater than the amount of parent's benefits.[633] A parent may, however, become re-entitled to parent's benefits if a re-marriage ends by death, divorce, or annulment.[634]

Who is entitled to receive Social Security children's benefits?

A child may be eligible to receive Social Security children's insurance benefits based on a parent's work record if the parent is eligible for Social Security retirement or disability benefits, or has died, and:

1. The child files an application for child's benefits;
2. The child is unmarried;[635]
3. The child is either under age 18 or under age 19 and a full-time elementary or secondary school student, or became disabled before turning age 22; and
4. The child is dependent on the parent.[636]

The term "child" for Social Security purposes includes a child or legally adopted child; a stepchild in that relationship for at least a year; or a grandchild or step-grandchild if there was no natural or adoptive parent living at the time, other than a parent who is disabled.[637]

A child who becomes disabled before age 22 qualifies for children's benefits based on that disability.[638] The importance of qualifying as a disabled child is that benefits continue into adulthood so long as the person remains disabled.[639] By contrast, children's benefits for nondisabled children cease at age 18 or at age 19 if the recipient is a full-time student.[640] If a child was disabled before age 22, but subsequently loses disability status, the child may become re-entitled to children's benefits if a disability recurs within seven years.[641]

Children's benefits are capped at 50 percent of a living parent's primary insurance amount and 75 percent of a deceased parent's primary insurance amount.[642] The benefit to the child may be lower than these percentages if multiple family members are receiving benefits on the parent's earnings record. A child may receive benefits based on only one parent's work record; whichever record will yield a higher level of benefits for the child.[643]

Who is eligible for a lump-sum death benefit?

A one-time, lump-sum Social Security death benefit is payable on the death of a fully or currently insured individual to that individual's surviving spouse or children. The payment is three times the insured's primary insurance amount or $255, whichever is smaller.[644] The claimant must file an application for the lump-sum payment within two years of the insured individual's death, except when the claimant is a surviving spouse who already was entitled to spousal benefits based on the deceased's Social Security record.[645]

Who is entitled to receive Social Security spouse's benefits?

An individual may receive Social Security retirement benefits based on the earnings history of the person's spouse. The Social Security Administration calls these "wife's or husband's benefits."[646] Spouses who never worked outside the home or who do not have a sufficient work history to qualify on their own may receive retirement benefits on this basis. Generally,, the amount of this benefit is 50 percent of the insured spouse's primary insurance amount (PIA). The benefit can fall to as low as 32.5 percent of the spouse's PIA if claimed prior to the claimant's full retirement age, unless the claimant is caring for a child under conditions described below.[647]

Married Spouses

The spouse of an insured individual entitled to Social Security retirement or disability benefits (the insured sometimes is called the "primary beneficiary") may qualify for spousal benefits based on the individual's earnings record if:

1. The spouse files an application for spousal benefits;
2. The spouse is at least age 62 at the time of application, or is caring for a child under age 16 who is entitled to benefits based on the primary beneficiary's Social Security record; and
3. The spouse is not entitled to retirement benefits that are equal to or greater than the primary beneficiary's primary insurance account.[648]

The Social Security Administration looks to state law to determine whether a spousal relationship is valid for Social Security purposes;[649] however, the U.S. Constitution requires states to recognize same-sex marriages on the same terms as other marriages,[650] and bars discrimination against same-sex spouses in the provision of governmental benefits.[651] Same-sex couples, therefore, qualify for Social Security spouse's benefits on the same basis as other couples as a matter of federal law.[652]

In addition to these requirements, a spouse claiming spousal benefits must: (1) have been married to the primary beneficiary for at least one continuous year immediately prior to applying for benefits; or (2) be the parent of the primary beneficiary's child; or (3) have been entitled or potentially entitled to certain specified benefits under the Social Security Act or Railroad Retirement Act of 1974 in the month prior to the month of marriage to the primary beneficiary.[653]

Divorced Spouses

A divorced spouse of an insured individual entitled to Social Security retirement or disability benefits may qualify for spousal benefits based on the individual's earnings record if:

1. The divorced spouse files an application for spousal benefits;
2. The divorced spouse was married to the primary beneficiary for at least 10 years;
3. The divorced spouse is at least age 62 at the time of application;
4. The divorced spouse is not married; and
5. The divorced spouse is not entitled to retirement benefits that are equal to or greater than the primary beneficiary's primary insurance amount.[654]

In addition, a divorced spouse who meets all five of these eligibility criteria can qualify for spousal benefits even if the primary beneficiary is not yet eligible for retirement or disability benefits, if (1) the primary beneficiary is at least age 62; and (2) the couple has been divorced for at least two years.[655]

Are Social Security benefits subject to reductions or offsets?

The amount of a Social Security benefit is based on a statutory formula that takes account of the earnings history of the insured worker, and the benefit amount may be subject to reduction under the circumstances described below.[656]

Reductions When Multiple Family Members Receive Benefits

When multiple family members receive Social Security benefits based on the earnings record of the same insured worker, the combined monthly benefit to the family is subject to a family maximum.[657] The family maximum for retirement and survivors' benefits is typically 150 to 188 percent of the worker's primary insurance amount.[658] The family maximum for benefits paid based on the earnings record of a disabled worker is 100 to 150 percent of the disabled worker's primary insurance amount.[659] When necessary, the Social Security Administration will reduce the benefits of each family member proportionately—other than those of the worker (who receives the full primary insurance amount)—to keep the total family amount within the family maximum.[660] Benefits paid to a divorced spouse are not subject to the family maximum.[661]

Reductions When a Person Receives Multiple Types of Benefits

When one person is entitled to multiple types of Social Security benefits, generally only the higher benefit will be paid.[662] However, an individual simultaneously entitled to retirement and disability benefits may elect to receive the smaller of those benefits if doing so would result in a larger total family benefit.[663] Since the combined maximum family benefit payable on a retired worker's account is higher than that payable on a disabled worker's account, the family's combined benefits sometimes will be higher if the worker elects retirement benefits, even if those benefits are lower than disability benefits.[664]

Social Security retirement benefits also will be reduced if an individual under age 65 concurrently receives certain public disability benefits.[665] These public benefits include workers' compensation, but not Veterans Administration benefits or Supplemental Security Income.[666] The total amount of such benefits is capped at 80 percent of the beneficiary's average current earnings before the person became disabled.

Reduction for Certain Pension Payments

Social Security benefits will be reduced to reflect a pension obtained through employment on which Social Security taxes were not paid because the employment was not covered by Social Security. This is known as the Windfall Elimination Provision.[667] The reduction does not apply to workers who have 30 or more years of substantial earnings covered by Social Security.[668]

Deductions for Earned Income and Other Reasons

In some cases, deductions from Social Security benefits may be made if the recipient or the primary insured has "excess earnings." The common scenario is where an individual is receiving retirement benefits before reaching full retirement age, is working, and has "excess earnings"; those earnings reduce the retirement benefit. Employment earnings received after attainment of full retirement age do not affect Social Security benefits.[669] A deduction penalty may be imposed if the individual failed to report certain information used in calculating benefits, although good cause may excuse such a failure.[670] Spousal and parent's benefits may be subject to deduction if the child-in-care requirement is not met.[671]

Nonpayments
Benefits are not payable to an individual who, for more than 30 consecutive days is (1) confined in a correctional facility; (2) a fugitive; or (3) violating conditions of probation or parole.[672]

Are Social Security benefits taxable?

A portion of an individual's Social Security benefits are taxable, but whether a tax needs to be paid depends on the person's other income (such as wages, interest, or dividends).[673] No recipient pays federal income tax on more than 85 percent of the Social Security benefit, and for many only a smaller percentage of benefits counts as taxable income.[674]

Are Social Security benefits payable only to U.S. citizens?

Social Security benefits may be paid to non-U.S. citizens, but the noncitizens must meet additional requirements.

Eligibility. The Social Security Protection Act of 2004 imposed additional requirements on non-U.S. citizens to receive Social Security benefits.[675] These requirements relate to the worker's ability to work lawfully in the United States.

Not lawfully present in the United States. The Social Security Act bars payment of benefits to noncitizens who are "not lawfully present in the United States."[676] The ban is enforced even as against unauthorized workers who are required to, and do, pay Social Security taxes on their wages.[677]

Not present in the United States. Benefits are not payable when a non-U.S. citizen leaves the United States for six or more consecutive months,[678] unless the receiving country has an international Social Security agreement (or a "totalization agreement") with the United States.[679] Any non-U.S. citizen living in a "restricted country" (such as North Korea) may not receive benefits, subject to certain exceptions.[680] No payment is made to a person who is deported, subject to some exceptions.[681]

No Social Security number. No payment is made if the claimant fails to apply for or to provide satisfactory proof of having a Social Security number.[682]

Can a claimant challenge the denial or reduction of Social Security disability benefits?

Yes. A claimant can challenge the denial or reduction of Social Security disability benefits through an appeal process that consists of a series of administrative decisions, followed by federal court review.[683] During the pendency of an appeal, a claimant may request to continue receiving benefits if (1) appealing a termination of disability benefits based on a finding that a medical condition is not disabling, and (2) the request is made within 10 days of receipt of the determination. In most respects, the Social Security appeal process is identical to the process that applies to Supplemental Security Income, which is discussed in detail in chapter 1. Only an abbreviated discussion of the appeal process is presented here.

What are the procedures for challenging a denial or reduction in Social Security disability benefits?

The process of appealing a negative decision goes through four levels of review. If after all of those levels the claimant is still negatively impacted by the agency's decision, then the claimant may file a lawsuit in district court. The claimant has the right to be represented by an attorney or other "qualified individual," but the representative must file a fee agreement or fee petition with the Social Security Administration.[684] Requests for appeals within the Social Security system may be filed at a Social Security office or online at https://www.ssa.gov/benefits/disability/appeal.html.

Initial Determinations
After a claimant files an application for Social Security disability benefits, an initial determination will be reached on that claim.

Reconsiderations
The first step in the appeals process is reconsideration, which involves a complete review of the evidence conducted by a person who was not involved in the initial determination.[685] A request must be made to the Social Security Administration in writing within 60 days of receipt of a determination notice. Claimants are presumed to have received a letter of determination five days after the date on the letter, unless they can show otherwise.[686] Disability claimants may request reconsiderations and hearings online.[687] A late request may be accepted if the claimant can show good cause for the failure to make a timely request.[688] A claimant may submit additional evidence.[689] Once the reconsideration is complete, the Social Security Administration will send a written determination to all appropriate parties.[690]

Administrative Hearings
A claimant who disagrees with a reconsideration decision may request a hearing. Hearings are held before administrative law judges (ALJs) and allow

claimants to submit new evidence, examine the evidence used to make the prior determinations under review, and present and question witnesses.[691] Effective May 2017, the claimant or the claimant's representative must submit any new evidence or provide notice to the Social Security Administration about it at least five business days from the date of the hearing, unless an exception applies. Examples of good cause exceptions may include death of an immediate family member, or the claimant can show diligence in having sought to obtain the evidence.[692] The ALJ will consider all issues that arose in previous determinations and has discretion to consider new issues, but must give the claimant written notice about including the new issue at least 20 days before the hearing. [693]

The hearing typically is held in person or by video (occasionally by telephone), and the claimant has 30 days to object to a video hearing if an in-person hearing is desired.[694] In some circumstances the Social Security Administration may pay certain travel expenses.[695] A claimant also may waive an oral hearing and ask the ALJ to make a decision based on filed and newly submitted evidence.[696]

The ALJ will issue a written decision based on all the evidence.[697] If the claimant fails to appear, the ALJ may dismiss the request for a hearing.[698] If the claimant believes the ALJ has engaged in unfair treatment, a written complaint may be filed outside of the appeals process.[699]

Appeals Council Review

The final step in the administrative appeals process is review by the SSA's Appeals Council.[700] The Appeals Council will review a case if there is (1) the appearance of an abuse of discretion by the ALJ, (2) an error of law, (3) lack of support by substantial evidence, or (4) a broad policy or procedural issue that may affect the general public interest.[701] The claimant or representative has an ongoing obligation to provide evidence of disability and must submit all evidence that relates to a disability claim even if the information is not favorable.[702]

Federal Court Review

If the claimant disagrees with the Appeals Council's decision or the Appeals Council refuses a request for review, the claimant may file a civil action in a federal district court.[703] The action must be filed within 60 days of receipt of the Appeals Council decision or denial of review.[704]

While a claimant ordinarily must exhaust administrative remedies before filing for judicial review, an expedited appeals process exists that allows Social Security claimants to go directly to federal court.[705] The expedited appeals process may be used if all parties to a determination, including the Social Security Administration, agree that the only factor preventing determination in the claimant's favor is a provision in the law that the claimant challenges as unconstitutional.[706] A written request for expedited appeal must be made to the SSA within 60 days of receipt of a determination notice.[707]

Notes

1. *See* R. George Wright, Towards a Federal Constitutional Right to Employment, 38 Seattle U.L. Rev. 63 (2014); *see also* William E. Forbath, The Distributive Constitution and Worker's Rights, 72 Ohio St. L.J. 1115 (2011); William E. Forbath, Constitutional Welfare Rights: A History, Critique and Reconstruction, 69 Fordham L. Rev. 1821 (2001); Kenneth Karst, Coming Crisis of Work in Constitutional Perspective, 82 Cornell L. Rev. 523 (1997). *See also* Cynthia Estlund, What Should We Do After Work? Automation and Employment Law, 128 Yale L.J. 254, 320 (2018) (arguing for "a shift away from employment as the platform for entitlements and their funding"). The first item on the Economic Bill of Rights proposed by President Franklin Delano Roosevelt in his 1944 State of the Union Address was the "Right to a useful and remunerative job." Franklin Delano Roosevelt, State of the Union Address (Jan. 11, 1944), http://www.fdrlibrary.marist.edu/archives/stateoftheunion.html.
2. U.S. Const. Amend. XIII ("Neither slavery nor involuntary servitude, except as a punishment for crime whereof the party shall be been duly convicted, shall exist within the United States, or any place subject to their jurisdiction.").
3. U.S. Const. Amends. V and XIV.
4. International Covenant on Economic, Social and Cultural Rights, Part III, Art. 6 (recognizing "the right to work, which includes the right of everyone to the opportunity to gain his living by work which he freely chooses or accepts"); *see also* Universal Declaration of Human Rights, Art. 23.1 ("Everyone has the right to work, to free choice of employment, to just and favourable conditions of work and to protection against unemployment.").
5. *See* Annette Bernhardt, The Role of Labor Market Regulation in Rebuilding Economic Opportunity in the U.S. (Mar. 25, 2014), http://rooseveltinstitute.org/wp-content/uploads/2014/03/214249508-The-Role-of-Labor-Market-Regulation-in-Rebuilding-Economic-Opportunity-in-the-U-S.pdf.
6. "Title VII" is the shorthand reference to the federal statute that remedies workplace discrimination based on race, gender, or national origin. *See* Civil Rights Act of 1964 § 703, 42 U.S.C. § 2000e-2(a). In addition, the Equal Pay Act of 1963, which is part of the Fair Labor Standards Act, protects men and women who do substantially the same work in the same workplace from sex-based wage discrimination. *See* 29 U.S.C. § 206(d).

    Title VII created the Equal Employment Opportunity Commission (EEOC) to enforce Title VII and protect employees from workplace discrimination. *See* 42 U.S.C. § 2000e-4(a). An individual who believes that an employer has engaged in impermissible discrimination may file a claim with the EEOC. The EEOC investigate the charge to determine whether there is "reasonable cause" to believe the employer has violated Title VII, and at the start of the investigation will inform the employer if it is eligible for mediation. *See* U.S. Equal Employment Opportunity Commission, https://www.eeoc.gov/employers/process.cfm; *see also* 42 U.S.C. § 2000e-5(b) (requiring the EEOC to have "reasonable cause" to believe the charge is true).

If the EEOC does find reasonable cause that the claim is true, then the agency must attempt to settle the dispute. *See* Mach Mining LLC v. E.E.O.C., 575 U.S. ___, 135 S. Ct. 1645 (2015). If mandatory conciliation fails, then the EEOC may file a suit on behalf of the harmed individual. In deciding whether to file a suit, the EEOC will consider "the seriousness of the violation, the type of legal issues in the case, the wider impact the lawsuit could have on the agency's efforts to combat workplace discrimination, and the resources available to litigate the case effectively." *See* U.S. Equal Employment Opportunity Commission, What You Should Know: The EEOC, Conciliation, and Litigation, https://www.eeoc.gov/eeoc/newsroom/wysk/conciliation_litigation.cfm.

If the EEOC fails to fund reasonable cause or decides not to bring suit, the harmed individual nevertheless may file a lawsuit within 90 days of receiving a "Notice of Right to Sue" from the EEOC. *See* U.S. Equal Employment Opportunity Commission, Filing a Lawsuit, https://www.eeoc.gov/employees/lawsuit.cfm.

7. Age Discrimination in Employment Act of 1967 § 7, 29 U.S.C. § 623. The act protects persons who are 40 years and older from discrimination in the workplace.

8. Americans with Disabilities Act of 1990 § 107, 42 U.S.C. § 12112. The act bars workplace discrimination against qualified individuals with disabilities and requires employers to make "reasonable accommodations" to facilitate employment by a person with a disability unless doing so would cause undue hardship on the business.

9. Albermarle Paper Co. v. Moody, 422 U.S. 405, 421 (1975), the rulings of which were codified in the Civil Rights Act of 1991, Pub. L. No. 102-166, 105 Stat. 1071 (codified as amended in scattered sections of 42 U.S.C.).

10. For information on how and where to file a charge of employment discrimination, *see* U.S. Equal Employment Opportunity Commission, Filing a Charge of Employment Discrimination, https://www.eeoc.gov/employees/charge.cfm.

11. For example, the California Fair Employment and Housing Act extends protection against discrimination on the basis of sexual orientation, gender identity, marital status, and medical condition. *See* Cal. Gov't Code § 12940 (effective Jan. 2019). The New York City Human Rights Law authorizes the Commission on Human Rights to eliminate and prevent discrimination in employment based on a person's "actual or perceived differences, including those based on race, color, creed, age, national origin, alienage or citizenship status, gender, sexual orientation, disability, marital status, partnership status, caregiver status, sexual and reproductive health decisions, uniformed service, any lawful source of income, status as a victim of domestic violence or status as a victim of sex offenses or stalking, whether children are, may be or would be residing with a person or conviction or arrest record." N.Y.C. Adm. Code § 8-101; *see also* § 8-502 (civil actions by persons aggrieved by unlawful discriminatory practices). New York City also makes it illegal for employers to ask an applicant about prior salary during the hiring process; to discriminate based on an

applicant's credit history; or to revoke a job automatically based on the existence of a criminal record. *See* New York City Commission on Human Rights, In NYC, Your Salary History Won't Hold Back Your Next Salary; You Are More than Your Credit Score; and Criminal Record? You Can Work with That, https://www1.nyc.gov/site/cchr/media/publications.page.

12. 8 U.S.C. § 1324b(a)(1)(B).

13. Immigration Reform and Control Act of 1986, Pub. L. No. 99-603, 100 Stat. 3359 (codified at 8 U.S.C. § 1324a). Section 274(a) of the Immigration Reformed Control Act makes it unlawful to "hire, or to recruit or refer for a fee, for employment in the United States an alien knowing the alien is an unauthorized alien." 8 U.S.C. § 1324a(a) (1)(A). The statute imposes a fine on an employer that violates this ban. For the first violation of law, the fine can range between $250 and $2,000 for each undocumented worker that the employer has hired. 8 U.S.C. § 1324a(e)(4)(A)(i).

14. Undocumented workers are protected against racial and ethnic discrimination under Title VII of the Civil Rights Act of 1964. *See* Espinoza v. Farah Mfg. Co., 414 U.S. 86, 96 (1973).

15. The I-9 form, with instructions and a list of acceptable documents for proving identity and eligibility to work, can be accessed on the U.S. Citizenship and Immigration Services website, at https://www.uscis.gov/i-9. Verification requirements do not apply to independent contractors or persons providing intermittent or irregular domestic services. *See* 8 C.F.R. § 274a.1. For a fuller explanation of the I-9 verification process, *see* National Immigration Law Center, The I-9 Process and Antidiscrimination Protections in the INA (Sept. 2009), https://www.nilc.org/issues/workersrights/i-9-process-and-ina-antidiscrimination-protections/.

16. *See* U.S. Citizenship and Immigration Services, How to Correct a Tentative Nonconfirmation (Feb. 23, 2016), https://www.uscis.gov/e-verify/employees/how-correct-tentative-nonconfirmation.

17. Studies indicate that these reports frequently include outdated and erroneous information. *See* Federal Trade Commission, Report to Congress Under Section 319 of the Fair and Accurate Credit Transactions Act of 2003 (2015), https://www.ftc.gov/system/files/documents/reports/section-319-fair-accurate-credit-transactions-act-2003-sixth-interim-final-report-federal-trade/150121factareport.pdf. *See also* Alison Cassidy & Edmund Mierzwinski, Mistakes Do Happen: A Look at Errors in Consumer Credit Reports, U.S. Public Interest Research Group (2004), http://www.uspirg.org/reports/usp/mistakes-do-happen.

18. Fair Credit Reporting Act, 15 U.S.C. §§ 1681–81x. Regulations implementing the statute were originally published by the Federal Trade Commission and appear at Title 16 of the Code of Federal Regulations Part 600. They have been republished by the Consumer Financial Protection Bureau at Title 12 of the Code of Federal Regulations, Part 1022 (Fair Credit Reporting, Regulation V).

19. Federal Trade Commission [File No. 112 3195], Filiquarian Publishing, LLC; Choice Level, LLC; and Joshua Linsk; Analysis of Proposed Consent Order to Aid Public Comment, 78 Fed. Reg. 3425 (Jan. 16, 2013). *See also* Federal Trade Commission, Marketers of Criminal Background Screening Reports to

Settle FTC Charges They Violated Fair Credit Reporting Act (Jan. 10, 2013), https://www.ftc.gov/news-events/press-releases/2013/01/marketers-criminal-background-screening-reportsto-settle-ftc.

20. 15 U.S.C. § 1681a(d)(1) (defining consumer report).

21. 15 U.S.C. § 1681a(e) (defining investigative report).

22. Federal Trade Commission, Background Checks: What Employers Need to Know (Feb. 2014), https://www.ftc.gov/tips-advice/business-center/guidance/background-checks-what-employers-need-know. *See also* Federal Trade Commission, David Lincicum, Background checks on prospective employees: Keep required disclosures simple (Apr. 28, 2017), https://www.ftc.gov/news-events/blogs/business-blog/2017/04/background-checks-prospective-employees-keep-required.

23. 15 U.S.C. § 1681b(b)(2)(A)(i).

24. 15 U.S.C. § 1681b(b)(2)(A)(i).

25. 15 U.S.C. § 1681b(b)(2)(A)(ii).

26. 15 U.S.C. § 1681b(b)(2)(A)(ii).

27. 15 U.S.C. § 1681b(b)(1)(A)(i)–(ii).

28. 15 U.S.C. § 1681a(k) (defining adverse action).

29. 15 U.S.C. § 1681b(b)(3)(A).

30. Brown v. Lowe's Cos., 52 F. Supp. 3d 749, 755 (W.D.N.C. 2014) ("The statute does not provide a specific amount of time for which notice must be given to the prospective employees. Instead, it merely requires that notice is given *before* an adverse action is taken against them by the potential employer."); Reardon v. ClosetMaid Corp., No. 2:08-CV-01730, 2013 WL 6231606, at *13 (W.D. Pa. Dec. 2, 2013) (denying employer's motion for summary judgment because "exactly 4 business days" was not reasonable notice before taking an adverse action, "especially where" that notice provided the applicant "five business days" to dispute her credit report).

   The trucking industry requires that notice must be given within three business days of taking an adverse action. *See* 15 U.S.C. § 1681b(3)(B)(i). In other industries, five days' notice has become an unofficial norm. *See* Brett E. Coburn & Brooks A. Suttle, The Fair Credit Reporting Act Can Be a Trap, Entrepreneur (May 19, 2015), https://www.entrepreneur.com/article/246375.

31. 15 U.S.C. § 1681m(a)(3)–(4).

32. Studies suggest that employers frequently violate the FCRA, through such acts or omissions as failing to get permission to obtain a consumer or investigative report; or failing to give the applicant or employee an opportunity to correct inaccurate information contained in a report; and failing to give a worker sufficient notice before taking an adverse action. *See* Michael Carlin & Ellen Frick, Criminal Records, Collateral Consequences, and Employment: The FCRA and Title VII in Discrimination Against Persons with Criminal Records, 12 Seattle J. for Social Justice 109, 127–129 (2013). Violations of this sort have led to the filing of class action suits against national employers including Food Lion and Michaels. *See* David N. Anthony & Julie D. Hoffmeister, The Fair Credit Reporting Act: Not Just About Credit, American Bar Association: Business Law Today (June 2016), http://www.americanbar.org/publications/blt/2016/06/13_anthony.html.

33. Society for Human Resource Management, "Background Checking: Conducting Criminal Background Checks" (Mar. 2010), http://www.slideshare.net/shrm/background-check-criminal?from=shair_email. For further discussion, *see* Eisha Jain, Arrests as Regulation, 67 Stan. L. Rev. 809 (2015).

34. *See* Stephen J. Tripodi, Johnny S. Kim, & Kimberly Bender, Is Employment Associated with Reduced Recidivism?: The Complex Relationship Between Employment and Crime, 54 Int'l J. Offender Therapy & Comp. Criminology 706 (2010).

35. Kimani Paul-Emile, Beyond Title VII: Rethinking Race, Ex-offender Status, and Employment Discrimination in the Information Age, 100 Va. L. Rev. 893 (2014).

36. Peter Wagner & Bernadette Rabuy, Mass Incarceration: The Whole Pie 2016, Prison Policy Initiative (Mar. 14, 2016), http://www.prisonpolicy.org/reports/pie2016.html.

37. Tiffany R. Nichols, Where There's Smoke, There's Fire?: The Cloud of Suspicion Surrounding Former Offenders and the EEOC's New Enforcement Guidance on Criminal Records under Title VII, 30 Ga. St. U.L. Rev. 591 (2014).

38. 15 U.S.C. § 1681c(a)(2).

39. 15 U.S.C. § 1681c(b)(3).

40. States with such restrictions include:

Alaska: Alaska Stat. Ann. § 12.62.160.
California: Cal. Labor Code § 432.7.
Connecticut: Conn. Gen. Stat. Ann. § 31-51i.
Hawaii: Haw. Rev. Stat. Ann. § 378-2.
Illinois: 775 Ill. Comp. Stat. Ann. 5/2-103.
Indiana: Ind. Code Ann. 34-28-5-15.
Massachusetts: Mass. Gen. Laws Ann. ch. 151B, § 4.
New York: N.Y. Exec. Law § 296 (16).
Pennsylvania: 18 Pa. Stat. and Cons. Stat. Ann. § 9125.
Rhode Island: 28 R.I. Gen. Laws Ann. § 28-5-7.
Wisconsin: Wis. Stat. Ann. § 111.335.

Some states also prohibit employers from inquiring about, obtaining, or considering records of youthful offender convictions, or certain sealed convictions. *See, for example*, N.Y. Exec. Law § 296(16).

41. California: Cal. Civil Code 1786.18; Montana: Mont. Code Ann. § 31-3-112; New Mexico: N.M. Stat. Ann. § 56-3-6. *But see* Jennifer Mora & Rod Fliegel, Background Screening Companies May Now Report Convictions Older Than Seven Years in Nevada, Littler Workplace Policy Institute (June 24, 2015), https://www.littler.com/publication-press/publication/background-screening-companies-may-now-report-convictions-older-seven.

42. *See* Beth Avery & Phil Hernandez, Ban the Box: U.S. Cities, Counties, and States Adopt Fair-Chance Policies to Advance Employment Opportunities for People with Past Convictions, National Employment Law Center (Sept. 2018), https://s27147.pcdn.co/wp-content/uploads/Ban-the-Box-Fair-Chance-State-and-Local-Guide-September.pdf.

43. *Id.* This publication contains a useful and comprehensive list of state and local fair chance policies, with descriptions of the coverages and policies, and links to primary

resources. For an important resource on the related issue of professional licensing for people with a criminal history, *see* Beth Avery, Phil Hernandez, & Maurice Emsellem, Fair Chance Licensing Reform: Opening Pathways for People with Records to Join Licensed Professions, National Employment Law Center (Nov. 26, 2018), https://www.nelp.org/publication/fair-chance-licensing-reform-opening-pathways-for-people-with-records-to-join-licensed-professions/ (noting that one in four jobs requires a license to work). The Restoration of Rights Project also maintains a directory of state laws regulating the use of criminal records for employment and licensing purposes. Restoration of Rights Project, 50-State Comparison: Consideration of Criminal Records in Licensing and Employment (updated Aug. 2018), https://ccresourcecenter.org/state-restoration-profiles/50-state-comparisoncomparison-of-criminal-records-in-licensing-and-employment/.

44. Federal Trade Commission, "Background Checks: What Employers Need to Know" (Feb. 2014), https://www.ftc.gov/tips-advice/business-center/guidance/background-checks-what-employers-need-know.

45. U.S. Equal Employment Opportunity Commission, No. 915.002, Consideration of Arrest and Conviction Records in Employment Decisions Under Title VII of the Civil Rights Act of 1964 (2012), chap. V.B.2 n.103, https://www.eeoc.gov/laws/guidance/arrest_conviction.cfm. *See* National Employment Law Project, Fact Sheet: The 2012 EEOC Guidance on the Consideration of Arrest & Conviction Records in Employment Decisions (Aug. 23, 2017), https://www.nelp.org/publications/2012-eoc-guidance-consideration-arrest-conviction-records-employment-decisions/. In 2013, the state of Texas challenged the EEOC's policy on the use of arrest and conviction records as procedural invalid under the Administrative Procedure Act because it was issued without the EEOC having undertaken "notice and comment." The suit has a complex litigation history. *See* Texas v. EEOC, 838 F.3d 511 (5th Cir. 201) (per curiam), withdrawing opinion and remanding.

46. Collateral Consequences Resources Center, Restoration of Rights Project, State Specific Guides to Restoration of Rights, Pardon, Sealing & Expungement, https://ccresourcecenter.org/state-restoration-profiles/50-state-comparisonjudicial-expungement-sealing-and-set-aside/.

47. 11 U.S.C. § 525(a).

48. 11 U.S.C. § 525(b).

49. *Compare* Leary v. Warnaco, Inc., 251 B.R. 656, 659 (S.D.N.Y. 2000) (holding that the statute's antidiscrimination provisions extend to "*all* aspects of employment, including hiring"), *with* In re Martin, 2007 WL 2893431, at *4 n.21 (D. Kan. 2007) (collecting negative federal cases).

50. *See* Robert J. Landry & Benjamin Hardy, Bankrupts Need Not Apply: Sound Hiring Policy or Dangerous Proposition, 7 Va. L. & Bus. Rev. 47, 54–56 (2012); U.S. Equal Employment Opportunity Commission, Pre-Employment Inquiries and Financial Information (Aug. 15, 2016), http://www.eeoc.gov/laws/practices/financial_information.cfm.

51. The EEOC identifies financial information to include "current or past assets, liabilities, or credit rating, bankruptcy or garnishment, refusal or cancellation of bonding,

car ownership, rental or ownership of a house, length of residence at an address, charge accounts, furniture ownership, or bank accounts." U.S. Equal Employment Opportunity Commission, Pre-Employment Inquiries and Financial Information, http://www.eeoc.gov/laws/practices/financial_information.cfm.

52. U.S. Department of Labor, Bureau of Labor Statistics, Long-term unemployed, https://www.bls.gov/bls/cps_fact_sheets/ltu_mock.htm.

53. E. Ericka Kelsaw, Help Wanted: 23.5 Million Unemployed Americans Need Not Apply, 34 Berkeley J. Emp. & Lab. L. 1, 13–18, 46 (2013).

54. U.S. Department of Labor, Bureau of Labor Statistics, Economic News Release, Table 12: Unemployed persons by duration of unemployment (Feb. 1, 2019), https://www.bls.gov/news.release/empsit.t12.htm. *See* Rodrigo J. Torres, Unemployed as a Protected Class: The Promise of Equal Opportunity, 21 Tex. Hisp. J.L. & Pol'y 63, 65–66 (2015).

55. Seth Katsuya Endo, Neither Panacea, Placebo, nor Poison: Examining the Rise of Anti-Unemployment Discrimination Laws, 33 Pace L. Rev. 1007, 1022–24 (2013).

56. U.S. Equal Employment Opportunity Commission, Pre-Employment Inquiries and Unemployed Status, https://www.eeoc.gov/laws/practices/unemployed_status.cfm.

57. *See* National Conference of State Legislatures, Discrimination Against the Unemployed, http://www.ncsl.org/research/labor-and-employment/discrimination-against-the-unemployed.aspx; Jennifer Jolly Ryan, Repairing Damaged Goods: Federal and State Legislation Prohibiting Employers from Making Current Employment a Job Requirement, 14 Rutgers Race & L. Rev. 54, 73–79 (2013).

58. 42 U.S.C. § 2000e(k).

59. Young v. United Parcel Service, Inc., 575 U.S. ___, 135 S. Ct. 1338, 1343–44 (2015).

60. *Id.*, 135 S. Ct. at 1354.

61. Pregnancy Discrimination Act Coverage, EEOC Compliance Manual ¶ 4802 ("[a]n employer may not discriminate against a woman with a medical condition relating to pregnancy or childbirth and must treat her the same as others who are similar in their ability or inability to work but are not affected by pregnancy, childbirth, or related medical conditions."). *See* Deborah A. Widiss, The Interaction of the Pregnancy Discrimination Act and the Americans with Disabilities Act After *Young v. UPS*, 50 U.C. Davis L. Rev. 1423 (2017).

62. For an overview of the statute, *see* Congressional Research Service, Gerald Mayer, Benjamin Collins, & David H. Bradley, The Fair Labor Standards Act (FLSA): An Overview (June 4, 2013), https://www.fas.org/sgp/crs/misc/R42713.pdf. *See also* Kate Andrias, An American Approach to Social Democracy: The Forgotten Promise of the Fair Labor Standards Act, 128 Yale L.J. 616 (2019).

63. 29 U.S.C. § 202(a).

64. Brooklyn Savings Bank v. O'Neil, 324 U.S. 697, 707 n. 18 (1945) (citations omitted).

65. Quoted in U.S. Department of Labor, Jonathan Grossman, Fair Labor Standards Act of 1938: Maximum Struggle for a Minimum Wage, https://www.dol.gov/general/aboutdol/history/flsa1938.

66. *See* William Forbath, Caste, Class and Equal Citizenship, 98 Mich. L. Rev. 1, 76–80 (1999) (discussing the negative racialized impact of the "Southern Veto" on the New

Deal); Cybelle Fox, Three Worlds of Relief: Race, Immigration, and the American Welfare State from the Progressive Era to the New Deal (Princeton 2012) (showing how the New Deal preserved white economic interests at the expense of workers of color). *See also* Daniel E. Slotnik, Overlooked No More: Dorothy Bolden, Who Started a Movement for Domestic Workers, N.Y. Times (Feb. 20, 2019), https://www.nytimes.com/2019/02/20/obituaries/dorothy-bolden-overlooked.html.

67. *See* U.S. Department of Labor, Wage and Hour Division, Minimum Wage Laws in the States (last updated Jan. 1, 2019), https://www.dol.gov/whd/minwage/america.htm. *See also* William M. Rodgers III & Amanda Novello, Making the Economic Case for a $15 Minimum Wage, The Century Foundation (Jan. 2019), https://tcf.org/content/commentary/making-economic-case-15-minimum-wage/?agreed=1 (analyzing inadequacy of federal minimum wage).

68. Pope Leo XIII, Rerum Novarum: Encyclical of Pope Leo XIII on Capital and Labor (May 15, 1891), http://w2.vatican.va/content/leo-xiii/en/encyclicals/documents/hf_l-xiii_enc_15051891_rerum-novarum.html.

69. Presidential Statement on N.I.R.A., quoted in The Public Papers and Addresses of Franklin D. Roosevelt, Volume II, 251 (No. 81) (Random House 1938).

70. In 1938, the minimum hourly wage was 25 cents and the standard workweek was 44 hours before overtime compensation was due. Fair Labor Standards Act of 1938, 75 P.L. 718, 52 Stat. 1060, 75 Cong. Ch. 676.

71. *See* David Cooper, The Minimum Wage Used to Be Enough to Keep Workers out of Poverty—It's Not Anymore, Economic Policy Institute (Dec. 14, 2013), https://www.epi.org/publication/minimum-wage-workers-poverty-anymore-raising/.

72. 29 U.S.C. § 206(a).

73. Christopher Ingraham, Here's How Much the Federal Minimum Wage Fell This Year, Washington Post (Dec. 27, 2018), https://www.washingtonpost.com/business/2018/12/26/heres-how-much-federal-minimum-wage-fell-this-year/?utm_term=.45dfa4a7dec8. According to the Pew Research Center, the current minimum wage has lost 9.6% of its purchasing power since 2009 when it was last increased. Drew DeSilver, 5 Facts about the Minimum Wage, Pew Research Center (Jan. 4, 2017), http://www.pewresearch.org/fact-tank/2017/01/04/5-facts-about-the-minimum- wage/.

74. *See* Ben Zipperer, The Erosion of the Federal Minimum Wage has Increased Poverty, Especially for Black and Hispanic Families, Economic Policy Institute (June 13, 2018), https://www.epi.org/publication/the-erosion-of-the-federal-minimum-wage-has-increased-poverty-especially-for-black-and-hispanic-families/. One consequence of inadequate minimum wage protections is that large numbers of low-wage workers must turn to public benefit programs to subsist. Notably, substantial proportions of public benefit recipients are low-income workers. *See, for example*, Ken Jacobs, Ian Perry, & Jenifer MacGillvary, The High Public Cost of Low Wages: Poverty-Level Wages Cost U.S. Taxpayers $152.8 Billion Each Year in Public Support for Working Families, U.C. Berkeley Labor Center (Apr. 2015), http://laborcenter.berkeley.edu/pdf/2015/the-high-public-cost-of-low-wages.pdf; Brynne Keith-Jennings & Vincent Palacios, SNAP Helps Millions of Low-Wage Workers: Crucial Financial Support

Assists Workers in Jobs with Low Wages, Volatile Income, and Few Benefits, Center For Budget and Policy Priorities (May 10, 2017), https://www.cbpp.org/research/ food-assistance/snap-helps-millions-of-low-wage-workers;   Kalena   Tomhave, Food Stamps Aren't a Substitute for Work. They're How Low-Wage Workers Avoid Hunger, American Prospect (Mar. 28, 2018), https://prospect.org/article/ food-stamps-arent-substitute-work-theyre-how-low-wage-workers-avoid-hunger.

75. *See* U.S. Department of Labor, Wage and Hour Division, Minimum Wage Laws in the States (last updated Jan. 1, 2019), https://www.dol.gov/whd/minwage/america.htm.

76. *See* Sarah Jones, For Low-Wage Workers, the Fight For 15 Movement Has Been a Boon, New York Magazine (Dec. 1, 2018), http://nymag.com/intelligencer/2018/12/ fight-for-15-movement-boon-for-low-wage-workers.html.

77. *See* Matthew Desmond, The $15 Minimum Wage Doesn't Just Improve Lives. It Saves Them, N.Y. Times Mag. (Feb. 21, 2019), https://www.nytimes.com/ interactive/2019/02/21/magazine/minimum-wage-saving-lives.html;   Tsu-Yu Tsao, Kevin J. Konty, Gretchen Van Wye, Oxiris Barbot, James L. Hadler, Natalia Linos, & Mary T. Bassett, Estimating Potential Reductions in Premature Mortality in New York City from Raising the Minimum Wage to $15, American Journal of Public Health (June 2016), https://ajph.aphapublications.org/doi/full/10.2105/ AJPH.2016.303188.

78. U.S. Department of Labor, Bureau of Labor Statistics, BLS Reports: Characteristics of minimum wage workers, 2017 (Report 1072) (Mar. 2018), https://www.bls.gov/ opub/reports/minimum-wage/2017/home.htm.

79. *See* U.S. Department of Labor, Wage and Hour Division, Minimum Wage Laws in the States (last updated Jan. 1, 2019), https://www.dol.gov/whd/minwage/america.htm.

80. U.S. Department of Labor, Bureau of Labor Statistics, BLS Reports: Characteristics of minimum wage workers, 2017 (Report 1072) (Mar. 2018), https://www.bls.gov/ opub/reports/minimum-wage/2017/home.htm.

81. *Id.* at Table 3.

82. U.S. Department of Labor, Bureau of Labor Statistics, Economic News Release: Union affiliation of employed workers by state (last modified Jan. 18, 2019), https:// www.bls.gov/news.release/union2.toc.htm.

83. U.S. Department of Labor, Wage and Hour Division, Minimum Wage Laws in the States (last updated Jan. 1, 2019), https://www.dol.gov/whd/minwage/america.htm.

84. *See, for example*, Matt Bruenig, Universal Health Care Might Cost You Less Than You Think: We don't think of the premiums we already pay as taxes, but maybe we should, N.Y. Times (Apr. 29, 2019), https://www.nytimes.com/2019/04/29/ opinion/medicare-for-all-cost.html (comparing health care cost for workers in the United States to those in other advanced nations); Mark V. Pauly, Health Benefits at Work: An Economic and Political Analysis of Employment-Based Health Insurance 15–16 (1997) (outlining economic theory that the cost of health insurance is passed on to workers in the form of lower wages).

85. *See* 29 C.F.R. § 516.4.

86. The poster is available in downloadable form at: https://www.dol.gov/whd/regs/ compliance/posters/flsa.htm.

87. *See* Charlotte S. Alexander, Transparency and Transmission: Theorizing Information's Role in Regulatory and Market Responses to Workplace Problems, 48 Conn. L. Rev. 177 (2015).

88. 17 C.F.R. Parts 229, 240, 249. *See* Recent Regulation, Securities Regulation—Dodd-Frank Wall Street Reform and Consumer Protection Act—SEC Finalizes Regulations Requiring Companies to Disclose Pay Ratio Between the CEO and Median Employee—Pay Ratio Disclosure, 80 Fed. Reg. 50,104 (Aug. 18, 2015) (to be codified at 17 C.F.R. Parts 229, 240, 249), 129 Harv. L. Rev. 1144 (2016).

89. *See* U.S. Securities and Exchange Commission, Public Statement of Acting Chairman Michael S. Piwowar, Reconsideration of Pay Ratio Rule Implementation (Feb. 6, 2017), https://www.sec.gov/news/statement/reconsideration-of-pay-ratio-rule-implementation.html. *See also* Jordan Vallinsky, Disney heir calls on company to give 50% of exec bonuses to lowest-paid employees, CNN (Apr. 24, 2019), https://www.cnn.com/2019/04/24/media/abigial-disney-executive-pay/index.html (reporting that pay package of Disney's CEO is $66 million, or 1,424 times the median salary of a Disney employee of $46,127).

90. Edward Helmore, CEOs don't want this released: US study lays bare extreme pay-ratio problem, The Guardian (May 16, 2018), https://www.theguardian.com/us-news/2018/may/16/ceo-worker-pay-ratio-america-first-study.

91. 29 U.S.C. §§ 203(s)(1); 209(a)(1).

92. 29 U.S.C. § 209(f).

93. 29 U.S.C. §§ 203(a), (d), (e); 209(a)(1). As discussed in text, certain entities and types of employment have been exempted from FLSA coverage through amendments to the act. *See* 29 U.S.C. § 213 for a list of these exemptions.

94. 29 U.S.C. § 203(e)(1).

95. 29 U.S.C. § 203(g).

96. *See, for example*, Zheng v. Liberty Apparel Co., 355 F.3d 61, 66 (2d Cir. 2003) (stating that the FLSA's definition of employ in 29 U.S.C. § 203(g) is " 'the broadest definition [of 'employ'] that has ever been included in any one act' "), quoting United States v. Rosenwasser, 323 U.S. 360, 363 n.3 (1945), quoting 81 Cong. Rec. 7675 (1937) (statement of Sen. Hugo L. Black).

97. The FLSA contains other exemptions that are difficult to classify: the statute does not cover, for example, persons who make wreaths at home, certain switchboard operators, and workers who catch "aquatic forms of animal and vegetable life." 29 U.S.C. §§ 213(d); 213(a)(5), (10).

98. Mitchell H. Rubinstein, Employees, Employers, and Quasi-employers: An Analysis of Employees and Employers Who Operate in the Borderland Between an Employer-and-Employee Relationship, 14 U. Pa J. Bus. L. 605 (2012) (citing Elaine Bernard & Robert Herrick, The Social and Economic Costs of Employee Misclassification in Maine Construction Industry 1–2 (2005)).

99. *See, for example*, Brock v. Superior Care, Inc., 840 F.2d 1054, 1058–61 (2d Cir. 1988).

100. Katherine S. Newman, The Great Recession and the Pressure on Workplace Rights, 88 Chi.-Kent L. Rev. 529 (2013).

101. U.S. Department of Labor, Misclassification of Employees as Independent Contractors, The DOL Misclassification Initiative, http://www.dol.gov/whd/workers/misclassification/. *See* Catherine Ruckelshaus & Ceilidh Gao, Independent Contractor Misclassification Imposes Huge Costs on Workers and Federal and State Treasuries, National Employment Law Project (Dec. 19, 2017), https://www.nelp.org/publication/independent-contractor-misclassification-imposes-huge-costs-on-workers-and-federal-and-state-treasuries-update-2017/.

102. *See* Francois Carre, (In)dependent Contractor Misclassification, Economic Policy Institute (June 8, 2015), https://www.epi.org/publication/independent-contractor-misclassification/.

103. U.S. Department of Labor, Administrator's Interpretation No. 2015-1, The Application of the Fair Labor Standard's Act's "Suffer or Permit" Standard in the Identification of Employees Who Are Misclassified as Independent Contractors (July 15, 2015), https://www.dol.gov/whd/opinion/administrprtnflsa.htm. *See also* U.S. Department of Labor, Fact Sheet #13: Am I an Employee: Employment Relationship Under the Fair Labor Standards Act (May 2014), http://www.dol.gov/whd/regs/compliance/whdfs13.pdf.

104. *See, for example*, Keller v. Miri Microsystems LLC, 781 F.3d 799 (6th Cir 2015) (satellite dish installers); In re FedEx Ground Package System, Inc. Employment Practices Litig., 792 F.3d 818 (7th Cir. 2015) (delivery drivers). For a fuller discussion of this issue and strategies to address it, *see* Sarah Leberstein & Catherine Ruckelshaus, Independent Contractor vs. Employee: Why independent contractor misclassification matters and what we can do to stop it, National Employment Law Project (May 2016), https://s27147.pcdn.co/wp-content/uploads/Policy-Brief-Independent-Contractor-vs-Employee.pdf.

105. U.S. Department of Labor, Secretary of Labor Thomas E. Perez, Remarks at the Department of Labor Future of Work Symposium, Washington, D.C., Dec. 10, 2015, http://www.dol.gov/newsroom/speech/20151210.

106. The courts have not agreed on the status of ride-hail drivers. *See, for example*, Razak v. Uber Technologies, Inc., 186 Lab. Cas. P 36,614 (E.D. Pa. Apr. 11, 2018) (Uber drivers are independent contractors); Cotter v. Lyft, Inc., 60 F. Supp. 3d 1067, 1069 (N.D. Cal. 2015) ("Lyft drivers don't seem much like independent contractors"). *See* Kati Griffith, The Fair Labor Standards Act at 80: Everything Old Is New Again, 104 Cornell L. Rev. 557, 562 (2019) (explaining that "the rise of work procured through online platforms, such as Uber and TaskRabbit, has raised questions about whether those who contract to perform services for such companies are statutory employees or independent contractors").

107. New York City Administrative Code § 19-548 (added by Local Law 150 of 2018 (Aug. 14, 2018)), https://legistar.council.nyc.gov/LegislationDetail.aspx?ID=3487613&GUID=E47BF280-2CAC-45AE-800F-ED5BE846EFF4. *See* Mark Matiusek, New York City just became the first US city to set a minimum wage for Uber and Lyft drivers, Business Insider (Dec. 4, 2018), https://www.businessinsider.com/nyc-sets-minimum-wage-for-uber-and-lyft-drivers-2018-12.

108. 29 U.S.C. § 213(a)(1).

109. 29 C.F.R. § 541.600. On May 23, 2016, the U.S. Department of Labor promulgated a new rule, which was to be effective on December 1, 2016, raising to $47,476 the minimum annual salary that could satisfy the salary test component of the white-collar exemptions. Before that rule took effect, a federal court in Texas issued a nationwide preliminary injunction against the Department of Labor's enforcement of it on the ground that the Department had exceeded its authority by increasing the minimum salary for exempt employees. *See* Nevada v. U.S. Dept. of Labor, 218 F. Supp. 3d 520 (E.D. Tex. 2016). The court later converted its order into a final judgment and the Department filed a notice of appeal. The court of appeals then stayed the appeal pending rulemaking by the Trump administration's Department of Labor, which advised the court that it intended to revisit the salary level set by the 2016 rule and defended its authority to adjust the FLSA exemption requirements. The proposed rule would increase the white-collar exemption to $35,308 annually, and the comment period closed in May 2019. *See* U.S. Department of Labor, Wage & Hour Division, Defining and Delimiting the Exemptions for Executive, Administrative, Professional, Outside Sales and Computer Employees, 84 Fed. Reg. 1090 (Mar. 22, 2019).
110. Gretchen Agena, What's So "Fair" About It? The Need to Amend the Fair Labor Standards Act, 39 Hous. L. Rev. 1119, 1126 (2002). *See* U.S. Department of Labor, Wage & Hour Division, Fact Sheet 17A: Exemption for Executive, Administrative, Professional, Computer & Outside Sales Employees Under the Fair Labor Standards Act (FLSA) (revised July 2008), https://www.dol.gov/whd/overtime/fs17a_overview.htm.
111. 29 C.F.R. § 541.100.
112. 29 C.F.R. § 541.200. *See* 29 C.F.R. § 541.202 for more details on what constitutes "discretion and independent judgment."
113. 29 C.F.R. § 541.300. The FLSA exempts various other categories of employees from the act's protections. *See* 29 U.S.C. § 213. *See, for example*, Encino Motorcars, LLC v. Navarro. 136 S. Ct. 2117 (2016) (holding car dealership "service advisors" to be outside the FLSA's overtime protections.).
114. *See* Farmworker Justice, Unfinished Harvest: The Agricultural Worker Protection Act at 30 (2013), https://www.farmworkerjustice.org/sites/default/files/Farmworker JusticeUnfinishedHarvest.pdf (description and brief history and critique of farmworker labor legislation in the United States).
115. 29 U.S.C. § 213(a)(6) & (b)(12). *See generally* Marc Linder, Farm Workers and the Fair Labor Standards Act: Racial Discrimination in the New Deal, 65 Tex. L. Rev. 1335 (1987).
116. U.S. Department of Labor, Wage & Hour Division, Fact Sheet 20: Employees Paid Commissions by Retail Establishments Who Are Exempt Under Section 7(i) Overtime Under the FLSA (2008), https://www.dol.gov/whd/regs/compliance/whdfs20.htm.
117. 29 U.S.C. § 213(a)(1).
118. U.S. Department of Labor, Wage & Hour Division, Fact Sheet 17F: Exemption for Outside Employees under the Fair Labor Standards Act (FLSA) (2008), https://www.dol.gov/whd/overtime/fs17f_outsidesales.htm. *See also* Christopher v. SmithKline Beecham Corp. d/b/a/ GlaxoSmithKline, 132 S. Ct. 2156 (2012).

119. Fair Labor Standards Amendments of 1974, Pub. L. No. 93-259, 88 Stat. 55, codified at 29 U.S.C. §§ 206(f), 207(l).

120. U.S. Department of Labor, Wage and Hour Division, Fact Sheet 79: Companionship Services Under the Fair Labor Standards Act (FLSA) (2013), https://www.dol.gov/whd/regs/compliance/whdfs79a.htm.

121. 29 U.S.C. § 213(a)(15).

122. 29 C.F.R. § 552.6.

123. U.S. Department of Labor, Wage and Hour Division, Fact Sheet 79: Companionship Services Under the Fair Labor Standards Act (FLSA) (2013), https://www.dol.gov/whd/regs/compliance/whdfs79a.htm.

124. 29 U.S.C. § 213(b)(21); 29 C.F.R. § 552.100(a)(1).

125. 29 C.F.R. § 552.109(a) (companionship services) and (c) (live-in domestic service). In 2013, the U.S. Department of Labor, recognizing the dramatic expansion of the home health care industry and the widespread practice of underpaying home health workers, amended its regulations to narrow the definition of "companionship services" and to extend minimum wage, overtime, and notice protections to any domestic workers employed by such agencies. *See* 78 Fed. Reg. 60454 (Oct. 1, 2013). The rule became effective in 2015. The Court of Appeals for the District of Columbia Circuit upheld the rule as a valid exercise of the Department of Labor's authority. *See* Home Care Association of America v. Weil, 799 F.3d 1084 (D.C. Cir. 2015), cert. denied, 136 S. Ct. 2506 (U.S. 2016).

126. Benjamin F. Burry, Testing Economic Reality: FLSA and Title VII Protection for Workfare Participants, 1 U. Chi. Legal F. 561 (2009).

127. The lower federal courts in the Second Circuit have held that "work experience" public assistance recipients are employees for purposes of the FLSA, relying on circuit precedent that public assistance recipients performing workfare activities are employees for purposes of Title VII. United States v. City of New York, 359 F.3d 83 (2d Cir. 2004); Elwell v. Weiss, 2007 WL 2994308 (W.D.N.Y. 2006); Stone v. McGowan, 308 F. Supp. 2d 79 (N.D.N.Y. 2004). The New York Court of Appeals, the state's highest court, likewise has held that the FLSA covers workfare workers. *See* Matter of Carver v. State of New York, 26 N.Y.3d 272 (2015).

   The U.S. Court of Appeals for the Tenth Circuit held that workers in a state welfare program who received interim assistance pending resolution of SSI applications are not employees entitled to the minimum wage. Johns v. Stewart, 57 F.3d 1544 (10th Cir. 1995). For a criticism of excluding participants in workfare programs from labor protection, *see* Bridgette Baldwin, Shadow Works and Shadow Markets: How Privatization of Welfare Services Produces an Alternative Market, 34 W. New Eng. L. Rev. 445 (2012).

128. Ross Perlin, Intern Nation: How to Earn Nothing and Learn Little in the Brave New Economy xvii (Verso Books 2011).

129. U.S. Department of Labor, Wage & Hour Division, Fact Sheet # 71, Internship Programs Under the Fair Labor Standards Act (Apr. 2010), http://www.dol.gov/whd/regs/compliance/whdfs71.pdf.

130. Primary beneficiary test: Benjamin v. B&H Educ., 877 F.3d 1139 (9th Cir. 2017); Schumann v. Collier Anesthesia, P.A., 803 F.3d 1199 (11th Cir. 2015); Glatt v. Fox Searchlight Pictures, Inc., 791 F.3d 376 (2d Cir. 2015); Solis v. Laurelbrook Sanitarium & Sch., Inc., 642 F.3d 518 (6th Cir. 2011).

Totality of the circumstances test: Reich v. Parker Fire Protection Dist., 992 F.2d 1023 (10th Cir. 1993).

Economic realities test: Hollins v. Regency Corp., 867 F.3d 830 (7th Cir. 2017).

131. Lynn's Food Stores, Inc. v. United States, 679 F.2d 1350, 1352 (11th Cir. 1982) ("Recognizing that there are often great inequalities in bargaining power between employers and employees, Congress made the FLSA's provisions mandatory."). *See* James Reif, "To Suffer or Permit to Work": Did Congress Say What They Meant and Mean What They Said?, 6 Northeastern U. L.J. 347, 391–392 (2014).

132. Tony & Susan Alamo Found. v. Sec'y of Labor, 471 U.S. 290 (1985).

133. Barrentine v. Arkansas-Best Freight Sys., Inc., 450 U.S. 728, 740 (1981).

134. Tony & Susan Alamo Found. v. Secretary of Labor, 471 U.S. 290, 295 (1985) (citing Walling v. Portland Terminal Co., 330 U.S. 148 (1947)).

135. 29 C.F.R. § 553.101.

136. *For example*, Doyle v. City of New York, 91 F. Supp. 3d 480 (S.D.N.Y. 2015); Vaughn v. Phoenix House Programs of New York, 2015 WL 5671902 (S.D.N.Y. 2015).

137. *For example*, Lucas v. Jerusalem Cafe, LLC, 721 F.3d 927 (8th Cir. 2013). *See* Michael T. Tusa, Jr. & Vanessa A. Spinazola, Wage Claims of Undocumented Workers and the Fair Labor Standards Act, 58 LA Bar J. 370, 371 (2011) ("The provisions of the Fair Labor Standards Act (FLSA) . . . apply to all workers regardless of immigration or citizenship status. . . . The rationale for this approach is quite simple. If the FLSA did not apply, unscrupulous employers would hire such workers, refuse to pay them after getting the benefits of their labor, and there would be no remedy.").

138. *See* Eric Cortellessa, How Trump Made Wage Theft Routine, The American Prospect (June 5, 2017), http://prospect.org/article/how-trump-made-wage-theft-routine. *See also* Annette Bernhardt, Ruth Milkman, Nik Theodore, Douglas A. Heckathorn, Mirabai Aner, James DeFilippis, Ana Luz González, Victor Narro, Jason Perelshteyn, Diana Polson, & Michael Spiller, Broken Laws, Unprotected Workers: Violations of Employment and Labor Laws in America's Cities, National Employment Law Project (2009), https://www.nelp.org/content/uploads/2015/03/BrokenLawsReport2009.pdf?nocdn=1.

139. Revised Memorandum of Understanding between the Departments of Homeland Security and Labor Concerning Enforcement Activities at Worksites (Dec. 7, 2011), https://www.dol.gov/asp/media/reports/dhs-dol-mou.pdf; Addendum to the Revised Memorandum of Understanding between the Departments of Homeland Security and Labor Concerning Enforcement Activities at Worksites, Modification of 2011 DOL DHS Deconfliction MOV to include the NLRB and the EEOC (May 2016), https://www.hlrb.gov. *See* National Employment Law Project & National Immigration Law Center, Immigration and Labor Enforcement in the Workplace: The Revised Labor Agency—DHS Memorandum of Understanding, https://www.nilc.org/wp-content/uploads/2015/11/ImmigrationLaborEnforcementWorkplace.pdf.

140. *See, e.g.,* Amy Donaldson, With or without threatened ICE raids, undocumented immigrants live with fear in Utah, Desert News (July 13, 2019), https://www.deseretnews.com/article/900079528/utah-undocumented-immigrants-ice-raids.html; Sarah Ruiz-Grossman, ICE Arrests Hundreds in Largest Workplace Raid in Over a Decade, Huffpost (Apr. 4, 2019), https://www.huffpost.com/entry/ice-largest-workplace-raid-immigrants_n_5ca54796e4b0409b0ec34df1.

141. *See, for example,* National Employment Law Project, What to Do If Immigration Comes to Your Workplace (July 17, 2017), https://www.nelp.org/publication/what-to-do-if-immigration-comes-to-your-workplace/.

142. 29 U.S.C. § 206(g)(1). *See* U.S. Department of Labor, Wage & Hour Division, Handy Reference Guide to the Fair Labor Standards Act, http://www.dol.gov/whd/regs/compliance/hrg.htm#7.

143. 29 U.S.C. § 214(c). *See* U.S. Department of Labor, Wage & Hour Division, Field Assistance Bulletin 2012-2 (Feb. 29, 2012), https://www.dol.gov/whd/FieldBulletins/fab2012_2.htm; Handy Reference Guide to the Fair Labor Standards Act, http://www.dol.gov/whd/regs/compliance/hrg.htm#6.

144. 29 U.S.C. § 203(m)(2).

145. *Id.*

146. Driver v. Apple Illinois, LLC, 739 F.3d 1073 (7th Cir. 2014).

147. For more information about tipped employees under the FLSA, *see* U.S. Department of Labor, Wage & Hour Division, Fact Sheet 15: Tipped Employees Under the Fair Labor Standards Act (FLSA) (2011), http://www.dol.gov/whd/regs/compliance/whdfs15.pdf. The Consolidated Appropriations Act of 2018, Pub. L. No. 115-141 (2018), reaffirmed administrative rulings that tips are property of the workers and that employers may not retain any of these funds for any purpose, whether or not the employer claims a tip credit. 29 U.S.C. § 203(m)(2)(B), as amended. The statute also overrode existing Department of Labor regulations that limited tip pooling. *See* U.S. Department of Labor, Wage & Hour Division, Field Assistance Bulletin 2018-3 (Apr. 6, 2018), https://www.dol.gov/whd/FieldBulletins/fab2018_3.htm#2. New regulations proposed by the Trump administration, 82 Fed. Reg. 57395 (Dec. 5, 2017), have been criticized as facilitating misappropriation of tips by employers. *See,* for example, Christine Owens, NELP Blasts Trump DOL's Proposed Rules as Allowing Tip Theft, Nat'l Employment Law Project (Dec. 4, 2017), https://www.nelp.org/news-releases/nelp-responds-to-tip-credit-rule/. As of this writing, final regulations have yet to be issued.

148. *See* Charlotte Alexander, Anna Haley-Lock, & Nantiya Ruan, Stabilizing Low-Wage Work, 50 Harv. C.R.-C.L. L. Rev. 1 (2015).

149. 29 C.F.R. § 516.5.

150. 29 C.F.R. § 516.6.

151. U.S. Department of Labor, Wage & Hour Division, Fact Sheet 21: Recordkeeping Requirements under the Fair Labor Standards Act (FLSA) (July 2008), https://www.dol.gov/whd/regs/compliance/whdfs21.pdf.

152. 29 C.F.R. § 516.1.

153. Bailey v. Titlemax of Georgia, Inc., 776 F.3d 797 (11th Cir. 2015).

154. *See, for example*, Nicole Hallett, The Problem of Wage Theft, 37 Yale L. & Pol'y Rev. 93 (2018).

155. The U.S. Supreme Court acknowledged this problem in *Anderson v. Mt. Clemens Pottery Co.*, 328 U.S. 680 (1946), where it held that an employer's failure to keep time records must not be permitted to hinder the employee's right to sue for unpaid wages; in these situations, an employee need only present "sufficient evidence to show the amount and extent of [the uncompensated work] as a matter of just and reasonable inference," *id.* at 687, a standard that some courts have held can be met entirely "through estimates based on [the worker's] own recollection." Kubel v. Black & Decker, Inc., 643 F.3d 352 (2d Cir. 2011). Nevertheless, workers would be well advised to keep contemporaneous records of their hours.

156. U.S. Department of Labor, DOL Mobile Applications, http://www.dol.gov/general/apps.

157. U.S. v. Rosenwasser, 323 U.S. 360 (1945).

158. 29 U.S.C. § 207(g).

159. U.S. Department of Labor, Wage & Hour Division, Handy Reference Guide to the Fair Labor Standards Act, http://www.dol.gov/whd/regs/compliance/hrg.htm.

160. Regulations are set out in Title 29 of the Code of Federal Regulations, Part 778.

161. California, New York, and a few other states impose a daily maximum and require a higher wage rate or bonus payment for hours worked in excess of the daily maximum. *See* U.S. Department of Labor, Wage & Hour Division, Minimum Wage Laws in the States, http://www.dol.gov/whd/minwage/america.htm.

162. Sandifer v. U.S. Steel Corp., 134 S. Ct. 870, 875 (2014).

163. Anderson v. Mt. Clemens Pottery Co., 328 U.S., 680, 690–691 (1946).

164. Johnson v. Heckmann Water Resources, Inc., 758 F.3d 627 (5th Cir. 2014).

165. 29 C.F.R. § 785.18.

166. 29 C.F.R. § 785.21.

167. 29 C.F.R. § 785.22(a).

168. 29 C.F.R. § 785.22(b).

169. 29 C.F.R. § 785.35.

170. 29 C.F.R. § 785.38.

171. *See* Mid-Continent Petroleum Corp. v. Keen, 157 F.2d 310, 317 (8th Cir. 1946).

172. 29 C.F.R. § 785.43.

173. *See* National Partnership for Women and Families, Paid Sick Days—State and District Statutes (updated Oct. 2018), http://www.nationalpartnership.org/our-work/resources/workplace/paid-sick-days/paid-sick-days-statutes.pdf; National Conference of State Legislatures, Paid Sick Leave (May 29, 2018), http://www.ncsl.org/research/labor-and-employment/paid-sick-leave.aspx.

174. *See* 29 C.F.R. § 785.26. *See also, for example*, Castaneda v. JBS USA, LLC, 819 F.3d 1237 (10th Cir. 2016) (walk times to work areas from the locker room where workers put on and took off clothing, and walk times to the locker room from the washing station were not compensable before plug times were added to employees' collective bargaining agreement). The compensability of time spent washing or changing

clothes is a subject that may be resolved by collective bargaining if the employment site is unionized. *See* Sandifer v. U.S. Steel Corp., 134 S. Ct. 870, 876 (2014).

175. Integrity Staffing Solutions, Inc. v. Busk, 135 S. Ct. 513 (2014).

176. 29 C.F.R. § 785.19(a) ("The employee is not relieved if he is required to perform any duties, whether active or inactive, while eating."); .19(b) ("It is not necessary that an employee be permitted to leave the premises. . . .").

177. *See, for example*, Havrilla v. United States, 125 Fed. Cl. 454, 463–464 (2016) (collecting cases). *Compare* Kohlheim v. Glynn Cty., 915 F.2d 1473, 1477 (11th Cir. 1990) ("complete relief" test), *with* Babcock v. Butler Cty., 806 F.3d 153, 155 (3d Cir. 2015) ("predominant benefit" test). *See* John A. Le Blanc, *But see* Kohlheim: The Third Circuit Muddies the Water on the Compensability of Employee Meal Periods under the Fair Labor Standards Act in Babcock v. Butler County, 58 B.C. L. Rev. E-Supplement 91 (2017) (arguing that the predominant benefit test "mischaracterized the status of the law on whether the U.S. Courts of Appeals uniformly apply the predominant benefit test when determining the compensability of an employee's meal period under the FLSA").

178. Naylor v. Securiguard, Inc., 801 F.3d 501 (5th Cir. 2015). *But see* Myracle v. General Electric Co., 33 F.3d 55 (Table) (6th Cir. 1994) (employee bears burden).

179. 29 U.S.C. § 207(r). *See* 75 Fed. Reg. 80073 (Dec. 21, 2010) ("Where an employer already provides paid breaks, an employee who uses that break time to express milk must be paid in the same way that other employees are compensated for break time."). An employer that employs fewer than 50 workers may be exempted from providing facilities for expressing breast milk "if such requirements would impose an undue hardship by causing the employer significant difficulty or expense when considered in relation to the size, financial resources, nature, or structure of the employer's business." 29 U.S.C. § 207(r)(3).

180. 29 C.F.R. § 785.17.

181. 29 C.F.R. § 785.17.

182. Skidmore v. Swift, 323 U.S. 134, 137 (1944).

183. 29 C.F.R. § 785.14.

184. Integrity Staffing Solutions, Inc. v. Busk, 574 U.S. 27 (2014).

185. 29 C.F.R. § 785.32.

186. For an overview of these mechanisms, *see* Nantiya Ruan, Same Law, Different Day: A Survey of the Last Thirty Years of Wage Litigation and Its Impact on Low-wage Workers, 30 Hofstra Lab. & Emp. L.J. 355 (2013).

187. 29 U.S.C. § 216.

188. 29 U.S.C. § 215(a)(3).

189. U.S. Department of Labor, Wage & Hour Division, Fiscal Year Data for WHD, https://www.dol.gov/whd/data/datatables.htm#panel1.

190. *See* Nicole Hallett, The Problem of Wage Theft, 37 Yale L. & Pol'y Rev. 93, 121–141 (2018).

191. *See* Brock v. Superior Care, Inc., 840 F.2d at 1062–63 for discussion of differences between § 216 and § 217.

192. *See* National Employment Law Project, Winning Wage Justice: An Advocate's Guide to State and City Policies to Fight Wage Theft (Jan. 2001), https://www.nelp.org/wp-content/uploads/2015/03/WinningWageJustice2011.pdf.

193. *See, for example*, Hosking v. New World Mortgage, Inc., 602 F. Supp. 2d 441, 447 (E.D.N.Y. 2009).

194. 29 U.S.C. § 216(b).

195. 29 U.S.C. § 215(a)(3). Regrettably, retaliation by employers is not uncommon. *See, for example*, Laura Hulzar, Exposing Wage Theft Without Fear: States Must Protect Workers from Retaliation, Nat'l Employment Law Project (June 2019), https://s27147.pcdn.co/wp-content/uploads/Retal-Report-6-26-19.pdf. Adverse actions that constitute prohibited retaliation include discharge, demotion, change in hours or schedule, harassment, threats to report the worker or family members to immigration authorities, and the like. *Id. See* Burlington Northern and Santa Fe Ry. Co. v. White, 548 U.S. 53 (2006) (holding that retaliation prohibited by federal employment laws is not limited to "employment-related or workplace actions.").

196. 29 U.S.C. § 216(b) ("Any employer who [engages in retaliation] shall be liable for such legal or equitable relief as may be appropriate . . . including without limitation employment, reinstatement, promotion, and the payment of wages lost and an additional equal amount as liquidated damages."). At least one court has held that an employer's attorney could be held liable for retaliatory actions since 29 U.S.C. § 215(a)(3) prohibits retaliation by "any person." Arias v. Raimondo, 860 F.3d 1185 (9th Cir. 2017). *See also* Pineda v. JTCH Apartments, LLC, 843 F.3d 1062 (5th Cir. 2016) (holding damages for mental and emotional distress are available on a FLSA retaliation claim).

197. Kasten v. Saint-Gobain Performance Plastics Corporation, 563 U.S. 1, 14 (2011).

198. *See, for example*, Greathouse v. JHS Security Inc., 784 F.3d 105 (2d Cir. 2015) (holding that internal complaint is protected from retaliation); Minor v. Bostwick Laboratories, Inc., 669 F.3d 428, 439 (4th Cir. 2012) (worker's complaint must meet "some degree of formality" and cannot simply be the " 'letting off steam' " to the employer). *But see* Brock v. Richardson, 812 F.2d 121, 124–125 (3d Cir.1987) (finding that, because of the FLSA's remedial purpose, "a retaliatory firing based on an employer's belief that an employee had filed a complaint—even when he had not—is prohibited by § 215(a)(3).").

199. 29 U.S.C. § 215(a)(3). *See* U.S. Department of Labor, Wage & Hour Division, Fact Sheet # 77A: Prohibiting Retaliation Under the Fair Labor Standards Act (Dec. 2011), https://www.dol.gov/whd/regs/compliance/whdfs77a.htm.

200. 29 U.S.C. § 2612(d)(2)(A).

201. 139 Cong. Rec. S1108-01, S1116 (Feb. 03, 1993) (statement of Sen. Dodd, sponsor).

202. *See* 29 U.S.C. § 2601. Subsection (a) has these findings:

1. the number of single-parent households and two-parent households in which the single parent or both parents work is increasing significantly;
2. it is important for the development of children and the family unit that fathers and mothers be able to participate in early childrearing and the care of family members who have serious health conditions;

3. the lack of employment policies to accommodate working parents can force individuals to choose between job security and parenting;

4. there is inadequate job security for employees who have serious health conditions that prevent them from working for temporary periods;

5. due to the nature of the roles of men and women in our society, the primary responsibility for family caretaking often falls on women, and such responsibility affects the working lives of women more than it affects the working lives of men; and

6. employment standards that apply to one gender only have serious potential for encouraging employers to discriminate against employees and applicants for employment who are of that gender.

See also Nevada Dept. of Human Resources v. Hibbs, 538 U.S. 721, 736-738 (2003) ("By creating an across-the-board, routine employment benefit for all eligible employees, Congress sought to ensure that family-care leave would no longer be stigmatized as an inordinate drain on the workplace caused by female employees, and that employers could not evade leave obligations simply by hiring men.");139 Cong. Rec. H396-03, H402-03 (Feb. 3, 1993) (statement of Rep. Stokes) ("Greater numbers of women with young children are now wage earners, and nearly half of all two-parent families in America have both parents working to make ends meet . . . the changes sweeping the American work force, it is becoming increasingly difficult for working parents to perform the basic functions of a traditional family, including caring for young children, family members who are seriously ill, or a seriously ill parent."); 139 Cong. Rec. H447-06 (Feb. 3, 1993) (statement of Rep. Richardson) ("Passage of this legislation recognizes the reality of working Americans, that most American families are headed either by two working parents or by single women, and that women are now the fastest-growing segment of the labor market."); 139 Cong. Rec. S1259-01, S1259 (statement of Sen. Lautenberg) ("Recent data show that over 80% of working women are in their prime childbearing years. In addition, less than 10% of all families are two parent families where the father is the breadwinner and the mother stays at home to care for the family. The Congress needs to recognize these remarkable changes in our society and pass this legislation to provide minimal job security to new parents and people who are forced to deal with family medical emergencies.").

203. *For example*, 139 Cong. Rec. S1108-01, S1110 (Feb. 3, 1993) (statement of Sen. Metzenbaum) ("[T]he bill's small business exemption nearly swallows the rule, exempting 95% of the businesses in this country. As a result, 60% of our work force will not be protected by this bill.").

204. *For example*, 139 Cong. Rec. H366-03, H368 (Feb. 3, 1993) (statement of Rep. Dreier) ("[T]his discriminates against the people who really do need to deal with the question of leave. This favors those who can take unpaid leave because not every worker can afford to do that.").

205. 29 U.S.C. § 2611(4)(A)(i); 29 C.F.R. § 825.104(a).

206. 29 C.F.R. § 825.104(a).

207. 29 U.S.C. § 2611(2)(B)(ii).

208. 29 C.F.R. § 825.105(e). To "employ" under the FMLA, is the same as under the Fair Labor Standards Act (FLSA): "to suffer or permit to work." The test for an employment relationship under the FLSA and the FMLA is broader than under the common law master/servant test. 29 C.F.R. § 825.105(a).
209. 29 C.F.R. § 825.104(c).
210. As to joint employers: 29 C.F.R. § 825.106(a) states that where two or more businesses exercise some control over the work or working conditions of the employee, the businesses may be joint employers under the FMLA. *See, for example,* Grace v. USCAR, 521 F.3d 655 (6th Cir. 2008) (design firm and staffing agency that provided employee to design firm held to be joint employers where staffing agency managed her pay and benefits but design firm supervised her day-to-day activities and set her schedule and pay).

   As to integrated employers: 29 C.F.R. § 825.104(c)(2) prescribes a four-factor test for when otherwise separate entities will be deemed "integrated employers" whose combined total number of employees is used to determine whether the 50-employee minimum is met. The four factors are: (1) common management; (2) interrelation between operations; (3) centralized control of labor relations; and (4) degree of common ownership/financial control. The regulation states that no single factor controls; "the entire relationship is to be viewed in its entirety."
211. 29 C.F.R. § 825.600(a)–(b). Certain limitations on FMLA rights apply to very small school districts (those employing fewer than 50 people in a 75-mile radius). 29 C.F.R. § 825.600(c).
212. 29 C.F.R. § 825.110(b)(1).
213. The principles of what constitutes a compensable hour are drawn from the Fair Labor Standards Act. 29 C.F.R. § 825.110(c)(1) (citing 29 C.F.R. § 785) ("The determining factor is the number of hours an employee has worked for the employer within the meaning of the FLSA.").
214. *See, for example,* Sepe v. McDonnell Douglas Corp., 176 F.3d 1113 (8th Cir. 1999), cert. denied, 528 U.S. 1062 (1999) (time off for medical leave did not count toward the 1,250 hours worked requirement).
215. 29 C.F.R. § 825.110(b)(3).
216. 29 U.S.C. § 2612 (a)(1)(A–B).
217. 29 U.S.C. § 2612(a)(2).
218. 29 U.S.C. § 2612(b)(1).
219. 29 U.S.C. § 2612(a)(1)(D).
220. U.S. Department of Labor, Office of Disability Employment Policy, Employment Laws: Medical and Disability Related Leave, http://www.dol.gov/odep/pubs/fact/employ.htm ("FMLA's definition of a serious health condition is broader than the definition of a disability, encompassing pregnancy and many illnesses, injuries, impairments, or physical or mental conditions that require multiple treatments and intermittent absences.").
221. 29 C.F.R. § 825.113(a).
222. 29 C.F.R. § 825.113(b).

223. 29 C.F.R. § 825.113(d).

224. 29 C.F.R. § 825.113(a), (d).

225. 29 C.F.R. § 825.113(b).

226. 29 C.F.R. § 825.115(b); 29 C.F.R. § 825.120(a)(4).

227. 29 C.F.R. § 825.113(f); 29 C.F.R. § 825.120(a)(4) (stating, as an example, that "[a]n employee who is pregnant may be unable to report to work because of severe morning sickness").

228. However, one court noted in dictum that the FMLA could apply to an employee wishing to take time off to care for grandparents who had acted as parents to the employee. *See* Sherrod v. Philadelphia Gas Works, 57 Fed. App'x 68, 72 (3d Cir. 2003) ("FMLA leave does not extend to leave to care for grandparents unless the grandparent served as the employee's parent."). *See* 29 U.S.C. § 2611(7) (defining parent to include individuals who stand in loco parentis to an employee.)

229. 29 U.S.C. § 2612(a)(1)(C).

230. *Compare* Ballard v. Chicago Park District, 741 F.3d 838, 842 (7th Cir. 2014) ("so long as the employee attends to a family member's basic medical, hygienic, or nutritional needs, that employee is caring for the family member, even if that care is not part of ongoing treatment of the condition") (citing 29 C.F.R. § 825.114(a)(2)(iv)), *with* Marchisheck v. San Mateo County, 199 F.3d 1068, 1076 (9th Cir. 1999) (some level of participation in treatment required).

231. 29 U.S.C. § 2611(12).

232. 42 U.S.C. § 12102(2).

233. U.S. Department of Labor, Wage & Hour Division, Fact Sheet 28K: "Son or Daughter" 18 years of age or older under the Family and Medical Leave Act (Jan. 2013), https://www.dol.gov/whd/regs/compliance/whdfs28k.pdf.

234. 29 C.F.R. §§ 825.122(b); 825.102.

235. *See* Obergefell v. Hodges, 576 U.S. ___, 135 S. Ct. 2584 (2015).

236. 29 C.F.R. Part 825 (defining spouse).

237. U.S. Department of Labor, Wage & Hour Division, Fact Sheet 28B: FMLA leave for birth, placement, bonding, or to care for a child with a serious health condition on the basis of an "in loco parentis" relationship (July 2015), https://www.dol.gov/whd/regs/compliance/whdfs28B.pdf.

238. 29 U.S.C. § 2612(b)(1).

239. National Defense Authorization Act of 2008, 110 Pub. L. No. 181, § 585, 122 Stat. 3, 129 (codified as amended at 29 U.S.C. § 2612 (2008)). Provision of qualifying exigency leave is meant to "reflect an understanding of and appreciation for the unique circumstances facing military families when a service member is deployed in support of a contingency operation or injured in the line of duty on active duty." The Family and Medical Leave Act of 1993, Part II, 73 Fed. Reg. 67,934, 67,936 (Nov. 17, 2008) (codified at 29 C.F.R. Part 825). The 2008 amendment covered immediate family members of members of the National Guard and Reserves, and limited qualifying exigency leave by family members for "short notice deployment, military events and related activities, childcare and school activities, financial and legal arrangements, counseling, rest and recuperation, post-deployment activities, and

additional activities." *Id.* at 67,959; 29 U.S.C. § 2612(a)(1)(E). The 2010 amendments broadened the state's coverage and when leave may be taken.

240. National Defense Authorization Act of 2010, 111 P.L. 84, § 565, 123 Stat. 2190, 2309 (codified as amended at 29 U.S.C. §§ 2611–12 (2009)).

241. *See* U.S. Department of Labor, Wage & Hour Division, Fact Sheet 28M(c): Qualifying Exigency Leave under the Family and Medical Leave Act (Feb. 2013), https://www.dol.gov/whd/regs/compliance/whdfs28mc.pdf (listing qualifying exigencies and defining covered duty).

242. *See* U.S. Department of Labor, Wage & Hour Division, Fact Sheet 28M(b): Military Caregiver Leave for a Veteran under the Family and Medical Leave Act (Feb. 2013), https://www.dol.gov/whd/regs/compliance/whdfs28mb.pdf.

243. 29 U.S.C. § 2614(a)–(b). *See* U.S. Department of Labor, Wage & Hour Division, Fact Sheet 28E: Employee Notice Requirements under the Family and Medical Leave Act (Feb. 2013), https://www.dol.gov/whd/regs/compliance/whdfs28e.pdf.

244. 29 U.S.C. § 2614(c)(1) (defining coverage).

245. 29 C.F.R. § 825.220(d).

246. Paylor v. Hartford Fire Insurance Co., 748 F.3d 1117, 1124 (11th Cir. 2014).

247. *For example,* Seeger v. Cincinnati Bell Tel. Co., 681 F.3d 274, 281–282 (6th Cir. 2012) ("Employers who violate the FMLA are liable to the employee for damages and such equitable relief as may be appropriate. . . . Our court has recognized two discrete theories of recovery under the FMLA: (1) the so-called 'interference' or 'entitlement' theory . . . and (2) the 'retaliation' or 'discrimination' theory."); Wallace v. FedEx Corp., 764 F.3d 571, 585 (6th Cir. 2014); Pagán-Colón v. Walgreens of San Patricio Inc., 697 F.3d 1, 11 (1st Cir. 2012).

248. 29 U.S.C. § 2617(c)(1)–(2). The statute provides for judicial relief—including money damages—against private as well as public employers. 29 U.S.C. § 2617(a)(1). The U.S. Supreme Court held that "state sovereign immunity" prevents individuals from receiving money damages against a state employer under the FMLA self-care provision, but that individuals can sue state employers for money damages under the FMLA family leave provisions. Coleman v. Court of Appeals of Maryland, 566 U.S. 30 (2012) (Congress cannot abrogate state sovereign immunity under the FMLA self-care provision). *Compare* Nevada Dept. of Human Resources v. Hibbs, 538 U.S. 721, 735 (2003) (money damages available to remedy FMLA family care provision).

249. National Labor Relations Act of 1935, Pub. L. No. 74-198, § 1, 49 Stat. 449.

250. President Franklin D. Roosevelt, Statement on Signing the National Labor Relations Act (July 5, 1935), https://www.presidency.ucsb.edu/documents/statement-signing-the-national-labor-relations-act.

251. 29 U.S.C. §§ 152(5), 158(d).

252. 29 U.S.C. §§ 157, 163.

253. Richard B. Freeman & James L. Medoff, What Do Unions Do? 7–11 (Basic Books 1984).

254. U.S. Bureau of Labor Statistics, Monthly Labor Review, George I. Long, Differences between union and nonunion compensation, 2001–2011 (Apr. 2013), 15, https://www.bls.gov/opub/mlr/2013/04/art2full.pdf; U.S. Bureau of Labor Statistics,

Compensation and Working Conditions, John W. Budd, The Effect of Unions on Employee Benefits: Recent Results from the Employer Costs for Employee Compensation Data (June 29, 2005), https://www.bls.gov/opub/mlr/cwc/the-effect-of-unions-on-employee-benefits-recent-results-from-the-employer-costs-for-employee-compensation-data.pdf.

255. *See* Henry S. Farber, Daniel Herbst, Ilyana Kuziemko, & Suresh Naidu, Unions and Inequality Over the Twentieth Century: New Evidence from Survey Data, Working Paper #620, Princeton University Industrial Relations Section (May 2, 2018), http://arks.princeton.edu/ark:/88435/dsp01gx41mm54w.

256. *See* Matthew Walters & Lawrence Mishel, How Unions Help All Workers, Economic Policy Institute (Aug. 26, 2003), https://www.epi.org/publication/briefingpapers_bp143/.

257. *See, e.g.,* Beatrix Hoffman, Health Care Reform and Social Movements in the United States, 93 Am. J. Pub. Health 75 (Jan. 2003).

258. *See* Congressional Research Service, Gerald Mayer, Union Membership in the United States (2004), http://digitalcommons.ilr.cornell.edu/cgi/viewcontent.cgi?article=1176&context=key_workplace.

259. U.S. Bureau of Labor Statistics, Economic News Release, Union Members Summary (Jan. 18, 2019), https://www.bls.gov/news.release/union2.nr0.htm.

260. *Id.* at Table 5.

261. Drew Desilver, Most Americans view unions favorably, though few workers belong to one, The Pew Research Center (Aug. 30, 2018). *See also* Harold Meyerson, The State of the Unions, The American Prospect (July 8, 2013), http://prospect.org/article/state-unions-0 (noting even higher support for unions among people under age 30).

262. Jake Rosenfeld, Patrick Denice, & Jennifer Laird, Union decline lowers wages of nonunion workers: The overlooked reason why wages are stuck and inequality is growing, Economic Policy Institute (Aug. 30, 2016), http://www.epi.org/publication/union-decline-lowers-wages-of-nonunion-workers-the-overlooked-reason-why-wages-are-stuck-and-inequality-is-growing/. *See also* Economic Policy Institute, Today's labor unions give workers the power to improve their jobs and unrig the economy (Aug. 24, 2017), https://www.epi.org/press/todays-labor-unions-give-workers-the-power-to-improve-their-jobs-and-unrig-the-economy/.

263. 29 U.S.C. § 157.

264. 29 U.S.C. § 158(a). *See generally* John E. Higgins, Jr., ed., The Developing Labor Law (7th ed. 2017).

265. 29 U.S.C. § 158(b).

266. 29 U.S.C. § 159(a).

267. 29 U.S.C. § 153(a).

268. National Labor Relations Board, Basic Guide to the National Labor Relations Act: General Principles of Law Under the Statute and Procedures of the National Labor Relations Board 3 (1997), https://www.nlrb.gov/sites/default/files/attachments/basic-page/node-3024/basicguide.pdf.

269. 29 U.S.C. § 152(3).

270. *Id.*
271. 29 U.S.C. § 164(a).
272. 29 U.S.C. § 152(11).
273. *See* Nationwide Mutual Insurance Co. v. Darden, 503 U.S. 318 (1992); Community for Creative Non-Violence v. Reid, 490 U.S. 730 (1989); NLRB v. United Insurance Co., 390 U.S. 254 (1968). *See also* U.S. Department of Labor, Wage & Hour Division, Fact Sheet 13: Employment Relationship Under the Fair Labor Standards Act (rev. 2008), http://www.dol.gov/whd/regs/compliance/whdfs13.htm.
274. *See generally* Jason E. Pirruccello, Contingent Worker Protection from Client Company Discrimination: Statutory Coverage, Gaps, and the Role of the Common Law, 84 Tex. L. Rev. 191 (2005).
275. *See* Katherine V. W. Stone, Legal Protections for Atypical Employees: Employment Law for Workers Without Workplaces and Employees Without Employers, 27 Berkeley J. Emp. & Lab. L. 251 (2006).
276. Browning-Ferris Industries of California, Inc. v. National Labor Relations Board, 911 F.3d 1195 (D.C. Cir. 2018) (discussing joint employer standard).
277. *Id. See generally* Restatement of Employment Law § 1.04.
278. *See* Milla Sanes & John Schmitt, Regulation of Public Sector Collective Bargaining in the States, Center for Economic and Policy Research (Mar. 2014), http://cepr.net/publications/reports/regulation-of-public-sector-collective-bargaining-in-the-states; Vijay Kapoor, Public Sector Labor Relations: Why It Should Matter to the Public and to Academia, 5 U. Pa. J. Lab. & Emp. L. 401 (2003) (citing Richard Kirschner, Labor Management Relations in the Public Sector: An Introductory Overview of Organizing Activities, Bargaining Units, Scope of Bargaining and Dispute Resolution Techniques in ALI-ABA Course of Study Materials (1997)).

In Janus v. American Federation of State, County and Municipal Employees, Council 31, 585 U.S. ___, 138 S. Ct. 2448 (2018), the U.S. Supreme Court held that the First Amendment barred states from compelling public employees to pay fees to public unions to cover the cost of collective bargaining. Research confirms that public sector unions play a positive role in state governance by reducing labor unrest. *See* Janet Currie & Sheena McConnell, The Impact of Collective-Bargaining Legislation on Disputes in the U.S. Public Sector: No Legislation May Be the Worst Legislation, 37 J.L. & Econ. 519 (1994); *see also* Charlotte Garden, Why Some States Want Strong Public-Sector Unions, The Atlantic (Jan. 17, 2016), http://www.theatlantic.com/business/archive/2016/01/friedrichs-state/424434/. However, some state politicians have attempted to dismantle public sector unions and threatened to eliminate wage and pension rights. *See* Steven Greenhouse, Wisconsin's Legacy for Unions, N.Y. Times (Feb. 22, 2014), http://www.nytimes.com/2014/02/23/business/wisconsins-legacy-for-unions.html?_r=0. *See generally* Julia Wolfe & John Schmitt, A profile of union workers in state and local government, Economic Policy Institute (June 7, 2018), https://www.epi.org/publication/a-profile-of-union-workers-in-state-and-local-government-key-facts-about-the-sector-for-followers-of-janus-v-afscme-council-31/.

279. *See* 29 U.S.C. § 159(a), (c); International Ladies' Garment Workers Union (Bernhard-Altman Texas Corp.) v. NLRB, 366 U.S. 731 (1961) (unlawful for employer to recognize union that lacks majority support).

280. A number of unions offer information and strategy advice for workers thinking about organizing a union. *See, for example*, AFL-CIO, Form a Union, https://aflcio. org/formaunion; United Electrical, Radio, and Machine Workers of America, The Five Basic Steps to Organizing a Union, https://www.ueunion.org/org_steps.html; Communications Workers of America, How to Organize, https://cwa-union.org/ join-union/how-organize.

281. 29 U.S.C. § 159(b). If the employer voluntarily recognizes a union as the representative of a group of its employees, no formal determination of the appropriateness of the bargaining unit is required. However, if the unit is not appropriate under the law, the union will be unable to enforce the employer's duty to bargain in good faith through the Board's unfair labor practice procedures. *See* NLRA §§ 158(a)(5); 159(a).

282. *See* NLRB v. Action Automotive, Inc., 469 U.S. 490, 494 (1985); United Operations, Inc., 338 NLRB 123, 123 (2002). The statute and the case law impose limitations on grouping certain types of employees with others. For detailed discussions on these and other issues relating to whether a unit may be appropriate, *see* National Labor Relations Board, An Outline of Law and Procedure in Representation Cases, updated by Terence G. Schoone-Jongen (2017), https://www.nlrb.gov/sites/default/ files/attachments/basic-page/node-1727/OutlineofLawandProcedureinRepresen tationCases_2017Update.pdf. *See generally* National Labor Relations Board, Basic Guide to the National Labor Relations Act: General Principles of Law Under the Statute and Procedures of the National Labor Relations Board (1997), https://www. nlrb.gov/sites/default/files/attachments/basic-page/node-3024/basicguide.pdf.

283. NLRB v. Gissel Packing Co., 395 U.S. 575, 614 (1969).

284. *See, for example*, N.Y. Comp. Codes R. & Regs. Tit. 4, § 201.8(c)(1) ("Certification without an election").

285. Congressional Research Service, RS 21887, Jon O. Shimabukuro, The Employee Free Choice Act (2011), http://digitalcommons.ilr.cornell.edu/key_workplace/783/.

286. 29 U.S.C § 159(c).

287. 29 U.S.C. § 159(c); *see* National Labor Relations Board, Final Rule, Representation— Case Procedures, 79 Fed. Reg. 74308, 74469 (Dec. 15, 2014) (Statement of the General Course of Proceedings Under Section 9(c) of the Act), https://www.gpo. gov/fdsys/pkg/FR-2014-12-15/pdf/2014-28777.pdf.

288. Roger C. Hartley, Freedom Not to Listen: A Constitutional Analysis of Compulsory Information Through Workplace Captive Audience Meetings, 31 Berkeley J. Emp. & Lab. L. 65, 67 (2010).

289. 79 Fed. Reg. 74308 (Dec. 15, 2014). *See* National Labor Relations Board, Rules & Regulations, https://www.nlrb.gov/reports-guidance/rules-regulations. *See also* National Labor Relations Board, NLRP Representation Case-Procedures Fact Sheet, https://www.nlrb.gov/news-publications/publications/fact-sheets/nlrb- representation-case-procedures-fact-sheet.

290. 29 U.S.C. §157 (employees "have the right . . . to engage in other concerted activities for the purpose of . . . mutual aid or protection").

291. *See, for example*, NLRB v. Washington Aluminum Co., 370 U.S. 9 (1962).

292. *See, for example*, Summit Healthcare Regional Medical Center, 357 NLRB 1614 (2011).

293. *See, for example*, Kelly's Taproom, 364 NLRB No. 153 (2016).

294. *See, for example*, Amglo Kemlite Laboratories, Inc., 360 NLRB 319, 322 (2014), enf'd, 833 F.3d 824 (7th Cir. 2016); Igramo Enterprise, Inc., 351 NLRB 1337 (2007).

295. 29 U.S.C. §157.

296. Meyers Industries, Inc., 281 NLRB 882, 885, 887 (1986) (Meyers II), *aff'd sub nom.* Prill v. NLRB, 835 F.2d 1481 (D.C. Cir. 1987).

297. 29 U.S.C. § 157.

298. *See* Eastex, Inc. v. NLRB, 437 U.S. 556, 565 (1978).

299. *See* Meyers II, 281 NLRB at 887.

300. Fresh and Easy Neighborhood Market, Inc., 361 NLRB 151 (2014).

301. 29 C.F.R. §§ 102.9, 102.10.

302. 29 C.F.R. §§ 102.15, 102.16.

303. 29 C.F.R. § 102.45(a); 29 U.S.C. § 160(c).

304. 29 C.F.R. § 102.46.

305. 29 U.S.C. § 10(c).

306. 29 U.S.C. § 10(f).

307. *See* Susannah Camic Tahk, The Tax War on Poverty, 56 Ariz. L. Rev. 791 (2014); Jason Furman, Poverty and the Tax Code, democracyjournal.org (Spring 2014), https://obamawhitehouse.archives.gov/sites/default/files/docs/democracy_article_on_poverty_and_the_tax_code_jf.pdf; David Kamin, Reducing Poverty, Not Inequality: What Changes in the Tax System Can Achieve, 66 Tax L. Rev. 593 (2013).

308. *See* Franchie J. Lipman, (Anti)Poverty Measures Exposed, 21 Fla. Tax. Rev. 389 (2017). For an overview of relevant programs, *see* U.S. Government Accountability Office, Federal Low-Income Programs: Eligibility and Benefits Differ for Selected Programs Due to Complex and Varied Rules (June 2017), https://www.gao.gov/assets/690/685551.pdf.

309. For an account of tax policy as an antipoverty tool, *see* Susannah Camic Tahk, The New Welfare Rights, 83 Brooklyn L. Rev. 875, 876 (2018).

310. There is one exception, namely, the Premium Tax Credit. *See* 26 U.S.C. § 36B. This credit is designed to help low-income families cover the premiums for certain qualified health insurance plans, and it applies to "taxpayer[s] whose household income for the taxable year equals or exceeds 100% but does not exceed 400% of an amount equal to the poverty line for a family of the size involved." 26 U.S.C. § 36(c)(1). This tax credit is discussed in chapter 4, "Health."

311. Starting in 2018, there are seven federal tax brackets: 10%, 12%, 22%, 24%, 32%, 35%, and 37%. *See* Tax Cuts and Jobs Act, Pub. L. No. 115-97, § 11001(a), 131 Stat. 2054, 2054-58 (2017) (amending I.R.C. § 1 by changing the rate tables for each filing type); 26 U.S.C. § 1(j). These new tax rates, however, are set to expire in 2025. *See*

Joint Committee on Taxation, List of Expiring Federal Tax Provisions 2016–2027, JCX-1-18, 15 (Jan. 9, 2018).

312. The eligibility cutoff for one of the most important tax credits for low-income working taxpayers, the Earned Income Tax Credit, is $49,194 for single taxpayers, and $54,884 for married taxpayers, filing jointly, in 2018.

313. *See* Kayla Fontenot, Jessica Semega, & Melissa Kollar, U.S. Census Bureau Current Population Reports, P60-263, Income and Poverty in the United States: 2017 (Sept. 2018), https://www.census.gov/content/dam/Census/library/publications/2018/demo/p60-263.pdf; *see also* United States Census Bureau, Poverty: How the Census Bureau Measures Poverty (Aug.16, 2018), https://www.census.gov/topics/income-poverty/poverty/guidance/poverty-measures.html.

314. Since 2009, the federal minimum wage has been $7.25 per hour. *See* U.S. Department of Labor, Minimum Wage, https://www.dol.gov/general/topic/wages/minimumwage (visited Mar. 10, 2018). To have earnings above the poverty threshold, a person earning the minimum wage would have to work at least 4,136 hours annually—which means approximately 80 hours a week—to keep a family of five above poverty. *See* Center for Poverty Research University of California, Davis, What Are The Annual Earnings For A Full-Time Minimum Wage Worker? Minimum Wage Basic Calculations and Its Impact on Poverty (Jan. 12, 2018), https://poverty.ucdavis.edu/faq/what-are-annual-earnings-full-time-minimum-wage-worker.

315. *See* 26 U.S.C. § 6012. The major exceptions to the tax filing requirement are for persons claimed as a dependent on another's tax return, and persons whose income does not exceed a certain threshold amount, usually the standard deduction amount.

316. *See* George K. Yin, John Karl Scholz, Jonathan Barry Forman, & Mark J. Mazur, Improving the Delivery of Benefits to the Working Poor: Proposals to Reform the Earned Income Tax Credit Program, 11 Am. J. Tax Pol'y 225, 230 (1994).

317. Before 2018, the federal tax system provided an additional tax benefit in the form of a "personal exemption" which was an amount that a taxpayer could exclude from his or her taxable income; a taxpayer could take a personal exemption on behalf of herself, her spouse, and her children or dependents. Beginning in 2018, however, the personal exemption is no longer available, and it is suspended until 2025. *See* 26 U.S.C. § 151(d)(5)(B); *see* also Pub. L. No. 115-97, 131 Stat. 2054 (2017).

318. Almost all low-income workers are subject to the payroll tax, and for families in the lowest income brackets, the payroll tax is the largest tax burden. Tax credits, however, are only allowed against income tax liability. *See* Linda Sugin, The Social Meaning of the Tax Cuts and Jobs Act, 128 Yale L.J. Forum 403, 410–411 (2018); Frank Sammartino & Aravind Boddupalli, The Tax Policy Center Briefing Book: A Citizens' Guide to the Tax System and Tax Policy: Taxes and the Poor, Tax Policy Center (2018) (finding that about 11% of families in the lowest brackets will pay federal income tax in 2018, whereas 62% of those families will pay payroll taxes), https://www.taxpolicycenter.org/briefing-book/how-does-federal-tax-system-affect-low-income-households.

319. *See* Susannah Camic Tahk, Everything Is Tax: Evaluating the Structural Transformation of U.S. Policymaking, 50 Harv. J. on Legis. 67, 69–70 (2013).

320. *See* Leslie Book, David Williams, & Krista Holub, Insights from Behavioral Economics Can Improve Administration of the EITC, 37 Va. Tax Rev. 177, 179 (2018).

321. *See* Internal Revenue Service, Taxable and Nontaxable Income, Publication 525 (2018), https://www.irs.gov/forms-pubs/about-publication-525.

322. *See* Does the Tax System Support Economic Efficiency, Job Creation and Broad-Based Economic Growth? Hearing on Tax Reform Before the S. Fin. Comm., 111th Cong. 10 (2011) (statement of Michael J. Graetz, Isidor and Seville Sulzbacher Professor of Law, Columbia Law School) ("[O]ur current individual income tax is a mess largely because our presidents and the Congress ask it to do too much. The result is a level of complexity that baffles experts, let alone ordinary Americans at tax time. Presidents and members of Congress from both political parties have come to believe that an income tax credit or deduction is the best prescription for virtually every economic and social problem our nation faces. In the process, we have turned the Internal Revenue Service from a tax collector into the administrator of many of the nation's most important spending programs.").

323. *See, for example*, Brishen Rogers, Justice at Work: Minimum Wage Laws and Social Equality, 92 Tex. L. Rev. 1543, 1548 (2014) ("Minimum wages might force employers to pay 'efficiency wages,' or above-market wages that tend to encourage greater effort by employees and greater attachment between employers and employees, which may also reduce turnover."); Christine Jolls, Fairness, Minimum Wage Law, and Employee Benefits, 77 N.Y.U. L. Rev. 47 (2002) (arguing that "fairness considerations will tend to drive the wage up"); Elise Gould, Commentary, Increasing Wages is an Effective Poverty Reduction Tool, Even for Kids, Economic Policy Institute (June 18, 2014), https://www.epi.org/publication/increasing-wages-effective-poverty-reduction/.

324. *See, for example*, Felicia Kornbluh, Is Work the Only Thing That Pays? The Guaranteed Income and Other Alternative Anti-Poverty Policies in Historical Perspective, 4 Nw. J. L. & Soc. Pol'y 61 (2009); Anne L. Alstott, Work vs. Freedom: A Liberal Challenge to Employment Subsidies, 108 Yale L.J. 967, 971–972 (1999) ("A program of unconditional cash grants would enhance the freedom and economic security of the least advantaged.").

325. *See* Congressional Research Service, Molly F. Sherlock & Donald J. Marples, The 2017 Tax Revision (P.L. 115-97): Comparison to 2017 Tax Law (Feb. 6, 2018), https://fas.org/sgp/crs/misc/R45092.pdf; Ben Steverman, Dave Merrill & Jeremy C.F. Lin, A Year After the Middle Class Tax Cut, the Rich Are Winning, Bloomberg (Dec. 18, 2018), https://www.bloomberg.com/graphics/2018-tax-plan-consequences/; William Gale et al., Effects of the Tax Cuts and Jobs Act: A Preliminary Analysis, Tax Policy Center (June 13, 2018), https://www.taxpolicycenter.org/publications/effects-tax-cuts-and-jobs-act-preliminary-analysis (concluding that the law primarily benefits the wealthy and that "[w]hen it is ultimately financed with spending cuts or other tax increases, as it must be in the long run, TCJA will, under the most

plausible scenarios, end up making most households worse off than if TCJA had not been enacted.").

326. *See* Internal Revenue Service, Tax Reform Basics for Individuals and Families: Tax Year 2018, Publication 5307 (10-2018), https://www.irs.gov/pub/irs-pdf/p5307.pdf.

327. *See* Nicole Kaeding, The Tax Cuts and Jobs Act after a Year, Tax Foundation (Dec. 17, 2018), https://taxfoundation.org/tcja-one-year-later/; Frank Sammartino, Philip Stallworth, & David Weiner, The Effect of the TCJA Individual Income Tax Provisions Across Income Groups and Across the States 2, Tax Policy Center (Mar. 28, 2018), http://www.taxpolicycenter.org/sites/default/files/publication/154006/the_effect_of_the_tcja_individual_income_tax_provisions_across_income_groups_and_across_the_states.pdf.

328. Moreover, the tax cuts are expected to decline over time. For instance, in 2018, the after-tax income for taxpayers in all income groups will increase, on average, by 2.3%, but in 2015 only by 1.6%. For a more detailed explanation of the effects, *see* Huaqun Li & Kyle Pomerleu, The Distributional Impact of the Tax Cuts and Jobs Act over the Next Decade, Tax Foundation (June 28, 2018), https://taxfoundation.org/the-distributional-impact-of-the-tax-cuts-and-jobs-act-over-the-next-decade/.

329. *See* Internal Revenue Service, Statistics of Income, David J. Kautter, Jeffrey J. Tribiano, Benjamin D. Herndon, Barry W. Johnson, Laura R. Rasmussen, & Timothy S. Castle, Fiscal Year Return Projections for the United States, Publication 6292 (2018), https://www.irs.gov/pub/irs-pdf/p6292.pdf.

330. By way of background, employers must withhold federal income taxes on employee pay, and employees can claim allowances to exclude part of their pay from such withholding. The Internal Revenue Service publishes withholding tables to inform employers how much to withhold. The TCJA gave the Treasury discretion to set the value of the withholding allowance for 2018. If taxpayers did not otherwise review their modified withholdings and change their W-4 forms for 2018, less money was being withheld. *See* Internal Revenue Service, Withholding Tables Frequently Asked Questions (Nov. 5, 2018), https://www.irs.gov/newsroom/irs-withholding-tables-frequently-asked-questions.

331. *See* Jeff Sommer & Keith Collins, Why a Tax Cut Might Not Mean a Bigger Refund, N.Y. Times (Feb. 22, 2019), https://www.nytimes.com/interactive/2019/02/22/your-money/tax-cuts-refund-return.html. *See also* Michael Cohn, Taxpayers take to Twitter to voice frustration over tax refunds, Accounting Today (Feb. 6, 2019), https://www.accountingtoday.com/news/taxpayers-take-to-twitter-to-voice-frustration-over-lack-of-tax-refunds.

332. *See* U.S. General Accountability Office, James R. McTigue, Jr., Federal Tax Withholding: Treasury and IRS Should Document the Roles and Responsibilities for Updating Annual Withholding Tables (July 31, 2018), https://www.gao.gov/products/GAO-18-548; *see also* Laura Davison, The U.S. Cut Taxes. Why Will Fewer Folks Get Refunds?, Bloomberg (Feb. 9, 2019), online at https://www.bloomberg.com/news/articles/2019-02-09/the-u-s-cut-taxes-why-will-fewer-folks-get-refunds-quicktake.

333. *See* Federal Tax Refund 2019: Tax Cuts and Jobs Act Changes Leave Colorado Family With $8,000 Tax Bill, CBS News (Feb. 21, 2019), https://www.cbsnews.com/news/

federal-tax-refund-2019-tax-cuts-and-jobs-act-changes-isadora-bielsk-colorado-8000-tax-bill/.

334. According to the study, "middle-class households (earning between $40,000 and $110,000) receive $2.75 a day from the Tax Cuts and Jobs Act. White households in the top 1% of earners receive $143 a day." *See* Emmauel Nieves, Jeremie Greer, David Newville, & Meg Wiehe, Race, Wealth and Taxes: How the Tax Cuts and Jobs Act Supercharges the Racial Wealth Divide, Prosperity Now (Oct. 2018), https://prosperitynow.org/resources/race-wealth-and-taxeshttps://itep.org/race-wealth-and-taxes-how-the-tax-cuts-and-jobs-act-supercharges-the-racial-wealth-divide/ (relying on data from the Institute of Taxation and Economic Policy and "provid[ing] the first quantitative analysis to examine the racial implications of the Tax Cuts and Jobs Act and how these tax cuts reward existing White wealth at the expense of the economic security of households of color, poor households and a stalling middle class").

335. *See* Frank Sammartino, Philip Stallworth, & David Weiner, The Effect of the TCJA Individual Income Tax Provisions Across Income Groups and Across the States 2–4, Tax Policy Center (Mar. 28, 2018), http://www.taxpolicycenter.org/sites/default/files/publication/154006/the_effect_of_the_tcja_individual_income_tax_provisions_across_income_groups_and_across_the_states.pdf ("In the bottom income-quintile, 27% will receive a tax cut and about 1% will have a tax increase, with the rest having no material change in their income tax.").

336. Edward McCaffery, The Burdens of Benefits, 44 Vill. L. Rev. 445, 483 (1999).

337. 26 U.S.C. § 21.

338. 26 U.S.C. § 22.

339. 26 U.S.C. § 24. A portion of the Child Tax Credit is refundable, but it is listed under subpart A "Nonrefundable Personal Credits" under the tax code.

340. 26 U.S.C. § 25A. While the Lifetime Learning Credit is a nonrefundable credit, the American Opportunity Tax Credit permits a partially refundable credit.

341. 26 U.S.C. § 25B.

342. 26 U.S.C. § 31.

343. 26 U.S.C. § 32.

344. 26 U.S.C. §§ 35, 36B.

345. 26 U.S.C. § 36.

346. Generally, tax deductions serve four main functions under the tax system: first, they "can account for large, unusual, and necessary personal expenditures, such as the deduction for extraordinary medical expenses"; second, they can encourage certain types of activities, such as homeownership; third, they can "account for and ease the burden of paying for non-federal forms of taxes, such as state and local taxes"; and fourth, they "adjust for the expenses of earning income, such as deductions for work-related employee expenses." Congressional Research Service, Sean Lowry, Tax Deductions for Individuals: A Summary (Mar. 17, 2017), https://fas.org/sgp/crs/misc/R42872.pdf. Deductions are classified as either: above-the-line deductions, which are also called adjustments to income because they represent costs incurred to earn income, and below-the-line deductions, which come in the form of either

the standard deduction or itemized deductions. The "line" here refers to the place on the tax forms, that is, Form 1040: U.S. Individual Income Tax Return, where such items are entered. *See* Brian H. Jenn, The Case for Tax Credits, 61 Tax Law. 549, 571 (2008). Above-the-line deductions "typically relate to the measurement of income or exist to address disparities affecting the tax treatment of the self-employed or employees whose employers do not offer certain tax-favored benefits." *See id. See also* 26 U.S.C. §§ 62, 162, 212. The vast majority of deductions are below-the-line deductions.

347. 26 U.S.C. § 64(d).

348. An additional standard deduction amount may be available for taxpayers who are age 65 or over or who are blind.

349. *See* Internal Revenue Service, Tax Topics: Topic Number 501—Should I itemize? (Jan. 28, 2019), https://www.irs.gov/taxtopics/tc501.

350. 26 U.S.C. § 63(c)(6).

351. *See* Center on Budget and Policy Priorities, Policy Basics: Tax Exemptions, Deductions, and Credits (Apr. 10, 2018), https://www.cbpp.org/research/federal-tax/policy-basics-tax-exemptions-deductions-and-credits.

352. Scholars and policymakers have long advocated making all tax credits refundable. *See* Jacob Nussim & Avraham Tabbach, Tax-Loss Mechanisms, 81 U. Chi. L. Rev. 1509, 1527–28 (2014); Lily L. Batchelder, Fred T. Goldberg, Jr., & Peter R. Orszag, Efficiency and Tax Incentives: The Case for Refundable Tax Credits, 59 Stan. L. Rev. 23, 34–35 (2006).

353. Deductions are generally worth more to higher bracket taxpayers, since deductions are tied to their marginal tax rates. *See* Thomas D. Griffith, Theories of Personal Deductions in the Income Tax, 40 Hastings L.J. 343, 353 (1989). The most common deductions claimed by taxpayers across all income brackets include deductions for state and local taxes, medical expenses, student loan interest, self-employment and home office expenses, and gambling losses. *See* 26 U.S.C. §§ 162(a), 164, 213, 221, 223; *see also* Ron Carson, Ready, Set, File! Seven Tax Deductions You Can Take Even If You Don't Itemize, Forbes (Jan. 20, 2019), https://www.forbes.com/sites/rcarson/2019/01/20/ready-set-file-seven-tax-deductions-you-can-take-even-if-you-dont-itemize/#31fde0b27573. For a list of all of the credits and deductions available for individuals, *see* Internal Revenue Service, Credits and Deductions for Individuals (Mar. 8, 2019), https://www.irs.gov/credits-deductions-for-individuals.

354. Among the average 30% of taxpayers who itemized their deductions, a significant portion were high-income taxpayers—those in the highest tax bracket with income over $500,000. *See* Internal Revenue Service, Statistics of Income— 2016 Individual Income Tax Returns Complete Report: 2016 (Publication 1304) (Rev. 09-18) (2018), https://www.irs.gov/pub/irs-pdf/p1304.pdf; *see also* Frank Sammartino & Aravind Boddupalli, The Tax Policy Center Briefing Book: A Citizens' Guide to the Tax System and Tax Policy: Taxes and the Poor, Tax Policy Center (2018), https://www.taxpolicycenter.org/briefing-book/how-does-federal-tax-system-affect-low-income-households.

355. Only 10% of all taxpayers are expected to itemize their deductions for the 2018 tax year. *See* Erica York, Nearly 90% of Taxpayers Are Projected to Take the TCJA's Expanded Standard Deduction (Tax Foundation, Sept. 26, 2018), https://taxfoundation.org/90-percent-taxpayers-projected-tcja-expanded-standard-deduction/.

356. This is an above-the line deduction. 26 U.S.C. § 219. *See generally* Vada Waters Lindsey, Encouraging Savings Under the Earned Income Tax Credit: A Nudge in the Right Direction, 44 U. Mich. J.L. Reform 83, 91 (2010) ("Although not targeted at low-income workers, the deferral of income for contributions to 401(k) plans and traditional IRAs is the most significant tax incentive that promotes retirement saving under the Code."). There is also a Savers' Tax Credit, which is designed to directly address the difficulty of saving for low-income families. *See* 26 U.S.C. § 25B. For more information on the Savers' Tax Credit, *see* Adi Libson, Confronting the Retirement Savings Problem: Redesigning the Saver's Credit, 54 Harv. J. on Legis. 207, 228 (2017).

357. *See generally* 26 U.S.C. § 219. *See also* Internal Revenue Code, IRA Deduction Limits (Nov. 2, 2018), https://www.irs.gov/retirement-plans/ira-deduction-limits. Married couples with two-wage earners may deduct a portion of the salary of one of the spouses. *See* 26 U.S.C. § 221.

358. *See* 26 U.S.C. § 219(b)(5)(A). The maximum deductible amount was $7,000 for taxpayers age 50 or older by the end of 2019.

359. If only one spouse is eligible for a company plan, the combined income cannot exceed $189,000 in 2019. *See* Internal Revenue Service, Retirement Topics—IRA Contribution Limits (Nov. 2, 2018), https://www.irs.gov/retirement-plans/2019-ira-deduction-limits-effect-of-modified-agi-on-deduction-if-you-are-not-covered-by-a-retirement-plan-at-work.

360. Hilary Hoynes & Jesse Rothstein, Tax Policy Toward Low-Income Families, National Bureau of Economic Research, NBER Working Paper No. 22080 (Mar. 2016), https:www.nber.org/papers/w22080. *See also* Michele Estrin Gilman, The Return of the Welfare Queen, 22 Am. U. J. Gender Soc. Pol'y & L. 247, 278 (2014).

361. 26 U.S.C. § 32. Additional resources about the federal EITC are available online from the Internal Revenue Service: http://www.eitc.irs.gov. *See also* Congressional Research Service, Margot L. Crandall-Hollick, The Earned Income Tax Credit (EITC): A Brief Legislative History (Mar. 20, 2018), https://fas.org/sgp/crs/misc/R44825.pdf.

362. *See* Sorenson v. Sec'y of Treasury of U.S., 475 U.S. 851 (1986); S. Rept. 94–36, at 11 (1975), 1975-1 C.B. 590, 595; 136 Cong. Rec. S15632, S15684-S15685 (daily ed. Oct. 18, 1990) (Explanatory Material Concerning Committee on Finance 1990 Reconciliation Statement). Congress first enacted the EITC in 1975 and expanded it in 1978, 1984, 1986, 1990, 1993, 2001, and 2015.

363. According to the Internal Revenue Service, the national EITC participation rate ranged from 78% to 80% for the 2015 tax year, estimated in cooperation with the Census Bureau. *See* Internal Revenue Service, EITC Participation Rates by States (Dec. 20, 2018), https://www.eitc.irs.gov/eitc-central/participation-rate/eitc-participation-rate-by-states. There is a rich literature on the EITC. *See, for example,*

Anne Alstott, The Earned Income Tax Credit and the Limitations of Tax-Based Welfare Reform, 108 Harv. L. Rev. 533 (1995); George K. Yin, John Karl Scholz, Jonathan Barry Forman, & Mark J. Mazur, Improving the Delivery of Benefits to the Working Poor: Proposals to Reform the Earned Income Tax Credit Program, 11 Am. J. Tax Pol'y 225 (1994); *see also* Wendy A. Bach, The Hyperregulatory State: Women, Race, Poverty, and Support, 25 Yale J.L. & Feminism 317, 374–375 (2014); Sara Sternberg Greene, The Broken Safety Net: A Study of Earned Income Tax Credit Recipients and A Proposal for Repair, 88 N.Y.U. L. Rev. 515, 588 (2013).

364. *See* Jennifer E. Spreng, When "Welfare" Becomes "Work Support": Exempting Earned Income Tax Credit Payments in Consumer Bankruptcy, 78 Am. Bankr. L.J. 279, 281 (2004) (internal citation omitted).

365. *See* Jon Lavamore, The Future of Access to Justice, 51 Ind. L. Rev. 19, 24 (2018) ("EITC does not address the worst poverty because it's the poverty of people without earned income, and they cannot participate in the program."); Dorothy A. Brown, The Tax Treatment of Children: Separate But Unequal, 54 Emory L.J. 755, 826 (2005) ("Contrary to what the academic analysis would suggest, being poor and Black makes you less likely to qualify for the EITC given the earned income requirement of the EITC.").

366. Maha Sadek, The Earned Income Tax Credit: The Means Tested Welfare that Works, 23 Pub. Int. L. Rep. 97 (2018).

367. For more information on tax returns with EITC, *see* Internal Revenue Service, Statistics for Tax Returns with EITC (Dec. 12, 2018), https://www.eitc.irs.gov/eitc-central/statistics-for-tax-returns-with-eitc/statistics-for-tax-returns-with-eitc.

368. *See* Internal Revenue Service, 2017 Statistics for Tax Returns with EITC (Dec. 12, 2018), https://www.eitc.irs.gov/eitc-central/statistics-for-tax-returns-with-eitc/statistics-for-2017-tax-returns-with-eitc; Leo P. Martinez, A Critique of Critical Tax Policy Critiques (or, You've Got to Speak Out Against the Madness), 28 Berkeley La Raza L.J. 49, 60 (2018) (citation omitted).

369. This finding was based on 2016 data. *See* Elaine Maag, Refundable Credits: The Earned Income Tax Credit and the Child Tax Credit, Tax Policy Center (Mar. 23, 2017), https://www.taxpolicycenter.org/publications/refundable-credits-earned-income-tax-credit-and-child-tax-credit/full.

370. *See* National Conference of State Legislatures, Tax Credits for Working Families: Earned Income Tax Credit (EITC) (Apr. 17, 2018), http://www.ncsl.org/research/labor-and-employment/earned-income-tax-credits-for-working-families.aspx. *See also* Megan Newman, The Low-Income Tax Group: The Hybrid Nature of the Earned Income Tax Credit Leads to Its Exclusion from Due Process Protection, 64 Tax Law 719, 721 (2011) ("The EITC has been described as one of the most complicated provisions in the tax code [ ]").

371. *See* Robert Greenstein, The Earned Income Tax Credit: Boosting Employment, Aiding the Working Poor, Center on Budget and Policy Priorities (Aug. 17, 2005), http://www.cbpp.org/archives/7-19-05EITC.htm.

372. Center on Budget and Policy Priorities, Policy Basics: The Earned Income Tax Credit (Apr. 19, 2018), https://www.cbpp.org/research/federal-tax/policy-basics-the-earned-income-tax-credit.

373. Leslie Book, David Williams, & Krista Holub, Insights from Behavioral Economics Can Improve Administration of the EITC, 37 Va. Tax. Rev. 177, 190–191 (2018).
374. *See* Hilary Hoynes & Ankur J. Patel, Effective Policy for Reducing Inequality? The Earned Income Tax Credit and the Distribution of Income, National Bureau of Economic Research, NBER Working Paper 21340 (July 2015), http://www.nber.org/papers/w21340).
375. Hilary Hoynes, Doug Miller, & David Simon, Income, the Earned Income Tax Credit, and Infant Health, 7 Am. Econ. J. 172 (2015) (". . . part of the mechanism for this improvement in birth outcomes is the result of more prenatal care, and less negative maternal health behaviors (smoking)" as well as "a change in the quality and, for some, quantity of insurance.").
376. *See* Anne L. Alstott, Why the EITC Doesn't Make Work Pay, Law & Contemp. Probs., Winter 2010, at 285, 312 (arguing that "the EITC does not make a large reduction in poverty, construed as a socially decent minimum measured relative to the prevailing standard of living"; "does not enable a minimum-wage worker to support herself and even one child at a socially decent minimum"; and "even together with other social-welfare programs, the EITC does not ensure a decent minimum standard of living to willing workers who suffer involuntary unemployment, health limitations, or family emergencies."). *See also* Conor Colasurdo, Welfare on Fire: The Earned Income Tax Credit Is Not Enough to Extinguish Poverty, 54 J. Cath. Legal Stud. 1, 19 (2015) ("The EITC is not consistent with the need to protect our most vulnerable precisely because it operates in, and is devised from, a culture that values work and profit over human dignity.").
377. Mark J. Van Ryzin, Diana Fishbein, & Antony Biglan, The Promise of Prevention Science for Addressing Intergenerational Poverty, 24 Psychol. Pub. Pol'y & L. 128, 131 (2018) ("supporting research to identify ways to reconfigure and/or streamline existing family-based programs to enhance their ability to integrate with existing service contexts").
378. *See* Vada Waters Lindsey, Encouraging Savings Under the Earned Income Tax Credit: A Nudge in the Right Direction, 44 U. Mich. J.L. Reform 83 (2010). *See also* Nancy E. Shurtz, Long-Term Care and the Tax Code: A Feminist Perspective on Elder Care, 20 Geo. J. Gender & L. 107 (2018).
379. Several scholars have argued that the approach of combining the EITC and a higher minimum wage is "both efficient and redistributive." *See, for example,* Matthew Dimick, Should the Law Do Anything About Economic Inequality?, 26 Cornell J.L. & Pub. Pol'y 1, 29 (2016) ("In the context of the EITC, which drives down wages and increases labor supply away from its efficient level, setting the minimum wage at the market-clearing level can restore efficiency in the labor market. Furthermore, by establishing a wage floor, low-wage workers now capture all of the EITC subsidy: $1 of EITC spending would increase low-wage workers' income by $1.") (internal citations omitted); *see also* Stephen F. Befort, The Declining Fortunes of American Workers: Six Dimensions and an Agenda for Reform, 70 Fla. L. Rev. 189 (2018); Erica Williams & Samantha Waxman, State Earned Income Tax Credits and Minimum Wages Work Best Together, Center on Budget and Policy Priorities (Feb. 7, 2018),

https://www.cbpp.org/research/state-budget-and-tax/state-earned-income-tax-credits-and-minimum-wages-work-best-together. Other scholars have analyzed the two as separate mechanisms. *See, for example*, Daniel Shaviro, The Minimum Wage, the Earned Income Tax Credit, and Optimal Subsidy Policy, 64 U. Chi. L. Rev. 405, 471 (1997) (arguing that the EITC is a better approach than a higher minimum wage, because the EITC better targets low-income individuals, and it does not tax or reduce employment); Lawrence Zelenak, Redesigning the Earned Income Tax Credit as a Family-Size Adjustment to the Minimum Wage, 57 Tax. L. Rev. 301, 302 (2004) (arguing that the "EITC can and should be revised to function as an adjustment to the minimum wage based on family size, designed to ensure that no family headed by a working parent lives in poverty, regardless of the number of children in the family.").

380. Dorothy A. Brown, Race and Class Matters in Tax Policy, 107 Colum. L. Rev. 790 (2007).

381. The TCJA changed the measure used for inflation-indexing from the Consumer Price Index (CPI) to the "chained CPI." *See* Congressional Research Service, Margot Crandall-Hollick, The Earned Income Tax Credit (EITC): A Brief Legislative History (Mar. 20, 2018), https://fas.org/sgp/crs/misc/R44825.pdf.

382. *See* Center for Budget and Policy Priorities, GOP Tax Law Erodes Federal and State EITCs Over Time by Slowing Their Inflation Growth (Mar. 7, 2019), https://www.cbpp.org/gop-tax-law-erodes-federal-and-state-eitcs-over-time-by-slowing-their-inflation-growth-0; Jesse Drucker & Alan Rappeport, The Tax Bill's Winners and Losers, N.Y. Times (Dec. 16, 2017), https://www.nytimes.com/2017/12/16/business/the-winners-and-losers-in-the-tax-bill.html.

383. *See* 26 U.S.C. § 32; Leslie Book, David Williams, & Krista Holub, Insights from Behavioral Economics Can Improve Administration of the EITC, 37 Va. Tax Rev. 177, 187–188 (2018); Congressional Research Service, Gene Falk & Margot L. Crandall-Hollick, The Earned Income Tax Credit (EITC): An Overview (Apr. 18, 2018), https://fas.org/sgp/crs/misc/R43805.pdf. The IRS also provides information on EITC eligibility for taxpayers. *See* Internal Revenue Service, Do I qualify for EITC? (last updated Jan. 22, 2019), https://www.irs.gov/credits-deductions/individuals/earned-income-tax-credit/do-i-qualify-for-earned-income-tax-credit-eitc.

384. A taxpayer's filing status cannot be married, filing separately. *See* 26 U.S.C. § 32(d) (stating that married individuals must file a joint return to claim the EITC). Also, an individual who is claimed as a dependent on another person's tax return is ineligible for the EITC.

385. *See* 26 U.S.C. § 32(a)(1). The total earned income must be at least $1.

386. The statute uses the term "adjusted gross income," which means a taxpayer's total income minus any above-the-line deductions (for example, student loan deduction or IRA deduction).

387. 26 U.S.C. § 32(a)(2) & (b). The IRS maintains an online EITC calculator that provides income guidelines by tax year, available at https://www.irs.gov/credits-deductions/individuals/earned-income-tax-credit/use-the-eitc-assistant.

388. The threshold amount was $3,500 in 2018 and increased to $3,600 in 2019. See 26 U.S.C. § 32(i)(1) ("disqualified income").

389. *See* 26 U.S.C. §32(c)(1)(D) (stating that an eligible individual does not include any individual who is a nonresident alien for any part of the year, unless the taxpayer elects to be treated as a resident alien under Section 6013).

390. 26 U.S.C. § 32(c)(1)(E) & (M).

391. 26 U.S.C. § 32(c)(1)(C) (stating that an eligible individual does not include any individual who claims the benefits of I.R.C. § 911).

392. 26 U.S.C. § 32(k)(1). Taxpayers who have been denied an EITC under Section 32(k) must demonstrate eligibility for the EITC by attaching Form 8862 to their return. Failure to attach Form 8862 to the return will result in denial of the EITC. *See* I.R.C. § 32(k)(2).

393. 26 U.S.C. § 32(c)(1).

394. 26 U.S.C. § 32(c)(1)(B).

395. 26 U.S.C. § 32(c)(1)(A)(i). An individual is treated as living in the United States during any period stationed outside the United States on extended active duty (90 days or more) in the U.S. Armed Forces. *See* 26 U.S.C. § 32(c)(4).

396. 26 U.S.C. § § 32(c)(1)(A)(ii)(II).

397. 26 U.S.C. § § 32(c)(1)(A)(ii)(III).

398. 26 U.S.C. § 32(c)(1)(B).

399. 26 U.S.C. §§ 32(c)(3); 152(c).

400. 26 U.S.C. §§ 32(c)(3)(C); 152(c)(1)(B).

401. For purposes of the EITC, a foster child is an individual who is placed with the taxpayer by an authorized placement agency or by judicial decree, or other order by any court of competent jurisdiction.

402. 26 U.S.C. §§ 152; 32(c)(3)(B).

403. 26 U.S.C. § 152(c)(3).

404. 26 U.S.C. § 32(c)(3)(D) & (m). *See* Internal Revenue Service, U.S. Taxpayer Identification Number Requirement, https://www.irs.gov/individuals/international-taxpayers/u-s-taxpayer-identification-number-requirement.

405. Internal Revenue Service, Earned Income Credit (EITC), Publication 596 (2018), https://www.irs.gov/publications/p596.

406. U.S. Social Security Administration, Application for a Social Security Card, https://www.ssa.gov/forms/ss-5.pdf.

407. 26 U.S.C. §§ 32(c)(3)(D) & (m).

408. *See* 26 U.S.C. §§ 32(c)(3), 152(c)(4); Prop. Reg. § 1.32-2(c)(3). Unless the special rule in 26 U.S.C. § 152(e) applies (applicable to divorced and separated taxpayers), the tiebreaking rule in 26 U.S.C. § 152(c)(4) applies to the head of household filing status (26 U.S.C. § 2(b)), the child and dependent care credit (26 U.S.C. § 21), the child tax credit (26 U.S.C. § 24), the EITC, and the dependency deduction as a group, rather than on a section-by-section basis. Notice 2006-86, 2006-41 I.R.B. 680.

409. 26 U.S.C. § 32(c)(2)(A); Carina Bryant, Earned income credit—Calculation of earned income, 8 Mertens Law of Fed. Income Tax'n § 32:48 (citations omitted).

410. *See* Internal Revenue Service, Divorced and Separated Parents (Feb. 6, 2019), https://www.eitc.irs.gov/tax-preparer-toolkit/frequently-asked-questions/divorced-and-separated-parents/divorced-and.

411. *See* 26 U.S.C. § 152(e) ("Special Rule for Divorced Parents, etc."); Internal Revenue Service, Divorced and Separated Parents, https://www.eitc.irs.gov/tax-preparer-toolkit/frequently-asked-questions/divorced-and-separated-parents/divorced-and.

412. *See* Chuck Marr, Chye-Ching Huang, Cecile Murray, & Arloc Sherman, Strengthening the EITC for Childless Workers Would Promote Work and Reduce Poverty, Center on Budget and Policy Priorities (Apr. 11, 2016), https://www.cbpp.org/research/federal-tax/strengthening-the-eitc-for-childless-workers-would-promote-work-and-reduce; *see also* Chuck Marr & Yixuan Huang, Childless Adults Are Lone Group Taxed into Poverty, Center on Budget and Policy Priorities (June 10, 2019), https://www.cbpp.org/research/federal-tax/childless-adults-are-lone-group-taxed-into-poverty; Center on Budget and Policy Priorities, Childless Adults Taxed into Poverty: Earned Income Tax Credit (EITC) Proposal Would Help Address Problem, https://www.cbpp.org/childless-adults-taxed-into-poverty-earned-income-tax-credit-eitc-proposal-would-help-address.

413. 26 U.S.C. § 32(a)(1).

414. Rev. Rul. 78-191 (IRS RRU), 1978-1 C.B. 8, 1978 WL 42248.

415. *See* Internal Revenue Service, Publication 596, Earned Income Credit (EITC) (2018), https://www.irs.gov/publications/p596.

416. 26 U.S.C. § 32(c)(2)(B)(i).

417. 26 U.S.C. § 32(c)(2)(B)(iv). The site where the services are performed (i.e., inside or outside the prison walls) is irrelevant. Rogers v. C.I.R., T.C. Memo. 2004-245, T.C.M. (RIA) P 2004-245 (2004). Instead, what is relevant is whether a taxpayer provides services while the taxpayer is incarcerated. Taylor v. C.I.R., T.C. Memo. 1998-401, T.C.M. (RIA) P 98401, 76 T.C.M. (CCH) 808 (1998). Therefore, compensation for work performed while in a work release program or while in a halfway house is not earned income. Tramble-Bey v. C.I.R., T.C. Summ. Op. 2001-23, 2001 WL 1922017 (T.C. 2001); IRS Pub. 596 (2006).

418. 26 U.S.C. § 32(c)(2)(B)(ii); Treas. Reg. § 1.32-2(c)(2).

419. Treas. Reg. § 1.32-2(c)(2).

420. Treas. Reg. § 1.32-2(c)(2).

421. 26 U.S.C. § 32(c)(2)(B)(v). Workfare payments generally include cash payments certain individuals receive from a state or local agency that administers public assistance programs funded under the federal Temporary Assistance for Needy Families program in return for certain work activities such as: (1) work experience activities (including remodeling or repairing public housing) if sufficient private sector employment is unavailable; or (2) community service program activities. Workfare is discussed in chapter 1.

422. 26 U.S.C. § 32(c)(2)(B)(i).

423. *See* Jacob Goldin & Zachary Liscow, Beyond Head of Household: Rethinking the Taxation of Single Parents, 71 Tax L. Rev. 367, 375–379 (2018).

424. *See* Internal Revenue Service, Earned Income Credit, Publication 596 (2018), https://www.irs.gov/pub/irs-pdf/p596.pdf.

425. *See id.* (includes any federal program or state or local program financed in whole or in part with the federal funds above); *see also* 26 U.S.C. § 32 (". . . any refund made to

an individual (or the spouse of an individual) by reason of this section shall not be treated as income (and shall not be taken into account in determining resources for the month of its receipt and the following month")).

426. The list is provided by the IRS. *See* Internal Revenue Service, Claiming Earned Income Tax Credit EITC: How Do I Claim EITC (Mar. 8, 2019), https://www.irs.gov/credits-deductions/individuals/earned-income-tax-credit/claiming-earned-income-tax-credit-eitc.

427. Internal Revenue Service, Claiming EITC for Prior Tax Years (Feb. 28, 2019), https://www.irs.gov/credits-deductions/individuals/earned-income-tax-credit/claiming-eitc-prior-years.

428. *See* Kate Leifeld, Creating Access to Tax Benefits: How Pro Bono Tax Professionals Can Help Low-Income Taxpayers Claim the Earned Income Tax Credit, 62 Me. L. Rev. 543, 546 (2010). According to the Center on Budget and Policy Priorities, "[t]he IRS instructions for the [EITC] are nearly three times as long as the 15 pages of instructions for the Alternative Minimum Tax, which is widely viewed as difficult." Robert Greenstein, John Wancheck, & Chuck Marr, Reducing Overpayments in the Earned Income Tax Credit, Center on Budget and Policy Priorities (Jan. 31, 2019), https://www.cbpp.org/research/federal-tax/reducing-overpayments-in-the-earned-income-tax-credit#_ftnref10.

429. Internal Revenue Service, Use the EITC Assistant (Jan. 22, 2019), http://www.irs.gov/Credits-&-Deductions/Individuals/Earned-Income-Tax-Credit/Use-the-EITC-Assistant.

430. *See* Internal Revenue Service, Let Us Help You, https://www.irs.gov/help/telephone-assistance.

The Hotline number of individuals is: 1-800-829-1040 (7 a.m. to 7 p.m. local time. For other resources, *see* Internal Revenue Service, EITC Publications, Forms, Brochures and Other Resources, https://www.irs.gov/credits-deductions/individuals/earned-income-tax-credit/eitc-publications-forms-brochures-and-other-resources.

431. *See* Emily Cauble, Accessible Reliable Tax Advice, 51 U. Mich. J.L. Rev. 589, 589 (2018) ("Unsophisticated taxpayers who lack financial resources are disadvantaged by a shortage of adequate tax advice. The IRS does not have the resources to answer all questions asked, and the IRS's informal advice comes with no guarantee as to its accuracy and offers the taxpayer no protection when it is mistaken.").

432. *See* Pippa Browde, A Consumer Protection Rationale for Regulation of Tax Return Preparers, 11 Marq. L. Rev. 527 (2017).

433. *See* Linda Sugin, The Social Meaning of the Tax Cuts and Jobs Act, 128 Yale L.J. Forum 403, 409–410 (2018) (citing Campbell Robertson, Tax Preparers Targeting Poor with High Fees, N.Y. Times (Apr. 7, 2014), https://www.nytimes.com/2014/04/08/us/tax-season-brings-big-refunds-and-preparers-clamoring-for-a-slice.html); *see generally* Maggie R. Jones, Tax Preparers, Refund Anticipation Products, and EITC Noncompliance (U.S. Census Bureau, CARRA Working Paper No. 2017-10, 2017), https://www.census.gov/content/dam/Census/library/working-papers/2017/adrm/carra-wp-2017-10.pdf [https://perma.cc/BU8T-SGJB]).

434. *See* Danshera Cords, Paid Tax Preparers, Used Car Dealers, Refund Anticipation Loans, and the Earned Income Tax Credit: The Need to Provide More Free Alternatives, 59 Case W. Res. L. Rev. 351 (2009).

435. Internal Revenue Service, Consequences of Errors on Your EITC Returns (Mar. 29, 2019), https://www.irs.gov/credits-deductions/individuals/earned-income-tax-credit/consequences-of-eitc-errors.

436. *See* Internal Revenue Service, Watch out for These Common EITC Errors! (July 24, 2018), https://www.irs.gov/credits-deductions/individuals/earned-income-tax-credit/watch-out-for-these-common-eitc-errors.

437. The IRS relied on tax returns from 2006 to 2008. Internal Revenue Serv., Compliance Estimates for the Earned Income Tax Credit Claimed on 2006–2008 Returns (2014), https://www.irs.gov/pub/irs-soi/EITCComplianceStudyTY2006-2008.pdf.

438. *See* Robert Greenstein, John Wancheck, & Chuck Marr, Reducing Overpayments in the Earned Income Tax Credit, Center on Budget and Policy Priorities (Jan. 31, 2019), https://www.cbpp.org/research/federal-tax/reducing-overpayments-in-the-earned-income-tax-credit. *See also* Leslie Book, David Williams, & Krista Holub, Insights from Behavioral Economics Can Improve Administration of the EITC, 37 Va. Tax. Rev. 177, 193–194 (2018) ("The upper estimates assume that all of the nonresponders were ineligible to claim the EITC, while the lower estimate assumes that the nonresponders had a similar rate of noncompliance as the taxpayers who were audited and participated in the Service's NRP audits.").

439. 26 U.S.C. § 6402(m), added by the Protecting Americans from Tax Hikes Act of 2015, Pub. L. No. 114-113, § 201(b).

440. 26 U.S.C. § 6402(m) (the second month following the close of the tax year, which is February 15, for calendar year taxpayers).

441. *See* Stephen D. Holt, Keeping It in Context: Earned Income Tax Credit Compliance and Treatment of the Working Poor, 6 Conn. Pub. Int. L.J. 183, 201 (2007) (stating that "the tendency to see low-income persons as less trustworthy has extended to working poor claimants of the EITC. Findings of high error rates are indeed a concern, but the sense of alarm and special attention given appear to be disproportionate in the context of tax compliance generally.").

442. *See* Paul Kiel & Jesse Eisinger, Gutting the IRS: Who's More Likely to Be Audited: A Person Making $20,000—or $400,000, ProPublica (Dec. 12, 2018), https://www.propublica.org/article/earned-income-tax-credit-irs-audit-working-poor.

443. *See* I.R.C. § 32(k)(2).

444. Lawrence Zelenak, *Tax or Welfare? The Administration of the Earned Income Tax Credit,* 52 UCLA L. Rev. 1867, 1894 (2005); *see also* Wendy A. Bach, Poor Support/Rich Support (Re)Viewing the American Social Welfare State, 20 Fla. Tax Rev. 495, 543 (2017).

445. *See* Eric Williams & Samantha Waxman, States Can Adopt or Expand Earned Income Tax Credits to Build a Stronger Future Economy, Center on Budget and Policy Priorities (Mar. 7, 2019), https://www.cbpp.org/research/state-budget-and-tax/states-can-adopt-or-expand-earned-income-tax-credits-to-build-a#_ftn1.

See also Internal Revenue Service, EITC and Other Refundable Credits, States and Local Governments with Earned Income Tax Credits (Feb. 28, 2019), https://www.irs.gov/credits-deductions/individuals/earned-income-tax-credit/states-and-local-governments-with-earned-income-tax-credit; National Conference of State Legislatures, Tax Credits for Working Families: Earned Income Tax Credit (EITC) (Mar. 25, 2019), https://www.ncsl.org/research/labor-and-employment/earned-income-tax-credits-for-working-families.aspx.

446. Sorenson v. Sec'y of Treasury of U.S., 475 U.S. 851 (1986).

447. *See* Jennifer E. Spreng, When "Welfare" Becomes "Work Support": Exempting Earned Income Tax Credit Payments in Consumer Bankruptcy, 78 Am. Bankr. L.J. 279 (2004). *See also* Boris I. Bittker & Lawrence Lokken, Federal Taxation of Income, Estates and Gifts, ¶ 37.1 Earned Income Credit, 1997 WL 439678.

448. All legal permanent residents qualify as "resident aliens" as do individuals who meet the "substantial presence" test. *See* Internal Revenue Service, U.S. Tax Guide for Aliens, Pub. 519 (2018), at 3–5, https://www.irs.gov/pub/irs-pdf/p519.pdf.

449. 26 U.S.C. §§ 32(c)(1)(D); 6013(g). *See also* 26 U.S.C. § 6013(h) (treating as a resident a taxpayer who is a nonresident alien at the beginning of the tax year and a resident at the close of the year, is married to a U.S. citizen or resident, and has made the necessary election). *See* Internal Revenue Service, EITC and Other Refundable Credits, Basic Qualifications, https://www.eitc.irs.gov/Tax-Preparer-Toolkit/faqs/basicquals.

450. 26 U.S.C. § 32(m). *See* Internal Revenue Service, Social Security Number and Claiming EITC (updated July 2018), https://www.irs.gov/credits-deductions/individuals/earned-income-tax-credit/social-security-number-and-claiming-eitc.

451. 26 U.S.C. § 152(c)(1)(B).

452. *See* 26 U.S.C. § 21. *See also* S. Rep. No. 94-938, at 132 (1976), *as reprinted in* 1976 U.S.C.C.A.N. 3438, 3565 (changing the structure of dependent care expenses from an itemized deduction to a tax credit because "the committee believes that such expenses should be viewed as a cost of earning income for which all working taxpayers may take a claim").

453. *See* 26 U.S.C. § 21.

454. *See* 26 U.S.C. § 21(a)(1)-(b)(2) (stating that the credit is only applicable toward "employment-related expenses . . . incurred to enable the taxpayers to be gainfully employed").

455. "Persons who can't dress, clean, or feed themselves because of physical or mental problems are considered not able to care for themselves. Also, persons who must have constant attention to prevent them from injuring themselves or others are considered not able to care for themselves." Internal Revenue Service, Topic 602—Child and Dependent Care Credit (2018), https://www.irs.gov/taxtopics/tc602.html; Internal Revenue Service, Child and Dependent Care Expenses, Pub. 503 (2016), https://www.irs.gov/publications/p503/index.html.

456. *Id.*

457. *See* Leila Schochet, Rachel West, & Katie Hamm, Trump's Plan for the Child Tax Credit Does Not Meet Working Families' Needs, Center for American Progress (Oct.

25, 2017), https://www.americanprogress.org/issues/early-childhood/news/2017/
10/25/441368/trumps-plan-for-the-child-tax-credit-does-not-meet-working-
families-needs/.

458. 26 U.S.C. § 21(a)(2).

459. 26 U.S.C § 21(d)(1)(A) & (B). *See* Internal Revenue Service, Topic 602—Child and
Dependent Care Credit (2018), https://www.irs.gov/taxtopics/tc602.html; Internal
Revenue Service, Child and Dependent Care Expenses, Pub. 503 (2016), https://www.
irs.gov/publications/p503/index.html. Special rules treat the earned income of a student to be $250 if the household includes one qualifying child. 26 U.S.C. § 21(d)(2).

460. 26 U.S.C. § 24(a).

461. 26 U.S.C. § 24(h). *See* Internal Revenue Service, Get Ready for Taxes: Here's how the
new tax law revised family tax credits (Nov. 2018), https://www.irs.gov/newsroom/
get-ready-for-taxes-heres-how-the-new-tax-law-revised-family-tax-credits.

462. 26 U.S.C. § 24. *See* Internal Revenue Service, Five Things to Know About the
Child Tax Credit (Feb. 2017), https://www.irs.gov/newsroom/five-things-to-
know-about-the-child-tax-credit.

463. *See* Internal Revenue Service, Divorced and Separated Parents, https://www.eitc.
irs.gov/tax-preparer-toolkit/frequently-asked-questions/divorced-and-separated-
parents/divorced-and.

464. *See* Elaine Maag, Who Benefits from the Child Tax Credit Now? Tax Policy Center
(Feb. 15, 2018), https://www.taxpolicycenter.org/publications/who-benefits-child-
tax-credit-now.

465. *See* Center on Budget and Policy Priorities, Policy Basics: The Child Tax Credit
(Apr. 8, 2019), https://www.cbpp.org/research/federal-tax/policy-basics-the-
child-tax-credit.

466. *See* Robert Greenstein, Elaine Maag, Chye-Ching Huang, Emily Horton, & Chloe
Cho, Improving the Child Tax Credit for Very Low-Income Families, US Partnership
on Mobility from Poverty (Center on Budget and Policy Priorities, Apr. 2018), https://
www.cbpp.org/sites/default/files/atoms/files/urban_ctc_paper.pdf (estimating that
"the credit—including both the longstanding child tax credit for children under age
17 and the new nonrefundable component of the credit for dependents age 17 and
older that the 2017 tax law created—will deliver $128 billion in benefits to 48 million
families with children, reaching just over 90% of all families with children, in 2018").

467. *See* 42 U.S.C. § 604; 45 C.F.R. § 260.31.

468. U.S. Department of Health & Human Services, Office of Family Assistance, Help
for Families, http://www.acf.hhs.gov/programs/ofa/help. For a state-by-state listing
of TANF expenditures on work-related benefits, *see* U.S. Department of Health
& Human Services, Office of Family Assistance, Federal TANF and State MOE
Expenditures Summary by ACF-196R Spending Category (Aug. 15, 2016), https://
www.acf.hhs.gov/ofa/resource/tanf-moe-spending-and-transfers-definitions.

469. 42 U.S.C. § 604(h).

470. U.S. Department of Health & Human Services, Office of Family Assistance, Q &
A: Individual Development Accounts (IDAs) (Apr. 11, 2010), https://www.acf.hhs.
gov/ofa/resource/q-a-individual-development-accounts-idas.

471. 42 U.S.C. § 604(h)(4).

472. 42 U.S.C. § 604(h)(2)(B)(i).

473. 42 U.S.C. § 604(h)(2)(B)(ii).

474. 42 U.S.C. § 604(h)(2)(B)(iii).

475. U.S. Department of Health & Human Services, Office of Family Assistance, Q & A: Individual Development Accounts (Apr. 11, 2010), https://www.acf.hhs.gov/ofa/resource/q-a-individual-development-accounts-idas.

476. 42 U.S.C. §§ 501–502. *See* U.S. Department of Labor, State Unemployment Insurance Benefits, https://workforcesecurity.doleta.gov/unemploy/uifactsheet.asp.

   The National Employment Law Project offers an important online resource about unemployment insurance. *See* Rebecca Dixon, Rick McHugh, Claire McKenna, & George Wentworth, Unemployment Insurance Policy Advocate's Toolkit, National Employment Law Project, http://www.nelp.org/publication/unemployment-insurance-policy-advocates-toolkit-2015/.

477. *See* Daniel Price, Unemployment Insurance, Then and Now, 1935–1985, 48 Social Security Bulletin 22 (Oct. 1985), https://www.ssa.gov/policy/docs/ssb/v48n10/v48n10p22.pdf.

478. 42 U.S.C. § 503(a)(12).

479. *See* Chad Stone & William Chen, Introduction to Unemployment Insurance, Center on Budget and Policy Priorities (July 30, 2014), https://www.cbpp.org/research/introduction-to-unemployment-insurance#_ftn11.

480. George Wentworth, Closing Doors on the Unemployed: Why Most Jobless Workers Are Not Receiving Unemployment Insurance and What States Can Do About It, National Employment Law Center (Dec. 2017), https://s27147.pcdn.co/wp-content/uploads/Closing-Doors-on-the-Unemployed12_19_17-1.pdf (hereinafter "Closing Doors").

481. Contact information for filing a claim may be found at: CareerOneStop: Careers and Career Information, Toolkit, https://www.careeronestop.org/LocalHelp/UnemploymentBenefits/unemployment-benefits.aspx.

482. Closing Doors, at 1, 24.

483. *See* Litigation of Disqualification from Unemployment Compensation Benefits Based on Allegations of Misconduct, 158 Am. Jur. Trials 105 (2019).

484. 42 U.S.C. § 503(a)(3).

485. U.S. Department of Labor, Handbook for Measuring Unemployment Insurance Lower Authority Appeals Quality, ET Handbook No. 382 (3d ed. Mar. 2011), https://wdr.doleta.gov/directives/attach/UIPL/UIPL20-11.pdf.

486. Center on Budget and Policy Priorities, Policy Basics, How Many Weeks of Unemployment Compensation Are Available? (updated Feb. 25, 2019), https://www.cbpp.org/research/economy/policy-basics-how-many-weeks-of-unemployment-compensation-are-available. The states providing more than 26 weeks of coverage are Montana (28) and Massachusetts (30). In addition to Florida and North Carolina, the states providing less than 26 weeks of coverage are Idaho (21); Arkansas, Michigan, and South Carolina (20); Kansas (16); Georgia (14); Missouri (13).

487. U.S. Department of Labor, Continued Eligibility, State Unemployment Insurance Benefits, http://workforcesecurity.doleta.gov/unemploy/uifactsheet.asp.
488. P.L. 113-128, 128 Stat. 1425 (2014). The WIOA replaced the Workforce Investment Act of 1998, Pub. L. No. 105-220, 112 Stat. 936 (1998).
489. *See* Congressional Research Service, David H. Bradley, The Workforce Innovation and Opportunity Act and the One-Stop Delivery System (Oct. 27, 2015), https://crsreports.congress.gov/product/pdf/R/R44252.
490. *Id.*
491. 29 U.S.C. §§ 2101-09. Regulations governing the WARN Act appear at 20 C.F.R. Part 639.
492. 29 U.S.C. § 2102.
493. *See* Congressional Research Service, Benjamin Collins, Worker Adjustment and Retraining Notification (WARN) Act, (Sept. 4, 2012) (explaining that the "purpose of notice is to allow workers to seek alternative employment, arrange for retraining, and otherwise adjust to employment loss," and for states and localities "to promptly provide services to the dislocated workers and otherwise prepare for changes in the local labor market").
494. *See* Congressional Research Service, Linda Levine, Unemployment Through Layoffs: What Are the Underlying Reasons (2005), https://digitalcommons.ilr.cornell.edu/key_workplace/188/.
495. *See* Congressional Research Service, Linda Levin, The Workers Adjustment and Retraining Notification Act (WARN) (updated Sept. 26, 2007), https://digitalcommons.ilr.cornell.edu/key_workplace/321/; Howard J. Shatz & Jeffrey D. Sachs, Trade and Jobs in U.S. Manufacturing, Brookings, Papers on Economic Activity, No. 1 (1994), https://www.brookings.edu/bpea-articles/trade-and-jobs-in-u-s-manufacturing/.
496. *See* Clyde W. Summers, Worker Dislocation: Who Bears the Burden: A Comparative Study, 70 Notre Dame L. Rev. 133, 1034 (1995):

> Instability of employment, often in the form of mass dislocation, is a painful fact of our modern market economy, beyond the reach of any country to prevent or even influence significantly. Indeed, for a country to prosper it must embrace and accelerate changes which introduce new products and increase production. These changes, however, with their dislocation of workers, inevitably bring substantial personal and social costs. The costs must be borne either by the workers, the employer, or by society in general. How we distribute those costs implicitly expresses our social values, and may in the long run affect our readiness and ability to absorb those changes rather than to attempt to resist them.

497. Bruce C. Fallick, A Review of the Recent Empirical Literature on Displaced Workers, 50 Indus. & Lab. Rel. Rev. 5, 8 (Oct. 1996).
498. *See generally* William Lazonick, The Financialization of the U.S. Corporation: What Has Been Lost, and How It Can Be Regained, 36 Seattle U.L. Re. 857 (2013); *see also* Fran Ansley, Standing Rusty and Rolling Empty: Law, Poverty, and America's Eroding Industrial Base, 81 Geo. L.J. 1757 (1993).

499. *See* Zamira M. Djabarova, Improving Corporate Accountability by Strengthening Employment Law, Brooklyn J. Int'l L. 917, 926 (2015):

> The United States ranks last on the Organization for Economic Cooperation and Development ("OECD") Employment Protection Strictness index. This index measures the complex of processes that are in place before an employee can be terminated In other words, out of thirty-four OECD member states, it is easiest to be fired or laid off in the United States, since with some narrow exceptions, immediate notice of termination is effective there without any limitation.

500. *See* Anne Marie Lofaso, Talking Is Worthwhile: The Role of Employee Voice in Protecting, Enhancing, and Encouraging Individual Rights to Job Security in a Collective System, 14 Employee Rts. & Emp. Pol'y 55, 72 (2010) (explaining that "the WARN Act buys into a unitary system of industrial relations—a system of industrial relations in which the employer is the main, if not sole, authority of workplace decision-making").

501. Richard W. McHugh, Fair Warning or Foul? An Analysis of the Worker Adjustment and Retraining Notification (WARN) Act in Practice, 14 Berkeley J. Emp. & Lab. L. 1, 9 (1993).

502. Laura B. Bartell, Why WARN: The Worker Adjustment and Retraining Notification Act in Bankruptcy, 18 Bank Dev. J. 243, 244 (2002).

503. 29 U.S.C. § 2101(a)(1).

504. 20 C.F.R. § 639.3(a)(1).

505. 20 C.F.R. § 639.3(a)(3).

506. 20 C.F.R. § 639.5(a)(2).

507. 20 C.F.R. § 639.3(a)(2).

508. Pearson v. Component Tech. Corp., 247 F.3d 471, 477 (3d Cir. 2001).

509. *See* Jonathan M. Horne, You've Been Warned, 33-Feb. Am. Bankr. Inst. J. 18 (2014) (explaining that each factor is assigned weight "based on the facts and circumstances of the case," and that de facto control "is considered the most important and therefore is given the most weight").

510. *See* Woolery v. Matlin Patterson Global Advisers LLC, 2013 WL 1750429 (D. Del. 2013).

511. *See* 54 Fed. Reg. 16042, 16045 (Apr. 10, 1989).

512. *See, e.g.*, In re World Marketing Chicago, LLC, 54 B.R. 587 (N.D. Ill. 2017); In re United Healthcare System, Inc., 200 F.3d 170 (3d Cir. 1999), cert. denied, 530 U.S. 1204 (2000). *See also* Frederick F. Rudzik, A WARN Act Claim's Impact on the Equitable Distribution of Assets, 37-JUN Am. Bankr. Inst. J. 14 (2018).

513. *See* Brett Amron, Director & Officer Liability for WARN Act Claims in Light of Stanziale, 2017-JUL Bus. L. Today 1 (2017) (discussing Stanziale v. MILK072011, LLC (In re Golden Guernsey Dairy, LLC), 548 B.R. 410 (Bankr. D. Del. 2015).

514. *See, e.g.*, Cruz v. Robert Abbey, Inc., 778 F. Supp. 605 (E.D.N.Y. 1991).

515. U.S. Department of Labor, Frequently Asked Questions, What notices must be given before an employee is terminated or laid off?, http://webapps.dol.gov/dolfaq/go-dol-faq.asp?faqid=328. For a guide to worker rights under the WARN Act, *see* U.S. Department of Labor, Education and Training Division,

Worker Adjustment and Retraining Notification (WARN) Act: Worker's Guide to Advance Notice of Closings and Layoffs, https://www.doleta.gov/layoff/pdf/WorkerWARN2003.pdf.

516. 29 U.S.C. § 2101(a)(2).

517. 29 U.S.C. § 2101(a)(3).

518. 20 C.F.R. § 639.7.

519. Guippone v. BH S & B Holdings LLC, 2010 WL 2077189 (S.D.N.Y. 2010), citing 20 C.F.R. § 639.7(d)(1)–(4).

520. 29 U.S.C. § 2102(b)(3); see Allen v. Sybase, 468 F.3d 642, 645–646 (10th Cir. 2006).

521. 29 U.S.C. § 2102(b)(1). See, for example, Carpenters District Council of New Orleans & Vicinity v. Dilolard Depart. Stores, Inc., 15 F.3d 1275 (5th Cir. 1994); Angles v. Flexible Flyer Liquidating Trust (In re FF Acquisition Corp.), 438 B.R. 886 (Bankr. N.D. Miss. 2010).

522. 20 C.F.R. § 639.9(b)(2); Worker Adjustment and Retraining Notification, 54 Fed. Reg. 16,042, 16,062 (April 20, 1989).

523. 29 U.S.C. § 2102(b)(2)(A). See Calloway v. Caraco Pharmaceutical Laboratories, Ltd., 800 F.3d 244 (6th Cir. 2015) (rare mass seizure of company's products by Food and Drug Administration was not unforeseen circumstance to excuse noncompliance).

524. See, e.g., In re AE Liquidation, 866 F.3d 515 (3d Cir. 2017); Halkias v. General Dynamics Corp., 137 F.3d 333(5th Cir. 1998).

525. 29 U.S.C. § 2102(c). See Michele Floyd, The Scope of Assistance for Dislocated Workers in the United States and the European Community: WARN and Directive 75/129 Compared, 15 Fordham Int'l L.J. 436, 456 & n.133 (1992).

526. 29 U.S.C. § 2102(b)(2)(B).

527. 29 U.S.C. § 2103(1)–(2).

528. 29 U.S.C. § 2101(b)(2).

529. See N.Y. Labor Law § 860-a & -b.

530. 20 C.F.R. § 639.1(g).

531. U.S. General Accounting Office, The Worker Adjustment and Retraining Act: Revising the Act and Education Materials Could Clarify Employer Responsibilities and Employee Rights (Sept. 2003), https://www.gao.gov/assets/240/239817.pdf.

532. 29 U.S.C. § 2104. 29 C.F.R. § 639.1(d).

533. See United Food & Commercial Workers Union Local 751 v. Brown Grp., 517 U.S. 544, 548 (1996).

534. 29 U.S.C. § 2104; 29 C.F.R. § 639.1(d).

535. In re APA Transport Corp Consol. Litig., 541 F.3d 233 (3d Cir. 2008).

536. 20 C.F.R. § 639.1(d).

537. See, e.g., Philip L. Bartlett II, Disparate Treatment: How Income Can Affect the Level of Employer Compliance with Employment Statutes, 5 N.Y.U. J. Legis. & Pub. Pol'y 419 (2001–2002).

538. Richard W. McHugh, Fair Warning or Foul? An Analysis of the Worker Adjustment and Retraining Notification (WARN) Act in Practice, 14 Berkeley J. Emp. & Lab. L. 1, 59 (discussing the lack of government enforcement of the WARN Act as a major shortcoming of the law).

539. *See* Jonathan D. Glater, Layoffs Herald a Heyday for Employee Lawsuits, N.Y. Times (Jan. 30, 2009), http://www.nytimes.com/2009/01/31/business/economy/31employ.html?pagewanted=all.

540. United Steel Workers of America Local 2660 v. U.S. Steel Corp., 683 F.3d 882 (8th Cir. 2012).

541. *See* Michael Luo & Karen Ann Cullotta, Even Workers Surprised by Success of Factory Sit-In, N.Y. Times (Dec. 12, 2008), http://www.nytimes.com/2008/12/13/us/13factory.html?pagewanted=all ("But when closing time came, the workers refused to leave. Union organizers demanded that the workers be given their lawful due: 60 days' pay and compensation for earned vacation time. For six days and nights, they occupied the silent factory, drawing national media attention and winning the support of the President. In the end, their demands were met.").

542. 29 U.S.C. § 2104(a).

543. In re Dewey & LeBoeuf LLP, 487 B.R. 169, 176–177 (Bankr. S.D.N.Y. 2013).

544. Local Joint Executive Bd. of Culinary/Bartender Trust Fund v. Las Vegas Sands, Inc., 244 F.3d 1152, 1157 (9th Cir. 2001).

545. *Compare* Local Joint Executive Bd. of Culinary/Bartender Trust Fund v. Las Vegas Sands, Inc., 244 F.3d 1152 (9th Cir. 2001) (work days), *with* United Steelworkers of America v. North Star Steel Co., 5 F.3d 39 (3d Cir.1993), cert. denied, North Star Steel Co., Inc. v. United Steelworkers of America, 510 U.S. 1114 (1994) (calendar days).

546. 29 U.S.C. § 2104(a)(2)(B). Under this standard, the Third Circuit Court of Appeals declined to reduce the damages owed by severance payments that the company was required to make under an ERISA-regulated pension agreement. Ciarlante v. Brown & Williamson Tobacco Corp., 143 F.3d 139 (3d Cir. 1998).

547. 29 U.S.C. § 2104(a)(3).

548. 29 U.S.C. § 2104(a).

549. 29 U.S.C. § 2104(b).

550. N. Star Steel Co. v. Thomas, 515 U.S. 29, 33 (1995).

551. 29 U.S.C. § 2104(a)(6).

552. *See, e.g.*, Bledsoe v. Emery Worldwide Airlines, Inc., 635 F.3d 836 (6th Cir. 2011) (relying on authorization of judicial discretion as a basis for characterizing relief as equitable and so denying plaintiffs' civil jury trial request). *See* Noah Yavitz, The Right to Trial by Jury under the WARN Act, 79 U. Chi. L. Rev. 1629 (2012).

553. *See* U.S. Department of Labor, The Worker Adjustment and Retraining Act, https://www.doleta.gov/layoff/warn.cfm.

554. *See* U.S Department of Labor, Rapid Response Services for Laid-Off Workers, http://www.doleta.gov/layoff/workers.cfm. *See also* 20 C.F.R. 631.30(b).

555. John T. Addison & McKinley L. Blackburn, A Puzzling Aspect of the Effect of Advance Notice on Unemployment, 1 Indus. & Lab. Rel. Rev. 268 (Jan. 1997). According to one early study, notification of a pending layoff or plant closing at least two months in advance decreased the probability that workers would experience unemployment or be forced to take a lower-paying job following their displacement. Later studies confirmed that the advance notification of job displacement empowered workers to better avoid post-layoff unemployment. *See* Stephen Nord

& Yuan Ting, The Impact of Advance Notice of Plant Closings on Earnings and the Probability of Unemployment, 45 Indus. & Lab. Rel. Rev. 665 (July 1991). However, the Bureau of Labor Statistics found that advanced notice of layoff has little effect on the ability of long-tenured workers to secure re-employment. U.S. Department of Labor, Bureau of Labor Statistics, Worker Displacement 2015–17 (2018), https://www.bls.gov/news.release/pdf/disp.pdf. *See generally* Rachel Arnow-Richman, Just Notice: Re-Reforming Employment at Will, 58 UCLA L. Rev. 1 (2010) (discussing U.S. employment termination law and calling for notice or wages and benefits during a notice period to ensure workers a "window of income security" while they search for other employment).

556. *See, e.g.*, Shedrick v. District Bd. of Trustees of Miami-Dad College, 941 F. Supp. 2d 1348 (S.D. Fla. 2013) (race); Vuona v. Merrill Lynch & Co., 919 F. Supp. 2d 359 (S.D.N.Y. 2013) (gender); Gary Minda, Opportunistic Downsizing of Aging Workers: The 1990s Version of Age and Pension Discrimination in Employment, 48 Hastings L.J. 511 (1997) (age).

557. 29 U.S.C. § 626.

558. *See* U.S. Equal Employment Opportunity Commission; Understanding Waivers of Discrimination Claims in Employee Severance Agreements (July 15, 2009), http://www.eeoc.gov/policy/docs/qanda_severance-agreements.html. *See also* Gilmer v. Interstate/Johnson Lane Corp., 500 U.S. 20 (1991); U.S. Equal Employment Opportunity Commission, Enforcement Guidance on nonwaivable employee rights under Equal Employment Opportunity Commission enforced statutes, EEOC Notice 915.002 (Apr. 10, 1997), http://www.eeoc.gov/policy/docs/waiver.html.

559. Anne Marie Lofaso, The Relevance of the Wagner Act for Resolving Today's Job-Security Crisis (W. Va. Univ. Coll. of Law Legal Studies, Research Paper No. 2012-01, 2012), http://ssrn.com/abstract=2051104.

560. NLRB v. Truitt Manufacturing Co., 351 U.S. 149, 153 (1956).

561. Fibreboard Paper Products v. NLRB, 379 U.S. 203, 209 (1964).

562. First National Maintenance Corp. v. National Labor Relations Board, 452 U.S. 666 (1981).

563. Dubuque Packing Co., 303 N.L.R.B. 386 (1991); *see* Shelby Silberman, Outsourcing and Collective Bargaining: A "Win-Win" for Employers and Employees, 13 Cardozo J. Int'l & Comp. L. 601 (2005).

564. Pub. L. No. 74-271, 49 Stat. 620, Tit. II (1935). *See* Franklin Delano Roosevelt Presidential Statement Signing the Social Security Act of 1935, http://www.ssa.gov/history/fdrsignstate.html.

565. *See* Nancy J. Altman, The Striking Superiority of Social Security in the Provision of Wage Insurance, 50 Harv. J. on Legis. 109 (2013).

566. *See* Kathleen Romig, Social Security Lifts More Americans Above Poverty Than Any Other Program, Center on Budget and Policy Priorities (updated Nov. 5, 2018), https://www.cbpp.org/research/social-security/social-security-lifts-more-americans-above-poverty-than-any-other-program.

567. *See* 42 U.S.C. § 401(a) (Pub. L. No. 114-219). There is a fund dedicated to retirement and survivor benefits and a separate fund dedicated to disability insurance. *See* 42 U.S.C. § 401(b) (Pub. L. No. 114-219).

568. 20 C.F.R. § 404.310 (old age benefits).
569. 20 C.F.R. § 404.390.
570. A "quarter of coverage" is a legal term defined in 42 U.S.C. § 413(a)(2)(A). Social Security Administration publications sometimes refer to "quarters of coverage" as "credits." *See, for example*, U.S. Social Security Administration, Social Security Handbook § 200.2 (Aug. 1, 2006), http://ssa.gov/OP_Home/handbook/handbook.02/handbook-0200.html.
571. U.S. Social Security Administration, Quarters of Coverage, https://www.ssa.gov/oact/COLA/QC.html.
572. 20 C.F.R. §§ 404.140, 404.143.
573. *See* 42 U.S.C. § 414(a)(2). Persons born before 1929 are subject to a lower requirement. *Id.* Special rules apply for workers who are self-employed, in the military, or engaged in domestic work, farmwork, or work for a religious organization that does not pay Social Security taxes.
574. 20 C.F.R. § 404.130(a)–(e). A table showing the quarters of coverage needed at each age of disability onset appears in U.S. Social Security Administration, How Your Earn Credits, Pub. No. 05-10072 (Jan. 2019), at 3, https://www.ssa.gov/pubs/EN-05-10072.pdf.
575. 42 U.S.C. § 414(b).
576. These rulings may be found online at: http://www.ssa.gov/OP_Home/rulings/rulings-toc.html.
577. Research, statistical, and policy reports published by the Social Security Administration can be found online at: http://www.ssa.gov/policy/index.html.
578. 42 U.S.C. § 402(a) (through Pub. L. No. 114-219).
579. 42 U.S.C. § 402(a).
580. 42 U.S.C. § 402(a)(3).
581. *See* U.S. Social Security Administration, Social Security Handbook § 301, https://www.ssa.gov/OP_Home/handbook/handbook.html.
582. *See* U.S. Social Security Administration, Program Operations Manual System § RS 00201.003 (last modified Jan. 23, 2015), https://secure.ssa.gov/apps10/poms.nsf/lnx/0300201003.
583. U.S. Social Security Administration, Normal Retirement Age, https://www.ssa.gov/oact/progdata/nra.html.
584. 42 U.S.C. § 402(q)(1). Early retirement occurs "if the first month for which an individual is entitled to an old-age, wife's, husband's, widow's, or widower's insurance benefit is a month before the month in which such individual attains retirement age."
585. 20 C.F.R. § 404.401(b)(1). The deduction is either $1 for every $2 earned above the limit if the beneficiary is under full retirement age for the full calendar year or $1 every $3 earned above the limit if the beneficiary reaches full retirement age during that year. The deduction is eventually repaid after the beneficiary reaches full retirement age. *See* U.S. Social Security Administration, How Work Affects Your Benefits, Pub. No. 05-10069 (Jan. 2019), https://www.ssa.gov/pubs/EN-05-10069.pdf.
586. 42 U.S.C. § 402(q)(1) & (w).
587. 42 U.S.C. § 402(w).

588. *See* 20 C.F.R. §§ 404.204 et seq.; U.S. Social Security Administration, Retirement Benefits, Pub. No. 05-10035 (Jan. 2019), https://www.ssa.gov/pubs/EN-05-10035. pdf.

589. U.S. Social Security Administration, Frequently Asked Questions, How can I get a Social Security Statement that shows a record of my earnings and an estimate of my future benefits? (last modified May 19, 2018), https://faq.ssa.gov/en-US/Topic/article/KA-01741.

590. U.S. Social Security Administration, Retirement Benefits: Learn About Social Security Programs, https://www.ssa.gov/planners/retire/r&m6.html. Financial experts estimate that 70–80% of pre-retirement income provides a comfortable retirement. With the demise of employer-provided retirement plans and the precarious economic circumstances that have prevailed for all but the wealthy, this goal will be out of reach for most retirees absent major policy changes. *See* Jennifer Erin Brown, Joelle Saad-Lessler, & Diane Oakley, Retirement in America: Out of Reach for Working Americans?, National Institute on Retirement Security (Sept. 2018), https://www.nirsonline.org/wp-content/uploads/2018/09/SavingsCrisis_Final. pdf.

591. Average monthly earnings, indexed to the national average wage index, are calculated according to statute. 42 U.S.C. § 415(a).

592. *Id. See* U.S. Social Security Administration, Your Retirement Benefit: How It Is Figured, http://www.ssa.gov/pubs/10070.pdf.

593. U.S. Social Security Administration, Retirement Estimator, http://www.socialsecurity. gov/estimator/.

594. 42 U.S.C. § 402(a).

595. *See* Kathy Ruffing, Women and Disability Insurance: Five Facts You Should Know, Center on Budget and Policy Priorities (Mar. 14, 2018), https://www. cbpp.org/research/social-security/women-and-disability-insurance-five-facts-you-should-know.

596. Benjamin W. Veghte, Elliot Schreur, & Mikki Waid, Social Security and the Racial Gap in Retirement Wealth, National Academy of Social Insurance (Dec. 2016), https://www.nasi.org/sites/default/files/research/SS_Brief_48.pdf.

597. 42 U.S.C. § 423(a)(1).

598. U.S. Social Security Administration, Program Operations Manual System § DI 10105.070 (last modified April 18, 2013), https://secure.ssa.gov/apps10/poms.nsf/ lnx/0410105070.

599. 42 U.S.C. § 423(a)(1) & (c)(2).

600. 42 U.S.C. § 423(a)(1).

601. *See* U.S. Social Security Administration, Disability Benefits 7 (2015), https://www. ssa.gov/pubs/EN-05-10029.pdf.

602. 20 C.F.R. § 404.130.

603. 20 C.F.R. § 404.130(b). In identifying the 40-quarter period, the Social Security Administration generally does not count any quarters in which an individual was previously determined to be disabled, unless doing so would result in a higher benefit payment. 20 C.F.R. § 404.130(f).

604. 20 C.F.R. § 404.130(c)–(d).
605. 20 C.F.R. § 404.130(e). Blindness is statutorily defined as having "central visual acuity of 20/200 or less in the better eye with the use of a correcting lens" or having a better eye "which is accompanied by a limitation in the fields of vision such that the widest diameter of the visual field subtends an angle no greater than 20 degrees." 42 U.S.C. § 416(i)(1).
606. 42 U.S.C. § 423(d)(1)(A).
607. 42 U.S.C. § 423(d)(5)(A). The Social Security Administration describes the kinds of evidence it may require, along with the responsibilities of claimants to furnish evidence and the responsibility of the SSA to develop claimants' medical histories. *See* 20 C.F.R. § 404.1512.
608. An activity is significant if it is "useful in the accomplishment of a job or the operation of a business" and has "economic value." U.S. Social Security Administration, Program Operations Manual System § DI 10501.001 (last modified Jan. 5, 2007), https://secure.ssa.gov/poms.nsf/lnx/0410501001.
609. 20 C.F.R. § 404.1510. Part-time work can qualify as substantial gainful activity *See* 20 C.F.R. § 404.1572.
610. 42 U.S.C. § 423(d)(2)(B).
611. 42 U.S.C. § 1382c(a)(3)(H)(i).
612. 20 C.F.R. Ch. III, Part 404, subpart D. *See* U.S. Social Security Administration, Survivors Benefits, https://www.ssa.gov/survivors/.
613. 42 U.S.C. § 402(d)(1); 20 C.F.R. § 404.350 (children); 42 U.S.C. § 402(e)(1), (f)(1); 20 C.F.R. §§ 404.335–336 (spouses and divorced spouses); 42 U.S.C. § 402(g)(1); 20 C.F.R. § 404.370 (parents).
614. *See* U.S. Social Security Administration, Program Operations Manual System § RS 00202.000-00202.100, https://secure.ssa.gov/apps10/poms.nsf/subchapterlist!open view&restricttocategory=03002.
615. 20 C.F.R. § 404.335. A claimant who was married to the deceased person for fewer than nine months can qualify for survivors' benefits if the claimant (a) is the biological parent of the deceased person's child; or (b) legally adopted the deceased person's child during their marriage and before the child turned age 18; or (c) has a child who was legally adopted by the deceased person during their marriage and before the child turned age 18; or (d) is entitled to certain specified benefits based on the deceased's record under the Social Security Act or certain specified benefits under the Railroad Retirement Act. *Id. See* 42 U.S.C. § 416(c), (g). The nine-month requirement is also relaxed if the deceased spouse died in an accident. 42 U.S.C. § 416(k)(1) (describing the exception for accidental deaths and the conditions needed for a death to be considered accidental).
616. 20 C.F.R. § 404.336(a)(2).
617. Eligibility for survivors' benefits also extends to a surviving spouse who remarried between ages 50 and 60 if the person (a) is now age 60 or over, and at the time of remarriage was entitled to survivors' benefits as a disabled surviving spouse; or (b) is now between 50 and 60 years old, and met statutory disability criteria at the time of remarriage. 20 C.F.R. § 404.335(e).
618. 20 C.F.R. §§ 404.335(c), 404.336(c). *See* 42 U.S.C. § 416(d)(2) & (d)(4).

619. There are exceptions to the application-filing requirement for surviving spouses who were previously entitled to certain other benefits. 20 C.F.R. § 404.335(b).
620. 42 U.S.C. § 402(e)(1), (f)(1); 20 C.F.R. § 404.335. *See* U.S. Social Security Administration, Social Security Handbook § 405.1 (last modified Mar. 12, 2009), https://www.ssa.gov/OP_Home/handbook/handbook.04/handbook-0405.html.
621. 42 U.S.C. § 402(e)(2)(A), (f)(2)(A).
622. 42 U.S.C. § 402(e)(1), (f)(1).
623. 42 U.S.C. § 402(g)(1).
624. U.S. Social Security Administration, Social Security Handbook § 415 (last modified Mar. 12, 2009), http://ssa.gov/OP_Home/handbook/handbook.04/handbook-0415.html.
625. 42 U.S.C. § 402(g)(2).
626. 42 U.S.C. § 402(g)(1).
627. 20 C.F.R. § 404.366(b) (definition of "one-half support"). Support can be in the form of money, goods, or services and must be provided for "a reasonable period of time."
628. 42 U.S.C. § 402(h)(1). *See* U.S. Social Security Administration, Social Security Handbook § 421 (last modified Sept. 1, 2009), http://ssa.gov/OP_Home/handbook/handbook.04/handbook-0421.html.
629. 20 C.F.R. § 404.374. A parent may be a biological, adoptive, or stepparent.
630. 42 U.S.C. § 402(h)(2)(A).
631. 42 U.S.C. § 402(h)(2)(B).
632. U.S. Social Security Administration, Program Operations Manual System § RS 00209.015(A)(1) (last modified Nov. 8, 2012), https://secure.ssa.gov/apps10/poms.nsf/lnx/0300209015.
633. 42 U.S.C. § 402(h)(1).
634. 42 U.S.C. § 402(h)(4). *See* U.S. Social Security Administration, Social Security Handbook § 417.2 (last modified Mar. 12, 2009), http://ssa.gov/OP_Home/handbook/handbook.04/handbook-0417.html.
635. Under certain, very limited, circumstances, a child may marry and continue to receive children's insurance benefits. 42 U.S.C. § 402(d)(5).
636. 42 U.S.C. § 402(d)(1). *See* U.S. Social Security Administration, Social Security Handbook § 323 (last modified Feb. 6, 2003), https://ssa.gov/OP_Home/handbook/handbook.03/handbook-0323.html. An insured worker's "natural child" is generally assumed to meet the dependency requirement without further proof. 20 C.F.R § 404.361.
637. 42 U.S.C. § 416(e). The U.S. Supreme Court of the United States has held that posthumously conceived children are eligible to receive Social Security benefits only if they are deemed legal heirs under a state's intestacy laws. Writing for a unanimous Court, Justice Ginsburg stated that despite the "[t]ragic circumstances" of the case, the Social Security Act is meant to "benefit primarily those supported by the deceased wage earner in his or her lifetime." Astrue v. Capato ex rel. B.N.C., 566 U.S. 541, 559, 545 (2012).
638. 42 U.S.C. § 402(d)(1)(B). Disability for purposes of children's insurance benefits has the same meaning and is determined in the same manner as for SSI disability

and Social Security Disability Insurance (SSDI). Unlike Social Security disability benefits, though, there is no five-month waiting period for children's insurance benefits awarded to a disabled child. 42 U.S.C. § 402(d)(1)(C). *See* U.S. Social Security Administration, Program Operations Management System, RS 00203.080(A)(2) (last modified Feb. 19, 2013), https://policy.ssa.gov/poms.nsf/lnx/0300203080.

639. 42 U.S.C. § 402(d)(1)(G)(i).

640. 42 U.S.C. § 402(d)(1)(E)–(F).

641. 42 U.S.C. § 402(d)(6)(B). Re-entitlement is allowed after a seven-year period if the child's prior benefits were terminated because the child was able to work for a period of time. *Id. See* U.S. Social Security Administration, Program Operations Management System, RS 00203.080(A)(1) (last modified Feb. 19, 2013), https://policy.ssa.gov/poms.nsf/lnx/0300203080.

642. 42 U.S.C. § 402(d)(1)–(2).

643. 20 C.F.R. § 404.353(b).

644. 42 U.S.C. § 402(i).

645. 42 U.S.C. § 402(i). Under some circumstances, the Social Security Administration may extend the two-year filing period. *See id.* at § 402(p).

646. 20 C.F.R. § 404.330.

647. 42 U.S.C. § 402(b)(2), (c)(2), (q)(1) & (7)(b).

648. 42 U.S.C. § 402(b)(1) & (c)(1). *See* U.S. Social Security Administration, Social Security Handbook § 312 (last modified Feb. 4, 2008), http://ssa.gov/OP_Home/handbook/handbook.03/handbook-0312.html.

649. 42 U.S.C. § 416(h); 20 C.F.R. § 404.345. *See* U.S. Social Security Administration, Social Security Handbook § 306.1 (last modified Aug. 25, 2016), http://ssa.gov/OP_Home/handbook/handbook.03/handbook-0306.html.

650. Obergefell v. Hodges, 576 U.S. ___, 135 S. Ct. 2584 (2015).

651. *See* Pavan v. Smith, 582 U.S. ___, 137 S. Ct. 2075 (2017) (states must afford same-sex couples the full "constellation of benefits that the States have linked to marriage"); United States v. Windsor, 570 U.S. 744 (2013) (federal tax benefits must be afforded to same-sex couples on the same basis as other couples).

652. *See* U.S. Social Security Administration, Program Operations Manual System, GN 00210.100 Same-Sex Relationships—Spouse's Benefits (Sept. 30, 2016), https://secure.ssa.gov/poms.nsf/lnx/0200210100. For more complete information about access to Social Security benefits for same-sex couples, *see* U.S. Social Security Administration, What Same-Sex Couples Need to Know, Pub. No. 05-10014 (Jan. 2017), https://www.ssa.gov/pubs/EN-05-10014.pdf.

653. 42 U.S.C. § 416(b)–(c). *See* U.S. Social Security Administration, Social Security Handbook § 305 (last modified Sept. 1, 2009), http://ssa.gov/OP_Home/handbook/handbook.03/handbook-0305.html.

654. 42 U.S.C. § 402(b)(1), (c)(1), (d)(1)–(4); 20 C.F.R. § 404.331.

655. 42 U.S.C. § 402(b)(4)(A) & (c)(4)(A); 20 C.F.R. § 404.331. *See* U.S. Social Security Administration, Retirement Benefits, Pub. 05-10035 (Jan. 2019), https://www.ssa.gov/pubs/EN-05-10035.pdf.

656. 20 C.F.R. § 404.401. For a comprehensive Chart on Reduced Benefits, *see* Social Security, Program Operations Manual System, RS 00615.010 (Mar. 29, 2017), https://secure.ssa.gov/poms.NSF/lnx/0300615010.

657. 42 U.S.C. § 403(a).

658. *See* 42 U.S.C. § 403(a)(1). An explanation of the SSA's calculation of family maximums can be found at U.S. Social Security Administration, Understanding the Social Security Family Maximum Benefit, https://www.ssa.gov/policy/docs/ssb/v75n3/v75n3p1.html.

659. *See* 42 U.S.C. § 403(a)(6). The family maximum for benefits paid on the account of a disabled worker is 85% of the worker's Averaged Indexed Monthly Earnings, provided, however, that the maximum is no less than 100% and no more than 150% of the worker's primary insured amount (PIA). *Id. See* U.S. Social Security Administration, Maximum Benefit for a Disabled-Worker Family, http://www.ssa.gov/oact/cola/dibfamilymax.html.

660. U.S. Social Security Administration, Social Security Handbook § 732.1 (last modified Sept. 22, 2003), https://ssa.gov/OP_Home/handbook/handbook.07/handbook-0732.html.

661. 42 U.S.C. § 403(a)(3)(C).

662. *See* 20 C.F.R. § 404.407(e).

663. 20 C.F.R. § 404.407.

664. U.S. Social Security Administration, Social Security Handbook § 734.2 (last modified Sept. 22, 2003), https://ssa.gov/OP_Home/handbook/handbook.07/handbook-0734.html.

665. *See* 20 C.F.R. § 404.408.

666. U.S. Social Security Administration, How Workers' Compensation and Other Disability Payments May Affect Your Benefits, https://www.ssa.gov/pubs/EN-05-10018.pdf.

667. 42 U.S.C. § 415(a)(7)(A)(i), (ii). *See* U.S. Social Security Administration, Windfall Elimination Provision, https://www.ssa.gov/pubs/EN-05-10045.pdf.

668. 42 U.S.C. § 415(a)(7)(i)-(ii). For an explanation and critique of the Windfall Elimination Provision, *see* Francine Lipman & Alan Smith, The Social Security Benefits Formula and the Windfall Elimination Provision: An Equitable Approach to Addressing "Windfall" Benefits, 39 J. Legis. 181 (2013).

669. 20 C.F.R. §§ 404.401(b)(1) & (3); 404.415. "Excess earnings" for these purposes means the individual's earned income, minus an annually calculated exemption, divided by two. 20 C.F.R. §§ 404.430, 430, 434. For updated annual exemption amounts, *see* U.S. Social Security Administration, Exempt Amounts Under the Earnings Test, https://www.ssa.gov/oact/cola/rtea.html. For a fuller explanation of how employment earnings may impact Social Security benefits, *see* U.S. Social Security Administration, How Work Affects Your Benefits, Pub. No. 05-10069 (Jan. 2019), https://www.ssa.gov/pubs/EN-05-10069.pdf.

670. U.S. Social Security Administration, Social Security Handbook, § 1832, http://www.socialsecurity.gov/OP_Home/handbook/handbook.18/handbook-1832.html.

671. 20 C.F.R. § 404.421.

672. 42 U.S.C. § 402(x)(1)(A).

673. 26 U.S.C. § 86.

674. *Id. See* U.S. Social Security Administration, Benefits Planner: Income Taxes And Your Social Security Benefits, https://www.ssa.gov/planners/taxes.html; Social Security, Withholding Income Tax From Your Benefits, https://www.ssa.gov/planners/taxwithold.html (providing access to Form W-4V, Voluntary Withholding Request).

675. § 211 of Pub. L. No. 108-203, 42 U.S.C. § 414, § 423. *See* U.S. Social Security Administration, Program Operations Manual RS 00301.102 Additional Requirements for Alien Workers—Social Security Protection Act of 2004, https://secure.ssa.gov/apps10/poms.nsf/lnx/0300301102.

   For a discussion of the legislative history, *see* Social Security Office of Retirement and Disability Policy, Erik Hansen, A Legislative History of the Social Security Protection Act of 2004, 66 Social Security Bulletin No. 4 (2008), https://www.ssa.gov/policy/docs/ssb/v68n4/v68n4p41.html.

676. 42 U.S.C. § 402(y).

677. For a criticism of this rule, *see* Francine J. Lipman, Bearing Witness to Economic Injustices of Undocumented Immigrant Families: A New Class of "Undeserving" Poor, 7 Nev. L.J. 736, 753 (2007).

678. 42 U.S.C. § 404.460.

679. U.S. Social Security Administration, Social Security Handbook 107, Totalization Agreements, http://www.socialsecurity.gov/OP_Home/handbook/handbook.01/handbook-0107.html.

680. U.S. Social Security Administration, Social Security Handbook 1847, Residence in a Restricted Country, http://www.socialsecurity.gov/OP_Home/handbook/handbook.18/handbook-1847.html. *See* U.S. Social Security Administration, Your Payments While You Are Outside the United States, Pub. 05-10137 (June 2018), https://www.ssa.gov/pubs/EN-05-10137.pdf.

681. 20 C.F.R. § 404.464. *See* U.S. Social Security Administration, Social Security Handbook 1841.2 Are There Any Exceptions to Nonpayment Under the Deportation/removal Provisions? (last revised May 10, 2004), https://www.ssa.gov/OP_Home/handbook/handbook.18/handbook-1841.html.

682. 20 C.F.R. § 404.469.

683. U.S. Social Security Administration, The Appeals Process (2017), https://www.ssa.gov/pubs/EN-05-10041.pdf.

684. U.S. Social Security Administration, Your Right to Representation (June 2017), https://www.ssa.gov/pubs/EN-05-10075.pdf. *See* U.S. Social Security Administration, Program Operations Manual Systems, GN 03910.010 Rules of Conduct and Standards of Responsibility for Representatives (last modified Dec. 7, 2015), https://secure.ssa.gov/poms.nsf/lnx/0203970010. Any individual who is "generally known to have a good character and reputation" and "capable of giving valuable help" may be appointed. 20 C.F.R. § 404.1705(b).

685. U.S. Social Security Administration, Program Operations Manual System, GN 03102.100 Reconsideration (last modified Aug. 29, 2012), https://secure.ssa.gov/poms.nsf/lnx/0203102000.

686. U.S. Social Security Administration, Hearings and Appeals, Time Limits for Appeal, https://www.ssa.gov/appeals/hearing_process.html.

687. U.S. Social Security Administration, Request for Reconsideration—Form SSA-561, https://www.ssa.gov/forms/ssa-561.html.

688. U.S. Social Security Administration, Program Operations Manual System GN 03101.020 Good Cause for Extending the Time Limit to File an Appeal (last modified Oct. 20, 2014), https://secure.ssa.gov/poms.nsf/lnx/0203101020.

689. 20 C.F.R. § 404.913.

690. 20 C.F.R. § 404.922.

691. 20 C.F.R. § 404.929.

692. 20 C.F.R. §§ 404.935(b), 416.1435(b)(2).

693. 20 C.F.R. § 404.953. See U.S. Social Security Administration, Program Operations Manual System, GN 03103.140 Issues Decided by ALJ (last modified Apr. 15, 2011), https://secure.ssa.gov/poms.nsf/lnx/0203103140.

694. 20 C.F.R. §§ 404.950, 404.936(d).

695. 42 U.S.C. § 401(j).

696. 20 C.F.R. § 404.929.

697. 20 C.F.R. § 404.953. See U.S. Social Security Administration, SSA Handbook § 2012 (last modified Nov. 30, 2010), http://www.socialsecurity.gov/OP_Home/handbook/handbook.20/handbook-2012.html.

698. U.S. Social Security Administration, Social Security Administration Handbook § 2008 ALJ Actions (last modified Aug. 8, 2011), https://www.ssa.gov/OP_Home%2Fhandbook/handbook.20/handbook-2008.html.

699. U.S. Social Security Administration, How to File an Unfair Treatment Complaint (Nov. 2015), https://www.ssa.gov/pubs/EN-05-10071.pdf.

700. See 20 C.F.R. § 404.967.

701. 20 C.F.R. § 404.970.

702. 80 Fed. Reg. 14828 (effective Apr. 2015).

703. See 42 U.S.C. § 405(g).

704. U.S. Social Security Administration, Program Operation Manual System GN 03106.005 Court Review (last modified July 18, 2012), https://secure.ssa.gov/poms.nsf/lnx/0203106005.

705. See 20 C.F.R. § 404.923.

706. 20 C.F.R. § 404.924. Even without invoking the expedited appeals process, a claimant may be able to file an action directly in federal court without first going through the administrative appeals process if the claimant is arguing that a regulation, policy, or procedure of the Social Security Administration is illegal or unconstitutional, or that a provision of the Social Security Act violates the U.S. Constitution. See, for example, Mathews v. Eldridge, 424 U.S. 319, 326–332 (1976).

707. 20 C.F.R. § 404.925.

3
Food Assistance

Introduction

Does the federal Constitution guarantee
a right to food or potable water?

The U.S. Supreme Court has never found an enforceable right to food or potable water in the federal Constitution, even for a person who is hungry or thirsty because of a lack of income.[1] Some advocates have argued that food-and-water rights can be grounded in international law.[2] In particular, the United Nations Resolution on the Right to Food encourages nations to take steps to achieve "the full realization of the right to food, including steps to promote the conditions for everyone to be free from hunger and, as soon as possible, to enjoy fully the right to food,"[3] and the United Nations International Covenant on Economic, Social, and Cultural Rights recognizes that a "right to water" is "fundamental" for survival.[4]

Is there a statutory right to food?

Although there so far is no constitutionally recognized guarantee to food assistance in the United States, the United States has established and founded food programs by statute and executive order, authorizing the provision of important benefits to poor and low-income persons.[5] Some of these programs create "entitlements," meaning that every person who applies and meets the eligibility criteria has a legal right to the benefits. The benefits provided, however, are not guaranteed to meet the recipient's nutritional needs. However, the federal Constitution requires that the government administer these programs fairly and not exclude people for arbitrary reasons unrelated to financial need.[6] This chapter describes the most important federal programs, including the Supplemental Nutrition Assistance Program (SNAP) and the Special Supplemental Nutritional Program for Women, Infants, and Children (WIC), focusing on the benefits provided, eligibility, and conditions for participation.

Getting By. Helen Hershkoff and Stephen Loffredo, Oxford University Press (2020). © Helen Hershkoff & Stephen Loffredo.
DOI: 10.1093/oso/9780190080860.001.0001

Supplemental Nutrition Assistance Program
(SNAP, Formerly Known as Food Stamps)

What is the Supplemental Nutrition Assistance Program?

The Supplemental Nutrition Assistance Program (SNAP) is the most important food program currently run by the federal government. Better known as food stamps, SNAP helps low-income people obtain nutritious and adequate diets. Eligibility is based largely on financial need, without regard to age, disability, parenting, or employment. However, SNAP excludes certain categories of poor persons from the program, including some people who are not U.S. citizens; limits how long some persons may receive benefits; and generally imposes "work requirements" as a condition of receiving benefits.[7]

SNAP, which began as a pilot program in 1939, is intended to boost the food-purchasing power of participants. As originally designed, the program sold coupons ("food stamps") to income-eligible households, which recipients could use to buy food in grocery stores, and for every dollar of coupons purchased, the household received a bonus of 50 cents in its purchasing power.[8] Congress stopped the program in 1943.[9] In 1961, President John F. Kennedy issued an executive order reviving the program, again on a pilot basis, spurred to action by having witnessed shocking conditions of hunger while on the campaign trail in West Virginia.[10] Congressional research later confirmed that the pilot program was effective in reducing hunger among participants, but that some families were too poor to buy the coupons and so did not benefit at all. The Food Stamp Act of 1964 established the program on a permanent basis.[11] Later amendments expanded participation in two ways: the program was established nationwide in 1974, and the coupon-purchase requirement was dropped in 1977.[12] These changes resulted in expanded participation, but during the 1980s, Congress cut back on the program, and 1996 legislation barred many noncitizens and persons with certain criminal convictions from participating.[13] In 1998 and 2002, Congress began to lift some of these restrictions, and in 2008 Congress renamed the program SNAP to put the focus on nutrition.[14]

Who administers SNAP?

SNAP is administered at two levels. At the national level, the federal government, through the Food and Nutrition Service of the U.S. Department of Agriculture (USDA), sets national rules and regulations and also gives states discretion to seek waivers or modifications of these rules (called state "options").[15] State and local offices run the program on a day-to-day basis, and the federal government pays the full cost of benefits and shares administrative costs. As a condition of receiving this funding, states must establish and obtain federal approval of a "state plan" addressing programmatic matters such as outreach, applications, interviews, and benefits.

How many people receive SNAP benefits?

In 2017, 38.5 million Americans in 19.4 million households participated in SNAP.[16] This was the lowest level of participation in the program in over six years and is attributable in part to incremental improvements in the U.S. economy and reduced unemployment since the 2008 recession. But declining participation does not necessarily reflect decreased need in all regions and among all population groups.[17] As explained later in this chapter, the government limits the number of months certain "able-bodied" adults may participate, so some households that are financially eligible—and out of work—are nevertheless barred from assistance.[18] Studies report that half of all children in the United States at some point in their lives will live in a household that receives SNAP benefits.[19]

For those households that participate, SNAP has been called "a success story."[20] The program has improved the health, diet, and life chances of those who receive assistance, while also supporting agriculture and generating revenue for local economies.[21] Children who receive SNAP benefits more often complete high school and less often suffer from stunting and anemia.[22] Moreover, SNAP has a wide-ranging positive impact on communities; every dollar of SNAP benefit produces $1.79 in local economic activity.[23] In 2016, SNAP lifted 3.6 million individuals out of poverty and mitigated poverty's impact on millions of others; it has played an essential role in helping millions of low-wage workers avoid hunger.[24] Still, the program could be improved: the method of calculating SNAP benefits is outdated (discussed later in this chapter), and because the level of benefits does not match the actual cost of living in some regions, not all participants have enough money to buy adequate amounts of food to meet nutritional needs.[25] Moreover, about one out of every five eligible individuals receives no SNAP benefits for reasons that range from perceptions of stigma to a complicated application process.[26] Table 3.1 shows the basic demographic characteristics of households receiving SNAP.

What benefits does SNAP provide?

SNAP benefits are designed to increase the food-purchasing power of eligible households. Benefits are provided through an Electronic Benefit Transfer (EBT) card that functions like a debit card and is used to buy food for home

Table 3.1 | 2016 and 2017 SNAP Household Characteristics: Distribution by Race, Gender, and Age[1]

Category	2016	2017
Female [*]	56.7%	57.2%
Male [*]	43.3%	42.8%
Children	42.9%	41.7%
Non-elderly	78.2%	75.9%
Elderly	21.8%	24.1%
White, not Hispanic [*]	31.7%	38.6%
African American [*]	24.2%	24.8%
Hispanic [*]	11.9%	11.5%
Asian, not Hispanic [*]	2.5%	2.9%
Native American, not Hispanic [*]	1.3%	1.2%

[*] Distribution by head of household characteristic

[1] U.S. Department of Agriculture, Food and Nutrition Service, Characteristics of Supplemental Nutrition Assistance Program Households: Fiscal Year 2016 (Nov. 2017), https://fns-prod.azureedge. net/sites/default/files/ops/Characteristics2016.pdf; U.S. Department of Agriculture, Supplemental Nutrition Assistance Program, Characteristics of Supplemental Nutrition Assistance Program Households: Fiscal Year 2017, Table A-1; A-21; A-23 (Feb. 2019), https://www.fns.usda.gov/snap/ characteristics-supplemental-nutrition-assistance-program-households-fiscal-year-2017.

consumption.[27] (SNAP no longer uses paper "food stamps.") Participants do not pay for the EBT card,[28] and a participating household must be allowed to select a personal identification number (PIN) for the card.[29] The card can be used at any approved retailer, including grocery stores, corner stores, farmers' markets, and other food outlets. In addition, the USDA is testing use of SNAP benefits for purchases online and may expand authorized retailers beyond brick-and-mortar stores.[30] A household also can use SNAP to buy other authorized goods, such as seeds and plants that produce food for home consumption.[31] In Alaska, participants who live too far from stores selling food can use SNAP benefits to purchase equipment (for example, nets, hooks, rods, harpoons, and knives, but not firearms or explosives) to fish and hunt for food for home consumption. SNAP benefits cannot be used to buy alcohol, tobacco, medicines, vitamins, soap, paper products, diapers, pet food, grooming items, or cosmetics.[32]

A SNAP participant is not required to spend the entire amount on the EBT card in a single purchase or in a single month. The participant spends just what is needed for the purchase being made. The remainder of the benefit—called the "allotment"—rolls over from one month to another. Unused benefits remain in the household's EBT account for one year, but if an account is inactive for three months, the state agency may "store" the benefits offline, making them inaccessible through the EBT card. Before taking that step, however, the agency must first make affirmative efforts to contact the recipient.[33] Benefits must be restored if the participant contacts the SNAP office or reapplies. Benefits not used for one year are removed from the account.[34]

Can SNAP benefits be used to buy prepared foods?

SNAP benefits generally cannot be used to buy prepared meals. The statute defines prepared meals as "hot foods or hot food products ready for immediate consumption."[35] This means SNAP benefits generally cannot be used to purchase hot prepared foods from grocers or to buy meals from fast-food outlets, diners, or restaurants. However, there are exceptions to this rule.

Participants who can use SNAP benefits to buy prepared meals at authorized centers include:

- Individuals age 60 or older or who receive SSI benefits because they are disabled or blind (and their spouses) can buy prepared meals served and eaten at senior citizens' centers, at apartment buildings occupied primarily by seniors or the disabled, at public or private nonprofit centers that feed seniors or the disabled, or at federally subsidized housing for seniors;[36]
- Individuals who are receiving treatment at a drug treatment or rehabilitation center and eating meals there;[37]
- Individuals who are homeless and are eating meals at a certified shelter;[38]
- Women and children temporarily living in a public or private nonprofit shelter and eating their meals there;[39] and
- Disabled or blind persons residing in authorized group living settings.[40]

In addition, SNAP has long allowed states to operate a SNAP "Restaurant Meals Program," which allows SNAP participants who are elderly, have disabilities, or are homeless to purchase meals at approved outlets.[41] There also is a pilot program designed to allow government agencies and nonprofits to accept SNAP as payment for meal deliveries.[42] Finally, in times of disasters, the federal government may grant waivers to states to allow SNAP retailers to redeem SNAP benefits for hot prepared foods.[43]

Can SNAP participants spend their benefits at any food retailer?

No, but about 260,000 grocery stores currently participate in the program, and "larger stores" redeem about 80 percent of all SNAP benefits.[44] A growing number of farmers' markets (over 7,000 in 2017) also accept SNAP.[45] Frequently, a food retailer that participates in the program will post a sign that says, "We accept food stamps or EBT cards"; the retailer also must display information about how to report program abuse.[46] Stores can accept purchases with SNAP benefits only if they have been approved by the federal government, which ensures that they stock a variety of staple foods.[47] Authorized stores are expected to treat SNAP participants fairly and politely. SNAP participants cannot be made to wait in a separate line to buy groceries, pay higher than the regular price, or be treated differently than other customers.[48] The store cannot charge sales tax on food bought with an EBT card, and SNAP participants cannot be required to pay "bag" fees.[49]

Will receiving SNAP benefits reduce a household's grant under other government programs or increase the amount of taxes to be paid?

No. SNAP benefits may not be counted as income or as a resource under any federal, state, or local law or program. Therefore, receipt of SNAP benefits will not reduce the amount of assistance that an eligible household receives, say, for SSI or TANF. SNAP benefits also do not count as income for tax purposes and do not increase a household's taxable income.[50]

What is a SNAP household?

SNAP applications are filed by a "household," a functional group made up of individuals who live together, buy food together, and prepare meals together.[51] Federal rules govern who must be included in a household and who may not be included. Individuals who live together may choose to form a single SNAP household even if they are not members of the same family or legally related.[52] Conversely, family members residing together generally must be part of the same SNAP household, with some exceptions noted below. These rules are important because the composition of the household affects eligibility, benefit levels, and any sanctions that might be imposed if a household member does not comply with program rules. It is usually more advantageous for people residing together to apply as separate SNAP households if the law permits it. SNAP benefits increase with household size, but the calculation of benefit amounts assumes economies of scale. For example, the SNAP allotment for a household of two is about 1.8 times the allotment for a household of one, so two separate SNAP households with one member each will generally receive higher total benefits than a single household with two members. Also, an individual will not be cut off from SNAP if a member of a separate household fails to meet program requirements or begins to earn too much money to qualify for assistance. By contrast, if a member of a household is disqualified from receiving benefits, the income of the disqualified member continues to be counted against the household members who remain eligible, reducing their SNAP benefits.

How is household membership determined?

Three questions help decide who must be included in a SNAP household:

1. Do you live together?
   - If the answer is no, the person is not a part of your household.
   - If the answer is yes, ask the next question.
2. Do you live with your spouse, your child who is under age 22, or a child under the age of 18 who is under your control?
   - If the answer is yes, these individuals are a part of your household whether or not you purchase food and prepare meals together.[53]
   - If the answer is no, ask the next question.
3. Do you customarily purchase and prepare food together?
   - If the answer is no, the person is not a part of your household, (except, as noted earlier, if the person is your spouse, your child under age 22, or a child under age 18 who is under your control.)
   - If the answer is yes, the person is a part of your household unless you are at least 60 years old and are unable to purchase and prepare meals independently because of a disability; in that case, you and your spouse may apply for SNAP as a household separate from the other people with whom you live, unless their income exceeds 165 percent of the federal poverty level.[54]

As the answers to these questions indicate, some people who live together are treated as one household whether or not they purchase food and prepare meals together. These people include:

- Spouses;[55]
- Parents and their children under age 22;[56] and
- Children (other than a foster child) under age 18 who live with and are under the parental control of a person other than their parent.[57]

What is the "head of a household"?

The head of the household is the adult member chosen by the other household members to complete the SNAP application, to attend interviews, to select the household's PIN, to make purchases, and to recertify benefits.[58]

What is an authorized representative?

An authorized representative is a person who has permission to apply for SNAP benefits on behalf of a household.[59] The authorized representative can attend interviews for the household, pick up the EBT card, and even purchase groceries for the household. An authorized representative can be a friend, a relative, or a government worker. A household member can designate an authorized representative on the application for SNAP, or later by making the request in writing to the SNAP office.[60]

Must a household have a fixed address to participate in SNAP?

No. An applicant must reside in the state in which benefits are sought, but cannot be denied benefits because of homelessness, the lack of a fixed mailing address, or lack of access to a kitchen or a place to store food.[61] (However, as described in the answer to the next question, certain living arrangements will bar an applicant from SNAP.) Eligibility does not depend on how long the household has lived in the state, but being on vacation in a state does not count as residence.[62]

Can a boarder participate in SNAP?

A boarder is a person who rents a room in a private house and pays the landlord for meals served at the house (federal law defines a boarding house as an establishment that offers "meals and lodging for compensation"). A boarder cannot participate in SNAP as a single-member household or as a household made up of the other boarders in the house.[63] If the provider of the meals and lodging applies to SNAP and asks the boarder to be a part of its household, then the boarder may do so, along with any spouse and children also residing in the boarding house.[64] In addition, if the boarder pays less than "reasonable compensation" for board, then the boarder must be considered a part of the provider's SNAP household.[65] An individual who simply rents a room in a house but does not buy meals is a "roomer" and may participate in SNAP, presumably as a single-member household.[66]

Does a household include children in foster care?

Children receiving foster care and living in the home of relatives or other approved individuals are considered boarders and cannot participate in SNAP independently of the household providing the services.[67]

Can a household include a person who lives in a shelter, group home, or some other institutional setting?

It depends. A person who lives in an institution that provides more than half of the day's meals is ineligible for SNAP.[68] However, certain congregate settings are not considered institutions, and residents may participate in SNAP as single-member households even if meals are provided. These residences include:

- Federally subsidized public housing for seniors;[69]
- A drug or alcohol treatment center;[70]
- A licensed group-living arrangement if the individual is disabled or blind;[71]
- A shelter for battered women or children;[72] and
- A shelter for people who are homeless.[73]

Is participation in SNAP limited to U.S. citizens?

SNAP is not limited to U.S. citizens, but only certain categories of immigrants qualify for benefits. People in the United States unlawfully, visitors, tourists, diplomats, students who reside in the United States temporarily, and individuals with "U visas" are all categorically ineligible for SNAP.[74] Other noncitizens may be eligible if they meet specific immigration classifications and other conditions described below. Conditions related to immigration status have changed over time.

The 1964 Food Stamp Act provided benefits to almost all otherwise eligible immigrants residing lawfully in the United States. Congress altered that policy in 1996 through the adoption of the Personal Responsibility and Work Opportunity Reconciliation Act (sometimes referred to as federal welfare reform), which sharply narrowed the eligibility of persons who are not U.S. citizens.[75] Thus, although noncitizens as a group are poorer than citizens, they accounted for a disproportionately smaller share of SNAP recipients (4.5 percent) in 2016,[76] and participation by eligible immigrant families declined to an even lower level following the presidential election of that year.[77] Then, in August 2019, the Trump administration published a controversial new rule that requires consideration of

SNAP receipt in determining whether certain immigrants are "likely to become a public charge," a determination that could affect admissibility into the United States and disqualify an immigrant from obtaining lawful permanent resident (green card) status.[78] The new rule alters long-standing law, under which receipt of noncash public benefits, such as SNAP or Medicaid, had no bearing on "public charge" status. It is important to note the limitations on this rule, as misinformation about "public charge" had already deterred many eligible immigrants—and their U.S. citizen family members—from accessing nutritional assistance, even before the new rule was published. First, receipt of SNAP still has no effect on whether an immigrant may be considered deportable. Second, the new public charge rule does not apply to lawful permanent residents while in the United States, or when re-entering the United States after an absence of 180 days or less. Third, the public charge rule does not apply to immigrants in the "humanitarian" categories (e.g., refugees, asylees, certain survivors of trafficking and domestic violence, or VAWA self-petitioners), or to immigrants in the U.S. armed forces (or their family members). Fourth, receipt of nutritional assistance through other programs, such as WIC or school meals, has no impact on the public charge determination.[79] There are other exceptions as well, and the new rule is complex and subject to interpretation, so it is advisable to consult immigrants' rights groups, including the National Immigration Law Center (nilc.org) and the Immigrant Legal Resource Center (ilrc.org), for the most recent developments. The new rule is scheduled to become effective on October 15, 2019, but lawsuits have been filed to stop it.

Which noncitizens are eligible for SNAP?

Some noncitizens who are lawfully in the United States and otherwise eligible for SNAP can qualify for benefits as soon as they apply. Other noncitizens can qualify for SNAP only after a five-year waiting period; in other words, they must reside in the United States in lawful status for five years before becoming eligible.
  Immigrants who can qualify for SNAP immediately include:[80]

- Lawful permanent residents ("green card" holders) who are (1) under 18 years of age; or (2) disabled; or (3) have earned, or can be credited with, 40 quarters of qualifying employment in the United States;[81] or (4) have a military connection (veteran, active duty service, or spouse or child of either);[82] or (5) were born on or before August 22, 1931, and were lawfully residing in the United States on August 22, 1996;[83]
- Persons granted asylum under Section 208 of the Immigration and Nationality Act;[84]

- Refugees admitted to the United States under Section 207 of the Immigration and Nationality Act;[85]
- Persons whose deportation or removal is being withheld under Section 243(h) or Section 241(b)(3) of the Immigration and Nationality Act;[86]
- Cuban or Haitian entrants as defined in Section 501(e) of the Refugee Education Assistance Act of 1980;[87]
- Iraqi and Afghan Special Immigrants as defined in Section 101(a)(27) of the Immigration and Nationality Act;[88]
- American Indians born in Canada, living in the United States under Section 289 of the Immigration and Nationality Act;[89]
- Members of a federally recognized tribe under Section 4(e) of the Indian Self-Determination and Education Assistance Act;[90]
- Persons lawfully residing in the United States and a member of a Hmong or Highland Laotian tribe that gave assistance to the United States during the Vietnam era (August 5, 1964 through May 7, 1975), or the member's spouse or unmarried dependent children;[91] and
- Victims of severe trafficking under the Trafficking Victims Protection Act of 2000, and certain family members.[92]

Immigrants who must be in lawful status in the United States for five years before they can qualify for SNAP include:[93]

- Legal permanent residents ("green card" holders) age 18 or older who do not meet one of the conditions described above;[94]
- Persons granted conditional entry under Section 203(a)(7) of the Immigration and Nationality Act as in effect before April 1, 1980;[95]
- Persons paroled into the United States under Section 212(d)(5) of the Immigration and Nationality Act for at least one year;[96] and
- Persons considered to be a battered spouse or child, a noncitizen parent of a battered child, or a noncitizen child of a battered parent.[97]

Can states provide SNAP benefits to noncitizens who are legally in the United States but ineligible under federal law?

Yes. In 1997, Congress authorized states, at their own expense, to provide SNAP (then known as food stamps) to immigrants lawfully in the country but barred from assistance under the 1996 Personal Responsibility and Work Opportunity Act.[98] This option declined in importance as later legislation eased the immigrant eligibility rules for SNAP.[99] Nevertheless, a small number of states have maintained state-funded SNAP alternatives for certain immigrants who do not qualify under federal law.[100]

Can persons convicted of a crime receive SNAP benefits?

Having a criminal record can affect eligibility for SNAP. Persons convicted of a crime and currently serving a sentence in prison,[101] or fleeing to avoid prosecution or to avoid custody or confinement after conviction, or violating a condition of probation or parole,[102] may not participate in SNAP. Persons convicted of murder, aggravated sexual abuse, or the kidnap, killing, or assault of certain federal officials are under a lifetime ban and cannot participate in SNAP.[103] Since 1996, persons convicted of a felony drug crime are under a lifetime ban, but states may enact statutory waivers to lift the restriction, and some have done so.[104] Arizona, Guam, Mississippi, South Carolina, the Virgin Islands, and West Virginia have not lifted the ban; 26 other states have modified but not lifted the disqualification.[105]

Are SNAP participants subject to drug testing?

Drug testing is not a condition of SNAP eligibility, and any across-the-board testing requirement would be unconstitutional.[106] Some of the states with federal waivers allowing them to provide SNAP to persons convicted of drug felonies condition eligibility for those persons on drug testing.[107]

Does failure to pay court-ordered child support affect SNAP eligibility?

States are permitted to terminate or deny SNAP to noncustodial parents who have not paid their child-support obligations.[108] Relatedly, states are permitted to require parents—both custodial and noncustodial—to cooperate in securing child support for a child and to terminate or deny benefits to a parent who does not cooperate.[109]

Can students receive SNAP benefits?

It depends. A student who is enrolled at least half-time in "an institution of higher education"—defined as a college or university, or a business, technical, trade, or vocational school that usually requires a high school diploma or its equivalent—cannot participate in SNAP, unless the student meets at least *one* of the following conditions (note especially that a student can acquire eligibility for SNAP by obtaining a work-study position):[110]

- The student is under age 18 or over age 49;[111]
- The student is "physically or mentally unfit";[112]
- The student is receiving benefits under the Temporary Assistance for Needy Families program;[113]
- The student is enrolled in SNAP as part of a Job Opportunities and Basic Skills program;[114]
- The student is employed for at least 20 hours per week and is paid for such employment or, if self-employed, is working a minimum of 20 hours per week and receiving weekly earnings at least equal to the federal minimum wage multiplied by 20 hours;[115]
- The student is participating in a state or federally financed work-study program during the regular school year and was approved for work-study at the time of applying for SNAP (SNAP eligibility continues until the end of the month in which the school term ends but does not continue between terms if the break is a full month or longer unless the student participates in work-study or employment during that time);[116]
- The student is participating in an on-the-job training program conducted by the employer;[117]
- The student is responsible for the care of a dependent household member under age six;[118] or the student is responsible for the care of a dependent household member who is older than age six but younger than age 12 and the state agency has determined that adequate child care is not available to enable the student to attend class and comply with SNAP's work requirements;[119]
- The student is a single parent enrolled in an institution of higher education on a full-time basis;[120] or
- The student is assigned to or placed in an institution of higher education through specified job-training programs.[121]

Does SNAP require a Social Security number to participate?

Yes. All members of a household must provide a Social Security number to be eligible for SNAP benefits. The state agency is required to inform the applicant that a refusal or failure to provide a Social Security number without good cause is grounds for disqualification. If the applicant does not have a Social Security number, the state must explain where to apply for one and what information will be needed to get a number.[122]

Who is financially eligible to receive SNAP benefits?

SNAP provides benefits only to those households "whose incomes are determined to be a substantial limiting factor in permitting them to obtain a more nutritious diet."[123] A household can show its financial eligibility for SNAP in one of two ways: "traditional eligibility" or "categorical (automatic) eligibility."

Traditional eligibility. The household must meet a gross income test (generally 130 percent of the federal poverty level (FPL), a net income test (generally 100 percent of FPL), and an assets test, all described below. Households with an elderly (age 60 or over) or disabled member are excused from the gross income test and have a higher asset limit.

Categorical eligibility. A household composed entirely of members who receive or qualify for cash assistance from Supplemental Security Income (SSI), a TANF-funded program, or a state general assistance program is automatically eligible for SNAP without meeting any additional asset or income test. However, since income is always considered in determining benefit amount, a household that is categorically eligible may receive only a very small benefit amount or even none at all. At state option, categorical eligibility may be extended to households that receive TANF-funded (or TANF maintenance of efforts funded) noncash services—such as child care or counseling.[124] This option is known as broad-based categorical eligibility (BBCE) and as of October 2018 42 states and the District of Columbia had elected to adopt the practice.[125] The use of BBCE streamlines a state's administrative process and indirectly encourages work, asset formation, and reduced food insecurity among affected households that do not need to meet SNAP's gross income or asset-cap tests at the eligibility stage.[126]

What are the income limits for SNAP benefits?

Households that are not "categorically eligible" and do not have an elderly or disabled member must meet two income tests to qualify for SNAP: the gross income test and the net income test. Households that are not "categorically eligible" but do have an elderly or disabled member are excused from the gross income test, but must still meet the net income test.[127]

"Gross income" includes most income to any member of the household, before deduction of taxes, union dues, or other work expenses.[128] A household subject to the gross income test generally does not qualify for SNAP if its gross income exceeds

130 percent of the federal poverty level. (In FY 2019, the cap was $1,316/month for a one-person household and $2,720/month for a four-person household.)[129]

"Net income" is the household's gross income minus deductions that the SNAP program allows for certain employment and living expenses.[130] To qualify for SNAP, a household's net income may not exceed 100 percent of the federal poverty level (in FY 2019, the net income cap was $1,021/month for a one-person household and $2,092/month for a four-person household).[131]

What counts as gross income?

Gross income is defined as "all income from whatever source,"[132] including earned income and "unearned" income (i.e., benefit payments); gross income does not include the value of in-kind donations to the household (such as clothes or furniture),[133] or any income "excluded" by the statute.[134]

Earned income includes:

- All wages and salaries of an employee;[135]
- Gross income from self-employment, including all of the gain from the sale of any capital goods or equipment related to the business, excluding the costs of doing business, as described later in this chapter;[136]
- Payments from boarders (except if the boarder is a child receiving foster care);[137]
- Training allowances (unless they are reimbursements) from vocational and rehabilitative programs, except if paid under the Job Training Partnership Act;[138]
- Payments from on-the-job training programs under the Workforce Investment Act, except if the money is paid to a household member under age 19 who is under the parental control of a household member;[139] and
- Certain educational assistance with a work requirement (such as an assistantship) unless used for educational expenses or dependent care.[140]

Unearned income includes:

- Assistance payments from federal or federally aided public assistance programs, such as Supplemental Security Income or Temporary Assistance for Needy Families; from general assistance programs; or from other assistance programs based on need. Payments count even if made to a third party, such as a landlord, on behalf of the household, subject to exclusions described later in this chapter. In addition, money withheld from a public assistance payment as a sanction for failure to comply with program requirements comparable to SNAP program requirements may be counted as income, even though not actually received by the household.[141]

- Annuities; pensions; retirement, veteran's or disability benefits; workers' or unemployment compensation; old-age, survivors, or Social Security benefits; strike benefits; and foster care payments for children or adults who are considered members of the household;[142]
- Support or alimony payments made directly to the household from nonhousehold members;[143]
- Payments from government-sponsored programs, dividends, interest, royalties, and all other direct money payments from any source "which can be construed to be a gain or benefit";[144] and
- Monies which are withdrawn or dividends which are or could be received by a household from trust funds considered to be excludable resources as discussed later in this chapter.[145]

Gross income does not include:

- Money withheld from an assistance payment or other income source to repay a prior overpayment from that same source (unless the overpayment was excluded from income when the household received it);[146] and
- Child-support payments received by TANF recipients that are transferred to the state agency to maintain TANF eligibility.[147]

Moreover, federal law excludes 19 categories of income from gross income:[148]

1. Benefits not in the form of money directly payable to the household (for example, in-kind benefits and certain kinds of "vendor payments," described in the answer to the next question);[149]
2. Income received too infrequently or irregularly to be reasonably anticipated, so long as it does not exceed $30 a quarter;[150]
3. Educational assistance, including grants, scholarships, fellowships, work-study, educational loans on which payment is deferred, veterans' educational benefits, and the like, if the household member is enrolled in a recognized institution of higher learning, or a vocational educational program, or a program to complete a high school diploma, but only to the extent that the educational assistance does not exceed the amount determined by the institution to be necessary for educational expenses, including, but not limited to tuition, fees, books, computers, origination fees, insurance premiums, and dependent care;[151]
4. All other loans on which repayment is deferred;[152]
5. Reimbursements that do not exceed expenses incurred (for example, reimbursement given to migrant farmworkers for the cost of travel);[153]

6. Moneys received or paid for care and maintenance of a third party, including a child, who is not a member of the household;[154]

7. Income earned by a household member who is age 17 or younger and attends elementary or secondary school;[155]

8. Money received as a nonrecurring lump-sum payment (for example, tax refunds, lump-sum insurance settlements, retroactive SSI payments, etc.); these sums count as resources in the month received, unless another federal law prohibits such treatment;[156]

9. The cost of producing self-employed income;[157]

10. Income specifically excluded by another federal statute for the purpose of determining SNAP eligibility;[158]

11. Payments and allowances made under federal or state law for energy assistance;[159]

12. Cost-of-living adjustments made after a certain date under the Social Security Act and other specified federal programs;[160]

13. Earned income tax credits under Section 3507 the Internal Revenue Code;[161]

14. Payments made under specified pilot programs for work-related and dependent-care expenses;[162]

15. Amounts needed to achieve a plan for self-support under the Social Security Act;[163]

16. At state option, educational loans not already excluded if exclusion is allowed under Title XIX of the Social Security Act;[164]

17. At state option, assistance payments excluded for the purpose of determining eligibility for medical assistance under Section 1931 of the Social Security Act;[165]

18. At state option, any types of income excluded for the purpose of determining eligibility under specified assistance programs;[166] and

19. Payments received by or from a servicemember deployed in a combat zone.[167]

Which vendor payments are excluded from gross income?

Vendor payments are payments made on behalf of a household to a third party. The following vendor payments are excluded from gross income:

– Public assistance (PA) vendor payments for medical assistance, child care assistance, or specified energy assistance; housing assistance made through a state or local housing authority; emergency and special assistance that is "over and beyond the normal PA grant or payment" or "cannot normally be provided as part" of that grant or payment; and emergency assistance to migrant or seasonal farmworker households while "in the job stream."[168]

- General assistance payments or reimbursements to a third party if made for housing assistance from a state or local housing authority; emergency or special payments (on the same terms as PA third-party payments); emergency assistance for migrant or seasonal farmworker households while "in the job stream"; and assistance in a state in which general assistance cash payments may not be made directly to the household.[169]
- Rent or mortgage payments or reimbursements to landlords or mortgagees by the federal Department of Housing and Urban Development;[170]
- Educational assistance provided to a third party;[171]
- Vendor payments that are reimbursements;[172]
- Vendor payments made under federally authorized demonstration projects;[173] and
- Other third-party payments from funds that are not owed to the household (for example, if a friend gratuitously uses personal funds to pay the household's rent, the vendor payment is excluded from income; by contrast if a portion of court-ordered monthly support is diverted to a creditor, the third-party payment is included as income).[174]

What is net income?

Net income is the household's gross income minus deductions that are permitted by law to account for household expenses. Generally, SNAP allows the following deductions in calculating a household's net income:

- *Earned Income Deduction*. Twenty percent of gross earned income (not counting earnings excluded, other than income used to pay child support).[175]
- *Standard Deduction*. A standard deduction based on household size as set out in Table 3.2.[176]

Table 3.2 SNAP: Standard Deduction as of October 1, 2018, through September 30, 2019

Region	1–3 members	4 members	5 members	6 or more members
48 contiguous states and District of Columbia	$164	$174	$204	$234
Alaska	$281	$281	$281	$292
Hawaii	$232	$232	$234	$269
Guam	$331	$348	$408	$467

- *Medical Deduction.* Medical expenses not paid by someone else that exceed $35/month incurred by a household member who is elderly or disabled, including recipients who receive emergency SSI based on presumptive eligibility.[177] Allowable medical expenses are:
  - Medical and dental care, including psychotherapy and rehabilitation services provided by a licensed practitioner;
  - Hospitalization or outpatient treatment, nursing care, and nursing home care payments by the household for an individual who was a household member immediately prior to entering a hospital or nursing home;
  - Prescription drugs when prescribed by a licensed practitioner and other over-the-counter medication (including insulin) when approved by a qualified health professional;
  - Costs of medical supplies, sick-room equipment, or other prescribed equipment;
  - Health and hospitalization insurance policy premiums;
  - Medicare premiums related to coverage under Title XVIII of the Social Security Act and Medicaid cost-sharing expenses;
  - Dentures, hearing aids, and prosthetics;
  - Securing and maintaining a Seeing Eye or hearing dog, including the cost of dog food and veterinarian bills;
  - Reasonable cost of transportation and lodging to obtain medical treatment; and
  - Employing an attendant, homemaker, home health aide, or child care services, necessary due to age, infirmity, or illness. In addition, an amount equal to the SNAP allotment for one person shall be deducted if the household furnishes the majority of the attendant's meals.[178]

INFORMATION BOX: STANDARD MEDICAL DEDUCTION DEMONSTRATION PROJECT

Twenty-one states have implemented standard medical deduction demonstration projects, under which a standard deduction representing the average medical expenses for senior or disabled SNAP households is automatically deducted from the net income of an eligible household that can show medical expenses of over $35 a month.[179] Under the demonstration program, households that previously claimed medical deductions below the standard deduction would see their deductions rise to the standard deduction. Households with medical expenses greater than the standard deduction may continue to claim actual expenses instead of the standard medical deduction, but to claim the actual deduction, the household must show that its medical expenses exceeded the standard deduction plus the $35 threshold.[180]

- *Dependent Care Deduction.* A household is entitled to deduct the actual cost of dependent care if the care enables a household member to accept or to continue employment or training or education that is in preparation for employment. The costs of care provided by a relative may be deducted if the relative providing the care is not part of the same SNAP household as the child or dependent receiving the care.[181]
- *Child Support Deduction.* A state may choose to treat legally obligated child-support payments made by a household member to a nonhousehold member as an exclusion; otherwise such payments count as a deduction.[182]
- *Shelter Deduction.* A deduction for housing costs (including rent, mortgage, condo and association fees, property taxes, utilities, and repairs resulting from damage to the home due to a natural disaster) that exceed 50 percent of the household's income after all deductions have been subtracted from gross income.[183] As of October 1, 2018, and through September 30, 2019, the shelter deduction was capped at $525 for the 48 contiguous states.[184] This cap does not apply to households that include a senior or disabled member.[185] States may use a standard amount for utility expenses (known as the "standard utility allowance") in calculating the shelter deduction, or else may allow households to claim actual documented utility expenses.[186]
- *Homeless Deduction.* States may elect to provide a deduction (capped at $147.55/month in FY 2019) for households in which all members are homeless and do not receive free shelter during the month.[187]

Are there special income rules for noncitizens?

A special rule may apply for determining the income of certain "sponsored" immigrants. A sponsored immigrant is a noncitizen for whom another person (the "sponsor") signed an affidavit agreeing to provide financial support to maintain the immigrant at a level above 125 percent of the federal poverty level.[188] (Such affidavits are sometimes required as part of an application for an immigrant visa.) If a sponsored immigrant applies for SNAP in a household separate from the sponsor's household, a portion of the sponsor's income is counted as income of the immigrant for purposes of determining SNAP eligibility and benefit amount. This is known as the "sponsor deeming rule." The rule applies until the immigrant becomes a citizen, or the immigrant has accumulated (or can be credited with) 40 qualifying quarters of employment in the United States, or the sponsor dies.[189] The deemed amount is equal to the sponsor's gross income reduced by (1) 20 percent of the sponsor's earned income;[190] and (2) an amount equal to SNAP's monthly gross income eligibility limit for a household that includes the sponsor plus the sponsor's spouse, and any person who could be claimed as a dependent by the sponsor for federal income tax purposes.[191] If the sponsor is sponsoring other persons, then the amount of the sponsor's income deemed to the immigrant is subject to proportionate reductions.[192]

Sponsor deeming does not apply to children under age 18.[193] If sponsored adult immigrants live in a household with their minor children (whether the children are U.S. citizens or immigrants), only a pro rata portion of the sponsor's deemed income will count as income to the household. For instance, in a household with two sponsored immigrant parents and two children under age 18, only one-half of the deemed income (the parents' share) will count as income to the household.

In addition, sponsor deeming does not apply to immigrants sponsored by an organization,[194] to certain survivors of domestic violence and their family members,[195] or to immigrants determined to be indigent, meaning that the immigrant's income plus any income contributed by the sponsor is insufficient to obtain adequate food and shelter.[196]

Can a household own assets—such as a home, bank accounts, cars, or other resources—and still receive SNAP benefits?

Yes, households that own assets may still qualify for SNAP benefits. First, there is no assets test at all for "categorically eligible" households; that is, households whose members all qualify for SSI, TANF-funded cash assistance, or a state general assistance program. In addition, as described earlier, there is no assets test for most low-income families in states that have adopted the "broad based categorical eligibility" (BBCE) option.[197] In July 2019, the Trump administration proposed to eliminate the BBCE option, a move that, if ultimately implemented, would terminate food assistance to over three million people, mostly working families with children, seniors, and people with disabilities.[198]

The assets test, when it applies, sets a resource limit of $2,250 per household, or $3,500 if the household includes a person age 60 or older.[199] Resources are "liquid and nonliquid assets" and generally include cash on hand or in the bank, stocks, bonds, money from insurance settlements, rebates, and inheritances.[200]

Not all of a household's assets count as resources for SNAP eligibility.[201] Here are some of the assets a household can own that do not count as resources:

- The household's home and surrounding property, or, a plot of land on which a household intends to build a home.[202]

– Personal and household goods, such as clothes, furniture, and appliances.[203]
– Burial plots.[204]
– Licensed vehicles: States may not count vehicles that are (1) used to produce earned income;[205] (2) needed to transport a physically disabled household member;[206] (3) needed for long-distance travel other than a daily commute or to carry water or heating fuel for home use;[207] or (4) have an equity value (fair market value minus debt owed for the vehicle) of less than $1,500.[208] Otherwise, the amount by which a vehicle's fair market value exceeds $4,650 may be counted as a resource, but all states have adopted more generous rules. Currently 39 states exclude the entire value of all vehicles, and 11 others exclude the entire value of at least one vehicle per household.[209]
– Other resources excluded by federal law for SNAP eligibility.[210]
– Earned income tax credits for one year after receipt if the household was participating in SNAP at the time of receipt and participates continuously during that 12-month period other than breaks of participation of one month or less due to administrative reasons.[211]

How much assistance does SNAP provide?

SNAP benefits levels are calculated with reference to the "Thrifty Food Plan" (TFP), a measure initially developed during the Great Depression for how much money households of different sizes needed to prepare meals at minimal cost.[212] A large body of research has established that the TFP is a deeply flawed and inadequate metric that leaves many families without sufficient means to purchase food throughout the month.[213] In fiscal year 2018, the average monthly SNAP benefit per person was about $136, the equivalent of $1.40 per person per meal.[214] The minimum monthly benefit to which all eligible households are entitled was $15.[215] Benefit levels largely depend on household income and size. Effective October 2018, maximum SNAP allotments for households residing in the contiguous 48 states and the District of Columbia were as listed in Table 3.3.[216]

Benefit levels are higher in Hawaii, Alaska, Guam, and the Virgin Islands.[217]

What's the process for applying to SNAP?

A household seeking SNAP benefits must submit an application form.

Every state has its own application form, but the forms generally elicit certain standard information, and must inform the applicant that information will be verified and that violating SNAP rules may result in criminal penalties.[218]

Table 3.3 SNAP: Maximum Allotments by Household Size, FY 2019

Household Size	48 Contiguous States and the District of Columbia
1	$192
2	$353
3	$505
4	$642
5	$762
6	$914
7	$1,011
8	$1,155
Each additional person	+ $144

Most states make the application form available at one of the many local SNAP or public assistance offices.[219] Applications also often can be gotten at local legal services and legal aid offices, community organizations, shelters, and soup kitchens. Some states make the application forms available online. The U.S. Department of Agriculture website provides links to online applications in states in which they are available: http://www.fns.usda.gov/snap/apply. Many states also have a toll-free hotline, which is a telephone number that can be called without charge to get information about SNAP and to ask that an application be mailed to the household.

A state agency is required under federal law to encourage a household to apply for benefits the same day that the household contacts the agency (for example, to obtain an application form or for information about the program).[220] States also must provide timely and accurate information about the application process, and must ensure that households with special needs, including the elderly, disabled, homeless, limited English proficiency, and working, are served by the program.[221] It is important to submit the application at the earliest possible date because once a household has been found eligible, benefits will be given for the month in which the application was submitted.[222] States can speed up the applications process and provide "expedited service" if a household faces an immediate need (discussed later in this chapter). A household may file an incomplete application—and eventually get benefits for the month in which it was submitted—as long as the application contains at least the applicant's name and address and is signed by a member of the household.[223] A final determination of eligibility requires a completed and signed application form; the household or its authorized representative must be interviewed; and certain information on the application must be verified.[224]

Is an applicant's information kept confidential?

Information provided in a SNAP application can be disclosed only to persons involved with administration of the program or of related programs.[225] For example, state agencies processing SNAP applications may contact federal immigration authorities to verify applicants' immigration status, since that factor is relevant to SNAP eligibility. However, if a noncitizen does not want the state agency to make this contact, the agency "must give the household the option of withdrawing its application or participating [in SNAP] without that member."[226]

What is an application interview?

An application interview is a meeting between the head of the household applying for benefits (or the household's authorized representative) and a state agency employee. The interview takes place after the application has been submitted and before eligibility is determined.[227] At the interview, the agency employee will ask questions about living arrangements, income and resources, and the need to fulfill work requirements. Interviews may be conducted in person or over the phone. Persons can request a telephone interview if an in-person interview would be a hardship. Hardship includes illness, transportation difficulties, care of a household member, prolonged severe weather, or work or training hours.[228] An interview can be scheduled as early as the day the household submits the application. The state agency can ask the applicant to come back on a different day, but in that event the interview should be scheduled within 30 days. If the household misses the first interview, the household must reschedule another one. If the household misses two interviews, the state agency can deny the application, and the household will then have to reapply if it still wants assistance.[229]

What documents must an applicant bring to a SNAP interview?

At the interview, the applicant will be expected to produce documents that verify household eligibility. Generally, proof of the following will be required:

- Identity;
- Income;
- The immigration status of noncitizen household members who are applying for benefits;
- Housing and utility expenses;
- Social Security numbers of household members;

- Medical expenses (incurred by household members who are seniors or persons with disabilities);
- Dependent care expenses;
- Child-support payments;
- Where the household lives;
- Disability benefits.

At the time the agency schedules the interview, the agency must tell the applicant what documents to bring and must give the applicant at least 10 days' notice prior to the scheduled date.[230] The state agency is responsible for helping the household obtain required documents or contacting third parties to verify eligibility factors, but the household must cooperate in the verification process.[231] Documents may include such items as pay stubs, utility bills, a driver's license, and medical bills.[232] To ensure that the household timely receives benefits, the state agency may also allow a household to verify information through collateral contacts instead of documents.[233]

Will the agency inspect the applicant's home as part of the application process?

Federal law allows the agency to inspect the applicant's home—this is known as a "home visit"—but only when eligibility cannot be determined through documents and only with advance notice to the household. The agency's characterization of an applicant as an "error-prone household" is not grounds for a home visit.[234]

How long does it take for an application to be processed?

The SNAP office must grant or deny an application within 30 days of the date of application.[235] If a household's application is approved, it is entitled to benefits "from the date of application."[236] If the applicant's household includes a member who filed a joint application for SSI and SNAP while still a resident of a public institution, SNAP for that individual begins in the month the person is discharged from the institution.[237]

What is expedited service?

Under certain circumstances, an applicant is entitled to get SNAP benefits within seven days of applying—a process known as "expedited service."[238]

SNAP agencies are required to screen all applicants to see if they may qualify for expedited service,[239] but applicants should also request it directly. To qualify, the applicant must provide identification and meet one of these conditions:

- The household has a gross monthly income of less than $150 and liquid resources of less than $100 (liquid resources are cash in hand, checking or savings accounts, savings certificates, and lump-sum payments such as income tax refunds or retroactive SSI benefits);[240] or
- The household's total monthly shelter cost (which includes rent, mortgage payments, utilities, and heat) is more than the household's gross income plus liquid resources;[241] or
- The household is made up of migrant or seasonal farmworkers, and its liquid resources do not exceed $100.[242]

The state agency will determine expedited eligibility at the time of the application.[243] State agencies must attempt to verify eligibility for SNAP expedited service, but may not delay issuance of benefits beyond the seven-day time frame to applicants whose identity has been verified, even if verification of other factors is not complete.[244]

Does SNAP require household members to work to receive benefits?

Yes, in some cases. SNAP has two categories of work-related provisions:[245] (1) "basic" work requirements; and (2) time limits that are imposed on certain persons who are deemed "able-bodied without dependents" unless they work a sufficient number of hours per week.

Basic Work Requirement
Generally, to receive SNAP benefits, a household member who is older than age 15 and younger than age 60 and "physically and mentally fit" must register for employment at the time of the household's SNAP application, and every 12 months afterward.[246] "Registering for employment" means (1) signing up with the SNAP office or a state employment service office to be notified about any available jobs;[247] (2) agreeing to participate in a state-run employment and training program or workfare program;[248] and (3) agreeing to accept a bona fide offer of suitable employment.[249] In addition, a household member who leaves a job or reduces work to less than 30 hours per week without good cause will not be eligible to receive SNAP benefits.[250]

The combined monthly hours of a SNAP household's members participating in an employment, training or workfare program may not exceed the number of hours equal to the household's SNAP benefits for the month divided by the higher of the applicable federal or state minimum wage.[251] For example, a household that receives a monthly SNAP allotment of $250 in a state where the minimum wage is $10 per hour cannot be required to participate in an employment or training or workfare program for more than 25 hours per month (about 5.75 hours per week).

Good Cause to Decline a Job Offer

Good cause to decline a job offer exists when the job is shown to be not suitable for the person.[252] A number of factors can make a job offer not suitable. They include:

- The wage offered is lower than the higher of the state or federal minimum wage or, if the minimum wage does not apply, is lower than 80 percent of the federal minimum wage; or the job offered is on a piece-rate basis and the average hourly yield the applicant would be expected to earn is less than the applicable minimum wage;[253]
- The applicant is required to join, resign from, or not join a legitimate labor organization, or the job is at a site subject to a strike or lockout, unless the strike has been enjoined by a court;[254]
- The job puts the applicant at an unreasonable degree of risk to health and safety;[255]
- The applicant is not physically or mentally fit to do the job;[256]
- The job is offered within the first 30 days of SNAP registration and is not within the applicant's major field of experience;[257]
- The commute is unreasonable given the expected wage and cost of commuting (for example, if a commute is two hours or more, the job would not be considered suitable);[258]
- The job, either because of its nature or hours of work, would interfere with religious observance;[259]
- The job fails to meet other standards of suitability that the state has established.[260]

Exemptions from Basic Work Requirements

Certain persons are exempt from SNAP's basic work requirements. They are:

- A person younger than age 16 or older than age 59;[261]
- A person between ages 16 and 18 who is not the head of a household; or who is attending school, or is enrolled in an employment training program on at least a half-time basis;[262]
- A person who is physically or mentally unfit for unemployment;[263]

- A person who is subject to and complying with work requirements under Title IV of the Social Security Act (TANF);[264]
- A parent or other household member who is responsible for the care of a dependent child under age six or of an incapacitated person;[265]
- A student enrolled at least half-time in an authorized educational institution;[266]
- A regular participant in a drug addiction or alcohol treatment program;[267]
- A person who is employed a minimum of 30 hours a week or receiving weekly earnings equal to the minimum wage multiplied by 30.[268]

Time Limits on Able-Bodied Persons without Dependents

SNAP limits the time period during which certain households may receive benefits. The time limits apply to persons between the ages of 18 and 49 who are considered "able-bodied," and who do not have dependents. The rule is referred to as the ABAWD (able-bodied without dependents) time limit, and a person subject to the rule may not receive benefits for longer than three months in any 36-month period unless:

- The person works an average of at least 20 hours a week;[269] or
- The person participates 20 hours a week in an employment or training program;[270] or
- The person participates in a state "workfare" program (the number of hours required varies from state to state, but effective SNAP benefits must come out to greater than or equal to the minimum wage);[271] or
- The person is medically certified as physically or mentally unfit for employment, or is receiving disability benefits;[272] or
- The person is responsible for a dependent child or resides in a household with a child younger than 18, even if the child is not receiving SNAP;[273] or
- The person is pregnant;[274] or
- The person is a student enrolled in a high-school, vocational, or postsecondary educational program or college and meets the SNAP student rules described earlier in the chapter.[275]

A person who loses SNAP eligibility because of the ABAWD rule can regain it by meeting the ABAWD work requirement for 30 consecutive days (or qualifying for an exemption from the rule).[276] Federal law allows states to extend the ABAWD time limit by one month for up to 15 percent of the SNAP caseload subject to the ABAWD rule.[277]

In 2016, households barred from receiving SNAP benefits by the ABAWD rule were very poor—on average, their gross income was only 17 percent of the poverty level and their job prospects were very limited.[278] States have discretion to seek waivers of the ABAWD rule in areas where the unemployment rate is more than 10 percent or there is a demonstrated insufficiency of available jobs.[279] As of late 2018, seven states had statewide ABAWD waivers, and 29 states had area-specific waivers.[280] A person who is notified that SNAP benefits are time-barred under the ABAWD rule should explore whether state waivers exist and whether any exemption applies. Advocates and organizations should press their states to seek ABAWD waivers.

Can workers who are on strike participate in SNAP?

Maybe. An individual who would have been eligible for SNAP before going out on strike can receive or continue to receive benefits, but the household's benefit amount will not increase to compensate for any reduction in income due to the strike. In other words, the household's SNAP benefit will be calculated as if the striking worker was still receiving a paycheck. This rule does not apply if the person who is on strike:

- Is "locked out";
- Is out of work because of someone else's strike;
- Is a part of a different bargaining unit than the striking workers and is afraid to cross a picket line;
- Has been permanently replaced; or
- Is exempt from work requirements (unless the reason for the exemption was that the individual was working).[281]

What happens if a household member fails to register for work or meet another basic work requirement?

In most cases, a household member who fails without "good cause" to register for work or to meet other SNAP-related work requirements will be disqualified from receiving benefits for a period of time.[282] Good cause includes any circumstance beyond the person's control, including, but not limited to, illness of the person or a household member, a family emergency, lack of transportation, or lack of adequate child care.[283] States set their disqualification periods within federal guidelines. For a first violation, the disqualification is one to three months; for a second violation, the disqualification is three to six months; and for a third or subsequent violation, the disqualification is six months to permanent disqualification.[284] If the disqualified member is the head of the household, the state can choose to bar the entire household from benefits for the duration of the member's ineligibility or 180 days, whichever is less.[285] During the sanction pe-riod, the disqualified member's income will continue to count as income to the household for determining SNAP eligibility and benefit amount. In this situa-tion, household members who are not *required* to be in the same SNAP house-hold as the disqualified individual (for example, household members who are not the disqualified person's spouse or child) should explore applying to be sepa-rate SNAP household, as that may increase the amount of benefits received.

What happens if a SNAP applicant or participant quits a job?

An individual who quits a job or reduces work effort without "good cause" is sub-ject to the same disqualification sanctions as individuals who fail without good cause to comply with other SNAP work requirements, as described above.[286] "Good cause" means that the worker was not at fault for the job termination and encompasses a range of circumstances, including, but not limited to:[287]

- Any reason that constitutes good cause for noncompliance with other SNAP work requirements (as discussed earlier in the chapter);
- Discrimination by the employer based on age, race, color, national origin, sex, handicap, religion, or political beliefs;[288]
- Unreasonable or dangerous work conditions (including the employer's failure to pay lawfully required wages or to pay the wages on time);
- Enrollment by the individual in any recognized school, training program, or institution of higher education on at least a half-time basis that requires the individual to leave employment.[289]

What happens if a SNAP participant is fired from a job?

If a recipient is fired from a job and is not at fault, SNAP benefits will continue, provided the recipient continues to comply with SNAP's work-registration conditions.[290] A worker who is dismissed for participating in a strike against the government is deemed to have quit without good cause.[291]

What is a certification period?

A certification period means the period of time during which an eligible house-hold will receive SNAP benefits before it must reapply for benefits. The state SNAP agency must notify a household as it approaches the end of its certification

Table 3.4 SNAP: Certification Periods

Household Type	Recommended Certification Period
Households in Which All Members Are Elderly or Disabled	Up to 24 months
Households with Stable Income and Stable Membership	12 months if circumstances are not expected to change
Households Experiencing Homelessness	6 months
Household with Frequent Changes in Membership or Income	"Shorter" certification periods
Household with Zero Income but with Circumstances Verified to Be Stable	Generally no less than 3 months
Households with Zero Income with Unstable Circumstances	1–2 months
Self-employed Household with Fluctuating Income	Shorter certification periods consistent with fluctuations in income

period and schedule the household for a recertification interview in time to avoid interruption of benefits.[292] The length of a household's certification period varies depending on how long its eligibility factors (income, household composition, residency, etc.) are expected to remain stable, as shown in Table 3.4. Federal law sets guidelines for certification periods and requires states to "assign the longest certification period possible based on the predictability of the household's circumstances."[293] For most households the certification period is 12 months.[294]

What procedural rights do SNAP applicants and recipients have?

All households applying for or receiving SNAP have a due process right to written notice and an opportunity to appeal any action that affects their eligibility for or participation in the SNAP program.[295] The notice must describe the action the agency proposes to take, the reasons for the action, and when the action takes effect. The notice must list a telephone number that can be called to get more information about the agency's decision. The notice also must provide the name of a legal aid or legal services office in the household's neighborhood that provides free representation. Finally, the notice must explain that the household has a right to a "fair hearing" and that—in the case of a proposed reduction or termination—it can continue to receive benefits unchanged pending completion of the hearing process.[296] A notice proposing to reduce or terminate SNAP during a certification period must be mailed no later than 10 days before the action is to take effect; that means that the SNAP agency may not reduce or cut off benefits during the 10-day period following the mailing of the notice.[297]

Does a household have the right to continue receiving SNAP during its appeal?

Yes. A SNAP household has the right to continue receiving its benefits unchanged through the conclusion of the hearing process, so long as the household's certification period has not ended.[298] This is known as "aid continuing." To invoke this right, the household must request a hearing during the initial 10-day period following the mailing of the adverse action notice; this ordinarily means the household must request the hearing before the "effective date" of the proposed action listed on the notice.[299] If the last day to request a hearing with aid continuing falls on a weekend or holiday, the request will be timely if made on the first following business day. Keep in mind that if the household loses the appeal, it may have to pay back the extra amount of SNAP benefits that it received while the appeal was pending. If the household's certification period for eligibility ends while it is waiting for a fair hearing to be decided, the household should reapply for benefits. Otherwise, the household may not receive SNAP benefits beyond the end date of the certification period, even if it wins the hearing.[300]

Why and how does a household request a "fair hearing"?

A SNAP household may request a hearing whenever the agency takes or proposes to take an action that affects its eligibility, benefit levels, or other matters involving the program.[301] Hearing requests may be made in writing, in person, by telephone, and in some cases online.[302] It is advisable to make the request in a manner that leaves the household with a record of the request, such as a receipt from the SNAP office, a copy of a letter request, or an online confirmation. The government's notice telling the household of the adverse action must include the address and telephone number of the office for the household to contact to request a hearing. The household may request a hearing anytime within 90 days of the decision that it disputes, but, as discussed earlier, the request must be made with 10 days of the date the agency mails notice of the adverse action in order for the household to continue to receive benefits unchanged pending the outcome of the hearing process.[303]

What is a fair hearing and how does the hearing process work?

A fair hearing is an informal legal proceeding that gives the household an opportunity to dispute the agency's decision to reduce or stop benefits. The hearing takes place at the agency, not at a court. A "hearing officer" runs the hearing, and the officer is required to be impartial and cannot have played any role in the agency's decision to reduce or stop benefits.[304] Before the hearing, the household has the right to examine the contents of its case file and any documents that the agency intends to present at the hearing.[305] The agency must make all of this material available sufficiently in advance of the hearing so that the household has adequate time to prepare. The household also can request a copy, free of charge, of any documents needed to prepare its case.[306]

At the hearing, the agency will be asked to show that its action has a basis in law and fact.[307] A nonlawyer representative or other agency staff member typically presents the agency's case. The hearing officer must give the household an opportunity to confront and cross-examine any adverse witnesses.[308] The household also has the right to present its own witnesses and documents, testify at the hearing, talk freely to the hearing officer, and reply to any statements that agency staff might present. The hearing officer must ensure that the household has a full opportunity to present its case and advance any arguments without undue interference or interruption.[309] The household may attend the fair hearing alone, or accompanied by a friend or relative, a paralegal, a lawyer, or any other person whom the household chooses to assist it.[310]

What happens after the hearing ends?

After the hearing ends, the household is entitled to a decision from the hearing officer based on the testimony and documents submitted at the hearing.[311] The state agency must issue a decision within 60 days of the hearing request.[312] The decision must be in writing and must explain the legal and factual reasons for the decision. If the decision is in favor of the household, it is binding on the SNAP agency, and the agency must promptly comply with the ruling, including issuing any retroactive benefits.[313] If the household disagrees with the hearing officer's decision, the household can challenge the decision by filing a lawsuit in court. To decide whether to take this action, the household should consider consulting a legal services or legal aid office for advice and to seek possible representation.

School-Based Food Programs for Children

Are there federal food-assistance programs for school-age children?

Yes. The federal government has established programs that provide funding to enable schools to provide breakfast, lunch, snacks, and suppers to students during the school year and meals during the summer, when school is not in session.[314] As described in this section, the programs operate onsite at participating schools and centers, and is open to every child at the site. Generally the price of the meal depends on whether the student is categorically eligible to receive free meals because of participation in another means-tested program; whether the student's household's income is below a poverty threshold; or whether the school has received certification as within a high-poverty area. Receipt of free or reduced-price meals does not reduce SNAP benefits to the child's household.[315]

When did Congress establish school-based food programs?

Federal assistance for school meals dates back at least to the Great Depression in the 1930s.[316] By 1942, on any given school day six million children were receiving school meals funded in part through federal assistance, and in 1944 Congress amended the Agricultural Act of 1935 to authorize funding to maintain school lunch and school milk programs.[317] Despite these efforts, childhood hunger persisted. Indeed, during World War II, the armed services rejected many military recruits who had medical conditions associated with childhood malnutrition.[318] Ultimately, President Harry Truman encouraged Congress to pass the National School Lunch Act in 1946.[319] The school breakfast program began later as a pilot program with passage of the Child Nutrition Act of 1966.[320] Amendments adopted in 1970 were designed to encourage expansion of the school lunch program and to ensure that all poor children were provided with assistance.[321] In 1975, the school breakfast program became permanent, and in 1998, Congress expanded the school lunch program to include snacks in certain after-school programs.[322] The Healthy, Hunger-Free Kids Act of 2010 made major changes to these programs by revising the nutrition standards and by changing the types of meals and snacks that are offered, requiring more fruits and vegetables per week, setting new caloric ranges, banning trans fats, and limiting sodium levels. Moreover, the 2010 act includes a "community eligibility" provision that allows schools attended by 40 percent or more "identified students" (which includes homeless students, migrant students, and students whose households receive SNAP benefits or TANF-funded assistance) to provide free meals to all students without having to process individual house-hold applications.[323]

National School Lunch Program

What is the National School Lunch Program?

The National School Lunch Program began in 1946 as a way to provide whole-some meals to school-age children and to help dispose of surplus agricultural production.[324] The U.S. Department of Agriculture administers the program, and national guidelines have been in effect since 1970. The lunch program provides reimbursement and in-kind assistance to schools that participate,[325] and about 95 percent of all public schools in the nation now do participate.[326] The National School Lunch Program is the second largest food-assistance pro-gram in the United States. On an average day in school year 2016–17, 30.4 mil-lion children overall, and 21.5 million low-income students, participated in the program; and in 2017–18, almost 13.6 million of the low-income students participated through the "community eligibility" provision of the 2010 Healthy, Hunger-Free Kids Act.[327] Not surprisingly, students from households living in poverty or on low incomes were far more likely to rely upon the program than students from households with higher disposable income.[328]

Which students can participate in the school lunch program?

Every student who attends a school that participates in the program can receive lunch, but the price of the lunch may depend on the student's family's income.

Is the school lunch program limited to students who are U.S. citizens?

Every student who is eligible to attend a public school can qualify for the school lunch program, and in the 1982 decision of *Plyler v. Doe*, the U.S. Supreme Court made clear that states cannot constitutionally exclude children who are not U.S. citizens from public schools.[329] In the decades since *Plyler*, some states have tried to bar children who could not document their immigration status,[330] and reports indicate that the Trump administration's anti-immigration policies have deterred immigrant families from signing up their children for school lunches.[331]

How does a student apply to the school lunch program?

The application process for the school lunch program depends on the school that the child attends and the child's circumstances. If the child attends a school that participates in the school lunch program through the community eligibility provision (CEP), then the student is not required to submit an individual application to participate. Any school, group of schools, or school district with a high proportion of low-income students can elect to participate in the CEP program.[332] A "community eligible" school provides free lunch (and breakfast) to all students. Information is available online identifying schools that participate through the community eligible provision.[333]

In all other schools, children are "categorically eligible" for free lunch—meaning, the household is not required to submit an individual application to participate—if the child's household receives assistance through SNAP, TANF-funded programs, or the Food Distribution Program on Indian Reservations (FDPIR), or the child is in foster care, lives in a migrant household, is homeless, is a runaway, or participates in Head Start. The school is required to directly certify students who are categorically eligible for school lunch by matching information in the other programs' databases. If for some reason the child nevertheless is not enrolled in the school lunch program even though categorically eligible, the household should submit an individual application signed by an adult household member, responding to two questions only: the child's name and the SNAP, TANF, or FDPIR case number (the adult's Social Security number is not required).[334]

Children who are not categorically eligible must apply to participate in the school lunch program. At the beginning of each academic year, schools must provide parents with information about how to apply for free and reduced-price meals (although a household can submit an application at any time during the school year).[335] Only one application is required per household, even if the household has multiple students.[336] A successful application qualifies the student for an entire school year plus 30 days.[337] Eligible students who change schools within the same district, remain eligible for free school meals without filing a new application;[338] when an eligible child transfers to a new school district, the new school may enroll the child in the meal program without a new application.[339]

The application form for school meals asks for:

- The names of household members;
- The household's income and source of income (for example, wages or unemployment benefits);
- The signature of an adult member of the household; and

– The last four digits of the Social Security number of the adult signing the application (if the household does not have a number, "none" should be written on the form).[340]

Schools are required to limit third-party access to information contained in the applications, and the form itself must tell applicants the extent to which the information will be disclosed.[341]

How much does a school lunch cost a student who participates in the program?

The price of the meal generally depends on the school the child is attending or the child's household's financial circumstances. Meals may be free, reduced-price, or full-price.

Free meals. Students who attend "community eligible" schools receive free meals. In addition, students who are categorically eligible to participate in the school lunch program because their households receive assistance through SNAP, TANF-funded programs, or the Food Distribution Program on Indian Reservations; and students who are in foster care, or are migrant, homeless, or runaway, or are in Head Start, receive free meals. In addition, students whose families have income at or below 130 percent of the federal poverty level receive free meals.

Reduced-price meals. Students whose households have incomes that range between 130 percent and 185 percent of the federal poverty level are eligible for reduced-price meals and cannot be charged more than 40 cents a meal for lunch (and 30 cents for breakfast).[342]

Full-price meals. Students whose households have incomes above 185 percent of the federal poverty level pay for meals at a price set by the school. If household income drops below the income limit, the student can be certified for free or reduced-price meals upon application to the program.[343]

What are the nutrition requirements for school lunches?

Federal law requires that participating schools serve lunches that are "nutritious, well-balanced, and age-appropriate."[344] Meals must meet quantity and nutritional requirements, and potable water must be offered at no charge.[345] Among other things, meals must have zero trans fat (unless it is naturally occurring, and then only of a minimal amount), and the saturated fat content must be less than

10 percent of the meal's total calories.[346] In addition, meat and meat substitutes must be included in the meals.[347]

Before President Obama's administration, some commentators criticized school lunches for serving children too many processed and "fast foods." Reforms adopted in 2010 included establishing an "organic food pilot program" to increase the amount of organic food in children's diets.[348] The Healthy, Hunger-Free Kids Act of 2010 also aligned school meals more closely with the Dietary Guidelines for Americans by requiring more fruits and vegetables in meals and setting requirements for what types of vegetables can be served, setting caloric ranges for meals based on grade groups, setting sodium limits, and banning naturally occurring trans fats.[349]

Can a school treat students who receive free or reduced-price meals differently than other students?

No. A school cannot discriminate against a child who receives a free or reduced-price breakfast, or who participates in the National School Lunch Program. A school cannot assign students to a different lunch line or cafeteria entrance, serve different meals, or use different-color meal tickets. The school must serve these meals at the same time as students who pay for meals and in the same dining room.[350] A school cannot force children who receive free or reduced-price meals to work or to perform chores as a condition of participation.[351]

What happens if a child who is expected to pay for a meal is unable to do so?

Unfortunately, some children's households will not be able to pay for school lunch, even at a reduced rate. School districts have responded differently to the problem. Some have handled these situations in ways that reasonable people would regard as hurtful to the child, for example, refusing to give the child any food, taking away an approved meal and giving the child only a cheese sandwich, or stamping the child's hand with a temporary tattoo that says, "I owe lunch money"—practices now known as "food shaming" or "lunch shaming."[352] As of the 2017 school year, the federal government recommended that participating states and school districts develop policies at the state or local level to address the situation of students who cannot pay meal fees or have accounts that are in arrears: however, this is left to the discretion of state and local agencies.[353]

Best practices suggest that the school should not publicly identify children unable to pay; should direct communications regarding payment to the parents, not to the children; must not take away food already served to children; should attempt to assist families in applying for free or reduced-price meals; and should weigh the cost of collecting school meal debt versus the value owed to the school.[354] In addition, those schools that are located in districts with high percentages of low-income children should consider enrolling in the school lunch program through the "community eligible" provision discussed earlier in the chapter.[355] Finally, some states are beginning to address the problem of lunch shaming in constructive, rather than stigmatizing and punitive ways.[356]

What can a family or student do if the school withholds a free or reduced-price lunch?

If the school participates in the program and refuses to provide a free or reduced-price meal, a family may challenge the decision to show that it meets eligibility requirements.[357] If the school believes that the child should be removed from the program and the family requests a hearing, the school must continue to give the student lunch until the dispute is resolved.[358]

Are the parents of participating students required to work or volunteer in the school lunch program?

A school may not require a parent or guardian of a student to work or volunteer in the school lunch program as a condition of the child's eligibility. However, federal law requires schools to invite participation of parents and community representatives in addressing issues such as planning of menus, improvement of the eating environment, and encouragement of good nutrition practices.[359]

Does the lunch program also serve snacks?

Participating schools may choose to provide snacks at after-school care programs.[360] In addition, schools may choose to provide suppers at after-school care programs through the Child and Adult Care Food Program described later in this chapter. An after-school care program means a program that provides "care and supervision" to students after school, and is not the same as an extracurricular program such as sports or music clubs.[361]

School Breakfast Program

What is the School Breakfast Program?

The School Breakfast Program provides federal funding to participating schools to enable them to serve breakfast to all students. The breakfasts are designed to deliver to children at least one-fourth of the daily recommended dietary allowances over the week.[362] Initially, the program focused on children who lived in poor areas or had to travel a great distance to school. Congress has since permanently authorized the program, and 93.2 percent of the schools that participate in the National School Lunch Program also serve breakfast. Participation in the School Breakfast Program has grown steadily over the years. In 1970, a half million students participated; in 2017–18, 12.5 million did.[363]

How does a student apply and how much does breakfast cost?

The application process for school breakfast is the same as for school lunch and households need apply once to qualify for both programs. The eligibility rules also are the same. Children eligible for reduced-price meals because family income is between 130 percent and 185 percent of the federal poverty level cannot be charged more than 30 cents a meal for breakfast.[364] However, fewer children participate in the school breakfast program than in school lunch—57 for every 100—and some advocates urge that schools consider serving breakfast in the classroom and "after the bell," rather than in the cafeteria or before the school day starts.[365]

The Afterschool Nutrition Program

What is the Afterschool Nutrition Program?

The Afterschool Nutrition Program is a federal program that allows participating schools, community and recreation centers, Boys & Girls Clubs, YMCAs, and other sites to provide free meals and snacks at after-school programs. Funding comes through the National School Lunch Program (and also the Child and Adult Care Food Program). The meals and snacks that are served must meet nutritional standards and contain at least two of the following four food groups: milk; fruit or vegetable; whole grain; and protein. Foods that meet these requirements include low-fat milk, apples, peanut butter, and cereal. More than

25,000 schools nationwide participate in a snack program, and 1.2 million children received after school supper in 2017.[366]

How much do the snacks cost?

As with school lunch, the price of the snack may be free or at a reduced price depending on the school and the child's household's financial circumstances. If the participating school is in an area in which 50 percent of the students are eligible for free or reduced-price meals, then the snacks are free.[367] If the school is not area-eligible, a child may still be eligible for free or reduced-price snacks based on lunch-program status. Families with income above 185 percent of the poverty level may have to pay full price for the snacks (approximately 91 cents) unless the after-school program waives the charge and pays the cost itself.[368]

The Child and Adult Care Food (CACPF) Program

The Child and Adult Care Food Program provides funding for student lunch and also for snacks and supper at community-based enrichment programs, such as those held at child care centers, family child care homes, Head Start programs, and homeless shelters in areas in which at least 50 percent of the children are eligible for free and reduced-price meals.[369] In 2018, CACFP funded meals to 4.5 million children. Community programs also may use funding to provide breakfast and lunch when school is not in session (namely, holidays, weekends, and school breaks).[370]

Summer Nutrition Programs

What food assistance programs are available during the summer for school-age children?

Congress currently funds several summer food programs for school-age children: the Summer Food Service Program,[371] the National School Lunch Program Seamless Summer Option,[372] and the Summer Electronic Benefit Transfer for Children Grant Program.[373] As with the school lunch and breakfast programs, the summer food programs give federal money to states, which in turn fund authorized centers to provide free meals and snacks to school-age children during the summer. Generally, funding is available for centers located in areas in which at least 50 percent of the children are eligible for free or reduced-price meals, centers in which 50 percent of the participating children are eligible for free or reduced-price meals, and centers that serve primarily migrant children.[374] Summer camps can receive funding under this program, as can schools that provide meals to students attending summer school.[375]

The expansion of summer food programs recognizes that poor and low-income children face higher rates of hunger when school is not in session.[376] In 1991, only 1.8 million children received summer meals. By 2018, 2.9 million children received summer lunch, but only 1.5 million received summer breakfast.[377] However, only one in seven low-income children who received school lunch during the school year 2017 received a summer lunch. Moreover, children's participation in summer lunch has declined in the three years since 2015. Advocates report that participation levels can increase (and in some communities have increased) through targeted outreach, strategic partnerships, and increased use of mobile meal sites. One important proposal recommends that the site-qualification poverty threshold be reduced from 50 percent of the student body eligible for free or reduced-price meals to 40 percent, to aid children who live in areas that have dispersed rather than concentrated poverty.[378] Ensuring children access to nutritious meals during the summer months not only relieves food insecurity but also has been shown to enhance educational achievement.[379]

How do students enroll in the Summer Food Service Program?

All children up to age 18 who attend a center participating in the program receive a free meal, regardless of income.[380] No application is required. To find out which centers participate in the summer program, contact the National Hunger Hotline at 1-866-3-HUNGRY or 1-877-8-HAMBRE, or visit https://www.fns.usda.gov/summerfoodrocks.

Summer EBT

Summer EBT is another important initiative developed by the U.S. Department of Agriculture to deal with the prevalence of childhood hunger when school is not in session. Since summer 2011, the Department of Agriculture has piloted a program that adds funds to the EBT cards of households enrolled in SNAP or Women, Infants and Children (discussed later in this chapter) that have children enrolled in free or reduced-price meals during the school year.[381] Evaluations of the pilot programs showed that the EBT summer supplement reduced very low food insecurity by one-third.[382] The EBT summer supplement has particularly utility in areas where children face transportation and other logistical barriers to accessing meal sites during the summer.[383]

Fresh Fruit and Vegetable Program

What is the Fresh Fruit and Vegetable Program?

The Fresh Fruit and Vegetable Program (FFVP) provides fresh fruits and vegetables for free to students who attend eligible schools. The program began on a pilot basis in 2002,[384] and now operates nationwide.[385] The program is administered at the national level by the U.S. Department of Agriculture and at the local level by the state agency that administers the National School Lunch Program.

Do all schools participate in the FFVP program?

Not all schools participate in the fruit and vegetable program. Appropriations for the program are limited, and priority for participation is given to elementary schools with the highest free and reduced-price school lunch enrollment. Before selecting schools, a state must do outreach and must ensure that the school is capable of administering the program.[386] Once a school has been selected to participate, it must provide free fruits and vegetables to all students in the school.

Special Milk Program

What is the Special Milk Program?

The Special Milk Program was established in 1954 and reimburses states for each half pint of milk served to students at participating schools and eligible child care institutions and camps. The program is administered by schools at the state level and children must apply every year to participate.[387] Children who are eligible for free lunch under the National School Lunch Program may, at state option, also receive free milk.[388] In addition, again at state option, free milk may be made available under the program to children attending half-day pre-kindergarten. Milk may include flavored or unflavored, and whole, low-fat, skim, or cultured buttermilk.[389] A listing of state agencies by state is available on the U.S. Department of Agriculture website.[390]

Special Supplemental Nutrition Program for Women, Infants, and Children (WIC)

What is WIC?

WIC refers to the Special Supplemental Nutrition Program for Women, Infants and Children. WIC is a program that provides supplemental food assistance to a special population—low-income pregnant, postpartum, or breastfeeding women, infants, and children up to age five.[391] WIC serves as an "adjunct" to other programs and provides participants with supplemental food and access to nutrition counseling and health care during formative periods of pregnancy and childhood development.[392] Receipt of WIC does not reduce a household's SNAP or any other nutritional assistance. The federal government establishes rules for WIC, and states administer the program at the local level using federal grants to fund benefits and administrative costs.[393]

When did the federal government establish WIC?

WIC began as a two-year pilot program in 1972, following recommendations by the White House Conference on Food, Nutrition, and Health that greater efforts be made to prevent hunger and malnutrition among poor pregnant women and infants.[394] Two years later, WIC was established on a permanent basis, initially called the Special Supplemental Food Program for Women, Infants, and Children. WIC is the third largest food-assistance program in the United States.[395]

How many people participate in WIC?

In 2018, a monthly average of 6.87 million people received WIC, marking the lowest participation rate in 15 years.[396] In an average month in 2018, WIC provided benefits to 1.6 million women, 1.7 million infants, and 3.5 million children up to age five.[397] For those who participate, WIC has had an excellent track record of improving diet and life chances.[398] Repeated studies show that WIC has reduced the likelihood of premature birth, low birthweight, infant mortality, and fetal death among participants.[399] Moreover, by reducing the incidence of anemia among children (low-income children are three to four times more likely to have low-iron blood levels, which causes anemia), WIC has prevented developmental delay and cognitive impairment.[400] Since 2007, when the program revised its available food package, WIC also has increased the likelihood of healthy diets and decreased the likelihood of stillbirths and obesity among participants.[401] In addition, studies have consistently confirmed the program's cost effectiveness.[402] In particular, WIC saves money by making long-term improvements in the cognitive and health outcomes of women and children who participate.[403]

How do WIC participants obtain their supplemental foods?

Generally, WIC participants receive checks, vouchers, or Electronic Benefit Transfer (EBT) cards to purchase foods in grocery stores. By 2020, "paper" benefits will be phased out and all recipients will receive EBT cards, which work like debit cards. Participants do not pay for the checks, vouchers, or EBT cards, and so obtain the supplemental foods for free.[404]

Participating grocery stores, "WIC-only," and "A50" stores (those with 50 percent or greater of sales from WIC), as well as direct delivery, home delivery, military commissaries, and pharmacies selling formula, must be authorized by the federal government, and often post a sign that says "WIC Accepted Here." The majority of states use retail food vendors.[405]

How does a participant know what food to purchase?

Authorized foods are identified in "food packages" that have been specially designed for different groups of participants, and there currently are seven food packages.[406] The amount of food that a WIC household may purchase does not turn on the household's income but rather on its nutritional and medical needs. Generally, the WIC food package is intended to provide recipients with high levels of protein, iron, calcium, and vitamins A and C—nutrients that are typically missing from the diets of low-income women and children. The packages include various amounts of infant formula, juice, milk or yogurt, cereal, eggs, cheese, fruits and vegetables, whole wheat bread, fish, and beans or peanut butter. The food packages take cultural differences into account; for example, brown rice, whole wheat tortillas, or whole wheat macaroni may be substituted for bread. The composition of the food packages is intended to encourage healthier eating habits and the breastfeeding of infants.[407]

A nutritionist will evaluate the household members and help choose the right food package. In addition, participants meet regularly with a nutritionist, so, as nutritional needs change during pregnancy, postpartum, breastfeeding, infancy, and childhood, so will the preferred food package. In addition, WIC participants can attend two classes in nutrition education during each certification period. Classes discuss the specific nutritional needs of mothers, infants, and children, and stress the importance of regular medical care, the dangers of using alcohol or drugs during pregnancy, and the advantages of breastfeeding during infancy. They also offer homemaking tips, such as how to shop for nutritious foods and how to prepare economical, well-balanced meals. Nutrition counseling can be done one-on-one, in groups, or through online courses, but supplemental foods will not be withheld if a participant declines to take part in nutrition education activities.[408]

What kind of medical care does WIC provide?

WIC provides access to ongoing, routine pediatric and obstetric care, or referral for treatment. WIC centers are generally located at or near clinics that provide prenatal or other medical services. In addition, WIC sometimes maintains joint medical records with health clinics, allowing WIC nutritionists and health professionals to share information and coordinate services. WIC clinics must ensure the confidentiality of participants' medical and other records.[409]

Who is eligible for WIC?

WIC has four eligibility requirements:

Requirement 1: Women, Infants, and Children

Participants must be either:

- A pregnant woman, or
- A new mother up to six months' postpartum, or
- A breastfeeding mother up to the infant's first birthday, or
- An infant or child up to age five.[410]

Parents or guardians who are not pregnant, postpartum, or breastfeeding can receive WIC benefits on behalf of eligible infants. Although fathers cannot apply on their own behalf, some states, for example, Massachusetts, encourage fathers to apply so they can accompany a child to a health appointment.[411]

Requirement 2: Income Limits

Participants must meet income limits:[412]

- Applicants are automatically income-eligible as an adjunct to participation in (or certification for) SNAP, Medicaid, TANF, or state-administered need-based programs, or if a family member is certified eligible, but the agency will require verification of the program-eligibility that makes the applicant income-eligible.[413]

– Applicants also are income-eligible if they meet the income standard set by the state in which they live, which must be between 100 percent and 185 percent of the federal poverty level and often is the same as the eligibility standard for the National School Lunch Program.[414] Table 3.5 lists maximum income levels effective July 1, 2017, through June 30, 2018 for determining WIC eligibility.[415]

Requirement 3: Residence and Proof of Identity

WIC is a national program, but eligibility is determined on a state-by-state basis, and an applicant can apply only in the household's state of residence. States cannot reject applicants because they are recent arrivals who have not lived in the state or locality for a set amount of time.[416]

Requirement 4: Nutritional Risk

WIC eligibility is limited to applicants who are at "nutritional risk."[417] Every applicant will be assessed by a competent professional who will make the decision and may base the decision on referral data. Factors to be considered include height and weight, anemia, pregnancy, breastfeeding, and dietary disorders.[418]

Table 3.5 WIC: Income Levels

Household Size	Annual Income 48 Contiguous States	Annual Income Alaska	Annual Income Hawaii
1	$22,459	$28,083	$25,826
2	$30,451	$38,073	$35,021
3	$38,443	$48,063	$44,215
4	$46,435	$58,053	$53,410
5	$54,427	$68,043	$62,604
6	$62,419	$78,033	$71,799
7	$70,411	$88,023	$80,993
8	$78,403	$98,013	$90,188
Each additional family member	+ $7,992	+ $9,990	+ $9,195

What counts as income for purposes of WIC eligibility?

States are permitted to use the income guidelines of the National School Lunch Program. If the state so chooses, then income means "gross cash income before deductions for income, taxes, employees' social security taxes, insurance premiums, bonds, etc."[419] Federal regulations list a dozen categories of income that are counted:[420]

1. Monetary compensation, including wages, commissions, or fees;
2. Net income from farm and nonfarm self-employment;
3. Social Security benefits;
4. Dividends or interest on savings accounts;
5. Public assistance or welfare payments;
6. Unemployment compensation;
7. Government retirement payments, including veterans' payments;
8. Private pensions or annuities;
9. Alimony or child support;
10. Regular contributions from third parties who are not members of the applicant's household;
11. Net royalties;
12. Other cash income.

What categories of payment do not count in determining WIC eligibility?

Certain categories of payments do not count as "income" for purposes of determining WIC eligibility, including the following:

1. The value of in-kind housing and other in-kind benefits;
2. Loans, other than portions of loans to which the household has unlimited or constant access;
3. Federal student financial aid used to pay for educational expenses;
4. Payments made through certain federal programs, such as SNAP, that are statutorily excluded from WIC income-eligibility determinations;
5. At state option, basic housing allowances received by military service-members residing off installation or in private housing; and
6. At state option, cost-of-living allowances received by military service-members under 37 U.S.C. Section 405.[421]

Can a household own assets and still be eligible for WIC?

WIC does not disqualify applicants because of resources that they own. Resources include such things as cars, homes, and savings.

Is participation in WIC limited to U.S. citizens?

Federal law does not disqualify noncitizens from participating in WIC, but permits states, at their option, to limit WIC to U.S. citizens, U.S. nationals, and "qualified aliens" as defined in the immigration and nationality laws.[422] A qualified applicant who is not a U.S. citizen is not required to meet a durational residence test as a condition of WIC participation.[423] Receiving WIC does not make the noncitizen a public charge or affect immigration status.[424]

Does every eligible applicant receive WIC?

No. WIC is not an "entitlement" program, and does not guarantee assistance to every eligible household that applies. Rather, Congress appropriates only a fixed sum to the program each year. Among eligible households, WIC uses a priority system to select participants. The priority system is based on an assessment of nutritional risk and health concerns, and directs benefits to those most in need if funds are insufficient to assist all applicants.[425] Applicants who are at nutritional risk because of medical conditions are ranked higher than those who have inadequate diets; pregnant and breastfeeding women are ranked higher than children. Applicants who are not in the highest priority category nevertheless should apply to the program. Different WIC clinics have different levels of funding and so may be able to enroll more applicants. In addition, clinics maintain waiting lists. Also, WIC clinics will try to coordinate applications with those of other health programs, and can provide useful information about available alternative health and nutrition services in in the locality.

What is the process for applying to WIC?

The process for applying to WIC—called "certification"—typically is integrated with procedures for other health programs that the state agency administers.[426]

Certification generally takes place at a local WIC clinic and includes an assessment of the applicant's nutritional risk and health need, done at no cost to the applicant.[427] States usually post toll-free numbers that an interested person can call to obtain information about where WIC clinics are located. Contact information for each state's WIC agency also is available online through the U.S. Department of Agriculture, Food and Nutrition Service, at http://www.fns.usda.gov/wic/toll-free-numbers-wic-state-agencies.

The WIC clinic is expected to advise a potential applicant about eligibility requirements and what information must be documented. Generally, but not always, documents are used to verify the following information:

Proof of income for adults. Applicants who participate in SNAP, Medicaid, or TANF-funded programs are considered "adjunctively income eligible" for WIC once they document their participation in one of these other programs and are not required to document income. Otherwise, income can be verified through such documents as a pay stub, an income tax return, or an employer's letter stating wages.[428]

Proof of residence. An applicant can document residence through a letter addressed to the applicant in the state of application. Moreover, if the applicant lacks proof of residence (or of identity) for a good reason, such as theft, disaster, loss, homelessness, or the applicant is a migrant farmworker, certification can still be done. In that case, the applicant will be required to confirm residence (or identity) in writing. A fixed address is not a condition of eligibility and a person who is homeless may participate in WIC.[429]

Proof of identity. The applicant must document identity and provide the Social Security numbers of adults in the household if they have such numbers.

Proof of pregnancy. In some states, the applicant must document that the person is pregnant. However, eligibility nevertheless may be certified without documented proof for a 60-day period.[430]

What is a certification interview?

The WIC clinic will schedule an appointment, called a certification interview, to ask the applicant questions relevant to eligibility conditions. The applicant is expected to bring documentation to that interview, and generally must attend in person. However, in some circumstances the applicant can be excused, for example, for reasons such as infancy, disability, a serious illness or medical condition, or interference with health care or work.[431]

What is a "certification form"?

A certification form is the official document that tells the applicant about the WIC program and states the consequences of intentionally providing false information.[432] It also is the document the WIC clinic uses to record application information about the household. The form will include such information as the applicant's name and address, the date of the initial visit to apply to WIC, whether the applicant was physically present at the certification interview (and if not, why not), a description of the documents used to verify income and identity, and medical information (height, weight, and so forth). The certification form is signed by a professional who is competent to make assessments about nutritional risk and health needs.

Can the WIC agency disclose any of the information contained in the certification form?

Information obtained from a WIC applicant and participant is confidential, and the state agency must restrict the use and disclosure of confidential applicant and participant information to persons directly connected with the WIC program.[433] State agencies may ask applicants and participants to sign release forms that give consent for disclosure of confidential information for other purposes, but consent is not a condition of eligibility for the program.[434] Federal law gives the state agencies the option of disclosing confidential information to other programs, government and private, that serve persons eligible for WIC,[435] but must comply with rules governing the protection of such confidential information.[436] In addition, state agencies may disclose confidential information concerning suspected incidents of child abuse and neglect if required to do so under state law.[437] Finally, state agencies may disclose confidential information in response to subpoenas and search warrants but must follow specified federal procedures to protect privacy.[438]

How does a household's lack of a fixed address or permanent home affect WIC participation?

A person who is homeless can participate in the WIC program. Moreover, participants who reside in a homeless facility must be treated equally with other WIC participants. The WIC agency must take steps to ensure that the homeless facility does not reduce its food expenditures for the WIC participant and that it does not restrict the household from accessing the facility's services or benefits, including supplemental foods, nutrition counseling, and breastfeeding support, because the household is receiving WIC.[439]

How long can a person participate in the WIC program and receive benefits?

Persons who are certified to participate in the WIC program receive benefits for a length of time called a "certification period." The length of the certification period depends on whether the individual is pregnant, postpartum, breastfeeding, an infant, or a child. Typically a certification period runs for six months to one year, and then the household must be recertified. However, pregnant women usually are certified for the length of their pregnancy plus up to six weeks postpartum. At recertification, the same questions will be asked as at the initial application: questions about income, residence, nutritional risk, and so forth, and a certification interview will again be scheduled.[440]

Can a household receive SNAP benefits and also participate in WIC?

Yes. Because WIC serves as an adjunct to other programs that provide supplemental food and services, a household can participate in SNAP and still receive WIC benefits. In addition, even if a household is not income-eligible for SNAP, it may be eligible for WIC. WIC participation does not preclude children from receiving free breakfast, lunch, and snacks as part of a school-based program.

What is the WIC Farmers' Market Nutrition Program?

The WIC Farmers' Market Nutrition Program was established in 1992 and provides grants to states to increase the ability of WIC households to buy fresh, locally grown fruits and vegetables. Participants (other than infants younger than four months), and those on the WIC waiting list, are given free coupons that can be used to buy produce at authorized farmers' markets.[441] The benefit is no less than $10 and no more than $30 a year.[442] The value of the coupons is not counted as income or resources for any purpose under federal, state, or local law.[443]

Senior Nutrition Programs

Are there any federal food programs for elder low-income Americans?

The federal government funds food-assistance programs that benefit elder low-income Americans, filling important nutritional gaps.[444] In 2017, 21.4 million, or 42 percent of seniors over 65, had incomes below 200 percent of the Supplemental Poverty Measure (which, unlike the official poverty measure, incorporates information about financial resources such as liabilities, in-kind benefits, out-of-pocket medical expenses, and geographic variations in housing), and half of Medicare recipients had incomes of less than 200 percent of the standard federal poverty level.[445] As discussed earlier in this chapter, seniors can participate in the Supplemental Nutrition Assistance Program, and although SNAP is open to persons of all ages, the program has special rules to benefit people age 60 and older and people with disabilities. Nevertheless, only about 40 percent of low-income seniors who are eligible for SNAP actually participate in the program, in part because seniors may attach a stigma to using assistance publicly in a grocery store or find applying for benefits to be difficult.[446] Additional programs are available that provide food or meals in different settings. The U.S. Department of Agriculture funds and administers the Commodity Supplemental Food Program and the Senior Farmers' Market Nutrition Program, specifically for seniors, and the U.S. Department of Health and Human Services administers Elder Nutrition Services Programs, funded under Title III of the Older Americans Act. Studies show that these food programs yield important results: they reduce hunger; they promote social interactions; they encourage good health; and they delay the onset of medical conditions; all of which reduce health care utilization, such as nursing home use, hospital use, and Medicare/Medicaid costs.[447]

What is the Congregate Meals Program?

The Congregate Meals Program, established under the Older Americans Act,[448] provides meals to elders once a day, Monday through Friday, at a community center, including religiously affiliated sites such as neighborhood churches or synagogues. Some sites may offer weekend meals. The program is intended to provide seniors with food and fellowship, offering a nutritious meal and a chance to talk to other people. Many of the locations serving congregate meals provide transportation to and from the site; information and referral for health and welfare counseling; nutrition education; and help with shopping and recreation.

Fifty-four percent of participants reported that a congregate meal supplied half or more of their total food for a day.[449]

Centers are required to serve adults who are functionally impaired or over age 60, to provide community-based programs and nonresidential services, and to be licensed or approved to provide adult day care service.[450] Additionally, nutrition service providers must ensure that meals meet the most recent Dietary Guidelines for Americans.[451] Program participants must be age 60 or older. Participants' spouses and caregivers accompanying the participant to the site may also participate no matter how old they are. There is no financial eligibility test, but services are targeted to older individuals "in greatest social and economic need," including those with low incomes, from minority communities, residing in rural areas, lacking English proficiency, or at risk of institutionalization.[452] State-based diversity initiatives have aimed to encourage participation by seniors who are members of racial and ethnic minorities and the LGBTQ community.[453]

What is the Home-Delivered Meals Program?

The Home-Delivered Meals Program, known as "Meals on Wheels," was established by Section 336 of the federal Older Americans Act.[454] The Home-Delivered Meals Program delivers a free, nutritious meal, Monday through Friday, to the homes of vulnerable older Americans. Some programs also provide two additional frozen meals in the Friday delivery for use on the weekend. Meals must provide at least one-third of the recommended Dietary Reference Intakes and adhere to the current Dietary Guidelines for Americans. Some programs are able to provide meals that meet special dietary needs, such as low-sodium, or for people with diabetes. Information about local programs, by zip code, is available online at Meals on Wheels America, http://www.mealsonwheelsamerica.org/.

Participants must be at least age 60 and frail (or recovering from illness, injury, or surgery), homebound, isolated, or the spouse of a person with disabilities who lives with a participating senior; must live in the program's service area; and must be unable to prepare meals. While there is no means test for participation, preference is given to those with the greatest economic and social needs, with particular attention to low-income older individuals, including those who are low-income minorities, have limited English proficiency, or reside in rural areas.[455] (Note that some "Meals on Wheels" programs offered throughout the country rely in whole or part on nongovernmental funds, and may have different criteria for participation.) The Home-Delivered Meals Program has been shown to improve diet quality and increase nutritional intake among recipients.[456] In 2017 the program served over 835,000 seniors in their homes, and provided over 137 million home-delivered meals.[457]

What is the Senior Farmers' Market Nutrition Program?

The Senior Farmers' Market Nutrition Program (SFMNP) provides financial assistance for low-income seniors to buy food at farmers' markets, community agriculture programs, and roadside stands.[458] The federal government offers funds to states, territories, and Indian Tribal Organizations to operate the program; most states administer a SFMNP program, but not every state runs the program on a statewide basis. The program reached 811,809 people in 2017.[459]

Seniors age 60 and over are eligible for SFMNP if their household income does not exceed 185 percent of the federal poverty level.[460] At state option, Native Americans 55 years of age or older and certain disabled individuals residing in congregate facilities occupied primarily by the elderly may qualify.[461] Applications for SFMNP are typically available from the local agency on aging. Contact information for state agencies accepting applications may be found on the U.S. Department of Agriculture web page at http://www.fns.usda.gov/sfmnp/sfmnp-contacts. Participants receive coupons that can be exchanged for eligible foods (fruits, vegetables, honey, and fresh-cut herbs) at participating farmers' markets, roadside stands, and community-supported agriculture programs. Benefit levels vary, but generally may not be less than $20 or more than $50 for each farmers' market calendar year.[462] Participants also are given access to nutritional counseling. The program operates during the harvest season, which varies by location.

Commodity Supplemental Food Program (CSFP)

The Commodity Supplemental Food Program (CSFP), established in 1969, is a program that distributes food to supplement the diets of its recipients.[463] In 1999, the program operated in 17 states, the District of Columbia, and two Indian Tribal Organizations; in 2019, the program operated in all states, in the District of Columbia, Puerto Rico, and five Indian Tribal Organizations.[464] An application requires, among other things, the applicant's name and address and "some form of identification"; household income; household size; and age.[465] Eligibility currently is limited to people age 60 or older with household income not more than 130 percent of the federal poverty level.[466] Participants must reside the state in which they wish to receive benefits, and some states require a certification of nutritional risk.[467] (Children or pregnant women who were certified and have continually received benefits as of February 6, 2014, may continue to participate in CSFP if the household's income is at or below 185 percent of the poverty level or the household receives SNAP, TANF-funded benefits, or Medicaid.)[468] CSFP participation is limited by annual appropriations, and so not every eligible applicant is able to receive assistance.[469] If the number of applications exceeds caseload limits, the agency must maintain a waiting list.[470] The program served nearly 700,000 people in fiscal year 2018 and 630,000 in 2017.[471] Seniors who participate in CSFP also may be entitled to receive SNAP assistance.[472]

Program participants receive a monthly food package containing items such as canned fruit and vegetables, cheese, milk, cereals, potatoes, grains, peanut butter, and dried beans.[473] The food package is designed for persons who can independently prepare meals. Beginning in 2007, when the food package was adapted to align with the 2005 Dietary Guidelines for Americans, the foods that are distributed have lower fat, lower sodium and sugar, and include more whole grains. The Food and Nutrition Service conducted a comprehensive review of the food package in 2017, and effective November 1, 2019, foods offered will double the amount of vegetables, include lentils and brown rice as an option, and will reduce package size of certain grains to allow for more food offerings.[474]

Contact information for state agencies accepting CSFP applications may be found on the U.S. Department of Agriculture web page, at https://www.fns.usda.gov/csfp/csfp-contacts.

Notes

1. For a critical perspective, *see* Jesse Burgess, Let Them Eat Cake: Constitutional Rights to Food, 18 Willamette J. Int'l L. & Disp. Resol. 256 (2010). On the distinction between a right to food and a right to nutrition, *see* Paul A. Diller, Combating Obesity with a Right to Nutrition, 101 Geo. L.J. 969 (2013).
2. *See* Nadia Lambek & Priscilla Claeys, Institutionalizing a Fully Realized Right to Food: Progress, Limitations, and Lessons Learned from Emerging Alternative Policy Models, 40 Vt. L. Rev. 743 (2016); Note, What Price for the Priceless? Implementing the Justiciability of the Right to Water, 120 Harv. L. Rev. 1067 (2007).
3. U.N. General Assembly, The right to food: resolution, adopted by the General Assembly, 7 March 2016, A/RES/70/154, http://ap.ohchr.org/documents/E/HRC/resolutions/A_HRC_RES_7_14.pdf.
4. International Covenant on Economic, Social and Cultural Rights, GA Res. 2200A (XXI), 21 UN GAOR Supp. (No. 16) at 49, UN Doc. A/6316 (1966); 993 UNTS 3; 6 ILM 368 (1967), http://www.ohchr.org/EN/ProfessionalInterest/Pages/CESCR.aspx. *See* Martha F. Davis, Bringing It Home: Human Rights Treaties and Economic, Social, and Cultural Rights in the United States, American Bar Association (Sept. 26, 2018), https://www.americanbar.org/groups/crsj/publications/human_rights_magazine_home/2015--vol--41-/vol--41--no--2---human-rights-at-home/bringing-it-home--human-rights-treaties-and-economic--social--an/ (observing that the United States has never ratified the ICESCR).

5. In addition, federal law regulates aspects of water quality, *see, for example*, the 1972 Clean Water Act, 33 U.S.C. § 1251, and the 1974 Safe Drinking Water Act, 42 U.S.C. § 300f. For a discussion of the right to water, *see* Martha F. Davis, Let Justice Roll Down: A Case Study of the Legal Infrastructure for Water Equality and Affordability, 23 Geo. J. on Poverty L. & Pol'y 355, 357 n.13 (2016) (noting that neither statute "recognizes a right to safe drinking water"). Federal law requires schools participating in the school lunch program to provide potable water to students. 42 U.S.C. § 1758(a)(5).

6. *See* U.S. Dept. of Agriculture v. Moreno, 413 U.S. 528 (1973) (holding invalid under the Due Process Clause the statutory exclusion from the Food Stamp Program of households composed of persons not related to each other; "a bare congressional desire to harm a politically unpopular group cannot constitute a legitimate governmental interest"); U.S. Dept. of Agriculture v. Murry, 413 U.S. 508 (1973) (holding invalid under the Due Process Clause the statutory exclusion from the Food Stamp Program of any person claimed as a tax dependent by a different household). *But see* Lyng v. International Union, UAW, 485 U.S. 360 (1988) (upholding statutory exclusion of households that became financially eligible for food stamps because a member was on strike).

7. For an overview of SNAP eligibility and benefits, *see* Congressional Research Service, Randy Alison Aussenberg, Supplemental Nutrition Assistance Program (SNAP): A Primer on Eligibility and Benefits, CRS Report Prepared for Members and Committees of Congress (June 9, 2013–Apr. 11, 2018), https://www.fas.org/sgp/crs/misc/R42505.pdf.

8. *See* U.S. Department of Agriculture National Agricultural Library, Dennis Roth, Food Stamps 1932–1977: From Provisional and Pilot Programs to Permanent Policy (2000), https://pubs.nal.usda.gov/sites/pubs.nal.usda.gov/files/foodstamps.html.

9. Instead, Congress authorized the distribution of surplus commodities to the poor. At the time, efforts to re-establish the Food Stamp Program were unsuccessful. *See* Janet Poppendieck and Marion Nestle, Breadlines Knee-Deep in Wheat: Food Assistance in the Great Depression (California, 2014), http://www.jstor.org/stable/10.1525/j.cttbwqbmq.

10. *See* Providing for an Expanded Program of Food Distribution to Needy Families, Executive Order No. 10914 (1961). Senator Kennedy's 1960 speech, Food for West Virginia, criticized the failure of the Republican administration to provide an adequate food surplus program to hungry Americans. Speech John F. Kennedy Presidential Library and Museum, https://www.jfklibrary.org/Asset-Viewer/Archives/JFKCAMP1960-1032-005.aspx. *See* Ardith L. Maney, Still Hungry After All These Years: Food Assistance Policy from Kennedy to Reagan, Studies in Social Welfare Policies and Programs Number 11 (Greenwood 1989).

11. Food Stamp Act of 1964, Pub. L. No. 88-525 (1964) (codified as amended at 7 U.S.C. §§ 2011–2036(a) et seq.). The statute's aim was to "alleviate . . . hunger and malnutrition" due to a household's "limited food purchasing power," and to give indirect support to the agricultural economy. 7 U.S.C. § 2011; 7 C.F.R. § 271.1.

12. Food Stamp Act of 1977, Pub. L. No. 108-269 (1977) (codified as amended at 7 U.S.C. §§ 2011–2036(a)). For a history of the statute, *see* Matthew Gritter & Iain MacRobert, The Policy and Politics of Food Stamps and SNAP (Palgrave 2015), http://www.palgrave.com/us/book/9781137520913.

13. Personal Responsibility and Work Opportunity Reconciliation Act, Pub. L. No. 104-193, 110 Stat. 2105 (1996).
14. The Food, Conservation, and Energy Act of 2008, Pub. L. No. 110-246 (2008).
15. SNAP is codified at 7 U.S.C. §§ 2011–2036(a), and implementing regulations are published in Title 7 of the Code of Federal Regulations, §§ 271.1–285.5. A list of state options can be found online. *See* U.S. Department of Agriculture, Food and Nutrition Service, State Options Report Supplemental Nutrition Assistance Program (May 2018), https://www.fns.usda.gov/snap/state-options-report. States also publish their own local rules.
16. U.S. Department of Agriculture, Food and Nutrition Service, Food and Nutrition Service, Supplemental Nutrition Assistance Program Data as of July 7, 2017, https://www.fns.usda.gov/sites/default/files/pd/34SNAPmonthly.pdf.
17. *See* Food Research & Action Center, SNAP Monthly Data—2017, SNAP Over-the-Year Participation Down Nearly Two million People in April 2017, the Lowest Level in Over Six Years, http://frac.org/research/resource-library/snap-monthly-data-2017. The trend continued through 2018. *See* Center on Budget and Policy Priorities, Policy Basics: The Supplemental Nutrition Assistance Program (updated June 25, 2019), https://www.cbpp.org/research/food-assistance/policy-basics-the-supplemental-nutrition-assistance-program-snap (reporting that "SNAP caseloads have been falling for five years; about 7 million fewer people participated in SNAP in 2018 than in 2013"). On regional and demographic differentials, *see* Food Research & Action Center, SNAP Map: SNAP Matters in Every State, Interactive Data Tool, https://frac.org/research/resource-library-snap-map-snap-matters-every-state (providing household participation rates by state, indicating shares with workers, children, or TANF participation, and metropolitan, rural, or small town).
18. *See* Dottie Rosenbaum and Brynne Keith-Jennings, SNAP Caseload and Spending Declines Accelerated in 2016: Return of Three-Month Time Limit a Factor in Many States, Center on Budget and Policy Priorities (Jan. 2017), https://www.cbpp.org/research/food-assistance/snap-caseload-and-spending-declines-accelerated-in-2016. In 2015 participation rates increased among the elderly and working households.
19. *See* Steven Carlson, Dottie Rosenbaum, Brynne Keith-Jennings, & Caitlin Nchako, SNAP Works for America's Children, Center on Budget and Policy Priorities (Sept. 29, 2016), https://www.cbpp.org/research/food-assistance/snap-works-for-americas-children (reporting shares of children who participate in SNAP each month based on 2014 data); *see also* Mark R. Rank & Thomas A. Hirschl, Estimating the Risk of Food Stamp Use and Impoverishment During Childhood, 163 (11) Pediatrics and Adolescent Medicine 994–999 (2009), https://jamanetwork.com/journals/jamapediatrics/fullarticle/382364.
20. Peter Edelman, So Rich, So Poor: Why It's So Hard to End Poverty in America 8 (New Press 2012).
21. Office of the President of the United States, Long-term Benefits of the Supplemental Nutrition Assistance Program (Dec. 2015), https://obamawhitehouse.archives.gov/sites/whitehouse.gov/files/documents/SNAP_report_final_nonembargo.pdf.

22. Center on Budget and Policy Priorities, Chart Book: SNAP Helps Struggling Families Put Food on the Table (Jan. 8, 2015), http://www.cbpp.org/cms/?fa=view&id=3744.

23. Food Research & Action Center, October 2015 Marked Fifth Straight Monthly Decline in SNAP Participation, http://frac.org/reports-and-resources/snapfood-stamp-monthly-participation-data/.

24. *See* Food Research & Action Center, The Role of the Supplemental Nutrition Assistance Program in Improving Health and Well-Being (Dec. 2017), http://www.frac.org/wp-content/uploads/hunger-health-role-snap-improving-health-well-being.pdf; Kalena Thomhave, Food Stamps Aren't a Substitute for Work. They're How Low-Wage Workers Avoid Hunger, The American Prospect (Mar. 28, 2018), https://prospect.org/article/food-stamps-arent-substitute-work-theyre-how-low-wage-workers-avoid-hunger (citing studies showing that "[m]ost adults on SNAP are workers, but they turn to the program when they're between jobs or making too little.").

25. *See, for example*, Craig Gunderson, Brent Kreider, & John V. Pepper, Reconstructing the Supplemental Nutrition Assistance Program to More Effectively Alleviate Food Insecurity in the United States, 4 Russell Sage J. of Soc. Sci. 113 (2018), Project MUSE, muse.jhu.edu/article/687578 (finding an increase in weekly benefits of $42 for SNAP households would produce 62% decline in food insecurity); Patricia M. Anderson & Kristin F. Butcher, The Relationships Among SNAP Benefits, Grocery Spending, Diet Quality, and the Adequacy of Low-Income Families' Resources, Center on Budget and Policy Priorities (June 14, 2016), https://www.cbpp.org/research/food-assistance/the-relationships-among-snap-benefits-grocery-spending-diet-quality-and-the; Adam Drewnowski & Petra Eichelsdoerfer, Can Low-Income Americans Afford a Healthy Diet?, 44 Nutrition Today 246 (Nov. 2010), https://www.ncbi.nlm.nih.gov/pmc/articles/PMC2847733/.

26. *See, for example*, Sasha-Ann Simons, "It's About Perception": Eligible Maryland Residents Aren't Participating in Food Stamp Benefit Program, WAMU (Jan. 21, 2019), https://wamu.org/story/19/01/21/its-about-perception-eligible-maryland-residents-arent-participating-in-food-benefit-program/; Anna Gorman & Harriet Rowan, Why Millions of Californians Eligible for Food Stamps Don't Get them, NPR (May 1, 2018), https://www.cnn.com/2019/04/24/media/abigial-disney-executive-pay/index.html; Eli Saslow, In Florida, a food-stamp recruiter faces would-be recipients' wrenching choices, Washington Post (Apr. 24, 2013), https://www.pulitzer.org/winners/eli-saslow.

27. 7 U.S.C. § 2012(i).

28. Congress eliminated the coupon purchase requirement with enactment of the Food Stamp Act of 1977. For a discussion of how eliminating the purchase requirement affected the program, *see* Mark Winne, Closing the Food Gap: Resetting the Table in the Land of Plenty xxi (Beacon Press 2008).

29. 7 C.F.R. § 274.2(f)(2).

30. 7 U.S.C. § 2016(k)(1)–(2); U.S. Department of Agriculture, Food and Nutrition Service, Supplemental Nutrition Assistance Program: Online Purchasing Pilot, https://www.fns.usda.gov/snap/online-purchasing-pilot. The Agricultural Improvement Act

of 2018 removed the sunset provision for these programs. P.L. 115-334, 132 Stat. 4490, 4624 (2018).

31. 7 C.F.R. § 271.2 (eligible food includes seeds and plants to grow foods for personal consumption). *See* U.S. Department of Agriculture, Nikki Salzman, Using SNAP Benefits to Grow Your Own Food (July 6, 2011), https://www.usda.gov/media/blod/2011/07/06/using-snap-benefits-grow-your-own-food.

32. 7 U.S.C. § 2012(k); *see* U.S. Department of Agriculture, Supplemental Nutrition Assistance Program, What Can SNAP Buy? (Sept. 4, 2013), https://www.fns.usda.gov/snap/eligible-food-items.

33. 7 C.F.R. § 274.2(h).

34. 7 C.F.R. § 274.2(h)(ii).

35. 7 U.S.C. § 2012(k).

36. 7 U.S.C. § 2012(k)(3) & (4).

37. 7 U.S.C. § 2012(k)(5).

38. 7 U.S.C. § 2012(k)(9). The household cannot be required to use SNAP benefits, and cannot be charged more than the average cost of the food purchased by the homeless provider. *See* 7 C.F.R. § 278.2(b).

39. 7 U.S.C. § 2012(k)(8).

40. 7 U.S.C. § 2012(k)(7).

41. For example, California used the RMP to give homeless college students access to meals. *See* California EBT Project, California Restaurant Meals Program, http://www.ebtproject.ca.gov/clientinformation/calfreshrmp.shtml.

42. U.S. Department of Agriculture, USDA Launches SNAP Online Purchasing Pilot (Apr. 18, 2019), https://www.fns.usda.gov/pressrelease/2019/fns-0003. *See also* Brad Weinstein, Illinois House Bill Would Allow Fast-Food Restaurants to Accept Food Stamps, Illinois Policy (May 10, 2019), https://www.illinoispolicy.org/illinois-house-bill-would-allow-fast-food-restaurants-to-accept-food-stamps/.

43. *See* Food Research & Action Center, Disaster Relief: Nutrition Programs Respond, http://frac.org/hunger-natural-disasters; U.S. Department of Agriculture, Food Assistance for Disaster Relief, https://www.fns.usda.gov/disaster/disaster-assistance.

44. Center on Budget and Policy Priorities, SNAP Retailers Database, https://www.cbpp.org/snap-retailers-database. Larger stores include superstores, supermarkets, and grocery stores.

45. *See* U.S. Department of Agriculture, Comparison of SNAP Authorized Farmers Markets FY2012 and FY2017, https://fns-prod.azureedge.net/sites/default/files/snap/SNAP-Farmers-Markets-Redemptions.pdf.

46. 7 C.F.R. § 278.1(s).

47. 7 U.S.C. § 2016(b); 7 C.F.R. § 278.1.

48. 7 C.F.R. § 278.2(b).

49. 7 U.S.C. § 2013(a) (state and local taxes); 7 C.F.R. §§ 272.1(b) (taxes) and 278.2 (taxes). For a chart that sets outs state-by state consumer bag legislation and whether bags are free for SNAP recipients, *see* Retail Compliance Center, Consumer Bag Legislation, http://www.retailcvc.org/RegGuidance/rcracompliance/Pages/bagMatrix.aspx.

50. 7 U.S.C. § 2017(b); 7 C.F.R. § 272.1(a).

51. 7 U.S.C. § 2012(i); 7 C.F.R. § 273.1.

52. *See* 7 U.S.C. § 2012(m); 7 C.F.R. § 273.1.

53. 7 C.F.R. § 273.1(b).

54. 7 C.F.R. § 273.1(b)(2).

55. 7 C.F.R. § 273.1(b)(1)(i).

56. 7 C.F.R. § 273.1(b)(1)(ii). Parents include natural, adoptive, and stepparents.

57. 7 C.F.R. § 273.1(b)(1)(iii).

58. 7 C.F.R. § 273.1(d)(1).

59. 7 C.F.R. § 273.2(c).

60. For more information on designating an authorized representatives, *see* AARP Foundation & FRAC, Combatting Food Insecurity: Tools for Helping Older Adults Access SNAP, http://frac.org/wp-content/uploads/senior_snap_toolkit_aarp_frac-1.pdf.

61. 7 C.F.R. § 273.3(a). "Homeless individual" is defined in 7 U.S.C. § 2012(l)(1)–(2) and 7 C.F.R. § 271.2.

62. 7 C.F.R. § 273.3(a).

63. 7 C.F.R. § 273.1(b)(3).

64. 7 C.F.R. § 273.1(b)(3)(ii).

65. Reasonable compensation is defined by statute to be "an amount that equals or exceeds two-third of the maximum foot stamp allotment for the appropriate size of the boarder household," assuming the board arrangement is "for two meals or less per day." 7 C.F.R. § 273.1(3)(ii)(B).

66. 7 C.F.R. § 273.1(b)(5).

67. 7 C.F.R. § 273.1(b)(4).

68. 7 C.F.R. § 273.1(b)(7)(vi).

69. 7 C.F.R. § 273.1(b)(7)(vi)(A).

70. 7 C.F.R. § 273.1(b)(7)(vi)(B).

71. 7 C.F.R. § 273.1(b)(7)(vi)(C).

72. 7 C.F.R. § 273.1(b)(7)(vi)(D).

73. 7 C.F.R. § 273.1(b)(7)(vi)(E).

74. 7 U.S.C. § 2015(f).

75. Congressional Research Service, Ruth Ellen Wasem, Noncitizen Eligibility for Federal Public Assistance: Policy Overview and Trends (Sept. 24, 2014), https://www.fas.org/sgp/crs/misc/RL33809.pdf.

76. U.S. Department of Agriculture, Food and Nutrition Service, Characteristics of Supplemental Nutrition Assistance Program Households: Fiscal Year 2016 (Nov. 2017), https://fns-prod.azureedge.net/sites/default/files/ops/Characteristics2016.pdf.

77. *See* Caitlin Dewey, Immigrants are going hungry so Trump won't deport them, *The Washington Post* (Mar. 16, 2017), https://www.washingtonpost.com/news/wonk/wp/2017/03/16/immigrants-are-now-canceling-their-food-stamps-for-fear-that-trump-will-deport-them/?utm_term=.5b1da4e85d97.

78. The new rule appears at 84 Fed. Reg. 41292 (Aug. 14, 2019), and the government's summary of the rule is available at https://www.uscis.gov/legal-resources/final-rule-public-charge-ground-inadmissibility. Receipt of SNAP does not automatically render an immigrant "likely to become a public charge." Instead, receipt of designated

public benefits (cash public assistance, SNAP, and certain forms of Medicaid and public housing assistance) is considered a negative factor or a "heavily weighted negative factor" in a "totality of the circumstances" test. 84 Fed. Reg. 41298–41299. The central impact of the new rule will be on immigrants with approved family-based petitions who are applying for lawful permanent resident status (green cards). For discussions of the deterrent effect on immigrant access to nutritional assistance, *see* American Public Health Association, Study: Following 10-year gains, SNAP participation among immigrant families dropped in 2018 (Nov. 12, 2018), https://www.apha.org/news-and-media/news-releases/apha-news-releases/2018/annual-meeting-snap-participation; Allison Bovell-Ammon, Stephanie Ettinger de Cuba, Sharon Coleman, Nayab Ahmad Maureen M. Black, Deborah A. Frank, Eduardo Ochoa, Jr., & and Diana B. Cutt, Trends in Food Insecurity and SNAP Participation among Immigrant Families of U.S.-Born Young Children, 6 no. 4 Children (2019), https://www.mdpi.com/2227-9067/6/4/55?_ga=2.66363049.641720268.156453235 3-23054786.1551631682.

79. For a concise explanation of the "public charge" concept, *see* Em Puhl, Erin Quinn, & Sally Kinoshita, An Overview of Public Charge, Immigrant Legal Resource Center (Dec. 2018), https://www.ilrc.org/overview-public-charge.

80. 7 U.S.C. § 2015(f).

81. An immigrant is entitled to credit for quarters of work by a parent (while the immigrant was under 18 years of age) or by a spouse. Quarters of employment are determined in the same manner as for calculation of Social Security benefits, except work not covered by the Social Security system may count toward the required 40 quarters. 7 C.F.R. § 273.4(a)(6)(ii)(A).

82. 7 C.F.R. § 273.4(a)(6)(i)(A).

83. 7 C.F.R. § 273.4(a)(6)(ii)(I).

84. 7 C.F.R. § 273.4(a)(6)(i)(B).

85. 7 C.F.R. § 273.4(a)(6)(i)(C).

86. 7 C.F.R. § 273.4(a)(6)(i)(E).

87. 7 C.F.R. § 273.4(a)(6)(i)(H).

88. Department of Defense Appropriations Act of 2010, Pub. L. No. 111-118, § 8120, 123 Stat. 3457.

89. 7 C.F.R. § 273.4(a)(3)(i).

90. 7 C.F.R. § 273.4(a)(3)(ii).

91. 7 C.F.R. § 273.4(a)(4)(i)–(iii).

92. 7 C.F.R. § 273.4(a)(5)(i)–(iv).

93. 7 C.F.R. § 273.4(a)(6)(iii).

94. 7 C.F.R. § 273.4(a)(6)(ii).

95. 7 C.F.R. § 273.4(a)(6)(i)(F) & (iii)(D).

96. 7 C.F.R. § 273.4(a)(6)(i)(D) & (iii)(B).

97. 7 C.F.R. § 273.4(a)(6)(i)(G) & (iii)(D).

98. *See* Congressional Research Service, Ruth Ellen Wasem, Unauthorized Aliens' Access to Federal Benefits: Policy and Issues (Sept. 17, 2012), https://fas.org/sgp/crs/homesec/RL34500; Congressional Research Service, Ruth Ellen Wasem,

Unauthorized Aliens' Access to Federal Benefits: Policy and Issues (updated Sept. 24, 2014 and Oct. 28, 2016), https://www.everycrsreport.com/reports/RL34500.html.

99. The 2002 Farm Bill broadly restored SNAP eligibility to most lawfully present noncitizens, including individuals who resided in the United States for five years, children under 18, and individuals receiving disability-related assistance or benefits. *See* U.S. Department of Agriculture, Food and Nutrition Service, Assessing Implementation of the 2002 Farm Bill's Immigrant Food Stamp Restorations, https://fns-prod.azureedge.net/sites/default/files/ImmigrantFSPRestorationSummary.pdf.

100. *See* National Immigration Law Center, State-Funded Food Assistance Programs, https://www.nilc.org/issues/economic-support/state_food/ (noting that as of August 2016, California, Connecticut, Illinois, Maine, Minnesota, and Washington State maintained food assistance programs for certain immigrants who do not meet federal eligibility guidelines).

101. 7 U.S.C. §§ 2020(q); 2020(e)(18)(b).

102. 7 U.S.C. § 2015(n).

103. 7 U.S.C. § 2015(s).

104. 7 C.F.R. § 2015(m).

105. Congressional Research Service, Maggie McCarty, Gene Falk, Randy Alison Aussenberg, & David H. Carpenter, Drug Testing and Crime-Related Restrictions in TANF, SNAP, and Housing Assistance (Nov. 28, 2016), at 15, Table 1, https://fas.org/sgp/crs/misc/R42394.pdf. *See also* Molly Born, In Some States, Drug Felons Still Face Lifetime Ban on SNAP Benefits, NPR (June 20, 2018), https://www.npr.org/sections/thesalt/2018/06/20/621391895/in-some-states-drug-felons-still-face-lifetime-ban-on-snap-benefits.

106. *See* Lebron v. Florida Dept. of Children and Families, 772 F.3d 1352 (11th Cir. 2014) (affirming injunction to halt drug-testing of public assistance applicants without any suspicion). *See also* Maria E. Valencia, Supplemental Nutrition Assistance Program (SNAP) Formerly Known as Food Stamps: The Unfair Target of Constitutionally Suspect Conditions, 27 San Joaquin Agric. L. Rev. 223 (2017–2018). The Agriculture Act of 2014, Pub. L. No. 113-79, rejected proposed changes that would have permitted states to require drug testing as part of the SNAP application, whether or not the applicant had been convicted of a drug-related crime. *See* Congressional Research Service, Randy Alisson Aussenberg, SNAP and Related Nutrition Provisions of the 2014 Farm Bill (P.L. 113-79) (Apr. 24, 2014), http://nationalaglawcenter.org/wp-content/uploads/assets/crs/R43332.pdf. Wisconsin now requires drug testing for all food stamp applicants. *See* H. Claire Brown, Buried in Wisconsin Republicans' Lame-Duck Legislation: Drug Testing Requirements for Food Stamp Applicants, The Intercept (Dec. 6, 2018), https://theintercept.com/2018/12/06/wisconsin-food-stamps-drug-testing/. Other states have proposed various other drug-testing regimes. *See generally* Victoria Palacio, Drug Testing SNAP Applicants Is Ineffective and Perpetuates Stereotypes, Center for Law and Social Policy (July 2017), https://www.clasp.org/publications/report/brief/drug-testing-snap-applicants-ineffective-and-perpetuates-stereotypes.

107. Congressional Research Service, Maggie McCarty, Gene Falk, Randy Alison Aussenberg, & David H. Carpenter, Drug Testing and Crime-Related Restrictions in TANF, SNAP, and Housing Assistance (Nov. 28, 2016), at 11, https://fas.org/sgp/crs/misc/R42394.pdf.

108. 7 C.F.R. §§ 273.1(b)(x); 7 C.F.R. §273.11(o), (p), (q).

109. *See* Elizabeth Wolkomir & Stacy Dean, Child Support Cooperation Requirements in SNAP Are Unproven, Costly, and Put Families at Risk, Center on Budget and Policy Priorities (Feb. 7, 2019), https://www.cbpp.org/research/food-assistance/child-support-cooperation-requirements-in-snap-are-unproven-costly-and-put.

110. 7 C.F.R. § 273.5(a), (b).

111. 7 C.F.R. § 273.5(b)(1).

112. 7 C.F.R. § 273.5(b)(2).

113. 7 C.F.R. § 273.5(b)(3).

114. 7 C.F.R. § 273.5(b)(4).

115. 7 C.F.R. § 273.5(b)(5).

116. 7 C.F.R. § 273.5(b)(6).

117. 7 C.F.R. § 273.5(b)(7).

118. 7 C.F.R. § 273.5(b)(8).

119. 7 C.F.R. § 273.5(b)(9).

120. 7 C.F.R. § 273.5(b)(10).

121. 7 C.F.R. § 273.5(b)(11). These job-training programs include those offered through the Job Training Partnership Act of 1974; an employment and training program assigned by the state agency under the Food Stamp Act; a program under § 236 of the Trade Act of 1974; and, an employment or training program for low-income households operated by state or local government as long as the state agencies have determined that the program qualifies.

122. 7 C.F.R. § 273.6. For information on how to apply for a Social Security number, *see* U.S. Social Security Administration, Application for a Social Security Card, https://www.ssa.gov/forms/ss-5.pdf.

123. 7 C.F.R. § 273.9(a).

124. 7 C.F.R. § 273.9(a)(1). *See* U.S. Department of Agriculture, Memo to Regional Directors, Clarification on Characteristics of Broad-Based Categorical Eligibility Programs (Dec. 27, 2016). For a list of SNAP Broad-Based Categorical Eligibility by State, *see* Congressional Research Service, Gene Falk & Randy Alison Aussenberg, The Supplemental Nutrition Assistance Program (SNAP): Categorical Eligibility (July 22, 2014), at Table 1.

125. *See* Congressional Research Service, Gene Falk & Randy Alison Aussenberg, The Supplemental Nutrition Assistance Program (SNAP): Categorical Eligibility (updated Jan. 4, 2019), https://crsreports.congress.gov/product/pdf/R/R42054.

126. *See* Elaine Waxman, The Importance of Broad-Based Categorical Eligibility (BBCE) in SNAP, Testimony before the Committee on Agriculture, U.S. House of Representatives, Urban Institute (June 20, 2019), https://www.urban.org/sites/default/files/publication/100429/the_importance_of-bbce_in_snap_2.pdf.

127. 7 C.F.R. §§ 2014(c) (gross income test); § 273.9(a)(1).

128. 7 U.S.C. § 2014(c) (gross income); § 2014(d) (exclusions from income); § 2014(e) (deductions from income); 7 C.F.R. § 273.9(a)(1) (gross income standard).

129. U.S. Department of Agriculture, Food and Nutrition Service, Supplemental Nutrition Assistance Program (SNAP): FY 2019 Income Eligibility Standards, https://fns-prod.azureedge.net/sites/default/files/snap/FY19-Income-Eligibility-Standards.pdf. Note that the federal poverty income guidelines are higher in Alaska and Hawaii than in the continental United States.

130. 7 C.F.R. § 2014(d) (deductions from income); 7 C.F.R. § 273.9(a)(2).

131. U.S. Department of Agriculture, Food and Nutrition Service, Supplemental Nutrition Assistance Program (SNAP):, SNAP Eligibility, Table 1: SNAP Income Eligibility Limits—October 1, 2018, through September 30, 2019, https://www.fns.usda.gov/snap/recipient/eligibility.

132. 7 U.S.C. § 2014(d); 7 C.F.R. § 273.9(b).

133. 7 C.F.R. § 273.9(c)(1).

134. 7 U.S.C. § 2014(d) (exclusions from income).

135. 7 C.F.R. § 273.9(b)(1)(i).

136. 7 C.F.R. § 273.9(b)(1)(ii). Self-employment income includes the ownership of rental property if a household member is actively engaged in the property's management at least an average of 20 hours a week (otherwise the income counts as unearned income and equals gross income less the cost of doing the business).

137. 7 C.F.R. § 273.9(b)(1)(ii).

138. 7 C.F.R. § 273.9(b)(1)(iii).

139. 7 C.F.R. § 273.9(b)(1)(v).

140. 7 C.F.R. §§ 273.9(b)(1)(vi), 273.9(c)(3)(ii), 273.9(b)(5), 273.11(k) (defining comparable sanctions under other means-tested programs).

141. 7 C.F.R. § 273.9(b)(2)(i).

142. 7 C.F.R. § 273.9(b)(2)(ii).

143. 7 C.F.R. § 273.9(b)(2)(iii).

144. 7 C.F.R. § 273.9(b)(2)(v).

145. 7 C.F.R. § 273.9(b)(2)(vi).

146. 7 C.F.R. § 273.9(b)(5).

147. 7 C.F.R. § 273.9(b)(5)(ii).

148. 7 U.S.C. § 2014(d); 7 C.F.R. § 273.9(c).

149. 7 U.S.C. § 2014(d)(1); 7 C.F.R. § 273.9(c)(1).

150. 7 U.S.C. § 2014(d)(2); 7 C.F.R. § 273.9(c)(2).

151. 7 U.S.C. § 2014(d)(3); 7 C.F.R. § 273.9(c)(3)(i)–(v).

152. 7 U.S.C. § 2014(d)(4); 7 C.F.R. § 273.9(c)(4).

153. 7 U.S.C. § 2014(d)(5); 7 C.F.R. § 273.9(c)(5).

154. 7 U.S.C. § 2014(d)(6); 7 C.F.R. § 273.9(c)(6).

155. 7 U.S.C. § 2014(d)(7); 7 C.F.R. § 273.9(c)(7).

156. 7 U.S.C. § 2014(d)(8); 7 C.F.R. § 273.9(c)(8).

157. 7 U.S.C. § 2014(d)(9); 7 C.F.R. § 273.9(c)(9).

158. 7 U.S.C. § 2014(d)(10); 7 C.F.R. § 273.9(c)(10) (identifying programs). Payments under the Alaska Native Claims Settlement Act and payments made to volunteers under the Foster Grandparents Program are excluded.

159. 7 U.S.C. § 2014(d)(11); 7 C.F.R. § 273.9(c)(11).
160. 7 U.S.C. § 2014(d)(12); 7 C.F.R. § 273.9(c)(12).
161. 7 U.S.C. § 2014(d)(13); 7 C.F.R § 273.9(c)(13).
162. 7 U.S.C. § 2014(d)(14); 7 C.F.R. §§ 273.9(c)(14) (educational and training costs) & 273.7(d)(3)(i) (dependent care services). Notwithstanding provisions of the Workforce Innovation and Opportunity Act, 29 U.S.C. 3241(a)(2), earnings to individuals participating in on-the-job training programs under the act are earned income except for dependents younger than age 19. 7 U.S.C. § 2014(l).
163. 7 U.S.C. § 2014(d)(15); 7 C.F.R. § 273.9(c)(16).
164. 7 U.S.C. § 2014(d)(16); 7 C.F.R. § 273.9(c)(18).
165. 7 U.S.C. § 2014(d)(17); 7 C.F.R. § 273.9(c)(19).
166. 7 U.S.C. § 2014(d)(18); 7 C.F.R. § 273.9(c)(18)–(19).
167. 7 U.S.C. § 2014(d)(19); 7 C.F.R. § 273.9(c)(20).
168. 7 U.S.C. § 2014(k); 7 C.F.R. § 273.9(c)(1)(i)(A)–(F).
169. 7 C.F.R. § 273.9(c)(1)(ii)(A)–(E). Energy assistance payments are considered money payable to the household. 7 U.S.C. § 2014(k)(4)(A).
170. 7 C.F.R. § 273.9(c)(1)(iii).
171. 7 C.F.R. § 273.9(c)(1)(iv).
172. 7 C.F.R. § 273.9(c)(1)(v).
173. 7 C.F.R. § 273.9(c)(1)(vi).
174. 7 C.F.R. § 273.9(c)(1)(vii).
175. 7 U.S.C. § 2014(e)(2); 7 C.F.R. § 273.9(d)(2).
176. 7 U.S.C. § 2014(e)(1); 7 C.F.R. § 273.9(d)(1). See U.S. Department of Agriculture, Food and Nutrition Service, SNAP—Fiscal year 2019 Cost-of-Living Adjustments, Memorandum (July 27, 2018), https://fns-prod.azureedge.net/sites/default/files/snap/FY19-Maximum-Allotments-Deductions.pdf.
177. 7 U.S.C. § 2014(e)(5); 7 C.F.R. § 273.9(d)(3). See Ty Jones, SNAP'S Excess Medical Expense Deduction: Targeting Food Assistance to Low-Income Seniors and Individuals with Disabilities, Center for Budget and Policy Priorities (Aug. 2014), https://www.cbpp.org/sites/default/files/atoms/files/8-20-14fa.pdf (discussing underutilization of the SNAP medical expense deduction and suggesting measures to remove barriers).
178. 7 C.F.R. § 273.9(d)(3)(i)–(x). Expenses for medical marijuana may not be counted toward this deduction. 7 U.S.C. § 2014(e)(5)(C).
179. See U.S. Department of Agriculture, Food and Nutrition Service, State Options Report (Fourteenth Edition, May 31, 2018), at 27, https://fns-prod.azureedge.net/sites/default/files/snap/14-State-Options.pdf.
180. See Food Research & Action Center, U.S. Hunger Solutions: Best Practices for Capturing Allowable Medical Expense Deductions for SNAP (May 2019), https://frac.org/research/resource-library/u-s-hunger-solutions-best-practices-for-capturing-allowable-medical-expense-deductions-for-snap.
181. 7 U.S.C. § 2014(e)(3); 7 C.F.R. § 273.9(d)(4). See Food Research & Action Center, U.S. Hunger Solutions: Best Practices for Using the Dependent Care Deduction to Maximize SNAP Benefits for Working Families (Nov. 2016), https://www.frac.org/wp-content/uploads/best-practice-using-dependent-care-deduction.pdf.

182. 7 U.S.C. § 2014(e)(4); 7 C.F.R. § 273.9(d)(5).

183. 7 U.S.C. § 2014(e)(6); 7 C.F.R. § 273.9(d)(6)(ii).

184. U.S. Department of Agriculture, Food and Nutrition Service, Supplemental Nutrition Assistance Program: Am I Eligible for SNAP?, SNAP Excess Shelter Cost Deductions [current for Oct. 1, 2018 through Sept. 30, 2019], https://www.fns.usda.gov/snap/eligibility#SNAP%20Excess%20Shelter%20Costs%20Deduction.

185. U.S. Department of Agriculture, Food and Nutrition Service, Supplemental Nutrition Assistance Program (SNAP), SNAP Special Rules for the Elderly or Disabled [current for Oct. 1, 2018 through Sept. 30, 2019], https://www.fns.usda.gov/snap/snap-special-rules-elderly-or-disabled.

186. 7 U.S.C. § 2014(e)(6)(C); 7 C.F.R. § 273.9(d)(6)(iii). The standard utility allowance is updated annually. See U.S. Department of Agriculture, Food and Nutrition Service, Supplemental Nutrition Assistance Program (SNAP), Standard Utility Allowances (Feb. 14, 2019), https://www.fns.usda.gov/snap/standard-utility-allowances.

187. 7 C.F.R. § 273.9(d)(6)(i). U.S. Department of Agriculture, Food and Nutrition Service, FY19 Homeless Shelter Deduction Memo (Feb. 8, 2019), https://www.fns.usda.gov/snap/fy19-homeless-shelter-deduction-memo. Twenty-eight states had elected this option as of FY2018. See U.S. Department of Agriculture, Food and Nutrition Service, State Options Report (Fourteenth Edition, May 31, 2018), at 14, https://fns-prod.azureedge.net/sites/default/files/snap/14-State-Options.pdf.

188. 7 U.S.C. § 2014(i); 7 C.F.R. § 273.4(c)(3). "Sponsored" is defined as "an alien for whom a person (the sponsor) has executed an affidavit of support (INS Form I-864 or I-864A) on behalf of the alien" under § 213A of the Immigration and Nationality Act. 7 C.F.R. § 273.4(c).

189. 7 C.F.R. § 273.4(c)(2).

190. 7 C.F.R. § 273.4(c)(2)(i)(A).

191. 7 C.F.R. § 273.4(c)(2)(i)(B).

192. 7 C.F.R. § 273.4(c)(2)(v).

193. 7 C.F.R. § 273.4(c)(2)(v)–(vi).

194. 7 C.F.R. § 273.4(c)(3)(2).

195. 7 C.F.R. § 273.4(c)(3)(v).

196. 7 C.F.R. § 273.4(c)(3)(iv). If an immigrant is determined to be indigent under this exception, then the only sponsor income deemed to the immigrant is income the sponsor actually provides. This exemption from sponsor deeming lasts for 12 months and is renewable for additional 12-month periods. Note that, given the current uncertainty surrounding the Trump administration's proposed "public charge" regulations, the immigration consequences of obtaining an indigency designation are unclear. The public charge issue is discussed earlier in this chapter.

197. See Congressional Research Service, Gene Falk & Randy Alison Aussenberg, The Supplemental Nutrition Assistance Program (SNAP): Categorical Eligibility (updated Jan. 4, 2019). For a list of states that have adopted SNAP broad based categorical eligibility and eliminated the assets test for families, see U.S. Department of Agriculture, Broad-Based Categorical Eligibility (Oct. 2018), https://fns-prod.azureedge.net/sites/default/files/snap/BBCE.pdf. See generally Jessica Gehr, Elimination of Asset Limits: Creating Savings for Families and State Governments, CLASP (updated Apr.

2018),   https://www.clasp.org/publications/report/brief/eliminating-asset-limits-creating-savings; Caroline Ratcliffe, Reviving SNAP asset limits could backfire on families' finances, Urban Institute, Urban Wire: Poverty, Vulnerability, and the Safety Net (May 14, 2018), https://www.urban.org/urban-wire/reviving-snap-asset-limits-could-backfire-families-finances (reporting that "in states that removed or relaxed asset limits, families' financial security improved through increased savings and connections to banks, and families were less likely to cycle on and off SNAP" and arguing against proposed federal changes that would narrow state discretion to relax SNAP asset limits).

198. 84 Fed. Reg. 35570 (July 24, 2019). *See* Robert Greenstein, Misguided Trump Administration Rule Would Take Basic Food Assistance from Working Families, Seniors, and People with Disabilities, Center on Budget and Policy Priorities (July 23, 2019), https://www.cbpp.org/press/statements/misguided-trump-administration-rule-would-take-basic-food-assistance-from-working. For a description of how states have implemented the BBCE and its impact of low-income families, *see* Dottie Rosenbaum, SNAP's "Broad-Based Categorical Eligibility" Supports Working Families and Those Saving for the Future, Center on Budget and Policy Priorities (updated July 23, 2019), https://www.cbpp.org/research/food-assistance/snaps-broad-based-categorical-eligibility-supports-working-families-and.

199. 7 U.S.C. § 2014(g)(1); 7 C.F.R. § 273.8(b). *See* U.S. Department of Agriculture, Food and Nutrition Service, Supplemental Nutrition Program: Resources (Oct. 2, 2017), https://www.fns.usda.gov/snap/resources-rules-resource-limits.

200. 7 U.S.C. § 2014(g)(1) (general definition) & (g)(2) (listing "included assets").

201. 7 C.F.R. § 273.8(e) (exclusions from resources).

202. 7 C.F.R. § 273.8(e)(1).

203. 7 C.F.R. § 273.8(e)(2).

204. 7 C.F.R. § 273.8(e)(2).

205. 7 C.F.R. § 273.8(e)(3)(i)(A).

206. 7 C.F.R. § 273.8(e)(3)(i)(E).

207. 7 C.F.R. § 273.8(e)(3)(C).

208. 7 C.F.R. § 273.8(e)(3)(i)(G).

209. *See* U.S. Department of Agriculture, Food and Nutrition Service, Supplemental Nutrition Program: Resources (Oct. 2, 2017), https://www.fns.usda.gov/snap/resources-rules-resource-limits.

210. 7 C.F.R. § 273.8(e)(11).

211. 7 C.F.R. § 273.8(e)(12)(ii). The 12-month rule applies to federal, state, and local earned income tax credits. If the credit is received as a lump sum or under Internal Revenue code § 3507 when the taxpayer is not participating in the Food Stamp Program, it counts as a resource for the month of receipt and the following month for the taxpayer and taxpayer's spouse.

212. *See* Food Research & Action Center, Replacing the Thrifty Food Plan in Order to Provide Adequate Allotments for SNAP Beneficiaries (Dec. 2012), http://frac.org/research/resource-library/replacing-thrifty-food-plan-order-provide-adequate-allotments-snap-beneficiaries.

213. *See* Executive Office of the President of the United States, Long-term Benefits of the Supplemental Nutrition Assistance Program 31–35 (Dec. 2015). *See also* Elaine Waxman, How reevaluating the Thrifty Food Plan can improve SNAP, Urban Institute, Urban Wire: Poverty Vulnerability and the Safety Net (June 12, 2018), https://www.urban.org/urban-wire/how-reevaluating-thrifty-food-plan-can-improve-snap (reporting that the average cost of a low-income meal is $2.36, 27% higher than the SNAP maximum benefit of $1.86).

214. Center on Budget and Policy Priorities, A Quick Guide to SNAP Eligibility and Benefits (Oct. 16, 2018), https://www.cbpp.org/research/food-assistance/a-quick-guide-to-snap-eligibility-and-benefits.

215. U.S. Department of Agriculture, Supplemental Nutrition Assistance Program (SNAP) Fiscal Year 2019 Maximum Allotments and Deductions (Oct. 1, 2018), https://fns-prod.azureedge.net/sites/default/files/snap/FY19-Maximum-Allotments-Deductions.pdf.

216. The Department of Agriculture announces household benefit levels every October. *See* U.S. Department of Agriculture, Food and Nutrition Service, SNAP—Fiscal Year 2019 Cost-of-Living Adjustments, https://www.fns.usda.gov/snap-fy-2019-cost-living-adjustments.

217. *See* U.S. Department of Agriculture, Supplemental Nutrition Assistance Program (SNAP) Fiscal Year (FY) 2019 Maximum Allotments and Deductions (Oct. 1, 2018), https://fns-prod.azureedge.net/sites/default/files/snap/FY19-Maximum-Allotments-Deductions.pdf.

218. 7 C.F.R. § 273.2(b)(i)–(ix).

219. 7 C.F.R. § 273.2(c)(3). For links to state SNAP agencies, *see* https://www.fns.usda.gov/snap/snap-application-and-local-office-locators.

220. 7 C.F.R. § 273.2(c)(2)(i).

221. 7 C.F.R. § 273.2(a)(1).

222. 7 C.F.R. § 273.2(c)(1)(iv).

223. 7 C.F.R. §§ 273.2(c)(1)(iii); 273.2(g)(1).

224. 7 C.F.R. §§ 273.2(a)(2); 7 C.F.R. § 273.2(b).

225. 7 C.F.R. § 272.1(c). The application must state the program's privacy and confidentiality rules. 7 C.F.R. § 273.2(b)(4). Also, interviews must be conducted "as an official and confidential discussion" and facilities "must be adequate to preserve the privacy and confidentiality of the interview." 7 C.F.R. § 273.2(e)(1).

226. 7 C.F.R § 273.2(f)(1)(ii)(A).

227. 7 C.F.R. § 273.2(e)(3).

228. 7 C.F.R. § 273.2(e)(2).

229. 7 C.F.R. § 273.2(e)(3).

230. 7 C.F.R. §§ 273.2(c)(5); 273.2(f).

231. 7 C.F.R. §§ 273.2(d)(1); 273.2(c)(5).

232. 7 C.F.R. § 273.2(f)(4)(i).

233. 7 C.F.R. § 273.2(e)(2)(ii). *See also* 7 C.F.R. § 273.8(c)(3)(F) (documentation for vehicle exception if "questionable").

234. 7 C.F.R. § 273.2(f)(4)(iii).

235. 7 C.F.R. § 273.2(g)(1). Audits by the Department of Agriculture have confirmed that "too many households applying for SNAP do not receive the benefits within the statutory timeframes." U.S. Department of Agriculture, Food and Nutrition Service, Timeliness in the SNAP Application Process (Summer 2013), http://www.fns.usda.gov/sites/default/files/timeliness_app_process.pdf. *See, for example*, Alexia Elejalde-Ruiz, Delays in processing food stamp applications land Illinois in hot water with the feds, Chicago Tribune (Mar. 27, 2019), https://www.chicagotribune.com/business/ct-biz-illinois-food-stamps-processing-delays-20190327-story.html; Harmony Jones, Federal Court Permits Class Action Lawsuit Alleging Unlawful Food Stamps Processing Delays to Proceed, Legal Aid Society of the District of Columbia, Making Justice Real Blog (Aug. 28, 2018), https://www.makingjusticereal.org/federal-court-permits-class-action-lawsuit-alleging-unlawful-food-stamps-processing-delays-to-proceed (discussing case status of *Garnett v. Zeilinger*, 323 F. Supp.3d 58 (D.D.C. 2018)).

236. 7 C.F.R. § 273.10(a)(1)(ii).

237. 7 C.F.R. §§ 273.2(g)(2); 273.10(a)(1)(ii); 273.11(i).

238. 7 C.F.R. § 273.2(i)(3)(i).

239. 7 C.F.R. § 273.2(i)(2).

240. 7 C.F.R. § 273.2(i)(1)(i).

241. 7 C.F.R. § 273.2(i)(1)(ii).

242. 7 C.F.R. § 273.2(i)(1)(iii).

243. 7 C.F.R. § 273.2(i)(2).

244. 7 C.F.R. § 273.2(i)(4)(i)(B).

245. 7 U.S.C. §§ 2015(d) & (o); 7 C.F.R. § 273.7. *See generally* U.S. Department of Agriculture, Food and Nutrition Service, SNAP Work Requirements (May 29, 2019), https:www.fns.usda.gov/snap/work-requirements; National Conference of State Legislatures, SNAP Work Requirements Fact Sheet (May 16, 2018), http://www.ncsl.org/research/human-services/snap-work-requirements-fact-sheet.aspx (including state-by-state work rules).

246. 7 U.S.C. § 2015(d)(1); 7 C.F.R. § 273.7(a)(1)(i).

247. 7 C.F.R. § 273.7(a)(1)(iv).

248. 7 C.F.R. § 273.7(a)(1)(iii).

249. 7 C.F.R. § 273.7(a)(1)(v)–(vi).

250. 7 C.F.R. § 273.7(a)(1)(vii).

251. 7 C.F.R. § 273.7(e)(3)(ii).

252. 7 C.F.R. § 273.7(h).

253. 7 C.F.R. § 273.7(h)(1)(i).

254. 7 C.F.R. § 273.7(h)(iv). A court may enjoin a strike under Section 208 of the Labor-Management Relations Act, 29 U.S.C. § 78, known as the Taft-Hartley Act, or under Section 10 of the Railway Labor Act, 45 U.S.C. § 160.

255. 7 C.F.R. § 273.7(h)(2)(i).

256. 7 C.F.R. § 273.7(h)(2)(ii).

257. 7 C.F.R. § 273.7(h)(2)(iii).

258. 7 C.F.R. § 273.7(h)(2)(iv).

259. 7 C.F.R. § 273.7(h)(2)(v).
260. 7 C.F.R. § 273.7(h)(1)(v).
261. 7 U.S.C. § 2015(d)(1)(A); 7 C.F.R. § 273.7(b)(1)(i).
262. 7 U.S.C. § 2015(d)(2)(F); 7 C.F.R. § 273.7(b)(1)(i).
263. 7 U.S.C. § 2015(d)(1)(A); 7 C.F.R. § 273.7(b)(ii).
264. 7 U.S.C. § 2015(d)(2)(A); 7 C.F.R. § 273.7(b)(iii).
265. 7 U.S.C. § 2015(d)(2)(B); 7 C.F.R. § 273.7(b)(iv).
266. 7 U.S.C. § 2015(d)(2)(C); 7 C.F.R. § 273.7(b)(viii).
267. 7 U.S.C. § 2015(d)(2)(D); 7 C.F.R. § 273.7(b)(vi).
268. 7 U.S.C. § 2015(d)(2)(E); 7 C.F.R. § 273.7(b)(vii).
269. 7 U.S.C. § 2015(o)(2); 7 C.F.R. § 273.24(a)(1)(i). The requirement is excused for employed individuals who "would have worked an average of 20 hours per week but missed some work for good cause . . . if the absence from work is temporary and the individual retains his or her job. Good cause shall include circumstances beyond the individual's control, such as, but not limited to, illness, illness of another household member requiring the presence of the member, a household emergency, or the unavailability of transportation." 7 C.F.R. § 273.24(b)(2).
270. 7 C.F.R. § 273.24(a)(ii). The exemption also applies to "[a]ny combination of working and participating in a work program 20 hours per week, as determined by the State agency." 7 C.F.R. § 273.24(a)(1)(iii).
271. 7 C.F.R. § 273.24(a)(1)(iv).
272. 7 C.F.R. § 273.24(c)(2).
273. 7 C.F.R. § 273.24(c)(3)–(4).
274. 7 C.F.R. § 273.24(c)(6).
275. 7 C.F.R. § 273.24(c)(5). ABAWD time limits do not apply to SNAP-eligible students because they are exempt from work requirements. 7 C.F.R. § 273.7(b)(viii) (student exemption).
276. *See* U.S. Department of Agriculture, Food and Nutrition Service, Guide to Serving ABAWDs Subject to Time-limited Participation: A Guide to Serving Able-Bodied Adults without Dependents (ABAWDs) (2015), http://www.fns.usda.gov/sites/default/files/Guide_to_Serving_ABAWDs_Subject_to_Time_Limit.pdf.
277. 7 U.S.C. § 2015(o)(6).
278. *See* Ed Bolen, Dottie Rosenbaum, Stacy Dean, & Brynne Keith-Jennings, More Than 500,000 Adults Will Lose SNAP Benefits in 2016 as Waivers Expire, Center on Budget and Policy Priorities (Mar. 18, 2016), http://www.cbpp.org/research/food-assistance/more-than-500000-adults-will-lose-snap-benefits-in-2016-as-waivers-expire; Jen Fifield, New Work Requirements Put Food Stamps at Risk, The Pew Charitable Trusts (Jan. 19, 2016), http://www.pewtrusts.org/en/research-and-analysis/blogs/stateline/2016/01/19/new-work-requirements-put-food-stamps-at-risk. For further discussion, *see* Andrew Hammond & MacKenzie Speer, SNAP's Time Limit: Emerging Issues in Litigation and Implementation, Clearinghouse Community (Apr. 2017), https://povertylaw.org/clearinghouse/article/timelimit.
279. 7 U.S.C. § 2015(o)(4).

280. U.S. Department of Agriculture, Supplemental Nutrition Assistance Program (SNAP): Status of State Able-Bodied Adult without Dependents (ABAWD) Time Limit Waivers—Fiscal Year 2019—1st Quarter (Oct. 1, 2018), https://www.fns.usda.gov/snap/abawd-waivers.
281. 7 U.S.C. § 2015(d)(3); 7 C.F.R. § 273.1(e).
282. 7 C.F.R. § 273.7(f)(1).
283. 7 C.F.R. § 273.7(i).
284. 7 C.F.R. § 273.7(f)(2)(i)–(iii).
285. 7 C.F.R. § 273.7(f)(5)(ii)(B).
286. 7 C.F.R. § 273.7(j)(3)(vi). *See* U.S. Department of Agriculture, Food and Nutrition Service, Clarifications on Work Requirements, ABAWDS and E&T (May 2018), https://fns-prod.azureedge.net/sites/default/files/snap/Clarifications-on-WorkRequirements-ABAWDs-ET-May2018.pdf.
287. 7 C.F.R. § 273.7(i).
288. 7 C.F.R. § 273.7(i)(3)(i).
289. 7 C.F.R. § 273.7(i)(3)(ii).
290. 7 C.F.R. §§ 273.7(j)(3)(ii) (unsuitable work demands); 273.7(i)(3)(iii) (educational training).
291. 7 U.S.C. § 2015(d)(1)(D)(iv); 7 C.F.R. § 273.7(j)(3)(ii).
292. 7 C.F.R. § 273.14.
293. 7 C.F.R. § 273.10(f).
294. *See* U.S. Department of Agriculture, Food and Nutrition Service, FNS Handbook 501, Chapter V—Certification Procedures (Rev. 4/2014), https://fns-prod.azureedge.net/sites/default/files/FNSHANDBOOK_501_Chap5_4_2014_new.pdf.
295. *See* 7 C.F.R. § 273.13 (notice of adverse action). *See also* 7 C.F.R. §§ 273.2(g)(3), 273.10(g)(1)(ii) (denial notices); 7 C.F.R. § 273.13(a)(2) (reduction or termination notices); 7 C.F.R. § 273.15 (hearing rights).
296. 7 C.F.R. §§ 273.13(a)(2); 273.15(k)(1)–(2).
297. 7 C.F.R. § 273.13(a)(1). In certain cases, the state agency may provide notice of an adverse action no later than the date the action would take effect, but the household retains its right to request a hearing and receive unreduced SNAP benefits pending the outcome of the hearing process. 7 C.F.R. § 273.13(a)(3).
298. 7 C.F.R. § 273.15(k).
299. 7 C.F.R. § 273.15(k)(1). If a household fails to request a hearing within the initial 10 days, but can show good cause for its failure, the state must reinstate lost SNAP benefits and continue to provide benefits pending the outcome of the hearing. *Id.*
300. 7 C.F.R. § 273.15(k)(2)(i).
301. 7 C.F.R. § 273.15(a).
302. 7 C.F.R. § 273.15(h).
303. 7 C.F.R. § 273.15(g).
304. 7 C.F.R. § 273.15(m).
305. 7 C.F.R. § 273.15(p)(1).
306. *Id.*
307. 7 C.F.R. § 273.15(a).

308. 7 C.F.R. § 273.15(p)(5).

309. 7 C.F.R. § 273.15(p)(1)–(5).

310. 7 C.F.R. § 273.15(p)(2).

311. 7 C.F.R. § 273.15(q)(1).

312. 7 C.F.R. § 273.15(c)(1).

313. *Id.* The agency must issue any benefits due to the household within 10 days of the fair hearing decision, unless it elects to pay the past-due benefits with the household's normal SNAP issuance, but may not make that election if it would delay issuance of benefits beyond 60 days from the date of the fair hearing request. *Id.* Moreover, if the hearing is at the local level, then within 45 days of the request, the state agency "shall assure that the hearing is conducted, and that a decision is reached and reflected in the SNAP benefit allotment." 7 C.F.R. § 273.15(c)(2).

314. *See* Rebecca Wolozin, Feeding Hungry Mouths: Getting Healthy Food to the Kids [Who] Need It Most, 19 U.C. Davis J. Juv. L. & Pol'y 232 (2015) (providing a history of children's food programs and urging that programs account for the needs of children who do not attend school).

315. 7 C.F.R. § 245.2. *See* Food Research & Action Center, School Meal Eligibility and Reimbursements, http://frac.org/school-meal-eligibility-reimbursements.

316. At the time, states and localities funded the meals, and a Federal Reconstruction Finance Corporation made loans to towns that could not otherwise pay the personnel costs of serving the meals. In another Depression-era development, the federal Department of Agriculture gave schools surplus foods through the Federal Surplus Commodities Corporation, and funded personnel costs through the Community Service Division of the Works Project Administration. *See* Patti Landers, The Food Stamp Program: History, Nutrition, Education and Impact, 107 J. Am. Dietetic. Assoc. 1945 (2007).

317. U.S. Department of Agriculture, Food and Nutrition Service, Gordon W. Gunderson, National School Lunch Program (NSLP): Background and Development (2014), http://www.fns.usda.gov/nslp/history.

318. U.S. Department of Agriculture, Economic Research Service, Mary Kay Fox, William Hamilton, & Biing-Hwan Lin eds., Effects of Food Assistance and Nutrition Programs on Nutrition and Health: Vol.3, Literature Review (Oct. 2004), https://www.ers.usda.gov/publications/pub-details/?pubid=46574.

319. The National School Lunch Act, Act of June 4, 1946, ch. 281, §§ 2–11, 60 Stat. 230. The act currently is codified at 42 U.S.C. §§ 1751–69. Regulations are published in Title 7 of the Code of Federal Regulations, §§ 210.1–.30, § 245.

320. 42 U.S.C. § 1773.

321. Joseph DeGiuseppe, Jr., The National School Lunch Act: An Unfulfilled Mandate, 4 Fordham Urb. L.J. 3 (1975).

322. 42 U.S.C. §§ 1751–69e.

323. Pub. L. No. 111-296, 124 Stat. 3183 (2010). The community eligibility provision appears as § 104(a) of the Healthy, Hunger-Free Kids Act, which amended § 11(a) of the Richard B. Russell National School Lunch Act. *See* Ethan A. Bergman, Tim Englund, Katie Weigt Taylor, Tracee Watkins, Stephen Schepman, & Keith

Rushing, School Lunch Before and After Implementation of the Healthy Hunger-Free Kids Act, 38 J. Child Nutrition & Mgmt. 1 (2014), https://schoolnutrition.org/uploadedFiles/5_News_and_Publications/4_The_Journal_of_Child_Nutrition_and_Management/Fall_2014/SchoolLunchBeforeandAfterImplementationHealthy HungerFreeKidsAct.pdf.

324. Susan Levine, School Lunch Politics: The Surprising History of America's Favorite Welfare Program (Princeton, 2008).

325. 7 C.F.R. § 210.1(a). Schools may operate federally funded lunch programs through the federal Commodity School Program. 7 C.F.R. §§ 210.2, 210.4(c).

326. Food Research & Action Center, FRAC Quick Facts: National School Lunch Program, http://frac.org/wp-content/uploads/cnnslp.pdf.

327. U.S. Department of Agriculture, National School Lunch Program (NSLP) Fact Sheet, https://www.fns.usda.gov/nslp/nslp-fact-sheet; Food Research & Action Center, National School Lunch Program: Quick Facts, http://frac.org/programs/national-school-lunch-program; Food Research & Action Center, More Low-Income Students Receive Free School Meals in the 2018–2019 School Year Through Community Eligibility (June 1, 2019), https://frac.org/news/more-low-income-students-receive-free-school-meals-in-the-2018-2019-school-year-through-community-eligibility.

328. U.S. Department of Agriculture, Elizabeth Potamites & Anne Gordon, Children's Food Security and Intakes from School Meals: Final Report 97, Mathematica Policy Research, Inc., Contractor and Cooperator Report No. 61 (May 2010), http://naldc.nal.usda.gov/download/42320/PDF.

329. Plyler v. Doe, 457 U.S. 202 (1982). See, for example, Illinois Legal Aid Online, School Meal Programs for Undocumented Kids, https://www.illinoislegalaid.org/legal-information/school-meal-programs-undocumented-kids (states cannot deny school lunch to children who cannot document their immigration status or do not have a Social Security number).

330. Priya Konings, Protecting Immigrant Children's Right to Education, American Bar Association (Mar. 2017), https://www.americanbar.org/groups/public_interest/child_law/resources/child_law_practiceonline/child_law_practice/vol-36/mar-apr-2017/protecting-immigrant-childrens-right-to-education-/ (discussing barriers immigrant children face when trying to attend public school, including "laws aimed at attempting to curtail the education rights of immigrant children to local administrators seeking to institute ad hoc mechanisms to bar immigrant children from receiving an education").

331. See America's Voice, Betsy DeVos is Wrong: Schools May NOT Contact ICE Regarding Immigration Children (May 23, 2018), https://americasvoice.org/press_releases/betsy-devos-is-wrong-schools-may-not-contact-ice-regarding-immigrant-children/ (reporting that the Secretary of Education, "directly contradicting" Plyler, "argued that individual schools can decide to report students and families to immigration enforcement"); Olga Khazan, Some Immigrants Choose Between Food Stamps and a Green Card: A Trump proposal is scaring legal immigrants away from essential health programs, The Atlantic (Apr. 25,

2019), https://www.theatlantic.com/health/archive/2019/04/trumps-immigration-proposal-hurting-immigrant-health/587908/ (reporting that although the Trump administration's proposed change to the public charge rule does not affect the school lunch program, "advocates say some immigrant families are avoiding signing up for them just in case").

332. 7 C.F.R. § 245.9(f)(2)(i). *See also* Jessie Hewins, Madeleine Levin, Becca Segal, & Zoë Neuberger, The Community Eligibility Provision: Alternatives to School Meal Applications, Food Research & Action Center & Center on Budget and Policy Priorities (June 19, 2014), http://frac.org/wp-content/uploads/cep_and_eliminating_school_meal_applications-1.pdf.

333. U.S. Department of Agriculture, Food and Nutrition Service, Community Eligibility Provision Status of School Districts and Schools by State (Mar. 30, 2019), https://www.fns.usda.gov/school-meals/community-eligibility-provision-status-school-districts-and-schools-state; Food Research & Action Center, Community Eligibility (CEP) Database, Interactive Data Tool (May 30, 2019), https://frac.org/research/resource-library/community-eligibility-cep-database.

334. 7 C.F.R. § 245.6. *See* Food Research & Action Center, Certifying Low-Income Children for Free & Reduced-Price Meals, Categorical Eligibility, https://frac.org/school-meal-eligibility-reimbursements.

335. 7 C.F.R. §§ 245.5(a)(1)(vi), 245.6(c)(1). *See* Food Research & Action Center, Certifying Low-Income Children for Free & Reduced-Price Meals, Categorical Eligibility, https://frac.org/school-meal-eligibility-reimbursements.

336. 7 C.F.R. § 245.6(a)(1).

337. 7 C.F.R. § 245.6(c)(1).

338. 7 C.F.R. § 245.6(a)(1).

339. 7 C.F.R. § 245.6(a)(4).

340. 7 C.F.R. §§ 245.2; 245.6(a).

341. Under federal law, the applicant's name and eligibility status may be disclosed without the household's consent only to federal education programs administered by a state or local agency (such as a Title I program), representatives of state or local agencies tasked with assessing the program, and means-tested nutrition programs. In addition, all eligibility information about the household may be disclosed without the household's consent to the Comptroller General of the United States, federal, state, and local agencies tasked with investigating program violations, and persons charged with administering or enforcing various other food-assistance programs. *See* U.S. Department of Agriculture, Food and Nutrition Service, Disclosure of Children's Free and Reduced Price Meals and Free Milk Eligibility Information in the Child Nutrition Programs (Mar. 12, 2007), https://www.fns.usda.gov/school-meals/fr-031207.

342. 7 C.F.R. § 245.2.

343. 7 C.F.R. §§ 245.3, 245.6.

344. 7 C.F.R. § 210.10(a)(1).

345. 7 C.F.R. § 210.10(a)(1)(i).

346. 7 C.F.R. § 210.10(b).

347. 7 C.F.R. § 210.10(c)(2)(i).

348. *See* Reed Troutman, Health Food Advocacy and the National School Lunch Program, 40 J.L. & Educ. 383 (2011).

349. Ethan A. Bergman, Tim Englund, Katie Weigt Taylor, Tracee Watkins, Stephen Schepman, & Keith Rushing, School Lunch Before and After Implementation of the Healthy Hunger-Free Kids Act, 38 J. Child Nutrition & Mgmt. 2 (2014), https://schoolnutrition.org/uploadedFiles/5_News_and_Publications/4_The_Journal_of_Child_Nutrition_and_Management/Fall_2014/SchoolLunchBeforeandAfterImplementationHealthyHungerFreeKidsAct.pdf.

350. 7 C.F.R. § 245.8(b) & (d).

351. 7 C.F.R. § 245.8(c).

352. *See* Candice Choi, How "lunch shaming" is facing scrutiny around the US, AP (May 16, 2019), https://www.apnews.com/21d02ce0aff444508ca427508ac1580; *see generally* William Moreau & Jessamine Pilcher, The Incentives Behind Lunch Shaming, American Bar Association, https://www.americanbar.org/groups/young_lawyers/publications/tyl/topics/access-to-education/incentives-behind-lunch-shaming/ (noting that although the federal government uses the term to apply only to "overt identification" of students who are eligible for free or reduced lunch, "in practice legal lunch shaming occurs against students whose family income exceeds free or reduced lunch eligibility thresholds").

353. *See* U.S. Department of Agriculture, Food and Nutrition Service, Memorandum No. SP 46-2016 to Regional Directors and Others Regarding Unpaid Meal Charges: Local Meal Charge Policies (July 8, 2016), https://www.fns.usda.gov/unpaid-meal-charges-local-meal-charge-policies.

354. *See* U.S. Department of Agriculture, Food and Nutrition Service, Unpaid Meal Charges, https://www.fns.usda.gov/school-meals/unpaid-meal-charges; Food Research & Action Center, Establishing Unpaid Meal Fee Policies: Best Practices to Ensure Access and Prevent Stigma (Jan. 3, 2018), http://www.frac.org/wp-content/uploads/frac-unpaid-meal-fees-policy-guide.pdf.

355. *See* Victoria Palacio, Community Eligibility: A Remedy for Lunch Shaming in Some School Districts, Center for Law and Social Policy (May 24, 2017), https://www.clasp.org/blog/community-eligibility-remedy-lunch-shaming-some-school-districts.

356. Jessie Hewins, The End of School Lunch Shaming?, Food Research & Action Center (Apr. 12, 2017), http://frac.org/blog/end-school-lunch-shaming.

357. 7 C.F.R. § 245.7(a).

358. 7 C.F.R. § 245.7(b)(1).

359. 7 C.F.R. § 210.12(a).

360. 7 C.F.R. § 210.10(o).

361. 7 C.F.R. § 210.2.

362. 42 U.S.C. § 1773, as amended by Pub. L. No. 104-193, 110 Stat. 2105 (1996).

363. Food Research & Action Center, School Breakfast Scorecard: School Year 2017–2018, at 6 (Feb. 2019), http://www.frac.org/wp-content/uploads/school-breakfast-scorecard-sy-2017-2018.pdf.

364. 7 C.F.R. § 226.23(c)(6).

365. *See* Food Research & Action Center, School Breakfast: Making it Work in Large School Districts (Feb. 2019), https://www.frac.org/research/resource-library/school-breakfast-making-it-work-in-large-school-districts-2017-2018-school-year-february-2019; *see also* Food Research & Action Center & National Association of School Principals, School Breakfast After the Bell: Equipping Students for Academic Success: Secondary School Principals Share What Works (Nov. 2015), https://www.frac.org/research/resource-library/afterschool-suppers-snapshot-participation-october-2018.

366. U.S. Department of Agriculture, Food and Nutrition Service, The School-Based Afterschool Snack Program (Sept. 2013), http://www.fns.usda.gov/sites/default/files/AfterschoolFactSheet.pdf; Food Research & Action Center, Afterschool Suppers: A Snapshot of Participation (Oct. 2018), https://www.frac.org/research/resource-library/afterschool-suppers-snapshot-participation-october-2018 (suppers). The majority of schools that provide after-school snacks are elementary schools in poor urban areas. *See* U.S. Department of Agriculture, Economic Research Service, Clare Cho & Joanne Guthrie, USDA's After-School Snack Program More Common in Elementary Schools in Poor Urban Areas (2016), https://www.ers.usda.gov/amber-waves/2016/januaryfebruary/usda-s-after-school-snack-program-more-common-in-elementary-schools-in-poor-urban-areas/.

367. U.S. Department of Agriculture, Food and Nutrition Service, Afterschool Snacks: USDA Food and Nutrition Service Programs for Out-of-School-Time Providers (Oct. 4, 2017), https://www.fns.usda.gov/school-meals/afterschool-snacks.

368. U.S. Department of Agriculture, Food and Nutrition Service, The School-Based Afterschool Snack Program (Sept. 2013), http://www.fns.usda.gov/sites/default/files/AfterschoolFactSheet.pdf; National School Lunch, Special Milk, and School Breakfast Programs, National Average Payments/Maximum Reimbursement Rates, 83 Fed. Reg. 34105, 34107 (July 19, 2018), https://www.govinfo.gov/content/pkg/FR-2018-07-19/pdf/2018-15465.pdf.

369. Food Research& Action Center, FRAC Facts: The Child and Adult Care Food Program (CACFP), http://frac.org/wp-content/uploads/cacfp-fact-sheet.pdf.

370. Reimbursement rates are adjusted each year in July. For current rates, *see* U.S. Department of Agriculture, Food and Nutrition Service, Child and Adult Care Food Program (CACFP) Reimbursement Rates (Aug. 17, 2018), https://www.fns.usda.gov/cacfp/reimbursement-rates.

371. U.S. Department of Agriculture, Food and Nutrition Service, Summer Food Service Program (June 21, 2018), http://www.fns.usda.gov/sfsp/summer-food-service-program.

372. U.S. Department of Agriculture, Food and Nutrition Service, School Meals: An Opportunity for Schools (Jan. 9, 2017), http://www.fns.usda.gov/school-meals/opportunity-schools.

373. U.S. Department of Agriculture, Food and Nutrition Service, FY 2019 Summer Electronic Benefit Transfer for Children (Summer EBT) Grant Program, https://www.fns.usda.gov/school-meals/fy-2019-summer-electronic-benefit-transfer-children-summer-ebt-grant-program.

374. See Food Research & Action Center, Facts: The Summer Food Service Program (Feb. 2019), https://www.frac.org/wp-content/uploads/sfsp_fact_sheet.pdf. To locate centers that participate in summer meal programs for children, see U.S. Department of Agriculture, Food and Nutrition Service, Find Summer Meals in Your Community, https://www.fns.usda.gov/summerfoodrocks or contact the National Hunger Hotline at 1-866-3-HUNGRY or 1-877-8-HAMBRE.

375. See 7 C.F.R. § 225.14.

376. Mark Nord & Kathleen Romig, Hunger in the Summer: Seasonal Food Insecurity and the National School Lunch and Summer Food Service Programs, 12(2) J. Children & Poverty 141 (2006), http://www.tandfonline.com/doi/pdf/10.1080/10796120600879582.

377. Food Research & Action Center, Hunger Doesn't Take a Vacation: Summer Breakfast Status Report (June 2019), https://www.frac.org/research/resource-library/hunger-doesnt-take-a-vacation-summer-breakfast-status-report-2019. For information on program trends, 1986–2002, see U.S. Department of Agriculture, Food and Nutrition Service, Anne Gordon, Ronette Briefel, Karen Needels, Nancy Wemmerus, Teresa Zavitsky, Randy Russo, Tania Tasse, Laura Kalb, Anne Peterson, Darryl Creel, & Jane E. Allshouse. Mathematica Policy Research, Inc., Feeding Low-Income Children When School Is Out-The Summer Food Service Program: Final Report (Mar. 2003), https://www.ers.usda.gov/publications/pub-details/?pubid=43229.

378. See Food Research & Action Center, Hunger Doesn't Take a Vacation: Summer Nutrition Status Report 2019 (July 2019), https://frac.org/research/resource-library/hunger-doesnt-take-a-vacation-summer-nutrition-status-report-2019; Food Research & Action Center, Hunger Doesn't Take a Vacation: Summer Nutrition Status Report (June 2018), http://frac.org/wp-content/uploads/2018-summer-nutrition-report.pdf. See also Zachary Sherwood & Brandon Lee, What to Know in Washington: Participation in Summer Meals Program, Bloomberg Government (July 20, 2019), https://about.bgov.com/news/what-to-know-trump-trump-readies-kidney-care-revamp/?eType=EmailBlastContent&eId=2033ba82-15d6-4c63-aeca-56fb9b4e1db7 (reporting FRAC's proposal).

379. See generally Seth Cline, Is Summer Breaking America's School?, U.S. News (June 7, 2018), https://www.usnews.com/news/education-news/articles/2018-06-07/summer-exacerbates-the-divide-between-rich-and-poor-students (discussing the importance of summer school meals and access to summer educational programs for low-income students).

380. 7 C.F.R. § 225.6(e)(3).

381. For the 2019 funding priorities, see U.S. Department of Agriculture, Food and Nutrition Service, Summer Electronic Benefit Transfer for Children (Summer EBT) Grant Program, Fiscal year Request for Applications (Oct. 21, 2018), https://www.fns.usda.gov/grant/fy-2019-summer-electronic-benefit-transfer-children-summer-ebt-grant-program.

382. See U.S. Department of Agriculture, Food and Nutrition Service, Nutrition Assistance Program Report Summer Electronic Benefit Transfer for Children (SEBTC) Demonstration: A Summary Report (May 11, 2016), https://www.fns.

usda.gov/sfsp/summer-electronic-benefit-transfer-children-sebtc-demonstration-summary-report (reporting on the differential impact of supplementing the EBT card with $30 or $60 per child per month, and concluding that for all outcomes related to food security and nutrition other than very low food security among children, "the impact of a $60 benefit was clearly greater than that of a $30 benefit"); *see also* Food Research & Action Center, Summer EBT: Availability of SNAP Retailers Compared to WIC Vendors (May 2019), https://frac.org/research/resource-library/summer-ebt-availability-of-snap-retailers-compared-to-wic-vendors; Eillie Anzilotti, Why Kids Go Hungry in the Summer, CityLab (May 20, 2016), https://www.citylab.com/equity/2016/05/why-kids-still-go-hungry-in-the-summer/483755/.

383. *See* No Kid Hungry, Summer EBT: An Efficient and Effective Way to End Summer Hunger, https://www.nokidhungry.org/sites/default/files/2019-05/Summer%20 EBT_0.pdf.

384. The Farm Security and Rural Investment Act of 2002 authorized the pilot program in four states and one Indian Tribal Organization. Four more states and 13 schools in tribal areas were added to the pilot program by the Children Nutrition and WIC Reauthorization Act of 2004. The program continued to be a success, and in 2006, the Agriculture, Rural Development, Food and Drug Administration, and Related Agencies Appropriations Act of 2006, P.L. No. 109-97, expanded the program, and further expansion came in 2008. That year, the Food Conservation and Energy Act of 2008 amended the Richard B. Russell National School Lunch Act by adding a new section permanently authorizing the program throughout the nation.

385. 42 U.S.C. § 1769.

386. *See* U.S. Department of Agriculture, Fresh Fruit and Vegetable Program: A Handbook for Schools (Dec. 2010), http://www.fns.usda.gov/sites/default/files/handbook.pdf.

387. Child Nutrition Act of 1966, 42 U.S.C. § 1771. *See* U.S. Department of Agriculture, Food and Nutrition Service, Special Milk Program Fact Sheet (Aug. 2012), https://fns-prod.azureedge.net/sites/default/files/SMPFactSheet.pdf.

388. 7 C.F.R. § 215.1(6).

389. 7 C.F.R. § 215.2.

390. U.S. Department of Agriculture, Food and Nutrition Service, School Meals Contacts, http://www.fns.usda.gov/office-type/child-nutrition-programs.

391. The law governing WIC is codified at 42 U.S.C. § 1786; federal regulations are codified at Title 7 of the Code of Federal Regulations, § 246.

392. 7 C.F.R. § 246.1.

393. 7 C.F.R. § 246.3(a) & (b).

394. The program was created by an amendment to § 17 of the Child Nutrition Act of 1966, P.L. 92-433, which was sponsored by Senator Hubert Humphrey. *See* Helen Hershkoff, David Super, & Ellen Teller, Introduction to the WIC and CSFP Programs, 24 Clearinghouse Rev. 820 (1990).

395. U.S. Department of Agriculture, Economic Research Service, Victor Oliveira & Elizabeth Frazão, The WIC Program: Background, Trends, and Economic Issues

(Jan. 2015), https://www.aap.org/en-us/advocacy-and-policy/federal-advocacy/ Documents/USDAWIC2015Report.pdf.

396. U.S. Department of Agriculture, Food and Nutrition Service, WIC Program Participation and Costs (Data as of Feb. 22, 2019), https://fns-prod.azureedge.net/ sites/default/files/pd/wisummary.pdf. *See also* Victor Oliveira, WIC Participation Continues to Decline, U.S. Department of Agriculture, Econ. Research Serv. (June 5, 2017), https://www.ers.usda.gov/amber-waves/2017/june/wic-participation-continues-to-decline/.

397. U.S. Department of Agriculture, Food and Nutrition Service, WIC Program, https:// www.fns.usda.gov/pd/wic-program (*see* FY 2018, Monthly Data—State Level Participation by Category and Program Costs).

398. *See* Food Research & Action Center, Impact of the Revised WIC Food Packages on Nutrition Outcomes and the Retail Food Environment 2 (Sept. 2014), http://frac. org/pdf/frac_brief_revised_wic_food_package_impact_nutrition_retail.pdf.

399. Steven Carlson & Zoë Neuberger, WIC Works: Addressing the Nutrition and Health Needs of Low-Income Families for 40 Years, Center on Budget & Policy Priorities (Mar. 29, 2017), http://www.cbpp.org/research/food-assistance/wic-works-addressing-the-nutrition-and-health-needs-of-low-income-families.

400. U.S. Department of Agriculture, Food and Nutrition Service, Women, Infants and Children (WIC): About WIC—How WIC Helps, https://www.fns.usda.gov/ wic/about-wic-how-wic-helps. *See also* L. Sonchak, The Impact of WIC on Birth Outcomes: New Evidence from South Carolina, 20 Matern. Child Health 1518 (2016), https://www.ncbi.nlm.nih.gov/pubmed/26976280.

401. *See* M. Angley, V.R. Thorsten, C. Drews-Botsch, R.L. Goldenberg, R.M. Silver, B.J. Stoll, H. Pinar, & C.J.R. Hogue, Association of participation in a supplemental nutrition program with stillbirth by race, ethnicity, and maternal characteristics, 18 BMA Pregnancy Childbirth 306 (2018), https://www.ncbi.nlm.nih.gov/pubmed/ 30041624; Molly Warren, Stacy Beck, & Jack Rayburn, The State of Obesity, Woman, Infants and Children: Better Polices for a Healthier America, Trust for America's Health (Sept. 2018), at 28, https://stateofobesity.org/wp-content/uploads/2018/09/ stateofobesity2018.pdf; M.A. Chiasson, S.E. Findley, J.P. Sekhobo, R. Scheinmann, L.S. Edmunds, A.S. Faly, & N.J. McLeod, Changing WIC Changes What Children Eat, 21(7) Obesity 1423 (Jan. 2013), http://onlinelibrary.wiley.com/doi/10.1002/ oby.20295/full.

402. Victor Oliveira & Elizabeth Frazão, Painting a More Complete Picture of WIC: How WIC Impacts Nonparticipants (Apr. 6, 2015), https://www.ers.usda.gov/amber-waves/2015/april/painting-a-more-complete-picture-of-wic-how-wic-impacts-nonparticipants/.

403. Roch A. Nianogo, May C. Wang, Ricardo Basurto-Davila, Tabashir Z. Nobari, Michael Prelip, Onyebuchi A. Arah, & Shannon E. Whaley, Economic evaluation of California prenatal participation in the Special Supplemental Nutrition Program for Women, Infants and Children (WIC) to prevent preterm birth, 124 Preventive Medicine 42 (2019), https://doi.org/10.1016/j.ypmed.2019.04.011 (reporting that $1 invested in WIC saves about $2.48 in medical, educational, and productivity costs);

Margot I. Jackson, Early Childhood WIC Participation, Cognitive Development and Academic Achievement, 126 Soc. Sci. Med. 145 (2015), https://www.ncbi.nlm.gov/pmc/articles/PMC4703081/.

404. 7 C.F.R. § 246.12(a).

405. *See* U.S. Department of Agriculture, Stacy Gleason, Jennifer Pooler, Loren Bell, Leslie Erickson, Celia Eicheldinger, Jeremy Porter, & Amy Hedershott, 2013 WIC Vendor Management Study, Final Report 8 (Nov. 2013), https://fns-prod.azureedge.net/sites/default/files/2013WICVendor.pdf. *See also* Vermont Department of Health, Shopping with WIC (Feb. 1, 2019), http://www.healthvermont.gov/family/wic/shopping-wic (explaining Vermont's 2016 shift to retail food vender-based services).

406. 7 C.F.R. § 246.10(e)(9)–(10).

407. 7 C.F.R. § 246.10(e)(9)–(12).

408. 7 C.F.R. § 246.11(a).

409. 7 C.F.R. § 246.26(d).

410. 7 C.F.R. § 246.7(g)(5). These are referred to as "categorical eligibility" requirements. 7 C.F. R. § 246.2.

411. Women, Infants and Children Offices, How To Apply For WIC In Massachusetts: Who Is WIC For?, https://www.womeninfantschildrenoffice.com/apply-for-wic-in-massachusetts-wa21.

412. 7 C.F.R. §§ 246.7(c)(ii) & (d).

413. 7 C.F.R. § 246.7(d)(2)(vi)(A).

414. 7 C.F.R. § 246.7.

415. U.S. Department of Agriculture, Food and Nutrition Service, Child Nutrition Programs: Income Eligibility Guidelines, 83 Fed. Reg. 20788, 20789 (May 8, 2018).

416. 7 C.F.R. § 246.7(c)(1)(i).

417. 7 C.F.R. § 246.7(c)(1)(iii) & (e).

418. 7 C.F.R. §§ 246.7(e).

419. 7 C.F.R. § 246.7(d)(2)(ii).

420. 7 C.F.R. § 246.7(d)(2)(ii)(A)–(L).

421. 7 C.F.R. §§ 246.7(d)(2)(iv)(A) (state options); 246.7(d)(2)(iv)(B)–(D) (mandatory income exclusions).

422. 7 C.F.R. § 246.7(c)(1) & (3). "Qualified aliens" include all of the immigrant categories discussed earlier in this chapter under the question "Which noncitizens are eligible for SNAP?"

423. 7 C.F.R. § 246.7(p). *See* U.S. Department of Agriculture, Food and Nutrition Service, Supplemental Nutrition Assistance Program: Guidance on Non-Citizen Eligibility 3 (June 2011), https://fns-prod.azureedge.net/sites/default/files/snap/Non-Citizen_Guidance_063011.pdf.

424. The U.S. Department of Homeland Security has proposed changes to the "public charge" test for immigration status. The proposed rule does not list WIC among the benefits that could impact an immigrant's status. *See* 83 Fed. Reg. 51,114 (Oct. 10, 2018). *See also,* National WIC Association, Breaking News: Public Charge Rule Moves Forward (Sept. 24, 2018), https://www.nwica.org/blog/

breaking-news-public-charge-rule-moves-forward#.XTDpT3spCM8; National
Immigration Law Center, Frequently Asked Questions Proposed Changes to
the Public Charge Rule (Nov. 2018), https://www.nilc.org/issues/economic-
support/pubcharge/proposed-changes-to-public-charge-rule-faq/#27 ("Under
both the current public charge policy and the proposed rule, it is ok to get help
from WIC . . . . Receiving WIC should not hurt your ability to adjust your immigration status.").

425. Data do not exist on how many eligible applicants do not participate in the WIC
program because of inadequate funding, and there is some suggestion that in recent
years funding has been sufficient to enroll eligible applicants. *See* U.S. Department
of Agriculture, Victor Oliveira & Elizabeth Frazão, The WIC Program: Background,
Trends, and Economic Issues, Economic Information Bulletin No. 134 (Jan. 2015),
https://papers.ssrn.com/sol3/papers.cfm?abstract_id=2709086.

426. 7 C.F.R. § 246.7(a).

427. 7 C.F.R. § 246.7(c)(4).

428. 7 C.F.R. § 246.7(d)(2)(vi)(A).

429. 7 C.F.R. § 246.7(c)(2). *See* 7 C.F.R. § 246.7(m) (WIC receipt in homeless shelters).

430. 7 C.F.R. § 246.7(c)(2)(ii).

431. 7 C.F.R. § 246.7(o)(2)(i)–(iv).

432. 7 C.F.R. § 246.7(i).

433. 7 C.F.R. § 246.26(d)(1).

434. 7 C.F.R. § 246.26(d)(4).

435. 7 C.F.R. § 246.26(d)(2).

436. 7 C.F.R. § 246.26(h).

437. 7 C.F.R. § 246.26(d)(3).

438. 7 C.F.R. § 246.26(i).

439. 7 C.F.R. § 246.7(m).

440. 7 C.F.R. § 273.14.

441. 7 C.F.R. § 248.6(a).

442. 7 C.F.R. § 248.8(b). *See generally* Allison Karpyn, Nicky Uly, Katy Wich, & Jonathan
Glyn, Farmers markets in low income communities: impact on community environment, food programs and public policy, 42(2) Community Development 208
(2011), https://doi.org/10.1080/15575330.2010.551663. *See also* Christina Grace,
Thomas Grace, Nancy Becker, & Judy Lyden, Barriers to Using Farmers' Markets: An
Investigation of Food Stamp Clients' Perceptions, 2(1) J. Hunger & Envtl. Nutrition
55 (2008), https://doi.org/10.1080/19320240802080916 (reporting that WIC
farmers' market motivated farmers' market use).

443. 7 C.F.R. § 248.24(a).

444. For an overview of food programs for seniors, *see* Food Research & Action
Center, Federal Nutrition Programs and Emergency Food Referral Chart for
Older Adults, https://www.frac.org/research/resource-library/federal-nutrition-
programs-emergency-food-referral-chart-older-adults.

445. Juliette Cubanski, Wyatt Koma, Anthony Camico, & Tricia Neuman, How Many
Seniors Live in Poverty?, Kaiser Family Foundation (Nov. 19, 2018), http://files.kff.
org/attachment/Issue-Brief-How-Many-Seniors-Live-in-Poverty.

446. Food Research & Action Center, SNAP Map: SNAP Matters to Seniors, https://frac. org/research/resource-library/snap-map-snap-matters-to-seniors (indicating that only 43% of eligible seniors use SNAP benefits each month); Heather Hartline-Grafton, SNAP Misses Millions of Eligible Older Adults, Food Research & Action Center, https://www.frac.org/blog/older-americans-month-part-3-addressing-food-insecurity-among-older-adults (stating that only 42% of eligible seniors participate in SNAP).

447. *See* Niranjana Kowlessar, Kristen Robinson, & Claudia Schur, Older Americans Benefit from Older Americans Act Nutrition Programs, Administration on Aging, Research Brief No. 8, at 2 (Sept. 2015), https://acl.gov/sites/default/files/programs/2016-11/AoA-Research-Brief-8-2015.pdf (discussing programs funded under the Older Americans Act, Title III-C). *See also* Ginger Zielinskie, Laura Samuel, Sarah Szanton, Charles Betley, & Rachel Cahill, Access to Public Benefits Among Dual Eligible Seniors Reduces Risk of Nursing Home and Hospital Admission and Cuts Costs, The National Resource Center on Nutrition and Aging (Apr. 11, 2018), https://nutritionandaging.org/access-to-public-benefi-ts-among-ddual-eligible-seniors-reduces-risk-of-nursing-home-and-hospital-admission-and-cuts-costs/.

448. 42 U.S.C. § 3030e. The federal government provides grants to states, territories, and eligible tribal organizations through the Congregate Nutrition Services and Home-Delivered Nutrition Services grant or the Nutrition Services Incentive Program, using a formula based on each state's share of the U.S. population age 60 and over, or the state's percentage of total meals served in the prior fiscal year. Admin. for Community Living, Nutrition Services: Federal Grants for Nutrition Services (Jan. 18, 2019), https://www.acl.gov/programs/healh-wellness-nutrition-services.

449. Admin. for Community Living, Congregate Meal Programs: A Value Proposition, https://www.acl.gov/programs/healh-wellness-nutrition-services. *See also* Juliette Cubanski, Kristen Robinson, & Claudia Schur, Older Americans Benefit from Older Americans Act Nutrition Programs, National Research Center on Nutrition and Aging (Sept. 2015), https://www.acl.gov/sites/default/files/programs/2016-11/AoA-Research-Brief-8-2015.pdf. *See also* James Mabli, Arkadipta Ghosh, Bob Schmitz, Marisa Shenk, Erin Panzarella, Barbara Carlson, & Mark Flick, Final Report: Evaluation of the Effect of the Older Americans Act Title III-C Nutrition Services Program on Participants' Health Care Utilization, Mathematic Policy Research, Submitted to U.D. Department of Health and Human Services (Sept. 14, 2018).

450. U.S. Department of Agriculture, Food and Nutrition Service, Adult Day Care: A Child and Adult Care Food Program Handbook (Jan. 2014), https://fns-prod.azureedge.net/sites/default/files/CACFPAdult%20DayCareHandbook.pdf.

451. Niranjana Kowlessar, Kristen Robinson, & Claudia Schur, Older Americans Benefit from Older Americans Act Nutrition Programs, Administration on Aging & Aging Services Network (Sept. 2015), https://www.acl.gov/sites/default/files/programs/2016-11/AoA-Research-Brief-8-2015.pdf.

452. U.S. Department of Health and Human Services, Administration for Community Living Older Americans Act Nutrition Programs 2, https://www.acl.gov/sites/default/files/news%202017-03/OAA-Nutrition_Programs_Fact_Sheet.pdf.

453. Kristen E. Porter & Sean Cahill, A State-Level Review of Diversity Initiatives in Congregate Meal Programs Established Under the Older Americans Act, 37(7) Research on Aging 719 (2014), http://www.ncbi.nlm.nih.gov/pubmed/25651589.

454. 42 U.S.C. § 3030f.

455. Congressional Research Service, Older Americans Act: Nutrition Services Program: Administration (Aug. 7, 2018), https://fas.org/sgp/crs/misc/IF10633.pdf.

456. See Huichen Zhu & Ruopeng An, Impact of Home-Delivered Meal Programs on Diet and Nutrition Among Older Adults: A Review, 22(2) Nutrition & Health 89 (2014), https://journals.sagepub.com/doi/pdf/10.1177/0260106014537146.

457. Meals on Wheels America, 2017 United States Fact Sheet 2 (2017), http://www.mealsonwheelsamerica.org/docs/default-source/fact-sheets/2017/mealsonwheelsamerica-2017usfactsheet.pdf?sfvrsn=2.

458. The federal regulations governing SFMNP appear at 7 C.F.R. Part 249.

459. U.S. Department of Agriculture, Seniors Farmers' Market Nutrition Program 1 (July 2018), https://fns-prod.azureedge.net/sites/default/files/sfmnp/SFMNPFactSheet.pdf.

460. 7 C.F.R. § 249.6(a)(3). See U.S. Department of Agriculture, Seniors Farmers' Market Nutrition Program 1 (July 2018), https://fns-prod.azureedge.net/sites/default/files/sfmnp/SFMNPFactSheet.pdf.

461. 7 C.F.R. § 249.6(a)(1).

462. 7 C.F.R. § 249.8(b).

463. CSFP is authorized under Section 4(a) of the Agriculture and Consumer Act of 1973, and its eligibility requirements were changed as of February 6, 2014, pursuant to the Agricultural Act of 2014, Pub. L. No. 113-79 generally to include only seniors. Federal regulations governing the program appear at 7 C.F.R. Parts 247 and 250.

464. See National Commodity Supplemental Food Program Association, State Participation Timeline, http://www.ncsfpa.org/history-of-csfp-expansion/.

465. 7 C.F.R. § 247.8(a). The state agency has options regarding its calculation of household income. See 7 C.F.R. § 247.9(e). Further, the agency must ensure that appropriate languages are used in communities in which "a significant proportion of the population . . . is comprised of non-English or limited-English persons with a common language." § 247.13(b).

466. 7 C.F.R. § 247.9(c).

467. 7 C.F.R. § 247.2(f)(1) & (2).

468. 7 C.F.R. § 247.2(b)(1)(i) & (ii).

469. 7 C.F.R. § 247.2(b) (caseload limits).

470. 7 C.F.R. § 247.11(a) & (b).

471. U.S. Department of Agriculture, Food and Nutrition Service, Commodity Supplemental Food Program (CSFP), https://www.fns.usda.gov/csfp/commodity-supplemental-food-program-csfp (2018); U.S. Department of Agriculture, Food and Nutrition Service, Nutrition Program Fact Sheet, Commodity Supplemental Food Program (Apr. 2018), https://fns-prod.azureedge.net/sites/default/files/csfp/programFactSheet-csfp.pdf.

472. *See* Food Research & Action Center, U.S. Hunger Solutions: Best Practices for Connecting Seniors Participating in the Commodity Supplemental Food Program (CSFP) to SNAP (2017), https://www.frac.org/wp-content/uploads/best-practice-snap-and-csfp.pdf.

473. U.S. Department of Agriculture, Food and Nutrition Service, Commodity Supplemental Food Program 2 (Apr. 2018), https://fns-prod.azureedge.net/sites/default/files/csfp/programFactSheet-csfp.pdf.

474. U.S. Department of Agriculture, Food and Nutrition Service, CSFP Food Package: What You Need to Know, Webinar (July 12, 2019), https://www.fns.usda.gov/csfp/csfp-food-package-what-you-need-know.

4

Health

Introduction

Is there a federal constitutional right to health care?

No. The U.S. Supreme Court has never found a right to health care in the federal Constitution. While acknowledging medical care to be "a basic necessity of life,"[1] the Court has declined to hold that the government has any affirmative constitutional obligation to provide or subsidize health services,[2] except in the narrow case where an individual is in the custody of the state.[3]

Is there a statutory right to health care?

In some cases, yes. A number of federal and state laws create various rights to health care for different groups of people. This chapter addresses the principal sources of these rights: the Medicaid and Medicare programs, the Children's Health Insurance Program, and the Patient Protection and Affordable Care Act of 2010. But these programs do not cover everyone. The United States, virtually alone among developed nations, does not offer universal access to health care.[4] The only universal right to health care in the United States is the right to emergency medical treatment, but only to the point of stabilizing the individual's condition.[5] Strikingly, per capita health care expenditures in the United States far exceed those of comparable countries[6] and yet our nation achieves worse outcomes.[7] For example, disease burden and "amenable mortality" (deaths that could have been prevented with proper medical care) are higher in the United States than in other developed countries, as are rates of infant mortality and low birth weight.[8]

What is health care reform (or "Obamacare")?

In 2010, Congress enacted landmark health care reform legislation called the Patient Protection and Affordable Care Act, popularly known as the "ACA" or "Obamacare." Perhaps the most significant anti-poverty legislation in the last

Getting By. Helen Hershkoff and Stephen Loffredo, Oxford University Press (2020). © Helen Hershkoff & Stephen Loffredo.
DOI: 10.1093/oso/9780190080860.001.0001

40 years, the ACA was designed to address the growing crisis in the nation's health care system, which had left nearly 50 million Americans without health insurance and millions more with inadequate access to health care.[9] The Medicaid program, enacted in 1965, had served as the largest provider of health care to people living at or below the poverty line, but its restrictive eligibility requirements excluded many low-income people who had no other means of obtaining medical care. At the same time, diminished employment-based health coverage, skyrocketing health costs, and restrictions in the private insurance market (such as the exclusion for "preexisting conditions") placed adequate care beyond the reach of many working people. As of 2010, the year Congress enacted federal health care reform, approximately one in six Americans had no health insurance. The ACA extended health coverage to millions of Americans, principally by: (1) expanding the Medicaid program to cover all U.S. citizens and certain lawful resident immigrants with incomes below 138 percent of the federal poverty level (FPL);[10] (2) creating incentives for employers to provide health coverage to their workers;[11] and (3) providing subsidies for households with income below 400 percent of the FPL to purchase coverage through Health Insurance Exchanges ("Exchanges")—online marketplaces for affordable insurance plans meeting ACA requirements.[12] The ACA also expanded access to health care by prohibiting private insurance companies from denying coverage for preexisting medical conditions (or increasing premiums for people with such conditions), requiring that insurance policies cover a defined package of essential health services, and requiring that they provide dependent coverage for children up to age 26.[13]

The Congressional Budget Office estimated that the ACA would extend health coverage to 34 million people by 2021, resulting in projected coverage for approximately 95 percent of nonelderly citizens (as compared to about 83 percent before the ACA went into effect).[14] By the end of 2016, the number of uninsured individuals had dropped dramatically, from 50 million to 28 million.[15] That trend reversed itself after the 2016 national elections, with the number of uninsured individuals increasing by seven million during the first two years of the Trump administration.[16] Republicans strenuously opposed enactment of the ACA and have repeatedly attempted to repeal the legislation.[17] Although repeal efforts have failed, the Trump administration turned to other measures to undermine the vitality of the ACA Exchanges, contributing to lower enrollment and a 1.3 percentage point increase in the uninsured rate between 2018 and 2019. Moreover, as this book goes to press, yet another lawsuit brought by Republicans to challenge the constitutionality of the ACA is making its way through the federal courts and may result in the elimination of some or all of the rights and protections created by the statute.[18]

Access to the benefits conferred by the ACA is discussed later in this chapter under the sections on Medicaid and Health Insurance Exchanges.

Who does the Affordable Care Act leave out?

Although the ACA extended health insurance to millions of people who previously could not afford it, important gaps in health coverage for low-income people still remain, including: (1) many categories of noncitizens who are ineligible for Medicaid, Medicare, and/or subsidized health insurance; (2) low-income people who remain ineligible for Medicaid because they reside in a state that refused to adopt expanded ACA Medicaid; (3) working poor families that cannot afford health insurance even with ACA subsidies; and (4) transgender and gender-nonconforming or nonbinary people whose medical needs are not adequately covered by existing health insurance.

In addition, people with employer-sponsored, self-funded insurance plans that are governed by the federal Employee Retirement Income Security Act (ERISA) do not enjoy certain ACA protections, such as the guaranteed coverage of essential health benefits or the medical loss ratio requirement, which places limits on insurance premiums.[19] Similarly, people who opt for inexpensive temporary coverage in the form of short-term, limited duration health plans (an option opened by federal regulations under the Trump administration)[20] may not enjoy the consumer protections required by the ACA, including coverage of preexisting conditions and limits on out-of-pocket costs.[21] As of 2018, these short-term plans can last up to 12 months, with the possibility of extending coverage for up to 36 months.[22] Some states have passed legislation restricting the availability of short-term plans.[23]

As this chapter explains, the federal laws expanding health care coverage go far, but not far enough, in ensuring that low income people have access to adequate medical services. Still, knowing the rules and the best methods for obtaining care under existing law is of critical importance.

Medicaid

What is Medicaid?

Medicaid is a program that provides health insurance and services to eligible low-income individuals. It currently serves over 70 million people, making it the largest source of health care in the United States. Congress enacted Medicaid in 1965 as part of the "War on Poverty" and "Great Society" programs of that time. The Medicaid statute offers federal matching funds to states that agree to operate a Medicaid program in accordance with federal guidelines. All 50 states currently operate a Medicaid program with federal financial assistance.[24] As first enacted, Medicaid required states to cover certain groups of low-income people, including elderly people, disabled people, and certain low-income families with minor children.[25] Over the following decades, Congress steadily enlarged eligibility for Medicaid, most recently with the enactment of the Affordable Care Act, which extended the program to most people with income below 138 percent of the federal poverty level. States have some discretion in the design of their Medicaid programs—including the choice of whether to accept the ACA's expanded eligibility guidelines—and so the rules and administration of Medicaid differ from state to state.

In addition to Medicaid, the Children's Health Insurance Program (CHIP) allows states to cover uninsured children in households with incomes greater than Medicaid eligibility limits, but too low to afford health insurance coverage.[26] CHIP is discussed in more detail later in this chapter.

Medicaid also works in concert with the Medicare program. Medicare is a public health insurance benefit for people age 65 or older and some people with disabilities. Unlike Medicaid, Medicare is funded and operated entirely by the federal government and is not means-tested (i.e., there is no income eligibility cutoff for Medicare). Low-income individuals at least 65 years old or disabled, may qualify for both Medicare and Medicaid, in which case Medicaid will pay for some expenses associated with Medicare, such as deductibles and copays, and for some expenses that Medicare does not cover, such as nursing home services. The Medicare program is discussed in detail later in this chapter.

Medicaid is not charity. It is a right to which eligible persons are entitled by law—like the right of a child to attend public school. State and federal laws determine who qualifies for Medicaid, what services Medicaid covers, and how to appeal decisions about coverage and eligibility. Federal laws set some basic requirements that each state must meet in order to receive federal matching funds to help pay for Medicaid. Federal Medicaid grants to states constitute the single largest federal financial outlay to states of any federal program.[27]

Who runs Medicaid?

Medicaid is a partnership between the federal, state, and local governments. States usually administer the program through their health and social services department. Locally, county departments of social services often play a role in administering the program, particularly in processing applications for coverage and determinations of eligibility. The Centers for Medicare & Medicaid Services

(CMS), a division of the U.S. Department of Health and Human Services (HHS), is in charge of Medicaid at the federal level.[28]

The cost of the Medicaid program is shared by federal, state, and local governments. The federal government pays between 50 percent and 75 percent of the cost of regular, pre-ACA Medicaid, with less affluent states receiving greater federal funding.[29] The federal government paid 100 percent of the cost of the ACA Medicaid expansion from 2014 through 2017. The federal share of that cost declined incrementally to 90 percent in 2020 and thereafter.[30]

How did the Affordable Care Act impact Medicaid?

Prior to adoption of the ACA in 2010, Medicaid's eligibility rules excluded a large percentage of low-income people who could not afford health care. Federal law required states to provide Medicaid only to certain categories of very low-income people, including minor children, parents, pregnant women, the elderly, and those who are blind or disabled (known as "Mandatory Categorically Needy" groups).[31] States also had the option to use federal matching funds to cover other, limited categories of low-income people (known as "Optional Categorically Needy" groups).[32] But the Medicaid law prohibited states from using federal Medicaid funds to provide health care to nondisabled people between ages 18 and 65 unless they were caretakers of minor children. Moreover, many people who fit into one of Medicaid's eligibility categories were nevertheless disqualified by stringent income eligibility cutoffs, which many states set far lower than the federal poverty level, leaving millions of desperately poor families and individuals without access to health care.[33] Before the ACA, the median state Medicaid income eligibility cutoff was just 61 percent of the federal poverty level.[34]

The ACA dramatically expanded Medicaid by eliminating categorical eligibility requirements, raising the income limits, and requiring states to extend Medicaid to *all* citizens (and certain immigrants) with incomes below 138 percent of the federal poverty level. In 2017, an estimated 12 million individuals had gained access to Medicaid coverage through the ACA's eligibility expansions.[35]

Did every state adopt the ACA's expanded Medicaid program?

No. Although the ACA required all states to adopt expanded Medicaid eligibility as a condition of continuing to receive federal Medicaid funds, a number of Republican-led states filed legal challenges against this requirement, and in 2012 the U.S. Supreme Court struck down the ACA's Medicaid expansion mandate.[36]

The Court held that the ACA had unconstitutionally "coerced" states into expanding their Medicaid programs, an odd conclusion, since the statute provided that the federal government would fund between 90 percent and 100 percent of Medicaid expansion, giving states a windfall in expanded health care for their citizens and substantial infusions of federal funds into state health systems and economies. As a result of the Supreme Court's ruling, states were allowed the option not to expand Medicaid eligibility and not to accept the increased federal funding.

Twenty-six states initially decided to forgo Medicaid expansion, leaving millions of their residents without health coverage.[37] Republican political opposition to the ACA played the central role in keeping states from adopting expanded Medicaid.[38] Over time, that political opposition increasingly gave way to sound policy and concern for the public well-being, with seven new states signing on to ACA Medicaid between 2014 and 2016.[39] More recently, citizens in four states, Maine in 2017, and Idaho, Nebraska, and Utah in 2018, adopted ballot initiatives to force their state governments to adopt ACA-expanded Medicaid.[40] As of May 2019, 37 states including the District of Columbia had decided to expand Medicaid as allowed under the ACA, while more than a dozen states had decided not to expand Medicaid.[41] The U.S. CMS HealthCare. gov website maintains current information on which states have elected ACA Medicaid expansion.[42]

Not surprisingly, expansion states have experienced larger health care coverage gains and lower uninsured rates than nonexpansion states.[43] In 2017, for example, the average uninsured rate in states that expanded Medicaid was 7.6 percent, whereas the average uninsured rate in nonexpansion states was 14.3 percent.[44] Studies indicate that Medicaid expansion has had a positive impact on access to health care, utilization of services, and affordability of care among the low-income population.[45]

What are the major ways Medicaid varies from state to state?

Federal law prescribes baseline requirements that all state Medicaid programs must meet, but states retain significant discretion within these federal guidelines. Most importantly, states may choose whether or not to adopt the ACA Medicaid expansion described above. States also have a variety of other design choices for their Medicaid programs, some of which only affect states that did not adopt ACA Medicaid expansion and some of which apply in all states. These include the following.

"Optional Categorically Needy"

While states *must* cover "mandatory categorically needy" populations, including pregnant women, people 65 or older, and people with disabilities, states have the option of covering other individuals who qualify under an "optional categorically needy" group.[46] These groups range from independent foster care adolescents to individuals receiving hospice care to individuals receiving home- and community-based services.[47]

Income Limits

Income eligibility cutoffs (as percentages of the federal poverty level) will vary from state to state depending on a range of factors, including whether the state adopted Medicaid expansion and the eligibility group of the person seeking coverage. States may extend Medicaid eligibility to children, pregnant women, and families with incomes above the mandatory income threshold. For instance, most states extend coverage to pregnant women beyond 138 percent of the federal poverty level. Income eligibility is discussed in more detail below.

Immigrant Access

Medicaid is generally available to "qualified" immigrants who are lawful permanent residents (LPRs) and meet a five-year waiting period, or who qualify as "humanitarian immigrants." States have the option to expand coverage to immigrant populations in a variety of ways.[48] First, states can eliminate the five-year waiting period for children and/or pregnant women, and as of 2018, over half of states have opted to do so.[49] Second, states may provide prenatal care to women regardless of immigration status using CHIP funds. Third, states can use state-only funding, without any federal contribution, to extend coverage to categories of noncitizens otherwise ineligible under federal law. Immigrant eligibility for Medicaid is discussed in more detail below.

Managed Care Plans

Most states choose to administer Medicaid coverage through managed care plans, meaning that private insurance companies manage benefits for people enrolled in Medicaid and Medicaid long-term care programs.[50] Over three-quarters of Medicaid beneficiaries across the country are covered through a Medicaid managed care plan.[51] Between 2012 and 2013, a total of 40 states adopted new managed care policies that expanded managed care to reach new geographic areas or additional eligibility groups.[52] In some states, Medicaid managed care is mandatory for certain populations, such as "dual-eligibles," who are people who receive health care through both Medicare and Medicaid.

Long-Term Care

States are encouraged under the ACA to offer long-term care programs designed to keep aging and disabled people in their communities.[53] States may pursue waivers from federal requirements in order to experiment with programs for long-term care and other Medicaid services.

Covered Services

States may elect to provide optional services, beyond those required by federal law, as part of their Medicaid programs. These optional covered services include, but are not limited to: prescription drugs, dental services, optometrist services, hospice care, physical therapy, and case management services.[54] For both mandatory and optional services, states may exercise discretion in determining the amount, duration and scope of covered benefits.

Waivers and Demonstration Projects

Under Section 1115 of the Social Security Act,[55] a state may ask the federal Centers for Medicare and Medicaid Services (CMS) to waive certain federally mandated program requirements and allow the state to experiment with the design of its Medicaid program. The CMS may grant such a request only if the proposed waiver is budget neutral and "likely to assist in promoting the objectives" of the Medicaid program.[56]

More recently, rather than pursuing approaches to expand or improve Medicaid, some states have begun seeking waivers to impose restrictions on Medicaid that include work requirements and the elimination of retroactive eligibility.[57] But not all recent waivers have been regressive; some states continue to experiment with innovative projects to expand benefits, such as programs to address the opioid crisis and improve access to substance abuse treatment and mental health services.[58] The number and kind of Medicaid waivers are constantly in flux. Several important categories of actual or proposed waivers are discussed later in this chapter. For a current list of waivers and pending waiver applications, consult the CMS online list of state waivers.[59]

Work Requirements

Several states have sought waivers allowing them to impose work requirements on people who enroll in Medicaid, and in January 2018, the Trump administration issued guidance supporting these state efforts.[60] States have proposed a variety of work conditions, some allowing imposition of so-called "lockout penalties," which would bar individuals from receiving Medicaid coverage during a period of three to nine months for noncompliance with work requirements.[61] As of early 2019, the CMS had granted waivers to seven states, although federal trial courts have struck down work requirements in Arkansas and Kentucky on grounds that appear applicable to, and could invalidate, the other state waivers.[62]

Health policy experts have argued that conditioning Medicaid coverage on work activity is counterproductive; such restrictions threaten to deny individuals who face serious employment barriers the health care that would improve their chances of becoming and staying employed.[63] The work conditions have also been criticized as unnecessary; over half of Medicaid-eligible adults already work full- or part-time, and 72 percent have at least one full-time or part-time worker in their family.[64] Studies project that the primary effect of work requirements will be decreased Medicaid enrollment and worsened health outcomes.[65] In Arkansas, the first state to impose work requirements on Medicaid in the 60-year history of the program, 83 percent of low-income Medicaid beneficiaries who were expected to log onto a website and report their work activity did not do so, and the state dropped over 4,000 people from the program in a single month.[66]

Medicaid to Purchase Private Insurance
Some states have received waivers that allow the use of Medicaid funds to purchase private health plans through an ACA Exchange, or to enroll people in private Medicaid managed care plans.[67]

Cost Sharing and Premiums
Some states have received waivers permitting them to charge premiums to Medicaid beneficiaries, but thus far the waivers have not permitted states to deny coverage to beneficiaries who do not pay their share of the premiums if they are living below the federal poverty line. In addition, HHS has required states that want to charge newly eligible Medicaid beneficiaries' cost sharing (such as copayments and coinsurance) to meet the existing "criteria for cost-sharing waivers set forth in the Medicaid statute."[68] Research has shown that charging premiums and other cost sharing to low-income people result in many of those people forgoing or delaying coverage, and from accessing the health care they need.[69]

Payment Reform
States may also seek "waivers"[70] from federal Medicaid requirements to experiment with payment reform,[71] coverage of specialized services such as behavioral health, or expansion of managed care.[72] One trend in most states is to shift people with Medicaid from state-administered "fee-for-service" coverage to managed care plans.[73]

Who can get Medicaid?

As noted earlier, Medicaid coverage differs from state to state and turns significantly on whether or not the state has adopted the ACA Medicaid expansion.

In all states, the applicant must be a U.S. citizen or be in a lawful immigration status that meets the state's Medicaid eligibility guidelines. In addition, the applicant must reside in the state from which Medicaid is sought.

In all states, the applicant must have limited income. The income eligibility guidelines for Medicaid and method of calculating income vary from state to state.

In ACA Medicaid expansion states, any person who is a U.S. citizen or meets the state's immigration eligibility guidelines qualifies for Medicaid if the person's income does not exceed 138 percent of the federal poverty level (FPL) for the applicable household size. As discussed later, states have the option to extend Medicaid coverage to individuals and households with incomes that exceed 138 percent of the FPL. Note also that children in families whose income exceeds Medicaid limits can still receive coverage through the Child Health Insurance Program (CHIP).

In states that have not adopted ACA Medicaid expansion, low-income individuals can qualify for Medicaid only if they fall within one of the pre-ACA eligibility categories. States must cover certain categories, including minor children and their parents or caretaker relatives, pregnant women, people age 65 or older, and people with disabilities,[74] but the income limits vary by state. At a minimum, all states must provide Medicaid to pregnant women and children under age six in households with income below 138 percent of the FPL; children aged six to 18 must be covered if their family's income is under 100 percent of the FPL.[75] Many states have expanded Medicaid eligibility to children beyond these federal minimums.[76] States also must cover children who are enrolled in or recently aged out of foster care, up to age 26, with no income limit.[77] States have the option to cover additional individuals who fall within an "optional categorically eligible group."[78]

The U.S. Centers for Medicare & Medicaid Services (CMS) website, HealthCare.gov, has a useful tool to help individuals and families determine whether they qualify for medical assistance in their state.[79]

Can people who are not U.S. citizens qualify for Medicaid?

It depends. Immigrants who are not lawfully present in the United States are not eligible for Medicaid, except for emergency services.[80] Most immigrants who lawfully reside in the United States can qualify for Medicaid, if otherwise eligible, after they have lived in the United States in lawful status for five years,[81] though certain immigrants are excused from the five-year waiting period as described below.

Immigrants who may receive Medicaid if otherwise eligible—referred to in the federal statutes and regulations as "qualified aliens"—include:

- Lawful permanent residents (LPRs/green card holders),
- Asylees;
- Refugees;
- Cuban/Haitian entrants;
- Persons paroled into the United States for at least one year;
- Persons granted conditional entrant status before 1980;
- Certain domestic violence survivors and their children or parents;
- Certain victims of trafficking and their spouse, child, sibling, or parent, or individuals with a pending application for a victim of trafficking visa;
- Persons granted withholding of deportation; and
- Members of a federally recognized Indian tribe or American Indian born in Canada.

Federal law eliminates the five-year waiting period for certain qualified noncitizens, including:

- Refugees, asylees, and LPRs who used to be refugees or asylees;
- Veterans or active duty military (and their dependents);
- People who have worked (or can be credited with) 40 quarters of covered employment in the Social Security system.[82]

In addition, the Attorney General has discretion to require states to provide Medicaid without a waiting period to immigrants who have been "battered or subjected to extreme cruelty" in the United States.

States have the option to provide Medicaid immediately to otherwise eligible children up to age 21 and pregnant women who are "lawfully present" in the United States.[83] As of January 2019, 25 states had elected this option for pregnant women, and 34 states had elected this option for children under age 21.[84]

States may also waive the immigrant waiting period for other groups at their own expense.[85] New York, Massachusetts, and California, for example, extend coverage to noncitizens considered "permanently residing under color of law" (PRUCOL) regardless of whether they have legal permanent resident status.[86] California uses state funds to cover low-income children under age 19 regardless of immigration status.[87] At least some courts have ruled that state exclusion of lawful permanent resident immigrants from state Medicaid programs violates the Equal Protection Clause of the Fourteenth Amendment to the U.S. Constitution and/or violates equal protection and social welfare guarantees of state constitutions.[88] States may also extend health care (albeit not Medicaid assistance) to noncitizens by creating a Basic Health Program under the Affordable Care Act.[89] A Basic Health option allows low-income persons, who are citizens or lawfully present noncitizens and do not otherwise qualify for Medicaid, to purchase a lower-cost plan in their state's Health Insurance Exchange.[90]

Additional issues facing immigrants seeking access to health care are discussed later in this chapter.

How much income can a family or individual have and still get Medicaid?

Medicaid is a "means-tested" program, which means that eligibility is limited to people with low incomes.[91] The amount of income a family or individual may have and still qualify for Medicaid depends on a number of factors, including family size and the eligibility limits in the individual's state. In ACA Medicaid expansion states, people with household income below 138 percent of the federal poverty level generally qualify for benefits, but states may elect to extend Medicaid to people with higher incomes, and federal law *requires* higher limits for certain groups, such as children and pregnant women.[92] Income eligibility guidelines in states that refused ACA Medicaid expansion vary more widely and are significantly lower than in expansion states. Table 4.1 summarizes income limits by group for expansion states and nonexpansion states.[93]

How is income calculated for determining Medicaid eligibility?

Financial eligibility for most categories of Medicaid is determined using a tax-based measure of income and household size known as Modified Adjusted Gross Income (MAGI). The ACA introduced this method of evaluating financial eligibility, and it applies not only to Medicaid but also to CHIP and to federal subsidies for qualified health plans purchased through health marketplaces.[94] The MAGI rules apply in all states –whether or not the state has adopted ACA Medicaid expansion–but certain groups of people are exempt from these rules, principally people whose eligibility for Medicaid is based on old age, disability, or status as a child in foster care.[95] Financial eligibility for those groups is evaluated under the state's eligibility rules as they existed prior to enactment of the ACA.[96]

There are three basic steps for calculating income and determining Medicaid eligibility under the MAGI rules. First, the composition of the applicant's

Table 4.1 State Medicaid and CHIP Income Eligibility Limits by Group and by Expansion Status
(Income limits are expressed as percentages of the federal poverty level based on state decisions as of April 2018)[1]

	Children Ages 0–1		Children Ages 1–5		Children Ages 6–18		Children Separate CHIP		Pregnant Women Medicaid		Non-Disabled Adults 19–64 (family of three)	
	Low	High	Low	High	Low	High	Low	High	Low	High	Low	High
ACA Expansion States (including Washington, D.C.)	147%	380%	138%	324%	138%	324%	175%	405%	138%	380%	138%	215%
Nonexpansion States	144%	306%	144%	218%	138%	213%	190%	317%	138%	306%	18%	101%

[1] For state-specific data, visit U.S. Centers for Medicare & Medicaid Services, Medicaid.gov, Medicaid, Children's Health Insurance Program, & Basic Health Program Eligibility Levels, https://www.medicaid.gov/medicaid/program-information/medicaid-and-chip-eligibility-levels/index.html; Kaiser Family Foundation, Where Are States Today? Medicaid and CHIP Eligibility Levels for Children, Pregnant Women, and Adults, https://www.kff.org/medicaid/fact-sheet/where-are-states-today-medicaid-and-chip/.

Medicaid household (i.e., who is included in the household) is determined according to the rules that govern federal income tax filings. Second, the Modified Adjusted Gross Income (MAGI) of each included household member is calculated and added together to arrive at the household's MAGI. Third, the MAGI of the applicant's household is compared to the federal poverty level (FPL) for a household of that size to determine eligibility for Medicaid (and for other health insurance programs, such as CHIP or Health Exchange subsidies, if income exceeds Medicaid limits). The MAGI rules are complex, so only a basic overview is provided here. A comprehensive explanation may be found in "The Advocate's Guide to MAGI," published by the National Health Law Project.[97]

How is Medicaid household composition determined and whose income is included in the calculation of a household's MAGI?

As already noted, the composition of an applicant's Medicaid household is important for two reasons: first, it affects whose income counts in determining the Modified Adjusted Gross Income (MAGI) of the applicant's household; and second it affects the amount of income the applicant's household may have and still qualify for Medicaid: the larger the household size, the higher the income limit. Financial eligibility for Medicaid is determined by comparing the MAGI of the applicant's "household" to the Medicaid income eligibility limit for a household of that size.

This calculation is not as straightforward as it seems, though, because "household" for these purposes does not necessarily include everyone who lives with the applicant; and a household's MAGI does not necessarily include the income of every household member.

Rather, since Medicaid household composition is determined by following the IRS rules for federal income tax filing, a Medicaid household for MAGI purposes generally consists only of the tax filer plus the tax filer's spouse and other "dependents" as defined by the Internal Revenue Code.[98] Relatives residing under the same roof may or may not be in the same "household" for purposes of determining Medicaid eligibility. For instance, households with grandparents and other relatives who are not considered dependents under IRS rules will be screened separately for Medicaid eligibility because they are not part of the same tax-filing unit.[99]

As to whose income counts, the general rule is that a household's MAGI is calculated by adding the MAGI of the tax filer and spouse to the MAGI of any dependent child who is required to file a tax return.[100] But a dependent child's income is only included if the dependent is *required* to file a tax return; if the

dependent child files taxes for another reason, but had no legal filing requirement, the child's income is not included.[101]

If an adult in a household without a tax filer applies for Medicaid, the household consists of the applicant and the applicant's spouse and children if living
with the applicant. If a child in a household without a tax filer applies for
Medicaid, the household consists of the applicant and the applicant's parents,
siblings, spouse, and children if living with the applicant. For purposes of these
rules, "child" means an individual under age 19 or under age 24 for full-time
students, at state option.[102]

How is household size determined for a household
that includes a pregnant woman?

When a pregnant woman applies for Medicaid, she counts as one person plus
the number of children expected to be delivered.[103] This is important because
financial eligibility for Medicaid is measured with reference to the federal poverty level (FPL), which varies by household size; increasing the household size
of a pregnant women means that her Medicaid income eligibility limit will be
higher. If another person in a pregnant women's household applies for Medicaid,
the state may, at its option, calculate the applicant's household size by counting
the pregnant women as one person, two people, or one plus the number of children expected.[104]

What is Modified Adjusted Gross Income (MAGI)
and what types of income are included in it?

Modified Adjusted Gross Income (MAGI) is the measure generally used to determine income eligibility for Medicaid; it consists of "Adjusted Gross Income,"
as defined by federal tax law, plus any nontaxable Social Security benefits, tax-
exempt interest, or nontaxable foreign income. Adjusted Gross Income (AGI)
is the taxpayer's income from any source minus (1) income exempt from federal
taxation, and (2) allowable tax deductions. Income not taxable under federal law,
and therefore not included in AGI, includes:

- TANF and other government cash assistance;
- Child support received;
- Supplemental Security Income (SSI);
- Workers' compensation payments;
- Veterans' benefits;

- Earned income tax credits, other federal tax credits, and income tax refunds;
- Pretax deductions from wages, such as health premiums, retirement contributions, or flexible spending accounts;
- Proceeds from life insurance, accident insurance, or health insurance; and
- Gifts, loans, and inheritances.

Allowable deductions are those listed on the first page of IRS Form 1040 (the individual tax return) and include:

- interest on student loans;
- higher education expenses;
- self-employment taxes;
- business expenses;
- alimony payments; and
- certain contributions to an Individual Retirement Account (IRA) or Health Savings Account.[105]

Example of a MAGI eligibility determination: Ms. A lives alone, earns gross wages of $1,400 per month, and has interest income of $10 per month. She pays $60 per month interest on her student loans. Ms. A's gross monthly income is $1,410 (wages plus interest income). Her monthly AGI is $1,350, because the $60 per month she pays for student loan interest is an allowable deduction ($1,410 − $60 = $1,350). Her MAGI is also $1,350 because she does not receive any of the income types (Social Security, nontaxable interest, or nontaxable foreign income) that are added to AGI to arrive at MAGI. Ms. A's financial eligibility for Medicaid is determined by comparing her MAGI of $1,350 to the applicable income limit—which, in an ACA Medicaid Expansion state, would be 138 percent of the FPL for a household of one.

What are other differences between MAGI and Non-MAGI Medicaid?

As already mentioned, individuals whose eligibility for Medicaid is based on old age, disability, or status as a foster care child generally are not subject to the MAGI rules. In shorthand, they are said to receive "Non-MAGI" Medicaid. A few important differences between MAGI and Non-MAGI Medicaid deserve special emphasis. First, there is no resource test for MAGI Medicaid; individuals may qualify for MAGI Medicaid regardless of the value of their assets. A resource test will apply, however, if a MAGI Medicaid recipient seeks long-term institutional care or nursing home care. By contrast, a resource test *always* applies to

Non-MAGI Medicaid, irrespective of the type of health services sought. Second, MAGI Medicaid income limits are higher than the income limits applicable to Non-MAGI Medicaid. Third, MAGI Medicaid recipients receive coverage for a full 12-month interval once they qualify, even if their income increases above the income eligibility limit during that period. Non-MAGI Medicaid recipients, on the other hand, can lose coverage at any time if income increases beyond the income eligibility maximum (although some states may extend coverage for such individuals for up to a year through a program called "Transitional Medicaid"). Each of these issues is discussed in more detail later in this chapter.

Can people choose between MAGI and Non-MAGI Medicaid?

Not usually. Only the following groups may qualify for either MAGI or Non-MAGI Medicaid:

- Disabled adults under age 65 who are not yet receiving Medicare;
- Disabled parent/caretaker relatives of any age (even if receiving Medicare) caring for a child up to age 18, or age 19 if the child is a student; and
- Disabled children, unless they are in a waiver program.

Generally, applicants are more likely to qualify for Medicaid under the MAGI rules because of the higher income eligibility limits and absence of an assets test. However, for households with significant earned income, the more generous deductions used for determining Non-MAGI eligibility (including deductions for child care expenses) may be more advantageous. Disabled adults under age 65 whose income exceeds MAGI and Non-MAGI Medicaid limits may still access coverage if their state operates a Medicaid Buy-In Program for Working People with Disabilities.[106] This program allows people to purchase Medicaid coverage through payment of modest monthly premiums. In New York, for example, the income limit for the Medicaid buy-in program is 250 percent of the FPL, but half of the applicant's gross earned income is initially disregarded in determining eligibility (meaning that New York's program is in effect open to people with income up to 500 percent of the FPL).[107]

Can Medicaid recipients continue getting benefits after their income increases above the Medicaid financial eligibility limit?

Maybe. MAGI Medicaid coverage continues through the end of the 12-month eligibility period, even if the household's countable income increases beyond the income limit during that period. By contrast, recipients of Non-MAGI Medicaid can lose eligibility as soon as their countable income exceeds the financial eligibility cap. In states that have not adopted ACA Medicaid expansion, income limits for Medicaid remain well below the poverty level and so loss of Medicaid due to a small increase in income could leave desperately poor families without access to health coverage. However, families with children who lose Medicaid eligibility because of increased earned income may qualify for continuing coverage through the federal Transitional Medical Assistance (TMA) program. States must provide at least six months of TMA coverage to families that lose Medicaid eligibility due to increased income from employment, as well as to families that lose eligibility due to the loss of a time-limited earned income disregard.[108] TMA benefits may come in the form of continued Medicaid coverage or state payments of premiums for health insurance offered through the recipient's employer. After the initial six-month period, a family is entitled to continued coverage for an additional six months if its countable income, minus child care costs, does not exceed 185 percent of the FPL; states have the option to waive this income limit.[109] During the second six-month period, states may require families with incomes at or above 100 percent of the FPL to pay a premium for the additional coverage.[110]

Congress enacted TMA to remove a powerful barrier—loss of Medicaid coverage—that stood in the way of families trying to increase their earned income and work their way out of poverty. The program, which Congress made permanent in 2015,[111] has proven to be a success, providing critical coverage to nearly four million working families annually. Regrettably, the Trump administration has approved several state waivers limiting the availability of TMA and undermining the program's effectiveness.[112]

What options are there for people whose income exceeds the state's Medicaid eligibility limit?

The principal health coverage options for people with income above their state's Medicaid limit are: (1) subsidized health insurance obtained through a state Health Exchange for people with incomes between 100 percent and 400 percent of the FPL; (2) coverage through CHIP for children in families with income below the state CHIP limit (ranging between 175 percent and 405 percent of the FPL); or (3) assistance with high medical bills through a Medicaid "medically needy program" in states that offer this program. Each of these options is discussed later in this chapter, but a few things are worth noting here.

First, in states that refused to adopt ACA expanded Medicaid, many adults with incomes below 100 percent of the FPL will fall into a coverage gap because their incomes are too high for Medicaid but too low for Health Exchange subsidies. Specifically, even though poor, most such individuals will not qualify for Medicaid because eligibility limits in nonexpansion states run far below the poverty level;[113] these individuals also will not qualify for subsidies on the Health Exchanges because eligibility for that benefit requires income of at least 100 percent (but no more than 400 percent) of the FPL.[114] The ACA restricted eligibility for Health Exchange subsidies to people with incomes above 100 percent of the FPL on the assumption that all persons at or below that income level would be covered by Medicaid. The continuum of coverage created by the ACA guaranteed health care to very low income people by requiring states to extend Medicaid to all adults with income below 138 percent of the FPL, and provided subsidies to those with somewhat higher incomes. Under the statutory scheme, coverage was available at all income levels through at least 400 percent of the FPL. The U,S. Supreme Court ruptured that arrangement—and created the coverage gap—when it ruled that Congress could not require states to accept ACA expanded Medicaid. As a result, over two million low-income adults in nonexpansion states have been left without affordable care.[115]

Second, because the income limits for children seeking Medicaid and CHIP substantially exceed the Medicaid income limits for adults, children in a household may be eligible for Medicaid or CHIP coverage even if their parents do not qualify.

Lastly, under the ACA's "single streamlined application" requirement, whenever an individual applies for health coverage, the state must check to see whether the person could qualify for Medicaid, CHIP or health insurance subsidies; people need not know in advance the program for which they may qualify.[116]

Can people with high medical bills get help from Medicaid even if their income is too high to qualify for ongoing Medicaid benefits?

Yes, in most states. People who would otherwise qualify for Medicaid except that their incomes or resources exceed eligibility limits can receive help with high medical costs through the "medically needy program," a component of the Medicaid program that states may elect to operate.[117] Each state that participates in this program sets a "medically needy income level" based on family size. If a family's expenditures on health care during a set period of time (known as the "spend down period") bring its income down to the "medically needy" level, Medicaid will cover any additional health costs the family incurs for the balance of that period. States may set the spend down period at anywhere from one month to six months. The spend down acts like an insurance deductible that must be met before coverage begins.

Eligibility workers often do not explain the medically needy program to applicants who are denied Medicaid because of excess income. People who may need assistance through that program should ask the state Medicaid agency for the state's "medically needy level" and "spend down period," then keep track (and records) of their medical expenses. Once the family has spent down to the medical needy level, it must file an application for assistance through this program.

Here is an example of how the medically needy program's spend down works: Suppose the state's medically needy income level is $500 per month, and the spend down period is one month. If an individual's income is $700, then the individual will have to incur a total of $200 in medical bills during the one-month spend down period before becoming eligible for Medicaid coverage.

States do not have to offer Medicaid to the medically needy, but most states have elected to do so.[118] States choosing to cover the medically needy must, at a minimum, cover pregnant and postpartum women and children under age 18.[119]

What bills count toward the medically needy spend down?

Almost any bill for "medical or remedial care" counts toward the medically needy spend down, including health insurance premiums, doctor bills, hospital bills, medical tests, physical therapy, home health care, prescriptions, dentures, eyeglasses, hearing aids, and mental health bills.[120] Also included are over-the-counter drugs, bandages, needles, and the like. Bills for treatments considered nontraditional, such as vitamin supplements, do not count. Medical costs incurred by family members also count toward the spend down, as do some costs incurred before filing of the Medicaid application, but applicants must provide documentation for all claimed expenses. Medical expenses count toward the spend down as soon as they are incurred, even if the individual has not yet paid the bill.

Is there a limit on the assets a person can have and still qualify for Medicaid?

It depends. States may not apply any asset or resource limit to people whose financial eligibility for Medicaid is determined under the MAGI rules described earlier in this chapter.[121] Before the ACA, people could be disqualified from Medicaid if their assets (such as cash, savings, or property) exceeded program maximums. As a result, people who needed access to medical care frequently had to sell off their assets and spend their savings in order to qualify for Medicaid. The ACA essentially eliminated the assets test for MAGI Medicaid.[122] As a general rule, individuals can receive MAGI Medicaid regardless of the value of their assets and resources. One important exception is that MAGI Medicaid will not cover long-term care services, such as nursing home care, unless the individual's assets are less than the maximum set by the state's Medicaid program.[123]

People who are not covered by the MAGI Medicaid rules—principally those whose eligibility for Medicaid is based on old age, disability, or status as a child in foster care[124]—do not qualify for Medicaid if their assets exceed the state's eligibility limits.[125] For these categories of people, states may use their own tests to calculate eligibility based on income, assets, and exceptions.[126]

Can an individual transfer assets to someone else in order to qualify for Medicaid?

If an individual gives away assets in order to receive Medicaid, a transfer-of-assets penalty may apply.[127] The transfer-of-assets penalty only affects Medicaid eligibility for long-term services in a nursing home or other nursing care facility and to home or community care services provided to individuals who would otherwise require long-term care in a nursing facility.[128] States have the option to apply the penalty to additional long-term services. Other services covered by Medicaid are not affected by the penalty.[129]

When a Medicaid applicant or recipient requests Medicaid for long-term care services, the agency will examine any asset transfers by the individual and individual's spouse during the 60-month period immediately preceding the request.[130] Any gifts made or assets transferred for less than fair market value during that 60-month look-back period will be used to calculate a disqualification penalty—a number of months during which Medicaid will not pay for long-term services.[131] The disqualification period is calculated by dividing the amount of uncompensated asset transfers by the private pay cost of a nursing home for one month. For example, assume that Ms. A gives a $50,000 certificate of deposit to a friend within 60 months of the day she enters a nursing home, and that the private pay nursing home rate in the state is $5,000 a month. Medicaid will not cover Ms. A's nursing facility services for 10 months (the $50,000 uncompensated asset transfer divided by the $5,000 monthly private pay nursing home rate). During those months Ms. A will have to pay the nursing home out of pocket.[132]

Some transfers are not penalized. An individual may transfer a home, without penalty, to a spouse, to a child who is under age 21 or disabled, to a sibling who has an equity interest in the home and was residing there for at least one year prior to the application for long-term care, or to a child of any age who resided in the home for at least two years prior to the application for long-term care and who provided care that permitted the applicant to remain at home rather than in an institution.[133]

Other assets may be transferred without penalty to a spouse or to a blind or disabled child.[134] Finally, the penalty will not apply if the applicant can show the transfer was made exclusively for reasons other than to qualify for Medicaid.[135]

Can assets be transferred into a trust fund in order to qualify for Medicaid?

Yes. There are several types of trusts that an individual may use to help qualify for Medicaid.

Individual Trusts for Persons with Disabilities under Age 65

A person with a disability under age 65 may transfer assets into an individual trust established solely for that person's benefit.[136] This kind of trust is commonly known as a "supplemental needs trust" and is usually designed to pay for goods and services not covered by government benefits. The trust must be established by the person's parent, grandparent, or legal guardian, or by court order.[137] Assets placed into a properly structured supplemental needs trust do not count as a resource for purposes of Medicaid eligibility and are not subject to any transfer-of-assets penalty.[138] Transferring excess assets into a properly structured trust may also allow the individual to qualify for Supplemental Security Income if otherwise eligible.[139]

There are a few disadvantages to transferring resources into a supplemental needs trust. First, a trust document must be drafted, which usually requires the assistance of a legal professional.[140] Second, a trustee is needed to manage the trust property. Third, ordinarily the individual can receive only small sums from the trust at any one time because cash distributions count as income for purposes of Medicaid and SSI eligibility and may reduce the amount of any SSI grant. Finally, any amount remaining in the trust when the individual dies will be used first to repay the Medicaid program for medical assistance received during the individual's lifetime.

Pooled Trusts for Persons with Disabilities of Any Age

Individuals with disabilities, regardless of age, may transfer excess resources into a "pooled trust" to establish Medicaid eligibility. A pooled trust is established by a not-for-profit organization and supplements a person's government benefits in the same way as an individual supplemental needs trust. Pooled trusts have separate accounts for each individual beneficiary. Assets in a qualifying pooled trust do not count as resources for purposes of Medicaid eligibility.[141]

One advantage of a pooled trust is that an individual can set up an account within the trust directly; there is no requirement that the account be established by a parent, grandparent, legal guardian, or court, as is the case with an individual trust. Another advantage of a pooled trust is that the individual may choose to have the funds remaining at death stay in the trust for the benefit of other people with disabilities, rather than being used to repay the state for Medicaid the individual received.

A disadvantage is that in some states a transfer of assets into a pooled trust by an individual age 65 or over is subject to the transfer-of-asset penalties described in the preceding question and so may result in a period of ineligibility.

Individual Irrevocable Trusts

Any person, regardless of age, and whether or not disabled, may transfer assets into an individual irrevocable trust. This is an "income-only" trust, which means that the trustee can use only the income generated by the trust (for example, interest payments or dividends) to provide for the individual beneficiary's needs, but may not withdraw trust assets during the individual's lifetime. Assets placed into an individual irrevocable trust do not count as resources for purposes of Medicaid eligibility.[142]

The major advantage of an individual irrevocable trust is that the beneficiary decides who will receive the trust assets upon the beneficiary's death; the Medicaid payback provisions do not apply. The disadvantages of this type of trust are that the beneficiary does not have access to the principal of the trust, and transfers into the trust are subject to the transfer-of-assets penalty described above, and so may result in a period of Medicaid ineligibility.

Can the state Medicaid agency take a recipient's home or property to recoup amounts it has paid for care?

Under certain circumstances, a state may recoup the cost of services provided to a Medicaid recipient. States must attempt to recover from the estate of a deceased Medicaid recipient the cost of any long-term care services provided to the individual at age 55 and thereafter. States have the option to recover payments for all other Medicaid services provided to these individuals, except for Medicare cost sharing paid on behalf of Medicare Savings Program beneficiaries. States may not recover from the estate of a deceased Medicaid recipient who is survived by a spouse, child under age 21, or blind or disabled child of any age. States must also establish procedures for waiving estate recovery when recovery would cause an undue hardship.[143]

States may place a lien on a living recipient's property if a court has ruled that Medicaid benefits were incorrectly paid for that individual.[144] States may also impose liens on real property during the lifetime of a Medicaid recipient who is permanently institutionalized,[145] except if any of the following people resides in the home: the spouse, child under age 21, blind or disabled child of any age, or sibling who has an equity interest in the home. States must remove any such lien if the Medicaid enrollee is discharged from the facility and returns home.[146]

States may also attempt to seek repayment from individuals alleged to have received Medicaid benefits in error. In some instances, agency officials may try to obtain an admission that the individual committed fraud in obtaining Medicaid. Fraud is a serious charge and not the same thing as making a mistake in the Medicaid application or in reporting information to the state agency. Individuals contacted by a Medicaid agency regarding incorrect Medicaid payments, should contact a local legal aid or legal services office for assistance.

What happens to a family's savings if a spouse has to go into a nursing home?

Federal laws ensure that the costs of nursing home care do not cause the at-home spouse to live without reasonable income or resources.[147] These "spousal impoverishment" protections extend to couples where one spouse is likely to remain in a hospital or nursing facility for more than 30 days. Without these protections, a couple would have to spend nearly all of its joint assets and use all of its income before the spouse requiring long-term care could qualify for Medicaid. The ACA reinforces protection against spousal impoverishment by making it mandatory in each state.[148]

Income of the noninstitutionalized spouse (known as the "community spouse") is not counted at all in in determining the institutionalized spouse's eligibility for Medicaid. In addition, some of the institutionalized spouse's income may be retained by the couple, including an allowance for the community spouse. The income deductions for the institutionalized spouse are made in the following order:

1. A personal needs allowance of at least $30 per month (for extra food, magazines, clothing);[149]
2. A minimum monthly needs allowance for the community spouse of at least $2,057.50 but not exceeding $3,160 in 2019 (adjusted annually based on cost-of-living increases) if the spouse's own income is below this amount;[150]
3. An allowance for each family member;
4. Deductions for medical or remedial care not covered by Medicaid.[151]

The monthly needs allowance for the community spouse can be increased if the couple can demonstrate at a Medicaid fair hearing that "exceptional circumstances" require higher deductions or if a court orders that the community spouse receive increased support.[152]

The spousal impoverishment protections also shield some of the couple's assets and resources. When an institutionalized person applies for Medicaid, the eligibility worker will consider all countable (i.e., nonexempt) resources owned by the institutionalized spouse, the community spouse, or both, at the beginning of the period of institutionalization. Exempt resources, including the home, household goods, an automobile, and a burial fund, are not considered in the eligibility determination. From the total countable resources, the community spouse is allowed to retain a minimum of $25,284 or one-half of the total resources, whichever is greater, up to a maximum of $126,420 (in 2019).[153] These amounts are adjusted annually based on cost-of-living increases and vary by state. The resource allowance can be increased by a fair hearing if it can be demonstrated that "exceptional circumstances" require higher deductions, or by a court order that the community spouse receive increased support.[154]

States must apply the spousal impoverishment protections when a spouse would be institutionalized in a nursing facility or an intermediate care facility if not for the state's provision of home- and community-based services.[155] States must apply the spousal impoverishment protections to households with children with AIDS or drug dependence at birth.[156]

What health costs must Medicaid cover?

State Medicaid programs must pay for the following types of care:

1. Inpatient and outpatient hospital services;
2. Early and periodic screening, diagnostic, and treatment services;
3. Nursing facility services;
4. Home health services;
5. Physician services;
6. Rural health clinic services;
7. Laboratory and x-ray services;
8. Family planning and nurse midwife services;
9. Certified pediatric and family nurse practitioner services;
10. Transportation to medical care;
11. Federally qualified health center services
12. Freestanding birth center services; and
13. Tobacco cessation counseling and pharmacotherapy for pregnant women.[157]

States are required to cover the services included in the definition of "Medical Assistance,"[158] including the categories of services above. Federal regulations do not specify all the services that Medicaid must cover within each category, but require that "each service must be sufficient in amount, duration, and scope to reasonably achieve its purpose."[159] State Medicaid agencies may not arbitrarily deny or reduce the amount, duration, or scope of a required service solely because of the diagnosis, type of illness, or condition.[160] For instance, a state could not categorically refuse to cover antiretroviral drugs for people with AIDS.[161]

Can Medicaid programs cover additional services at state option?

Yes. States may elect to expand Medicaid coverage beyond the list of services mandated by federal law. These optional services include prescription drugs, clinic services, physical therapy, occupational therapy, speech and hearing disorder services, respiratory care services, podiatry services, optometry services, dental services, dentures, prosthetics, eyeglasses, chiropractic services, private duty nursing services, personal care, hospice, and case management.[162] All services, even those that the state provides at its option, must be covered in sufficient amount, duration, and scope. States may not arbitrarily deny or reduce optional services because of the diagnosis, type of illness, or condition.[163]

States may place reasonable limits on the amount, duration, and scope of services it covers for adults.[164] The state can also make a service subject to prior authorization, preadmission screening, or second opinion.[165] These types of "utilization controls" mean that the provider will have to get the state's agreement that the service is medically necessary before Medicaid will cover the service.

Does Medicaid cover additional health services for children?

Yes. Federal law requires states to cover a comprehensive set of health services for individuals under the age of 21. This package of services, known as Early and Periodic Screening, Diagnostic, and Treatment (EPSDT), includes the full range of medically necessary services, plus regularly scheduled health and developmental screenings and preventive care, mental health care, dental care, hearing and vision screenings, and access to the health care services required to treat any conditions revealed by these screenings.[166] The EPSDT program has dramatically improved health outcomes and well-being for children and has been documented as a "critical tool to reduce racial and ethnic health inequality."[167]

Nevertheless, federal audits show that some states have not complied fully and consistently with the program's requirements.[168]

Can Medicaid pay for Medicare premiums and expenses?

There are several programs, including the Qualified Medicare Beneficiary (QMB) program, through which Medicaid will pay an individual's Medicare Part A and Part B premiums, deductibles, and coinsurance.[169] Medicare beneficiaries who have incomes at or below the federal poverty level and resources that do not exceed twice the SSI resource eligibility standards can qualify for the QMB program.[170] Advocates report that beneficiaries and providers have sometimes been unaware of the availability the QMB program or did not understand or abide by the rule that QMB participants may not be asked to make any copayment or pay any coinsurance.[171]

How did the ACA change the health care benefits covered by Medicaid?

Following the enactment of the ACA, Medicaid coverage must be at least equal to the state's "benchmark coverage."[172] "Benchmark coverage" means, at state option, the package of services covered by the state or federal employee health plans available in that state, or by the largest commercial plan, or by another plan that has been selected as a benchmark by the Secretary of Health and Human Services. This requirement ensures that Medicaid coverage will be consistent with the "essential health benefits" covered by plans sold through the state Health Insurance Exchanges.[173]

In addition, the ACA expands Medicaid coverage in several respects including the following.

Preventive Care
Under the ACA, Medicaid must cover all preventive services that are recommended by the U.S. Preventive Services Task Force. For adults, these services include routine screenings for blood pressure and cholesterol, as well as screenings for alcoholism and depression. For women, preventive care includes screenings for breast cancer and cervical cancer. For children, preventive care includes screenings for autism, hearing, and vision. Preventive care for all people includes immunizations. For a full list, check the Healthcare.gov website.[174]

Family Planning Services and Supplies

Family planning has been mandatory under Medicaid since 1976. As noted above, "medical assistance" must include family planning services and supplies furnished to individuals of childbearing age, including minors who may be sexually active, who are eligible under the state plan, and who desire such services and supplies.[175]

The ACA also opens a new pathway for states to offer family planning as a "state option" for people who might not otherwise qualify for Medicaid.[176] States now have the flexibility to set the income limit for family planning up to the highest limit for pregnant women under Medicaid or CHIP (185 percent of the FPL), and to consider only the income of the person seeking family planning services in determining eligibility. Additionally, states have the option to provide presumptive eligibility for family planning.[177] The ACA did not change the long-standing rule—known as "the Hyde Amendment"—that bars use of federal funds for abortion services except in cases of rape, incest, or danger to the life of the woman, though some states use their own funds to provide medically necessary abortion services through their Medicaid programs.[178]

Freestanding Birth Centers

Freestanding birth centers are facilities separate from hospitals that are licensed by the state to provide prenatal, labor and delivery, and postpartum care. Under the ACA, services provided at freestanding birth centers qualify as "medical assistance" and are reimbursable under Medicaid.[179] On average, freestanding birth centers have lower costs of care than traditional hospitals.[180] The ACA includes a provision allowing pregnant women enrolled in Medicaid to choose to deliver at birth centers rather than hospitals if birth centers are available in their state. A woman's access to a birth center may depend on her state's scope of practice rules for birth centers; for example, birth centers generally may not handle high-risk pregnancies.

Are states required to pay for home health services?

States may choose to cover home health services for persons entitled to receive nursing home services. On enacting the ACA, Congress made explicit its desire to increase access to home- and community-based services (HCBS), and to decrease dependence on institutional care.[181] States have the option to expand the use of HCBS through a state plan amendment, and may expand income eligibility for these services (otherwise capped under federal Medicaid law at 150 percent of the FPL) to as high as three times the federal SSI rate.[182] Individuals who are eligible for nursing facility services but who wish to remain at home should ask the state Medicaid agency which home health services it covers.[183]

What are case management services?

Medicaid broadly defines "case management" as services that will assist individuals "in gaining access to needed medical, social, educational, and other services."[184] Case management involves a wide range of activities, including providing transportation and appointment-scheduling assistance for medical visits, securing prior authorization of medical services, obtaining referrals to special education programs, managing complex treatment plans, and counseling. Trained professionals, such as social workers and Medicaid eligibility workers, provide case management services. Some states place additional limits on the scope of case management services provided as well as the populations eligible for them. For example, Missouri places daily quantity limits on services, whereas Pennsylvania limits case management services to individuals in designated high-risk groups, such as those with serious mental illness.[185]

Must a health care provider accept Medicaid?

Doctors, nurses, medical clinics, pharmacies, and other health care providers are not required to participate in the Medicaid program. Rather, provider participation in Medicaid is, for the most part, voluntary. Medicaid recipients must find providers that have agreed to participate in the program. This may be difficult because, in some areas, few providers will accept Medicaid. Providers complain that Medicaid rates are too low, and in many states payment is indeed inadequate. Although federal law requires states to pay providers reasonable rates for health services,[186] many states have failed, without legal consequences, to comply with the law.[187] Increased state reliance on health management organizations to deliver services to Medicaid recipients has ameliorated some of the shortage problems, but Medicaid beneficiaries still face difficulty obtaining certain kinds of care.[188]

Will Medicaid pay a recipient's full health care bill?

Federal law allows states to require Medicaid recipients to make "nominal" copayments for their health care (sometimes referred to as "cost sharing"), and most states now impose this requirement for at least certain Medicaid services.[189] Copayments usually range from 50 cents to $5, but may exceed these amounts, and recipients make the payments directly to the health care provider. Copayments may not be charged for children under age 18 (or under 21 at state option), except for infants under the age of one in a family with income exceeding 150 percent of the FPL.[190] Nor may copayments be required for nursing facility residents, services related to pregnancy, emergency services, family planning services, services furnished to individuals enrolled in managed care, or hospice services.[191] Some states, such as New York, allow copayments for all services to be waived in cases of hardship.

Aside from these limited circumstances, a Medicaid provider must accept the Medicaid reimbursement as payment in full and may not seek any additional payment from the recipient. The state or the managed care plan makes payments directly to the provider. Finally, Medicaid is always the last payor: Medicaid will cover only those costs not covered by any other available insurance.

What happens if a Medicaid recipient cannot afford to travel to the doctor?

Every state must provide some suitable method of transportation to and from hospitals, clinics, and doctors' offices for people receiving Medicaid. For example, the state may provide ambulance or medi-van services, public transport tokens, or money to allow people to use a taxi or a private car.[192] Medicaid agencies must offer a full description of transportation services.

What is "presumptive eligibility"?

Presumptive eligibility is a Medicaid option that permits states to authorize certain entities, including qualified health centers, hospitals, and schools, to make on-the-spot eligibility determinations and temporarily enroll low-income children, pregnant women, or both in Medicaid or the Children's Health Insurance Program (CHIP).[193] Presumptive eligibility serves the important purpose of affording immediate access to health care, rather than delaying care until after the full application process and formal eligibility determination.

The ACA extended presumptive eligibility beyond children and pregnant women and expanded the role of hospitals in determining eligibility presumptively. Specifically, states that adopted presumptive eligibility for children or pregnant women now have the option to extend it to parents and other adults. Moreover, the ACA directly authorizes hospitals to make presumptive eligibility determinations, regardless of whether the state has an established presumptive eligibility program.[194]

Will Medicaid pay for medical services received even before the individual applied for benefits?

Yes. States must pay for medical services provided to an individual during the three months before a Medicaid application is filed, provided that the individual was otherwise eligible for Medicaid at the time the medical services were received.[195] Retroactive coverage is available even if the person had become ineligible for Medicaid as of the date of the application. Retroactive coverage is also available regardless of whether the recipient is alive when the application for Medicaid is submitted.

What is Medicaid managed care?

Traditionally, Medicaid recipients had a right to choose any health care provider that accepted Medicaid. This was called "fee-for-service" Medicaid. In theory, this arrangement had the advantage of affording recipients some measure of choice in selecting their health care providers. As a practical matter, though, so few providers accepted Medicaid that the promise of choice was largely illusory. In the 1980s, a significant number of states began to encourage or require Medicaid recipients to enroll in a Medicaid managed care program operated by a private, state-designated health maintenance organization (HMO) or managed care organization (MCO). After enactment of the ACA in 2010, states that adopted expanded Medicaid have generally relied on managed care organizations to serve the newly eligible, mostly adult population.[196] An increasing number of states have also extended managed care to people with disabilities and to those needing behavioral and mental health care.[197] In many states, enrollment in managed care is "mandatory," meaning that people may not choose to remain in traditional, fee-for-service Medicaid. Eighty-one percent of all Medicaid recipients in the United States were enrolled in managed care plans in 2016.[198]

Medicaid recipients assigned to a managed care plan may use only the doctors, hospitals, and other providers in that plan. Moreover, the assigned primary care physician or a "care manager" will serve as a gatekeeper whose permission the beneficiary must seek in order to access services. Managed care plans employ extensive "utilization review,"[199] meaning that the plans closely track beneficiary use of Medicaid services and attempt to limit usage and costs. Supporters of managed care argue that it saves money and increases access. Advocates criticize managed care because it creates pressure on doctors to limit services. Researchers have found that managed care may not significantly reduce costs or improve the quality of health care.[200]

Many states have created special managed care plans for long-term care (LTC) services under Medicaid.[201] LTC includes the nursing services and home- and community-based services described above. LTC accounts for a significant portion of each state's Medicaid costs, and by contracting with managed care plans, which employ extensive utilization review, states attempt to reduce these costs, but the savings can come at the expense of reduced services to people who are medically fragile.[202] Managed care presents particular challenges for people receiving LTC as they typically require assistance with activities of daily living and may find it difficult to self-advocate with managed care plans to get the care they need.[203]

What should a Medicaid recipient consider in choosing a managed care plan?

In some states, Medicaid beneficiaries will have a number of health plans from which to choose. The checklist below can be used in conjunction with other state-specific checklists to help identify the managed care plan that best serves the family's or individual's needs:[204]

- Are the family's doctors, clinics, and hospital part of the health plan?
- Are any conveniently located pharmacies part of the plan?
- Does the plan provide a list of participating doctors, hospitals, and pharmacies and a member booklet that explains how the plan works?
- Does that plan have doctors, nurses, and other staff who speak the family's language?
- Can the family choose from among doctors in the plan and change doctors if dissatisfied? Can the family change plans?
- Is there a 24-hour phone line that allows access to medical assistance during and after office hours?
- Does the plan provide immediate access to doctors in emergencies and access within two weeks for a checkup or for special care?
- Does the plan cover all of the family's known health care needs (for example, necessary medications, mental health services, physical therapy) and does the plan put any limits on these services?
- If a doctor decides against providing requested care, does the plan allow for the patient to seek a second opinion from another doctor?
- If the patient does not agree with the plan's decision about care, will the plan handle the problem quickly in all cases, within 24 hours for severe illness and immediately in potentially life-threatening cases?

- Does the plan offer a staffed 800 number or other efficient means for answering questions?
- Does the plan provide transportation to the doctor or hospital even in nonemergency situations?
- Does the plan require copayments from patients, and if so, does it set limits on patients' out-of-pocket expenses?
- Has the plan agreed not to place a limit on what it will cover if someone in the family becomes disabled?

It is important to know the answers to as many of these questions as possible before selecting a managed care plan. The National Committee for Quality Assurance (https://www.ncqa.org) examines and provides reviews of health plans. Many state legislatures have adopted "bills of rights" that require managed care plans to afford some or all of the services and rights discussed in the checklist.[205]

What other legal rights do Medicaid recipients have?

Persons who meet the eligibility criteria for Medicaid have a legally enforceable right to the benefits prescribed by law, as well as a right to appeal any decision that denies, terminates, or reduces those benefits. This includes the right to receive covered health services as they are needed; to receive emergency care immediately from the nearest emergency room; to be free from discrimination based on disability, race, sex, ethnicity, national origin, religion, sexual orientation, or age; to obtain copies of medical records; to have medical information kept confidential; to receive clear and comprehensive information about rights and benefits within the Medicaid program, including a clear explanation of how to file a complaint or request a state hearing, as described below; and to participate fully in all decisions related to health care treatment.[206]

What due process rights apply to Medicaid?

Medicaid applicants and recipients have a right to notice of any adverse action taken in their case and an opportunity to contest that action at a state "fair hearing." Adverse actions that may be appealed include a denial of an application, a termination or reduction of benefits, or a refusal to authorize or to pay for services. [207] The state, directly or through the managed care plan, must provide written notice to the applicant or recipient describing the action, the reason for the action, and how to appeal.[208] Such notice must be provided at least

10 days before any proposed termination, reduction, or other negative change in benefits.[209] In order to continue receiving Medicaid benefits unchanged pending the outcome of an appeal, the recipient must request the appeal within 10 days of the notice date.[210] This is sometimes called "aid to continue." Once the 10-day period elapses, the recipient may still appeal any time within 60 days of the notice, but will not receive benefits during the appeals process, which may take months to resolve. If a recipient receives Medicaid "aid-to-continue" and ultimately loses the hearing, the state may seek recovery of those benefits.

Recipients challenging a denial of coverage for a treatment or medication may request an expedited hearing if the time otherwise permitted for a hearing "could jeopardize the individual's life, health or ability to attain, maintain, or regain maximum function."[211] If a request for an expedited hearing is granted on an issue of benefits or treatment coverage, the state agency must issue its decision within three business days after the agency receives the individual's request. For eligibility issues, the agency must issue its decision no later than seven working days after the agency receives the request.[212]

Individuals who appeal a decision on their Medicaid case must be given an opportunity to review their Medicaid file and any documents the Medicaid agency will use at the hearing.[213] At the hearing, the individual has the right to testify, to present witnesses, documents, and other evidence, to cross-examine the agency's witnesses, to present arguments, and to be represented by counsel (at their own expense) or other representative of their choice.[214]

By law, the Medicaid agency must issue a decision no later than 90 days from the date of the hearing request.[215] A negative decision after fair hearing may be appealed to court (as described below), but the process is complex, so assistance should be sought from a legal aid or legal services office.

Medicaid Managed Care Appeals

Medicaid managed care plans must provide an initial grievance system and an appeals system, in addition to the state fair hearing system described above.[216] An "appeal" is a request to review any "adverse benefit determination,"[217] such as a denial or limited authorization of a service; a reduction, suspension, or termination of a previously authorized service; a denial, in whole or in part, of payment for a service; or a failure to provide services in a timely manner.[218] A "grievance" is a complaint about the managed care plan for any other reason.[219]

Managed care plans must provide reasonable assistance to individuals who wish to file a grievance or an appeal.[220] Grievances and appeals may be made orally or in writing[221] (though it is best to submit a written appeal) and must ordinarily be filed within 60 days from the action complained of, though some plans allow more time.[222] The managed care plan is required to provide a written acknowledgment of all grievance and appeal requests.[223]

As with state fair hearings, managed care plans must provide the claimant or that person's representative an opportunity before and during the appeals process to examine the case file (including medical records), and any other documents or records the plan will consider in processing the appeal. The complaining party also has the right to present evidence, and arguments, in person as well as in writing.[224] Appeals based on medical necessity and grievances involving clinical issues must be reviewed by a health care professional with appropriate clinical expertise.[225] The plan must reach its decision "as expeditiously as the enrollee's health condition requires" and no later than 90 days for grievances, 30 days for appeals, and 72 hours for expedited appeals, where the enrollee's health may be at risk.[226] A managed care enrollee must exhaust the grievance or appeal process before requesting a state fair hearing, unless the managed care plan fails to provide adequate notice of its actions or fails to resolve the appeal within the time frames set by law; in those cases, the enrollee may seek relief directly through the state fair hearing process.[227]

How can people apply for Medicaid?

Applications for Medicaid may be made online through the state's Health Insurance Exchange (accessible through HealthCare.gov) or by applying directly to the state's Medicaid agency.[228] Contact information for state Medicaid agencies can be obtained from the CMS website.[229] Some states automatically enroll people in Medicaid when they apply for other public benefits, such as SNAP (food stamps) or cash public assistance. States may also authorize hospitals and other health care providers (or even schools) to provisionally enroll people in Medicaid. (See "What is 'presumptive eligibility'?" earlier in this chapter.) States must accept and process Medicaid applications for pregnant women and children at locations other than welfare offices, including public hospitals, community and migrant health clinics, and other facilities serving large numbers of poor pregnant women and children.[230]

The ACA requires each state to establish a streamlined access point for Medicaid, CHIP, and Health Insurance Exchanges, meaning that states must determine an individual's eligibility for all these programs through a single application.[231] Even if an individual only "applies for Medicaid," the state must also screen to see if the person may instead qualify for CHIP or health insurance subsidies. On request, Medicaid agencies must assist individuals in completing the application process.

Applicants may be asked to verify information relating to eligibility, so it is wise to gather documentation of identity, residency, citizenship or immigration status, and income. In many states, applicants can receive real-time eligibility determinations within a few days without having to submit pay stubs or paper documentation if the state can verify eligibility information electronically.

All applicants have the right to apply for Medicaid on the day assistance is sought. The state has 45 days to process a Medicaid application in nondisability cases (unless state law sets a shorter deadline), and 90 days to process a Medicaid application that requires a determination of disability. Approved applicants will receive a card showing the name and Medicaid number, plus the name of the managed health plan if one has been assigned.

Does Medicaid have any state residency requirements?

Yes. States can limit Medicaid benefits to persons who are residents of that state. However, federal law defines the state of residence broadly. For example, for an adult who is not in an institution, the state of residence is the state in which the person is living with the intention of remaining permanently or indefinitely, or where the person is living, having entered with a job commitment or seeking employment.[232] Moreover, a state may not discontinue Medicaid benefits for someone who leaves the state temporarily.[233] States cannot exclude an otherwise eligible person because the person does not have a permanent dwelling or a fixed mailing address. Rather, states are required to have a process for making Medicaid cards available even to people who cannot supply a permanent address. This requirement is designed to ensure that people who are underhoused or homeless have access to medical assistance.

The Children's Health Insurance Program (CHIP)

What is CHIP?

The Children's Health Insurance Program (CHIP) is a government-funded health insurance program for children in households with too much income to qualify for Medicaid but not enough to afford health insurance.[234] Congress created the program in 1997 to plug a hole in the nation's social safety net that had left millions of children without access to health care. By 2000, every state and the District of Columbia had elected to establish a state-based CHIP plan. States may incorporate CHIP into their existing Medicaid programs (extending Medicaid to children at income levels that otherwise exceed Medicaid eligibility caps) or may operate a separate CHIP program. The program now covers more than 9.5 million children from low-income households, and has succeeded not only in achieving substantial gains in health access and health outcomes but also in reducing the broader impacts of child poverty.[235]

Income eligibility caps for CHIP vary by state, ranging from 175 percent to 405 percent of the federal poverty level (FPL) ($37,327 to $86,386 for a family of three in 2019.).[236] The services covered by CHIP also vary from state to state. In states that incorporated CHIP into their existing Medicaid programs, CHIP must cover the same services covered by Medicaid; for children, that coverage includes the comprehensive benefit package known as Early and Periodic Screening, Diagnostic, and Treatment (EPSDT), described earlier in this chapter.[237] States that created CHIP programs independent of Medicaid have discretion to cover a different package of services that is less comprehensive.[238] Some states require copayments for certain services provided through CHIP. Details of each state's CHIP coverage may be found on the CMS website.[239]

A major policy failure is that Congress has thus far declined to make the CHIP program permanent or to ensure that it has enough funding to cover all eligible children. Like Medicaid, CHIP is financed by a combination of federal and state funds and is administered by each state's health or social services department. Unlike Medicaid, CHIP is not an entitlement program, and so its funding does not increase with increased need; rather, CHIP is a block grant program that provides states with a fixed sum of federal funds, based on the state's recent levels of CHIP spending. States are required to match a percentage of the federal grants with state funds. This financing arrangement means that there may not be sufficient CHIP funding in a given year to enroll every eligible child.

The ACA required states to maintain their Medicaid-based CHIP programs through 2019 as a condition of receiving federal matching funds for Medicaid.[240] Nevertheless, in 2018, a Republican Congress threatened to allow CHIP funding to expire, ultimately extending the program at the last moment for six years.[241] That extension included a "maintenance of effort" provision, requiring states to maintain their CHIP coverage rules for children from 2019 through 2023. After October 1, 2019, though, this requirement applies only to children in families with incomes at or below 300 percent of the federal poverty level. Congress later extended CHIP funding through 2027 as part of the Bipartisan Budget Act of 2018.[242]

How can a parent enroll children in CHIP?

Children may be enrolled in CHIP at any time; there is no special enrollment period. Applications for CHIP may be filed through the state's online Health Exchange or directly with the state Medicaid agency. Parents can find out if their children qualify for CHIP by visiting https://www.insurekidsnow.gov or calling 1-800-318-2596 (TTY: 1-855-889-4325).

Health Insurance Exchanges

What are Health Insurance Exchanges and why did the ACA create them?

Health Insurance Exchanges are online marketplaces through which families and individuals can compare, shop for, and select from a variety of "quali-fied health plans" (QHPs) that offer comprehensive benefits as defined by the Affordable Care Act (ACA).[243] Each state has an Exchange (sometimes referred to as a "Marketplace") approved by the U.S. Department of Health and Human Services. The Exchanges are operated by a state agency or, if the state declines to run an Exchange, by the federal government.[244] Exchanges for every state may be accessed through HealthCare.gov. As described below, individuals with incomes between 100 percent and 400 percent of the federal poverty level (FPL) are gen-erally eligible for premium tax credits to defray the cost of a QHP purchased through an Exchange; people with incomes between 100 percent and 250 per-cent of the FPL are also eligible for cost-sharing reductions, which limit out-of-pocket expenses for copayments and the like.

Before the ACA, the business model for most health insurance companies was to enroll and renew coverage for healthy people, whose costs of coverage were low, but decline to enroll people with illnesses (or charge them extremely high premiums), refuse to cover treatment for "preexisting medical conditions," impose annual and lifetime caps on medical expenditures, and terminate or refuse to renew policies of people who became ill.[245] The ACA largely outlawed these practices. To advance the goal of universal access to adequate health care, the ACA barred insurance companies from denying coverage on account of a person's medical condition or medical history, and prohibited insurers from charging higher premiums to people with preexisting conditions.

The quid pro quo for removing these barriers was a provision in the ACA known as the "individual mandate," which required all uninsured individuals to purchase an ACA-complaint policy or pay a modest tax penalty (known as a "shared responsibility payment"). The reasoning was that without the individual mandate, the ACA's requirement that insurers cover preexisting conditions would remove any incentive for healthy (low-cost) individuals to obtain in-surance until after they became ill. And if healthy individuals did not purchase insurance until they required medical care, the insurers' risk pools would be composed predominantly of people with high health expenditures, making it impossible to spread costs and driving premiums to unaffordable levels.[246]

The ACA established the Health Exchanges to create markets for insurance plans that comply with the new rules, and to ensure that people have access to an affordable plan, irrespective of their age or health condition. The Exchanges, along with tax subsidies for insurance premiums, were designed to make plans available to people who previously could not buy health insurance, either because of a preexisting health condition or excessive cost. The future viability of the Exchanges is in doubt because of actions by the Trump administration and ongoing assaults by Republican politicians at the federal and state levels. In 2018, the Republican-dominated Congress, after failing in repeated efforts to repeal the ACA outright, eliminated the incentive effect of the "individual mandate" by reducing to zero the tax penalty for failure to maintain health coverage.[247] The Trump administration, for its part, slashed funds for ACA outreach (in an effort to reduce voluntary enrollment through Health Exchanges), has threatened to curtail funding meant to hold down QHP premium costs, and—in a remarkable dereliction of executive duty—directed the Department of Justice not to defend the constitutionality of the ACA in pending litigation by Republican state attorneys general.[248] The ultimate impact of these efforts to undermine the ACA remains to be seen.

What is a qualified health plan?

A qualified health plan (QHP) is a health insurance plan issued by a private or nonprofit company that meets ACA requirements and that has been certified by and made available through an Exchange.[249] QHPs must cover the benefits offered by the state's "benchmark plan," and must cover the "essential health benefits" required by the ACA.[250] (Each state designates a "benchmark plan"—from among a list of health plans prescribed by the ACA—to serve as the standard for all health plans in the state's Exchange.)[251] Plans must cover care and services in categories required by the Exchange, and they must offer adequate coverage networks. Each plan must have a sufficient number and geographic distribution of doctors and other providers to ensure reasonable and timely access, specifically for low-income and medically underserved individuals in each service area.[252]

QHPs must secure approval from the Exchange for any increase in premiums.[253] In an effort to contain the cost of health care coverage, the ACA requires that QHPs spend at least 80 percent of insurance premiums on actual health care services.[254] QHPs must also make information about their claims payment policies and enrollment data public.[255]

What are the "essential health benefits"
that qualified health plans must cover?

Before the ACA, a major shortcoming of private health plans was that they either failed to cover many essential services or charged exorbitant rates for such coverage. For example, less than 12 percent of the health insurance plans sold in the individual markets in the United States covered maternity care benefits.[256]

The ACA ensures that private health insurance plans will cover health care services that are "essential." Without this protection, people could buy health insurance only to find that it does not cover the actual health care they need.

The essential health benefits (EHB) requirement in the ACA means that health insurance plans must cover services in the following categories of care:

- ambulatory patient services
- emergency services
- hospitalization
- maternity and newborn care
- mental health and substance use disorder services, including behavioral health treatment
- prescription drugs
- rehabilitative and habilitative services and devices
- laboratory services
- preventive and wellness services and chronic disease management
- pediatric services, including oral and vision care.[257]

Qualified health plans must provide coverage of benefits in each of the categories that is "substantially equal" to the state benchmark plan.[258] For example, each QHP must include a prescription drug benefit that covers at least one drug in every category in the United States Pharmacopeia, or the same number of drugs in each category and class as the benchmark plan.[259] For people whose doctor recommends a drug that is not covered, plans must provide a process that allows patients to request access, similar to the internal and external appeal processes described below.[260]

Federal regulations allow QHPs some flexibility to make "actuarily equivalent substitutions" for benefits offered by the state's benchmark plan, provided that the QHP provides a "substantially equal package of benefits with regard to both the scope of benefits offered and any limitations on those benefits," such as limits on doctor's visits.[261] This flexibility may reduce costs to the QHP, but may also leave plan enrollees with fewer treatment options. Moreover, the danger arises that QHP discretion may result in unacceptable discrimination if coverage packages are tailored to reduce expensive services needed by specific groups, such as HIV/AIDS patients, people with disabilities, or other vulnerable individuals. Advocates may challenge any such actions by QHPs by filing complaints with the U.S. Department of Health and Human Services Office of Civil Rights, or in court.[262]

How much of a person's health care costs does a qualified health plan pay for?

Qualified health plans are sold on the Exchange in different categories corresponding to the percentage of overall health care costs paid by the plan and the percentage of costs the enrollee must shoulder through copayments or deductibles. The plan categories are called "platinum," "gold," "silver," and "bronze" and cover 90, 80, 70, and 60 percent of health costs, respectively.[263] Of course, the more comprehensive plans charge higher premiums. Individuals under age 30 and those who establish a "hardship exemption" may buy a less expensive, less comprehensive "catastrophic" health plan that mainly protects against very high medical costs.[264]

How can people apply for a qualified health plan through an Exchange?

For those with internet access, the easiest way to file an application may be through each Exchange's website, all of which are linked to HealthCare.gov. The ACA requires every Exchange to maintain both a call center and an internet website with information about premiums, cost sharing, benefits, and ratings for each plan.[265] Exchanges must accept applications through the website, by telephone, and by mail.[266] Information about the plans must be in plain language and provided in a manner that is accessible and timely for individuals with disabilities and individuals with limited English proficiency.[267] Contact information for every state Exchange can be found on HealthCare.gov.

Under the ACA's "no wrong door" provision, any application submitted to an Exchange must be evaluated under the eligibility criteria for Medicaid and CHIP, as well as for QHP tax premium credits and cost-reduction subsidies.[268] For example, if an applicant for a QHP appears to be eligible for Medicaid, the Exchange must redirect the application to the state Medicaid agency for processing.[269] In addition, states must ensure that applicants have the opportunity to enroll in the most beneficial program for which they qualify—typically, the program with the most comprehensive coverage and lowest costs possible.[270]

The Exchange must determine eligibility "promptly and without undue delay"[271] and must provide timely written notice of its determination, including an explanation of the applicant's right to appeal.[272]

What are health care navigators and what assistance can they provide to people seeking to enroll in a qualified health plan through the Exchange?

The ACA requires each Exchange to provide health care "navigators" to assist individuals—especially those from underserved and vulnerable populations—enroll in a health plan or program though the Exchange.[273] Navigators are public or private entities or individuals who are certified by the Exchange as experts in health insurance eligibility and enrollment,[274] and who receive federal grants to provide free, accurate, and impartial information and one-on-one assistance to people who wish to obtain health coverage through the Exchange.[275] Navigators should be community-based entities familiar with the uninsured or underinsured communities they have been engaged to assist.[276] Navigators must provide information that is culturally and linguistically appropriate for the needs of the population being served, including people who speak limited English.[277] Individuals should ask their social service and health care providers about navigators available in the locality. The U.S. CMS maintains a list of certified organizations that have received federal grants to serve as navigators in each state.[278]

Who can get coverage through an Exchange and how is eligibility determined?

There is no income-based eligibility restriction on the use of a Health Exchange to enroll in a plan. Income levels affect only eligibility for premium tax credits and cost-sharing reductions, as explained below. However, the ACA imposes restrictions based on immigration, incarceration, and residency that disqualify some people from purchasing health insurance through an Exchange at all.[279]

Immigration Status
Noncitizens must be lawfully present in the United States in order to obtain health coverage through an Exchange.[280] Exchanges will verify immigration status electronically, either with a Social Security number, or by verification with

records of the Department of Homeland Security.[281] If the Exchange identifies inconsistencies with a Social Security number, it must give the applicant notice of the inconsistency and time to clarify the inconsistency without delaying the application.[282] Importantly, the Exchange may not request Social Security numbers or information regarding the immigration status of relatives or household members who are not seeking coverage for themselves.[283]

Incarcerated Individuals

People who are incarcerated, other than incarceration pending the disposition of charges (i.e., pretrial detention), may not enroll in a health plan through an Exchange.[284] This rule recognizes that the government has a direct legal obligation to provide adequate medical care to people it holds in custody.[285] People held in prison pending their trials are not disqualified from seeking insurance through an Exchange, but many qualified health plans exclude coverage for those in jail.[286]

State Residency

Adults may enroll only through the Exchange in their state of "residency."[287] "Residency" for these purposes means the place in which a person is living *and* (1) intends to reside, or (2) has entered with a job commitment or is seeking employment.[288] People under age 21 may enroll where they reside, or in the state of a parent or caretaker with whom they reside.[289] Applicants for enrollment in a health plan need not have a fixed address in the service area in which they seek to be enrolled.[290] The Exchange may accept an applicant's sworn statement or attestation of residency, or it may "examine electronic data sources" to verify residency. If the Exchange finds inconsistencies regarding an address provided by an applicant, it must notify the applicant and allow time to clarify the inconsistency without delaying the application.[291]

The Exchange may not require an applicant to provide information beyond the minimum necessary to support the eligibility and enrollment process.[292]

When can people enroll in a health plan through an Exchange?

Typically, people must apply for health insurance during the annual "open enrollment" period, which generally begins on October 15 of the year before the insurance would begin, and ends on December 7. So, for example, in order to have health insurance coverage beginning on January 1, 2022, the individual would have to apply between October 15 and December 7 of 2021. Some state Exchanges may extend the open enrollment period, so it is wise to check the Exchange's website.

People may apply for a health plan outside of the open enrollment period if they experience a "qualifying life event" that changes their eligibility or needs for health insurance.[293] Qualifying life events include a change in the number of people in the family (such as having a baby, adopting a child, placing a child in foster care, or getting married), loss of employer-provided health care coverage on leaving a job, or loss of Medicaid eligibility (for example, because of increased income).[294] Individuals do not get this special chance to enroll through an Exchange if they voluntarily drop out of an individual or employment-based insurance plan.[295]

Note that applications for Medicaid or CHIP may be filed at any time.

Can an employee obtain health insurance through an Exchange instead of enrolling in the employer's health plan?

Yes, an employee may decline health insurance offered by an employer and enroll for coverage through an Exchange. However, the employee should consider the financial consequences. First, employers pay part of the premiums for job-related health insurance but do not contribute to the premiums for coverage obtained through an Exchange. In addition, employees who decline job-related insurance cannot qualify for premium tax credits (the ACA subsidy that helps low-income families pay health care premiums) if the job-related insurance is deemed "affordable" and meets minimum quality standards.[296] Job-related insurance is considered "affordable" if the employee's share of the premiums for the lowest-cost self-only coverage that meets the "minimum value standard" (pays at least 60 percent of health costs) is less than 9.56 percent of household income.[297] This is a harsh and unrealistic measure of affordability for families; premiums for family coverage vastly exceed those for self-only coverage and family coverage through job-related insurance could easily exceed 30 percent of total household income. Moreover since the "minimum value" standard only requires that the job-related insurance pay 60 percent of health costs, it leaves the employee responsible for the remaining 40 percent, on top of premium payments.[298] Because most employer plans meet these minimal requirements, many low-income workers are put to the choice of paying unaffordable premiums for family coverage through an employer plan, or declining employer coverage, but being denied any tax subsidies to defray the costs of health insurance from an Exchange.[299] The dilemma created by these rules is known as the "family glitch" and has left millions of people without health insurance or in dire financial straits.[300] This harsh and counterproductive shortcoming of the ACA urgently requires correction.

What financial assistance does the government offer to defray the cost of health insurance premiums?

A central goal of the ACA was to make health care affordable to individuals and families at all income levels. Recognizing that the cost of premiums would place health care out of reach for most low-income households, the ACA provided two forms of financial assistance: "premium tax credits" and "cost-sharing reductions." These subsidies are discussed in turn below.

What are premium tax credits and who qualifies for them?

Premium tax credits are subsidies distributed by the Internal Revenue Service to tax filers who have enrolled, or whose family members have enrolled, in a qualified health plan (QHP) through an Exchange. The purpose of the credit is to offset the costs of QHP premiums. When individuals or families apply to an Exchange for a QHP, the Exchange must also determine whether they qualify for a premium tax credit. Eligible individuals or families can receive the credit in one of two ways. First, they may opt for advance payments of the premium tax credit (APTC), which means the Exchange computes the applicant's estimated monthly tax credit and the government pays that amount directly to the insurance carrier each month, lowering the applicant's premium payments throughout the year. Alternatively, the family or individual may pay the full monthly premiums out of pocket during the year and receive the credit as a lump sum after filing their tax return.

To qualify for a premium tax credit, a household's income must be at least 100 percent, but not more than 400 percent, of the federal poverty level (FPL).[301] A special rule applies to noncitizens who are lawfully present in the United States but who are ineligible for Medicaid by reason of immigration status; such individuals may qualify for the premium tax credit even if household income is below 100 percent of the FPL.[302] In addition, an individual in a household with income below 100 percent of the FPL qualifies for the credit if at the time of enrollment in a QHP, the Exchange estimated the household's income would exceed 100 percent of the FPL and the IRS has made APTC premium payments to the individual's health plan.[303]

Premium tax credits are available only for individuals who lack access to other adequate health insurance. Individuals cannot receive premium tax credits for any month in which they qualify for "minimum essential coverage," including coverage through Medicare Part A or C, Medicaid, CHIP, or most job-related health insurance.[304]

Premium tax credits are calculated based on ACA guidelines setting the percentage of household income that families or individuals are expected to contribute toward the cost of health care. This contribution level is determined on a sliding scale, from a low of 2 percent to a high of 9.5 percent of household income, as illustrated in Table 4.2.

"Initial percentage" and "Final percentage" refer to the lower and upper incomes in each row: for example, a family with income of 150 percent of the FPL would be expected to devote 4 percent of its income to health premiums; a family at 200 percent of the FPL would be expected to devote 6.3 percent of its income to health care. Household composition and income for these purposes generally follows federal tax law and is calculated according to the Modified Adjusted Gross Income (MAGI) rules discussed earlier in the Medicaid section of this chapter.

The amount of the premium tax credit is generally equal to the lesser of (1) the premium for the second lowest cost silver plan available through the Exchange that applies to the members of the household, or (2) the premium for a QHP in which the household members are already enrolled, *minus* the percentage of household income determined to be its contribution level as described above.[305]

Example: Maria projects that her Modified Adjusted Gross Income (MAGI) for 2019 will be $31,170, which equals 150 percent of the FPL. Based on that income level, she is expected to contribute 4 percent of her income—about $104 per month—toward the cost of health premiums. Maria is not currently enrolled in a QHP. If the premium for the second lowest cost silver QHP available to her through the Exchange is $704 per month, Maria would qualify for a premium tax credit of $600 per month ($704 – $104 = $600).

The Exchange will do these calculations when an individual or family applies for health coverage.

Table 4.2 Premium Tax Credits: Maximum Family Contribution

Household income percentage of federal poverty level (FPL)	Initial percentage	Final percentage
Less than 133%	2.0	2.0
At least 133% but less than 150%	3.0	4.0
At least 150% but less than 200%	4.0	6.3
At least 200% but less than 250%	6.3	8.05
At least 250% but less than 300%	8.05	9.5
At least 300% but less than 400%	9.5	9.5

What are cost-sharing reductions and who qualifies for them?

A cost-sharing reduction (CSR) is a discount that lowers the amount of money low-income families or individuals may be charged for health care through deductibles, copayments, or other cost-sharing measures. Insurers must provide CSRs to households with income below 250 percent of the FPL that enroll in a silver qualified health plan. Here is an example of how CSRs affect affordability: generally, the "actuarial value" of a silver plan is 70 percent (meaning that the plan will cover 70 percent of health care costs, and the enrollee must pay for the remaining 30 percent through copayments and deductibles). But the CSR provision of the ACA requires insurers to increase the "actuarial value" of silver plans (and correspondingly reduce the policyholder's costs) on a sliding scale for very low-income households. For households with income between 100 percent and 150 percent of the FPL, actuarial value must be 94 percent (which yielded an average deductible of about $300 in 2017). For households with income between 150 percent and 200 percent of the FPL, actuarial value must be 87 percent (which yielded an average deductible of about $800 in 2017); and for households with income between 200 percent and 250 percent of the FPL, actuarial value must be 73 percent (which yielded an average deductible of about $2,900 in 2017).[306]

The Trump administration announced in 2017 that it would no longer reimburse insurers for the cost-sharing payments they are obligated to make to qualifying individuals.[307] While insurers are still expected to provide the required cost-sharing assistance, the Congressional Budget Office projects higher premiums for silver plan enrollees as a result of the termination.[308]

Is there a right to appeal eligibility or coverage determinations made by an Exchange?

Yes. People have a right to appeal any adverse action taken by an Exchange, including denial of eligibility, termination, reduction, or suspension of services, and determinations affecting premium or cost-sharing amounts.[309] The Exchange must provide written notice of any such actions, and generally it must issue that notice at least 10 days before the effective date of the action.[310] The notice must include a statement of the action the Exchange intends to take, a clear and specific statement of the reasons for the action, and instructions for requesting an appeal.[311] Appeals are heard by the state agency that administers the Medicaid program. In some states, Exchanges may provide their own appeals process, but individuals may still demand review at a "fair hearing" conducted by the state.[312] Individuals challenging decisions by an Exchange have the same due process and fair hearing rights as those described earlier in this chapter with respect to Medicaid appeals.[313]

Insurance Reforms and Patient Rights under the ACA

What rights did the ACA insurance reforms create?

The Affordable Care Act's reform of private insurance markets forms one of three main pillars in the statute's blueprint for expanding health care coverage. The architects of the ACA regarded these reforms as a "patient's bill of rights"[314] that extends robust, legally enforceable protections to millions of families and individuals.[315] Although these rights and protections generally apply to all forms of private insurance, some of the new provisions do not apply to certain "grandfathered plans," health policies purchased on or before March 23, 2010.[316]

The Secretary of the U.S. Department of Health and Human Services (HHS) has authority to enforce the ACA's insurance market reforms, though the Act contemplates that states, as traditional regulators of private insurance, would take the lead in ensuring compliance, and most states have undertaken this enforcement role.[317] In the small number of states that lack legal authority or ability to fully enforce ACA insurance reforms, the Centers for Medicare and Medicaid Services (CMS) of the HHS has taken charge of this enforcement function. As described below, individuals may directly seek enforcement of their own rights under the ACA. These rights include the following:

1. The Right to Coverage Regardless of Pre-existing Conditions
Health plans may not impose a preexisting condition exclusion to deny coverage, nor charge higher premiums because of a person's medical history. Plans may not establish rules for eligibility or exclude beneficiaries based on any health factor, including current health status, medical history, or claims history.[318] Premiums may only be different for each person based on age, geographic area, tobacco use, and whether the coverage is for an individual or family.[319] Before this reform took effect, millions of people with chronic illnesses, including cancer and HIV/AIDS, were effectively barred from obtaining any private health insurance.[320]

2. The Right to Guaranteed Availability and Guaranteed
   Continuing Coverage
An insurance company that offers a health plan in the group or individual market in a state must offer coverage to all employers and all individuals in that state.[321] The insurer must renew coverage unless the enrollee fails to pay premiums or the plan ceases to offer coverage.[322] Insurers may no longer refuse to renew coverage

for people who become ill. The plan may not cancel coverage retroactively unless the enrollee has committed fraud or misrepresentation.[323]

3. The Right to Keep Children on the Parent's Health Plan until Age 26

Health plans and insurance issuers offering group or individual coverage that includes family coverage must allow children to remain on the parent's health plan until the day before their twenty-sixth birthday. This right applies regardless of the child's income, marital status, employment or student status, residence (the child need not live with the parent or in the health plan's service area), eligibility for other coverage, or whether the child is financially dependent on the parent. [324]

4. The Right to Coverage for Needed Health Services without Dollar Limits

Health insurance plans may no longer impose annual or lifetime dollar limits on coverage of essential health benefits.[325] Before this reform, millions of people with expensive medical conditions lost coverage once the cost of treatment hit an annual or lifetime maximum set by their insurance companies. Because of these restrictions, many people were forced into poverty and/or went without necessary health care.[326] After the ACA, health plans must cover all essential health services, even if the cost of care runs into the millions of dollars, as long as the individual continues to pay premiums and remains enrolled. However, a plan may limit coverage of benefits that do not fall within the definition of "essential health benefits," such as eyeglasses or braces.

5. The Right to Affordable Care

The ACA imposes a cost-control measure requiring individual and small-group health plans to spend at least 80 percent and large-group health plans to spend at least 85 percent of premium dollars on medical care—and if they fail to do so, they must rebate the difference to enrollees.[327] The purpose of the measure is to limit insurer's use of premiums for overhead, executive salaries, and profits. In addition, health plans may not raise premiums unless they successfully justify the increase to the CMS (and, in some cases, to state authorities).[328] Although these provisions have placed some restraints on the cost of health insurance, they have not made care truly affordable for many families and individuals.[329]

6. The Right to Cost-Free Preventive Care

Health plans must cover a range of preventive care services without imposing cost-sharing requirements, such as copayments, coinsurance, or deductibles.[330] Preventive care covered by this provision include:

- Services that are recommended as effective, with a rating of "A" or "B" from the U.S. Preventive Services Task Force (USPSTF).[331]

- Immunizations recommended by the Advisory Committee on Immunization Practices of the Centers for Disease Control and Prevention for children, adolescents, and adults.[332]
- Preventive services and screenings recommended for infants, children, and adolescents in guidelines from the Health Resources and Services Administration (HRSA).[333]
- Preventive services for women recommended in guidelines by HRSA (this is intended to add coverage for women's preventive services not already recommended by the USPSTF).[334] This provision gives women the right to coverage for contraception without copayment, coinsurance, or deductible.[335]

7. The Right to Choose a Doctor

Health plans must allow enrollees to designate any available participating primary care provider as their provider. Parents have a right to choose any available participating pediatrician to be their children's primary care provider.[336]

8. The Right to Be Free from Discrimination

Section 1557 of the ACA prohibits discrimination based on race, color, national origin, sex, age, or disability under "any health program or activity" that receives financial assistance from the federal government. It also prohibits such discrimination by any agency or entity created under Title I of the ACA, such as a Health Insurance Exchange.[337] The Office for Civil Rights of the Department of Health and Human Services is charged with enforcement of these antidiscrimination provisions. Anyone who believes that a health care program, plan, or entity has discriminated against them based on race, color, national origin, sex, age, or disability may file a complaint with the Office of Civil Rights within 180 days of the discriminatory act.[338]

9. Women's Right to Health Care Access without Higher Premiums

Before the ACA, many women had to pay as much as 84 percent more for the same health insurance as men, depending on their age and location.[339] The ACA prohibits health insurance plans from charging higher premiums based on gender, and bars insurers and employer plans from requiring pre-authorization or referral for obstetrical or gynecological (OB-GYN) care. Women have a right to direct access to such care.[340]

10. The Right to Coverage without an Excessive Waiting Period

A group health care plan may not impose a waiting period of more than 90 days before coverage comes into effect.[341]

Are insurance plans required to cover benefits for mental health and substance use treatment?

Yes. As discussed earlier, the ACA designates mental health services, including coverage for substance use disorder treatment, as an "essential health benefit" that must be covered by all qualified health plans. In addition, the Mental Health Parity and Addiction Equity Act (MHPAEA) of 2008 prohibits all insurance plans from discriminating between mental health services and other services with respect to cost, coverage, or limitations.[342] For instance, plans may not impose financial requirements such as deductibles, copayments, coinsurance, or out-of-pocket expenses on mental health or substance abuse benefits that are more costly than the financial requirements applied to substantially all medical and surgical benefits.[343]

How is health care information protected?

In 1996, Congress passed the Health Insurance Portability and Accountability Act (HIPAA). Under HIPAA, every person has the right to access, inspect, and obtain a copy of the person's own health information, except for certain instances in which an individual may not access psychiatric records.[344] Health care entities, including doctors, hospitals, and insurance companies, may disclose personal health information without the patient's express written authorization in order to facilitate treatment, payment, and operations, but they may only disclose the minimum amount of information necessary.[345] All other use of personal health information requires the patient's written authorization.[346] A person who believes that a health care entity has violated these privacy protections should file a complaint with the Department of Health and Human Services' Office for Civil Rights[347] within 180 days of the infraction.[348]

Can people choose not to enroll in a health plan?

Yes. As originally enacted, the ACA required most individuals to maintain ACA-compliant health coverage or pay a modest tax penalty, known as a "shared responsibility payment."[349] That requirement lost practical force in 2018 after the Republican-dominated Congress reduced the "shared responsibility payment" to zero dollars,[350] in an effort to undermine the ACA by reducing enrollments and potentially causing premiums to balloon.[351]

Do ACA protections apply to student health plans?

Yes, although a small number of schools that have self-insured student health plans are exempt from the ACA. In general, student health plans must comply with the same consumer protections as other plans, including no longer imposing annual or lifetime limits on benefits, covering preventive services, meeting minimum percentage of premiums spent on health care (medical loss ratio), and following coverage explanation documentation requirements.[352]

Are employers required to provide health care coverage?

Employers with more than 50 full-time employees must offer their employees access to affordable health care coverage or pay penalties of $2,000 each year for each employee.[353] To meet this requirement, an employer health plan must (1) cover the cost of at least 60 percent of essential health benefits;[354] and (2) must be "affordable," meaning that the premiums for the lowest cost individual health plan offered may not exceed more than 9.56 percent of the employee's Modified Adjusted Gross Income (as discussed earlier in this chapter).[355] If an employer chooses not to offer coverage, or offers coverage that is not "affordable," the worker may seek coverage from a Health Insurance Exchange and the employer must pay the $2,000 penalty to the government.[356]

Under the ACA, employers are no longer permitted to discriminate between different classes of employees in their offers of health insurance.[357] Any person who works full-time for three months and reasonably expects to work full-time on an annual basis, must be offered coverage under the employer's group health plan, and must be enrolled within three months of becoming eligible for coverage.[358]

Is there a right to appeal a health plan's decision that denies or restricts coverage?

Individuals have a right to appeal any decision by a qualified health plan or employer-sponsored plan that denies, restricts, or rescinds coverage for medical treatment, services, or medication.[359] An appeal must first be presented to the plan itself and is known as an "internal claim" or "internal appeal."[360] Individuals dissatisfied with a plan's decision after the internal appeal have a right to an independent review, known an "external review," conducted by an "Independent Review Organization" in accordance with state and federal standards.[361] Determinations issued after an external review may be appealed to court.

Notice and Internal Appeal

Health plans must provide timely written notice of any "adverse action"—including determinations to deny, reduce, or restrict an individual's coverage or care.[362] The written notice must include a description of the determination, the specific reason for the determination, the plan provisions on which the determination is based, a description of any additional information needed to approve the claim along with an explanation of why that information is necessary, and a description of the plan's review procedures, how to request review, and the time limits applicable to such requests.[363] Plans must allow at least 60 days from the notice for the filing of an internal appeal.[364]

As part of the internal appeals process, the health plan must, upon request and free of charge, provide the claimant copies of all documents, records, and other information relevant to the claim for benefits.[365] The claimant has the right to submit comments, documents, and records in support of the appeal.[366] The plan must undertake a "full and fair review," meaning that it must consider the evidence and arguments advanced by the claimant and base its decision on medical judgment.[367] If the plan proposes to restrict or terminate an ongoing course of treatment that it previously approved, it must continue to cover that treatment until it decides the internal appeal.[368]

Normally, the plan must issue a notice of determination within 60 days of the request for internal review.[369] If the regular time frame for an internal review may jeopardize the claimant's health, a request for an urgent care claim should be made. Where the claimant documents an urgent circumstance, the plan must issue a determination within three business days.[370]

External Review

Individuals dissatisfied with the outcome of an internal appeal have a right to an "external review" conducted by an Independent Review Organization (IRO) that is accredited by a nationally recognized private accrediting organization.[371] All denied claims are eligible for external review, even if the dollar amount is small.[372] The state may charge a nominal fee for the review, but any such fee may not exceed $25, should be waived in cases of hardship, and must be refunded if the claimant prevails on the appeal.[373]

A request for an external review must be filed within four months of the health plan's final decision after an internal appeal.[374] The claimant may submit additional medical or other documentation to the IRO with the request for the external review, and must be given at least an additional five business days to do so.[375] The IRO reviewing the appeal must base its decision on the plan's requirements for medical necessity, appropriateness, health care setting, level of care, and effectiveness of a covered benefit.[376]

The IRO must issue its determination within 45 days of the request for external review.[377] In urgent cases—where delay may endanger the claimant's health—the IRO must decide the appeal "as expeditiously as possible" and no later than 72 hours after it receives the request for review.[378] The external review process is binding, meaning that the health plan must promptly comply with an external review decision awarding benefits.[379]

Medicare

What is Medicare?

Medicare is a federal health insurance program that pays some of the costs of hospital, doctor, skilled nursing, home health, and outpatient care, and prescription drugs for people age 65 and older and for some disabled persons. There are no financial eligibility restrictions for Medicare; people of any income level may receive Medicare if otherwise qualified.

Congress enacted the Medicare program in 1965 as part of the same landmark legislation that created the Medicaid program.[380] National health insurance had been the subject of policy discussion since the early twentieth century, but efforts to adopt any such program repeatedly failed, fiercely opposed by the American Medical Association and the health insurance industry as "un-American" and "socialistic." These same interest groups, joined by political conservatives, derided the proposed Medicare statute itself as "socialized medicine."[381] But by the 1960s, the failure of the existing system to provide reasonable access to health care had acquired an unmistakable urgency, with nearly 60 percent of the nation's elderly bereft of means to obtain necessary medical services. Large majorities in Congress adopted Medicare and Medicaid, and these programs soon became popular, universally recognized pillars of the social contract. Periodic attempts by Republicans to undermine or privatize these programs have been met with sharp and sustained public rebuke.[382] By 2018, Medicare covered over 60 million people, including 51.3 million people age 65 or older, and 8.7 million non-elderly people with a permanent disability.[383]

Medicare has four parts. Part A provides insurance for hospitalizations. Part B provides insurance for outpatient health care expenses. Part C allows Medicare beneficiaries to forgo Medicare Part A and Part B and instead enroll in a commercial "Medicare Advantage Plan" that is required to provide coverage at least equivalent to that included under Part A and Part B. Medicare pays a fixed monthly amount to the private companies offering Medicare Advantage Plans, and the beneficiaries are responsible for the balance of the premiums. Medicare Part D, added in 2003, provides optional prescription drug coverage.[384] The

CMS's website, Medicare.gov, has useful information and advice about how to choose among the various Medicare options.

Most Medicare beneficiaries elect "original" Part A and Part B benefits, meaning that the federal government pays their medical providers directly. As of 2018, over 20 million Medicare beneficiaries (about 34 percent) opted to enroll in a Part C Medicaid Advantage Plan, meaning that a private insurer contracts with health care providers and pays them for approved services.[385] Part C plans closely manage individual use of medical services and tend to restrict the choice of medical providers and drugs. Enrollees in each part of the Medicare program generally report that they receive timely, appropriate care.[386]

How and when can people apply for Medicare?

Applications for Medicare may be made in person at district offices of the Social Security Administration, by mail, by calling 1-800-772-1213, or online at https://www.ssa.gov/benefits/medicare/. The "initial enrollment period" for people who qualify for Medicare at age 65 is the seven-month period that includes the month the applicant turns 65 and the three months before and after that month. In most cases, failure to enroll in Medicare Part B during the initial enrollment period will result in a late enrollment penalty that adds 10 percent to monthly premiums for each year of delay. This penalty does not apply to people who delay enrollment because they are still working and covered by their employer's insurance. (Coverage of retired employees through COBRA, though, does not excuse late enrollment in Medicare.) For those without health coverage, it is advisable to apply for Medicare at the very beginning of the initial enrollment period to account for the application processing time.

On approval of an application, the CMS issues a Medicare card with the beneficiary's name and Medicare claim number. The claim number has nine digits and a letter, and must be used on all Medicare claims and correspondence. The CMS annually publishes a guide, "Medicare and You," with detailed practical information for Medicare beneficiaries.[387]

Is assistance available to defray the cost of Medicare premiums and copays?

Medicare was designed to extend health care to people who could not otherwise afford it, but the program does not fully cover medical expenses.[388] Part A requires copays; Part B requires monthly premiums, copays, and an annual deductible; Parts C and D also typically require copays, premiums, and deductibles, depending on the plan. Taken together, these out-of-pocket expenses often impose a heavy financial burden. Very low-income Medicare beneficiaries may qualify for assistance from their state Medicaid program to reduce or eliminate these costs.[389] Most importantly, the Qualified Medicare Beneficiary (QMB) Program will pay the Medicare premiums, deductibles, and coinsurance costs for certain low-income, elderly, and disabled individuals.[390] A similar Medicare Savings Program serves qualified disabled and working individuals. Application for these must be made to the state Medicaid agency. The CMS web page includes current income eligibility standards for these programs, as well as contact information for filing applications with each state Medicaid agency.[391]

Medicare Part A Hospital Insurance Benefits

Who is eligible for Medicare Part A?

Medicare Part A is automatic and free to most people age 65 or older who are citizens or legal permanent residents (LPRs).[392] To qualify, LPRs must reside in the United States continuously for five years immediately before the Medicare application.[393] Three groups are automatically eligible for free Part A hospital insurance:

- Anyone age 65 or older, if the person or spouse has worked long enough (generally 10 years) in Social Security–covered employment, the Railroad Retirement system, or a federal, state, or local government and paid taxes;
- Anyone under age 65 who has been receiving Social Security disability benefits for 24 months;
- Any worker, spouse, or dependent of any age with kidney failure requiring dialysis or a kidney transplant.[394]

People age 65 or older who are still working, and not receiving Social Security Benefits qualify for Part A without paying premiums, but must affirmatively enroll. Other persons 65 or older who have not worked 40 quarters and paid Medicare taxes can enroll in Medicare Part A upon payment of a monthly premium, which is adjusted annually.[395]

What are the Part A benefits?

Medicare Part A helps pay for four health services: inpatient hospital services, skilled nursing services, home health services, and hospice care.[396] A doctor must certify the need for these services.

Medicare's inpatient hospital coverage is based on the "benefit period,"[397] sometimes called a "spell of illness." The benefit period is a way of measuring Medicare beneficiaries' use of hospital services covered by Medicare Part A. A benefit period begins on the first day the beneficiary is hospitalized and ends after the patient has been out of the hospital for 60 days in a row. If the beneficiary is hospitalized again after 60 days have elapsed, a new benefit period begins.

In each benefit period, the Medicare beneficiary is responsible for paying a Part A deductible ($1,364 in 2019).[398] In addition, the patient is responsible for a daily co-payment for hospital care received from the sixty-first through the nine-tieth day of each benefit period ($341 per day in 2019).[399] There is no limit on the number of benefit periods a person can have. However, regular Medicare coverage for hospital care ends after ninetieth day within a benefit period. If the hospitalization lasts more than 90 days, the patient can choose to use one or more of his or her 60 "lifetime reserve days." There is a daily co-payment charge for each reserve day, equal to one-half of the Part A deductible ($682 per day in 2019).[400] The average length of Medicare hospital stay is about five days,[401] so it is unusual for a Medicare patient to exhaust the 90 days of inpatient coverage available during each benefit period.

If a beneficiary does exhaust the 90 days available during the benefit period, the financial impact could be disastrous. The beneficiary would be forced to cover the additional hospital stay out of pocket. The beneficiary may reduce the risk of exhausting benefits by purchasing a Medigap policy or enrolling in a Part C plan that covers extended hospital stays or limits total out of pocket expenses.

Here is an example of how the benefit period works. Suppose Ms. A was admitted to the hospital on January 1 and discharged on January 15, only to be readmitted on February 15. Since 60 days have not passed between the January 15 discharge and the February 15 readmission, Ms. A is still in the same benefit period and does not have to pay another deductible for the new hospital stay. However, she is now in the fifteenth day of covered hospital care for the benefit period. Suppose instead that Mr. A was readmitted to the hospital on May 3. In that case, more than 60 days would have passed since her prior discharge on January 15, so she would be in a new benefit period. She would again have to pay the Part A deductible, but she would be in the first day of covered hospital care for the new benefit period.

During the inpatient hospital stay, Medicare will pay for a semiprivate room, meals (including special diets), regular nursing services, and intensive care. Medicare also covers drugs, blood, laboratory tests (including x-rays and radiology), medical supplies and equipment, operating and recovery room costs, and rehabilitation services (such as physical therapy). Medicare will not pay for private duty nurses, "luxury items" (for example, TV or radio), and hospital stays that Medicare determines are not medically necessary. Medicare will pay the hospital directly and send the beneficiary a statement. Hospitals may not require a Medicare beneficiary to pay a deposit before being admitted for treatment.[402]

What is a DRG?

Medicare pays for inpatient hospital care using "diagnosis-related groupings" (DRGs).[403] This means that the hospital gets paid a fixed amount of money based on the doctor's diagnosis of the patient's medical problem. If the patient's care costs more than the amount of money received, the hospital loses money on that patient. If the care costs less than the amount received, the hospital makes money. Some patient advocates are concerned that DRGs cause hospitals to discharge patients too early, discharge them without adequate post-hospital care, or otherwise limit the care they provide.[404]

What discharge planning accompanies Medicare inpatient hospital services?

Hospitals must provide Medicare beneficiaries with a discharge plan and planning services whenever needed to avoid adverse health consequences.[405] The hospital must identify such patients at an early stage of hospitalization. Other Medicare patients have a right to such services upon request. The discharge plan must be discussed with the patient and made a part of the patient's medical record.

Also, before a hospital discharges a patient, it must provide a notice called "An Important Message from Medicare" that explains post-hospital services, including discharge planning and appeal rights regarding the denial of Medicare-covered services. The notice should be given to the patient or to the patient's next of kin if the patient may not be unable to comprehend the notice.

Patients who believe that a hospital is discharging them too soon or that the discharge plan is inadequate, should contact the local Quality Improvement Organization[406] and file a complaint. Patients may have a right to appeal a hospital's discharge decision (as described later in this chapter under "Medicare Appeals"). A local legal aid or legal services office or local Older Americans Act–funded legal assistance program may be available to assist in filing discharge related complaints or appeals.

Will Medicare cover nursing home care?

Nursing home coverage under Medicare Part A is very limited.[407] Medicare will cover only care received at Medicare-certified skilled nursing facilities. These nursing facilities have the staff and equipment qualified to provide skilled nursing care and a full range of rehabilitation therapies. Custodial care—the type of care provided by most nursing homes—is not covered by Medicare.

Medicare caps the duration of skilled nursing facility coverage. Part A will cover up to 100 days of medically necessary skilled nursing care per benefit period. The care must be preceded by a hospital stay of at least three days. The first 20 days of skilled care are covered in full, but the patient has to pay coinsurance for care received from the twenty-first through the one-hundredth day in each benefit period ($170.50 per day in 2019).[408] Medicare will cover a semiprivate room, meals (including special diets), nursing services, rehabilitation services, drugs, and medical equipment and supplies used during the skilled nursing facility stay. Private duty nurses, luxury items, and services determined not to be medically necessary are not covered.

Will Medicare pay for home health care services?

Medicare Part A will pay for home health visits if the patient needs intermittent, skilled nursing care.[409] The patient must be at least temporarily confined to the home, and the patient's doctor has to prescribe a home health treatment plan. The home health agency must be Medicare certified. Medicare will pay the full cost of medically necessary home health, which includes skilled nursing services, physical therapy, speech therapy, and home health aides. Medicare will not pay for custodial or around-the-clock home care.

Will Medicare cover hospice care?

A hospice is an agency that provides support services, pain relief, and counseling to terminally ill patients and their families. Medicare Part A will pay for hospice care.[410] To get the coverage, a doctor and the hospice medical director must certify that the patient is terminally ill. The patient must choose hospice care, and the care must be provided by a Medicare-certified hospice. Medicare coverage is limited to a maximum of 210 days. Medicare will cover nursing and physician services, drugs, therapy, home health aides and homemaker services, medical supplies, and counseling.

Medicare Part B Medical Insurance

Who is eligible for Medicare Part B?

Everyone enrolled in Medicare Part A is eligible for and presumed to want Part B, and premiums are automatically deducted from the Social Security check. In 2019 the premium was $135.50/month or higher depending on income.[411] Individuals may opt out of Part B coverage, but this makes sense only for people whose health care, including copays and deductibles, is covered entirely by third-party insurance.

People who are not automatically enrolled in Part B can choose to do so during their initial enrollment period (the month of their sixty-fifth birthday and the three months before and after) and at the beginning of each calendar year. As noted earlier, failure to enroll in Part B during the initial enrollment period may result in a late enrollment penalty.

What are the Part B benefits?

The Part B medical insurance program covers doctors' services, outpatient hospital care, ambulance services, and medical equipment and prosthetic devices.[412]

Doctors' Services
Medicare covers medically necessary doctors' services. The services can be furnished in the doctor's office, a clinic, a hospital, a skilled nursing facility, or at home. The doctors' services that are covered by Medicare include medically necessary visits to a doctor, hospital visits and consults, surgery, anesthesia, diagnostic tests, drugs, and medical supplies.

Outpatient Services
Part B covers services received as an outpatient of a hospital. These services include medical and surgical services in an emergency room or outpatient clinic, lab tests, medical supplies, and drugs. Part B also covers outpatient physical therapy, occupational therapy, and speech therapy.

Ambulance Services
Medicare will pay for ambulance services if the ambulance, equipment, and personnel meet Medicare requirements, and transportation by other means would endanger the patient's health. Medicare will pay for transport to or from

a hospital or skilled nursing facility. Medicare will not pay for ambulance transportation from your home to a doctor's office.

Medical Equipment

Medicare will pay for medically necessary "durable medical equipment" such as wheelchairs, walkers, oxygen services, beds, and other equipment the doctor prescribes for use in the home.[413] Beneficiaries can choose between renting and purchasing such equipment, and should consider how long the equipment will be needed and the difference between purchase price and rental payments for that period of time.

Medicare will also cover prostheses such as artificial limbs, cardiac pacemakers, colostomy supplies, and breast prostheses following mastectomy.

What new preventive services does Medicare cover under the ACA?

The ACA added new provisions for Medicare to provide cost-free preventive services,[414] including an "Annual Wellness Visit" at which the doctor creates a personalized preventive care plan based on the beneficiary's medical history and risk factors.[415] In addition to removing copayments and coinsurance for most of the preventive services covered by Medicare,[416] the ACA added Medicare Part B coverage without copay and without coinsurance for services that get an "A" or a "B" recommendation from the U.S. Preventive Services Task Force (USPSTF).[417] This means that the beneficiary will not be charged additional fees for these preventive services.[418]

The USPSTF regularly updates and make new recommendations. As a result, the preventive services covered by Medicare could change as new preventive services are developed and evaluated.[419] A current list of covered preventive services appears in the "Medicare & You Handbook," or at http://www.medicare.gov/coverage/preventive-and-screening-services.html.

What services are not covered by Medicare Part B?

Medicare Part B does not cover many of the services that older and disabled people especially need. For instance, Medicare will not pay for eyeglasses or eye exams (except after cataract surgery), hearing aids or hearing exams, routine dental care, long-term nursing home care, custodial care, full-time nursing care in the home, naturopathy, acupuncture, and drugs and medications taken at home.[420]

How much of a beneficiary's medical expenses does Part B cover?

Medicare Part B uses deductibles and coinsurance. Part B will pay 80 percent of "approved amounts" for covered medical services that exceed the annual deductible. (In 2018 the deductible was $183.)[421] Most beneficiaries are responsible for the remaining 20 percent of the bill, known as the "coinsurance" payment. However, people eligible for both Medicaid and Medicare, and who are enrolled in the Qualified Medicaid Beneficiary (QMB) program (discussed earlier), have no coinsurance obligation: Medicaid is responsible for all deductibles and copayments.[422]

Some people purchase supplemental "Medigap" insurance or choose a Part C plan to cover these costs. People who elect a Part C plan do not need and may not be sold a Medigap policy. CMS has approved a number of Medigap policies with differing coverages and premiums that cover deductibles, copayments, and gaps at different levels.[423]

What is the Medicare-approved amount?

Medicare Part B payments are limited by a "fee schedule" that lists a payment amount for every covered medical service. This amount is often less than what the doctor or supplier has charged the patient for the service. The Medicare-approved amount is the lesser of the actual charge submitted by the provider and fee schedule amount. Part B pays 80 percent of the Medicare-approved amount.

How much can a doctor bill a Medicare beneficiary?

It depends. A doctor (or other health care provider) who "accepts assignment" has agreed to accept the Medicare-approved amount as payment in full. The doctor submits the claim directly to the insurance carrier,[424] and the carrier will pay the doctor 80 percent of the approved amount. The doctor may then bill the patient no more than the remaining 20 percent of the approved amount—regardless of the actual charge. There is an important exception to this rule for people enrolled in the QMB program. The state Medicaid program—not the individual—is responsible for any Part B deductibles, coinsurance, or copayments, and Medicare providers may not bill the QMB enrollee for these amounts, even if the state failed to pay. Many doctors ignore this restriction and unlawfully bill QMB enrollees (who by definition have very low incomes) for coinsurance.[425] Patients should alert their providers each time they receive care that they have QMB and cannot be charged for Medicare deductibles, coinsurance, and copayments. If the provider persists in making these charges, the patient should report the problem to 1-800-MEDICARE.

Here is an example of a claim for a patient who is not enrolled in the QMB program and whose doctor accepts assignment (assuming that the patient has already met the annual Part B deductible):

Doctor's actual charge:	$600
Medicare-approved amount:	$500
Medicare pays the doctor:	$400
(80 percent of approved amount)	
Patient pays the doctor:	$100
(20 percent of approved amount)	

Doctors who agree in advance to accept assignment on all Medicare claims are called "Medicare-participating doctors." Medicare-participating doctors (and suppliers) can be found online.[426]

If the doctor does not accept assignment, then Medicare still pays 80 percent of the approved amount. The doctor can bill the patient for the 20 percent coinsurance and up to (but not more than) 15 percent above the Medicare-approved amount. This is called the "limiting charge rule." Here is an example of a claim for a patient who is not enrolled in the QMB program and whose doctor does not accept assignment:

Doctor's actual charge:	$600
Medicare-approved amount:	$500
Medicare pays the doctor:	$400
(80 percent of approved amount)	
Patient pays the doctor:	$175
(20 percent coinsurance + 15 percent of approved amount)	

It is unlawful for a doctor or other provider to charge a Medicare beneficiary more than the amount permitted by the 15 percent limited charge rule or to bill patients in the QMB program. Anyone subjected to illegal billing should report the practice to their Medicare carrier or call 1-800-MEDICARE.

Medicare Part C Advantage Plans

What is a Part C Medicare Advantage Plan?

Part C Medicare Advantage Plans are private insurance plans, approved by the Centers for Medicare and Medicaid Services, that people may choose in place of Medicare Part A and Part B. Advantage plans must offer at least the same level of coverage as Part A and Part B and frequently cover additional services.[427] Most Medicare Advantage Plans also include Part D prescription drug coverage. Most Advantage Plans are health maintenance organizations (HMOs).

People choose Medicare Advantage Plans in order to obtain particular benefits, such as vision, hearing, or dental care, not covered by Part B; or to ensure coverage beyond the benefit periods allowed under Part A; or to limit other out-of-pocket expenses. Medicare pays part of the beneficiary's premium directly to the Medicare Advantage Plan, and the beneficiary is responsible for any balance. Part C plans have some disadvantages. For example, most plans are HMOs that require recipients to see certain providers or to fill prescriptions at certain pharmacies, whereas people who opt for regular Medicare can choose any provider that accepts Medicare. Keep in mind that Advantage Plans are operated by for-profit insurance companies that receive a fixed, per-person payment from the government, no matter how much or how little the company spends on providing health services to its members. Premiums for Part C plans vary and may be higher or lower than the cost for Medicare Part B.[428]

What restrictions are there on out-of-pocket costs in Medicare Advantage Plans?

The ACA bars Medicare Advantage Plans from imposing higher out-of-pocket costs than Medicare Part A and Part B for certain services designated by CMS, and requires Medicare Advantage Plans to cover preventive services without coinsurance or copayment to the same extent as Medicare Part B.[429] Each year through regulation, the CMS can add to the list of services that Medicare Advantage Plans must cover without charging more in coinsurance or copayments than regular Medicare.[430]

In addition, while this does not directly impact out-of-pocket costs, the ACA now requires Medicare Advantage Plans to meet an 85 percent medical loss ratio, which means that at least 85 percent of the premiums paid to the insurance companies must be used to pay for health care and services for Medicare beneficiaries.[431]

How can people enroll in a Part C Medicare Advantage Plan?

People may elect a Medicare Part C Advantage Plan during their initial enroll-ment period or when they otherwise become eligible for Medicare Part B.[432] Those already enrolled in Part B may switch to a Part C plan during the open en-rollment period, from October 15 through December 7 of each year. Applications for a Medicare Advantage Plan may be made at a Social Security district office, by calling any insurance company that provides a Part C plan, or online at Medicare. gov. Important factors to consider in choosing a plan include whether it covers visits to the beneficiary's existing health care providers and whether it covers the prescription drugs the beneficiary takes or is likely to need. Some people choose plans that have no premiums except the Part B premium. Others choose plans with higher premiums that limit out-of-pocket expenses. Medicare.gov includes a tool to help people evaluate these options and choices.

Medicare Part D Prescription Drug Coverage

What is Part D prescription drug coverage?

Medicare Part D is insurance that pays some of the cost of prescription drugs.[433] Enrollment in Part D coverage is optional.[434] Beneficiaries choose from a list of plans offered by private insurance companies and approved by the CMS. Prescription drug coverage is often included in Part C Medicare Advantage Plans. Part D plans pay a share of prescription drug costs: higher premium plans offer greater coverage, lower-premium plans offer less coverage. Each Part D plan covers a different list of drugs, and some may require prior authorizations or step therapy before approving certain prescriptions drugs. Beneficiaries should care-fully review each plan's rules and benefit formularies before choosing a plan.[435]

What is the "doughnut hole" and how does it affect out-of-pocket costs for prescription drugs?

The "doughnut hole" is the popular term for the coverage gap in Medicare Part D Plans. Each Part D plan is different, but they all cover the majority of prescription drug expenses until the costs in a particular calendar reach an annually revised statutory amount ($3820 in 2019). After that point, the beneficiary pays 25 per-cent of the cost of prescription drugs until out-of-pocket expenditures reach the threshold for "catastrophic coverage" ($5,100 in 2019). Medicare then kicks in again and covers any additional drug expenses for the rest of the year, subject only to a small copay or coinsurance for each prescription.[436]

The issue of prescription drug prices and affordability has drawn intense political and congressional attention in recent years, so the rules governing Medicare Part D are likely to change.[437]

Can low-income beneficiaries get additional assistance to pay Medicare drug costs?

The Low Income Subsidy program, also known as "Extra Help," will pay most premiums, deductibles, and coinsurance of Medicare Part D for people with very low income and resources.[438] The financial guidelines for the program change annually and may be found at http://www.ssa.gov/medicare/prescriptionhelp/. People whose Medicare Part B premiums are paid by Medicaid, and people who receive Supplemental Security Income (SSI) from the Social Security Administration automatically qualify for Extra Help. Applications for Extra Help may be filed online (https://www.socialsecurity.gov/extrahelp), by telephone (1-800-722-1213), or at a Social Security district office.

When and how can people enroll for Part D coverage?

Individuals are eligible to obtain Part D prescription drug coverage as soon as they become eligible for Medicare Part B. People who do not enroll in Part D within 63 days of becoming eligible must pay a late enrollment penalty, in the form of higher Part D premiums, if they later opt in to Part D.[439] This is different from the Part B late enrollment penalty discussed earlier in this chapter. Applications for Part D may be filed online (https://www.medicare.gov), by telephone (1-800-MEDICARE), at a Social Security district office, or by calling any insurance company that provides a Part D plan.

Medicare Appeals

Is there a right to appeal decisions regarding a Medicare claim?

Yes. Individuals have the right to appeal any decision by Medicare, a Medicare Advantage Plan, or a Part D prescription drug plan regarding services, coverage, or amount of payment.[440] These entities must provide written notice to the beneficiary that describes the action taken on every claim, the basis for the action, and how to appeal. Part B beneficiaries will receive a "Medicare Summary Notice" every three months summarizing all claims.[441] Private insurers participating in Medicare Parts C or D must also issue summary of benefits notices. People who do not receive notice regarding a determination, or do not understand a notice, should contact the local Social Security office, the Quality Improvement Organization in their state,[442] or a local legal aid or legal services office.

The Medicare appeals process has five levels. At each level, the beneficiary will receive written notice of the decision, together with instructions on how to appeal to the next level if the beneficiary disagrees with the determination. The time limits for filing appeals are different at each level, and those wishing to appeal should take care not to miss the deadline. At any stage of this process, beneficiaries should consider enlisting the assistance of their doctor to supply evidence and medical explanations to support the appeal. (Practical instructions on how to file Medicare appeals may be found at https://www.medicare.gov/claims-appeals/how-do-i-file-an-appeal.)

The first level of appeal is called "redetermination" and is essentially an internal review.[443] Redetermination must be requested within 120 days of receipt of the Medicare Summary Notice or other written notification of the disputed benefits determination. Redetermination requests regarding Parts A and B are reviewed by a Medicare intermediary. Those regarding Parts C and D are reviewed by the private insurance company that administers the beneficiary's Medicare plan. In either case, a redetermination decision must be issued within 60 days of the request, unless the health of the beneficiary is at immediate risk, in which case a decision must be made within 72 hours.[444]

The second level of appeal is "reconsideration,"[445] which must be requested within 180 days of receipt of the redetermination decision.[446] Panels from independent entities engaged by Medicare—a Qualified Independent Contractor (QIC) for Parts A and B or an Independent Review Entity (IRE) for Parts C and D—conduct reconsideration reviews. Members of these panels must have "sufficient medical, legal, and other expertise, including knowledge of the Medicare program," to decide appeals properly and must be physicians where the claim involves the medical necessity of treatment or other items or services.[447] Beneficiaries have the right to review their entire files, and should submit with their appeal any additional documentation or evidence (including letters from doctors or other providers) that supports their claim. This is especially important because evidence not submitted before a reconsideration decision is issued will not be considered at later levels of appeal unless the beneficiary shows good cause for not presenting the evidence on time.[448] The QIC or IRE must decide these appeals within 60 days for standard requests, or within 72 hours for expedited requests.

The third level of appeal is a hearing with an administrative law judge (ALJ),[449] which must be requested in writing from the Office of Medicare Hearings and Appeals within 60 days of receipt of the reconsideration decision.[450] Appeals to an ALJ are available only if the dollar amount of the claim exceeds a statutory threshold ($160 in 2019).[451] The beneficiary has the right to bring an attorney or other representative to present witnesses and evidence, to examine any other evidence presented, and to question witnesses brought by other parties.[452]

The fourth level is a written appeal to the Medicare Appeals Council,[453] which must be requested within the time frame specified in the ALJ decision. The fifth level of appeal is federal court.[454] Claims that meet the statutory dollar amount ($1,630 in 2019)[455] may be appealed to federal court. At these last two levels of the appeals process, it is especially advisable to seek legal assistance.

Are there special rules for Part C and Part D appeals?

In addition to the appeals process described above, Part C and Part D plans are required to establish internal grievance procedures to resolve complaints about issues[456] that do not arise from formal benefit or payment determinations included in determinations, such as hours of service, location of facilities, and treatment by personnel.[457] The plan must provide information to members regarding this grievance process in the plan's written rules, along with timetables and information about the steps necessary to utilize the grievance process.[458]

Is there a right to appeal a hospital's decision to discharge a Medicare patient?

Yes. Patients have a right to an expedited appeal to contest a discharge decision by a Medicare-participating hospital.[459] The Quality Improvement Organization (QIO) assigned to the hospital conducts these appeals.[460] QIOs are certified by and work with the U.S. Department of Health and Human Services.[461] The right to contest a discharge (together with other rights of hospital patients) is explained in a notice entitled "An Important Message from Medicare" that the hospital must give to every patient within two days of admission.[462] This notice will provide the contact information for the QIO assigned to the hospital.

A patient may appeal a hospital discharge by contacting the QIO orally or in writing no later than the day the discharge is to take place.[463] Once such an appeal is made, the hospital must provide the patient a detailed notice explaining the medical and legal bases for its discharge decision.[464] The QIO will review the patient's hospital records and must give the patient or the patient's representative, an opportunity to explain the reasons for opposing a discharge. The hospital bears the burden of demonstrating that its discharge decision is correct.[465] The QIO must notify the patient of its determination by the end of the first business day after it receives all requested information pertinent to the appeal.[466]

Health Care Coverage for People Living with HIV/AIDS

More than a million people are living with HIV in the United States, and Medicaid has generally been their most significant source of health care, but Medicaid does not reach all those in need. In 1990, Congress passed the Ryan White Comprehensive AIDS Resources Emergency (CARE) Act, which provided subsidized health care for low-income, uninsured people affected by HIV/AIDS.[467] Nevertheless, many people living with HIV/AIDS were still unable to obtain health insurance because private companies refused to sell policies to them, or charged them exorbitant premiums, or excluded essential care, or imposed annual or lifetime limits on coverage.[468]

How does the ACA impact health care access for people living with HIV/AIDS?

The ACA's insurance reforms, discussed earlier in this chapter, outlawed many of the insurance company practices that prevented people living with HIV/AIDS from securing coverage. Most importantly, health plans may no longer set higher premiums or limit or deny coverage because of a person's medical condition.[469] This means that people living with HIV/AIDS should no longer face higher premiums or barriers to obtaining health insurance because of the disease.[470] The ACA's Medicaid expansion and subsidized health care through the Exchanges also opened health care access to many people living with HIV/AIDS who previously relied on Ryan White for health care services or did not have adequate access.[471]

How does the ACA impact the Ryan White HIV/AIDS health care program?

About two-thirds of the people served by the Ryan White HIV/AIDS Program had incomes below the federal poverty level, and almost 90 percent had incomes below 200 percent of the federal poverty level. This means that most Ryan

White beneficiaries became eligible for health coverage through an Exchange or for ACA-expanded Medicaid in states that adopted it. As a result, Ryan White programs may shift their funding to fill gaps in Medicaid or Health Exchange services, or provide care for people in states that do not expand Medicaid.[472] Unlike Medicare and Medicaid, Ryan White programs depend on federal funds that must be passed in appropriations bills each year, so the amount of funding available for Ryan White programs could change.

Can people who qualify for health coverage through Medicaid or an Exchange receive assistance from a Ryan White program?

Maybe. Ryan White programs provide "coverage of last resort," meaning that people eligible for Medicaid or affordable insurance through an Exchange may not forgo that coverage and choose to get health care from Ryan White instead.[473] However, low-income individuals enrolled in Medicaid or a qualified health plan may still qualify for Ryan White assistance to cover out-of-pocket health expenses, such as insurance premiums, copayments, deductibles, other services that are either limited or not covered by Medicaid or insurance obtained through an Exchange, and the cost of AIDS drugs under the AIDS Drug Assistance Program.[474] The local Ryan White provider should be consulted about current programs and eligibility guidelines, which will vary from state to state.

Immigration Status and Access to Health Care

Eligibility for Medicaid and Medicare, Health Exchange access, and premium tax credits is restricted to U.S. citizens and certain immigrants lawfully residing in the United States, as discussed earlier in this chapter.[475] The following questions address several general issues affecting immigrants seeking access to health care.

What medical assistance is available to immigrants who do not qualify for Medicaid, Medicare, or insurance from a Health Exchange?

Emergency Medical Care at Hospitals

State Medicaid programs must cover emergency medical treatment for any legal immigrant or undocumented person living in the state if the person meets the other eligibility requirements for Medicaid. An emergency is "a medical condition (including severe pain) such that the absence of immediate medical attention could reasonably be expected to result in (A) placing the patient's health in serious jeopardy, (B) serious impairment of bodily function, or (C) serious dysfunction of any bodily organ or part."[476] A Social Security number is not needed to obtain emergency Medicaid.

In addition, the Emergency Medical Treatment & Labor Act (EMTALA) requires hospitals that receive Medicare or Medicaid payments to treat any person—regardless of immigration status or ability to pay—who presents with an "emergency medical condition."[477] Hospitals must provide "examination and such treatment as may be required to stabilize the medical condition."[478]

Routine Medical Care at a Federal Qualified Health Center or Other Free Clinic

Federally Qualified Health Centers (FQHCs) are community-based clinics that serve populations with limited access to health care, such as migrant farmworker families.[479] These clinics are funded under the Public Health Safety Act, as expanded by the ACA, and their services are available to people regardless of immigration status.[480] A list of FQHCs by location may be found at https://www.findahealthcenter.hrsa.gov. In addition, the National Association for Free and Charitable Clinics (NAFCC) operates a network of safety net clinics that provide medical and dental care to families and individuals, irrespective of immigration status or ability to pay. Local NAFCC clinics may be found at https://www.nafcclinics.org/find-clinic. Immigrants may also receive public health services (such as immunization, mental health, and screening for communicable diseases) and may be able to obtain services at public hospitals. As these resources vary from state to state and locality by locality, it is advisable to consult with local social services providers, an immigration advocacy group, or a health advocacy organization.

Can members of an immigrant family receive health coverage even if some members of the family are ineligible because of immigration status?

Yes. Any individual who meets the eligibility requirements for Medicaid, CHIP, or health subsidies through an Exchange is entitled to that benefit whether or not other family members qualify. Moreover, a family member who is not eligible for health care, such as an undocumented parent, may complete an application for a U.S. citizen or lawfully residing child, or any other family member who is eligible for coverage. Neither the Exchange nor a state Medicaid agency may ask about the immigration status of any family member who is not applying for health care coverage for themselves.[481]

Does applying for health coverage place immigrants at risk?

Federal privacy protections restrict the use of information provided by people applying for health care coverage. Such information (including information relating to immigrant status) must be kept confidential and may be used only to determine eligibility for health care coverage.[482] As of 2019, federal policy guidance acknowledging that the government may not use information submitted with a health care application for immigration enforcement purposes was still in effect.[483] As noted earlier, people applying for health coverage cannot be asked about—and should not discuss—the immigration or citizenship status of any family member who is not seeking benefits for themselves.[484]

A second question is whether an immigrant's receipt of government-subsidized health insurance can have any effect on the person's immigration status or admissibility to the United States. For at least the past 50 years, the answer to that question has been "no." However, in August 2019, the Trump administration adopted a harsh and legally questionable new rule that expands the government's authority to deem certain immigrants ineligible for lawful permanent resident (green card) status and inadmissible to the United States on the ground that they are "likely to become a public charge" (that is, likely to become primarily dependent on government for subsistence). Under prior law, receipt of noncash public benefits had no bearing on "public charge" status. The new rule, by contrast, permits the government to consider receipt of most forms of Medicaid, as well as SNAP and housing assistance, in making "public charge" determinations.

It is important to note the limitations on this rule, as misinformation about the receipt of government benefits already has deterred many eligible immigrants—and U.S. citizen family members—from accessing needed medical care. First, receipt of Medicaid still has no effect on whether an immigrant may be considered deportable. Second, the rule does not apply to lawful permanent residents while in the United States, or when re-entering the United States after an absence of 180 days or less. Third, the public charge rule does not apply to immigrants in the "humanitarian" categories (e.g., refugees, asylees, certain survivors of trafficking and domestic violence, and VAWA self-petitioners) or to immigrants in the U.S. armed forces (or their family members). Fourth, Medicaid received by children under age 21, by pregnant women through 60 days postpartum, or for treatment of an emergency medical condition, is not considered in the public charge calculus. Fifth, Medicaid received by a family member does not count against an immigrant for purpose of the public charge determination.[485] There are other exceptions as well, and the new rule is complex and subject to interpretation, so it is advisable to consult immigrants' rights groups, including the National Immigration Law Center (nilc.org) and the Immigrant Legal Resource Center (ilrc.org), for the most recent developments. The new rule is scheduled to become effective on October 15, 2019, but lawsuits have been filed to stop it.

Health Care Access for Transgender, Gender Nonconforming, and Nonbinary People

In most states, transgender, gender nonconforming, and nonbinary people face barriers to obtaining necessary care.[486] Some states explicitly exclude gender-related care in the statutes and regulations that govern their Medicaid benefits. In other states, the discrimination flows from policy determinations by the state government. In the past, most private insurers excluded gender-related care. However, some states have begun to enforce requirements to cover health care related to gender transition as part of antidiscrimination statutes governing health insurance coverage.[487] As of 2018, 13 states and the District of Columbia have made it illegal to deny coverage for transgender health care and have offered transgender inclusive benefits to state employees.[488] In addition, Medicare has ended a long-standing provision that excluded coverage for some services related to gender transition, and several state Medicaid programs have followed that precedent.[489]

Notes

1. Memorial Hospital v. Maricopa County, 415 U.S. 250, 259 (1974).
2. *See, for example*, Harris v. McRae, 448 U.S. 297 (1980) (no constitutional duty to fund abortions for indigent women).
3. Youngberg v. Romeo, 457 U.S. 307 (1982) (institutions for the disabled); Estelle v. Gamble, 429 U.S. 97 (1976) (prisons); *see* LaShawn v. Dixon, 762 F. Supp. 959 (D.D.C. 1991), aff'd in part and remanded in part, 990 F.2d 1319 (D.C. Cir. 1994), cert. denied, 510 U.S. 1044 (1994) (foster care). Violations of this constitutional mandate are not uncommon, as illustrated most recently by the appalling treatment of refugees placed into detention camps at the Mexican border, including children the government forcibly separated from their parents. *See, for example*, Elora Mukherjee, Let the Doctors In, Slate (June 30, 2019), https://slate.com/news-and-politics/2019/06/child-detention-border-sick-quarantine-doctors.html (firsthand report of rampant illness and disease in U.S. Border Patrol detention facilities for children, and inadequacy of medical care). *See also* Chloe Reichel, How detention centers affect the health of immigrant children: A research roundup, Journalist's Resource (July 22, 2019), https://journalistsresource.org/studies/government/immigration/health-effects-immigration-detention-children/; Julie M. Linton, Marsha Griffin, & Alan J. Shapiro, Detention of Immigrant Children, 139 Pediatrics

4 (Apr. 2017), https://pediatrics.aappublications.org/content/pediatrics/139/5/e20170483.full.pdf (policy statement of the American Academy of Pediatrics).

4. Max Fisher, Here's a Map of the Countries That Provide Universal Health Care (America's Still Not on It), The Atlantic (June 28, 2012), https://www.theatlantic.com/international/archive/2012/06/heres-a-map-of-the-countries-that-provide-universal-health-care-americas-still-not-on-it/259153/.

5. 42 C.F.R. § 440.255 (emergency Medicaid); Emergency Medical Treatment and Active Labor Act (EMTALA), 42 U.S.C. § 13955dd.

6. Bradley Sawyer & Cynthia Cox, How Does Health Care Spending in the U.S. Compare to Other Countries?, Kaiser Family Foundation (Dec. 7, 2018), https://www.healthsystemtracker.org/chart-collection/health-spending-u-s-compare-countries/. For an argument that U.S. workers effectively pay as much or more in health taxes than counterparts in countries that offer universal health care, see Matt Bruenig, Universal Health Care Might Cost You Less Than You Think, N.Y. Times (Apr. 29, 2019), https://www.nytimes.com/2019/04/29/opinion/medicare-for-all-cost.html.

7. Bradley Sawyer & Selena Gonzales, How Does the Quality of the U.S. Healthcare System Compare to Other Countries?, Kaiser Family Foundation (Mar. 28, 2019), https://www.healthsystemtracker.org/chart-collection/quality-u-s-healthcare-system-compare-countries/.

8. Id.; Cynthia Cox & Bradley Sawyer, What do we know about the burden of disease in the U.S.?, Kaiser Family Foundation (May 22, 2017), https://www.healthsystemtracker.org/chart-collection/know-burden-disease-u-s/?_sf_s=burden#item-start;   OECD Data, Infant mortality rates (2017), https://data.oecd.org/healthstat/infant-mortality-rates.htm#indicator-chart; OECD Family Database, CO1.3: Low birth weight (Oct. 31, 2018), http://www.oecd.org/els/family/database.htm.

9. U.S. Census Bureau, Income, Poverty, and Health Insurance Coverage in the United States: 2009, at 23 Table 8 (2010), http://www.census.gov/prod/2010pubs/p60–238.pdf.

10. 42 U.S.C. § 1396a. The ACA sets the income cutoff at 133% of the FPL, but the formula for determining eligibility includes a 5% income disregard, placing the effective income eligibility limit at 138% of the FPL. 42 U.S.C. § 1396a(a)(10)(A)(i)(VIII).

11. 26 U.S.C. § 4980H.

12. 45 C.F.R. § 155. An Exchange is a government or nonprofit entity that oversees a marketplace for qualified health insurance plans. 26 C.F.R. Part 1 § 1.36B.

13. 29 C.F.R. § 2590.715-2714.

14. Congressional Budget Office, Analysis of the Major Health Care Legislation Enacted in March 2010 at 18 Table 3 (2011), https://www.cbo.gov/sites/default/files/03-30-healthcarelegislation.pdf.

15. Key Facts About the Uninsured Population, Kaiser Family Foundation (Dec. 8, 2018), https://www.kff.org/uninsured/fact-sheet/key-facts-about-the-uninsured-population/.

16. Dan Witters, U.S. Uninsured Rate Rises to Four-Year High, Gallup (Jan. 23, 2019), https://news.gallup.com/poll/246134/uninsured-rate-rises-four-year-high.aspx.

17. See, for example, Steven Schwinn, The Strange Politics of Medicaid Expansion, 47 J. Marshall L. Rev. 947 (2014).

18. Margot Sanger-Katz, After Falling Under Obama, America's Uninsured Rate Looks to Be Rising, N.Y. Times (Jan. 23, 2019), https://www.nytimes.com/2019/01/23/upshot/rate-of-americans-without-health-insurance-rising.html. For the current litigation challenging the ACA's constitutionality, *see* Texas v. United States, 430 F. Supp. 3d. 579 (N.D. Tex. 2018) (appeal pending).

19. The medical loss ratio provision requires insurance companies to use at least 80% of premiums on medical care (85% in the large group market), and when a company fails to do so, the law requires the company to refund to consumers the difference between the 80% (or 85%) it was required to spend on medical services the amount it actually spent on such services. 42 C.F.R. § 438.8; 45 C.F.R. § 158.210 (delineating the medical loss ratios for the large, small, and individual group markets).

20. 83 Fed. Reg. 38212 (Aug. 3, 2018) (to be codified at 26 C.F.R. Part 54, 29 C.F.R. Part 2590, 45 C.F.R. Parts 144, 146, 148).

21. *See* Margot Sanger-Katz, What to Know Before You Buy Short-Term Health Insurance, N.Y. Times (Aug. 1, 2018), https://www.nytimes.com/2018/08/01/upshot/buying-short-term-health-insurance-what-to-know.html.

22. 83 Fed. Reg. 38212 (Aug. 3, 2018).

23. *See* Claire McAndrew, State Strategies to Prevent the Harmful Impact of Short-Term Health Plans, Families USA (Aug. 2018), https://familiesusa.org/product/state-strategies-prevent-harmful-impact-short-term-health-plans.

24. *See* Robin Rudowitz & Rachel Garfield, 10 Things to Know about Medicaid: Setting the Facts Straight, Kaiser Family Foundation (Apr. 12, 2018), https://www.kff.org/medicaid/issue-brief/10-things-to-know-about-medicaid-setting-the-facts-straight/.

25. 42 U.S.C. §§ 1396a et seq.

26. Robin Rudowitz, Samantha Artiga, & Rachel Arguello, Children's Health Coverage: Medicaid, CHIP and the ACA, Kaiser Family Foundation (Mar. 26, 2014), http://kff.org/health-reform/issue-brief/childrens-health-coverage-medicaid-chip-and-the-aca/.

27. Robin Rudowitz, Medicaid Financing: The Basics, Kaiser Family Foundation (Dec. 22, 2016), http://www.kff.org/report-section/medicaid-financing-the-basics-issue-brief/.

28. *See* U.S. Centers for Medicare & Medicaid Services, https://www.CMS.gov.

29. 81 Fed. Reg. 80080 (Nov. 15, 2016). The percentage of costs borne by the federal government is determined by the Federal Medical Assistance Percentage (FMAP), which is calculated using per capita income, squared.

30. 42 U.S.C. §§ 1396b, 1396b(a)(3).

31. 42 U.S.C. § 1396a.

32. 42 U.S.C. § 1396a(a)(10)(A)(ii).

33. Before the ACA took effect, 70% of low-income children had Medicaid coverage, and only 30% of low-income, nonelderly adults had coverage. The overall uninsured rate among the low-income, nonelderly population was about 40%, double the national average. *See* Alison Mitchell, Congressional Research Service, the ACA Medicaid Expansion *2 (Dec. 30, 2014), https://fas.org/sgp/crs/misc/R43564.pdf.

34. *See* Julia Paradise, Medicaid Moving Forward, Kaiser Family Foundation (Mar. 9, 2015), https://www.kff.org/health-reform/issue-brief/medicaid-moving-forward/.

35. Congressional Research Service, Overview of the ACA Medicaid Expansion, https://fas.org/sgp/crs/misc/IF10399.pdf (last updated Dec. 3, 2018).

36. National Federation of Independent Business v. Sebelius, 567 U.S. 519 (2012).

37. Congressional Research Service, Overview of the ACA Medicaid Expansion, https://fas.org/sgp/crs/misc/IF10399.pdf (last updated Dec. 3, 2018).

38. For example, three Democratic governors in Virginia, Missouri, and Montana, each of whom sought to expand Medicaid, were repeatedly rebuffed by Republican-controlled state legislatures. *See* Kyle Cheney & Jennifer Haberkorn, Dem Trio Stuck in Medicaid Morass, Politico (Apr. 27, 2014), https://www.politico.com/story/2014/04/medicaid-obamacare-democrats-106051. *See also* Steven Schwinn, The Strange Politics of Medicaid Expansion, 47 J. Marshall L. Rev. 947 (2014).

39. Those seven states are: Michigan, New Hampshire, Pennsylvania, Indiana, Alaska, Montana, and Louisiana. *See* Congressional Research Service, Overview of the ACA Medicaid Expansion, https://fas.org/sgp/crs/misc/IF10399.pdf (last updated Dec. 3, 2018).

40. *Id.*

41. *See* Kaiser Family Foundation, Status of State Action on the Medicaid Expansion Decision (May 13, 2019), https://www.kff.org/health-reform/state-indicator/state-activity-around-expanding-medicaid-under-the-affordable-care-act/ (reporting 37 states including the District of Columbia have expanded Medicaid, and 14 states are not expanding Medicaid). States that have chosen to expand Medicaid may still change their mind and rescind the expansion. One state has passed laws such that Medicaid expansion must be renewed every year, and other states have included a trigger in their state law so the expansion will be repealed if the federal government decreases the matching rate for funding that covers care for the new eligible Medicaid beneficiaries. *Id.*

42. U.S. Centers for Medicare & Medicaid Services, HealthCare.gov, Medicaid & CHIP Coverage, https://www.healthcare.gov/medicaid-chip/getting-medicaid-chip/.

43. A 2014 report showed disparities in Medicaid enrollment growth between states that initially expanded (12.9% growth) and states that did not expand (2.6%). *See* Vikki Wachino, Samantha Artiga, & Robin Rudowitz, How Is the ACA Impacting Medicaid Enrollment, Kaiser Family Foundation (May 5, 2014), https://www.kff.org/medicaid/issue-brief/how-is-the-aca-impacting-medicaid-enrollment/.

44. Kaiser Family Foundation, Key Facts about the Uninsured Population (Dec. 7, 2018), https://www.kff.org/uninsured/fact-sheet/key-facts-about-the-uninsured-population/.

45. *See* Larisa Antonisse et al., The Effects of Medicaid Expansion under the ACA: Updated Findings from a Literature Review, Kaiser Family Foundation (Mar. 28, 2018), https://www.kff.org/medicaid/issue-brief/the-effects-of-medicaid-expansion-under-the-aca-updated-findings-from-a-literature-review-march-2018/ (collecting studies showing the positive impact of Medicaid expansion).

46. 42 U.S.C. § 1396a(a)(10)(A)(ii); 42 C.F.R. §§ 435.210–236.

47. For a list of optional categorically needy groups, consult U.S. Centers for Medicare & Medicaid Services, Medicaid.gov, List of Medicaid Eligibility Groups, https://www.medicaid.gov/medicaid-chip-program-information/by-topics/waivers/1115/downloads/list-of-eligibility-groups.pdf.

48. *See* National Immigration Law Center, Medical Assistance Programs for Immigrants in Various States (Jan. 2018), https://www.nilc.org/wp-content/uploads/2015/11/med-services-for-imms-in-states.pdf.

49. Kaiser Family Foundation, Medicaid/CHIP Coverage of Lawfully-Residing Immigrant Children and Pregnant Women (Jan. 1, 2018), https://www.kff.org/health-reform/state-indicator/medicaid-chip-coverage-of-lawfully-residing-immigrant-children-and-pregnaht-women/.

50. Laura Snyder & Robin Rudowitz, Trends in State Medicaid Programs: Looking Back and Looking Ahead, Kaiser Family Foundation (June 21, 2016), http://www.kff.org/report-section/trends-in-state-medicaid-programs-section-5-managed-care-and-delivery-system-reform/ (all states except Alaska, Connecticut, and Wyoming reported operating comprehensive Medicaid managed care programs as of June 2016).

51. Kaiser Family Foundation, Total Medicaid Managed Care Enrollment (2016), http://kff.org/medicaid/state-indicator/total-medicaid-mc-enrollment/.

52. Kaiser Family Foundation Medicaid: 3 Issues to Watch in 2013 (Feb. 22, 2013), http://kff.org/medicaid/fact-sheet/quick-take-medicaid-3-key-issues-to-watch-in-2013/.

53. 42 C.F.R. § 441.545.

54. *See* U.S. Centers for Medicare & Medicaid Services, Medicaid.gov, Mandatory & Optional Medicaid Benefits, https://www.medicaid.gov/medicaid/benefits/list-of-benefits/index.html (listing the mandatory and optional covered Medicaid services).

55. 42 U.S.C. § 1315.

56. *Id.*

57. *See* National Health Law Program, Section 1115 Waiver Tracking Chart,.

58. *See* U.S. Centers for Medicare & Medicaid Services, Medicaid.gov, Substance Use Disorder Demonstrations, https://www.medicaid.gov/state-resource-center/innovation-accelerator-program/program-areas/reducing-substance-use-disorders/1115-sud-demonstrations/index.html.

59. U.S. Centers for Medicare & Medicaid Services, Medicaid.gov, State Waiver List, https://www.medicaid.gov/medicaid/section-1115-demo/demonstration-and-waiver-list/index.html.

60. Department of Health and Human Services, State Medicaid Director Letter, Opportunities to Promote Work and Community Engagement Among Medicaid Beneficiaries (Jan. 11, 2018), https://www.medicaid.gov/federal-policy-guidance/downloads/smd18002.pdf.

61. National Acad. for State Health Policy , A Snapshot of State Proposals to Implement Medicaid Work Requirements Nationwide (last updated May 31, 2019), https://nashp.org/state-proposals-for-medicaid-work-and-community-engagement-requirements/.

62. *See* Section 1115 Waiver Tracking Chart, National Health Law Program, https://healthlaw.org/resource/sec-1115-waiver-tracking-chart-3-2/. The federal district court for the District of Columbia permanently enjoined Kentucky's Medicaid work requirement, ruling that the CMS had unlawfully granted the waiver without accounting for the harms Kentucky's program was likely to inflict. Stewart v. Azar, 366 F. Supp. 3d 125 (D.D.C. 2019). *See also* Gresham v. Azar, 363 F. Supp. 3d 165 (D.D.C. 2019) (invalidating Arkansas Medicaid work requirement.). Both of these cases are on appeal.

63. *See, for example*, Jared Bernstein & Hannah Katch, Trump's Medicaid Work Requirement Will Backfire, N.Y. Times (Jan. 11, 2018), https://www.nytimes.com/2018/01/11/opinion/trumps-medicaid-backfire.html.

64. Jessica Schubel & Judith Solomon, States Can Improve Health Outcomes and Lower Costs in Medicaid Using Existing Flexibility, Center on Budget & Policy Priorities (Apr. 9, 2015), http://www.cbpp.org/cms/index.cfm?fa=view&id=5301.

65. Rachel Garfield, Robin Rudowitz, & Mary Beth Musumeci, Implications of a Medicaid Work Requirement: National Estimates of Potential Coverage Losses, Kaiser Family Foundation (June 27, 2018), https://www.kff.org/medicaid/issue-brief/implications-of-a-medicaid-work-requirement-national-estimates-of-potential-coverage-losses/ (estimating that coverage losses may range from 1.4 to 4 million nonelderly Medicaid adults).

66. Joan Alker & Maggie Clark, After Two Months Under New Work Requirements, Thousands of Arkansans May Lose Medicaid Without Even Realizing the Rules Changed, Georgetown University Health Policy Institute (Aug. 15, 2018), https://ccf.georgetown.edu/2018/08/15/after-two-months-under-new-work-requirements-thousands-of-arkansans-may-lose-medicaid-without-even-realizing-the-rules-changed/. *See* Robert Pear, Federal Panel Alarmed as Thousands Are Dropped from Medicaid in Arkansas, N.Y. Times (Sept. 14, 2018), https://www.nytimes.com/2018/09/14/us/politics/arkansas-medicaid-work-requirements.html?module=inline.

67. Robin Rudowitz & MaryBeth Musumeci, The ACA and Medicaid Expansion Waivers, Kaiser Commission on Medicaid and the Uninsured, Kaiser Family Foundation (Nov. 20, 2015), http://kff.org/medicaid/issue-brief/the-aca-and-medicaid-expansion-waivers/.

68. Jessica Schubel & Judith Solomon, States Can Improve Health Outcomes and Lower Costs in Medicaid Using Existing Flexibility, Center on Budget & Policy Priorities (Apr. 9, 2015), http://www.cbpp.org/cms/index.cfm?fa=view&id=5301.

69. *Id.*

70. 42 U.S.C. § 1315. The CMS maintains an online database of pending and approved waivers application at https://www.medicaid.gov/medicaid/section-1115-demo/demonstration-and-waiver-list/index.html.

71. Some states have adopted payment reform waivers that allow them to distribute Medicaid funds to health organizations based on whether they achieve performance goals related to quality of care and outcomes. *See, for example*, U.S. Centers for Medicare & Medicaid Services, Medicaid.gov, Examining New York's Delivery System Reform Incentive Payment Demonstration: Achievements at the Demonstration's

Midpoint and Lessons for Other States (Apr. 2018), https://www.medicaid.gov/medicaid/section-1115-demo/downloads/evaluation-reports/ny-dsrip-case-study.pdf.

72. *See, for example*, New York State Department of Health, Medicaid and Managed Care, https://www.health.ny.gov/health_care/managed_care/mamctext.htm.

73. U.S. Centers for Medicare & Medicaid Services, Medicaid.gov, National Summary of Medicaid Managed Care Programs and Enrollment (June 2011), http://www.medicaid.gov/Medicaid-CHIP-Program-Information/By-Topics/Data-and-Systems/Downloads/2011-Medicaid-MC-Enrollment-Report.pdf (reporting that managed care enrollment increased from 23 million people and 58% of Medicaid enrollees in 2002 to 42 million people and 74% of enrollees in 2011). In 2017, managed care enrollment rose to 65.8 million individuals and 82% of total Medicaid enrollees. U.S. Centers for Medicare & Medicaid Services, Medicaid.gov, 2017 Managed Care Enrollment Summary, https://data.medicaid.gov/Enrollment/2017-Managed-Care-Enrollment-Summary/uw3d-3r25.

74. States must provide Medicaid to most aged, blind, and disabled individuals or couples who are receiving or are deemed to be receiving Supplemental Security Income (which provides cash payments to low-income seniors and people with disabilities who have limited resources and need assistance paying for essential needs such as food, clothing, and shelter). 42 C.F.R. § 435.120. SSI receipt does not guarantee eligibility for Medicaid, however. Some states elected an option provided by Section 209(b) of the Social Security Amendments of 1972 (P.L. 92-603), and set income limits on Medicaid for aged and disabled people that are more restrictive than the SSI income limits. *See* Alison Mitchell, The ACA Medicaid Expansion, Congressional Research Service (Dec. 30, 2014), https://fas.org/sgp/crs/misc/R43564.pdf.

75. *Id.*

76. *See* Kaiser Family Foundation, Where Are States Today? Medicaid and CHIP Eligibility Levels for Children, Pregnant Women, and Adults, http://www.kff.org/medicaid/factsheet/where-are-states-today-medicaid-and-chip/. In addition, a majority of states offer CHIP coverage to children in families with incomes up to 250% of the FPL. *Id.*

77. 42 U.S.C. § 1396a(a)(10)(A)(i)(IX); 42 C.F.R. § 435.150.

78. 42 C.F.R. §§ 435.300–435.350.

79. U.S. Centers for Medicare & Medicaid Services, HealthCare.gov, "Medicaid & CHIP Coverage," https://www.healthcare.gov/medicaid-chip/getting-medicaid-chip/.

80. 42 C.F.R. § 440.255 (emergency medical services); 42 C.F.R. § 435.139.

81. 8 U.S.C. § 1612; 42 C.F.R. § 435.406.

82. Quarters worked by parents when the immigrant was a dependent child, or by a spouse while married to the immigrant, count toward the immigrant's 40 quarters. 8 U.S.C. § 1631(b)(2)(A).

83. *See* U.S. Centers for Medicare & Medicaid Services, Letter to State Health Officials, Re: Medicaid and CHIP Coverage of "Lawfully Residing" Children and Pregnant Women, (July 1, 2010), https://www.medicaid.gov/federal-policy-guidance/downloads/sho10006.pdf.

84. Kaiser Family Foundation, Medicaid/CHIP Coverage of Lawfully-Residing Immigrant Children and Pregnant Women (last updated Jan. 1, 2019), https://

www.kff.org/health-reform/state-indicator/medicaid-chip-coverage-of-lawfully-residing-immigrant-children-and-pregnant-women/.

85. A current state-by-state compilation of medical assistance benefits available to immigrants is maintained by the National Immigration Law Center at https://www.nilc.org/issues/health-care/medical-assistance-various-states/.

86. *Id. See also* NY Health Access, Medicaid for Immigrants Who Are Not Permanent Residents http://www.wnylc.com/health/entry/33/. Individuals are considered PRUCOL if federal immigration agencies are aware they are in the country but are not contemplating their removal. *Id.*

87. *See* Cal. Welf. & Inst. Code § 14007.8 (West 2018) ("[A]n individual who is under 19 years of age and who does not have satisfactory immigration status . . . shall be eligible for the full scope of Medi-Cal benefits . . .").

88. *See, for example*, Aliessa v. Novello, 96 N.Y.2d 418 (N.Y. 2001). *See also* Helen Hershkoff & Stephen Loffredo, Tough Times and Weak Review: The 2008 Economic Meltdown and Enforcement of Socio-Economic Rights in U.S. State Courts, in Aoife Nolan ed., Economic and Social Rights After the Global Financial Crisis 234, 250 (Cambridge 2014).

89. *See* 42 C.F.R. § 600.110. *See also* U.S. Centers for Medicare & Medicaid Services, Medicaid.gov, Basic Health Program, https://www.medicaid.gov/basic-health-program/index.html (listing New York and Minnesota as two states to use a Basic Health Program).

90. *Id.*

91. 42 U.S.C. § 1396a.

92. 42 C.F.R. § 435.116 (pregnant women); 42 C.F.R. § 435.118 (infants and children).

93. 42 U.S.C. § 1396a(e)(14)(I)(i). For state-by-state eligibility levels for Medicaid beneficiaries, *see* Kaiser Family Foundation, Where Are States Today? Medicaid and CHIP Eligibility Levels for Children, Pregnant Women, and Adults (last updated Mar. 31, 2019), http://www.kff.org/medicaid/fact-sheet/where-are-states-today-medicaid-and-chip/.

94. 42 U.S.C. § 1396a(e)(14); 26 U.S.C. § 36B(d)(2)(B); 42 C.F.R. § 435.603.

95. *See* 42 C.F.R. § 435.603(j) (listing groups excluded from MAGI methodology).

96. 42 U.S.C. § 1396a(e)(14)(D).

97. National Health Law Program, Advocate's Guide to MAGI (last updated Aug. 22, 2018), https://healthlaw.org/resource/advocates-guide-to-magi-updated-guide-for-2018/.

98. 26 U.S.C. § 36B(d)(2)(A); 42 C.F.R. § 435.603(f).

99. *See* Bryon Gross, Modified Adjusted Gross Income (MAGI): A Primer, National Health Law Program (Apr. 1, 2013), https://9kqpw4dcaw91s37kozm5jx17-wpengine.netdna-ssl.com/wp-content/uploads/2018/09/2013_04_Vol_12_Health_Advocate.pdf.

100. 42 C.F.R. § 435.603(d).

101. 42 C.F.R. § 435.603(d)(2)(i). As of 2018, dependents must file a tax return if they received at least $12,000 in earned income; $1,050 in unearned income; or if the earned and unearned income together totals more than the greater of $1,050 or

earned income (up to $12,000) plus $350. In general, unearned income is defined as investment income.

102. 42 C.F.R. § 435.603(f)(3).

103. 42 C.F.R. § 435.603(b).

104. *Id.*

105. *See* 42 C.F.R. § 435.603. Federal law also excludes from MAGI "scholarships, awards, or fellowship grants used for education purposes and not for living expenses," and certain distributions to Native Americans. 42 C.F.R. § 435.603(e)(2)–(3).

106. For a list of state programs, *see* Kaiser Family Foundation, Medicaid Eligibility through Buy-In Programs for Working People with Disabilities, https://www.kff.org/other/state-indicator/medicaid-eligibility-through-buy-in-programs-for-working-people-with-disabilities/?currentTimeframe=0&sortModel=%7B%22colI d%22:%22Location%22,%22sort%22:%22asc%22%7D.

107. New York Department of Health, Medicaid Buy-in Program for Working People with Disabilities, https://www.health.ny.gov/health_care/medicaid/program/buy_in/index.htm.

108. 42 U.S.C. § 1396r-6(a)(1).

109. 42 U.S.C. § 1396r-6(b)(3)(A)(iii). *See* National Health Law Program, The Advocate's Guide to MAGI (last updated Apr. 2018), https://healthlaw.org/resource/advocates-guide-to-magi-updated-guide-for-2018/.

110. 42 U.S.C. § 1396r-6(b)(5).

111. Medicare Access and CHIP Reauthorization Act of 2015, Pub. L. No. 114-10, 129 Stat. 87 (2015).

112. *See* Andy Schneider, Gutting Medicaid Transitional Medical Assistance: Watch What We Waive, Not What We Say, Georgetown University Health Policy Institute (Mar. 15, 2018), https://ccf.georgetown.edu/2018/03/15/gutting-medicaid-transitional-medical-assistance-watch-what-we-waive-not-what-we-say/.

113. *See* Kaiser Family Foundation, Where Are States Today? Medicaid and CHIP Eligibility Levels for Children, Pregnant Women, and Adults (Mar. 31, 2019), https://www.kff.org/medicaid/fact-sheet/where-are-states-today-medicaid-and-chip/.

114. 45 C.F.R. § 155.305(f)(2).

115. Rachel Garfield, Anthony Damico, & Kendal Orgera, The Coverage Gap: Uninsured Poor Adults in States that Do Not Expand Medicaid, Kaiser Family Foundation (Mar. 21, 2019), https://www.kff.org/report-section/the-coverage-gap-uninsured-poor-adults-in-states-that-do-not-expand-medicaid-issue-brief/.

116. 42 U.S.C. § 18083.

117. 42 U.S.C. § 1396a(a)(10)(C).

118. Kaiser Family Foundation, The Medicaid Medically Needy Program: Spending and Enrollment Update (Dec. 2012), https://www.kff.org/wp-content/uploads/2013/01/4096.pdf.

119. 42 C.F.R. §§ 435.300 et seq.

120. 42 U.S.C. § 1396a(a)(17)(D).

121. 42 U.S.C. § 1396a(e)(14)(C); 42 C.F.R. § 435.603(g).

122. *Id.*
123. 42 C.F.R. § 435.603(j)(4).
124. *See* 42 C.F.R. § 435.603(j) (listing groups excluded from MAGI methodology).
125. 42 U.S.C. § 1396a(e)(14)(D); 42 C.F.R. § 435.603(j).
126. *See id.* (authorizing states to apply an asset test to Non-MAGI populations); 42 C.F.R. 435.601(d) (allowing states to use less restrictive income-counting methodologies for Non-MAGI populations). State asset limits for Non-MAGI Medicaid vary widely. New York, for example, sets a total resource limit of $22,800 for a household of two (excluding the primary residence, IRAs, and certain other assets). *See* http://www.wnylc.com/health/entry/15/. In many states, the asset limit for a household of two is only $3,000. *See* American Council on Aging, State Specific Medicaid Eligibility Requirements, https://www.medicaidplanningassistance.org/state-specific-medicaid-eligibility.
127. 42 U.S.C. § 1396p(c).
128. *Id. See, for example,* New York State Department of Health, Administrative Directive 06 OMM/ADM-5 (July 20, 2006), http://www.health.ny.gov/health_care/medicaid/publications/docs/adm/06adm-5.pdf.
129. 42 U.S.C. § 1396p(c)(1)(C). *See* Western New York Law Center, Transfer of Assets Rules in Medicaid—the Deficit Reduction Act of 2005, http://wnylc.com/health/pdf/38/ (last updated Aug. 26, 2014).
130. One state, California, limits the look-back period to only 30 months. *See* John A. Miller, Medicaid Planning for Long-Term Care: California Style, 41 ACTEC L.J. 331, 343–344 (2015).
131. 42 U.S.C. § 1396p(c)(1)(B). *See also* Enclosures in Letter to State Directors, New Medicaid Transfer of Assets Rules Under the Deficit Reduction Act of 2005 (July 26, 2006), http://www.canhr.org/medcal/PDFs/TOAEnclosure.pdf.
132. The penalty period does not begin to run until the applicant is in the nursing home, is otherwise eligible for Medicaid (i.e., is below the asset limit), and has submitted an application for Medicaid (which will inevitably be denied, because of the transfers). 42 U.S.C. § 1396p(c)(1)(B)(ii).
133. 42 U.S.C. § 1396p(c)(2)(A).
134. 42 U.S.C. § 1396p(c)(2)(B).
135. 42 U.S.C. § 1396p(c)(2)(C).
136. 42 U.S.C. § 1396p(d)(4)(A).
137. 42 U.S.C. § 1396p(d)(2).
138. 42 U.S.C. §§ 1396p(c)(2)(B)(iv), 1396p(d)(4)(A).
139. Keep in mind that trusts are treated somewhat differently under the SSI and Medicaid programs, depending on the structure of the trust and how it is treated under the relevant state law. *See* U.S. Social Security Administration, Spotlight on Trusts (2012), http://www.ssa.gov/ssi/spotlights/spot-trusts.htm.
140. Some legal aid and legal services organizations and bar associations provide this service at no charge.
141. 42 U.S.C. § 1396p(d)(4)(C).
142. 42 U.S.C. § 1396p(d)(3)(B).

143. 42 U.S.C. § 1396p(a).

144. 42 U.S.C. § 1396p(a)(1).

145. Before imposing such a lien, the state must first give the individual notice and an opportunity to contest at a hearing the state's finding that the individual "cannot reasonably be expected to be discharged from the medical institution and to return home." 42 U.S.C. § 1396p(a)(1)(B)(ii).

146. 42 U.S.C. § 1396p(a)(3).

147. 42 U.S.C. § 1396r-5.

148. 42 U.S.C. § 1395r-5(h)(1)(A). *See* U.S. Centers for Medicare & Medicaid Services, Medicaid.gov, Letter to State Medicaid Directors, Re: Affordable Care Act's Amendments to the Spousal Impoverishment Statute (May 7, 2015), https://www.medicaid.gov/federal-policy-guidance/downloads/smd050715.pdf.

149. U.S. Centers for Medicare & Medicaid Services, Medicaid.gov, Spousal Impoverishment, https://www.medicaid.gov/medicaid/eligibility/spousal-impoverishment/index.html.

150. *Id.*

151. 42 U.S.C. § 1396r-5(d)(1).

152. 42 U.S.C. § 1396r-5(d)(5).

153. U.S. Centers for Medicare & Medicaid Services, Medicaid.gov, Spousal Impoverishment, https://www.medicaid.gov/medicaid/eligibility/spousal-impoverishment/index.html.

154. 42 U.S.C. §§ 1396r-5(e)(2), 1396r-5(f)(3).

155. 42 U.S.C. § 1396n(c)–(d).

156. 42 U.S.C. § 1396n(e).

157. 42 U.S.C. § 1396d. *See also* Medicaid.gov, Mandatory & Optional Medicaid Benefits, https://www.medicaid.gov/medicaid/benefits/list-of-benefits/index.html   (listing mandatory and optional services for state Medicaid programs).

158. 42 U.S.C. § 1396d.

159. 42 C.F.R. § 440.230(b).

160. 42 C.F.R. § 440.230(c).

161. *See* Weaver v. Reagan, 886 F.2d 194 (8th Cir. 1989).

162. U.S. Centers for Medicare & Medicaid Services, Medicaid.gov, List of Medicaid Benefits, https://www.medicaid.gov/medicaid/benefits/list-of-benefits/index.html.

163. 42 C.F.R. § 440.230(c).

164. *See* 42 C.F.R. § 440.230. *See also* Charleston Memorial Hospital v. Conrad, 693 F.2d 324 (4th Cir. 1982); *see generally* Alexander v. Choate, 469 U.S. 287 (1985). *But see* Bontrager v. Indiana Family & Social Services Administration, 697 F.3d 604 (7th Cir. 2012).

165. 42 U.S.C. § 1396a(a)(30).

166. 42 U.S.C. § 1396d(r). *See also* U.S. Centers for Medicare & Medicaid Services, Medicaid.gov, Early and Periodic Screening, Diagnostic and Treatment, https://www.medicaid.gov/medicaid/benefits/epsdt/index.html.

167. Families USA, Medicaid's Children's Benefit—EPSDT—Supports the Unique Needs and Healthy Development of Children (Nov. 2018), https://familiesusa.org/sites/

default/files/product_documents/Report-EPSDT_Supports_the_Unique_Needs_
and_Healthy_Development_of_Children.pdf.

168. *See* Office of Inspector General, Department of Health & Human Services, Most
Medicaid Children in Nine States Are Not Receiving All Required Preventive
Screening Services (May 2010), https://oig.hhs.gov/oei/reports/oei-05-08-
00520.pdf (reporting 76% of children sampled in nine states did not receive
one or more required EPSDT service); Medicaid's Health Care Benefit Package
for Children: EPSDT, National Conference of State Legislatures (May 2, 2014),
http://www.ncsl.org/research/health/medicaids-early-and-periodic-screening-
diagnostic-and-treatment-epsdt-participation-rates-2011.aspx (finding only 60%
of the 37 million children eligible for EPSDT services received them in fiscal year
2012).

169. U.S. Centers for Medicare & Medicaid Services, Dual Eligible Beneficiaries
Under Medicare and Medicaid, (May 2018), http://www.cms.gov/Outreach-
and-Education/Medicare-Learning-Network-MLN/MLNProducts/downloads/
Medicare_Beneficiaries_Dual_Eligibles_At_a_Glance.pdf.

170. 42 U.S.C. § 1396d(p).

171. Center for Medicare Advocacy, The QMB Benefit: How to Get It, How to Use It (June
2010), http://www.medicareadvocacy.org/old-site/Projects/AdvocatesAlliance/
IssueBriefs/10_06.14.QMB.pdf.

172. 42 U.S.C. § 1396b(i)(26).

173. 42 U.S.C. § 1396u-7(b)(5). Linking essential health benefits and benchmark equivalence creates room for advocacy to raise the floor by expanding "essential health
benefits." *See* U.S. Centers for Medicare & Medicaid Services, Medicaid.gov, Letter
to State Medicaid Director, Re: Essential Health Benefits in the Medicaid Program
(Nov. 2012), http://www.medicaid.gov/Federal-Policy-Guidance/Downloads/
SMD-12-003.pdf.

174. *See* U.S. Centers for Medicare & Medicaid Services, Healthcare.gov, Preventive
Health Services, https://www.healthcare.gov/coverage/preventive-care-benefits/.

175. 42 U.S.C. § 1396d(a)(4)(C).

176. 42 U.S.C. § 1396a(a)(10)(A)(ii).

177. 42 U.S.C. § 1396r-1c.

178. The U.S. Supreme Court upheld the Hyde Amendment against constitutional
challenge in *Harris v. McRae*, 448 U.S. 297 (1980). For a detailed analysis and critique of this restriction on low-income women's reproductive choice, *see* Center
for Reproductive Rights, Whose Choice? How the Hyde Amendment Harms
Poor Women (2010), https://reproductiverights.org/sites/crr.civicactions.net/
files/documents/Hyde_Report_FINAL_nospreads.pdf. For current state policies
on Medicaid coverage for abortion, *see* Kaiser Family Foundation, State Health
Facts: State Funding of Abortions Under Medicaid (as of June 21, 2019), https://www.
kff.org/medicaid/state-indicator/abortion-under-medicaid/?currentTimeframe=0&
sortModel=%7B%22colId%22:%22Location%22,%22sort%22:%22asc%22%7D.

179. 42 U.S.C. § 1396d.

180. *See generally* https://www.birthcenters.org.

181. Patient Protection and Affordable Care Act (PPACA), Public Law No. 111-148, 124 Stat. 119, § 2406.

182. 42 U.S.C. § 1396n(i).

183. 42 C.F.R. § 441.15.

184. 42 U.S.C. § 1396n(g)(2).

185. Kaiser Family Foundation, Medicaid Benefits: Targeted Case Management (last updated 2018), https://www.kff.org/medicaid/state-indicator/targeted-case-management/.

186. 42 U.S.C. § 1396a(a)(30)(A).

187. *See* Armstrong v. Exceptional Child Center, Inc., 135 S. Ct. 1378 (2015) (holding that the Medicaid Act does not authorize private rights of action by Medicaid providers against a state for failure to comply with the reimbursement-rate standard in § 1396a(a)(30)(A)). *But see* Hoag Memorial Hospital Presbyterian v. Price, 866 F.3d 1072 (9th Cir. 2017) (finding the CMS's approval of California's 10% reduction in rates for outpatient services a violation of the Administrative Procedure Act).

188. *See, for example*, Esther Hing et al., Acceptance of New Patients with Public and Private Insurance by Office-Based Physicians: United States, 2013, National Center for Health Statistics, Center for Disease Control & Prevention (Mar. 2015), https://www.cdc.gov/nchs/data/databriefs/db195.pdf (documenting physician reluctance to accept Medicaid patients). *See also* Kaiser Family Foundation, Medicaid Managed Care Tracker, https://www.kff.org/data-collection/medicaid-managed-care-market-tracker/ (noting that Medicaid managed care plans serve a growing majority of Medicaid beneficiaries nationally).

189. 42 U.S.C. § 1396o(a)(3). *See* Federal Requirements and State Options: Premiums and Cost Sharing, Medicaid and CHIP Payment and Access Commission *2 (Nov. 2017), https://www.macpac.gov/wp-content/uploads/2017/11/Federal-Requirements-and-State-Options_Premiums-and-Cost-Sharing.pdf (noting 27 states impose cost sharing on adults for nonpreventive physician care, and 38 states require it for prescription drugs). Total expenses for cost sharing and premiums may not exceed 5% of one's quarterly or monthly household income. *Id.*; 42 C.F.R. § 447.56.

190. 42 U.S.C. § 1396r-6.

191. 42 C.F.R. § 447.56.

192. *See* 42 U.S.C. § 1396a(a)(70).

193. 42 U.S.C. § 1396r-1. For a list of states that offer presumptive eligibility, *see* U.S. Centers for Medicare & Medicaid Services, Presumptive Eligibility for Medicaid and CHIP Coverage, https://www.medicaid.gov/medicaid/outreach-and-enrollment/presumptive-eligibility/index.html.

  See also Tricia Brooks, Medicaid Presumptive Eligibility Coming to a Hospital Near You, Georgetown University Health Policy Institute (Mar. 28, 2013), http://ccf.georgetown.edu/all/medicaid-presumptive-eligibility-coming-to-a-hospital-near-you/.

194. *See* 42 U.S.C. § 1396r-1(e).

195. 42 U.S.C. § 1396a(a)(34).

196. *See* Kaiser Family Foundation, Medicaid Managed Care Market Tracker, http://www.kff.org/data-collection/medicaid-managed-care-market-tracker/.

197. *See* Kaiser Family Foundation, People with Disabilities and Medicaid Managed Care: Key Issues to Consider (Feb. 2012), http://www.kff.org/medicaid/upload/8278.pdf.

198. Kaiser Family Foundation, Total Medicaid Managed Care Enrollment, http://kff.org/medicaid/state-indicator/total-medicaid-mc-enrollment/. The federal government encourages states to seek Section 1115 demonstration project waivers to create specialize managed care plans for specific groups, including managed care plans for aged and disabled Medicare beneficiaries by pursuing "waivers," which allow states to create specialized managed care plans for certain populations, including people who are eligible for both Medicaid and Medicare. Half the states have managed care plan waivers to cover these "dual eligibles." *See* Kaiser Family Foundation, Medicaid Managed Care: Key Data, Trends, and Issues (Feb. 2012), http://www.kff.org/medicaid/upload/8046-02.pdf.

199. 42 U.S.C. § 1396a(a)(30).

200. Michael Sparer, Managed Care: Costs, Access, and Quality of Care, Robert Wood Johnson Foundation (Sept. 2012), http://www.rwjf.org/content/dam/farm/reports/reports/2012/rwjf401106.

201. The acronym used by Centers for Medicare & Medicaid Services is MLTSS (Managed Long Term Services and Supports).

202. *See, for example*, New York State Department of Health, 2007 MLTC Model Contract (Jan. 2011), https://www.health.ny.gov/health_care/managed_care/mltc/pdf/mltc_contract.pdf.

203. *See* Virgil Dickson, Managed-Care Plans Increasingly Taking Over Medicaid Long-Term Care. Not Everyone Is Happy About It, Modern Healthcare (Nov. 26, 2016), https://www.modernhealthcare.com/article/20161126/MAGAZINE/311269984.

204. *See, for example*, New York State Department of Health, Consumer Checklist: Asking the Right Questions About Medicaid Managed Care Options, https://www.health.ny.gov/health_care/managed_care/living_with_hiv/docs/consumer_checklist.pdf.

205. *See, for example*, N.Y. Soc. Serv. Law § 364-j (McKinney 2012). *See also* New York State Department of Health, Managed Care Bill of Rights, http://www.health.ny.gov/health_care/managed_care/billofrights/bill.htm.

206. U.S. Department of Health & Human Services, Consumer Bill of Rights and Responsibilities (last revised 1998), https://archive.ahrq.gov/hcqual/cborr/exsumm.html. In 1997, President Clinton created the Advisory Commission on Consumer Protection and Quality on the Health Care Industry. This committee, consisting of consumers, businesses, labor, health care providers, health plans, and health care quality and financing experts, wrote the Consumer Bill of Rights in health care. *Id.*

207. 42 C.F.R. §§ 431.200 et seq.

208. 42 C.F.R. § 431.210.

209. 42 C.F.R. § 431.211.

210. 42 C.F.R. § 431.230.

211. 42 C.F.R. § 431.224.

212. 42 C.F.R. § 431.244.

213. 42 C.F.R. § 431.242.

214. *Id.*

215. 42 C.F.R. § 431.244.

216. 42 C.F.R. § 438.402. *See* 81 Fed. Reg. 27498 (May 6, 2016), https://www.gpo.gov/fdsys/pkg/FR-2016-05-06/pdf/2016-09581.pdf.

217. 42 C.F.R. § 438.402.

218. 42 C.F.R. § 438.400.

219. *Id.*

220. 42 C.F.R. § 438.406.

221. *Id.*

222. 42 C.F.R. § 438.402.

223. 42 C.F.R. § 438.406.

224. *Id.*

225. *Id.*

226. 42 C.F.R. § 438.408.

227. 42 C.F.R. § 438.408(f).

228. 42 U.S.C. § 18083.

229. The CMS lists each state's Medicaid program contact information at https://www.medicaid.gov/about-us/contact-us/contact-state-page.html.

230. 42 C.F.R. § 435.904.

231. 42 U.S.C. § 18083.

232. 42 C.F.R. § 435.403.

233. 42 C.F.R. § 435.403(j).

234. 42 C.F.R. Ch. IV, Subch. D, Part 457.

235. *See, for example*, Dee Mahan, G.M. Kenney, & B.D. Sommers, The Children's Health Insurance Program, Families USA (Sept. 2017), https://familiesusa.org/product/children-health-insurance-program-chip; Laura Wherry et al., The Role of Public Health Insurance in Reducing Child Poverty, 16 Academic Pediatrics S98 (Apr. 2016), https://www.academicpedsjnl.net/article/S1876-2859(15)00384-8/fulltext.

236. For a list of CHIP income eligibility standards by state, *see* Kaiser Family Foundation, Where Are States Today? Medicaid and CHIP Eligibility Levels for Children, Pregnant Women, and Adults, http://kff.org/medicaid/fact-sheet/where-are-states-today-medicaid-and-chip/.

237. 42 U.S.C. § 1396d(r). The EPSDT is a much more robust benefit package than the Medicaid services available for adults, and includes enhanced protections for children's access and coverage for benefits that they need. *See* U.S. Centers for Medicare & Medicaid Services, Medicaid.gov, Early and Periodic Screening, Diagnostic, and Treatment, https://www.medicaid.gov/medicaid/benefits/epsdt/index.html.

238. 42 U.S.C. § 1396u-7.

239. For information about state CHIP eligibility and benefits, *see* https://www.healthcare.gov/medicaid-chip/childrens-health-insurance-program/.

240. 42 C.F.R. § 457.609.

241. Healthy Kids Act, Pub. L. No. 115-120, 132 Stat. 28 (2018). *See* Kelly Whitener, HEALTHY KIDS ACT (Helping Ensure Access for Little Ones, Toddlers and Hopeful Youth by Keeping Insurance Delivery Stable Act), Georgetown Univ. Health Policy Inst. (Jan. 24, 2018), https://ccf.georgetown.edu/2018/01/24/healthy-kids-act-helping-ensure-access-for-little-ones-toddlers-and-hopeful-youth-by-keeping-insurance-delivery-stable-act/. The Republican Congress refused to reauthorize CHIP until the eleventh hour, creating administrative chaos for the states and causing needless distress for thousands of low-income families, many of whom received notices that their children's health insurance would be canceled. *See, for example*, Jordan Weismann, The Fight Over CHIP Has Reached New Heights of Absurdity (or Depths of Cruelty), Slate (Jan. 9, 2018), https://slate.com/business/2018/01/chip-is-about-to-run-out-of-funding-again.html; Maureen Hensley-Quinn, December Is the Most Critical Month Yet for States' CHIP Funding, National Academy for State Health Policy (Dec. 5, 2017), https://nashp.org/december-is-the-most-critical-month-yet-for-states-chip-funding/.
242. Bipartisan Budget Act of 2018, Pub. L. No. 115-123, 132 Stat. 64 (2018).
243. 45 C.F.R. § 155.20.
244. 45 C.F.R. § 155.105.
245. *See* U.S. Department of Health and Human Services, Coverage Denied: How the Current Health Insurance System Leaves Millions Behind 1 (2009); Peter Harbage, Too Sick for Health Care, Center for American Progress (July 2009), http://cdn.americanprogress.org/wp-content/uploads/issues/2009/07/pdf/too_sick.pdf.
246. *See* Sara Rosenbaum, The Patient Protection and Affordable Care Act: Implications for Health Policy and Practice Public Health Rep. 2011 Jan.–Feb.; 126(1): 130–135, https://www.ncbi.nlm.nih.gov/pmc/articles/PMC3001814/.
247. *See* Thomas Rice, L.Y. Unruh, E. van Ginneken, P. Rosenau, & A.J. Barnes, Universal Coverage Reforms in the USA: From Obamacare through Trump, 122 Health Policy 398 (July 2018), https://www.sciencedirect.com/science/article/pii/S0168851018301544#sec0015.
248. *See* Congressional Budget Office, The Effects of Terminating Payments for Cost-Sharing Reductions (Aug. 2017), https://www.cbo.gov/system/files?file=115th-congress-2017-2018/reports/53009-costsharingreductions.pdf. The current challenge to the ACA's constitutionality is Texas v. United States, 430 F. Supp. 3d. 579 (N.D. Tex. 2018) (appeal pending). *See also* Nicholas Bagley, Why Trump's New Push to Kill Obamacare Is So Alarming, N.Y. Times (Mar. 27, 2019), https://www.nytimes.com/2019/03/27/opinion/trump-obamacare-affordable-care-act.html (criticizing Trump administration refusal to defend the ACA in court.).
249. 45 C.F.R. § 155.20 (definitions, including QHP); 45 C.F.R. § 156.200 (QHP standards).
250. *See* 45 C.F.R. §§ 147.150, 156.110EHB, 156.111.
251. *See* 45 C.F.R. §§ 156.100, 156.111. A state may choose its benchmark plan from, among others, "the largest health plan by enrollment in any of the three largest small group insurance products by enrollment," or any of the three largest health benefit plan options offered to state employees, or the largest HMO in the state. *Id.*

252. 45 C.F.R. § 156.230 (network adequacy standard); *see also* 45 C.F.R. § 156.235. (essential community providers.)

253. 45 C.F.R. § 156.210.

254. 45 C.F.R. § 158.210.

255. 45 C.F.R. § 156.220.

256. Danielle Garrett, Turning to Fairness: Insurance Discrimination against Women Today and the Affordable Care Act, National Women's Law Center (Mar. 2012), https://www.nwlc.org/sites/default/files/pdfs/nwlc_2012_turningtofairness_report.pdf.

257. 45 C.F.R. § 156.110.

258. 45 C.F.R. § 156.115.

259. 45 C.F.R. § 156.122.

260. 78 Fed. Reg. 12834, 12846 (Feb. 25, 2013).

261. 45 C.F.R. § 156.115(b). *See* U.S. Centers for Medicare & Medicaid Services, Frequently Asked Questions on Essential Health Benefits Bulletin 5 (Feb. 17, 2012), http://www.cms.gov/CCIIO/Resources/Files/Downloads/ehb-faq-508.pdf.

262. *See* Aids Institute, National Health Law Program, Administrative Complaint, Discriminatory Pharmacy Benefits Design in Select Qualified Health Plans in Florida, filed May 29, 2014, with Office of Civil Rights, U.S. Department of Health and Human Services, https://healthlaw.org/resource/nhelp-and-the-aids-institute-complaint-to-hhs-re-hiv-aids-discrimination-by-fl/.

263. 45 C.F.R. § 156.140. The Centers for Medicare & Medicaid Services website offers advice on how to evaluate and choose a health plan through the Marketplace at https://www.healthcare.gov/choose-a-plan/.

264. 45 C.F.R. §§ 156.135, 156.155.

265. 45 C.F.R. § 155.205(a)–(b).

266. 45 C.F.R. § 155.405.

267. 45 C.F.R. § 155.205(c).

268. 45 C.F.R. § 155.405. The federal government is required to design a single, streamlined form. 42 U.S.C. § 18083(b)(1)(A). States can develop their own form as long as it meets federal standards. 42 U.S.C. § 18083(b)(1)(B).

269. 45 C.F.R. § 155.302.

270. 45 C.F.R. § 155.305. *See* 42 U.S.C. § 1396w-3(b)(1)(C).

271. 45 C.F.R. § 155.310(e).

272. 45 C.F.R. §§ 155.310(f), 155.355.

273. 45 C.F.R. § 155.210.

274. Navigators play an important role in educating consumers about open enrollment and their various coverage options. *See* Anne Markus, Jessica Sharac, Jennifer Tolbert, Sara Rosenbaum, & Julia Zur, Community Health Centers' Experiences in a More Mature ACA Market, Kaiser Family Foundation (Aug. 23, 2018), https://www.kff.org/medicaid/issue-brief/community-health-centers-experiences-in-a-more-mature-aca-market/.

275. 45 C.F.R. § 155.210(e).

276. 45 C.F.R. § 155.210.

277. 45 C.F.R. § 155.210(e).

278. https://www.cms.gov/CCIIO/Programs-and-Initiatives/Health-Insurance-Marketplaces/Downloads/2018-Navigator-Grant-Recipients.PDF. Many states maintain their own website for accessing navigators. *See, for example,* New York State Department of Health, Navigators, https://nystateofhealth.ny.gov/agent/navigators; DC.gov, Health Benefit Exchange Authority, https://hbx.dc.gov/page/navigator-program.

279. 45 C.F.R. § 155.305(a).

280. 45 C.F.R. § 155.305(a)(1).

281. 45 C.F.R. § 155.315(c).

282. 45 C.F.R. § 155.315(f).

283. 45 C.F.R. § 155.310(a)(2)–(3).

284. 45 C.F.R. § 155.305(a)(2).

285. *See* Estelle v. Gamble, 429 U.S. 97 (1976).

286. *See* Kathy Rowings & Maeghan Gilmore, The Affordable Care Act and County Jails, National Association of Counties (Oct. 2014), http://www.naco.org/sites/default/files/documents/QandA-ACA%20Inmate%20Healthcare-OCT2014%20(2).pdf.

287. 45 C.F.R. § 155.305(a)(3)(i). The regulations require residency in the "service area of the exchange," but since all Exchanges currently operate on a statewide basis, the "service area of the exchange" means in effect the state in which the Exchange operates.

288. *Id.*

289. 45 C.F.R. § 155.305(a)(3)(ii).

290. 45 C.F.R. § 155.305(a)(3).

291. 45 C.F.R. § 155.315(f).

292. 45 C.F.R. § 155.315(i).

293. 45 C.F.R. § 155.420.

294. *Id.*

295. *Id.*

296. 26 U.S.C. § 36B.

297. 26 C.F.R. § 1.36B-2 (c)(3)(v)(A)(2). The "affordability" standard is adjusted annually to reflect changes in the ratio of income growth to premium growth. 26 C.F.R. § 1.36B-2 (c)(3)(v)(C). In 2019 the rate was 9.56% of household income. Changes to this percentage will appear on HealthCare.gov at https://www.healthcare.gov/have-job-based-coverage/change-to-marketplace-plan/.

298. 26 U.S.C. § 36B.

299. *See* HealthCare.Gov, https://www.healthcare.gov/have-job-based-coverage/change-to-marketplace-plan/.

300. *See* Shefali Luthra, Fixing Obamacare's Family Glitch Depends on the Outcome of November's Elections, Kaiser Health News (Oct. 23, 2018), https://khn.org/news/fixing-obamacares-family-glitch-hinges-on-outcome-of-november-elections/.

301. 26 C.F.R. § 1.36B-2.

302. 45 C.F.R. § 155.305(f)(2).

303. For IRS's description of premium tax credit eligibility and filing requirements, *see* https://www.irs.gov/affordable-care-act/individuals-and-families/eligibility-for-the-premium-tax-credit.

304. *See* HealthCare.Gov, https://www.healthcare.gov/have-job-based-coverage/change-to-marketplace-plan/.

305. *See* 26 C.F.R. § 1.36B-3(d). *See also* National Health Law Program, The Advocate's Guide to MAGI *79 (last updated 2018), https://healthlaw.org/resource/advocates-guide-to-magi-updated-guide-for-2018/.

306. Congressional Budget Office, The Effects of Terminating Payments for Cost-Sharing Reductions (Aug. 2017), https://www.cbo.gov/system/files?file=115th-congress-2017-2018/reports/53009-costsharingreductions.pdf.

307. *See* Letter from Jefferson B. Sessions III, Attorney General, to Steven Mnuchin, Secretary of U.S. Department of Treasury, and Don Wright, Acting Secretary of U.S. Department of Health and Human Services (Oct. 11, 2017), https://www.hhs.gov/sites/default/files/csr-payment-memo.pdf.

308. Congressional Budget Office, The Effects of Terminating Payments for Cost-Sharing Reductions (Aug. 2017), https://www.cbo.gov/system/files?file=115th-congress-2017-2018/reports/53009-costsharingreductions.pdf.

309. 42 C.F.R. §§ 431.201, 431.205, 431.220.

310. 42 C.F.R. § 431.206.

311. 42 C.F.R. § 431.210.

312. 42 C.F.R. § 431.220.

313. 42 C.F.R. §§ 431.200, 431.205.

314. *See* U.S. Centers for Medicare & Medicaid Services, The Affordable Care Act's New Patient's Bill of Rights, https://www.cms.gov/CCIIO/Resources/Fact-Sheets-and-FAQs/aca-new-patients-bill-of-rights.html.

315. *See, for example*, 45 C.F.R. § 146.121 (prohibiting insurers from discriminating against participants based on a health factor); 26 U.S.C. § 35(e)(2) (listing consumer protection requirements for coverage in qualified health plans); 42 U.S.C. § 1395dd(g)–(h) (prohibiting hospitals from discriminating against individuals or inquiring into method of payment and insurance status before providing emergency care).

316. *See* 75 Fed. Reg. 34538 (June 17, 2010). A list of protections that are and are not enforced for grandfathered plans is available at https://www.healthcare.gov/health-care-law-protections/grandfathered-plans/. A plan may lose its "grandfathered" status if it makes changes that significantly reduce overage or increase costs. *Id.*

317. *See* U.S. Centers for Medicare & Medicaid Services, Ensuring Compliance with the Health Market Reforms, http://cciio.cms.gov/programs/marketreforms/Compliance/index.html.

318. 45 C.F.R. §§ 146.121, 147.108. Certain patient protection provisions of the ACA were implemented concurrently through regulations of the Departments of Health and Human Services, Treasury (IRS) and Labor. *See* 75 Fed. Reg. 37187 (June 28, 2010), https://www.federalregister.gov/articles/2010/06/28/2010-15278/

patient-protection-and-affordable-care-act-preexisting-condition-exclusions-lifetime-and-annual.

319. 45 C.F.R. § 147.102. Employers may also charge differential premiums based on employee participation in a nondiscriminatory wellness program. 45 C.F.R. § 146.121(f). *See* Workplace Wellness Programs (Health Affairs, May 16, 2013), http://healthaffairs.org/healthpolicybriefs/brief_pdfs/healthpolicybrief_93.pdf.

320. Gary Claxton, Cynthia Cox, Anthony Damico, Larry Levitt, & Karen Politz, Pre-existing Conditions and Medical Underwriting in the Individual Insurance Market Prior to the ACA, Kaiser Family Foundation (Dec. 12, 2016), https://www.kff.org/health-reform/issue-brief/pre-existing-conditions-and-medical-underwriting-in-the-individual-insurance-market-prior-to-the-aca/.

321. 45 C.F.R. § 147.104(a) (exempting plans with networks in certain areas, which may limit coverage to people who live within those areas). *See* 47 C.F.R. § 147.104(c).

322. 45 C.F.R. § 147.106.

323. 45 C.F.R. § 147.128.

324. 45 C.F.R. § 147.120.

325. 45 C.F.R. § 147.126.

326. *See* U.S. Centers for Medicare & Medicaid Services, The Affordable Care Act's New Patient Bill of Rights, https://www.cms.gov/CCIIO/Resources/Fact-Sheets-and-FAQs/aca-new-patients-bill-of-rights.html.

327. *See* 45 C.F.R. § 158.210.

328. 45 C.F.R. § 154.215.

329. Sara R. Collins, Americans' Confidence in Their Ability to Pay for Health Care Is Falling, Commonwealth Fund (May 10, 2018), https://www.commonwealthfund.org/blog/2018/americans-confidence-their-ability-pay-health-care-falling.

330. 45 C.F.R. § 147.130. *See* 75 Fed. Reg. 41726 (July 19, 2010).

331. U.S. Preventive Services Task Force, Recommendations A and B, http://www.uspreventiveservicestaskforce.org/uspstf/uspsabrecs.htm.

332. U.S. Centers for Disease Control and Prevention, General Recommendations on Immunization: Recommendations of the Advisory Committee on Immunization Practices (ACIP) (Jan. 28, 2011), http://www.cdc.gov/mmwr/pdf/rr/rr6002.pdf.

333. Preventive services recommended by the Health Resources and Services Administration Bright Futures Program are available at http://www.aap.org/en-us/professional-resources/practice-support/Periodicity/Periodicity%20Schedule_FINAL.pdf. A list of preventive services covered for children is available at https://www.healthcare.gov/preventive-care-children/.

334. *See* 78 Fed. Reg. 39870 (July 2, 2013).

335. Although the U.S. Supreme Court held that certain employers could refuse to provide contraception coverage if it violated their religious beliefs, Burwell v. Hobby Lobby, 134 S. Ct. 2751 (2014), the government devised a method to ensure that women employees would nevertheless have no-cost access to these benefits. *See* 45 C.F.R. §§ 147.131, 147.132; 79 Fed. Reg. 51092 (Aug. 27, 2014).

336. 45 C.F.R. § 147.138.

337. 45 C.F.R. Part 92 sets forth the ACA's antidiscrimination provisions and enforcement mechanisms.

338. The U.S. Department of Health and Human Services website provides instructions on how to file a discrimination complaint (including an online complaint) with the Office of Civil Rights. *See* https://www.hhs.gov/civil-rights/for-individuals/section-1557/index.html.

339. National Women's Law Center, Still Nowhere to Turn: Insurance Companies Treat Women Like a Pre-existing Condition (2009), http://www.nwlc.org/sites/default/files/pdfs/stillnowheretoturn.pdf.

340. 45 C.F.R. § 147.138(a).

341. 42 U.S.C. § 300gg-7.

342. 29 U.S.C. § 1185a. The MHPAEA amended the Mental Health Parity Act of 1996.

343. 29 U.S.C. § 1185a(a)(3)(i).

344. 45 C.F.R. § 164.524(a).

345. 45 C.F.R. § 164.524.

346. 45 C.F.R. § 164.508.

347. U.S. Department of Health and Human Services, Health Information Privacy, http://www.hhs.gov/ocr/privacy/.

348. 45 C.F.R. § 160.306. *See* https://www.hhs.gov/civil-rights/for-individuals/section-1557/index.html for instructions and online portal for filing a complaint.

349. 26 C.F.R. § 1.5000A-1.

350. Tax Cuts and Jobs Act, Pub. L. No. 115-97, 121 Stat. 2025 (2017).

351. *See* Thomas Rice, L.Y. Unruh, E. van Ginneken, P. Rosenau, & A.J. Barnes, Universal Coverage Reforms in the USA: From Obamacare through Trump, 122 Health Policy 398 (July 2018), https://www.sciencedirect.com/science/article/pii/S0168851018301544#sec0015.

352. American College Health Association, Frequently Asked Questions (Apr. 21, 2014), https://www.acha.org/ACA_FAQ#Q3. *But see* 83 Fed. Reg. 16930, 16972 (Apr. 17, 2018) (final rule to exempt student health plans from the federal rate review requirement).

353. 26 U.S.C. § 4980H. Full-time employees are defined as employees who work at least 30 hours per week. The calculation of the number of employees for the purposes of deciding whether or not a business is subject to the employer responsibility requirement takes account of part-time employees in accordance with a formula set forth at 26 U.S.C. § 4980H(c)(2)(E).

354. 26 U.S.C. § 36B.

355. 26 C.F.R. § 601.105. The percentage of income used to determine "affordability" is subject to annual adjustment. *Id.* The current percentage may be found on HealthCare.Gov at https://www.healthcare.gov/have-job-based-coverage/change-to-marketplace-plan/. The MAGI method of calculating income is discussed earlier in this chapter. *See also* Internal Revenue Service, Questions and Answers on the Premium Tax Credit, https://www.irs.gov/affordable-care-act/individuals-and-families/questions-and-answers-on-the-premium-tax-credit.

356. This option is discussed earlier in the chapter under "Can an employee obtain health insurance through an Exchange instead of enrolling in the employer's health plan?"

357. 42 U.S.C. § 300gg-16.

358. *See* Internal Revenue Service, Frequently-Asked-Questions from Employers Regarding Automatic Enrollment, Employer Shared Responsibility, and Waiting Periods (2012), https://www.irs.gov/pub/irs-drop/n-12-17.pdf.

359. Additional resources on health plan appeals may be found on the CMS website at https://www.healthcare.gov/appeal-insurance-company-decision/appeals/.

360. 29 C.F.R. § 2590.715-2719(a)(2).

361. 29 C.F.R. § 2560.503-I(h).

362. 29 C.F.R. § 2560.503-I(f).

363. 29 C.F.R. § 2560.503-1(g).

364. 29 C.F.R. § 2560.503-1(h)(2)(i).

365. 29 C.F.R. § 2590.715-2719 (b)(2)(ii)(B).

366. 29 C.F.R. § 2590.715-2719 (b)(2)(ii)(C).

367. *Id.*; 29 C.F.R. § 2560.503-1(h).

368. 29 C.F.R. § 2590.715-2719 (b)(2)(iii); 29 C.F.R. § 2560.503-1(f)(2)(ii).

369. 29 C.F.R. § 2560.503-1(i)(1).

370. 29 C.F.R. § 2590.715-2719 (b)(2)(ii)(B); 29 C.F.R. 2560-503-1(f)(2)(i).

371. 29 C.F.R. §§ 2590.715-2719(c)(2)(iv), et seq. The IRO must have no connection with or interest in the claimant's health plan, nor any other conflicts of interest. 29 C.F.R. § 2590.715-2719(c)(2)(ix).

372. 29 C.F.R. § 2590.715-2719(c)(2)(v).

373. 29 C.F.R. § 2590.715-2719(c)(2)(iv).

374. 29 C.F.R. § 2590.715-2719(c)(2)(vi).

375. 29 C.F.R. § 2590.715-2719(c)(2)(x).

376. 29 C.F.R. § 2590.715-2719(c)(2)(i).

377. 29 C.F.R. § 2590.715-2719(c)(2)(xii).

378. 29 C.F.R. § 2590.715-2719(c)(2)(xiii).

379. 29 C.F.R. § 2590.715-2719(c)(2)(xi).

380. 42 U.S.C. §§ 1395–95ccc.

381. *See* Julian Zelizer, How Medicare Was Made, The New Yorker (Feb. 15, 2015), https://www.newyorker.com/news/news-desk/medicare-made.

382. *See* Teresa Ghilarducci, Republicans' Public Opposition to Social Security and Medicare, Forbes (Nov. 2, 2018), https://www.forbes.com/sites/teresaghilarducci/2018/11/02/republican-public-opposition-to-social-security-and-medicare/#6a0ebf9a4e71.

383. U.S. Centers for Medicare & Medicaid Services, CMS Fast Facts (July 2019), https://www.cms.gov/Research-Statistics-Data-and-Systems/Statistics-Trends-and-Reports/CMS-Fast-Facts/index.html.

384. Medicare Prescription Drug, Improvement, and Modernization Act of 2003, Pub. L. No. 108-173, 117 Stat. 2066 (2003). *See* 42 U.S.C. §§ 1395w-27, 1395w-101.

385. Gretchen Jacobson, Anthony Damico, & Tricia Neuman, Medicare Advantage 2019 Spotlight: First Look, Kaiser Family Foundation (Oct. 16, 2018), https://www.kff. org/medicare/issue-brief/medicare-advantage-2019-spotlight-first-look/.

386. Juliette Cubanski, Christina Swoope, Cristina Boccuti, Gretchen Jacobson, & Giselle Casillas, A Primer on Medicare: Key Facts About the Medicare Program and the People It Covers, Kaiser Family Foundation (Mar. 20, 2015), https://www.kff.org/ report-section/a-primer-on-medicare-how-do-medicare-beneficiaries-fare-with-respect-to-access-to-care/.

387. U.S. Centers for Medicare & Medicaid Services, Medicare and You, https://www. medicare.gov/sites/default/files/2018-11/10050-Medicare-and-You.pdf. The most recent "Medicare & You Handbook" may be accessed at Medicare.gov, under the Useful Links heading at the bottom of the home page.

388. Lisa Potetz, Juliette Cubanski, & Tricia Neuman, Medicare Spending and Financing: A Primer, Kaiser Family Foundation (Jan. 31, 2011), http://www.kff.org/ medicare/upload/7731-03.pdf (reporting that in 2006, Medicare paid only 48% of the cost of enrollees' health care, with the balance paid by Medicaid, third-party coverage, or out of pocket).

389. 42 C.F.R. § 431.625. See U.S. Centers for Medicare & Medicaid Services, Medicare Savings Programs, https://www.medicare.gov/your-medicare-costs/get-help-paying-costs/medicare-savings-programs#collapse-2625.

390. See U.S. Centers for Medicare & Medicaid Services, Medicare Savings Programs, https://www.medicare.gov/your-medicare-costs/get-help-paying-costs/medicare-savings-programs#collapse-2625.

391. Id.

392. 42 U.S.C. § 1395o.

393. Id.; 8 U.S.C. § 1612.

394. 42 U.S.C. § 426.

395. In 2019 the Part A premium for people with less than 30 quarters of covered employment was $437/month; the premium for people with 30 to 39 quarters of covered employment was $240/month. U.S. Centers for Medicare & Medicaid Services, Medicare Costs at a Glance, https://www.medicare.gov/your-medicare-costs/medicare-costs-at-a-glance.

396. 42 U.S.C. § 1395d.

397. See 42 U.S.C. § 1395x.

398. U.S. Centers for Medicare & Medicaid Services, Medicare Costs at a Glance, https:// www.medicare.gov/your-medicare-costs/medicare-costs-at-a-glance.

399. Id.

400. Id.

401. See MEDPAC, Report to Congress: Medicare Payment Policy *235 (Mar. 2011), http://www.medpac.gov/docs/default-source/reports/Mar11_EntireReport. pdf?sfvrsn=0.

402. U.S. Centers for Medicare & Medicaid Services, Medicare Claims Processing Manual § 10.3, https://www.cms.gov/Regulations-and-Guidance/Guidance/Manuals/downloads/ clm104c02.pdf.

403. *See* 42 U.S.C. § 1395ww.

404. *See* Dina Fine Maron, Why You Should Care About New Major Changes in Billing, Scientific American (Sept. 2015), https://www.scientificamerican.com/article/why-you-should-care-about-the-new-major-changes-in-medical-billing/.

405. 42 U.S.C. §§ 1395x(ee); 42 C.F.R. §§ 482 et seq.

406. *See* U.S. Centers for Medicare & Medicaid Services, Quality Improvement Organizations, https://www.cms.gov/medicare/quality-initiatives-patient-assessment-instruments/qualityimprovementorgs/index.html.

407. *See* 42 C.F.R. §§ 409 et seq.

408. U.S. Centers for Medicare & Medicaid Services, Your Medicaid Coverage: Skilled Nursing Facility (SNF) Care, https://www.medicare.gov/coverage/skilled-nursing-facility-snf-care.

409. *See* 42 C.F.R. §§ 484 et seq.

410. *See* 42 C.F.R. §§ 418 et seq.

411. U.S. Centers for Medicare & Medicaid Services, Medicare Costs at a Glance, https://www.medicare.gov/your-medicare-costs/medicare-costs-at-a-glance.

412. 42 U.S.C. § 1395k.

413. *See* U.S. Centers for Medicare & Medicaid Services, What Medicare Covers, https://www.medicare.gov/what-medicare-covers/part-b/durable-medical-equipment.html.

414. 42 U.S.C. § 1395x(ww); 42 C.F.R. § 405.2449.

415. 42 U.S.C. § 1395x(s)(2); 42 C.F.R. § 405.2449.

416. *See* 75 Fed. Reg. 73,169 (Nov. 29, 2010), amending 42 C.F.R. §§ 410.152 and 410.160. Table 65 includes a chart of the complete list of codes for preventive services that indicates whether the services are subject to cost sharing.

417. 42 U.S.C. § 1395l (elimination of coinsurance); 42 U.S.C. § 1395w-4(j)(3) (elimination of coinsurance in the physician fee schedule); 42 U.S.C. § 1395l (elimination of coinsurance in outpatient hospital settings).

418. 42 C.F.R. § 410.152. It is important to note that doctors must accept assignment in order for copayment or coinsurance to be waived. In addition, in some cases, such as with a colonoscopy, if the screening test includes a treatment, such as the removal of a polyp, then it is considered diagnostic or treatment procedure and then coinsurance or copayment may apply.

419. Authority of the Secretary to update coverage to conform with USPSTF recommendations is codified at 42 U.S.C. § 1395m.

420. 42 U.S.C. § 1395y(a); U.S. Centers for Medicare & Medicaid Services, What's Not Covered by Part A & Part B?, https://www.medicare.gov/what-medicare-covers/whats-not-covered-by-part-a-part-b.

421. For the current deductible amount, *see* Centers for Medicare & Medicaid Services, Your Medicare Costs, https://www.medicare.gov/your-medicare-costs/part-b-costs/part-b-costs.html.

422. *See* U.S. Centers for Medicare & Medicaid Services, Medicare Savings Plans, https://www.medicare.gov/your-medicare-costs/get-help-paying-costs/medicare-savings-programs#collapse-2625.

423. *See* U.S. Centers for Medicare & Medicaid Services, Medigap (Medicare Supplement Health Insurance), http://www.cms.hhs.gov/Medicare/Health-Plans/Medigap/index.html?redirect=/Medigap/.

424. Medicare Part B payments are made by "carriers," insurance companies such as Cigna or Wellpoint, which have agreements with Medicare to handle Part B payments. For an updated listed of Part B carriers by state, *see* U.S. Centers for Medicare & Medicaid Services, Medicare Contacts, https://www.medicare.gov/Contacts/#searchresult&searchType=org&stateCode=ALL%7CAll%20States&orgTypeByName=A%7CCarrier.

425. Robert Pear, Doctors Are Improperly Billing Some on Medicare, U.S. Says, N.Y. Times (July 30, 2016), https://www.nytimes.com/2016/07/31/us/politics/doctors-are-improperly-billing-some-on-medicare-us-says.html.

426. U.S. Centers for Medicare & Medicaid Services, Find Medicare Physicians & Other Clinicians, http://www.medicare.gov/find-a-doctor/provider-search.aspx.

427. 42 U.S.C. § 1395w-22.

428. According to the Congressional Research Service, Part C Medicare Advantage Plans generally "offer additional benefits or require smaller co-payments or deductibles than original Medicare. Sometimes beneficiaries pay for these additional benefits through a higher monthly premium, but sometimes they are financed through plan savings." Patricia Davis, Scott R. Talaga, Cliff Binder, Jim Hahn, Suzanne M. Kirchhoff, Paulette C. Morgan, & Sibyl Tilson, A Medicare Primer, Congressional Research Service Report R40425 (Aug. 2, 2017), https://fas.org/sgp/crs/misc/R40425.pdf.

429. 42 C.F.R. §§ 417.454, 422.100 (cost sharing for in-network preventive services, as defined in 20 C.F.R. § 410.152(l)).

430. 42 C.F.R. § 417.454.

431. 42 U.S.C. § 1395w-27(e)(4).

432. 42 U.S.C. § 1395w-21.

433. 42 U.S.C. § 1395w-102.

434. 42 U.S.C. § 1395w-101.

435. CMS offers links to Part D Plan lists of covered drugs. *See* https://www.medicare.gov/index.php/drug-coverage-part-d/what-drug-plans-cover.

436. 42 U.S.C. § 1395w-114a; 42 C.F.R. § 423.104. A more detailed guide for calculating prescription drug costs in the coverage gap ("doughnut hole") is available at https://www.medicare.gov/drug-coverage-part-d/costs-for-medicare-drug-coverage/costs-in-the-coverage-gap.

437. *See* Juliette Cubanski, Summary of Recent and Proposed Changes to Medicare Prescription Drug Coverage and Reimbursement, Kaiser Family Foundation (Feb. 15, 2018), https://www.kff.org/medicare/issue-brief/summary-of-recent-and-proposed-changes-to-medicare-prescription-drug-coverage-and-reimbursement/. *See also* Bipartisan Budget Act, Pub. L. No. 115-123, 132 Stat. 64, 305 (2018).

438. 42 U.S.C. § 1395w-114 (premium and cost-sharing subsidies for low-income individuals); 42 C.F.R. § 423.34.

439. The late enrollment penalty is calculated by multiplying 1% of the "national base beneficiary premium" ($33.19 in 2019) times the number of full, uncovered

months the individual was eligible but did not join a Medicare drug plan and went without other creditable prescription drug coverage. The final amount is rounded to the nearest 10 cents and added to the individual's monthly premium. *See* U.S. Centers for Medicare & Medicaid Services, Part D late enrollment penalty, https://www.medicare.gov/drug-coverage-part-d/costs-for-medicare-drug-coverage/part-d-late-enrollment-penalty.

440. 42 U.S.C. § 1395ff.

441. For a sample notice, *see* http://www.medicare.gov/pubs/pdf/SummaryNoticeA.pdf.

442. 42 C.F.R. § 478 et seq. Quality Improvement Organizations are independent agencies contracted by Medicare to protect Medicare Beneficiaries. Contact information may be found at https://www.cms.gov/medicare/quality-initiatives-patient-assessment-instruments/qualityimprovementorgs/index.html.

443. 42 C.F.R. § 405.940.

444. 42 C.F.R. § 405.950.

445. 42 C.F.R. § 405.960.

446. 42 C.F.R. § 405.962.

447. 42 C.F.R. § 405.968.

448. 42 C.F.R. § 405.966(a)(2).

449. 42 C.F.R. § 405.1000.

450. 42 C.F.R. § 405.1004. The request form for an ALJ appeal, together with filing instructions, may be found at https://www.medicare.gov/claims-appeals/file-an-appeal/original-medicare-appeals/appeals-level-3-hearing-before-administrative-law-judge. The law presumes these notices are received within five days of the reconsideration notice date, so it is wise to file no later than 65 days after that date.

451. *See* U.S. Centers for Medicare & Medicaid Services, Appeals Level 3: Hearing before Administrative Law Judge, https://www.medicare.gov/claims-appeals/file-an-appeal/original-medicare-appeals/appeals-level-3-hearing-before-administrative-law-judge.

452. 42 C.F.R. § 405.1000.

453. *Id.*

454. 42 C.F.R. § 1136.

455. U.S. Centers for Medicare & Medicaid Services, Appeals Level 5: Federal District Court Judicial Review, https://www.medicare.gov/claims-appeals/file-an-appeal/appeals-level-5-federal-district-court-judicial-review.

456. 42 C.F.R. §§ 422.560, 422.564.

457. 42 C.F.R. § 422.564(b).

458. 42 C.F.R. § 422.111(b)(8).

459. 42 C.F.R. § 405.1206.

460. 42 C.F.R. § 476.78.

461. *See* U.S. Centers for Medicare & Medicaid Services, Quality Improvement Organizations, https://www.cms.gov/medicare/quality-initiatives-patient-assessment-instruments/qualityimprovementorgs/index.html.

462. 42 C.F.R. § 405.1205 (for Traditional Medicare); 42 C.F.R. § 422.620 (for Medicare Advantage).

463. 42 C.F.R. § 405.1206(b)(1).

464. 42 C.F.R. § 405.1206(e).

465. 42 C.F.R. § 405.1206(c).

466. 42 C.F.R. § 405.1206(e)(5).

467. Ryan White CARE Act, Pub. L. 101-381, 104 Stat. 576 (1990); 42 U.S.C. Ch. 6A, Subch. XXIV.

468. *See* Erika G. Martin & Bruce R. Schackman, What Does U.S. Health Reform Mean for HIV Clinical Care?, 60 J. Acquired Immune Deficiency Syndromes 72 (2012).

469. Insurance market reforms for individual and small group markets are codified at 42 U.S.C.A. § 300gg-(1)-(28), et seq.; 42 U.S.C. § 300gg-4 specifically prohibits discrimination in health insurance eligibility or premiums based on health status.

470. 42 U.S.C. § 18116.

471. Jennifer Kates, Rachel Garfield, Katherine Young, Kelly Quinn, Emma Frazier, & Jacek Skarbinski, Assessing the Impact of the Affordable Care Act on Health Insurance Coverage of People with HIV, Kaiser Family Foundation (Jan. 7, 2014), https://www.kff.org/report-section/assessing-the-impact-of-the-affordable-care-act-on-health-insurance-coverage-of-people-with-hiv-issue-brief/ ("One of the most important components of the ACA for people with HIV is the expansion of Medicaid eligibility.").

472. Health Resources and Services Administration, Bureau of HIV/AIDs, Policy Clarification Notice (PCN) #13-06, Clarifications Regarding Use of Ryan White HIV/AIDS Program Funds for Premium and Cost-Sharing Assistance for Medicaid (revised June 6, 2014), http://hab.hrsa.gov/manageyourgrant/pinspals/pcn1306me dicaidpremiumcostsharing.pdf.

473. The Ryan White Program does not pay for services "to the extent that payment has been made, or can reasonably be expected to be made, with respect to that item or service" by another payment source. *See* 42 U.S.C. §§ 300ff-15(a)(6), 300ff-27(b)(7) (F), 300ff-64(f)(1); Health Resources and Services Administration, Bureau of HIV/ AIDS, Policy Clarification Notice (PCN) #13-02, Clarifications on Ryan White Program Client Eligibility Determinations and Recertifications Requirements, https://hab.hrsa.gov/sites/default/files/hab/Global/pcn1302clienteligibility.pdf.

474. 45 C.F.R. § 156.1250; 79 Fed. Reg. 40763 (July 14, 2014).

475. *See* 8 U.S.C. § 1612. *See also* 42 C.F.R. § 435.406. Additional, up-to-date information on health care reform and immigrants is available at https://www.healthcare.gov/ immigrants/.

476. 42 U.S.C. § 1396b(v)(3); 42 C.F.R. § 440.255(b)(1).

477. 42 U.S.C. § 1395dd.

478. 42 U.S.C. § 1395dd(b)(1)(a); 42 C.F.R. § 489.24(a)(1)(ii).

479. 32 U.S.C. § 1395x.

480. 42 U.S.C. § 254b.

481. *See* U.S. Centers for Medicare & Medicaid Services, More Information for Immigrant Families, https://www.healthcare.gov/immigrants/immigrant-families/.

482. 45 C.F.R. § 155.260(b).

483. Immigration and Customs Enforcement. Clarification of Existing Practices Related to Certain Health Care Information (Oct. 25, 2013), https://www.ice.gov/doclib/ero-outreach/pdf/ice-aca-memo.pdf.

484. *See* National Immigration Law Center, Know Your Rights: Is It Safe to Apply for Health Insurance or Seek Health Care? (Nov. 30, 2016), https://www.nilc.org/issues/health-care/health-insurance-and-care-rights/.

485. The new rule appears at 84 Fed. Reg. 41292 (Aug. 14, 2019) and the government's summary of the rule is available at https://www.uscis.gov/legal-resources/final-rule-public-charge-ground-inadmissibility. Receipt of Medicaid does not automatically render an immigrant "likely to become a public charge." Instead, receipt of designated public benefits (cash public assistance, SNAP, and certain forms of Medicaid and housing assistance) is considered a negative factor or a "heavily weighted negative factor" in a "totality of the circumstances" test. 84 Fed. Reg. 41298–41299. The central impact of the new rule will be on immigrants with approved family-based petitions who are applying for lawful permanent resident status (green cards). For a concise explanation of the "public charge" concept in general, *see* Em Puhl, Erin Quinn, & Sally Kinoshita, An Overview of Public Charge, Immigrant Legal Resource Center (Dec. 2018), https://www.ilrc.org/overview-public-charge. For a discussion of the new rule's deterrent effect on immigrant access to medical care, *see, for example*, Kaiser Family Foundation, Changes to "Public Charge" Inadmissibility Rule: Implications for Health and Health Coverage (Aug. 12, 2019), https://www.kff.org/disparities-policy/fact-sheet/public-charge-policies-for-immigrants-implications-for-health-coverage/.

486. *See* Kellan Baker & Andrew Cray, Ensuring Benefits Parity and Gender Identity Nondiscrimination in Essential Health Benefits, Center for American Progress (Nov.15, 2012), https://www.americanprogress.org/wp-content/uploads/2012/11/BakerHealthBenefits-2.pdf.

487. New York State Issues Guidance Requiring Health Insurance Companies to Cover Transgender Health Care, Transgender Legal Defense & Education Fund (Dec. 10, 2014), http://www.tldef.org/press_show.php?id=425; Anemona Hartocollis Insurers in New York Must Cover Gender Reassignment Surgery, Cuomo Says, N.Y. Times (Dec. 10, 2014), http://www.nytimes.com/2014/12/11/nyregion/in-new-york-insurance-must-cover-sex-changes-cuomo-says.html.

488. Human Rights Campaign, State Maps of Laws & Policies: Transgender Healthcare (Mar. 29, 2018), https://www.hrc.org/state-maps/transgender-healthcare.

489. U.S. Centers for Medicare & Medicaid Services Pub. 100-03 Medicare National Coverage Determinations Change Request 8825 (June 27, 2014), https://www.cms.gov/Regulations-and-Guidance/Guidance/Transmittals/Downloads/R169NCD.pdf.

5

Education

Introduction

Does the federal Constitution guarantee a right to education?

The federal Constitution does not list education as a protected right. The U.S. Supreme Court has acknowledged the "supreme importance" of education to democratic life,[1] but it so far has declined to treat free, quality public schooling as a fundamental right that deserves implicit constitutional protection.[2] The absence of a federal constitutional right to education contrasts with the status of education under the constitutions of most other liberal, democratic nations.[3] It also runs counter to the spirit of Article 26 of the Universal Declaration of Human Rights, which proclaims: "Everyone has the right to education. Education shall be free, at least in the elementary and fundamental stages. . . . Education shall be directed to the full development of the human personality and to the full strengthening of respect for human rights and fundamental freedoms."[4]

Instead, the provision of public schooling in the United States is left largely to the states. States generally fund public schooling from property taxes that are paid by the residents of the neighborhood or district in which a school is located.[5] Because of racial and economic housing segregation, property wealth is unevenly distributed throughout a state, leaving some school districts disadvantaged in the revenue they can raise to support local education. In consequence, the quality of public schooling differs considerably within states and across states,[6] and educational disparities track family wealth and race.[7] The U.S. Supreme Court has held that the federal Equal Protection Clause does not require the states to ensure that students in low-income districts receive public schooling of "equal quality" to that of wealthier students.[8] However, the Court has left open whether the Constitution requires the states to provide "some identifiable quantum of education" to all students, regardless of financial status—at the least, opportunities for receiving a minimally adequate education—as a prerequisite to a person's democratic rights to "effective speech" or to "informed electoral choice."[9]

Although not recognizing a right to public schooling, the federal Constitution does bar states from withholding education on the basis of race, a principle that was first established in 1954, when the U.S. Supreme Court decided *Brown*

Getting By. Helen Hershkoff and Stephen Loffredo, Oxford University Press (2020). © Helen Hershkoff & Stephen Loffredo.
DOI: 10.1093/oso/9780190080860.001.0001

v. Board of Education.[10] In addition, a state must have a strong reason for taking race into account when designing a public school system.[11] Moreover, a state may not constitutionally withhold public schooling from students who are not citizens or cannot document their immigration status, even if their parents are in the United States illegally.[12] In addition, Congress has enacted statutes that authorize funding to states for specific educational purposes, and educational programs that are supported by these federal funds have an obligation not to discriminate against students because of disabilities,[13] ethnicity,[14] or sex.[15]

It would be difficult to overstate the importance of quality education to the development and life chances of children, the economic opportunities of individuals and families, and the health of the nation's democracy.[16] Higher levels of education lead to higher income, they provide a basis for more stable employment, and they offer a pathway from poverty to the middle class.[17] Yet this pathway is closed to many. Ultimately, it is public policy that determines the degree to which education reproduces and reinforces inequality, or instead promotes the social and economic mobility that is a cornerstone of a democratic society. Congress has enacted some laws that provide funding for educational programs designed to improve and equalize educational opportunity for poor and low-income children, but these measures do not go far enough. Potentially, a mobilized public will persuade Congress to support a federal statutory right to quality education that will benefit students in all states, wherever they live.[18] Over time, the U.S. Supreme Court may see the wisdom in revisiting its earlier reading of the Constitution and identify and protect a federal education right that is consistent with the requirements of free speech, the right to vote, and personal autonomy.[19] Or, influenced by the constitutional provisions of liberal democratic countries abroad, a social movement may develop in favor of amending the Constitution to guarantee free quality public schooling for all.[20] Until then, securing even a minimally adequate education depends on the patchwork of programs and protections, both state and federal, described in this chapter.

Do state constitutions guarantee a right to public schooling?

Every state in the United States has its own constitution, and each refers to public schooling, although there are broad differences in language and guarantees.[21] The Montana Constitution, for example, declares, "It is the goal of the people to establish a system of education which will develop the full educational potential of each person."[22] The New Hampshire Constitution recognizes "[k]nowledge and learning, generally diffused through a community, [to be] essential to the preservation of a free government. . . ."[23] Given existing federal constitutional doctrine, advocates have turned to state constitutions as a lever to improve public schooling in low-wealth communities. In all but a handful of states, lawsuits have been filed in state courts challenging the equity and adequacy of a state's funding system and seeking relief under the state's constitution. In a majority of the cases, state courts have found a violation of the state constitutional duty, either with respect to specific students and localities or in the state overall.[24] Nevertheless, broad disparities in educational quality persist, with manifest racial impacts, causing preventable harms to children, communities, and the nation at large.

Preschool Programs

Does the federal government offer preschool programs for low-income children?

"Preschool" refers to educational programs for children who are not yet old enough to attend a state's public schools and who usually are below age five.[25] The United States funds two preschool programs: Head Start (which includes Early Head Start) and Early Intervention Services. These programs are designed to overcome some of the developmental delays that are associated with poverty by helping to prepare children to be ready to learn once they are old enough to enroll in school. Head Start serves toddlers who are at least age three and no older than the age of compulsory school attendance.[26] Early Head Start serves infants and toddlers under age three.[27] Early Intervention Services are geared to children under age three who have disabilities.[28] Services in both programs are provided free of charge.[29]

Research confirms that a toddler's participation in a preschool program can have many beneficial effects. In the short run, developmentally appropriate preschool programs can help a child acquire the cognitive skills needed to learn to read and write once public school officially begins, thereby lessening the prospect of retention in grade or placement in special education programs.[30] Additionally, these programs promote healthy development of social-emotional skills and executive function.[31] In the longer run, participation can improve a child's life chances by encouraging high school graduation, making college more likely, and reducing the risk of poverty because of better employment options.[32] Quality preschool programs thus are a cost-effective social investment because they positively affect earnings and tax payment, and reduce the likelihood of teenage pregnancy and encounters with the criminal justice system.[33] Studies also have shown that participants in Head Start programs are more likely to invest in their own children, creating positive generational effects.[34]

What is the process for applying to Head Start?

Application to Head Start is done at the local level and through local programs. Each program has its own set of enrollment criteria and admission decisions are made at the site where the program takes place, but general selection is aimed at children in families with income below the federal poverty level, children whose families are homeless, and children in foster care.[35] Applications can be submitted at any time during the program year and a family can apply to more than one program at a time (but enroll in only one).[36] The application is separate from an application for Supplemental Security Income (SSI), Temporary Assistance for Needy Families (TANF), WIC, or SNAP (food stamps). Head Start is not an entitlement program, meaning the government does not guarantee funding for all eligible children who want to participate. In the 2016–17 program year, Head Start and Early Head Start cumulatively served 1,070,000 children and pregnant women.[37]

Generally, the Head Start application will ask for the name of the child's parent or guardian, the family's address, the name of the child, the child's birthday, and family income. Applicants will be asked to verify income through such documents as an income tax return, pay stubs, written statements from an employer, or documentation of the family's receipt of TANF or SSI benefits. It is possible that an application will require a copy of the child's immunization records, or proof from a social worker if the family is homeless. An applicant can get help from the Head Start center to gather together the necessary paperwork.

Federal regulations require that at least 90 percent of the children enrolled be from low-income families,[38] and generally 10 percent of the participants must be children with disabilities or children who are experiencing developmental delays.[39] If a local program no longer has available places, the applicant can ask to have the child's name placed on a waiting list and to be contacted if a vacancy occurs.[40] The waiting list is not ranked on a first-come, first-served basis. Rather, selection is made according to the criteria the agency uses to administer the local program. Vacancies that open during the enrollment year must be filled within 30 days.[41]

Information about local Head Start programs is available from the regional office of the Administration for Children and Families, which is part of the U.S. Department of Health and Human Service (HHS).[42] The HHS hosts an online Head Start Locator, which provides information about local programs.[43]

After being accepted into the Head Start program, how long can a child participate?

Once a child is enrolled in Head Start, participation can continue until a local kindergarten or first-grade program is available, assuming certain conditions are met.[44] A child's eligibility for Head Start is determined once per year, and it lasts through the end of the next enrollment year.[45] The responsible adult must make sure that an enrolled child attends the program on a regular basis. If the child repeatedly misses class, the program must contact the parent or guardian, find out the reasons for the absenteeism, and provide family support services if appropriate.[46] If after such a contact the absenteeism persists, the agency is permitted to consider the child's slot to be vacant and to make it available to another child.[47]

What services does Head Start provide?

Head Start programs generally run for a half-day, that is, three and a half hours, or for a full day, and classes meet four or five days a week (for 128 days per year).[48] Programs are offered in a variety of learning environments, and can include a classroom in a local public school,[49] the child's home,[50] a family-like setting,[51] or a combination of settings.[52] In home-based programs, the child must receive at least one teacher-visit per week (with makeups for cancellations available) and two group activities per month.[53] Programs provide participating children with nutritious foods and access to comprehensive health services, including preventive medical, dental, mental health, and nutrition services.[54] In some programs, the parent or guardian is eligible for health and other services, which can include prenatal education, services to prevent maternal depression, reproductive services, and help with maintaining insurance coverage. If a local program serves children with disabilities, it must specifically address the needs of such children.[55] A child with disabilities who is placed in a Head Start program must be given an Individualized Education Program (discussed later in this chapter), developed with full parent participation, consistent with the requirements of the federal Individuals with Disabilities Education Act.[56] Federal law requires Head Start services to be of high quality, and the federal government has a duty to review the programs and, every three years, to issue a performance review.[57]

What is Early Head Start?

Early Head Start is a federally funded program which serves infants and toddlers under the age of three, and helps children transition to Head Start or to another preschool program. Like Head Start, Early Head Start provides enrichment opportunities and social services for low-income children, and includes services for low-income pregnant women and fathers, as well as an option to provide services in the family's home. Early Head Start is run by the same agencies that run Head Start, and must meet many of the same programmatic requirements, with distinct rules on specific features, such as hours of attendance and class ratios. Studies report favorable benefits for all participants.[58]

Can a parent participate in Head Start?

Head Start recognizes that positive parental involvement helps children to develop, and a program must offer parents activities that support the parent-child relationship.[59] Federal regulations require a program to implement intake and family assessment procedures to identify a family's strengths and areas that could be improved.[60] However, a parent is not required to participate in the program, and parental participation is not a condition of the child's enrollment.[61] Parents are the sole members of a program's Parent Committee, which is responsible for working with the program's staff to develop and implement policies, activities, and services. Parents also make up half the members of the Head Start Policy Council or Policy Committee, which is responsible for making personnel decisions, setting eligibility criteria, and approving local centers.[62] A parent can work in the program as a volunteer, observer, or paid employee and interact with other program parents.[63] Information about participating is available from the director of the local program.

What are Early Intervention Services?

Early Intervention Services is a federally funded program authorized by the federal Individuals with Disabilities Education Act (IDEA).[64] The program is geared to preschool children under age three who have disabilities or are at risk of experiencing developmental delays. The program is intended to support the child's development of skills to mitigate physical, learning, and other difficulties a child might otherwise experience.[65] Generally, the program is open only to infants and toddlers, from birth to age three, who have disabilities in one or more of the following five developmental areas:[66] physical development, cognitive development, communication development, social or emotional development, or adaptive development. Programs currently are offered in almost every state, although each state or territory's standard for eligibility differs.

What is the process for applying to Early Intervention Services?

The application process for Early Intervention Services depends upon the state in which the program is located. Every state must keep a directory, updated every year, of the programs that are offered, and typically the programs are run by a state's department of education, health, mental health, human services, or public assistance. Each state has its own eligibility criteria. A family interested in these services can talk to the child's pediatrician or a state-assigned social worker and ask that the child be referred to a program. If the family receives WIC benefits (discussed in chapter 3), staff from that program can help to make a referral. In addition, a parent or guardian can contact the local agency that runs the program and ask for the child to be evaluated for services. If the child qualifies, the entire family will be entitled to free services, but participation is voluntary.[67]

What services are provided to participating children?

The Early Intervention Services program is built on the idea that providing certain kinds of services to children early in their lives can help prevent cognitive disabilities that might otherwise develop.[68] The services provided vary by state but may include physical therapy, speech therapy, nursing and health services, early education services, nutritional planning, family training and counseling, and transportation.[69] The child and family are paired with a service coordinator, who works with the family to create a written Individualized Family Service Plan (IFSP) that details the therapies or services the child and family will receive. A parent must consent to services before services may start.[70] The program is required to review the IFSP with a parent or guardian at least once every six months, or more frequently at the family's request, to determine whether the child is making progress and the plan needs to be modified. The service coordinator and the family also will meet annually to review any new evaluations the child has had and to determine if additional services are needed. If a child is about to age out of Early Intervention Services, the service coordinator must discuss a transition plan with the child's family, and the IFSP must include details for how the child will transition into a preschool program, such as Head Start, or into kindergarten.

Do states offer preschool programs?

Forty-three states plus the District of Columbia fund preschool programs, but because of funding caps not all eligible children can enroll and participation is not mandated. Vermont and a few other states do offer universal preschool programs, and several other states offer mostly universal preschool.[71] A few cities also offer universal preschool.[72] However, in academic year 2016–17, only 5 percent of three-year-olds and 33 percent of four-year-olds attended state-funded preschool programs. [73]

Public Schooling—Kindergarten through High School

Must a child attend school?

Yes. Every state, as well as the District of Columbia, Puerto Rico, Guam, the Northern Mariana Islands, American Samoa, and the U.S. Virgin Islands, has enacted a compulsory school attendance law requiring parents and guardians to send school-age children to school.[74] The term "school age" differs from state to state but generally starts at between five and seven years and ends at between 16 and 18 years. A parent or guardian can choose to send a child to public school, including a charter school,[75] or to private school, including a parochial school.[76] In addition, some states permit parents and guardians to educate their children at home,[77] as long as the "home schooling" program meets state requirements.[78] States must permit home-schooled children to access public school courses and activities if they wish to participate.[79]

Do states provide kindergarten programs?

State-funded kindergarten programs are not universally available. Thirteen states (plus the District of Columbia) require a school district to offer full-day kindergarten programs.

Seventeen states (plus the District of Columbia) require kindergarten attendance, but the eligibility age and length of the school day vary by state and, in some instances, by school district within a state.[80]

How do states enforce school attendance requirements?

Students are required to attend school and to arrive at school on time. Failure to meet these requirements without good cause is referred to as truancy. Most states treat truancy as a status offense—noncriminal activity that is illegal only when done by a minor—and a school may refer a truant student to the juvenile justice system.[81] Traditionally juvenile courts at least in principle were oriented toward service interventions such as counseling that aimed at rehabilitation. However, since at least the 1980s, the use of juvenile courts by school systems has increasingly become the first step in what commentators call a school-to-prison pipeline that steers children from low-income families, especially children of color, out of the public schools and into the criminal justice system, at an age when educational and other services are critical to growth and development.[82]

Under the federal Juvenile Justice Reform Act of 2018,[83] which reauthorized the Juvenile Justice Delinquency and Prevention Act,[84] a minor adjudicated for a status offense and found in "violation of a valid court order"—which can include an order that the child regularly attend school—may be held in detention for no longer than seven days. If the court determines the minor should be placed in a detention or correctional facility, it must issue a written order, which may not be renewed or extended, that: (1) "identifies the valid court order that has been violated"; (2) "specifies the factual basis for determining that there is reasonable cause to believe that the status offender has violated such order"; (3) "includes findings of fact to support a determination that there is no appropriate less restrictive alternative available to placing the status offender in such a facility, with due consideration to the best interest of the juvenile"; and (4) "specifies the length of time, not to exceed 7 days, that the status offender may remain in a secure detention facility or correctional facility, and includes a plan for the status offender's release from such facility."[85]

Some states refer status offenses to municipal courts and criminalize truancy as a misdemeanor, punishable by fine or jail.[86] Incarceration of a child for truancy causes a severe disruption of a student's education. Juvenile justice facilities are not exempt from the state constitutional requirement of providing free public schooling, but the quality of education that minors receive has been criticized as substandard, and the child's re-entry into the regular school classroom must hurdle legal and practical barriers.[87] In addition, states hold parents and guardians responsible for a child's school attendance, and some may impose penalties, including fines, as a punishment for the child's school absence. For example, Texas decriminalized truancy in 2015, but parents whose children are excessively absent may be prosecuted for a Class C misdemeanor with a first offense punishable by a fine of $100.[88] California's truancy law, enacted in 2011, imposes fines on parents of up to $2,000 and a year in jail if a child is absent 10 percent of the school year.[89] The consequences of truancy charges can be severe, and it is important to seek legal representation if a child faces discipline for school absence.

Does a child's school attendance affect a family's eligibility for assistance from TANF-funded programs?

Federal law bars states from using federal funds under the Temporary Assistance for Needy Families program to provide assistance to unmarried teen parents whose children are older than 12 weeks unless the teen parent successfully completes high school or its equivalent, or works toward a high school diploma or its equivalent, or participates in an alternative education or training program. A teen parent is a parent under age 18.[90] Otherwise, whether a child's absence from school affects a family's eligibility for TANF-funded assistance depends on the state in which the family lives. This is because federal law gives the states discretion to adopt policies that withhold some or all of a family's assistance payment if the family's child does not regularly attend school; states also may exercise their discretion to provide bonus payments as an incentive to encourage school attendance. As of July 2017, 37 states linked eligibility for assistance to some kind of attendance requirement.[91] If a household faces a sanction or reduction in TANF-funded benefits because of a student's truancy, it is important to contact the applicable school or a social worker to discuss how to achieve compliance with program rules and to encourage school attendance.

Must a child live in a state to attend its public schools for free?

The U.S. Supreme Court has held that states can limit tuition-free education to state residents, but only if the residence requirement is "bona fide," "appropriately defined," and "uniformly applied" to further "a substantial state interest."[92] In approving residence requirements, the Supreme Court recognized their importance to "the proper planning and operation" of a state's school system.[93] A majority of states impose in-state residence requirements as a condition of attending their public schools for free.[94] Generally these laws presume that a child has the same place of residence as the parent or guardian, but allow the child to establish an independent residence if the family can document that the child is not in a different district solely to attend its public schools.[95] For example, if a child comes from a different state to live in New Jersey with a New Jersey resident who intends to act as the child's legal guardian, the child will be treated as a resident of New Jersey for education purposes, provided the adult files a guardianship application within the time period prescribed by state law.[96] Some states require the parent or guardian to provide written documentation of the child's living arrangements.[97] A state may not invoke residence requirements to exclude otherwise eligible homeless children from school (as discussed later in this chapter).[98]

Is a child required to attend public school in the district where the child resides?

Most states require students to attend the public school in the district in which the child's family lives.[99] Some states make it a crime to supply false information for the purpose of enabling a child to attend a public school outside the district of the family's residence. The laws provide for a combination of fines, imprisonment, or probation as a punishment.[100] In some highly publicized cases, school districts have arrested parents and charged them with felonies for misstating their household address as a way to send a child to a better public school in a different district.[101]

Can a family choose to send a child to private school or parochial school rather than the public school in its district of residence?

A family can choose to send a child to a private school or parochial school but will be responsible for the payment of tuition, fees, and expenses. Some states have established voucher programs to enable a family to send a child to a school of choice,[102] but financial barriers remain because the vouchers subsidize only a portion of the costs.[103] As set out in Table 5.1, at least 14 states and the District of Columbia have programs providing state-funded vouchers to eligible students.[104] Of these states, Indiana, Louisiana, North Carolina, Ohio, Wisconsin, and Washington, D.C., limit voucher-subsidies to families with earnings that do not exceed specified limits (and meet other eligibility criteria).[105] Additionally, many programs are for students with disabilities and require eligible students to have an identified disability.[106]

Table 5.1 School Vouchers: State Income Limits

State	Income Limit for School Voucher
Indiana	150% of free lunch guideline
Louisiana	250% of federal poverty guideline
North Carolina	133% of free lunch guideline
Ohio	200% of federal poverty guideline
Wisconsin	300% of federal poverty guideline
District of Columbia	185% of federal poverty guideline

Note: 2017 federal poverty guideline for family of four was $24,600

Can a student transfer from one school
to another in the same district?

Generally, school assignment within a district is based on residence, and a student cannot elect to attend a different school even in the same district. However, the No Child Left Behind Act and its successor statute, the Every Student Succeeds Act (ESSA), enacted in 2015, require states that receive federal funding under the statute to establish a process for students otherwise enrolled in an unsafe school to transfer to a different school in the same district—called the "unsafe school choice option."[107] However, during the Trump administration, the U.S. Department of Education, in August 22, 2018, removed and reserved regulations pertaining to the unsafe school choice option, and on December 3, 2018, announced its intent to conduct a study of state implementation of the program.[108]

Maintaining an unsafe school choice option would permit a family to request a transfer from a local public school to another public school in two circumstances: (1) if the child's school is "persistently dangerous" as determined by the state in consultation with local educational agencies; and (2) if the student becomes a victim of a violent criminal offense, as determined by state law, while at the elementary or secondary school that the student attends.[109] Second, ESSA-funded schools may choose to allow students who attend academically struggling schools to request a transfer to a higher-performing school in the district.[110] A struggling school is one that needs improvement based on academic and other outcomes,[111] and typically would fall in the bottom 5 percent of state school performance.[112] So far only three states—Louisiana, New Mexico, and New York—have mandated struggling-school transfer options.[113] It is vital that schools in all districts and throughout a state provide children with safe learning environments.

Can public schools charge fees for tuition, instructional
material, and other school-related activities or products?

Generally, in states with a constitution that provides for "free" public schooling, districts cannot charge "tuition"[114]—that is, fees for an educational service or activity relating to a core curricular function, such as schoolbooks[115]—but can charge for school-related activities that are considered optional. The rules governing school fees vary from state to state,[116] and so far the federal Constitution has not been applied to limit the fees that states can charge.[117] In the majority of states, fees for sports and arts programs are legal, with a minority of the states treating sports as essential and barring fees for athletics.[118] Some state courts have upheld fees for summer school[119] and for nonacademic courses (such as behind-the-wheel sessions of driver-education courses).[120] All-day kindergarten is another program for which some school districts charge fees.[121]

A number of states have statutes that authorize school-fee waivers.[122] Some state courts have upheld school fees, even for essential services such as instructional material, provided the state has a waiver procedure for families that cannot afford to pay.[123] Eligibility for fee waivers generally is based on family income. Presumptively, a school should waive its fee if a child is eligible for free or reduced-price school meals or SNAP benefits, or the household receives TANF-funded assistance. Moreover, the school should treat a family's request for a waiver as confidential.[124] If a child will be prevented from accessing a particular service or activity because of a school fee, consider asking the principal or administrator whether a waiver is available and how to request a waiver. If a waiver is not available, the next step would be to consult a legal aid or legal services lawyer.

Can a public school penalize a student who cannot pay a fee for books or another core educational material or service?

If a student cannot pay a fee for core educational material such as books, the school cannot suspend the child, lower a course grade, or otherwise treat the student unfavorably. This is not to suggest that students who cannot pay fees do not face stigma, humiliation, and barriers to learning.[125] Apart from the question of whether a particular fee is unlawful or must be waived, constitutional rights may be violated if a school punishes a child for parental indigence or for family actions that the student cannot control, or if these practices have disparate racial impacts.[126]

Can a district exclude resident children from its public schools?

In the 1954 decision in *Brown v. Board of Education*, the U.S. Supreme Court held that the Equal Protection Clause of the Fourteenth Amendment to the U.S. Constitution bars states from maintaining separate public schools for white children and children of color. [127] Since *Brown*, federal law, by statute and judicial decision, has extended the principle of equal educational access broadly to include children who are living in a school district but are homeless;[128] children who were born or whose family members were born outside the United States;[129] children whose immigration status is not documented;[130] children who have only limited proficiency in the English language;[131] children of a particular gender;[132]

children who are pregnant or parenting;[133] and children who have mental or physical disabilities.[134] Nevertheless, exclusionary school practices persist, and they entrench structural inequalities that impede social mobility, personal development, and democratic participation.

Can a school district exclude a child who is homeless from attending its public schools?

No. The federal Every Student Succeeds Act allows a child who is considered homeless to attend the school in the district where the child previously was housed if it is in the children's best interest, or in the district where the child is currently staying.[135] Federal law provides assistance to children who are homeless and who face legal or administrative barriers to enrolling or remaining in school;[136] logistical barriers to getting to school for lack of transportation;[137] or psychological barriers that accompany the stress and instability of homelessness.[138]

The ESSA amended and strengthened the Education for Homeless Children and Youth Program under Title VII of the McKinney-Vento Assistance Act, which provides funding to states to guarantee the educational rights of children who are homeless and "to provide urgently needed assistance."[139] The statute also requires states to establish mechanisms for resolving disputes about school selection, eligibility, or enrollment of homeless students.[140] Under federal law, a student is considered homeless if:

- The student lacks a "fixed, regular, and adequate nighttime residence";
- The student's "primary nighttime residence [is] a public or private place not designed for or ordinarily used as a regular sleeping accommodation for human beings, including a car, park, abandoned building, bus or train station, airport, or camping ground"; or
- The student lives "in a temporary public or private shelter" (including hotels or motels paid for by government or charitable organizations);
- The student "resided in a shelter or place not meant for human habitation and . . . is exiting an institution where he or she temporarily resided";
- The student is facing imminent loss of housing, has "no subsequent residence identified," and has no means of obtaining new permanent housing;
- The student shares the housing of, or is doubled-up with, other persons due to loss of housing, economic hardship, or similar reason; or
- The student is an unaccompanied minor.[141]

In addition, the U.S. Department of Education has issued a "Nonregulatory Guidance" that defines other students who qualify as homeless under the

McKinney-Vento Act.[142] Nationwide almost 1.4 million students were homeless during academic year 2015–16.[143]

States and school districts that receive federal funds under the McKinney-Vento Act must establish an administrative mechanism to carry out the statute's protections. The mechanism includes:

- Liaison: Every school district must designate a homelessness liaison who is responsible for such services as ensuring that children are enrolled in school and receive necessary referrals, including transportation or preschool; that parents are given opportunities to participate in decisions about their children's education; and that disputes are mediated, taking into account the interests of the child and family.[144]
- Coordinator: Each state must designate a State Coordinator to ensure that the act is implemented in coordination with other agencies providing services to homeless youth and families.[145]
- Policy Review: State departments of education, county offices of education, and school districts must review and revise their policies and practices to eliminate barriers to the enrollment and retention of homeless children and youth.[146]

How does federal law help children who are homeless receive free public schooling?

The McKinney-Vento Act gives children who are homeless statutory rights to ensure that they are not denied free public schooling. These protections are: (1) the right to remain in the school of their original home district (even while the district makes a best-interest determination, unless the child's parents or guardian objects), or to enroll in the school of their temporary home district; (2) the right to transportation to allow them to attend their original or new school; and (3) the right not to be educated in classes that are segregated from students who are housed.[147]

1. Right to Remain in Home District School or to Enroll in the School of the Temporary Home District

A child who is homeless has a right to remain at the school of origin, even if the child remains homeless for a number of years, and even if the child is temporarily living outside the district.[148] A student who is considered homeless under the McKinney-Vento Act who moves into permanent housing during the school year can continue attending the school of origin for the remainder of the school year.[149] However, the local education agency may enroll the child in a public school in the district where the homeless child is temporarily living,[150] except when doing so is not in the best interests of the child or is contrary to the wishes of the child's parent or guardian.[151]

The U.S. Department of Education has provided guidance about how the state agency is to determine the best interests of the child. Factors that appropriately may be considered include: the child's age; the length of the commute; personal safety issues; special education needs; the anticipated length of homelessness or transient shelter; and time remaining in the academic year.[152] The agency must provide a written explanation if it chooses a school other than the school of origin or the school requested by the parent or guardian, and must include a statement about the family's right to appeal.[153] If the student is an unaccompanied youth, the agency must ensure that the homelessness liaison assists in enrollment decisions, considers the views of the student, and provides notice about the right to appeal.[154]

The school selected must "immediately enroll the homeless child or youth, even if the child or youth is unable to produce records normally required for enrollment, such as previous academic records, medical records, proof of residency, or other documentation."[155] Enrollment is defined as including "attending classes and participating fully in school activities."[156] It is the responsibility of the new school, not the child or parent or guardian, to "immediately contact the school last attended by the child or youth to obtain relevant academic and other records."[157] Parental consent is not required to transfer academic records to the new school.[158] If the child needs immunizations or immunization records, the school must immediately refer the family to the homelessness liaison, who is required to assist.[159] Schools may not require proof of residency as a condition of enrollment,[160] and federal laws protecting the privacy of students' records bar schools from contacting the landlords of host families or other third parties to discuss a student's living arrangements without permission.[161]

If the school disputes the child's eligibility to enroll, the McKinney-Vento Act requires that the child or youth be immediately enrolled in the school in which enrollment is sought, pending resolution of the dispute.[162] Homeless children and youth can enroll in the school and begin attending immediately, even without documentation that usually is required.[163]

The child's parent or guardian must be provided with a written explanation of the school's decision, including the rights of the parent, guardian, or student to appeal the decision.[164] The student, parent, or guardian then must be referred to the homelessness liaison, who is required to carry out a dispute resolution process as expeditiously as possible,[165] using procedures set out by the State Coordinator.[166] If the school district fails to do this, the family should contact the State Coordinator, the state department of education, or a legal services lawyer.

2. Right to Transportation

States that receive McKinney-Vento funding must develop plans to assure that transportation is provided at the request of the parent or guardian, or the homelessness liaison (in the case of unaccompanied youth).[167] The transportation must be to and from the school of origin, and be comparable to transportation used for students who are not homeless, although a particular type of transport is not required.[168] Moreover, transportation must be provided even if the district does not provide such services to students who are housed.[169]

3. Right Not to Be Segregated in "Homeless-Only" Schools

The McKinney-Vento Act prohibits—with very limited exceptions—districts from enrolling students in "homeless-only" schools or using "homeless-only" programs within schools.[170] Rather, the statute requires full integration of students who are homeless into the school.[171] The act states that "in providing a free public education to a homeless child or youth, no State receiving funds under this subtitle shall segregate such child or youth in a separate school, or in a separate program within a school, based on such child's or youth's status as homeless."[172] An exception is available for short periods of time if it is necessary for health or safety emergencies, or if it is necessary to provide temporary, special, and supplementary services to meet the unique needs of students who are homeless.[173] McKinney-Vento funds can be used to provide supplemental programs exclusively for students who are homeless, but the programs must be implemented in a way that does not stigmatize participants.[174]

Can a public school exclude a child who lives in the district if family members were not born in the United States or cannot document their immigration status?

No. In the 1982 decision in *Plyler v. Doe*, the U.S. Supreme Court held that the Fourteenth Amendment to the federal Constitution prohibits states from denying undocumented school-age children the same education they provide to children who are citizens or lawfully admitted aliens. Any other result, the Court explained, would mark the excluded immigrant children with "[t]he stigma of illiteracy" and create a permanent "underclass."[175] About one million children living in the United States do not have a documented status, and about five million children who were born in the United States have a parent who lacks documented status.[176] Children who arrive in the United States as unaccompanied children and are in temporary custody in shelters run by the U.S. Department of Health and Human Services are not enrolled in public schools but are required to be given basic education services.[177] However, once the minor is residing with a sponsor, a school district may not discourage or refuse enrollment.[178]

During the Obama administration, the United States issued guidelines confirming that children with undocumented immigration status are entitled under the federal Constitution to attend public school. The guidelines included the following:[179]

- School districts may request proof of residency within the district, but questions about immigration status may not be asked to establish residency. A parent's state-issued identification card or driver's license cannot be required to document residency.
- School districts may request proof of the child's age to show eligibility for school, but a school district may not bar a child whose birth certificate lists birth in a foreign country.
- A school district may not bar a child from its schools for lack of a Social Security number or for the family's refusal to provide a Social Security number.
- A school district may ask information about race or ethnicity, but cannot bar a child if the family refuses to provide this information.

However, the Obama administration also increased enforcement actions aimed at detaining and deporting nondocumented immigrants, which discouraged children from attending school.[180] These enforcement actions continued with even greater force during the Trump administration.[181]

Can a public school refuse to enroll or otherwise discriminate against a child who does not speak English?

No. In *Lau v. Nichols*, the U.S. Supreme Court held that the federal Civil Rights Act of 1964 required public schools that receive federal financial assistance to provide English-language instruction to non-English speakers.[182] Congress codified the *Lau* requirements in the Equal Educational Opportunity Act of 1974 (EEOA),[183] which requires public schools to develop a plan to serve English-language learners and take "appropriate action" for students to overcome language barriers.[184] The EEOA applies to all schools whether or not they receive federal funding.[185] In addition, the Every Student Succeeds Act, adopted in 2015, seeks to ensure "that children who are limited English proficient, including immigrant children and youth, attain English proficiency, develop high levels of academic attainment in English, and meet the same challenging

State academic content and student achievement standards as all children are expected to meet."[186] States have broad discretion to choose an instructional method, "based on scientifically based research . . . , that the agencies believe to be the most effective for teaching English";[187] the use of different instructional models, including pullout, bilingual, and structured immersion programs, have broad implications for ensuring educational equality, promoting cultural respect, and promoting achievement.[188] The number of English-language learners in the United States has increased over the last decade, but funding and programming have has not kept pace.[189] The U.S. Department of Education maintains an interactive web page that provides data about "English Learner" students.[190]

Can a public school refuse to enroll or otherwise discriminate against a child because of sex?

No. A federal statute known as Title IX of the Education Amendments of 1972 prohibits discrimination on the basis of sex in any educational program or activity receiving federal financial assistance.[191] Title IX has been interpreted to bar three types of sex-related discrimination:

- Disparate treatment, meaning actions that treat similar individuals differently on the basis of sex;[192]
- Disparate impact, meaning policies or practices that do not explicitly require different treatment of males and females, but in practice disproportionately hurt individuals on the basis of sex;[193] and
- Retaliation, meaning actions that penalize an individual for trying to enforce rights under the statute.[194]

During the Obama administration, the U.S. Department of Education's Office for Civil Rights issued guidance to schools advising that their responsibilities under Title IX include addressing the problem of sex-based violence and sex-based harassment.[195] Moreover, the Department's stance was that although Title IX does not directly prohibit discrimination on the basis of sexual orientation or gender non-conformity, sexual harassment directed at LGBTQ students may violate the statute. The Trump administration shifted policy, both with respect to protection against sex-based harassment and transgender equality.[196] If a school fails to take steps to stop bullying, harassment, or other discrimination based on sexuality, gender, or gender non-conformity, a family should consult a lawyer and consider filing a complaint with the Office for Civil Rights.[197]

Can a public school refuse to enroll or otherwise discriminate against a student who is pregnant or is a parent?

Pregnancy and parenting are significant reasons that students drop out of school.[198] Reports indicate that in some cases, the student is "pushed out" of school because absences are unexcused and the student is treated as a truant.[199] Title IX prohibits discrimination against pregnant or parenting students and requires school districts to provide accommodations to help such students remain in school.[200] Impermissible discrimination includes refusing to enroll a student or penalizing a student because of pregnancy or family status.[201]

Federal regulations make clear that public schools cannot exclude students because they are pregnant, have given birth to a child, terminated a pregnancy, experienced a "false" pregnancy, are recovering from one of these conditions, or are parenting.[202] These protections apply to all aspects of a student's education, including advanced placement programs, extracurricular activities, and other scholastic pursuits. The U.S. Department of Education has issued guidelines how Title IX protects the rights of pregnant or parenting students. These protections extend to parenting fathers as well as mothers.[203]

A school may not ask a pregnant student to provide medical documentation that she is able to participate in educational activities unless it requires similar medical documentation from all students with physical or emotional conditions that require medical treatment. Nor may a school require pregnant students to participate in a separate program for such students; attendance in any separate program must be entirely voluntary, and the program must be comparable to regular instruction.[204]

Can a school penalize a student who is pregnant or a new parent for missing class or not taking a test or completing a project on time?

Federal law bars public schools from penalizing a student because of pregnancy-related conditions or family status and requires them to prevent and address verbal harassment. However, most schools and school districts do not have general policies in place to carry out federal requirements, and the nature of the accommodation is up to the discretion of the individual classroom teacher.[205] In consequence, pregnant and parenting students face many barriers to continuing their education. Students generally can make up work only if an absence is excused. If a student is unable to attend class, say, because the student has a doctor's appointment or has been prescribed bed rest, the student or student's parent or guardian is advised to contact the classroom teacher to ask to make up the work that will be missed and to see whether an alternative project can earn necessary credit. In this situation, students should be prepared to provide medical documentation.[206]

Some new mothers may wish to take a leave of absence, comparable to maternity leave in the workplace.[207] Only New Mexico has a statewide parental leave policy for students.[208] As a first step, an inquiry should be made to a school administrator to find out whether the school has a leave policy.[209] If there is no leave policy, Title IX regulations require the school to treat pregnancy and related conditions as bases for granting a leave as long as it is "medically necessary"—a term that the statute leaves open-ended and that the regulations do not define. (Ordinary pregnancy-related conditions are not considered a disability under the Americans with Disability Act.)[210] Moreover, if a student is granted a leave of absence, Title IX requires that the school "reinstate" the student, with the expectation that reinstatement is to the same academic and extracurricular status as when the leave began.[211] Again, medical documentation is important, and a doctor's note certifying the medical condition will be useful.[212] If the student participates in WIC (discussed in chapter 3), that program should be helpful in providing referrals and in meeting paperwork requirements.[213] On a principle of gender equality, new fathers seeking leave would be within the protected status if they meet the "medically necessary" requirement, but leaves for infant care would raise different issues.

What should a student do if excluded or otherwise discriminated against because of pregnancy or parenting status?

Every school district that receives federal financial support must establish procedures that enable students to file complaints of sex-based discrimination.[214] In addition, every school district must designate at least one employee as its Title IX Coordinator to ensure that the statute is enforced. The school district is required to notify students of the name and contact information or the Title IX Coordinator.[215] Title IX does not require a school district to develop policies dealing with pregnancy and parenting, but the U.S. Department of Education recommends that school districts make clear that discrimination on these grounds is barred.[216]

A student who feels that educational opportunities are being denied for reasons related to pregnancy or parenting should keep notes about the incident and report them in confidence to the Title IX Administrator and see if the school's grievance procedures can achieve an acceptable resolution.[217] However, a student is not required to use the school's procedures, and may immediately file a complaint with the federal Office for Civil Rights (OCR).[218] The filing must be done within 180 days of the incident that forms the basis of the complaint. Filing a complaint is free and can be submitted online. A student also can write to the OCR enforcement office responsible for the state in which the public school is located.[219] It is not lawful for a school to retaliate against a student who seeks to enforce Title IX rights. The OCR is expected to investigate the incident and issue a determination; if the OCR finds that the school violated rights, and the school does not come into compliance, it risks losing federal funding.

A student also can file a lawsuit in federal court, and can do so without invoking the school's grievance procedures or filing a complaint with the OCR. If the student complains first to the OCR and files a lawsuit while the OCR procedure is pending, the OCR will close the complaint. The OCR complaint can be reinstated if the court case terminates without a judicial decision or settlement. Filing a lawsuit often involves expenses; it is important to talk with a lawyer.[220]

If the student wins in federal court, two kinds of relief can be ordered: injunctive relief and damages. Injunctive relief is the most common type of relief in a lawsuit seeking to enforce Title IX and the Department of Education's regulations.[221] This means that the court can order the school to correct its discriminatory or exclusionary actions.[222] Courts also have authority to order the school to pay the student damages, which are monetary awards that compensate for loss and injury suffered from the violation of Title IX, and to pay legal costs and attorney's fees.[223]

Can a public school refuse to enroll or otherwise discriminate against a student who has mental or physical disabilities?

Federal laws prohibit public schools from discriminating against children with disabilities, regardless of the nature or severity of their disability. The Individuals with Disabilities Education Act (IDEA) is the primary federal vehicle for protecting the rights of students with disabilities.[224] Federal law defines "child with a disability" as a child "with intellectual disabilities, hearing impairments (including deafness), speech or language impairments, visual impairments (including blindness), serious emotional disturbance . . . , orthopedic impairments, autism, traumatic brain injury, other health impairments, or specific learning disabilities."[225] Congress enacted the IDEA in 1975 in response to its findings that millions of disabled students received inferior instruction in segregated classrooms or were totally excluded from public schools. The IDEA enacted a new national policy of ensuring equal educational opportunity to students between the ages of three and 21 who have disabilities covered by the statute.

To that end, IDEA requires public schools to identify students with disabilities and to provide them with a free appropriate public education (FAPE).[226]

A FAPE includes special education and related services designed to meet a student's unique needs, and is individually tailored to allow the student to progress in the curriculum under the state's educational standards.[227] The FAPE mandate extends to students who are disabled even if they are homeless or in foster care; suspended or expelled from school; placed in hospitals, mental health institutions, or correctional institutions; or referred to private education settings.[228]

The FAPE to which a student with disabilities is entitled is designed and delivered through that student's Individualized Education Program (IEP).[229] An IEP is a personalized learning plan that, among other things, documents a student's present levels of achievement, frames "measurable annual goals," and details the services the school will provide to help the student advance toward those goals.[230]

When developing an IEP, schools must meet a number of procedural and substantive requirements that protect the rights afforded by the IDEA. Procedurally, the IDEA safeguards the parent's prerogative to serve as the school district's equal partner throughout the life of an IEP.[231] For instance, the school must establish an IEP team for each student, made up of parents and educators,[232] and the team generally must meet at least once yearly to review and revise the plan as necessary.[233] Parents are further entitled to examine their child's educational records,[234] to give or deny informed consent to disability screening,[235] and to receive notice prior to the school's making or refusing adjustments to their child's educational services.[236] Substantively, the IDEA guarantees IEPs that are (1) "reasonably calculated to enable [the student] to make progress appropriate in light of [the child's] circumstances"; (2) "appropriately ambitious" in light of the student's unique abilities; and (3) complete with "challenging objectives."[237] In addition, the IDEA requires that the FAPE be provided in the least restrictive environment (LRE) possible for the student, which means including students with disabilities in regular classrooms, alongside nondisabled peers, "to the maximum extent appropriate."[238] A student's LRE is dictated by individuated educational needs[239] and exists along a "continuum of alternative placements."[240] For any particular child, the least restrictive environment may be placement in regular, homebound, or special education settings, or some combination of the approaches.

Inquiries into the appropriateness of a student's IEP, and whether it provides a FAPE, are twofold.[241] First, parents may contest whether the school district satisfactorily observed the IDEA's procedural requirements when crafting the IEP.[242] To mount a successful claim, the complainant must demonstrate that a procedural error (1) "impeded the child's right to a [FAPE]," (2) "significantly impeded the parents' opportunity to participate in the decisionmaking process," or (3) "caused a deprivation of educational benefits."[243] For example, a school might neglect to include at least one regular education teacher on an IEP team, as required by the IDEA;[244] that procedural error might impede a child's right to a FAPE if the IEP team refuses to place the child in a regular education classroom without first seeking the specialized input of a regular education teacher, in violation of the statute.[245] Conversely, trivial procedural violations do not warrant relief.[246] Second, parents may challenge the IEP as substantively inadequate for failing to provide the student an appropriate level of educational benefit; the school violates the IDEA if the educational benefits that it delivers are merely minimally adequate.[247]

Parents may file complaints (pursuant to state procedures) against public school districts for failing to provide their children a FAPE through their IEPs.[248] Complaints must be filed within two years from the time that the parent or school district should have been aware of the alleged IDEA violation.[249] Complainants are entitled to relief from substantively defective IEPs.[250] When an IEP is disputed, a school district must offer "cogent" reasoning as to how the IEP satisfies each of the IDEA's requirements.[251] Note, however, that the U.S. Supreme Court has interpreted the IDEA to require only that IEPs be "reasonable"; IEPs need not reflect what the parents or the court would regard as "ideal."[252] Common forms of relief for successful claims include compensatory education and private school tuition reimbursement; a parent can also secure injunctive relief directing a school district to promptly develop an IDEA-compliant IEP.

IDEA protections complement two other civil rights statutes: Title II of the Americans with Disabilities Act of 1990 (ADA)[253] and Section 504 of the Rehabilitation Act of 1973 (Section 504).[254] The ADA and Section 504 guarantee nondiscriminatory access to public institutions for all people with disabilities (for example, through accommodations like wheelchair ramps, service animals, and screen readers). Parents may bring concurrent claims under each of these statutes as necessary.[255] Before filing suit on behalf of an IDEA-eligible student under a statute other than the IDEA, but seeking relief essentially for the denial of a FAPE, complainants must exhaust the full panoply of the IDEA's administrative remedies.[256] Exhaustion of the IDEA's due process procedures is *not* required in ADA or Section 504 suits, however, "when the gravamen of the plaintiff's suit is something other than the denial of [a FAPE]."[257]

For more information about the rights of students with disabilities, readers may contact the Office for Civil Rights in the U.S. Department of Education.[258]

Can a school punish a student for misconduct?

Public schools may discipline and suspend students for misconduct. Over the last 30 years, schools in some communities have moved from treating school misconduct as an administrative matter and instead as a criminal matter to be referred to the police for prosecution.[259] In practice, studies show that schools disproportionately discipline children whose families are poor or low-income, who are African American, or are enrolled in special education classes.[260] The problem of disparate disciplinary practices meted out by race and class begins as early as preschool, contributing to what now is called the school-to-prison pipeline.[261] Students who are suspended or expelled face tremendous barriers to receiving schooling and often fall behind, making their return to the regular classroom even more difficult. Eleven states have statutes that mandate alternative education in certain disciplinary contexts,[262] but analysts question the quality of the schooling provided.[263] Moreover, of the 100,000 students expelled from school in 2011–12, 50 percent received no education during that period.[264] Responding to concerns that high rates of suspension produce negative outcomes for students, a few school districts have begun to experiment with no-suspension policies that provide services to prevent disruptive behaviors at the outset.[265] In addition, some school districts have implemented restorative-justice programs.[266] A student who faces discipline or suspension can invoke a few rights, as follows.

Due Process Rights

The U.S. Supreme Court has held that a child's right to public schooling "may not be taken away for misconduct without adherence to the minimum procedures" consistent with the Due Process Clause of the federal Constitution. Any anticipated suspension that is more than "trivial"—usually measured by length of time—triggers procedural rights.[267] However, transfer to an alternative school has been held not to trigger due process protections unless "the education received at the alternative school is significantly different from or inferior to that received" at the student's regular school.[268]

At the least, before the school district punishes a student for misbehavior it must (1) have procedures governing when and how discipline is to be imposed; (2) make the procedures available to students; and (3) follow the procedures in deciding whether punishment is appropriate. These procedures typically require that the school give the student written notice of the impermissible misbehavior and the range of punishments, and an opportunity for the student to make a statement or present the testimony of witnesses to show, for example, that misbehavior did not take place or punishment is not warranted. A student should ask for a copy of the district's procedures, sometimes called a Code of Conduct or Discipline Code or "*Goss*" procedures (the name comes from the decision of the U.S. Supreme Court establishing the constitutional right to process in this context).[269] The procedures may vary depending on whether the suspension is short- or long-term. A student who faces a disciplinary hearing should consider requesting free legal assistance from a local legal services office.[270] In general, "*Goss*" procedures set a low bar and commentators note that schools have suspended students based on very limited proof.[271]

Individuals with Disabilities Education Act (IDEA)

A child who has been classified as disabled and is charged with misbehavior may invoke protection under the Individuals with Disabilities Education Act (IDEA).[272] Moreover, these protections apply to a student who has not yet been determined eligible for special education if the school district knew or should have known that the student was a "child with a disability" when the misconduct took place. The district should have known of the disability—thus triggering the IDEA's protections—if the parent "expressed concern in writing" to the child's teacher that special education and related services were needed, or requested that the child be evaluated for such services, or if the child's teacher or other personnel "expressed specific concerns about a pattern of behavior" by the child "directly to the director of special education or other supervisory personnel."[273]

First, the IDEA provides procedural protection to the child, including notice and hearing rights, for any change in placement that exceeds 10 days. Second, while disciplinary procedures are pending, a "stay-put" provision is triggered. Under this provision, the child remains in the current educational placement unless the child's parents and the educational agency otherwise agree to a change. Third, if the educational agency proposes a change in placement, the school district, parent, and members of the Individualized Education Program (IEP) team must meet within 10 days to determine if the misbehavior is a manifestation of the disability. Manifestation refers to instances in which misbehavior "was caused by, or had a direct and substantial relationship to, the child's disability" or the misbehavior "was the direct result" of the school district's failure to implement the child's IEP. If the misbehavior is a manifestation of the child's disability, the child is not subject to discipline; instead, the school must perform a "functional behavioral assessment" and develop a "behavioral intervention plan" that must be added to the child's IEP. If the misbehavior is not a manifestation of the child's disability, the child is subject to the same discipline as students without disabilities, but remains entitled to receive the services mandated in the IEP, even if provided in an alternative setting.[274] It is important that a parent or responsible adult monitor the quality of the education that is provided during a period of suspension and inform the IEP team of concerns.[275] Finally, special circumstances, usually involving violence or weapons, permit placement in an interim alternative placement for up to 45 days.[276] An appeal may be taken from these determinations.[277]

What is a Title I school?

Title I, which is part of the Elementary and Secondary Education Act, refers to a federal law that provides funding to local educational agencies to provide extra services to students who are falling below grade level or are at risk of doing so. The amount of funding and the formula for providing it has changed since the statute was first enacted in 1965, as have the authorizing statute's methods of ensuring school accountability.[278] Public schools can qualify for one of two types of Title I programs: schoolwide or targeted assistance.[279] In a schoolwide program, at least 40 percent of the school's students must come from low-income families.[280] A schoolwide program can use its Title I funds in combination with other federal, state, and local funds to improve the school's entire educational program, thereby serving all children in the school.[281] By contrast, a targeted assistance school can use its Title I funds only for eligible students, defined as those who are identified as "failing, or most at risk of failing, to meet . . . challenging State academic standards" as measured by multiple criteria.[282]

Title I funds are meant to supplement, not supplant, state or local educational funds,[283] and must be used to provide extra educational services to eligible students.[284] Schools can do this in many ways.[285] Additional services have included hiring teachers, aides, and tutors to work with children; providing family literacy programs; training school personnel; purchasing materials and equipment; and providing before- and after-school, weekend, or summer school programs.[286] In particular, Title I programs are expected to make use of effective instructional practices that avoid the "pullout" of students during regular school hours[287] and assist in meeting state performance standards.[288] Schools must provide qualified teachers[289] who will coordinate and support the regular education program.[290] In addition, schools are required to integrate their Title I programs with other federal, state, and local assistance programs and services, including violence prevention services, nutritional aid, vocational and technical training, and job-training programs.[291]

Can a parent participate in activities at a Title I school?

Yes. Schools that receive Title I funds are required to involve parents who wish to participate in school activities,[292] and must set aside 1 percent of total Title I funds received to support parental involvement activities.[293] Title I requires participating schools and school districts to work with parents in an organized, ongoing, and timely way on all aspects of the Title I program,[294] including decisions about how to allocate the funds.[295] School and district staff are expected to write to parents about the school's parental involvement policy,[296] and must develop a school-parent compact jointly with the parents of participating children,[297] aimed at implementing parental activities, identifying children most in need of services, and developing a Title I school plan.[298] Also, every year a school must convene a meeting to inform the parents of participating children about Title I and to explain parental involvement rights.[299] The school may provide transportation, child care, home visits, and other services to improve parental involvement and enable parents to attend meetings about Title I.[300] Schools must make every effort to accommodate parents with disabilities and parents who are learning English as a second language, including providing information and school profiles in languages and forms that can be understood.[301] By becoming involved in school activities, parents can advocate using Title I funds for programs that will most effectively encourage student success. For example, Title I funds can be used to develop policies of curative discipline—providing intervention services to children who misbehave rather than using punitive "push-out" policies or "zero-tolerance" approaches that increase the likelihood of involvement with the juvenile justice system.[302] Title I funds also can be used to develop services for mobile children, for example, those who are homeless or transitioning out of foster care.[303]

Skills and Job-Training Programs for Youth

Does the federal government fund voluntary skills and job-training programs for poor and low-income youth?

Yes. The federal government funds a number of voluntary programs that provide skills training to poor and low-income youth. These programs include the following:

Perkins Act—Vocational and Technical Education Programs
The Carl D. Perkins Vocational and Technical Education Act is a federal statute that provides funding to increase the quality and availability of vocational and technical education in the United States.[304] Most vocational and technical schools receive Perkins Act funds, and cannot refuse to enroll students on the basis of income, previous low grades, disability, limited English proficiency, or desire to be in a program that is gender unconventional. Moreover, they must provide information about their program and, if needed, help in applying to the program.

Job Corps

Job Corps is a free and voluntary vocational and academic training program aimed at enabling poor and low-income youth to acquire skills needed to obtain a job, to enter advanced training programs, to enroll in higher education programs, or to join the armed forces.[305] Job Corps is administered by the U.S. Department of Labor's Office of Job Corps. The program consists of 125 Job Corps centers throughout the United States and Puerto Rico. Most Job Corps centers provide services in a residential setting, but some offer the option of living off campus. Contracts to run Job Corps centers are awarded by the Department of Labor on a competitive basis to government agencies, area vocational education schools, residential vocational schools, and private organizations.

Center-offered services include career technical training in over 100 occupational areas; academic training including basic reading and math skills, GED attainment, college preparatory courses, and Limited English Proficiency courses; work-based learning, including on-the-job training; and counseling and other residential support, including driver's education, health and dental care, a biweekly basic living allowance and clothing allowance, and, in select centers, child care programs for single parents.

These services generally are administered in four phases.

- Phase 1: Outreach and Admission—A potential participant learns what the program is about and what vocational programs are available at the chosen center.
- Phase 2: Career Preparation Period—A student begins skill-building and creates a personal career development plan with the help of a Job Corps staff member. This phase takes place during the first 60 days of participation in Job Corps.
- Phase 3: Career Development Period—A participant learns the technical and academic skills necessary to fulfill an individualized career plan. The length of this phase depends on each individual student, but students are allowed to participate in Job Corps for up to two years.
- Phase 4: Career Transition Period—The student receives placement services to help connect to full-time jobs, advanced training programs, or higher education programs.

In order to qualify for Job Corps, a participant must be between 16 and 24 years of age,[306] be a U.S. citizen or legal resident, meet low-income requirements, and (1) need additional career technical training, education, counseling, and related assistance to complete regular schoolwork or to secure and hold meaningful employment; or (2) have dropped out of school; or (3) be a runaway, a foster child, a parent, or homeless.[307]

YouthBuild

YouthBuild is a full-time program designed to assist youth between 16 and 24 years of age to work toward acquiring a GED or high school diploma while learning job skills at construction sites building and rehabilitating housing for homeless and low-income individuals. In order to qualify, the applicant must meet the age condition, have dropped out of school, and fall into one of the following categories: (1) a member of a low-income family; (2) a youth in foster care; (3) a youth offender; (4) a person with a disability; (5) the child of a current or formerly incarcerated individual; or (5) a migrant youth.[308]

The Employment and Training Administration (ETA), which is a part of the U.S. Department of Labor, administers the program, and makes grants directly to local sponsors on a competitive basis; these grantees receive technical and data management assistance.[309] The program lasts from six months to two years depending on the individual participant.[310] Participants must spend at least 50 percent of their time in educational programming and services or activities related to education.[311]

Eligible educational activities include: (1) basic skills instruction and remedial education; (2) language instruction education programs for individuals with limited English proficiency; (3) secondary education services and activities designed to lead to the attainment of a high school diploma or its equivalent; (4) counseling and assistance in obtaining postsecondary education and required financial aid; (5) alternative secondary school services; (6) counseling services, including counseling on drug and alcohol abuse; (7) activities designed to develop employment and leadership skills; and (8) supportive services, for up to 12 months following the completion of the program, to assist individuals in retaining employment or applying for and transitioning to postsecondary education.[312]

Participants also must spend at least 40 percent of their time in work and skill development activities. These activities can include: (1) work experience and skills training coordinated, to the extent feasible, with pre-apprenticeship and registered apprenticeship programs in areas relating to the rehabilitation or construction of low-income housing or community/public facilities; (2) occupational skills training; (3) paid and unpaid work experience, including internships and job shadowing; and (4) job search assistance.[313] For information about applying, contact the local YouthBuild program.[314]

One-Stop Career Centers

Federal law authorizes job-training services to unemployed and underemployed individuals through programs that are primarily run by the U.S. Department of Labor through its Employment and Training Administration.[315] Federal law also requires the formation of a One-Stop delivery system, which coordinates state, local, and partner programs' training and employment activities and brings job-related services under one roof.[316] Anyone aged 18 and older is eligible for core services, and some centers have special programs for youth aged 14 and older who are part of a group that traditionally has faced serious barriers to being employed, such as living in low-income circumstances or having a disability. For more information about the program, contact the local American Job Center.[317]

Summer Youth Employment Programs

Many states and localities operate summer youth employment programs that provide opportunities for employment or educational experience. The programs often depend on state or city funding, so program availability may vary year to year. Eligibility requirements usually relate to age, income, household size, single parenthood status, and other family circumstances.[318]

Is a school-age person required to participate in work activities as a condition of receiving TANF-related benefits?

As a general matter, TANF work requirements do not apply to a "minor child," defined as an individual under age 18 or an individual under age 19 who is a full-time student in a secondary school or its vocational equivalent.[319] However, a minor who is the head of the household or married must meet work requirements to receive TANF-funded benefits. The work requirement can be satisfied by maintaining satisfactory attendance at a secondary school or the equivalent, or by participating in education directly related to employment for an average of at least 20 hours per week.[320] In addition, other educational activities may satisfy some or all of an individual's work requirement, including:[321]

1. Vocational associate degree programs;
2. Instructional certificate programs;
3. Industry skill certifications;
4. Noncredit course work;
5. Education leading to a baccalaureate or advanced degrees; and
6. Basic education and English as a Second Language (ESL) programs if they are a necessary and regular part of the work activity and as long as they are taught alongside vocational education or training and not as stand-alone activities.

Keep in mind that within these federal guidelines, each state has authority to determine its own eligibility and work requirements.[322] TANF work requirements, and the opportunities for satisfying them with educational activities, are discussed in chapter 1.

Postsecondary Education

Are there federal programs to help prepare
students with low income for college?

Yes. The federal government has a number of programs to encourage and help prepare students who have low income for college. Two important federal programs are Upward Bound[323] and Talent Search.[324]

Upward Bound
Upward Bound is funded by the U.S. Department of Education and is aimed at students in grades 9 through 12. Colleges and universities that participate in Upward Bound become partners with local high schools in year-round educational programs. While the programs vary from school to school, students generally receive tutoring, homework assistance, enrichment classes, and SAT or ACT preparation.[325] During the summer, students participate in a full academic program, usually on a college campus.[326] Some Upward Bound programs give students an opportunity to live on campus for the summer.[327] Participating students receive guidance on how to apply to college and to obtain scholarships and financial aid. A student who wants more information should talk to a school guidance counselor or, if none is available, consult the Upward Bound website.[328]

Talent Search
Talent Search is a federal program designed to assist poor and low-income students to finish high school and receive postsecondary education.[329] Talent Search is also open to individuals who dropped out of school and want to re-enter or to pursue an alternative educational opportunity.[330] Talent Search provides a range of services, including academic counseling, tutoring, and assistance in completing college and financial aid applications.[331] To be eligible, students must have completed at least five years of elementary school and be between ages 11 and 27.[332] For more information about Talent Search, talk to a guidance counselor at a local school, contact the state department of education, or consult the Talent Search website.[333]

Federal Assistance for Higher Education

Does the federal government provide assistance
to enable persons with low income to attend college?

The federal government provides different kinds of assistance to help pay for college. The assistance may be described as grants, loans, work-study, or tax credits.

The nature of the assistance significantly affects the student's legal responsibilities, ability to save money, and mobility out of poverty. A grant lowers the cost of education and does not have to be repaid. A loan does not lower the cost of education but makes education accessible on easier credit terms; however, the student then faces debt plus interest payments. Work-study provides term-time employment while a person attends college.[334] Getting a work-study grant is especially important for certain low-income students because, as discussed in chapter 3, it allows them to qualify for SNAP (food stamps) benefits when they would otherwise be excluded from participation.[335] Finally, the United States makes various tax credits available to households with low income; the credits do not lower the cost of education but they may increase the amount of money available to pay for tuition and other expenses. All of these loan and grant programs must be viewed in context: since 1964, the average cost of attending a four-year public college in the United States has increased by 3,819 percent, and student loan debt is now almost $1.6 trillion. In particular, debt burden for low-income students has become a national crisis that exacerbates poverty and blocks mobility. Programs that support higher education should provide affordable and quality opportunities that provide a pathway out of poverty, and not require students to mortgage their futures. A number of states are taking the lead in offering tuition-free public higher-education.[336]

INFORMATION BOX: STATES THAT OFFER TUITION-FREE HIGHER EDUCATION

Over the past several years, a number of states and cities have moved toward providing free college education to students. Tennessee in 2015 began allowing students to attend community colleges tuition-free. New York in 2017 became the first state to make its four-year colleges tuition-free. Oregon and the city of San Francisco have enacted similar policies, while Arkansas, Minnesota, and South Dakota offer free tuition for high-demand fields (computer science or welding). By last count, 20 states offered some type of tuition-free college program. Each of these programs is subject to different eligibility requirements, such as family income, established residence in state, and maintaining a minimum grade point average.[337]

What grants does the federal government offer to help pay the cost of college?

The two most important federal grant programs for higher education are Pell Grants and Federal Supplemental Educational Opportunity (FSEO) grants. In fiscal year 2018, the U.S. Department of Education disbursed $28.2 billion in Pell Grants and $750 million in FSEO grants; looking at all grants, more than eight million students received scholarships.[338] These programs have played a key role in expanding access to higher education. Nevertheless, according to the College Board, the average Pell Grant in 2018–18 covered 60 percent of the average public four-year in-state tuition and fees, down from 92 percent in 1998–99.[339] Moreover, not all of the recipients are poor or low-income; since 1978, students from middle-income families have been eligible for Pell Grants, and their share of federal disbursements has steadily increased.[340]

Pell Grant

A Pell Grant is scholarship money that the federal government awards to help a student of modest means pay for education after high school.[341] How much money an eligible student receives depends on the student's financial circumstances, tuition and other costs, and whether attendance is full-time or part-time. Since 2012, receipt of a Pell Grant is limited to 12 semesters (the equivalent of six years). The size of the grant changes from year to year; for academic year 2019–20, the largest grant was $6,195. The U.S. Department of Education directly runs the program and accepts applications through online submission of the Free Application for Federal Student Aid (FAFSA) form.[342] Persons who are incarcerated are generally barred from the Pell Grant program, as are individuals subject to an involuntary civil commitment after incarceration for a forcible or nonforcible sexual offense. The Obama administration initiated a pilot program in 2016 to address this harsh and racialized collateral consequence of incarceration.[343] Students convicted of a drug offense while receiving federal financial assistance for higher education are temporarily or permanently disqualified from receiving federal financial aid, but this restriction may be lifted if the individual successfully completes a drug rehabilitation program.[344]

Federal Supplemental Educational Opportunity Grant

A Federal Supplemental Educational Opportunity (FSEO) grant is money that the federal government gives to students with "exceptional" financial need to help pay for education after high school.[345] Each educational institution, and not the U.S. Department of Education, runs the program for its own students, but not all schools participate in the program, and funding is limited, so not every eligible applicant receives an FSEO grant. If a student receives an FSEO grant, the amount of the award is determined by financial need, the amount of other financial aid the student will receive, and the availability of funds at the student's school, subject to a cap that changes each year. Pell Grant recipients are given priority for these supplemental grants; in 2019–20 the maximum grant was $4,000.

Students who are interested in this program should complete the FAFSA form and apply for the grant at their school as early as possible.[346]

What loan programs does the United States offer to pay for college?

The federal government offers loans to help students pay for college. The term "federal loan" may be used to refer to (1) loans issued directly through the federal government ("direct loans"), or (2) loans issued through private lenders or state agencies and guaranteed by the federal government under the Federal Family Education Loan (FFEL) Program ("guaranteed loans").[347] In 2010, Congress ended the FFEL Program, from which private lenders were making over $6 billion per year in fees, and directed that all federal educational loans be made directly by the U.S. Department of Education under the Higher Education Act.[348]

Although all federal loans are now "direct loans" administered by the Department of Education, private lenders continue to issue educational loans without federal guarantees. Federal loans offer many advantages but also a few disadvantages relative to private loans. Federal loans are preferable to private loans because they carry fixed and lower interest charges; may be subsidized (the government may pay the interest while the student is in school); always offer income-based repayment plans; may be forgiven in certain circumstances; and interest is deferred under certain circumstances. In addition, although a student must provide financial information as part of the federal student loan application, the approval process does not include a credit check.[349] However, federal law caps the amounts that a student can borrow, and also makes it easier for the federal government to recover an unpaid loan—wages can be garnished without a court order, tax refunds can be intercepted, and there is no statute of limitations for the collection process. (Consumer protections for borrowers with private student loans are discussed in chapter 6.)

What are federal Direct Loans?

The William D. Ford Federal Direct Loan Program offers four types of loans, all administered by the federal U.S. Department of Education:[350]

1. Direct Subsidized Loans. These loans are available for eligible college students who demonstrate financial need.

2. Direct Unsubsidized Loans. These loans are available to eligible college, graduate, and professional students without regard to financial need.
3. Direct PLUS Loans. These loans are available to graduate and professional students and parents of dependent college students for education expenses not covered by other financial aid.
4. Direct Consolidation Loans. These loans allow a student-debtor to combine all eligible student loans into one loan with a single loan servicer.

What are Perkins loans?

The Perkins loan is a school-based loan for eligible college and graduate students who demonstrate exceptional financial need. Unlike direct loans, the educational institution functions as the lender.[351]

What is the process to apply for a federal student loan?

The first step to apply for a federal student loan is to complete the "Free Application for Federal Student Aid" (FAFSA) form. The form is available online with a guide that explains how to fill in the information and submit the form.[352]

What are the rates and terms of federal loans?

The rates and terms of federal student loans are standardized. The Bipartisan Student Loan Certainty Act of 2013 indexes the interest rates for new student loans issued on or after July 1, 2013 to the rates for 10-year U.S. Treasury notes.[353] Under this act, interest rates are determined each June for new loans being made for the upcoming award year, which runs from July 1 to the following June 30. Each loan will have a fixed interest rate for the life of the loan. The interest rate for undergraduate student loans issued in 2019–20 was 4.53 percent.[354] By contrast, the rates and terms of private loans are largely unregulated, and vary widely.

When must a borrower start to repay a federal student loan?

Most federal student loans require the first payment to be made six months after the borrower leaves school.[355] Financial institutions, including those that provide loan servicing, are required to give exit counseling for borrowers. Such counseling must include, among other items, information on repayment plans.[356]

What is the standard repayment plan for a federal student loan?

The standard repayment plan for direct and guaranteed federal student loans carries a fixed payment of at least $50 per month for 10 years (unless the loan is "consolidated"—discussed later in this chapter—and then the payment term can extend to 30 years, depending on the amount of the loan). Loans covered by the standard repayment plan are:

- Direct subsidized loans
- Direct unsubsidized loans
- Direct PLUS loans
- Direct consolidation loans
- Subsidized Stafford loans
- Unsubsidized Stafford loans
- FFEL PLUS loans
- FFEL consolidation loans

What happens if a federal student borrower cannot meet the terms of the standard repayment plan?

If a federal student borrower cannot meet the terms of the standard repayment plan, the borrower should immediately consider switching to an income-driven plan, which reduces monthly loan payments to bring them in line with the borrower's income. It is important to elect this alternative, if needed, before the loan goes into default, because a loan in default status cannot be repaid under an income-driven plan. However, a defaulted loan can become eligible for income-driven repayment through a process called "loan rehabilitation," which requires the borrower to make a number of payments based on the borrower's income.[357]

Federal law offers a variety of income-driven repayment plans for federal loans (both direct loans and guaranteed loans). These plans are designed to make student loan debt more manageable by reducing monthly payments to an amount intended to be affordable for the debtor, given income and family size.[358] Keep in mind that although payments will be lower, the repayment period may be extended, causing larger payments in interest over time. However, some income-driven repayment plans provide for cancellation of any loan balance remaining after 20 or 25 years. An applicant for an income-driven repayment plan submits an online or paper "Income-Driven Repayment Plan Request" application.[359] Along with the application, the applicant will be asked to provide information about income in the form of a tax return or an acceptable alternative documentation of income. These repayment options do not apply to private loans. The four income-driven repayment plans are income-based repayment, pay as you earn, revised pay as you earn, and income-contingent repayment plans.

Income-Based Repayment Plan Option

The Income-Based Repayment plan (IBR plan) is available for all federal direct loans,[360] except Federal PLUS or Direct PLUS loans taken out on behalf of a dependent student, and "consolidation" loans taken out to repay PLUS loans made to parents.[361] The IBR plan is open to borrowers who can show "partial financial hardship." For loans made after July 1, 2014, partial financial hardship exists whenever the annual amount the borrower owes under the standard 10-year repayment plan is greater than 10 percent of the amount by which the borrower's annual income exceeds 150 percent of the federal poverty income guideline. For example, suppose Graduate's yearly income exceeds 150 percent of the federal poverty line by $12,000; Graduate qualifies for an Income-Based Repayment plan if the annual amount due on Graduate's loan is more than $1,200 (10 percent of $12,000).[362] In that case, Graduate's loan repayment would be reduced to $1,200 per year (10 percent of the amount by which her income exceeds 150 percent of the poverty line), or $100 per month.[363] Notice that for borrowers with annual income near, at, or below 150 percent of the poverty line, application of the IBR formula will reduce the repayment amount to zero. However, whenever a borrower's reduced monthly payment is less than the amount of interest due on the loan, the unpaid interest is added to the principal amount that must be repaid if the borrower leaves the Income-Based Repayment plan or no longer qualifies for it.[364] On the other hand, borrowers who make payments according to the plan for 25 years, may have some or all of their remaining loan balance cancelled.[365]

INFORMATION BOX: INCOME-BASED REPAYMENT CALCULATOR

The U.S. Department of Education provides an Income-Based Repayment (IBR) calculator to help determine eligibility for the income-based repayment program.[366] The Consumer Financial Protection Bureau's website provides a chart that sets approximate monthly payments adjusting for income and family size.[367]

Pay as You Earn Repayment

The Pay as You Earn (PAYE) plan caps the monthly loan payment at 10 percent of the borrower's income.[368] The amount of the payment never exceeds what would be paid under the standard plan, based on the amount owed at the time the borrower elects the PAYE option. Also, under PAYE, any student debt that remains after 20 years of monthly payments will be forgiven—meaning the debt no longer needs to be repaid or repaid in its entirety. The PAYE option is available only to borrowers who took out their first federal student loan after October 1, 2007, received a disbursement of a Direct Loan or Direct Consolidation Loan after October 1, 2011, and can demonstrate "partial financial hardship."[369] The loan may be prepaid without penalty at any time.

Revised Pay as You Earn Repayment

The Revised Pay as You Earn repayment plan (REPAYE) is open to all borrowers with direct loans except Parent PLUS loans and consolidated loans taken out to repay Parent PLUS loans. REPAYE has no income restrictions, and the monthly payment generally is 10 percent of discretionary income.[370] Unlike PAYE, REPAYE does not cap the monthly payment at the amount that would be owed under a standard repayment plan (meaning that the payment could be higher than the standard monthly payment for a borrower with higher income). Unpaid amounts for undergraduate loans are forgiven after 20 years of qualifying payments. If the monthly payment does not cover the full amount of the accrued interest, the government pays the full amount of the difference for the first three years and half the difference after the first three years.[371]

Income-Contingent Repayment

The Income-Contingent Repayment (ICR) plan covers all direct loan borrowers except Parent PLUS loans or consolidated loans (after July 1, 2006) taken to repay Parent PLUS loans. The ICR has no income limits on participation, and the repayment amount generally is the lesser of 20 percent of "discretionary income" or the fixed payment under a 12-year term.[372] However, as with REPAYE, the monthly payment may be more than under a standard repayment plan for borrowers with higher income. If the payment does not cover the interest that accrues, the unpaid amount goes into the principal to be repaid, limited to 10 percent of the original loan at the time the borrower elected to participate in the ICR plan. After 25 years of qualifying payments, the outstanding loan balance is forgiven.[373]

Can a borrower defer repayment of a federal student loan?

In certain circumstances, a federal Direct Loan borrower facing hardship may obtain a "deferment" of repayment, which temporarily suspends the obligation to make monthly payments of interest or interest and principal on the student loan.[374] Loans that are in default generally do not qualify for deferment, so it is important that an eligible borrower apply for deferment before a default occurs. There are several categories of deferment, including the following:

Unemployment deferment. This may be granted for periods of unemployment, not to exceed an aggregate of three years, if the borrower is actively seeking but unable to locate a full-time job.

Economic hardship deferment. This may be granted for periods, not to exceed an aggregate of three years, during which the borrower (1) receives public assistance (including SSI, SNAP, TANF, state assistance); (2) works full-time but earns less than 150 percent of the federal poverty income guideline applicable to the borrower's family; or (3) serves as a volunteer in the Peace Corps.

Military service deferment. This is available to borrowers serving on active duty or certain qualifying National Guard duty during a war or other defined military operation or national emergency.

Can federal student loans ever be "forgiven"?

If a loan is forgiven, the remaining debt no longer has to be repaid or repaid in its entirety. Federal student loans can be "forgiven" under certain income-based repayment plans, discussed above. In addition, certain federal direct loans can be forgiven if the borrower engages in a public service career after graduation and meets loan repayment requirements.[375]

Loans that can be forgiven. Federal Direct Subsidized or Unsubsidized loans, Direct PLUS loans, and Direct Consolidation Loans.

Repayment requirement. The borrower must not be in default on the loan and generally must have made 120 separate monthly payments after October 1, 2007, though a standard repayment plan or one of the income-driven repayment plans.

Amounts that can be forgiven. The loan principal and accrued interest that remains after the borrower makes the required 120 monthly payments (as of March 2019, the average amount forgiven was over $59,000).[376]

Public service work. The borrower must work full-time for a qualifying public service organization or private organization. Eligible public service jobs include firefighters, teachers, nurses, lawyers, and public safety officers.[377] Borrowers must have made a required number of monthly payments and have made payments through a standard or income-contingent repayment plan (a program known as Temporary Expanded Public Service Loan Forgiveness, introduced in 2018, is available to some qualifying borrowers whose repayments were not made through a qualifying repayment plan).[378] In 2018, the program had a rejection rate of 99 percent—41,000 borrowers applied for forgiveness, and only 206 had their loans discharged.[379] At least one lawsuit has been filed against the U.S.

Department of Education challenging its administration of the Public Service Loan Forgiveness program.[380]

Special loan forgiveness program for teachers. The federal government offers two forgiveness programs for teachers who incurred federal student debt. These programs are loan forgiveness for Direct Subsidized Loans, Direct Unsubsidized Loans, Subsidized Stafford Loans, and Unsubsidized Federal Stafford loans. In addition, Federal Perkins Loans are eligible for cancellation. (PLUS loans are not eligible for either program.)

Teachers are eligible for forgiveness of up to $17,500 of their federal loans if they teach full-time for at least five consecutive years at designated low-income schools or educational agencies, and meet other conditions,[381] including being certified as "highly qualified."[382] Different rules and amounts of forgiveness apply, depending whether the qualifying teaching service began before or after October 30, 2004.[383]

INFORMATION BOX: 9/11 AND LOAN DISCHARGE

Federal student loans are discharged for police officers, firefighters, other safety and rescue personnel, or members of the armed forces who died or became "permanently and totally disabled" in the terrorist attacks that took place on September 11, 2001, as well as for their spouses and parents who endorsed loans on their behalf.[384] The U.S. Department of Education does not provide an application for this program. Interested parties should contact FedLoan Servicing, available at https://myfedloan.org/borrowers/forgiveness-discharge.

Does a borrower's disability affect repayment or discharge of a federal student loan?

A borrower's disability may affect repayment or discharge of a federal student loan (discharge means the debt is canceled and does not have to be paid).[385] The U.S. Department of Education provides three mechanisms for loan discharge depending on the kind of federal loan.

Permanent and Total Disability

For applications filed on or after July 1, 2013, a showing of total and permanent disability will discharge a William D. Ford Federal Direct Loan, a Federal Perkins Loan, or a Federal Family Education Program Loan.[386] A debtor is eligible for a disability discharge upon submission of a certification from a physician of total and permanent disability[387] and that the debtor is unable to engage in any gainful activity because of an impairment that can be expected to result in death; has lasted for a continuous period of not less than 60 months; or can be expected to last for a continuous period of 60 months.[388]

Veterans' Disability Discharge

A veteran is eligible for discharge upon a showing that the U.S. Department of Veterans Affairs has determined that the veteran is unemployable due to a service-connected condition; additional medical documentation is not required.[389]

Disability Benefits (SSDI or SSI) Discharge

A recipient of Social Security Disability Insurance or Supplemental Security Income is eligible for discharge upon submission of the notice of benefits from the Social Security Administration stating that the next scheduled disability review is within five to seven years from the date of the most recent disability determination.[390]

Are student loans discharged if the borrower's school closed?

Over 100 for-profit and career colleges and 20 nonprofit colleges have closed since 2016 alone. School closures in 2018 and 2019 by just three companies have affected tens of thousands of students.[391] Student borrowers may be eligible for a discharge of their student loans if they attended a school that closed while they were enrolled or within 120 days of the student's enrollment ending.[392] Closed school debt relief offers a 100 percent discharge of federal Direct Loans, Federal Family Education Loans, or Federal Perkins Loans. The request must be made through the student's loan servicer.[393] The discharge is not available if the borrower completed a comparable course of study through a "teach-out" agreement or similar means.[394]

Is there any relief for a borrower with federal student loans whose school engaged in fraud or misrepresentation, but remains open?

Student-borrowers under federal loan programs may be eligible for a "borrower's defense" if the enrolling school engaged in misconduct harmful to the student. Misconduct can be fraud or misrepresentation (such as inducing enrollment based on inflated job-placement statistics). Studies have documented systematic predatory behavior by for-profit colleges (discussed in chapter 6).[395] Existing regulations recognize the borrower defense when the school engaged in an act or omission that would violate state law. Students who incurred federal debt to attend schools that engaged in fraud or misrepresentation are eligible for a defense to repayment based on acts or omissions that the school committed.[396] Debtors seeking "defense to payment" relief may apply online.[397] The Trump administration has proposed regulations that limit the ability of student-loan borrowers to obtain this remedy, and the Department of Education has failed to process pending applications.[398]

What happens if a borrower defaults on a federal student loan?

A borrower who does not make payments on a federal student loan may be in default, and face serious consequences.[399] For this reason, borrowers should make every effort to avoid default (including through applying for an income-driven repayment plan that reduces monthly payments, as discussed earlier); and if the loan does go into default, the borrower should immediately attempt to remove the loan from default status.[400] If a borrower defaults, the entire balance of the loan (principal and interest) may become due in a single payment. This is called acceleration. Once a loan is accelerated, the holder of the loan may place it with a collection agency. The United States has important litigation advantages when it seeks to collect federal student loans from a borrower who is in default. Above all, the federal government is not bound by the Fair Debt Collection Practices Act and is exempt from the Telephone Consumer Protection Act.[401] Borrowers must be alert to four practices associated with student debt collection by the federal government:

- The United States is not constrained by a statute of limitations on the time to bring suit to enforce the debt, and can file suit decades after a default.
- The United States can impose fees on the borrower.
- The United States can garnish the wages of the borrower without a court order.
- The United States can intercept tax refunds to collect the debt.

Statute of Limitations
There is no time limit on the collection of federal student loans; unlike other forms of debt, which a collector must collect within a certain time span, federal student loans can be collected at any time.[402] The government collects loans years after the debt originated, payment stopped, or default occurred. This means that older low-income people are vulnerable to debt collection decades after the debt was incurred.

Collection Fees
The government may charge "reasonable collection costs" to the borrower from whom a debt is being collected.[403] Collection costs can include but are not

limited to attorney's fees, collection agency charges, and court costs.[404] The total amount of collection costs must be the lesser of the amount the Department of Education would charge if it held the loan, or an amount calculated by a formula in 34 C.F.R. § 30.60.[405]

If the government uses a third-party collection agency to collect the debt, the collection cost will be the amount charged to the government for collection services.[406] If a borrower enters into a repayment or settlement agreement in order to pay off a student loan, the collection costs charged will be those specified in the agreement.[407] To learn more about collection and collection costs, visit the Federal Student Aid website.[408]

Garnishment of Wages without Court Order

The government may collect unpaid federal student loans through wage garnishment if the debtor is not making payments required under a repayment agreement, and may do so without a court order.[409] The following restrictions apply:

1. The government may not deduct more than 15 percent of a paycheck (unless it obtains written consent from the debtor);[410]
2. The debtor must be mailed a written notice of the garnishment and an explanation of legal rights, at least 30 days before the garnishment proceedings begin;[411]
3. The debtor must be given the opportunity to look at records of the debt,[412] to enter into a payment agreement with the government,[413] and to have a hearing in court on the existence of the debt and/or the payment agreement.[414]

Once an administrative order for garnishing wages is issued, the garnished wages are paid directly to the government by the employer.[415] If the wages are not paid, the government can take legal action against the employer itself, and the employer can be held liable.[416] The debtor does not have to be included in the lawsuit.[417] If the debtor is fired, and starts a new job within one year of being fired, the government will not begin to garnish wages until the debtor has been continuously employed at the new job for one year.[418] Employers cannot refuse to hire, and may not fire or otherwise discipline, an employee because of the garnishment.[419] If an employer takes such an action, the employee can sue the employer; if successful in the suit, the employee will be awarded attorney's fees, and can be awarded job reinstatement, back pay, and other damages.

Interception of Tax Refunds

Federal law permits the U.S. Department of Treasury to transfer a taxpayer's tax refund to another federal agency to pay a past due debt,[420] including a student loan. The interception process is not covered by the Fair Debt Collection Practices Act and is not limited by state laws that might afford the borrower greater protection. Moreover, some federal courts have held that the fact that the refund consisted primarily of an Earned Income Tax Credit does not bar the offset.[421]

Social Security Offset

The federal government also may offset a debtor's Social Security benefits to collect on a student loan debt, even when that debt has been outstanding for more than 10 years.[422]

What is consolidation?

Consolidation is the term for combining different federal student loans into one loan. The federal government charges no fee to consolidate loans, and it is important not to be tricked into paying a consolidation fee by a private company. Consolidation has advantages and disadvantages, depending on the borrower's circumstances. The upside of consolidation is that the borrower makes only one monthly payment, rather than payments on each loan, and extends the payment term to 30 years. The downside of consolidation is that it could result in the loss of various benefits (for example, the loss of credits made toward an income-driven repayment plan forgiveness). Almost all federal student loans are eligible for consolidation, but a student cannot consolidate loans with any Direct PLUS Loans borrowed by a parent.[423]

What is work-study?

Federal work-study programs provide jobs for undergraduate and graduate students who need financial aid.[424] Payment is made directly to the students, who are expected to use the earnings to help pay their educational expenses. Each school runs its own work-study program for its own students, and because funding is limited, not every eligible student is able to participate. Students who are interested in participating in federal work-study programs should apply at their school as early as possible. As noted earlier, securing a work-study grant is especially important for certain low-income students because it allows them to qualify for SNAP (food stamps) benefits when they would otherwise be excluded.[425] If a student is accepted into a program, the total amount of money that can be earned through the work-study job is determined by financial need, the amount of other financial aid the student will receive, and the availability of funds at the student's school. Work-study jobs, which can be on campus or off campus, pay at least the current federal minimum wage, and may have higher minimum pay rates, depending on the applicable state's minimum wage laws.

What is the National Service Trust Program?

The National Service Trust Program provides a living allowance, salary, and health and child care benefits to students who undertake up to two years of community service in the fields of education, human services, the environment, or public safety as part of the AmeriCorps program. [426] Participants must work 1,700 hours a year. This money can be used to pay tuition or financial-aid loans.[427]

Does the federal tax code help offset the cost of postsecondary education?

Under the Internal Revenue Code, some kinds of educational assistance are tax-free if they meet specified statutory conditions.[428] A scholarship or grant does not count as taxable income if the student is a candidate for a degree at an eligible educational institution, the scholarship or grant does not exceed the student's qualified educational expenses, the funds are not earmarked for other purposes, and the funds are not payment for teaching, research, or other services required as a condition of the scholarship or grant (with some exceptions).[429] Pell Grants and other federal needs-based grants, for example, are treated as scholarships that are tax-free to the extent they are used to meet qualified educational expenses.[430]

Tax benefits for education also come in the form of deductions and credits, and their applicability depends on whether the taxpayer is currently attending college, is liable for student loan payments, or is saving for college.[431] First, there are two credits available for higher education expenses: (1) the American Opportunity Tax Credit (AOTC) and (2) the "Lifetime Learning" Credit (LLC).[432] Both are subject to numerous qualifying conditions and limitations, but one of the most important conditions is that a taxpayer may not claim both credits with respect to the same student for the same tax year.[433] Second, there is a deduction for the payment of interest on a student loan. The deduction is capped at $2,500 and phases out at higher income levels.[434] And third, contributions to certain savings accounts for qualified tuition programs (for example, Coverdell) may be made on a tax-deferred basis. In 2017, a Republican Congress passed the Tax Cuts and Jobs Act of 2017 (TCJA), which dramatically reduced taxes on corporations and wealthy individuals and limited deductibility of state and local taxes in ways that will likely impede public funding for education. The TCJA did not directly change either of the two education tax credits (the AOTC or LLC) or eliminate the student loan interest deduction.[435] However, it allowed the tax deduction for college tuition and fees to expire,[436] and eliminated the deduction for work-related education expenses as miscellaneous itemized deductions subject to a 2 percent of income floor.[437] The following discussion describes tax credits that may be beneficial to low-income taxpayers pursuing postsecondary education.[438]

What is the American Opportunity Tax Credit?

The American Opportunity Tax Credit (AOTC), formerly known as the Hope Scholarship Credit,[439] is a partially refundable credit of up to $2,500 per eligible student per year for qualified tuition, related expenses, and course materials covering the first four years of the student's postsecondary education in a degree or certification program.[440] Students receive a credit of 100 percent against the first $2,000 of expenses, plus a credit of 25 percent against the next $2,000. Forty percent, or $1,000, of the AOTC is refundable, but none of it is refundable if the taxpayer claiming the credit is: (1) under age 18; or (2) under age 24 and a student providing less than one-half self-support who has one living parent and does not file a joint return.[441] The AOTC is phased out at certain income levels. For 2018, the phaseout for unmarried individuals is $80,000 to $90,000; for married couples filing jointly, $160,000 to $180,000.

What is the Life Learning Credit?

The Lifetime Learning Credit (LLC) is a nonrefundable credit equal to 20 percent of qualified tuition and related expenses for any postsecondary education expenses, up to a maximum annual credit of $2,000 for the taxpayer, the taxpayer's spouse, or any dependent of the taxpayer.[442] Unlike the AOTC, which is calculated on a *per-student* basis, the maximum allowable LLC per year is $2,000 *per taxpayer* regardless of the number of students reported on the taxpayer's return.[443] Additionally, the amount of the credit is not adjusted for inflation. Similar to the AOTC, the LLC is phased out at certain income levels. For 2018, the phase out for unmarried individuals is $57,000 to $67,000; and for married couples filing jointly, $114,000 to $134,000.

What are "qualified tuition and related expenses"?

Qualified tuition and related (QTR) expenses generally refer to tuition and fees required for the enrollment or attendance of the taxpayer, the taxpayer's spouse, or any dependent of the taxpayer at an eligible educational institution for courses of instruction of such individual at such institution. QTR expenses include fees for books, supplies, and equipment only if the fees must be paid to the educational institution as a condition of the student's enrollment or attendance.[444] For the AOTC, QTR also covers course materials.[445]

Can a taxpayer claim both education credits?

A taxpayer may not claim "double benefits." Specifically, a taxpayer may not do any of the following:[446]

1. Deduct higher education expenses and also claim an American Opportunity Credit or Lifetime Learning Credit based on those same expenses;
2. Claim an American Opportunity Credit and Lifetime Learning Credit based on the same qualified education expenses;
3. Claim an American Opportunity Credit or Lifetime Learning Credit based on the same expenses used to figure the tax-free portion of a distribution from a qualified tuition program under Section 529 or a Coverdell education savings account under Section 530; or
4. Claim an American Opportunity Credit or Lifetime Learning Credit based on qualified education expenses paid with a tax-free scholarship, grant, or employer-provided educational assistance.

Adult Education Programs

Does the United States fund programs to help adults retrain and acquire new skills?

The federal government funds a number of programs that encourage adults to retrain and develop new workplace skills.[447] These programs include the following:

1. One-Stop Career Centers
One-Stop Career Centers, established under the Work Investment Act, offer a tiered-system of services.

- Core Services: All adults, regardless of their current employment status, can access "core services," which include initial assessments, job search assistance, information about access to supportive services, and employment counseling.

- Intensive Services: Adults and dislocated workers who are not able to obtain employment or who remain underemployed after utilizing core services may access intensive services. An individual must have received at least one core service such as an initial assessment that determines that individual's need for these services. Intensive services include comprehensive assessments of skill levels and in-depth evaluation of employment barriers, development of individual employment plans, short-term prevocational services, work experience activities, and case management.
- Training Services: Adults and dislocated workers who are unable to obtain or retain employment through intensive services and unable to obtain grant assistance from other sources such as Pell Grants are eligible to receive training services. Training services include occupational skills training, on-the-job training, combination workplace and related instruction training, skills upgrading and retraining, job-readiness training, adult education, and literacy activities combined with other authorized services.

Centers can be found in major population areas in every state, but in many states and cities these centers are not called One-Stop Centers. The easiest way to find a One-Stop Center is to visit the One-Stop Career website at https://www. careeronestop.org/ or America's Service Locator at https://www.servicelocator. org.

2. Registered Apprenticeship

Registered Apprenticeship connects job seekers with employers. Participants earn a paycheck right away and receive on-the-job training. Participants can also potentially earn college credit or an associate or bachelor's degree and can earn a nationally recognized certificate of completion. The U.S. Department of Labor runs the Registered Apprenticeship System through the Office of Apprenticeship.[448] The Office of Apprenticeship provides leadership, guidance, information, and technical support to employers, labor management organizations, and workers interested in developing apprenticeship programs. A network of State Apprenticeship Agencies exists in 25 states and the District of Columbia. An operator of an apprenticeship program is called a program sponsor. Program sponsors include single employer sponsors, groups of employers in partnership with organized labor (called a Joint Apprenticeship Training Committee), or an industry or employer association. Some registered apprenticeships have agreements with postsecondary institutions, such as community colleges, for academic credit. Some apprenticeship programs award associate degrees upon completion or have links to other degree programs. Registered apprenticeship program sponsors identify the minimum qualifications to qualify for their apprenticeship program. The eligible starting age can be no less than 16; however, in order to work in certain hazardous programs an individual must usually be at least 18. Program sponsors may also identify additional minimum qualifications and credentials, including education, ability to physically perform the essential functions of the occupation, and proof of age.[449]

Educational Opportunities for Incarcerated People and Ex-Offenders

Is federal educational assistance available for people who are incarcerated or have re-entered the community?

People who are incarcerated and those who have served their sentence and are re-entering the community face many legal and practical barriers to accessing education, especially higher education.[450] These barriers trace in part to federal policies. Some of these are policies of omission. For example, federal law does not require youth over age 16 to return to school after incarceration.[451] Others are conscious and counterproductive policies designed to block ex-offenders from accessing education. In 1994, for instance, Congress eliminated Pell Grant eligibility for students incarcerated in state or federal prisons, with predictable consequences for educational access.[452] To take one example, the Prisoner Reentry Institute reported that the number of prison postsecondary education programs in New York during the period 1994 to 2008 plummeted from 70 to 8.[453] In 2012, the Obama administration, noting the devastating impact of mass incarceration on many low-income communities, especially communities of color, and the strongly positive effects of education and training on re-entry outcomes, issued guidelines encouraging states to strengthen educational opportunities for ex-offenders.[454] Some states have taken the initiative to increase education access for incarcerated people and those transitioning back into the community.[455]

The story on the federal level is less encouraging. Recent federal criminal justice legislation (the First Step Act of 2018) adopted some modest though important measures to reduce incarceration rates, and recognized the need to study and improve reentry outcomes. However, the statute did almost nothing to enhance educational access and left restrictions on federal educational aid in place.[456] It is worth re-emphasizing that these restrictions (discussed earlier in this chapter) are not always a categorical bar. First, the general bar on federal student aid for people incarcerated in state or federal correctional facilities does not apply to people confined in a local facility or a juvenile justice facility.[457] Also, the limitations on federal student aid for people convicted of drug offenses apply only if the offense was a felony or misdemeanor that occurred while the student was receiving such aid. Moreover, the student can regain eligibility for financial aid by successfully completing an approved drug rehabilitation program.[458] Finally, in one hopeful development, the Obama administration initiated a pilot program in 2016 known as "Second Chance Pell," which has made federal financial aid available to over 10,000 inmates, enabling them to work toward college degrees, which have been shown to increase the likelihood of successful reentry into the community. As of 2019, the program had been extended through June 2020, but its continuation depends on enabling legislation or annual administrative renewals.[459]

Notes

1. Meyer v. Nebraska, 262 U.S. 390, 400 (1923). *See also* Brown v. Board of Education of Topeka, Shawnee County, Kan., 347 U.S. 483, 493 (1954), in which the Court stated:

   Today, education is perhaps the most important function of state and local governments. Compulsory school attendance laws and the great expenditures for education both demonstrate our recognition of the importance of education to our democratic society. It is required in the performance of our most basic public responsibilities, even service in the armed forces. It is the very foundation of good citizenship. Today it is a principal instrument in awakening the child to cultural values, in preparing him for later professional training, and in helping him to adjust normally to his environment. In these days, it is doubtful that any child may reasonably be expected to succeed in life if he is denied the opportunity of an education. Such an opportunity, where the state has undertaken to provide it, is a right which must be made available to all on equal terms.

2. San Antonio Independent School District v. Rodriguez, 411 U.S. 1, 19 (1973). For arguments that the federal Constitution guarantees a right to public schooling, *see* Derek W. Black, The Constitutional Compromise to Guarantee Education, 70 Stan. L. Rev. 735 (2018); Derek Black, Unlocking the Power of State Constitutions with Equal Protection: The First Step Toward Education as a Federally Protected Right, 51 Wm. & Mary L. Rev. 1343 (2010); Goodwin Liu, Education, Equality, and National Citizenship, 116 Yale L.J. 330, 345 (2006); Erwin Chemerinsky, The Deconstitutionalization of Education, 36 Loy. U. Chi. L.J. 111 (2004); Susan H. Bitensky, Theoretical Foundations for a Right to Education Under the U.S. Constitution: A Beginning to the End of the National Education Crisis, 86 Nw. U.L. Rev. 550 (1992); David A.J. Richards, Equal Opportunity and School Financing: Towards a Moral Theory of Constitutional Adjudication, 41 U. Chi. L. Rev. 32 (1973).

3. *See* Nicole Lawler, The Right to Education in the United States and Abroad: A Comparative Analysis, Fed. Law. 34 (Mar. 2018).

4. Universal Declaration of Human Rights, G.A. Res. 217(A)(III), U.N. Doc. A/810 at 76 (1948). *See* Emily H. Wood, Economic, Social, and Cultural Rights and the Right to Education in American Jurisprudence: Barriers and Approaches to Implementation,

19 Hastings Women's L.J. 303 (2008); Connie de la Vega, The Right to Equal Education: Merely a Guiding Principle or Customary International Legal Right?, 11 Harv. Blackletter L.J. 37 (1994); Ann I. Park, Comment, Human Rights and Basic Needs: Using International Human Rights Norms to Inform Constitutional Interpretation, 34 UCLA L. Rev. 1195 (1987).

5. Two notable exceptions are Vermont and Hawaii. Vermont employs a statewide funding system following a 1997 decision by its supreme court that funding based on local property taxes led to unequal education opportunities and violated the state constitution. Brigham v. State, 166 Vt. 246 (1997); see also Vt. Stat. Ann. Tit. 16, § 4025. Hawaii has a statewide public education system, which is funded primarily by state general funds. Hawaii State Department of Education, The Department's Budget, http://www.hawaiipublicschools.org/ConnectWithUs/Organization/Budget/Pages/home.aspx.

6. See James E. Ryan, Five Miles Away, a World Apart: One City, Two Schools, and the Story of Educational Opportunity in Modern America (Oxford 2010). See also Bruce D. Baker, David G. Sciarra, & Danielle Farie, Is School Funding Fair? A National Report Card, Education Law Center (7th ed. Feb. 2018), http://www.edlawcenter.org/assets/files/pdfs/publications/Is_School_Funding_Fair_7th_Editi.pdf.

7. See Gary Orfield, Jongyeon Ee, Erica Frankenberg, & Genevieve Siegel-Hawley, Brown at 62: School Segregation by Race, Poverty, and State, The Civil Rights Project/ Proyecto Derechos Civile at UCLA (May 16, 2016), https://www.civilrightsproject.ucla.edu/research/k-12-education/integration-and-diversity/brown-at-62-school-segregation-by-race-poverty-and-state/Brown-at-62-final-corrected-2.pdf. The report discussed "the striking rise in double segregation by race and poverty for African American and Latino students who are concentrated in schools that rarely attain the successful outcomes typical of middle class schools with largely white and Asian student populations."

8. San Antonio Independent School District v. Rodriguez, 411 U.S. 1, 24 (1973).

9. Id. at 36. See Kristine L. Bowman, Education Reform and Detroit's Right to Literacy Litigation, 75 Wash. & Lee L. Rev. Online 61 (2018).

10. Brown v. Board of Education, 347 U.S. 483 (1954). See Goodwin Liu, Rethinking Constitutional Welfare Rights, 61 Stan. L. Rev. 203, 241 (2008) (explaining Brown's "temporally situated understanding" that "educational 'opportunity, where the state has undertaken to provide it, is a right which must be made available to all on equal terms'"), citing Brown, 349 U.S. at 493.

11. Parents Involved in Community Schools v. Seattle School Dist. No. 1, 551 U.S. 701 (2007) (rejecting "racial balancing as a compelling state interest"). For a critique of Parents Involved as legally flawed and unnecessarily destructive of local efforts to avoid racially segregated public schools, see Wendy Parker, Limiting the Equal Protection Clause Roberts Style, 63 U. Miami L. Rev. 507 (2009).

12. Plyler v. Doe, 457 U.S. 202 (1982) (holding that Texas policy of denying free public school education to undocumented children violates the Equal Protection Clause of the U.S. Constitution).

13. See, for example, the Individuals with Disabilities Education Act, 20 U.S.C. §§ 1400 et seq.; Section 504 of the Rehabilitation Act of 1973, as amended, 29 U.S.C. § 794.

14. *See* Title VI of the Civil Rights Act of 1964, 42 U.S.C. §§ 2000d et seq.

15. *See* Title IX of the Education Amendments of 1972, 20 U.S.C. § 1681.

16. *See, for example*, Emma Garcia & Elaine Weiss, Education inequalities at the school starting gate: Gaps, trends, and strategies to address them, Economic Policy Institute (Sept. 2017), https://www.epi.org/publication/education-inequalities-at-the-school-starting-gate/; Philip Trostel, It's Not Just the Money: The Benefits of College Education to Individuals and to Society, Lumina Foundation (2015), https://www.luminafoundation.org/files/resources/its-not-just-the-money.pdf.

17. *See* Elise Gould, Julia Wolfe, & Zane Mokhiber, Class of 2019: High School Edition, Economic Policy Institute (June 6, 2019), https://www.epi.org/publication/class-of-2019-high-school-edition/ (reporting that two-thirds of workers over age 21 do not have a college degree and that their average wage rate is $12.26 per hour, and women and people of color experience a 10.2% and 11.1% wage penalty, respectively). Some public universities have served as powerful engines of upward mobility. *See, for example*, Raj Chetty, John Friedman, Emmanuel Saez, Nicholas Turner, & Danny Yagan, Mobility Report Cards: The Role of Colleges in Intergenerational Mobility, Opportunity Insights (Dec. 2017), https://opportunityinsights.org/paper/mobilityreportcards/; David Leonhardt, America's Great Working-Class Colleges, N.Y. Times (Jan. 18, 2017), https://www.nytimes.com/2017/01/18/opinion/sunday/americas-great-working-class-colleges.html?searchResultPosition=1; Susan Scrivener, Michael J. Weiss, Timothy Rudd, Colleen Sommo, & Hannah Fresques, Doubling Graduation Rates: Three-Year Effects of CUNY's Accelerated Study in Associate Programs (ASAP) for Developmental Education Students, MRDC (Feb. 2015), https://www.mdrc.org/publication/doubling-graduation-rates.

18. The trend has been for the federal government to leave educational policies to the states, despite the significant inequalities that result for children who come from low-wealth households or are children of color. *See* Derek W. Black, Abandoning the Federal Role in Education: The Every Student Succeeds Act, 105 Cal. L. Rev. 1309 (2017). For arguments in favor of an expanded federal role in education to achieve greater educational equity, *see* Kimberly Jenkins Robinson, Disrupting Education Federalism, 92 Wash. U. L. Rev. 959 (2015).

19. *See* Joshua E. Weishart, Reconstituting the Right to Education, 67 Ala. L. Rev. 915, 918 (2016) (setting forth academic arguments in favor of a federal educational right).

20. *See* Anna Williams Shavers, Using International Human Rights Law in School Finance Litigation to Establish Education as a Fundamental Right, Kan. J.L. & Pub. Pol'y 457 (Summer 2018).

21. The Education Law Center, a nonprofit organization that advocates for educational justice in the United States, maintains a website with state-by-state information about state constitutional education provisions and state court suits seeking to secure equitable and quality schooling, *see* Education Law Center, State Profiles, http://www.edlawcenter.org/states. *See also* Allen W. Hubsch, The Emerging Right to Education Under State Constitutional Law, 65 Temple L. Rev. 1325, 1343–48 (1992).

22. Mont. Const. Art. X, § 1.

23. N.H. Const. Art. 83.

24. *See* Molly Hunter, School Funding Litigation from Coast to Coast, Education Law Center (Mar. 26, 2018), http://www.edlawcenter.org/news/archives/school-funding-national/school-funding-litigation-from-coast-to-coast.html. For a discussion of "next-generation" educational finance litigation, *see* William S. Koski, Beyond Dollars? The Promises and Pitfalls of the Next Generation of Educational Rights Litigation, 117 Colum. L. Rev. 1897 (2017).

25. *See* W. Steven Barnett & Donald J. Yarosz, Who Goes to Preschool and Why Does it Matter?, National Institute for Early Education Research, Rutgers University (Nov. 2007), http://nieer.org/policy-issue/policy-brief-who-goes-to-preschool-and-why-does-it-matter-updated.

26. 45 C.F.R. § 1302.12(b).

27. 45 C.F.R. § 1302.12(b).

28. 20 U.S.C. §§ 1432(4)(C)(i)–(v) & 1432(5).

29. 45 C.F.R. § 1302.18 (2016).

30. *See* William T. Gormley, Jr., Deborah Phillips, & Ted Gayer, Preschool Programs Can Boost School Readiness, 320 Science 1723–24 (June 27, 2008), http://citeseerx.ist.psu.edu/viewdoc/download?doi=10.1.1.621.4481&rep=rep1&type=pdf. Studies such as those of New Jersey's Abbott Preschool Program have tracked the beneficial results of participation in preschool programs. *See, for example*, Education Law Center, Preschool http://www.edlawcenter.org/issues/preschool.html.

31. Michael Yogman, Andrew Garner, Jeffrey Hutchinson, Kathy Hirsh-Pasek, & Roberta Michnick Golinkoff, The Power of Play: A Pediatric Role in Enhancing Development in Young Children, 142 Pediatrics 3 (Sept. 2018), http://pediatrics.aappublications.org/content/pediatrics/142/3/e20182058.full.pdf.

32. *See* Greg J. Duncan & Katherine Magnuson, Investing in Preschool Programs, 27(2) J. Econ. Persp. 109 (Spring 2013), https://www.jstor.org/stable/23391693; *see also* Greg J. Duncan, Jens Ludwig, & Katherine A. Magnuson, Reducing Poverty through Preschool Interventions, 17(2) The Future of Children, The Next Generation of Antipoverty Policies 143, 147 (Fall 2007), https://futureofchildren.princeton.edu/publications.

33. *See* Lynn A. Karoly, The Economic Returns to Early Childhood Education, 26(2) The Future of Children, Starting Early: Education from Pre Kindergarten to Third Grade 37 (Fall 2016), https://www.jstor.org/stable/43940580; The White House, The Economics of Early Childhood Investments (Dec. 2014), https://obamawhitehouse.archives.gov/sites/default/files/docs/early_childhood_report1.pdf.

34. Diane Whitmore Schanzenbach & Lauren Bauer, The Long-Term Impact of the Head Start Program, Brookings (Aug. 19, 2016), https://www.brookings.edu/research/the-long-term-impact-of-the-head-start-program/. *See also* Andrew Barr & Chloe R. Gibbs, Breaking the Cycle? Intergenerational Effects of an Anti-Poverty Program in Early Childhood, J. Pol. Econ. (Aug. 2017), https://static1.squarespace.com/static/563b95a2e4b0c51a8b87767c/t/59b2e1d259cc681cdd587b22/1504895485410/Barr.

35. 45 C.F.R. §§ 1302.12 & 1302.14(a)(1).

36. 45 C.F.R. § 1302.14(a)–(c) (detailing selection criteria and requiring wait lists).

37. *See* U.S. Department of Health and Human Services, Administration for Children and Families, Office of Head Start, Head Start Program Facts: Fiscal Year 2017,

https://eclkc.ohs.acf.hhs.gov/about-us/article/head-start-program-facts-fiscal-year-2017. The report defines "cumulative enrollment" as "the actual number of children and pregnant women that Head Start programs serve throughout the entire program year, inclusive of enrollees who left during the program year and the enrollees who filled those empty places."

38. 45 C.F.R. § 1302.12(c)(2).

39. 42 U.S.C. § 9835(d); 45 C.F.R. § 1302.14(b).

40. 45 C.F.R. § 1302.14(c).

41. 45 C.F.R. §§ 1302.11, 1302.14, 1302.15(a).

42. A list of Regional Offices is available at http://www.acf.hhs.gov/programs/oro/regional-offices.

43. The Head Start Locator is available at http://eclkc.ohs.acf.hhs.gov/hslc/HeadStartOffices.

44. 45 C.F.R. § 1302.12(b).

45. 45 C.F.R. § 1302.12(j)(1).

46. 45 C.F.R. § 1302.16(a)(2).

47. 45 C.F.R. § 1302.16(a)(3).

48. 45 C.F.R. § 1302.21(c).

49. In a center-based program, services take place in a classroom setting. The classroom can be located at a local public or private nonprofit agency, for example, a community center or a faith-based organization. 42 U.S.C. § 9836; 45 C.F.R. § 1306.3(a). For more information on class size requirements and other guidelines for a center-based program, *see* 45 C.F.R. § 1302.21. By August 1, 2019, Head Start programs must gradually increase the number of hours/day they provide services to families to 1,020 annual hours of "planned operations over the course of at least eight months per year for at least 5% of its Head Start center-based funded enrollment." *See* 42 U.S.C. § 1302.21(c)(2)(iii).

50. Home-based programs provide services in the child's home. 45 C.F.R. § 1302.22.

51. A family child care program provides services in a family child care provider's home or other family-like setting, such as a space in a public housing complex. 45 C.F.R. § 1302.23.

52. A locally designed program provides services both in a classroom setting and at a child's home. 45 C.F.R. § 1302.24(b). For example, a child in a combination program might go to a classroom setting two times a week and receive two home visits a month from teachers.

53. 45 C.F.R. § 1302.22(b). Each home visitor is allowed to serve no more than 12 families.

54. 45 C.F.R. § 1302.45–46.

55. 45 C.F.R. §§ 1302.60–61.

56. 20 U.S.C. §§ 1414(d), 1415; 34 C.F.R. §§ 300.320–328.

57. Any program deemed to have one or more deficiencies by an official from the Department of Health and Human Services must apply and compete with other programs to receive its next five years of funding. 45 C.F.R. § 1304.11. Furthermore, each local Head Start program is required to conduct a community-needs assessment

every three years and use the results to shape the program for younger children. 45
C.F.R. § 1302.21. Class size for 4 and 5 year olds in double session programs—in
which a single teacher is employed to teach two half-day programs, with one group of
students in the morning and a different group in the afternoon—may not exceed 17.
45 C.F.R. § 1302.21(b)(4).

58. *See* U.S. Department of Health and Human Services, Office of Planning, Research &
Evaluation, Early Head Start Research and Evaluation Project, 1996–2010, https://
www.acf.hhs.gov/opre/research/project/early-head-start-research-and-evaluation-
project-ehsre-1996-2010. *See also* U.S. Department of Health and Human Services,
Administration for Children and Families, Early Head Start Benefits Children and
Families (2006), http://www.acf.hhs.gov/sites/default/files/opre/research_brief_
overall.pdf.

59. 42 U.S.C. § 9833 (opportunity for parent participation in Head Start programs required as condition of federal funding); § 9836(d)(2)(J) (significant parent and
community involvement required in selection of Head Start agencies); § 9837(b)
(mandating that the program foster parental involvement including decision-making
and implementation). *See* Arya Ansari & Elizabeth Gershoff, Parent Involvement
and Children's Development: Indirect Effects Through Parenting, 78(2) J. Marriage
Fam. 562 (Apr. 2016), https://www.ncbi.nlm.nih.gov/pmc/articles/PMC4807601/; U.S.
Department of Health and Human Services, FACES Findings: New Research on
Head Start Outcomes and Program Quality (Dec. 2006), http://www.acf.hhs.gov/
sites/default/files/opre/faces_findings.pdf.

60. 45 C.F.R. § 1302.52(b). *See* U.S. Department of Health and Human Services,
Administration for Children and Families, Head Start Parent, Family, and Community Engagement Framework (2018), https://eclkc.ohs.acf.hhs.gov/publication/
head-start-parent-family-community-engagement-framework.

61. 45 C.F.R. § 1302.15(f).

62. 34 C.F.R. § 303.13.

63. *Id.*

64. 20 U.S.C. § 1412(a)(1)(A).

65. *See* Kathryn A. Kuhlenberg, The Uncertainties of Educating a Preschooler with
Special Needs: Who Makes the Important Determinations? And, Who Should?, 10
Seattle J. for Soc. Just. 585 (Fall/Winter 2011).

66. The Individuals with Disabilities Act defines "at-risk infant or toddler" as "an individual under 3 years of age who would be at risk of experiencing a substantial developmental delay if early intervention services were not provided to the individual."
20 U.S.C. § 1432(1). Some states offer Early Intervention Services to children older
than age three. See 20 U.S.C. § 1432(5)(B)(ii); 34 C.F.R. § 303.211. Compare Cal.
Gov't Code § 95014 (defining "risk conditions" as "conditions of known etiology or
conditions with established harmful developmental consequences"), with Haw. Rev.
Stat. § 321–351 (defining risk to include "environmental risk[s]" such as having a
parent less than age 16 or having a primary caregiver who has a disability).

67. The Centers for Disease Control maintains a contact list of state Early Intervention
programs at https://www.cdc.gov/ncbddd/actearly/parents/states.html#textlinks.

See 34 C.F.R. § 303.520(c) (prohibiting denial of services based on family's ability to pay).

68. *See* Joseph R. Jenkins, Philips Dale, Paulette E. Mills, Kevin Nicole, Constance Pious, & Joan Ronk, How Special Education Preschool Graduates Finish: Status at 19 Years of Age, 43 Am. Educ. Res. J. 737 (Winter 2006).

69. 20 U.S.C. § 1432(4)(E).

70. 20 U.S.C. § 1436; 34 C.F.R. § 303.342.

71. *See* The State of Preschool 2017, National Institute for Early Education Research, http://nieer.org/wp-content/uploads/2018/04/YB2017_Executive-Summary.pdf. Oklahoma provides free preschool for all four-year-olds. Simon Workman & Jessica Troe, Early Learning in the United States: 2017, Center for American Progress (July 20, 2017), https://www.americanprogress.org/issues/early-childhood/reports/2017/07/20/436169/early-learning-united-states-2017/.

72. New York City offers universal preschool, and Boston and Chicago are both in the process of implementing universal preschool programs. Taylor Swaak, As Universal Pre-K Struggles to Secure a Nationwide Platform, It Finds Hope in Cities Like Chicago (July 17, 2018), https://www.the74million.org/article/universal-pre-k-chicago-national-platform/.

73. State-by-state information, including the name of the state agency running the preschool program, is available from the National Institute for Early Education Research, a part of the Rutgers University Graduate School of Education. *See* The State of Preschool 2017, National Institute for Early Education Research, http://nieer.org/state-preschool-yearbooks/yearbook2017.

74. *See* Mark G. Yudof, Betsy Levin, Rachel Moran, James E. Ryan, & Kristi L. Bowman, Educational Policy and the Law at 1 (Cengage 5th ed. 2012).

75. Charter schools are considered public schools and cannot charge tuition to students. Charter schools are governed by the rules set out in the school charter. They are exempt from many state laws and regulations, but are often—although not universally—subject to the health and safety, civil rights, and student assessment laws that other public schools must follow. *See* Education Commission of the States, Charter Schools: What Rules Are Waived for Charter Schools? (Jan. 2018), http://ecs.force.com/mbdata/mbquestNB2C?rep=CS1713. The Education Commission of the States is a national education policy organization founded in 1967 through an interstate compact approved by Congress that partners with state education policymakers.

76. Pierce v. Society of Sisters, 268 U.S. 510 (1925).

77. In 2007, the number of homeschooled students in the United States was about 1.5 million. Students in families with annual earnings of $25,000–$75,000 were more likely to be homeschooled than children in families with annual earnings of less than $25,000. The most-cited reason for homeschooling children was a desire to provide religious or moral instruction (36% of students) followed by a concern about public school environment (21%). *See* National Center for Education Statistics, The Condition of Education (2009), https://nces.ed.gov/pubs2009/2009081.pdf. In 2016, the number of homeschooled students had increased to 1.69 million. *See* National Center for Education Statistics, Digest of Education Statistics 2017, Table 206.10,

https://nces.ed.gov/programs/digest/d17/tables/dt17_206.10.asp. The National Center for Education Statistics is located in the U.S. Department of Education and the Institute of Education Sciences. Among its projects, it collects and maintains statistics about the condition of education in the United States.

78. *See, for example*, N.Y. Educ. Law §§ 3204, 3210; N.Y. Comp. Codes R. & Regs. Tit. 8, § 100.10.

79. *See* Home School Legal Defense Association, State Laws Concerning Participation of Homeschool Students in Public School Activities (Mar. 21, 2016), http://www.hslda. org/docs/nche/Issues/E/Equal_Access.pdf.

80. *See* National Center for Education Statistics, State Education Reforms, Table 5.3, http://nces.ed.gov/programs/statereform/tab5_3.asp; Louisa Diffey, 50-State Comparison: State Kindergarten-Through-Third-Grade Policies, Education Commission of the States (June 4, 2018), https://www.ecs.org/kindergarten-policies/.

81. *See* Aaron J. Curtis, Tracing the School-to-Prison Pipeline from Zero-Tolerance Policies to Juvenile Justice Dispositions, 102 Geo. L.J. 1251, 1260 (2014).

82. The role of anti-truancy rules in creating a school-to-prison pipeline has drawn increased attention and criticism. *See* Meredith S. Simons, Giving Vulnerable Students Their Due: Implementing Due Process Protections for Students Referred from Schools to the Justice System, 66 Duke L.J. 943 (2017); Judith A.M. Scully, Examining and Dismantling the School-to-Prison Pipeline: Strategies for a Better Future, 8 Ark. L. Rev. 959 (2016); Jonathon Arellano-Jackson, But What Can We Do? How Juvenile Defenders Can Disrupt the School-to-Prison Pipeline, 13 Seattle J. for Soc. Just. 751 (2015); Dana Goldstein, Inexcusable Absences: Skipping School Is a Problem. But Why Is It a Crime?, The Marshall Project & The New Republic (Mar. 6, 2015), https://www.themarshallproject.org/2015/03/06/inexcusable-absences#. MqO3MqgS3.

83. Juvenile Justice Reform Act of 2018, Pub. L. No. 115-385 (2018).

84. Juvenile Justice and Delinquency Prevention Act, Pub. L. No. 93-415 (1974) (codified at 42 U.S.C. §§ 5601 et seq.). In 2002, Congress reauthorized the act, *see* 21st Century Department of Justice Appropriations Authorization Act, Pub. L. No. 107-273, 116 Stat. 1758.

85. For criticisms of the use of VCO as a sanction for truancy, *see* Jay D. Blitzman, Are We Criminalizing Adolescence?, 32(5) GPSolo 72 (Sept./Oct. 2015), https://www-jstor-org.proxy.library.nyu.edu/stable/24634371?seq=1#metadata_info_tab_contents. *See also* Use of the Valid Court Order: State-by-State Comparisons, Coalition for Juvenile Justice, http://www.juvjustice.org/sites/default/files/resource-files/State%20 VCO%20usage%202.18.15.pdf; *see also* Rachel Spaethe, Survey of School Truancy Intervention and Prevention Strategies, 9 Kan. J.L. & Pub. Pol'y 689 (2000).

86. Until 2015, Texas was one of two states that treated truancy as a crime. *See* Sarah Orman & Cristina Blanton, Truancy Transformed: How House Bill 2398 Decriminalized Failure to Attend School, 78 Tex. B.J. 870 (2015). In 2001, Texas codified a status offense known as "Failure to Attend School," which was categorized as a Class C misdemeanor to be adjudicated in municipal courts. Truant students also could be referred to juvenile courts for the lesser charge of "Conduct in Need of Supervision."

See Elizabeth A. Angelone, Comment, The Texas Two-Step: The Criminalization of Truancy Under the Texas "Failure to Attend" Statute, 13 Scholar 433 (2010). Effective September 1, 2015, Texas amended its Education Code, Family Code, Government Code, Local Government Code, and Code of Criminal Procedure to require truancy to be treated as a civil matter in specialized truancy courts. Act of May 30, 2015, 84th Leg., R.S., ch. 935, 2015 Tex. Gen. Laws 3224. As a part of that change, the legislature repealed Section 25.094 of the Education Code, which previously had made the failure to attend school by a person within the compulsory school attendance age a Class C misdemeanor. *Id.* at § 41(2), 2015 Tex. Gen. Laws at 3255. *See* Steven E. Gilmore, Education and Its Discontents: The Decriminalization of Truancy and the School-to-Prison Pipeline in Texas, 18 Scholar: St. Mary's L. Rev. & Soc. Just. 229 (2016).

87. *See* Sonia Pace, From Correctional Education to School Reentry: How Formerly Incarcerated Youth Can Achieve Better Educational Outcomes, 23 Tex. J. on C.L. & C.R. 12 (2018); *see also* Molly McCluskey, What If This Were Your Kid?, The Atlantic (Dec. 24, 2017), https://www.theatlantic.com/politics/archive/2017/12/juvenile-solitary-confinement/548933/.

88. *See* Andrea L. Dennis, Decriminalizing Childhood, 45 Fordham Urb. L.J. 1 (2017). *See also* Nadja Popovich, Do US Laws That Punish Parents for Truancy Keep Their Kids in School?, The Guardian, U.S. Edition (June 23, 2014), http://www.theguardian.com/education/2014/jun/23/-sp-school-truancy-fines-jail-parents-punishment-children.

89. Cal. Penal Code § 270.1(a). *See* Adriane Kayoko Peralta, An Interrogation and Response to the Predominant Framing of Truancy, 62 UCLA L. Rev. Discourse 42 (2014); Alison Cardova, California Penal Code § 270.1: A Constitutionally Impermissible Attempt to Combat Truancy, 39 Hastings Const. L.Q. 539 (2012).

90. Pub. L. No. 104-193, 110 Stat. 2105, § 103 (1996). Section 103 added a new section to Title IV of the Social Security Act, allowing states to "sanction welfare recipients for failing to ensure that minor dependent children attend school." 42 U.S.C. § 604(i). *See* Kelley O'Dell, Teen Parents and the Reauthorization of Welfare Reform, Advocates for Adolescent Mothers (June 2017), http://advocatesforadolescentmothers.com/article/teen-parents-reauthorization-welfare-reform/.

91. U.S. Department of Health and Human Services, Administration for Children and Families, Welfare Rules Databook: State TANF Policies as of July 2017, at Table A.III.1, 136–137, https://www.acf.hhs.gov/opre/resource/welfare-rules-databook-state-tanf-policies-as-of-july-2017.

92. Martinez v. Bynum, 461 U.S. 321, 328–330 (1983). *See also* Horton v. Marshall Pub. Sch., 769 F.2d 1323 (8th Cir. 1985) (finding school district's application of Arkansas residency requirement to violate the Due Process and Equal Protection Clauses of the U.S. Constitution); In re White, 715 N.E.2d 203 (Ohio Ct. App. 1998).

93. Martinez v. Bynum, 461 U.S. at 329.

94. *See, for example*, Ariz. Rev. Stat. Ann. § 15-823; Colo. Rev. Stat. Ann. § 22-1-102; Mass. Gen. Laws Ann., c. 76, §§ 5–6; R.I. Gen. Laws § 16-64-1; Utah Code Ann. §§ 53A-2-201, 53A-2-202.

95. *See* Major v. Nederland Indep. Sch. Dist., 772 F. Supp. 944 (E.D. Tex. 1991); Nancy M. v. Scanlon, 666 F. Supp. 723 (E.D. Pa. 1987).

96. *See* Education Law Center, Understanding Public School Residency Requirements: A Guide for Advocates, at 3 (2005), http://www.edlawcenter.org/assets/files/pdfs/publications/ResidencyRequirementsGuide.pdf.

97. *See, for example*, Indiana Legal Services, Inc., Enrolling a Child in School When You Are Not the Child's Custodial Parent (Mar. 2003), https://www.indianalegalservices.org/node/32/enrolling-child-school-when-you-are-not-childs-custodial-parent.

98. *See* McKinney-Vento Homeless Assistance Act, 42 U.S.C. §§ 11431–35, as amended by Improving America's Schools Act of 1994 (detailing states' responsibility to educate homeless children in public school notwithstanding residency requirements); U.S. Department of Education, Education For Homeless Children and Youths Program, Non-Regulatory Guidance (Mar. 2017), https://www2.ed.gov/policy/elsec/leg/essa/160240ehcyguidance072716updated0317.pdf.

99. Kern Alexander & M. David Alexander, The Law of Schools, Students and Teachers in a Nutshell, at 8–9 (West 4th ed. 2009).

100. *See* State of Connecticut, James Orlando, Criminal Penalties for Falsely Claiming Residency Within a School District (May 5, 2011), https://www.cga.ct.gov/2011/rpt/2011-R-0214.htm. State laws that criminalize claiming false residence include:

> Ark. Code Ann. § 6-18-202(f) (fine up to $1,000 for knowingly giving false residential address for public school enrollment);
> D.C. Code § 38-312 (providing false school residency information punishable by 90 days in jail, retroactive tuition, and a fine of up to $500);
> Ill. Comp. Stat. 5/10-20.12b (Class C misdemeanor for providing false information for publish school enrollment);
> Mich. Comp. Laws. Serv. § 380.1812 (misdemeanor to give false residence information punishable by 20 days' imprisonment and $50 maximum fine);
> Mo. Rev. Stat. § 167.020 (Class A misdemeanor punishment by up to one year of imprisonment and $1,000 fine, or both);
> Okla. Stat. Tit. 70, § 1-113(A) (making knowingly false statement in affidavit to establish school residence punishable as a misdemeanor by $500 fine and one year of imprisonment);
> 24 Pa. Cons. Stat. § 13-1302 (making knowingly false statement in sworn statement to establish school residence punishable as summary offense punishable by payment of back tuition, fine of up to $300, and community service).

101. *See* Kelly Phillips Erb, Would You Lie About Where You Live to Get Your Child Into A Better School?, Forbes (Nov. 6, 2018), https://www.forbes.com/sites/kellyphillipserb/2016/11/06/would-you-lie-about-where-you-live-to-get-your-child-into-a-better-school/#3f033aa2f483; Inimai Chettiar & Rebecca McCray, Sending Your Kid to the Wrong School Could Land You Five Years Behind Bars, ACLU (Jan. 28, 2011), https://www.aclu.org/blog/speakeasy/sending-your-kid-wrong-school-could-land-you-five-years-behind-bars; Rania Khalek, 20 Years in Prison for Sending Your Kids to the Wrong School? Inequality in School Systems Leads Parents to Big Risks, AlterNet (Oct. 18, 2011), http://www.alternet.org/story/152737/20_years_in_prison_for_sending_your_kids_to_the_wrong_school_inequality_in_school_systems_leads_parents_to_big_risks.

102. Zelman v. Simmons-Harris, 536 U.S. 639, 643–644 (2002) (vouchers may be used to pay tuition of religiously affiliated school).

103. For example, Wisconsin established a voucher program that allows low-income students to attend private school at government expense. Wis. Stat. Ann. § 119.23 (2012) (describing application process for vouchers to private schools). As of 2009, approximately 60,000 students were participating in publically funded voucher programs (out of the approximately 49 million students attending public schools in the United States). Questions and Answers about Educational Vouchers: Facts, Figures, and a Summary of the Research, Research for Action (2010), http://www.researchforaction.org/wp-content/uploads/2015/10/Educational-vouchers-Facts-figures-and-a-summary-of-the-research.pdf.

104. Micah Ann Wixom, 50-State Comparison: Vouchers, Education Commission of the States (Mar. 6, 2017), https://www.ecs.org/50-state-comparison-vouchers/.

105. School Voucher Laws: State-by-State Comparison, National Conference of State Legislatures, http://www.ncsl.org/research/education/voucher-law-comparison.aspx.

106. Micah Ann Wixom, 50-State Comparison: Vouchers, Education Commission of the States (Mar. 6, 2017), https://www.ecs.org/50-state-comparison-vouchers/.

107. Every Student Succeeds Act (ESEA), 20 U.S.C. § 7912(a). The unsafe school option appears in Title IX, § 9532 of the ESEA. The ESEA replaced the No Child Left Behind Act of 2001 and reauthorized the 1965 Elementary and Secondary Education Act, 20 U.S.C. chs. 28 and 70. The unsafe-transfer option existed under the earlier law. *See* U.S. Department of Education, Unsafe School Choice Option: Non-Regulatory Guidance (May 2004), https://www2.ed.gov/policy/elsec/guid/unsafeschoolchoice.pdf; U.S. Department of Education, No Child Left Behind, Public School Choice Non-Regulatory Guidance (Jan. 2009), https://www2.ed.gov/policy/elsec/guid/schoolchoiceguid.pdf. *See also* Congressional Research Service, Gail McCallion & Rebecca R. Skinner, School and Campus Safety Programs and Requirements in the Elementary and Secondary Education Act and Higher Education Act (Dec. 19, 2012), https://www.hsdl.org/?view&did=729503. *See* Lindsey Burke & Jennifer Marshall, The "Safe Student" Scholarship—Expanding Education Choice Options to Improve School Safety, The Heritage Foundation (June 8, 2018) (calling this option "overlooked" and urging state policymakers to implement the transfer options).

Forty-three states obtained waivers to exempt themselves from portions of the act and its requirements. U.S. Department of Education, ESEA Flexibility, http://www2.ed.gov/policy/elsec/guid/esea-flexibility/index.html. *See also* U.S. Department of Education, Office of Inspector General, An OIG Perspective on the Unsafe School Choice Option (Aug. 2007), https://www2.ed.gov/policy/elsec/leg/esea02/pg112.html.

108. *See* U.S. Department of Education, Outdated or Superseded Regulations: Title I, Parts A through C; Christa McAuliffe Fellowship Program; and Empowerment Zone or Enterprise Community—Priority, 83 Fed. Reg. 42438, 42440 (Aug. 22, 2018); U.S. Department of Education, Agency Information Collection Activities; Comment Request; Study of State Implementation of the Unsafe School Choice Option, 83 Fed. Reg. 6231 (Dec. 3, 2018).

109. 20 U.S.C. § 7912(a). In A.H. v. Paramount Unified School Dist., 2014 WL 3955168 (C.D. Cal. 2014), a student who had been stabbed by another student while on the school campus sued for a violation of his civil rights after his request to transfer was denied. The district court held that the statutory "unsafe school choice option" did not confer a "federal right to transfer to a different school" that is enforceable in court by an individual student; it requires only that the school establish a plan for transferring a victim to another school under the federal civil rights law.

110. 20 U.S.C. § 6315; 34 C.F.R. § 200.37(b)(4)(iv). Effective July 7, 2017, the U.S. Department of Education removed this and certain other regulations relating to the Every Student Succeeds Act from the Code of Federal Regulations. *See* 82 Fed. Reg. 31690 (July 7, 2017).

111. *See* Linda Darling-Hammond, Soung Bae, Channa M. Cook-Harvey, Livia Lam, Charmaine Mercer, Anne Podolsky, & Elizabeth Leisy Stosich, Pathways to New Accountability Through the Every Student Succeeds Act, Learning Policy Institute (Apr. 2016), https://learningpolicyinstitute.org/product/pathways-new-accountability-through-every-student-succeeds-act.

112. Alyson Klein, States Give Short Shrift to School Choice Option in ESSA Plans, Education Week (Apr. 24, 2018), https://www.edweek.org/ew/articles/2018/04/25/states-give-short-shrift-to-school-choice.html.

113. *Id.*

114. *See, for example*, Concerned Parents v. Caruthersville Sch. Dist. 18, 548 S.W.2d 554 (Mo. 1977); Dowell v. Sch. Dist. 1, 250 S.W.2d 127 (Ark. 1952); Batty v. Board of Educ., 269 N.W. 49 (N. Dak. 1936); Special Sch. Dist. v. Bangs, 221 S.W. 1060 (Ark. 1920); Board of Educ. v. Dick, 78 P. 812 (Kan. 1904).

115. *See* Union Free Sch. Dist. v. Jackson, 403 N.Y.S.2d 621 (N.Y. Sup. Ct. 1978); Granger v. Cascade Co. Sch. Dist., 499 P.2d 780 (Mont. 1972); Paulson v. Minidoka Co. Sch. Dist., 463 P.2d 935 (Idaho 1970); Bond v. Public Schools of Ann Arbor Sch. Dist., 178 N.W.2d 484 (Mich. 1970).

116. Christine Kiracofe, Isn't School Supposed to Be Free?: An Analysis of State Constitutional Language and School Fees, 253 Ed. Law Rep. 1 (2010).

117. Kadrmas v. Dickinson School District, 487 U.S. 450 (1988) (no federal constitutional obligation to provide free school bus service).

118. Evan D. Feldman, A Temporary Band-Aid, 29 Ent. & Sports Law. 4 (Fall 2011) (discussing majority position). *But see* Hartzell v. Connell, 35 Cal.3d 899, 907–908, 911 (Cal. 1984). *See* Micah Bucy, The Costs of the Pay-To-Play Model in High School Athletics, 13 U. Md. L.J. Race, Religion, Gender & Class 278 (2013).

119. Crim v. McWhorter, 252 S.E.2d 421 (Ga. 1979).

120. Parsippany-Troy Hills Educ. Ass'n v. Board of Educ., 457 A.2d 15 (N.J. Super. 1983). *But see* Driving Sch. Ass'n of Cal. v. San Mateo Union High Sch. Dist., 11 Cal. App. 4th 1513 (Cal. 1st Dist. 1992) (finding that driver education is an integral part of high school education and thus prohibiting fees).

121. *See* Luke van Houwelingen, Tuition-Based All-Day Kindergartens in the Public Schools: A Moral and Constitutional Critique, 14 Geo. J. on Poverty L. & Pol'y 367 (2007).

122. *See, for example*, Illinois State Board of Education, School Fee Waivers and Verification Process, https://www.isbe.net/pages/school-fee-waivers.aspx (state waiver policy); Lorenc v. Call, 789 P.2d 46 (Utah 1990) (local waiver could not be less generous than state waiver). A 2011 report found that even when fee waivers were available, children in families with annual earnings of less than $60,000 a year were four times more likely than children from wealthier families to be unable to participate in school sports because the school charged "pay-to-play" fees that the family could not afford. Pay-to-Play Sports Keeping Lower-Income Kids Out of the Game, 15(3) C.S. Mott Children's Hospital, National Poll on Children's Health (May 14, 2012), http://www.mottnpch.org/reports-surveys/pay-play-sports-keeping-lower-income-kids-out-game.

123. Fee statutes survived a facial constitutional challenge in: Arcadia Unified Sch. Dist. v. State Department of Education, 825 P.2d 438 (Cal. 1992) (transportation fees); Crim v. McWhorter, 252 S.E.2d 421 (Ga. 1979) (summer school tuition); Gohn v. Akron Sch., 562 N.E.2d 1291 (Ind. Ct. App. 1990) (textbook rental fee); Attorney Gen. v. East Jackson Public Sch. 372 N.W.2d 638 (Mich. 1985) (interscholastic sports fee); Vandevender v. Cassell, 208 S.E.2d 436 (W. Va. 1974) (textbooks, workbooks, and required materials fee).

124. *See* Attorney Gen. v. East Jackson Public Sch., 372 N.W.2d 638, 639 (Mich. 1985) (example of fee waiver provision with confidential process).

125. *See* Amanda Harmon Cooley, An Efficacy Examination and Constitutional Critique of School Shaming, 79 Ohio St. L.J. 319 (2018); *see, for example*, Bettina Elias Siegel, New Mexico Outlaws School "Lunch Shaming," N.Y. Times (Apr. 7, 2017), https://www.nytimes.com/2017/04/07/well/family/new-mexico-outlaws-school-lunch-shaming.html?_r=0.

126. *See* Carder v. Michigan City Sch. Corp., 552 F. Supp. 869, 870 (N.D. Ind. 1982) ("suspension of a student from school for a parent's failure to pay textbook fees or sign waiver request form amounts to a denial of equal protection"); Chandler v. South Bend Comm. Sch. Corp., 312 N.E.2d 915 (Ind. App. 1974) (enjoining school system from suspending students, withholding report cards, or taking other disciplinary action based on parents' nonpayment of school fees).

127. Brown v. Board of Education, 347 U.S. 483 (1954). *But see* Parents Involved in Community Schools v. Seattle School District, 551 U.S. 701 (2007) (striking down voluntary school integration plans in Seattle, Washington, and Louisville, Kentucky); Milliken v. Bradley, 418 U.S. 717 (1974) (striking down interdistrict busing remedy for segregation in Detroit, Michigan, school system).

128. McKinney-Vento Homeless Assistance Act of 1987, 42 U.S.C. § 11432.

129. Keyes v. School Dist. No. 1, 413 U.S. 189 (1973) (*Brown* principle extended to "Hispanos"); 42 U.S.C. § 2000d (prohibiting discrimination based on race, color, or national origin by programs receiving federal funds).

130. Plyler v. Doe, 457 U.S. 202 (1982).

131. Lau v. Nichols, 414 U.S. 563 (1974).

132. Title IX of the Education Amendments of 1972, 20 U.S.C. § 1681, prohibits discrimination on the basis of sex by any program receiving federal funds. During the

Obama administration, the U.S. Department of Education and the Department of Justice released a joint guidance to help schools ensure the civil rights of transgender students, providing an interpretation of Title IX. *See* U.S. Department of Justice and U.S. Department of Education, Dear Colleague Letter on Transgender Students (May 13, 2016), archived at https://www2.ed.gov/about/offices/list/ocr/letters/colleague-201605-title-ix-transgender.pdf. The Trump administration withdrew that guidance. *See* U.S. Department of Justice and U.S. Department of Education, Dear Colleague Letter (Feb. 22, 2017), https://www2.ed.gov/about/offices/list/ocr/letters/colleague-201702-title-ix.docx. *See generally* Ariane de Vogue, Mary Kay Mallonee, & Emanuella Grinberg, Trump Administration Withdraws Federal Protections for Transgender Students, CNN (Feb. 23, 2017), http://www.cnn.com/2017/02/22/politics/doj-withdraws-federal-protections-on-transgender-bathrooms-in-schools/index.html.

133. 34 C.F.R. § 106.40.
134. *See* 29 U.S.C. § 1400 (IDEA).
135. *See* 42 U.S.C. §§ 11431 et seq. *See* U.S. Department of Education, Education for Homeless Children and Youth Program Non-Regulatory Guidance, Title VII-B of the McKinney-Vento Homeless Assistance Act, as Amended by the Every Student Succeeds Act (July 27, 2016), https://www2.ed.gov/policy/elsec/leg/essa/160240ehcyguidance072716updated0317.pdf.
136. Evan S. Stolove, Pursuing the Educational Rights of Homeless Children: An Overview for Advocates, 53 Md. L. Rev. 1344, 1347 (1994).
137. Andrea B. Berkowitz, Homeless Children Dream of College Too: The Struggle to Provide America's Homeless Youth with a Viable Education, 31 Hofstra L. Rev. 515, 521 (2002).
138. *See* Jennifer A. Na, For Better or for Worse?: A Closer Look at the Federal Government's Proposal to Provide Adequate Educational Opportunities for Homeless Children, 51 How. L.J. 863, 866–868 (2008).
139. Pub. L. No. 115-338, 101 Stat. 525 (codified at 42 U.S.C. § 11431), later reauthorized as part of the No Child Left Behind Act, Pub. L. No. 107-110, 115 Stat. 1425. For additional information, *see* Barbara Duffield, Patricia Julianelle, & Michael Santos, The Most Frequently Asked Questions on the Education Rights of Children and Youth in Homeless Situations, National Association for the Education of Homeless Children and Youth & National Law Center on Homelessness & Poverty (Sept. 2016), http://nlchp.org/wp-content/uploads/2018/10/McKinney-Vento_FAQs.pdf.
140. *See* U.S. Department of Education, Education for Homeless Children and Youth Program Non-Regulatory Guidance, Title VII-B of the McKinney-Vento Homeless Assistance Act, as Amended by the Every Student Succeeds Act (updated Mar. 2017), https://www2.ed.gov/policy/elsec/leg/essa/160240ehcyguidance072716updated0317.pdf.
141. *See* 42 U.S.C. §§ 11302 & 11434a. Immigrant students and migrant students are covered by the McKinney-Vento Act's protections. More generally, states cannot deny students the right to a free public education based on their immigration status, Plyler v. Doe, 457 U.S. 202 (1982), and any inquiry into a student's immigration status may

violate federal law. More information on acceptable enrollment policies and what information may or may not be requested of families can be found later in this chapter. *See also* U.S. Department of Justice, Civil Rights Division, Fact Sheet: Information on the Rights of All Children to Enroll in School (May 8, 2014), https://www.justice.gov/sites/default/files/crt/legacy/2014/05/08/plylerfact.pdf

Under the McKinney-Vento Act, schools must make special efforts to ensure that unaccompanied youth receive appropriate credit for coursework completed in prior schools. 42 U.S.C. § 11432(g)(6)(A)(x)(II). Although the policy for awarding credit to unaccompanied immigrant students may vary by school or district, the process should involve interviewing the student regarding the student's educational background; researching or referencing the origin country's educational system; and evaluating and translating the transcript. *See, for example*, New York City Department of Education, Office of Youth Development & School-Community Services, Evaluating Foreign Transcripts: The A-Z Manual, http://www.uft.org/files/attachments/evaluating-foreign-transcripts.pdf; Minnesota Department of Education, Working with Refugee Students in Secondary Schools (2010), https://dpi.wi.gov/sites/default/files/imce/english-learners/pdf/counselors-companion.pdf.

For additional educational resources regarding immigrant students, *see* U.S. Department of Education, Educational Resources for Immigrants, Refugees, Asylees and other New Americans, https://www2.ed.gov/about/overview/focus/immigration-resources.html; U.S. Department of Education, Resource Guide: Supporting Undocumented Youth (Oct. 20, 2015), https://www2.ed.gov/about/overview/focus/supporting-undocumented-youth.pdf; ACLU, FAQ for Educators on Immigrant Students in Public Schools, https://www.aclu.org/other/faq-educators-immigrant-students-public-schools.

142. *See* U.S. Department of Education, Education for Homeless Children and Youths Program Non-Regulatory Guidance: Title VII-B of the McKinney-Vento Homeless Assistance Act, as amended by the Every Student Succeeds Act (updated Mar. 2017), https://www2.ed.gov/policy/elsec/leg/essa/160240ehcyguidance072716updated0317.pdf. *See also* 42 U.S.C. § 11434a(2)(B)(i).There is limited case law interpreting the word "homeless" under the McKinney-Vento Act. *See, for example*, G.S. By J.S. v. Rose Tree Media School District, 914 F.3d 206 (3d Cir. 2018) (student living with grandmother in doubled-up arrangement is "homeless" within the meaning of the McKinney-Vento Act, even after residing with the grandmother for four years). *See also* D.C. on behalf of C.C. and M.C. v. Wallingford-Swarthmore School District, 2018 WL 3968866, *33–35 (E.D. Pa. 2018) (collecting cases).

143. *See* Philip T.K. Daniel & Jeffrey C. Sun, Falling Short in Sheltering Homeless Students: Supporting the Student Achievement Priority through the McKinney-Vento Act, 312 Ed. L. Rep. 489 (2015); *See also* National Center for Homeless Education, Federal Data Summary School Years 2014–15 to 2016–17 Education for Homeless Children and Youth (Feb. 2019), https://nche.ed.gov/data-and-stats/.

144. 42 U.S.C. § 11432 (3)(e).

145. 42 U.S.C. § 11432(f).

146. 42 U.S.C. § 11432(i).

147. *See* Candace Crook, Educating America's Homeless Youth Through Reinforcement of the McKinney Vento Homeless Assistance Act, 6 Faulkner L. Rev. 395 (2014).

148. 42 U.S.C. § 11432(g)(3)(A)(i). For example, in *N.J. v. New York*, 872 F. Supp. 2d 204, 215 (E.D.N.Y. 2011), the federal court ordered a school district not to "disenroll" students whose family's house had burnt down and who had gone to live, temporarily, with family friends in a different district.

149. 42 U.S.C. § 11432(g)(3)(A).

150. 42 U.S.C. § 11432(g)(3)(A).

151. 42 U.S.C. § 11432(g)(3)(B)(i).

152. U.S. Department of Education, Education for Homeless Children and Youths Program Non-Regulatory Guidance at 16 (July 27, 2016), https://www2.ed.gov/policy/elsec/leg/essa/160240ehcyguidance072716.pdf.

153. 42 U.S.C. § 11432(g)(3)(B)(iii).

154. 42 U.S.C. § 11432(g)(3)(B)(iv).

155. 42 U.S.C. § 11432(g)(3)(C)(i).

156. 42 U.S.C. § 11434a(1).

157. 42 U.S.C. § 11432(g)(3)(C)(ii).

158. Family Educational Rights and Privacy Act of 1974, 20 U.S.C. § 1232g; 34 C.F.R. § 99.31(a)(3).

159. 42 U.S.C. § 11432(g)(3)(C)(iii).

160. 42 U.S.C. § 11432(g)(3)(C).

161. The privacy of student records is protected by the Family Educational Rights and Privacy Act, 20 U.S.C. § 1232g; 34 C.F.R. Part 99. *See* National Law Center on Homelessness & Poverty, Education of Homeless Children & Youth: The Guide to Their Rights (June 2011), at 20 (stating that schools and districts may not call third parties and reveal that a student is homeless without parental permission, and that "[a] parent always has the right to say no. If the parent says no, the student can still attend school."), https://www.nlchp.org/Education_of_Homeless_Children_and_Youth.

162. 42 U.S.C. § 11432(g)(3)(E)(i).

163. 42 U.S.C. § 11432(g)(3)(C)(i).

164. 42 U.S.C. § 11432(g)(3)(E)(ii).

165. 42 U.S.C. § 11432(g)(3)(E)(iii).

166. 42 U.S.C. § 11432(g)(1)(C).

167. 42 U.S.C. § 11432(g)(1)(J)(iii).

168. 42 U.S.C. § 11432(g)(4)(A).

169. 42 U.S.C. § 11432(g)(1)(J)(iii).

170. 42 U.S.C. § 11432(e)(3).

171. *See* Eric S. Tars, Separate & Unequal in the Same Classroom: Homeless Students in America's Public Schools, 14 Pub. Int. L. Rep. 267, 274–275 (2009).

172. 42 U.S.C. § 11432(e)(3).

173. 42 U.S.C. § 11433(a)(2)(B)(ii).

174. *See* U.S. Department of Education, Education for Homeless Children and Youths Program Non-Regulatory Guidance at 17 (July 27, 2016), https://www2.ed.gov/policy/elsec/leg/essa/160240ehcyguidance072716.pdf ("In some

circumstances . . . it may be appropriate to provide additional services to homeless children and youth in a separate setting. In doing so, a district should be careful not to stigmatize these students. If a district does implement a supplemental program exclusively for homeless children, such as a shelter-based evening tutoring program, it should not be called, for example, 'the homeless tutoring program' or the 'shelter tutoring program.' Instead, the district should use an alternative name such as 'Discovery Club' or 'Homework Club' to avoid stigmatization.").

175. Plyler v. Doe, 457 U.S. 202, 223, 234 (1982). *See also* María Pabón López & Diomedes J. Tsitouras, From the Border to the Schoolhouse Gate: Alternative Arguments for Extending Primary Education to Undocumented Alien Children, 36 Hofstra L. Rev. 1243 (2008).

176. Mary Tamer, The Education of Immigrant Children: As the Demography of the U.S. Continues to Shift, How Can Schools Best Serve Their Changing Population?, Harvard Graduate School of Education (Dec. 11, 2014), https://www.gse.harvard. edu/news/uk/14/12/education-immigrant-children. *See also* Randy Capps, Michael Fix, & Jie Zong, A Profile of U.S. Children with Unauthorized Immigrant Parents, Migration Policy Institute (Jan. 2016), http://www.migrationpolicy.org/research/ profile-us-children-unauthorized-immigrant-parents.

177. U.S. Department of Education, Educational Services for Immigrant Children and Those Recently Arrived to the United States, http://www2.ed.gov/policy/rights/ guid/unaccompanied-children.html. *See* Julie M. Linton, Marshal Griffin, & Alan J. Shapiro, Detention of Immigrant Children, American Academy of Pediatrics Council on Community Pediatrics, 139(5) Pediatrics (2017), https://pediatrics. aappublications.org/content/139/5/e20170483 ("School facilities should be safe settings for immigrant children to access education. School records and facilities should not be used in any immigration enforcement action."). For a description of the education actually provided to immigrant children held in detention, *see, for example*, Lizzie O'Leary, Children Were Dirty, They Were Scared, and They Were Hungry, The Atlantic (June 25, 2019), https://www.theatlantic.com/family/archive/ 2019/06/child-detention-centers-immigration-attorney-interview/592540/; Camilo Montoya-Galvez, Trump administration nixes educational, recreational activities for migrant children in U.S. custody, CBS News (June 25, 2019), https:// www.cbsnews.com/news/trump-administration-nixes-educational-recreational-activities-for-migrant-children-in-u-s-custody/.

178. U.S. Department of Justice, U.S. Department of Education, and U.S. Department of Health & Human Services, Information on the Rights of Unaccompanied Children to Enroll in School and Participate Meaningfully and Equally in Educational Programs, https://www2.ed.gov/about/overview/focus/rights-unaccompanied-children-enroll-school.pdf. *See also* Jeanette M. Acosta, The Right to Education for Unaccompanied Minors, 43 Hastings Const. L.Q. 649 (2016).

179. U.S. Department of Justice, Fact Sheet: Information on the Rights of All Children to Enroll in School (Aug. 6, 2015), https://www.justice.gov/crt/fact-sheet.

Prior to the Obama guidelines, some states had attempted to bar noncitizen students. *See* Paul Easton, School Attrition through Enforcement: Title VI Disparate

Impact and Verification of Student Immigration Status, 54 B.C. L. Rev. 313 (2013). For example, in 2011, Alabama passed an immigration law that required state officials to check the immigration status of students in public schools. *See* Beason-Hammon Alabama Taxpayer and Citizen Protection Act, 2011 Alabama Laws Act 2011-535 (H.B. 56). It was reported that the law discouraged noncitizen children from attending school. *See* Campbell Robertson, After Ruling, Hispanics Flee an Alabama Town, N.Y. Times (Oct. 3, 2011), http://www.nytimes.com/2011/10/04/us/after-ruling-hispanics-flee-an-alabama-town.html. A lawsuit was filed to challenge the constitutionality of the law, and a federal appeals court blocked its enforcement, citing *Plyler v. Doe. See* Hispanic Interest Coalition of Alabama v. Governor of Alabama, 691 F.3d 1236 (11th Cir. 2012).

During the Trump administration, some states reaffirmed their commitment to the Obama guidelines. *See, for example*, State of Connecticut, State Board of Education, Guidance for Districts Regarding Refugee Students (Jan. 30, 2017), https://portal.ct.gov/-/media/SDE/Digest/2016_17/Guidance_for_Districts_Regarding_Refugee_Students.pdf.

180. *See* Statement by Secretary Jeh C. Johnson on Southwest Border Security (Jan. 4, 2016), archived at https://www.dhs.gov/news/2016/01/04/statement-secretary-jeh-c-johnson-southwest-border-security; Statement by Secretary Jeh C. Johnson on Southwest Border Security (Mar. 9, 2016), archived at https://www.dhs.gov/news/2016/03/09/statement-secretary-jeh-c-johnson-southwest-border-security. *See also* Georgetown Law Human Rights Institute Fact-Finding Project, Ensuring Every Undocumented Student Succeeds: A Report on Access to Public Education for Undocumented Children (2016), https://www.law.georgetown.edu/human-rights-institute/our-work/fact-finding-project/ensuring-every-undocumented-student-succeeds-a-report/.

181. *See* Tory Johnson, New Government Data Reveals Immigration Arrests and Deportations Increased in 2018, American Immigration Council (Dec. 20, 2018), http://immigrationimpact.com/2018/12/20/new-government-data-reveals-immigration-arrests-and-deportations-increased-in-2018/. *See also* Lisette Partelow & Philip E. Wolfin, The Trump Administration's Harsh Immigration Policies Are Harming Schoolchildren, Center for American Progress (Nov. 30, 2018), https://www.americanprogress.org/issues/education-k-12/news/2018/11/30/461555/trump-administrations-harsh-immigration-policies-harming-schoolchildren/.

182. Lau v. Nichols, 414 U.S. 563 (1974).

183. *See* 20 U.S.C. § 1703, which provides that "[n]o State shall deny equal educational opportunity to an individual on account of his or her race, color, sex, or national origin, by . . . the failure by an educational agency to take appropriate action to overcome language barriers that impede equal participation by its students in its instructional programs."

184. *See* Daniel B. Weddle, An American Tune: Refugee Children in U.S. Public Schools, 27 Kan. J.L. & Pub. Pol'y 434 (Summer 2018).

185. The Equal Educational Opportunities Act, Pub. L. No. 93-380, § 204, 88 Stat. 484 515 (the language barrier provision is codified at 20 U.S.C. § 1703(f)). *See*

Rosemary C. Salomone, Educating English Learners: Reconciling Bilingualism and Accountability, 6 Harv. L. & Pol'y Rev. 115 (2012).

186. Pub. L. No. 114-95, 129 Stat. 1802 (codified as amended at 20 U.S.C. § 6812).

187. 20 U.S.C. § 6812(9). The Fifth Circuit in *Castaneda v. Pickard*, 648 F.2d 989, 1010 (5th Cir. 1981), set out an influential but criticized three-prong analysis that accorded deference to the school's programmatic choice but required the school's program to rest on a sound educational theory, to implement effectively the theory, and to produce results that actually overcome language barriers. *See* Jessica R. Berenyi, "Appropriate Action," Inappropriately Defined: Amending the Equal Educational Opportunities Act of 1974, 65 Wash. & Lee L. Rev. 639 (2008) (arguing that the *Castaneda* factors ignore the EEOA's nonprogrammatic requirements such as monitoring and administration). *See, for example*, U.S. v. Texas, 601 F.3d 354 (5th Cir. 2010) (finding that there was insufficient evidence to support a determination that the schools' failure to monitor limited English proficiency programs caused achievement gaps). For a criticism of the decision, *see* Cristin Lee Hedman, School Law—The Fifth Circuit Prolongs Educational Inequalities in *United States v. Texas*, 64 SMU L. Rev. 779 (2011). On the other hand, the Third Circuit, affirming an order of a preliminary injunction on behalf of refugee children, applied the *Castaneda* factors, and explained further that the EEOA does not require a showing of intentional discrimination; rather what is required is a showing of a "nexus between the lost educational opportunity alleged and an EEOA-protected characteristic." Issa v. School District of Lancaster, 847 F.3d 121, 140 (3d Cir. 2017). *See* Abigail Flores, Redefining How to Speak "American": *Issa v. School District of Lancaster*, the Equal Educational Opportunities Act of 1974, and Their Impact, 68 DePaul L. Rev. 635 (2019). *See* Marie C. Scott, Resegregation, Language, and Educational Opportunity: The Influx of Latino Students into North Carolina Public Schools, 11 Harv. Latino L. Rev. 123 (2008). *See also* Karlie Love Hudson, Leandro's Left Behind: How North Carolina's English Learners Have Been Denied Their Fundamental Right to a Sound Basic Education, 39 Campbell L. Rev. 457 (2017).

188. Catherine E. Lhamon, Assistant Sec'y for Civil Rights, U.S. Department of Education, and Vanita Gupta, Acting Assistant Attorney Gen. for Civil Rights, U.S. Department of Justice, Dear Colleague Letter: English Learner Students and Limited English Proficient Parents (Jan. 17, 2015), http://www2.ed.gov/about/offices/list/ocr/letters/colleague-el-201501.pdf.

189. These funding resources include: Improving Basic Programs Operated by Local Education Agencies, Title I, Part A of the Elementary and Secondary Education Act, 20 U.S.C. §§ 6301 et seq.; Individuals with Disabilities Education Act, 20 U.S.C. §§ 1400 et seq.; McKinney-Vento Homeless Assistance Act, 42 U.S.C. §§ 11301 et seq. *See* U.S. Department of Education, Educational Services for Immigrant Children and Those Recently Arrived to the United States, http://www2.ed.gov/policy/rights/guid/unaccompanied-children.html. *See also* Brentin Mock, How U.S. Schools Are Failing Immigrant Children, Citylab (July 1, 2015), https://www.citylab.com/equity/2015/07/how-us-schools-are-failing-immigrant-children/397427/. In *Horne v. Flores*, 557 U.S. 433 (2009), the U.S. Supreme Court held that it was an error

for the district court to focus on funding levels as evidence of a continuing EEOA violation. *See* Jeffrey Mongiello, The Future of Equal Educational Opportunities Act § 1703(f) after *Horne v. Flores*: Using No Child Left behind Proficiency Levels to Define Appropriate Action Towards Meaningful Educational Opportunity, 14 Harv. Latino L. Rev. 211 (2011) (offering alternative litigation strategies in the light of *Horne's* approach to the EEOA); *see also* Kevin Golembiewski, Compensatory Education Is Available to English Language Learned under the EEOA, 9 Ala. Civil Rights & Civil Liberties L. Rev. 57 (2018) (urging suits to compel compensatory education programs as an EEOA remedy).

190. U.S. Department of Education, U.S. Department of Education Launches New English Learner Data Story (Jan. 29, 2018), https://www.ed.gov/news/press-releases/us-department-education-launches-new-english-learner-data-story; Office of English Language Acquisition, https://www2.ed.gov/about/offices/list/oela/index.html; National Clearinghouse for English Language Acquisition, https://www.ncela.ed.gov/.

191. 20 U.S.C. §§ 1681–88. Title IX states that: "No person in the United States shall, on the basis of sex, be excluded from participation, be denied the benefits of, or be subject to discrimination under any education program or activity receiving Federal financial assistance." Title IX does not apply to educational institutions controlled by religious organizations where the application of Title IX would violate their religious tenets. 34 C.F.R. § 106.12.

192. *See, for example,* Cohen v. Brown University, 101 F.3d 155 (1st Cir. 1996) (holding that demoting two women's sports teams from "university-sponsored" status to "donor-sponsored" status constituted discrimination under Title IX).

193. *See, for example,* Jackson v. Birmingham Bd. of Educ., 544 U.S. 167 (2005) (explaining that Title IX prohibits retaliation against an individual who has made a complaint of sex discrimination).

194. *See, for example,* Emeldi v. University of Oregon, 698 F.3d 715 (9th Cir. 2012) (holding that a professor's resignation as a student's faculty dissertation chair may have been retaliatory action that penalized student for reporting alleged gender-based institutional bias).

195. U.S. Department of Education, Office for Civil Rights, Revised Sexual Harassment Guidance: Harassment of Students by School Employees, Other Students, or Third Parties, Title IX (Jan. 19, 2001), https://www2.ed.gov/about/offices/list/ocr/docs/shguide.html; *see also* U.S. Department of Education, Dear Colleague Letter (Oct. 26, 2010), http://www2.ed.gov/about/offices/list/ocr/letters/colleague-201010.pdf. *See* Aaron J. Curtis, Conformity or Nonconformity?: Designing Legal Remedies to Protect Transgender Students from Discrimination, 53 Harv. J. on Legis. 459 (2016).

196. In February 2017, the U.S. Department of Education withdrew the earlier administration's guidance on transgender students, pending consideration of the legal issues. *See* U.S. Department of Justice, Civil Rights Division, U.S. Department of Education, Office for Civil Rights, Dear Colleague Letter (Feb. 22, 2017), https://www2.ed.gov/about/offices/list/ocr/letters/colleague-201702-title-ix.pdf. The letter nevertheless asserted that "[a]ll schools must ensure that all students, including

LGBTQ students, are able to learn and thrive in a safe environment." In addition, the Department of Education announced that it would no longer investigate or take action on complaints by transgender students who are banned from bathrooms and other facilities that align with their gender identity. *See* Logan Casey & Elizabeth Mann Levesque, LGBTQ students face discrimination while Education Department walks back oversight, Brookings (Apr. 18, 2018), https://www.brookings.edu/blog/ brown-center-chalkboard/2018/04/18/lgbtq-students-face-discrimination-while- education-department-walks-back-oversight/.

197. To learn more about the complaint process, go to U.S. Department of Education, How to File a Discrimination Complaint with the Office for Civil Rights, http:// www2.ed.gov/about/offices/list/ocr/docs/howto.html?src=rt.

198. For statistics about teen pregnancy in the United States, *see* Centers for Disease Control and Prevention, Reproductive Health: Teen Pregnancy (Mar. 1, 2019), https://www.cdc.gov/teenpregnancy/about/index.htm.

   The birth rate among school-age children has declined over the last two decades. Birth rates among adolescents are higher among African American and Hispanic females than white females, and higher among adolescents living in poor and low-income neighborhoods. About half of the female students in the United States who become pregnant do not earn a high school diploma by age 22, and are more likely to have lower earnings and earnings below the poverty line. *See id*; Two Sides of the Same Coin: Teen Pregnancy Prevention and Dropout Prevention, National Women's Law Center (June 2009), http://www.nwlc.org/ sites/default/files/pdfs/TwoSidesofSameCoin.pdf; Madeline E. McNeeley, Title IX and Equal Educational Access for Pregnant and Parenting Girls, 22 Wis. Women's L.J. 267, 269 (2007).

199. Tiffany Sala, SB 1014: Parental Leave for Parenting Pupils, 48 U. Pac. L. Rev. 608, 622 (2017).

200. Title IX of the Education Amendments of 1972, 20 U.S.C. §§ 1681 et seq. *See* U.S. Department of Justice, Overview of Title IX of the Education Amendments of 1972, 20 U.S.C. §§ 1681 et seq., https://www.brookings.edu/blog/brown-center-chalkboard/ 2018/04/18/lgbtq-students-face-discrimination-while-education-department- walks-back-oversight/ (compiling statute, regulations, other legal resources, and complaint form). *See* U.S. Department of Education, Know Your Rights: Pregnant or Parenting?: Title IX Protects You from Discrimination at School, https://www2. ed.gov/about/offices/list/ocr/docs/dcl-know-rights-201306-title-ix.html.

201. 34 C.F.R. § 106.40. For more information, *see* U.S. Department of Education, Office for Civil Rights, Supporting the Academic Success of Pregnant and Parenting Students: Under Title IX of the Education Amendments of 1972 (June 2013), http:// www2.ed.gov/about/offices/list/ocr/docs/pregnancy.pdf.

202. 34 C.F.R. § 106.40(b)(1).

203. U.S. Department of Education, Office for Civil Rights, Supporting the Academic Success of Pregnant and Parenting Students Under Title IX of the Education Amendments of 1972 (June 2013), http://www2.ed.gov/about/offices/list/ocr/docs/ pregnancy.pdf.

204. 34 C.F.R. § 106.40(b)(1) & (3). For a criticism of the comparability regulations, *see* Kendra Fershee, Hollow Promises for Pregnant Students: How the Regulations Governing Title IX Fail to Prevent Pregnancy Discrimination in School, 43 Ind. L. Rev. 79 (2009).

205. *See* Victoria Ryan, Eliminating the Element of Chance: School District Title IX Implementation to Support Pregnant and Parenting Students, 32 Berkeley J. Gender L. & Just. 73 (2017).

206. 34 C.F.R. § 106.40(b)(2).

207. *See* Brittany L. Grome, The Four-Week Challenge: Student Mothers, Maternity Leaves, and Pregnancy-Based Sex Discrimination, 4 Alb. Gov't L. Rev. 538 (2011).

208. *See* Tiffany Sala, SB 1014: Parental Leave for Parenting Pupils, 48 U. Pac. L. Rev. 608 (2017).

209. 34 C.F.R. § 106.40(b)(5).

210. *See* Hogan v. Ogden, 2008 WL 2954245, at *4–5 (E.D. Wash. July 30, 2008) (finding a prima facie case of discrimination and holding that whether plaintiff's pregnancy-related complications constituted a disability under the ADA was a question for the jury); Darian v. Univ. of Massachusetts Boston, 980 F. Supp. 77, 91 (D. Mass. 1997) (finding that plaintiff suffered complications severe enough to be a disability but that "no reasonable fact-finder could find the University [to have] failed to make a reasonable accommodation merely because it did not offer [plaintiff] what she wanted").

211. 34 C.F.R. § 106.40(b)(5).

212. 29 C.F.R. Part 1630, App. § 1630.9.

213. 34 C.F.R. § 106.40(b)(5).

214. 34 C.F.R. § 106.8(b).

215. 34 C.F.R. § 106.8(a).

216. *See* U.S. Department of Education, Pregnant or Parenting? Title IX Protects You from Discrimination at School (June 2013), https://www2.ed.gov/about/offices/list/ocr/docs/dcl-know-rights-201306-title-ix.pdf.

217. 65 Fed Reg. 52867 at § .135(a).

218. U.S. Department of Education, Office for Civil Rights, Online Complaint Form, http://www.ed.gov/ocr/complaintintro.html.

219. To locate contact information, telephone 1-800-421-3481 or *see* the OCR website, https://wdcrobcolp01.ed.gov/CFAPPS/OCR/contactus.cfm.

220. Information about how to file a complaint with OCR is available at https://www2.ed.gov/about/offices/list/ocr/docs/howto.pdf.

221. *See* U.S. Department of Justice, Title IX Legal Manual, http://www.justice.gov/crt/about/cor/coord/ixlegal.php.

222. Courts have considered whether it is a violation of Title IX for a school to bar a student from the National Honor Society because of pregnancy, and whether reinstatement is the appropriate remedy. *See* Cazares v. Barber, 959 F.2d 753 (9th Cir. 1992); Wort v. Vierling, 778 F.2d 1233 (7th Cir. 1985); Chipman v. Grant Cnty. Sch. Dist., 30 F. Supp. 2d 975 (E.D. Ky. 1998). The courts in *Cazares, Wort,* and *Chipman* held that

the school district violated Title IX in expelling a pregnant student from the honor society and ordered the school to reinstate the members. However, a school was found not to have violated Title IX when it expelled a pregnant student from honor society not because she was pregnant but rather because she had engaged in premarital sex. *See* Pfeiffer v. Marion Center Area Sch. Dis., 917 F.2d 779, 784 (3d Cir. 1990).

223. *See* Cannon v. University of Chicago, 441 U.S. 677, 705 (1979). Damages can compensate, for example, for lost income due to a delayed graduation or lost potential income because a student's grades have fallen due to the failure of a school to accommodate the absence. Students should keep in mind that there have not been many cases seeking to enforce pregnancy-related rights under Title IX, and very few of them have ordered damages. *See* Michelle Gough, Parenting and Pregnant Students: An Evaluation of the Implementation of the "Other" Title IX, 17 Mich. J. Gender & L. 211 (2011). Franklin v. Gwinnett County Public Schools, 503 U.S. 60 (1992) (holding that a damage remedy is available to redress violations of Title IX). Title IX was modeled after Title VI of the Civil Rights Act of 1964, which bars race discrimination in programs receiving federal funds. In Alexander v. Sandoval, 532 U.S. 275 (2001), the Court held that a private right of action did not exist to enforce disparate impact regulations under Title VI. However, the Court emphasized that regulations enforcing the Title VI "ban on intentional discrimination are covered by the cause of action to enforce that section." *Id.* at 284. For further discussion, *see* Kendra Fershee, An Act for All Contexts: Incorporating the Pregnancy Discrimination Act into Title IX to Help Pregnant Students Gain and Retain Access to Education, 39 Hofstra L. Rev. 281, 288–292 (2010).

224. 20 U.S.C. § 1400(c).

225. 20 U.S.C. §1401(3)(A).

226. 20 U.S.C. § 1412(a)(1)(A).

227. 20 U.S.C. § 1401(9).

228. 20 U.S.C. §§ 1412(a)(3)(A), 1414(a)(1)(D)(iii)(II)(bb), 1412(a)(1)(A), 1401(29)(A), 1412(10)(B)(ii).

229. 20 U.S.C. § 1414(d).

230. 20 U.S.C. § 1414(d)(A).

231. *See, for example,* 20 U.S.C. § 1415; 34 C.F.R. §§ 300.148, 300.151–153, 300.300, 300.502–518, 300.530–536, 300.610–625.

232. 20 U.S.C. § 1414(d)(B).

233. 20 U.S.C. § 1414(a)(4)(A). *Cf.* 20 U.S.C. § 1414(d)(5) (discussing multiyear IEPs).

234. 34 C.F.R. §§ 300.501(a), 300.613.

235. 20 U.S.C. § 1414(a)(1)(D).

236. 34 C.F.R. § 300.503(a)–(b).

237. Endrew F. ex rel. Joseph F. v. Douglas Cty. Sch. Dist. RE-1, 580 U.S. ___, 137 S. Ct. 988, 992, 1000–01 (2017). *See also* F.L. v. Bd. of Educ. of Great Neck Union Free Sch. Dist., 735 Fed. Appx. 38, 40–41 (2d Cir. 2018); Z. B. v. District of Columbia, 888 F.3d 515, 517 (D.C. Cir. 2018).

238. 20 U.S.C. § 1400(c)(5)(D). *See also* 34 C.F.R. § 300.114(a)(2).

239. 20 U.S.C. § 1412(5)(B)(i).

240. 34 C.F.R. § 300.115. *See also* Oberti ex rel. Oberti v. Bd. of Educ. of Borough of Clementon Sch. Dist., 995 F.2d 1204, 1218 (3d Cir. 1993) ("IDEA and its regulations do not contemplate an all-or-nothing educational system in which handicapped children attend either regular or special education.") (internal quotations omitted) (citations omitted).

241. 20 U.S.C. § 1415(f)(3)(E); Bd. of Educ. of the Hendrick Hudson Cent. Sch. Dist. v. Rowley, 458 U.S. 176, 206–207 (1982).

242. 20 U.S.C. § 1415.

243. 20 U.S.C. § 1415(f)(3)(E)(ii); 34 C.F.R. § 300.513.

244. 20 U.S.C. § 1414(d)(1)(B)(ii).

245. M.L. v. Fed. Way Sch. Dist., 394 F.3d 634, 648–649 (9th Cir. 2005) ("[T]he record supports an inference that [the student could have been] placed in a regular educa-tion classroom. So long as this was a possibility, participation of a regular education teacher in the IEP team was [procedurally] required by the IDEA.").

246. Compare MM ex rel. DM v. Sch. Dist. of Greenville Cty., 303 F.3d 523, 533 (4th Cir. 2002) (holding that "mere technical contravention[s]of the IDEA" do not give rise to claims warranting relief), with Leggett v. District of Columbia, 793 F.3d 59 (D.C. Cir. 2015) (holding that the failure to timely develop an IEP violated the IDEA's proce-dural safeguards and warranted relief), and R.E. v. N.Y.C. Department of Education, 694 F.3d 167, 190 (2d Cir. 2012) (holding that the cumulative effect of numerous procedural violations may amount to a denial of FAPE—even where those errors fail to do so when considered individually).

247. Endrew F. ex rel. Joseph F. v. Douglas Cty. Sch. Dist. RE-1, 580 U.S. ___, 137 S. Ct. 988, 1001 (2017) (rejecting a "de minimis" standard for IDEA sufficiency); Bd. of Educ. of the Hendrick Hudson Cent. Sch. Dist. v. Rowley, 458 U.S. 176, 200–201 (1982).

248. 20 U.S.C. § 1415(b)(6)(A).

249. 20 U.S.C. § 1415(b)(6)(B).

250. R.E. v. N.Y.C. Dept. of Educ., 694 F.3d 167, 190 (2d Cir. 2012).

251. Endrew F. ex rel. Joseph F. v. Douglas Cty. Sch. Dist. RE-1, 580 U.S. ___, 137 S. Ct. 988, 1002 (2017).

252. Endrew F., 137 S. Ct. at 99. *See also* M.E. v. N.Y.C. Department of Education, 2018 WL 582601, *3 (S.D.N.Y. Jan. 26, 2018) (explaining that FAPE does not require pro-viding all "that might be thought desirable by loving parents") (citations omitted).

253. 42 U.S.C. §§ 12131 et seq.

254. 29 U.S.C. § 794.

255. 20 U.S.C. § 1415(l) (explaining that the IDEA does not restrict or limit the rights conferred on children with disabilities by the ADA or Section 504).

256. 20 U.S.C. § 1415(l). *See also* Fry v. Napoleon Community Schools, 580 U.S. ___, 137 S. Ct. 743, 754–755 (2017).

257. Fry v. Napoleon Community Schools, 580 U.S. ___, 137 S. Ct. 743, 754–755 (2017).

258. *See* U.S. Department of Education, Disability Discrimination: Overview of the Laws, https://www2.ed.gov/about/offices/list/ocr/disabilityoverview.html. Other resources include: AFC's Guide to Special Education (June 2016), Advocates for

Children, https://www.advocatesforchildren.org; Arc Guide to Special Education Evaluation (Aug. 2018), https://arcminnesota.org/wp-content/uploads/2019/06/Arc-Guide-to-Special-Education-Evaluations.pdf; The Right to Special Education in New Jersey, Education Law Center, https://edlawcenter.org/assets/files/pdfs/publications/Rights_SpecialEducation_Guide%20TL.pdf.

259. *See* Jason P. Nance, Dismantling the School-to-Prison Pipeline: Tools for Change, 48 Ariz. St. L.J. 313 (2016). For statistics on criminal referrals, *see* U.S. Department of Education, Office for Civil Rights, Civil Rights Data Collection, Data Snapshot: School Discipline, Issue Brief No. 1 (Mar. 21, 2014), https://ocrdata.ed.gov/Downloads/CRDC-School-Discipline-Snapshot.pdf.

260. *See* U.S. Government Accountability Office, K–12 Education: Discipline Disparities for Black Students, Boys, and Students with Disabilities, GAO-18-258 (Mar. 2018), https://www.gao.gov/assets/700/692095.pdf; Daniel J. Losen & Tia Elena Martinez, Out of School and Off Track: The Overuse of Suspensions in American Middle and High Schools, The Civil Rights Project/*Proyecto Derechos Civiles* at UCLA (Apr. 8, 2013), http://civilrightsproject.ucla.edu/resources/projects/center-for-civil-rights-remedies/school-to-prison-folder/federal-reports/out-of-school-and-off-track-the-overuse-of-suspensions-in-american-middle-and-high-schools; *see also* Alia Wong, How School Suspensions Push Black Students Behind, The Atlantic (Feb. 8, 2016), http://www.theatlantic.com/education/archive/2016/02/how-school-suspensions-push-black-students-behind/460305/.

261. *See* Rocío Rodríguez Ruiz, School-to-Prison Pipeline: An Evaluation of Zero Tolerance Policies and their Alternatives, 54 Hous. L. Rev. 803 (2017).

262. *See* Robyn K. Bitner, Exiled from Education: Plyler v. Doe's Impact on the Constitutionality of Long-term Suspensions and Expulsions, 101 Va. L. Rev. 763, 783 n.115 (2015) (listing states as: Arkansas, California, Connecticut, Georgia, Maryland, Missouri, New Jersey, Ohio, Rhode Island, Texas, Utah). *See also* Cathe A. v. Doddridge County Board of Education, 490 S.E.2d 340, 351 (W. Va. 1997) (recognizing right to alternative education as component of state "constitutionally mandated" right to education). For further discussion about alternative schooling, *see* Leah Porter, Educational Obligations to Delinquent Youth: The Role of Public Schools, 7 Northeastern U. L.J. 211 (2015).

263. Barbara Fedders, Schooling at Risk, 103 Iowa L. Rev. 871 (2018).

264. *Id.* at 890–891.

265. *See* Jenni Owen, Jane Wettach, & Katie Claire Hoffman, Instead of Suspension: Alternative Strategies for Effective Discipline, Duke University Center for Child and Family Policy and Children's Law Clinic (2015), https://law.duke.edu/childedlaw/schooldiscipline/downloads/instead_of_suspension.pdf.

266. *See* Mary Louise Frampton, Finding Common Ground in Restorative Justice: Transforming Our Juvenile Justice Systems, 22 U.C. Davis J. Juv. L. & Pol'y 101, 103 (2018) ("The restorative justice model focuses on the responsibility of young people to repair the damage that their misbehavior has caused, so that the needs of victims are satisfied and the community itself becomes safer."); *see also* Erin R. Archerd, Restoring Justice in Schools, 5 U. Cin. L. Rev. 761 (2017); Jon Powell,

Making Space for Good Things to Happen: A Restorative Approach to the School-to-Prison Pipeline, 17 Fla. Coastal L. Rev. 83 (2015).

267. Goss v. Lopez, 419 U.S. 565 (1975).

268. Buchanan v. City of Bolivar, Tenn., 99 F.3d 1352, 1359 (6th Cir. 1996); *see also* Chyma v. Tama Cnty. Sch. Bd., 2008 WL 4552942, at *3 (N.D. Iowa 2008) ("It appears to be the consensus of the circuits, however, that placement in an alternative school does not implicate procedural due process rights unless there is a showing that the education provided by the alternative school is substantially inferior."). In E.S. by and through D.K. v. Brookings School District, 2018 WL 2338796 (D. S. Dak. 2018), the district court held that due process protections were triggered because the alternative education to which the disciplined student was consigned—consisting of one online class for a six-week period—was significantly different from or inferior to that of the education at the student's regular school.

269. Goss v. Lopez, 419 U.S. 565 (1975).

270. For a summary of protections available in New York, *see* New York Civil Liberties, Know Your Rights: Students' Rights and Responsibilities When Facing a Suspension, http://www.nyclu.org/content/know-your-rights-students-rights-and-responsibilities-when-facing-suspension.

271. For a discussion of the minimal nature of the *Goss* hearing and the insufficiency of its procedural protections for the student, *see* Derek W. Black, The Constitutional Limit of Zero Tolerance in Schools, 99 Minn. L. Rev. 823 (2015); *see also* Peter H. Schuck, Matthew Matera, & David I. Noah, What Happens to the "Bad Apples": An Empirical Study of Suspensions in New York City Schools, 87 Notre Dame L. Rev. 2063 (2012).

272. The comments to regulations implementing the IDEA emphasize that the statute "recognizes that a child with a disability may display disruptive behaviors characteristic of the child's disability and the child should not be punished for behaviors that are a result of the child's disability." Assistance to States for the Education of Children with Disabilities and Preschool Grants for Children with Disabilities, 71 Fed. Reg. 46,540, 46,720 (Aug. 14, 2006) (codified at 34 C.F.R. Parts 300 & 301). *See* Trisha Kreson, The Conflict Between Preserving the Rights of Students with Disabilities and Promoting Safe Schools—Will the Procedural Safeguards of the Individuals with Disabilities Education Act Survive the Era of School Violence?, 47 U. Tol. L. Rev. 515 (2016).

273. 20 U.S.C. § 1415(k)(5)(B)(ii); 34 C.F.R. § 300.534(a).

274. 20 U.S.C. § 1415(k)(1)(B); 34 C.F.R. § 300.530(b).

275. *See* Sarah Lusk, The Dimming Light of the IDEA: The Need to Reevaluate the Definition of a Free Appropriate Public Education, 36 Pace L. Rev. 292 (2015).

276. 20 U.S.C. § 1415(k)(1)(G); 34 C.F.R. § 300.530(g).

277. 20 U.S.C. § 1415(k)(3)(A); 34 C.F.R. § 300.532(a).

278. 20 U.S.C. § 6313(a). During its first 20 years, Title I focused essentially on remedial education and the development of basic skills, relying on "pullout" programs that separated participating children from the regular classroom. Responding to criticisms of the statute, Congress amended Title I in 1988 to ensure that schools receiving funds help eligible children to attain grade level, to succeed in the regular

classroom, and to achieve the basic and more advanced skills expected of all children. 20 U.S.C. § 2701(b), as amended and replaced by Improving America's Schools Act of 1994, 20 U.S.C. §§ 6301–8962. Later amendments, including Goals 2000: Educate America Act, Pub. L. No. 103-227, and the No Child Left Behind Act, Pub. L. No. 107-110, have been repealed and replaced by the Every Student Succeeds Act, Pub. L. No. 114-95. For an assessment of Goals 2000, *see* The National Educational Goals Report: Building a Nation of Learners (U.S. Gov. Printing Office 1999), https://babel.hathitrust.org/cgi/pt?id=mdp.39015077158429;view=1up;seq=3.

The core of the No Child Left Behind Act was found in its testing and accountability standards. The NCLB required states to test students in reading and mathematics annually in grades 3–8 and once in grades 10–12. States were also required to test students in science, although less frequently: only once in grades 3–5, 6–8, and 10–12. Results from these tests had to be made public both generally and for specific student subgroups, including low-income students, students with disabilities, non-English speaking students, and major racial and ethnic groups. When No Child Left Behind was passed in 2001, it set the nationwide goal of achieving 100% proficiency in math and reading based on accountability tests by the year 2014. The 2011 National Assessment of Educational Progress at Grades 4 and 8 found that 40% of students in grade 4 and 35% of students in grade 8 achieved proficiency in mathematics; reading scores were similar, with 34% of students in grade 4 and 8 testing proficient. *See* U.S. Department of Education, Institute of Education Sciences, The Nation's Report Card, Reading 2011, National Assessment of Educational Progress at Grades 4 and 8, http://nces.ed.gov/nationsreportcard/pdf/main2011/2012457. pdf. The statute was criticized on multiple grounds including its use of outcomes-based determinative funding, which negatively affected communities with low-wealth students and children of color. For a summary of criticisms, *see* Frederick M. Hess, Michael J. Petrilli, & Andrew J. Rotherham, No Child Left Behind Primer 4–6, 23–25, 124–126 (Peter Lang 2006). Although the ESSA retains the NCLB's testing requirements, it provides states with greater flexibility in determining what the testing looks like in practice and established pilot programs for states wishing to experiment with innovative ways to evaluate student success. It also moves away from the NCLB's high-stakes emphasis on testing, no longer requiring states to consider schools failing if students do not score high enough. *See* U.S. Department of Education, Every Student Succeeds Act (ESSA), https://www.ed.gov/essa.

279. 20 U.S.C. §§ 6314–15.
280. 20 U.S.C. § 6314(a)(1).
281. 20 U.S.C. § 6314(a)(1).
282. 20 U.S.C. § 6315(b).
283. 20 U.S.C. § 6321(b).
284. 20 U.S.C. § 6321(b)–(c).
285. 20 U.S.C. § 6315. Schools largely have used Title I funds for instruction. *See* U.S. Government Accountability Office, Disadvantaged Students: School Districts Have Used Title I Funds Primarily to Support Instruction (July 15, 2011), http://www.gao.gov/products/GAO-11-595.

286. 20 U.S.C. §§ 6314–15.

287. 20 U.S.C. § 6315(b)(g)(ii).

288. 20 U.S.C. §§ 6314(b)(1)(C), 6315(c)(1)(E).

289. 20 U.S.C. § 6314(b)(1)(C).

290. 20 U.S.C. § 6315(c).

291. 20 U.S.C. §§ 6314(b)(5), 6315(c)(1)(H).

292. 20 U.S.C. § 7861(c)(6).

293. 20 U.S.C. § 6318(a)(3)(A).

294. 20 U.S.C. § 6318(c)(3).

295. 20 U.S.C. § 6318(a)(3)(B).

296. 20 U.S.C. § 6318(d).

297. 20 U.S.C. § 6318(a)(2)(B). The School-Parent Compact is an important part of the school-level parental involvement policy designed to give parents a clear understanding of what a school is doing to improve its students' educational experience. The school must develop the compact jointly with parents of students receiving Title I services. The compact describes how parents, school staff, and students will share responsibility for ensuring improved student achievement and student success at meeting state performance standards. Among its specific requirements, the compact must describe the school's responsibility to provide high quality curriculum and instruction in a supportive and effective learning environment. In addition, the compact should list the parent's responsibility with respect to such activities as the child's attendance, homework, and television viewing habits. The compact requires parents and school officials to communicate regularly, ensuring the compact is being obeyed. At least once a year, parents of elementary school students and their teachers should meet to discuss the children's achievement, how the compact is working toward ensuring progress, and whether or not the compact needs to be updated. Further, schools, at a minimum, should provide frequent reports on a child's progress, as well as reasonable access to school staff, including opportunities to visit, participate, observe, and volunteer in a child's classroom.

298. 20 U.S.C. § 6318.

299. 20 U.S.C. § 6318(c)(1).

300. 20 U.S.C. § 6318(c)(2).

301. 20 U.S.C. § 6318(f).

302. *See, for example*, Rachel Klein, Keeping Our Kids in School and Out of Court: Rooting Out School Suspension Hearings and a New Alternative, 17 Cardozo J. Conflict Resol. 633 (2016). *See generally* Jacob Kang-Brown, Jennifer Trone, Jennifer Fratello, & Tarika Daftary-Kapur, A Generation Later: What We've Learned about Zero Tolerance in Schools, Vera Institute of Justice, Center on Youth Justice (Dec. 2013), http://www.vera.org/sites/default/files/resources/downloads/zero-tolerance-in-schools-policy-brief.pdf.

303. Carolyn Weisman, Giving Credit Where Credit Is Due: Advancing the Highly Mobile Student Population Toward High School Graduation, 50 Fam. Ct. Rev. 527 (2012).

304. The Carl D. Perkins Vocational and Technical Education Act was first authorized in 1984, and again in 1998 and 2006, when it was renamed the Carl D. Perkins Career

and Technical Education Improvement Act of 2006. *See* 20 U.S.C. §§ 2321 et seq., Pub. L. No. 109-270. The program was reauthorized in 2018 as the Strengthening Career and Technical Education for the 21st Century Act (known as Perkins V), Pub. L. No. 115-224. It increased funding and gave states greater authority to set "Career Technical Education" goals. Perkins V also changed the process for setting performance targets and required disaggregation of student data, allowing the Secretary of Education to sanction states with reduced funding if they fail to meet 90% of performance targets for two consecutive years. For a description of innovative programs funded through the Perkins Act, *see* Michael Selmi, Unions, Education, and the Future of Low-Wage Workers, 1 U. Chi. Legal F. 147 (2009).

305. The program was created in 1964 by the Economic Opportunity Act and, most recently, was authorized as the Workforce Investment Act (WIA) of 1998, Pub. L. No. 105-220, Title 1, Subtitle C, Section 141. Although the WIA's authorization of appropriation expired after FY 2003, Congress has continued to appropriate funds for Job Corps. For more information, *see* Job Corps, https://www.jobcorps.gov.

306. 20 C.F.R. § 670.400.There is no upper age limit for students with disabilities. *Id.*; U.S. Department of Labor, Office of Job Corps, Job Corps' Eligibility Criteria, https://www.jobcorps.gov/reports/eligibility-fact-sheet.

307. 20 C.F.R. § 670.400. States and localities have discretion to define "requires additional assistance to complete an educational program, or to secure and hold employment." 20 C.F.R. § 664.210.

308. *See* 20 C.F.R. § 100 (program description); 20 C.F.R. § 672.300 (basic eligibility criteria). The definitions of low-income and migrant youth appear in 20 C.F.R. § 672.110.

309. YouthBuild Transfer Act, Pub. L. No. 109-281. YouthBuild was authorized as a federal program in 1992 under Subtitle D of Title IV of the Cranston-Gonzalez National Affordable Housing Act and is currently authorized by Title I, Subtitle D, Section 173 of the Workforce Investment Act. In 2006, the program was transferred from the U.S. Department of Housing and Urban Development to the Department of Labor. *See* 20 C.F.R. §§ 672.200 & 672.210. For additional information, *see* YouthBuild, https://www.youthbuild.org.

310. 20 C.F.R. § 672.315.

311. 20 C.F.R. § 672.320.

312. 20 C.F.R. § 672.310(a).

313. 20 C.F.R. § 672.310(b).

314. A directory of Youth Build programs is available at https://www.youthbuild.org/program-directory.

315. The Workforce Innovation and Opportunity Act reauthorized the Adult Education and Family Literacy Act with several revisions. Pub. L. No. 113-128.

316. *See* 20 C.F.R. §§ 662.100 et seq. For more information, *see* the CareerOneStop website, http://www.careeronestop.org/. CareerOneStop is sponsored by the U.S. Department of Labor.

317. Contact information for local American Job Center offices may be found at https://www.careeronestop.org/LocalHelp/AmericanJobCenters/american-job-centers.aspx.

318. *See, for example*, Growing Up NYC, Summer Work for Youth, https://growingupnyc. cityofnewyork.us/programs/summer-youth-employment-program/.

319. 45 C.F.R. §§ 260.30 & 261.2(n).

320. 45 C.F.R. § 261.33(b)(1). *See* Elizabeth Lower-Basch, Education and Training Opportunities for TANF Recipients: Opportunities and Challenges under the Final Rule, Center for Law & Soc. Policy 5 (Mar. 18, 2008), https://www.clasp.org/sites/ default/files/publications/2017/04/0406.pdf.

321. *See* 45 C.F.R. §§ 261.30, 261.33; 73 Fed. Reg. 6772, 6780-95 (Feb. 5, 2008).

322. *See* U.S. Department of Health and Human Services, Administration for Children and Families, Welfare Rules Databook: State TANF Policies as of July 2017, https:// www.acf.hhs.gov/sites/default/files/opre/2017_welfare_rules_databook_final_10_ 31_18_508_2.pdf.

323. 20 U.S.C. § 1070a-13.

324. 20 U.S.C. § 1070a-12. For more information about TANF education and training options, *see* Randi Hall, Expanding Education and Training Opportunities under TANF, CLASP (July 2016), https://www.clasp.org/tanf-education-and-training-resources.

325. 20 U.S.C. § 1070a-13(b); 34 C.F.R. §§ 645.1 et seq.

326. 34 C.F.R. § 645.13(a).

327. 20 U.S.C. § 1070a-13(d)(3).

328. U.S. Department of Education, Upward Bound Program, http://www2.ed.gov/ programs/trioupbound/index.html.

329. 20 U.S.C. § 1070a-12(a); 34 C.F.R. §§ 643.1 et seq.

330. 20 U.S.C. § 1070a-12(b)(5)(B).

331. 20 U.S.C. § 1070a-12(b)–(c).

332. 20 U.S.C. § 1070a-12(d)(2).

333. U.S. Department of Education, Talent Search Program, https://www2.ed.gov/ programs/triotalent/index.html. For an example of a state application for Talent Search *see* http://nacee.net/wp-content/uploads/2012/11/2016-17-ETS-Application.pdf.

334. The U.S. Department of Education maintains a useful online resource detailing available grants and loans, eligibility requirements, and application procedures at https://studentaid.ed.gov/sa/. *See also* U.S. Department of Education, The Guide to Federal Student Aid: Funding Your Education, https://studentaid.ed.gov/sa/sites/ default/files/funding-your-education.pdf.

335. *See* 7 C.F.R. § 273.5(b)(6).

336. Data are set out in: College Board, Trends in College Pricing 2018, https://trends. collegeboard.org/college-pricing; National Center for Education Statistics, Digest of Education Statistics, Table 320, https://nces.ed.gov/programs/digest/d07/ tables/dt07_320.asp. On overall student debt, *see* Association of Public & Land-Grant Universities, What is the typical debt load for graduates of four-year public universities?, https://www.aplu.org/projects-and-initiatives/college-costs-tuition-and-financial-aid/publicuvalues/student-debt.html.

337. *See* Tuition-free college is now a reality in nearly 20 states, CNBC (Mar. 12, 2019), https://www.cnbc.com/2019/03/12/free-college-now-a-reality-in-these-states.

html (identifying Oregon, Nevada, Arkansas,, New Jersey, Maryland, Tennessee, New York, Rhode Island, Delaware, Kentucky, and Indiana). *See also* Marsha Mercer, Why Free College Tuition Is Spreading from Cities to States, Pew (Jan. 5, 2018), https://www.pewtrusts.org/en/research-and-analysis/blogs/stateline/2018/ 01/05/why-free-college-tuition-is-spreading-from-cities-to-states. For advocacy on this issue, *see* Campaign for Free College Tuition, https://www.freecollegenow.org/.

338. U.S. Department of Education, Federal Student Aid Office, Fiscal Year 2018 Annual Report, https://studentaid.ed.gov/sa/sites/default/files/FSA-FY-2018-Annual-Report-Final.pdf.

339. *See* College Board, Trends in Higher Education: Maximum Pell Grant and Published Prices at Four-Year Institutions over Time, Figure 21B, https:// trends.collegeboard.org/student-aid/figures-tables/maximum-pell-grant-and-published-prices-four-year-institutions-over-time; *see also* Spiros Protopsaltis & Sharon Parrott, Pell Grants—A Key Tool for Expanding College Access and Economic Opportunity—Need Strengthening, Not Cuts, Center on Budget and Policy Priorities (July 2017), https://www.cbpp.org/research/federal-budget/ pell-grants-a-key-tool-for-expanding-college-access-and-economic-opportunity.

340. *See* Susan Dynarski & Judith Scott-Clayton, Financial Aid Policy: Lessons from Research, Working Paper 1870, National Bureau of Economic Research (Jan. 2013), http://www.nber.org/papers/w18710 (reporting that the middle-class share of Pell grants increased from 6% to 9% between 2008 and 2011); Preston Cooper, Pell Grants Are Now A Middle Class Benefit, Forbes (Feb. 2, 2018), https://www. forbes.com/sites/prestoncooper2/2018/02/02/pell-grants-are-now-a-middle-class-benefit/#34d67b7b4a1f.

341. 20 U.S.C. § 1070a. Regulations governing the federal Pell Grant program appear at 34 C.F.R. Part 690. The grant program began as part of the Higher Education Act of 1965 (called the Educational Opportunity Grant program) and provided funds to colleges that were expected to recruit students with "exceptional financial need." In 1972, the United States divided the grant program into two separate programs, the Supplemental Educational Opportunity Grant program, continuing to give direct grants to colleges, and the Basic Educational Opportunity Grant program, giving grants directly to students. In 1980, the direct student grant program was renamed the Pell Grant program, in honor of Senator Claiborne Pell, who expanded the program to include part-time students, students attending community colleges, and students enrolled in vocational educational programs. The Middle Income Student Assistance Act of 1978 extended the program to include students who are not poor or low-income. Pub. L. No. 95-566.

342. *See* U.S. Department of Education, Federal Student Aid Office, https://studentaid. ed.gov/sa/types/grants-scholarships/pell.

343. In 2016, the Obama administration initiated a pilot program known as "Second Chance Pell," which has made financial aid grants available to over 10,000 inmates in its first two years. As of 2019, the pilot program had been extended through the 2019–20 cycle, but its continuation depends upon future renewals. *See* U.S. Department of Education, Answering Your Frequently Asked Questions about Second Chance Pell

(Apr. 2019), https://blog.ed.gov/2019/04/answering-frequently-asked-questions-second-chance-pell/. *See generally* Jason L. Mallory, Denying Pell Grants to Prisoners: Race, Class, and the Philosophy of Mass Incarceration, International Soc. Sci. Rev. Vol. 90, Issue 1, article 2, http://digitalcommons.northgeorgia.edu/issr/vol90/iss1/2.

344. *See* 34 C.F.R. § 668.40; U.S. Department of Education, Federal Student Aid Office, https://studentaid.ed.gov/sa/eligibility/criminal-convictions.

345. 20 U.S.C. § 1070b. Regulations governing the Federal Pell Grant Program appear at 34 C.F.R. Part 676.

346. For more information, *see* U.S. Department of Education, Federal Student Aid Office, Federal Student Grant Programs, https://studentaid.ed.gov/sa/sites/default/files/federal-grant-programs.pdf.

347. For more information, *see* U.S. Department of Education, Federal Family Education Loan (FFEL) Program, http://www2.ed.gov/programs/ffel/index.html.

The federal government's role as subsidized lender traces back to 1958, when Congress enacted the National Defense Education Act, authorizing federal loans to financially needy "talented young men and women" interested in careers in science, math, engineering, or foreign languages, seen as important to national defense. *See* Act of September 2, 1958, Pub. L. No. 85-864. 72 Stat. 1580, codified at 20 U.S.C. Chapter 17. Regulations appeared in Title 34 of the Code of Federal Regulations Part 144.

The Guaranteed Student Loan Program (GSLP), adopted as part of the Higher Education Act of 1965, extended this approach to low-income students generally, responding to concerns that post-secondary schooling was financially out of reach for students of limited financial means. *See* Higher Education Act of 1965, 20 U.S.C. § 431. Under the GSLP, financially eligible students obtained loans from private lenders, and the loans were guaranteed by the federal government (or by a state or private lending agency). Payment of the loan was deferred until after the student's graduation—called a grace period—and the rate of interest was subsidized, with the federal government providing an allowance to the lender. If the student defaulted on the loan, the federal government reimbursed the lender.

In 1978 the program was expanded to include students of any income, *see* Middle Income Student Assistance Act, 20 U.S.C. § 1087, and then in 1982 the program was cut back to include only students with family incomes below $30,000.

The 1990s saw the introduction of nonsubsidized student loans for students from higher-income families that also were guaranteed by the government. For further discussion, *see* Elizabeth Popp Berman & Abby Stivers, Student Loans as Pressure on U.S. Higher Education, 46 Research in the Sociology of Organizations, 129–160 (2016), http://www.emeraldinsight.com/doi/abs/10.1108/S0733-558X20160000046005.

Student loans are no longer available as "guaranteed loans" because the Healthcare and Education Reconciliation Act of 2010 does not permit new student loans issued after June 30, 2010, to be issued under the FFELP, the guaranteed loan program. Pub. L. No. 111-152, 124 Stat. 1071; *see* 20 U.S.C. § 1001.

348. Health Care and Education Reconciliation Act of 2010, Pub. L. No. 111-152, 124 Stat. 1071. *See* David M. Herszenhorn & Tamar Lewin, Student Loan Overhaul Approved by Congress, N.Y. Times (Mar. 25, 2010), https://www.nytimes.com/2010/03/26/us/politics/26loans.html.

349. For more information, *see* U.S. Department of Education, Federal Student Aid Office, https://studentaid.ed.gov/sa/resources.

350. *See* 20 U.S.C. §§ 1087a et seq.; 34 C.F.R. Part 685.

351. *See* 20 U.S.C. §§ 1070g, 1087aa-1087hh; 34 C.F.R. Part 674.

352. *See* U.S. Department of Education, Federal Student Aid Office, Filling Out the FAFSA, https://studentaid.ed.gov/sa/fafsa/filling-out.

353. 20 U.S.C. §1087e(b).

354. *Id.* For current interest rates on federal student loans, *see* U.S. Department of Education, Federal Student Aid Office, Interest Rates for New Direct Loans, https://studentaid.ed.gov/About/announcements/interest-rate.

355. U.S. Department of Education, Federal Student Aid Office, Federal Student Loans: Repaying Your Loans, https://studentaid.ed.gov/sa/sites/default/files/repaying-your-loans.pdf.

356. 20 U.S.C. § 1092b(1)(A)(i).

357. *See* U.S. Department of Education, Federal Student Aid Office, Getting Out of Default, https://studentaid.ed.gov/sa/repay-loans/default/get-out#loan-consolidation.

358. U.S. Department of Education, Federal Student Aid Office, Income-Driven Repayment Plans for Federal Student Loans, https://studentaid.ed.gov/sa/repay-loans/understand/plans/income-driven.

359. *See* U.S. Department of Education, Federal Student Aid Office, Income-Driven Repayment (IDR) Plan Request, https://studentloans.gov/myDirectLoan/ibrInstructions.action?source=15SPRRPMT#.

360. 20 U.S.C. § 1098e; 34 C.F.R. § 685.221.

361. 20 U.S.C. § 1098e(b)(1); U.S. Department of Education, Federal Student Aid Office, Loan Consolidation, https://studentaid.ed.gov/sa/repay-loans/consolidation.

362. 20 U.S.C. §§ 1098e(a), 1098e(e). For loans made *before* July 1, 2014, partial financial hardship exists whenever the annual loan repayment is greater than *15%* of the amount by which the borrower's annual income exceeds 150% of the federal poverty line. 20 U.S.C. § 1098e(a); 34 C.F.R. § 682.215. For purposes of this calculation "income" means "Adjusted Gross Income" as reported on the borrower's IRS tax return; if the borrower is married and files a joint return, the spouse's income counts into the calculation of hardship, as does the repayment cost of the spouse's federal student loans, if any. 20 U.S.C. § 1098e(a)(3); 34 C.F.R. § 682.215(a). The federal poverty guideline varies by family size, is recalculated annually and published by the Department of Health and Human services. *See* https://aspe.hhs.gov/2019-poverty-guidelines. For additional information and guidance on income based repayment options, *see* U.S. Department of Education, Federal Student Aid Office, https://studentloans.gov/myDirectLoan/index.action.

363. 20 U.S.C. § 1098e(b)(1); 34 C.F.R. § 682.215(a)(4).

364. 34 C.F.R. § 682.215(b).

365. 34 C.F.R. § 682.215(f).
366. U.S. Department of Education, Federal Student Aid Office, Repayment Estimator https://studentloans.gov/myDirectLoan/repaymentEstimator.action. To access the estimator, click "Use the Repayment Estimator," which appears under the repayment and consolidation tab. *See also* Student Loan Income-Based Repayment (IBR) Calculator, Student Loan Hero, https://studentloanhero.com/calculators/student-loan-income-based-repayment-calculator/.
367. Consumer Financial Protection Bureau, Repay Student Debt, https://www.consumerfinance.gov/paying-for-college/repay-student-debt/.
368. *See* 34 C.F.R. § 685.209(a). For a contextualized discussion of PAYE and its origins as a response to the student debt crisis, *see* Eryk J. Wachnik, The Student Debt Crisis: The Impact of the Obama Administration's "Pay As You Earn" Plan on Millions of Current and Former Students, 24 Loyola Consumer Law Rev. 442 (2012).
369. "Partial financial hardship" means the same thing for purposes of PAYE as it does for purposes of Income-Based Repayment plans, as described in the prior question and endnotes. *See* 34 C.F.R. § 685.209(a)(1)(v) (PAYE); 34 C.F.R. § 682.215(a)(4) (IBR); U.S. Department of Education, Federal Student Aid Office, Income-Driven Plans, https://studentaid.ed.gov/sa/repay-loans/understand/plans/income-driven.
370. *See* 34 C.F.R. § 685.209(c). Loan payments are capped at 10% of the amount by which the borrower's Adjusted Gross Income, as reported to IRS, exceeds 150% of the federal poverty guideline applicable to the borrower's family size. 34 C.F.R. § 685.209(c)(2)(i).
371. *See* U.S. Department of Education, Federal Student Aid Office, Income-Contingent Repayment Plan, https://studentaid.ed.gov/sa/repay-loans/understand/plans/income-driven. The Income-Contingent Plan is distinct from the Income-Sensitive Repayment Plan offered for FFELP loans. *See* U.S. Department of Education, Federal Student Aid Office, Income-Sensitive Plan, https://studentaid.ed.gov/sa/repay-loans/understand/plans/income-sensitive.
372. *See* 34 C.F.R. § 685.209(b). "Discretionary income" for purposes of ICR means the amount by which the borrower's Adjusted Gross Income, as reported to the IRS, exceeds the federal poverty guideline applicable to the borrower's family. 34 C.F.R. § 685.209(b)(1)(iii).
373. *See* 34 C.F.R. § 685.209(b)(3)(iii)(D).
374. *See* 34 C.F.R. § 685.204. A similar but less advantageous alternative for temporarily suspending loan repayments is called "forbearance." *See* 34 C.F.R. § 685.205. For more detail on eligibility and application requirements, and an explanation of the difference between deferment and forbearance, *see* U.S. Department of Education, Federal Student Aid Office, Deferment and Forbearance, https://studentaid.ed.gov/sa/repay-loans/deferment-forbearance#differences.
375. 20 U.S.C. § 1078-11.
376. 34 C.F.R. § 685.219(c). A borrower can keep track of payments by using an Employment Certification for Public Service Loan Forgiveness Form. The form for the Federal Direct Loan Program is available at https://studentaid.ed.gov/sa/sites/default/files/public-service-employment-certification-form.pdf; *see* Ryan Lane,

Don't Give Up on Public Service Loan Forgiveness, Nerdwallet (May 16, 2019), https://www.nerdwallet.com/blog/loans/student-loans/dont-give-up-on-public-service-loan-forgiveness/.

377. 20 U.S.C. §§ 1078–11; 34 C.F.R. § 685.219(b) & (c). Eligible public service occupations include: nurses; foreign language specialists; librarians; teachers at low-income or limited English proficiency schools; child welfare workers; speech-language pathologists and audiologists; school counselors, in a school that qualifies for loan cancellation for Perkins loan recipients; public safety occupations, such as firefighters, police officers, and other public safety officers; emergency management occupations; public health or public interest legal careers; nutrition professionals who work for a supplemental nutrition program for women and children; certain medical specialties, in which the person participates in a graduate program or fellowship to provide health care services which requires more than five years of graduate medical training; mental health professionals providing mental health services to children, adolescents, or veterans; dentists who have either completed residency training in pediatric dentistry, general dentistry, or dental public health, or are employed on faculty of an accredited dental school; individuals employed full-time in applied sciences, technology, engineering, or mathematics; physical therapists who provide physical therapy services to children, adolescents, or veterans; superintendents, principles, and administrators at schools in low-income communities; occupational therapists who provide physical therapy services to children, adolescents, or veterans; allied health professionals who work for a public health agency and work in medically underserved areas or communities. For more information, *see* U.S. Department of Education, Federal Student Aid Office, Public Service Loan Forgiveness, https://studentaid.ed.gov/sa/repay-loans/forgiveness-cancellation/public-service.

378. *See* U.S. Department of Education, Federal Student Aid Office, Temporary Expanded Public Service Loan Forgiveness, https://studentaid.ed.gov/sa/repay-loans/forgiveness-cancellation/public-service/temporary-expanded-public-service-loan-forgiveness.

379. U.S. Department of Education, Federal Student Aid Office, Public Service Loan Forgiveness Data, https://studentaid.ed.gov/sa/about/data-center/student/loan-forgiveness/pslf-data. *See also* Gregory Korte, More Than 41,000 Public Service Workers Sought Federal Student Loan Forgiveness. The Government Approved Just 206, USA Today (Dec. 27, 2018), https://www.usatoday.com/story/news/nation/2018/12/27/student-loan-debt-department-education-public-service-loan-forgiveness-denial/2366589002/; Stephanie Frances Ward, Few qualify for public service loan forgiveness, often due to bad information, lawsuit says, ABA Journal (July 18, 2019), http://www.abajournal.com/web/article/few-qualify-for-public-service-loan-forgiveness-often-due-to-bad-information-says-lawsuit.

380. In December 2016, the American Bar Association and others sued the Department of Education alleging that the agency had changed the eligibility requirements for public service loan forgiveness after approving the work. *See* American Bar Ass'n v. U.S. Dep't of Education, 370 F. Supp. 3d 1 (D.D.C. 2019) (granting partial relief

on cross-motions for summary); American Bar Association, Issue Resources: Public Service Loan Forgiveness (Jan. 28, 2019), https://www.americanbar.org/advocacy/governmental_legislative_work/aba-day/resources/pslf/.

381. 34 C.F.R. § 685.217. *See* U.S. Department of Education, Federal Student Aid Office, Teacher Loan Forgiveness, https://studentaid.ed.gov/sa/repay-loans/forgiveness-cancellation/teacher. The school must be listed in the Directory of Low-Income Schools for Teacher Cancellation Benefit, https://studentloans.gov/myDirectLoan/tcli.action, or be operated by the Bureau of Indian Education (BIE) or located on Indian reservations by Indian tribal groups under contract with the BIE.

382. To be highly qualified, the teacher is required to hold a bachelor's degree, and new teachers are required to pass state requirements tests (for example, for elementary school, the teacher is required to pass a test in every subject area of the basic elementary school curriculum; for middle school, a teacher is required to pass a test on each subject taught). Experienced teachers are required to demonstrate competency in all subjects taught, according to a uniform state evaluation. Regulations defining "highly qualified teacher" were removed from the Code of Federal Regulations effective July 7, 2017. 82 Fed. Reg. 31,690, 31,707 (July 7, 2017). However, they continue to appear on the website of the Department of Education as of July 2019, https://studentaid.ed.gov/sa/repay-loans/forgiveness-cancellation/teacher#highly-qualified.

383. If the qualifying teaching service began before October 30, 2004, the borrower may qualify to receive up to $5,000 in loan forgiveness, if they either (1) demonstrated knowledge and teaching skills in reading, writing, mathematics, and other areas of the elementary school curriculum; or (2) taught in a subject area that is relevant to the borrower's academic major. *See* 34 C.F.R. § 685.217(c)(4)(i). If the qualifying teaching service began after October 30, 2004, the borrower may qualify to receive up to $5,000 in loan forgiveness if they were certified as a "highly qualified" full-time elementary or secondary school teacher. 34 C.F.R. § 685.217(c)(5)(i).

384. *See* 34 C.F.R. § 685.218(a)–(b).

385. 34 C.F.R. §§ 674.61; 682.402; 685.213.

386. For further information, and a Discharge Application, *see* https://www.disabilitydischarge.com. The debtor is expected to contact the Nelnet Total and Permanent Disability Servicer which manages the discharge website. To do so, call 1-888-303-7818; email at disabilityinformation@nelnet.net. Note that loans under the Federal Family Education Program have not been offered since 2010, but repayments still must be made. *See* U.S. Department of Education, Federal Student Aid Office, FFEL Program Lender and Guaranty, https://studentaid.ed.gov/sa/about/data-center/lender-guaranty.

387. 34 C.F.R. §§ 674.61(b)(3)(i); 682.402(c)(2)(iv), (v), & (vii); 685.213(b)(2)(i).

388. 34 C.F.R. §§ 674.51(aa)(1); 682.200; 685.102.

389. 34 C.F.R. §§ 674.61(c)(3)(ii); 682.402(c)(9)(v); 685.213(c)(1).

390. 34 C.F.R. §§ 674.61(b)(2)(iv)(B); 682.402(c)(2)(iv)(B); 685.213(b)(2)(ii).

391. Education Dive, A Look at trends in college and university consolidation since 2016 (June 24, 2019), https://www.educationdive.com/news/how-many-colleges-

and-universities-have-closed-since-2016/539379/; U.S. Department of Education, Federal Student Aid Closed School Search Page (July 22, 2019), https:/www2. ed.gov/offices/OSFAP/PEPS/docs/closedschoolsearch.xlsx.

392. *See* 34 C.F.R. § 685.214. During the Obama administration, the U.S. Department of Education took special steps to deal with the closing of particular private schools, referred to as Corinthian schools and ITT Technical Institutes. *See* U.S. Department of Education, Federal Student Aid Office, Information About Debt Relief for Corinthian Colleges Students, https://studentaid.ed.gov/sa/about/announcements/corinthian; U.S. Department of Education, Federal Student Aid Office, Closure of ITT Technical Institutes, https://studentaid.ed.gov/sa/about/announcements/itt.

393. The identity of the loan servicer can be obtained by logging into My Federal Student Aid, available at https://studentaid.ed.gov/sa/?log-in#nslds-login-block, or by calling 1-800-4-FED-AID.

394. *See* U.S. Department of Education, Federal Student Aid Office, Closed School Discharge, https://studentaid.ed.gov/sa/repay-loans/forgiveness-cancellation/closed-school#criteria.

395. *See, for example*, Yan Cao & Tariq Habash, College Complaints Unmasked: 99 Percent of Student Fraud Claims Concern For-Profit Colleges, The Century Fund (2017), https://tcf.org/content/report/college-complaints-unmasked/; College Fraud Claims Up 29 Percent Since August 2017 (2019), https://tcf.org/content/commentary/college-fraud-claims-29-percent-since-august-2017/.

396. *See* Higher Education Act of 1965, § 455(h), 20 U.S.C. § 1087e; 34 C.F.R. § 685.206(c).

397. U.S. Department of Education, Federal Student Aid Office, Borrower Defense to Loan Repayment, https://studentaid.ed.gov/sa/repay-loans/forgiveness-cancellation/borrower-defense.

398. Federal regulations announced in November 2016 set forth a federal process and federal standard for determining when the borrower defense is available. *See* 81 Fed. Reg. 75926 (Nov. 1, 2016), amending 34 C.F.R. Parts 30, 668, 674, 682, 685, and 686, effective July 1, 2017. Before the regulations were to take effect, the U.S. Department of Education announced that it would delay their enforcement. 82 Fed. Reg. 27621 (June 16, 2017). A federal court held that the Department of Education acted arbitrarily and capriciously in staying implementation of the regulations. Bauer v. DeVos, 325 F. Supp. 3d 74 (D.D.C. 2018). In July 2018, the Department proposed a new set of regulations addressing misrepresentation and fraud. *See* U.S. Department of Education, U.S. Department of Education Takes Action to Protect Student Borrowers, Hold Higher Education Institutions Accountable for Deceptive Practices (July 25, 2018), https://www.ed.gov/category/keyword/borrower-defense. For a criticism of the proposed rules, *see* Bruce McClary, What the Proposed Borrower Defense Rules Mean, U.S. News & World Report (Sept. 19, 2018), https://www.usnews.com/education/blogs/student-loan-ranger/articles/2018-09-19/what-the-proposed-borrower-defense-rules-mean-for-student-loans. In March 2019, the Department of Education issued a guidance on the borrower defense. *See* https://ifap.ed.gov/eannouncements/030719GuidConcernP rov2016BorrowerDefensetoRypmtRegs.html. As of April 2019, the Department

of Education had neither approved nor denied borrower-defense claims since June 2018, although there were more than 158,000 claims pending. *See* Andrew Kreighbaum, Data Show No Action on Borrower-Defense Claims, Inside Higher Ed (Apr. 1, 2019), https://www.insidehighered.com/quicktakes/2019/04/01/data-show-no-action-borrower-defense-claims.

399. *See* U.S. Department of Education, Federal Student Aid Office, Understanding Delinquency and Default, https://studentaid.ed.gov/sa/repay-loans/default.

400. *See* U.S. Department of Education, Federal Student Aid Office, Getting Out of Default, https://studentaid.ed.gov/sa/repay-loans/default/get-out#loan-consolidation.

401. Congress amended the Telephone Consumer Protection Act, effective November 2, 2015, to provide an exception for calls "made solely to collect a debt owed to or guaranteed by the United States." Bipartisan Budget Act of 2015, Pub. L. No. 114–74, § 301(a)(1)(A), 129 Stat. 584, 588; 47 U.S.C. § 227(b)(1)(A)(iii). In *Duguid v. Facebook, Inc.*, 926 F.3d 1146 (9th Cir. 2019), the appeals court invalidated the exception as a violation of the First Amendment's ban on speech restrictions that are not content neutral. As a result, debt collection companies cannot make robocalls to cell phones to collect a government-based debt. *See also* American Association of Political Consultants, Inc. v. Federal Communications Commission., 923 F.3d 159 (4th Cir. 2019).

402. 20 U.S.C. § 1091a(a)(2)(D).

403. 20 U.S.C. § 1091a(b)(1).

404. 34 C.F.R. § 682.410(b)(2). *See* U.S. v. Vilus, 419 F. Supp. 2d 293, 300 (E.D.N.Y. 2005) (allowing a collection fee award of 2% of the total debt, noting that the Department of Education typically charges or can charge 2% of the total debt under 34 C.F.R. § 30.60 (b)).

405. 34 C.F.R. § 682.410(b)(2)(i).

406. 34 C.F.R. § 30.60(b).

407. 34 C.F.R. § 30.60(e).

408. U.S. Department of Education, Federal Student Aid Office, Collections, https://studentaid.ed.gov/sa/repay-loans/default/collections.

409. 20 U.S.C. § 1095a.

410. 20 U.S.C. § 1095a(a)(1).

411. 20 U.S.C. § 1095a(a)(2).

412. 20 U.S.C. § 1095a(a)(3).

413. 20 U.S.C. § 1095a(a)(4).

414. 20 U.S.C. § 1095a(a)(5).

415. 20 U.S.C. § 1095a(a)(6).

416. *See* Walsh v. Wal-Mart Stores, Inc., 836 F.2d 1152, 1153 (8th Cir. 1988); Savage v. Scales, 310 F. Supp. 2d, 122, 137 (D.D.C. 2004).

417. *See* Educational Credit Management Corp. v. Central Equipment Co., 477 F. Supp.2d 783, 786 (E.D. Ky. 2006) (holding that debtor is not an indispensable party to an action between the creditor and the debtor's employer in regards to garnishment of debtor's account for repayment of student loan debt).

418. 20 U.S.C. § 1095a(a)(7).

419. 20 U.S.C. § 1095a(a)(8).

420. U.S. Department of Treasury Offset Program, 26 U.S.C. § 6402(d); 31 U.S.C. § 3720A.

421. Bosarge v. U.S. Department of Education, 5 F.3d 1414 (11th Cir. 1993), cert. denied, 512 U.S. 1226 (1994).

422. Lockhart v. United States, 546 U.S. 142 (2005).

423. *See* U.S. Department of Education, Federal Student Aid Office, Loan Consolidation, https://studentaid.ed.gov/sa/repay-loans/consolidation#should-i.

424. 20 U.S.C. § 1087-53; 34 C.F.R. Part 676.

425. *See* 7 C.F.R. § 273.5(b)(6).This issue is discussed in chapter 3.

426. 42 U.S.C. § 12601.

427. For more information on how to apply and a copy of the application form, *see* https://www.nationalservice.gov/sites/default/files/documents/AmeriCorps_Enrollment_Form_May%202016.pdf.

428. *See* Internal Revenue Service, Publication 970: Tax Benefits for Education for use in preparing 2018 Returns (Jan. 17, 2019), https://www.irs.gov/pub/irs-pdf/p970.pdf.

429. *Id.* at 5.

430. *Id.* at 7.

431. *Id.*at 9–39; *see also* Stuart Lazar, Schooling Congress: The Current Landscape of the Tax Treatment of Higher Education Expenses and a Framework for Reform, 2010 Mich. St. L. Rev. 1047, 1080 (2010).

432. 26 U.S.C. § 25A(a). The amount of the education credit is actually the sum of the AOTC and the LLC. For more background on the underlying policy of educational credits, *see* Kerry A. Ryan, Access Assured: Restoring Progressivity in the Tax and Spending Programs for Higher Education, 38 Seton Hall L. Rev. 1 (2008).

433. 26 C.F.R. § 1.25A-1(b)(1).

434. Internal Revenue Service, Publication 970: Tax Benefits for Education for use in preparing 2018 Returns (Jan. 17, 2019), at 31, https://www.irs.gov/pub/irs-pdf/p970.pdf. Beginning in tax year 2019, the student-loan interest deduction phases out for taxpayers with modified adjusted gross income of $70,000. 26 U.S.C. § 1, Note, Section 3, 2019 Adjusted Items, .31.

435. *See* Apirta A. Shroff, The Tax Cuts and Jobs Act—Individual Tax Reform, 129 J. Tax'n 30, 34, 2018 WL 3618389 (Aug. 2018).

436. *See* 26 U.S.C. § 222.

437. *See* Internal Revenue Service, Miscellaneous Deductions, Publication 529 (2018), https://www.irs.gov/publications/p529.

438. Congress enacted these education tax credits to "encourage[] the pursuit of higher education and provide[] aid to students from low-income households." *See* Jacob Nussim & Avraham Tabbach, Tax-Loss Mechanisms, 81 U. Chi. L. Rev. 1509, 1527–28 (2014) (citation omitted). Using the tax system to enhance access to higher education has certain benefits. Students do not have to fill out the Free Application for Federal Student Aid (FAFSA) form, and everyone who is eligible for the benefit should receive it. *See* Tax Policy Center, What Tax Incentives Exist to Help Families Pay for College (2018), https://www.taxpolicycenter.org/briefing-book/

what-tax-incentives-exist-help-families-pay-college-0. However, commentators have questioned whether these tax credits have actually boosted enrollment rates of low-income students in higher education. At least one report suggested that nonrefundable tax credits primarily benefit "middle- and upper-income families, whose decision on whether to send their kids to college is unlikely to be affected by a tax benefit that is relatively small in relation to their income or the costs of college attendance." Another explanation was that "the credits are delivered too late to affect enrollment," especially for low-income families. *See* Susan M. Dynarski & Judith Scott-Clayton, The Tax Benefits for Education that Don't Increase Education, Brookings (Apr. 26, 2018), https://www.brookings.edu/research/the-tax-benefits-for-education-dont-increase-education/ (citing Caroline Hoxby & George Bulman, The Returns to the Federal Tax Credits for Higher Education, Vol. 29 (Tax Policy and the Economy, 2015)); Caroline M. Hoxby & George B. Bulman, The Effects of the Tax Deduction for Postsecondary Tuition: Implications for Structuring Tax-Based Aid, Economics of Education Review (2015); Susan Dynarski & Judith Scott-Clayton, Tax Benefits for College Attendance, The Economics of Tax Policy (Alan Auerbach & Kent Smetters eds.) (Oxford 2017).

439. American Recovery and Reinvestment Act of 2009, Pub. L. No. 111-5, § 1004(a), 123 Stat. 115, 313-14. The AOTC is considered to be more generous than the prior Hope Scholarship Credit; the AOTC "increase[ed] the maximum credit amount to $2,500 per eligible student per year for QT&R expenses; expand[ed] the definition of QT&R expenses to include course materials; allows[ed] the credit for the first four years of the student's post-secondary education in a degree or certificate program; increase[ed] the modified adjusted gross income (AGI) range at which the credit is phased-out; permit[ed] the credit to be claimed against alternate minimum tax (AMT) liability; and allow[ed] 40% of the credit to be refundable." Tax Advisors Planning Systems, 10.06 Education Credits, 2000 WL 243616.

440. 26 U.S.C. § 25A(b); 26 C.F.R. § 1.25A-3(c).

441. 26 U.S.C. § 25A(i). For example, assume that a taxpayer is eligible to claim an American Opportunity Tax Credit of $2,500. Forty percent of that amount ($1,000) is refundable, and the remaining 60% ($1,500) is nonrefundable. Assume also that the taxpayer owes $1,900 in federal taxes. The nonrefundable $1,500 portion of the credit is used first and reduces the taxpayer's tax bill to $400. Next, the first $400 of the refundable credit is used to reduce the tax bill to zero. Then the remaining $600 of the refundable credit is paid to the taxpayer as a tax refund. If the taxpayer owed $4,500 in taxes, the $1,500 nonrefundable portion of the credit reduces the tax bill to $3,000, and the $1,000 refundable credit further reduces the tax bill to $2,000.

442. 26 U.S.C. § 25A(c).

443. 26 U.S.C. § 25A(c)(1)(A).

444. 26 U.S.C. § 25A(f)(1)(A); 26 C.F.R. § 1.25A-2(d).

445. 26 U.S.C. § 25A(f)(1)(D); 26 C.F.R. § 1.25A-2(d).

446. *See* Carina Bryant, Credits For Higher Education, 8 Mertens Law of Fed. Income Tax'n § 32:38 (2019).

447. *See* U.S. Department of Education, Office of Career, Technical, and Adult Education, http://www2.ed.gov/about/offices/list/ovae/index.html.

448. The National Apprenticeship Act of 1937, 50 Stat. 664; 29 U.S.C. § 50, authorizes the Department of Labor to issue regulations protecting the health, safety, and general welfare of apprentices. The standards governing apprenticeship programs are located in 29 C.F.R. § 29.

449. To find apprenticeship opportunities in a specific area, visit the Department of Labor's Office of Apprenticeship website which provides links to each state's apprenticeship program, http://www.doleta.gov/OA/eta_default.cfm. The Career One-Stop website also has an apprenticeship search function, which can be accessed at http://www.careeronestop.org/educationtraining/find/apprenticeshipoffices.aspx.

450. *See* Diana Brazzell, Anna Crayton, Debbie A. Kumamal, Amy L. Solomon, & Nicole Lindahl, The Urban Institute & John Jay College of Criminal Justice, From the Classroom to the Community: Exploring the Role of Education during Incarceration and Reentry (2009), https://files.eric.ed.gov/fulltext/ED508246.pdf; Todd A. Berger & Joseph A. DaGrossa, Overcoming Legal Barriers to Reentry: A Law School–Based Approach to Providing Legal Services to the Reentry Community, 77-JUN Fed. Probation 3 (2013).

451. *See* Sonia Pace, From Correctional Education to School Reentry: How Formerly Incarcerated Youth Can Achieve Better Educational Outcomes, 23 Tex. J. on C.L. & C.R. 127, 130 (2018) ("There is no federal policy on school reentry regarding formerly incarcerated youth").

452. *See* Patrick Oakford, Cara Brumfield, Casey Goldvale, Laura Tatum, Margaret diZerga, & Fred Patrick, Investing in Futures: Economic and Fiscal Benefits of Postsecondary Education in Prison, 4 Vera Institute of Justice (Jan. 2019), https://www.vera.org/publications/investing-in-futures-education-in-prison.

453. John Jay College of Criminal Justice, Prisoner Reentry Institute, Mapping the Landscape of Higher Education in New York State Prisons (Feb. 2019), http://johnjaypri.org/category/research-and-publications/. The elimination of Pell Grant funds also negatively impacted the availability of prison educational programs. *See* Keesha M. Middlemass, Convicted and Condemned: The Politics and Policies of Prisoner Reentry 118 (New York University Press 2017) (reporting that prior to 1994, prison education programs were available in 40 states, and that by 2002 only 22 states "had instituted mandatory education for prisoners").

454. *See* U.S. Department of Education, Michelle Tolbert & Laura Rasmussen Foster, Reentry Education Framework: Guidelines for Providing High-Quality Education for Adults Involved in the Criminal Justice System (2012), https://www2.ed.gov/about/offices/list/ovae/pi/AdultEd/reentry-model.pdf. A substantial body of evidence confirms that providing educational access in prisons significantly reduces recidivism, increases employment outcomes, benefits communities, is highly cost-effective, and "can truly disrupt mass incarceration and break the cycle of poverty that comes with it." *See* Patrick Oakford, Cara Brumfield, Casey Goldvale, Laura Tatum, Margaret diZerega, & Fred Patrick, Investing in Futures: Economic and Fiscal Benefits of Postsecondary Education in Prison, Center on Poverty &

Inequality and Vera Institute of Justice (Jan. 2019), https://storage.googleapis. com/vera-web-assets/downloads/Publications/investing-in-futures-education-in-prison/legacy_downloads/investing-in-futures.pdf; Lois M. Davis, Robert Bozick, Jennifer L. Steele, Jessica Saunders, & Jeremy Miles, Evaluating the Effectiveness of Correctional Education, RAND (2013), https://www.rand.org/pubs/research_reports/RR266.html. For an evaluation of demonstration projects under the guidelines, *see* Wendy Erisman, Reentry Education Model Implementation Study, RTI International, Prepared for U.S. Department of Education, Office of Career, Technical, and Adult Education (June 2015).

455. *See, for example*, Ruth Delaney, Fred Patrick, & Alex Boldin, Unlocking Potential: Pathways from Prison to Postsecondary Education, Vera Institute for Justice (May 2019), https://storage.googleapis.com/vera-web-assets/downloads/ Publications/unlocking-potential-prison-to-postsecondary-education/legacy_ downloads/unlocking-potential-prison-to-postsecondary-education-report. pdf (describing the foundation-funded Pathways project and its implementation in New Jersey, Michigan, and North Carolina); John Jay College of Criminal Justice, Prisoner Reentry Institute, Mapping the Landscape of Higher Education in New York State Prisons (Feb. 2019), http://johnjaypri.org/wp-content/uploads/ 2019/06/Mapping-the-Landscape-of-Higher-Ed-in-NYS-Prisons-6.10.19.pdf.

456. First Step Act of 2018, Pub. L. No. 115-391, 132 Stat. 5194 (Dec. 21, 2018). One section of the act directs the attorney general to "develop recommendations regarding evidence-based recidivism reduction programs." *See* 18 U.S.C. § 3631. As noted earlier, a growing body of evidence has documented the effectiveness of higher education as method of improving reentry outcomes. Nevertheless, the attorney general's only action on that issue thus far has been to direct the Bureau of Prisons to send "guidance to Wardens as to how to enter into partnerships with nonprofits and other private organizations; institutions of higher education; private vocational training entities; and industry-sponsored organizations . . . to enable BOP to expand the opportunities for evidence-based recidivism reduction programs." U.S. Department of Justice, First Step Implementation Fact Sheet (July 19, 2019), https:// www.justice.gov/opa/press-release/file/1184766/download.

457. *See* U.S. Department of Education, Federal Student Aid Office, Students with criminal convictions have limited eligibility for federal student aid, https://studentaid. ed.gov/sa/eligibility/criminal-convictions.

458. *See* 34 C.F.R. § 668.40; U.S. Department of Education, Federal Student Aid Office, Federal Student Aid for Students in Adult Correctional and Juvenile Justice Facilities, https://studentaid.ed.gov/sa/sites/default/files/aid-info-for-incarcerated-individuals.pdf. For additional resources, *see* The National Reentry Resource Center, https://csgjusticecenter.org/nrrc.

459. *See* U.S. Department of Education, Answering Your Frequently Asked Questions about Second Chance Pell (Apr. 2019), https://blog.ed.gov/2019/04/answering-frequently-asked-questions-second-chance-pell/; Erica L. Green, A "Second Chance" to Choose a Diploma over a Rap Sheet, N.Y. Times (July 8, 2019), https:// www.nytimes.com/2019/07/08/us/politics/criminal-justice-education.html.

6

Consumer Rights and Credit Protection

Introduction

Does the federal Constitution guarantee consumer rights?

The federal Constitution nowhere refers to consumers.[1] However, the Constitution contains a Due Process and an Equal Protection clause, and the U.S. Supreme Court has interpreted these provisions as affording protection against some unfair commercial practices.[2] In addition, the Eighth Amendment, which protects against cruel and unusual punishment, increasingly is understood as protection against civil proceedings that result in punitive consequences, such as jailing a consumer who has committed no crime.[3] Moreover, the Constitution authorizes Congress to regulate interstate commerce,[4] and federal laws have been enacted that protect against some unfair and abusive commercial practices. For example, federal laws bar companies from discriminating against consumers because of their race or gender (and, in some instances, whether they receive public benefits).[5] They guarantee fair procedures when creditors seek to collect unpaid debts.[6] And they protect consumers' privacy by limiting access to personal information.[7] Admittedly, federal laws do not go far enough in recognizing the importance of financial security to personal autonomy, political equality, or democratic participation.[8] Indeed, federal consumer law may harm low-income people by making it more difficult to find housing or a job and so exacerbate problems of poverty.[9] Some commentators have urged reframing consumer issues in the language of human rights to make clear the connection between economic justice, structural inequality, and individual dignity.[10]

Nevertheless, it is important for persons who are poor or have low income to know about federal laws that may help them when they apply for credit, jobs, and housing, or find themselves pushed into the criminal justice system by court-imposed fines and fees for unpaid traffic tickets, or confront a debt collector about a loan that was long ago repaid. Low-income people, disadvantaged in conventional capital markets, are vulnerable to predatory lending practices that exploit financial insecurity, and the chapter discusses the "debt trap" that fringe financing, such as payday lending, auto title loans, and online lending, may create for consumers.[11] The laws described in this chapter are extremely

Getting By. Helen Hershkoff and Stephen Loffredo, Oxford University Press (2020). © Helen Hershkoff & Stephen Loffredo.
DOI: 10.1093/oso/9780190080860.001.0001

complicated and technical, and the materials offer only an overview of some of the statutes and regulations that govern in this field.[12]

Fair Debt Collection Practices Act

What is the Fair Debt Collection Practices Act?

The Fair Debt Collection Practices Act (FDCPA, or "the act") is a federal statute that regulates the ways debt collectors may seek to collect alleged debts.[13] The act recognizes that abusive collection practices add to financial distress by increasing personal bankruptcies, putting jobs at risk, imposing emotional tolls, and invading consumer privacy. The FDCPA applies in 49 states (Maine has an exemption, but a separate and similar law applies there).[14]

The act is important because at least 60 percent of American families have outstanding credit accounts at any one time, making them vulnerable to debt collection practices.[15] In 2017, the average indebted household owed about $8,000 in credit card debt,[16] and credit card debt rose by $55 billion from the 2016 level of more than $800 billion.[17] Studies show that debt collectors tend to target their contacts at consumers who have low income or are African American.[18] Among other things, the FDCPA bars debt collectors from using unfair, false, and misleading tactics when trying to collect a debt. In addition, the act gives the consumer an opportunity to challenge the amount of money allegedly owed and the validity of the debt.[19] And it permits the consumer to stop the debt collector from communicating with the consumer and family members. Some of the act's protections are triggered only if the consumer specifically asks—making it critical to know what the act guarantees and how to invoke those protections.

What kinds of debt does the FDCPA cover?

The FDCPA covers consumer debt, defined as "any obligation or alleged obligation of a consumer to pay money arising out of a transaction . . . primarily for personal, family, or household purposes."[20] The act does not cover debts relating to business.[21] Courts generally have held that a consumer debt is debt based on a "consensual transaction,"[22] for example, a credit card agreement or a consumer purchase agreement. Typically, consumer debt would not include an employee's overpaid salary that the employer seeks to recover.[23] But it would include recovery of unpaid residential rent.[24] An important question is whether the FDCPA covers debts that are owed to the government for such things as unpaid fines[25] or taxes.[26] It is now well known that states and localities excessively rely on fines and fees to fund government services, and that this practice disproportionately impacts persons with low income and of color.[27] The FDCPA covers moneys owed to the government only if the payment involves a consensual transaction. The facts and circumstances of the government-imposed payment thus matter, and in some cases the courts of appeals have held that the FDCPA's protections do apply to the collection of such a debt.[28]

Which debt collectors does the FDCPA regulate?

The FDCPA regulates the collection activities of a "debt collector," defined as a person or business that "regularly collects or attempts to collect . . . debts owed or due."[29] The term "debt collector" also may include collection lawyers,[30] suppliers of deceptive forms,[31] mortgage servicing companies that obtain rights after the debtor's default,[32] and debt buyers whose principal purpose is the collection of debts.[33] Process servers engaged in the service of process are not treated as debt collectors; however, the Second Circuit Court of Appeals has recognized that a process server engaged in a fraudulent scheme to obtain default judgments through the filing of false affidavits of service may be liable under the act (the problem of "sewer service" is discussed in chapter 9).[34] Nonprofit organizations that provide "bona fide" consumer credit counseling are not treated as debt collectors.[35] Nor does the FDCPA cover federal or state officers or employees "to the extent that collecting or attempting to collect any debt is in the performance of his official duties."[36] However, in some states, the government outsources its debt collection activities to independent contractors; the independent contractor is not exempt.[37]

Be aware that a debt collector is not necessarily the same person or business as the creditor, which the act defines as the party that "offers or extends credit creating a debt or to whom a debt is owed."[38] The FDCPA does not cover a creditor that "regularly collects" its own debts,[39] but the act does apply when the person has received an assignment or transfer of a debt "solely for the purpose of facilitating collection of such debt for another,"[40] or uses a false name.[41]

Whom does the FDCPA protect?

The FDCPA protects "consumers" and "persons." A consumer is "any natural person"—meaning, not a corporation or a partnership—who owes a debt incurred for personal, family, or household purposes.[42] A person who takes out a bank loan for household use is a consumer. A person who owes money on a credit card used for household purposes is a consumer. The act also protects a consumer's family member, roommate, neighbor, and any other person who did not incur the debt but is the target of the collection action;[43] it protects the consumer's spouse, parents (if a minor), guardian, administrator, or executor from some communications with or from the debt collector;[44] and it protects a person who is wrongly targeted for collection.[45]

What rights does a consumer have if a debt collector wants to collect a debt?

The FDCPA recognizes that debt collectors may try to collect a debt that the consumer has not incurred or that the consumer already has paid.[46] Indeed, in enacting the statute, Congress found "abundant evidence of the use of abusive, deceptive, and unfair debt collection practices by many debt collectors."[47] To deal with the problem, the FDCPA gives the consumer a right to dispute the validity of a debt that a debt collector wants to collect. Federal courts have held that the FDCPA bars a debt collector from collecting a debt from the time the consumer requests that the debt be validated and until the collector has done so.[48] The consumer also has a right to certain disclosures from the collector. It is important to know what disclosures are required and what steps must be taken in response to the disclosures in order to stop an impermissible collection action.

The debt collector will contact the consumer in writing or orally. In that first contact, the collector must disclose that it is seeking to collect a debt "and that any information obtained will be used for that purpose."[49] Within five days of the first contact, the debt collector must give the consumer a written notice (unless the collector's first communication contained the required information).[50] The written notice must disclose:

1. The amount of the debt and the name of the creditor to whom the debt is owed.[51]
2. The fact that the debt collector will assume the debt to be valid unless the consumer disputes the validity of the debt or any portion of the debt within 30 days of receiving the notice.[52]
3. That if the consumer in writing disputes the validity of the debt or any portion of the debt within 30 days of receiving the notice, the debt collector will obtain and mail to the consumer a copy of verification of the debt or a judgment against the consumer.[53]
4. That if the consumer makes a written request to the debt collector within 30 days of receiving the notice, the debt collector will provide the consumer

"the name and address of the original creditor, if different from the current creditor."[54]

The act does not prescribe a form or mode of notice for the debt collector to use when it gives the required notice. Courts have held that the notice must effectively convey the required information,[55] and many courts assess effectiveness from the perspective of the "least sophisticated consumer."[56] This test turns on such factors as the layout of the notice, the size of the text, and the words used to convey the information.[57] An effective notice is not one that leaves the consumer uncertain of rights or options, as for example, if the notice includes unnecessary information that overshadows or contradicts the required disclosures or if it fails to convey information about each of the consumer's rights.[58] The fact that a collector does not intentionally mean to mislead the consumer is not relevant to whether the notice is effective.[59] Moreover, the required notice cannot be combined with other required disclosures (for example, about data security breaches or privacy).[60] To illustrate: the act was violated when a collector's letter included disclosures about the dispute process on one side of the letter, but on the other side advised the consumer to "please call"—giving the misimpression that disputing a debt orally carried the same legal effect as disputing a debt in writing.[61] The debt collector is not required to repeat the required disclosures in its later communications, but may not contradict its earlier information.[62]

What are the consumer's options after receiving a "validation" notice?

After receiving the notice about the debt—called a validation notice—the consumer must take a number of steps to stop an impermissible debt collection from going forward. In particular, the consumer must act within 30 days of receiving the notice. It is important to read the validation notice carefully and to mark when the 30-day period begins. Although the notice is supposed to "effectively convey" information about the consumer's rights, studies have found that disclosures do not always meet this standard (indeed, even disclosures that federal courts have upheld as legally sufficient).[63]

In particular, the consumer must decide whether to dispute the validity of the debt that the collector seeks to collect. Certainly, if the consumer has paid all or part of the debt, the consumer should dispute the debt's validity. Moreover, if the consumer does not recognize the creditor's name, the consumer should request the name of the original creditor. A written request for information stops the collection process until the collector mails the consumer verification of the debt or identifies the original creditor.[64] Sending a dispute letter also is an opportunity for the consumer to inform the debt collector about possible defenses (for example, the debt is past the statute of limitations) or that the consumer is "collection-proof" because income is exempt under the act (explained later in the chapter). If the consumer does not dispute the debt or ask for information about the identity of the creditor within the 30-day period, the debt collector may assume that the debt is valid.[65] Moreover, until the consumer disputes the debt, the collector is permitted to take some collection activities that do not "overshadow" and are not "inconsistent" with the consumer's right to dispute the debt or request the name and address of the original creditor.[66]

To stop the collection process, the safe approach is for the consumer to dispute the debt in writing.[67] The Consumer Financial Protection Bureau has sample dispute letters on its website that a consumer can use as a model when responding to a validation notice. [68]

Can the debt collector contact the consumer or third parties about the debt?

Unless the consumer gives consent directly to the debt collector,[69] the debt collector is barred from certain kinds of communications "in connection with the collection of any debt" with the consumer,[70] as well as with the consumer's spouse, parent (if the debtor is a minor), guardian, executor, or administrator.[71] The act defines communicating as "the conveying of information regarding a debt directly or indirectly to any person through any medium."[72] Impermissible nonconsensual contacts include:

1. Communications at "an unusual time or place" or "a time or place known or which should be known to be inconvenient" to the consumer. The presumption is that calling within the hours of 8 a.m. and 9 p.m. is convenient "[i]n the absence of knowledge of circumstances to the contrary."[73]
2. Communicating with the consumer if the debt collector knows that the consumer is represented by counsel.[74]
3. Communicating with the consumer at the consumer's place of employment if the collector knows or has reason to know that the employer bars the consumer from receiving such communications.[75]

In addition, the consumer can demand "no contact"—that the debt collector stop any further communication with the consumer and with designated third parties.[76] The request must be in writing. The debt collector is not required to tell the consumer of the right to demand no-contact, but the right to make the request—and to have it enforced—is clear.[77] A federal court has held that a letter that says, "Kindly don't bother me anymore," is a sufficient communication to stop further contact.[78] No-contact begins once the debt collector has received the letter.[79] The only exceptions to the no-contact rule are:

1. To advise the consumer the collection efforts are being ended;
2. To notify the consumer that the debt collector or creditor may invoke "specified remedies which are ordinarily invoked"; or
3. To notify the consumer that the debt collector or creditor "intends to invoke a specified remedy."[80]

Courts have disagreed whether the act is violated if, after receiving a no-contact letter, the debt collector places an unanswered phone call,[81] or leaves a voice message that does not specifically refer to the debt.[82] Likewise, case law is mixed as to whether the debt collector can send the consumer a repayment plan after having received a no-contact request. On the one hand, the collector's request for a repayment plan arguably falls within the collector's right to invoke "specified remedies."[83] On the other hand, the request may give the false impression of offering a settlement, and so should be barred as deceptive (discussed later in this chapter).[84]

Can a debt collector contact persons other than the consumer to learn the consumer's whereabouts?

The debt collector can contact third persons to try to acquire location information about the consumer. However, in that communication, the collector cannot reveal that the consumer owes a debt. Nor can the collector use language or symbols indicating that the speaker or sender is in the debt collection business.[85]

What collection activities does the FDCPA cover?

The FDCPA covers a debt collector's express demand for payment and other activity used "in connection with the collection of any debt."[86] Communications that are a part of a collection activity are covered by the act; communications that are only informational are not.[87] The courts do not have a bright-line rule to distinguish between these two situations.[88] A letter advising that a company had assumed mortgage servicing responsibilities related to a debtor's mortgage loan, followed by a payment statement some months later, was a treated as a collection activity, and not as an informational notice advising that servicing of the debt had been transferred.[89] Similarly, a lawyer's filing of an assignment of judgment in state court was treated as a collection activity, and not simply as informational.[90]

Abusive Practices Barred

The FDCPA bars abusive collection practices. The statute takes a broad approach to what is barred, recognizing that abusive practices can take many forms.[91] The act prohibits debt collectors from:

- Harassing consumers with obscene language and threats in an abusive manner;[92]
- Making false representations;[93]
- Contacting consumers at inconvenient times and places;[94]
- Giving consumers misleading forms;[95] and
- Using various other unfair practices.[96]

Harassment Barred

The FDCPA bars the collector from harassing the consumer.[97] It is illegal for a debt collector:

- To use or threaten to use violence or other criminal means to harm a person or the person's reputation or property;[98]
- To use obscene or profane language in an abusive manner;[99]
- To call a consumer repeatedly, whether or not the calls are answered, intending to annoy, abuse, or harass the person being called;[100] and
- To call a consumer without disclosing that the call is from a debt collector.[101]

A court can ban a collector's action as harassment even if the specific act is not listed in the statute.[102] The determination is to be made from the consumer's perspective.[103]

False and Misleading Statements Barred

The FDCPA bars the debt collector from making statements that are false or misleading.[104] For example, saying or implying that the debt collector is associated with the government—if the debt collector is not associated with the government—is false and misleading, and so illegal.[105] Likewise, a false statement about how much money is owed is barred;[106] a false statement about work a collector has performed, or compensation that the collector will receive if the debt is paid, is barred.[107] Other examples of false and misleading statements include:

1. Saying or implying that the collector is an attorney or is speaking on behalf of an attorney;[108]

2. Threatening arrest of the consumer;[109]
3. Threatening to garnish wages or property that the collector cannot or does not intend to garnish (garnishment is discussed later in this chapter);[110]
4. Threatening legal action that the collector cannot or does not intend to take;[111]
5. Saying or implying that a consumer has committed a crime, in an attempt to embarrass the consumer;[112]
6. Giving or threatening to give false information to third parties about the consumer's credit;[113]
7. Sending documents that simulate government-issued documents, or are falsely represented as being "authorized, issued, or approved" by a court or government official,[114] or are falsely represented as being official legal documents;[115]
8. Saying or implying that actual legal documents are not legal documents, or falsely stating that a consumer does not need to take legal action;[116] and
9. Using a false name of the collection company[117] or falsely stating that the collector represents a credit reporting agency.[118]

This list is not exhaustive; other statements can be barred as false and misleading representations depending on the facts and circumstances, as viewed from the consumer's perspective.[119] For example, a creditor, who otherwise would not be covered by the act when collecting its own debt, violates the act by sending a letter that creates a false belief that it has hired a third-party collection agency to handle collection when no third party is involved.[120] Thus, when the creditor uses a "false name" to collect a debt, it becomes liable for misleading practices under the FDCPA.[121]

"Flat rating" is another practice that in some cases may be illegal under the FDCPA.[122] Flat-rating involves a creditor's purchase of a collection company's letters—often at a flat-rate per letter, giving the practice its name—misleading the consumer into thinking that someone other than the creditor is collecting the debt.[123] The Ninth Circuit Court of Appeals has held that whether the bar on flat-rating applies depends on whether the company that sent letters demanding payment of a debt "meaningfully participated" in the collection process.[124]

Unfair and Unconscionable Acts Barred
The FDCPA bars unfair or unconscionable practices.[125] Examples include:

– Collection of an amount that is not authorized by the loan agreement or by law;[126]
– Accepting a check postdated by more than five days, unless the collector gives written notification of an intent to deposit the check, not more than 10 days nor less than three business days prior to the deposit;[127]

- Depositing or threatening to deposit a postdated check prior to the date on the check;[128] and
- Using a postcard to communicate with the consumer about a debt,[129] or an envelope with a symbol or other sign indicating that a letter pertains to debt collection.[130]

Does the FDCPA bar a debt collector from trying to collect a debt that is "stale"?

A stale debt is a debt for which the statute of limitations has expired so that the creditor no longer has a right to payment. The Federal Trade Commission (which has power to enforce the FDCPA) has taken the position that a debt collector is not permitted to sue a consumer on a debt that is time-barred.[131] So have the majority of federal circuit courts of appeals.[132] Threatening to sue on a stale claim likewise violates the FDCPA.[133] On the other hand, a debt collector may seek the consumer's voluntary payment of a time-barred debt. However, if a debt collector contacts a consumer about a stale debt, it must provide the consumer with a validation notice, described earlier in this chapter, and the consumer can dispute the validity and amount of the debt. The U.S. Supreme Court has held that it does not violate the FDCPA for a debt collector to file a proof of claim for a stale claim in a proceeding brought by the debtor to declare bankruptcy. However, the Court's decision was limited to the bankruptcy context, where, among other things, the consumer is protected by a trustee who determines whether a proof of claim is enforceable and the statute of limitations is an affirmative defense.[134]

Whether or not a debt collector can collect on a stale debt (for example, by contacting the consumer), separate questions are raised under the FDCPA if the collector threatens to report a stale debt to a consumer reporting agency.[135] Consumer reports are discussed later in this chapter.

What can a consumer do if a debt collector seems to be violating the FDCPA?

A consumer who believes that a debt collector is engaging in abusive or other invalid collection practices has two options: to file an administrative complaint with the federal agency that monitors and enforces the act; or to file a federal court action.

Administrative Complaints

A consumer can file a complaint with the Consumer Financial Protection Bureau (CFPB).[136] The complaint can be filed online, or by telephone, mail, email, and fax and does not require paying a fee or any other expense.[137]

The CFPB screens the complaints that it receives to make sure information is complete and that the complaint is not duplicative, and then forwards the complaint to the company at which the complaint is directed. The company then will review the complaint and determine what action to take in response. If the company needs to contact the consumer, it will do so through the CFPB's secure website, so consumers do not have to worry about the company directly contacting them. A company's response could be anything from an explanation seeking to justify the conduct that triggered the complaint, to an offer of monetary or nonmonetary relief.[138] Consumers then provide the CFPB with feedback and may choose to dispute the response if they are unhappy with it.[139]

Court Actions

The FDCPA also gives the consumer a right of action to sue a debt collector in court.[140] The statute of limitations is one year from the violation, but courts are divided on whether the date begins to run from when the alleged violation took place or when the consumer discovers it.[141] Generally, debt collectors that violate the act are "strictly liable," meaning "a consumer need not show intentional conduct . . . to be entitled to damages." However, the debt collector may raise as a defense and "escape liability if it can demonstrate by a preponderance of the evidence" that its violation "was not intentional and resulted from a *bona fide* error notwithstanding the maintenance of procedures reasonably adapted to avoid any such error."[142] A plaintiff who wins a lawsuit may receive an award of actual damages, additional damages of up to $1,000, and attorney's fees.[143] In appropriate cases, a lawsuit also can be filed as a class action, in which an individual represents the interests of a group of consumers who have been similarly injured by the debt collector.[144]

Actual damages in a successful suit include compensation for the harm the consumer experienced as a result of the collector's actions.[145] This harm can be financial harm, such as a harm suffered in the form of a lower credit rating if the creditor wrongly reported credit issues that did not exist.[146] Harm also can be emotional or physical; for example, if a collector used obscene or profane language and a consumer experienced anxiety and stress as a result.[147] With a class action lawsuit, the court will consider the frequency and persistence of the collector's noncompliance, how many people were affected by the violations, whether the violations were intentional, and the collector's financial ability to compensate the consumers.[148] Additional damages, sometimes called "statutory damages," are damages awarded to remedy a violation of the act not linked to the consumer's actual harm, and their award is a matter of the court's discretion.[149]

An award of attorney's fees consists of the payments to the lawyer who provided representation in a winning lawsuit—as the statute puts it, "any successful action."[150] Some courts award attorney's fees as long as a consumer proves some violation of the act, even if the consumer is not awarded any money (for example, the consumer did not prove actual damages and the court did not award additional damages although it found a violation).[151] However, some courts have refused to award fees if the consumer does not win monetary relief.[152] In addition, if a court finds that the consumer's lawsuit was brought in bad faith or for purposes of harassing the debt collector, a consumer may be required to pay the defendant's attorney's fees.[153]

Keep in mind that filing a lawsuit can be expensive, and a plaintiff will not be reimbursed for expenses if the suit is lost or if the court decides not to award attorney's fees (as discussed in chapter 9). Attorneys who specialize in debt collection cases can provide guidance about a lawsuit's likelihood of success, but consumers must be careful that the attorney they talk to offers a sensible assessment. Consumers can search for lawyers in their area by visiting the website for the National Association of Consumer Advocates.[154]

Do any state laws protect against abusive debt collection practices?

States and localities may have laws that provide different and more generous protections than those available under the FDCPA. A consumer may contact the state Attorney General's office to report objectionable collection actions and to obtain help in determining what legal rights exist under the laws of that state.[155] Information about how to locate the Attorney General of a particular state is available at https://www.naag.org.

Fair Credit Reporting Act

What is the consumer reporting industry and why is it important to low-income consumers?

Consumer reporting is a multi-billion dollar industry that collects and reports consumer-specific information to third parties.[156] The entities that purchase consumer reports rely on the information when a consumer applies for financial and other services: for example, to evaluate a consumer's personal credit history before extending credit; to assess a job applicant's criminal past before extending a job offer; to investigate a potential tenant's character and mode of living before renting an apartment; or to assess a consumer's medical history before offering insurance. Consumer reports involve different kinds of reporting (and, as explained later, different kinds of reports have different names), but reports about credit, although only one type of report, are used for purposes other than securing credit. The use of a consumer report of any type raises privacy concerns for the consumer.[157] In addition, consumer reports function as gatekeepers, and the consumer may be disadvantaged or disqualified if a report contains negative information that is incomplete, out of date, or inaccurate[158] (and repeated studies show that a high percentage of reports of every type do indeed contain significant errors[159]). However, even when a report is accurate—correctly stating a criminal record or a history of loan defaults—its use as a presumptive reason for rejecting the consumer's application may work to amplify past disadvantages and so function as an insuperable and arbitrary barrier to financial stability and upward mobility.[160] Congress has adopted a federal law that tries to deal with some (but not all) of the problems that consumer reporting may raise, but the statute's enforcement is uneven.[161]

What is the Fair Credit Reporting Act?

The Fair Credit Reporting Act (FCRA) is a federal statute that aims to protect consumers from some of the harmful consequences of consumer reporting.[162] A consumer means an identifiable individual, and not a corporation or a cooperative.[163] The FCRA requires consumer reporting agencies to follow "reasonable procedures to assure maximum possible accuracy" of the information reported about a consumer.[164] It regulates those who furnish information to agencies.[165] It generally requires the users of consumer reports to make certain disclosures to consumers when planning to take an adverse action based at least in part on information contained in a consumer report[166] and it limits how consumer reports can be used.[167] It entitles consumers to get copies of their consumer files, to dispute and exclude information contained in reports because it is inaccurate, incomplete, stale, or protected from disclosure, and to know who sees reports about themselves.[168] The FCRA also authorizes remedies when rights are violated.[169] What follows is an overview of how the FCRA regulates the major players in the consumer reporting industry—consumer reporting agencies, furnishers of information, and users of reports—and how a consumer can invoke the statute to prevent consumer reporting from becoming a bar to future opportunity. Consumer reporting creates lots of problems for low-income people,[170] and although the statute is incomplete and imperfect, it nevertheless can provide important protection.[171]

What is a consumer reporting agency?

The FCRA regulates consumer reporting agencies—companies that are in the business of collecting and distributing information about consumers. A "consumer reporting agency" is a "person" (which includes a corporation) that for a fee, dues, or on a nonprofit basis regularly gathers or evaluates consumer credit information or other consumer information "for the purpose of furnishing consumer reports to third parties."[172] A consumer reporting agency can include a tenant screening bureau, a criminal background screening agency, or a check-approval service company. "Applicant Tracking Systems," which use automated methods to assess employability, also can be consumer reporting agencies regulated by the FCRA.[173] Keep in mind that many companies that routinely buy, sell, access, or share consumer information do not come within the FCRA's definition of a consumer reporting agency.[174]

The largest consumer reporting agencies in the United States are Experian, Equifax Information Services, and TransUnion—the "Big Three"—which are "nationwide" agencies and have special obligations under the FCRA (discussed later this chapter). A nationwide consumer reporting agency collects and maintains public records and credit account information about consumers "on a nationwide basis."[175] There also are specialty nationwide consumer reporting agencies which collect and maintain consumer files on a nationwide basis in a specialty area such as insurance claims or tenant history.[176] Every year the Consumer Financial Protection Bureau publishes an online list of consumer reporting companies with contact information.[177]

What is a consumer report?

A consumer report is a communication by a consumer reporting agency about a consumer made to third parties. Most people are the subject of multiple consumer reports. However, not every statement about a person's personal or financial information is considered a consumer report that has to meet the requirements of the FCRA. Moreover, the information that a consumer reporting agency has on file about a consumer is not a consumer report—it becomes a report only when made available to third parties. A communication about a consumer is covered by the FCRA as a consumer report if it:

1. Consists of information communicated by a consumer reporting agency to a third party, whether written, oral, or in another form (such as an electronic communication);[178]
2. Bears upon a consumer's "credit worthiness, credit standing, credit capacity, character, general reputation, personal characteristics, or mode of living"—known as the "seven factors";[179] and
3. Is used or expected to be used, or collected to serve, as a factor in establishing the consumer's eligibility for credit or insurance primarily for personal or household purposes or employment purposes, and other statutorily permissible purposes (which include complying with a court order; at the consumer's written instruction; determining eligibility for a license or benefit granted by the government; or a legitimate business need in connection with a transaction initiated by the consumer).[180]

A consumer report typically will list current and past credit accounts, including when the account was opened and closed, payment history, the name of the creditor, and account balances. It might identify matters that are in collection, and financial activities that are a matter of public record, such as liens, foreclosures, and civil judgments. The report will list "inquiries," meaning, information about which companies have asked to see the credit report.[181] Finally, it might include the consumer's credit score (explained later in this chapter).

The FCRA also regulates investigative reports, which are a type of consumer report (discussed later in this chapter). An investigative report contains information about a consumer's character, reputation, personal characteristics, or mode of living, and it relies upon interviews with third parties, such as neighbors, friends, or associates for the information that it discloses.[182]

What is a "credit header"?

"Credit header" information accompanies a consumer report and typically includes the consumer's name, previous names used, address, former addresses, telephone number, date of birth, and Social Security number (technically known as nonpublic personal information).[183] The Federal Trade Commission has taken the position that information in a credit header is not a consumer report. However, consumer reporting agencies that receive this information from financial institutions may not distribute it in any form other than a consumer report, and, as a result, its communication is regulated under the FCRA.[184]

Are there communications about a consumer that the FCRA does not treat as a consumer report, even if the communications are used for employment, credit, or other financial purposes?

The FCRA exempts certain kinds of communications from treatment as a consumer report. Exempt communications include:

1. Experience Information—The FCRA excludes communications by a person based solely on the person's firsthand experience with the consumer.[185] However, once the information is furnished to a third party, and the third party discloses the information, the communication becomes a consumer report. For example, if Retailer sells a consumer a product, and furnishes information solely about that transaction to a consumer reporting agency, the communication is not itself a consumer report.

2. Communications Among Affiliates—The FCRA excludes communications of reports "containing information solely as to transactions or experiences between the consumer and furnisher"[186] among companies that have common ownership or are affiliated by corporate control, known as related companies (for example, a bank might be affiliated with an insurance company), and of other information communicated among related companies, but only if the consumer is told about the information sharing and given an opportunity to opt out,[187] and special rules apply to information shared for marketing purposes.[188]

3. Employment Agency Communications—The FCRA excludes communications by an employment agency, but only if the communication would otherwise be part of an investigative consumer report; the consumer has given consent for the communication; the consumer has received certain disclosures from the agency; and the information is used only for the procurement of employment.[189]

4. Employee Misconduct and Compliance Investigations—The FCRA excludes communications made to an employer in connection with an investigation of employee misconduct or compliance with certain policies and regulations.[190]

5. Credit Card Authorization—The FCRA excludes communications by a credit card company to a merchant to honor a transaction.[191]

Exempting a communication from the definition of a consumer report is important because it affects whether the consumer will know whether a user of the information relied on the information to make a negative decision about the consumer. Generally, a consumer will not have a right to know that an adverse decision was based on an exempt communication.[192] However, an employer that bases an adverse decision, even in part, on a communication that is exempt because part of an investigation must provide the consumer with a summary of the communication (but does not have to reveal its sources).[193]

Are there limits on the information that a consumer report may contain?

Certain topics are off limits for a consumer report, and the consumer reporting agency must exclude information about them from the reports that it provides. The FCRA also imposes time limits on the information that may be included.[194] In addition, a consumer report may not include information sourced from personal interviews unless the agency complies with special rules that govern investigative reports.[195]

Substantive limits. A consumer report must exclude "medical information," meaning information or data from the consumer or a health care provider that relates to health conditions, health care, and payment of health care. The report cannot contain the name and contact information of a "medical information furnisher" unless the information is restricted or reported in code. The only exception is for medical information provided to an insurance company for a purpose relating to insurance other than for property or casualty.[196] "Medical information" does not include the consumer's age, gender, or demographic information such as residence.[197] The point of the exclusion is to protect the consumer's legitimate privacy interest.

In addition, under a settlement reached in July 2017, the "Big Three" consumer reporting agencies may no longer include information about tax liens or outstanding debt owed to the Internal Revenue Service in a consumer report, unless the information has been verified with the consumer's name, address, and either the Social Security number or date of birth. (Prior to the rule, information about unpaid liens remained in a report for up to 10 years, and fully paid liens, for up to seven years.)[198]

Consumer reporting agencies also are subject to content restrictions specific to members of the armed services and veterans. The Servicemembers Civil Relief Act (SCRA) regulates the enforcement of claims against servicemembers who are on active duty.[199] A consumer report may not include information on whether a servicemember tried to invoke or did receive protection under the SCRA.[200] In addition, effective May 2019, the FCRA bars nationwide consumer reporting agencies from reporting a veteran's medical debt if the debt was fully paid or settled, characterized as delinquent, charged off, or in collection, or if the medical debt is recent—less than one year from the date when health care was provided, on condition that the consumer reporting agency has actual knowledge that the medical debt is that of a veteran and that the agency checked the Veteran's Administration database that identifies veterans' medical debt.[201]

Time limits. The FCRA limits the use of information that is too old and so presumptively is misleading, unfair, or inaccurate.[202] A report must exclude information about bankruptcy cases that "antedate the report by more than 10 years."[203] A report cannot include information about civil lawsuits, civil judgments, paid tax liens, and any other "adverse item of information, other than records of convictions of crimes" that "antedate the report by more" than seven years (and keep in mind restrictions on "Big Three" reporting already mentioned).[204] Accounts placed in collection may be included in the report for seven years and 180 days after the first delinquency.[205] In addition, prescreening inquiries (not initiated by a consumer) from the preceding year must be disclosed to the consumer upon request, but they cannot be included in a consumer report furnished to a third party.[206]

Be aware that there is no time limit on reporting criminal convictions.[207] However, arrests, like civil suits, are subject to the seven-year limit (or until the statute of limitations runs, whichever is longer).[208]

In addition, the Higher Education Act imposes special rules on the reporting of government-backed student loans as set forth in Table 6.1.[209]

Table 6.1

Type of Student Loan	Reporting Period
Federal Family Education Loan (FFEL), including: Stafford Loans Unsubsidized Stafford Loans PLUS Loans	Defaults may be included for 7 years from the latest of 3 dates: When Secretary of Education or guaranty agency pays claim to loan holder on the guaranty; When Secretary of Education, guaranty agency, lender, or any other loan holder first reported account to the consumer reporting agency; When debtor reenters payment after defaulting and then goes into default.
Direct Student Loan	Same time limits as FFEL.
Perkins Loan	No time limit. Perkins institutions must report to consumer reporting agency when debtor has made 6 consecutive payments on a defaulted loan.

The FCRA's exclusion of stale information from consumer reports is very important; otherwise, consumers become permanently trapped by a past cycle of disadvantage. However, although the FCRA shields stale information from disclosure in a consumer report, a prospect employer or landlord is free to search the internet—a Google search is likely to reveal out-of-date personal information, and the use of such information sidesteps the FCRA's protections.[210]

How does the FCRA regulate the preparation and use of investigative reports?

The FCRA imposes a few special requirements on "investigative reports," a subset of consumer reports that contain information obtained in whole or in part through personal interviews with the consumer's neighbors, friends, or associates and describes sensitive details about character, reputation, personal characteristics, and mode of living. A consumer reporting agency preparing such a report must verify its information within 30 days before releasing an investigative report.[211] Moreover, the agency may not report information that is adverse to the consumer's interest and obtained through a personal interview with someone with whom the consumer is acquainted, unless the person interviewed "is the best possible source of the information," or the agency has followed "reasonable procedures to obtain confirmation of the information."[212]

The requester who wants to use an investigative report must meet several requirements that do not apply to ordinary consumer reports. No later than three days after requesting an investigative report, the user, in writing, "clearly and accurately" must mail or otherwise provide the consumer with a disclosure that it has requested an investigative report about the consumer. The disclosure must inform the consumer of the right to request information about "the nature and scope" of the requested report. In addition, the user must certify to the consumer reporting agency from which the report is requested that it has complied with the disclosure requirement; the agency cannot prepare the report without the requestor's certification.[213]

The user must give the consumer a second notice if the user takes an adverse action based on the report.[214] The notice must tell the consumer of the adverse action; it must provide the name and address of the consumer reporting agency; and it must explain that the consumer may request a free copy of the report from the consumer reporting agency within 60 days and that the consumer may dispute the report with the agency.[215]

How does the FCRA regulate consumer reports
used for employment purposes?

The vast majority of employers conduct background checks on job applicants, and some of them purchase consumer reports to make their decisions.[216] The FCRA does not require that the information contained in a consumer report be related to the qualifications needed for a job, and critics have questioned whether a good credit history—among the information included in a consumer report—ought to be an across-the-board job requirement.[217] Given barriers that low-income people face in credit markets, linking employment with credit history works to compound a lifetime of disadvantage, and often with racialized and gendered consequences.[218] Moreover, the FCRA's regulation of consumer reports used for employment purposes has many gaps: as already discussed, it does not regulate an employer's own investigation about a job applicant (as, for example, talking to co-workers or doing a Google search);[219] it does not regulate many reports prepared by employment agencies for prospective employers; and once the employee is hired, it does not cover reports prepared in connection with alleged misconduct. What the FCRA does do is impose special duties on consumer reporting agencies that prepare particular types of consumer reports for employers. Because of the act, a job applicant is alerted to the fact that a prospective employer will request a consumer report. Central to the FCRA's protections is a set of special disclosure and authorization requirements.

The FCRA defines a consumer report for "employment purposes" as "a report used for the purpose of evaluating a consumer for employment, promotion, reassignment or retention as an employee"; as with all consumer reports governed by the FCRA, the report must be prepared by a consumer reporting agency.[220]

The FCRA imposes special obligations on the consumer reporting agency that furnishes a report to an employer if, for the purpose of the report, the agency "compiles and reports items of information" about the consumer that are matters of "public record and are likely to have an adverse effect on the consumer's ability to obtain employment."[221] The consumer reporting agency must take one of two actions: either "maintain strict procedures designed to ensure" that the public record information compiled and reported is "complete and up to date," or concurrent with giving the report to the employer, notify the consumer of the name and address of the person receiving the report and of fact that it is reporting public record information.[222]

The FCRA also imposes duties on the user of a consumer report for employment purposes whether or not it contains public record information. Before a prospective employer "procure[s]" a consumer report from a consumer reporting agency, or causes a report "to be procured," it must give the consumer a written document "solely" providing "a clear and conspicuous disclosure" that a consumer report "may be obtained for employment purposes." The consumer must authorize in writing the report's "procurement"—in other words, give written consent to the employer to obtain a consumer report as part of the background check. Authorization may be given in the same document as the disclosure.[223] In an issue of first impression, the Ninth Circuit Court of Appeals held that the disclosure given to the consumer may not include "extraneous information"—in particular, a request that the consumer concurrently release the employer from liability for obtaining inaccurate information.[224] Clearly a consumer who withholds consent to the procurement will forfeit a job offer, but the disclosure puts the consumer on notice that a report is to be obtained. If the employer then plans to deny employment based on information contained in the report, the employer must give the consumer a copy of the report and a summary of the consumer's rights under the FCRA.[225]

Many employers also rely upon investigative reports prepared by employment agencies in making their hiring decisions. In 1996, Congress amended the FCRA to make such reports "excluded" communications from its protections provided certain disclosure and consent requirements are met. The basic exclusion applies when an employment agency prepares what would be considered an investigative report—meaning, a report about a consumer's character and reputation and sourced on interviews—for a prospective employer and the report is used only for that purpose.[226] First, the employment agency in conducting its inquiry is subject to federal and state equal opportunity law as if the inquiry were "made by a prospective employer of the consumer."[227] Second, the employment agency must make certain disclosures and secure consent from the consumer before it begins its investigation or provides the report to the employer, and, if consent is given orally, there must be written consent within three days. Third, the consumer must be told that it has a right to request and may request from the employment agency information about the "nature and substance of all information in the consumer's file" at the time of the request (but not about "the sources of information" acquired "solely" for the report provided to the employer and used for that purpose), and the employment agency must provide the disclosure in response to the consumer's request in writing "not later than 5 business days after receiving the request."[228] Realistically, a consumer who refuses to consent to the investigation will not be hired for the job; however, the FCRA does give an opportunity to know what is being said about the consumer.[229]

Finally, the FCRA excludes from its coverage consumer reports prepared to investigate an employee's alleged misconduct. For further discussion, see chapter 2.

Why is it important for consumers
to review their consumer files?

The FCRA requires a consumer reporting agency to use reasonable procedures to ensure the maximum accuracy of consumer reports, yet reports continue to contain inaccurate, misleading, and outdated information. In some situations, information may be technically accurate but is not complete and so presents a misleading picture of the consumer's credit worthiness.[230] Another kind of inaccuracy can result from the "re-aging" of a debt that occurs when a debt collector reports the existence of a debt that it has purchased, even though it is required to use the date of delinquency.[231] Common errors include reporting incorrect payment history, wrong information due to identity theft, and misstating a criminal record. One study found that half of the criminal records in the FBI's database were incomplete, and that the failure of states to update criminal records (to show that an arrest did not result in a conviction) negatively impacted 600,000 persons a year.[232] It therefore makes good sense for a consumer to review information in a consumer file:

1. Regularly, and at least once a year.
2. Before starting a job or apartment search, or applying for a car loan or mortgage.
3. Whenever a company has used the report to make a decision that negatively affects the consumer.
4. Whenever the consumer suspects fraud or identity theft.

Can a consumer get a free copy of a consumer file?

Every consumer has a right to a free annual disclosure from each of the Big Three nationwide consumer reporting companies—TransUnion, Equifax, and Experian.[233] Technically, the consumer is requesting a copy of the consumer's file, not of a credit report. This is because a communication is not a report unless it has been given to a third party other than the consumer. A consumer file thus is not identical to a consumer report, and to avoid confusion, the information provided sometimes is called a "required disclosure." The disclosure includes not only the information in the consumer file but also must identify the sources of the information,[234] as well as the names of all third parties to whom the consumer's report was provided within the year prior to the consumer's request (this information is known as "inquiries").[235] The request is made to a centralized source, which is available on the internet at https://www.AnnualCreditReport.com, the only authorized federal source online.[236] The Consumer Financial Protection

Bureau also states that a report can be requested by calling 1-877-322-8228, or by downloading, printing, and completing the Annual Credit Request form, available online, and mailing it to:[237]

Annual Credit Report Request Service
P.O. Box 105281
Atlanta, GA 30348-5281

If the report is made online, it should be immediately accessible; if requested via phone or mail, the disclosure should be processed and mailed within 15 days of receipt.[238] Be aware that the Big Three actively promote credit-monitoring products that are not free and might try to sell a product to a consumer who is requesting a free annual disclosure. The consumer does not have to buy a product to get the free disclosure.[239]

Every consumer also has a right to request a free annual copy of a disclosure from a specialty nationwide consumer reporting agency. The agency must designate a toll-free number for this purpose.[240]

Under the FCRA, special circumstances trigger rights to additional free copies:

Public Assistance Recipient. Every consumer who is a recipient of public assistance has a right to get a free disclosure.[241]

Unemployed. A consumer who is unemployed and intends to apply for employment within 60 days has a right to request a free copy.[242]

Fraud Victim. A consumer who suspects fraud has a right to a free copy. The consumer should visit IdentityTheft.gov, which will guide the consumer through the steps that should be taken, including contacting consumer reporting agencies and placing a fraud alert on credit reports.[243] The consumer reporting agency must tell the consumer of the right to request a free report and provide the report within three business days of the request.[244] In addition, it must include a fraud alert in the consumer's file, and, if it is a nationwide agency, it must notify the other nationwide agencies and they, too, must include a fraud alert in the consumer's file.[245] If the consumer already has submitted an identity theft report to law enforcement and submits proof of that report to a nationwide consumer reporting agency, the consumer has the right to two free copies of the consumer report. The nationwide consumer reporting agency must include a fraud alert in the consumer's file, and the alert may remain in the file for up to seven years.[246]

Adverse Action. A consumer who has received notice of a decision denying credit, insurance, or employment or experienced any other "adverse action" based on a consumer report has a right to a free copy of the consumer report from the consumer reporting company identified in the report. The request must be made within 60 days after the notice.[247]

Reinvestigation. A consumer has a right to a revised consumer disclosure as a result of a consumer reporting agency's reinvestigation of a disputed report (reinvestigation is further discussed later in this chapter). In addition, under the terms of a settlement, the "Big Three" consumer reporting agencies are required to provide an additional free copy of the annual file disclosure to any consumer who commenced a dispute and requested and obtained a change.[248]

Additionally, every consumer has a right to request a disclosure upon payment of a fee. Consumer reporting agencies are subject to caps on the amount they can charge a consumer, and currently they can charge no more than $12.50 for a copy.[249] The act does not specify the time period within which the report must be provided.

When making a request, whether free or paid, the consumer will be asked to verify identity.[250] "Regulation V" regulates what kind of information can be required and includes sample forms that may be used to request a report.[251] The standardized form requires the consumer's name, address, contact phone numbers, Social Security number, and date of birth. A consumer may authorize a representative to request the report, but the authorization must be in writing, and a consumer reporting agency has been held not to violate the act if it does not comply with the instruction.[252]

How can a consumer find out the "credit score"?

A "credit score" is a number based on information, such as a consumer report, that summarizes a consumer's credit worthiness.[253] A higher credit score indicates the consumer is a strong, low-risk candidate for credit cards, auto loans, and mortgages, which means the consumer is more likely to get credit or insurance, or get it more cheaply. Studies find that a large percentage of credit scores contain inaccuracies.[254] A consumer reporting agency is not required to include the credit score in the consumer report that it provides upon request from the consumer.[255] However, the agency must tell the consumer that it has a right to request the credit score, separately or together with the report, but must pay a "fair and reasonable fee" for the score.[256] The Federal Trade Commission has interpreted "fair and reasonable" to mean that the agency may not charge an amount that significantly exceeds the market rate for credit scores (currently between $4 and $8).[257]

In response to a request, the agency must provide the most current score available, the date the score was calculated, the entity that created the score, and the range of possible scores. In addition, the agency must list the four top factors that negatively affected the consumer's credit score in their order of importance.[258] When the score is purchased, it often comes with information about how to improve it. The Consumer Financial Protection Bureau advises that there are four ways to get a credit score.[259] First, a consumer can purchase a score.[260] Second, free credit scores can be gotten from nonprofit credit counselors.[261] Third, the trend has been for credit card companies to provide consumers with free copies of their credit scores.[262] Finally, mortgage lenders must provide a free copy if they use the scores in connection with an application for residential real estate secured credit.[263]

How does the FCRA limit access to a consumer report?

A consumer report can be provided to a user only for certain purposes. The FCRA allows the consumer reporting agency to provide a report in response to a court order or a federal subpoena, or pursuant to the consumer's written instructions. Otherwise, the agency may furnish the report only to a person that the agency believes will use the report for employment purposes; in connection with a credit transaction or the underwriting of insurance; to determine the consumer's eligibility for a license or government benefit if financial responsibility is a legal requirement; to a potential investor or servicer; or to a person with a legitimate business need for the information (for example, in connection with a business transaction or at the request of a state or local child support agency).[264] As already discussed, these disclosures may be subject to specific certification procedures by the user.

Generally, the user of a consumer report is not required to tell the consumer that it has requested access to the report, but must disclose if it plans to take an adverse action based in whole or in part of the information contained in a consumer report.[265] (Keep in mind the special rules about investigative reports and consumer reports used for employment purposes.)[266] The disclosure of the adverse action can be oral, written, or electronic; it must tell the consumer the name and contact information of the consumer reporting agency that provided the consumer report.[267] The notice must state that the consumer reporting agency did not make the adverse decision, and that it cannot explain the reasons for the decision. It also must tell the consumer of the right: (1) to obtain a free copy of the consumer report from the consumer reporting agency, explaining that the request for the report must be made within a 60-day period; and (2) to dispute the accuracy or completeness of the information in the report that the agency provides.[268] The right to get a free copy after an adverse action is additional to the right to get a free annual report from a nationwide consumer reporting agency, and this requirement applies to all consumer reporting agencies.[269]

Can a consumer get help in reviewing
and understanding a consumer file?

The consumer's role regarding the accuracy and completeness of a consumer file has been likened to that of "a quality control inspector" whose job is to identify wrong information, stale information, incomplete information, and exempt information.[270] However, a consumer file may be highly detailed and difficult to understand. Be aware that resources are available to help review and analyze a consumer file. The FCRA requires that consumer reporting agencies (not just the "Big Three") provide trained personnel "to explain . . . any information furnished."[271] Moreover, with the consumer's written permission, the agency can discuss the file with the consumer and a companion.[272]

What should a consumer do if the report
appears to be inaccurate?

The FCRA permits the consumer to dispute the accuracy or completeness of the information contained in a consumer report. A significant minority of consumer reports contain errors—the Federal Trade Commission reported to Congress that 21 percent of consumer reports had verified errors.[273] Indeed, the Consumer Financial Protection Bureau in its first four years of operation received over 170,000 complaints about credit reports.[274] However, the monitoring-and-correction process may require persistence.[275]

If a consumer believes that the report is not accurate, it can lodge a dispute with the consumer reporting agency that issued the report. The agency is required to reinvestigate and to delete or modify the information if it is inaccurate; the agency must also delete the information if it does not conduct an investigation within 30 days of notice of the dispute.[276] Following the reinvestigation, the agency must provide the consumer with written notice of the results of the investigation, and give the consumer an opportunity to request information about the procedure used to do the investigation.[277] The agency cannot charge the consumer to investigate the disputed information. Within five days of receiving notice of the dispute, the agency must provide notification of the dispute to any person who provided any item of the disputed information.[278] The furnisher of the information must participate in the reinvestigation process and may be liable to the consumer if the furnisher does not comply with its duty to reinvestigate.[279]

As a second step, the consumer can file a complaint with the Consumer Financial Protection Bureau (CFPB), the federal agency that enforces the act.[280] The complaint form and a fact sheet, entitled "A Summary of Your

Rights under the Fair Credit Reporting Act," are available online.[281] The CFPB will forward the complaint to the agency, and the agency must respond within 15 days. The CFPB expects most complaints to be resolved within 60 days.[282]

Federal law also allows a consumer to sue in federal court to redress some violations of the statute by the consumer reporting agency. If the consumer wins, the consumer might recover damages if the court finds that the defendant's violation was negligent or willful.[283] Actual damages along with attorney's fees may be awarded for negligent violations of the FCRA; actual and/or punitive damages, along with attorney's fees, may be awarded for company's willful noncompliance with the statute. To show willful noncompliance, the consumer must establish that the defendant knowingly or recklessly violated a provision of the act, and reckless means more than "merely careless."[284]

How does the FCRA regulate persons who furnish information to reporting agencies?

The FCRA regulates parties, such as a bank or an institution of higher education, that provide information about a consumer to a consumer reporting agency.[285] Consumer reporting agencies rely on tens of thousands of furnishers for information. Furnishers are required to establish and implement "reasonable written policies and procedures regarding the accuracy and integrity" of information provided to a consumer reporting agency and to reinvestigate information when disputed by a consumer.[286] For these purposes, "accuracy" requires that the information furnished about an account or other relationship with a consumer correctly:

1. "Reflects the terms of and liability for the account or other relationship";
2. "Reflects the consumer's performance and other conduct with respect to the account or other relationship"; and
3. "Identifies the appropriate consumer."[287]

In addition, the information furnished must conform to standards of "integrity," which means, in part, that the furnisher's records substantiate the information at the time it is furnished to the consumer reporting agency.[288] If the consumer has a credit account with the furnisher and voluntarily closes the account, the furnisher must notify the consumer reporting agency that the account has voluntarily been closed.[289] If the information pertains to an account placed for collection, delinquency, or charge-off, the furnisher must, within 90 days, notify the consumer reporting agency of the "date of delinquency."[290] This date is important because the report must exclude accounts that are considered stale (as discussed earlier in this chapter).[291]

<h2 style="text-align:center">How can a consumer get a furnisher to correct
information or to stop providing inaccurate
information to a consumer reporting agency?</h2>

The FCRA bars a furnisher from furnishing information to a consumer reporting agency that it "knows or has reasonable cause to believe . . . is inaccurate."[292] Two simultaneous strategies are available to a consumer to get the furnisher to correct information about the consumer that the furnisher has provided to a consumer reporting agency. One strategy involves contacting the furnisher itself and pursuing, if available, a direct dispute with the furnisher. The other strategy involves filing a dispute about the information with the consumer reporting agency.

Contacting the furnisher is important because the furnisher "shall not furnish information" to a consumer reporting agency if the consumer has notified the furnisher, at an address provided by the furnisher, that "specific information is inaccurate" and "the information is, in fact, inaccurate."[293] A furnisher has reasonable cause to believe that information is inaccurate if it has specific knowledge of the inaccuracy, "other than solely allegations by the consumer."[294] Thus, when the consumer disputes the information with the furnisher, the consumer should take care to be specific in describing the information that is not accurate and to provide supporting documentation. Once contacted, the furnisher may not furnish the information without notifying the agency that the consumer has disputed its accuracy.[295]

Some consumers also may file a "direct dispute" with the furnisher which triggers the furnisher's duty to conduct an investigation of the disputed information.[296] The furnisher is required to have policies and procedures in place to enable such direct disputes by consumers.[297] This option is available if the information pertains to an account or other relationship that the furnisher had or has with the consumer—for example, a credit card account.[298] The consumer must send the dispute notice to the address that the furnisher has provided for this purpose, and if no address is provided, then to the furnisher's business address.[299] Here, again, it is important for the consumer to be specific in the notice of dispute and to include documentation; the FCRA permits the furnisher to treat a dispute as "frivolous or irrelevant" if the consumer fails to provide "sufficient information to investigate the disputed information." The furnisher must notify the consumer no later than five days after deciding a dispute is frivolous or irrelevant, and must disclose the reasons for the determination and identify any information that the furnisher needs to investigate the dispute.[300] Otherwise, the furnisher must conduct an investigation that is reasonable, must review all "relevant" information provided by the consumer, and generally must complete the investigation in 30 days.[301] If the information is found to be inaccurate, the furnisher must "promptly notify" each consumer reporting agency to which the information was furnished, together with any correction to make the information accurate.[302]

On a parallel track, contacting the consumer reporting agency about the disputed information is important because, among other things, the agency then must send notice of the dispute to the furnisher, which triggers the furnisher's general duty to investigate the accuracy of the disputed information. The furnisher's duty is to conduct an investigation that is reasonable, which one court has characterized as requiring "an inquiry likely to turn up information about the underlying facts and positions of the parties, not a cursory or sloppy review of the dispute."[303] The duty to investigate includes the duty to review information provided by the consumer reporting agency, to report the results of the investigation to the consumer reporting agency, and—if the investigation finds that the information is incomplete or not accurate—to report the results "to all other reporting agencies" to which the information was furnished.

What are the furnisher's duties regarding information related to identity theft?

The FCRA requires the furnisher of information to a consumer reporting agency to establish "reasonable procedures" to respond to an agency's notification of information related to identity theft, "to prevent that person from refurnishing" information that has been blocked.[304] Moreover, if a consumer directly submits an identity theft report to the furnisher, the furnisher may not furnish information purporting to relate to the consumer, unless the furnisher "subsequently knows or is informed by the consumer that the information is correct."[305] These requirements are substantially weaker than some that have been proposed, as for example, requiring a consumer reporting agency to mail an adverse investigative report to a consumer before sending it to the requester so the consumer could have a chance to correct or remove any inaccurate, obsolete, incomplete, or exempt information before its use influenced a third party's decision.[306]

Can a consumer sue a furnisher who fails to correct, modify, or block disputed information?

The FCRA requires the furnisher to provide accurate information.[307] However, the consumer does not have a right of action to sue in court to redress a violation of the furnisher's duty to provide accurate information. Instead, the consumer's right to sue is limited to actions seeking to redress the furnisher's failure to carry out its general duty to investigate disputed information—and then only if the consumer has disputed the information with the consumer reporting agency.[308]

What are the duties of government agencies that furnish information to consumer reporting agencies?

A federal agency may furnish information about debt to a consumer reporting agency, but it must establish and follow procedures in connection with the reporting. The information can include only the debtor's name, address, Social Security number, and the amount, status, and history of the claim.[309] For example, the U.S. Department of Education is required to enter into an agreement with each consumer reporting agency "to exchange information concerning student borrowers," and may report information about student loans, such as the remaining balance, the repayment status, and any default.[310]

In addition, a consumer reporting agency "shall include in any consumer report" information about a consumer's failure to pay overdue child support, provided the information is furnished directly by a state or local child support enforcement agency.[311] Information about overdue child support from any other furnisher must be verified by a local, state, or federal government agency.[312] State law may require that the enforcement agency establish and comply with procedures notifying the delinquent parent that information about the overdue support is being furnished to the consumer reporting agency.

Equal Credit Opportunity Act

What is the Equal Credit Opportunity Act?

Credit helps consumers purchase goods and services on the promise that they will pay for them later. For many poor and low-income persons, credit is a necessary lifeline. In 2017, a person working a full-time job at the minimum wage earned an income that was less than the federal poverty line for a family of two.[313] Lacking meaningful support from the government, it is challenging to meet every day needs.[314] Access to credit is not a solution to the problem of low wages, it is not a substitute for a meaningful social welfare system, and it does not redress systemic inequalities that block opportunity and mobility.

However, low-income households depend on credit to get through medical emergencies, to purchase a large consumer good like a car, or are temporarily out of work.[315]

Creditors are in the business of choosing which applicants for credit are likely to be able to repay their loans and which are not.[316] To make these decisions, creditors rely on consumer reports and credit scores, and increasingly in the last decade depend on information drawn from "big data" that are algorithmically driven.[317] Low-income persons face an uphill struggle when they try to access mainstream credit products, because they may lack a bank account, cannot establish a credit record, or have a credit history (depicted, correctly or not, in the person's consumer report) that makes them seem credit unworthy. In addition, mainstream credit companies may steer low-income households to higher loan rates than legal, or push them into the more expensive "fringe" financing market like payday loans (discussed later in this chapter).[318]

The Equal Credit Opportunity Act (ECOA) addresses some of the barriers confronting low-income households when they seek credit. The ECOA's goal is not to require creditors to provide credit to persons creditors regard as not credit worthy, but rather to prevent the withholding of credit on the basis of factors that are irrelevant to equal access to credit. As originally adopted, the ECOA barred creditors from discriminating against women.[319] The statute was later amended, and it now protects persons from credit discrimination on the basis of race,[320] color,[321] religion,[322] national origin,[323] sex,[324] marital status,[325] age,[326] receipt of public assistance benefits,[327] and the exercise of rights under the statute itself.[328] Regulations enforcing the ECOA are known as Regulation B,[329] and they make plain that a creditor "may not consider in its evaluation of creditworthiness any information that is barred."[330]

What kinds of credit transactions does the ECOA regulate?

The ECOA broadly defines credit as the right given by a creditor to a debtor (1) to defer payment of debt, (2) to incur debts and defer its payment, or (3) to purchase property or services and defer payment for them.[331] Credit transactions thus do not involve only a conventional loan or application for a credit card. Rather, a bill that allows the consumer to defer payment is a credit transaction, even though it does not involve a loan; by contrast, an application for an ATM card does not meet the definition.[332]

The ECOA applies to any part of the credit transaction—not just the application stage, but also servicing and modification.[333] The creditor may not withhold information about credit services to a person in a protected group; may

not offer different credit terms because of membership in a protected group; and
may not provide differential servicing of a loan because the debtor is a member
of protected group.[334] For example, American Express violated the ECOA
when it charged higher fees and interest rates, offered fewer promotional offers,
and imposed lower credit limits to consumers who lived in Puerto Rico and
U.S. territories.[335]

The ECOA and Regulation B set out limited exceptions for two kinds of
transactions of significance to households with low income: "public-utilities
credit" and "incidental credit."[336] The exception for public-utilities credit
applies to credit for the purchase of utility service such as gas, electricity, or
telephone service. The exception does not apply if the public utility is offering
credit for some other good or service (such as the purchase of a gas dryer for
home use).[337] The exception for incidental credit includes the deferral of payment to a service provider (such as a doctor or retailer) that is not payable
by agreement in more than four installments and are not subject to a finance
charge.[338]

The exceptions affect, among other things, the kinds of information
that the creditor may consider in connection with the credit transaction.
Transactions involving public utilities credit are not subject to the prohibition concerning information about marital status.[339] Transactions involving
incidental credit are not subject to the prohibition concerning information
about sex, but only to the extent necessary for medical records or similar
purposes;[340] information about a spouse or former spouse;[341] information
about marital status;[342] and information about income derived from alimony, child support, or separate maintenance payment.[343] In addition, incidental credit transactions are not subject to notification rules provided in
connection with other transactions or the furnishing of credit information to
consumer reporting agencies.[344]

Can a person who receives public assistance
be denied credit on that basis?

The ECOA bars a creditor from considering whether a consumer's income
derives "from any public assistance program"[345] in the "evaluation of creditworthiness."[346] Moreover, a credit-scoring system may not consider public assistance
status as a factor.[347] However, if the creditor uses a "judgmental"[348] system to
assess creditworthiness, then questions about public assistance status may be
permitted.[349] Regulation B defines a public assistance program as "[a]ny federal,
state, or local governmental assistance program that provides a continuing, periodic income supplement, whether premised on entitlement or need."[350] Many of

the public assistance programs described in this volume come within the ECOA definition: Temporary Assistance for Needy Families, SNAP ("food stamps"), SSI, and unemployment compensation. The official interpretation of Regulation B states, "Only physicians, hospitals, and others to whom the benefits are payable need consider Medicare and Medicaid as public assistance." The ECOA also bars creditors from discriminating against consumers who associate with persons who receive benefits under a public assistance program.[351]

What are special purpose credit programs?

Special purpose credit programs are programs intended to benefit persons who would otherwise be denied credit or offered credit on less favorable terms.[352] An example is an energy conservation program for seniors, or programs under the Minority Enterprise Small Business Investment Corporation.[353] The creditor may request and consider information regarding an otherwise impermissible basis (such as race, national origin, or sex) if this characteristic is necessary for eligibility for the program.[354]

Who enforces the Equal Credit Opportunity Act?

The ECOA can be enforced by the government and by individual consumers whose rights are violated. Currently the Consumer Financial Protection Bureau is the federal agency responsible for developing regulations and enforcing the ECOA.[355] A person who believes rights have been violated can report the conduct or file an online complaint with the CFPB. The CFPB also enforces the statute by monitoring fair lending compliance and creditors' reporting requirements.

An individual also can file a lawsuit to enforce rights under the ECOA. A person thinking about filing a lawsuit should consider consulting a lawyer. Applicants generally have five years from the time of the violation to file suit.[356] An individual who wins a lawsuit may be awarded actual and punitive damages. Punitive damages are capped at $10,000 in individual actions, and in class actions, $500,000 or 1 percent of the creditor's net worth, whichever is less. Applicants also can sue for equitable relief, which stops the creditor from continuing to engage in the illegal practice, and for declaratory relief that conduct is illegal. A winning plaintiff also may seek the costs (including attorney's fees) of the lawsuit. Keep in mind that courts consistently have held that the ECOA bars disparate impact discrimination, as well as intentional discrimination.[357]

Telephone Consumer Protection Act

What is the Telephone Consumer Protection Act?

Congress enacted the Telephone Consumer Protection Act (TCPA) in 1991 to protect consumers from unwanted telemarketing calls. The statute bars the use of "any automatic telephone dialing system or an artificial or prerecorded voice" to call or text messages to cell phones, pagers, or similar devices without the recipient's prior express consent.[358] The banned calls do not only have a nuisance value; they impose a cost on the receiver of the call, who, absent protection, likely would be charged for the call or the call would count against minutes under a monthly phone plan.[359]

Does the TCPA bar a debt collector from contacting a consumer?

The TCPA ban on using autodialing systems or prerecorded messages to make calls to pagers, cell phones, and similar devices or any service for which the consumer is charged applies to debt collectors unless the consumer has given express consent to receive phone calls.[360] The TCPA is violated even when the collector places an autorecorded or predialed call to the wrong cell phone. The reason for this rule is simple: most consumers have to pay for incoming cell phone calls, and the cost of an erroneous call should be on the creditor, not the innocent consumer.

The TCPA also bans calls to residential phone lines using artificial or prerecorded voice messages without the recipient's express consent; however, calls by debt collectors who have an established business relationship with the intended recipient of the prerecorded calls are exempt.[361] A consumer's failure to object to the phone call is not the same thing as consent to the automated call.[362] However, in some cases a consumer's consent to be called by the debt collector has been treated as consent to receive automated calls.[363] By contrast, a consumer's giving a phone number to a vendor or service provider has been found not to be consent to debt-collection calls for unpaid bills.[364]

Consumers need to take note of the written agreements they sign with vendors and service providers; they may include terms by which the consumer consents to autodial or prerecorded messages for debt collection purposes. Courts have upheld the validity of these agreements' consent terms, even if the consumer did not read the agreement—and most consumers do not—before signing.[365]

A consumer can revoke consent that was already given. Federal regulations have been interpreted to allow for oral revocation. However, to be safe, and because some courts have taken this position,[366] it is best to make the revocation in writing. In addition, the statute allows a consumer to partially revoke consent to receive future automated calls.[367]

Consumer Credit Protection Act

What is the Consumer Credit Protection Act?

The Consumer Credit Protection Act (CCPA) is a federal law that regulates the credit relationship of borrowers and lenders.[368] Among other things, the CCPA protects consumers from some of the harmful effects of "garnishment"—a legal procees that allows a creditor to collect a debt by diverting assets of a debtor that are held by a third party. Assets that are subject to garnishment include wages held by the debtor's employer and cash held in a bank account.[369]

Congress enacted the CCPA in part out of concern that making wage garnishment too easily available to creditors encouraged them to engage in predatory lending prices, to which poor and low-income people were especially vulnerable. Garnishment hurt workers by reducing or eliminating take-home earnings that were needed for everyday expenses. Garnishment also imposed administrative burdens upon employers, who tended to respond by firing the worker whose wages had been garnished. Many policymakers opposed the use of wage garnishment as a debt collection device, urging its elimination. The CCPA adopted a compromise position, allowing wage garnishment but restricting its use. As the CCPA's legislative history explains, the act was designed "to relieve countless honest debtors driven by economic desperation from plunging into bankruptcy in order to preserve their employment and insure a continued means of support for themselves and their families."[370] Today, declaring bankruptcy is less of an affordable option for low-income persons,[371] and wage garnishment, even as regulated by the CCPA, can exacerbate financial insecurity by pushing workers below the poverty line and saddle them with additional debt from interest on judgments.[372] Still, knowing about the limits on garnishment, especially as they affect wages and public benefits (such as Social Security), is very important even if the statute provides incomplete protection. In addition, the CCPA's protections may be supplemented by state law protections.[373] Also, the Servicemembers Civil Relief Act sets out special rules for the garnishment of servicemembers' earnings.[374] Finally, separate rules govern the garnishment of funds for unpaid federal taxes and other debts owed to the United States (discussed later in this chapter).

How does the CCPA limit the creditor's use
of wage garnishment to collect a debt?

Wage garnishment operates as a deduction from the debtor's wages—money is diverted from the worker and instead paid to the creditor. A creditor can garnish wages as a way to get a debtor to repay a debt, but only by going to court and getting a court order that establishes the debt is owed. When the CCPA was adopted, some states allowed "prejudgment garnishment," meaning, the creditor was permitted to take a deduction from the worker's wages even before a court had established that a debt was owed. The U.S. Supreme Court held that the practice of prejudgment wage garnishment violated the Due Process Clause. As a result, a court cannot order that a worker's wages be diverted to a creditor unless the worker is given notice of the garnishment proceeding and an opportunity to contest the debt or the amount owed.[375]

The CCPA limits wage garnishment as a debt collection device, in two ways: (1) it caps the amount of earnings that can be diverted from the worker to the creditor; and (2) it limits the employer's authority to fire a worker whose earnings are subject to garnishment. Moreover, it authorizes financial sanctions on creditors and employers who violate the law.

How much of a worker's earnings does the CCPA
allow to be diverted through garnishment?

The CCPA caps the amount of the worker's disposable earnings that can be garnished by court order in any pay period.[376] The caps do not apply to wage assignment (which is contractual) unless it is pursuant to court order.[377] The garnishment order may not divert more than 25 percent of the worker's "disposable earnings" in any workweek, capped at an amount that is 30 times the federal minimum wage.[378] Disposable earnings are those earnings left after taxes and other amounts that the law requires the employer to withhold.[379] The cap is intended to ensure that workers receive at least 75 percent of earnings per weekly pay period.[380] One problem with the amount of the cap is that it was set in 1968 and tied to the minimum wage, and has not been updated. As a result, some low-wage workers, already making annual earnings that are less than the federal poverty line for their households, are further impoverished.[381]

Are there exceptions to the CCPA's earnings cap?

The CCPA earnings cap on wage garnishment does not apply to support orders; "Chapter 13" bankruptcy proceedings;[382] and debts due for state or federal taxes.[383]

In support cases, whether spousal or child, the garnished amount for a person supporting a spouse or child is capped at 50 percent of disposable earnings for the weekly pay period, and 55 percent if the debtor is 12 weeks or more in arrears.[384] If the person is not supporting a spouse or child, the cap increases to 60 percent of disposable earnings, subject to other exceptions, and 65 percent if the debtor is 12 weeks or more in arrears.[385]

Can an employer fire a worker whose earnings are subject to garnishment?

One of the main reasons for enacting the CCPA was to stop the practice of employers firing workers whose earnings are subject to garnishment.[386] Federal law now bars an employer from firing a worker "by reason of the fact that his earnings have been subjected to garnishment for any one indebtedness."[387] The expression "one indebtedness" apparently means a single debt, and multiple debts joined in a single court judgment count as one indebtedness. However, lower federal courts have held that the protection against being fired does not apply if there are multiple garnishments for multiple debts,[388] but first the earnings must be withheld pursuant to the garnishment order before the employer may discharge the worker.[389] Willful violations of the statute are subject to criminal sanctions of not more than $1,000 or imprisonment for not more than one year, or both.[390] The Secretary of Labor, a federal official, is responsible for enforcing the statute.[391]

Can a creditor garnish moneys other than earnings to collect a debt?

Yes. A creditor may seek to garnish money that the debtor has deposited into a bank account. Once the creditor has gotten a court order and served that order upon a bank where the debtor has an account, the bank will divert funds from the account and pay that money to the creditor without seeking permission from the debtor. Different rules apply depending on the source of the moneys.

Earnings. Some courts have taken the position that earnings, once they have been deposited into a bank account, are not subject to the garnishment caps set by the statute for earnings.[392]

Income tax refunds. Income tax refunds can be garnished. Moreover, the U.S. Supreme Court has held that the CCPA's limits on wage garnishment do not apply to tax refunds.[393] Similarly, state courts have held that state tax refunds are not exempt from garnishment.[394] The rationale for these decisions is that wage earners typically do not rely upon tax refunds as a means of support to the same extent that they rely upon wages, and so garnishment of these funds does not cause the debtor to suffer the kind of hardship that the CCPA was enacted to avoid. However, this rationale needs to be reconsidered; a majority of low-income consumers do indeed depend upon their tax refunds to cover basic necessities or to pay off debt.[395]

Government benefits. Federal law protects specific government benefits from garnishment even if they have been paid to the recipient and deposited in a bank account, but the funds must be traceable and available to the consumer for daily living expenses.[396]

Social Security benefits are exempt from garnishment,[397] except when the garnishment is to pay outstanding alimony or child support,[398] to pay debts to the federal government (including student loans),[399] or to pay taxes owed to the federal government.[400] Supplemental Security Income (SSI) is exempt from garnishment,[401] and the ban is not subject to any exception.[402] Other exempt benefits include assistance payments under the Temporary Assistance for Needy Families Program and other needs-based state or local government assistance programs,[403] Veterans' Benefits,[404] Federal Civil Service Retirement Benefits,[405] and Federal Railroad Retirement Benefits.[406] A minority of states also exempt the wages of current and former recipients of certain means-tested programs.[407]

Are public assistance benefits protected from garnishment after they have been deposited in a bank account?

In 2011, the U.S. Department of Treasury issued rules to protect against the garnishment of public assistance benefits, which are exempt from garnishment, when they are held in a bank account with nonexempt funds.[408] The rules protect only exempt funds that are directly deposited into a bank account by the benefit agency and only in an amount equal to two months of benefits.[409]

The Treasury Rule protects these benefits: Social Security benefits; SSI; Veteran's Benefits; Federal Railroad Retirement, unemployment, and sickness benefits; Federal Civil Service Retirement System Benefits; and Federal Employee Retirement System Benefits. (These benefits are not protected: military benefits, state benefits, workers' compensation benefits, and unemployment compensation.) The Treasury Rule provides two important protections: (1) it requires notice before funds can be diverted; and (2) it sets dollar amounts that are automatically exempt.[410]

Under the Treasury Rule, a bank must take the following steps when it receives a garnishment order:

- Within two business days, the bank must determine if the garnishment relates to a collection effort by the United States or for child support. If so, the bank follows its usual procedures.[411]

- If the garnishment is not by the United States or for child support, the bank must review the debtor's account history during a two-month "lookback" period to determine whether the account has received direct deposit of protected government benefits.[412]
- If protected benefits were direct-deposited into the account during the two-month period, the bank must give the account holder unrestricted access to a "protected amount," which is essentially twice the account holder's monthly benefit.[413] If the account contains less than the protected amount, it may not be garnished. If the account contains more than the protected amount, it may be garnished.
- The bank is not allowed to charge a garnishment fee against this protected amount.[414] The amount is calculated separately for each account in the name of an account holder.[415]
- If the account contains protected benefits, then, within three days of the account review,[416] the bank must give notice to the account holder.[417] The notice must state "in readily understandable language":[418]

1. That the bank received an order garnishing the account;[419]
2. The date on which the bank got the order;[420]
3. A succinct explanation of garnishment;[421]
4. That the bank is required to review the account and make sure that exempt benefits are made available to the account holder;[422]
5. Which account the order relates to, and what "protected amount" the bank has found;[423]
6. That the bank is obligated by state law to freeze the nonexempt funds in the account;[424]
7. The amount of any garnishment fee charged to the account;[425]
8. A list of the federal benefits exempt under the regulations;[426]
9. That the account holder has the right to take legal action against the creditor (what actions are available will vary by state);[427] and
10. The creditor's name and the creditor's contact information, if it was included in the order.[428]

It is the bank's duty to make the exempt funds deposited within the prior two-month period accessible to the consumer; the consumer is not required to assert the exemption. Moreover, the bank must tell affected consumers that they have a right to consult an attorney to raise other exemptions for amounts above the protected amount.[429]

Keep in mind that the Treasury Rule does not protect government benefits that are deposited into a bank account by check rather than by direct deposit; funds deposited into the account more than two months before the bank received the garnishment order; and exempt funds transferred from another bank account into the account that is subject to garnishment. If a debtor believes that any garnishment rights have been violated, it is important to seek legal advice, to read any notice that the bank sends, and to respond by the stated deadlines. Additional information is available from the Federal Trade Commission FTC (https://www.ftc.gov) and the state's Attorney General (contact information can be found at https://www.naag.org).[430]

How much do banks charge the account holder to process a garnishment?

Federal regulations bar banks from charging and debiting fees for processing garnishment against the protected amount of exempt funds. Otherwise, banks typically charge fees for processing a garnishment application, and these fees are taken from the debtor's account.[431] The National Bank Act, a federal statute, gives financial institutions "[a]uthority to impose charges and fees," and this includes authority to impose fees to process the garnishment of a bank account.[432] Banks have a lot of discretion over how much they charge.[433] The top 15 banks in the United States (making up more than half of deposits for all banks in the country),[434] charge between $75 and $125 to process the garnishment.[435] If debiting the fee causes the account to become overdrawn, the bank is permitted to impose another fee for an overdrawn account. Find out what a bank charges and consider other banking options, including smaller institutions such as credit unions. Credit unions and credit development credit unions are nonprofits formed to serve their communities, and most operate under a recommended 36 percent interest rate cap for small loans. Many will offer small loans even for borrowers with poor credit scores. Moreover, they typically charge fewer and less costly fees on accounts.[436]

Truth in Lending Act and Private Student Loans

What is the Truth in Lending Act?

The Truth in Lending Act (TILA) was enacted as part of the Consumer Credit Protection Act.[437] The TILA is implemented by "Regulation Z."[438] Both the statute and the regulation have been amended a number of times since 1969, when they became effective.[439] In the wake of the Great Recession, Congress amended the TILA in a number of ways, including as it relates to private education loans. Despite this reform, many commentators express concerns that indebtedness from student loans will be the next "bubble" causing severe economic dislocation.[440]

Student loan debt is indeed the highest category of consumer debt aside from mortgage debt, with close to $1.5 trillion dollars outstanding as of 2018.[441] Student-loan indebtedness presents a particular problem for persons who are poor or have low income and have had to borrow at higher levels to pay for postsecondary education.[442] The cost of postsecondary education is higher than a generation ago; tuition even at public institutions rose 34 percent between 2003– 04 and 2013–14.[443] Moreover, for-profit proprietary schools, which offer career-specific programs, charge higher tuition than public secondary schools,[444] and it is known that they targeted their recruitment efforts at low-income and especially African American males.[445] In the past, it was assumed that a college graduate would be able to repay student debt because of higher earnings. Although college can promote mobility (as discussed in chapter 5), private loans taken out to attend some proprietary schools may have made some students worse off.[446]

Borrowers of private student loans lack most of the protections that attach to federal student loans (discussed in chapter 5). By amending the TILA, Congress aimed to help students become informed consumers before they became responsible for such loans. The TILA and Regulation Z impose a series of disclosure requirements on private lenders who make student loans on the view that borrowers will better understand the terms and conditions of their indebtedness; the disclosure regime also assumes that well-informed consumers will influence the market to offer better terms. In practice, disclosure is a limited form of consumer protection; strong arguments have been made for imposing substantive limits on private student loans, such as requiring repayment options.[447] Still, it is very important to know the scope of the private-loan obligation and the limits of the protections that are provided should a borrower find that repayment is not feasible.

Who must comply with the disclosure rules about private education loans?

Regulation Z requires any creditor who makes a loan to a consumer to attend a "covered educational institution,"[448] "expressly, in whole or in part,"[449] for postsecondary educational expenses, to give information about the loan's terms and costs before the student takes out the loan ("solicitation" disclosure);[450] when the loan is approved ("approval" disclosure);[451] and when the loan becomes final ("final" disclosure).[452] Educational expenses are defined by federal law to include such things as tuition and fees, an allowance for books and supplies, and an allowance for room and board.[453] A private education loan is a loan that is not insured under Title IV of the Higher Education Act of 1965. The rule by definition excludes open-end credit and real-estate-secured loans. It also exempts an extension of credit given by a covered institution of higher education for a term of 90 days or less, or loans for which the covered institution does not charge interest and the term is for a year or less.[454] The disclosures must be given to any person who requests information about private student loans or is applying for a private student loan and are in addition to other disclosures required under Regulation Z.[455]

What is the form and content of a solicitation disclosure?

The solicitation disclosure must be in writing and in a form that the consumer can keep;[456] further, the disclosures must be separate from other kinds of information given to the consumer.[457] Electronic formats are allowed but must meet special requirements.[458] The disclosure must make clear that the information is not about federal loans,[459] and must "clearly and conspicuously" state:[460]

1. The potential range of rates of interest applicable to the loan;[461]
2. Whether the interest rate will be fixed or variable;[462]
3. How many times and to what degree the lender may adjust the interest rate;[463]
4. Any requirements for a co-borrower, including changes in the applicable interest rates which may occur if the student does not have a co-borrower;[464]
5. "[P]otential finance charges, late fees, penalties, and adjustments to principal, based on defaults or late payments";[465]
6. Fees or range of fees applicable to the loan;[466]
7. The period for which the loan will last;[467]
8. Whether the borrower will be charged interest while attending school;[468]
9. The options the borrower will have for deferring payments;[469]
10. The "general eligibility criteria" for the loan;[470]
11. An example of the total cost of the loan with the interest factored in, as well as all applicable finance charges, and calculated for each payment option;[471]
12. "[T]hat a covered educational institution may have school-specific education loan benefits and terms not detailed on the disclosure form";[472]
13. That the borrower may qualify for a federal student loan or grant,[473] the interest rates available for a federal student loan,[474] and the fact that federal loan terms may be better for borrowers than private loan terms;[475]
14. That the borrower has 30 days from the date of approval to accept the private loan;[476]

15. That in order to accept the loan, the borrower must fill out a loan acceptance form from the school;[477] and

16. That additional information about federal student loans is available from
the school, or at the U.S. Department of Education website.[478]

What is the content of the approval disclosure?

The approval disclosure is transaction-specific and must give the borrower information about:[479]

1. The interest rate, including whether it is fixed or variable and whether the
rate can change after the loan becomes final;

2. Fees and default or late payment costs;

3. Repayment terms, including the principal, the term, a description of the
payment deferral option that the borrower has chosen, whether payments
are required while the borrower attends school, the accrual of interest while
the student is enrolled, a statement that repayment may be required even
if the student declares bankruptcy, and an estimate of the total payments
due, given the applicable interest rate and estimates of the maximum
interest rate;

4. Alternatives to private loans, including interest rates for loans available
under Title IV of the Higher Education Act, and a statement that additional information is available from the covered institution or through the
specified website of the U.S. Department of Education; and

5. That the borrower has 30 days to accept the terms, and that other than interest rate and "other changes permitted by law," the rates and terms of the
loan must stay the same during that period.

What is the content of the final disclosure?

After the borrower has accepted the loan,[480] the lender must provide most of
the information contained in the approval disclosure,[481] specific to the loan that
is about to be signed. Significantly, the lender must disclose that the borrower
has the right to cancel the loan at any time before midnight of the third business
day following receipt of the final disclosure.[482] The notice must state how the
borrower can cancel the loan and that if cancellation by mail is permitted, the
request is timely if mailed not later than the date specified in the disclosure.[483]
No loan disbursement may be made until the cancellation period lapses.[484]

What disclosures must an educational
institution make about student loans?

Schools, as eligible institutions under the statute,[485] are required to provide all prospective and enrolled students with information about student loans. Schools sometimes enter into agreements with individual private lenders, under which the school promotes certain private loans. If a school enters into such an agreement, federal law requires that the school must disclose on its website and in any materials that describe or discuss student loans that it will process loans from any lender the student chooses for borrowing.[486]

The disclosure must provide information about:

1. Financial assistance available at the school for enrolled students;[487]
2. The methods by which such assistance is distributed to student recipients;[488]
3. The means by which students are to apply for financial assistance, including providing students with the forms;[489]
4. The rights and responsibilities of students who receive financial assistance;[490]
5. The cost of attending the institution, including tuition, fees, books, supplies, typical room and board expenses, and any additional costs of programs in which a student is enrolled or has expressed an interest;[491]
6. The requirements for loan refunds and for officially withdrawing from the school;[492]
7. The academic program offered at the institution;[493]
8. Contact information for the financial assistance information personnel of the institution;[494]
9. The standards which students must maintain in order to be considered to be "making satisfactory progress" in order to continue receiving aid, which is either a cumulative C average or the academic standing determined by the school to be sufficient for graduation;[495] and
10. The terms of the loans students receive.[496]

The school also must provide exit counseling to the student prior to completing the course of study.[497] Counseling is required to address such topics as repayment plans, debt-management strategies, prepayment options, loan forgiveness plans, applicable deferment options, consequences of default, consolidation, tax benefits available to borrowers, and the availability of the National Student Loan Data system.[498]

INFORMATION BOX: LEARNING MORE ABOUT PAYING FOR COLLEGE

A person thinking about financing postsecondary education can visit the Consumer Financial Protection Bureau's website. The CFPB's "Paying for College" project provides many tools that are helpful when deciding how to pay for higher education.[499] The website provides information about the benefits and risks of different types of student loans. The site also allows parents and students to compare costs at different colleges, some of which may offer financial aid, learn about college money and loan options, and learn about repayment options. Additional information about private loans is available at FinAid's website.[500]

Private Student Loan Repayment

What happens if a consumer cannot repay a private student loan?

Estimates in 2018 put more than 10 percent of outstanding student debt as delinquent or in default, and the average household student debt is $39,400.[501] A consumer who cannot repay a private student loan may face default. Under the federal direct loan program, generally default does not take place until the borrower has not made a payment for nine months;[502] however, with a private education loan, default may happen after only one missed payment.[503]

A borrower who has entered into a private student loan is not entitled to the statutory protections that attach to federal student loans (discussed in chapter 5). Instead, the consumer's options depend on the terms and conditions of the loan. For loans taken out after the TILA's disclosure requirements became mandatory, a borrower will have some information about payment and deferral options. It is very important to find out information about the specific transaction. Here are some options that might be available depending on the contractual terms:

> Partial Payment—Check to see if the loan permits a graduated repayment or extended payment plan. The upside of partial payment is that the action avoids default; the downside is that interest payments increase over the life of the loan, making the total amount to be repaid larger.
>
> Temporary Halt on Payment—Another option involves a temporary halt on payment, called "deferment" or "forbearance." The upside of a halt period is that the borrower has breathing room; the downside is that a halt period is not a

grace period—interest continues to pile up and so the total amount to be repaid becomes larger.

In addition, reforms adopted in 2018 allow a consumer to request that a consumer reporting agency remove from the consumer's report a previously reported default on a private education loan if the lender offers and the consumer meets the requirements of a "loan-rehabilitation program that requires a number of consecutive on-time monthly payments demonstrating renewed ability and willingness to repay the loan." Rehabilitation benefits are available only once per loan.[504]

How can a borrower find out more information about the borrower's student loans?

To find out more information about the borrower's student loans, the borrower can contact the "servicer" that manages the credit account. The servicer is a company that handles the borrower's account and processes payment. The servicer is often not the lender; moreover, the current servicer of a loan may not be the same as the original servicer. The servicer communicates between the borrower and the lender. The education amendments to the TILA also impose obligations on servicers.[505] The servicer must provide the borrower with copies of the original loan document on request and may not charge a fee. In addition, the servicer must provide the borrower with the loan history—a detailed list of payments, charges, and fees—either through a secure website or on written request. In addition, the TILA imposes substantive requirements on the servicer. The servicer cannot charge a late payment fee or payment charge if a payment is late because of a change in the servicer's handling procedures or address. Moreover, payments are to be applied first to interest and fees, and then to the principal of the loan with the highest interest rate, unless the borrower has given other instructions.

If the servicer does not respond to a request for information (for example, the name of the original creditor) or the disclosure is not clear or seems incomplete, a complaint may be registered with the Consumer Financial Protection Bureau either online,[506] or by telephone, at: 855-411-2372. The agency will forward the complaint to the company for a response.[507] In other contexts, courts have considered whether the Regulation Z disclosure requirements are judicially enforceable.[508]

Does the Fair Debt Collection Practices Act apply to collectors who seek to collect student loans?

A collector who seeks to collect a student debt on behalf of a creditor is subject to the Fair Debt Collection Practices Act, discussed earlier in this chapter. This means, among other things, that the consumer can insist that the creditor stop its collection activity until it verifies the existence and amount of the debt, and demand that the collector stop contact with the debtor, even if the debt is valid.

Can collectors seek to collect from a private student loan borrower who is in the armed services?

The Servicemembers Civil Relief Act provides some protections to borrowers who are serving on active duty in the armed services.[509] The servicemember's rights include: a reduction in interest to a cap of 6 percent;[510] a halt in payment; deferment;[511] and cancellation of the debt due to a permanent and total disability.[512] Each of these options affects the borrower in different ways; for example, a deferment does not stop the accrual of interest, and the total amount of the debt becomes much larger over time.[513] As a first step, the borrower must contact the servicer of the loan. If the servicer does not respond or if the information provided is not clear or seems incomplete, contact the Consumer Financial Protection Bureau and file an online complaint or call the agency at 1-855-411-2372.[514] Many members of the armed services have reported problems with the enforcement of their rights under the Servicemembers Civil Relief Act.[515]

What are "student loan debt relief companies"?

Student loan debt relief companies are private companies that offer services to lower debt payments.[516] Their services are not free; the fees they charge may be recurring and expensive; in practice, the service may not provide the borrower anything of benefit.[517] The Consumer Financial Protection Bureau has sued to stop some of these companies from operating and has issued an advisory warning to student borrowers to beware of "scams" from these relief companies and to resist their too-good-to-be-true offers.[518]

What is consolidation?

Loan consolidation is the process of combining multiple loans into one loan.[519] Consolidation often is done to simplify a consumer's loan repayment by giving the debtor a single loan with just one monthly bill. Borrowers, if they want, can consolidate their federal student loans for free by applying for a Direct Consolidation Loan (some companies offer loan consolidation services for a fee). Combining federal student loans into a Direct Consolidation Loan often lowers a consumer's monthly payment by extending the length of the repayment plan. However, by extending the repayment period, interest payments over the life of the loan may increase. Consolidation also may cause the borrower to lose benefits that existed under the preconsolidated loans. For example, consolidation of federal loans with private loans will result in losing benefits and protections associated with the federal loans.[520] Thus, the advantages of consolidation must be weighed carefully against their disadvantages. More information about consolidation can be obtained from the U.S. Department of Education's Loan Consolidation Information Call Center, which can be reached at 1-800-557-7392.

Can student loans be discharged through bankruptcy?

Even with repayment and deferral options—and most private education loans do not have these terms—a borrower might not be able to make payments as required by the loan agreement.[521] Default rates among student borrowers differ, depending on the type of loan, the educational institution, and characteristics of the borrower. In particular, higher default rates reflect a borrower's low earnings, a trend that continues over a lifetime even for college graduates, and earnings are especially low for students who attended or dropped out of some "for-profit" proprietary schools (which predominately targeted African American men).[522]

Bankruptcy is a federal procedure designed to enable "honest but unfortunate debtors" to get a "fresh start" by discharging their debts.[523] Many borrowers believe that student loans are not dischargeable in bankruptcy.[524] Moreover, without access to counsel, borrowers of student loans are deterred by the sheer complexity of the process from seeking relief.[525] However, there is no categorical bar on the dischargeability of student loans in bankruptcy. Indeed, a federal court held that it was a violation of federal law for a debt collection agency to tell a consumer that a student loan could not be discharged in bankruptcy.[526] Student loans are dischargeable, but only through an adversary proceeding in which the borrower must show that repayment will cause "undue hardship"—a requirement that does not apply to other unsecured debts.[527] Keep in mind (as discussed later in this section) that not every private loan related to schooling is an education loan subject to the "undue hardship" requirement.[528]

The decision to file for bankruptcy is a serious matter that involves consideration of many legal, personal, and financial factors.[529] The proceeding is very complex, and there are multiple pathways to relief, and the pathway has important consequences, such as the ability to retain assets or to halt debt collection activity while the proceeding is pending. Moreover, despite the Bankruptcy Code's "fresh start" philosophy, declaring bankruptcy potentially carries negative consequences for a debtor in terms of future access to credit or employment.[530] However, for some student loan debtors, lacking access to repayment or other options, filing a bankruptcy action and a related adversary proceeding to seek discharge of a private education loan may be a reasonable option to explore, even though the standard for discharge is tough to meet and there are downsides to meeting it.[531] This section focuses only on issues pertinent to the dischargeability of private education loans.

Does filing for bankruptcy automatically put a private education loan into default?

Prior to 2018, lenders automatically were able to declare a private education loan in default (or demand acceleration of payment) if a signer or cosigner on the loan filed for bankruptcy. Reforms adopted in 2018 do not permit the lender to trigger a default solely on this ground for a loan "involving a student obligor and 1 or more cosigners."[532] However, this provision applies only to students loans consummated 18 days or more after enactment of the law.

Are all student loans subject to the "undue hardship" rule?

The Bankruptcy Code singles out specific categories of loans for disfavorable discharge treatment. Not all school-related loans come within the statutory definition. Although there is disagreement, some courts have held that "private loans for a variety of educational expenses including bar review, study abroad, elementary education, private tutoring, and many trade schools are discharged at the conclusion of a debtor's bankruptcy case."[533] When considering whether bankruptcy is an option, an important first step is identifying the loan and how it is characterized for discharge purposes.

Under what circumstances might a private education loan be dischargeable in bankruptcy?

The Bankruptcy Code makes certain categories of student loans not dischargeable unless the exception "would impose an undue hardship on the debtor and the debtor's dependents."[534] A separate action, called an adversary proceeding, must be filed in order to request a discharge of student loans.[535] The statute does not define what circumstances constitute "undue hardship," and the federal courts have exercised their equitable discretion to determine whether the debtor has adequately met the requirement. Two leading tests have developed.

The majority of the federal circuit courts of appeals, taking the lead of the Second Circuit Court of Appeals in *Brunner v. New York State Higher Education Services Corp.*,[536] look to three factors, each of which must be satisfied by a preponderance of the evidence:[537] (1) the debtor must show an inability to maintain, based on current income and expenses, a "minimal" standard of living for self and dependents if forced to repay the loans; (2) the debtor must show additional, exceptional circumstances indicating that this state of affairs is likely to persist for a significant portion of the repayment period of the student loans; and (3) the debtor must show good-faith efforts to repay the loans.[538] The Eighth Circuit looks to the "totality of circumstances" in determining whether undue hardship exists.[539] The First Circuit has not endorsed either test.[540]

In determining whether repayment will block the borrower from maintaining a minimal standard of living, the debtor typically is required to show "more than tight finances,"[541] or "mere hardship," or "even considerable hardship."[542] The situation must be that of "more than temporary financial adversity, but typically stop short of utter hopelessness."[543] However, some commentators assert that courts interpret "undue hardship" as meaning "the most hopeless of hardship circumstances"—"what some cases have described as an 'existential despair' made up of a certainty of hopelessness or total incapacity."[544]

The additional circumstances prong requires a showing that the debtor's financial circumstances are not likely to improve for a significant period of time. A medical condition, for instance, may constitute such an additional circumstance if it impairs the debtor's ability to earn a living and persists for a significant period of time.[545] The Ninth Circuit Court of Appeals has looked to a nonexhaustive list of "objective factors" that may evidence the debtor's long term inability:

> (1) serious mental or physical disability of the debtor or the debtor's dependents; (2) the debtor's obligation to care for dependents; (3) lack of or severely limited education; (4) poor quality of education; (5) lack of usable or marketable job skills; (6) underemployment; (7) maximized income potential in the debtor's chosen educational field and no other lucrative job skills; (8) a limited number of years remaining in the debtor's work life to allow repayment; (9) age or other factors that prevent retraining or relocation that would facilitate repayment; (10) lack of assets to repay the loans (whether exempt or not); (11) potentially increasing expenses that outweigh potential appreciation in the value of the debtor's assets and/or likely increases in the debtor's income; and (12) the lack of better financial options elsewhere.[546]

Other courts have interpreted "additional circumstances" to include a "certainty of hopelessness" requirement, requiring a showing of unique or extraordinary circumstances beyond inability to pay before relief is granted.[547]

The good-faith prong generally looks to the debtor's efforts to obtain employment, maximize income, and minimize expenses.[548] A debtor who minimizes expenses without maximizing income or making adequate efforts to obtain employment will likely not show good faith for purposes of the test. Another factor that courts may consider is the debtor's efforts to negotiate repayment of the debt. Nevertheless, failure to pursue such a plan does not automatically preclude the debtor from establishing good faith.[549]

Are student debtors eligible for a partial discharge of the loan?

Some courts have held that a student borrower may be eligible for a partial discharge. To be sure, the Bankruptcy Code nowhere authorizes a partial discharge for private education loans. Courts that offer this form of relief take the position that "an all-or-nothing approach" to dischargeability is inconsistent with the Bankruptcy Code and with the court's equitable authority to fashion a remedy.[550] Those courts that recognize the possibility of a partial discharge disagree whether the debtor must show undue hardship,[551] or whether the court has authority to grant relief "where facts and circumstances require intervention in the financial burden on the debtor."[552] Courts have taken account of a borrower's ineligibility for repayment plans when considering the appropriateness of partial discharge.[553]

Can an employer fire a worker for declaring bankruptcy?

Federal law protects debtors who have declared bankruptcy from adverse actions by employers.[554] In any particular case, an employer will try to defend a decision to terminate an employer by arguing that the decision was not based "solely" on the filing of a bankruptcy petition and that other factors were at play.[555] Moreover, although the U.S. Supreme Court has not addressed the issue, lower courts have held that the antidiscrimination protection does not apply to the hiring stage of the employment relation.[556]

How did the 2017 tax act affect private student loan borrowers and what else might Congress do?

The Tax Cuts and Jobs Act of 2017, discussed in chapter 2, affected borrowers of student loans by excluding student loan balances from taxable income arising from the total permanent disability or death of the borrower.[557] The 2017 act retained the deductibility of student loan interest up to $2,500 per return gradually reduced depending on adjusted gross income (but the deduction has been moved to a new schedule on IRS form 1040).[558] However, the act did not address the arbitrary treatment of private student loans in bankruptcy, the racialized effects of student debt, or the broader impact that student loan debt has on the economy or the life choices of student borrowers.[559] Proposed legislative reforms range from allowing student loans to be dischargeable in bankruptcy on a par with other debts, affording broad-scale debt cancellation outside of the bankruptcy context, and making college free.[560]

Fringe Financing

What is fringe financing?

Fringe financing refers to alternative financial services that operate outside of federally insured banks and are said to have a simple business model: make predatory loans to low-income people.[561] The fringe financing industry targets people who are "unbanked"—those who do not have access to checking or savings accounts—or "underbanked"—borrowers who rely on a mix of traditional and alternative financial services—because they generally have lacked access to ordinary credit markets.[562] Fringe lenders charge annual percentage rates of interest (APRs) of over 30 percent and that may be higher than 400 percent. Transaction, rollover, and refinancing fees also are exorbitantly high and drive up debt burden. Fringe financing is said to meet the short-term financial needs of low-income households that, subsisting below the poverty line even if a member works a full-time job at the minimum wage, cannot save and cannot get conventional credit when emergencies arise. In practice, fringe financing multiplies the cost of borrowing and exacerbates financial insecurity, trapping low-income borrowers in a vicious and calculated "debt trap."[563]

What are payday loans?

Payday loans are the most prevalent fringe financing option.[564] Payday lenders provide small, short-term loans, typically of amounts that range between $100 and $500 with extremely high interest rates—the national average APR for a payday loan is about 400 percent and can be as high as 700 percent—and repayment terms range from two weeks to one month although the loans are frequently refinanced or rolled over and so in any meaningful sense are long-term debt.[565] Payday loans also are known as payday advances, deferred deposit loans, cash advance loans, check advance loans, postdated check loans, and delayed deposit loans.

To apply for a payday loan, a borrower typically needs a driver's license, pay stub, bank statement, telephone bill, and checkbook.

A payday loan is made without any assessment of the consumer's ability to repay, and is borrowed against the borrower's future income. The future earnings can be employment earnings or recurring public benefits (such as Social Security payments). At the time of the loan, lenders generally take a postdated check for the loan amount plus a fee. At the time of the agreed-upon repayment, the lender will attempt to cash the check unless the borrower repays the loan in full and reclaims the postdated check. The borrower can also be required to pay a fee to roll over or extend the loan. Some states prohibit rollovers, in which case, the lender will have the borrower refinance and impose another but different fee. Some lenders will not accept a postdated check and instead require that the borrower authorize a debit to the consumer's bank account. This allows the lender to automatically withdraw any payments that are due and additional fees, diverting funds from the consumer without even the protections of garnishment.

Payday lenders generally do not accept partial payments on the original principal. This balloon-payment structure means that a borrower must repay the loan and often in a short period of time. By effect, borrowers get trapped in a cycle of rollovers, and the resulting fees can amount to much greater than the original loan amount. This cycle of debt is worsened if a lender has the ability to debit payments directly, resulting in overcharges or related fees from the borrower's bank.[566]

The payday industry every year lends to about 12 million Americans who spend $9 billion on loan fees, and payday loans often are concentrated in communities where people of color live.[567] One study found that, on average, borrowers have 10 to 12 transactions with a payday lender each year.[568] Another study found that 90 percent of payday lending revenues draws from fees "stripped from trapped borrowers," and that most payday lenders "earn a return on assets between ten and twenty times greater than traditional banks."[569]

How do payday loans trap low-income borrowers into deeper financial trouble?

Payday loans have been called a "debt trap" because they saddle financially marginalized people with debt that carries exorbitant rates of interest as well as additional fees that drive up indebtedness. To best protect themselves, borrowers considering a payday loan—which are illegal in some states—should know about the following features:

- *Annual percentage rates.* These interest rates are usually in the triple digits. For example, a rate of 300 percent APR would amount to 25 percent of the loan amount per month. Some states have statutory caps of 36 percent APR.[570]
- *Repayment period.* Payday loans typically have a short repayment period that results in rollovers, fees, and more interest that has to be paid.[571]
- *Balloon- or multiple-payment structure.* Balloon payments by effect trap the borrower into repeat loans that multiply fees and interest.
- *Origination fee.* The origination fee for taking out a loan will vary among lenders. Some do not charge any, while others may charge $5 per $50 loan, or more. Some states regulate the imposition of origination fees.[572]
- *Rollover fees.* The availability of renewing or rolling over debt is one of the easiest ways for a borrower to slide into default, incur more fees, and fall into a cycle of debt.
- *Refinancing options.* Refinancing provides the lender with another opportunity to impose fees on the borrowers.
- *State laws.* Payday loans are illegal in some states.[573] Other states have laws that regulate usury. Some states place caps on payday loan rates, but some states do not.[574] Moreover, some payday lenders sidestep state regulation by partnering with banks in a practice called rent-a-bank or charter renting. In states where there are no caps on consumer loans, the banks underwrite the loans while the payday lenders act as loan originators and collection agents.[575]
- *Online payday lending.* Online payday lending makes it very easy to apply for and obtain a loan. Online loans often result in even steeper fees. Half of online borrowers who failed a payment request were charged an average of $185 in overdraft and other fees. Resulting bank fees caused one-third of borrowers having their accounts closed involuntarily.[576]

In short, the payday loan industry seeks to make the borrower a habitual customer and engage in repeat borrowing. Lenders have an economic incentive to make the borrowing process seem as easy as possible while obscuring the interest rate and other state regulations. These lenders might also not ask the borrower the purpose of the loan and get only partial information on the borrower's ability to pay. Some lenders offer reward programs, offering $5 or $10 off the next loan through points systems. At many places, clerks may try to "upsell" borrowers, persuading them to borrow more than they need. Keep in mind that there are alternative credit options to payday lending, and they are cheaper.[577]

What is an "account advance"?

Some banks and credit unions offer "account advances," which in reality are loans that share many of the same harmful characteristics of payday loans. Often banks will offer "account advances" to customers who have their wages or benefit checks deposited directly into their checking accounts. If customers sign up for these plans, the bank automatically repays itself the advance when the next deposit is received. However, in the process, the bank may overdraw the account and trigger overdraft fees. At U.S. Bank, Wells Fargo, and Fifth Third, these loans carry an APR with fees of approximately 240 percent.[578] Like payday lending, these account advances have a balloon-payment structure; moreover, the bank sidesteps legal protections through its contract with the consumer permitting it to seize portions of the borrower's paycheck or exempt funds and without regard to whether the borrower needs the account funds for necessities.[579]

INFORMATION BOX: PAYDAY LOAN DEFAULTS

Important things to remember if a borrower defaults on a payday loan—and one study found that 46 percent of payday borrowers defaulted in their first year of borrowing:[580]

- Remember that payday loans are unsecured debt. This means that the debt is not tied to any assets such as a house or car. If a borrower defaults, the lender has no legal claim on any of the borrower's assets, even if debt collectors threaten such actions.
- Some payday lenders may bring civil lawsuits to collect on the debt. Some states permit a court to award treble damages in favor of a winning creditor. Moreover, if the borrower loses, the action may appear in a credit report and affect the consumer's credit score.
- Even without going to court, falling behind on payday loans or defaulting can affect the consumer's ability to borrow in the future. While payday loans generally do not show up on credit reports, lenders can access specialty credit reporting services like Teletrack (a credit reporting agency that caters specifically to payday lenders, auto title lenders, rent-to-own agencies, and similar fringe financing businesses) when considering future loans. In addition, if the lender sells the borrower's debt to a debt collector, the collector may report the debt to a major credit reporting agency, which would then risk affecting the borrower's credit score.

What federal laws regulate payday loans?

Many of the federal statutes discussed in this chapter cover payday loans.[581]

The Truth in Lending Act (TILA) applies to payday loans.[582] The purpose of the TILA is to promote the informed use of consumer credit through the requirement of disclosures about terms and costs, and protects consumers in certain situations. The TILA desires to standardize how terms of consumer credit agreements are communicated, and provides for statutory and actual damages. Under the TILA, payday loans are classified as "closed-end" credit because the loan requires a single payment or installment payments.[583] This is opposed to "open-end credit" where the loan may be used repeatedly until a certain limit, such as "lines of credit" or "revolving lines of credit."

As a type of closed-end credit, payday loans are subject to disclosure requirements of Section 1638 of the TILA.[584] Disclosure requirements include:

- The interest charge as a dollar amount ("finance charge") as well as an "annual percentage rate," using this term (if the loan is over $75 and if the finance charge is over $5).
- The number, amount, and due dates or period of payments scheduled to repay the total (original loan amount plus any charges).
- Descriptive explanations for terms such as "amount financed," "finance charge," "annual percentage rate," "total of payments," and "total sale price."
- Any dollar charge or percentage amount imposed on account of late payment.

Furthermore, the Board of Governors of the Federal Reserve Board has promulgated a comprehensive set of rules, Regulation Z, as a companion to the TILA, imposing still other disclosure requirements:[585]

- Lenders must provide correct responses to oral inquiries about the cost of credit, including the annual percentage rate (APR). Lenders might say that they do not know the APR but only the short-term interest rate. However, the borrower should know that lenders can often easily obtain the APR by using simple computer programs.
- Similarly, if a lender advertises the finance charges by posting a fee schedule, the lender must include the APR, using the term "annual percentage rate."
- Before signing an agreement, the lender must also disclose both the dollar amount of the cost of credit (finance charge) and the APR. TILA regulations require the disclosures to be made "clearly and conspicuously in writing, in

a form that the consumer may keep" and that such disclosures shall be made "before the consummation of the transaction."[586]

Statutory damages are available once a violation of the TILA has been established without regard to whether actual injury has occurred.[587] Actual compensatory damages are also available, although much harder to prove. Damages are usually sought through class actions.

Payday loans may be vulnerable under the Equal Credit Opportunity Act, if the lender discourages or discriminates against credit applicants on an impermissible basis, such as race or public assistance status. In addition, the Fair Credit Reporting Act requires the lender to provide notice to a consumer when it declines a credit application or takes an adverse action based on information received from a consumer reporting agency (such as a bad-check list).[588] The Fair Debt Collection Practices Act would not apply to debts collected by the creditor, but if the bank provides payday loans through a third party, the third party may become liable under the FDCPA if it collects defaulted loans on behalf of the bank.

Finally, the federal Consumer Financial Protection Bureau (CFPB) has broad power to regulate fringe financing markets.[589] These powers include creation of a research unit to study the impact of alternative financing on underserved communities and underbanked consumers; monitoring and supervision;[590] rulemaking to enforce federal consumer protection laws and to identify "unlawful, unfair, deceptive, or abusive acts or practices"; and enforcement power through civil penalties. The act also establishes a consumer hotline for violations, which will allow the CFPB to gather information and better seek out violations. The CFPB's enforcement activities have been tied up in litigation.[591]

In 2017, the CFPB published a payday lending rule, which was to be effective January 2018.[592] With some exceptions,[593] the rule covers short-term loans with terms of 45 days or less, short-term auto title loans, and longer-term loans if they require balloon payments or meet other conditions.[594] Generally, the rule requires a lender to determine a borrower's ability to repay before making the loan. The rule also seeks to prevent abusive practices by capping the number of short-term loans that can be made in succession, curbing additional withdrawals after a certain number of failed attempts to obtain payment by the lender, and making it more difficult for lenders to push for reborrowing or refinancing.[595] On February 6, 2019, the CFPB under the Trump administration proposed to amend the rule and to delay portions of its implementation.[596]

In particular, requiring an assessment of a consumer's ability to pay as a condition of extending a payday loan is an essential feature of any fair and reasonable debt instrument; withdrawing that requirement is a green light for lenders to target low-income consumers with unfair and abusive predatory lending practices that have, and will continue to cause, extreme harm.[597]

What are auto title loans?

Auto title loans are secured by a lien on the borrower's vehicle. Like a pawn shop loan, this loan is completely asset-based, and the ability to repay is not part of the vetting process. Lenders usually request a copy of the borrower's car keys. Some lenders may require due diligence such as job history and a proven ability to repay the loan, but most are simply interested in a clean title.[598]

Title loans are extremely oversecured loans. This means that the value of the vehicle (the collateral) that secures the loan is much greater than the actual amount the borrower may receive. Lenders may claim that they lend up to 50 percent of the value of the borrower's vehicle, but, according to one survey of New Mexico, the reality is that the loan is typically between 25 percent and 40 percent of the vehicle's value.[599]

Much like payday loans, rollovers for title loans result in high profits for lenders and great harm for borrowers. The resulting fees and interest may result in the borrower quickly repaying as much as they borrowed without paying off any of the principal. Lenders with alternative models that structure repayments in installments over a period of time may be more forgiving. Some lenders may claim to charge no fee for early repayment. However, the borrower should be cautious about the actual terms, as the lender may still require that the repayment include all the interest that would have been due had the loan not been repaid early. There also may be a lien fee for the purpose of registering the lien with the state's Department of Motor Vehicles (DMV).

Finally, the borrower's car may be repossessed. A 2016 study found that 20 percent of borrowers have their vehicle seized when they do not pay the loan in full. Furthermore, four out of five title loans are reborrowed because borrowers cannot afford the single balloon repayment required by lenders. In this way, more than half of auto title loan borrowers take out four or more consecutive loans trying to repay the initial loan and reborrowing fees.[600]

What are pawn shops?

Pawn dealers give borrowers a loan based on an item of personal property. When the loan is repaid, the personal property is returned. If the debtor defaults, the property is forfeited.[601] In other words, the debt is self-liquidating.

Will a default on a title loan or the pawn shop be included on a credit report?

With secured loans that use assets as collateral (such as pawning items and title loans), lenders typically will not check the consumer's credit history, and loans are not reported to credit bureaus. These loans are based on the value of the assets and not based on the debtor's credit (as banking loans are). However, a debtor must be careful that, in prioritizing these secured loans (so as not to lose a car), the debtor does not fall behind on payments that *can* affect a credit report (such as payday loans).

Keep in mind, however, that if a debtor falls behind in payment, or a car is repossessed but does not cover the full amount of the debt, the pawn shop or lending company may choose to sue for the remaining amount in a civil action court. If the court rules against the debtor and the debtor fails to pay the amount determined by the court, this information—the "judgment debt"—will be appear in a credit report.[602]

Are there other kinds of fringe financing?

Other examples of fringe financing include:

- Rent-to-own companies allow borrowers to rent goods, such as appliances or furniture, through installment payment plans at extremely inflated prices. Repayment installments range from one week to monthly or more, and can be aligned with the borrower's paydays. Many states treat the transaction as a lease and not a credit sale. If the consumer can no longer finish paying the installments, the consumer returns the good and terminates the agreement, forfeiting all payments without having built up any equity interest.[603]
- Refund anticipation loans (RALs) or simply, tax refund loans, are short-term loans in anticipation of the borrower's tax refunds and are extremely costly to the borrower. These loans are made by commercial tax preparers who have a contractual arrangement with a bank. The bank extends the loan and opens a temporary bank account in which the borrower will arrange for the IRS to direct-deposit the refund. The banks charge interest subject to state interest rate caps (or lack of) and also charge a tax preparation fee, an electronic tax refund filing fee, and a loan fee to the bank making the loan. Changes in IRS rules have reduced the availability of refund anticipation loans.[604]

Tax Collection by the United States

What rules govern the collection of unpaid taxes by the United States?

The Fair Debt Collection Practices Act (discussed earlier in this chapter) does not govern the United States when it seeks to collect unpaid taxes. However, federal law requires tax collection practices to be "fair." Taxpayers cannot be contacted at unusual, inconvenient times or places, or at work if the Secretary of the Internal Revenue Service (acting as collector) knows that their employer prohibits such contact.[605] If a taxpayer is known to be represented by an attorney, the Secretary generally must contact that attorney rather than the taxpayer directly.[606]

The Secretary also is prohibited from engaging in harassment or abuse of taxpayers during the debt collection process. Harassment or abuse includes:

1. The use or threat of use of violence or other criminal means to harm the physical person, reputation, or property of any person;
2. The use of obscene or profane language or language the natural consequence of which is to abuse the hearer or reader;
3. Causing a telephone to ring or engaging any person in telephone conversation repeatedly or continuously with intent to annoy, abuse, or harass any person at the called number; and
4. Placing telephone calls without meaningful disclosure of the caller's identity.[607]

If a taxpayer experiences any of these activities, the taxpayer may file a claim with the Internal Revenue Service.[608] The claim should be in writing and addressed "to the Area Director, Attn: Compliance Technical Support Manager of the area in which the taxpayer currently resides."[609] The claim must include:

1. The name, current address, current home and work telephone numbers and any convenient times to be contacted, and taxpayer identification number of the taxpayer making the claim;
2. The grounds, in reasonable detail, for the claim (include copies of any available substantiating documentation or correspondence with the Internal Revenue Service);
3. A description of the injuries incurred by the taxpayer filing the claim (include copies of any available substantiating documentation or evidence);
4. The dollar amount of the claim, including any damages that have not yet been incurred but which are reasonably foreseeable (include copies of any available substantiating documentation or evidence); and

5. The signature of the taxpayer or duly authorized representative. For purposes of this paragraph, a duly authorized representative is any attorney, certified public accountant, enrolled actuary, or any other person permitted to represent the taxpayer before the Internal Revenue Service who is not disbarred or suspended from practice before the Internal Revenue Service and who has a written power of attorney executed by the taxpayer.[610]

If the administrative process does not provide the requested relief, the taxpayer can file a lawsuit against the United States in a federal district court,[611] and the lawsuit must be filed within two years of the first violation.[612] If the taxpayer wins the lawsuit, damages may be awarded in the amount of "actual, direct economic damages" the taxpayer suffered, plus the cost the taxpayer incurred in the process of bringing the lawsuit; however, the amount awarded to the taxpayer cannot exceed $1 million, or $100,000 if the government's violations were unintentional.[613] The damages available to taxpayers do not include emotional or physical damages that might result from harassment, only economic damages (like higher interest rates as the result of a poor credit rating).

Can the government file a lien on property to collect taxes?

Yes, the government can file a lien on property to collect taxes, but it must comply with certain requirements when doing so.[614] If the Secretary files a notice of lien, written notice must be given to the taxpayer.[615] The notice must state:

1. The amount of unpaid tax;
2. The right of the person to request a hearing during the 30-day period beginning on the day after the five-day period after the filing of the notice of lien;
3. The administrative appeals available to the taxpayer with respect to the lien and the procedure relating to such appeals; and
4. Information about release of liens on the property.[616]

Federal law makes specific property exempt from a tax lien. These properties include wearing apparel and schoolbooks; fuel, provisions, furniture, and personal effects, not to exceed $500 in value; and books and tools of a trade, business, or profession, not to exceed $250 in value. Federal law does not specifically exempt Social Security benefits for Old Age and Survivor's Insurance from a tax levy. However, any levy is limited to 15 percent of the monthly Social Security payment.[617]

Will the government offer repayment options to the taxpayer?

A taxpayer who cannot afford to pay the taxes due can pursue three different alternatives with the Internal Revenue Service.[618]

The IRS can approve a monthly installment agreement for payment. This option is almost always available through a streamlined process for a taxpayer who owes less than $50,000.[619] Penalties and fees continue to accrue until the taxes due are paid in full. A waiver of penalties is available. If the amount owed is less than $25,000 and the installment agreement contemplates full payment in six years or less, the IRS will not file a lien and, in any event, generally will not take an enforcement action while the plan is in effect.

Another option is to negotiate a reduced payment through the IRS's "offer-in-compromise" program. Generally, a taxpayer who can pay the liability through an installment agreement does not qualify for this option.[620]

In addition, the taxpayer may be eligible for "currently not collectible" status, which halts collection, although interest and penalties continue to accrue. CNC status defers payment if, after payment, the taxpayer would not have any income in light of allowable monthly living expenses.[621] While the taxpayer has CNC status, the IRS may file a tax lien if the taxpayer owes more than $10,000.[622]

Where can taxpayers get help with tax problems?

For assistance in finding the area director's contact information, and other assistance with tax problems, taxpayers can contact the Office of the Taxpayer Advocate. The Office of the Taxpayer Advocate is an independent office within the IRS, which provides free assistance to qualifying taxpayers who are struggling to resolve a tax problem through normal IRS channels.[623] In addition, help may be available through legal services clinics that specialize in tax matters.[624] Keep in mind that persons with earned income may be eligible for the Earned Income Tax Credit, discussed in chapter 2, which requires that a tax return be filed even if no tax is due.

Notes

1. The U.S. Constitution refers to government debt, but that is different from a consumer's personal debt. *See, for example*, U.S. Const. Amend. XIV, § 4 ("[t]he validity of the public debt of the United States . . . shall not be questioned"). Moreover, the Constitution prevents the states from passing any law "impairing the Obligation of Contracts" or "make any Thing but gold and silver Coin a Tender in Payment of Debts." U.S. Const. Art. I, § 10, cl. 1.

2. *See, for example*, Sniadach v. Family Finance Corp., 395 U.S. 337 (1969).

3. *See, for example*, Timbs v. Indiana, 586 U.S. ___, 139 S. Ct. 682 (2019 (discussing Eighth Amendment problems raised by civil forfeiture).

4. *See* U.S. Const. Art. I, § 8, cl. 3 (authorizing Congress "To regulate Commerce with foreign Nations, and among the several States, and with the Indian Tribes").

5. *See, for example*, 42 U.S.C. § 1981 ("All persons . . . shall have the same right . . . to make and enforce contracts . . . and to the full and equal benefit of all laws and proceedings for the security of persons and property as is enjoyed by white citizens").

6. *See* the discussion of the Fair Debt Collection Practices Act in this chapter.

7. *See* the discussion of the Fair Credit Reporting Act in this chapter. *See generally* Christine A. Varney, Consumer Privacy in the Information Age: A View from the United States, Federal Trade Commission (Oct. 9, 1996), https://www.ftc.gov/public-statements/1996/10/consumer-privacy-information-age-view-united-states; *see also* Federal Trade Commission, Privacy and Data Security Update: 2018, https://www.ftc.gov/system/files/documents/reports/privacy-data-security-update-2018/2018-privacy-data-security-report-508.pdf.

8. Chrystin Ondersma, A Human Rights Approach to Consumer Credit, 90 Tulane L. Rev. 373, 378 (2015) (stating that a human rights approach to financial security "provides a powerful, universal floor of protection for consumer debtors that cannot be circumvented on efficiency grounds"); *see also* Chrystin Ondersma, Consumer Financial Protection and Human Rights, 50 Cornell Int'l L.J. 543 (2017).

9. *See* Mechele Dickerson, Vanishing Financial Freedom, 61 Ala. L. Rev. 1079 (2010). *See, for example*, Michael S. Barr, Credit Where It Counts: The Community Reinvestment Act and Its Critics, 80 N.Y.U. L. Rev. 513 (2005) (historically credit markets have excluded low-income communities and minority households and advocates argue that credit, when extended, is offered on predatory terms); Cassandra Jones Havard, Democratizing Credit: Examining the Structural Inequities of Subprime Lending, 56 Syracuse L. Rev. 233 (2006). The potential criminal consequences of civil indebtedness are discussed in Tamar R. Birckhead, The New Peonage, 72 Wash. & Lee L. Rev. 1595 (2015); Kary L. Moss, Debtors' Prison in Michigan: The ACLU Takes Up the Cause, 89-Jul. Mich. B. J. 40 (2010).

10. *See* Iris Benöhr, EU Consumer Law and Human Rights (Oxford University Press 2013).

11. The Center for Responsible Lending has a "Stop the Debt Trap" campaign to encourage regulation of the payday and fringe financing industry. *See* Center for Responsible Lending, https://www.responsiblelending.org/.

12. The National Consumer Law Center publishes print and online resources on consumer and debtor issues. The NCLC offers Consumer Education Brochures free of charge that can be downloaded from its website, https://www.nclc.org/for-consumers/nclcs-consumer-education-brochures.html. The NCLC also publishes 21 consumer law treatises which offer up-to-date and detailed information about the programs discussed in this chapter. For information about the NCLC digital library, accessible through a fee-paid subscription, *see* https://library.nclc.org.

13. The statute is codified in Title VII of the Consumer Credit Protection Act, 15 U.S.C. §§ 1692–92p.

14. Maine Fair Debt Collection Practices Act, Me. Rev. Stat. Ann. § 11003.

15. *See* Thomas A. Durkin, Gregory Elliehausen, & Todd J. Zywicki, Consumer Credit and the American Economy: An Overview, 11 J.L. Econ. & Pol. 279, 280 (2015).

16. Consumer Financial Protection Bureau, Annual Report 2017, 13 (Mar. 20, 2017), https://files.consumerfinance.gov/f/documents/201703_cfpb_Fair-Debt-Collection-Practices-Act-Annual-Report.pdf. *See also* Federal Reserve Bank of New York, Quarterly Report on Household Debt and Credit (Feb. 2017), https://www.newyorkfed.org/medialibrary/interactives/householdcredit/data/pdf/HHDC_2016Q4.pdf.

17. Consumer Financial Protection Bureau, Annual Report 2018, 12–13 (Mar. 20, 2018), https://s3.amazonaws.com/files.consumerfinance.gov/f/documents/cfpb_fdcpa_annual-report-congress_03-2018.pdf.

18. *See* Consumer Financial Protection Bureau, Consumer Experiences with Debt Collection: Findings from the CFPB's Survey of Consumer Views on Debt, Table 3 Distribution of the Number of Debts Consumers Were Contacted About, by Annual Household Income (Percent); Table 6 Distribution of the Number of Debts Consumers Were Contacted About by Race and Ethnicity (Percent) (Jan. 12, 2017), https://s3.amazonaws.com/files.consumerfinance.gov/f/documents/201701_cfpb_Debt-Collection-Survey-Report.pdf. *See also* Catherine Ruetschlin & Dedrick Asante-Muhammad, The Challenge of Credit Card Debt for the African American Middle Class, Demos & NAACP 20 (Dec. 2013), https://www.demos.org/sites/default/files/publications/CreditCardDebt-Demos_NAACP_0.pdf.

19. Debt collectors make many mistakes. According to the Consumer Financial Protection Bureau, "More than half of consumers (fifty-three percent) who were contacted about a debt in collection in the past year indicated that the debt was not theirs, was owed by a family member, or was for the wrong amount." Consumer Financial Protection Bureau, Annual Report 2017, 62 (Mar. 20, 2017), https://s3.amazonaws.com/files.consumerfinance.gov/f/documents/201703_cfpb_Fair-Debt-Collection-Practices-Act-Annual-Report.pdf.

20. 15 U.S.C. § 1692a(5).

21. *See, for example*, Miller v. McCalla, Raymer, Padrick, Cobb, Nichols and Clark, L.L.C., 214 F.3d 872 (7th Cir. 2000).

22. For a discussion of what constitutes a consensual transaction for purposes of a covered debt, *see* Bass v. Stolper, Koritzinsky, Brewster & Neider, S.C., 111 F.3d 1322, 1326 (7th Cir. 1997).

23. *See, for example*, Orenbuch v. Leopold, Gross, & Sommers, P.C., 586 F. Supp. 2d 105 (E.D.N.Y. 2008). *See* Jim Hawkins, Law's Remarkable Failure to Protect Mistakenly Overpaid Employees, 99 Minn. L. Rev. 89 (2014).

24. In Romea v. Heiberger & Associates, 163 F.3d 111 (2d Cir. 1998), the Second Circuit Court of Appeals held that a three-day notice to pay rent or vacate the premises signed by an attorney was a debt covered by the FDCPA. *See* Eric M. Steven, From Landlord/Tenant to Debt Collector/Consumer and Back Again, 35 Gonzaga L. Rev. 175 (2000).

25. *See, for example*, Gulley v. Markoff & Krasny, 664 F.3d 1073 (7th Cir. 2011) (fines for violating real property provisions of a municipal code were not debts). However, in

Franklin v. Parking Revenue Recovery Services, Inc., 832 F.3d 741, 744 (7th Cir. 2016), the court found that parking "fines" were within the scope of the FDCPA. The district court had characterized the $45 nonpayment penalty assessed by the public parking lot as a "fine" and analogized the nonpayment to theft. *Id.* at 743. The court of appeals reversed, determining the source of the obligation to be "the contract that is formed when a customer parks in the lot." *Id.* at 744. Somewhat similarly, a district court in Brown v. Transurban USA, Inc., 144 F. Supp. 3d 809, 842 (E.D. Va. 2015), found that collection for toll violations was covered by the FDCPA. This determination turned on the fact that the violations were the result of faulty E-ZPass equipment, so the ultimate source of the obligation was the consensual transaction entered into when plaintiffs joined the E-ZPass program. According to the court, defendant's characterization of the assessment as fines "[did not] alter the nature of the underlying debt."

26. *See, for example*, Staub v. Harris, 626 F.2d 275 (3d Cir. 1980). The *Staub* court focused on the "transaction" requirement in the FDCPA definition of debt, holding that "at a minimum, the statute contemplates that the debt has arisen as a result of the rendition of a service or purchase of property or other item of value. The relationship between taxpayer and taxing authority does not encompass that type of pro tanto exchange which the statutory definition envisages." *Id.* at 278. In *Beggs v. Rossi*, 145 F.3d 511, 512 (2d Cir. 1998), the court declined to distinguish a property tax from the per capita tax at issue in *Staub*. In rejecting the argument that the tax on the plaintiff's vehicle was a "transaction-based tax," the court upheld the basic principle of *Staub* in excluding taxes from FDCPA protections.

27. *See, for example*, Torie Atkinson, A Fine Scheme: How Municipal Fines Become Crushing Debt in the Shadow of the New Debtors' Prisons, 51 Harv. C.R.-C.L. L. Rev. 189 (2016) (discussing fees and fines as a revenue-raising device and the disproportionate and negative impact of this practice on the poor and persons of color).

28. *Compare* Pollice v. National Tax Funding, L.P., 225 F.3d 379, 400 (3d Cir. 2000) (water and sewer charges owed to the government were debt), *with* Boyd v. J.E. Robert Co., Inc., 765 F.3d 123, 126 (2d Cir. 2014) ("the relationship between plaintiffs and the City with respect to such charges is akin to 'taxpayer and taxing authority'") (quoting Staub v. Harris, 626 F.2d 275 (3d Cir. 1980) (citing Beggs v. Rossi, 145 F.3d 511, 512 (2d Cir. 1998)); Betts v. Equifax Credit Information Services, Inc., 245 F. Supp.2d 1130, 1133 (W.D. Wash. 2003) (impoundment and towing fees were not debt).

29. 15 U.S.C. § 1692a(6).

30. An earlier version of the statute contained an express exemption for lawyers, but Congress later repealed that provision. *See* Heintz v. Jenkins, 514 U.S. 291 (1995). A lawyer who collects debts, like other debt collectors, may not mislead consumers, as described later in this chapter. In particular, a lawyer must make clear that any contact with the consumer is in the lawyer's capacity as debt collector, and not as attorney. *See* Jones v. Dufek, 830 F.3d 523, 527 (D.C. Cir. 2016) ("a prominent and clear disclaimer stating that an attorney is acting as a debt collector is enough, but a hidden or confusing disclaimer is not"); Greco v. Trauner, Cohen & Thomas, LLP, 412 F.3d 360, 364 (2d Cir. 2005) (language must make clear that the lawyer was not, "at the time of the letter's transmission, acting as an attorney").

31. 15 U.S.C. §1692j.
32. *See* Carter v. AMC, LLC, 645 F.3d 840 (7th Cir. 2011). A loan servicing company handles the billing of a loan, arranges for repayment options, and collects the interest and principal on the loan.
33. Barbato v. Greystone Alliance LLC, 916 F.3d 260 (3d Cir. 2019) (finding that debt purchaser that had collection of purchased debt as its principal business purpose was a debt collector regardless of whether it hired third-party services to collect debts).
34. 15 U.S.C. § 1692a(6)(D). *See* Sykes v. Mel S. Harris and Associates LLC, 780 F.3d 70, 84–87 (2d Cir. 2015).
35. 15 U.S.C. § 1692a(6)(E).
36. 15 U.S.C. §1692a(6)(C).
37. The U.S. Supreme Court had the opportunity to consider this question, but declined to rule, assuming for the sake of argument that special counsel were not exempt government officers (because even if, in this case, they were not officers, defendants would prevail). *See* Sheriff v. Gillie, 578 U.S. ___, 136 S. Ct. 1594, 1600 (2016). *See also* Brannan v. United Student Aid Funds, Inc., 94 F.3d 1260, 1263 (9th Cir. 1996) ("This exemption applies only to an individual government official or employee who collects debts as part of his government employment responsibilities. USA Funds is a private nonprofit organization with a government contract; it is not a government agency or employee"); Pollice v. National Tax Funding, L.P., 225 F.3d 379, 386, 406 (3d Cir. 2000) (exclusion did not apply to private company that had "contractual relationship with the government," even though the government "retain[ed] some measure of control" over the company's collection activities).
38. 15 U.S.C. § 1692a(4).
39. Henson v. Santander Consumer USA Inc., 582 U.S. ___, 137 S. Ct. 1718 (2017) (construing 15 U.S.C. § 1692a(6) "regularly collects" language but not addressing alternative "principal purpose" language).
40. 15 U.S.C. § 1692a. *See* Federal Trade Commission, The Structure and Practices of the Debt Buying Industry 3 (Jan. 2013), https://www.ftc.gov/sites/default/files/documents/reports/structure-and-practices-debt-buying-industry/debtbuyingreport.pdf.
41. 15 U.S.C. §1692a(6). *See, for example*, Vincent v. The Money Store, 736 F.3d 88, 91 (2d Cir. 2013) ("Where a creditor, in the process of collecting its own debts, hires a third party for the express purpose of representing to its debtors that the third party is collecting the creditor's debts, and the third party engages in no *bona fide* efforts to collect those debts, the false name exception exposes the creditor to FDCPA liability.").
42. 15 U.S.C. § 1692a(3) & (5).
43. *See, for example*, Muir v. Navy Federal Credit Union, 529 F.3d 1100 (D.C. Cir. 2008) (act applied to debtor's son).
44. 15 U.S.C. § 1692c(d).
45. *See, for example*, Todd v. Collecto, Inc., 731 F.3d 734, 737 (7th Cir. 2013):

> In enacting the FDCPA, Congress specified that a "group of people who do not owe money, but who may be deliberately harassed are the family, employer and

neighbors of the consumer. These people are also protected by this bill." H.R. Rep. No. 95-131, at 8 (1977).

This intent to extend protection beyond consumers is clearly embodied in § 1692k(a), the liability provision, which specifies that "any debt collector who fails to comply with any provision of this subchapter *with respect to any person* is liable to such person." (Emphasis added.) Similarly, § 1692d says that a "debt collector may not engage in any conduct the natural consequence of which is to harass, oppress, or abuse *any person* in connection with the collection of a debt." (Emphasis added.) [Alterations in original.]

> *See also* Dunham v. Portfolio Recovery Associates, LLC, 663 F.3d 997, 1002 (8th Cir. 2011), citing FTC Staff Commentary, 53 Fed. Reg. 50097-02, 50106 (Dec. 13, 1988) ("[a] debt collector must verify a disputed debt even if he has included proof of the debt with the first communication, because the section is intended to assist the consumer when a debt collector inadvertently contacts the wrong consumer at the start of his collection efforts").

46. *See* Elwin Griffith, The Role of Validation and Communication in the Debt Collection Process, 43 Creighton L. Rev. 429, 433 (2010) (stating that the FDCPA "responds to the possibility that the collector may be pursuing the wrong person or seeking to collect a debt that the consumer has already paid").

47. 15 U.S.C. §1692(a).

48. *See* Shimek v. Forbes, 374 F.3d 1011, 1104 (11th Cir. 2004).

49. 15 U.S.C. § 1692e(11).

50. 15 U.S.C. § 1692g. Using a court pleading as the collector's first contact does not eliminate the requirement of providing the validation notice. *See* 15 U.S.C. § 1692g(d). For a discussion of this rule, *see* Brian Koontz, Creditor Certainty and Consumer Protection: Complaints as Initial Communications under the Fair Debt Collection Practices Act, 11 N.C. Banking Inst. 289 (2007).

51. 15 U.S.C. § 1692g(a)(1) & (2).

52. 15 U.S.C. § 1692(g)(a)(3). This section does not specify whether the consumer must raise the dispute in writing. A circuit split exists on whether oral disputes stop the collection process. *See* Daniel O'Connell, Confounded Collectors, Confused Consumers: Time to Close the Circuit Split on Whether the Fair Debt Collection Practices Act Requires a Consumer to Dispute a Debt in Writing, 64 Cath. U. L. Rev. 1075 (2015).

53. 15 U.S.C. § 1692g(a)(4).

54. 15 U.S.C. § 1692g(a)(5).

55. Swanson v. Southern Oregon Credit Service, Inc., 869 F.2d 1222, 1225 (9th Cir. 1988) ("the notice must be conveyed effectively to the debtor").

56. Clomon v. Jackson, 988 F.2d 1314, 1318 (2d Cir. 1993). *But see* Blackwell v. Professional Business Services, of Georgia, Inc., 526 F. Supp. 535, 538 (N.D. Ga. 1981) (applying a "reasonable consumer" standard), criticized by Wright v. Credit Bureau of Georgia, Inc., 555 F. Supp. 1005, 1007 (N.D .Ga. 1983):

> This court has not rejected out-of-hand the "reasonable consumer" standard. Instead, this court declined to follow the *Blackwell* court only to the extent that

the *Blackwell* reasonable consumer standard may be applied in a manner that does not take into account that the recipients of a debt collector's letters include both unsophisticated and sophisticated consumers. This court considers the term "reasonable consumer" an appropriate appellation for the objective standard to be applied, so long as that standard encompasses protection for "the unsophisticated or uneducated consumer." *See Bustamante v. First Federal Savings & Loan Ass'n*, 619 F.2d 360, 364 (5th Cir. 1980).

57. *See, for example*, Muha v. Encore Receivable Management, Inc., 558 F.3d 623, 630 (7th Cir. 2009) (reversed dismissal of action and remanded for further proceedings where "confusing statement did not appear in or adjacent to the notice of the plaintiffs' right to challenge the debt" and was not "a flat-out contradiction of anything in the letter, though this depends on just what an unsophisticated consumer would understand it to mean"); Terran v. Kaplan, 109 F.3d 1428 (9th Cir. 1997) (no violation where notice used same-size font and did not require immediate payment).

58. Swanson v. Southern Oregon Credit Service, Inc., 869 F.2d 1222, 1225–27 (9th Cir. 1988).

59. Sims v. GC Services, L.P., 445 F.3d 959, 964 (7th Cir. 2006).

60. 15 U.S.C. § 1692g(e).

61. Caprio v. Healthcare Revenue Recovery Group, LLC, 709 F.3d 142 (3d Cir. 2013); Miller v. Payco-General American Credits, Inc., 943 F.2d 482 (4th Cir. 1991).

62. *See, for example*, Durkin v. Equifax Check Services, Inc., 406 F.3d 410 (7th Cir. 2005). Some advocates have urged that the Consumer Financial Protection Bureau adopt regulations setting out a simplified notice. *See* National Consumer Law Center Comments to the Bureau of Consumer Financial Protection (Feb. 28, 2014), https://www.nclc.org/news-archive/comments.html. The CFPB has not done so. Instead, during the Trump administration, the CFPB published a proposed rule that would permit a debt collector, among other things, to place "a telephone call to a person . . . seven times within a seven-day period" about each debt. *See* Consumer Financial Protection Bureau, Proposed Rule—Debt Collection Practices (Regulation F), 84 Fed. Reg. 23274 (May 21, 2019). *See also* National Consumer Law Center, Protect Consumers from Harassing and Abusive Debt Collection Tactics, https://www.nclc.org/take-action/take-action-debt-collection-rule.html. The comment period was scheduled to close August 19, 2019.

63. *See* Jeff Sovern & Kate E. Walton, Are Validation Notices Valid? An Empirical Evaluation of Consumer Understanding of Debt Collection Validation Notices, 70 SMU L. Rev. 63 (2017). The authors surveyed consumers by showing them the validation notice that the Seventh Circuit Court of Appeals had upheld in Zemeckis v. Global Credit & Collection Corp., 679 F.3d 632 (7th Cir. 2012), cert. denied, 568 U.S. 999 (2012), and concluded that under standards set out by the Federal Trade Commission, the notice would have been found deceptive.

64. 15 U.S.C. § 1692g(b).

65. 15 U.S.C. § 1692g(a)(3). However, if the debt collector sues the consumer in court, the consumer's failure to dispute the debt will not count as an admission of liability. 15 U.S.C. § 1692g(c). Rather, the debt collector will have the burden to verify the debt's validity and the amount owed before the court may enter judgment against the consumer. 15 U.S.C. § 1692g(b).

66. 15 U.S.C. § 1692g(b). *See* Elwin Griffith, The Challenge of Communicating with the Consumer and Validating the Debt Under the Fair Debt Collection Practices Act, 55 U. Kan. L. Rev. 61 (2006), explaining that § 1692g requires:

> . . . a debt collector to notify the consumer that if the consumer disputes the debt in writing, the debt collector will seek verification thereof from the creditor. . . . There is nothing in the statute that requires the collector to suspend its activities during the thirty days granted to the consumer for disputing the debt, because that period is not a grace period.

Id. at 65 & n.23 (citing Mezines, FTC Advisory Opinion (Mar. 31, 2000)). *See, for example*, Jacobson v. Healthcare Financial Services, Inc., 516 F.3d 85, 91 (2d Cir. 2008), in which the appeals court explained that although "a debt collector is, as a general matter, entitled to demand immediate payment of a debt, and to threaten further action in the event of non-payment," in some contexts "such demands may cause confusion about the right to dispute, and will sometimes, in that way, lead debt collectors to run afoul of the Act."

67. 15 U.S.C. § 1692g(b); *but compare* 15 U.S.C. § 1692g(a)(3). *See* Elwin Griffith, The Role of Validation and Communication in the Debt Collection Process, 43 Creighton L. Rev. 429, 433–434 n.28 (2010):

> If the consumer disputes the debt in writing, the debt collector must suspend its collection activities until it gives the consumer written verification of the debt. If the consumer disputes the debt orally, the collector does not have any obligation to verify the debt, but the collector cannot thereafter assume that the debt is valid. Although a consumer's oral dispute of the debt does not impose any obligation on the debt collector to respond to the consumer, at least it signals to the collector that there may be something wrong with its claim and that it may want to investigate the matter further.

And further noting:

> Despite the omission of a writing requirement in section 1692g(a)(3), some courts have held that the section does require a consumer to dispute the debt in writing. See Graziano v. Harrison, 950 F.2d 107, 112 (3d Cir. 1991); Wallace v. Capital One Bank, 168 F. Supp. 2d 888, 894–895 (D. Md. 2001); Sturdevant v. Jolas, 942 F. Supp. 426, 429 (W.D. Wis. 1996). However, the Ninth Circuit and the majority of district courts have found that section 1692g(a)(3) does not require a writing. See Camacho v. Bridgeport Financial, Inc., 430 F.3d 1078, 1081–82 (9th Cir. 2005); Register v. Reiner, Reiner & Bendett, PC, 488 F. Supp. 2d 143, 147 (D. Conn. 2007); Jerman v. Carlisle, McNellie, Rini, Kramer & Ulrich, 464 F. Supp. 2d 720 (N.D. Ohio 2006); Rosado v. Taylor, 324 F. Supp. 2d 917 (N.D. Ind. 2004); Sambor v. Omnia Credit Servs., Inc. 183 F. Supp. 2d 1234, 1240 n. 4 (D. Haw. 2002); Sanchez v. Robert E. Weiss, Inc., 173 F. Supp. 2d 1029 (N.D. Cal. 2001); Ong v. Am. Collections Enter., Inc., No. 98-CV-5117 (JG), 1999 WL 51816 (E.D.N.Y. Jan. 15 1999).

68. Consumer Financial Protection Bureau, Ask CFPB/ Debt Collection, What should I do when a debt collector contacts me? (Feb. 2, 2017), http://www.consumerfinance.gov/askcfpb/1695/ive-been-contacted-debt-collector-how-do-i-reply.html. Sample letters also are contained in National Consumer Law Center, Surviving Debt: Expert Advice for Getting Out of Financial Trouble (2019).

69. 15 U.S.C. § 1692c(a). A court can give permission for collection-related contact. *See id.*
70. 15 U.S.C. § 1692c(a).
71. 15 U.S.C. § 1692c(d).
72. 15 U.S.C. § 1692a(2).
73. 15 U.S.C. § 1692c(a)(1).
74. 15 U.S.C. § 1692c(a)(2). Communication with the consumer is permitted if the attorney fails "within the reasonable period of time" to respond to the collector's contact. *Id.*
75. 15 U.S.C. § 1692c(a)(3).
76. 15 U.S.C. § 1692c(c).
77. *See, for example,* Szczurek v. Professional Management Inc., 627 Fed. Appx. 57 (3d Cir. 2015).
78. Isham v. Gurstel, Staloch & Chargo, P.A., 738 F. Supp. 2d 986, 994 (D. Ariz. 2010). *See* Hilgenberg v. Elggren & Peterson, 2015 WL 4077765, *6 (D. Utah 2015) (finding a violation when the consumer's letter stated that the law firm should not make any more phone calls and that all communications "need to be by mail"; the consumer did not need to quote the language of the statute); Bishop v. I.C. System, Inc., 713 F. Supp. 2d 1361, 1363, 1367–68 (M.D. Fla. 2010) (holding consumer's letter stating "Any further correspondence from your organization or any other collection agency will be discarded or returned to you unopened" was sufficient to notify the collector that it should cease communications).
79. 15 U.S.C. § 1692c(c).
80. 15 U.S.C. § 1692c(c)(1), (2), & (3).
81. *See* Rush v. Portfolio Recovery Associates, 977 F. Supp. 2d 414 (D. N.J. 2013) (collecting cases).
82. *Compare* Edwards v. Niagara Credit Solutions, Inc., 586 F. Supp. 2d 1346 (N.D. Ga. 2008), aff'd, 584 F.3d 1350 (11th Cir. 2009) (prerecorded phone messages left on consumer's answering machine, which did not reveal they were from a debt collector, violated the FDCPA), *with* Biggs v. Credit Collections, Inc., 2007 WL 4034997, at *4 (W.D. Okla. 2007) (voicemails did not constitute "communication" because they did not convey information regarding a debt).
83. Lewis v. ACB Business Services, Inc., 135 F.3d 389 (6th Cir. 1998).
84. Evory v. RJM Acquisitions Funding L.L.C., 505 F.3d 769 (7th Cir. 2007); Goswami v. American Collections Enterprise, Inc., 377 F.3d 488 (5th Cir. 2004).
85. 15 U.S.C. § 1692b. In any communication with a third party to obtain "location information about the consumer," the debt collector must:

   (1) identify himself, state that he is confirming or correcting location information concerning the consumer, and, only if expressly requested, identify his employer;
   (2) not state that such consumer owes any debt;
   (3) not communicate with any such person more than once unless requested to do so by such person or unless the debt collector reasonably believes that the earlier response of such person is erroneous or incomplete and that such person now has correct or complete location information;

(4) not communicate by post card;

(5) not use any language or symbol on any envelope or in the contents of any communication effected by the mails or telegram that indicates that the debt collector is in the debt collection business or that the communication relates to the collection of a debt[.]

See also 15 U.S.C. § 1692b(1)–(5).

86. 15 U.S.C. §1692e.

87. *Compare* Bailey v. Security National Servicing Corp., 154 F.3d 384 (7th Cir. 1998) (letter advising of the status of account and amounts due was informational where respondents were servicing a current payment plan and not demanding payment on a defaulted loan), *with* Mennes v. Capital One, N.A., 2014 WL 1767079 (W.D. Wis. 2014) (at the pleading stage, allegations that letter advised consumer of unpaid balance sufficiently stated a claim that the communication was sent in connection with an attempt to collect a debt).

88. Gburek v. Litton Loan Servicing LP, 614 F.3d 380, 384 (7th Cir. 2010) ("Neither this circuit nor any other has established a bright-line rule for determining whether a communication from a debt collector was made in connection with the collection of any debt.").

89. Hart v. FCI Lender Services, Inc., 797 F.3d 219 (2d Cir. 2015).

90. Powell v. Palisades Acquisition XVI, LLC, 782 F.3d 119 (4th Cir. 2014).

91. The legislative history states:

> Collection abuse takes many forms, including obscene or profane language, threats of violence, telephone calls at unreasonable hours, misrepresentation of a consumer's legal rights, disclosing a consumer's personal affairs to friends, neighbors, or an employer, obtaining information about a consumer through false pretense, impersonating public officials and attorneys, and simulating legal process.
>
> S. Rep. No. 382, 95th Cong., 1st Sess. (1977), reprinted in 1977 U.S.C.C.A.N. 1695, 1696.

92. 15 U.S.C. § 1692d.

93. 15 U.S.C. § 1692e.

94. 15 U.S.C. § 1692c(a)(1).

95. 15 U.S.C. § 1692j.

96. 15 U.S.C. § 1692f.

97. 15 U.S.C. § 1692d.

98. 15 U.S.C. § 1692d(1).

99. 15 U.S.C. § 1692d(2).

100. 15 U.S.C. § 1692d(5).

101. 15 U.S.C. § 1692d(6). *See also* Costa v. National Action Financial Services, 634 F. Supp. 2d 1069, 1075 (E.D. Cal. 2007) (holding that "meaningful disclosure" under § 1692d(6) is disclosure of the collector's identity and the nature of the business about which the collector is calling).

102. Diaz v. D.L. Recovery Corp., 486 F. Supp. 2d 474, 477 (E.D. Penn. 2007) (refusing to grant a defendant's motion to dismiss for failure to state a claim, saying that even if

the defendant's alleged conduct did not fall under § 1692d(1), it might still be harassment and be prohibited by § 1692d generally).

103. "[C]laims under § 1692d should be viewed from the perspective of a consumer whose circumstances makes him relatively more susceptible to harassment, oppression, or abuse." Jeter v. Credit Bureau, Inc., 760 F.2d 1168, 1179 (11th Cir. 1985).

104. 15 U.S.C. § 1692e.

105. 15 U.S.C. § 1692e(1): "The false representation or implication that the debt collector is vouched for, bonded by, or affiliated with the United States or any State, including the use of any badge, uniform, or facsimile thereof."

106. 15 U.S.C. § 1692e(2)(A). *See, for example,* Pacheco v. Joseph McMahon Corp., 698 F. Supp. 2d 291, 296 (D. Conn. 2010) (holding that a statement that the consumer would incur "a 'fortune in legal fees,'" when legal fees were actually capped at $300 was a violation of § 1692e(2)).

107. 15 U.S.C. § 1692e(2)(B).

108. 15 U.S.C. § 1692e(3). *See also* Rosenau v. Unifund Corp., 539 F.3d 218, 223 (3d Cir. 2008) (holding that collector's letter which stated that it came from the "Legal Department" may violate § 1692e(3) because it is possible that it would mislead a reasonable consumer into believing a lawyer was involved in the case).

109. 15 U.S.C. § 1692e(4).

110. 15 U.S.C. § 1692e(4).

111. 15 U.S.C. § 1692e(5).

112. 15 U.S.C. § 1692e(7).

113. 15 U.S.C. § 1692e(8).

114. 15 U.S.C. § 1692e(9).

115. 15 U.S.C. § 1692e(13).

116. 15 U.S.C. § 1692e(15).

117. 15 U.S.C. § 1692e(14).

118. 15 U.S.C. § 1692e(16).

119. 15 U.S.C. § 1692e.

120. For example, the Third Circuit Court of Appeals found that a law firm violated the FDCPA by sending collection letters on firm letterhead, for it falsely implied that an attorney, acting as an attorney, was involved in the collection process. *See* Lesher v. Law Offices of Mitchell N. Kay, PC, 650 F.3d 993 (3d Cir. 2011), cert. denied, 565 U.S. 1185 (2012). However, the Third Circuit later distinguished *Lesher,* finding no violation by the lawyer when a collection letter, although on law firm letterhead, was not reviewed by a lawyer, was not signed by a lawyer, and stated it was from a debt collector. Daniels v. Solomon & Solomon P.C., 751 Fed. Appx. 254 (3d Cir. 2018).

121. *See* 15 U.S.C. §1692j (barring the design, compiling, and furnishing of a form "used to create the false belief in a consumer that a person other than the creditor . . . is participating" in collection of the debt, "when in fact such person is not so participating"). *See, for example,* Sokolski v. Trans Union Corp., 53 F. Supp. 2d 307, 312 (E.D.N.Y. 1999) ("[A] creditor participating in [a] flat-rating arrangement can be liable under the [false name exception].").

122. Courts look to a number of factors to determine whether "flat rating" is misleading and so barred:

- If the collection agency is only a mailing service or performs only ministerial functions;
- If the letters state that if the debtor does not pay, the debt "will be referred for collection";
- If the collection agency is paid only for sending the letters, and not a percentage of debts collected;
- If the collection agency does not receive any payments or forwards payments to the creditor;
- If the collection agency has no contact with the debtor even if the debtor fails to respond to the letter;
- If the collection agency does not receive the files of the debtors;
- If the collection agency never discussed the collection process with the creditor or steps pertinent to specific debtors;
- If the collection agency forwards correspondence to the creditor;
- If the collection agency has no authority to negotiate the collection of debts;
- If the letters do not state the collection agency's telephone number or address or direct questions or payments to the creditor; and
- If the creditor has substantial control over the content of the letters.

See Burns v. Ross Stuart & Dawson, Inc., 2016 WL 7013007 (E.D. Mich. 2016); Larson v. Evanston Northwestern Healthcare Corp., 1999 WL 518901 (N.D. Ill. 1999). When a debt collector is involved in ways more significant than just selling its letterhead, then the activities no longer are considered to be flat rating.

123. See White v. Goodman, 200 F.3d 1016, 1018 (7th Cir. 2000) ("The element of deception lies less in the misrepresentation that a third-party debt collector is involved than in the signal, conveyed by turning over a debt for collection, that the creditor does not intend to drop the matter. . . . [S]uch deception might induce debtors to abandon legitimate defenses.").

124. Echlin v. PeaceHealth, 887 F.3d 967 (9th Cir. 2018).

125. 15 U.S.C. § 1692f.

126. 15 U.S.C. § 1692f(1).

127. 15 U.S.C. § 1692f (2).

128. 15 U.S.C. § 1692f(4).

129. 15 U.S.C. § 1692f(7).

130. 15 U.S.C. § 1692f(8).

131. See Federal Trade Commission, Consumer Information: Time-Barred Debts (July 2013), https://www.consumer.ftc.gov/articles/0117-time-barred-debts. See also Federal Trade Commission, Under FTC Settlement, Debt Buyer Agrees to Pay $2.5 Million for Alleged Consumer Deception (Jan. 30, 2012), https://www.ftc.gov/news-events/press-releases/2012/01/under-ftc-settlement-debt-buyer-agrees-pay-25-million-alleged.

132. Kaiser v. Cascade Capital LLC, 2017 WL 2332856, *7 (D. Or. 2017) ("The majority of circuits agree that when the debt collector either threatens to sue or actually sues on a clearly time-barred debt, the debt collector violates the FDCPA. Daugherty v. Convergent Outsourcing, Inc., 836 F.3d 507, 511 (5th Cir. 2016).").

133. Huertas v. Gallery Asset Management, 641 F.3d 28, 33 (3d Cir. 2011).

134. See Midland Funding, LLC v. Johnson, 137 S. Ct. 1407 (2017) (quoting Freyermuth v. Credit Bureau Services, Inc., 248 F.3d 767, 771 (8th Cir. 2001)).

135. *See* Cole v. Truelogic Financial Corp., 2009 WL 261428 (W.D.N.Y. 2009). *See generally* Mary Spector, Where the FCRA Meets the FDCPA: The Impact of Unfair Collection Practices on the Credit Report, 20 Geo. J. on Poverty L. & Pol'y 479 (2013).

136. The CFPB was created by the Dodd-Frank Wall Street Reform and Consumer Protection Act, Pub. L. No. 111-203, §§ 1001–1100H, 124 Stat. 1376, 1955 (2010), codified at 12 U.S.C. § 53. The act transferred all duties and powers relating to consumer financial protection to the CFPB from agencies which previously had regulatory power with respect to consumer finance. 12 U.S.C. § 5581. The CFPB began to accept collection complaints in the second half of 2013. In its first year, the CFPB processed 88,300 collection complaints. The most common type of complaint— 37%—concerned the collector's continued effort to collect a debt that the consumer did not owe. *See* Consumer Financial Protection Bureau, Annual Report 2015, 12 (Mar. 2015), http://www.consumerfinance.gov/data-research/research-reports/fair-debt-collection-practices-act-annual-report-2015/. In 2018, attempts to collect a debt not owed increased to 39% of collection complaints. Consumer Financial Protection Bureau, Annual Report 2018, Table 1 (Mar. 2018), https://www.consumerfinance.gov/data-research/research-reports/fair-debt-collection-practices-act-annual-report-2018/.

137. Before the CFPB, the Federal Trade Commission (FTC) had primary responsibility over consumer matters. *See* Federal Trade Commission, About the Bureau of Consumer Protection, https://www.ftc.gov/about-ftc/bureaus-offices/bureau-consumer-protection/about-bureau-consumer-protection. The FTC hosts an online complaint system that addresses credit and debt issues, as well as scams, rip-offs, unwanted telemarketing, text, or spam, mobile devices or telephones, internet services, and other topics. A consumer who believes that a collection agency is engaged in abusive practices can upload a complaint and inform the FTC of the problem. Filing a complaint with the FTC will not stop the abusive practice or produce individual relief. Rather, the FTC relies upon filed complaints to identify patterns that it investigates and seeks to prosecute in a systemic way. The online complaint system can be accessed through http://www.ftccomplaintassistant.gov.

138. *See* Consumer Financial Protection Bureau, Semi-Annual Report, 20, 42–43 (May 2014), http://files.consumerfinance.gov/f/201405_cfpb_semi-annual-report.pdf.

139. Consumer Financial Protection Bureau, Consumer Response: A Snapshot of Complaints Received 4 (Oct. 10, 2012), http://files.consumerfinance.gov/f/201210_cfpb_consumer_response_september-30-snapshot.pdf. In addition to helping resolve individual complaints, the CFPB is also tasked with redressing systemic problems with debt collection practices. During the Obama administration, the CFPB uncovered and put a halt to serious violation by "larger participants"— debt collection firms with receipts of more than $10 million annually—that included excessive phone calls, use of misleading representations, and false threats of litigation. The CFPB also can bring enforcement actions, and in 2015, those actions resulted in more than $360 million returned to consumers and more

than $79 million in fines. Consumer Financial Protection Bureau, Annual Report 2016, 24–25, 27 (Mar. 2016), http://files.consumerfinance.gov/f/201603_cfpb-fair-debt-collection-practices-act.pdf. The CFPB's enforcement activities on behalf of consumers declined "sharply" during the Trump administration. *See* Christopher L. Peterson, Dormant: The Consumer Financial Protection Bureau's Law Enforcement Program in Decline, Consumer Federation of America (Mar. 11, 2019), https://consumerfed.org/reports/dormant-the-consumer-financial-protection-bureaus-law-enforcement-program-in-decline/. *See also* Patricia A. McCoy, Inside Job: The Assault on the Structure of the Consumer Financial Protection Bureau, 103 Minn. L. Rev. 2543 (2019); Nicholas Confessore, Mick Mulvaney's Master Class in Destroying a Bureaucracy from Within, N.Y. Times Magazine (Apr. 16, 2019), https://www.nytimes.com/2019/04/16/magazine/consumer-financial-protection-bureau-trump.html; Ted Knutson, Ex-CFPB Chief Cordray Attacks Trump Administration for Retreating on Consumer Financial Protection, Forbes (Mar. 21, 2019), https://www.forbes.com/sites/tedknutson/2019/03/21/ex-cfpb-chief-cordray-attacks-trump-administration-for-retreating-on-consumer-financial-protection/#2b83d2de184c.

140. 15 U.S.C. § 1692k(d).
141. 15 U.S.C. § 1692k(d) ("an action . . . may be brought . . . within one year from the date on which the violation occurs"). *See* Rotkiske v. Klemm, 890 F.3d 422 (3d Cir. 2018), cert. granted, 139 S. Ct. 1259 (2019). Argument is scheduled for October 2019. The Third Circuit held that the FDCPA's one-year limitations period begins to run when a putative defendant violates the act, not when the consumer discovers or should have discovered the violation. By contrast, the Fourth and Ninth Circuits have held that the time begins to run when the consumer discovers the violation. *See* Lembach v. Bierman, 528 Fed. Appx. 297 (4th Cir. 2013); Mangum v. Action Collection Serv., Inc., 575 F.3d 935 (9th Cir. 2009). The Third Circuit's analysis did not foreclose the availability of equitable tolling of the limitations period if the violation involved "fraudulent, misleading, or self-concealing conduct." *See* Consumer Protection, 30 No. 9 Bus. Torts Rep. 221 (July 2018).
142. Marisco v. NCO Financial Systems, Inc., 946 F. Supp. 2d 287, 291 (E.D.N.Y. 2013) (quoting Easterling v. Collecto, Inc., 692 F.3d 229, 234 (2d Cir. 2012), quoting Russell v. Equifax A.R.S., 74 F.3d 30 (2d Cir. 1996) (internal quotations omitted) and 15 U.S.C. § 1692k(c) (emphasis added in original)).
143. 15 U.S.C. § 1692k(a). The U.S. Supreme Court addressed a plaintiff's standing to seek statutory damages in Spokeo, Inc. v. Robins, 578 U.S. ___, 136 S. Ct. 1540 (2016).
144. 15 U.S.C. § 1692k(a)(2)(B).
145. 15 U.S.C. § 1692k(a)(1).
146. *See, for example*, Myers v. LHR, Inc., 543 F. Supp. 2d 1215 (S.D. Cal. 2008) (awarding $90,000 in actual damages where collector erroneously reported debt to credit agencies, plaintiff did not owe the debt, plaintiff incurred medical expenses from stress, and the error affected plaintiff's ability to purchase a home). However, where the illegal conduct and emotional and physical effects "lasted only three days," and plaintiff suffered "no concrete effect on her professional life," the court awarded

$1,500 in actual damages. Thomas v. Smith, Dean & Associates, 2011 WL 2730787, at *4 (D. Md. 2011).

147. A court will consider the collector's specific violations, how many violations were committed, and whether the violations were intentional. 15 U.S.C. § 1692k(b)(1). *See, for example*:

> A consumer was awarded $2,500 in actual damages when she received multiple harassing calls from a collector, and "became upset, anxious, and distressed" after each call. She did not experience any physical injury or lasting psychological harm and did not have to pay any out-of-pocket expenses. *See* Sweetland v. Stevens & James, Inc., 563 F. Supp. 2d 300, 303–304 (D. Me. 2008).
>
> A consumer was awarded $1,000 in actual damages and $1,000 in additional damages when a collector obtained the consumer's home phone number from the consumer's employer by falsely stating that the consumer's family was undergoing an emergency overseas. The collector misrepresented that he was the Marshal and threatened to remove furniture from the consumer's mother's home, where the consumer was staying, and "auction it off." *See* Teng v. Metropolitan Retail Recovery, Inc., 851 F. Supp. 61, 63, 71 (E.D.N.Y. 1994).

148. 15 U.S.C. § 1692k(b)(2) ("[T]he frequency and persistence of noncompliance by the debt collector, the nature of such noncompliance, the resources of the debt collector, the number of persons adversely affected, and the extent to which the debt collector's noncompliance was intentional.").

149. 15 U.S.C. § 1692k(a)(2).

150. 15 U.S.C. § 1692k(a)(3).

151. *See* Graziano v. Harrison, 950 F.2d 107, 113 (3d Cir. 1991) ("Given the structure of the section, attorney's fees should not be construed as a special or discretionary remedy; rather, the Act mandates an award of attorney's fees as a means of fulfilling Congress's intent that the Act should be enforced by debtors acting as private attorneys general.").

152. *See* Johnson v. Eaton, 80 F.3d 148, 151 (5th Cir. 1996).

153. 15 U.S.C. § 1692k(a)(3).

154. National Association of Consumer Advocates, https://www.consumeradvocates.org/find-an-attorney.

155. Consumer Information, Debt Collection, Federal Trade Commission, https://www.consumer.ftc.gov/articles/debt-collection-faqs.

156. Federal Trade Commission, 40 Years of Experience with the Fair Credit Reporting Act: An FTC Staff Report with Summary of Interpretations (July 2011), https://www.ftc.gov/reports/40-years-experience-fair-credit-reporting-act-ftc-staff-report-summary-interpretations (identifying consumer reporter industry). *See, for example*, Ken Sweet, Equifax makes money by knowing a lot about you, USA Today (Oct. 6, 2017), https://www.usatoday.com/story/money/personalfinance/2017/10/06/equifax-makes-money-knowing-lot-you/738824001/ (the "Big Three" consumer reporting agencies, Equifax, Experian, and TransUnion, had revenue of $3.1 billion, $4.3 billion, and $1.7 billion, respectively, in 2016).

157. *See* The Sedona Conference Data Privacy Primer, a Project of The Sedona Conference Working Group on Data Security and Privacy Liability, 19 Sedona Conf.

J. 273, 292 (2018) (explaining that privacy laws usually apply "only to individually identifiable personal information," but that this "narrow definition may be insufficient from the perspective of consumers, for instance where such information is used for data analytics purposes").

158. *See* Alexandra P. Everhart Sickler, The (Un)fair Credit Reporting Act, 28 Loy. Consumer L. Rev. 238, 240–241 (2016) ("Accuracy in consumer credit reporting is fundamental to an individual consumer's access to credit at fair rates as well as other services and opportunities.").

159. *See* Aaron Klein, The Real Problem with Credit Reports Is the Astounding Number of Errors, CNBC (Sept. 27, 2017), https://www.cnbc.com/2017/09/27/the-real-problem-with-credit-reports-is-the-astounding-number-of-errors-equifax-commentary.html; Meredith Schramm-Strosser, The "Not So" Fair Credit Reporting Act: Federal Preemption, Injunctive Relief, and the Need to Return Remedies for Common Law Defamation to the States, 14 Duq. Bus. L.J. 165, 168 (2012) ("The individual consumers' lack of control over the content of these files is documented by numerous studies that nearly eighty percent of consumer reports contain errors, twenty-five percent of which contained errors serious enough to cause a denial of credit.").

160. *See* Luke Herrine, Credit Reporting's Vicious Cycles, 40 N.Y.U. Rev. L. & Soc. Change 305, 336 (2016) ("Through the widespread use of credit reports, a bad credit history has become a barrier to access to everything from a cell phone to an apartment to acceptance to the bar. Credit reports have become debt rap sheets[.]").

161. *See, for example*, U.S. General Accountability Office, Consumer Data Protection: Actions Needed to Strengthen Oversight of Consumer Reporting Agencies (Feb. 2019), https://www.gao.gov/assets/700/697026.pdf.

162. 15 U.S.C. § 1681. Congress enacted the FCRA in 1970, effective 1971, and has amended it a number of times. One important set of amendments was enacted as the Consumer Credit Reporting Reform Act of 1996, which significantly revised and strengthened the FCRA by, among other things, extending obligations to furnishers of information. *See* Omnibus Consolidated Appropriations Act for Fiscal Years, Pub. L. No. 104-208, 110 Stat. 3009, 3444, codified as amended at 15 U.S.C. § 1681c. Another set of amendments, adopted in 2003 as part of the Fair and Accurate Credit Transactions Act, Pub. L. No. 108-159, 117 Stat. 1952, codified at 15 U.S.C. §§ 1681–81x, which, among other things, addressed identity theft. The 2007 Credit and Debit Card Receipt Clarification Act, Pub. L. No. 108-159, § 113, 117 Stat. 1952, 1959–60, codified as amended at 15 U.S.C. § 1681c(g), amended rules about the printing of consumer information on electronically printed receipts provided at the point of sale. The 2009 Credit Card Accountability, Responsibility and Disclosure Act added provisions dealing with deceptive practices in the marketing of credit reports. *See* Pub. L. No. 111-24, § 205, 123 Stat. 1734, 1747, codified as amended at 15 U.S.C. § 1681j(g). Then, in 2011, the Dodd-Frank Wall Street Reform and Consumer Protection Act, Pub. L. No. 111-203, 124 Stat. 1376, established the Consumer Financial Protection Bureau, which now is primarily responsible for enacting rules to enforce the FCRA. The Federal Trade Commission and the Securities and

Exchange Commission, as well as banking regulators, also have authority to enforce the FCRA. The 2018 Economic Growth, Regulatory Relief, and Consumer Protection Act, Pub. L. No. 115-174, 132 Stat. 1296, portions to be codified at 15 U.S.C. § 1681c, made changes affecting requests for the "security freeze" of a consumer report in the event of fraud; limited the reporting of certain medical collection debts of a veteran; required nationwide consumer reporting agencies to provide free electronic credit monitoring to active duty military consumers; and mandated the U.S. Comptroller General to submit a report on consumer reporting agencies to the Committee on Banking, Housing, and Urban Affairs of the U.S. Senate and to the Committee on Final Services of the U.S. House of Representatives by May 25, 2019.

163. 15 U.S.C. § 1681a(c). *See, for example,* McCready v. eBay, Inc., 453 F.3d 882, 889 (7th Cir. 2006) (eBay's Feedback forum did not involve an identifiable person and was not a consumer report because not about a consumer).

164. 15 U.S.C. § 1681e(b).

165. 15 U.S.C. § 1681s-2(a)(1)(A) ("A person shall not furnish any information relating to a consumer to any consumer reporting agency if the person knows or has reasonable cause to believe that the information is inaccurate.").

166. 15 U.S.C. § 1681m(a) & (b).

167. 15 U.S.C. § 1681b(f).

168. *See, for example,* 15 U.S.C. § 1681j(a)(1(A).

169. 15 U.S.C. §§ 1681n & 1681o.

170. *See, for example,* Dalton v. Capital Associated Industries, 257 F.3d 409 (4th Cir. 2011) (finding that an error in a criminal background check violated the FCRA when the employer withdrew a job offer based at least in part on a report that erroneously stated the applicant had been convicted of a felony). For a discussion of consumer reports, criminal records, and unemployability, *see* Elizabeth Westrope, Employment Discrimination on the Basis of Criminal History: Why an Anti-Discrimination Statute Is a Necessary Remedy, 108 J. Crim. L. & Criminology 367 (2018).

171. Online resources are available from the National Consumer Law Center, https://www.nclc.org/for-consumers/for-consumers.html (hub of consumer resources) and https://www.nclc.org/for-consumers/nclcs-consumer-education-brochures.html (brochures and other information on issues including correcting report errors); and from the Electronic Privacy Information Center, https://www.epic.org/privacy/fcra. In addition, the Consumer Financial Protection Bureau publishes online "A Summary of Your Rights Under the Fair Credit Reporting Act," which is available for free. For access and additional information, go to https://www.consumerfinance.gov/learnmore.

172. 15 U.S.C. § 1681a(f). In addition, the "consumer reporting agency" operates in interstate commerce, "us[ing] any means or facility of interstate commerce for the purpose of preparing or furnishing consumer reports." *Id.*

173. *See* Mary Madden, Michele Gilman, Karen Levy, & Alice Marwick, Privacy, Poverty, and Big Data: A Matrix of Vulnerabilities for Poor Americans, 95 Wash. U. L. Rev.

53, 79, 83 (2017) (explaining that Applicant Tracking Systems software "is designed to simplify the hiring process and automate the review of resumes and applications for employers," and that they "qualify as consumer reporting agencies").

174. The major examples are Facebook and Google. *See* Lindsey Barrett, Confiding in Con Men: U.S. Privacy Law, the GDPR, and Information Fiduciaries, 42 Seattle U.L. Rev. 1057, 1070 (2019).

175. 15 U.S.C. § 1681a(p) ("The term 'consumer reporting agency that compiles and maintains files on consumers on a nationwide basis' means a consumer reporting agency that regularly engages in the practice of assembling or evaluating, and maintaining, for the purpose of furnishing consumer reports to third parties bearing on a consumer's credit worthiness, credit standing, or credit capacity, each of the following regarding consumers residing nationwide: (1) Public record information. (2) Credit account information from persons who furnish that information regularly and in the ordinary course of business.").

176. 15 U.S.C § 1681a(x).

177. *See* Consumer Financial Protection Bureau, 2019 List of Consumer Reporting Companies, https://www.consumerfinance.gov/f/documents.cfpb_consumer-reporting-companies-list.pdf .

178. 15 U.S.C. § 1681a(d)(1). The Federal Trade Commission has taken the position during investigations that the FCRA applies to reports based on information drawn from social media. Federal Trade Commission, Lesley Fair, The Fair Credit Reporting Act & social media: What businesses should know (June 23, 2011), https://www.ftc.gov/news-events/blogs/business-blog/2011/06/fair-credit-reporting-act-social-media-what-businesses. *See also* Pauline T. Kim & Erika Hanson, People Analytics and the Regulation of Information Under the Fair Credit Reporting Act, 61 St. Louis U. L.J. 17 (2016).

179. 15 U.S.C. § 1681a(d)(1). For the communication to be considered a consumer report, the information that is disclosed must bear upon at least one of the seven factors, but it does not have to address all of the factors. *See, for example*, Cortez v. Trans Union, LLC, 617 F.3d 688, 707 (3d Cir. 2010) (consumer reporting agency's disclosure of information from the Treasury Department's Office of Foreign Assets Control as an add-on to a credit report was a credit report because the information is used to bar credit to a person on the antiterrorism list).

180. 15 U.S.C. §§ 1681a(d)(1)(a)–(c), 1681b(a). *See, for example*, Williams v. AT&T Wireless Serv., Inc., 5 F. Supp. 2d 1142 (W.D. Wash. 1998) (wireless service obtained credit report for a permissible purpose under 15 U.S.C. § 1681b(a)(3)(E), to determine whether consumer could pay for cell phone).

181. 15 U.S.C. § 1681g(a)(3).

182. 15 U.S.C. § 1681a(e).

183. 15 U.S.C. § 6809(4); Federal Trade Commission, How To Comply with the Privacy of Consumer Financial Information Rule of the Gramm-Leach-Bliley Act at 4–5, https://www.ftc.gov/system/files/documents/plain-language/bus67-how-comply-privacy-consumer-financial-information-rule-gramm-leach-bliley-act.pdf.

184. 16 C.F.R. § 313.11(a)(1). This limitation on the use by credit reporting agencies of credit header information is based on the Gramm-Leach-Bliley Act, 15 U.S.C. § 6809(4)(A), which responded in part to problems of identity theft caused by the bulk sale of credit header information. *See* Trans Union, L.L.C. v. Federal Trade Commission, 295 F.3d 42 (D.C. Cir. 2002) (explaining the background of and upholding the validity of the Gramm-Leach-Bliley Act).

185. 15 U.S.C. § 1681a(d)(2)(A)(i). *See, for example,* American Bankers Ass'n v. Gould, 412 F.3d 1081, 1084 (9th Cir. 2005) (defining experience information as "information obtained by financial institutions from their own dealings with their customers"); Mirfasihi v. Fleet Mortgage Corp., 551 F.3d 682 (7th Cir. 2008) (consumer names obtained from the bank's mortgage files sold to telemarketers were not credit reports because the information was obtained from the bank's personal experiences with the consumers); Knox v. Quest Diagnostics, Inc., 2012 WL 400333 (D. V.I. 2012) (report provided by drug-testing company was not a consumer report because the information was based on the drug-testing company's firsthand experience with the consumer).

186. 15 U.S.C. § 1681a(d)(2)(A)(ii).

187. *See* 15 U.S.C. §1681a(d)(2)(A)(iii).

188. *See* 15 U.S.C. §1681s-(3)(a)(1). The marketing opt-out is subject to exceptions, 15 U.S.C. §1681s-3(a)(4), and runs for five-year renewable periods, *id.* at § 1681s-3(a) (3).

189. 15 U.S.C. § 1681a(o). An employment agency is a company that regularly engages in employment procurement. The exclusion was adopted by amendment in the Omnibus Consolidated Appropriations Act, Pub. L. No. 104-208, §2402, 110 Stat. 3009, 3436 (Sept. 30, 1996).

190. 15 U.S.C. § 1681a(y).

191. 15 U.S.C. § 1681a(d)(2)(B).

192. *See* National Consumer Law Center, Fair Credit Reporting ¶ 2.4.2 (explaining that "users (except for creditors and certain affiliated companies) of experience information not furnished to a CRA will not have to inform consumers that a denial or other adverse action was based on information reported directly from the company involved in the transaction with the consumer").

193. *See* 15 U.S.C. § 1681a(y)(2).

194. 15 U.S.C. § 1681c(a)(1)–(5). Other federal statutes that limit the information that a consumer file may permissibly include are the Fair Debt Collection Practices Act and the Equal Credit Opportunity Act, discussed in this chapter.

195. 15 U.S.C. § 1681a(d).

196. 15 U.S.C. § 1681c(a)(6)(A)–(B).

197. 15 U.S.C. § 1681a(i)(2).

198. *See* Consumer Financial Protection Bureau, Quarterly Consumer Credit Trends: Public Records (Feb. 2018), https://www.google.com/url?sa=t&rct=j&q=&esrc= s&source=web&cd=11&ved=2ahUKEwjM8rXHh9PjAhWhrVkKHYSMCWsQFjAKegQ IARAC&url=https%3A%2F%2Ffiles.consumerfinance.gov%2Ff%2Fdocuments%2Fcfpb_ consumer-credit-trends_public-records_022018.pdf&usg=AOvVaw14OkurtGIOgC

ywxaOhYvDl. *See also* Consumer Financial Protection Bureau, Jasper Clarkberg & Michelle Kambara, Removal of public records has little effect on consumers' credit scores (Feb. 22, 2018), https://www.consumerfinance.gov/about-us/blog/removal-public-records-has-little-effect-consumers-credit-scores/ (noting, however, that the report cannot yet assess "scoring-model accuracy" because at least two years of data are required for that analysis).

199. 50 U.S.C. §§ 3901–4043.

200. 50 U.S.C. § 3919(3).

201. The FCRA was amended by § 301 of the Economic Growth, Regulatory Relief, and Consumer Protection Act, Pub. L. No. 115-174, § 302, 132 Stat. 1296 (2018), codified at 15 U.S.C. §§ 1681c(a)(8) (fully paid or settled); 1681c(a)(7) (less than one year); 1681c(a)(7) & (8) (actual knowledge and duty to check VA-data base). Veteran medical debt is defined in 15 U.S.C. § 1681a(aa). *See* Consumer Financial Protection Bureau, Patrick Campbell & Brian Levin, New protections for servicemembers and veterans alert (Feb. 7, 2019), https://www.consumerfinance.gov/about-us/blog/new-protections-servicemembers-and-veterans-alert/.

202. 15 U.S.C. § 1681c. Staleness is determined by the date of the event's occurrence, not the date that the information was furnished to the consumer reporting agency. The statute of limitations is relevant only to determining the staleness of civil judgments, civil lawsuits, and arrest records. 15 U.S.C. § 1681c(a).

203. 15 U.S.C. § 1681c(a)(1).

204. 15 U.S.C. § 1681c(a)(2)–(5). *See, for example*, Serrano v. Sterling Testing Sys., Inc., 557 F. Supp. 2d 688 (E.D. Pa. 2008) (disclosure of the existence of an outdated arrest record, even without production of the record, violated 15 U.S.C. § 1681c(a)(5) and possibly (a)(2)).

205. 15 U.S.C. § 1681c(c)(1). *See, for example*, Slick v. Portfolio Recovery Assoc., 111 F. Supp. 3d 900, 904 (N.D. Ill. 2015).

206. 15 U.S.C. § 1681g(a)(5) (agency must maintain record of inquiries received by agency during one-year period preceding request "that identified the consumer in connection with a credit or insurance transaction that was not initiated by the consumer"); 15 U.S.C. § 1681b(c)(3) (except as provided in § 1681g(a)(5), agency shall not furnish a "record of inquiries in connection with a credit or insurance transaction that is not initiated by a consumer").

207. The Consumer Reporting Employment Clarification Act of 1998 amended the FCRA to exclude criminal convictions from the general seven-year rule that applies to most information under the act. As a result, reports can include criminal convictions without any time limit. Pub. L. No. 105-347, 112 Stat. 3208 (1998).

208. National Consumer Law Center, Fair Credit Reporting ¶ 5.2.3.7.2 (citing Fite v. Retail Credit Co., 386 F. Supp. 1045 (D. Mont. 1975), aff'd, 537 F.2d 384 (9th Cir. 1976)).

209. 20 U.S.C. § 1087cc(c)(3). *See* National Consumer Law Center, Fair Credit Reporting ¶ 5.2.3.10. Federal student loans are discussed in chapter 5.

210. *See* Ravi Antani, The Resistance of Memory: Could the European Union's Right to Be Forgotten Exist in the United States?, 30 Berkeley Tech. L.J. 1173, 1190

(2015); *see also* W. Gregory Voss & Kimberly A. Houser, Personal Data and the GDPR: Providing a Competitive Advantage for U.S. Companies, 56 Am. Bus. L.J. 287 (2019) (explaining that U.S. law accords less protection to personal data than does European law).

211. 15 U.S.C. § 1681d(d)(3).

212. 15 U.S.C. § 1681d(d)(4). The agency must obtain information "from an additional source that has independent and direct knowledge of the information."

213. 15 U.S.C. § 1681d(a).

214. 15 U.S.C. § 1681b(b)(3)(A).

215. *Id.*; 15 U.S.C. §§ 1681m(a) & 1681j(b).

216. *See* Eisha Jain, Capitalizing on Criminal Justice, 67 Duke L.J. 1381, 1397 (2018) ("Virtually all employers conduct background checks on some or all employees, including in ways that are overbroad.").

217. *See* Kelly Gallagher, Rethinking the Fair Credit Reporting Act: When Requesting Credit Reports for "Employment Purposes" Goes Too Far, 91 Iowa L. Rev. 1593, 1595 (2006) (questioning the use of a good credit score as a proxy for honesty or productivity).

218. *See* Jordan Bartley Mack, Born in the Red: How Affirmative Action Could Cure the Race-Credit Divide, 55 Hous. L. Rev. 1157, 1168 (2018) ("the poor and minority communities" are "those most lacking access to traditional forms of credit").

219. *See* Mary Madden, Michele Gilman, Karen Levy, & Alice Marwick, Privacy, Poverty, and Big Data: A Matrix of Vulnerabilities for Poor Americans, 95 Wash. U. L. Rev. 53, 84 (2017). The authors report that "estimates are that one-fifth to one-quarter of employers research job applicants themselves, using social networks and search engines." *See also* Robert Sprague, Googling Job Applicants: Incorporating Personal Information into Hiring Decisions, 23 Lab. Law. 19, 36 (2007) ("Due to the restrictions facing employers in investigating the background of applicants, it is no wonder they have turned to the Internet to investigate prospective employees.").

220. 15 U.S.C. §§ 1681a(h) (employment purposes); 1681a(d)(1)(B) (consumer report); 1681b(b)(2)(A)(i)–(ii)(disclosure requirements prior to procurement).

221. 15 U.S.C. § 1681k.

222. 15 U.S.C. § 1681k(a)(1), (2).

223. *See* 15 U.S.C. § 1681b(b)(2)(A)(i)(ii).

224. *See* Syed v. M-1, LLC, 853 F.3d 492 (9th Cir. 2017), cert. denied, 138 S. Ct. 447 (2017*). See also* Lowell Ritter, On Issue of First Impression, Ninth Circuit Holds No Extraneous Information Allowed in Fair Credit Reporting Act Disclosure; Such Violation Is Willful Under Statute, 92 Notre Dame L. Rev. Online 159, 171 (2017) (commenting that the "court did not address whether a liability waiver could be provided separate from the disclosure and authorization").

225. 15 U.S.C. §1681b(b)(3)(A).

226. 15 U.S.C. §§ 1681a(o), as amended by Pub. L. No. 104-208, 110 Stat. 3009 (1996); 1681a(e) (investigative report).

227. 15 U.S.C. § 1681a(o)(5)(B).

228. 15 U.S.C. § 1681a(o)(5)(C).

229. *See, for example*, Investopedia, How do credit reports and investigative consumer reports differ? (updated June 25, 2019), https://www.investopedia.com/ask/answers/110614/whats-difference-between-credit-reports-and-investigative-consumer-reports.asp ("Per federal law, no investigation may be conducted without your approval. However, failure to accept the investigation likely means automatic denial for whatever you may have been applying for, such as tenancy, licensing, employment, etc.").

230. Dalton v. Capital Associated Indus., Inc., 257 F.3d 409, 415 (4th Cir. 2001) (technically accurate information may still be misleading).

231. *See, for example*, Jack v. Midland Credit Mgmt., 2011 WL 4387556 (S.D. Ind. 2011). Amendments to the FCRA adopted in 2003 regulate how debt collectors are to report the age of debt, providing that the collector must use the date of delinquency of the original credit and, if that date is not available, must use reasonable procedures to find out the date. 15 U.S.C. § 1681s-2(a)(5)(B).

232. *See* Jeffrey Selbin, Justin McCrary, & Joshua Epstein, Unmarked? Criminal Record Clearing and Employment Outcomes, 108 J. Crim. L. & Criminology 1, 18 (2018) (citing Madeleine Neighly & Maurice Emsellem, Wanted: Accurate FBI Background Checks for Employment, The National Employment Law Project 7 (July 2013), http://www.nelp.org/content/uploads/2015/02/Report-Wanted-Accurate-FBI-Background-Checks-Employment-1.pdf).

233. 15 U.S.C. § 1681j(a)(1)(A).

234. 15 U.S.C. § 1681g(a)(2).

235. 15 U.S.C. § 1681g(a)(3). There is an exception for FBI and government security requests. 15 U.S.C. § 1681g(a)(3)(c).

236. AnnualCreditReport.com, https://www.annualcreditreport.com/index.action. *See also* Consumer Financial Protection Bureau, Ask CFPB, https://www.consumerfinance.gov/ask-cfpb/i-tried-to-check-my-credit-report-online-but-the-site-wanted-to-charge-me-a-fee-or-get-me-to-sign-up-for-other-services-arent-credit-reports-free-en-1285/ ("AnnualCreditReport.com is the only authorized website for the free annual credit reports that you are guaranteed by law.").

237. Consumer Financial Protection Bureau, Ask CFPB, https://www.consumerfinance.gov/ask-cfpb/how-do-i-get-a-copy-of-my-credit-reports-en-5/.

238. Federal Trade Commission, Consumer Information, Free Credit Reports, https://www.consumer.ftc.gov/articles/0155-free-credit-reports.

239. *See, for example*, Joint Consent Order, Order for Restitution, and Order to Pay Civil Money Penalty, In the Matter of Discover Bank, Greenwood, DE, No. FDIC-11-548b (F.D.I.C./C.F.P.B. Sept. 24, 2012), https://files.consumerfinance.gov/f/201209_cfpb_consent_order_0005.pdf (settlement of lawsuit by Consumer Financial Protection Bureau regarding deceptive marketing of credit monitoring products).

240. 15 U.S.C. § 1681j(1)(C)(i). *See* Consumer Financial Protection Bureau, Bulletin 2012-09, The FCRA's "Streamlined Process" Requirement For Consumers to Obtain Free Annual Reports From Nationwide Specialty Consumer Reporting Agencies, https://files.consumerfinance.gov/f/201211_cfpb_NSCRA_Bulletin.pdf.

241. 15 U.S.C. § 1681j(c)(2). The statute does not define public assistance.

242. 15 U.S.C. § 1681j(c)(1). Federal Trade Commission, Consumer Information—Free Credit Reports, https://www.consumer.ftc.gov/articles/0155-free-credit-reports.

243. IdentityTheft.gov, https://www.identitytheft.gov/.

244. 15 U.S.C. § 1681c-1(a)(2)(B).

245. 15 U.S.C. § 1681c-1(a)(1).

246. 15 U.S.C. § 1681c-1(b)(1)(A) & 2(A).

247. 15 U.S.C. § 1681m(a)(3)(A) & (B).

248. 15 U.S.C. § 1681i(a)(6)(B)(ii); National Consumer Law Center, Fair Credit Reporting § 4.6.1.2 (citing Assurance of Voluntary Compliance/Assurance of Voluntary Discontinuance, In the Matter of Equifax Info. Serv. L.L.C., Experian Info. Solutions, Inc., and TransUnion L.L.C., § IV (F)(5) (May 20, 2015)).

249. 15 U.S.C. § 1681j(f); Consumer Financial Protection Bureau, Fair Credit Reporting Act Disclosures, Annual Adjustments, https://www.consumerfinance.gov/policy-compliance/rulemaking/final-rules/fair-credit-reporting-act-disclosures/.

250. 15 U.S.C. § 1681h(a)(1).

251. 12 C.F.R. § 1022.137; 12 C.F.R. Part 1022, App. L.

252. 15 U.S.C. § 1681b(a)(2). *See, for example*, Oses v. Corelogic SafeRent, L.L.C., 171 F. Supp. 3d 775 (N.D. Ill. 2016) (consumer reporting agency was not required to respond to consumer's attorney's request for disclosure).

253. 15 U.S.C. § 1681g(f)(2)(A)(i). *See* Federal Trade Commission, Consumer Information, Credit Scores, https://www.consumer.ftc.gov/articles/0152-credit-scores.

254. Vlad A. Hertza, Fighting Unfair Classifications in Credit Reporting: Should the United States Adopt GDPR-Inspired Rights in Regulating Consumer Credit?, 93 N.Y.U. L. Rev. 1707, 1710 (2018) ("a large percentage of credit scores nationwide contain inaccuracies").

255. 15 U.S.C. § 1681g(a)(1)(B).

256. 15 U.S.C. § 1681g(a)(6) & (f)(8).

257. National Consumer Law Center, Fair Credit Reporting, ¶ 3.3.4.5 (discussing fees for a credit score).

258. 15 U.S.C. § 1681g(f)(1). In addition, the agency must disclose if the score was affected by the number of inquiries in the file. 15 U.S.C. § 1681g(f)(9).

259. Consumer Financial Protection Bureau, Where can I get my credit score? (updated Aug. 4, 2016), https://www.consumerfinance.gov/ask-cfpb/where-can-i-get-my-credit-score-en-316/.

260. *See, for example*, https://wwwmyfico.com.

261. *See* Consumer Financial Protection Bureau, How do I find a credit counselor?, https://www.consumerfinance.gov/ask-cfpb/where-can-i-get-my-credit-score-en-316/.

262. *See* Ellen Cannon, Which Credit Cards Give Free FICO Scores?, NerdWallet (July 8, 2016), https://www.nerdwallet.com/blog/credit-cards/credit-cards-give-free-fico-scores/ ("In 2013, Fair Isaac Corp., the company that created the FICO score, launched its FICO Score Open Access program, which allowed lenders to give their customers free FICO scores. More than 50 now do so."); Consumer Financial Protection Bureau, CFPB Calls on Top Credit Card Companies to Make Credit

Scores Available to Consumers (Feb. 27, 2014), https://www.consumerfinance.gov/about-us/newsroom/cfpb-calls-on-top-credit-card-companies-to-make-credit-scores-available-to-consumers/.

263. 15 U.S.C. § 1681g(g)(1)(A).
264. 15 U.S.C. § 1681b.
265. 15 U.S.C. § 1681m(a).
266. 15 U.S.C. § 1681m(a)(3)(B).
267. 15 U.S.C. § 1681m(a)(3)(A).
268. 15 U.S.C. § 1681m(a)(4).
269. 15 U.S.C.A. § 1681j(b). The report provided directly to the consumer by the consumer reporting agency is a disclosure and includes information in the consumer file as well as information provided to the user. 15 U.S.C. § 1681a(d). The report obtained from the consumer reporting agency may not be identical to the report upon which the company based the adverse decision. Moreover, only the report provided by the consumer reporting agency to the user is a consumer report.
270. Michael E. Staten & Fred H. Cate, Accuracy in Credit Reporting, in Building Assets, Building Credit: Creating Wealth in Low-Income Communities 237, 243 (Nicolas P. Retsinas & Eric S. Belsky, eds.) (Brookings 2005), https://www.jstor.org/stablr/10.7864/jctt128175.18.
271. 15 U.S.C. § 1681h(c).
272. 15 U.S.C. §1681h(d).
273. Federal Trade Commission, Report to Congress Under Section 319 of the Fair and Accurate Credit Transactions Act of 2003 i (Dec. 2012), https://www.ftc.gov/sites/default/files/documents/reports/section-319-fair-and-accurate-credit-transactions-act-2003-fifth-interim-federal-trade-commission/130211factareport.pdf.
274. Consumer Financial Protection Bureau, Monthly Complaint Report, Vol. 18, tbl. 2 (Dec. 27, 2016), https://www.consumerfinance.gov/data-research/research-reports/monthly-complaint-report-vol-18/.
275. *See, for example*, Tara Siegel Bernard, An $18 Million Lesson in Handling Credit Report Errors, N.Y. Times (Aug. 2, 2013), https://www.nytimes.com/2013/08/03/your-money/credit-scores/credit-bureaus-willing-to-tolerate-errors-experts-say.html?module=inline.
276. 15 U.S.C. § 1681i(a)(1)(A).
277. 15 U.S.C. § 1681i(a)(6).
278. 15 U.S.C. § 1681i(a)(2).
279. 15 U.S.C. § 1681s-2(b).
280. The site is available at http://www.consumerfinance.gov/learnmore/.
281. Consumer Action, The CFPB Consumer Complaint Database 2 (Aug. 2016), https://www.consumer-action.org/downloads/english/cfpb_full_dbase_report.pdf.
282. To file a claim with the CFPB, go to https://www.consumerfinance.gov/complaint, or call: 855-411-2372. The U.S. Department of Justice also enforces the act, but takes up cases where there is a pattern of discrimination, so individuals have to first file a claim with whichever regulatory agency is relevant to their situation. These are: Department of Housing and Urban Development (HUD), Consumer Financial

Protection Bureau (CFPB), Comptroller of Currency (OCC), Federal Reserve Board (FRB), Federal Deposit Insurance Corporation (FDIC), National Credit Union Association (NCUA), and Federal Trade Commission (FTC).

283. 15 U.S.C. §§ 1681o(a)(1), 1681n(a)(1)–(3).

284. Safeco Ins. Co. of America v. Burr, 551 U.S. 47, 69 (2007); Pedro v. Equifax, Inc., 868 F.3d 1275, 1280 (11th Cir. 2017).

285. 16 C.F.R. § 660.2(c). *See, for example*, Seamans v. Temple University, 744 F.3d 853, 861 (3d Cir. 2014) (Temple University was a "furnisher of consumer credit"). The statute sets out exceptions from the definition of furnisher, including related companies that share information.

286. 16 C.F.R. §§ 660.3(a)–4.

287. The FCRA does not define accuracy or integrity. The definitions are set forth in regulations known as "Regulation V." 12 C.F.R. § 1022.41(a). *See also* 74 Fed. Reg. 31,484, effective July 1, 2010. The Consumer Financial Protection Bureau restated these regulations at 12 C.F.R. Part 1022. *See* 76 Fed. Reg. 79308 (Dec. 21, 2011).

288. *See* 12 C.F.R. § 222.41(e) (defining integrity).

289. 15 U.S.C. § 1681s-2(a)(4).

290. 15 U.S.C. § 1681s-2(a)(5)(A).

291. 15 U.S.C. § 1681c(a).

292. 15 U.S.C. § 1681s-2(a)(1)(A).

293. 15 U.S.C. § 1681s-2(a)(1)(B)(i) & (ii).

294. 15 U.S.C. § 1681s-2(a)(1)(D).

295. 15 U.S.C. § 1681s-2(a)(3).

296. 15 U.S.C. § 1681s-2(a)(8).

297. *See* 12 C.F.R. § 1022.42(a). The Consumer Financial Protection Bureau in 2017 reported failures on the part of furnishers to establish policies and procedures for direct disputes. *See* Consumer Financial Protection Bureau, Supervisory Highlights Consumer Reporting Special Edition (Issue 14, Winter 2017), http://files.consumerfinance.gov/f/documents/201703_cfpb_Supervisory-Highlights-Consumer-Reporting-Special-Edition.pdf.

298. 12 C.F.R. § 1022.41(b). For exceptions, *see, for example*, 12 C.F.R. §. 1022.43(b)(1)(i) (identifying information and past employers).

299. 12 C.F.R. § 1022.43(c)(1).

300. 15 U.S.C. § 1681s-2(a)(8)(F)(i)(I)–(II) & (ii).

301. 12 C.F.R. § 1022.43(a).

302. 15 U.S.C. § 1681s-2(a)(8)(E)(iv).

303. Gorman v. Wolpoff & Abramson, LLP, 584 F.3d 1147 (9th Cir. 2009).

304. 15 U.S.C. §§ 1681s-2(a)(6)(A) (procedures); 1681c-2(b) (agency's notification).

305. 15 U.S.C. § 1681s-2(a)(6)(B).

306. *See* Bonnie G. Camden, Fair Credit Reporting Act: What You Don't Know May Hurt You, 57 U. Cin. L. Rev. 267, 287 n.152 (1988) (describing efforts to amend the FCRA to require prior written permission and a chance to correct an investigative report before its release to third parties).

307. 15 U.S.C. § 1681s-2(a).

308. *See, for example*, Boggio v. USAA Federal Sav. Bank, 696 F.3d 611 (6th Cir. 2012); Hrebal v. Sterus, Inc., 598 B.R. 252, 265 (D. Minn. 2019). For a proposal to reform the statute to give the consumer a private right of action against the furnisher that fails to furnish accurate information, *see* Jeffrey Bils, Fighting Unfair Credit Reports: A Proposal to Give Consumers More Power to Enforce the Fair Credit Reporting Act, 61 UCLA L. Rev. Discourse 226 (2013).

309. 31 U.S.C. § 3711(e)(1)(F)(i)–(ii).

310. 20 U.S.C. § 1080a.

311. 15 U.S.C. § 1681s-1(1)(A).

312. 15 U.S.C. § 1681s-1(1)(B).

313. Ben Zipperer, The erosion of the federal minimum wage has increased poverty, especially for black and Hispanic families, Economic Policy Institute (June 13, 2018), https://www.epi.org/publication/the-erosion-of-the-federal-minimum-wage-has-increased-poverty-especially-for-black-and-hispanic-families/; *see also* David Cooper, The Minimum Wage Used to Be Enough to Keep Workers Out of Poverty—It's Not Anymore, Economic Policy Institute (Dec. 4, 2013), https://www.epi.org/publication/minimum-wage-workers-poverty-anymore-raising/. *See generally* Willy E. Rice, Race, Gender, "Red-lining," and the Discriminatory Access to Loans, Credit, and Insurance: An Historical and Empirical Analysis of Consumers Who Sued Lenders and Insurers in Federal and State Courts, 1950–1995, 22 San Diego L. Rev. 583, 584 (1996) (stating that "[p]ersistent unemployment is likely to develop among members of any racial or socioeconomic group when members of that group are regularly and systemically denied access to capital and credit").

314. *See* Erica Williams & Samantha Waxman, State Earned Income Tax Credits and Minimum Wage Work Best Together, Center on Budget and Policy Priorities (Feb. 7, 2018), https://www.cbpp.org/research/state-budget-and-tax/state-earned-income-tax-credits-and-minimum-wages-work-best-together:

> Low wages make it hard for working families to afford basics like decent housing in safe neighborhoods, nutritious food, reliable transportation, and quality child care, as well as educational opportunities that can move working families toward the middle class. But the wages of workers paid the least are not much higher than they were over 40 years ago, after adjusting for inflation.

315. *See* Andrea Freeman, Racism in the Credit Card Industry, 95 N.C. L. Rev. 1071, 1077 (2017) (stating that "[o]ver several decades, credit cards have evolved into an essential tool for lower- and middle-class families to maintain financial stability"); *see also* Sara Sternberg Greene, The Bootstrap Trap, 67 Duke L.J. 233, 262 (2017) ("Several studies have found that, post-welfare reform, low-income parents increasingly rely on credit to weather emergencies.").

316. *See* Martha J. Svoboda, The Evolution of Redlining Post-Financial Crisis and Best Practices for Financial Institutions, 22 N.C. Banking Inst. 67, 69 (2018) (stating that "[i]n the broadest sense, every successful lender 'discriminates,' in that such a lender will avoid those potential borrowers who are unlikely to repay the obligation and instead favor (i.e., provide loans to) those most likely to repay.").

317. *See* Solon Barocas & Andrew D. Selbst, Big Data's Disparate Impact, 104 Cal. L. Rev. 671 (2016).

318. *See generally* Michael S. Barr & Rebecca M. Blank, Savings, Assets, Credit, and Banking Among Low-Income Households: Introduction and Overview, in Insufficient Funds: Savings, Assets, Credit, and Banking Among Low-Income Households (Rebecca M. Blank & Michael S. Barr eds.) (Russell Sage Foundation 2009).

319. *See* Susan Smith Blakely, Credit Opportunity for Women: The ECOA and Its Effects, 1981 Wis. L. Rev. 655; Gail R. Reizenstein, A Fresh Look at the Equal Credit Opportunity Act, 14 Akron L. Rev. 215 (1980); John W. Cairns, Credit Equality Comes to Women: An Analysis of the Equal Credit Opportunity Act, 13 San Diego L. Rev. 960 (1976).

320. 15 U.S.C. § 1691(a)(1); Reg. B, 12 C.F.R. §§ 1002.2(z), 1002.6(b)(9).

321. 15 U.S.C. § 1691(a)(1); Reg. B, 12 C.F.R. §§ 1002.2(z), 1002.6(b)(9).

322. 15 U.S.C. § 1691(a)(1); Reg. B, 12 C.F.R. §§ 1002.2(z), 1002.6(b)(9).

323. 15 U.S.C. § 1691(a)(1); Reg. B, 12 C.F.R. §§ 1002.2(z), 1002.6(b)(9). Under 12 C.F.R. § 1002.5(e), a creditor may inquire about a person's permanent residency and immigration status.

324. 15 U.S.C. § 1691(a)(1); Reg. B, 12 C.F.R. §§ 1002.2(z), 1002.6(b)(9). *See also* Laura Eckert, Inclusion of Sexual Orientation Discrimination in the Equal Credit Opportunity Act, 103 Com. L.J. 311 (1998); Taylor Flynn, Transforming the Debate: Why We Need to Include Transgender Rights in the Struggles for Sex and Sexual Orientation Equality, 101 Colum. L. Rev. 392 (2001).

325. 15 U.S.C. § 1691(a)(1); Reg. B, 12 C.F.R. §§ 1002.2(z), 1002.6(b)(8).

326. 15 U.S.C. § 1691(a)(1); Reg. B, 12 C.F.R. §§ 1002.2(z), 1002.6(b)(2)(i). However, the applicant must be able to enter into a binding contract, and age can be used as a predictive variable to determine creditworthiness. *See* 15 U.S.C. § 1691(b)(2)–(4); Reg. B, 12 C.F.R. § 1002.6(b)(2).

327. 15 U.S.C. § 1691(a)(2); Reg. B, 12 C.F.R. § 1002.2(z). Whether an applicant derives income from a public assistance program may be used to evaluate a pertinent element of creditworthiness. *See* 15 U.S.C. § 1691(b)(2); Reg. B, 12 C.F.R. § 1002.6(b)(2)(iii).

328. 15 U.S.C. § 1691(a)(3); Reg. B, 12 C.F.R. § 1002.2(z).

329. Reg. B, 12 C.F.R. § 1002. Currently the Consumer Financial Protection Bureau is authorized to issue Regulation B. 15 U.S.C. § 1691b. In 2013, the CFPB amended Regulation B requiring creditors to provide applicants for credit with free copies of all appraisals and other written valuations developed in connection with credit applications to be secured by a first lien on a dwelling. The amendment also requires the creditor to give applicants written notice that the copies will be promptly provided. *See* Reg. B, 12 C.F.R. § 1002.14; Marko Stojkovic, The Dodd-Frank Solution to Predatory Lending, 22 Pub. Int. L. Rep. 106, 112–113 (2017) (discussing amendments).

330. Official Interpretation of Reg. B, 12 C.F.R. § 1002, Supp. I, § 1002.6(a).

331. 15 U.S.C. § 1691a(d) (defining credit). A "creditor" means "any person who regularly extends, renews, or continues credit; any person who regularly arranges for the

extension, renewal, or continuation of credit; or any assignee of an original creditor who participates in the decision to extend, renew, or continue credit." 15 U.S.C. § 1691a(e). The regulations exclude from the definition of creditor a merchant who honors a credit card. *See* Reg. B, 12 C.F.R. § 1002.2(l).

332. Dunn v. American Express Co., 529 F. Supp. 633, 634 (D. Colo. 1982).

333. 15 U.S.C. § 1691 ("any aspect of a credit transaction").

334. *See* Scott J. Hyman & Erin S. Kubota, Predatory Servicing, 72 Consumer Fin. L.Q. Rep. 43, 50 (2018).

335. *Id.* at 55, discussing Consent Order, In re American Express Centurion Bank, CFPB No. 2017-CFPB-0016 (Aug. 23, 2017).

336. Regulation B partially exempts specified categories of credit from certain procedural requirements. Relevant here are: public utility credit, Reg. B, 12 C.F.R. § 1002.3(a); and incidental consumer credit, Reg. B, 12 C.F.R. § 1002.3(c).

337. A telephone company comes within the exception only if the company is regulated by a government unit or the company files its charges for service, delayed payment, or a prompt-payment discount with the government. Reg. B., 12 C.F.R. § 1002.3(a).

338. Official interpretation of 3(c) incidental credit, Reg. B, 12 C.F.R. § 1002.3(c). *See, for example*, Williams v. AT & T Wireless Servs., Inc., 5 F. Supp. 2d 1142, 1147 (W.D. Wash. 1998) (application for cell phone service was incidental consumer credit).

339. Reg. B, 12 C.F.R. § 1002.3(a)(1)(2) (providing exception from Reg. B, 12 C.F.R. § 1002.5(d)(1) (limiting inquiries about marital status).

340. Reg. B, 12 C.F.R. § 1002.3(c)(2)(1) (providing exception from Reg. B, 12 C.F.R. § 1002.5(b)).

341. Reg. B, 12 C.F.R. § 1002.3(c)(2)(ii) (providing exception from Reg. B, 12 C.F.R. § 1002.5(c)).

342. Reg. B, 12 C.F.R. § 1002.3(c)(2)(iii) (providing exception from Reg. B, 12 C.F.R. § 1002.5(d)(1)).

343. Reg. B, 12 C.F.R. § 1002.3(c)(2)(iv) (providing exception from Reg. B, 12 C.F.R. § 1002.5(d)(2)).

344. Reg. B, 12 C.F.R. § 1002.3(c)(2)(vi)–(vii) (providing exception from Reg. B, 12 C.F.R. §§ 1002.9 and 1002.10).

345. 15 U.S.C. § 1691(a)(2); Reg. B, 12 C.F.R. § 1002.2(z).

346. Official Interpretation of Reg. B, 12 C.F.R. Part 1002, Supp. I, § 1002.6(a) (explaining the general rule concerning use of information that is barred).

347. Reg. B, 12 C.F.R. § 1002.6(b)(2)(i).

348. A judgmental system of evaluating applicants is a "system for evaluating the creditworthiness of an applicant other than an empirically derived, demonstrably and statistically sound, credit scoring system." Reg. B, 12 C.F.R. § 1002.2(t), (y).

349. Reg. B, 12 C.F.R. § 1002.6(b)(2)(iii). *See, for example*, Bowman v. Bank of Am. N.A., 2016 WL 8943266, at *5 (D.S.C. June 16, 2016) ("Under the ECOA, inquiries directed at the continuance of public assistance income, such as SSDI income, are not discriminatory."), aff'd, 676 Fed. Appx. 216 (4th Cir. 2017).

350. Official Interpretations of Reg. B, 12 C.F.R. Part 1002, Supp. I, § 1002.2(z)(3).

351. Official Interpretations of Reg. B, 12 C.F.R. Part 1002, Supp. I, § 1002.2(z)(1).

352. Reg. B, 12 C.F.R. § 1002.8(a). Creditors can extend special purpose credit only to applicants who are involved in a federal or state credit assistance program, a credit assistance program offered by a nonprofit, or a special purpose credit program offered by a for-profit organization if that program meets additional requirements.

353. Reg. B, 12 C.F.R. Part 1002, Supp. I, § 1002.8(c)(2).

354. Reg. B, 12 C.F.R. § 1002.8(c).

355. Reg. B, 12 C.F.R. § 1002.16(a)(2).

356. Reg. B, 12 C.F.R. § 1002.16(b)(2) (extending statute of limitations from two to five years).

357. Reg. B, 12 C.F.R. § 1002.16(b)(1). *See* Francesca Lina Procaccini, Stemming the Rising Risk of Credit Inequality: The Fair and Faithful Interpretation of the Equal Credit Opportunity Act's Disparate Impact Prohibition, 9 Harv. L. & Pol'y Rev. 543 (2015).

358. 47 U.S.C. § 227(b)(1)(A)(iii). Text messages are included. *See* Satterfield v. Simon & Schuster, Inc., 569 F.3d 946, 954 (9th Cir. 2009). *But see* Dominguez on Behalf of Himself v. Yahoo, Inc., 894 F.3d 116 (3d Cir. 2018) (consumer failed to establish that text messaging system was autodialer within meaning of TCPA). The TCPA also bans a company's faxing unsolicited advertisements, but fax machines are not a typical household item. The Federal Communications Commission issued an order clarifying various aspects of the ban on using automated dialing services. *See* In re Rules & Regulations Implementing the TCP Act of 1991, 2015 WL 4387780 (July 10, 2015) (clarifying ban on robocalls and autodialers, consumer's right of revocation, and limit of one call to reassigned wireless numbers without recipient's consent). The D.C. Court of Appeals held that the order was unreasonable for treating smartphones as autodialers; that a one-call safe harbor under the provision prohibiting automated calls to cellular telephones without the called party's consent was arbitrary; that the treatment of reassigned numbers had to be set aside; and that the FCC was not compelled to interpret "called party" to mean "intended recipient," rather than the current subscriber. *See* ACA International v. Federal Communications Commission, 885 F.3d 687 (D.C. Cir. 2018). In the wake of *ACA International*, the Ninth Circuit clarified that an autodialer is "equipment which has the capacity—(1) to store numbers to be called or (2) to produce numbers to be called, using a random or sequential number generator—and to dial such numbers automatically." *See* Marks v. Crunch San Diego, LLC., 904 F.3d 1041, 1053 (9th Cir. 2018).

359. *See, for example*, Soppet v. Enhanced Recovery Co., 679 F.3d 637, 638–639 (7th Cir. 2012).

360. Provision of a telephone number in a credit application is considered express consent. *See* S. David Smith, Michael D. Ferachi, Gregg D. Stevens, & Mark H. Tyson, Impact of the TCPA and the FDCPA on Debt Collection: Current Issues and Recent Developments, 66 Consumer Finance L.Q. Rep. 15, 18 (2012).

361. *See* Meadows v. Franklin Collection Serv., 414 Fed. Appx. 230, 235 (11th Cir. 2011).

362. McCaskill v. Navient Solutions, Inc., 178 F. Supp. 3d 1281, 1290 (M.D. Fla. 2016) (finding a loan borrower's mother who allowed her cell phone to ring over 700 times without attempting to stop the calls was insufficient consent under the TCPA).

363. Ebling v. ClearSpring Loan Servs., Inc., 106 F. Supp. 3d 1002, 1005 (D. Minn. 2015) (recipient of debt collection calls gave prior express consent for debt collector to call her cellular phone, and thus debt collector's automated calls to that phone did not violate the TCPA, even though recipient did not specifically consent to be contacted via automated calls).

364. For example, after the death of a parent, a family member likely will call the National Grid to discontinue service on the parent's account. A federal appeals court has held that the family member's giving that phone number did not qualify as consent to receive autodialed or prerecorded calls in connection with amounts owed by the decedent on the account. Nigro v. Mercantile Adjustment Bureau, 769 F.3d 804, 806 (2d Cir. 2014).

365. *See, for example*, Baisden v. Credit Adjustments, Inc., 813 F.3d 338 (6th Cir. 2016) (debtors' provision of their cellular phone numbers to a hospital when completing form authorizations as part of their hospital admissions constituted giving of "prior express consent" to receive debt collection calls from the hospital's anesthesiology provider's debt collector); Baird v. Sabre Inc., 995 F. Supp. 2d 1100 (C.D. Cal. 2014) (found consent to calls from an automated dialing machine when a consumer included her cell phone number in an online flight reservation), aff'd, 636 Fed. Appx. 715 (9th Cir. 2016); Jordan v. ER Solutions, Inc., 900 F. Supp. 2d 1323 (S.D. Fla. 2012) (consumer gave express consent to automated collection calls and prerecorded messages from debt collector as term and condition of purchase).

366. *Compare* Gutierrez v. Barclays Grp., 2011 WL 579238, at *4 (S.D. Cal. 2011) (consent can be revoked orally under the TCPA), *with* Moltz v. Firstsource Advantage, LLC, 2011 WL 3360010, at *3 (W.D.N.Y. 2011) (FDCPA, not TCPA, governed and required written request).

367. Schweitzer v. Comenity Bank, 866 F.3d 1273 (11th Cir. 2017).

368. Pub. L. No. 90-321, 82 Stat. 146, codified at 15 U.S.C. ch. 41 § 1601.

369. *See* Edward L. Rubin, Legislative Methodology: Some Lessons from the Truth-in-Lending Act, 80 Geo. L.J. 233 (1991).

370. H.R. Rep. No. 90 (1967), reprinted in 1968 U.S.C.C.A.N. 1962, 1979.

371. *See* Hon. Henry Callaway & Jonathan Petts, Too Broke for a Fresh Start, 38-Feb. Am. Bankr. Inst. J. 24 (2019):

> Consumer bankruptcy was designed to provide a "new opportunity in life and a clear field for future effort." In addition to erasing unsecured debt and stopping wage garnishment, chapter 7 [a kind of bankruptcy proceeding] increases debtors' employment outcomes by 12 percent, and often improves access to credit after discharge. In short, the fresh start is a powerful poverty-fighting tool.
>
> However, over the last decade, chapter 7's fresh start has become steadily less accessible for low-income Americans. Since the financial crisis, the number of individual chapter 7 filings has steadily decreased.... In many markets, the cost of filing has more than doubled, putting a chapter 7 discharge outside the reach of many low-income debtors.

Debtors who cannot afford a chapter 7 attorney might file a deficient *pro se* petition, fall prey to an unscrupulous bankruptcy petition preparer, or file a "no-money-down" chapter 13 case that is (in some jurisdictions) likely to be dismissed without any lasting debt relief. Lacking funds for the filing and attorney fees, these financially stressed debtors might not be able to file at all in some cases. In turn, they suffer from the lack of housing, food and basic utilities that often accompany severe debt.

372. *See* Stephen L. Willborn, Wage Garnishment: Efficiency, Fairness, and the Uniform Act, 49 Seton Hall L. Rev. 847, 848 (2019) (reporting that annually 11 million Americans have wages garnished, and their wages "are reduced, on average, by over $2,000 each year even though those most likely to be garnished only earn between $25,000 and $40,000" per year).

373. States that bar wage garnishment include Texas, North Carolina, South Carolina, and Pennsylvania. A list of each state's garnishment procedures can be found at http://www.fair-debt-collection.com/state-garnishment-laws.html. *See, for example*, New York State Exempt Income Protection Act, L. 2008, ch. 575, and codified throughout Article 52 of the N.Y. Civil Practice Law and Rules. For further information, *see* National Consumer Law Center, Collection Actions, ¶ 14.2.4 (discussing the relation between federal and state wage garnishment protection). If an account is wrongfully garnished, the consumer may have a state-law cause of action against the creditor for wrongful garnishment, which generally requires a showing that the garnishment was sought although no debt was owed to the party seeking the garnishment and that the party subject to the garnishment owned a beneficial interest in the property being garnished. *See, for example*, Vanover v. Cook, 260 F.3d 1182, 1189 (10th Cir. 2001) (defining claim for wrongful garnishment under Kansas law, and holding it does not apply to excessive garnishment); *see also* Todd v. Weltman, Weinberg & Reis Co., 434 F.3d 432, 443–444 (6th Cir. 2006) ("As with the tort of malicious prosecution, two of the necessary elements of a cause of action for wrongful garnishment are (1) an absence of probable cause for such proceeding, and (2) the presence of legal malice, which 'may be inferred entirely from a lack of probable cause.'") (citations omitted); Calahan v. Scottsdale Ins. Co., 903 So. 2d 1251, 1260 (La. Ct. App. 3d Cir. 2005) ("A wrongful garnishment by a judgment creditor is answerable in damages."). Other cases are collected in 38 C.J.S. Garnishment §§ 453–456.

374. 50 U.S.C. §§ 3901–4026. A creditor can enforce a civil judgment against a military member by applying for an involuntary allotment from the member's military pay. However, applications for involuntary allotments cannot be based on garnishments. *See* 32 C.F.R. § 113.6(b)(1)(iii) ("A garnishment summons or order is insufficient to satisfy the final judgment requirement of § 113.6(b)(1)(ii) and is not required to apply for an involuntary allotment under this part"). Moreover, under the Servicemembers Civil Relief Act, 50 U.S.C. § 3934, a court may stay or vacate garnishment of a servicemember's property. Garnishment is permitted only for child and spousal support. *See* U.S. Courts, Servicemembers' Civil Relief Act, https://uscourts.gov/services-forms/bankruptcy/bankruptcy-basics/servicemembers-civil-relief-act-scva.

375. Sniadach v. Family Finance Corp., 395 U.S. 337 (1969).
376. "Earnings" means "compensation paid or payable for personal services, whether denominated as wages, salary, commission, bonus, or otherwise, and includes periodic payments pursuant to a pension or retirement program." 15 U.S.C. § 1672(a). Some courts have held that tips paid directly from the customer to the worker are not earnings subject to wage garnishment. *See* National Consumer Law Center, Collection Actions, ¶ 14.2.1.4.3 (discussing tips and wage garnishment).
377. *See, for example*, Voss Prods., Inc. v. Carlton, 147 F. Supp. 2d 892, 897 (E.D. Tenn. 2001).
378. 15 U.S.C. § 1673(a)(1)–(2).
379. 15 U.S.C. § 1672(b). "The term 'disposable earnings' means that part of the earnings of any individual remaining after the deduction from those earnings of any amounts required by law to be withheld."
380. *See* Kokoszka v. Belford, 417 U.S. 642, 648–651 (1974).
381. *See* Faith Mullen, Another Day Older and Deeper in Debt: Mitigating the Deleterious Effect of Wage Garnishments orl Appalachia's Low-Wage Workers, 12 W. Va. L. Rev. 973, 978–979 (2018):

> Kentucky is typical of the states in the Appalachian Region that have adopted the federal formula for calculating the amount of a wage garnishment. In Kentucky, the median annual household income is $45,000. A single person with no dependents who earned that amount would have an annual after-tax income of approximately $34,500. Garnishment would reduce such a wage earner's annual income to approximately $25,900.
>
> Although that reduction of income would be disruptive to someone who earns the median income, the effect of wage garnishment on a worker who earns minimum wage is potentially catastrophic. A worker in Kentucky who earns minimum wage would have an annual after-tax income of approximately $15,800 (based on 2017 tax rates). The allowable weekly wage garnishment would be $76, leaving an annual income of approximately $11,900. Wage garnishment would cause this worker's income to drop below the federal poverty level. The effect is even more pronounced when the household includes more than one person; the income of a single parent raising two children would dip almost to 50% of the poverty level.
>
> States can ensure that wage garnishment will not drive low-wage workers into poverty by protecting more wages from garnishment. This can be done by adjusting one or both parts of the two-part federal formula (first, the amount by which disposable earnings exceed 30 times the federal minimum hourly wage, and second, 25% of disposable earnings). Federal law allows garnishment of the lesser of these numbers.

382. 15 U.S.C. § 1673(b)(1)(B).
383. 15 U.S.C. § 1673(b)(1)(C).
384. 15 U.S.C. § 1673(b)(2)(A)–(B).
385. 15 U.S.C. § 1673(b)(2)(B).
386. 15 U.S.C. § 1671(a)(2). *See also* Stewart v. Travelers Corp., 503 F.2d 108, 113 n.14 (9th Cir. 1974) (noting that Congress enacted the Consumer Credit Protection Act out of concern over the "unscrupulous and unfair use of wage garnishments," and

that "in a vast number of cases the debt is a fraudulent one, saddled on a poor igno-rant person who is trapped in an easy credit nightmare").

387. 15 U.S.C. § 1674(a).

388. *See, for example*, Newby v. Wal-Mart Stores, Inc., 659 F. Supp. 879 (D.C. Ill. 1987); Dull v. Advance Mepco Cent. Lab, Inc., 151 Wis.2d 524, 444 N.W.2d 463 (1989 Wis. App. 1989).

389. *See* National Consumer Law Center, Collection Actions ¶ 14.2.1.6.1 (discussing the discharge prohibition) (citing United States Department of Labor, Wage & Hour Division, Field Operations Handbook Ch. 16, § 16c03(a)–(b), https://www.dol.gov/whd/FOH/FOH_Ch16.pdf).

390. 15 U.S.C. § 1674(b).

391. 15 U.S.C. § 1676. *Compare* Stewart v. Travelers Corp., 503 F.2d 108 (9th Cir. 1974) (implying a private civil remedy under the statute), *with* LeVick v. Skaggs Companies, Inc., 701 F.2d 777 (9th Cir. 1983) (declining to imply a private civil remedy).

392. *See, for example*, United States v. Tripodis, 2016 WL 5389142, at *4 (N.D. Ga. 2016) (CCPA does not protect "[w]ages that have been voluntarily converted into savings"). *See* Chris Arnold, With Debt Collection, Your Bank Account Could be at Risk, NPR (Sept. 16, 2014), http://www.npr.org/templates/transcript/transcript.php?storyId=348709389; Jason C. Walker, Wyoming's Statutory Exemption on Wage Garnishment: Should It Include Deposited Wages?, 6 Wyo. L. Rev. 53 (2006) (urging protection of wages even after deposit in bank).

393. Kokoszka v Belford, 417 U.S. 642 (1974). *See also* In re Trudeau, 237 B.R. 803, 806 (10th Cir. 1999) (a tax refund is not "earnings" within the meaning of the Consumer Credit Protection Act).

394. Funk v. Utah State Tax Com., 839 P.2d 818, 821 (Utah 1992).

395. *See* National Retail Federation, Tax Returns: Consumer Filing Plans, https://nrf.com/tax-returns-data-center; *see also* Haley Sweetland Edwards, Do Tax Refunds Boost the Economy?, Time (Apr. 15, 2016), http://time.com/4293090/tax-refunds-tax-day-economic-stimulus/; Janie Boschma, Some Americans Depend on Their Tax Refunds to Survive, The Atlantic (Mar. 16, 2015), http://www.theatlantic.com/business/archive/2015/03/some-americans-depend-on-their-tax-refunds-to-survive/425427/.

396. *See* Porter v. Aetna Casualty & Surety Co., 370 U.S. 159, 162 (1962) (holding that veteran disability benefits as exempt benefits remain exempt after deposit in a bank account, provided they are traceable, have not been converted into a "permanent investment," and "retain the qualities of moneys").

397. 42 U.S.C. § 407(a).

398. Social Services Amendments of 1974, Pub. L. No. 93-647, § 459, 88 Stat. 2337, 2357–58 (1975) (amending 42 U.S.C. § 659 to allow legal process upon federal benefits to recover child support and alimony payments).

399. 31 U.S.C. § 3716(c)(3)(A).

400. 26 U.S.C. § 6334(c).

401. 42 U.S.C. § 1383(d)(1).

402. Allen C. Myers, Untangling the Safety Net: Protecting Federal Benefits from Freezes, Fees, and Garnishment, 66 Wash. & Lee L. Rev. 371, 383 n.62 (2009). However, as discussed earlier in this volume, the Social Security Administration may withhold an SSI recipient's retroactive SSI award to reimburse a state for public assistance provided while the SSI application was pending. 42 U.S.C. § 1383(g).

403. 26 U.S.C. § 6334(a)(11).

404. 38 U.S.C. § 5301(a)(1).

405. 5 U.S.C. § 8346(a).

406. 45 U.S.C. § 231m(a). Also exempt are: military annuities and survivors' benefits; student assistance; merchant seamen's wages; longshoremen's and harbor workers' death and disability benefits; foreign service retirement and disability benefits; compensation for injury, death, or detention of employees of U.S. contractors outside the United States; and federal emergency management agency federal disaster assistance. See Federal Trade Commission, Consumer Information, Garnishing Federal Benefits, https://www.consumer.ftc.gov/articles/0114-garnishing-federal-benefits.

407. National Consumer Law Center, Collection Actions ¶ 14.3.2 (discussing public assistance benefits and identifying Rhode Island, Minnesota, Vermont, New York, Connecticut, and Wisconsin as states with laws that protect workers in this situation).

408. A 2010 report of the Federal Trade Commission documented that illegal garnishment of exempt public benefits occurred when the recipient deposited the funds in a bank account with nonexempt funds. The garnishment was found to have caused "considerable hardship"—banks froze accounts up to the amount of the garnishment order, regardless of the source of the funds; banks imposed fees on the consumer; the consumer could not access funds; checks bounced, generating more fees; and the consumer lacked sufficient funds for the purchase of basic necessities. See Federal Trade Commission, Repairing a Broken System: Protecting Consumers in Debt Collection Litigation and Arbitration 31–32 (2010), https://www.ftc.gov/sites/default/files/documents/reports/federal-trade-commission-bureau-consumer-protection-staff-report-repairing-broken-system-protecting/debtcollectionreport.pdf.

409. 31 C.F.R. §§ 212.1–12. See Margot F. Saunders & Johnson Tyler, Past, Present and Future Threats to Federal Safety Net Benefits in Bank Accounts, 16 N.C. Banking Inst. 43 (2012) (identifying gaps in the regulations).

410. 31 C.F.R. §§ 212.4–6.

411. 31 C.F.R. § 212.4(a).

412. 31 C.F.R. §§ 212.4–6.

413. "The financial institution shall immediately calculate and establish the protected amount for an account. The financial institution shall ensure that the account holder has full and customary access to the protected amount, which the financial institution shall not freeze in response to the garnishment order." 31 C.F.R. § 212.6(a). "Protected amount means the lesser of the sum of all benefit payments posted to an account between the close of business on the beginning date of the lookback period

and the open of business on the ending date of the lookback period, or the balance in an account when the account review is performed." 31 C.F.R. § 212.3.

414. 31 C.F.R. § 212.6(h).
415. 31 C.F.R. § 212.6(b).
416. 31 C.F.R. § 212.7(f).
417. 31. C.F.R. §§ 212.6(e), 7(a).
418. 31 C.F.R. § 212.7(b).
419. 31 C.F.R. § 212.7(b)(1).
420. 31 C.F.R. § 212.7(b)(2).
421. 31 C.F.R. § 212.7(b)(3).
422. 31 C.F.R. § 212.7(b)(4).
423. 31 C.F.R. § 212.7(b)(5).
424. 31 C.F.R. § 212.7(b)(6).
425. 31 C.F.R. § 212.7(b)(7).
426. 31 C.F.R. § 212.7(b)(8).
427. 31 C.F.R. § 212.7(b)(9).
428. 31 C.F.R. § 212.7(b)(11).
429. 31 C.F.R. § 212.7(b)(10).
430. Federal Trade Commission, Consumer Information, Take Action, https://www.consumer.ftc.gov/. A fact sheet entitled "Garnishing Federal Benefits" is available free of charge, https://www.consumer.ftc.gov/articles/0114-garnishing-federal-benefits.
431. 31 C.F.R. 212.6(h), but allowing a fee "up to five days after the account review if funds other than a benefit payment are deposited to the account within this period, provided that the fee may not exceed the amount of the non-benefit deposited funds." *See* Monroe Retail, Inc. v. RBS Citizens, 589 F.3d 274, 284 (6th Cir. 2009) (federal National Banking Law preempted state restriction on fee deductions prior to garnishment payment processing).
432. 12 C.F.R. § 7.4002(a) & (b)(2) ("The establishment of non-interest charges and fees, their amounts, and the method of calculating them are business decisions to be made by each bank, in its discretion, according to sound banking judgment and safe and sound banking principles."). The Officer of the Comptroller of the Currency (OCC), which has regulatory and supervisory power over national banks, has defined this authority as an "incidental power" of a national bank; some federal courts have held that the National Bank Act preempts the power of the states to regulate garnishment fees. *See* Monroe Retail, Inc. v. Charter One Bank, 624 F. Supp. 2d 677, 686 (N.D. Ohio 2007) ("[A]ny interference with a national bank's right to assess service fees is necessarily preempted whether it directly affects a depositor's account, or indirectly affects the amount a garnishor will receive.").
433. 12 C.F.R. §§ 7.4002(b)(2)(i)–(iv). The factors are: (i) the cost incurred by the bank in providing the service; (ii) the deterrence of misuse by customers of banking services; (iii) the enhancement of the competitive position of the bank in accordance with the bank's business plan and marketing strategy; and (iv) the maintenance of the safety and soundness of the institution.

434. The largest three (Bank of America, J.P. Morgan Chase, and Wells Fargo) account for over 30% alone. *See* Alina Comoreanu, Bank Market Share by Deposits and Assets, WalletHub (Feb. 9, 2017), https://wallethub.com/edu/bank-market-share-by-deposits/25587.

435. *See* Bank of America, Personal Schedule of Fees (effective May 17, 2019), https://www.bankofamerica.com/deposits/resources/personal-schedule-fees.go; Chase Bank, Additional Services and Fees for Personal Accounts: Deposit Account Agreement (effective June 9, 2019), https://www.chase.com/content/dam/chasecom/en/checking/documents/how-your-transaction-will-work.pdf; John Aidan Byrne, Banks Introduce New Fees and Service Cuts, N.Y. Post (June 21, 2015), http://nypost.com/2015/06/21/banks-introduce-new-fees-and-service-cuts/ ("Wells Fargo charges $125 on money in an account garnished by a court order.").

436. *See, for example*, New Economy Project, Know Your Rights: Community Development Credit Unions, https://neweconomynyc.org/resources/credit-unions; Mandi Woodruff, Here's Why You're Better Off Using a Credit Union Rather Than a Big Bank, Business Insider (Jan. 30, 2014, 9:46 AM), http://www.businessinsider.com/should-you-use-credit-unions-or-big-banks-2014-1; Devan Goldstein, Credit Unions vs. Banks: How to Decide, NerdWallet (Nov. 26, 2018), https://www.nerdwallet.com/blog/banking/credit-unions-vs-banks/; Richie Bernardo, Credit Union vs. Bank: What's the Difference?, WalletHub (Mar. 17, 2015), https://wallethub.com/edu/credit-union-vs-bank/115/.

437. The Truth in Lending Act (TILA) is codified at 15 U.S.C. §§ 1601 et seq. and was enacted as Title I of the Consumer Credit Protection Act, Pub. L. No. 90-321.

438. Implementing regulations appear in Reg. 2, 12 C.F.R. § 1026.

439. TILA was amended in 1970 to bar unsolicited credit cards. Regulations implementing this reform can be found in 12 C.F.R. § 226.12(a). The TILA was amended in 1994 by the Home Ownership and Equity Protection Act (HOEPA) to regulate certain closed-end mortgage loans bearing rates above a certain amount. Regulations implementing this reform can be found in 12 C.F.R. § 226.32(a). The 2009 Credit Card Accountability Responsibility and Disclosure (CARD) Act further amended the TILA and added new protections involving consumer credit card accounts. *See* Credit Card Accountability Responsibility and Disclosure Act of 2009, Pub. L. No. 111-24, 123 Stat. 1734 (2009). The Dodd-Frank Wall Street Reform and Consumer Protection Act of 2010 granted rulemaking authority under the TILA to the Consumer Financial Protection Bureau (CFPB). *See* Dodd-Frank Wall Street Reform and Consumer Protection Act, Pub. L. No. 111-203, 124 Stat. 1376 (2010). In particular, Title XIV of the Dodd-Frank Act included a number of amendments to the TILA, which amends primarily consumer rights relating to mortgage loans and appraisals. *See* Title XIV, Mortgage Reform and Anti-Predatory Lending Act, 124 Stat. at 1400. For a history of amendments to the TILA, *see* Consumer Financial Protection Bureau, Laws and Regulations, Truth in Lending Act (Apr. 2015), http://files.consumerfinance.gov/f/201503_cfpb_truth-in-lending-act.pdf. *See also* Jeff Sovern, Preventing Future Economic Crises Through Consumer Protection Law or How the Truth in Lending Act Failed the Subprime Borrowers, 71 Ohio St. L.J. 761 (2010).

440. The Higher Education Opportunity Act of 2008, Pub. L. No. 110-315, 122 Stat. 3078, § 1011 (2008), reauthorized the Higher Education Act of 1965, as amended. *See* Vincent J. Roldan & Elizabeth L. Gunn, Trekking through the Quagmire: A Creative Discharge Solution to the Student Loan Crisis, 37-Dec. Am. Bankr. Inst. J. 36 (2018) ("Since 2008, student loan debt relative to overall household debt has grown from 5% to 30%. This growth has some commentators predicting that the student loan industry is the next economic 'bubble' that will burst."); *see also* Andrew A. Sexton, The Education Loan Bubble: How the Discharge Student Loans in Bankruptcy Act of 2017 and Legislation Alike Is the Only Answer to the Student Loan Crisis, 54 Cal. W. L. Rev. 323 (2018) (calling for reforms not related to the TILA to deal with the student loan "bubble").

441. *See* Andrew Wold, Alt-Remedies to Paying Student Loans, 76-Feb. Bench & B. Minn. 27 (2019) (stating that "[c]lose to $1.5 trillion in loans have been issued to students"). In 2017, student debt totaled $1.3 trillion. *See* Zack Friedman, Student Loan Debt in 2017: A $1.3 Trillion Crisis, Forbes (Feb. 21, 2017), https://www.forbes.com/sites/zackfriedman/2017/02/21/student-loan-debt-statistics-2017/#4f3139565dab.

442. *See* William G. Gale, Benjamin H. Harris, Bryan Renaud, & Katherine Rodihan, Student Loans Rising: An Overview of Causes, Consequences, and Policy Options *2, Tax Policy Center, Urban Institute and Brookings Institution (May 2014), https://www.brookings.edu/wp-content/uploads/2016/06/student_loans_rising_gale_harris_09052014.pdf.

443. National Center for Education Statistics, Fast Facts: Tuition Costs of Colleges and Universities, https://nces.ed.gov/fastfacts/display.asp?id=76.

444. *See* Aaron N. Taylor, "Your Results May Vary": Protecting Students and Taxpayers Through Tighter Regulation of Proprietary School Representations, 62 Admin. L. Rev. 729, 761 (2010). As a consequence, there are typically higher rates of default on loans at these schools. About 25% of student loans were in default or behind in payment as of August 2015, with default rates higher among students at for-profit schools than at public schools. *See* Consumer Financial Protection Bureau, Student Loan Servicing: Analysis of Public Input and Recommendations for Reform, *3 (Sept. 2015), http://files.consumerfinance.gov/f/201509_cfpb_student-loan-servicing-report.pdf. *See also* National Bureau of Economic Research, Lance Locher & Alexander Monge-Naranjo, Student Loans and Repayment: Theory, Evidence and Policy (Jan. 2015), http://www.nber.org/papers/w20849.

445. Tiffany F. Boykin, For Profit, For Success, For Black Men: A Review of Literature on Urban For-Profit Colleges and Universities, 52 Urban Educ. 1140 (2017). *See also* William Beaver, Fraud in For-Profit Higher Education, 49 Society 274 (May 2012); Adam Looney & Constantine Yannelis, A Crisis in Student Loans? How Changes in the Characteristics of Borrowers and in the Institutions They Attended Contributed to Rising Loan Defaults, Brookings Papers on Economic Activity, Brookings Institution (Sept. 2015), http://www.brookings.edu/~/media/projects/bpea/fall-2015_embargoed/conferencedraft_looneyyannelis_studentloandefaults.pdf.

446. Among other things, a school with a high rate of student default is subject to losing important sources of federal aid; for strategic reasons, proprietary schools may

sometimes pay off loans for students who have withdrawn from the school. But after paying the loans, the schools often aggressively pursued repayment from the debtors themselves, and students have ended up with less favorable repayment terms. Real job prospects also have tended to be lower than expected, in part because the employment statistics many for-profit schools published in advertising material turned out to be fabricated. *See* Maura Dundon, Students or Consumers? For-Profit Colleges and the Practice and Theoretical Role of Consumer Protection, 9 Harv. L. & Pol'y Rev. 375 (2015); Jonathan A. LaPlante, Congress's Tax Bomb: Income-Based Repayment and Disarming a Problem Facing Student Loan Borrowers, 100 Cornell L. Rev. 703, 704 (2015); Kamille Wolff Dean, Student Loans, Politics, and the Occupy Movement: Financial Aid Rebellion and Reform, 46 J. Marshall L. Rev. 105, 111 (2012).

447. *See* Jeffrey Davis, Revamping Consumer-Credit Contract Law, 68 Va. L. Rev. 1333, 1345–46 (1982) (remarking that the TILA disclosure statement is "nearly incomprehensible to the average consumer"); Edward L. Rubin, Legislative Methodology: Some Lessons from the Truth-In-Lending Act, 80 Geo. L.J. 233, 234–235 (1991) ("Our penchant for disclosure laws is in part a political compromise and in part a collective neurosis, but it is also an artifact of the current method- ology of statutory design."). The TILA education amendments have been criticized for not requiring lenders to set maximum interest rates or fees, provide affordable repayment plans, or cancel debts because of death, permanent disability, or school closure; borrowers often still find it nearly impossible to discharge private loans in bankruptcy; schools do not know when their students are taking out private loans; and policymakers lack basic information about who is borrowing and on what terms. The Institute for College Access & Success, The Project on Student Debt, Summary of New Disclosure Requirements for Private Student Loans (Aug. 2009), https://ticas.org/sites/default/files/pub_files/FRB_summary_aug09rules.pdf.   *See also* Ryan Bubb & Richard Pildes. How Behavioral Economics Trims Its Sails and Why, 127 Harv. L. Rev. 1593 (2014) (questioning the efficacy of disclosure to reg- ulate credit markets and considering the benefits of substantive regulation such as setting price caps).

448. 20 U.S.C. § 1001(a) (general definition of institution of higher education).

449. 12 C.F.R. § 1026.46(b)(5)(ii).

450. 12 C.F.R. §§ 226.46(d)(1) & 226.47(a).

451. 12 C.F.R. §§ 226.46(d)(2) & 226.47(b).

452. 12 C.F.R. §§ 226.46(d)(3) & 226.47(c).

453. 20 U.S.C. § 1087ll; 12 C.F.R. § 226.46(b)(3).

454. 12 C.F.R. § 1024.46.

455. 15 U.S.C. § 1638(e)(1); 12 C.F.R. § 226.47(a).

456. 12 C.F.R. § 226.46(c)(2)(i).

457. 12 C.F.R. § 226.46(c)(2)(i).

458. 12 C.F.R. § 226.46(c)(3); *see* Electronic Signatures in Global and National Commerce (E-Sign) Act, 15 U.S.C. §§ 7001 et seq.

459. 20 U.S.C. § 1019a (a)(1)(B)(iii).

460. 15 U.S.C. § 1638(e)(1); 12 C.F.R. § 226.46(c)(1).

461. 15 U.S.C. § 1638(e)(1)(A); 12 C.F.R. § 226.47(a)(1)(i).
462. 15 U.S.C. § 1638(e)(1)(B); 12 C.F.R. § 226.47(a)(1)(ii). A variable rate is based on a rate in the market, which may change over time. *See* Consumer Financial Protection Bureau, Private Student Loans, *108 (Aug. 29, 2012), https://files.consumerfinance. gov/f/201207_cfpb_Reports_Private-Student-Loans.pdf (noting that the variable rate may include a risk premium "based on the credit worthiness of a borrower").
463. 15 U.S.C. § 1638(e)(1)(C); 12 C.F.R. § 226.47(a)(1)(iii).
464. 15 U.S.C. § 1638(e)(1)(D); 12 C.F.R. § 226.47(a)(1)(iv).
465. 15 U.S.C. § 1638(e)(1)(E); 12 C.F.R. § 226.47(a)(2)(ii).
466. 15 U.S.C. § 1638(e)(1)(F); 12 C.F.R. § 226.47(a)(2)(i).
467. 15 U.S.C. § 1638(e)(1)(G); 12 C.F.R. § 226.47(a)(3)(i).
468. 15 U.S.C. § 1638(e)(1)(H); 12 C.F.R. § 226.47(a)(3)(iii)(A).
469. 15 U.S.C. § 1638(e)(1)(I); 12 C.F.R. § 226.47(a)(3)(ii)–(iii).
470. 15 U.S.C. § 1638(e)(1)(J); 12 C.F.R. § 226.47(a)(5).
471. 15 U.S.C. § 1638(e)(1)(K)(i)–(ii); 12 C.F.R. § 226.47(a)(4)(i)–(iii).
472. 15 U.S.C. § 1638(e)(1)(L).
473. 15 U.S.C. § 1638(e)(1)(M); 12 C.F.R. § 226.47(a)(6)(i).
474. 15 U.S.C. § 1638(e)(1)(N); 12 C.F.R. § 226.47(a)(6)(ii).
475. 20 U.S.C. § 1019a(a)(1)(B)(ii)(II).
476. 15 U.S.C. § 1638(e)(1)(O)(i); 12 C.F.R. § 226.47(a)(7).
477. 15 U.S.C. § 1638(e)(1)(P).
478. 15 U.S.C. § 1638(e)(1)(Q); 12 C.F.R. § 226.47(a)(6)(iii). The website is available at http://studentaid.ed.gov.
479. 12 C.F.R. § 1026.47(b).
480. 12 C.F.R. § 1026.48(c)(1)
481. 12 C.F.R. § 1026.47(c).
482. 15 U.S.C. § 1638(e)(4)(c); 12 C.F.R. §1026.47(c)(4)(i).
483. 12 C.F.R. § 126.47(c)(4)(ii).
484. 12 C.F.R. § 1026.47(c)(4)(ii).
485. 20 U.S.C. § 1092(a)(1).
486. 20 U.S.C. § 1019a(a)(1)(A)(i)(III). A private lender can never use a school's mascot, logo, emblem, or anything else that might lead a student to believe that the loan is being made by the school itself. 20 U.S.C. § 1019a(a)(2).
487. 20 U.S.C. § 1092(a)(1)(A).
488. 20 U.S.C. § 1092(a)(1)(B).
489. 20 U.S.C. § 1092(a)(1)(C).
490. 20 U.S.C. § 1092(a)(1)(D).
491. 20 U.S.C. § 1092(a)(1)(E).
492. 20 U.S.C. § 1092(a)(1)(F)(i)–(iii).
493. 20 U.S.C. § 1092(a)(1)(G). This information must include "(i) the current degree programs and other educational and training programs, (ii) the instructional, laboratory, and other physical plant facilities which relate to the academic program, (iii) the faculty and other instructional personnel, and (iv) any plans by the institution for improving the academic program of the institution."

494. 20 U.S.C. § 1092(a)(1)(H). Under 20 U.S.C. § 1092(c), each eligible institution must designate employee(s) to be available on a full-time basis to assist students or potential students in obtaining information about available financial aid.

495. 20 U.S.C. §§ 1092(a)(1)(K); 1091(c)(1)(B).

496. 20 U.S.C. § 1092(a)(1)(M). Along with the information listed relating to loans, schools are also required to provide information about services and facilities available to students with disabilities, information about the institutional accreditation, the graduation or completion rate of students entering the institution, information about the implications of studying abroad for financial assistance, campus crime rates, the institution's policies relating to copyright infringement, information about student body diversity at the institution, statistics on employment after graduation, the institution's fire safety report, the institution's retention rate, and information about required vaccinations. 20 U.S.C. § 1092(a)(1)(I)–(L), (N)–(V).

497. 20 U.S.C. § 1092(b)(1)(A).

498. 20 U.S.C. § 1092(b)(1)(A)(i)–(ix). The National Student Loan Data System allows students to access information about their student loans or grants, and is available at https://nsldsfap.ed.gov/nslds_FAP/.

499. *See* Consumer Financial Protection Bureau, Paying for College, http://www.consumerfinance.gov/paying-for-college.

500. *See* FinAid: The SmartStudent Guide to Financial Aid, http://www.finaid.org/loans/studentloans.phtml.

501. Vincent J. Roldan & Elizabeth L. Gunn, Trekking through the Quagmire: A Creative Discharge Solution to the Student Loan Crisis, 37-Dec. Am. Bankr. Inst. J. 36 (2018) (citing statistics); *see also* Nigel Chiwaya, These five charts show how bad the student loan debt situation is, NBC (Apr. 24, 2019), https://www.nbcnews.com/news/us-news/student-loan-statistics-2019-n997836.

502. U.S. Department of Education, Federal Student Aid, Don't ignore your student loan payments or you'll risk going into default, https://studentaid.ed.gov/sa/repay-loans/default.

503. *See* National Consumer Law Center, Surviving Debt: Expert Advice for Getting Out of Financial Trouble, Chapter 13: Student Loans (2019), https://library.nclc.org/SD; National Consumer Law Center, Student Loan Law, Chapter 6: Implications of Student Loan Defaults (2015), https://library.nclc.org/sl.

504. Pub. L. No. 115-174, Economic Growth, Regulatory Relief, and Consumer Protection Act, Title VI—Protection for Student Borrowers, § 602, amending the Fair Credit Reporting Act.

505. Helping Families Save Their Homes Act of 2009, Pub. L. No. 111-22, 123 Stat. 1632, § 404(g), codified at 15 U.S.C. § 1641(f)–(g).

506. Consumer Financial Protection Bureau, Submit a Complaint, http://www.consumerfinance.gov/complaint/#student-loancomplaint.

507. The Consumer Financial Protection Bureau brought enforcement actions against Navient, the largest student loan servicer in the United States, alleging improprieties in its treatment of student private and federal debtors. *See, for example*, Consumer Financial Protection Bureau v. Navient Corp., 2017 WL 3380530, *1 (M.D. Pa.

2017) (finding the CFPB had enforcement authority without first engaging in rulemaking; finding no constitutional defects in the structure of the CFPB; finding the complaint was adequately pleaded).

508. *See, for example*, Narais v. Chase Home Fin. LLC, 736 F.3d 711, 718–719 (6th Cir. 2013) (holding the servicer not liable for failing to identify the creditor in a suit involving Regulation Z and the Real Estate Settlement Procedures Act); Erickson v. PNC Mortgage, 2011 WL 1743875 (D. Nev. 2011) (denying motion to dismiss claim that servicer failed to make mandatory disclosure in in suit involving mortgage note).

509. *See* U.S. Department of Education, Federal Student Aid, Aid for Military Families, https://studentaid.ed.gov/sa/types/grants-scholarships/military#interest-and-deferment; *see also* U.S. Department of Defense, Servicemembers Civil Relief Act (SCRA) Website, https://scra.dmdc.osd.mil/scra/#/home.

510. 50 U.S.C. § 3937(a)(1), previously codified at 50 App. U.S.C. § 527.

511. 34 C.F.R. § 685.204(h).

512. 34 C.F.R. § 685.213(c)(1).

513. Hollister Petraeus & Rohit Chopra, The Next Front? Student Loan Servicing and the Cost to Our Men and Women in Uniform, Consumer Financial Protection Bureau, *2 (Oct. 18, 2012), http://files.consumerfinance.gov/f/201210_cfpb_servicemember-student-loan-servicing.pdf.

514. Consumer Financial Protection Bureau, Submit a Complaint, http://www.consumerfinance.gov/complaint/#student-loancomplaint.

515. *See* Hollister Petraeus & Seth Frotman, Overseas & Underserved: Student Loan Servicing and the Cost to Our Men and Women in Uniform, Consumer Financial Protection Bureau *3 (July 7, 2015), http://files.consumerfinance.gov/f/201507_cfpb_overseas-underserved-student-loan-servicing-and-the-cost-to-our-men-and-women-in-uniform.pdf.

516. Consumer Financial Protection Bureau, What are Debt Settlement/Debt Relief Services and Should I Use Them?, Ask CFPB (last updated Feb. 15, 2017), http://www.consumerfinance.gov/askcfpb/1457/what-are-debt-settlementdebt-relief-services.html.

517. *See* Deanne Loonin & Jillian McLaughlin, Searching for Relief: Desperate Borrowers and the Growing Student Loan "Debt Relief" Industry, 3–5, National Consumer Law Center (June 2013), http://www.studentloanborrowerassistance.org/wp-content/uploads/File/searching-for-relief-report.pdf.

518. *See* Rohit Chopra, Consumer Advisory: Student Loan Debt Relief Companies May Cost You Thousands of Dollars and Drive You Further into Debt, Consumer Financial Protection Bureau Blog (Dec. 11, 2014), http://www.consumerfinance.gov/blog/consumer-advisory-student-loan-debt-relief-companies-may-cost-you-thousands-of-dollars-and-drive-you-further-into-debt/.

519. U.S. Department of Education, Federal Student Aid, Loan Consolidation, https://studentaid.ed.gov/sa/repay-loans/consolidation.

520. *See* Federal Trade Commission Consumer Information, Student Loans (Oct. 2017), https://www.consumer.ftc.gov/articles/1028-student-loans#loan_consolidation.

521. *See* Comments of Bankruptcy Scholars on Evaluating Hardship Claims in Bankruptcy, 21 J. Consumer & Com. L. 114, 117 (2018) (in the context of federal loan repayment options, stating that "all the available empirical evidence indicates that" income-driven repayment options are "failing the most vulnerable borrowers").

522. *See* Judith Scott-Clayton, The looming student loan default crisis is worse than we thought, Economic Studies at Brookings, Evidence Speaks Reports, vol. 2, No. 34 (Jan. 10, 2018), https://www.brookings.edu/research/the-looming-student-loan-default-crisis-is-worse-than-we-thought/ (stating that "poorer labor market outcomes and for-profit enrollment at the graduate level contribute to high rates of default among black college graduates," and the default rate is "significantly higher than the default rate for first generation, low-income graduates").

523. Local Loan Co. v. Hunt, 292 U.S. 234, 244 (1934) (stating that a primary purpose of the Bankruptcy Code is to "relieve the honest debtor from the weight of oppressive indebtedness and permit him to start afresh free from all the obligations and responsibilities consequent upon business misfortunes"). *See* John Patrick Hunt, Help or Hardship?: Income-Driven Repayment in Student-Loan Bankruptcies, 106 Geo. L.J. 1287 (2018) (discussing the "fresh start" policy with respect to student-loan debtors).

524. *See* Kara J. Bruce, Recent Developments in Educational-Benefit Discharge Litigation, 38 No. 10 Bankruptcy Law Letter (Oct. 2018) ("According to the conventional wisdom, student loans are forever.").

525. *See* Jonathan D. Glater, The Other Big Test: Why Congress Should Allow Students to Borrow More Through Federal Aid Programs, 14 N.Y.U. J. Legis. & Pub. Pol'y 11, 47 (2011) (suggesting that the combination of uncertain outcomes and litigation costs may deter borrowers from trying to get rid of loan obligations, even when they have legitimate reasons to seek discharge). For a discussion of how to improve access to justice in bankruptcy proceedings, *see* Henry Callaway & Jonathan Petts, Too Broke for a Fresh Start, 38-Feb. Am. Bankr. Inst. J. 24 (2019).

526. *See* Easterling v. Collecto, Inc., 692 F.3d 229, 232–235 (2d Cir. 2012) (applying preponderance of evidence standard). In this case, a collection agency sent collection letters to a debtor in order to collect on her student debt. These letters included the statement, "your account is NOT eligible for bankruptcy discharge." The court found that this statement was both literally false and fundamentally misleading, and that its capacity to discourage debtors from fully availing themselves of their legal rights rendered the misrepresentation "exactly the kind of 'abusive debt collection practice []' that the FDCPA was designed to target."

527. 11 U.S.C. § 523(b).

528. 11 U.S.C. § 523(b).

529. For additional resources, *see* National Consumer Law Center, Consumer Bankruptcy Law and Practice (9th ed. 2009 and Supp.); National Consumer Law Center, Student Loan Law (4th ed. 2010 and Supp.).

530. Julapa Jagtiani & Wenli Li, Credit Access After Consumer Bankruptcy Filing: New Evidence, 89 Am. Bankr. L.J. 327 (2015) (discussing negative effects on credit access). *But see* In re Patterson, 967 F.2d 505, 514 (11th Cir. 1992).

531. *See* Daniel A. Austin, The Indentured Generation: Bankruptcy and Student Loan Debt, 53 Santa Clara L. Rev. 329, 331 (2013) ("education debt servitude will last a lifetime for tens of thousands" of borrowers).

532. Pub. L. No. 115-174, Economic Growth, Regulatory Relief, and Consumer Protection Act, Title VI—Protection for Student Borrowers (May 24, 2018), amending U.S.C. § 1650 to add a new provision, "With respect to a private education loan involving a student obligor and 1 or more cosigners, the creditor shall not declare a default or accelerate the debt against the student obligor on the sole basis of a bankruptcy or death of a cosigner."

533. Kara Bruce, Recent Developments in Student Loan Non-Dischargeability: Aggregating Discharge-Violation Claims, 39 No. 1 Bankruptcy Law Letter NL 1 (Jan. 2019). *See also* Kara Bruce, Recent Developments in Educational-Benefit Discharge Litigation, 38 No. 10 Bankruptcy Law Letter NL 1 (Oct. 2018) (collecting cases). The author explains:

> Congress drafted a new exception to discharge that targeted certain, but not all, for-profit student loans: section 523(a)(8)(B) excepts from discharge for-profit loans that meet the definition of "qualified education loans" under the Internal Revenue Code of 1986. If Congress intended subsection 523(a)(8)(A)(ii) to broadly except all education-related loans from discharge, there would be no purpose to drafting the more restrictive exception in section 523(a)(8)(B).

Id. Compare In re Campbell, 547 B.R. 49 (E.D.N.Y. 2016) (bar study loan was not an education loan), *with* In re Brown, 539 B.R. 853 (S.D. Cal. 2015) (bar study loan was an education loan).

534. 11 U.S.C. § 523(a)(8). Until 1976, student loans, like all unsecured loans, were dischargeable in bankruptcy. Their disfavored treatment came about through a number of statutory amendments. In 1976, § 439A of the Higher Education Act of 1965 introduced a student-loan exception, providing that federally insured or guaranteed loans could be discharged only after five years, absent a judicial determination that "payment from future income or other wealth will impose an undue hardship on the debtor or his dependents." Pub. L. No. 94-482, § 127(a), 90 Stat. 2081 (repealed 1978). The Bankruptcy Reform Act of 1978 likewise included an undue-hardship requirement subject to a five-year bar. Pub. L. No. 95-598, § 523, 92 Stat. 2549, 2590-91. In 1990, the five-year bar was enlarged to seven years in the Federal Debt Collection Procedures Act, adopted as part of Title XXXVI of the Crime Control Act of 1990. Pub. L. No. 101-647, §§ 3601–31, 104 Stat. at 4933–66. Then, in 1998, the Higher Education Amendments eliminated the seven-year bar. Pub. L. No. 105-244, § 971(a), 112 Stat. 1581, 1837. The undue-hardship requirement was extended to private educational loans under the Bankruptcy Abuse Prevention and Consumer Protection Act of 2005. Pub. L. No. 109-8, §220, 119 Stat. 23, 59 (amending § 523(a)(8) of the Bankruptcy Code). *See generally* Jason Iuliano, Student Loan Bankruptcy and the Meaning of Educational Benefit, 93 Am. Bankr. L. J. 277 (2019) (arguing that billions of dollars of loans are misclassified as student loans, preventings discharge).

535. An adversary proceeding is a civil action that is related to, but separate from, a bankruptcy proceeding. *See* Fed. R. Bankr. P. 7001. The plaintiff in an adversary

proceeding sues one or more defendants, just as in a regular civil action. Thus, for a borrower to discharge a student debt that is subject to the undue hardship standard, it is necessary to file a bankruptcy proceeding and also to sue the creditor of the private education loan. An adversary proceeding can be filed without an attorney.

536. Brunner v. New York State Higher Educ. Servs. Corp., 831 F.2d 395 (2d Cir. 1987). *See* Cheryl D. Cook, Should Congress Abrogate *Brunner's* Criteria for Determining "Undue Hardship" under § 523(A)(8)?, 38-MAR Am. Bankr. Inst. J. 18 (2019) (arguing that application of *Brunner* has blocked discharge and requires legislative attention).

537. Easterling v. Collecto, Inc., 692 F.3d 229, 232 (2d Cir. 2012).

538. *See* Student Loans and Bankruptcy: Recommendations for Reform, 37-Mar Am. Bankr. Inst. J. 8 (Mar. 2018) (stating that nine circuits follow the *Brunner* test, and some of those circuits require that the debtor "show a 'certainty of hopelessness'" in order to discharge a debt).

539. In re Long, 322 F.3d 549 (8th Cir. 2003).

540. In re Nash, 446 F.3d 188 (1st Cir. 2006).

541. In re Faish, 72 F.3d 298, 306 (3d Cir. 1995).

542. Matter of Rappaport, 16 B.R. 615, 616 (D.N.J. 1981).

543. In re Nascimento, 241 B.R. 440, 445 (9th Cir. 1999) (citing In re Hornsby, 144 F. 3d 433, 437 (6th Cir. 1998)).

544. *See* Susan Ingles, Representing Student Loan Debtors in the Changing World of Student Loan Law, 27 S.C. Law. 36, 40 (2016). Empirical studies shed some light on the differences between debtors who have received discharges and those who did not. One study reported that those who obtained discharges (1) had lower incomes, (2) had lower monthly expenses, and (3) were more likely to have a medical problem or a dependent with a medical problem. Of these characteristics, having a medical condition was the only statistically significant predictor of successful discharge. *See* Rafael I. Pardo & Michelle R. Lacey, The Real Student Loan Scandal: Undue Hardship Discharge Litigation, 83 Am. Bankr. L.J. 179, 223–229 (2009). Another study found that three variables were predicative of discharge: (1) whether the debtor is employed, (2) whether the debtor has a medical hardship, and (3) the debtor's income the year before filing bankruptcy. Jason Iuliano, An Empirical Assessment of Student Loan Discharges and the Undue Hardship Standard, 86 Am. Bankr. L.J. 495, 495 (2012).

545. In re Coco, 335 Fed. Appx. 224 (3d Cir. 2009) (finding the second prong of the *Brunner* test met by showing that debtor suffered chronic medical problems and cared for her elderly, disabled mother).

546. Educ. Credit Mgmt. Corp. v. Nys, 446 F.3d 938, 947 (9th Cir. 2006).

547. In re Barrett, 487 F.3d 353, 359 (6th Cir. 2007) ("To satisfy the second prong . . . [the debtor] must show that circumstances indicate a 'certainty of hopelessness, not merely a present inability to fulfill financial commitment.'").

548. In re Mason, 464 F.3d 878, 884 (9th Cir. 2006).

549. In re Mandighomi, 242 Fed. Appx. 401, 403 (9th Cir. 2007) (affirming the bankruptcy court's partial discharge of student debt under "undue hardship" text). *See*

also In re Coco, 335 Fed. Appx. 224, 228 (3d Cir. 2009) (debtor's refusal to enroll in an income-based repayment plan did not bar a finding of good faith where the debtor suffered from chronic medical problems that made it difficult for her to live above the poverty line and her inability to repay her loans largely was beyond her control).

550. In re Modeen, 586 B.R. 298 (W.D. Wis. 2018).

551. In re Saxman, 325 F.3d 1168, 1175 (9th Cir. 2003) (must show undue hardship).

552. In re Hornsby, 144 F.3d 433, 439 (6th Cir. 1998).

553. *See* Vincent J. Roldan & Elizabeth L. Gunn, Trekking through the Quagmire: A Creative Discharge Solution to the Student Loan Crisis, 37-Dec. Am. Bankr. Inst. J. 36 (2018).

554. Federal law explicitly protects debtors who have declared bankruptcy from adverse actions by employers. *See* 11 U.S.C.§ 525(b), which provides:

> No private employer may terminate the employment of, or discriminate with respect to employment against, an individual who is or has been a debtor under this title, a debtor or bankrupt under the Bankruptcy Act, or an individual associated with such debtor or bankrupt, solely because such debtor or bankrupt—
>> (1) is or has been a debtor under this title or a debtor or bankrupt under the Bankruptcy Act;
>> (2) has been insolvent before the commencement of a case under this title or during the case but before the grant or denial of a discharge; or
>> (3) has not paid a debt that is dischargeable in a case under this title or that was discharged under the Bankruptcy Act.

A similar prohibition applies to public employers. 11 U.S.C. § 525(a). Congress enacted § 525 to codify the Supreme Court's decision in Perez v. Campbell, 402 U.S. 637 (1971), which invalidated an Arizona law that rescinded a bankrupt's driving privileges.

555. *See, for example*, White v. Kentuckiana Livestock Market, Inc., 397 F.3d 420, 422 (6th Cir. 2005).

556. *See* Robert C. Yan, The Signs Says "Help Wanted, Inquire Within"—But It May Not Matter if You have Ever Filed (or Plan to File) for Bankruptcy), 10 Am. Bankr. Inst. L. Rev. 429 (2002). *Compare* In re Martin, 2007 WL 2893431 (D. Kan. 2007) (hiring not protected), *with* Leary v. Warnaco, Inc., 251 B.R. 656 (S.D.N.Y. 2000) (hiring protected). In some cases, a bankruptcy filing was a factor in the denial of an applicant's security clearance. *See* Lea Shepard, Toward a Stronger Financial History Antidiscrimination Norm, 53 B.C. L. Rev. 1695, 1697 (2012).

557. Tax Cuts and Jobs Act, Pub. L. No. 115-97, §§ 11031, 11032, 11041 (2017).

558. *See* IRS, Topic No. 456 Student Loan Interest Deduction, https://www.irs.gov/taxtopics/tc456; Kelly Phillips Erb, Back to School Myths: The Student Loan Interest Deduction Is Gone, Forbes (Aug. 20, 2018), https://www.forbes.com/sites/kellyphillipserb/2018/08/20/back-to-school-myths-the-student-loan-interest-deduction-is-gone/#1f7727d6fb28.

559. For a discussion of the negative social impact of student debt, *see, for example*, Center for Responsible Lending, Quicksand: Borrowers of Color & the Student Debt

Crisis (July 22, 2019), https://www.responsiblelending.org/research-publication/quicksand-borrowers-color-student-debt-crisis.

560. Legislative Update, The Student Borrower Bankruptcy Relief Act of 2019, 38-JUN Am. Bankr. Inst. J. 8 (2019); *see also* Robert Farrington, The 2020 Presidential Candidates' Proposals for Student Loan Debt, Forbes (Apr. 24, 2019), https://www.forbes.com/sites/robertfarrington/2019/04/24/the-2020-presidential-candidates-proposals-for-student-loan-debt/#1af29cf9520e.

561. *See* Kathleen C. Engel & Patricia A. McCoy, A Tale of Three Markets: The Law and Economics of Predatory Lending, 80 Tex. L. Rev. 1255, 1260 (2002) (defining predatory lending "as a syndrome of abusive loan terms or practices that involve one or more of the following five problems: (1) loans structured to result in seriously disproportionate net harm to borrowers, (2) harmful rent seeking, (3) loans involving fraud or deceptive practices, (4) other forms of lack of transparency in loans that are not actionable as fraud, and (5) loans that require borrowers to waive meaningful legal redress"). *See also* Ed Mierwinzki, The Poor Still Pay More, 44-SEP Trial 40 (2008) (explaining that the fringe financing industry has organized and grown through such devices as consolidating local firms; making campaign contributions to state legislators; using "crisis-management" public relations firms; and limiting consumer rights through use of mandatory arbitration clauses in lending agreements).

562. For more on the demographics of the unbanked and underbanked, *see* The Debt Resistors' Operations Manual, A Project of Strike Debt and Occupy Wall Street, 59–60 (Sept. 2012). *See also* Olufunmilayo B. Arewa, Investment Funds, Inequality, and Scarcity of Opportunity, 99 B.U. L. Rev. 1023, 1031 (2019) (referring to limited access "to finance on nonexploitative terms").

563. *See* Tobie Stranger, CFPB Proposes to Relax Payday Loan Regulation, Consumer Reports (Feb. 6, 2019), https://www.consumerreports.org/consumer-financial-protection-bureau/cfpb-bids-to-relax-payday-loan-regulation/ ("Consumer advocates voice concern about 'debt traps.'"); Susanna Montezemolo, Payday Lending Abuses and Predatory Practices, Center for Responsible Lending 2 (Sept. 2013), https://www.responsiblelending.org/state-of-lending/reports/10-Payday-Loans.pdf [https://perma.cc/6SN2-QP5H] ("Payday loans create a debt treadmill that makes struggling families worse off than they were before they received a payday loan.").

564. *See* Ronald J. Mann & Jim Hawkins, Just Until Payday, 54 UCLA L. Rev. 855, 857 (2007) (calling payday lenders the "most prominent and rapidly growing of" fringe providers).

565. *See* Center for Responsible Lending, The Debt Trap of Triple-Digit Interest Rate Loans: Payday, Car-Title, and High–Cost Installment Loans, https://www.responsiblelending.org/; PEW Charitable Trusts, Payday Loans Weigh Down Holiday Borrowers (Dec. 2015), https://www.pewtrusts.org/en/research-and-analysis/data-visualizations/2012/payday-loans-really-add-up (showing that a $375 payday loan could generate $520 in fees leading to an indebtedness of $895). In a 2014 study tracking payday borrowers over 10 months, the Consumer Financial Protection Bureau found that more than 80% of loans (or four out of five) taken by these borrowers were rolled over or reborrowed within 30 days, incurring additional renewal fees. Furthermore,

only 15% of the borrowers in the study repaid their debts without reborrowing within 14 days; 20% defaulted entirely; and 64% renewed a loan at least once. *See* Consumer Financial Protection Bureau, CFPB Data Point: Payday Lending (Mar. 2014), http://files. consumerfinance.gov/f/201403_cfpb_report_payday-lending.pdf.

566. Benjamin D. Faller, Payday Loan Solutions: Slaying the Hydra (and Keeping It Dead), 59 Case W. Res. L. Rev. 125 (2008). *See generally* Consumer Financial Protection Bureau, What is a payday loan? (June 2, 2017), https://www.consumerfinance.gov/ask-cfpb/what-s-a-payday-loan-en-1567/.

567. Pew Charitable Trust, Payday Loan Facts and the CFPB's Impact (Jan. 2016, updated May 2016), https://www.pewtrusts.org/en/research-and-analysis/fact-sheets/2016/01/payday-loan-facts-and-the-cfpbs-impact. The "marketing" of payday loans in communities of color in some places goes hand in hand with municipal misuse of fines and fees as a revenue-raising device discussed in chapter 9. *See* Jodi Rios, Racial States of Municipal Governance: Policing Bodies and Space for Revenue in North St. Louis County, Mo, 37 Law & Inequality: A Journal of Theory and Practice 235, 280–281 (2019) (reporting that "payday loan establishments and bail bondsmen have cropped up next to many municipal courts to take advantage of family members who do not have the resources to pay fines and fees of those jailed").

568. Karen E. Francis, Rollover, Rollover: A Behavioral Law and Economics Analysis of the Payday-Loan Industry, 88 Tex. L. Rev. 611, 617 (2010).

569. Christopher L. Peterson, Usury Law, Payday Loans, and Statutory Sleight of Hand: Salience Distortion in American Credit Pricing Limits, 92 Minn. L. Rev. 1110, 1127 (2008); *see also* Nathalie Martin, 1,000% Interest—Good While Supplies Last: A Study of Payday Loan Practices and Solutions, 52 Ariz. L. Rev. 563, 571(2010) ("While some scholars have questioned the profitability of the industry and the industry sometimes denies that its returns are excessive, the mere existence of such a large number of lenders belies the conclusion that these loans are not highly profitable."). As the industry develops, increasingly private equity firms have taken ownership stakes in companies engaged in payday lending, and lenders bundle their loans and sell them to investors as asset backed securities. *See* Center for Responsible Lending, Testimony Before the House Financial Services Subcommittee on Consumer Protection and Financial Services, at 5 (Apr. 30, 2019), https://www.responsiblelending.org/research-policy/testimony.

570. *See* Center for Responsible Lending, Map of U.S. Payday Interest Rates (Feb. 14, 2019), https://www.responsiblelending.org/research-publication/map-us-payday-interest-rates. *See also* Lauren K. Saunders, Why 36% The History, Use, and Purpose of the 36% Interest Rate Cap, National Consumer Law Center (Apr. 2013), https://www.nclc.org/issues/usury.html. Table 1 lists states that ban payday loans and states that impose a cap on the APR.

571. *See* National Consumer Law Center, Stopping the Payday Loan Trap: Alternatives That Work, Ones That Don't 14 (June 2010), https://www.nclc.org/images/pdf/high_cost_small_loans/payday_loans/report-stopping-payday-trap.pdf.

572. *See* Creola Johnson, Payday Loans: Shrewd Business or Predatory Lending?, 87 Minn. L. Rev. 1 (2002).

573. *See* National Conference of State Legislatures, Payday Lending State Statutes (May 29, 2019), http://www.ncsl.org/research/financial-services-and-commerce/payday-lending-state-statutes.aspx.

574. *See* National Consumer Law Center, Predatory Installment Lending in 2017: States Battle to Restrain High-Cost Loans (Aug. 2017) (stating that "nationally, for a $500 six-month loan," 21 states cap the annual percentage rate at 36% or less).

575. Christopher Konneker, How the Poor Are Getting Poorer: The Proliferation of Payday Loans in Texas via State Charter Renting, 14 Scholar 489 (2011).

576. In recent years, online lenders also have been proliferating and gaining a greater share of the payday loan market. While research on online lending is scarce, APRs can get as high as 800%–1,000% in the absence of legislation and exclusion from state payday loan regulations. Nathalie Martin, Online Payday Lenders Seek More Respect and Less Oversight: Call Them What You Like, They Are Still 1,000% Long-Term Loans, Credit Slips (July 26, 2012), http://www.creditslips.org/creditslips/2012/07/online-payday-lenders-seek-more-respect-and-less-oversight-call-them-what-you-like-they-are-still-10.html. *See also* Consumer Financial Protection Bureau, Online Payday Loan Payments (Apr. 2016), http://files.consumerfinance.gov/f/201604_cfpb_online-payday-loan-payments.pdf.

577. *See* Center for Responsible Lending, Fact v. Fiction: The Truth about Payday Lending Industry Claims (Jan. 1, 2001), https://www.responsiblelending.org/research-publication/fact-v-fiction-truth-about-payday-lending-industry-claims ("The typical payday loan is more than twice as expensive as a credit card late fee, and much more costly than paying bills late. Payday lenders routinely collect bounced check fees and late fees as well.").

578. National Consumer Law Center, Stopping the Payday Loan Trap: Alternatives That Work, Ones That Don't 24 (June 2010), https://www.nclc.org/images/pdf/high_cost_small_loans/payday_loans/report-stopping-payday-trap.pdf.

579. *See* Mike Calhoun, Bank deposit advances are payday loans in disguise, American Banker (Mar. 8, 2019), https://www.americanbanker.com/opinion/bank-deposit-advances-are-payday-loans-in-disguise (interest rates average 200%).

580. Susanna Montezemolo & Sarah Wolff, Payday Mayday: Visible and Invisible Payday Lending Defaults, Center for Responsible Lending (Mar. 2015), http://bit.ly/1QrE4bS.

581. During the Obama administration, the Consumer Financial Protection Bureau sued various payday lenders under the Truth in Lending Act and other statutes, resulting in a consent order that banned defendants from the industry, caused them to forfeit $14 million in assets, and imposed a judgment of $69 million to pay consumers (but during the Trump administration the CFPB effectively suspended the judgment). *See* Consumer Financial Protection Bureau, Bureau of Consumer Financial Protection Settles with Defendants in Hydra Group Payday Lending Case (Aug. 10, 2018), https://www.consumerfinance.gov/about-us/newsroom/bureau-consumer-financial-protection-settles-defendants-hydra-group-payday-lending-case (assessing $1 civil penalty and suspending $69 million jury award against payday lending company). The stipulated final judgment is available at https://files.consumerfinance.gov/f/documents/bcfp_hydra_stipulated-final-judgment-order_

2018-08.pdf. Relatedly, Google has established rules for online personal loan advertisements, requiring them to display the maximum APR, calculated in compliance with the Truth in Lending Act. *See* Sean Murray, Google's Payday Loan Ad Ban References the Truth in Lending Act (TILA) (Aug. 15, 2016), https://debanked. com/2016/08/googles-payday-loan-ad-ban-references-the-truth-in-lending-act-tila/.

582. Truth in Lending Act, Pub. L. No. 90-321, § 107, 82 Stat. 149 (codified at 15 U.S.C. § 1606).

583. Official Staff Interpretation, 12 C.F.R. Part 226, Supp. I, § 226.2(a)(14) cmt. 2 (2000).

584. 15 U.S.C. § 1638(b).

585. 12 C.F.R. Part 226.

586. 12 C.F.R. § 226.17. *See* Polk v. Crown Auto, Inc., 221 F.3d 691 (4th Cir. 2000) (holding that lender-car dealer violated the TILA disclosure requirements when the lender gave the consumer credit terms in a form that they could keep only a few minutes before signing the contract).

587. 15 U.S.C. § 1640(a)(2); Brown v. Payday Check Advance, Inc., 202 F.3d 987, 990–991 (7th Cir. 2000).

588. *See* Federal Deposit Insurance Corporation, Guidelines for Payday Lending, https:// www.fdic.gov/news/news/press/2003/pr7003a.pdf.

589. For a comprehensive but earlier account, *see* Jim Hawkins, The Federal Government in the Fringe Economy, 15 Chap. L. Rev. 23, 24 (2011).

590. Dodd-Frank empowers the monitoring of the fringe economy, potentially requiring registration or reports-filing, and specifically empowers the CFPB to supervise three types of lenders, including payday lenders. In addition, the CFPB can supervise two broad categories of lending activity that can be interpreted to include most other fringe financing activities beyond payday lending. These two categories are: (1) anyone who is a "larger participant" in a market for other consumer financial products or services (for example, large pawnbrokers and lenders), and (2) any person who is engaging, or has engaged, in "conduct that poses risks to consumers" (which, arguably, includes fringe financing).

591. *See, for example*, PHH Corporation v. Consumer Financial Protection Bureau, 839 F.3d 1 (D.C. Cir. 2016) (CFPB was unconstitutionally structured, in violation of Article II of the U.S. Constitution); Advance America v. Federal Deposit Insurance Corporation, 2017 WL 1497823 (D.D.C. 2017) (permitting payday lenders to proceed to trial on due process challenges to federal enforcement initiative called "Operation Choke Point").

592. Consumer Financial Protection Bureau, Press Release, Consumer Financial Protection Bureau Proposes Rule to End Payday Debt Traps (June 2, 2016), http:// www.consumerfinance.gov/about-us/newsroom/consumer-financial-protection-bureau-proposes-rule-end-payday-debt-traps/.

593. *See* Final Rule, 82 Fed. Reg. at 54,874 (to be codified at 12 C.F.R. § 1041.3(f)).

594. Consumer Financial Protection Bureau, 12 C.F.R. Part 1041, Payday, Vehicle Title, and Certain High-Cost Installment Loans, http://www.consumerfinance. gov/policy-compliance/rulemaking/rules-under-development/notice-proposed-rulemaking-payday-vehicle-title-and-certain-high-cost-installment-loans/.

595. For analyses of the CFPB rule, *see, for example*, Hannah Clayshulte, How Payday Loans Affect Domestic Violence Survivors and What the New CFPB Regulations Will Mean for Survivors in Wisconsin, 33 Wis. J.L. Gender & Soc'y 149 (2018); Recent Regulation, Consumer Financial Regulation—CFPB's Final Payday Lending Rule Deems It an "Unfair" and "Abusive" Practice to Make Payday Loans without Determining Borrower Ability to Repay—Payday, Vehicle Title, and Certain High-Cost Installment Loans, 82 Fed. Reg. 54,472 (Nov. 17, 2017) (to be codified at 12 C.F.R. Part 1041), 131 Harv. L. Rev. 1852 (2018).

596. Consumer Financial Protection Bureau, Summary of Proposed Rulemakings: 2019 Proposals to Amend the Payday Lending Rule (Feb. 6, 2019), https://files.consumerfinance.gov/f/documents/cfpb-Payday-Summary-of-2019-Proposed-Rulemakings. *See* PBS News Hour, Financial watchdog to gut its payday lending rules (Feb. 6, 2019), https://www.pbs.org/newshour/economy/financial-watchdog-to-gut-its-payday-lending-rules. *See also* Megan Leonhardt, Trump administration rolls back payday loan protections, which could affect millions of young people, CNBC (Feb. 6, 2019), https://www.cnbc.com/2019/02/06/trump-administration-rolls-back-payday-loan-protections.html. During the Trump administration the CFPB has all but stopped seeking redress for the victims of payday loans or predatory practices.

597. *See* Group Comments of the Center for Responsible Lending, Public Citizen, National Consumer Law Center (on behalf of its low-income clients), Consumer Federation of America, American Federation of Labor and Congress of Industrial Organizations, Americans for Financial Reform Education Fund, Leadership Conference on Civil and Human Rights, League of United Latin American Citizens, NAACP, National Association for Latino Community Asset Builders, National Coalition of Asian Pacific American Community Development, & U.S. PIRG to the Consumer Financial Protection Bureau, Docket No. CFPB-2019-0007, RIN 3170-AA495 (Mar. 18, 2019) and Docket No. CFPB-2019-0006, RIN 3170-AA80 (May 15, 2019), https://www.responsiblelending.org/research-policy/comment-letters.

598. *See* Ryan Baasch, Taming Title Loans, 101 Va. L. Rev. 1753, 1757 (2015) (stating that "proof of employment, income documentation, and other mechanisms designed to test the credit worthiness of the borrower" are "conspicuously absent" in this credit situation).

599. Nathalie Martin & Ozymandias Adams, Grand Theft Auto Loans: Repossession and Demographic Realities in Title Lending, 77 Mo. L. Rev. 41, 61 (2012).

600. Consumer Financial Protection Bureau, Single-Payment Vehicle Title Lending 4 (May 2016), http://files.consumerfinance.gov/f/documents/201605_cfpb_single-payment-vehicle-title-lending.pdf. *See also* Jim Hawkins, Credit on Wheels: The Law and Business of Auto-Title Lending, 69 Wash. & Lee L. Rev. 535 (2012) (reporting that consumers were over optimistic about the possibility of losing their cars).

601. Jim Hawkins, Regulating on the Fringe: Reexamining the Link Between Fringe Banking and Financial Distress, 86 Ind. L.J. 1361, 1388–89 (2011). Professor Jim Hawkins found the pawn loan the least harmful of fringe financing products because they can never cause direct financial distress. He explained: "One positive

feature of pawn credit is its tendency to be naturally short-term and terminal. Unlike payday loans where consumers often are forced to repay their loans over relatively long periods, a defaulting pawn debtor simply forfeits the personal item left with the pawnbroker as collateral." *See also* Jarret C. Oeltjen, Pawnbroking on Parade, 37 Buff. L. Rev. 751 (1988/1989).

602. Nathalie Martin & Ozymandias Adams, Grand Theft Auto Loans: Repossession and Demographic Realities in Title Lending, 77 Mo. L. Rev. 41, 51 (2012).

603. *See generally* Eligio Pimentel, Renting-to-Own: Exploitation or Market Efficiency, 13 Law & Ineq. 369 (1995); James P. Nehf, Effective Regulation of Rent-to-Own Contracts, 52 Ohio St. L.J. 751 (1991). *See also* David Ray Papke, Perpetuating Poverty: Exploitative Businesses, the Urban Poor, and the Failure of Reform, 16 Scholar: St. Mary's L. Rev. & Soc. Just. 223 (2014) (discussing treatment of transaction as lease and the racialized and gendered effects of the practice). States may have laws that regulate rent-to-own agreements. *See, for example,* N.Y. Attorney General, Rent-to-Own, https://ag.ny.gov/consumer-frauds/rent-own.

604. *See* Kathryn Smetana, Refund Anticipation Loans: Less Money for Consumers Entitled to Refunds, More Profit for H & R Block, 14 Loy. Consumer L. Rev. 371 (2002) (explaining IRS rules and how they impact taxpayers).

605. 26 U.S.C. § 6304(a)(1) & (3). *See generally* IRS, The IRS Tax Collection Process, Publication 594, https://www.irs.gov/pub/irs-pdf/p594.pdf.

606. 26 U.S.C. § 6304(a)(2).

607. 26. U.S.C. § 6304(b).

608. 26 U.S.C. § 7433(d)(1)–(2).

609. 26 C.F.R. § 301.7433-1(e)(1).

610. 26 C.F.R. § 301.7433-1(e)(2).

611. 26 U.S.C. § 7433(a).

612. 26 U.S.C. § 7433(d)(3).

613. 26 U.S.C. § 7433(b).

614. 26 U.S.C. § 6321.

615. 26 U.S.C. § 6320(a)(1).

616. 26 U.S.C. § 6320(a)(3).

617. 26 U.S.C. § 6331(h). *See* Social Security, SSR 79-4: Sections 207, 452(b), 459, and 462(f) (42 U.S.C. §§ 407, 652(b), 659, and 662(f)) Levy and Garnishment of Benefits, https://www.ssa.gov/OP_Home/rulings/oasi/41/SSR79-04-oasi-41.html.

618. For additional resources, *see* National Consumer Law Center, Surviving Debt 225–227 (2019) (options for paying tax debt).

619. *See* IRS, Apply Online for a Payment Plan, https://www.irs.gov/payments/online-payment-agreement-application. The site lists the costs. Setting up an installment agreement online carries a $31 setup fee, which is waived for low-income persons. *See* IRS Form 13844, Application for Reduced User Fee for Installment Agreements, https://www.irs.gov/pub/irs-pdf/f13844.pdf. If the taxpayer is ineligible for the Online Payment Agreement too, installment payment is still an option, but the fee is higher and must be requested through IRS Form 9465, Installment Agreement Request, https://www.irs.gov/pub/irs-pdf/f9465.pdf.

620. *See* IRS, Topic Number 24—Offers in Compromise, https://www.irs.gov/taxtopics/tc204.

621. *See* IRS Form 433-F, Collection Information Statement.

622. *See* IRS, Businesses and Self-Employed, Temporarily Delay the Collection Process, https://www.irs.gov/businesses/small-businesses-self-employed/temporarily-delay-the-collection-process.

623. *See* IRS, Local Taxpayer Advocate, https://www.irs.gov/advocate/local-taxpayer-advocate.

624. *See* IRS Publication 4134: Low Income Taxpayer Clinic List, https://www.irs.gov/pub/irs-pdf/p4134.pdf.

7

Housing

Introduction

Does the federal Constitution guarantee a right to housing?

The U.S. Supreme Court has held that the federal Constitution does not guarantee a right to housing.[1] Some scholars disagree with this reading of the Constitution.[2] Moreover, some analysts point to the United Nations International Covenant on Economic, Social, and Cultural Rights as a source for a domestic right to housing, but no American court has accepted this argument.[3] On the other hand, every state has its own constitution, and in New York, state courts interpreting that state's constitution have recognized a right to temporary emergency shelter for persons who cannot afford housing.[4]

Is there a federal statutory right to housing?

Although there is as yet no recognized federal constitutional right to housing, Congress has established programs aimed at making affordable and adequate housing accessible to poor and low-income households. The statutes that authorize these programs do not create a right—sometimes called an entitlement—to housing. Rather, even if an applicant meets the program's eligibility requirements, assistance may not be forthcoming. Indeed, only about 25 percent of families that qualify for housing assistance actually receive it because the programs are not adequately funded to meet the housing needs of families with low income.[5] Since 1996, federal spending on affordable housing has not matched a rise in applications, and relative to gross domestic product, funding has fallen 30 percent, with funding in 2019 less than in 2010, notwithstanding an overall increase in outlays over the last 30 years.[6] During this period, the United States has not funded new affordable housing that it owns and manages; instead it relies on private development, incentivized by tax credits, to expand the stock of housing and to keep it affordable for a set time. Moreover, for many decades the United States provided housing assistance on a racially segregated basis,[7] and racial stratification continues to characterize residential patterns, to block economic mobility, and to impede the achievement of housing justice.[8]

Getting By. Helen Hershkoff and Stephen Loffredo, Oxford University Press (2020). © Helen Hershkoff & Stephen Loffredo.
DOI: 10.1093/oso/9780190080860.001.0001

This chapter provides an overview of rental and homeownership programs administered by the U.S. Department of Housing and Urban Development. Some attention is given to rural housing programs administered by the U.S. Department of Agriculture.[9] In addition, the chapter focuses on the low-income tax credit program administered by the U.S. Department of the Treasury.[10] The emphasis is on the application process for HUD-supported rent programs and how tenants can maintain eligibility for assistance. The chapter also touches on issues critical to housing justice—including environmental displacement; the government's duty to affirmatively further fair housing; and tenant participation in decisions involving assisted housing programs. The statutory frameworks are complicated, and the chapter, which is not a substitute for legal advice, suggests resources for getting advice about particular housing opportunities.[11]

Federal Rental Assistance Programs

What is the U.S. Department of Housing and Urban Development?

The U.S. Department of Housing and Urban Development, Office of Public and Indian Housing, known as HUD, is the federal agency that administers most housing programs in the United States. Among other activities, these programs provide rental assistance and subsidize mortgages and insurance to increase the availability of affordable housing. HUD sets national standards in regulations and informal rules.[12] HUD has a national office located in Washington, D.C.[13] Locally, Public Housing Authorities (PHAs) administer some of the HUD-assisted programs described in this chapter. A PHA is an entity created by state law and is governed by a locally appointed board of commissioners.[14] Usually, the board of each PHA must include at least one tenant, although this requirement is subject to exception in some locales.[15] PHAs have broad authority to establish local policies for the application process and admission criteria, and these policies may vary among programs and even within a single PHA for different housing programs.[16]

The HUD-administered housing programs discussed in this chapter fall into three categories: (1) Public Housing, through which Public Housing Authorities, with federal support, constructed, own, and operate rental buildings; (2) Multifamily Programs, through which private developers, with federal support, constructed, own, and operate rental buildings; and (3) Housing Choice Vouchers, through which tenants rent apartments in private buildings and the government gives a direct subsidy to the landlord.[17]

What is Public Housing?

"Public Housing" is the oldest of the HUD-administered housing programs.[18] Public Housing is publicly owned and publicly financed. It is administered by local Public Housing Authorities. By the 1960s, insufficient federal funding had led to maintenance backlogs and severe capital needs.[19] Apart from a few replacement units, the federal government has not constructed new Public Housing in decades.[20] In addition, Public Housing Authorities are permitted to demolish Public Housing and to redevelop units with higher quality, mixed-income complexes.[21] This approach is reported to have led overall to a decline in the number of affordable units available for poor and low-income households,[22] with African American tenants disproportionately displaced from affordable units.[23] In 2011, Congress enacted the Rental Assistance Demonstration (RAD) with the stated goal of preserving and improving Public Housing (and certain other assisted multifamily) buildings, but with the clear potential to accelerate privatization.[24] Under RAD, the PHA (or owner) can convert a public housing property to a project-based voucher or project-based rental assistance program.[25] (RAD is discussed later in this chapter.)

Currently, there are about 1.03 million units of Public Housing. Tenants include 3.3 million children, and 31 percent are over the age of 62. Sixty-five percent of Public Housing residents are considered to have extremely low income, and the average income of Public Housing residents nationally is $14,496. African American families occupy 46.8 percent of Public Housing units.[26] Public Housing Authorities continue to accept applications, but in most communities the waiting list for an apartment is long.[27]

What are Multifamily Programs?

Multifamily Programs (also called Project Based Rental Assistance) refer to HUD assisted programs that leveraged private investment to construct affordable housing that the developer owns and manages.[28] Some programs provided mortgage subsidies; other programs provided direct subsidies to the developer for a set period of time. Tenants in Multifamily Program housing pay affordable rents based on their incomes. Rental subsidies are building-specific, which means tenants lose the below-market rent option if they move to a different building or if the building ceases to be a part of the HUD program. From the tenant's perspective, the programs are informally known by the section number of the federal law that established them, such as Section 221(d)(3) BMIR,[29] Section 236,[30] and Section 202 (generally now only for the elderly).[31] The Section 8 program, established in 1974, provided direct subsidies to the developers, but contracts for new multifamily construction have not been awarded since the 1980s.[32]

What is the Housing Choice Voucher program?

The Housing Choice Voucher program (also known as the Section 8 voucher or Section 8 existing housing program) is currently HUD's largest program for tenant rental assistance.[33] Housing Choice does not assign a tenant to an assisted unit. Rather, the program pays a subsidy to the tenant's private landlord. The subsidy is capped, based on the median rent in the area (called the "Fair Market Rent" or FMR), and is also known as the payment standard. FMRs are usually based on the fortieth percentile of rents in a region, but some Public Housing Authorities base rents on "Small Area FMRs," setting rents separately for each zip code in a region. A tenant who has a voucher is required to pay a minimum of 30 percent of the household's adjusted monthly income to the landlord, and HUD pays the rest up to the payment standard. Although the rent level must be reasonable, HUD does not guarantee that the subsidy will meet the entire rental cost, and the tenant must make up the difference. Section 8 vouchers are portable, meaning that if the tenant moves, the voucher may be used at the new apartment if the apartment meets HUD standards and the landlord agrees to participate in the Voucher program.[34] The Housing Choice Voucher program does not support the construction of new affordable units, and there is no guarantee that a tenant will find an owner willing to accept the subsidy.[35]

What is the Low-Income Housing Tax Credit?

Since 1986, the Low-Income Housing Tax Credit (LIHTC) has been the primary federal program for the construction, maintenance, and rehabilitation of new affordable housing in the United States. The LIHTC program has supported 70,000 affordable units a year and as of 2016 had helped create 3.05 million affordable units.[36] HUD does not administer the program, but income eligibility rules for prospective tenants are generally the same as for HUD-supported programs.[37] However, the LIHTC has unique features that affect tenant participation and benefits. Under the program, Congress allocates tax credits, and the Internal Revenue Service (a part of the U.S. Department of the Treasury) allocates the credits through state agencies. There are two different types of credits, subject to different criteria, and collectively, the states have been authorized to award about $8 billion in tax credits to housing developers each year.[38] To maintain the credit, developments generally must commit to affordability for 30 years, keep at least 20 percent of the units affordable ("rent-restricted") and rent them to tenants with household incomes at or below 50 percent of the HUD-calculated area median income, or keep at least 40 percent of the units affordable and rent them to tenants with household incomes at or below 60 percent of the area median income. The 2018 Omnibus Budget Act created a third option: keep at least 40 percent of units affordable and rent them to tenants with an average income at or below 60 percent of the area median income, with no tenant having an income exceeding 80 percent of the average median income. LIHTC-supported housing also must meet a rent-level test: rents cannot exceed 30 percent of the elected 50 or 60 percent of area media gross income; and the tenant's rent does not change with shifts in the tenant's income.[39]

Since 1997, HUD has maintained a database about the LIHTC program that is available to the public and is a source of valuable information for tenants, advocates, and analysts.[40] Although the program has increased the supply of affordable housing, some commentators argue that overall the program has discouraged integrated housing and failed to provide sufficient incentives to develop housing for the very poor.[41] In particular, because rents are set by income category and not by household income, there may be a mismatch between available units and households with the lowest incomes.[42] Looking forward, allowing developers the option of income averaging may cause rents to rise, which will create barriers for tenants seeking to use vouchers in an LIHTC-supported development.[43]

What housing assistance is provided to persons with low income in rural areas?

Both HUD and the U.S. Department of Agriculture (USDA), Rural Housing Services (an agency within the Rural Development division of the USDA, formerly known as the Farmers Home Administration) operate housing programs specifically for poor and low-income people in rural areas. HUD programs support affordable housing and community development in rural areas through capacity-building grants to local organizations.[44] HUD also provides housing stability grants aimed at assisting rural families who are homeless or in danger of becoming homeless.[45] The USDA offers a more comprehensive set of housing programs for rural households. Some of these programs assist owners of single-family homes, and others are geared toward tenants and developers of multifamily structures.[46] Income requirements vary by program and are often pegged to a percentage of area median income, adjusted for household size.[47] Through its single-family housing programs, the USDA provides direct loans or loan guarantees for homebuyers,[48] assists families in the construction of their own homes,[49] provides loans to nonprofit organizations to purchase and develop housing sites,[50] and provides loans or grants to homeowners to pay for necessary repairs or improvements.

How does a prospective tenant apply for federal rental assistance?

As a first step, a prospective tenant seeking rental assistance, whether in a HUD-supported program or the Low-Income Housing Tax Credit program, needs to find out what buildings and units are available in the state or community in which the tenant wants to live. The tenant can obtain information from a number of sources. HUD sponsors housing counseling agencies, and their staff can provide advice.[51] Also, the local Public Housing Authority or local HUD office can provide information about which federal developments in a community are accepting applications and which have open waiting lists. Some information on vacant affordable housing units is available online.[52] An applicant for a Public Housing or Multifamily Program unit must apply separately to each program,[53] and sometimes for each development.[54]

An applicant seeking rental assistance through the Housing Choice Voucher program files an application with the local PHA, which determines eligibility and issues the voucher. If a family receives a voucher, it then must find a private owner willing to rent an apartment, enter into a lease, and abide by the terms of the Section 8 Housing Choice Voucher program. As with other federal rental assistance programs, though, the fact that a family meets the eligibility criteria for a program is no guarantee of receiving aid. To the contrary, Congress's failure over many years to appropriate adequate funds has created a severe shortage of Section 8 vouchers, and in most areas the number of eligible applicants far exceeds the number of available vouchers.[55] Some PHAs maintain waiting lists, though the wait time for a Section 8 voucher often extends to many years. In some regions, PHAs are so oversubscribed that they select only a small subset of applicants to place on the waiting list, or have closed their waiting lists altogether.[56]

What questions will an applicant for rental assistance have to answer?

Generally, an application for federal rental assistance asks questions about financial circumstances, the people who live with the applicant, the names of previous landlords, and credit and criminal history. The applicant must sign a written consent form to permit verification of income through HUD's central database, the Enterprise Income Verification System (EIV).[57] In addition, the applicant must consent to disclosure of Social Security numbers for each household member,[58] and the processing entity must deny the application of any individual who does not comply with this requirement.[59] The application may ask for other information. For Public Housing, tenant screening guidelines are found in the "Admissions and Continued Occupancy Plan";[60] for Multifamily Housing programs, the guidelines are found in the "Tenant Selection Plan";[61] and for vouchers, in the PHA "Administrative Plan."[62] Additional questions might cover an applicant's prior eviction from federally assisted housing or contacts with the criminal justice system (as discussed later in this chapter). The application process is free.[63]

As mentioned earlier, applicants for Section 8 Housing Choice vouchers must be approved in two steps: first, by the Public Housing Authority administering the voucher program in their area, and second, by the private owner of the unit from whom they are seeking to rent. The PHA is responsible for verifying an applicant's income and eligible immigration status, as well as for ensuring the applicant has not committed certain disqualifying crimes (conditions that are discussed later in this chapter). In addition, the PHA will inspect the apartment[64] and determine whether the rent is reasonable, and the owner must sign a Housing Assistance Payment Contract with the PHA.[65]

What are the admission standards for federal rental assistance programs?

The admission standards common to all federal rental programs are (1) eligibility standards, (2) "preferences," and (3) tenant-selection criteria. Eligibility standards for rental assistance programs include income limits. "Preferences" (awarded on the basis of hardship and urgency, among other things) and the date of the application then determine an applicant's priority for consideration. The PHA or private owner chooses a tenant from among eligible applicants. Keep in mind that a property owner is not required to participate in the Voucher program and has no duty to accept the subsidy. Ordinarily, it is not illegal for a landlord to refuse to rent to voucher recipients for a neutral reason, such as a desire to avoid paperwork or the other administrative requirements associated with the Voucher program.[66] However, some states and localities have laws that bar housing discrimination based on "source of income," and a landlord's refusal to rent because the tenant's rent is assisted through the Voucher program could violate those statutes.[67] Moreover, as discussed later in this chapter, federal law bars refusals to rent based on a prospective tenant's race, ethnicity, religion, sex, or creed, or the fact that the household includes children, and selection practices that have a disparate impact on members of protected groups also may violate the law.[68]

What are the income limits for HUD-assisted rental programs?

Income limits for HUD rental programs are calculated as a percentage of the median income in the geographic area. Initial eligibility is limited to applicants whose household income is no more than 50 percent of area median income. Every year, HUD publishes estimated income limits, which are then subject to individual program guidelines.[69] The PHA will generally re-examine a recipient family's income every year, though families with fixed incomes have their incomes fully re-examined only every three years.[70] Either the family or the PHA may request an income re-examination before the next regular annual re-examination in accordance with the PHA's Administrative Plan.[71]

Income limits are adjusted further to account for family size, with a downward per capita reduction of 10 percent for households smaller than four and an upward per capita increase of 8 percent for households larger than four.[72] Federal law defines low-income families as those with income no greater than 80 percent of median family income in the area; very low-income families are those with income no greater than 50 percent of median family income in the area; and extremely low-income families are those with incomes not greater than 30 percent of the median family income for the area, or the federal poverty line, whichever is higher.[73] These categories determine income eligibility for various housing assistance programs.

By way of example, the national median family income in 2018 was $71,900, up 5.7 percent from 2017.[74] The 2018 median family income for selected states for a four-person household were as shown in Table 7.1.

What counts as income in determining eligibility for HUD-assisted rental programs?

The rules for determining income are complex, but a few general statements can be made. Most HUD programs define "income" the same way for determining eligibility for Section 8 public housing and rental assistance.[75] Income is total anticipated income from all sources received by or on behalf of every member of the household,[76] unless the income is specifically excluded by the program from

Table 7.1 FY 2018 Income Limits in Dollars for Public Housing and Section 8 Programs

State	Median Family Income	Very Low Income (50%) Limit	Extremely Low-Income (30%) Limit	Low-Income (80%) Limit
Alabama	60,200	30,100	18,050	48,150
California	77,500	34,900	23,250	62,000
Louisiana	62,100	31,050	18,650	49,700
Massachusetts	95,500	47,750	28,650	71,900
New York	77,800	38,900	23,350	62,250
Texas	68,800	34,400	20,650	55,050
Washington	81,100	40,550	24,350	64,900

the calculation of income.[77] The kinds of payments that count in gross annual income include:

1. Income from assets to which any household member has access;[78]
2. Gross wages and salaries, including overtime pay, tips, commissions, and bonuses;[79]
3. Net income from the operation of a business;[80]
4. Periodic payments from Social Security, insurance policies, retirement funds, disability payments, and other similar types of payments;[81]
5. Payments in lieu of earnings, such as unemployment compensation benefits;[82]
6. Assistance under the Temporary Assistance for Needy Families program;[83]
7. Periodic and "determinable" payments, such as alimony and child care, and regular contributions from persons or entities not living in the household;[84]
8. All regular and special pay and allowances received by a member of the armed forces (other than special pay for exposure to hostile fire);[85] and
9. For Section 8 programs only: financial assistance other than loans for educational expenses in excess of tuition and required fees and charges, except if the recipient is age 23 or over with dependent children. The assistance covered includes amounts received under Higher Education Act of 1965 (for example, Pell Grants, college work-study, and Supplemental Opportunity Grants); from private sources; and from a higher education institution (as defined by the Higher Education Act of 1965).[86]

What does not count as income in determining eligibility for HUD-assisted rental programs?

Federal law does not count certain payments received by an applicant-family as "income" for purposes of HUD-assisted rental programs. Currently excluded are:

1. Employment income of children younger than age 18 (including foster children);[87]
2. Payments received to care for foster children or foster adults;[88]
3. Lump-sum additions to family assets, such as insurance payments;[89]
4. Reimbursement for the cost of medical expenses;[90]
5. Income of a live-in aide, who lives in the rental unit but is not a regular household member;[91]
6. Special pay to armed forces members exposed to hostile fire;[92]
7. Payments received for participation in HUD training programs or qualifying state or local employment training programs;[93]
8. Temporary, nonrecurring payments, including gifts;[94]
9. Reparations payments by foreign governments for crimes committed during the Nazi era, including the Holocaust;[95]
10. Earnings in excess of $480 for each full-time student age 18 or older, other than the head of the household or spouse;[96]
11. Adoption assistance payments in excess of $480 per child;[97]
12. Deferred periodic payments that are received as a lump sum or in prospective monthly amounts, from SSI, Social Security, or Veterans Affairs disability benefits;[98]
13. Refunds or rebates under state or local law for property taxes paid on the dwelling unit;[99]
14. Payments made by a state agency to maintain a person with developmental disabilities in the home;[100] and
15. Amounts specifically excluded under other federal programs.[101]

Further, the applicant's income is adjusted by subtracting certain deductions. For Public Housing, Project-Based Section 8, and the Section 8 Housing Choice Voucher program, deductions include:

1. A standard deduction of $480 for each dependent. A dependent means any member of the tenant's household, other than a spouse or partner, who is younger than age 18 (excluding foster children); a person with disabilities; or a full-time student. A fetus does not count as a dependent.[102]
2. A standard deduction of $400 for an "elderly or disabled family." A family is elderly or disabled if the head of the household or the spouse is age 62 or

older, or is disabled. A household also qualifies if there are two or more elderly or disabled persons living together, or if there are one or more elderly or disabled persons living with one or more live-in aides.[103]

3. A deduction for medical expenses for an elderly or disabled family. An elderly or disabled family may take a deduction for unreimbursed medical expenses.[104]

4. A deduction for child care expenses. A tenant can take this deduction for money spent for the care of children under age 13, when such care is needed to allow the tenant or a family member to be employed or to continue education. The amount of the deduction cannot be more than the amount of employment income received.[105]

Additional deductions and exclusions apply to earned income.[106] Implementing regulations, with one exception, are limited to Public Housing tenants.[107]

Can a family own assets and still receive HUD rental assistance?

HUD-assisted housing has no asset test. However, this does not mean that the ownership of assets does not affect eligibility or rent levels. This is because any income generated by the assets (for instance, interest or dividends) counts as income in determining eligibility.[108] In addition, for net family assets over $ 5,000, income includes the greater of actual income generated by the assets or an imputed amount based on the current passbook saving rate.[109] The 2016 Housing Opportunity Through Modernization Act amended federal housing laws to permit Public Housing Authorities to make applicants and current tenants ineligible for Public Housing or other HUD rental assistance if they have more than $100,000 in net assets (with some adjustments) or have a right to live in suitable residential property (the statute provides an exception for victims of domestic abuse and families offering property for sale). In addition, the amendment requires HUD, as of October 1, 2017, to direct Public Housing Authorities to obtain information about assets needed to reach eligibility determinations. These requirements do not go into effect until HUD publishes rules.[110]

Can HUD rental assistance be withheld because of the applicant's race, color, religion, sex, familial status, national origin, or disability?

No. For many years, the government provided subsidized housing units to tenants on a racially segregated basis.[111] Although such policies have been declared illegal and Public Housing Authorities have officially renounced them, Public Housing continues to be racially stratified and residential patterns generally in the United States reflect entrenched patterns of racial segregation.[112] Federal law clearly bars housing discrimination on specified impermissible bases. In particular, Title VIII of the Civil Rights Act of 1968,[113] known as the Fair Housing Act, forbids discrimination in housing on the basis of race, color, religion, sex, familial status (meaning, minor children in the home as well as pregnant persons),[114] national origin, and disability.[115] (The Fair Housing Act does not bar discrimination due to a person's source of income.) HUD, during the Obama administration, published several notices to make clear that equal access to federally assisted housing extends to persons who are gender nonconforming.[116] These notices remain in effect until amended, superseded, or rescinded.[117] However, links to information about LGBTQ equal access no longer appear on the HUD website.[118]

Sometimes eligibilty rules or processes used to select tenants or award housing assistance do not explicitly rely on an impermissible criterion (such as gender, race, or nationality), but nevertheless have a negative disparate impact on members of a protected group. For example, a rule that gives preference to applicants who work full-time may disproportionately exclude persons with disabilities from housing opportunities. As another example, a rule that excludes persons who have had contacts with the criminal justice system may unintentionally exclude women who have been the victims of sexual battering or domestic abuse. The Fair Housing Act bars not only outright discrimination against a member of a protected group but also certain practices that are neutral on their face yet produce a negative disparate impact on members of those protected groups. The focus of disparate impact claims thus is not the perpetrator's intent to discriminate, but rather the consequences of the actions. HUD has codified regulations on disparate-impact liability,[119] and the U.S. Supreme Court has recognized the viability of a disparate impact claim under the Fair Housing Act.[120] Under the regulation, the party challenging a practice or policy first must show that it "actually or predictably results in a disparate impact on a group of persons or creates, increases, reinforces, or perpetuates segregated housing patterns because of race, color, religion, sex, handicap, familial status, or national origin."[121] Then, the defendant must prove that its policy or practice "is necessary to achieve one or more substantial, legitimate, nondiscriminatory interests," and that those interests "could not be served by another practice that has a less discriminatory effect."[122] In June 2018, the Trump administration published advance notice of proposed rulemaking to amend the disparate impact rule, and an amended rule could make it more difficult to prove non-intentional discrimination under the Fair Housing Act.[123]

Tenants, applicants, and others who believe they have been discriminated against in the provision of housing or subject to policies or practices in violation of the Fair Housing Act, may file a complaint with the U.S. Department of Housing and Development or the Department of Justice, both of which are tasked with investigating compliance with civil rights requirements as they apply to housing.[124]

What is the duty to affirmatively further fair housing?

The Fair Housing Act also requires all federal agencies and federal grantees to take action to undo entrenched patterns of segregation[125]—known as the duty to affirmatively further fair housing.[126] This duty has broad implications for the availability, siting, and eligibility for assisted housing. A federal court in 1973 explained that the duty involves taking action "to fulfill, as much as possible, the goal of open, integrated residential housing patterns and to prevent the increase of segregation, in ghettos, of racial groups whose lack of opportunities the Act was designed to combat."[127] For many years HUD regulations did not define the duty, other than to require program participants to certify that the grantee had analyzed "impediments" to fair housing within the relevant community, taken steps to overcome those impediments, and maintained records. Overall, commentators state that implementation of the duty was poorly monitored, weakly enforced, and inadequately implemented.[128] In 2010 the U.S. General Accountability Office recommended that HUD improve its oversight,[129] and in 2015, the Obama administration published a final rule setting out a regulatory approach "to overcome historic patterns of segregation, promote fair housing choice, and foster inclusive communities that are free from discrimination."[130] A key component of the rule is an Assessment of Fair Housing tool to be used by local government agencies, aimed at facilitating increased equal access to housing and to focus affirmative efforts on areas in which there is racial and poverty concentration.[131] In its wake, a Republican-dominated Congress introduced various legislative measures to block HUD from implementing the rule; in May 2018, the Trump administration withdrew the assessment tool, and in August 2018, HUD published advance notice of proposed rulemaking to amend the rule entirely.[132]

Who submits an application for federal rental assistance?

A "family" (which may consist of a single person) submits an application for federal housing assistance and constitutes the unit whose size, income, and resources are evaluated in determining eligibility and assistance level. Federal law does not limit the definition of a family to persons joined by blood relation, marriage, or the operation of law; HUD regulations also state that the definition of family shall not depend on actual or perceived sexual orientation, gender identity, or marital status.[133] A family consists of all of the people who reside in the unit, but federal law requires that certain individuals be treated as living together even if they do not.[134] A family includes, but is not limited to:

1. A family with children, even if the children are temporarily absent or placed in foster care;
2. A family without children;
3. A family with a spouse or head of household or sole member who is over age 62 (elderly), over age 50 but below age 62 (near-elderly), or disabled;
4. Two or more individuals living together who are over age 62 (elderly), over age 50 but below age 62 (near-elderly), or disabled;
5. A displaced family;
6. A disabled family;
7. An individual who is the remaining member of a tenant family that already is in residence; and
8. Any other single person who lives alone and does not qualify as an elderly family, a displaced person, or as the remaining member of a tenant family.[135]

The temporary absence of a child due to placement in foster care does not reduce a family's composition or size.[136]

Can noncitizens receive federal rental assistance?

Maybe. Section 214 of the Housing and Community Development Act of 1980 imposed restrictions on noncitizen eligibility for certain federal housing programs. These restrictions do not apply to housing assisted through the Low-Income Housing Tax Credit program, and the LIHTC program does not impose citizenship conditions. However, if the LIHTC development receives support from a HUD-assisted program, then the HUD citizenship restrictions likely will apply.[137]

Noncitizen eligibility for Public Housing, Section 8 Vouchers, Project-Based Section 8, and low-income housing under Section 236 is limited to certain categories of immigrants, including the following:[138]

1. People lawfully admitted for permanent residence ("green card" holders);
2. Political asylees;

3. People who entered the country before 1972, have continuously maintained residence in the United States since then, and have been "registered" by the Attorney General as lawfully admitted for permanent residence;
4. Refugees;
5. People granted withholding of deportation;
6. People "paroled" into the United States;
7. Victims of trafficking;[139]
8. Battered women who have self-petitioned for status under the Violence Against Women Act (VAWA);[140] and
9. Immigrants who are lawful residents in Guam (however, effective 2016, a preference or priority is given to citizens or nationals of the United States over aliens covered by compacts between the United States and Palau, Micronesia, and the Marshall Islands).[141]

Generally, a family is ineligible for housing programs covered by Section 214 unless all members meet the immigration eligibility criteria (or are U.S citizens).[142] Nevertheless, if a family is "mixed," in the sense of including members who are eligible and members who are not eligible because of their immigration status, the household can receive a prorated share of rental assistance.[143] However, in May 2019, the Trump administration published a proposed rule that would bar "mixed families" from living in Public Housing or receiving Section 8 benefits. In addition, the Trump administration published a new rule in August 2019 that allows the government in certain cases to consider an immigrant's use of housing assistance as part of a "totality of the circumstances test" for determining whether the immigrant may be inadmissible to the United States and ineligible for lawful permanent resident status on "public charge" grounds (the new public-charge rule is discussed in more detail in chapters 3 and 4).[144] As this book goes to press, family members are not required to establish immigration status if they are not applying for assistance or contending that they are eligible,[145] but the new public-charge rule is complex, and it is advisable to consult immigrants' rights groups, such as the National Immigration Law Center (nilc.org) or the Immigration Law Resource Center (ilrc.org), to remain current about the situation.

How is immigration status verified?

The housing provider (generally the Public Housing Authority) is responsible for verifying immigration status. The applicant is required to submit documentation of status, as follows.

U.S. citizen or U.S. national. Evidence consists of a signed declaration. However, the Public Housing Authority or subsidized owner may request verification (for example, presentation of a U.S. passport or other document).[146]

Noncitizens age 62 or older. Evidence consists of a signed declaration and proof of age.[147]

Noncitizens under age 62. Evidence consists of a signed declaration; original documents of the sort designated by the federal immigration services as evidence of immigration status; and a signed consent form permitting verification of status with the Department of Homeland Security.[148]

A Public Housing Authority, but not a subsidized owner, may provide rental assistance before beginning the verification process, but the verification must be completed before the family's annual re-examination.[149] Neither the PHA nor an owner may delay the grant of assistance while the verification process is pending if at least one family member's immigration status has been verified and that person is eligible to receive assistance.[150] Moreover, noncitizens petitioning for lawful permanent resident status under the Violence Against Women Act can receive federal housing assistance while verification of their eligible immigration status is pending.[151]

If an applicant's immigration status cannot be verified, the applicant must be informed in writing of the denial and told of the options to appeal.[152] Applicants may appeal to the U.S. Department of Homeland Security or to the PHA or owner (or to both).[153] Appeals to the PHA follow the grievance process (which applies only to Public Housing), described later in the chapter.

How does contact with the criminal justice system affect eligibility for HUD-supported rental assistance?

An applicant's contact with the criminal justice system—whether an arrest or a felony conviction—may affect eligibility for HUD rental assistance depending on the program and the nature of the contact. Federal law requires the Public Housing Authority and owner to ban from admission certain applicants who have engaged in specified criminal conduct. The mandatory bans are narrowly defined. For other kinds of criminal activity, federal law allows the PHA or owner to deny admission but also gives them authority to offer admission, after considering whether the applicant has undergone rehabilitation, usually by participating in or successfully completing a drug or alcohol treatment program and showing that the illicit conduct no longer continues. The rules governing treatment of an applicant's criminal history for admission to HUD-assisted housing generally are the same from program to program, but the regulations do differ, and it is important to check each program's requirements.[154] Keep in mind that some of the rules refer to admission of a person or applicant, while others refer to admission of a household. What follows are the rules governing admission for Public Housing, the Housing Choice Voucher program, and Section 8 moderate rehabilitation.

The PHA or owner must permanently ban any "household in which any member is a lifetime sex offender."[155] The PHA or owner also must permanently ban any "person" convicted of crimes related to the manufacture or production of methamphetamine on the premises of federally assisted housing.[156]

The PHA or owner must ban any "household" with a member determined to be "illegally using a controlled substance."[157]

The PHA or owner may impose a three-year ban on admission of any "tenant" evicted from HUD-assisted housing for "drug-related criminal activity," unless the tenant "successfully completes a rehabilitation program."[158]

The PHA or owner may ban a "household" if the PHA or owner has reasonable cause to believe that a household member's "illegal use (or pattern of illegal use)" of a controlled substance or abuse or pattern of abuse of alcohol "may interfere with the health, safety, or right to peaceful enjoyment of the premises by other residents," but may offer admission after considering whether the household member has been rehabilitated by, for example, the member's currently participating in or successfully completing a drug or alcohol program and is no longer engaged in illegal use of a controlled substance or alcohol.[159]

The PHA or owner may ban "an applicant" if the applicant or any member of the applicant's family is determined to have been, "during a reasonable time preceding the date" of the application, "engaged in any drug-related or violent criminal activity or other criminal activity which would adversely affect the health, safety, or right to peaceful enjoyment of the premises by other residents" or has a history of violent criminal activity, but after a "reasonable period" of time has passed since the offending activity, may admit the applicant upon consideration of evidence, submitted by the applicant, "sufficient . . . to ensure that the individual or individuals in the applicant's household who engaged in criminal activity for which denial was made . . . have not engaged in any criminal activity during such reasonable period."[160]

Special rules govern the admission of applicants whose encounters with the criminal justice system are the result of forms of sexual abuse. In Public Housing, Project-Based Section 8, and the Section 8 Housing Choice Voucher program, a PHA or owner may not ban an "applicant . . . on the basis that the applicant . . . is or has been a victim of domestic violence, dating violence, sexual assault or stalking."[161]

A generation has passed since Congress imposed these eligibility rules limiting access to HUD-assisted housing by persons who have had contact with the criminal justice system. Studies show that they have had harsh, arbitrary, and counterproductive effects on poor and low-income families, with disproportionate racial and gender impacts—causing homelessness, contributing to family breakup, and raising insuperable barriers to community reentry by those who had been incarcerated.[162] In many communities, the PHA and owner failed to consider whether an applicant had undergone rehabilitation and no longer engaged in the impermissible conduct;[163] rather, taking their lead from President Clinton's endorsement of a "one-strike" policy, housing providers applied a rigid, hard-edged ban on rental assistance to any applicant who had some prior contact with the criminal justice system.[164] During the Obama administration, HUD took steps to make clear that the mandatory ban on certain convicted criminals applies in only "limited instances,"[165] and in 2016 issued a specific Guidance on the use of criminal records—underscoring, moreover, that the use of criminal records as the exclusive basis for a decision to bar admission to assisted housing could violate the Fair Housing Act because of its disparate, negative effects on members of protected groups.[166] At least one federal court has held that tenant-screening services that interpret criminal records and provide information to housing providers must make decisions that comply with the Fair Housing Act (these services are a form of consumer reporting that is discussed in chapter 6).[167]

What is a "preference"?

"Preferences" are rules that allow Public Housing Authorities and subsidized owners to give priority to certain categories of applicants when selecting tenants. PHAs and owners may, but are not required, to adopt "preferences."[168] An eligible applicant who falls within the preference category will be ranked higher than an eligible applicant who does not. A PHA may adopt different preferences for different programs, limit the number of applicants under each preference, and "rank" preferences—that is, prefer applicants falling under one preference to those under another. Preferences for Public Housing and vouchers must be included in the PHA plan.[169]

EXAMPLE: Person 1 is unemployed, the caretaker of four children, and lives in the jurisdiction of the Public Housing Authority. Person 2 lives with a spouse and their three children; both adults work, but they do not live in the jurisdiction of the PHA. Each family applies for subsidized housing. If the local PHA has a residency preference, the PHA will rank Person 1's application higher on the waiting list. If it has a "working families" preference, then the application of Person 2 would receive priority. If the PHA has both preferences, the applications' positions on the waiting list would depend on how the PHA ranks the respective preferences. As discussed later, preferences are acceptable as long as they do not violate fair housing laws.

HUD has provided guidance for some, but not all, of the preferences that may be adopted. For example, a residency preference is permitted but a residency requirement is not.[170] Nor may a durational residency requirement be set—that is, the preference may not turn on whether the applicant has resided in an area for a certain time.[171] (Durational residence requirements are discussed further in chapter 8.) Applicants who are working or have been hired to work in the area must be considered residents for the purposes of a PHA's or owner's residency preference, and PHAs and owners have discretion to treat participants in or graduates of local job education or training programs as local residents as well.[172] Residency preferences must comply with the Fair Housing Act's nondiscrimination requirements, which include a ban on rules "that have the purpose or effect of delaying or otherwise denying [housing]" on the basis of race, ethnic origin, gender, or any other protected characteristic.[173] A PHA may not deny a preference to an applicant seeking a Section 8 voucher solely because the applicant currently lives in public housing.[174]

A preference also may be given to families in which the head of the household or spouse is employed. However, if this preference is adopted, a preference also must be given to families whose head of household and spouse or whose sole member is elderly (age 62 or older) or disabled.[175] However, a preference may not be given to persons with a particular disability or for persons without disabilities.[176] Another permissible preference is for persons who are homeless or displaced.

Until 1998, federal law mandated preferences for (1) people involuntarily displaced by disaster or government action (including domestic violence victims and persons subject to no-fault evictions); (2) people living in substandard housing or without housing; and (3) people paying more than 50 percent of their income for rent. PHAs and subsidized owners in some localities continue to apply these preferences or apply them with modifications to meet local needs. Given past siting decisions that located some assisted housing near toxic or adverse conditions, some commentators urge that the statutory duty to "affirmatively further fair housing" include consideration of preferences (and other initiatives) for tenants displaced by environmental disasters.[177]

What is income targeting and how does it affect the provision of rental assistance?

"Income targeting" is the federal government's current approach to focusing provision of rental assistance on people whose income is "extremely low."[178] "Extremely low" income means an amount that does not exceed the higher of the federal poverty guidelines or 30 percent of the area median income.[179] Income targeting requires that Public Housing, Project-Based Section 8, and the Section

8 voucher program provide a certain percentage of assistance to families whose income meets this condition.[180] The required minimum varies depending on the program; for example, the PHA must admit at least 75 percent extremely low-income families from the waiting list for Section 8 vouchers (with some exceptions).[181] The targeting requirement for Section 8 project-based housing applies to each project with a contract for Section 8 assistance.[182]

How many rooms will an apartment include?

The number of rooms in a HUD-assisted unit depends on the family's size and the particular development. Public Housing Authorities and owners must establish policies outlining their occupancy standards and comply with fair housing mandates and other civil rights requirements,[183] but they have discretion within these guidelines to assign families to units of particular sizes.[184] PHAs may have different policies establishing the relationship between family size and unit size.[185] Under the "Keating Memorandum,"[186] typically it is considered reasonable to require two persons to share a room. Qualified applicants with disabilities can request a larger unit size as a reasonable accommodation.[187] When a family using a voucher moves to a new jurisdiction, the family may find that the number of rooms in its apartment differs because it is subject to a different unit size policy.[188]

Generally, the first step to determine the appropriate unit size is to count the number of occupants. In answering that question, these family members count:

- Individuals who live with the applicant full-time;
- Children who are away at school, but live with the applicant at recess;
- Children under joint custody, who live with the applicant at least half-time;
- Foster children;
- Medically necessary live-in attendants; and
- Children temporarily away from home because of their placement in foster care.

Once the number of occupants is established, the policies governing unit size are considered.[189]

How does an applicant learn whether HUD-supported rental assistance has been granted or denied?

Applicants for HUD rental assistance are entitled to notice of their acceptance or rejection. If an application is accepted, and a unit of the right size is available, the applicant will receive assistance; if a unit is not available, the applicant's name will be placed on the waiting list. If the application is denied, the applicant is entitled to know the specific reasons for the denial,[190] and has a right to challenge the denial.

- If the application is for Public Housing, the applicant can request an "informal hearing."[191]
- If the application is for Section 8 voucher assistance, the applicant can ask to provide additional written information or request an "informal review" of the decision.[192] HUD has established different procedures to review the PHA's decision, depending on whether the person is classified as an "applicant" or a "participant" in the voucher program.[193] HUD must allow a participant an opportunity to request an informal hearing when it has made a decision affecting income, the assistance payment, the utility allowance, family size, or termination.[194] The opportunity to request the hearing must come before the PHA terminates the housing assistance payment under an existing contract.[195]
- If the application is for project-based rental assistance, the applicant can dispute the rejection in writing. The applicant also may request a meeting to dispute the rejection. In that case, the person conducting the meeting on behalf of the owner cannot have been involved in the original decision to deny admission to the applicant.[196]

What is a lease?

A lease is a legal document that defines the relationship between the tenant and the landlord, setting out their respective rights and responsibilities, and addressing such matters as rent, extra charges, pets, security deposits, rent redeterminations, evictions, and inspections. When a person becomes a tenant in a HUD-assisted property, the person will be required to sign a lease. To protect tenants' rights, HUD has advised PHAs and owners that copies of their leases may need to be available in languages other than English,[197] and housing providers (for example, under the Section 8 program) who receive federal funding must provide meaningful language access.[198] In addition to the lease, rights and obligations also are set out in "house rules," which span a variety of issues and must be reasonable.[199] For example, it is considered reasonable to prohibit the placing of bicycles on balconies or to restrict walking on the grass. It is considered unreasonable, and perhaps may be discriminatory, to prohibit children from playing in common areas.[200]

What information must a lease include?

The lease must provide the tenant with certain basic information. Required lease provisions vary somewhat by program and are codified in scattered sections. Private owners participating in project-based assistance programs are required to use certain HUD-issued model leases.[201] By law, lease terms must not be unreasonable, but in practice not all lease terms are reasonable.[202] A lease should include this information:

1. The name of the landlord and the name of the tenant;
2. The landlord's repair obligations and obligation to keep the premises in a safe, decent, and sanitary condition;[203]
3. The particular unit rented;
4. The length of the lease;
5. The amount of rent and when rent is due;
6. Approved household members, if a lease is for a public housing unit;[204]
7. Which utilities, services, and equipment require tenant payment in addition to rent;
8. Any policy regarding entry into the unit by the landlord during the tenancy, and notice requirements for such entry;
9. Provisions regarding late payment;
10. Provisions regarding eviction and grievance procedures, if a lease is for a public housing unit;[205] and
11. Procedures for reporting and recertifying household income and composition.[206]

Does federal law prohibit certain lease terms?

Federal law bars Public Housing and Multifamily Housing leases from including specified terms. Although these federal restrictions do not directly apply to leases for privately owned apartments in the Section 8 voucher program, to the extent that terms in such leases conflict with the "Tenancy Addendum" required by Section 8, they would be unenforceable. In addition, state and local law may prohibit the terms.[207]

The prohibited terms are:

1. Confession of judgment. The lease cannot require the tenant to consent to any judgment in favor of the landlord prior to the landlord's bringing a lawsuit.

2. Exculpatory clauses. The lease cannot require the tenant to agree to limit the landlord's liability for personal or property damage caused by the action or inaction of the landlord or the landlord's employees.

3. Waiver of legal notice. The lease cannot authorize the landlord to take important legal steps (like initiating an eviction or seeking a money judgment) without giving the tenant prior written notice that a suit has been filed.

4. Waiver of jury trial. The lease cannot require the tenant to give up the right to a jury if the landlord brings an eviction action or a suit for a money judgment.

5. Waiver of legal proceedings. The lease cannot require the tenant to give up the right to present a case in court before being evicted or having property removed.

6. Waiver of appeal rights. The lease cannot require the tenant to give up the right to go to court to appeal a judgment in favor of the landlord.

7. Distraint for rent or other charges. The lease cannot authorize the landlord to take the tenant's possessions, or to lock the tenant out of the apartment, to satisfy an alleged claim of unpaid rent.

8. Attorney's fees and costs. The lease cannot obligate the tenant to pay the landlord's legal costs under any circumstances—whether the tenant wins or loses a lawsuit. However, a court may order a tenant to pay the landlord's legal costs if the tenant is sued by the landlord and loses the case.[208]

How much rent does a tenant in HUD-supported housing pay?

Rent levels depend on the program providing assistance and the family's financial circumstances. Rent calculations are subject to different and complicated methodologies: minimum rent, flat rent, budget-based rents, and income-based rent.[209] The general guiding principle for HUD programs is that the amount payable by a tenant for rent and utilities should not exceed the higher of 30 percent of family monthly adjusted income or 10 percent of family monthly income.[210] The 30 percent cap does not apply to those Multifamily Programs that use a budget-based (rather than income-based) rent.[211] Additionally, in the Section 8 voucher program, on the initial lease, tenants can pay up to 40 percent of their adjusted income in rent if the rent in the new unit exceeds the payment standard.[212] Separate rules apply to rents under the Low-Income Housing Tax Credit program.

Public Housing. Once every year, Public Housing tenants elect between paying an income-based rent or a flat rent.[213] Income-based rent is the higher of 30 percent of the family's adjusted monthly income, or 10 percent of the family's unadjusted monthly income, or the portion of welfare payments intended for payment of rent. A tenant who elects the flat rent but experiences financial hardship (for example, loss of income, unemployment, increased medical costs) may immediately switch to an income-based rent.[214] Additionally, PHAs may set a minimum rental payment for Public Housing of no more than $50 per month, subject to a hardship suspension and waiver mandated by federal law.[215]

Section 8 Project-Based Assistance, Section 202, and Section 811. Tenants in units subsidized through Section 8 project-based programs, Section 202 programs, and Section 811 programs pay rent of 30 percent of adjusted monthly income toward rent and utilities, regardless of the actual cost of the unit, subject to a fixed minimum rent of $25 regardless of income.[216] Older Section 202 and Section 811 properties have budget-based rents if they do not have project-based Section 8 rental assistance.

Section 236. Rents for units without utility assistance in Section 236 projects are the higher of 30 percent of monthly adjusted income or a HUD-calculated basic rent, which reflects the owner's costs of operating the project with the mortgage subsidy. However, rents cannot exceed the Section 236 market rent, which represents the amount of rent the owner would have to charge if the mortgage were not subsidized. Tenants pay a percentage of their income toward rent, but never pay less than the basic rent or more than the market rent for the property.[217]

Section 221(d)(3) BMIR. Rents for units in Section 221(d)(3) BMIR projects are at a HUD-approved flat rent, regardless of income. If, after becoming a tenant, the family's income exceeds 110 percent of the income standard for a BMIR project, the tenant payment will be 110 percent of the flat rent.[218]

Low-Income Housing Tax Credit projects. As discussed earlier, rents in developments financed through the tax credit program are not based on the tenant's actual income, but rather are calculated using a formula that relies on area median income subject to restrictions.[219] The owner elects the restriction at the outset of the project. Although affordability options have differed in the past, at present the owner can choose one of three: (1) keep at least 20 percent of the units affordable ("rent-restricted") and occupied by tenants with income at or below 50 percent of the area median income; or (2) keep at least 40 percent of the units affordable and occupied by tenants with income at or below 60 percent of the area median income; or (3) keep at least 40 percent of the units affordable and occupied by tenants whose average income is no more than 60 percent of area median income, on condition no individual tenant's income exceeds 80 percent of area median income.[220]

Section 8 Housing Choice Vouchers. A tenant with a Section 8 voucher generally pays 30 percent of adjusted monthly income for rent and utilities (referred to as Total Tenant Payment) if the rent for the apartment does not exceed the "payment standard" established for a unit of similar size. The payment standard ordinarily is set at between 90 percent and 110 percent of the Fair Market Rent for the area, a figure that HUD calculates every year, generally at the fortieth per-centile of standard rents in the area.[221] In addition to the rent paid by the tenant, the PHA pays a subsidy directly to the landlord based on the "payment standard" that the PHA has established. The subsidy is the amount equal to the difference between the rental price of the unit and the tenant's rent contribution, capped by the payment standard. In certain circumstances, the "payment standard" can be based on zip codes instead of a metropolitan area, and a 2016 regulation requires agencies in certain urban areas to use "small area" Fair Market Rent.[222] Using small area FMRs as the basis for calculating voucher rent levels carries important benefits from the perspective of tenant mobility, deconcentration of poverty, and racial integration.[223]

A landlord renting to a tenant with a Section 8 voucher is permitted to charge a rent that is higher than the payment standard (which caps the PHA subsidy), as long as the rent charged is "reasonable" by comparison to rents of similar units available on the private market.[224] If the rent charged is higher than the payment standard, the tenant is responsible for paying both Total Tenant Payment plus the difference between the payment standard and the ac-tual rent. As a result, a Section 8 voucher holder may have to pay more than 30 percent of adjusted monthly income to rent the apartment. As explained earlier, when a voucher holder first signs a lease, the tenant contribution to-ward rent and tenant-paid utilities may reach, but not exceed, 40 percent of adjusted income.[225]

Can a rent change during the term of a tenancy?

Yes. A family's rent in HUD-assisted housing may change if family income or composition changes. Generally, every year the Public Housing Authority or owner will review the family's composition and income; the tenant will be required to submit documentation as part of the recertification process.[226] Moreover, the tenant is required to report changes affecting eligibility and assis-tance,[227] and a tenant in Public Housing or receiving a Section 8 voucher must report changes in family composition.[228] In addition, the tenant or the landlord may request an interim examination and recertification to account for changes in income and family composition. [229] A tenant's request for an interim review must be conducted in a timely manner.[230] Special rules govern Public Housing tenants when a family member has been unemployed for more than a year. In that situation, if the family member finds a job and begins to earn income, rent will remain the same for one year, and then later rent increases will be phased in.[231] Families on fixed income need to "recertify" this information once every three years.[232]

Rents in projects subsidized under the Section 236 or Section 221(d)(3) programs are exempt from state and local rent control,[233] but can increase if HUD approves a building-wide rent increase.[234] HUD will base its decision on whether the owner needs additional income to cover the building's operating expenses or to keep the building well maintained.

In addition, a housing provider must inform the tenants in writing of any proposed building-wide rent increase, and a tenant can challenge the rent increase, but must file written comments within 30 days of the written notice.[235] HUD will consider the tenants' comments in its decision regarding a rent change.[236]

Does a tenant in HUD-assisted housing pay utilities in addition to rent?

The rules governing utilities differ for each program, but some overall principles apply. The lease will say whether the tenant has to pay for utilities. Whether a tenant pays for utilities in addition to rent depends on where the tenant lives and how the apartment is metered. However, if a tenant pays separately for utilities, the Public Housing Authority or owner must offset a utility allowance against the tenant's share of the rent. A review of the utility allowance must be undertaken at least annually to account for changes in costs.[237] The term "utilities" generally includes electricity, gas, heating fuel, water and sewerage services, and trash and garbage collection services. "Utilities" does not include telephone service.[238] In Public Housing, most of the time utilities excludes air conditioning.[239]

Retail metered. An apartment is retail metered if it has its own utility meter and the tenant pays for utilities directly to the utility company. The Public Housing Authority or owner will reduce the rent the tenant would otherwise pay (if the owner paid all utilities) by an allowance for reasonable utility service.[240]

Check metered. An apartment is check metered if it has its own utility meter, but the landlord pays for utilities directly to the utility company. In Public Housing, an allowance for reasonable utility service will be included in the rent, and the PHA can impose a surcharge for excess consumption.[241] Check meters are not typical in Project-Based Section 8 housing.[242]

Master metered. An apartment is master metered if the building has a single utility meter and the landlord pays for utilities directly to the utility company. Under a master-meter system, the tenant is not charged for utility use except for utility consumption attributed to tenant-owned major appliances and optional use of PHA-furnished equipment, such as air conditioning, over and above the cost estimated for reasonable use of such equipment.[243]

In buildings financed through the Low-Income Housing Tax Credit, the gross rent includes an allowance for tenant-paid utilities. However, if the unit is retail metered, the allowance is deducted from the amount of rent payable to the project owner.[244] The utility allowance does not include internet service, cable television, or telephone costs.[245] If additional HUD subsidies apply to the development, then the utility allowance used in the other subsidy programs applies.[246]

Can a HUD-subsidized owner impose fees for services other than utilities?

No. A subsidized owner cannot charge fees for services that are necessary for tenancy, such as use of a stove or insect control. On the other hand, a lease can set extra fees for optional services, such as cable television or parking, and for such things as excessive damage to a tenant's unit.[247] An owner cannot base an eviction for nonpayment of rent on the tenant's nonpayment of these extra fees unless the lease makes nonpayment a material violation of the lease.[248] Likewise, an owner cannot base an eviction for nonpayment of rent on the tenant's non-payment of late charges.[249]

Does a tenant have to pay a security deposit?

Most leases in HUD-assisted housing provide for a security deposit. A security deposit is a payment by the tenant that the owner may use to remedy conduct by the tenant that breaches the lease agreement, such as tenant-caused damage to the apartment that exceeds so-called normal wear and tear.[250] Subsidized owners must comply with state laws regarding investment of security deposits and distribution of any earned interest.[251]

The amount of the security deposit depends on the kind of HUD housing in which the tenant lives and how much rent is paid:

Public Housing—The security deposit cannot exceed one month's rent or a reasonable amount fixed by the Public Housing Authority.[252]

Section 236 or Section 221(d)(3)-Assisted Housing—The security deposit cannot exceed one month's rent (this assumes that the project receives no additional HUD support).[253]

Vouchers—Property owners may require a security deposit; the Public Housing Authority may adopt a rule barring deposits in amounts that exceed those required from unsubsidized tenants.[254]

Can tenants have pets in HUD-assisted housing?

Whether a tenant can have a pet depends on the kind of subsidized unit and the terms of the lease. Generally, the rules are:

Public Housing—Tenants in Public Housing may have pets.[255]

Section 202 Housing—Tenants in HUD-assisted housing for the elderly or disabled may have pets.[256]

Other Assisted Housing—Tenants can have pets with the landlord's consent. Tenants who want a pet must be sure that the lease specifies that pets are allowed and whether fees will be charged.

A tenant who has a pet is required to comply with various rules. Every HUD-subsidized building will mandate registering the pet and pet vaccinations.[257] A PHA or owner also may impose discretionary pet rules, such as restrictions on pet size or the creation of no-pet areas.[258] Federal regulations make clear that pet rules must have a reasonable relation to legitimate interests in maintaining the property and be narrowly drawn to achieve those ends.[259] A tenant's violation of pet rules can result in the removal of a pet.[260] A property owner can charge a tenant who wants a pet a refundable deposit for repairs, fumigation, and other reasonable expenses related to the pet.[261]

It is important to emphasize that a service animal is not a pet, and that pet rules do not govern use of a service animal.[262] A service animal is an animal needed for assistance because of the tenant's disability. A property owner's refusal to permit a service animal in a HUD-assisted unit may violate federal law protecting persons with disabilities,[263] including 1988 amendments to the Fair Housing Act,[264] the Rehabilitation Act of 1973,[265] and the Americans with Disabilities Act.[266]

Is the landlord required to maintain the building in good repair?

Congress adopted federal housing laws in part to remedy "unsafe housing conditions."[267] HUD has published regulations setting forth physical condition standards that generally apply to all subsidized housing.[268] The regulations state that housing must be "decent, safe, sanitary and in good repair," and that owners must meet the published standards, which include:[269]

- Regular cleaning of all common areas;
- Maintaining common areas in safe condition;
- Arranging for trash and garbage removal;
- Keeping all equipment and appliances in working order;

- Making necessary repairs with reasonable promptness;
- Maintaining exterior lighting in good working order;
- Providing for extermination services; and
- Maintaining grounds and shrubs.

A tenant should bring maintenance issues to the attention of the owner or management company. However, it may be necessary to consider other strategies that are discussed later in this chapter.

Does federal law regulate the use of lead paint in federally subsidized buildings?

Exposure to lead paint can lead to serious adverse health conditions and developmental problems. Two statutes regulate the use of lead paint in HUD-assisted housing: the Lead-Based Paint Poisoning Prevention Act and the Residential Lead-Based Paint Hazard Reduction Act of 1992.[270] In 2017, HUD amended its regulations on lead paint to account for developments in the medical and scientific community underscoring the dangers of lead exposure.[271] Upon the identification of a child age six or younger with an elevated blood lead level (EBLL), the regulations require that the Environmental Protection Agency or the relevant state agency conduct an environmental investigation of the child's home. If the investigation finds lead-based paint hazards in the residence, the regulation requires that the owner or the Public Housing Authority eliminate the risk through abatement, interim controls, or paint stabilization. The regulation does not cover non-lead-paint-based hazards, and HUD has not developed regulations addressing the health hazards of lead in water.[272]

Are tenants who receive HUD-supported rental assistance required to do community service?

Adult tenants in Public Housing are required to do community service as a condition of their rental assistance. The requirement is eight hours of community service per month or participation in a range of education and training programs. Exemptions are available for tenants who are older than age 62, disabled or blind, engaged in specified work activities, or are part of a family receiving specified assistance. If the annual recertification shows that the nonexempt family member has failed to participate, there may be grounds not to renew the lease.[273] In this situation, the PHA must give notice to the tenant of the nature of the noncompliance, explaining that the lease will not be renewed unless the noncompliant member enters into a written agreement to cure the conduct and does cure the noncompliance. The tenant also is permitted to request a grievance hearing.[274]

Are tenants in HUD-assisted housing allowed to organize?

Democracy begins at home: the tenant's right to organize is critical to the ability of poor and low-income tenants to influence housing conditions in the communities in which they live. Tenants in HUD-assisted housing generally are permitted to organize and through a tenants' association can influence management policies, maintenance, and other important issues.[275] The rules governing organizing differ depending on the program, as described below.[276] State laws also protect tenant organizing.[277]

In Public Housing, residents have a right to organize and to elect a Resident Council.[278] The Resident Council is made up of Public Housing tenants only, and must have written rules, called bylaws, that describe its election and recall procedures, and the council must hold fair elections at least every three years.[279] A PHA that receives an operating subsidy is required to fund at least $25 per occupied unit per year for tenant participation activities, and at least $15 must go to the Resident Council for tenant participation activities (however, funding requires a written agreement between the PHA and the democratically elected Resident Council).[280] The funds can be used for activities including resident management, training of residents for programs, such as child care, resident surveys, elections and organizing, and reasonable refreshments for resident meetings. The funds cannot be used for the purchase of alcoholic beverages, trips to theme parks, or bowling nights.[281] A PHA resident cannot be evicted for organizing or joining a tenants' association, for talking to the press about conditions at the apartment complex, or for complaining to neighbors or to government agencies about the landlord.

In Multifamily Housing programs, tenants have a right to organize and to elect a group called a Resident Organization.[282] HUD's Model Lease specifically refers to the tenants' right to organize.[283] A Resident Organization is treated as legitimate and entitled to recognition if it "meets regularly, operates democratically, is representative of all residents in the development, and is completely independent of owners, management, and their representatives,"[284] but no particular structure is required. The tenants do not need permission for activities related to the establishment or operation of the Resident Organization, including: distribution of leaflets in common areas or under tenants' doors, holding meetings on site, and conducting tenant surveys.[285] Owners are required to provide meetings spaces; if a fee is charged, it must be "reasonable, customary and usual," and HUD must approve the fee.[286] Subsidized owners under Section 236, Section 202, and

Section 221(d)(3) are barred by federal regulation from impeding the reasonable efforts of tenants to organize.[287] HUD is authorized to sanction owners and their agents for impeding the tenants' right to organize.[288]

The tenants' right to engage in collective action enjoys other protections, as well. A Public Housing Authority is considered to be a government representative and is obliged to respect the First Amendment of the U.S. Constitution, which protects the tenant's right to speak, to associate with others, and to protest.[289]

Tenants can become involved, individually and collectively, in other ways, too. Indeed, HUD regulations require that the PHA include tenants in the development of an annual and five-year PHA Plan. Every PHA is required to have a Resident Board and to ensure tenant participation in the PHA Plan. Regulations governing the Resident Advisory Board require that there be reasonable representation of voucher households.[290]

HUD regulations also allow tenants to participate in the management of Public Housing and other assisted units.[291] The most extensive opportunities for tenant management are in Public Housing, where HUD has enacted a comprehensive program allowing a PHA to contract for resident management with qualifying tenant associations (called "resident management corporations").[292] Relatedly, tenants can participate in the development of lease provisions and building rules and regulations,[293] the review of proposed rent increases,[294] and the decision to convert from master-metered utility service to check-metered or retail-metered units.[295] Prior regulations requiring the PHA to consult resident organizations before appointing a hearing officer have been eliminated, but the PHA must include information about its selection policies in the tenant lease form, which is subject to a 30-day comment period.[296]

What is an eviction?

An eviction is a legal proceeding through which a Public Housing Authority or other housing provider terminates a tenant's lease and retakes possession of the apartment that the tenant is renting. Eviction is not the same as termination of assistance. Assistance may terminate, but the tenant will still have a right to remain in an apartment provided the tenant pays the full rent, including the share that had been paid through the rental assistance. Eviction is a very serious event: it means that the tenant will not be able to live in the apartment and will lose the rental assistance if it is project-specific. Depending on the circumstances, the tenant may face other legal consequences that can delay or even prevent receipt of future government rental assistance.[297]

Before an eviction takes place, the landlord is required to take a number of formal steps, which generally begins with notice to the tenant and must end with a court order. The procedures governing eviction vary from state to state, but some federal regulations apply to proceedings involving federally assisted housing. In addition, the landlord must show a legally permissible basis for the eviction. Overall, HUD-assisted tenants are protected by the requirement of "good cause"—the tenant cannot be removed from the apartment for arbitrary or unreasonable grounds.[298] Voucher tenants are protected by good cause, but the protection applies only during the term of the lease.[299] After the voucher lease has expired, the landlord must have a legal reason for eviction but is not required to state good cause; however, if the owner uses the HUD model lease, eviction may not be grounded on business reasons that do not relate to tenant misconduct.[300] A tenant who receives a notice of eviction should seek advice from a legal services or legal aid lawyer immediately.

Does a tenant's contact with the criminal justice system count as good cause for eviction?

Whether a tenant's contact with the criminal justice system counts as good cause for eviction depends on the program, as well as the nature of the criminal activity, where the activity occurred, and who engaged in the act. As already explained, termination of assistance occurs when the tenant is no longer eligible for assistance. Termination of tenancy, by contrast, is the first step toward eviction. Eviction takes place only after a judicial proceeding and court order. Eviction can be based on a tenant's material violation of obligations that are set out in the lease. Each program has different regulations, and it is important to consult the requirements for each program and to make sure that the lease provides the requisite notice.[301]

In Public Housing, the PHA lease must specify that alcohol abuse and criminal activity constitute "other good cause" for eviction.[302] The PHA "must immediately terminate the tenancy" if it "determines that any member of the household has ever been convicted of drug-related criminal activity for manufacture or production of methamphetamine on the premises."[303] The PHA may terminate the tenancy if a tenant is "fleeing to avoid prosecution, or custody or confinement after conviction . . . or violating a condition of probation or parole."[304] "Good cause" grounds for eviction do not require a criminal conviction, but rather—and more broadly—tenant activity in material violation of the lease, which by regulation may include: criminal activity "that threatens the health, safety or right to peaceful enjoyment of the premises by other residents"; any "drug-related criminal activity on the premises" engaged in "by any tenant, member of the tenant's household or guest," or "any such activity engaged in on the premises by any other person under the tenant's control"; and a failure to "assure that no member of the household engages in an abuse or pattern of abuse of alcohol that affects the health, safety, or right to peaceful enjoyment of the premises by other residents."[305]

In Multifamily Housing, HUD regulations (but not the statute) require owners to use leases that specify certain criminal activity as good cause for eviction, including:[306]

1. "Drug-related criminal activity" by the tenant, household member, or guest "on or near the premises" or by other persons under the tenant or household member's control "on the premises."[307]
2. Illegal drug use by a household member that interferes with the health, safety, or peaceful enjoyment of the premises by other residents.[308]
3. Criminal activity by a tenant, household member, guest, or other person under the tenant or household member's control that threatens the health, safety, or right to peaceful enjoyment of residents or other persons residing in the immediate vicinity of the premises.[309]
4. The tenant's fleeing to avoid prosecution, custody, or conviction for a felony or attempted felony, or in violation of a condition of probation or parole.[310]
5. A household member's alcohol abuse that threatens the health, safety, or right to peaceful enjoyment of other residents.[311]
6. Violent criminal activity.[312]

In the Section 8 Housing Choice Voucher program, an owner may evict a tenant who "threatens the health, safety, or right to peaceful enjoyment of the premises by other tenants, any criminal activity that threatens the health, safety, or right to peaceful enjoyment of their residences by persons residing in the immediate vicinity of the premises, or any drug-related criminal activity *on or near* such premises, engaged in by a tenant of any unit, any member of the tenant's household, or any guest or other person under the tenant's control."[313]

In 1992, the U.S. Supreme Court held it was constitutional for a Public Housing Authority to evict a tenant on the basis of criminal activity by a household member or guest, even if the tenant did not know or have reason to know about the activity and there was no conviction.[314] By effect, the Court sanctioned what some commentators saw as "no fault" eviction, which subjected the tenant to a regime of strict liability.[315] In the wake of that decision, many PHAs and owners interpreted the good cause requirements to allow and even encourage eviction for "one strike" by the tenant—any alleged criminal activity by the tenant or a person under the tenant's control on or near the premises.[316] Application of this interpretation led to consequences that were harsh, severe, and racialized in their impact.[317] In 2002 HUD provided guidance to PHAs and owners reminding, but not requiring, the housing providers to make a holistic assessment of the tenant's action before taking the drastic step of eviction, considering such factors as the "seriousness of the offending action, the extent of participation by the leaseholder in the offending action, the effects that the eviction would have on family members . . . and the extent to which the leaseholder has shown personal responsibility."[318] In 2011 HUD followed up with additional guidance[319] and in 2015 issued another Guidance that could not have been clearer: "HUD does not require that PHAs and owners adopt or enforce so-called 'one-strike' rules that . . . require automatic eviction any time a household member engages in criminal activity in violation of their lease." Rather, the Guidance stated, other than in the limited circumstances when eviction is required,[320] housing providers have discretion whether to evict. Moreover, the Guidance emphasized that a decision to evict must comply with the Fair Housing Act and ensure that the application of termination policies does not produce disparate negative impacts on protected groups that cannot be justified by legitimate business needs.[321]

Can a landlord base good cause for eviction on a tenant's reporting or being the target of domestic abuse?

Survivors of domestic violence, dating violence, sexual assault, or stalking who are applicants for or tenants in certain HUD-subsidized housing are protected from the denial of assistance or eviction based on the acts of abuse under a federal statute called the Violence Against Women Reauthorization Act of 2013 (VAWA) and later amendments.[322] VAWA 2017 continued and improved upon housing protection provided under the law as enacted in 2005.[323] Keep in mind that VAWA does not bar eviction or termination of assistance if the housing provider can show an "actual or imminent threat" to other residents or employees at the property. However, HUD regulations implementing VAWA in some circumstances require a housing provider to consider "lease bifurcation" as a way to keep the victim of abuse housed in an assisted unit but to evict the abuser for a violation of the lease.[324] In some localities, landlords have invoked local nuisance laws or "crime-free statutes" (barring multiple calls to the police for protection within a specified period) to seek to evict tenants who report or are the victims of domestic abuse.[325] In 2016, HUD issued a Guidance advising that the enforcement of such laws in ways that adversely impact domestic violence victims and survivors potentially violates the Fair Housing Act. Likewise, a locality's adoption of such laws for discriminatory reasons or its selective enforcement of such laws could violate the Fair Housing Act.[326]

Can a landlord base good cause for eviction on a tenant's having guests in the unit?

Tenants in HUD-assisted units have a right to host guests.[327] Public housing leases specifically state that the tenant's right to the use and occupancy of the unit includes "reasonable accommodation of their guests."[328] Further, HUD's model lease requires that any tenant restrictions be reasonable.[329] The reasonableness of having guests in the apartment typically turns on how long the guest is visiting and whether the guest is an unauthorized occupant whose presence requires written approval of the landlord and otherwise may constitute a violation of the lease.[330] In Multifamily Housing, HUD treats unauthorized occupants as a minor violation of the lease, which would not constitute good cause for eviction.[331]

Can a landlord base good cause on a tenant's refusal to permit management to inspect the apartment?

The lease details the scope of the tenant's obligation to permit management access to the apartment to do an inspection,[332] and state law also applies to inspections.[333] Leases in federal housing typically require the tenant to allow the landlord access to the apartment upon reasonable notice and during business hours.[334] This means that the landlord may enter the apartment, with prior notice, to inspect, to make repairs, or to show the apartment to prospective tenants. Generally no permission is required if an emergency exists.[335] Whether a violation of these terms counts as good cause depends on the facts and circumstances; the landlord's right to enter to inspect the apartment is intended to ensure safe living conditions,[336] and does not justify entering the apartment to harass or abuse the tenant. In addition, whether good cause exists may depend on whether the tenant has mental health or other disabilities and the landlord has engaged in effective communication.[337]

Can a landlord evict a tenant because the lease has expired?

Expiration of the lease is not a basis for eviction. A lease in subsidized housing automatically will renew unless the tenant has failed to participate in required community service or economic self-sufficiency programs.[338] Any of the grounds that would provide good cause for eviction would be sufficient grounds for a refusal to renew a lease, but the landlord must have good cause to refuse to renew the lease and to terminate the tenancy.[339] Good cause would include:

- The household failed to provide required information at the recertification stage, such as information about changes in family composition;
- The household failed to provide required forms, such as the verification form;
- The household failed to relocate to a different-size apartment assigned by the landlord within 30 days after the owner has given notification of the change.

Can a family remain in a HUD-assisted unit if the head of the household dies or moves out?

Family composition may change over time because of death, births, divorce, or other reasons. These changes in composition may affect program eligibility, rights to succeed to a lease, and continued lease rights. Whether remaining family members can stay in an assisted unit after the death or departure of the head of the household depends on the lease and program rules. The lease identifies the parties to the agreement, and parties to a lease usually remain as tenants.

Generally, when the head of the household dies or moves, remaining household members who are on the lease are still treated as tenants and are eligible for rental assistance although the size of the apartment might change.[340] A remaining family member in Public Housing is eligible for continued occupancy,[341] and, if refused, has a right to a grievance hearing.[342] Under all Section 8 programs, a remaining family member is eligible for continued assistance.[343] In the Voucher program, the Administrative Plan sets out the rules about continued occupancy and unit transfer.[344] A different rule applies if the household resides in housing for the elderly under Section 202 or for persons with disabilities under Section 811. Then, if the head of the household dies, household members who are on the lease may remain, but if the head of the household moves, and the other household members are not eligible for the program, they may not remain.[345] Nevertheless, in any particular case questions may arise whether a remaining household member succeeds to rights under the lease or the subsidy of the departed household head.[346] A remaining household member should consult a local legal aid or legal services attorney for advice.

What procedural protections does a tenant have
before an eviction from assisted housing?

Eviction is a serious event and federal law and HUD regulations guarantee the tenant various procedural protections. The protections vary depending on the program through which the tenant receives housing assistance. However, a few common themes may be noted. The housing provider must take certain formal steps under federal and state law and obtain a court order before a tenant can be evicted.[347] A court order is the last step in the process. If the PHA or owner does not take the requisite procedural steps before going to court, the tenant may be able to stop the eviction from happening.[348] A tenant who faces eviction should talk to a legal services or legal aid lawyer about the notice procedures that apply to the assisted unit and the household's circumstances.

First, the housing provider must give the tenant written notice of the grounds for the eviction.[349] The notice is not sufficient if it says merely that a provision of the lease has been violated; rather, it must state the specific factual circumstances that form the basis of the violation.[350] In Public Housing, the PHA must give the tenant notice of lease termination.[351] An opportunity to cure noncompliance is not required under federal regulations but may be required under state law.[352] The notice must tell the tenant of the right to examine PHA documents relevant to the eviction, of the right to respond, and the right, if provided, to ask for a grievance hearing (in certain cases, tenants have an absolute right to a grievance hearing if they make a timely request).[353] The notice to tenants in Multifamily Housing must state the date the tenancy terminates, the grounds for the eviction, that an eviction requires a court order, that the tenant has 10 days to discuss the matter with the landlord, and that persons with disabilities may request accommodations.[354] In Section 8 voucher programs, the owner must provide written notice of the grounds for the eviction.[355]

Second, the tenant must be given a reasonable amount of time to respond to the notice, but the time periods vary with the programs. In Public Housing, eviction that is based on nonpayment of rent requires a 14-day notice period; for an eviction based on conduct that threatens the health and safety of other tenants, or if any member of the household has been convicted of a felony or engaged in violent or drug-related criminal activity, the PHA must give reasonable notice of not more than 30 days.[356] In any other case, a 30-day notice by the PHA is required.[357] Delivery of the notice must be to an adult member of the tenant household or sent by prepaid first-class mail.[358] In Multifamily Housing, if the eviction is based on material noncompliance with the lease, the notice period is determined by state law;[359] for evictions based on other grounds, the notice period must be at least 30 days.[360] The owner must serve two copies of the eviction notice, one by prepaid first-class mail and the other by personal delivery to an adult at the apartment.[361] In Section 8 voucher programs, the notice period is determined by state law, and must be given "at or before" commencement of an eviction action; both the tenant and the landlord must give the PHA a copy of the notice.[362]

Third, depending on the program, the tenant may have a right to a grievance procedure, including a formal and informal grievance (as described in the answer to the next question). If the tenant loses the grievance, then the PHA or other housing provider will file an eviction proceeding with the court.

What is the grievance process?

The grievance process is a procedure that allows a tenant to challenge any action or inaction by their landlord involving either the tenant's lease or any PHA regulation that adversely affects the tenant's rights, duties, welfare, or status. The primary purpose of the grievance process is to resolve individual tenant complaints and protect tenants against arbitrary or illegal management practices. For example, if the PHA has not maintained the building in good repair, a tenant can use the grievance process to request repairs, to assert a claim for money damages, and to ask for a rent abatement for substandard conditions.[363] HUD originally established the grievance process for Public Housing tenants. In 1983, Congress passed legislation requiring PHAs to provide a grievance procedure, except in certain eviction disputes (discussed later in this chapter). Since then, the grievance procedure has been adapted and extended to other HUD-assisted tenants to give them protection against private owners.

A tenant's lease in Public Housing incorporates the grievance process. Generally, that process requires a PHA to:[364]

- Give the tenant written notice of the specific grounds of the proposed adverse action;
- Give the tenant an opportunity to present the tenant's views in person before an impartial hearing officer;
- Give the tenant an opportunity to examine documents, records, or regulations related to the proposed action, and provide that opportunity before the hearing takes place;
- Allow the tenant to be represented at the hearing by a person of the tenant's choice;
- Allow the tenant an opportunity to question witnesses at the hearing and to have others make statements on the tenant's behalf; and
- Give the tenant a written decision on whether the proposed action will go forward.

In other federally subsidized housing, the grievance process requires the owner to give the tenant notice of the adverse action and a chance to comment; however, a tenant does not have a right to a fair hearing or to present witnesses. Section 8 voucher tenants also are protected by a grievance process. Those tenants have a right to:[365]

- Receive written notice of the specific grounds of the proposed adverse action;
- Request a hearing before a decision maker who did not participate in the decision to propose the adverse action;
- Request, review, and copy any relevant PHA documents before any hearing;
- Be accompanied by a lawyer or other representative at the hearing;
- Have a hearing officer who is someone other than a person who made the decision being challenged, or a subordinate of this person;
- Question witnesses; and
- Receive a written decision stating the reasons for the action taken based on the facts presented at the hearing.

Can a Public Housing tenant use the grievance process to lodge a complaint against another tenant?

A tenant cannot use the grievance process to bring a complaint directly against another tenant.[366] However, a tenant can lodge a complaint about another tenant with the Public Housing Authority. It is useful to put the complaint in writing, and to provide details about the problem and to identify the individuals. Management then has a duty to take corrective action to resolve the complaint. If the PHA fails to take action, and the problem continues, then the tenant can use the grievance process to complain about management's failure to take reasonable action.

Does the Public Housing grievance process cover evictions?

The Public Housing grievance process covers evictions, but the Public Housing Authority has authority to make three exceptions: (1) evictions based on criminal activity that threatens health, safety, or the right to peaceful enjoyment of the premises; (2) evictions based on drug-related conduct "on or off" the premises; and (3) evictions based on criminal activity that results in a felony conviction.[367] The PHA may exempt these cases from the grievance process only if HUD has determined that state law will sufficiently protect the tenants' due process

rights.[368] The eviction notice must explain the reasons for skipping the grievance process and describe the state court procedures that are available.[369] The
PHA also has authority to establish expedited grievance processes for evictions
on these bases.[370]

How does a Public Housing tenant request and go through the grievance process?

A Public Housing tenant initiates the grievance process by filing a grievance
complaint. The complaint must be "personally presented" to the Public Housing
Authority or PHA apartment office and can be oral or in writing.[371] As a practical
matter, it is sensible to have a record of having filed a grievance, so it is best to file
a complaint by certified mail or to hand deliver it. The complaint should describe
the facts supporting the grievance. The complaint also should specify the kind
of relief that the tenant wants the PHA to give. Some PHAs require a tenant to
file the grievance complaint within a very short period of time—as short as five
days—after the unfavorable event has occurred.[372] These rules should be set out
in the PHA's Admissions and Continued Occupancy Plan and/or the grievance
process attached to the lease. If the complaint is late, the PHA has grounds to
refuse to hear the grievance.

The next step after the filing of the grievance complaint is that the tenant
attends an informal conference with management. The tenant can bring a friend,
lawyer, or other person to the discussion as a representative. After the conference,
the PHA must give the tenant a written summary of the conference, including
the names of the participants, the date of the meeting, the proposed decision, and
the reasons for the decision. The summary also must explain that the tenant has
a right to request a formal hearing if the tenant is not satisfied with the proposed
resolution and the steps that must be taken to obtain a formal hearing.[373] Then,
the tenant can request a formal hearing by submitting to the PHA or management
office a written statement of the reasons for the grievance and the relief requested.

The hearing officer is required to schedule the hearing promptly and at a time
and place reasonably convenient to both the tenant and management. Federal
law guarantees Public Housing tenants a number of procedural protections
during the formal hearing process. At a minimum, the tenant has these rights:[374]

- A right to be represented by counsel or accompanied by a lay representative;
- A right to present evidence and arguments, to controvert evidence, and to
  confront and cross-examine witnesses upon whose testimony the PHA or
  management relies;

– A right to have the hearing held in private, rather than in public; and

– A right to a decision based on the facts that are developed at the hearing.

What happens if a Public Housing tenant loses the formal hearing?

A tenant is not required to go through the grievance process before filing a court action or defending against an eviction proceeding. This means that if the tenant loses at the formal hearing, the tenant still has a right to go to court to challenge the unfavorable decision.[375] Although the regulations do not provide for any administrative appeal from an unfavorable grievance hearing, the tenant may ask to appear before the Public Housing Authority's Board of Commissioners and ask for review of the hearing officer's decision, which may be overruled if contrary to law or does not concern PHA action.[376]

Tenant Protections When Buildings Change Legal Status

What happens to tenants who live in Public Housing scheduled for demolition?

Federal law permits the demolition of Public Housing.[377] Between the mid-1990s and 2010, about 200,000 public housing units were demolished;[378] of those, 12 public housing projects were demolished in Chicago, causing the displacement of about 25,000 tenants, almost all African American, from their neighborhoods.[379] The Public Housing Authority must disclose any proposed demolition in the PHA Annual Plan, and must consult with tenants and tenant organizations before submitting an application for demolition to HUD. HUD must disapprove any proposal that is inconsistent with the Annual Plan or not developed in consultation with residents and resident groups.[380] Tenants must receive notice and are entitled to relocation on a nondiscriminatory basis to comparable housing in a neighborhood that is generally not less desirable.[381] The PHA is not required to ensure a one-for-one replacement of demolished units unless Community Development Block Grant or HOME funds are used in the demolition. In that situation, the PHA is subject to a one-to-one replacement requirement, and the tenants may be entitled to relocation assistance.[382] Under certain circumstances, an eligible Resident Organization or nonprofit group may purchase a development that the PHA seeks to demolish.[383]

What happens to tenants who live in Public Housing that comes under private management?

The Rental Assistance Demonstration (RAD) Program, established in 2011, seeks to convert Public Housing that is in need of significant repair to a Project-Based Section 8 model.[384] This means that RAD conversions allow certain Public Housing properties to convert to a different type of federal housing program.[385] Congress does not appropriate additional funding for repairs through RAD; instead, the program creates incentives for private developers to invest in the Public Housing properties through existing financial resources such as the Low-Income Housing Tax Credit. In many RAD-converted properties, a for-profit or nonprofit landlord will own and manage the property, but the Public Housing Authority must retain an interest in the property.[386] Congress authorized the RAD program because it recognized the crisis of substandard conditions in public housing, but was unwilling to appropriate the funds necessary to address the problem. Instead, the government has embarked on a process of privatizing public housing stock, but has failed to ensure that this transition does not inflict injury on tenants and their families.[387]

The law governing the RAD program formally guarantees tenants the same rights that they had in Public Housing, such as the grievance process, the right to organize, and the right to be funded each year for organizing activities at up to $25 per occupied unit.[388] Additionally, after the RAD conversion, the tenant's rent is set at 30 percent of the household's adjusted income.[389] The Public Housing Authority must hold informational meetings with tenants about the conversion.[390] However, tenant engagement with the RAD conversion process comes only after submission of the application for the conversion.[391]

What happens to tenants who live in a building constructed or operated with HUD subsidies when the owner leaves the HUD program?

Owners of properties built with HUD-subsidized mortgages are obligated to maintain affordable housing units only while the subsidized mortgage is in effect and the units are part of a federal program.[392] Once the mortgage that subsidized construction of the project matures or is prepaid, the owner is free to convert the property to market-rate housing, assuming the owner is not subject to any other agreements with HUD. For example, units that receive assistance through a Project-Based Section 8 remain subsidized until the Section 8 contract governing the arrangement expires or the owner "opts out" of the contract at the end of its term.

If the property owner converts the building to market-rate housing, tenant rents may be increased very substantially. The kind of assistance that the tenant receives at that stage, if any, mostly depends on two factors: (1) the type of project-based housing; and (2) whether the mortgage has expired or whether the property owner has prepaid the mortgage.

Section 221(d)(3) and Section 236 Housing. When a HUD mortgage reaches its originally scheduled end date, the mortgage "matures." Most HUD mortgages have a 40-year term, although some have a 30-year term. When a loan is fully repaid according to its original amortization schedule, the mortgage and accompanying regulatory agreement are extinguished. This means that the property loses its affordability restrictions and the owner can raise tenants' rents to the market rate, which in most cases will be unaffordable to low-income tenants. If there are no other contractual restrictions or applicable statutory restrictions, the owner is free to convert the property to market-rate use. In general, HUD does not provide additional rental support to help tenants confronting this situation, but certain at-risk households in "low-vacancy areas" may qualify for help under limited circumstances.[393]

If the landlord chooses to prepay the mortgage (i.e., repay the loan in full in advance of the original maturity date), income-eligible tenants who live in a Section 221(d)(3) or Section 236 property and do not already receive Section 8 vouchers are entitled to an "Enhanced Voucher."[394] (For most HUD-subsidized properties, owners must provide at least 150 but not more than 270 days' advance written notice to tenants, HUD, and the local government before taking this step.)[395]

Enhanced Vouchers have two key features that supplement the regular Section 8 vouchers. First, Enhanced Vouchers may exceed the Public Housing Authority's ordinary payment standard (used for regular Section 8 vouchers), allowing payment of any rent the PHA determines is "reasonable" by comparison with the rental market. So long as the rent remains "reasonable," the amount of the tenant's rental payment ordinarily should not increase. Second, an Enhanced Voucher provides the tenant with a right to remain in the unit after conversion to market rents, thus creating an obligation for the owner to accept the Enhanced Voucher. If the tenant elects to move, the voucher loses its enhancements and becomes a regular Section 8 Housing Choice Voucher. Federal laws do not guarantee preservation of federally supported affordable housing facing conversion, but some states and localities have enacted further protections for these properties through supplemental laws and policies, such as additional notice requirements and purchase opportunities. Occasionally, properties facing prepayment may have other restrictions constraining their use. These restrictions typically come from additional federal, state, or local subsidies provided to the property, or from local zoning or land use requirements.

Section 8 Housing. In addition to federally insured mortgages, HUD provides housing subsidies through "Project-Based Section 8" contracts with private owners. At the expiration of the contract, the owner can renew and continue its participation in the program, or it can "opt out" and end its participation. Federal law requires an owner to give a one-year written notice to both tenants and HUD of its intention either to renew or to "opt out."[396] Owners failing to give proper notice must either renew the contract for up to one year or permit tenants to remain while paying their former rent contributions until one year after proper notice is served. When an owner opts out of Project-Based Section 8, most tenants will receive Enhanced Vouchers that are intended to enable them to remain in their homes.

Nevertheless, in some situations, a tenant will find it difficult or impossible to obtain an Enhanced Voucher. For instance, the owner who removes a building from Project-Based Section 8 may choose not to rent certain apartments at all, in which case the tenants might be forced to leave. Under these circumstances, and others in which the tenant cannot remain in the unit, the Enhanced Voucher converts to a regular Section 8 voucher, and the family must find a new apartment to rent where the landlord will accept the voucher.

Keep in mind that subsidies under the Low-Income Housing Tax Credit program also are time-limited, and important questions about preserving affordable housing are raised at the end of the developer's commitment.[397]

What happens to tenants who live in a building that is subject to foreclosure?

Beginning in 2005, with enactment (and annual reenactments) of the "Schumer Amendment," federal law has required HUD to preserve Project-Based Section 8 contracts with owners of troubled properties (even those in foreclosure or disposition sale) unless "infeasible." HUD's prior policy was to terminate contracts at the outset of foreclosure proceedings, causing unnecessary dislocation. Federal law requires HUD to develop procedures to facilitate the orderly transfer of troubled properties, preferably to tenant-endorsed nonprofit or public owners, with a renewal of the Section 8 contract. In the event of an imminent disqualification of the project from the Section 8 program, tenants will usually receive a notice from HUD or a PHA that the building is being disqualified and they must move, and that the tenants should come in for a voucher-certification appointment.[398]

Tenants in foreclosed buildings also have rights under the Protecting Tenants at Foreclosure Act (PTFA). Initially enacted in 2009, in response to mass evictions accompanying the Great Recession, the legislation expired in 2014, but was re-enacted on a permanent basis in 2019. The PTFA gives tenants in foreclosed properties the right to remain in residence for the duration of their lease terms and the right to at least 90 days' notice before any eviction proceeding is commenced. Tenants with Section 8 vouchers have the right to retain their Section 8 leases, and PTFA requires the new owner of the building to assume the housing assistance payment contract associated with that lease.[399]

INFORMATION BOX: WHAT IS MORTGAGE FORECLOSURE?

A mortgage is a type of real estate conveyance that uses an interest in real property to secure payment of a financial obligation. In plain English, a mortgage is an agreement between a lender and a property owner that gives the lender the right to take the owner's property if the owner fails to repay the loan.[400] Mortgages secure the loans that most Americans use to buy houses. The borrower is called the mortgagor, and the lender is called the mortgagee. In most states, the mortgagor retains full ownership of the property, and the lender cannot take possession of the property without bringing a lawsuit. However, in some states, the borrower retains only an "equitable interest" in the property, and the lender has the right to possession and absolute ownership rights until the mortgage terms have been satisfied. Foreclosure is how a lender takes possession of a house when the borrower has not met the loan obligations under the mortgage. Foreclosure begins when a mortgagor misses a number of loan payments, and the lender determines that there has been a default. Foreclosure ends with the sale of the mortgaged property and, in some cases, the entry of a judgment against the borrower for the difference between the sale price and the amount owed. Generally, state law will govern the foreclosure and the procedures vary from state to state. The two most prevalent forms of foreclosure are judicial foreclosure and nonjudicial foreclosure (sometimes called foreclosure by power of sale). In states with judicial foreclosure, a mortgagee must bring a civil action in state court to commence a foreclosure. In nonjudicial foreclosure states, the mortgagee forecloses by exercising the "power of sale" contained in the mortgage agreement itself without first having to obtain judicial authority.[401]

As a formal matter, not all foreclosures extinguish the right that a tenant has under the lease. In many power of sale states, a lease made before the mortgage under foreclosure will survive foreclosure because the mortgage was conveyed subject to the pre-existing lease. As a practical matter, however, most leases include a clause that will "subordinate" the lease to any future mortgages, and therefore renters are rarely in a position to assert their rights against that of the foreclosing lender. Judicial foreclosure generally terminates a tenancy.[402] In order for foreclosure to terminate a tenancy, though, most judicial states require that the tenants be joined as a party to the foreclosure action and be given an opportunity to defend their interests in the property.[403] This proceeding will give tenants the opportunity to bring state law claims against their landlord, including claims for improvements, rent overcharges, back rent, and even breach of covenant and quiet enjoyment for the foreclosure-related eviction.[404] However, these claims generally will not prevent foreclosure from terminating the tenancy, and many landlords facing foreclosure are "judgment proof" because of insolvency.[405]

Overview of Homeownership Programs

Does the federal government help low-income families buy homes?

HUD has a few home-ownership programs for low-income people, although the programs are small in scale.

The first program permits Public Housing Authorities to make units in Public Housing available for purchase by low-income families.[406] PHAs wishing to sell units must submit a plan to the HUD Special Applications Center for approval, and have significant discretion in how they implement the program. Current residents of Public Housing units receive priority in purchasing the units.[407] The federal government provides no dedicated funding for the program, but PHAs may use other HUD assistance to help finance home sales.[408]

The second program is the Homeownership Voucher Program.[409] This program authorizes PHAs to provide vouchers, similar to Section 8 Housing Choice Vouchers, which are used for partial funding of a family's mortgage payments and other homeownership expenses. Under the program participants generally take out two mortgages, one based on the participant's income alone, and, another, usually originated by a nonprofit community group, to cover the remaining cost of the home. Information about participating Public Housing Authorities is available online.[410] Participation generally is limited to a first-time homeowner or cooperative member, and a family member must be working with an annual income of no less than the federal minimum hourly wage multiplied by 2,000 hours.[411]

Are there federal programs to help low-income families save to purchase a home?

Federal law allows states to establish "Individual Development Accounts" to help eligible participants purchase a first residence (or other uses, such as paying for education).[412] Individuals who work and receive benefits funded through the Temporary Assistance for Needy Families program are eligible to participate. The account takes the form of a trust and is funded through the individual's contributions of earned income that are then matched with money from the state's TANF funds. The trust allows the individual to save money because the funds that are deposited in the account are disregarded for purposes of determining eligibility or assistance levels under other federal programs. The states directly operate these accounts; HUD does not. For more information on how to set up an Individual Development Account, contact a local TANF office.

In addition, the Family Self-Sufficiency (FSS) program helps families save to purchase a home. The FSS program is a federal program that links subsidized housing with social services, education and training, and employment opportunities.[413] The program primarily is aimed at families receiving Section 8 vouchers, but also is open to tenants in Public Housing. Participation is not a condition of receiving housing assistance, and if a tenant decides not to participate, housing assistance may not be delayed.[414] PHAs generally are required to implement the program, but may be granted an exception by HUD.[415]

Tenant participation brings benefits and obligations.[416] Participating families sign a five-year contract specifying rights and responsibilities and are eligible to receive a broad range of services, including child care, service-related transportation, education and job training, substance abuse treatment, homemaking advice, and counseling. The head of the household is required to seek "suitable" employment. A key feature of the FSS program is that rent increases that would be imposed because of the household's increased earnings are placed in an escrow account for five years; the funds may be used for such activities as the purchase of a home, starting a business, or paying for education.[417]

Does federal law require private banks to lend to low-income families to help them to purchase homes?

Banks are not required to lend to low-income families; the extension of credit depends on a complex analysis of risk factors. However, banks are not permitted to discriminate against low-income families on the basis of race or other impermissible grounds (as discussed in chapter 6). Two federal laws help the government monitor banking practices, with an eye toward increasing credit for low-income communities.

The Community Reinvestment Act (CRA) was enacted during the Carter administration to deal with the lack of credit opportunities for low-income families and to reduce the refusal of banks to lend to residents of low-income neighborhoods, a practice otherwise known as redlining.[418] The CRA calls for the evaluation of banks regulated under the Federal Deposit Insurance Act based on lending practices, and each bank must meet "the convenience and needs of the communities in which they are chartered to do business."[419] The CRA does not mandate criteria, and it is not judicially enforceable. Rather, the act is enforced through data collection, federal examinations, and federal regulatory approvals; it authorizes the preparation of a report on every lending institution and the ranking of each institution, and that the information be made public. Prior to adoption of the CRA, the U.S. Commission on Civil Rights found that African Americans who took out loans often were subject to more severe terms for down payments and repayments than individuals of other races.[420] Evidence regarding the effectiveness of the statute has been mixed.[421]

In addition, the Home Mortgage Disclosure Act (HMDA), enacted in 1975, requires many financial institutions engaged in mortgage lending to maintain, report, and make public data on their mortgage loan activities. Since 2015, the Consumer Financial Protection Bureau has enforced the statute, aimed at improving the availability of data about mortgage lending practices and assessing whether financial institutions are serving needy communities.[422] The Trump administration has altered both the nature of the available data[423] and the institutions required to report under the HMDA.[424] Commentators note that in the wake of the Great Recession, lending to low-income people by the three largest banks (Bank of America, JP Morgan Chase, and Wells Fargo) has declined, with disproportionate impact on African Americans.[425]

How did the 2017 tax reform act affect prospects for community development?

The Tax Cuts and Jobs Act of 2017 contains provisions that affect community development and the construction of new affordable units in a number of crosscutting ways.[426] Currently, new construction for low-income communities is mostly funded through the Low-Income Housing Tax Credit (LIHTC). The 2017 act reduced the tax rate on corporations from 35 percent to 21 percent, which potentially could lower the effective value of the LIHTC.[427] Overall, although the 2017 tax act expanded the LIHTC program, those gains were not expected to offset the loss of more than 235,000 affordable units that will result from tax changes.[428] The 2017 act also weakened the Community Development Corporation tax credit.[429] However, the 2017 act also included provisions of the Investing in Opportunity Act, which is intended to encourage investment in "opportunity zones," which are drawn from among low-income communities. The legislation seeks to tap into unrealized capital gains on stocks and mutual funds, estimated at $2.3 trillion, and channel it toward new community development.[430] What none of these laws do is acknowledge housing as a fundamental right or promote the government's duty to affirmatively further fair housing.

Housing-Related Services for Homeless Individuals and Families

Does the federal government fund housing-related programs for persons who are homeless?

The federal government funds housing-related programs for persons who are homeless and to help persons avoid becoming homeless. States and localities administer the programs. Earlier statutory programs tended to define homelessness only as lack of a fixed address.[431] However, the 2009 Homeless Emergency Assistance and Rapid Transition to Housing (HEARTH) Act expands the definition of homeless persons to include those living in hotels or motels, transitional housing, and places of last resort, like cars, parks, abandoned buildings, train stations, and airports[432]—a population known as the "chronically homeless."[433] The HEARTH definition likewise includes as homeless persons who will "imminently lose their housing" and victims fleeing domestic violence, and HUD has enacted regulations implementing this definition.[434] A similar definition of homelessness—looking to conditions other than simply not having a fixed, regular address—appears in the Education for Homeless Children and Youths program[435] and the Violence Against Women Act.[436]

In addition to expanding the definition of homelessness, the HEARTH Act:

- Consolidated existing competitive grant programs, which had been called the Supportive Housing Program, the Shelter Plus Care (S+C) Program, and the Section 8 Moderate Rehabilitation for Single Room Occupancy (SRO) Program into a new program called "Continuum of Care" (CoC).[437]
- Renamed the existing Emergency Shelter Grants program, which operates through appropriated funds, as the Emergency Solutions Grants program. These programs provide grants to providers to make different services available, including transitional housing; development of more single-room occupancy units; rehabilitation of existing housing; rental assistance;

and improving emergency shelters. HUD maintains a website that provides information on which services are available in a locality and how to apply for benefits under a local program.[438]

Working through the HEARTH Act, in 2010, President Obama and Congress jointly tasked the U.S. Interagency Council on Homelessness to develop a strategic plan—called Opening Doors—to prevent and end homelessness. The Council amended the plan in 2012 and 2015, and again in 2018, when it renamed the plan Home Together; the plan seeks to ensure that every community has a response to prevent homelessness if possible or to mitigate its effects.[439]

Notes

1. Lindsey v. Normet, 405 U.S. 56, 74 (1972). The Court disclaimed a right "to dwellings of a particular quality" or "any recognition of a tenant to occupy the real property of his landlord beyond the terms of his lease without the payment of rent or otherwise contrary to the terms of the relevant agreement."
2. *See, for example*, Lisa T. Alexander, Occupying the Constitutional Right to Housing, 94 Neb. L. Rev. 245 (2015); Shelby D. Green, Imagining a Right to Housing, Lying in the Interstices, 19 Geo. J. on Poverty L. & Pol'y 393 (2012).
3. International Covenant on Economic, Social and Cultural Rights, GA Res. 2200A (XXI), 21 UN GAOR Supp. (No.16) at 49. UN Doc. A/6316 (1966); 993 UNTS 3; 6 ILM 368 (1967), http://www.ohchr.org/EN/ProfessionalInterest/Pages/CESCR. aspx. *See* Kirsten David Adams, Do We Need a Right to Housing?, 9 Nev. L.J. 275, 291 (2009) (positing that "the treaty's definitions and explanations" of the right to adequate housing "may provide guidance to the United States if it chooses to adopt a right to housing at some future time"). The United States has not ratified the treaty.
4. *Compare* McCain v. Koch, 484 N.Y.S.2d 985 (N.Y. Sup. Ct. 1984), aff'd as modified, 502 N.Y.S.2d 720 (N.Y. App. Div. 1986), rev'd in part, 70 N.Y.2d 109 (1987) (right of families to emergency shelter); Eldredge v. Koch, 459 N.Y.S.2d 960 (N.Y. Sup. Ct. 1983), rev'd, 98 A.D.2d 675 (N.Y. App. Div. 1983) (right of women to emergency shelter); Callahan v. Carey, No. 79-42582 (N.Y. Sup. Ct. Dec. 5, 1979) (right of men to emergency shelter), *with* Moore v. Ganim, 660 A.2d 742 (Conn. 1995) (Connecticut Constitution does not encompass a right to housing). *See* Susan Lyons, Publications on the Right to Housing, 63 Rutgers L. Rev. 1037 (2011); Robert Doughten, Filling Everyone's Bowl: A Call to Affirm a Right to Minimum Welfare Guarantees and Shelter in State Constitutions to Satisfy International Standards of Human Decency, 39 Gonz. L. Rev. 421 (2004).
5. *See* Alison Bell, 2019 Bill Largely Sustains 2018 HUD Funding Gains, Center on Budget and Policy Priorities (Feb. 15, 2019), https://www.cbpp.org/blog/2019-bill-largely-sustains-2018-hud-funding-gains. At one time, U.S. public policy embraced a far more expansive view of governmental obligation to secure adequate housing

for all. The "Declaration of National Housing Policy" set forth in the Housing Act of 1949, reads:

> The Congress hereby declares that the general welfare and security of the Nation and the health and living standards of its people require . . . the realization as soon as feasible of the goal of a decent home and a suitable living environment for every American family.

Housing Act of 1949, Pub. L. No. 81-171 (1949). *See also* Robert E. Lang & Rebecca R. Sohmer, Legacy of the Housing Act of 1949: The Past, Present, and Future of Federal Housing and Urban Policy, 11 Housing Policy Debate 291 (2000), https://www.tandfonline.com/doi/pdf/10.1080/10511482.2000.9521369.

6. For a comprehensive overview of appropriations for selected housing programs in FY 1980–2018, *see* Congressional Research Service, Maggie McCarty, Libby Perl, & Katie Jones, Overview of Federal Housing Assistance Programs and Policy (updated Mar. 27, 2019), https://crsreports.congress.gov/product/pdf/RL/RL34591. *See also* Will Fischer & Barbara Sard, Chart Book: Cuts in Federal Assistance Have Exacerbated Families' Struggles to Afford Housing, Center on Budget and Policy Priorities (Apr. 12, 2016), http://www.cbpp.org/research/housing/chart-book-cuts-in-federal-assistance-have-exacerbated-families-struggles-to-afford. Millions of Americans are "cost burdened"—meaning, they are tenants who pay more than 30% of their income for rent. Indeed, in no part of the United States can a household with one full-time worker earning the minimum wage afford the rent of a two-bedroom apartment. *See* U.S. Department of Housing and Urban Development, Affordable Housing, https://portal.hud.gov/hudportal/HUD?src=/program_offices/comm_planning/affordablehousing. In 2016, 11.4 million households paid more than half of household income for rent (an increase of over 53% since 2001), making them "severely cost burdened." *See* The Joint Center for Housing Studies of Harvard University, The State of the Nation's Housing 2016 (2016), http://www.jchs.harvard.edu/sites/jchs.harvard.edu/files/jchs_2016_state_of_the_nations_housing_lowres.pdf?_ga=1.140549554.1475906291.1466625845. Thousands of poor and low-income households live doubled or tripled up with relatives or in other substandard conditions. Thousands more—estimated at more than a half million individuals in 2015—are homeless, defined as sleeping outside, in an emergency shelter, or in a transitional housing program. *See* National Alliance to End Homelessness, The State of Homelessness in America 2016, http://www.endhomelessness.org/library/entry/SOH2016; National Low Income Housing Coalition, Out of Reach 2016: No Refuge for Low Income Renters (2016), http://nlihc.org/sites/default/files/oor/OOR_2016.pdf. The mortgage foreclosure crisis during the Great Recession exacerbated housing insecurities; by one estimate, renters made up 40% of families evicted following foreclosures in those years. *See* Shambhavi Manglik, Renters in Foreclosure: A Fresh Look at an Ongoing Problem, National Low Income Housing Coalition (2012), http://nlihc.org/sites/default/files/Renters_in_Foreclosure_2012.pdf.

7. *See* Richard Rothstein, Public Housing: Government-Sponsored Segregation, The American Prospect (Oct. 11, 2012), http://prospect.org/article/public-housing-government-sponsored-segregation. *See also* James H. Carr & Katrin B. Anacker,

The Complex History of the Federal Housing Administration: Building Wealth, Promoting Segregation, and Rescuing the U.S. Housing Market and the Economy, 34 No. 8 Banking & Financial Services Policy Report 10 (Aug. 2015) (discussing the segregation-promoting policies of the Federal Housing Administration).

8. Emily Rees Brown, Public-Private Partnerships: HUD's Lost Opportunities to Further Fair Housing, 21 Lewis & Clark L. Rev. 735, 741 (2017) (racial disparities in housing were "in large part created by decades of federal housing policy that contained and economically isolated black communities while financing the creation of upwardly-mobile white suburbs"). *See* Yvette N. Pappoe, Remedying the Effects of Government-Sanctioned Segregation in a Post-Freddie Gray Baltimore, 16 U. Md. L.J. of Race, Religion, Gender and Class 115 (2016).

9. The U.S. Department of Agriculture administers housing programs for poor and low-income households in rural areas. For a concise overview of USDA's rural housing programs, *see* Congressional Research Service, Tadlock Cowan, An Overview of USDA Rural Development Programs (Feb. 10, 2016), https://fas.org/sgp/crs/misc/RL31837.pdf.

10. The Department of the Treasury has a role in developing affordable housing in part through the Treasury's administration of the Low-Income Housing Tax Credit program. LIHTC has provided tax credits of about $8 billion annually for the acquisition, rehabilitation, or new construction of housing for low-income tenants. *See* U.S. Department of Housing and Urban Development, Low-Income Housing Tax Credits, https://www.huduser.gov/portal/datasets/lihtc.html.

11. The major sourcebook about federal housing programs is The National Housing Law Project, HUD Housing Programs: Tenants' Rights (5th ed. 2018) [hereinafter HUD Housing Programs]. *See also* Alex F. Schwartz, Housing Policy in the United States (3d ed. 2015); Navigating HUD Programs: A Practitioner's Guide to the Labyrinth (George Weidenfeller & Julie McGovern, eds.) (American Bar Association 2012).

12. Regulations relevant to programs administered by the U.S. Housing and Urban Development are published in Title 24 of the Code of Federal Regulations.

13. The address is 451 Seventh St., S.W., Washington, D.C. 20410. HUD also has 10 regional offices located around the country, and there are branch, division, and area offices within each region. HUD's website is located at http://www.hud.gov.

14. For an overview, *see* Peter W. Salsich, Jr., Does America Need Public Housing?, 19 George Mason L. Rev. 689 (2012).

15. 42 U.S.C. §§ 1437(b)(1)(A), 1437(b)(2); 24 C.F.R. § 964.415. *See* Housing Opportunity Through Modernization Act of 2016, Pub. L. No. 114-201, § 114, 130 Stat. 782 (2016), codified as amended at 42 U.S.C. § 1437.

16. *See* 42 U.S.C. § 1437(a)(1)(C) (2016) (granting PHAs "the maximum amount of responsibility").

17. For a list of HUD-assisted properties, *see* U.S. Department of Housing and Urban Development, HUD Resource Locator, https://resources.hud.gov.

18. *See* 42 U.S.C. § 1437. Tenant lease and grievance regulations for Public Housing are in 24 C.F.R. Part 966. *See also* U.S. Department of Housing and Urban Development, Public Housing Occupancy Guidebook (June 2003), https://www.hud.gov/offices/programs/ph/rhiip/phguidebook.cfm [hereinafter Public Housing Guidebook].

19. *See* Barbara Sard & Douglas Rice, Decade of Neglect Has Weakened Federal Low-Income Housing Programs, Center on Budget and Policy Priorities (Feb. 25, 2009), https://www.cbpp.org/research/decade-of-neglect-has-weakened-federal-low-income-housing-programs?fa=view&id=2691. Public Housing developed a negative image that was inextricably related to racism. *See* Rachel M. Cohen, We Can't Talk About Housing Policy Without Talking About Racism, The American Prospect (May 19, 2015), http://prospect.org/article/we-cant-talk-about-housing-policy-without-talking-about-racism. *See* Javon T. Henry, Low Income Housing Tax Credits and the Dangers of Privatization, 16 Pitt. Tax Rev. 247, 248 (2019) (explaining that "public housing has a long history of racial discrimination, poor management, and minimal financial support" and that this history "has made it easy for Congress to step away from state-controlled public housing and to look to the private market to provide affordable housing").

20. *See* Peter W. Salsich, Jr., Toward a Policy of Heterogeneity: Overcoming a Long History of Socioeconomic Segregation in Housing, 42 Wake Forest L. Rev. 459 (2007). The Nixon administration placed a moratorium on funding for new construction of public housing. *See* Cara Hendrickson, Racial Desegregation and Income Deconcentration in Public Housing, 9 Geo. J. Poverty L. & Pol'y 35 (2002).

21. Demolition is permitted under Section 18 of the United States Housing Act of 1937, which was amended by the Quality Housing and Work Responsibility Act of 1998 [hereinafter QHWRA], Pub. L. No. 105-276, Tit. V, §531, 112 Stat. 2461, 2570 (Oct. 21, 1998). Implementing regulations are found at 73 Fed. Reg. 3868 (Jan. 23, 2008). Redevelopment has taken place through the HOPE VI program under Section 24 of the United States Housing Act of 1937, amended by the QHWRA, and the Choice Neighborhood Initiative.

22. *See* Ben Austen, The Towers Came Down, and with Them the Promise of Public Housing, N.Y. Times Mag. (Feb. 6, 2018), https://www.nytimes.com/2018/02/06/magazine/the-towers-came-down-and-with-them-the-promise-of-public-housing.html; Dianna Douglas, When Public Housing Is Bulldozed, Families Are Supposed to Eventually Come Back. Why Don't They?, Slate (Aug. 11, 2016), https://slate.com/business/2016/08/why-families-don-t-return-to-redeveloped-communities-after-public-housing-is-demolished.html; Jasmine Coleman, Why is America pulling down the projects?, BBC News, Washington, D.C. (Apr. 14, 2016), http://www.bbc.com/news/magazine-35913577; Dani McClain, Former Residents of New Orleans's Demolished Housing Projects Tell Their Stories, The Nation (Aug. 28, 2015), https://www.thenation.com/article/former-residents-of-new-orleans-demolished-housing-projects-tell-their-stories/. *See also* Peter Dreier, Why American Needs More Social Housing, The American Prospect (Apr. 16, 2018), https://prospect.org/article/why-america-needs-more-social-housing (explaining how the problems of public housing resulted from political choices made by Congress and "local power brokers," and that many of these decisions resulted in economically isolated, racially segregated, and poor-quality housing).

23. Studies about the demolition of public housing, tenant displacement, and reduction in housing inventory for families that are poor or with low income, include: John N. Robinson III, Welfare as Wrecking Ball: Constructing Public Responsibility in Legal Encounters over Public Housing Demolition, 41 Law & Soc. Inquiry 670 (2016); Meagan Cahill, Samantha S. Lowry, & P. Mitchell Downey, Movin' Out: Crime and

HUD's HOPE VI Initiative, Urban Institute (2011), http://www.urban.org/publications/412385.html; Edward G. Goetz, Gentrification in Black and White: The Racial Impact of Public Housing Demolition in American Cities, Urban Stud. J. (first published Nov. 12, 2010), http://journals.sagepub.com/doi/abs/10.1177/0042098010375323; Herbert R. Giorgio, Jr., HUD's Obligation to "Affirmatively Further" Fair Housing: A Closer Look at HOPE VI, 25 St. Louis U. Pub. L. Rev. 183 (2006).

The Choice Neighborhood Initiative aimed to replace both Public Housing and Project-Based Housing developments with mixed-income complexes. Choice Neighborhoods required the PHA to replace each affordable unit that it demolished with at least one affordable unit, with some exceptions, and it provided funds for additional neighborhood improvements. *See* Urban Institute and MDRC, Choice Neighborhoods: Baseline Conditions and Early Progress (Nov. 2015), https://www.urban.org/research/publication/choice-neighborhoods-baseline-conditions-and-early-progress; Rolf Pendall & Leah Hendey, A Brief Look at the Early Implementation of Choice Neighborhoods, Urban Institute (Oct. 2013), http://www.urban.org/research/publication/brief-look-early-implementation-choice-neighborhoods/view/full_report; U.S. Department of Housing and Urban Development, Office of Policy Development and Research, Evidence Matters: Choice Neighborhoods: History and HOPE, Evidence Matters (Winter 2011), https://www.huduser.gov/portal/periodicals/em/EM-newsletter_FNL_web.pdf.

24. RAD is codified at 42 U.S.C. § 1437f. It was enacted as part of the Consolidated and Further Continuing Appropriations Act of 2012, approved Nov. 18, 2011, Pub. L. No. 112-55, as amended by Pub. L. No. 113-76, Pub. L. No. 113-235, Pub. L. No. 114-113, Pub. L. No. 115-31, and Pub. L. No. 115-141), Division C—Transportation, Housing and Urban Development, and Related Agencies Appropriations Act, 2012, Title II, Department of Housing and Urban Development, Rental Assistance Demonstration, Pub. L. No. 112-55, 125 Stat. 552, 673–675 (Nov. 18, 2011), https://www.gpo.gov/fdsys/pkg/PLAW-112publ55/pdf/PLAW-112publ55.pdf.

25. *See* National Housing Law Project, Resource Center: Rental Assistance Demonstration (RAD), https://www.nhlp.org/resources/rental-assistance-demonstration-rad/; *see also* U.S. General Accountability Office, Report to the Ranking Member, Committee on Financial Services, House of Representatives, Rental Assistance Demonstration: HUD Needs to Take Action to Improve Metrics and Ongoing Oversight (Feb. 2018), https://www.gao.gov/products/GAO-18-123.

26. *See* Frederick J. Eggers, Characteristics of HUD-Assisted Renters and Their Units in 2013, Econometrica, Inc. (July 2017), prepared for U.S. Department of Housing and Urban Development, Office of Policy Development & Research, https://www.huduser.gov/portal/publications/Characteristics-HUD-Assisted.html.

27. 42 U.S.C. § 1437d; *see, for example*, 24 C.F.R. §§ 903.7(b)(2) (annual report and waiting lists); 960.202 (tenant selection plans and waiting lists); 982.205 (merging waiting lists for different programs).

28. Section 8 of the U.S. Housing Act, 42 U.S.C. § 1437f(f)(1). Regulations are found at 24 C.F.R. Parts 880, 881, 883, 884, 886. *See* U.S. Department of Housing and Urban Development, HUD Handbook 4350.3 Occupancy Requirements of Subsidized

Multifamily Housing Programs (Nov. 2013), https://www.hud.gov/sites/documents/ 43503hsgh.pdf [hereinafter HUD Handbook]. *See* National Law Income Housing Coalition, Millions of Families on Voucher and Public Housing Waiting Lists (Apr. 30, 2019), https://nlihc.org/resource/millions-families-voucher-and-public-housing-waiting-lists (citing Public and Affordable Housing Research Corporation at HAI Group, Housing Agency Waiting Lists and the Demand for Housing Assistance, 2016 Research Spotlight (based on 2012 national survey, reporting 1.6 million families on Public Housing waiting lists)).

29. Section 221(d)(3) BMIR [Below Market Interest Rate] Program

Congress established the Section 221(d)(3) BMIR Program as part of the Housing Act of 1961, supporting housing for low- and middle-income households. The Federal Housing Administration insured the 3% "BMIR" mortgages, and the developers were required to pass the savings from the reduced interest rates on to tenants through decreased rents, typically about 75% to 80% of rents in comparable unsubsidized projects. The program produced about 159,000 affordable units. Over time, rising property taxes and operating costs made rentals in many Section 221(d)(3) properties no longer "affordable" to the tenant without the tenant receiving voucher assistance to pay the rent. (Section 221(d)(3) also authorized unsubsidized mortgages to projects which are not required to supply affordable housing; this chapter will use "Section 221(d)(3)" to refer to the Below Market Interest Rate program.) Most of the mortgages have now matured or been prepaid, and so the rent subsidies are no longer available. *See* HUD Handbook 4350.3 REV-1, CHG-4 (Nov. 2013), http://portal.hud.gov/ hudportal/documents/huddoc?id=43503HSGH.pdf. *See also* U.S. Department of Housing and Urban Development, Preservation Options for Section 236 Properties (Apr. 2016), https://www.hudexchange.info/resource/4973/preservation-options-for-section-236-properties/ ; HUD Housing Programs § 1.3.2.

30. Section 236 Program

Congress enacted the Section 236 Program as part of the Housing and Urban Development Act of 1968, replacing the Section 221(d)(3) BMIR Program for new projects. *See* 12 U.S.C. § 1715z-1. Tenant rights provisions are detailed in 12 U.S.C. §1715z-1b(b). Under the Section 236 program, private developers received market-rate mortgages insured by the Federal Housing Administration and were obligated to make loan payments to the lending institution as though the loan bore only a 1% interest rate. HUD made the remainder of the payment directly to the lender. *See* HUD Handbook 4350.3 REV-1, CHG-4, https://www.hud.gov/program-offices/ administration/hudclips/handbooks/hsgh/4350.3; U.S. Department of Housing and Urban Development, Preservation Options for Section 236 Properties (Apr. 2016), https://www.hudexchange.info/resource/4973/preservation-options-for-section-236-properties/; HUD Housing Programs § 1.3.3. Estimates are that the program helped finance creation of about 544,000 affordable housing units, although there is disagreement about the actual number built. *See* Alexander von Hoffman, To Preserve Affordable Housing in the United States: A Policy History, Harvard Joint Center for Housing Studies (Mar. 2016), http://jchs.harvard.edu/sites/jchs.harvard. edu/files/von_hoffman_to_preserve_affordable_housing_april16.pdf.

31. Section 202 Program

    Congress established the Section 202 program as part of the Housing Act of 1959. *See* 12 U.S.C. § 1701q. The program provided direct loans at below-market rates to consumer cooperatives, limited-profit sponsors, private nonprofit developers, and public agencies that agreed to provide housing and related facilities to tenants who were disabled or elderly. Congress restructured the Section 202 program in 1990, creating one program for elderly persons (which continues to be called Section 202) and one for handicapped persons (called Section 811), each of which has its own rental assistance authorization. *See* 12 U.S.C. § 1701q; 42 U.S.C. § 8013. Currently there are about 144,000 units under active Section 202 agreements. *See* Congressional Research Service, Maggie McCarty & Libby Perl, Preservation of HUD-Assisted Housing 36, Table 1 (2012), http://digital.library.unt.edu/ark:/67531/metadc807157/m1/1/. *See also* HUD Housing Programs § 1.3.4.

32. Congress established the Section 8 New Construction and Substantial Rehabilitation programs in 1974 to encourage the construction and renovation of privately owned affordable housing. *See* Pub. L. No. 93-383, § 201(a), 88 Stat. 633 (1974), formerly codified at 42 U.S.C. § 1437f(b)(2), repealed for future projects by Pub. L. No. 98-181, § 209, 97 Stat. 1153, 1183 (1983). *See also* HUD Housing Programs § 1.4.1.2. Congress expanded the project-based program in 1978, establishing the Section 8 Moderate Rehabilitation program to encourage the upgrading of existing lower-income housing. *See* 42 U.S.C. § 1437f(e)(2) (repealed 1990, except that it remains in effect with respect to single-room occupancy dwellings under Title IV of the McKinney Vento Homeless Assistance Act, Pub. L. No. 100-77, § 401, 101 Stat. 482 (1987)). Some properties constructed and rehabilitated with Section 8 project-based assistance remain subject to rent affordability constraints. Under these programs, HUD contracts with private owners and PHAs to pay rental assistance equal to the difference between the contract rent and the tenant's share of rent. Currently about 1.2 million households live in housing funded through this program. *See* Congressional Research Service, Maggie McCarty & Libby Perl, Preservation of HUD-Assisted Housing 2 (2012), http://digital.library.unt.edu/ark:/67531/metadc807157/m1/1/. Contracts for new construction ended during the Reagan administration. *See* U.S. Department of Housing and Urban Development, HUD Interactive Timeline, https://www.huduser.gov/hud_timeline/; U.S. Department of Housing and Urban Development, Multifamily Properties: Opting In, Opting Out and Remaining Affordable (Jan. 2006), http://www.huduser.org/Publications/pdf/opting_in.pdf. *See generally* William G. Johnson, Housing Policy under the Reagan Presidency: The Demise of an Iron-Triangle, 10 Policy Stud. Rev. 69 (1991/1992), https://onlinelibrary.wiley.com/doi/10.1111/j.1541-1338.1991.tb00280.x/pdf.

33. Congress established the Housing Choice Program in 1983 as a demonstration program. *See* Housing and Urban-Rural Recovery Act of 1983, Pub. L. No. 98-181, § 207, 97 Stat. 1153. Earlier, the Housing and Community Development Act of 1974, Pub. L. No. 93-383, codified at 42 U.S.C. § 1437f(o), had established two different voucher programs: Section 8 project-based assistance, for families assigned to live in specific buildings built or rehabilitated with HUD assistance, and the Section 8

existing housing program, which provided a "certificate" to families who could select an apartment and the certificate traveled with the tenant. These programs were followed by the Section 8 Existing Housing Program, which paid subsidies directly to the owner and set a cap on the unit's rent. The Housing Choice Program was revised and reauthorized in later years. The Quality Housing and Work Opportunity Reconciliation Act of 1998 merged the certificate and voucher programs, now called Housing Choice. *See* 42 U.S.C. § 1437f(o); 24 C.F.R. § 982. *See* U.S. Department of Housing and Urban Development, Housing Choice Voucher Program Guidebook 7420.10G (Apr. 2001). *See also* HUD Housing Programs § 1.5.1.

34. *See* Daniel Herriges, What Housing Vouchers Can and Can't Do, Strong Towns (Apr. 16, 2018), https://www.strongtowns.org/journal/2018/4/26/what-housing-vouchers-can-and-cant-do.

35. *See* E. Tammy Kim, The Section 8 Voucher Trap: For Yonkers families, the search for affordable housing is long and weary, New Republic (Feb. 18, 2016), https://newrepublic.com/article/130128/section-8-voucher-trap; Alana Semuels, How Housing Policy Is Failing America's Poor, The Atlantic (June 24, 2015), https://www.theatlantic.com/business/archive/2015/06/section-8-is-failing/396650/; Alicia Mazzara & Brian Knudsen, Where Families with Children Use Housing Vouchers, Center on Budget and Policy Priorities & Poverty & Race Research Action Council (Jan. 3, 2019), https://www.cbpp.org/research/housing/where-families-with-children-use-housing-vouchers; Alison Bell, Barbara Sard, & Becky Koepnick, Prohibiting Discrimination Against Renters Using Housing Vouchers Improves Results, Center on Budget and Policy Priorities (updated Dec. 20, 2018), https://www.cbpp.org/research/housing/prohibiting-discrimination-against-renters-using-housing-vouchers-improves-results.

36. *See* Corianne Payton Scally, Amanda Gold, & Nicole DuBois, The Low-Income Housing Tax Credit: How It Works and Who It Serves, Urban Institute (July 2018), https://www.urban.org/research/publication/low-income-housing-tax-credit-how-it-works-and-who-it-serves; Ali Foyt, Legal Obstacles to Affordable Housing Development, 56 Hous. L. Rev. 505 (2018); Poverty & Race Research Action Council, The Low Income Housing Tax Credit, https://prrac.org/fair-housing/the-low-income-housing-tax-credit/; *see also* Affordable Housing Resource Center, About the LIHTC, Novogradac, https://www.novoco.com/resource-centers/affordable-housing-tax-credits/lihtc-basics/about-lihtc.

37. *See* IRS Revenue Notice 88-80 (1988) (determination of income "to be made in a manner consistent with the determination of annual income and estimates for median family income" under HUD Section 8). LIHTC landlords cannot refuse to rent to tenants solely because they are receiving Housing Choice Vouchers, provided rents are reasonable, but the nondiscrimination principle is not a duty to rent. *See* 26 U.S.C. § 42(h)(6)(B)(iv); 26 C.F.R. § 1.42–5(c)(1)(xi).

38. *See generally* U.S. Department of Housing and Urban Development, Office of Policy Development and Research, Low-Income Housing Tax Credits (revised May 24, 2019), https://www.huduser.gov/portal/datasets/lihtc.html. Congress increased LIHTC credits by 12.5% in 2018. *See* Consolidated Appropriations Act, 2018, Pub. L. No. 115-141, div. T, § 102, 132 Stat. 348 (Mar. 23, 2018).

39. Internal Revenue Code, 42 U.S.C. §§ 42(g)(1) (income levels); 42(g)(2) (rent levels); Consolidated Appropriations Act, 2018, Pub. L. No. 115-141, Div. T, General Provisions, § 132 Stat. 348 (Mar. 23, 2018) (income averaging option).

40. The LIHTC database can be accessed at https://lihtchuduser.gov.

41. For discussions about LIHTC siting decisions and racial segregation, *see* Will Fischer, Low-Income Housing Tax Credit Could Do More to Expand Opportunity for Poor Families, Center on Budget and Policy Priorities (Aug. 28, 2018), https:// www.cbpp.org/research/housing/low-income-housing-tax-credit-could-do-more-to-expand-opportunity-for-poor-families; Philip Tegeler, Affirmatively Furthering Fair Housing in the LIHTC Program: Recent Progress, Poverty & Race Research Action Council (2017), https://prrac.org/pdf/Tegeler_HJN_LIHTC_presentation. pdf; Raquel Smith, A Seat at the Table: Changing the Governing Structure of Low Income Housing Tax Credit Administration to Reflect Civil Rights Values and Fair Housing, 6 Colum. J. Race & Law 193 (2016); Simon Kawitzky, Fred Freiberg, Diane L. Houk, & Salimah Hankins, Choice Constrained, Segregation Maintained: Using Federal Tax Credits to Provide Affordable Housing, Report on the Distribution of Low Income Housing Tax Credits in the New York City Region, Fair Housing Justice Center (Aug. 2013), https://www.fairhousingjustice.org/resources/publications/ (concluding that "10 years of LIHTC allocations by New York's three housing finance agencies to expand the supply of affordable housing opportunities in the region effectively reinforced, rather than reduced, residential racial segregation and poverty concentration"). *See generally* Michelle D. Layser, How Federal Tax Law Rewards Housing Segregation, 93 Ind. L.J. 915 (2018); Myron Orfield, Racial Integration and Community Revitalization: Applying the Fair Housing Act to the Low Income Housing Tax Credit, 58 Vand. L. Rev. 1747 (2005).

42. For discussion of LIHTC tenant selection and affordable housing for the very poor, *see* Katherine M. O'Regan & Keren M. Horn, What Can We Learn about the Low Income Housing Tax Credit Program by Looking at the Tenants?, New York University Furman Center for Real Estate & Urban Policy 4–5 (2012), http://furmancenter.org/ files/publications/LIHTC_Final_Policy_Brief_v2.pdf; U.S. Department of Housing and Urban Development, Michael Hollar, Understanding Whom the LIHTC Program Serves: Tenants in LIHTC Units as of December 31, 2012, 28–29 (2014), https://www. huduser.gov/portal/publications/pdf/2012-LIHTC-Tenant-Data-Report-508.pdf; Brandon M. Weiss, Locating Affordable Housing: The Legal System's Misallocation of Subsidized Housing Incentives, 70 Hastings L.J. 215 (2018); Cassandra Jones Havard, The Community Reinvestment Act, Banks, and the Low Income Housing Tax Credit Investment, 26 J. Affordable Housing & Community Dev. L. 415 (2017); Mark Lipschultz, Merging the Public and Private: The LIHTC Program and a Formula for More Affordable Housing, 36 Rev. Banking & Fin. L. 379 (2016).

43. Mark Schwartz, Dina Schlossberg, & Steven Sharpe, What Do Advocates Need to Know about the New Income Average Rules for LIHTC Properties?, https://www. nhlp.org/wp-content/uploads/2018/06/LIHTC-Properties-Webinar-Slides.pdf.

44. HUD granted $5 million in FY 2017 through the Rural Capacity Building for Community Development and Affordable Housing Program. *See* HUD Exchange,

Rural Capacity Building for Community Development and Affordable Housing Program, https://www.hudexchange.info/programs/rural-capacity-building/; *see also* Consolidated Appropriations Act of 2017, Pub. L. No. 115-31, 131 Stat. 135, 770.

45. Through HUD's Rural Housing Stability Assistance Program, grants are made to nonprofit organizations and local governments to provide a wide range of housing stabilization services to families, from rental assistance to short-term shelter and construction of new housing units. *See* 42 U.S.C. § 11408. More information can be found at U.S. Department of Housing and Urban Development, Rural Housing Stability Assistance Program, https://www.hud.gov/hudprograms/rural-housing.

46. *See* Title V of the Housing Act of 1949, codified at 42 U.S.C. §§ 1471 et seq. Regulations are found at 7 C.F.R. §§ 1804–2054 and 3550–75.

47. USDA housing programs generally define households with very-low incomes as those with incomes below 50% AMI. Households with low incomes range from 50% to 80% AMI, and those with moderate incomes make up to $5,500 above the low-income limit. *See* U.S. Department of Agriculture, Handbook HB-1-3550, Direct Single Family Housing Loans and Grants—Field Office Handbook, at Glossary 7–8, 13 (revised Jan. 6, 2017); U.S. Department of Agriculture, Handbook HB-2-3560, MFH Asset Management Handbook, at 6-1 (Feb. 24, 2005).

48. Section 502 loans (Single Family Direct Home Loans) subsidize, for a limited period of time, the mortgage payments of rural households with low or very-low incomes that meet eligibility requirements. *See* 7 C.F.R. Part 3550. More information can be found at U.S. Department of Agriculture, Single Family Housing Direct Home Loans, https://www.rd.usda.gov/programs-services/single-family-housing-direct-home-loans. Single Family Home Loan Guarantees are available to lenders that provide home loans to eligible rural households with low or moderate incomes. *See* 7 C.F.R. Part 3555. More information can be found at U.S. Department of Agriculture, Single Family Home Loan Guarantees, https://www.rd.usda.gov/programs-services/single-family-housing-guaranteed-loan-program.

49. Mutual Self-Help Housing Technical Assistance Grants support nonprofit organizations that supervise groups of families with low or very-low incomes as they help each other build their homes in rural areas. *See* 7 C.F.R. §§ 1944.401 et seq. More information can be found at U.S. Department of Agriculture, Mutual Self-Help Housing Technical Assistance Grants, https://www.rd.usda.gov/programs-services/mutual-self-help-housing-technical-assistance-grants.

50. Rural Housing Site Loans assist nonprofits with purchasing and developing sites that will either be used for self-help housing construction (Section 523 loans) or sold to families with low or moderate incomes, regardless of the construction method to be employed (Section 524 loans). *See* 7 C.F.R. Part 1822 and especially § 1822.261. More information can be found at U.S. Department of Agriculture, Rural Housing Site Loans, https://www.rd.usda.gov/programs-services/rural-housing-site-loans.

51. HUD counseling agencies can be contacted at a toll-free phone number: 1-800-569-428.

52. *See* U.S. Department of Housing and Urban Development, Low-Rent Apartment Search, http://www.hud.gov/apps/section8/index.cfm. For an unofficial list of Public

Housing waiting lists, *see* Affordable Housing Online, Open Public Housing and Project-Based Voucher Waiting Lists by State, http://affordablehousingonline.com/public-housing-waiting-lists.

53. *See* 24 C.F.R. § 960.202(a)(1) ("The PHA shall establish and adopt written policies for admission of tenants."). Tenant selection procedures for Public Housing can be found in the PHA's Admission and Continued Occupancy Policy (ACOP). A sample ACOP is appended to HUD's Public Housing Occupancy Guidebook. *See* U.S. Department of Housing and Urban Development, Public Housing Occupancy Guidebook (June 2003), App. III, https://www.hud.gov/sites/documents/DOC_10767.PDF. HUD-assisted and subsidized owners must adopt a written tenant selection plan, as well as an Affirmative Fair Housing Marketing Plan. *See* HUD Housing Programs § 2.8.2 and especially on the importance of advocates reviewing the plans.

54. These rules vary by locality. In New York City, for example, applicants for public housing apply with borough preferences but not to a specific development.

55. *See, for example*, Douglas Rice, Chart Book: Cuts in Federal Assistance Have Exacerbated Families' Struggles to Afford Housing, Center on Budget and Policy Priorities (Apr. 12, 2016), https://www.cbpp.org/research/housing/chart-book-cuts-in-federal-assistance-have-exacerbated-families-struggles-to-afford.

56. For an unofficial list of Section 8 waiting lists across the country, *see* Affordable Housing Online, http://affordablehousingonline.com/open-section-8-waiting-lists.

57. 24 C.F.R. §§ 5.230–233.

58. 42 U.S.C. § 3543(a).

59. 24 C.F.R. § 5.218(a).

60. *See* U.S. Department of Housing and Urban Development, Public Housing Occupancy Guidebook, App. III (June 2003), https://www.hud.gov/sites/documents/DOC_10767.pdf (providing sample admissions and continued occupancy plan).

61. *See* HUD Housing Handbook 4350 REV-1, Ch. 4, https://www.hud.gov/sites/documents/43503c4HSGH.pdf.

62. 24 C.F.R. § 982.54(d).

63. HUD Handbook 4350.3, ¶ 6-20.

64. 24 C.F.R. § 982.405. A PHA can issue rental assistance for up to 30 days if the initial inspection finds defects that are non-life-threatening. A PHA also can authorize occupancy before an initial inspection if the property met inspection requirements within a prior 24-month period. *See* U.S. Department of Housing and Urban Development, Housing Opportunity Through Modernization Act of 2016: Implementation of Various Section 8 Voucher Provisions, 82 Fed. Reg. 5458-01 (Jan. 18, 2017). Life-threatening defects must be fixed within 24 hours; other deficiencies generally must be fixed within 30 days. *See* 24 C.F.R. § 982.404(a)(3) ("If a defect is life threatening, the owner must correct the defect within no more than 24 hours. For other defects, the owner must correct the defect within no more than 30 calendar days (or any PHA-approved extension.)"). The 2016 Housing Opportunity Through Modernization Act, Pub. L. No. 114-201, 130 Stat. 782, amended the U.S. Housing Act of 1937 and other housing laws in ways that affect the initial inspection and enforcement of housing quality standards. An updated implementation notice, containing technical

corrections not relevant to the new inspection rules, was published six months later. *See* U.S. Department of Housing and Urban Development, Housing Opportunity Through Modernization Act of 2016: Implementation of Various Section 8 Voucher Provisions; Corrections, 82 Fed. Reg. 32461-01 (July 14, 2017).

65. 42 U.S.C. § 1437f(c). The PHA will perform follow-up inspections at least every two years, in order to ensure the unit meets housing quality standards. 24 C.F.R. § 982.405(a). Prior to March 2016, annual inspections were required. *See* U.S. Department of Housing and Urban Development, Streamlining Administrative Regulations for Public Housing, Housing Choice Voucher, Multifamily Housing, and Community Planning and Development Programs, 81 Fed. Reg. 12354 (Mar. 8, 2016); *see also* HUD Housing Programs, § 7.6.2.1.

66. A Minnesota court found no violation of the state's source-of-income discrimination statute when a property owner chose not to participate in Section 8 for any tenant. *See* Edwards v. Hopkins Plaza Ltd., 783 N.W.2d 171 (Minn. Ct. App. 2010). However, this result may be questioned in light of Texas Dept. of Housing and Community Affairs v. Inclusive Communities Project, Inc., 576 U.S. ___, 135 S. Ct. 2507 (2015) (holding disparate impact claims cognizable under the Fair Housing Act). *See* Philip Tegeler, Affirmatively Furthering Fair Housing and the Inclusive Communities Project Case: Bringing the Fair Housing Act into the 21st Century, in Facing Segregation: Housing Policy Solutions for a Stronger Society (Molly W. Metzger & Henry S. Webber eds.) (Oxford 2018).

67. States with laws barring source-of-income discrimination and so affording protection for families with Housing Choice vouchers denied housing on this basis are: California, Connecticut, Delaware, the District of Columbia, Maine, Massachusetts, Minnesota, New Jersey, North Dakota, Oklahoma, Oregon, Utah, Vermont, and Wisconsin. A number of cities and localities have passed their own statutes prohibiting source of income discrimination. *But see* Abraham Gutman, Katie Moran-McCabe, & Scott Burris, Health, Housing, and the Law, 11 Ne. U.L. Rev. 251, 301 (251) (three states with source-of-income bars exclude housing choice vouchers from the protection). For a complete list and details on each state or locality's law, *see* The Policy Surveillance Program, State Fair Housing Protections, Center for Public Health Law Research, Temple University Beasley School of Law (Aug. 1, 2018), http://lawatlas.org/datasets/state-fair-housing-protections-1498143743; *see also* Poverty & Race Research Action Council, Expanding Choice: Practical Strategies for Building A Successful Housing Mobility Program, Appendix B, http://www.prrac.org/pdf/AppendixB.pdf. In Connecticut and New Jersey, for example, courts have found that the state's antidiscrimination statute is not preempted by federal law, and requires property owners to enter into Section 8 leases with applicants with vouchers. *See* Commission on Human Rights and Opportunities v. Sullivan Assocs., 739 A.2d 238 (Conn. 1999); Franklin Tower One, LLC v. N.M., 725 A.2d 1104 (N.J. 1999). *See* Jessica Luna & Josh Leopold, Landlord Discrimination Restricts the Use of Rental Vouchers, Urban Institute (July 22, 2013), https://www.urban.org/urban-wire/landlord-discrimination-restricts-use-rental-vouchers; Kinara Flagg, Mending the Safety Net Through Source of Income Protections: The Nexus Between Antidiscrimination and

Social Welfare Law, 20 Colum. J. Gender & L. 201 (2011). *See also* Lisa L. Walker, The Fair Housing Act Turns 50 Years Old—Part 1: A Legal Retrospective from the Public & Affordable Housing World, 47 No. 2 Real Estate Rev. J. Art. 2 (2018) (reporting that in 2009 HUD recommended that the Fair Housing Act be amended to bar discrimination on the basis of source of income, and in 2010 required applicants for funding to show that they had not received a "cause determination" for violating state source-of-income requirements, but that since then "HUD has made no further efforts" to advocate for such protection). Finally, a 2018 pilot study of landlord acceptance of vouchers found some relation with state and local source-of-income laws. *See* U.S. Department of Housing and Urban Development, Office of Policy Development and Research, Mary K. Cunningham, Martha Galvez, Claudia L. Aranda, Robert Santos, Doug Wissoker, Alyse Oneto, Rob Pittingolo, & James Crawford, Urban Institute, A Pilot Study of Landlord Acceptance of Housing Choice Vouchers (Sept. 2018), https://www.huduser.gov/portal/pilot-study-landlord-acceptance-hcv.html.

68. Title VIII of the Civil Rights Act of 1968, Pub. L. No. 90-284, 82 Stat. 81, codified at 42 U.S.C. §§ 3601–31. *See* Maia Hutt, This House Is Not Your Home: Litigating Landlord Rejections of Housing Choice Vouchers under the Fair Housing Act, 51 Colum. J.L. & Soc. Probs. 391 (2018); *see also* Paula Beck, Fighting Section 8 Discrimination: The Fair Housing Act's New Frontier, 31 Harv. C.R-C.L. L. Rev. 155, 162 (1996).

69. *See* U.S. Department of Housing and Urban Development, Income Limits, https://www.huduser.gov/portal/datasets/il.html (setting forth income limits by year, effective Apr. 1, 2018).

70. 42 U.S.C. § 1437a(a)(1); 24 C.F.R. § 982.516. *See also* U.S. Department of Housing and Urban Development, Streamlining Administrative Regulations for Public Housing, Housing Choice Voucher, Multifamily, and Community Planning and Development Programs, 81 Fed. Reg. at 12355 (Mar. 8, 2016). Under HUD's Moving to Work demonstration program, many PHAs have implemented biennial or triennial income reexamination schedules for all tenants. *See* Congressional Research Service, Maggie McCarty, Moving to Work (MTW): Housing Assistance Demonstration Program 13 (2014), https://www.everycrsreport.com/files/20140103_R42562_6b34fc13366fbcdba6ace2841085b019d34e4b2e.pdf.

71. 24 C.F.R. § 982.516(c); *see also* HUD Housing Programs, § 4.6.1.

72. U.S. Department of Housing and Urban Development, FY 2018 Income Limits Documentation System, FY 2018 Income Limits Summary, https://www.huduser.gov/portal/datasets/il/il2018/2018summary.odn?inputname=STTLT*9999999999%2BU.S.+Non-Metropolitan+Total&selection_type=county&stname=U.S.+Non-Metropolitan+Total&statefp=99&year=2018; *see also* U.S. Department of Housing and Urban Development, FY 2018 HUD Income Limits Methodology, https://www.huduser.gov/portal/datasets/il/il18/IncomeLimitsMethodology-FY18.pdf.

73. 42 U.S.C. § 1437a(b)(1).

74. U.S. Department of Housing and Urban Development, Transmittal of Fiscal Year 2018 Income Limits for the Public Housing and Section 8 Programs, Notice PDR-2018-02 (Apr. 1, 2018), Transmittal of Fiscal Year 2018 Income Limits for the Public Housing and Section 8 Programs, https://www.huduser.gov/portal/datasets/il/il18/HUD-sec8-FY18r.pdf.

75. 24 C.F.R. § 5.601.

76. 24 C.F.R. § 5.609(a)(1)–(2).

77. 24 C.F.R. § 5.609(a)(3).

78. 24 C.F.R. § 5.609(a)(4).

79. 24 C.F.R. § 5.609(b)(1).

80. 24 C.F.R. § 5.609(b)(2).

81. 24 C.F.R. § 5.609(b)(4).

82. 24 C.F.R. § 5.609(b)(5).

83. 24 C.F.R. § 5.609(b)(6)(i); 45 C.F.R. § 260.31. If the TANF payment includes an amount specifically designated for shelter and utilities, and the payment is subject to adjustment to reflect the actual cost of shelter and utilities, then the portion of the TANF payment that is counted as income equals the total TANF payment exclusive of the amount designated for shelter and utilities, plus the maximum amount that the agency "could in fact allow the family for shelter and utilities." 24 C.F.R. § 5.609(b)(6)(ii).

84. 24 C.F.R. § 5.609(b)(7).

85. 24 C.F.R. § 5.609(b)(8) & (c)(7).

86. 24 C.F.R. § 5.609(b)(9). *See* U.S. Department of Housing and Urban Development, Amendment to the Definition of Tuition, Notice PIH 2015-21, H 2015-12 (Dec. 10, 2015), https://portal.hud.gov/hudportal/documents/huddoc?id=15-12hsgn. pdf (providing guidance as to what constitutes tuition and mandatory fees, and emphasizing that the full amount of financial assistance received for tuition and fees is to be excluded from the calculation of income in programs other than the Section 8 programs).

87. 24 C.F.R. § 5.609(c)(1).

88. 24 C.F.R. § 5.609(c)(2).

89. 24 C.F.R. § 5.609(c)(3).

90. 24 C.F.R. § 5.609(c)(4).

91. 24 C.F.R. § 5.609(c)(5).

92. 24 C.F.R. § 5.609(c)(7).

93. 24 C.F.R. § 5.609(c)(8)(i), (v).

94. 24 C.F.R. § 5.609(c)(9).

95. 24 C.F.R. § 5.609(c)(10).

96. 24 C.F.R. § 5.609(c)(11).

97. 24 C.F.R. § 5.609(c)(12).

98. 24 C.F.R. § 5.609(c)(14).

99. 24 C.F.R. § 5.609(c)(15).

100. 24 C.F.R. § 5.609(c)(16).

101. 24 C.F.R. § 5.609(c)(17); U.S. Department of Housing and Urban Development, Federally Mandated Exclusions from Income: Updated Listing, 79 Fed. Reg. 28938-01 (May 20, 2014).

102. 24 C.F.R. §§ 5.603(b), 5.611(a)(1).

103. 42 U.S.C. § 1437a(b)(5)(A)(i); 24 C.F.R. §§ 5.403, 5.611(a)(2). Congress authorized an increase in the deduction from $400 to $525 in the Housing Opportunity

Through Modernization Act of 2016, Pub. L. No. 114-201, 130 Stat. 782, but HUD must take implementing action. *See* HUD Housing Programs § 4.3.9.2.

104. 42 U.S.C. § 1437a(b)(5)(A)(ii)(III); 24 C.F.R. §§ 5.603(b), 5.611(a)(3). The deduction is equal to the amount by which those expenses exceed 3% of annual income. If a member of the family has a disability, "medical expenses" include the cost of attendant care and the cost of equipment (such as a wheelchair or an adapted van), to the extent that these expenses are necessary to allow another family member or the disabled family member to be employed. The amount of this deduction may not exceed the earned income of the family members rendered able to work. Congress authorized an increase in the deduction to 10% in the Housing Opportunity Through Modernization Act of 2016, Pub. L. No. 114-201, 130 Stat. 782, § 102, but HUD must take implementing action. *See* HUD Housing Programs, § 4.3.9.2.

105. 42 U.S.C. § 1437a(b)(5)(A)(iii); 24 C.F.R. §§ 5.603(b), 5.611(a)(4).

106. *See* HUD Housing Programs, § 4.3.8.4.

107. 24 C.F.R. § 960.255.

108. 24 C.F.R. § 5.609(b)(3). *See* HUD Handbook 4350.3 REV-1, Exhibit 5-2: Assets, https://www.hud.gov/sites/documents/DOC_35701.pdf.

109. 24 C.F.R. § 5.609(b)(3). The passbook savings rate, used to calculate the imputed income from assets, is adjusted periodically by HUD, and in 2016 was set at 0.06%. *See* U.S. Department of Housing and Urban Development, Passbook Savings Rate Effective February 1, 2016, Notice 2016-01 (Jan. 19, 2016), https://portal.hud.gov/hudportal/documents/huddoc?id=16-01hsgn.pdf.

110. Housing Opportunity Through Modernization Act of 2016, Pub. L. No. 114-201, § 104, 130 Stat. 782. *See* U.S. Department of Housing and Urban Development, Housing Opportunity Through Modernization Act of 2016: Initial Guidance, 81 Fed. Reg. 73030-01, 73033 (Oct. 24, 2016).

111. *See* Richard Rothstein, The Color of Law: A Forgotten History of How Our Government Segregated America (W.W. Norton 2017); *see also* Douglas Massey & Nancy Denton, American Apartheid: Segregation and the Making of the Underclass (Harvard 1993).

112. *See* Sam Fulwood III, The United States' History of Segregated Housing Continues to Limit Affordable Housing, Center for American Progress (Dec. 15, 2016), https://www.americanprogress.org/issues/race/reports/2016/12/15/294374/the-united-states-history-of-segregated-housing-continues-to-limit-affordable-housing/.

113. Title VIII of the Civil Rights Act of 1968, 42 U.S.C. §§ 3601–31; § 3604(a) provides that it shall be unlawful: "To refuse to sell or rent after the making of a bona fide offer, or to refuse to negotiate for the sale or rental of, or otherwise make unavailable or deny, a dwelling to any person because of race, color, religion, sex, familial status, or national origin."

114. The protections extended to tenants based on familial status under 42 U.S.C. § 3604(a) prohibit discrimination against households that include one or more minor children. These protections only apply to households where a child lives with a parent, with an individual who has legal custody of the child, or with the designee of the parent or individual who has custody (with written permission).

Individuals who are pregnant or in the process of securing legal custody of a child also are protected from discrimination based on familial status. *See* 42 U.S.C. § 3602(k).

115. Since 1988, the Fair Housing Act has barred discrimination based on the disability of the buyer, renter, resident, or associate of the buyer or renter. *See* Fair Housing Amendments Act of 1988, Pub. L. No. 100-430, 102 Stat. 1619. Under this section, an owner must allow "reasonable modifications" to a dwelling, made at the expense of the disabled tenant, to permit the tenant "full enjoyment of the premises." 42 U.S.C. § 3604(f)(3)(A). The owner must also make "reasonable accommodations in rules, policies, practices, or services" to allow a disabled tenant an equal opportunity to use and enjoy the dwelling. 42 U.S.C. § 3604(f)(3)(B). Before 1988, discrimination based on disability was prohibited, and the provision of reasonable accommodations was required, by Section 504 of Rehabilitation Act of 1973, 29 U.S.C. § 794(a), (b) (3)(A)(ii). *See* U.S. Department of Housing and Urban Development, Reasonable Accommodations and Modifications, https://www.hud.gov/program_offices/fair_housing_equal_opp/reasonable_accommodations_and_modifications.

116. Proposed and Final Rules pertinent to gender identity and equal access include:

U.S. Department of Housing and Urban Development, Final Rule, Equal Access to Housing in HUD Programs Regardless of Sexual Orientation or Gender Identity, 77 Fed. Reg. 5662 (Feb. 3, 2012), amending 24 C.F.R. Parts 5, 200, 203, 236, 400, 570, 574, 882, 891, and 982, with key protections set forth at 24 C.F.R. § 5.105(a)(2) and 24 C.F.R. § 200.300(a). The Equal Access Rule did not address how transgender and gender-nonconforming persons should be accommodated in emergency shelters. 77 Fed. Reg. at 5666. Further, the 2012 rule generally barred inquiries about a person's gender identity, and provided a limited exception for emergency shelters with shared bathrooms and sleeping areas. 77 Fed. Reg. at 5662.

U.S. Department of Housing and Urban Development, Proposed Rule, Equal Access in Accordance With an Individual's Gender Identity in Community Planning and Development Programs, 80 Fed. Reg. 72642-01 (Nov. 20, 2015). The proposed rule addressed equal access to emergency shelter and other community facilities based on a person's gender identity.

U.S. Department of Housing and Urban Development, Final Rule, Equal Access in Accordance with an Individual's Gender Identity in Community Planning and Development Programs, 81 Fed. Reg. 64763-01 (Sept. 21, 2016). The rule amended the definition of gender identity "to more clearly reflect the difference between actual and perceived gender identity and eliminates the prohibition on inquiries related to sexual orientation or gender identity, so that service providers can ensure compliance with this rule." *Id.* at 64764.

U.S. Department of Housing and Urban Development, Final Rule, Equal Access to Housing in HUD's Native American and Native Hawaiian Programs—Regardless of Sexual Orientation or Gender Identity, 81 Fed. Reg. 80989 (Nov. 17, 2016).

HUD Notices pertinent to gender identity and equal access include:

U.S. Department of Housing and Urban Development, Program Eligibility Regardless of Sexual Orientation, Gender Identity or Marital Status as Required by HUD's Equal Access Rule, Notice PIH 2014-20 (HA) (Aug. 20, 2014), https://www.hud.gov/sites/documents/PIH2014-20.PDF.

U.S. Department of Housing and Urban Development, Notice of Program Eligibility for HUD Assisted and Insured Housing Programs for All People Regardless of Sexual Orientation, Gender Identity or Marital Status as Required by HUD's Equal Access Rule [Section 232 and Section 242], Notice H 2015-01 (Feb. 6, 2015), https://www.hud.gov/sites/documents/15-01HSGN.PDF.

U.S. Department of Housing and Urban Development, Appropriate Placement for Transgender Persons in Single-Sex Emergency Shelters and Other Facilities, Notice CPD-15-02 (Feb. 20, 2015), https://www.hud.gov/sites/documents/15-02CPDN.PDF.

U.S. Department of Housing and Urban Development Notice, Program Eligibility in Multifamily Assisted and Insured Housing Programs in Accordance with HUD's Equal Access Rule, Notice H 2015-06 (July 13, 2015), https://www.hud.gov/sites/documents/15-06HSGN.PDF.

117. The Equal Access Rule makes it impermissible for Public Housing Authorities and private owners of subsidized projects to impose additional tenant-selection conditions that discriminate on the basis of sexual orientation, gender identity, or marital status. *See* 24 C.F.R. § 960.202–203 (PHAs); 24 C.F.R. § 5.655 (private landlords). Prior to the Equal Access Rule, some PHAs or owners had policies excluding families because couples were of the same sex, couples were not married, unmarried women were pregnant, and grandchildren were living with grandparents. When challenged as illegal, some courts struck down the conditions. *See, for example*, Hann v. Housing Authority of Easton, 709 F. Supp. 605 (E.D. Pa. 1989) (invalidating eligibility requirement limiting housing assistance to married heterosexual parents with children); Thomas v. Housing Authority of Little Rock, 282 F. Supp. 575 (E.D. Ark. 1967) (holding housing authority cannot automatically exclude unwed mothers from facilities). *But see* Freeman v. Sullivan, 954 F. Supp. 2d 730 (W.D. Tenn. 2013), aff'd (6th Cir. 13-5927 Dec. 27, 2013) (PHA could exclude nonmarried couple).

Moreover, the Fair Housing Act itself may prohibit some of these tenant-selection conditions by barring discrimination in housing on the basis of sex, which includes a tenant's failure to conform to sex stereotypes. *See* 42 U.S.C. §§ 3604–06; U.S. Department of Housing and Urban Development, Notice of Program Eligibility for HUD Assisted and Insured Housing Programs for All People Regardless of Sexual Orientation, Gender Identity or Marital Status as Required by HUD's Equal Access Rule, Notice H 2015-01 (Feb. 6, 2015), https://www.hud.gov/sites/documents/15-01HSGN.PDF ("[C]ourts have recognized that the Fair Housing Act's prohibition against discrimination because of sex includes discrimination based on non-conformance with sex stereotypes. Therefore, under certain circumstances, complaints involving sexual orientation or gender identity may be investigated under the Fair Housing Act."). In May 2019, the Trump administration announced a proposed rule that would effectively eliminate the equal access rule for transgender persons. *See* Executive Office of the President, Revised Requirements Under Community Planning and Development Housing Programs (FR-6152), https://www.reginfo.gov/public/do/eAgendaViewRule?pubId=201904&RIN=2506-AC53; *see* Tracy Jan, Proposed HUD rule would strip protections at homeless shelters, Washington Post (May 22, 2019), https://www. washingtonpost.com/business/2019/05/22/proposed-hud-rule-would-strip- transgender-protections-homeless-shelters/?utm_term=.6f87ccd9a2c7. In the context of employment discrimination, the Trump administration has opposed extending civil rights protection to persons who are gender nonconforming. *See generally* National Center for Transgender Equality, The Discrimination Administration: Trump's record of action against transgender people, https:// transequality.org/the-discrimination-administration.

118. *See* U.S. Department of Housing and Urban Development, with message stating, "The requested page '/program_offices/fair_housing_equal_opp/LGBT_Housing_ Discrimination' could not be found," https://www.hud.gov/program_offices/fair_ housing_equal_opp/LGBT_Housing_Discrimination (last accessed July 24, 2019).

119. U.S. Department of Housing and Urban Development, Implementation of the Fair Housing Act's Discriminatory Effects Standard, 78 Fed. Reg. 11460 (Feb. 15, 2013) (codified at 24 C.F.R. § 100.500(a)).

120. Texas Department of Housing and Community Affairs v. Inclusive Communities Project, Inc., 576 U.S. ___, 135 S. Ct. 2507 (2015).

121. 24 C.F.R. § 100.500(a).

122. 24 C.F.R. §§ 100.500(b)(1)(1)–(ii); 100.500(c) (burdens).

123. *See* U.S. Department of Housing and Urban Development, Reconsideration of HUD's Implementation of the Fair Housing Act's Disparate Impact Standard, 83 Fed. Reg. 28560-01 (June 18, 2018); *see also* Katy O'Donnell, HUD to propose more hurdles to prove housing discrimination, Politico (July 31, 2019) (reporting that HUD is considering a rule revision that would replace the three-part burden shifting approach to disparate impact claims with a five-step threshold rule), https://www. politico.com/story/2019/07/31/hud-prove-housing-discrimination-1629826.

124. *See* U.S. Department of Housing and Urban Development, Learn about the FHEO Complaint and Investigation Process, https://www.hud.gov/program_offices/ fair_housing_equal_opp/complaint-process. *See also* Consumer Action, Filing a Housing Discrimination Complaint, https://www.consumer-action.org/english/ articles/filing_a_housing_discrimination_complaint; *see also* U.S. Department of Justice, https://www.justice.gov/crt/how-file-complaint. For an analysis of trends in complaints filed pertinent to the Fair Housing Act, *see* Congressional Research Act, Libby Perl, The Fair Housing Act: HUD Oversight, Programs, and Activities (June 15, 2018), https://www.hud.gov/program_offices/fair_housing_equal_opp/ complaint-process.

125. *See generally* Natasha M. Trifun, Residential Segregation after the Fair Housing Act, American Bar Association (June 30, 2017), https://www.americanbar.org/groups/ crsj/publications/human_rights_magazine_home/human_rights_vol36_2009/ fall2009/residential_segregation_after_the_fair_housing_act/.

126. 42 U.S.C. § 3608.

127. *See* Otero v. New York City Housing Authority, 484 F.2d 1122, 1134 (2d Cir. 1973).

128. *See* Lawyers' Committee for Civil Rights, National Fair Housing Alliance & Poverty & Race Research Action Council, Affirmatively Furthering Fair Housing

at HUD: A First Term Report Card, Part II: HUD Enforcement of the Affirmatively Furthering Fair Housing Requirement (Mar. 2013), https://prrac.org/pdf/ HUDFirstTermReportCardPartII.pd; Jay Michael Patterson, Aggressively and Affirmatively Furthering Fair Housing: Grantees Obligated to Litigate, 87 Miss. L. Rev. 859, 865–867 (2018) (recounting weak oversight of HUD-assisted programs); Julia Garrison, Because Separate Is Not Equal: The Duty to Affirmatively Further Fair Housing, 23 Geo. J. on Poverty L. & Pol'y 571 (2016) (discussing litigation record); Jonathan J. Sheffield, At Forty-Five Years Old the Obligation to Affirmatively Further Fair Housing Gets a Face-Life, But Will It Integrate America's Cities?, 25 U. Fla. J.L. & Pub. Pol'y 51 (2014) (discussing failure to influence city and regional planning). *See also* Kara Brodfuehrer & Renee Williams, 27 J. Affordable Housing & Community Dev. L. 67, 71 (2018) (discussing inattention to duty in Low Income Housing Tax Credit program).

129. U.S. General Accountability Office, Housing and Community Grants: HUD Needs to Enhance Its Requirements and Oversight of Jurisdictions' Fair Housing Plans 32– 33 (Sept. 14, 2010), https://www.gao.gov/products/GAO-10-905.

130. U.S. Department of Housing and Urban Development, Affirmatively Furthering Fair Housing; Final Rule, 80 Fed. Reg. 42272 (July 16, 2015). For a summary of the rule and additional resources, *see* National Income Housing Coalition, HUD Releases Final Affirmatively Furthering Fair Housing Rule, https://nlihc.org/resource/hud-releases-final-affirmatively-furthering-fair-housing-rule; Poverty & Race Research Action Council, Affirmatively Furthering Fair Housing, https://prrac.org/fair-housing/affirmatively-furthering-fair-housing/; National Fair Housing Alliance, Furthering Fair Housing, https://nationalfairhousing.org/affirmatively-furthering-fair-housing/. *See also* HUD User, Officer of Policy Development and Research, Affirmatively Furthering Fair Housing, https://www.huduser.gov/portal/affht_ pt.html#affh (providing access to the final rule, the Assessment Tool, the AFFH Data and Mapping Tool, and previous documents pertinent to the AFFH duty).

131. U.S. Department of Housing and Urban Development, Affirmatively Furthering Fair Housing Assessment Tool: Announcement of Final Approved Document, 80 Fed. Reg. 81,840 (Dec. 31, 2015). *See* National Fair Housing Alliance v. Carson, 330 F. Supp. 3d 13 (D.D.C. 2018) (holding that the assessment tool was an information collection device not subject to notice-and-comment rulemaking when HUD withdrew the tool, and that HUD's withdrawal of the tool was not arbitrary and capricious).

132. U.S. Department of Housing and Urban Development, Affirmatively Furthering Fair Housing: Streamlining and Enhancements, Proposed Rule, 83 Fed. Reg. 40713 (Aug. 16, 2018). The comment period closed Oct. 15, 2018. *See* National Low Income Housing Coalition, HUD Indefinitely Suspends AFFH Rule, Withdraws Assessment Tool, https://nlihc.org/resource/hud-indefinitely-suspends-affh-rule-withdraws-assessment-tool.

133. 24 C.F.R. § 5.403.

134. 42 U.S.C. § 1437a(b)(3)(A)–(C); 24 C.F.R. § 5.403 (defining family).

135. 24 C.F.R. § 5.403. For Section 202 units, single persons and families qualify only if elderly or if they experience a disability. *See* 24 C.F.R. subpart B, § 891.205 (defining elderly and disabled).

136. 42 U.S.C. § 1437a(b)(3)(C).

137. Housing and Community Development Act of 1980, Pub. L. No. 96-399, Tit. II, § 214, 94 Stat. 1637 (codified at 42 U.S.C. § 1436a). Categories of eligible immigrants appear at 42 U.S.C. § 1436a(a). Housing assistance programs covered by the eligibility restrictions appear at 42 U.S.C. § 1436a(b). Implementing regulations appear at 24 C.F.R. §§ 5.500–528. The Personal Responsibility and Work Opportunity Reconciliation Act of 1996 (PRA), discussed in chapter 1 ("Cash Assistance"), imposed broad restrictions on noncitizen eligibility for federal benefits. The interaction of the PRA with Section 214 continues to cause uncertainty with respect to noncitizen eligibility for federal housing assistance. *See* Congressional Research Service, Maggie McCarty & Allison Siskin, Immigration: Noncitizen Eligibility for Needs-Based Housing Programs 4 (2015), https://fas.org/sgp/crs/homesec/RL31753.pdf. *See* National Housing Law Project, Resources, LIHTC Admissions, Rents, and Grievance Procedures (Apr. 27, 2018), https://www.nhlp.org/resources/lihtc-admissions-rents-grievance-procedures/.

138. 42 U.S.C. § 1436(a).The regulations also cover Section 235 Homeownership Housing, Housing Development Grants (low-income units only), and Section 23 Leased Housing Assistance Program. Section 214 does not apply to housing supported by the Low Income Housing Tax Credit, Section 202, the Section 515 Rural Rental Housing Program, McKinney-Vento and HEARTH Act programs, as well as other programs not discussed in this volume. For additional information, *see* HUD Housing Programs, Appendix 2A.

139. Victims of Trafficking and Violence Protection Act of 2000, Pub. L. No. 106-386, 114 Stat. 1464, § 107 (2000).

140. *See* U.S. Department of Housing and Urban Development, Notice PIH 2017-02, Violence Against Women Act (VAWA) Self Petition Verification Procedures (Jan. 19, 2017), https://www.hud.gov/sites/documents/17-02PIHN.PDF.

141. 42 U.S.C. § 1436a(a); Housing Opportunity Through Modernization Act of 2016, Pub. L. No. 114-201, § 113, 130 Stat. 782 (July 29, 2016).

142. *See* 24 C.F.R. § 5.506(a)(2).

143. *See* 24 C.F.R. § 5.520.

144. *See* U.S. Department of Housing and Urban Development, Housing and Community Development Act of 1980: Verification of Eligible Status, 84 Fed. Reg. 20589 (May 10, 2019). The comment period closed July 9, 2019. For criticisms of the proposed "mixed family" rule. *See, for example*, National Low Income Housing Coalition, Members of Congress Oppose HUD Mixed-Status Immigrant-Family Rule (June 24, 2019), https://nlihc.org/resource/members-congress-oppose-hud-mixed-status-immigrant-family-rule (discussing proposed "Keeping Families Together Act of 2019" introduced to block implementation of the HUD rule to evict mixed families). The new public charge rule was published at 84 Fed. Reg. 41292 (Aug. 15,

2019), and is due to take effect on October 15, 2019, though legal actions have been filed to stop it. The new rule does not change the grounds for deportability, does not apply to lawful permanent residents while in the United States or when re-entering the U.S. after an absence not exceeding 180 days, does not apply to immigrants in the "humanitarian" categories (e.g., refugees, asylees, certain survivors of trafficking and domestic violence, VAWA self-petitioners, etc.) or to immigrants in the U.S. armed forces (or their family members). *See* Archana Pyati, For housing authorities, "public charge" expected to sow confusion and add administrative costs, Urban Institute (Jan. 17, 2019), https://www.urban.org/urban-wire/housing-authorities-public-charge-expected-sow-confusion-and-add-administrative-costs ("While few noncitizens qualify for housing assistance, those who might become eligible because of a change in immigration status may be reluctant to apply, potentially increasing the risk of housing insecurity among immigrant households.").

145. 24 C.F.R. § 5.508(e).
146. 24 C.F.R. § 5.508(b)(1).
147. 24 C.F.R. § 5.508(b)(2).
148. 24 C.F.R. § 5.508(b)(3)(i)–(iii).
149. 42 U.S.C. § 1436a(i)(2)(A); 24 C.F.R. § 5.512(b). *See* U.S. Department of Housing and Urban Development, Quality Housing and Work Responsibility Act of 1998; Initial Guidance, 64 Fed. Reg. 8192, 8206 (Feb. 18, 1999).
150. 42 U.S.C. § 1436a(i)(1).
151. Guidance to PHAs on how to verify a VAWA's self-petitioner's immigration status appears in U.S. Department of Housing and Urban Development, Violence Against Women Act (VAWA) Self-Petitioner Verification Procedures, HUD Notice PIH 2017-02 (HA) (Jan. 19, 2017). *See* Leslye E. Orloff, Eligibility of Battered Immigrants Spouses and Children With Family Based Visa Petitioners for Public and Assisted Housing: Determinations of Battering or Extreme Cruelty, National Immigration Women's Advocacy Project of American University, Washington College of Law, http://library.niwap.org/wp-content/uploads/Eligibility-of-VAWA-Self-Petitioners-2016-12-14.pdf.
152. 24 C.F.R. § 5.514(d).
153. 24 C.F.R § 5.514(e)–(f).
154. The National Housing Law Center has prepared a comprehensive chart setting out the rules and regulations for all HUD-assisted programs. *See* HUD Housing Programs, Appendix 2B: Federally Assisted Housing Programs: Admissions for Applicants with Certain Criminal Backgrounds. Housing assistance for these purposes includes Public Housing, Section 8, Section 202, Section 811, Section 221(d)(3), Section 236, Section 515, and Section 514. HUD has imposed no specific requirements on the admission of individuals with criminal backgrounds to: Low-Income Housing Tax Credit housing, Shelter Plus Care, Supportive Housing Program, or Housing Opportunities for Persons with AIDS. *See* 24 C.F.R. §§ 582.325, 582.330 (Low-Income Housing Tax Credit and Shelter Plus Care), 583.325 (Supportive Housing Program), 574.603 (Housing Opportunities for Persons with AIDS). However, applicants for housing in these developments might also be

seeking assistance under HUD programs. *See generally* Lahny R. Silva, Criminal Histories in Public Housing, 2015 Wis. L. Rev. 375 (2015).

155. 42 U.S.C. § 13663(a) ("an owner of federally assisted housing shall prohibit admission to such housing for any household that includes any individual who is subject to a lifetime registration requirement under a State sex offender registration program"); 24 C.F.R. §§ 960.204(a)(4) (public housing), 982.553(a)(2)(i) (vouchers), 882.518(a)(2) (Section 8 moderate rehabilitation).

156. 42 U.S.C. § 1437n(f)(1) (a PHA "shall establish standards . . . that . . . permanently prohibit occupancy . . . and assistance . . . for, any person who has been convicted of manufacturing or otherwise producing methamphetamine on the premises in violation of any Federal or State law"); 24 C.F.R. §§ 960.204(a)(3) (public housing); 982.553(a)(1)(ii)(C) (vouchers), 882.518(a)(1)(ii) (Section 8 moderate rehabilitation).

157. 42 U.S.C. § 13661(b)(1) (a PHA or owner "shall establish standards that prohibit admission . . . for any household with a member . . . who the public housing agency or owner determines is illegally using a controlled substance"); 24 C.F.R. §§ 960.204(a)(2)(i)–(ii) (public housing), 982.553(b)(1)(i)(A) (vouchers), 882.518(a)(1)(iii) (Section 8 moderate rehabilitation).

158. 42 U.S.C. § 13661(a) ("Any tenant evicted from federally assisted housing by reason of drug-related criminal activity shall not be eligible . . . during the 3-year period beginning on the date of such eviction, unless the evicted tenant successfully completes a rehabilitation program approved by the public housing agency (which shall include a waiver of this subsection if the circumstances leading to eviction no longer exist)"); 24 C.F.R. §§ 960.204(a)(1) (public housing), 982.553(a)(1)(i) (vouchers), 882.518(a)(1)(i) (Section 8 moderate rehabilitation).

159. 42 U.S.C. § 13661(b)(1)(B) & (b)(2) (the PHA or owner "shall establish standards that prohibit admission . . . for any household with a member . . . whom the public housing agency or owner determines it has reasonable cause to believe that such household member's illegal use (or pattern of illegal use) of a controlled substance, or abuse (or pattern of abuse) of alcohol, may interfere with the health, safety, or right to peace enjoyment of the premises by other residents" and in determining whether to deny admission "may consider whether such household member" "has successfully completed" a rehabilitation program and is no longer engaging in the illegal use of a controlled substance or alcohol abuse or "has otherwise been rehabilitate successfully and is no longer engaging in the illegal use of a controlled substance or abuse of alcohol"); 24 C.F.R. §§ 960.203(c) (public housing), 982.553(a)(2)(ii)(A)(3)–(4) (vouchers), 882.518(b)(1)(iii)–(iv) (Section 8 moderate rehabilitation).

160. 42 U.S.C. § 13661(c) (the PHA or owner may deny admission to an applicant if it "determines that an applicant or member of the applicant's household is or was, during a reasonable time preceding the date when the applicant household would otherwise be selected for admission, engaged in any drug-related or violent criminal activity or other criminal activity which would adversely affect the health, safety, or right to peaceful enjoyment of the premises by other residents," and after a "reasonable period" after "expiration . . . of such activity, require the applicant, as a condition

of admission . . . to submit . . . evidence sufficient . . . to ensure that the individual or individuals in the applicant's household who engaged in criminal activity for which denial was made . . . have not engaged in any criminal activity during such reasonable period"); 24 C.F.R. §§ 960.203(c)(3) (public housing), 982.553(a)(2)(ii)(A)(2) (vouchers), 882.518(b)(1)(ii) (Section 8 moderate rehabilitation).

161. 34 U.S.C. § 12491.

162. *See* Afomeia Tesfai & Kim Gilhuly, The Long Road Home: Decreasing Barrier to Public Housing for People with Criminal Records, Human Impact Partners and the Ella Baker Center for Human Rights (2016), https://humanimpact.org/hipprojects/the-long-road-home-decreasing-barriers-to-public-housing-for-people-with-criminal-records/; Corinne A. Carey, No Second Chance: People with Criminal Records Denied Access to Public Housing, 36 U. Toledo L. Rev. 545 (2005).The effects on formerly incarcerated women have been severe. *See* Torrey McConnell, The War on Women: The Collateral Consequences of Female Incarceration, 21 Lewis & Clark L. Rev. 493, 506–507 (2017) ("President Bill Clinton's enthusiasm for a "one-strike" policy here only further demonstrated the large amount of discretion granted to public housing authorities . . . was and remains particularly problematic for female offenders upon release, as mothers are already twice as likely as fathers to have been homeless prior to incarceration.").

163. *See* Marie-Claire Tran-Leun, When Discretion Means Denial: A National Perspective on Criminal Records Barriers to Federally Subsidized Housing, Sargent Shriver National Center on Poverty Law (Feb. 2015), https://www.povertylaw.org/files/docs/discretion-denial.pdf. The author surveyed the criminal record policies of more than 100 properties participating in the Project-Based Section 8 program and found that housing providers (1) did not undertake individualized assessments of applicants; (2) presumed criminal activity from the fact of arrest; (3) placed no time limit on use of arrest records; and (4) used an overbroad definition of criminal activity.

164. President Clinton had stated: "In my State of the Union address I challenged local housing authorities and tenant associations to adopt this one strike and you're out policy, to restore the rule of law to public housing. To simply say, if you mess up your community you have to turn in your key; if you insist on abusing or intimidating or hurting other people you'll have to live somewhere else." President Bill Clinton, Remarks by the President at One Strike Crime Symposium (Mar. 28, 1996), http://clinton6.nara.gov/1996/03/1996-03-28-president-remarks-at-one-strike-crime-symposium.html.

165. U.S. Department of Housing and Urban Development, Notice PIH 2015-19, Guidance for Public Housing Agencies (PHAs) and Owners of Federally-Assisted Housing on Excluding the Use of Arrest Records in Housing Decisions (Nov. 2, 2015), citing 24 C.F.R. Part 5, subpart I; Part 960, subpart B; Part 966, subpart A; Part 982, subpart L. In 2011, HUD signaled its support for local housing policies that provide formerly incarcerated persons with "second chances." Letter from Shaun Donovan, Secretary, United States Department of Housing and Urban Development, to Public Housing Authority Executive Directors (June 17, 2011),

http://usich.gov/resources/uploads/asset_library/Rentry_letter_from_Donovan_to_PHAs_6-17-11.pdf. In 2013 HUD provided additional guidance that emphasized the relationship between homelessness and re-incarceration. *See* U.S. Department of Housing and Urban Development, Guidance on Housing Individuals and Families Experiencing Homelessness Though the Public Housing and Housing Choice Voucher Programs, HUD PIH Notice 2013-15 (HA), 8 (June 10, 2013), https://www.hud.giv/sites/documents?PIH2015-19.PDF.

166. U.S. Department of Housing and Urban Development, Office of General Counsel, Guidance on Application of Fair Housing Act Standards to the Use of Criminal Records by Providers of Housing and Real Estate-Related Transactions (Apr. 4, 2016), https://www.hud.gov/sites/documents/hud_ogcguidappfhastandcr.pdf.

167. Connecticut Fair Housing Center v. Corelogic Rental Property Solutions, LLC, 369 F. Supp. 3d 362 (D. Conn. 2019) (tenant stated claim for disparate treatment against tenant-screening company that used automated system and communicated nonspecific and out-of-date criminal records of an arrest said to be disqualifying).

168. *See* 24 C.F.R. §§ 5.655 (Section 8 project-based assistance), 960.206 (public housing), 982.207 (vouchers).

169. 42 U.S.C. §§ 1437d(c)(4)(A), 1437f(d)(1)(A), 1437f(o)(6)(A)(ii).

170. 24 C.F.R. §§ 5.655(c)(1)(i), 960.206(b)(1)(i), 982.207(b)(1)(i).

171. 24 C.F.R. §§ 960.206(b)(1)(iv) (public housing), 982.207(b)(1)(iv) (voucher), 5.655(c)(1)(v) (Project-Based Section 8).

172. 24 C.F.R. §§ 960.206(b)(1)(v) (public housing), 5.655(c)(1)(vi) (Project-Based Section 8), 982.207(b)(1)(v) (voucher).

173. 24 C.F.R. §§ 5.655(c)(3), (5) (Project-Based Section 8), 960.206(b)(1)(i) (public housing). *See* 24 C.F.R. § 100.500 (discriminatory effect prohibited).

174. 42 U.S.C. § 1437f(s); 24 C.F.R. § 982.207(a)(4).

175. 24 C.F.R. §§ 960.206(b)(2) (public housing), 5.655(c)(2) (Project-Based Section 8), 982.207(b)(2) (voucher).

176. 24 C.F.R. §§ 960.206(b)(3), (b)(5) (public housing); 5.655(c)(3) & (c)(5) (Project-Based Section 8); 982.207(b)(3) & (b)(5) (voucher).

177. HUD Housing Programs, § 2.3.5. *See generally* Brie Sherwin, After the Storm: The Importance of Acknowledging Environmental Justice in Sustainable Development and Disaster Preparedness, 29 Duke Envtl. L. & Pol'y 273 (2019); Megan Haberle, Fair Housing and Environmental Justice, 26 J. Affordable Housing & Community Dev. L. 271 (2017).

178. Quality Housing and Work Responsibility Act, Pub. L. No. 105-276, § 513, 112 Stat. 2461, 2543–47 (Oct. 21, 1998) (codified at 42 U.S.C. § 1437n).

179. 42 U.S.C. § 1437a(b)(2)(C).

180. 42 U.S.C. § 1437n(a)(2)(A), (b)(1), & (c)(3). For exclusions from income targeting, *see* HUD Handbook 4350.3 ¶ 4-5(A).

181. HUD Housing Programs § 2.4; 24 C.F.R. §§ 5.653(c), 960.202(b)(1), 982.201(b)(2).

182. *See* HUD Handbook 4350.3, ¶ 4-5(A). For a discussion of income targeting as a method to achieve housing justice and its effect on segregation, *see* John J. Infranca,

Housing Resource Bundles: Distributive Justice and Federal Low-Income Housing, 49 U. Rich. L. Rev. 1071 (2015).

183. 24 C.F.R. §§ 982.401(d), 982.402 (occupancy guidelines for Section 8 voucher programs); HUD Handbook 4350.3 ¶ 3-23 (occupancy guidelines for privately owned HUD-assisted properties); HUD Handbook 7465.1 REV-2 CHG-1, ¶ 5-1 (Aug. 1987) (PHA occupancy guidelines). *See also* U.S. Department of Housing and Urban Development, Public Housing Occupancy Guidebook §§ 5.0–5.5, 6.9 (2003), https://www.hud.gov/sites/documents/DOC_10760.PDF (guidance for compliance with civil rights requirements).

184. *See* 24 C.F.R. § 982.4 (granting discretion to PHAs to set a policy establishing the relationship between family size unit size). HUD has issued several Notices to PHAs advising against providing apartments larger than family size would warrant. *See, for example*, U.S. Department of Housing and Urban Development, Notice PIH 2014-25 (HA), Over Subsidization in the Housing Choice Voucher Program (Oct. 16, 2014), http://portal.hud.gov/hudportal/documents/huddoc?id=14-25pihn.pdf.

185. 24 C.F.R. § 982.4 (mandating that "family unit size" be defined by PHAs).

186. HUD published a statement of policy on the factors that it will consider when assessing a housing provider's occupancy policies and their validity under the Fair Housing Act's ban on discrimination on the basis of children in a family. *See* U.S. Department of Housing and Urban Development, Fair Housing Enforcement—Occupancy Standards; Notice of Statement of Policy, 63 Fed. Reg. 70,982 (Dec. 22, 1998), http://www.gpo.gov/fdsys/pkg/FR-1998-12-22/pdf/98-33568.pdf (reprinting Memorandum from Frank Keating to All Regional Counsel, HUD, Re Fair Housing Enforcement Policy: Occupancy Cases) (Mar. 20, 1991).

187. *See* Section 504 of the Rehabilitation Act of 1973, Pub. L. No. 93-112, 87 Stat. 344, codified at 29 U.S.C. §§ 701 et seq.; 24 C.F.R. §§ 8.1–8.58. *See also* 42 U.S.C. § 3601 et seq. (Fair Housing Act); 24 C.F.R. § 100.204 (reasonable accommodations).

188. HUD Housing Programs § 2.6.4.

189. 24 C.F.R. § 982.402(b)(4), (b)(6), & (b)(8); HUD Handbook 4350.3, ¶ 3-23.

190. 42 U.S.C. § 1437d(c)(3); 24 C.F.R. §§ 960.208(a) (public housing), 982.201(f)(1) (Section 8 voucher); HUD Handbook 4350.3, ¶ 4-9(C).

191. 24 C.F.R. § 960.208(a).

192. 24 C.F.R. § 982.201(f)(1).

193. *Compare* 24 C.F.R. § 982.554(a) (informal review for "applicants"), *with* 24 C.F.R. § 982.555(a)(1) (informal hearing for "participants"). "Participants" are families that have already been admitted to the PHA's program and who have had a Housing Assistance Payment contract made for them with an owner by the PHA. 24 C.F.R. § 982.4. Everyone else is an "applicant." *Id.*

194. 24 C.F.R. 982.555(a)(1)(i)–(v).

195. 24 C.F.R. 982.554(a)(2).

196. HUD Handbook 4350.3, ¶ 4-9(C)–(D).

197. U.S. Department of Housing and Urban Development, Final Guidance to Federal Financial Assistance Recipients Regarding Title VI Prohibition Against National

Origin Discrimination Affecting Limited English Proficient Persons, 72 Fed. Reg. 2732 (Jan. 22, 2007), https://www.lep.gov/guidance/HUD_guidance_Jan07.pdf.

198. 42 U.S.C. § 2000d; Executive Order 13166, Improving Access to Services for Persons with Limited English Proficiency, 65 Fed. Reg. 50121 (Aug. 16, 2000). *See also* Lau v. Nichols, 414 U.S. 563 (1974) (holding that failure to provide "meaningful" language access constitutes discrimination pursuant to under Title VI on the basis of national original). Other relevant HUD notices include: U.S. Department of Housing and Urban Development, Final Guidance to Federal Financial Assistance Recipients Regarding Title VI Prohibition Against National Origin Discrimination Affecting Limited English Proficient Persons, 72 Fed. Reg. 2732 (Jan. 22, 2007); U.S. Department of Housing and Urban Development, List of Federally Assisted Programs, 69 Fed. Reg. 68,700 (Nov. 24, 2004).

199. *See* 24 C.F.R. § 966.4(f)(4) (public housing); HUD Handbook 4350.3, ¶ 6-9 (Multifamily Programs). A lease under the Housing Choice Voucher program must include a tenancy addendum. 24 C.F.R. § 982.308(f).

200. *See, for example*, Pack v. Fort Washington II, 689 F. Supp. 2d 1237 (E.D. Cal. 2009) (finding that rule mandating adult supervision for children aged 10 and under constituted familial status discrimination under the FHA); Fair Housing Congress v. Weber, 993 F. Supp. 1286 (C.D. Cal. 1997) (holding that explicit prohibition on children playing in common areas violates the FHA).

201. *See* HUD Handbook 4350.3, Figures 6-2 & 6-3, ¶ 6-5(C)–(F). The Family Model Lease, which is the most widely employed model lease, is available in Appendix 4-A of the Handbook. For required provisions of leases for tenants receiving Section 8 voucher assistance, *see* 24 C.F.R. § 982.308(d). The PHA must approve the lease between the owner and tenant receiving assistance through the Section 8 voucher program. *See* 24 C.F.R. §§ 982.305(a), 982.308(c). The lease must contain a standard Section 8 Tenancy Addendum, which provides, among other things, that during the term of the lease the family may be evicted only for specified grounds (such as a serious violation of the lease) or for other good cause as provided in the addendum, distinguishing between good cause during the initial lease term and after the initial lease term. U.S. Department of Housing and Urban Development, Tenancy Addendum: Section 8 Tenant-Based Assistance Housing Choice Voucher Program (Sept. 30, 2017), https://www.hud.gov/sites/documents/52641-a.pdf. *See also* HUD Housing Programs § 4.2.2.5.

202. HUD Housing Programs § 3.1 (urging that "[n]egotiation of lease terms by a strong tenant organization is the most effective means of securing fair lease for all tenants").

203. *See, for example*, 24 C.F.R. § 966.4(e)(1).

204. 24 C.F.R. § 966.4(a)(1)(v).

205. 24 C.F.R. § 966.4(l)(1) & (n).

206. *See, for example*, 24 C.F.R. § 966.4(c). Federal law requires that a Public Housing lease state that it is the tenant's obligation to assure that "no tenant, member of the tenant's household, or guest" or "other person under the tenant's control" engages in: (a) any criminal activity that threatens the health, safety or right to peaceful

enjoyment of the premises by other residents; or (2) any drug-related criminal activity on or off the premises. 24 C.F.R. § 966.4(f)(12).

207. *See* HUD Housing Programs § 3.2.8.

208. HUD Handbook 4350.3, ¶ 6-5(C)(6) (project-based assistance programs); *see also* 24 C.F.R. § 966.6(h) (public housing).

209. For an overview of rent in HUD public and subsidized housing, *see* HUD Housing Programs, Appendix 4A.

210. 42 U.S.C. §§ 1437a(a)(1), 1437f(c)(3); 24 C.F.R. § 5.628(a).

211. This occurs when the units do not receive rental assistance. *See* 42 U.S.C. § 1437a(a)(2)(A)–(B).

212. 42 U.S.C. § 1437f(o)(3).

213. 42 U.S.C. § 1437a(a)(2)(A)(i); 24 C.F.R. § 960.253(a)(1).

214. For more on flat rent, which is established by the PHA, *see* 42 U.S.C. §§ 1437a(a)(2)(A)–(B); on switching to income-based rent due to financial hardship, *see* 42 U.S.C. § 1437a(a)(2)(C).

215. 42 U.S.C. § 1437a; 24 C.F.R. §§ 5.630, 960.253. The financial hardship exemption is set forth at 24 C.F.R. § 5.630(b).

216. 24 C.F.R. §§ 5.628, 5.630 (Section 8 project-based assistance); *see also* 24 C.F.R. § 891.440 (Section 202).

217. HUD Handbook 4350.3 ¶ 5-29.

218. *Id.*

219. Tax Reform Act of 1986, 26 U.S.C. § 42.

220. 26 U.S.C. § 42(g). *See* HUD Housing Programs § 4.2.13; *see also* Congressional Research Service, Mark P. Heightley, An Introduction to the Low-Income Housing Tax Credit (updated Feb. 27, 2019), https://fas.org/sgp/crs/misc/RS22389.pdf.

221. 42 U.S.C. § 1437f(o)(1)–(3); 24 C.F.R. §§ 982.451, 982.501–521. For regulations concerning Fair Market Rents, *see* 24 C.F.R. §§ 888.111–115. For the most recent Fair Market Rent calculations by HUD, *see* U.S. Department of Housing and Urban Development, Office of Policy Development and Research, Data Sets: Fair Market Rents, https://www.huduser.gov/portal/datasets/fmr.html.

222. *See* U.S. Department of Housing and Urban Development, Establishing a More Effective Fair Market Rent System; Using Small Area Fair Market Rents in the Housing Choice Voucher Program Instead of the Current 50th Percentile FMRs, 81 Fed. Reg. 221 (Nov. 16, 2016). *See also* U.S. Department of Housing and Urban Development, Guidance on Recent Changes in Fair Market Rent (FMR), Payment Standard, and Rent Reasonableness Requirements in the Housing Choice Voucher Program," PIH Notice 2018-01 (Jan. 17, 2018), https://www.hud.gov/sites/dfiles/PIH/documents/PIH-2018-01.pdf. At the start of the Trump administration HUD announced it would delay implementation of the small-area rent rule, and a nonprofit group and two Voucher recipients challenged the delay. A federal court held that plaintiffs were likely to succeed on their claim that HUD lacked authority to delay, and issued a preliminary injunction. *See* Open Communities Alliance v. Carson, 286 F. Supp. 3d 148 (D.D.C. 2017); *see generally* Olatunde C.A. Johnson, "Social Engineering," Notes on the Law and Political Economy of Integration, 40 Cardozo L. Rev. 1149, 1162 n.52 (2019).

223. *See* Center on Budget and Policy Priorities & Poverty & Race Research Action Council, A Guide to Small Area Fair Market Rents (SAFMRs): How State and Local Housing Agencies Can Expand Opportunity for Families in All Metro Area (May 4, 2018), https://www.cbpp.org/research/housing/a-guide-to-small-area-fair-market-rents-safmrs; Barbara Sard & Douglas Rice, Realizing the Housing Voucher Program's Potential to Enable Families to Move to Better Neighborhoods, Center on Budget and Policy Priorities (Jan. 12, 2016), https://www.cbpp.org/research/housing/realizing-the-housing-voucher-programs-potential-to-enable-families-to-move-to.

224. 42 U.S.C. § 1437f(o)(10)(A)–(C); 24 C.F.R. §§ 982.305(a)(4), 982.507. Note that if the rent for the unit is subject to regulation (for example, through rent control, or through the unit's participation in another federal or state subsidized housing program), the rent may not be greater than the level permitted or required by that regulation. *See* HUD Housing Programs § 4.9.3.8.

225. 42 U.S.C. § 1437f(o)(3); 24 C.F.R. § 982.508.

226. Housing Opportunity Through Modernization Act of 2016, Pub. L. No. 114-201, 130 Stat. 782, § 102 (July 29, 2016); 42 U.S.C. §§ 1437d(c)(2) (public housing), 1437f(c)(3), 1437f(o)(5) (Section 8); 12 U.S.C. §§ 1715z-1(e)(1) (Section 236), 1701s(e)(2) (Rent Supplement). Implementing regulations can be found at 24 C.F.R. §§ 5.657, 236.760, 960.257, 960.259, 982.516, 982.551. *See also* HUD Handbook 4350.3 ¶ 7-4, which outlines the recertification process for tenants of privately owned HUD-assisted projects.

227. 24 C.F.R. §§ 5.657(c), 960.257(b)(2), 966.4(c)(2), 982.516(d). *See also* HUD Handbook 4350.3 ¶ 7-10, which states that tenants must disclose to owners not only changes in family composition but also the employment of previously unemployed adults in the family and increases in family income of more than $200 per month.

228. 24 C.F.R. §§ 966.4(a)(1)(v), 982.551(h)(2)–(4).

229. 24 C.F.R. § 982.516(c)(1).

230. Housing Opportunity Through Modernization Act of 2016, Pub. L. No. 114-201, 130 Stat. 782, § 102 (2016); 24 C.F.R. §§ 5.657(c), 960.257(b)(1), 982.516(c)(2).

231. 42 U.S.C. § 1437a(d); 24 C.F.R. § 960.255(b).

232. *See* 42 U.S.C. § 1437a(a)(1).

233. 24 C.F.R. §§ 246.1(b), 246.20–.21.

234. *See* 24 C.F.R. §§ 245.305–330 (regulations on rent increase procedure).

235. 24 C.F.R. § 245.310(a). Part 245 of the HUD regulations also apply to additional programs. *See* 24 C.F.R. § 245.10(a).

236. 12 U.S.C. § 1715z-1b(b)(1); *see also* 24 C.F.R. § 245.10.

237. *See, for example*, 24 C.F.R. §§ 965.507(a) (requirement of annual PHA review of utility allowances), 982.517(c)(1) (requirement for PHAs regarding the Voucher program), 880.610 (Project-Based Section 8 programs); 264 C.F.R. § 1.42-10(c)(2) (LIHTC).

238. 24 C.F.R. § 5.603(b) (public housing and Project-Based Section 8 housing).

239. 24 C.F.R. § 965.505(e).

240. 24 C.F.R. §§ 960.253, 965.502(a), 965.505 (public housing); 24 C.F.R. §§ 5.634(a), 982.517(b) (Section 8). Under certain circumstances, a PHA will pay a retail

metered tenant's utilities directly or reimburse the tenant for utilities. *See* 24 C.F.R. §§ 5.632(b)(2), 960.253(c)(3)–(4), 982.514(b)–(c).

241. 24 C.F.R. §§ 965.502(a), 965.506(a).

242. HUD Housing Programs, § 5.5.1.

243. 24 C.F.R. §§ 965.501(b), 965.506(b). In public housing, if air conditioning is an option for residents and has been check metered, the use of air conditioning will not be included in the utility allowance—tenants will pay for what they use. 24 C.F.R. § 965.505(e). If air conditioning is an option but cannot be check metered, tenants will be billed under the master-metered concept of 24 C.F.R. § 965.506(b).

244. 26 U.S.C. § 42(g)(2)(B)(ii).

245. 26 C.F.R. § 1.42-10(a).

246. 26 C.F.R. § 1.42-10(b).

247. 24 C.F.R. §§ 966.4(b)(2)–(3), 982.510; HUD Handbook 4350.3, ¶ 6-25. For a comprehensive overview of the legal issues surrounding additional tenant charges, *see* HUD Housing Programs § 6.2.

248. *See, for example,* 24 C.F.R. §§ 247.3(c)(4), 880.607(b)(3), 966.4(l)(2)(i)(A). *See* Sager v. Housing Commission of Anne Arundel County, 957 F. Supp. 2d 627 (D. Md. 2013) (invalidating allocation clause in public housing lease providing that if tenant made payment that was not marked as rent or for rent, payment could be applied to maintenance charges, late fees, or legal fees before applying payment to rent).

249. HUD Handbook 4350.3, ¶ 6-23(F).

250. Survivors of domestic violence, dating violence, sexual assault, or stalking potentially may argue that under the Violence Against Women Act, damage that stems from the abuse (i.e., damage by the abuser) should not be assessed to the survivor. *See* 34 U.S.C. § 12471. Depending on the circumstances, arguments also may be available under the Fair Housing Act if the policy has a negative and disparate impact on the basis of gender. *See generally* Elizabeth J. Thomas, Building a Statutory Shelter for Victims of Domestic Violence: The United States Housing Act and Violence Against Women Act in Collaboration, 16 Wash. U. J.L. & Pol'y 289 (2004).

251. 24 C.F.R. § 982.313(c)–(d); HUD Handbook 4350.3, ¶ 6-17(A).

252. 24 C.F.R. § 966.4(b)(5).

253. HUD Handbook 4350.3, fig. 6-7.

254. 24 C.F.R. § 982.313(a)–(b).

255. 42 U.S.C. § 1437z-3; 24 C.F.R. § 960.707.

256. 12 U.S.C. § 1701r-1(a); 24 C.F.R. § 5.309.

257. 24 C.F.R. § 5.350(a), (d).

258. 24 C.F.R. §§ 5.318, 960.707(b).

259. 24 C.F.R. § 5.315(c).

260. 24 C.F.R. § 5.356(b)(2).

261. 24 C.F.R. §§ 5.318(d), 960.707(d). *See also* HUD Handbook 4350.3, ¶ 6-24, which discusses pets in further detail.

262. *See* 24 C.F.R. §§ 5.303, 960.705.

263. *See, for example,* Majors v. DeKalb Co. Housing Authority, 652 F.2d 454 (5th Cir. 1981) (PHA's refusal to allow mentally ill tenant to keep a pet could violate the Rehabilitation Act of 1973).

264. *See* 42 U.S.C. § 3604 (2012); 24 C.F.R. Part 100.

265. 29 U.S.C. § 794.

266. 42 U.S.C. § 12132.

267. 42 U.S.C. § 1437(a)(1)(A).

268. 24 C.F.R. §§ 5.701, 5.703, 902.21.

269. 24 C.F.R. § 5.703.

270. 42 U.S.C. §§ 4821, 4851.

271. 24 C.F.R. §§ 35.100 et seq. *See* U.S. Department of Housing and Urban Development, Requirements for Notification, Evaluation and Reduction of Lead-Based Paint Hazards in Federally Owned Residential Property and Housing Receiving Federal Assistance; Response to Elevated Blood Lead Levels, 82 Fed. Reg. 4151 (Jan. 13, 2017). Critically, Elevated Blood Lead Levels now are set in accordance with Centers for Disease Control and Prevention guidance. Until the amendment, HUD regulations had not been updated to reflect current scientific knowledge about acceptable blood lead levels. *See* Emily Benfer, Emily Coffey, Allyson E. Gould, Mona Hanna-Attisha, Bruce Lanphear, Helen Y. Li, Ruth Ann Norton, David Rosner, & Kate Walz, Duty to Protect: Enhancing the Federal Framework to Prevent Childhood Lead Poisoning and Exposure to Environmental Harm, 18 Yale J. Health Pol'y, L. & Ethics 1 (2019); Emily Benfer, Blame HUD for America's Lead Epidemic, N.Y. Times (Mar. 4, 2016), https://mobile.nytimes.com/2016/03/05/opinion/blame-hud-for-americas-lead-epidemic.html?mcubz=0. Certain housing is exempt from HUD's lead-paint regulations, including housing constructed after 1978. *See* 24 C.F.R. § 35.115.

272. Failure to address these harms also may implicate the duty to affirmatively further fair housing. *See generally* Sarah Fox, Environmental Gentrification, 90 U. Colo. L. Rev. 803, 814 (2019) (explaining that "[d]ue to a host of historic and socioeconomic factors, a disproportionate number of contaminated sites are concentrated in low-income communities and communities of color").

273. 42 U.S.C. § 1437j(c); 24 C.F.R. §§ 960.600–609.

274. *See* U.S. Department of Housing and Urban Development, Streamlining Administrative Regulations for Public Housing, Housing Choice Voucher, Multifamily Housing, and Community Planning and Development Programs, 81 Fed. Reg. 12354-01 (Mar. 8, 2016) (amending 24 C.F.R. §§ 960.605, 960.607 permitting tenant self-certification for community service requirements but subject to third-party verification procedures).

275. *See* Emily Coffey, Tenants' Right to Organize in HUD-Assisted Housing Must Be Enforced, Shriver Center on Poverty Law (Apr. 20, 2016), https://theshriverbrief.org/tenants-right-to-organize-in-hud-assisted-housing-must-be-enforced-4f0c59ee6e08; National Low Income Housing Coalition, Resident Engagement, https://nlihc.org/take-action/resident-engagement (providing resources about tenant organizing, tenant engagement, and an engagement Facebook group to empower tenant advocacy). *See generally* Christopher Bangs, A Union for All: Collective Associations Outside the Workplace, 26 Geo. J. on Poverty L. & Pol'y 47 (2018) (discussing funding for tenant associations); Michael Grinthal, Power with: Practice Models for Social Justice Lawyering, 15 U. Pa. J.L. & Soc. Change

25 (2011) (discussing representing groups in the process of organizing for power); Shekar Krishnan, Advocacy for Tenant and Community Empowerment: Reflections on My First Year in Practice, 14 CUNY L. Rev. 215 (2010) (discussing tenant empowerment generally as an aspect of legal advocacy); Scott L. Cummings & Ingrid V. Eagly, A Critical Reflection on Law and Organizing, 48 UCLA L. Rev. 443 (2001) (discussing the law and organizing model of social justice lawyering).

276. *See* 24 C.F.R. Part 964 (public housing). The right to organize by tenants in project-based rental assistance units is governed by 24 C.F.R. Part 245. *See* Ed Gramlich, Resident Participation in Federally Subsidized Housing, in Advocates Guide 2018: A Primer on Federal Affordable Housing & Community Development Programs, National Low Income Housing Coalition, ¶ 2-44

277. For an overview of state laws on tenant organizing, *see* Christopher Bangs, A Union for All: Collective Associations Outside the Workplace, 26 Geo. J. on Poverty L. & Pol'y 47, 58–62 & accompanying tables.

278. 24 C.F.R. § 964.11.

279. 24 C.F.R. § 964.130(a).

280. 42 U.S.C. § 1437g(e)(1)(E); 24 C.F.R. § 964.150. *See also* U.S. Department of Housing and Urban Development, Guidance On the Use of Tenant Participation Funds, PIH 2013-21 (HA) (Aug. 23, 2013).

281. PIH 2013-21, ¶¶ 7 & 8.

282. *See* 12 U.S.C. § 1715z-1b(a); 24 C.F.R. Part 245, which covers Project-Based Section 8 properties, properties with HUD-insured or mortgages assisted under Section 236, Section 221(d)(3) BMIR, properties that receive enhanced vouchers, Section 202 properties for the elderly, Section 811 properties for persons with disabilities, and some other properties. *See* HUD Housing Programs § 9.5.3.

283. *See* HUD Handbook REV-2, 4381.5.

284. 24 C.F.R. § 245.110.

285. 24 C.F.R. § 245.115.

286. 24 C.F.R. § 245.120(a), (c).

287. 24 C.F.R. § 245.105(b).

288. 24 C.F.R. Part 30. Notices pertaining to the tenant participation rights include:

U.S. Department of Housing and Urban Development, Notice H 2011-29, Implementation of Tenant Participation Requirements in accordance with 24 C.F.R. 245 subpart B and HUD Handbook 4381.5 REV-2 "The Management Agent Handbook" (Oct. 13, 2011).

U.S. Department of Housing and Urban Development, Implementation of Tenant Participation Requirements in accordance with 24 C.F.R. Part 245, Policy Notice H 2014-12 (Sept. 4, 2012).

U.S. Department of Housing and Urban Development, Implementation of Tenant Participation Requirements in accordance with 24 C.F.R. Part 245 subpart B and HUD Handbook 4381.5 REV-2 "The Management Agent Handbook," Policy Notice H 2012-21 (Oct. 17, 2012).

U.S. Department of Housing and Urban Development, Revision of Tenant Participation Requirements in accordance with 24 C.F.R. Part 245, Notice H 2016-05 (Mar. 31, 2016). The Notice expanded the property types that may be assessed civil penalties for noncompliance with the tenant-participation rules.

289. *See* Herring v. Chicago Housing Authority, 850 F. Supp. 694 (N.D. Ill. 1994) (PHA violated tenant's First Amendment right of association); Crowder v. Housing Authority, 990 F.2d 586 (11th Cir. 1993) (PHA's complete ban on tenant's Bible studies violated First Amendment). As Justice William O. Douglas, Jr. explained in Thorpe v. Housing Authority (a decision of the U.S. Supreme Court), "The recipient of a government benefit . . . [such as] a home in a public housing project, cannot be made to forfeit the benefit because he exercises a constitutional right." Thorpe v. Housing Auth., 386 U.S. 670, 678–679 (1967) (Douglas, J., concurring), rev'd on other grounds, 393 U.S. 268 (1969); *see also* Davis v. Village Park II Realty Co., 578 F.2d 461 (2d Cir. 1978); McQueen v. Druker, 438 F.2d 781 (1st Cir. 1971); Rudder v. United States, 226 F.2d 51 (D.C. Cir. 1955).

290. *See* 24 C.F.R. Part 903.

291. 24 C.F.R. § 964.11.

292. *See* 24 C.F.R. Part 964. Definition is at 24 C.F.R. § 964.7. Requirements are at 24 C.F.R. § 964.120.

293. 24 C.F.R. §§ 966.3, 966.5.

294. 24 C.F.R. § 966.4(c)(4) (providing for hearing to challenge rent increase).

295. 24 C.F.R. § 965.405(c).

296. *See* U.S. Department of Housing and Urban Development, Streamlining Administrative Regulations for Public Housing, Housing Choice Voucher, Multi-family Housing, and Community Planning and Development Programs—Final Rule, 81 Fed. Reg. 12374 (Mar. 8, 2016).

297. *See* 24 C.F.R. § 960.204.

298. 42 U.S.C. § 1437d(1)(5), 24 C.F.R. Part 966.4(1)(2)(iii) (public housing). HUD regulations set out in 24 C.F.R. § 247.3 extend good cause protections to tenants in buildings receiving subsidies under Section 221(d)(3) BMIR, Section 236, Section 202, Rent Supplement, and some but not all Project-Based Section 8 programs (Section 8 new construction, Section 8 substantial rehabilitation, Section 8 through state housing agencies, and Section 515 Rural Rental Housing set aside are excluded). However, subject to a few differences, these latter programs are subject as well to good cause rules. *See* HUD Housing Programs § 11.2.1.2.

299. *See* 24 C.F.R. § 982.310(a), (d). *See* HUD Housing Programs § 11.2.2.3.

300. *See* HUD Handbook 4350.3; HUD Housing Program § 11.2.2.3.

301. The National Housing Law Project has prepared a comprehensive chart of requirements for eviction in different HUD-assisted housing. *See* HUD Housing Programs, Appendix 11B.

    The rules governing eviction for criminal contacts developed in a series of statutes:

    The Anti-Drug Abuse Act of 1988, which amended the Housing Act of 1937, required Public Housing Authorities to use leases providing that no tenant or a person under the control of the tenant engage in criminal activity "on or near" public and other federally assisted low-income housing. *See* Anti-Drug Abuse Act of 1988, Pub. L. No. 100-690, 102 Stat. 4181 (codified as amended in various sections of 21 U.S.C. and 42 U.S.C.).

The Cranston-Gonzalez National Affordable Housing Act of 1990 imposed a three-year ban on housing assistance following a drug-related eviction. *See* Cranston-Gonzalez National Affordable Housing Act, Pub. L. No. 101-625, 104 Stat. 4079 (1990) (codified as amended in various sections of 42 U.S.C.).

The Housing Opportunity Program Extension Act of 1996—adopted in response to President Clinton's State of the Union Address calling for a "one-strike" rule to be enforced without exception (*see* 142 Cong. Rec. H768) (daily ed. Jan. 23, 1996) (State of the Union by the President of the United States—required public housing leases to "provide that any criminal activity that threatens the health, safety, or right to peaceful enjoyment of the premises by other tenants or any drug-related criminal activity on or off such premises, engaged in by a public housing tenant, any member of the tenant's household, or any guest or other person under the tenant's control, shall be cause for termination of tenancy." *See* Housing Opportunity Program Extension Act of 1996, Pub. L. No. 104-120, 110 Stat. 834 (1996) (codified as amended in various sections of 42 U.S.C., *see* 42 U.S.C. § 1437d(1)(6)).

In 1998, Congress extended these requirements to the Section 8 program. Quality Housing and Work Responsibility Act, Pub. L. No. 105-276, § 501, 112 Stat. 2461 (1998) (codified as amended in various sections of 42 U.S.C.).

302. 24 C.F.R. § 966.4(l)(2).
303. 24 C.F.R. § 966.4(l)(5)(i)(A).
304. 24 C.F.R. §966 4(l)(5)(ii)(B).
305. 24 C.F.R. § 966.4(l)(2)(iii). Since 2016, HUD also has banned smoking in subsidized housing. *See* Teresa Wiltz, A New Smoking Ban in Public Housing Roils Some Residents, Pew (Aug. 20, 2018), https://www.pewtrusts.org/en/research-and-analysis/blogs/stateline/2018/08/20/a-new-smoking-ban-in-public-housing-roils-some-residents.
306. Multifamily Housing includes Project-Based Section 8, Section 202, Section 211, Section 811, and some other subsidy programs. *See* 24 C.F.R. §§ 5.100, 5.858, 5.859.
307. 24 C.F.R. § 5.858.
308. 24 C.F.R. § 5.858. There is no specific regulation governing methamphetamine production.
309. 24 C.F.R. § 5.859(a).
310. 24 C.F.R. § 5.859(b).
311. 24 C.F.R. § 5.860.
312. 24 C.F.R. § 5.858 does not refer to violent criminal activity, but § 5.100 does. *See* HUD Housing Programs, Appendix 11B.
313. 42 U.S.C. §§ 1437f(d)(1)(B)(iii) (Section 8 Certificate); 1437f(o)(7)(D) (Section 8 Voucher); 24 C.F.R. § 982.310(c).ˋ
314. U.S. Department of Housing and Urban Development v. Rucker, 535 U.S. 125 (2002). The U.S. Supreme Court reversed the decision of the Ninth Circuit Court of Appeals, which had invalidated the one-strike rule for its "absurdity and unjustness." Rucker v. Davis, 237 F.3d 1113 (9th Cir. 2001) (en banc).

Studies confirm that these policies contributed to homelessness, recidivism, and family disruption, particularly in communities of color. *See* Lahny R. Silva,

Collateral Damage: A Public Housing Consequence of the "War on Drugs," 5 U.C. Irvine L. Rev. 783 (2015); Wendy J. Kaplan & David Rossman, Called "Out" at Home: The One Strike Eviction Policy and Juvenile Court, 3 Duke Forum for Law & Social Change 109 (2011); Human Rights Watch, No Second Chance (2004), https://www.hrw.org/reports/2004/usa1104/0.htm.

315. Nelson H. Mock, Punishing the Innocent: No-Fault Eviction of Public Housing Tenants for the Actions of Third Parties, 76 Tex. L. Rev. 1495 (1998).

316. *See* Barclay Thomas Johnson, The Severest Justice Is Not the Best Policy: The One-Strike Policy in Public Housing, 10-SPG J. Affordable Housing & Community Dev. L. 234 (2001).

317. *See* Emily Ponder Williams, Fair Housing's Drug Problem: Combatting the Racialized Impact of Drug-Based Housing Exclusions alongside Drug Law Reform, 54 Harv. C.R.-C.L. L. Rev. 769 (2019).

318. 24 C.F.R. § 966.4(l)(5)(vii)(B). *See also* Letter from Michael M. Liu, Assistant Secretary of HUD to Public Housing Directors (June 6, 2002), https://www.hud.gov/sites/documents/DOC_10888.PDF ("PHAs remain free, as they deem appropriate, to consider a wide range of factors in deciding whether, and whom, to evict as a consequence of such a lease violation."). For advocacy strategies, *see* Gerald S. Dickinson, Towards New Eviction Jurisprudence, 23 Geo. J. on Poverty L. & Pol'y 1 (2015); Robert Hornstein, Litigating Around the Long Shadow of Department of Housing and Urban Development v. Rucker: The Availability of Abuse of Discretion and Implied Duty of Good Faith Affirmative Defenses in Public Housing Criminal Activity Evictions, 43 U. Toledo L. Rev. 1 (2011).

319. U.S. Department of Housing and Urban Development, Letter from Shaun Donovan, Secretary, to Public Housing Authority Executive Directors (June 17, 2011), http://usich.gov/resources/uploads/asset_library/Rentry_letter_from_Donovan_to_PHAs_6-17-11.pdf.

320. For the rules on mandatory termination of assistance in Public Housing, Housing Choice Voucher program and Section 8 Multifamily programs, *see* 24 C.F.R. Part 5, subpart I; Part 960, subpart B; Part 966, subpart A; Part 982, subpart L.

321. U.S. Department of Housing and Urban Development, Notice PIH 2015–19 (Nov. 2, 2015), Guidance for Public Housing Agencies (PHAs) and Owners of Federally-Assisted Housing on Excluding the Use of Arrest Records in Housing Decisions, https://www.hud.gov/sites/documents/PIH2015-19.PDF.

322. *See* 34 U.S.C. § 12491. The Violence Against Women Act 2013 covers these HUD assisted-housing units: Public Housing, Section 8 Housing Choice Voucher programs; Section 8 project-based housing; Section 202 housing for the elderly; Section 811 housing for people with disabilities; Section 236 multifamily rental housing; Section 221(d)(3) BMIR housing; HOME; Housing Opportunities for People with AIDS; and McKinney-Vento Act homeless assistance programs. It also covers housing subsidized under the Low-Income Housing Tax Credit program administered by the Department of Treasury and Rural Development multifamily housing programs administered by the Department of Agriculture. *See* 34 U.S.C.A. §§ 12491(a)(3).

323. *See* Department of Justice, Office on Violence Against Women (OVW) VAWA 2013 Summary: Changes to OVW-Administered Grant Programs, https://www.justice.gov/sites/default/files/ovw/legacy/2014/06/16/VAWA-2013-grant-programs-summary.pdf.

324. *See* 24 C.F.R. § 966.4(e)(9) (public housing); U.S. Department of Housing and Urban Development, Notice H 2017-05, Violence Against Women Act (VAWA) Reauthorization Act of 2013—Additional Guidance for Multifamily Owners and Management Agents (June 30, 2017), https://www.hud.gov/sites/documents/17-05HSGN.PDF. *See also* Karlo Ng, Renee Williams, Sandra Park, & Kate Walz, HUD's Final Rule Implementing VAWA 2013, National Housing Law Project, Women's Rights Project, ACLU, & Shriver Center on Poverty Law (Mar. 1, 2017), nhlp.org/.../0%2017.3.1%20NHLP%20&%20Shriver%20HUD%20Final%20VAWA.

325. Annamarya Scaccia, Federal Agency Issues Guidance Shielding Abuse Survivors from Eviction for Calling Police, Rewire (Sept. 14, 2016), https://rewire.news/article/2016/09/14/federal-agency-issues-guidance-shielding-abuse-survivors-eviction-calling-police/.

326. U.S. Department of Housing and Urban Development, Office of General Counsel Guidance on Application of Fair Housing Act Standards to the Enforcement of Local Nuisance and Crime-Free Housing Ordinances Against Victims of Domestic Violence, Other Crime Victims, and Others Who Require Police of Emergency Services (Sept. 13, 2016), https://www.hud.gov/sites/documents/FINALNUISANCEORDGDNCE.PDF.

327. A "guest" for this purpose is defined as "a person temporarily staying in the unit with the consent of a tenant or other member of the household who has express or implied authority to so consent on behalf of the tenant." 24 C.F.R. § 5.100.

328. 24 C.F.R. § 966.4(d)(1). Courts have affirmed the constitutional right of a Public Housing tenant to host guests. *See, for example*, McKenna v. Peekskill Housing Authority, 647 F.2d 332 (2d Cir. 1981) (holding that a guest who stayed two or three nights was not subject to the guest-registry requirement). *See also* Norwich Housing Authority v. Majewski, 2000 WL 73034 (Conn. Super. Ct. 2000) (holding that a lease provision requiring tenants to register guests who would be present for a week with the PHA did not unconstitutionally chill tenants' rights to privacy and free association).

329. HUD Housing Programs § 3.2.8.

330. Public Housing lease regulations require a tenant to secure permission from the PHA before adding a new member to the lease. *See* 24 C.F.R. § 966.4(a)(1)(v).

331. HUD Housing Programs § 11.2.2.3, citing HUD Handbook 4350.3, ¶ 8-13.

332. Federal regulations require the lease for Public Housing to "set forth the circumstances under which the PHA may enter the dwelling unit during the tenant's possession." 24 C.F.R. § 966.4(j).

333. HUD Housing Programs § 3.2.6.

334. U.S. Department of Housing and Urban Development, Model Lease for Subsidized Programs, Form HUD-90105-A (12/207), ref. HUD Handbook 4350.3 REV-1, https://www.hud.gov/sites/dfiles/OCHCO/documents/90105a.pdf.

335. *See* 24 C.F.R. § 966.4(j) (public housing lease regulations).

336. *See* Suzy Khimm, Laura Strickler, Hannah Rappleye, & Stephanie Gosk, Under Ben Carson, more families live in HUD housing that fails health and safety inspections, MSNBC (Nov. 14, 2018), https://www.nbcnews.com/politics/white-house/under-ben-carson-more-families-live-hud-housing-fails-health-n935421.

337. *See* U.S. Department of Housing and Urban Development, Section 504: Frequently Asked Questions, hud.gov, https://www.hud.gov/program_offices/fair_housing_equal_opp/disabilities/sect504faq.

338. *See* 24 C.F.R. § 966.4(a)(2)(i)–(ii).

339. *See* 24 C.F.R. § 966.4(l)(2)(iii). For a discussion of the availability of good cause in the Voucher program after the lease term has ended, *see* HUD Housing Programs § 11.2.2.3.

340. 42 U.S.C. § 1437a(b)(3)(A); 24 C.F.R. §§ 982.4, 5.403(2)(vi) ("family" defined to include "remaining member of a tenant family") (public housing). *See* 42 U.S.C. § 1437d(k); 24 C.F.R. § 966.53(f)(2) (grievance hearing). *See also* HUD Handbook 4350.3 ¶ 3-16 B(1) (multifamily program).

341. 42 U.S.C. § 1437a(b)(3)(A).

342. 42 U.S.C. § 1437d(k); 24 C.F.R. § 966.53(f)(2).

343. 24 C.F.R. § 5.403 (defining "family" for Section 8 purposes).

344. 24 C.F.R. §§ 982.54(d)(11).

345. HUD Housing Programs § 2.2.3.13; 11.2.4.5. *See, for example*, Findlay Teller Housing Development Fund Corp. v. Chevere, 29 Misc. 3d, 958 N.Y.S.2d 307 (Civ. Ct. Bronx Co.).

346. *See* HUD Housing Programs, § 2.2.3.13 (remaining family member); § 3.4.2 (public housing).

347. *See, for example*, 24 C.F.R. §§ 247.6(a), (c); 982.310(f).

348. *See, for example*, Leake v. Ellicott Redevelopment Phase II, 470 F. Supp. 600 (W.D.N.Y. 1979).

349. 42 U.S.C. § 1437d(k)(l).

350. *See, for example*, Homestead Equities, Inc. v. Washington, 672 N.Y.S.2d 980 (N.Y. Civ. Ct. 1998).

351. 42 U.S.C. § 1437d(l)(4).

352. 24 C.F.R. § 966.4(l)(3).

353. 24 C.F.R. §§ 966.4(l)(3)(ii), (l)(3)(iv), (m), 966.54.

354. HUD Handbook 4350.3, ¶ 8-13 B 2 & 3 & app. 4-A; 24 C.F.R. §§ 247.3–6. Part 247 regulations do not apply to Section 8 new construction, Section 8 substantial rehabilitation, Section 8 through state housing agencies, and Section 8 new construction set aside for Section 515 rural housing. However, many of its requirements are included in the model lease used in these other programs. See HUD Housing Programs § 11.3.3.2.2.

355. 42 U.S.C. § 1437f(o)(7)(E); 24 C.F.R. § 982.310. Even if state law does not provide for notice prior to eviction, federal law creates a right to such notice. *See* 42 U.S.C. §§ 1437f(d)(1)(B)(iv), (o)(7)(E).

356. 42 U.S.C. § 1437d(l)(4)(A); 24 C.F.R. § 966.4(l)(3)(i)(B).

357. 42 U.S.C. § 1437d(l)(4)(C); 24 C.F.R. § 966.4(l)(3)(i)(C).

358. 24 C.F.R. § 966.4(k)(1)(i).

359. 24 C.F.R. § 247.4(c).

360. 24 C.F.R. § 247.4(c).

361. 24 C.F.R. § 247.4(b).

362. 42 U.S.C. § 1437f(o)(7)(E); 24 C.F.R. § 982.310(e).

363. *See* Samuels v. District of Columbia, 770 F.2d 184, 191 n.1 (D.C. Cir. 1986), on remand, 650 F. Supp. 482 (D.D.C. 1986).

364. 42 U.S.C. § 1437d(k)(1)–(6); 24 C.F.R. §§ 966.53, 966.56. *See* U.S. Department of Housing and Urban Development, Streamlining Administrative Regulations for Public Housing, Housing Choice Voucher, Multifamily Housing, and Community Planning and Development Programs, 81 Fed. Reg.12374 (Mar. 8, 2016).

365. 24 C.F.R. §§ 966.53, 966.56.

366. 24 C.F.R. § 966.51(b).

367. 42 U.S.C. § 1437d(k).

368. 42 U.S.C. § 1437d(k); 24 C.F.R. § 966.51(a)(2). *See* U.S. Housing and Urban Development, Public Housing Lease and Grievance Procedures; Notice of HUD Due Process Determinations, 61 Fed. Reg. 13,276 (Mar. 26, 1996); Public Housing Lease and Grievance Procedures; Notice of HUD Due Process Determinations, 61 Fed. Reg. 47,953 (Sept. 11, 1996); Public Housing Lease and Grievance Procedures; Notice of HUD Due Process Determinations, 62 Fed. Reg. 45, 434 (Aug. 27, 1997).

369. 24 C.F.R. § 966.4(l)(3)(v).

370. Cranston-Gonzalez National Affordable Housing Act, Pub. L. No. 101-625, § 503, 104 Stat. 4079, 4184 (1990), codified as amended at 42 U.S.C. § 1437d(k) (allowing "expedited grievance procedure" or no grievance procedure upon due process determination in drug-related criminal activity eviction cases); Quality Housing and Work Responsibility Act, Pub. L. No. 105-276, § 575, 112 Stat. 2261, 2634 (1998), codified as amended at 42 U.S.C. § 1437d(k) (expanding the exception to the mandatory grievance procedures to include tenants involved in "violent" criminal activity and "any activity resulting in a felony conviction").

371. 24 C.F.R. § 966.54.

372. One federal court held that a tenant filing a grievance in a noneviction situation must have a year to file the complaint. Samuels v. District of Columbia, 669 F. Supp. 1133, 1141 (D.D.C. 1987), on remand, 650 F. Supp. 482 (D.D.C. 1986).

373. 24 C.F.R. § 966.54.

374. 24 C.F.R. § 966.56(b).

375. 24 C.F.R. § 966.57(c).

376. 24 C.F.R. § 966.57(b).

377. The authority for most demolition is based on 42 U.S.C. §1437p, as amended by the Quality Housing and Work Responsibility Act of 1998, Pub. L. No. 105-276, Tit. V, §531, 112 Stat. 2461, 2570 (Oct. 21, 1998). Regulations governing the requirements for demolition projects were amended in 2006. *See* U.S. Housing and Urban Development, 71 Fed. Reg. 62,354, 62,362 (Oct. 24, 2006) (creating a revised 24 C.F.R. Part 970).

378. HUD Housing Programs § 12.2.

379. *See* Ryan D. Enos, What the Demolition of Public Housing Teaches Us about the Impact of Racial Threat on Political Behavior, 60 Am. J. Pol. Sci. 123 (2015), https://scholar.harvard.edu/files/renos/files/enoschicago.pdf.

380. U.S. Department of Housing and Urban Development, Demolition and/or disposition of public housing property, eligibility for tenant-protection vouchers and associated requirements, Notice PIH 2018-04 (Mar. 22, 2018; revised July 3, 2018 and Dec. 14, 2018); *see* 24 C.F.R. § 970.9(a) (consultation with affected residents, resident organizations, and the Resident Advisory Board).

381. 24 C.F.R. § 970.21(a). *See* HUD Issues Final Rule for the Demolition or Disposition of Public Housing, 36 Housing L. Bulletin 226, https://nhlp.org/files/10%20NHLP%20Bull%20Dec.%202006%20final_HUD%20final%20rule%20dispo%20demo.pdf.

382. *See* Housing and Community Development Act, 42 U.S.C. § 5304(d)(2). *But see* Darst-Webbe Tenant Association Board v. St. Louis Housing Authority, 339 F.3d 702 (8th Cir. 2003) (holding that the one-to-one replacement requirement would run counter to the congressional goal of reducing residential density). For a discussion of litigation concerning demolition, *see* John N. Robinson III, Welfare as Wrecking Ball: Constructing Public Responsibility in Legal Encounters over Public Housing Demolition, 42 Law & Soc. Inquiry 670 (2016).

383. 24 C.F.R. § 970.9(c).

384. RAD initially authorized conversion of 60,000 units, which was then expanded to 185,000 units, which was then expanded again in 2017 to 225,000. *See* Consolidated and Further Continuing Appropriations Act, 2015, Pub. L. No. 113-235, § 234, 128 Stat. 2130, 2757. HUD requires PHAs to submit a RAD application and fulfill certain criteria before the property can officially convert under RAD. HUD has announced its intention to convert all Public Housing to the Section 8 model through RAD. *See* U.S. Department of Housing and Urban Development, Remarks of Secretary Julián Castro, Bipartisan Policy Center 2014 Housing Summit (Sept. 16, 2014), http://portal.hud.gov/hudportal/HUD?src=/press/speeches_remarks_statements/2014/Speech_091614.

For criticisms of the RAD program, *see* Peter Schroeder, House Dem Questions WH Public Housing Relief Program, The Hill (Dec. 15, 2014), http://thehill.com/policy/finance/227143-house-dem-questions-wh-public-housing-relief-program. *See also* Jaime Alison Lee, Rights at Risk in Privatized Public Housing, 50 Tulsa L. Rev. 759 (2015).

385. RAD conversions allow Public Housing properties to convert to either Project-Based Vouchers or Project-Based Rental Assistance. *See* Consolidated and Further Continuing Appropriations Act, 2015, Pub. L. No. 113-235, § 234, 128 Stat. 2130, 2757.

386. *See* Andrew Balashov, Private Investment: Trojan-Horse or Shining Knight for America's Public Housing Stock, 4 U. Balt. J. Land & Devel. 165 (2015); Anne Marie Smetak, Private Funding, Public Housing: The Devil in the Details, 21 Va. J. Soc. Pol'y & L. 1 (2014).

387. *See* U.S. Government Accountability Office, Rental Assistance Demonstration: HUD Needs to Take Action to Improve Metrics and Ongoing Oversight (Feb. 2018), https://www.gao.gov/assets/700/690210.pdf. *See also* Danielle McLean, Trump's HUD wants to expand flawed program that is "privatizing public housing," Think Progress (Feb. 27, 2019), https://thinkprogress.org/a-flawed-public-housing-program-leaves-vulnerable-residents-at-the-mercy-of-developers-66a0ee5b2321/.

388. *See* National Housing Law Project, Don't Get RAD-dled: 30 Minute Trainings for Tenant Advocates on What You Need to Know about the Rental Assistance Demonstration (RAD), https://www.nhlp.org/webinars/dont-get-rad-dled-30-minute-trainings-tenant-advocates-need-know-rental-assistance-demonstration-rad/.

389. *See* National Housing Law Project, Rental Assistance Demonstration (RAD) (Sept. 7, 2017), https://www.nhlp.org/resources/rental-assistance-demonstration-rad/.

390. For a description of the process in New York City, *see* Community Service Society, Enterprise Community Partners, Inc. & The Legal Aid Society, Resident Handbook: A Guide to NYCHA RAD Conversion (Mar. 2018), https://www.cssny.org/publications/entry/resident-handbook-a-guide-to-nycha-rad-conversion.

391. *See* Rachel M. Cohen, The Hopes and Fears around Ben Carson's Favorite Public Housing Program, CityLab (Apr. 21, 2017), https://www.citylab.com/equity/2017/04/the-hopes-and-fears-around-ben-carsons-favorite-public-housing-program/523926/; Ed Gramlich, Resident Participation in Federally Subsidized Housing, in Advocates Guide 2018: A Primer on Federal Affordable Housing & Community Development Programs, National Low Income Housing Coalition, ¶ 2–44, https://nlihc.org/sites/default/files/AG-2018/2018_Advocates-Guide.pdf.

392. *See* Kaitlin J. Brown, A Dangerous Disappearing Act: Preserving Affordable Housing in the Face of Maturing Mortgages, 35 B.C. J.L. & Soc. Just. 59 (2015).

393. *See* U.S. Department of Housing and Urban Development, Notice PIH 2018-02, Funding Availability for Set-Aside Tenant-Protection Vouchers—Fiscal Year 2017 Funding (Feb. 8, 2018), https://www.hud.gov/sites/dfiles/OCHCO/documents/18-01hsgn.pdf; Jessica Cassella, Understanding HUD Mortgage Prepayments and Maturities, National Housing Law Project (May 3, 2018), https://www.nhlp.org/wp-content/uploads/2018/05/Saving-HUD-Homes-4-FINAL.pdf.

394. 42 U.S.C. § 1437f(t). HUD has notified PHAs that families receiving enhanced vouchers may not live in units with more bedrooms than the appropriate occupancy standards warrant. As a result, a family having fewer members than the occupancy standard for the family's current unit, under most circumstances, will have to move to a different unit within the converted project in order to receive the enhanced voucher. *See* U.S. Department of Housing and Urban Development, Enhanced Voucher Requirements for Over-housed Families, PIH-2016-02 (HA (Mar. 4, 2016).

395. Pub. L. No. 105-276, § 219(b), 112 Stat. 2487 (Oct. 21, 1998). State laws may require additional notice to tenants and other stakeholders.

396. 42 U.S.C. 1437f(c)(8).

397. *See generally* U.S. Housing and Urban Development, Office of Policy Development and Research, What Happens to LIHTC Properties After Affordability Requirements

Expire?, Edge https://www.huduser.gov/portal/pdredge/pdr_edge_research_
081712.html.

398. *See* 24 C.F.R. § 401.480; Ellen Lurie Hoffman, Project Based Rental Assistance, National Low Income Housing Coalition (2017), https://nlihc.org/sites/default/files/AG-2017/2017AG_Ch04-S06_Project-Based-Rental-Assistance.pdf.

399. *See* National Low Income Housing Coalition, Congress Permanently Authorizes the Protecting Tenants at Foreclosure Act (Apr. 30, 2019). In 2009, in response to the financial crisis, Congress enacted Helping Families Save Their Homes Act of 2009, Pub. L. No. 111-22, §§ 701–704, 123 Stat. 1632, 1660–62 (2009) to assist the great number of tenants being dispossessed by foreclosure. *See* Kathryn L.S. Pettit & Jennifer Comey, The Foreclosure Crisis and Children: A Three-City Study, Urban Institute (Mar. 1, 2012), http://www.urban.org/research/publication/foreclosure-crisis-and-children-three-city-study; Tony S. Guo, Tenants at Foreclosure: Mitigating Harm to Innocent Victims of the Foreclosure Crisis, 4 DePaul J. for Soc. Just. 215 (2011). State and local laws also offer some protections for tenants at foreclosure. *See* Elayne Weiss, Protecting Tenants at Foreclosure, National Low Income Housing Coalition, https://nlihc.org/sites/default/files/AG-2018/Ch06-S05_PTFA_2018.pdf; National Housing Law Project, Tenants at Foreclosure, https://www.nhlp.org/initiatives/foreclosure-and-tenants/. Conversely, some state laws that would have harmed tenants, by providing landlords with a way to terminate Section 8 tenancies after foreclosure, are preempted by federal law. *See, for example*, German v. Federal Home Loan Mortgage Corp., 899 F. Supp. 1155, 1162–63 (S.D.N.Y. 1995); *see also* U.S. Department of Housing and Urban Development, Protecting Tenants at Foreclosure: Notice of Responsibilities Placed on Immediate Successors in Interest Pursuant to Foreclosure of Residential Property, 74 Fed. Reg. 30106 (June 24, 2009).

400. *See* Consumer Financial Protection Bureau, What Is a Mortgage?, https://www.consumerfinance.gov/ask-cfpb/what-is-a-mortgage-en-99/. For more information about mortgages, *see* the excellent materials published by the National Consumer Law Center: Mortgage Servicing and Loan Modifications and Home Foreclosures, https://library.nclc.org/forc.

401. The U.S. Supreme Court has granted certiorari on whether entities engaged in non-judicial foreclosure proceedings are debt collectors under the Fair Debt Collection Act. *See* Obduskey v. Wells Fargo, 879 F.3d 1216 (10th Cir. 2018), cert. granted, 138 S. Ct. 2710 (2018).

402. John Rao, Odette Williamson, Tara Twomey, & Geoff Walsh, with contributions by Andrew G. Pizor, Foreclosures: Defenses, Workouts, and Mortgage Servicing § 14.7.2.1, National Consumer Law Center (3d ed. 2010) [hereinafter Rao].

403. *See, for example*, Citizens Bank & Trust v. Bros. Constr. & Mfg., Inc., 859 P.2d 394 (Kan. Ct. App. 1993); Metro. Life Ins. Co. v. Childs Co., 130 N.E. 295 (N.Y. 1921); Tappin v. Homecomings Fin. Network, Inc., 830 A.2d 711 (Conn. 2003).

404. *See* Rao, at § 14.7.2.1.

405. 1 Milton R. Friedman & James Charles Smith, Friedman on Contracts and Conveyances of Real Property § 8.1.1 (Practicing Laws Institute 7th ed. 2007).

406. The program is authorized by the Quality Housing and Work Responsibility Act and implemented through Section 32 of the Housing Act of 1937, Pub. L. No. 105-276, Tit. V, § 536, 112 Stat. 2461, 2586 (1998) (codified at 42 U.S.C. § 1437z-4). Implementing regulations are located at 24 C.F.R. Part 906 (2012). *See also* U.S. Department of Housing and Urban Development, Guidance for PHAs Developing a Section 32 Homeownership Plan (2003), http://portal.hud.gov/hudportal/documents/huddoc?id=DOC_8104.pdf.

407. 24 C.F.R. § 906.13.

408. 24 C.F.R. § 906.5.

409. The program is implemented by the Quality Housing and Work Responsibility Act, Pub. L. No. 105-276, Tit. V, § 555, 112 Stat. 2461, 2611–13 (1998) (codified as amended at 42 U.S.C. § 1437f(y)). Implementing regulations are located at 24 C.F.R. §§ 982.635–643. *See* U.S. Department of Housing and Urban Development, Voucher Homeownership Program Overview, https://www.hud.gov/sites/documents/22061_voucherprgm0405.pdf. HUD's Housing Choice Voucher Homeownership Program Guidebook can be accessed at https://www.hud.gov/program_offices/public_indian_housing/programs/hcv/homeownership.

410. U.S. Department of Housing and Urban Development, HCV Homeownership Enrollments, CY 2013–CY2017.

411. *See* U.S. Housing and Urban Development, Statement of Homeowner Obligations Housing Choice Homeownership Voucher Program (Apr. 30, 2018), https://www.hud.gov/program_offices/public_indian_housing/programs/hcv/homeownership.

412. 42 U.S.C. § 604(h)(2)(B).

413. Congress established the program in 1990 as part of the Cranston-Gonzalez National Affordable Housing Act, Pub. L. No. 101-625, Tit. V, § 554(a), 104 Stat. 4079, 4225 (1990) (codified as amended at 42 U.S.C. § 1437u). *See* U.S. Housing and Urban Development, Family Self-Sufficiency (FSS) Program, https://portal.hud.gov/hudportal/HUD?src=/program_offices/public_indian_housing/programs/hcv/fss. In 2017, Congress permanently authorized FSS for project-based rental assistance properties. *See* Economic Growth, Regulatory Relief, and Consumer Protection Act, Pub. L. No. 115-174, § 306, 132 Stat. 1296 (May 24, 2018), amending 42 U.S.C. § 1437u.

414. 42 U.S.C. § 1437u(b)(5).

415. 42 U.S.C. § 1437u(b)(2).

416. *See* Upward Mobility in the Family Self-Sufficiency Program: An Expert Q&A, How Housing Matters (May 31, 2018), https://howhousingmatters.org/articles/upward-mobility-family-self-sufficiency-program-expert-qa/.

417. *See* U.S. Department of Housing and Urban Development, Evaluation of the Family Self-Sufficiency Program: Prospective Study (2011), http://www.huduser.org/Publications/pdf/FamilySelfSufficiency.pdf; *see also* Barbara Sard & Jeff Lubell, The Family Self-Sufficiency Program: HUD's Best Kept Secret for Promoting Employment and Asset Growth, Center for Budget and Policy Priorities 13–18 (2001), http://www.cbpp.org/files/4-12-01hous.pdf.

418. The CRA was enacted as Title VIII of the Housing and Community Development Act of 1977, Community Reinvestment Act of 1977, Pub. L. No. 95-128, 91 Stat. 1111 (1977).

419. 12 U.S.C. § 2901(a)(1).

420. U.S. Commission on Civil Rights Report (1961), 30 http://www.law.umaryland. edu/marshall/usccr/documents/cr11961bk4.pdf. *See* Speech by Chairman Ben S. Bernanke, The Community Reinvestment Act: Its Evolutions and New Challenges (Washington, D.C., 2007), citing William Apgar and Mark Duda, The Twenty-fifth Anniversary of the Community Reinvestment Act: Past Accomplishments and Future Regulatory Challenges, 9 FRBNY Economic Policy Review 169 (June 2003), https://www.federalreserve.gov/newsevents/speech/Bernanke20070330a.htm.

421. *See* Oral Statement of Mark A. Willis, Before the Joint Public Hearing on the Community Reinvestment Act Regulation, Federal Reserve Bank of San Francisco, 2–3 (Aug. 17, 2010), http://furmancenter.org/files/testimonies/Willis_CRA_Oral_ Testimony_082510.pdf. There is some support for the view that the CRA was effective in encouraging banks to serve lower- to middle-income individuals, create complex affordable housing structures, and contribute to the growth of new government programs. However, some studies suggest that while overall loans to low- and middle-income households increased since the CRA, many of those loans fell outside the parameters of the act and so the act cannot be said to be responsible for the increase in low-income household loans. *See, for example*, Federal Reserve Bank, Elizabeth Laderman & Carolina Reid, CRA Lending During the Subprime Meltdown, in Revisiting the CRA: Perspectives on the Future of the Community Reinvestment Act, A Joint Publication of the Federal Reserve Banks of Boston and San Francisco (2009), http://www.frbsf.org/community-development/files/cra_ lending_during_subprime_meltdown11.pdf. Following the subprime mortgage crisis, critics argued that the CRA contributed to the housing bubble by encouraging banks to make loans to low-income households, who later defaulted. *See* John Carney, Here's How the Community Reinvestment Act Led to the Housing Bubble's Lax Lending (June 27, 2009), http://articles.businessinsider.com/2009-06-27/ wall_street/30009234_1_mortgage-standards-lending-standards-mortgage-rates; Chandra Mishra, The Professor: Yes, Community Reinvestment Act to blame for mortgage crisis (Oct. 14, 2011), http://articles.sun-sentinel.com/2011-10-14/news/ fl-cmcol-cra-failure-mishra-1014-20111014_1_soundness-act-fannie-mae-fannie- and-freddie; Yaaron Brook, The Government Did It (July 18, 2008), http://www. forbes.com/2008/07/18/fannie-freddie-regulation-oped-cx_yb_0718brook.html. However, a leading empirical study rebuts this critical view of the CRA's causative effect on the subprime mortgage crisis. In particular, a study conducted by Glenn Canner and Neil Bhutta at the Board of Governors of the Federal Reserve System found that most subprime mortgage loans were not covered by the CRA. Instead, the CRA accounted for "about half of all subprime originations." Furthermore, "about 60 percent of higher-priced loan originations went to middle- or higher- income borrowers or neighborhoods, populations not targeted by the CRA." Neil

Bhutta, Did the CRA cause the mortgage market meltdown? (Mar. 1, 2009), http://www.minneapolisfed.org/publications_papers/pub_display.cfm?id=4136.

422. *See* Consumer Financial Protection Bureau, Home Mortgage Disclosure (Regulation C), 80 Fed. Reg. 66128 (Oct. 28, 2015), https://www.consumerfinance.gov/data-research/hmda/; *see also* Consumer Financial Protection Bureau, Technical Corrections and Clarifying Amendments to the Home Mortgage Disclosure (Regulation C) October 2015 Final Rule, 82 Fed. Reg. 19142 (Apr. 25, 2017).

423. The CFPB issued final policy guidance that it would modify the HMDA loan data by excluding several data fields—including the credit score(s) relied on in making the loan decision and the principal reason(s) the financial institution denied the loan application—and by "reduc[ing] the precision of most of the values reported" for certain data fields. Consumer Financial Protection Bureau, Home Mortgage Disclosure (Regulation C) Adjustment to Asset-Size Exemption Threshold, 84 Fed. Reg. 649 (Jan. 31, 2019).

424. The Economic Growth, Regulatory Relief, and Consumer Protection Act, enacted in May 2018, amended the HMDA by partially exempting certain depository institutions and credit unions from its data reporting requirements. *See* Pub. L. No. 115-174, §104(a), 132 Stat. 1296 (2018), codified at 12 U.S.C. § 2803. The CFPB issued interpretive guidance clarifying the scope of these exemptions. *See* Consumer Financial Protection Bureau, Partial Exemptions from the Requirements of the Home Mortgage Disclosure Act Under the Economic Growth, Regulatory Relief, and Consumer Protection Act (Regulation C), 83 Fed. Reg. 45325 (Sept. 7, 2018).

425. *See* Amanda Abrams, Why Have Banks Stopped Lending to Low-Income Americans?, Talk Poverty (Dec. 5, 2017), https://talkpoverty.org/2017/12/05/banks-stopped-lending-low-income-americans/. *See generally* Urban Institute, Ten Years after the Crash, https://www.urban.org/features/ten-years-after-crash.

426. *See* The Tax Cuts and Jobs Act, Pub. L. No. 115-97, 131 Stat. 2054 (Dec. 2017).

427. *See* Conor Dougherty, Tax Overhaul Is a Blow to Affordable Housing Efforts, N.Y. Times (Jan. 18, 2018), https://www.nytimes.com/2018/01/18/business/economy/tax-housing.html.

428. *See* Michael Novogradac, Scott Keller, Peter Lawrence, & Mark Shelburne, Tax Reform and Its Consequences for Affordable Rental Housing, 27 J. Affordable Housing & Community Dev. L. 107 (2018) (citing Michael Novogradac, Final Tax Reform Bill Would Reduce Affordable Rental Housing by Nearly 235,000 Homes, Tax Reform Resource Center (Dec. 19, 2017), https://www.novoco.com/notes-from-novogradac/final-tax-reform-bill-would-reduce-affordable-rental-housing-production-nearly-235000-homes).

429. *See* Dina El Bogdady, How the New U.S. Tax Law Affects Community Development Projects, Urbanland (June 4, 2018), https://urbanland.uli.org/capital-markets/new-u-s-tax-law-affects-community-development-projects/; Community Development Tax Credits: Damaged, but not Devastated, Novogradac (Jan. 2, 2018), https://www.novoco.com/periodicals/articles/community-development-tax-credits-damaged-not-devastated. For background on the Community Development Corporation tax credit, *see* Carol Steinbach, The CDC Tax Credit: An Effective Tool for Attracting Private Resources to Community Economic Development, Brookings (Aug. 1, 1998),

https://www.brookings.edu/research/the-cdc-tax-credit-an-effective-tool-for-attracting-private-resources-to-community-economic-development/. *See* Matthew Goldstein & Jim Tankersley, Wall Street, Seeking Big Tax Breaks, Sets Sights on Distressed Main Streets, N.Y. Times (Feb. 20, 2019), https://www.nytimes.com/2019/02/20/business/taxes-hedge-funds-investors-opportunity-funds.html (reporting that "[t]he flood of capital is raising hopes as well as concerns," and that some impact investors are working with philanthropists trying "to establish accountability standards for the funds that the government does not yet require, to address issues like the quality of jobs created in poor areas").

430. *See* 2017 Tax Legislation Creates New Tool For Community Development, Novogradac (Feb. 1, 2018), https://www.novoco.com/periodicals/articles/2017-tax-legislation-creates-new-tool-community-development. *See also* Ann Carrns, "Opportunity Zones" Offer Tax Breaks and, Maybe, Help for Communities, N.Y. Times (Feb. 15, 2019), https://www.nytimes.com/2019/02/15/business/opportunity-zone-tax-break-controversy.html; Brett Theodos, A Little-Publicized Incentive in the New Tax Law Could Become America's Largest Economic Development Program, Tax Policy Center (Urban Institute & Brookings Institution) (Mar. 27, 2018), https://www.taxpolicycenter.org/taxvox/little-publicized-incentive-new-tax-law-could-become-americas-largest-economic-development.

431. *See, for example*, 42 U.S.C. § 254b(h)(5)(A). The statute defines homeless individual as "an individual who lacks housing (without regard to whether the individual is a member of a family), including an individual whose primary residence during the night is a supervised public or private facility that provides temporary living accommodations and an individual who is a resident in transitional housing." *Id. See* Congressional Research Service, Libby Perl, Erin Bagalman, Adrienne L. Fernandes-Alcantara, Elayne McCallion, Francis X. McCarthy, & Lisa N. Sacco, Homelessness: Targeted Federal Programs and Recent Legislation (May 6, 2015), https://fas.org/sgp/crs/misc/RL30442.pdf. HUD's Annual Homeless Assessment Report to Congress used the term homeless to describe "a person who lacks a fixed, regular, and adequate nighttime residence." *See* U.S. Department of Housing and Urban Development, The 2016 Annual Homeless Assessment Report, https://www.hudexchange.info/resources/documents/2016-AHAR-Part-1.pdf. The 2016 Report reported that 549,928 persons experienced homelessness on a single night in 2016. This number marked a 23% decline in homelessness among families, and a 27% among individuals, since 2010, when the Obama administration instituted new initiatives to deal with the problem of lacking a place to live.

432. 42 U.S.C. § 11302(a)(2).

433. *See* 24 C.F.R. § 578.3.

434. U.S. Department of Housing and Urban Development, Homeless Emergency Assistance and Rapid Transition to Housing: Defining "Chronically Homeless," 89 Fed. Reg. 75791 (Dec. 4, 2015); regulations are available at 24 C.F.R. Parts 91 and 578.

435. 42 U.S.C. § 11434a(2). The statute defines homeless children and youth as individuals "who lack a fixed, regular, and adequate nighttime residence" and includes:

- children and youths who are sharing the housing of other persons due to loss of housing, economic hardship, or a similar reason;

- are living in motels, hotels, trailer parks, or camping grounds due to the lack of alternative adequate accommodations;
- are living in emergency or transitional shelters;
- or are abandoned in hospitals;
- children and youths who have a primary nighttime residence that is a public or private place not designed for or ordinarily used as a regular sleeping accommodation for human beings . . . ;
- children and youths who are living in cars, parks, public spaces, abandoned buildings, substandard housing, bus or train stations, or similar settings;
- and migratory children . . . who qualify as homeless for the purposes of this part because the children are living in circumstances described [above].

436. 34 U.S.C. § 12473(6). The statute defines homeless as an individual "who lacks a fixed, regular, and adequate nighttime residence," and includes:

  (i) an individual who:
    (I) is sharing the housing of other persons due to loss of housing, economic hardship, or a similar reason;
    (II) is living in a motel, hotel, trailer park, or campground due to the lack of alternative adequate accommodations;
    (III) is living in an emergency or transitional shelter;
    (IV) is abandoned in a hospital; or
    (V) is awaiting foster care placement;
  (ii) an individual who has a primary nighttime residence that is a public or private place not designed for or ordinarily used as a regular sleeping accommodation for human beings; or
  (iii) migratory children . . . who qualify as homeless . . . because the children are living in circumstances described in this paragraph.

437. Prevent Mortgage Foreclosures and Enhance Mortgage Credit Availability, Pub. L. No. 111-22, Div. B, §§ 1002, 1301, 123 Stat. 1664 (May 20, 2009), codified at 42 U.S.C. § 11301. For more information about CoC grants, see U.S. Department of Housing and Urban Development, FY 2018 CoC Competition Grants, https://www.hudexchange.info/programs/coc/awards/.

See U.S. Department of Housing and Urban Development, HUD Exchange: HUD Awards and Allocations, https://www.hudexchange.info/grantees/allocations-awa rds/?params=%7B%22limit%22%3A20%2C%22COC%22%3Afalse%2C%22sort% 22%3A%22%22%2C%22min%22%3A%22%22%2C%22years%22%3A%5B%5D% 2C%22dir%22%3A%22%22%2C%22grantees%22%3A%5B%5D%2C%22state%22 %3A%22%22%2C%22programs%22%3A%5B6%5D%2C%22max%22%3A%22%2 2%2C%22searchTerm%22%3A%22%22%7D##granteeSearch

438. To find services, see U.S. Department of Housing and Urban Development, Homeless Services, http://resources.hud.gov/.

Special rules, discussed elsewhere in this volume, deal with access to food assistance, educational assistance, and medical care.

The U.S. Department of Agriculture has special rules to facilitate participation in the Supplemental Nutrition Assistance Program.

The Federal Emergency Management Agency administers the Emergency Food and Shelter Program, which provides funds to local jurisdictions, usually counties, for food, utilities, and shelter for homeless individuals and families in emergency situations, with funds disbursed according to a formula based on unemployment and poverty rates within a locality. *See* 42 U.S.C. §§ 11331–52.

The U.S. Department of Health and Human Services provides special grants to states and localities for outpatient medical facilities for homeless people, *see* Health Care for the Homeless, permanently authorized under the Patient Protection and Affordable Care Act, 42 U.S.C. §§ 18001 et seq.; to provide services to youth; and to victims of domestic abuse. *See* Traditional Housing Assistance for Victims of Domestic Violence, Stalking, or Sexual Assault, authorized by the Prosecutorial Remedies and Other Tools to End the Exploitation of Children Today Act of 2003, Pub. L. No. 108-21, 117 Stat. 650 (Apr. 30, 2003).

The U.S. Department of Veterans Affairs administers programs for veterans who are homeless. Programs include:

- Health Care for Homeless Veterans, Pub. L. No. 100-6, § 2, 101 Stat. 92 (1987);
- Grant and Per Diem Program, 38 U.S.C. §§ 2011–13;
- Domiciliary Care for Homeless Veterans Program, 28 U.S.C. § 2043;
- Compensated Work Therapy program, permanently authorized by the VA Special Therapeutic and Rehabilitation Activities Fund, 38 U.S.C. § 1718(c) (including a Therapeutic Transitional Housing component, codified by the Veterans Health Care Facilities Capital Improvement Act of 2011, 38 U.S.C. § 2031); and
- Supportive Services for Very Low-Income Veterans and their Families, 38 U.S.C. § 2044, authorized by the Veterans' Mental Health and Other Care Improvements Act of 2008, Pub. L. No. 110-387, 122 Stat. 4110 (Oct. 10, 2008).

Some of these programs are managed in collaboration with HUD. For example, through the HUD-VA Supported Housing Program, HUD provides Section 8 housing vouchers to homeless veterans, while the VA offers supportive services. The vouchers are allocated on a competitive basis to public housing authorities based on geographic need, administrative performance, and other factors. Some vouchers are project-based, which means they are designated to a specific unit of housing and do not move with the tenant. However, if a tenant lives in a project-based unit and wants to move, the public housing authority must provide the tenant with another voucher.

439. *See* U.S. Interagency Council of Homelessness, Opening Doors: Federal Strategic Plan to Prevent and End Homelessness (July 15, 2015), https://www.usich.gov/opening-doors. In terms of recent federal initiatives for those who are homeless, President Trump stated in 2019 that homelessness "started two years ago" and that the federal government "may intercede." *See* Elizabeth Thomas, Trump claims homelessness is "phenomenon that started 2 years ago," blames "liberal" mayors, ABC News (July 2, 2019), https://abcnews.go.com/Politics/trump-claims-homelessness-phenomenon-started-years-ago/story?id=64083965; *see also* Bill Press, Trump's disappearing homelessness, The Hill, Opinion (July 8, 2019), https://thehill.com/opinion/bill-press/452090-press-trumps-disappearing-homelessness.

8

Rights in Public Spaces

Introduction

What is a public space?

A public space is any place, indoor or outdoor, that is not privately owned. Typical examples of public spaces include streets and sidewalks, roads and highways, parks, train stations, government offices, and libraries. In some circumstances, shopping malls are treated as public spaces, even though they are privately owned and designed for commercial use. Public spaces benefit the community by providing services and amenities that are important and which many individuals otherwise might not be able to afford. For example, a library offers access to books, newspapers, and the internet; a park provides a bench for outdoor sitting and recreation; and a street offers a pathway for travel and a place to stand and talk with other people. Being able to use and access public spaces is a critical aspect of social citizenship.

For a variety of reasons, many communities have adopted "quality of life" rules that by effect block persons who are homeless or "look poor" from accessing public spaces.[1] In particular, some of these practices regulate or criminalize activities that are legal when done in the privacy of one's home (such as sitting, sleeping, or accepting food from another person), but have been made illegal when done in public.[2] Arresting a poor person who falls asleep on a park bench and has no other place to sleep is a serious invasion of personal autonomy and often results in the destruction of the person's few possessions. It also reinforces a vicious cycle of poverty, generating fines, jail time, a criminal record, and increased barriers to housing and employability.[3] Courts have not consistently ensured that persons with low income are not arbitrarily and harshly excluded from public spaces,[4] but knowing the rights that do exist is a critical step in giving them force on the ground.

Getting By. Helen Hershkoff and Stephen Loffredo, Oxford University Press (2020). © Helen Hershkoff & Stephen Loffredo.
DOI: 10.1093/oso/9780190080860.001.0001

The Right to Travel in the United States

Does the federal Constitution protect a person's right to travel throughout the United States?

It is now settled that the federal Constitution protects a person's right to travel from state to state throughout the country.[5] However, the U.S. Supreme Court did not always recognize that poor people have a right to interstate migration.[6] To the contrary, traditionally, states and localities, borrowing from the English Poor Laws, barred poor people from entering their communities or consigned them to the "work house" or "poor house" if present within their borders.[7] The Supreme Court endorsed these practices, on the view that poverty is a "moral pestilence" to be quarantined like a major illness.[8] Persons of color—whether or not poor—faced additional restrictions on their right to travel. After the Civil War and the end of formal racial slavery, many Southern states adopted "Black Codes" that were designed to maintain conditions of coerced labor among African Americans by imposing curfews and other restrictions that impeded geographic mobility.[9]

A legal shift for the poor came in 1941, when the U.S. Supreme Court invalidated a California law that made it a crime to bring a poor person into the state.[10] Some version of California's ban had been on the books since the 1860s. However, California started vigorously enforcing the statute in the 1930s, when agricultural workers needed to escape the devastation of the "Dust Bowl"—severe storms that destroyed the economy of the Southern Plains.[11] Striking down the law as unconstitutional, the Court explained that a state may not "isolate itself from difficulties common to all [states] . . . by restraining the transportation of persons . . . across its borders." The Court also stated that the traditional view of equating "[p]overty and immorality" was no basis for excluding "paupers" from a community.[12]

In later opinions, the Court has clarified that the right to travel protects three distinct rights:

1. "[T]he right of a citizen of one state to enter and to leave another State";
2. "[T]he right to be treated as a welcome visitor rather than an unfriendly alien when temporarily present"; and
3. "[F]or those travelers who elect to become permanent residents, the right to be treated like other citizens of that State."[13]

Does the federal Constitution protect the right to travel within a state?

The U.S. Supreme Court so far has declined to consider whether there is a federal constitutional right to travel within a state.[14] A few lower federal courts have held that the right to travel does include the right to travel "within a state,"[15] and some state courts likewise have recognized a right to intrastate travel.[16] However, whether or not there is a right to intrastate travel, the Court has held that the right to become a permanent resident of a state does not prevent a state or locality from using zoning laws that effectively bar persons with low income from living in a particular community.[17] Zoning laws affect who can permanently join a community by making the cost of housing too expensive (for example, limiting land use to one-family residential homes rather than multifamily apartment houses or mixed-use buildings).[18] Exclusionary zoning laws may be illegal under federal law if they have a negative disparate impact on persons of color or explicitly exclude persons on the basis of race or ethnicity.[19] (The duty to affirmatively further fair housing, which may involve assessing the impact of zoning laws, is discussed in chapter 7.)

INFORMATION BOX: MOBILE HOMES

The U.S. Supreme Court has not considered whether a locality can exclude persons in "mobile homes" from traveling to and establishing residence in a community, but a number of state courts have held that localities can regulate the location and use of mobile homes.

"Mobile home" is the old-fashioned term for housing that is delivered on wheels to a community. The stereotype of such housing was that of a trailer attached to the back of a car, lacking plumbing, and inhabited by persons who intended only temporary residence in a community.[20] Since the 1960s, "manufactured housing" that is not built on the site has become an important, low-cost source of affordable housing.[21] However, regulations that date to the earlier period continue to be on the books. For example, some localities have zoning laws that restrict where a manufactured home can be located; others require the owner to obtain a permit to "park" the home in a particular area.[22] Another kind of regulation allows the home to be located only as an accessory to a use permitted in the zone, such as farming.[23] Courts tend to view zoning laws as a legitimate way for a community to maintain property values and generate tax revenue.[24] Relatedly, courts have held it is permissible to exclude manufactured homes from a neighborhood if they do not meet laws regulating the size and dimension of lots and homes.[25] In practice, manufactured homes tend to concentrate in special zones or designated parks. A few states have begun to reconsider this approach, and some now bar localities from absolutely prohibiting mobile homes in residential communities.[26]

Does the federal Constitution mandate giving assistance to persons too poor to travel from state to state or within a state?

The right to travel assumes that a person is financially able to travel; the federal Constitution has not yet been interpreted to guarantee cash assistance to a poor person or mandate the provision of public transportation.[27] Arguably, the absence of assistance needed to use public transportation, to buy a car, to pay for a driver's license, or to pay a toll to access the public highways burdens the right of an indigent person to travel, but the Court has not yet endorsed this position or redressed its racially disparate impact.[28] Indeed, to the extent that federal law provides subsidies for personal transportation, it tilts in favor of more-resourced persons who are able to purchase automobiles and use highways.[29] Some public school districts will waive transportation fees, typically for students whose family's income qualifies for free or reduced lunch prices.[30] In other contexts, a court may require that the government waive a fee that impedes travel, but the test for requiring a waiver is very hard to meet.[31] Finally, limited transportation allowances to travel to work may be available through assistance programs described in this book. For example, benefits in programs funded through Temporary Assistance for Needy Families (TANF) may include transportation allowances to pay for the cost of going to and from required assignments within a state.[32] Contact the local TANF office to find out if these allowances are provided under the state's plan and what the eligibility rules are.

May a state or locality favor long-term residents over newcomers?

One of the benefits of interstate and intrastate travel is that it allows a person to relocate to a community that might have more job opportunities, better public schools, and affordable housing units. In a number of cases, the U.S. Supreme Court has held that the right to travel is violated if a state or locality discriminates in favor of long-term residents relative to newcomers by giving them better benefits. For example, in *Saenz v. Roe*, the Court struck down a law that gave state newcomers lower welfare benefits than those provided to long-term residents.[33] As the Court had earlier explained in *Shapiro v. Thompson*, "a state may no more try to fence out those indigents who seek higher welfare benefits than it may try to fence out indigents generally."[34] A law that classifies on the basis of residence implicates the right to travel when the law "actually deters such travel,"[35] "when impeding travel is its primary objective,"[36] or when it uses a classification which serves " 'to penalize the exercise of that right,' " such as length of the person's residence.[37]

The right to travel, although considered fundamental, is thus not absolute; a rule that impacts the distribution of benefits and indirectly affects interstate travel may be legal if the government can show it is "is necessary to accomplish a compelling state interest."[38] For example, a federal appeals court upheld a law that gave teachers less than full salary credit for out-of-state teaching experience, on the view that the classification focused on "the location of teaching experience, not duration of residency." On the other hand the U.S. Supreme Court held that New York could not give a civil service preference to veterans who entered the armed forces while residing in New York, but withhold that preference from veterans who entered the armed forces while residing in a different state and later moved to New York.[39]

Giving a resident a "preference" is especially when important when used to distribute a benefit that is not an entitlement and the number of eligible recipients exceeds the available pool of benefits; the applicant who is given the preference has priority over an applicant who does not.[40] Federal law allows localities to use residence preferences as a mechanism for distributing affordable housing units.[41] In some circumstances, the use of the preference may be illegal because of its adverse impact on persons of color.[42]

The Right to Access and Use Public Spaces

Does the federal Constitution protect a person's right to be on a street or sidewalk?

Streets and sidewalks typically are government-managed spaces that provide a pathway for movement within a locality. Moreover, they have special status in constitutional law as "traditional public forums" for expressive activity protected under the First Amendment of the federal Constitution.[43] It is settled that the federal Constitution protects a person's right to be on a street or sidewalk, alone or with others, to walk or stroll, to lounge or loaf—activities "not mentioned in the Bill of Rights," but which are, as the Court has explained, "unwritten amenities," which give Americans a "feeling of independence."[44]

The U.S. Supreme Court did not always recognize the right of poor persons to access public spaces on an equal basis with the rich. For centuries towns made it illegal for a person to be on a public street without any apparent purpose—a crime called vagrancy or loitering—and enforced these laws primarily against persons who "looked poor" and so out of place or were assumed to be engaged in criminal activity.[45] In 1972, the Court invalidated Florida's vagrancy statute, which punished walking outside at night, juggling on the streets, or wandering from place to place. The Court held that the statute violated the Due Process Clause of

the federal Constitution because it was impermissibly vague: it criminalized innocent conduct; failed to give ordinary people fair notice that their behavior was
illegal; and allowed the police to make arrests for arbitrary reasons, creating the
impermissible situation "in which the poor and the unpopular are permitted to
'stand on a public sidewalk . . . only at the whim of any police officer.' "[46]

Nevertheless, a wide gap persists between what the Constitution requires and
what happens in practice when persons who "look poor" wish to be physically
present in a public space. Anti-vagrancy laws remain on the books throughout
the United States but in many localities have been rewritten to address specific
conduct that is done in public. Of 187 U.S. cities surveyed in 2016, almost half
(47 percent) banned sitting or lying down in a public place, including in a park or
on a bench, and more than half (54 percent) banned loitering or loafing in particular places (as an example, Burlington, Vermont, banned "remaining idle in
essentially one location . . . or walking about aimlessly").[47] The restrictions give
the police excessive discretion to choose which individuals to arrest, and tend
to be enforced more vigorously against those who look poor or homeless; such
enforcement is unconstitutional, as are many of the restrictions themselves.[48]
Apart from due process concerns, enforcement of these bans against persons
with disabilities or persons of color raise additional issues of illegal or unconstitutional discrimination.[49]

May a person sleep in a public space?

The U.S. Supreme Court has not addressed whether it is constitutional to criminalize sleeping in public when the person cannot afford housing and the government does not provide free and safe space in a public shelter. In 2016, a third
of 187 cities surveyed banned camping in public, 18 percent banned sleeping in
public, and 27 percent banned sleeping in particular public places.[50]

In 2018, the Ninth Circuit Court of Appeals (which covers federal courts
in Alaska, Arizona, California, Hawaii, Idaho, Montana, Nevada, Oregon, and
Washington State, as well as the District of Guam and of the Northern Mariana
Islands) held that it violates the Eighth Amendment—which bars cruel and unusual punishment[51]—for a locality to impose criminal penalties for sleeping,
sitting, or lying outside on public property on an individual who is homeless and not able to access shelter.[52] The appeals court explained that " 'the
Eighth Amendment prohibits the state from punishing an involuntary act or
condition if it is the unavoidable consequence of one's status or being,' " and
" '[w]hether sitting, lying, and sleeping are defined as acts or conditions, they
are universal and unavoidable consequences of being human.' " Although the
appeals court declined to mandate that the locality provide sufficient shelter for

persons who are homeless, it held that "as long as there is no option of sleeping indoors, the government cannot criminalize indigent, homeless people for sleeping outdoors, on public property, on the false premise they had a choice in the matter."[53] Moreover, the court recognized that shelter may be unavailable both because shelters are full and there is no bed space, or because a homeless person has exhausted the number of days a locality will provide shelter during a defined period of time.[54] Not all courts have agreed with this analysis, at least when the ban applies to camping in public and not sitting, lying, or sleeping.[55] Relatedly, in *Clark v. Community for Creative Non-Violence*, the U.S. Supreme Court held that the United States Park Service did not violate the right to free expression protected by the First Amendment to the federal Constitution when it refused to permit demonstrators to sleep in temporary structures erected in public places (including on the National Mall) as part of a protest aimed at drawing attention to the lack of affordable housing.[56]

In addition, some localities make it a crime for a person to sleep in a car parked on a public street.[57] In 2014, the Ninth Circuit Court of Appeals invalidated Los Angeles' ban on car-sleeping as unconstitutionally vague, calling the ordinance "broad and cryptic." The court further stated, "The City of Los Angeles has many options at its disposal to alleviate the plight and suffering of its homeless citizens. Selectively preventing the homeless and the poor from using their vehicles for activities many other citizens also conduct in their cars should not be one of those options."[58] However, courts in other localities have found it permissible to ban a person from sleeping in a vehicle on a public street.[59]

May the police seize and immediately destroy the possessions of a person who is in a park or some other public space?

The Fourth Amendment to the federal Constitution protects against unreasonable searches and seizures. Since the landmark decision in *Katz v. United States*, the U.S. Supreme Court has "recognized that the Fourth Amendment protects people—and not simply [places]—against unreasonable searches and seizures."[60] Some courts have recognized that individuals who are homeless and stay in public parks or shelters have a reasonable expectation of privacy, and thus are protected under the Fourth Amendment against warrantless police searches.[61] Moreover, they acknowledge that it is unreasonable to expect a homeless person to retain physical control over possessions at all times when in a public park or shelter:

> As a practical matter, homeless people cannot stay with their property 24 hours per day because they, like people who have homes, have to use the bathroom,

shower, and conduct other necessary daily activities. Those who have jobs must leave their belongings while they work, recycle, or engage in other activities. They nonetheless have an expectation of continued ownership of their property and do not intend to abandon their property because they leave it in a cart or similar device, which is covered by or wrapped in a blanket, tarp, or tent, unattended for a period of time.[62]

On a similar rationale, a Florida federal court held that police violated Fourth Amendment rights when they conducted warrantless searches and seizures of property left by homeless people in Miami public parks.[63]

Nevertheless, some localities have instituted "homeless sweeps"—seizing and destroying without notice personal items that homeless people have temporarily left unattended in a public space, arguing that they are abandoned property.[64] For example, a federal court in Idaho held that a statute authorizing the seizure of property remaining or left unattended after the issuance of a citation for a person's violation of a statute that prohibited camping was valid under the "community caretaking" exception to the Fourth Amendment.[65] In contrast, the Ninth Circuit Court of Appeals affirmed a preliminary injunction that barred the City of Los Angeles from "seizure and summary destruction of . . . unabandoned, but momentarily unattended, personal property."[66]

The legal analysis differs if the police seize a homeless person's possessions while arresting the person.[67] The U.S. Supreme Court has interpreted the Constitution to permit the police to conduct even a warrantless search in order to preserve evidence of a crime if a prior valid arrest has been made. Thus, whether the police can search and seize a homeless person's property may in some circumstances turn on the legality of arresting the person in the first place (for example, for sleeping in a public space).[68]

If the police seize a person's possessions from a public space, it is important to find out how to get the items back, quickly and without paying a fee. In 2012, the Ninth Circuit Court of Appeals held that it was unconstitutional for the government to seize property temporarily left on the sidewalk by a homeless person unless the government offered a process to let the owner get the property back.[69]

Can the police search a person's car or mobile home when it is parked in a public space?

The Fourth Amendment requires that police obtain a warrant, based on probable cause, before conducting a search of private property. But the Fourth Amendment rule is subject to exceptions,[70] allowing warrantless searches that are incident to a lawful arrest,[71] or of a vehicle if it is reasonable for the police officer to believe it contains contraband or evidence of criminal activity.[72] Additionally, the U.S. Supreme Court has found that individuals have a more limited "reasonable expectation to privacy" in vehicles because of their inherent mobility and public use.[73] Thus, under the vehicle exception to the Fourth Amendment, whether a police officer has probable cause to search an entire vehicle will affect the legality of a warrantless search of every part of the vehicle and of its contents, including wrapped packages, even if they belong to a passenger and not the owner of the car.[74] However, the Court has emphasized that the exception does not permit a police officer, without a warrant, to enter a home or its curtilage (the land attached to a house) to search a vehicle parked in the enclosure, even if the vehicle can be seen by third parties from beyond the property.[75]

The exception for vehicles has been applied to searches of mobile homes and portable campers, even in cases when the mobile home or camper is not immediately mobile.[76] However, the Supreme Court has not extended the vehicular exception to "a motor home that is situated in a way or place that objectively indicates that it is being used as a residence."[77]

Police also may search a vehicle if consent to the search is given voluntarily by a person who is authorized to give it.[78] Voluntariness is assessed by measuring the totality of the circumstances, and includes such factors as the person's age, level of cooperation, understanding of the right to refuse consent, and intelligence.[79]

A related question is whether the police can obtain "location information" from a person's car or mobile home (or even a mobile phone) without a warrant. New devices have made it easier for the government to monitor a person's whereabouts, and courts have been slow to keep pace with these rapidly advancing technologies.[80] The. Supreme Court held that attaching a Global Positioning System tracking device to a vehicle to monitor the vehicle's movements is a search subject to the protections and restrictions of the Fourth Amendment.[81] The Court also has held that individuals maintain a legitimate expectation of privacy in their historical cell-site location information—records of their physical movements captured by cell phone towers.[82] Therefore, a search warrant is required to access cell phone location information spanning a period of at least seven days or longer.[83]

Can the police demand ID from a person who is standing on the street or in some other public place?

The U.S. Supreme Court has held that the police cannot stop a person on the street and demand identification without having a reasonable suspicion of criminal activity.[84] Moreover, the kinds of identification demanded cannot be arbitrary or vague. In *Kolender v. Lawson*, a 1983 decision, the Supreme Court invalidated a California law that allowed police to demand "credible and reliable" identification from a person on the street. In the Court's view, the statute was unconstitutionally vague because it did not define what identification would be sufficient, and instead gave the police "virtually complete discretion . . . to determine whether the suspect has satisfied the statute."[85] In 2004, the Court again considered whether the refusal to identify oneself when asked to do so by the police could be grounds for arrest. The Court held that Nevada's "stop and identify" statute—interpreted to require the police to have reasonable suspicion to make the stop and to ban the police from demanding production of an official ID such as a driver's license—did not violate the Fourth Amendment prohibition against unreasonable searches or the Fifth Amendment right against self-incrimination.[86] In practice, anecdotal reports indicate that the police arrest homeless persons when they are asked to produce an ID but are unable to do so because they lack documents.[87]

INFORMATION BOX: HOW TO GET AN "OFFICIAL" ID

"Official" identification cards can be obtained by filing an application with a state government office. The issuance of ID cards (including driver's licenses) is regulated by the federal REAL ID Act, enacted in 2005.[88] Almost all states now issue official IDs only if the applicant can present a photo ID (or a nonphoto ID stating the person's full legal name and date of birth), proof of date of birth, proof of Social Security number or that the person is not eligible for one, and proof of the person's name and principal residence.[89] Acceptable documentation includes a certified copy of a birth certificate or a valid unexpired passport or permanent residence card.[90] Many states charge a fee for the ID, although a majority of states will waive the fee based on factors such as age, indigence, or disability.[91] Requiring one form of ID to obtain another is problematic for people who have lost their papers, had them taken from them, or never had them to begin with.[92]

When applying for government benefits, it is helpful but not generally required to have a photo ID. Some federal programs have procedures to help an applicant who does not have a photo ID in verifying eligibility information:

SNAP: The Supplemental Nutrition Assistance Program, formerly known as the Food Stamp program, verifies identity through "documentary evidence, or if this is unavailable, through a collateral contact,"[93] such as a shelter worker or an employer.[94]

SSI: Applicants for Supplemental Security Income may verify their identity without presenting a photo ID, for example, by completing a written certification that they are who they say they are and by providing their name, Social Security number, date of birth, parents' names, mother's maiden name, and place of birth.[95]

TANF: The Temporary Assistance for Needy Families (TANF) program is administered in each state and allows states to make their own rules regarding identity verification, and so the identification requirements vary by state.[96] For example, Rhode Island's TANF program, called Rhode Island Works, requires applicants to provide a driver's license, school or work identification, immigration documents, birth certificate, U.S. passport, or any other documentation requested for citizenship, immigration status, or age.[97]

WIC: The Women, Infants and Children (WIC) program is administered in each state and allows states to make their own rules regarding identification verification, so, as with TANF, the requirements vary from program to program.[98] For example, in Texas the WIC program accepts such documents as a form or letter from a Medicaid, SNAP, or TANF program, or a crib card from a hospital.[99]

Can the police demand ID from a person believed not to be a citizen?

Federal law requires persons who are not citizens and are temporarily in the United States to carry and to present identification papers upon request. In particular, the Immigration and Nationality Act requires "[e]very alien, eighteen years of age and over, [to] carry with him and have in his personal possession any certificate of alien registration or alien registration receipt card issued to him."[100] However, if no registration card is provided to the person, then the statute does not require the person to carry or to present an ID. Persons falling into the latter category include those who entered the United States illegally; those who sought to regularize their immigration status after entry into the United States; and those who entered the country and applied for and were granted Temporary Protected Status or deferred action.[101] Advocates suggest that a person who is over age 18 and has immigration documents carry them at all times and show them upon request from an immigration officer or police.

Federal law permits immigration officers to interrogate an undocumented immigrant or person believed to be an undocumented immigrant, and to arrest the person if the officer has "reason to believe" that the person is in violation of specified immigration laws, but the person stopped for questioning has a right to remain silent.[102] In 2012, the U.S. Supreme Court considered the extent to which a state may permit police to make warrantless arrests of persons suspected of being removable from the United States because of their immigration status. The Court held that it was impermissible for the state of Arizona to authorize its police to make a unilateral decision to detain, on the basis of immigration status, an immigrant who is not lawfully present in the country, absent any request, approval, or other instruction from the federal government. However, the Court did uphold the state's power to check the immigration status of a person during the course of an authorized, lawful detention or after a detainee has been released.[103] In January 2017, President Trump signed executive orders expanding a program to deputize local law enforcement officers to double as federal immigration agents. Once trained, local officers are authorized to interview, arrest, and detain any person who may be in violation of federal immigration laws.[104] The Trump administration has undertaken aggressive anti-immigration policies, and it would be helpful to consult additional resources, available from immigrants' rights groups, on how to handle encounters with immigration authorities and the police.[105]

Can the police arrest a person who does not answer questions or runs away even before questions are asked?

The U.S. Supreme Court has held that the police may "approach individuals at random in airport lobbies and other public places" to ask questions "so long as a reasonable person would understand that he or she could refuse to cooperate." As the Court stated, "We have consistently held that a refusal to cooperate, without more, does not furnish the minimal level of objective justification needed for a detention or seizure."[106] However, the Court also has held that a police officer constitutionally may conduct a "brief, investigatory stop when the officer has a reasonable, articulable suspicion that criminal activity is afoot," and has upheld the constitutionality of such a stop when the person was present "in an area of heavy narcotics trafficking" and who engaged in "evasive behavior" through "[h]eadlong flight."[107] Some lower federal courts have held that although flight does not establish guilt, it creates ambiguity and "officers may stop the person to resolve the ambiguity."[108] The Black Lives Matter movement has drawn national attention not only to racial profiling in policing practices, but also to racialized police violence.[109] Some state judges, influenced by reports that police officers disproportionately "stop" persons of color even when reasonable suspicion is not present, have questioned whether it is appropriate to equate flight with guilt for Fourth Amendment purposes.[110]

INFORMATION BOX: RECORDING INTERACTIONS WITH POLICE

Smart phones, social media, and mobile apps (such as the ACLU's Mobile Justice app) have made it easier to record police activity on the street and in other public places.[111] Statutes prohibiting nonconsensual recording may operate to criminalize the recording of police activity. Federal law requires consent from one of the parties to a phone call or conversation for it to be audio recorded,[112] and a majority of states likewise have one-party consent statutes, but a minority of states bar audio recording unless consent is obtained from all parties to the conversation (known as two-party consent statutes).[113] However, these statutes typically do not criminalize nonconsensual recording unless the parties being recorded have a reasonable expectation of privacy, which the police do not have when they engage in enforcement activity in a public area. Some states also have statutes that criminalize interference with police activity, and police may attempt to invoke these statutes against persons seeking to record police activity, although until now their application has involved much more traditional forms of obstruction.[114] Nevertheless, persons who seek to record police interactions may face threats of arrest, actual arrest, demands to delete the contents of a recording device, or seizure or destruction of the device. The U.S. Supreme Court has not yet considered these specific issues.[115] But, so far, the majority of federal appeals courts have found that the First Amendment protects the right to record police activity in public, subject to reasonable restrictions[116] (although courts have not unanimously found this right to be clearly established in civil rights suits seeking damages for wrongful arrest).[117]

Can a person without a permanent home or a fixed address receive mail at the post office?

Persons who do not have a permanent home or a fixed address can apply for a post office box to be able to pick up mail at the post office.[118] In addition, the person can apply for general delivery service.

Post office boxes can be rented for a fee on a three- or six-month basis by a person who does not have a street address.[119] No-fee boxes are available only to individuals who have physical addresses but do not have carrier delivery.[120] Persons who are homeless may request general delivery service, which means that the postal service holds the mail until the recipient calls for it. Typically, general delivery service is used by customers who are transient or cannot receive mail at a post office box because a post office is not available. The service is available to an individual without a fixed address at the discretion of the postmaster if the individual is "personally known to the Postmaster or retail associate and [is] known as a person with no fixed address."[121] The postal service has discretion to determine where and how general delivery service will be provided.[122] A federal appeals court held that Seattle's policy of providing general delivery service at only one post office location was reasonable, and thus constitutional.[123] The post office will hold mail for only 30 days, but the 30-day period does not limit how long a person may use general delivery service; as one federal judge underscored, "homeless persons may use the service indefinitely."[124] Some advocates are pushing for "ban the address" rules that would bar employers from asking an applicant for a street address until after a provisional offer an employment is made; nevertheless, the ability to access mail through a post office box or general delivery service remains critical.[125]

May a public library refuse admission or expel a person who "looks" poor or homeless?

Public libraries do not charge a fee for admission and most books may be borrowed for free if the patron has a current library card. An individual is allowed to remain in the library as long as the person's behavior does not violate library regulations that govern patron conduct. The American Library Association, in its 2012 Policy Statement on Library Services to the Poor, explicitly called upon libraries to help reduce homelessness through "library engagement"—for example, by promoting networking between the library and social service agencies, sensitivity training for staff, and making it easy to obtain a library card even when required documentation is not readily available.[126]

However, a library may ban patrons if their behavior interferes with other people's reasonable use of the facility or is inconsistent with the library's purpose. In some localities, library regulations that require patrons to conform to certain standards of dress or hygiene may allow those communities to exclude persons who "look" poor or homeless.[127] Challenges to libraries' enforcement of "personal decorum" regulations have met with mixed results. Some federal courts have upheld these restrictions when challenged under the First Amendment and the Equal Protection and Due Process Clauses.[128] However, a federal district court invalidated a hygiene restriction that was neither "narrowly tailored" nor "specifically defined" by statute or case law, and so was found to have created an impermissible "potential for unlimited ad hoc determinations of the regulation's scope by Library guards, employees, supervisors, and outside police officers."[129]

Relatedly, the American Library Association's 2012 Policy Statement urged localities to reduce library fees for those who cannot afford to pay (typically charged for the late return of books or the failure to return a book at all).[130] In some localities, schoolchildren are barred from using the library if a member of their family has outstanding book fines.[131] Moreover, book fines could impair a household's credit rating.[132] Overall, public libraries are an important resource for poor and low-income people—providing access to books, magazines, and the internet, as well as a safe place to sit, read, do homework, write job applications, and plan. Nevertheless, the Trump administration's budget proposals consistently have eliminated the Institute of Museum and Library Services, which effectively would cut all federal funding for all public libraries. #FundLibraries is an important advocacy effort urging that funds for library resources be retained or increased.[133]

May a privately owned store exclude a person who "looks" poor or homeless?

Privately owned retail stores, including shopping malls, may post dress codes and enforce these codes to exclude individuals who "look" poor and are not expected to make purchases while on the premises.[134] Private property owners also may refuse to give the public at large access to their toilets or benches.[135] Property owners may seek to enforce these restrictions through the criminal justice system.[136] However, federal antidiscrimination law may be implicated if any policy of exclusion intentionally or disproportionally impacts racial or ethnic minorities or persons with disabilities.[137]

INFORMATION BOX: ACCESS TO PUBLIC TOILETS

In all states, public urination and defecation are illegal or restricted as public nuisances. Moreover, no federal law requires a locality to provide public toilets, even for those individuals who lack a home or access to minimal facilities for health and hygiene.[138] Most localities have declined to fund public toilets, opting instead for "quasi-public restrooms," located in restaurants or office buildings, and for the use only of tenants or tourists.[139] Police in these localities are authorized to arrest persons who use public spaces to engage in basic bodily acts, or to apply nuisance laws and impose fines which, if not paid, can result in jail time.[140]

Localities that do provide public toilets cannot segregate them on the basis of race,[141] but they may provide separate facilities on the basis of gender.[142] The rights of transgender individuals to access public toilets and other facilities based on their gender identity remains unresolved.[143] Federal law provides some basis for insisting that public toilets be accessible to persons with disabilities.[144]

INFORMATION BOX: ACCESS TO PUBLIC LACTATION PLACES

According to the National Conference of State Legislatures, 49 states, the District of Columbia, and the Virgin Islands have laws that specifically allow women to breastfeed in any public or private location.[145] Idaho is the only state that does not have a law specifically allowing women to breastfeed in public. Twenty-nine states, the District of Columbia, and the Virgin Islands additionally exempt breastfeeding from public indecency laws.[146] Some states prohibit individuals from interfering with a nursing mother's ability to breastfeed in public.[147]

The Right to Solicit Work, Sell Goods, or Request or Provide Charitable Assistance

Can a person stand on the street or in another public space and solicit work?

Many industries—primarily construction, agriculture, landscaping and, to a lesser extent, housekeeping, nail salons, and child care—rely on "day laborers."[148] Day laborers solicit work by standing on the street or other public spaces where employers expect applicants to gather.[149] Some localities have adopted ordinances that criminalize the act of standing on the sidewalk to solicit employment. Localities justify these bans as ways to avoid traffic congestion and to relieve a public nuisance.[150] The federal Constitution does not specifically address this practice, but it does protect rights to free speech and peaceful assembly under the First Amendment. A few lower federal courts have found that day-labor bans violate the First Amendment as impermissibly broad restrictions on speech and peaceful assembly.[151]

May a person perform in public?

Performing—such as singing, dancing, miming, or playing an instrument—is a form of expression protected under the First Amendment.[152] As with any form of speech, the government may regulate when, where, and how a person may perform in public, but the restrictions must be content neutral and leave open alternative channels of communication.[153] For example, the government can regulate specific problems that may arise with some performing, such as playing an instrument too loudly.[154] Performing in public for money also is considered expression and protected by the First Amendment.[155]

May a person sell things on the street or in another public place?

States and localities may regulate street vending in reasonable ways, and in many localities a person who wishes to sell things in a public space or from a mobile or portable device must obtain a license or permit to engage in the activity.[156] Special rules apply to the sale of expressive written matter or artwork and are discussed separately.

Street vending offers important entrepreneurial opportunities for low-income people who might otherwise be blocked from starting and running a small business. According to the Institute for Justice, two-thirds of street vendors in California are persons of color and over half are immigrants. Street vendors also contribute to the local economy in which they work. In New York, for example, street vendors in 2012 created an estimated 17,960 jobs and $292.7 million in added value.[157] Nevertheless, in many localities persons who want to start or run a street vending business face administrative obstacles and arbitrary policy actions.

Restrictions on street vending vary by locality. The Institute for Justice examined street-vending rules in the 50 highest-population cities in the United States, and sorted vending restrictions into categories: bans from certain public areas such as streets or sidewalks, bans from whole areas of a city, minimum distance requirements from other businesses, prohibitions on parking mobile vending units, and time limits on how long mobile vendors can stay in one place. Forty-five of the cities imposed at least one of these restrictions, and 31 of the cities imposed at least two. Vendors in some cities face barriers that fall outside these five categories, such as particularly burdensome licensing processes and bans on selling certain items. Here are some examples of local rules regulating street vending:

> Seattle, Washington prohibits selling anything but food and cut flowers in
>   public spaces, and food vendors must obtain a permit and comply with the

same health department laws imposed on conventional restaurants and food stores.[158]

Wichita, Kansas distinguishes sidewalk vending from street vending.[159]

New York imposes different licensing requirements depending on whether merchandise or food is sold, and also sets a cap on the number of general vendor and food licenses it issues.[160]

Chicago food truck owners must prepare all food at a designated commissary and change location every two hours.[161]

Los Angeles, until 2018, did not have a permit system for street vending,[162] and allowed mobile vending,[163] but otherwise made street vending illegal. That year, California enacted statewide legislation, effectively making street vending legal and requiring localities to adopt street vendor regulations or forfeit a chance to regulate street vending at all.[164]

Persons selling "expressive" material receive heightened protection from licensing requirements under the First Amendment to the U.S. Constitution.[165] Local ordinances generally have withstood First Amendment challenge if they are content-neutral and leave vendors at least some opportunity to sell their materials.[166] Selling newspapers, including "street papers" that focus on homelessness, thus is an expressive activity even though it also is commercial.[167] As such, the activity is entitled to First Amendment protection but is subject to reasonable time, place, and manner restrictions. Some localities regulate where newspapers can be sold; for example, prohibiting the sale of newspapers to motorists whose cars are stopped at an intersection. At least one federal appeals court has held that such a ban is permissible under the First Amendment if it applies to all newspapers and if the locality does not block all sales, but rather leaves other options open, such as going door to door or selling on the sidewalk.[168]

INFORMATION BOX: STREET VENDOR LICENSES IN NEW YORK CITY

The rules for becoming a street vendor vary from locality to locality; New York City's licensing regime is offered as an illustration.[169] Anyone who wants to sell merchandise on the streets of New York City must obtain a general vendor license from the New York City Department of Consumer Affairs. A general vendor license is not needed to sell written matter such as newspapers, periodicals, books, and pamphlets, or artwork such as paintings, photographs, prints, and sculptures. These items are protected from license requirements under the First Amendment to the U.S. Constitution.[170] However, whether other merchandise counts as protected matter is a question that may require judicial resolution in any given situation.[171] Vendors who believe their merchandise merits First Amendment protection cannot seek preapproval from the city, and thus risk penalties if they go forward without a license and it is ultimately determined that a license was required.[172] Application rules are set out in the appendix.

May a person beg or panhandle on the street or in another public space?

Begging and panhandling are both forms of speech through which a person requests an immediate donation of money. These forms of speech are protected by the First Amendment,[173] and thus the government may impose only reasonable "time, place, and manner" restrictions. Restrictions on speech are unconstitutional if based on the content of the speech or the identity of the speaker, and if they do not leave the speaker with alternative pathways for communication.[174]

Although the U.S. Supreme Court has not directly decided that the First Amendment of the federal Constitution protects an individual's right to solicit alms, it consistently has upheld the right of members of charitable organizations to do so.[175] Moreover, a number of lower courts have held that begging is a form of solicitation protected by the First Amendment, and have invalidated restrictions when not sufficiently narrowly tailored to afford alternative communicative pathways.[176] For example, the First Circuit Court of Appeals held that it was unconstitutional to arrest a person for begging under a statute that banned standing, sitting, staying, driving, or parking on a median strip. As the appeals court explained, the statute violated the First Amendment because it banned virtually all expressive activity by the speaker and was not narrowly tailored to protect public safety.[177]

Of 187 cities surveyed in 2016, 61 percent banned begging in some public places, a 7 percent increase since 2006, and some of these bans make begging or panhandling a crime.[178] A blanket ban on begging would violate the First Amendment.[179]

Some localities also ban "aggressive panhandling"—requests for donations that are accompanied by perceived intimidation or unwarranted physical contact.[180] Such bans impinge on both speech and conduct, but governments try to defend them as regulations of the non-expressive elements of begging, and argue that courts should uphold the regulations as serving a public interest, such as safety, that is unrelated to the speaker's expressive message.[181] The better view is that a ban of this sort regulates expressive conduct, is impermissibly content-based, and can be upheld only if the regulation is "the least restrictive means for achieving a compelling state interest."[182]

INFORMATION BOX: IN-KIND ASSISTANCE—
COLLECTION BINS AND FOOD SHARING

Some localities provide or rent space for collection bins where community members may drop off clothing, food, or household items to be distributed to those who need charitable assistance. The locality is permitted to impose reasonable time, place, and manner restrictions on the location and maintenance of the bins.[183] However, in some states, it is illegal to give money or food directly to a person who is standing or sitting in a public space, without regard to whether the person solicits charitable assistance. In particular, of 187 cities surveyed in 2016, 12 cities had restrictions on "food-sharing" designed to bar groups or individuals from feeding poor and homeless persons who are on the streets.[184] These restrictions generally take three forms: imposing a permit requirement on charity food providers, sometimes accompanied by payment of a substantial fee; enforcing food safety rules (that are designed for restaurants) against charity food providers; and limiting the geographic spaces in which charity food providers may serve those in need.[185] Legal challenges to these restrictions have had mixed results.[186]

Is it legal to scavenge?

Scavenging involves a person's searching through and removing items from garbage or recycling bins. Many localities ban scavenging. However, case law and anecdotal reports suggest that the enforcement of these anti-scavenging laws is spotty and inconsistent.[187]

The Right to Associate with Others in Public

Does the federal Constitution allow advocates and others to distribute information at or near a government office?

Advocates may wish to assemble at or near government offices in order to distribute "know your rights" leaflets, to talk to persons applying for benefits, or to provide other information or make referrals. A few lower courts have held that individuals may hand out leaflets or talk with individuals sitting in the waiting room of a welfare office because such activity is expressive, does not disrupt the business of the welfare office, and is protected by the First Amendment.[188] However, later decisions by the U.S. Supreme Court have given the government greater discretion to restrict speech on public property other than sidewalks, parks, town squares, or other public places deemed to be a "traditional public forum." The Court has held that government may reserve public property that is not a traditional public forum "for its intended purposes, communicative or otherwise, as long as the regulation on speech is reasonable and not an effort to suppress expression merely because public officials oppose the speaker's view."[189] The legality of any restriction or of an order to "move on" will depend on the facts and circumstances.

Does the federal Constitution protect the right of persons to assemble or protest in a public space?

Persons are permitted to associate in public spaces, but a locality may require permits for assemblies such as demonstrations and parades. Permit systems may raise constitutional problems if they fail to set forth clear standards for the granting of the permit. A permit system allows the government to anticipate and prepare for crowd control, street closings, and other consequences, and it also ensures that there will not be two groups congregating in a public space at the same time and place.[190] However, as the U.S. Supreme Court has explained, a regulation that allows a permit requirement to be applied in an arbitrary way is "inherently inconsistent with a valid time, place, and manner regulation because such discretion has the potential for becoming a means of suppressing a particular point of view."[191] Applying these principles, courts have considered the size of the group wishing to demonstrate, the specifics of the space, and the availability of other places for expression in assessing whether the denial of a permit, or imposing a permit requirement at all, is constitutional.[192]

In addition to requiring the sponsor to obtain a permit, a locality generally can charge a fee, provided the amount of the fee is genuinely related to the cost of processing a permit application, does not vary with the kind of demonstration, and is so small that it does not deter the exercise of free speech.[193] This is the case whether the charge is called an application fee, a cleanup fee, or an insurance fee. In 1941, the U.S. Supreme Court upheld the imposition of nominal fees on the sponsors or organizers of a demonstration to "meet the expense incident to the administration of the [licensing statute] and to the maintenance of public order in the matter licensed."[194] Two years later, the Court struck down a license fee that was "not a nominal fee imposed as a regulatory measure to defray the expenses of policing the activities in question."[195] However, in 1992 the Court struck down even a nominal fee as unconstitutional because the fee varied based on a discretionary assessment of the amount of hostility likely to be created by the speech based on its content.[196]

What is the "Homeless Bill of Rights"?

Several states have adopted a "Homeless Bill of Rights" to protect homeless people from some of the practices described in this chapter: arrest for sleeping or urinating in public when facilities are not available for these basic activities; exclusion from public services such as the public library; and being subjected to harassment on the street or in a park. Advocates also want to ensure that persons who lack housing are able to vote and to receive social services. The movement for adopting a "Homeless Bill of Rights" recognizes that individuals who lack a fixed and private place to reside are vulnerable to arrest, are exposed to dangerous conditions, and lose control over their lives.[197] As an example, in 2012, the Rhode Island General Assembly passed a "Homeless Bill of Rights," securing, among other protections, the right to move freely in public spaces and the right to equal treatment by state and municipal agencies.[198] Connecticut has a similar statute protecting movement in public spaces.[199] Similarly, the Illinois Homeless Bill of Rights protects homeless individuals' rights to move freely in public spaces, keep a job, vote, and access emergency medical care and municipal agencies without discrimination; it also protects the person's records, information, and privacy.[200] These protections are a critical step—together with advocacy to secure housing justice, jobs with living wages, and affordable health care.

Appendix: Street Vending Application in New York City
The application for a vendor's license requires: a completed application form; proof of eligibility (for veterans, proof of honorable discharge, and for surviving spouses or partners of veterans, proof of marriage or partnership, death certificate, and proof of honorable discharge); New York State Department of Taxation and Finance Certificate of Authority; general vendor questionnaire; residence form; license and clearance fees; and various additional forms where applicable. Applicants may file in person or online. General vendor licenses last up to one year and expire every year on September 30, before which vendors may apply to renew the license. The Department of Consumer Affairs puts a cap on the number of licenses that it will issue, and for many years the waiting list in New York has been closed. However, the cap does not cover veterans who were honorably discharged from the armed services and their surviving spouses or partners who live in New York.

Food vendors in New York do not need a general vendor license, but do need a license from the Department of Health and Mental Hygiene. New York has capped the number of general food vendor licenses, and there currently is a long waiting list. However, the city issues specific "Green Cart" licenses for vendors of fruits and vegetables.[201] Waiting lists for these licenses are created twice a year, making it slightly easier to get a license.[202] The city also issues mobile food vending permits for restricted areas, for which there is no waiting list.[203] Applicants for these permits must have permission to operate on certain private properties or Department of Parks and Recreation property. All food vendors must have a mobile food vending license, as well as a mobile food vending permit issued specifically for the intended vending unit, such as a truck or cart. Permissions and renewal requirements vary by the type of permit.[204] Even for licensed and permitted vendors, many New York streets are restricted or have specific times during which a vendor may sell,[205] and there are restrictions on where on the street the vendor's cart or truck may be.

Selling at street fairs does not require a general vendor license but does require a temporary street fair vendor permit.[206] Vendors rent street fair space directly from the private fair sponsor.[207] Flea market vendors also must coordinate space rental from the event sponsor and get applicable licenses and permits.[208]

Unlicensed street vendors can be fined up to $250,[209] be arrested, and have their goods confiscated.[210] Because the caps and restrictions on licenses make it difficult to start a vending business, many vendors rent licenses from former vendors who are no longer using their license,[211] but transferring licenses without authorization is illegal.[212] New York law also allows for vendors with disabilities to request authorization to enlist helpers for selling.[213]

Notes

1. *See* Timothy Zick, Property, Place, and Public Discourse, 21 Wash. U. J.L. & Pol'y 173, 175 (2006):

> Today, access to public places is treated as more of an indulgence than as a fundamental right. It can be balanced away in favor of a growing list of interests, such as in governmental proprietorship and management, public order, aesthetics, privacy, repose, and now increasingly interests relating to "security." This is so even in "quintessential" public places such as streets and parks.

> *See also* Brittany Scott, Is Urban Policy Making Way for the Wealthy? How a Human Rights Approach Challenges the Purging of Poor Communities from U.S. Cities, 45 Colum. Hum. Rts. L. Rev. 863, 879 (2014) ("City governments are increasingly dealing with the growing crises of poverty and homelessness by defining the people most impacted as the problem that needs to be addressed, rather than recognizing how they have been affected by inequitable and exclusionary policies and practices.").

2. Report of the Special Rapporteur on Extreme Poverty and Human Rights on His Mission to the United States of America, United Nations, General Assembly, Human Rights Council, Thirty-eighth session (May 4, 2018), at 12.

3. On the importance of housing to a person's ability to obey the law, *see* Terry Skolnik, Homelessness and the Impossibility to Obey the Law, 43 Fordham Urb. L.J. 741 (2016); Terry Skolnik, Rethinking Homeless People's Punishments, 22 New Crim. L. Rev. 73 (2016); Gregory S. Alexander, Property's Ends: The Publicness of Private Law Values, 99 Iowa L. Rev. 1257 (2014); Jeremy Waldron, Community and Property—For Those Who Have Neither, 10 Theoretical Inquiries L. 161 (2009). For a discussion of quality of life regulations, *see* Debra Livingston, Police Discretion and the Quality of Life in Public Places: Courts, Communities, and the New Policing, 97 Colum. L. Rev. 551 (1997); Robert Ellickson, Controlling Chronic Misconduct in Public Spaces, Of Panhandlers, Skid Rows, and Public Space Zoning, 105 Yale L.J. 1165 (1996).

4. David Rudin, "You Can't Be Here": The Homeless and the Right to Remain in Public Space, 42 N.Y.U. Rev. L. & Soc. Change 309, 311 (2018) (discussing inconsistent protection of the poor and homeless).

5. United States v. Guest, 383 U.S. 745, 757 (1966) (calling the right to travel from state to state "firmly established and repeatedly recognized"). *See also* Shapiro v. Thompson, 394 U.S. 618, 630 (1969) ("We have no occasion to ascribe the source of this right to travel interstate to a particular constitutional provision.").

6. *See* Prigg v. Pennsylvania, 41 U.S. 539, 625 (1842) (states have police power allowing them to "remove from their borders . . . idlers, vagabonds and paupers"). *See also* Gerald L. Neuman, The Lost Century of American Immigration Law, 93 Colum. L. Rev. 1833, 1846 (1993) ("In neither the eighteenth century nor the nineteenth century did American law concede the right of the poor to geographic mobility."); Caleb Foote, Vagrancy-Type Law and Its Administration, 104 U. Pa. L. Rev. 603, 615–616 (1956) (discussing feudal origins of American restrictions on poor people's mobility).

7. *See* Papachristou v. City of Jacksonville, 405 U.S. 156, 161 (1972):

> The history is an often-told tale. The break-up of feudal estates in England led to labor shortages which in turn resulted in the Statutes of Laborers, designed to stabilize the labor force by prohibiting increases in wages and prohibiting the movement of workers from their home areas in search of improved conditions. Later vagrancy laws became criminal aspects of the poor laws. The series of laws passed in England on the subject became increasingly severe.

8. Mayor of N.Y. v. Miln, 36 U.S. 102, 141, 143 (1837) (upholding New York statute passed to prevent the state "from being oppressed by the support of multitudes of poor persons, who come from foreign countries, without possessing the means of supporting themselves," on the ground that it is "as necessary for a state to provide precautionary measures against the moral pestilence of paupers, vagabonds, and possibly convicts" as it is to take preventive steps against "unsound and infectious articles imported" from abroad). The Articles of Confederation, which preceded the Constitution, specifically excluded "paupers" and "vagabonds" from the privileges and immunities guaranteed in Article IV. Article IV of the Constitution does not contain the exclusionary language, but as cases like *Prigg*

and *Miln* show, the U.S. Supreme Court for many generations grafted the omitted terms onto the text.

9. *See* Eric Foner, Reconstruction: America's Unfinished Revolution, 1863–77 (Perennial 2002). Further, until 1946, interstate buses and trains were permitted to segregate passengers by race. *See* Morgan v. Virginia, 328 U.S. 373 (1946). Laws enabling persons of color to access "public accommodations" were not enacted until 1964. *See* Civil Rights Act of 1964, 42 U.S.C. § 2000a.

10. Edwards v. California, 314 U.S. 160, 177 (1941).

11. *See* Stephen Loffredo, "If You Ain't Got the Do, Re, Mi": The Commerce Clause and State Residence Restrictions on Welfare, 11 Yale L. & Pol'y Rev. 147, 175 (1993). John Steinbeck's novel *The Grapes of Wrath*, published in 1939, described the plight of the Joad family, tenant farmers unable to remain in Oklahoma, who tried to relocate to California. *See generally* Abbe Smith, For Tom Joad and Tom Robinson: The Moral Obligation to Defend the Poor, 1997 Ann. Surv. Am. L. 869.

12. Edwards v. California, 314 U.S. at 173, 177.

13. Saenz v. Roe, 526 U.S. 489, 500 (1999); *see also* United States v. Guest, 383 U.S. 745, 757–759 (1966).

14. *See* Memorial Hospital v. Maricopa Cty, 415 U.S. 250, 255–256 (1974) (reserving the question of whether there is a constitutionally protected federal constitutional right to intrastate travel). The U.S. Supreme Court has noted that as early as the Articles of Confederation (the governance structure in the United States before the states adopted the Constitution), state citizens "possessed the fundamental right, inherent in citizens of all free governments, peacefully to dwell within the limits of their respective states, to move at will from place to place therein, and to have free ingress thereto and egress therefrom." United States v. Wheeler, 254 U.S. 281, 293 (1920). However, as earlier noted, the articles excluded the poor, *see* note 8.

15. *Compare* King v. New Rochelle Mun. Hous. Auth., 442 F.2d 646, 648 (2d Cir. 1971), cert. denied, 404 U.S. 863 (1971) ("It would be meaningless to describe the right to travel between states as a fundamental precept of personal liberty and not to acknowledge a correlative constitutional right to travel within a state."); Williams v. Town of Greenburgh, 535 F.3d 71, 75 (2d Cir. 2008) ("individuals possess a fundamental right to travel within a state"); Johnson v. City of Cincinnati, 310 F.3d 484, 498 (6th Cir. 2002) ("the Constitution protects a right to travel locally through public spaces and roadways"), *with* Eldridge v. Bouchard, 645 F. Supp. 749, 754 (W.D. Va. 1986) (rejecting a right to intrastate travel as outside the Privileges and Immunities Clause); Wardwell v. Bd. of Ed. of City Sch. Dist. of City of Cincinnati, 529 F.2d 625, 627 (6th Cir. 1976) (finding no federal constitutional right to intrastate travel). *See* Andrew M. Schnitzel, Comment, Balancing Police Action Against an Underdeveloped Fundamental Right: Is There a Right to Travel Freely on Public Fora?, 114 Penn. St. L. Rev. 667, 672–674 (2009) (arguing that in the absence of guidance from the U.S. Supreme Court, lower courts have not consistently treated the scope and existence of an intrastate travel right, but characterizing the circuit differences as a "split" is not warranted).

16. *See* Kathryn E. Wilhelm, Freedom of Movement at a Standstill? Toward the Establishment of a Fundamental Right to Intrastate Travel, 90 B.U. L. Rev. 2461 (2010). Examples:

> Hawaii: State v. Shigematsu, 483 P.2d 997, 1001 (Haw. 1971) (recognizing right to freedom of movement, which "include[s] the right of men to move from place to place, to walk in the fields in the country or on the streets of a city, [and] to stand under open sky").
> Minnesota: State v. Cuypers, 559 N.W.2d 435, 437 (Minn. Ct. App. 1997) ("Minnesota also recognizes the right to intrastate travel.").
> New York: City of N.Y. v. Andrews, 719 N.Y.S.2d 442, 452 (N.Y. Sup. Ct. 2000) ("There can be no doubt that our State Constitution, no less than the Federal Constitution, supports the right to travel freely within the State.").
> Wisconsin: Brandmiller v. Arreola, 544 N.W.2d 894, 899 (Wis. 1996) ("[W]e recognize that the right to travel intrastate is fundamental among the liberties preserved by the Wisconsin Constitution. This right to travel includes the right to move freely about one's neighborhood, even in an automobile.").
> Wyoming: Watt v. Watt, 971 P.2d 608, 615 (Wyo. 1999) ("The right to travel freely throughout the state is a necessary and fundamental aspect of our emancipated society, and it is retained by the citizens.").

17. *See* Village of Belle Terre v. Boraas, 416 U.S. 1, 7 (1974) (local zoning ordinance that restricted land use to one-family dwellings did not infringe a right to travel). *See also* Richard Briffault, Our Localism: Part I—The Structure of Local Government Law, 90 Colum. L. Rev. 1, 102 (1990) ("An outsider has no constitutionally protected right to make a home in a locality; the right to travel does not encompass the freedom to move into the community."). On the relation between zoning laws, policing, and "norms of order," *see* Nicole Stelle Garnett, Ordering (and Order in) the City, 57 Stan. L. Rev. 1 (2004).

18. *See* Charles M. Haar, The Wrong Side of the Tracks: A Revolutionary Rediscovery of the Common Law Tradition of Fairness in the Struggle Against Inequality (Simon & Schuster 1986) (discussing challenges to zoning laws as a violation of a common law antidiscrimination principle); *see also* Henry Grabar, Minneapolis Confronts Its History of Housing Segregation, Slate (Dec. 7, 2019), https://slate.com/business/2018/12/Minneapolis-single-family-zoning-housing-racism.html ("By doing away with single family zoning, the city takes on high rent, long commutes, and racism in one fell swoop.").

19. *See* Texas Dept. of Housing and Community Affairs v. Inclusive Communities Project, Inc., 576 U.S. ___, 135 S. Ct. 2507 (2015) (holding that a claim that the allocation of low income tax credits had a disparate impact on African Americans was cognizable under the Fair Housing Act). *See also* NAACP v. N. Hudson Reg'l Fire & Rescue, 665 F.3d 464, 486 (3d Cir. 2011), cert. denied, 132 S. Ct. 2749 (2012) (residence requirement for municipal firefighters violated Title VII of the 1964 Civil Rights Act).

20. *See* Richard W. Bartke & Hilda R. Gage, Mobile Homes: Zoning and Taxation, 55 Cornell L. Rev. 491, 495 (1970) ("The term 'trailer' has been replaced by 'mobile homes.'"); *see also* James F. Vernon, Mobilehomes: Present Regulation and Needed

Reforms, 27 Stan. L. Rev. 159 (1974) (discussing the earlier conception of mobile homes).

21. *See* James Milton Brown & Molly A. Sellman, Manufactured Housing: The Invalidity of the "Mobility" Standard, 19 Urb. Law. 367, 375–376 (1987) (explaining that manufactured housing includes two types: (1) all housing built in a factory and in compliance with state building codes; and (2) housing built to conform to national standards); *see also* Frequently Asked Questions, Manufactured Housing Institute, https://www.manufacturedhousing.org/faq/. Federal regulations define manufactured homes as transportable structures of a certain size built on a permanent chassis and designed to be used as a dwelling. *See* 24 C.F.R. Part 3280. Mobile homes are any such moveable dwellings constructed prior to the implementation of federal building regulations published by the U.S. Department of Housing and Urban Development in 1976.

22. *See, for example*, Pioneer Tr. & Sav. Bank v. McHenry Cty., 241 N.E.2d 454 (Ill. 1968). A local rule banning undocumented immigrants from obtaining such a permit was struck down as preempted by federal law. *See* Cent. Ala. Fair Hous. Center v. Magee, 835 F. Supp. 2d 1165, 1175–76 (M.D. Ala. 2011), vacated as moot sub nom. Cent. Ala. Fair Hous. Center v. Comm'r, Ala. Department of Revenue, 2013 WL 2372302 (11th Cir. 2013).

23. *See, for example*, Kendall Cty. v. Husler, 358 N.E.2d 1337 (Ill. App. Ct. 1977).

24. *See, for example*, Tex. Manufactured Hous. Ass'n, Inc. v. City of Nederland, 905 F. Supp. 371, 380 (E.D. Tex. 1995), aff'd, 101 F.3d 1095 (5th Cir. 1996) ("[T]here is a belief on the part of some property owners and the city council that mobile homes reduce land value."); State v. Murray, 471 S.W.2d 460, 463 (Mo. 1971) (mobile homes "may be confined to mobile home parks, or may be excluded from residential districts . . . on the ground that they tend to stunt the growth potential of the land"). *But see* S. Burlington Cty. NAACP v. Mount Laurel Twp., 391 A.2d 935, 956–957 (N.J. Super. Ct. Law. Div. 1978), aff'd in part, rev'd in part on other grounds, 456 A.2d 390 (1983) ("In view of the development of the attractive, well-constructed mobile home designed and intended for permanent year-round dwelling and capable of being set in attractive surroundings in harmony with conventional residential development, it appears that [a mobile home exclusion] is no longer supported by the facts.").

25. *For example*, McBride v. Town of Forestburgh, 388 N.Y.S.2d 940 (1976) (upholding a town zoning ordinance that required at least one-acre lots for homes).

26. *See* Daniel R. Mandelker, Zoning Barriers to Manufactured Housing, 48 Urb. Law. 233, 251–255 (2016). Examples include:

> Iowa: Iowa Code Ann. § 335.30 ("A county shall not adopt or enforce zoning regulations or other ordinances which disallow the plans and specifications of a proposed residential structure solely because the proposed structure is a manufactured home.").

> Maine: Me. Rev. Stat. Tit. 30-A, § 4358 ("Municipalities shall permit manufactured housing to be placed or erected on individual house lots in a number of locations on undeveloped lots where single-family dwellings are allowed, subject to the same requirements as single-family dwellings. . . .").

Michigan: Mich. Comp. Laws Ann. §125.2307 ("A local government ordinance shall not contain . . . special use zoning requirements that apply only to, or excludes, mobile homes. A local government ordinance shall not contain a manufacturing or construction standard that is incompatible with, or is more stringent than, a standard promulgated by the federal department of housing and urban development pursuant to the national manufactured housing construction and safety standards act of 1974, 42 USC 5401 to 5426.").

New Jersey: N.J. Stat. Ann. § 40:55D-104 ("A municipal agency shall not exclude or restrict, through its development regulations, the use, location, placement, or joining of sections of manufactured homes which are not less than 22 feet wide, are on land the title to which is held by the manufactured home owner, and are located on permanent foundations, unless those regulations shall be equally applicable to all buildings and structures of similar use.").

27. See Dandridge v. Williams, 397 U.S. 471 (1970) (stating that "the intractable economic, social, and even philosophical problems presented by public welfare assistance programs are not the business of this Court").

28. The Ninth Circuit Court of Appeals has stated that the right to travel is not impermissibly burdened if the government fails to equalize transportation opportunities for the rich and poor. Monarch Travel Servs. v. Associated Cultural Clubs, 466 F.2d 552, 554 (9th Cir. 1972) ("[H]igher air tariffs will limit travel of those who cannot pay the price. A rich man can choose to drive a limousine; a poor man may have to walk. The poor man's lack of choice in his mode of travel may be unfortunate, but it is not unconstitutional."). In a later case, the Ninth Circuit upheld a policy of refusing to grant a driver's license unless the applicant provided a Social Security number. The appeals court explained that there is no constitutional right to drive a car, and that "[b]urdens placed on travel generally, such as gasoline taxes, or minor burdens impacting interstate travel, such as toll roads, do not constitute a violation" of the right. Miller v. Reed, 176 F.3d 1202, 1205 (9th Cir. 1999); see also Mathew v. Honish, 233 Fed. Appx. 563 (7th Cir. 2007) (state driver licensing laws did not violate the right to travel).

29. See Timothy Baldwin, The Constitutional Right to Travel: Are Some Forms of Transportation More Equal than Others?, 1 N.W. J.L. & Soc. Pol'y 213 (2006). See also Roberta F. Mann, On the Road Again: How Tax Policy Drives Transportation Choices, 24 Va. Tax. Rev. 587 (2005); Paul Boudreaux, Vouchers, Buses, and Flats: The Persistence of Social Segregation, 49 Vill. L. Rev. 55 (2004).

30. For further information, contact the local school district. See, for example, Fee for Service Waiver Guidelines, Attleboro Public Schools, http://www.attleboroschools.com/central_office/transportation/fee_for_service_waiver_guidelines.

31. Fees that impede travel are constitutional so long as they are "based on some fair approximation of use of the facilities," are "not excessive in relation to the benefits conferred," and "do[] not discriminate against interstate commerce." Nw. Airlines, Inc. v. County of Kent, 510 U.S. 355, 369 (1994); see also Selevan v. N.Y. Thruway Auth., 584 F.3d 82, 102 (2d Cir. 2009) (ordering lower court to apply this test to assess the constitutionality of a highway toll).

32. *See* Nicole Stelle Garnett, The Road from Welfare to Work: Informal Transportation and the Urban Poor, 38 Harv. J. on Legis. 173, 192–194 (2001).
33. Saenz v. Roe, 526 U.S. 489 (1999).
34. Shapiro v. Thompson, 394 U.S. 618, 631 (1969).
35. Att'y Gen. of N.Y. v. Soto-Lopez, 476 U.S. 898, 903 (1986) (citing Crandall v. Nevada, 6 Wall. 35, 46 (1868)).
36. *Id.*, citing Zobel v. Williams, 457 U.S. 55, 62 n.9 (1982).
37. *Id.* (quoting Dunn v. Blumstein, 405 U.S. 330, 340 (1972), quoting Shapiro v. Thompson, 394 U.S. 618, 634 (1969)).
38. *Id.* at 903–904. *See, for example*, Sosna v. Iowa, 419 U.S. 393 (1975) (upholding one-year residence requirement for maintaining an action for divorce because of state's strong traditional interest in marriage and divorce). *See* Robert C. Farrell, Classifications that Disadvantage Newcomers and the Problem of Equality, 28 U. Rich. L. Rev. 547 (1994). Residency requirements for public schooling, including the validity of differential tuition for residents and nonresidents, are discussed in chapter 5 of this book.
39. Connelly v. Steel Valley School District, 706 F.3d 209, 214 (3d Cir. 2013) (teaching credit); Att'y Gen. of N.Y. v. Soto-Lopez, 476 U.S. 898 (1986) (state employment and veterans).
40. *See* Tim Iglesias, Threading the Needle of Fair Housing Law in a Gentrifying City with a Legacy of Discrimination, 27 J. Affordable Housing & Community Dev. L. 51 (2018) (reporting that a lottery for 26 units of affordable housing in a San Francisco neighborhood elicited 1,900 applicants).
41. *See* 24 C.F.R. §§ 5.655, 982.207.
42. *See* Texas Dept. of Housing and Community Affairs v. Inclusive Communities Project, Inc., 535 U.S. ___, 135 S. Ct. 2507 (2015). *See also* Zachary C. Freund, Perpetuating Segregation or Turning Discrimination on Its Head? Affordable Housing Residence Preferences as Anti-Displacement Measures, 118 Colum. L. Rev. 833 (2018).
43. *See* Hague v. CIO, 307 U.S. 496, 515 (1939) (explaining that streets and parks "have immemorially been held in trust for the use of the public, and, time out of mind, have been used for purposes of assembly, communicating thoughts between citizens, and discussing public questions").
44. Papachristou v. City of Jacksonville, 405 U.S. 156, 164 (1972).
45. *See* Harry Simon, Towns Without Pity: A Constitutional and Historical Analysis of Official Efforts to Drive Homeless Persons from American Cities, 66 Tulane L. Rev. 631, 633–634 (1992).
46. Papachristou v. City of Jacksonville, 405 U.S. 156, 162, 170 (1972) (quoting Shuttlesworth v. Birmingham, 382 U.S. 87, 90 (1976)). In a later case, the Court reiterated the unconstitutionality of anti-loitering ordinances that either fail to provide notice of what behavior is prohibited or authorize discretionary decision making likely to lead to arbitrary enforcement. City of Chicago v. Morales, 527 U.S. 41, 51 (1999) (striking down a gang loitering statute as void for vagueness).
47. *See* National Law Center on Homelessness & Poverty, Housing Not Handcuffs: Ending the Criminalization of Homelessness in U.S. Cities at 24 (2016), https://www.nlchp.

org/documents/Housing-Not-Handcuffs. From 2006 to 2016, the number of cities reporting these bans increased 52% and 88%, respectively.

48. Modern-day anti-vagrancy laws have been successfully challenged on First, Fifth, and Eighth Amendment grounds. However, some of these laws are more narrowly tailored, prohibiting specified activities only at certain times or in certain places, and thus may survive judicial scrutiny.

Cases invalidating ordinances:

City of Chicago v. Morales, 527 U.S. 41, 51 (1999) (holding a gang loitering statute void for vagueness because the "definition of 'loiter' did not assist in clearly articulating the proscriptions of the ordinance.").

Cutting v. City of Portland, Maine, 802 F.3d 79, 81 (1st Cir. 2015) (holding unconstitutional under the First Amendment a city ordinance prohibiting standing, sitting, or staying on median strips).

Jones v. City of Los Angeles, 444 F.3d 1118, 1138 (9th Cir. 2006), vacated, 505 F.3d 1006 (9th Cir. 2007) (holding that the Eighth Amendment prohibits punishing involuntary sitting, lying, or sleeping on public sidewalks that is an unavoidable consequence of being homeless; the Ninth Circuit vacated the decision after the parties settled the action and jointly sought dismissal of the appeal and withdrawal of the opinion). See Sarah Gerry, Jones v. City of Los Angeles: A Moral Response to One City's Attempt to Criminalize, Rather than Confront, Its Homelessness Crisis, 42 Harv. C.R.-C.L. L. Rev. 239 (2007).

Casale v. Kelly, 710 F. Supp. 2d 347, 351 (S.D.N.Y. 2010) (holding New York City in contempt for continuously enforcing three unconstitutional loitering statutes for decades following judicial invalidation of those laws and despite numerous court orders to the contrary).

Cases upholding ordinances:

City of Cleveland v. McCardle, 12 N.E.3d 1169 (Ohio 2014) (ordinance that barred staying in public square between 10 p.m. and 5 a.m. without permit did not violate First Amendment).

Occupy Fresno v. County of Fresno, 835 F. Supp. 2d 849 (E.D. Cal. 2011) (ordinance barring loitering or being in park between 12 a.m. and 6 a.m. did not violate First Amendment).

Joel v. City of Orlando, 232 F.3d 1353, 1358–59 (11th Cir. 2000) (upholding ordinance that prohibited sleeping as rationally related to city's interest in promoting aesthetics and public health and safety and not violative of the equal protection rights of the homeless).

Roulette v. City of Seattle, 97 F.3d 300 (9th Cir. 1996) (upholding ban on sitting or lying on a sidewalk during the day; the law did not ban this activity at night or in public parks).

Roulette v. City of Seattle, 850 F. Supp. 1442, 1450 (W.D. Wash. 1994), aff'd, 78 F.3d 1425 (9th Cir. 1996), opinion amended and superseded on denial of reh'g, 97 F.3d 300 (9th Cir. 1996), as amended on denial of reh'g and reh'g en banc (1996) (upholding ordinance that banned sitting or lying on public sidewalks in commercial areas during specified hours, finding no evidence that the city council "was targeting homeless people in a hostile and discriminatory fashion").

Joyce v. City & County of San Francisco, 846 F. Supp. 843 (N.D. Cal. 1994). The court refused to enjoin San Francisco's "Matrix Quality of Life Program," which criminalized such conduct as sitting on the sidewalk and sleeping in public. While an appeal from the trial court's decision was pending, the mayor directed the chief of police to suspend enforcement of the program. In response, all citations were dismissed and all warrants were recalled, and the appeal was dismissed as moot because it was assumed that the Matrix Program had officially ended and was unlikely to be resumed. *See* Joyce v. City & County of San Francisco, 87 F.3d 1320 (9th Cir. 1996)). For a discussion, *see* Nancy Wright, Not in Anyone's Backyard: Ending the "Contest of Nonresponsibility" and Implementing Long-Term Solutions to Homelessness, 2 Geo. J. on Fighting Poverty 163 (1995).

49. Congress has enacted legislation protecting the rights of persons with disabilities to access public services. These statutes are Title II of the Americans with Disabilities Act and Section 504 of the Rehabilitation Act. At least some federal courts have held that a sidewalk is a service that must be made accessible when the locality undertakes construction or alteration. Moreover, the U.S. Supreme Court has held that persons with disabilities may sue to enforce their right of physical access to a courthouse. *See* Tennessee v. Lane, 541 U.S. 509 (2004). Persons of color are protected from discrimination under the Equal Protection Clause of the federal Constitution and federal civil rights laws barring discrimination in public accommodations.

50. *See* National Law Center on Homelessness & Poverty, Housing Not Handcuffs: Ending the Criminalization of Homelessness in U.S. Cities, at 22–23 (2016), https://www.nlchp.org/documents/Housing-Not-Handcuffs.

51. The Eighth Amendment provides: "Excessive bail shall not be required, nor excessive fines imposed, nor cruel and unusual punishments inflicted." U.S. Const. Amend. VIII.

52. Martin v. City of Boise, 902 F.3d 1031 (9th Cir. 2018), superseded by 920 F.3d 585, 603 (9th 2019) (denying petition for panel rehearing and rehearing en banc, and concluding that "the Eighth Amendment's prohibition on cruel and unusual punishment bars a city from prosecuting people criminally for sleeping outside on public property when those people have no home or other shelter to go to"). The Obama administration filed a statement of interest in the lawsuit, arguing that the Eighth Amendment bars criminalizing sleeping on the street when beds in public shelters are not available. *See* U.S. Department of Justice, Justice Department Files Brief to Address the Criminalization of Homelessness (Aug. 16, 2015), https://www.justice.gov/opa/pr/justice-department-files-brief-address-criminalization-homelessness. Earlier, in Jones v. City of Los Angeles, 444 F.3d 1118, 1138 (9th Cir. 2006), vacated, 505 F.3d 1006 (9th Cir. 2007), the Ninth Circuit had concluded that "so long as there is a greater number of homeless individuals in Los Angeles than the number of available beds [in shelters]" for the homeless, Los Angeles could not enforce a similar ordinance against homeless individuals "for involuntarily sitting, lying, and sleeping in public," but that decision was vacated due to a settlement between the parties and so was not binding.

53. Martin v. City of Boise, 902 F.3d at 1048 (quoting Jones v. City of Los Angeles, 444 F.3d at 1135–38).

54. Martin v. City of Boise, 902 F.3d at 1040–41. Likewise, a lower federal court held that it is illegal to arrest a person who is sleeping in public if the person lacks a permanent home and the locality does not provide adequate temporary indoor shelter. The court reasoned that criminalizing sleeping in public places—a normal and involuntary human act—effectively criminalizes the status of being poor and violates the Eighth Amendment. *See* Pottinger v. City of Miami, 810 F. Supp. 1551, 1554 (S.D. Fla. 1992). In *Pottinger*, homeless people living in Miami, Florida, sued the city to stop a "policy of arresting, harassing and otherwise interfering with homeless people for engaging in basic activities of daily life—including sleeping and eating—in the public places where they are forced to live." Finding that the homeless in Miami "have no realistic choice but to live in public places," the district court held that it was a violation of the Eighth Amendment's prohibition to criminalize doing otherwise innocent activity in public. *Id.* at 1563, 1584. As the district court explained:

> [P]laintiffs have no place else to go and no place else to be. . . . This is so particularly at night when the public parks are closed. As long as the homeless plaintiffs do not have a single place where they can lawfully be, the challenged ordinances, as applied to them, effectively punish them for something for which they may not be convicted under the eighth amendment—sleeping, eating and other innocent conduct.

Id. at 1565. The district court further found that the city's policy was a form of banishment violating a homeless person's fundamental right to travel and to equal protection of the law. *Id.* at 1583.

55. Joel v. City of Orlando, 232 F.3d 1353, 1358–59 (11th Cir. 2000) (ban on camping on public property as applied to homeless person did not violate Eighth Amendment); Lehr v. City of Sacramento, 624 F. Supp. 2d 1218, 1234 (E.D. Cal. 2009) (enforcement of anti-camping ban against homeless persons did not violate Eighth Amendment). Results in other lawsuits have been mixed. *See, for example*:

Alabama: Davison v. City of Tucson, 924 F. Supp. 989 (D. Ariz. 1996) (denying motion for preliminary injunction in challenge to ban on camping on city-owned property).
Arizona: Seeley v. State, 655 P.2d 803 (Ariz. Ct. App. 1982) (city ban on lying, sleeping, or sitting on public rights of way not unconstitutional).
California: Joyce v. City and County of San Francisco, 846 F. Supp. 843 (N.D. Cal. 1994) (refused preliminary injunction to stop arrest of persons engaged in camping or sleeping in public parks).
California: People v. Davenport, 222 Cal. Rptr. 736 (Cal. App. Dept. Super. Ct. 1985), cert. denied, 475 U.S. 1141 (1986) (ban on sleeping in certain public areas not unconstitutional).
Oregon: City of Portland v. Johnson, 651 P.2d 1384 (Or. Ct. App. 1982) (ban on camping in or upon sidewalk, street, alley, lane, or any public place not unconstitutionally vague or overbroad).
Rhode Island: Whiting v. Town of Westerly, 942 F.2d 18 (1st Cir. 1991) (ban on sleeping on public beach not unconstitutional).

56. 468 U.S. 288 (1984). If sleeping in public is part of a demonstration protesting the lack of housing for poor people, First Amendment rights are implicated. In that case,

sleeping may be prohibited only if the prohibition is a reasonable restriction on the time, place, or manner of speech and alternative means of expression remain available. *Id.* at 293; *see also* Occupy Fort Myers v. City of Fort Myers, 882 F. Supp. 2d 1320, 1328–30 (M.D. Fla. 2011). Disputes about the legality of anti-camping laws increased during the "Occupy" demonstrations and often were upheld in that context. "Occupy Wall Street" is the name of a loosely organized global movement which began on September 17, 2011, in Lower Manhattan to draw attention to growing income inequality in the United States and the influence of corporations on government, particularly in financial regulation. Many of the protests included camping sites set up by demonstrators in city centers and most famously in Zuccotti Park in Manhattan. *See* Occupy Solidarity Network, About, OccupyWallStreet: We are the 99% (Aug. 13, 2017), http://occupywallst.org/about/; *see also* Colin Moynihan, Wall Street Protest Begins, with Demonstrators Blocked, City Room: Blogging from the Five Boroughs (Sept. 17, 2011 4:26 PM), https://cityroom.blogs.nytimes.com/2011/09/17/wall-street-protest-begins-with-demonstrators-blocked/; Erik Tarloff, The Occupation, The Atlantic (Oct. 16, 2011), https://www.theatlantic.com/national/archive/2011/10/the-occupation/246755/. For decisions involving Occupy and the right to be in public spaces, *see, for example*, Watters v. Otter, 955 F. Supp. 2d 1178 (D. Idaho 2013); Henke v. Department of the Interior, 842 F. Supp. 2d 54 (D.D.C. 2012); Occupy Minneapolis v. County of Hennepin, 866 F. Supp. 2d 1062 (D. Minn. 2011); Occupy Fresno v. County of Fresno, 835 F. Supp. 2d 849 (E.D. Cal. 2011).

57. These regulations take the form of "metered street parking zones, permit-only parking zones, time restrictions, restrictions on vehicle operability, restrictions regarding licensing and registration, and even prohibitions directed specifically at vehicle habitation." *See* T. Ray Ivey, The Criminalization of Vehicle Residency and the Case for Judicial Intervention via the Washington State Homestead Act, 42 Seattle U.L. Rev. 243, 244 (2018). Although the regulation may be civil, not criminal, the imposition of fees and fines could result in jail. *Id.* at 21 (discussing civil restrictions that allow for the conversion of unpaid, noncriminal violations into misdemeanors, having the compounding effect of dragging vehicle residents into the criminal justice system).

58. Desertrain v. City of Los Angeles, 754 F.3d 1147, 1157–58 (9th Cir. 2014). For further discussion, *see* Lindsay Walter, Judicial Limits in Addressing Homelessness: Desertrain v. City of Los Angeles, 6 Cal. L. Rev. Circuit 98 (2015). In 2016, it was estimated that at any point in time 11,000 people in Los Angeles, California, slept in cars, tents, or encampments for lack of better alternatives. *See* Los Angeles Homeless Services Authority, 2016 Homeless Count Results, at 12 (May 10, 2016), https://documents.lahsa.org/Planning/homelesscount/2016/factsheet/2016-HC-Results.pdf.

59. *See, for example*, Hershey v. City of Clearwater, 834 F.2d 937 (11th Cir. 1987); Allen v. City of Sacramento, 183 Cal. Rptr. 3d 654 (Ct. App. 2015); State v. Sturch, 82 Haw. 269 (Ct. App. 1996), as amended (June 27, 1996), cert. denied, 82 Haw. 360 (1996).

60. Katz v. United States, 389 U.S. 347, 353 (1967). *See* U.S. Const. Amend. IV ("The right of the people to be secure in their persons . . . shall not be violated."). For further discussion, *see* Kevin Bundy, "Officer, Where's My Stuff?": The Constitutional

Implications of a De Facto Property Disability for Homeless People, 1 Hastings Race & Poverty L.J. 57 (2003).

61. Courts currently employ a two-prong test to determine whether an individual has a reasonable expectation of privacy. Under this test, an individual has a constitutionally protected interest if the person has exhibited an actual, subjective expectation of privacy and if that expectation is one that society is prepared to recognize as reasonable. *See, for example,* Vernonia Sch. Dist. 47J v. Acton, 515 U.S. 646 (1995).

62. Kincaid v. City of Fresno, 2006 WL 35442732 (E.D. Cal. 2006). The court entered a preliminary injunction to halt the city's practice of seizing and destroying the possessions of homeless persons "on the spot" during sweeps of encampments variously located in a public space or on private property. The court later approved a $2.35 million class action settlement to create a medical and housing fund for 225 class members and to compensate those class members whose property had been destroyed. The settlement required the city to provide written notice "at least three days before the sweep of any encampment" and to store items that are seized for at least 90 days. *See* Farida Ali, Limiting the Poor's Right to Public Space: Criminalizing Homelessness in California, 21 Geo. J. on Poverty L. & Pol'y 197, 226–227 (2014).

63. Pottinger v. City of Miami, 810 F. Supp. 1551, 1583 (S.D. Fla. 1992). Relatedly, a federal court in Washington, D.C., held that federal marshals looking for a fugitive acted unconstitutionally when they entered a shelter without a warrant and demanded identification from the homeless people sleeping inside. Comm. for Creative Non-Violence v. Unknown Agents of the U.S. Marshals Serv., 797 F. Supp. 7 (D.D.C. 1992).

64. California v. Greenwood, 486 U.S. 35 (1988) (warrantless seizure of trash deposited curbside permissible under the Fourth Amendment because the owner left the trash in public view and so there was no expectation of privacy).

65. Watters v. Otter, 955 F. Supp. 2d 1178 (D. Idaho 2013) (involving "Occupy Boise's tent city"). *See also* Lyall v. Denver, 2018 WL 1470197 (D. Colo. 2018) (involving class action on behalf of homeless persons living on Denver's streets). *But see* Carr v. Oregon Department of Transportation, 2014 WL 3741934 (D. Ore. 2014) (dismissing due process challenge to seizure of homeless person's camping property). The community caretaking exception allows for the seizure of unattended property in public places when the seizure is made to protect the property rather than to investigate a crime. Additional exceptions to the Fourth Amendment are discussed later in this chapter.

66. Lavan v. City of Los Angeles, 693 F.3d 1022, 1024 (9th Cir. 2012), cert. denied, 570 U.S. 918 (2013). The preliminary injunction barred the City from:

    1. Seizing property in Skid Row absent an objectively reasonable belief that it is abandoned, presents an immediate threat to public health or safety, or is evidence of a crime, or contraband; and
    2. Absent an immediate threat to public health or safety, destruction of said seized property without maintaining it in a secure location for a period of less than 90 days.

67. *See, for example,* Pottinger v. City of Miami, 810 F. Supp. 1551, 1570 & n.30 (S.D. Fla. 1992) (holding that seizure of homeless person's belongings from public area

violated Fourth and Fifth Amendments). *But see* Stone v. Agnos, 960 F.2d 893 (9th Cir. 1992) (upholding constitutionality of seizure and destruction of homeless person's property during arrest for sleeping on park bench); *see also* Commonwealth v. Gordon, 640 A.2d 422 (Pa. Super. Ct. 1994), appeal granted, 655 A.2d 467 (1995), rev'd, 683 A.2d 253 (1996) (seizure of homeless person's belongings in abandoned building must comply with constitutional protections). The law is different if the person is sleeping on private property; then the person is considered to be a trespasser. *See* D'Aguanno v. Gallagher, 50 F.3d 877 (11th Cir. 1995).

68. Kentucky v. King, 563 U.S. 452 (2011) (police may not create grounds for warrantless search by violating the Fourth Amendment).

69. Lavan v. City of Los Angeles, 693 F.3d 1022, 1032 (9th Cir. 2012), cert. denied, 133 S. Ct. 2855 (2013). A settlement in Tucker v. Oregon Department of Transportation, No. 11-466 (D. Or. Apr. 15, 2011), required the Oregon Department of Transportation to enact regulations providing at least 10 days' notice before removing personal property from a state right of way. Even before the settlement, the state agency was required to store property taken from a state right of way for at least 30 days and permit property owners to schedule appointments to claim it. *See* Or. Admin. R. § 734-035-0030 (1990); *see also* Panzella v. Sposato, 863 F.3d 210 (2d Cir. 2017) (gun owner was entitled to prompt hearing before neutral decision maker following seizure of rifles in connection with temporary order of protection issued by family court).

70. The U.S. Supreme Court, when considering the reasonableness of a search, begins with the basic rule that "searches conducted outside the judicial process, without prior approval by judge or magistrate, are per se unreasonable under the Fourth Amendment—subject only to a few specifically established and well-delineated exceptions." Arizona v. Gant, 556 U.S. 332, 338 (2009), quoting Katz v. United States, 389 U.S. 347, 357 (1967). '

71. *See* Birchfield v. North Dakota, 579 U.S. ___, 136 S. Ct. 2160 (2016) (Fourth Amendment permitted warrantless breath tests but not warrantless blood tests incident to arrests for drunk driving).

72. Arizona v. Gant, 556 U.S. 332, 344 (2009) (warrantless search of vehicle not reasonable when suspect handcuffed in patrol car; vehicle search incident to arrest justified by the "possibility of access [by the arrestee] []or the likelihood of discovering offense-related evidence").

73. Carroll v. United States, 267 U.S. 132 (1925) (warrantless vehicular search was permissible during course of a lawful arrest); Rakas v. Illinois, 439 U.S. 128, 154 n.2 (1978) (Powell, J., concurring) ("There are sound reasons for this distinction: Automobiles operate on public streets; they are serviced in public places; they stop frequently; they are usually parked in public places; their interiors are highly visible; and they are subject to extensive regulation and inspection. The rationale of the automobile distinction does not apply, of course, to objects on the person of an occupant.").

74. United States v. Ross, 456 U.S. 798 (1982).

75. Collins v. Virginia, 584 U.S. ___, 138 S. Ct. 1663 (2018).

76. California v. Carney, 471 U.S. 386, 393 (1985) (because of their inherent mobility, the vehicular exception applies to motor homes, even when they are used as dwellings).

See, for example, United States v. Ervin, 907 F.2d 1534, 1538–39 (5th Cir. 1990) (warrantless search of defendant's mobile home was valid because the mobile home was not parked in a place regularly used for residential purposes, it was not occupied as a home, and it was readily mobile); United States v. Markman, 844 F.2d 366, 369 (6th Cir. 1988) (warrantless search of mobile home was valid because vehicle had out-of-state license plates, was parked in a state other than the owner's state of residence, and was parked in a driveway connected to a public street). *But see* State v. Durbin, 489 N.W.2d 655, 659 (Wis. Ct. App. 1992) (vehicular exception did not apply to an unhitched camper trailer in the owner's backyard that was not readily movable and appeared to be used as a home).

77. California v. Carney, 471 U.S. 386, 394 n.3 (1985). Factors that may be relevant to determine whether a warrant would be required include the mobile home's location, whether it is readily mobile or elevated on blocks, whether it is licensed, whether it is connected to utilities, and if it has convenient access to a public road.

78. Schneckloth v. Bustamonte, 412 U.S. 218, 219 (1973) (referring to consent as a well-settled exception to the requirements of a warrant or probable cause for a search).

79. The surrounding environment also is relevant, including whether the police threaten, intimidate, or make false promises or if the individual is in custody. United States v. Drayton, 536 U.S. 194, 207 (2002) (consent to search was voluntary because the officers were not coercive, even though the defendants were on a bus and they were not informed of their right to refuse); United States v. Bearden, 780 F.3d 887, 895 (8th Cir. 2015).

80. *See* Rachel Levinson-Waldman, Hiding in Plain Sight: A Fourth Amendment Framework for Analyzing Government Surveillance in Public, 66 Emory L.J. 527 (2017).

81. United States v. Jones, 565 U.S. 400, 404 (2012).

82. Carpenter v. United States, 585 U.S. ___, 138 S. Ct. 2206 (2018). The Court explicitly declined to extend the third-party doctrine, which holds that "a person has no legitimate expectation of privacy in information he voluntarily turns over to third parties," *id.* at 2216 (quoting Smith v. Maryland, 442 U.S. 735, 743–744 (1979)), to seven days' worth of historical cell phone location information. However, the Court emphasized that its decision was narrow, and it declined to consider whether a person would have a legitimate expectation of privacy in real-time cell-site location information.

83. Carpenter v. United States, 585 U.S. ___, 138 S. Ct. 2206 (2018).

84. Brown v. Texas, 443 U.S. 47 (1979); Erin Murphy, Manufacturing Crime: Process, Pretext, and Criminal Justice, 97 Geo. L.J. 1435, 1468–71 (2009). As of 2018, 26 states have enacted "stop and identify" statutes in some form. Immigrant Legal Res. Center, Chart of Stop-and-Identify State Statutes (Feb. 1, 2018), https://www.ilrc.org/chart-stop-and-identify-state-statutes. Some states additionally list "failure to identify" as a ground for an officer to have reasonable suspicion of criminal loitering. *Id.*

85. 461 U.S. 352, 358–361 (1983).

86. Hiibel v. Sixth Judicial Circuit Court of Nevada, Humboldt County, 542 U.S. 177, 184–185 (2006). A survey conducted in 2004 by the National Law Center on

Homelessness & Poverty recorded that 59.8% of homeless people who were stopped by police for minor offenses and could not produce ID suffered harassment or arrest. *See* National Law Center on Homelessness & Poverty, Photo Identification Barriers Faced by Homeless Persons: The Impact of September 11, at 5 (Apr. 2004), https://www.nlchp.org/documents/ID_Barriers.

87. The practice was enjoined in Los Angeles, California. *See* Justin v. City of Los Angeles, 2000 WL 1808426, at *13 (C.D. Cal. 2000). But it persists in many places. *See* Erika Aguilar, How having an ID card can make or break a homeless person's chances of recovery, Southern California Public Radio (June 3, 2015), http://www.scpr.org/news/2015/06/03/52147/how-an-id-card-can-make-or-break-a-homeless-person/.

88. REAL ID Act of 2005, Pub. L. No. 109-13, 119 Stat. 32, amending 8 U.S.C. ch. 12. In 2013, the U.S. Department of Homeland Security announced a phased-in enforcement of the act. *See* U.S. Department of Homeland Security, REAL ID, available at https://www.dhs.gov/real-id.

89. Emergency Supplemental Appropriations Act for Defense, the Global War on Terror, and Tsunami Relief, 2005, Pub. L. No. 109-113, May 11, 2005, 119 Stat. 231, § 202(c).

90. 6 C.F.R. § 37.11(c).

91. Niki Ludt, Justice Requires that Legal ID Be Affordable to All, Face to Face (Feb. 11, 2015), http://facetofacegermantown.org/news/justice-requires-legal-id-affordable-niki-ludt/ ("Thirty-three states . . . provide for waivers of non-driver's ID fees, usually based on age, indigence, homelessness, or some combination thereof.").

92. *See, for example*, Imani Gandy, Well Actually, It's Pretty Hard for Some People to Get a Photo ID So They Can Vote, Rewire (Oct. 16, 2014), https://rewire.news/ablc/2014/10/16/well-actually-pretty-hard-people-get-photo-id-just-vote/.

93. 7 C.F.R. § 273.2(f)(1)(vii).

94. Food Research & Action Center, SNAP/Food Stamp Program Rights for People Experiencing Homelessness, https://web.archive.org/web/20161018021005/http://frac.org/federal-foodnutrition-programs/snapfood-stamps/homeless-persons-rights-under-the-snapsnapfood-stamp-program/; 7 C.F.R. § 273.2(f)(4)(ii).

95. U.S. Social Security Administration, Program Operations Manual, Identity of Claimants, GN 00203.020 (Aug. 5, 2016), https://policy.ssa.gov/.

96. National Law Center on Homelessness & Poverty, Photo Identification Barriers Faced by Homeless Persons: The Impact of September 11, at 15 (Apr. 2004), https://www.nlchp.org/documents/ID_Barriers. *See* United States Department of Health and Human Services, Office of Family Assistance, Temporary Assistance for Needy Families (TANF), http://www.acf.hhs.gov/programs/ofa/programs/tanf.

97. State of Rhode Island Department of Human Services, RI Works Program Verification Checklist, http://www.dhs.ri.gov/assets/documents/RHODE%20ISLAND%20WORKS%20PROGRAM%20VERIFICATION%20CHECKLIST.pdf.

98. U.S. Department of Agriculture Food and Nutrition Service, Women, Infants and Children (WIC), http://www.fns.usda.gov/wic/who-gets-wic-and-how-apply.

99. Texas WIC, What to Bring to Your WIC Appointment, http://texaswic.dshs.state.tx.us/wiclessons/docs/What-to-bring-to-your-appointment_English.pdf.

100. 8 U.S.C. § 1304(e).

101. *See* Jonathan Weinberg, Demanding Identity Papers, 55 Washburn L.J. 197, 213–214 (2015).

102. 8 U.S.C. § 1357(g). *See* ACLU, Know Your Rights: Immigrants' Rights, https://www.aclu.org/know-your-rights/immigrants-rights/#ive-been-stopped-by-police-or-ice ("If you are not a U.S. citizen and an immigration agent requests your papers, you must show them if you have them with you. If you are over 18, carry your immigration documents with you at all times. If you do not have immigration papers, say you want to remain silent.").

103. Arizona v. United States, 567 U.S. 387, 410 (2012). *See* Jennifer M. Chacón, Policing Immigration After Arizona, 3 Wake Forest J.L. & Pol'y 231, 245 (2013) ("[T]he invitation to agents to police in this way will inevitably lead to the exercise of judgment in ways that are tainted by racial stereotypes."). That same year, a federal appeals court granted a preliminary injunction barring the county sheriff from detaining persons based solely on reasonable suspicion or knowledge of their unlawful presence in the country. Rather, an extended detention required further evidence of criminal activity because "unlike illegal entry, mere unauthorized presence in the United States is not a crime." Melendres v. Arpaio, 695 F.3d 990, 1000–01 (9th Cir. 2012).

104. Border Security and Immigration Enforcement Improvements, Executive Order No. 13767, 82 Fed. Reg. 8793, § 10 (Jan. 25, 2017); Enhancing Public Safety in the Interior of the United States, Executive Order No. 13768, § 10 (Jan. 25, 2017). The latter executive order also sought to withhold funding from "sanctuary jurisdictions" that "willfully refuse to comply" with 8 U.S.C. § 1373, which requires communication between government agencies and federal immigration officials. This portion of the executive order has been challenged in federal court. *See* City & Cty. of San Francisco v. Trump, 897 F.3d 1225 (9th Cir. 2018) (holding that the President could not constitutionally withhold funds appropriated by Congress but remanding to the district court to determine the proper scope of an injunction). *See* Amanda Sakuma, Donald Trump's Plan to Outsource Immigration Enforcement to Local Cops, The Atlantic (Feb. 18, 2017), https://www.theatlantic.com/politics/archive/2017/02/trump-immigration-enforcement/517071/.

105. *See, for example*, Immigrant Defense Project, Know Your Rights with ICE (Jan. 2018), https://www.immigrantdefenseproject.org/wp-content/uploads/2016/12/IDP-ICE-Raids-Flyer-ENG-Jan-13-2018.pdf; Catholic Immigration Network, Know Your Rights: A Guide to Your Rights When Interacting with Law Enforcement, https://cliniclegal.org/resources/know-your-rights-law-enforcement; ACLU, Know Your Rights: Immigrants' Rights, https://www.aclu.org/know-your-rights/immigrants-rights/#ive-been-stopped-by-police-or-ice.

106. Florida v. Bostick, 501 U.S. 429, 431, 437 (1991).

107. Illinois v. Wardlow, 528 U.S. 119, 123–124 (2000).

108. See, *for example*, United States v. Franklin, 323 F.3d 1298, 1302 (11th Cir. 2003).

109. *See, for example*, Garrett Chase, The Early History of the Black Lives Movement, and the Implications Thereof, 18 Nev. L.J. 1091 (2018).

110. *See, for example*, Commonwealth v. Warren, 475 Mass. 530, 538–540 (2016) (noting reports that "black males in Boston are disproportionately and repeatedly targeted. . . . Such an individual, when approached by the police, might just as easily be motivated by the desire to avoid the recurring indignity of being racially profiled as by the desire to hide criminal activity.").

111. ACLU Apps to Record Police Conduct, https://www.aclu.org/issues/criminal-law-reform/reforming-police-practices/aclu-apps-record-police-conduct.

112. 18 U.S.C. § 2511(2)(d).

113. The states are: California, Connecticut, Florida, Illinois, Maryland, Massachusetts, Montana, New Hampshire, Pennsylvania, and Washington. *See* Alexander Shaaban, Officer! You Are on Candid Camera: Why the Government Should Grant Private Citizens an Exemption from State Wiretap Laws When Surreptitiously Recording On-Duty Officers in Public, 42 Western St. L. Rev. 202 (2015).

114. *For example*, in Texas, persons may be charged who "with criminal negligence interrupt, disrupt, impede, or otherwise interfere with" the work of law enforcement as well as many other government officials. Tex. Penal Code Ann. § 38.15 (2015); *see* Berrett v. State, 152 S.W.3d 600, 604–605 (Tex. Ct. App. 2004) (moving one's arms and continuing to film during arrest constituted interference). Kansas and New Mexico have similar statutes. *See* Ky. Rev. Stat. Ann. § 21-5904(a)(3) (2014) (potential felony for "knowingly obstructing, resisting or opposing any person authorized by law to serve process in the service or execution or in the attempt to serve or execute any writ, warrant, process or order of a court, or in the discharge of any official duty"); N.M Stat. Ann. § 30-22-1 (1978) (misdemeanor for "knowingly obstructing, resisting or opposing any officer of this state or any other duly authorized person serving or attempting to serve or execute any process or any rule or order of any of the courts of this state or any other judicial writ or process").

115. Lower courts that do not protect the right to record police activity tend to rely on the 1972 decision in *Colten v. Kentucky*, where the Court rejected a First Amendment challenge to a conviction for disorderly conduct when the accused refused "to move on after being directed to do so," explaining that the accused "had no constitutional right to observe the issuance of a traffic ticket." 407 U.S. 104, 109 (1972). However, in 1987, the Court distinguished *Colten* when faced with a city ordinance that made it unlawful to interrupt a police officer "in the execution of his duty," finding the ordinance to be overbroad under the First Amendment because it impermissibly criminalized protected speech and could not be upheld as a regulation of disorderly conduct. The Court stated: "The freedom of individuals verbally to oppose or challenge police action without thereby risking arrest is one of the principal characteristics by which we distinguish a free nation from a police state." City of Houston, Texas v. Hill, 482 U.S. 451, 462–463 (1987).

During the Obama administration, the Civil Rights Division of the U.S. Department of Justice submitted a Statement of Interest in a pending criminal proceeding setting forth guidance on the right to record police activity. *See* Statement of Interest of the United States, Sharp v. Balt. City Police Department, No.

1:11-cv-02888-BEL, *1 (D. Md. Jan. 10, 2012), http://www.justice.gov/crt/about/spl/documents/Sharp_SOI_1-10-12.pdf.

116. The case law includes:

Fields v. City of Philadelphia, 862 F.3d 353 (3d Cir. 2017) ("Simply put, the First Amendment protects the act of photographing, filming, or otherwise recording police officers conducting their official duties in public.").

Gericke v. Begin, 753 F.3d 1, 8 (1st Cir. 2014) ("Importantly, an individual's exercise of her First Amendment right to film police activity carried out in public, including a traffic stop, necessarily remains unfettered unless and until a reasonable restriction is imposed or in place.").

American Civil Liberties Union of Illinois v. Alvarez, 679 F.3d 583, 595–596 (7th Cir. 2012), cert. denied, 568 U.S. 1027 (2012) (preliminary injunction entered blocking enforcement of state eavesdropping statute as applied to "people who openly record police officers performing their official duties in public" and, specifically, the ACLU's "Chicago-area 'police accountability program,' which includes a plan to openly make audiovisual recordings of police officers performing their duties in public places and speaking at a volume audible to bystanders").

Glik v. Canniffe, 655 F.3d 78 (1st Cir. 2011) (person on public street had clearly established First Amendment right to film police making arrest in a public space, and his Fourth Amendment right was violated by his arrest without probable cause).

Smith v. City of Cumming, 212 F.3d 1332, 1333 (11th Cir. 2000) (district court erred in finding no First Amendment right to videotape police enforcement action, but no showing right was violated).

Fordyce v. City of Seattle, 55 F.3d 436, 439 (9th Cir. 1995) (issue of material fact existed whether person seeking to record police activity "was assaulted and battered by a Seattle police officer in an attempt to prevent or dissuade him from exercising his First Amendment right to film matters of public interest").

Courts also have located protection of the right in the Fourth Amendment. *For example*, Williamson v. Mills, 65 F.3d 155 (11th Cir. 1995) (no qualified immunity from Fourth Amendment false arrest claim arising from arrest without probable cause of festival participant taking photos of police officers).

See Clay Calvert, The First Amendment Right to Record Images of Police in Public Places: The Unreasonable Slipperiness of Reasonableness & Possible Paths Forward, 3 Tex. A&M L. Rev. 131 (2015); Seth F. Kreimer, Pervasive Image Capture and the First Amendment: Memory, Discourse, and the Right to Record, 159 U. Pa. L. Rev. 335 (2011); *see also* American Civil Liberties Union of Pennsylvania, Know Your Rights When Taking Photos and Making Video and Audio Records, https://www.aclupa.org/issues/policepractices/your-right-record-and-observe-police/taking-photos-video-and-audio/.

117. Cases include:

Turner v. Lieutenant Driver, 848 F.3d 678 (5th Cir. 2017) (First Amendment protects recording of police activity, but detainee did not have clearly established right to videotape activity).

Kelly v. Borough of Carlisle, 622 F.3d 248, 262 (3d Cir. 2010) (was clearly established "that police officers do not have a reasonable expectation of privacy when recording conversations with suspects"; it was not clearly established that a person had "a right to videotape police officers during a traffic stop to put a reasonably competent officer on 'fair notice' that seizing a camera or arresting an individual for videotaping police during the stop would violate the First Amendment").

Szymecki v. Houck, 353 Fed. Appx. 852, 853 (4th Cir. 2009) (First Amendment right "to record police activities on public property was not clearly established in this circuit at the time of the alleged conduct").

Of course, once the federal courts in a jurisdiction hold that police interference with peaceful video recording of their activities violates the First Amendment, any later such interference by the police would subject them to money damages.

118. Form 1093, which is available at a local post office, is used for this purpose. The form is completed online or at the post office, and is available at https://about.usps.com/forms/ps1093.pdf.

119. The least expensive three-month fee is $11 per quarter. *See* United States Postal Service, Notice 123, Price List (2017), http://pe.usps.com/text/dmm300/notice123.htm#2568215.

120. United States Postal Service, Domestic Mail Manual § 508-4.1.1 (2014), http://pe.usps.com/cpim/ftp/manuals/dmm300/508.pdf. *See* Currier v. Potter, 379 F.3d 716, 730–731 (9th Cir. 2004).

121. United States Postal Service, Postal Operations Manual, Issue 9 § 843.1 (2013), https://www.apwu.org/sites/apwu/files/resource-files/POM%209%20Postal%20Operations%20Manual%20%5Bupdated%20through%2010-13%5D.pdf.

122. United States Postal Service, U.S. Postal Bulletin D930 (June 23, 1990); Postal Regulatory Commission, Report on Universal Postal Service and the Postal Monopoly (1996), http://www.prc.gov/docs/61/61628/USO%20Report.pdf ("[T]he Postal Service enjoys considerable discretion to determine the nature and location of postal facilities by which access will be provided."); United States Postal Service, Domestic Mail Manual 508, Section 6, http://pe.usps.com/text/dmm300/508.htm#wp1052038 ("General delivery is normally available at only one facility under the administration of a Post Office with multiple facilities.").

123. Currier v. Potter, 379 F.3d 716 (9th Cir. 2004). Relatedly, the County of San Francisco's use of single-point delivery (leaving a mailbag with building management to distribute among tenants), rather than centralized delivery (delivering mail directly to individual tenant mailboxes), was found not to violate the equal protection rights of tenants living in single-room-occupancy hotels. City & Cty. of San Francisco v. U.S. Postal Serv., 546 Fed. Appx. 697 (9th Cir. 2013).

124. Currier v. Potter, 379 F.3d 716, 722 (9th Cir. 2004).

125. *See* Sarah Golabek-Goldman, Ban the Address: Combating Employment Discrimination Against the Homeless, 126 Yale L.J. 1788 (2017).

126. American Library Association, Extending Our Reach: Reducing Homelessness Through Library Engagement, http://www.ala.org/aboutala/offices/extending-our-reach-reducing-homelessness-through-library-engagement. *See also* Ellyn Ruhlmann, A Home to the Homeless, American Libraries (Nov. 24, 2014), http://americanlibrariesmagazine.org/2014/11/24/a-home-to-the-homeless/; Richard Gunderman & David C. Stevens, How Libraries Became the Front Line of America's Homelessness Crisis, Washington Post (Aug. 19, 2015), https://www.

washingtonpost.com/posteverything/wp/2015/08/19/how-libraries-became-the-front-line-of-americas-homelessness-crisis/.

127. *See, for example,* Kreimer v. Bureau of Police for the Town of Morristown, 958 F.2d 1242, 1247 (3d Cir. 1992) (discussing library rules of Morristown Township, New Jersey, which provided that patrons must conform their "dress and personal hygiene . . . to the standard of the community for public places"); *see also* Madeleine R. Stoner, The Civil Rights of Homeless People: Law, Social Policy, and Social Work Practice, at 165 (Aldine 1995) (discussing removal of homeless persons from public libraries in Las Vegas); Sanford Berman, Jean E. Coleman Library Outreach Lecture, Classism in the Stacks: Libraries and Poverty, American Library Association (2005), http://www.ala.org/offices/olos/olosprograms/jeanecoleman/05berman.

128. Kreimer v. Bureau of Police, 958 F.2d 1242, 1264 (3d Cir. 1992); *see also* Neinast v. Board of Trustees of the Columbus Metropolitan Library, 346 F.3d 585 (6th Cir. 2003) (barring library users who did not wear shoes); Lu v. Hulme, 133 F. Supp. 3d 312, 321 (D. Mass. 2015) (barring library users from bringing "garbage" or "articles with a foul odor" into the facility).

129. Armstrong v. District of Columbia Public Library, 154 F. Supp. 2d 67, 78–79 (D.D.C. 2001) (barring patrons based on "objectionable" appearance violated Constitution).

130. Ruth Graham, Long Overdue: Why Public Libraries are Finally Eliminating the Late-Return Fine, Slate (Feb. 6, 2017), http://www.slate.com/articles/arts/culturebox/2017/02/librarians_are_realizing_that_overdue_fines_undercut_libraries_missions.html.

131. Carol Pogash, In San Jose, Poor Find Doors to Library Closed, N.Y. Times (Mar. 30, 2016), http://www.nytimes.com/2016/03/31/us/in-san-jose-poor-find-doors-to-library-closed.html?_r=0.

New York in 2017 announced a "forgiveness program" giving a library user a one-time amnesty to restore library privileges that had been stopped due to unpaid overdue fees. *See* New York Public Library, Get a New Start at NYC Libraries, http://nyclibraries.org/newstart/.

132. Anne Barnard & Jo Craven McGinty, How One Overdue Book Can Hurt a Credit Record, N.Y. Times (Dec. 26, 2007), http://www.nytimes.com/2007/12/26/nyregion/26library.html.

133. *See* American Library Association, President's budget proposal to eliminate federal library funding "counterproductive and short-sighted," ALA News (Apr. 16, 2017), http://www.ala.org/news/press-releases/2017/03/president-s-budget-proposal-eliminate-federal-library-funding; Loida Garcia-Febo, Federal Budget Includes Big Gains for Libraries, American Libraries (Sept. 28, 2018), https://americanlibrariesmagazine.org/blogs/the-scoop/federal-budget-includes-big-gains-libraries/ (reporting that "#FundLibraries advocacy succeeds at protecting vital programs"); American Library Association, White House budget proposal continues to miscalculate the values of libraries, ALA News (Feb. 12, 2018), http://www.ala.org/news/press-releases/2018/02/white-house-budget-proposal-continues-miscalculate-value-libraries; Andrew Albanese, In FY 2020 Budget Proposal, Trump Renews Bid to End Federal Library Funding, Publishers Weekly

(Mar. 11, 2019), https://www.publishersweekly.com/pw/by-topic/industry-news/libraries/article/79496-in-fy2020-budget-proposal-trump-renews-bid-to-end-to-federal-library-funding.html. *See generally* Amy K. Garner, Public Libraries in the Community, 13 I/S J.L. & Pol'y for Info. Soc'y 1 (2016) (discussing the democratic importance of public libraries and noting their increased use during the Great Recession).

134. *See, for example,* Amy Benfer, Policing Gangsta Fashion, Salon (May 29, 2002), https://www.salon.com/2002/05/29/nelly_2/.

135. The owners of private shopping centers may regulate expressive activities such as handbilling without running afoul of the First Amendment to the federal Constitution. The U.S. Supreme Court has reasoned that it would be an "unwarranted infringement of property rights to require them to yield to the exercise of First Amendment rights under circumstances where adequate alternative avenues of communication exist." Lloyd Corp. v. Tanner, 407 U.S. 551, 567 (1972).

Most state constitutions also permit private property owns to restrict speech. *See* Steven P. Aggergaard, When "Public Space" Isn't Public: Shopping Malls May be the New Town Squares in Many Respects, But in Minnesota and Many Other States, Citizens Leave Their Free Speech Rights at the Door, 72 Bench & B. Minn. 28, 29–30 (2015) (citing as examples State v. Wickland, 589 N.W.2d 793 (Minn. 1999), and Jacobs v. Major, 407 N.W.2d 832 (Wis. 1987)).

However, several state constitutions, including those of California and New Jersey, have been interpreted to protect a person's right to engage in some expressive activity in the common areas of privately-owned shopping centers. *See, for example,* N.J. Coalition Against War in the Middle East v. J.M.B. Realty Corp., 650 A.2d 757, 781 (N.J. 1994) (noncommercial leafleting); Bock v. Westminster Mall, 819 P.2d 55 (Colo. 1991) (distribution of pamphlets and solicitation of signatures regarding U.S. foreign policy); Batchelder v. Allied Stores Int'l, 445 N.E.2d 590, 595 (Mass. 1983) (distribution of material and solicitation of signatures in support of presidential candidate); Alderwood Associates v. Washington Environmental Council, 635 P.2d 108, 117 (Wash. 1981) (soliciting signatures to qualify an initiative for an upcoming election); Robins v. Pruneyard Shopping Center, 592 P.2d 341, 347 (Cal. 1979), aff'd, 447 US 74, 79 (1980) (solicitation of signatures for a petition to Congress). *See* Helen Hershkoff, "Just Words": Common Law and the Enforcement of State Constitutional Social and Economic Rights, 62 Stan. L. Rev. 1521, 1565 (2010) (discussing state law treatment of property owner's right to exclude speakers).

136. *See, for example,* Timothy Williams, Courts Sidestep the Law, and South Carolina's Poor Go to Jail, N.Y. Times (Oct. 12, 2017), https://www.nytimes.com/2017/10/12/us/south-carolina-jail-no-lawyer.html (reporting that police arrested a homeless man 270 times for trespassing because he was near or at a fast-food restaurant or convenience store).

137. *See, for example,* Erik Sherman, Another Starbucks Refused to Let a Black Customer Use the Bathroom, Inc. (Apr. 18, 2018), https://www.inc.com/erik-sherman/another-starbucks-racism-video-training-will-be-harder-than-management-expected.

html; Chad Oliver, Good Question: Restaurant Bathrooms for Customers Only?, NBC2 News (May 6, 2014), http://www.nbc-2.com/story/25446355/good-question-restaurant-bathrooms-for-customers-only.

138. *See* Jeremy Waldron, Homelessness and the Issue of Freedom, 39 UCLA Rev. 295, 312, 315 (1991):

> There is no law against urinating—it is a necessary and desirable human activity. However, there is a law against urinating in public, except in the specially designated premises of public restrooms. . . . If urinating is prohibited in public places (and if there are no public lavatories) then the homeless are simply unfree to urinate.

139. Mike Davis, Afterword—A Logic Like Hell's: Being Homeless in Los Angeles, 39 UCLA L. Rev. 325, 330 (1991). For further discussion, *see* Irus Braverman, Loo Law: The Public Washroom as a Hyper-Regulated Place, 20 Hastings Women's L.J. 45 (2009).

140. Marc L. Roark, Homelessness at the Cathedral, 80 Mo. L. Rev. 53, 109 (2015).

141. 42 U.S.C. § 2000a ("All persons shall be entitled to the full and equal enjoyment of the goods, services, facilities, privileges, advantages, and accommodations of any place of public accommodation, . . . without discrimination or segregation on the ground of race, color, religion, or national origin."); *see also* Angela D. Hooton, Constitutional Review of Affirmative Action Policies for Women of Color: A Hopeless Paradox?, 15 Wis. Women's L.J. 391, 406–407 (2000) ("[I]f an African-American is denied entrance to the . . . bathroom on the basis of race, there is public and judicial outrage.").

142. Kelly Levy, Equal, But Still Separate?: The Constitutional Debate of Sex-Segregated Public Restrooms in the Twenty-First Century, 32 Women's Rts. L. Rep. 248 (2011); *see also* G.G. v. Gloucester County School Board, 822 F.3d 709 (4th Cir. 2016), vacated and remanded, 137 S. Ct. 1239 (2017). In 2017, the Trump administration issued guidance documents on transgender access to public school bathrooms, reversing an earlier guidance issued by the Obama administration that supported civil rights protection for transgender children. *See* Emma Green, The Federal Government's Reversal: Let the States Deal with Transgender Kids, The Atlantic (Feb. 22, 2017), https://www.theatlantic.com/politics/archive/2017/02/transgender-guidance/517530.

143. *See, for example*, Carcaño v. McCrory, 203 F. Supp. 3d 615 (2016) (school preliminarily enjoined from restricting bathroom use based on persons' biological sex as defined by birth certificates).

144. *See, for example*, Gray v. City of Kern, 2015 WL 7352302 (E.D. Cal. Nov. 19, 2015), aff'd in part, rev'd in part and remanded, 704 Fed. Appx. 649 (9th Cir. 2017).

145. National Conference of State Legislatures, Breastfeeding State Laws (June 5, 2017), http://www.ncsl.org/research/health/breastfeeding-state-laws.aspx.

146. *See* Charity R. Clark & Elizabeth R. Wohl, Breastfeeding Laws in Vermont: A Primer, 34 Vt. Bar J. 36, 38 n.8 (2008).

147. Conn. Gen. State § 53-34b (1997) ("No person may restrict or limit the right of a mother to breast-feed her child"); Vt. Stat. Ann. Tit. 9 § 4502(j) (2002) ("Notwithstanding any other provision of law, a mother may breastfeed her child in any place of public accommodation in which the mother and child would otherwise have a legal right to be."); La. Rev. Stat. Ann. § 2247.1(C) (2001) ("It is discriminatory practice in connection with public accommodation for a person to deny an individual the full and equal enjoyment of the goods, services, facilities, privileges, advantages, and accommodations of a place of public accommodation . . . on the grounds that the individual is a mother breastfeeding her baby."); Wis. Stat. Ann. §253.165 (In a location where the mother and child are otherwise authorized to be ". . . no person may prohibit a mother from breast-feeding her child, direct the mother to move to a different location to breast-feed her child, direct a mother to cover her child or breast while breast-feeding, or otherwise restrict a mother from breast-feeding her child. . . .").

148. *See* Michelle Gilman & Rebecca Green, The Surveillance Gap: The Harms of Extreme Privacy and Data Marginalization, 42 N.Y.U. L. & Soc. Change 253, 266 (2018):

> On any given day in the United States, approximately 117,600 people seek work as day laborers in jobs such as construction, landscaping, roofing, and painting, as well as in restaurants and nail salons. Employers typically hire day laborers on a day-to-day basis at a public site (such as a gas station, street corner, or home improvement store parking lot), where as many as two hundred workers may gather. The employer and worker negotiate a verbal, short-term employment agreement. Day-labor markets are usually unregulated, and workers are paid in cash; this is "temporary work in which the work, and often the workers, lack documentation." Earnings are variable, but the median wage for day laborers is $10 per hour, meaning that most day laborers remain below the poverty level, as their annual earnings rarely exceed $15,000. The market for day labor is driven by employer demands for worker flexibility, a downtick in industrial and manufacturing jobs, and the number of migrant workers willing to accept payment below market and legally mandated rates.

149. *See* Elizabeth J. Kennedy, The Invisible Corner: Expanding Workplace Rights for Female Day Laborers, 31 Berkeley J. Emp. & Lab. L. 126, 132–133 (2010):

> Day labor markets exhibit fluid dimensions, with new workers entering the market and other workers leaving it each day. Day laborers primarily search for work on a full-time basis, and the vast majority (eighty-three percent) relies on day labor as their sole source of income. Those looking for work in the male-dominated construction and landscaping industries are organized informally in parking lots and on street corners, or formally by temporary agencies or day labor centers—often run by a non-profit or faith-based organization in partnership with local government agencies. Only twenty-one percent of day laborers search for work at a day labor worker center. The others find work by standing at informal sites, such as in front of businesses (24 percent), home improvement stores (22 percent), gas stations (10 percent) and on busy streets (8 percent).

150. *See* Scott L. Cummings, Litigation at Work: Defending Day Labor in Los Angeles, 58 UCLA L. Rev. 1617 (2011).

151. Cases preliminarily enjoining or invalidating "day laborer" bans:

> Arizona:
> Valle Del Sol Inc. v. Whiting, 709 F.3d 808 (9th Cir. 2013).
> Comite de Jornaleros de Redondo Beach v. City of Redondo Beach, 657 F.3d 936 (9th Cir. 2011).
>
> New York:
> Centro De La Comunidad Hispana De Locust Valley v. Town of Oyster Bay, 128 F. Supp. 3d 597 (E.D.N.Y. 2015), aff'd, 868 F.3d 104 (2d Cir. 2017). Doe v. Village of Mamaroneck, 462 F. Supp. 2d 520 (S.D.N.Y. 2006).
>
> Texas:
> Jornaleros de Las Palmas v. City of League City, 945 F. Supp. 2d 779 (S.D. Tex. 2013).

152. Ward v. Rock Against Racism, 491 U.S. 781, 790 (1989); Schad v. Borough of Mount Ephraim, 452 U.S. 61, 65 (1981); Goldstein v. Town of Nantucket, 477 F. Supp. 606, 608 (D. Mass. 1979). *But see* Barnes v. Glen Theatre, Inc., 501 U.S. 560 (1991) (city may ban nude dancing).

153. Pence v. City of St. Louis, Mo., 958 F. Supp. 2d 1079 (E.D. Mo. 2013) (granting injunction preventing the enforcement of a St. Louis ordinance requiring that street performers have a permit).

154. *See* Ward v. Rock Against Racism, 491 U.S. 781 (1989); Carew-Reid v. Metropolitan Transp. Auth., 903 F.2d 914 (2d Cir. 1990). *But see* Casey v. City of Newport, R.I., 308 F.3d 106 (1st Cir. 2002) (holding total ban on amplification violated First Amendment).

155. *See, for example*, Berger v. City of Seattle, 569 F.3d 1029, 1053 (9th Cir. 2009) (permit requirement before performing was not narrowly tailored and rule allowing performers passively but not actively to solicit donations was content neutral); Goldstein v. Town of Nantucket, 477 F. Supp. 606 (D. Mass. 1979) (transient vendor law as applied to musician infringed First Amendment rights).

156. *See, for example*, Philadelphia Code, Title 9, Chapter 9-203, http://www.phila.gov/ philacode/html/_data/title09/CHAPTER_9_200_COMMERCIAL_ACTIV/9_ 203_Street_Vendors_.html (defining a street vendor as "[a]ny person travelling by foot, wagon, motor vehicle or any other type of conveyance from place to place, house to house or street to street or on property owned or controlled by the City of Philadelphia carrying, conveying, or transporting goods, wares or merchandise and offering and exposing them for sale...").

157. *See* Rob Frommer & Alex Montgomery, Street vending and the American dream, Los Angeles Daily News (Aug. 6, 2018), https://www.dailynews.com/2018/08/ 05/street-vending-and-the-american-dream/; Dick M. Carpenter II, Street Vending in the United States: A Unique Dataset from a Survey of Street Vendors in America's Largest Cities, 20 Cityscape: A Journal of Policy Development & Research 245 (2018), https://www.huduser.gov/portal/periodicals/cityscpe/ vol20num3/article13.html; Institute for Justice, Street Vending in the United States: A Unique Dataset from a Survey of Street Vendors in America's Largest

Cities (Feb. 2018), https://ij.org/report/upwardly-mobile/street-vending-in-the-united-states-a-unique-dataset-from-a-survey-of-street-vendors-in-americas-largest-cities/.

158. *See* Erin Norman, Robert Frommer, Bert Gall, & Lisa Kuepper, Streets of Dreams: How Cities Can Create Economic Opportunity by Knocking Down Protectionist Barriers to Street Vending, Institute for Justice (2011).

159. City of Wichita, Kansas, Street and Sidewalk Vendors, http://www.wichita.gov/Licenses/Licenses/Street%20Sidewalk%20Vendor%20INFO.pdf.

160. For more information, *see* New York City Consumer Affairs, Apply, General, http://www1.nyc.gov/site/dca/businesses/license-checklist-general-vendor.page.

161. City of Chicago Business Affairs & Consumer Protection, Mobile Food Truck Licenses, http://www.cityofchicago.org/city/en/depts/bacp/supp_info/mobile_food_vendorlicenses.html.

162. Los Angeles Bureau of Street Services, Frequently Asked Questions, http://bss.lacity.org/InvestigationAndEnforcement/FAQs.htm.

163. County of Los Angeles Public Health, Plan Check Guidelines for Mobile Food Facilities and Mobile Support Unit, http://publichealth.lacounty.gov/eh/docs/vip/PLAN_CHECK_GUIDELINES_1.pdf. *See* Ernesto Hernandez-Lopez, LA's Taco Truck War: How Law Cooks Food Culture Contests, 43 U. Miami L. Rev. 233 (2011).

164. *See* Jibran Khan, Los Angeles Legalizes Street Vending, National Review (Dec. 6, 2018), https://www.nationalreview.com/corner/los-angeles-legalizes-street-vending/; Tim Arango, L.A. Street Sellers Outlawed No More, N.Y. Times (Jan. 11, 2019), https://www.nytimes.com/interactive/2019/01/11/multimedia/la-street-vendors.html.

165. *See, for example*, White v. City of Sparks, 500 F.3d 953 (9th Cir. 2007).

166. *See, for example*, Josephine Havlak Photographer, Inc. v. Vill. of Twin Oaks, 864 F.3d 905 (8th Cir. 2017), cert. denied, 138 S. Ct. 986 (2018) (ordinance prohibiting commercial activity in park without permit was constitutional as applied to photographer). *See* Christen Martosella, Refusing to Draw the Line: A Speech-Protective Rule for Art Vending Cases, 13 N.Y.U. J. Legis. & Pub. Pol'y 603, 619 (2010) ("Outside of [the Second and Ninth Circuits], no court has attempted to construct a comprehensive rule to employ in art vending cases.").

167. In 2010, it was reported that the sale of "street papers"—specialty newspapers sold by unemployed and often homeless persons—was a thriving industry, with circulation up 36% that year. Blake Farmer, "Street Papers" Sold by Homeless Are Thriving, National Public Radio (Dec. 23, 2010), http://www.npr.org/2010/12/23/132291799/Street-Papers-Sold-By-Homeless-Are-Thriving.

168. The Contributor v. City of Brentwood, Tenn., 726 F.3d 861, 866 (6th Cir. 2013).

169. For additional information about vendor licenses in New York City, *see*

    Department of Consumer Affairs, General Street Vendor License, https://www1.nyc.gov/nyc-resources/service/2938/general-street-vendor-license.

170. Street Vendor Project, FAQ, http://streetvendor.org/faq/. *See also* Bery v. City of New York, 97 F.3d 689, 695 (2d Cir. 1996) ("The City apparently looks upon visual

art as mere 'merchandise' lacking in communicative concepts or ideas. . . . [But v]
isual art is as wide ranging in its depiction of ideas, concepts and emotions as any
book, treatise, pamphlet or other writing, and is similarly entitled to full First
Amendment protection.").

171. For example, the court in *People v. Saul* determined that playing cards containing
the images and descriptive captions of Iraqi military or political personnel did not
merit protection because they did not "communicate[] ideas, opinions, emotions or
a point of view." People v. Saul, N.Y.S.2d 189, 193 (N.Y. Crim. Ct. 2004). The plaintiffs
in *Mastrovincenzo v. City of New York* challenged the license requirement for selling
items of clothing decorated with "oil paints, spray paints, markers, and permanent
paint pens." Mastrovincenzo v. City of New York, 435 F.3d 78, 86 (2d Cir. 2006). The
Second Circuit Court of Appeals disagreed that the items were "necessarily expressive" or "automatically entitled to First Amendment protection." *Id.* at 105. Rather
when items offered for sale straddle utility and expression, the First Amendment
applies only if "an object's dominant purpose is expressive." *Id.* at 95.

172. Answers About New York's Street Vendors, N.Y. Times (Oct. 9, 2009), http://
cityroom.blogs.nytimes.com/2009/10/07/answers-about-new-yorks-street-
vendors/.

173. Begging is clearly speech because of its expressive content. Restrictions on begging are not content neutral; they apply "to a particular speech because of the topic
discussed or the idea or message expressed." Norton v. City of Springfield, Ill., 806
F.3d 411,412 (7th Cir. 2015), quoting Reed v. Gilbert, 576 U.S. ___, 135 S. Ct. 2218,
2227 (2015).

In addition, bans on begging often restrict only an individual's request for alms,
and do not apply to requests by members of charitable organizations, and often
leave open no alternative way to request assistance. *See* Helen Hershkoff & Adam
S. Cohen, Begging to Differ: The First Amendment and the Right to Beg, 104 Harv.
L. Rev. 896 (1991); Paul G. Chevigny, Begging and the First Amendment: Young
v. New York City Transit Authority, 57 Brook. L. Rev. 525 (1991).

174. Reed v. Town of Gilbert, 576 U.S. ___, 135 S. Ct. 2218 (2015). In *Reed*, the Court
explained that the question of whether a restriction on speech impermissibly singles out particular kinds of speakers must be made before the government offers a
justification for the restriction. *See* Thayer v. City of Worcester, 755 F.3d 60 (1st Cir.
2014), judgment vacated in light of Reed v. Gilbert, 576 U.S. ___, 135 S. Ct. 2887
(2015); Norton v. City of Springfield, Ill., 806 F.3d 411 (7th Cir. 2015), cert. denied,
136 S. Ct. 1173 (2016) (collecting conflicting decisions on this question prior to
Reed, and interpreting the import of *Reed*). *See* Katie Pilgram Neidig, The Demise of
Anti-panhandling Laws in America, 48 St. Mary's L.J. 543 (2017).

175. Village of Schaumburg v. Citizens for a Better Environment, 444 U.S. 620 (1980); *see
also* Speet v. Schuette, 726 F.3d 867 (6th Cir. 2013).

176. Invalidating ban on panhandling:

Norton v. City of Springfield, Ill., 806 F.3d 411 (7th Cir. 2015), cert. denied, 136
S. Ct. 1173 (2016).
Speet v. Schuette, 726 F.3d 867 (6th Cir. 2013).

A.C.L.U. of Nevada v. City of Las Vegas, 466 F.3d 784 (9th Cir. 2006).
Loper v. New York City Police Department, 999 F.2d 699 (2d Cir. 1993).
McLaughlin v. City of Lowell, 140 F. Supp. 3d 177 (D. Mass. 2015).
Clatterbuck v. City of Charlottesville, 92 F. Supp. 3d 478 (W.D. Va. 2015), appeal dismissed (May 8, 2015).
People v. Hoffstead, 28 Misc. 3d 16 (N.Y. App. Term 2010).

Upholding ban on panhandling:

Smith v. City of Fort Lauderdale, Fla., 177 F.3d 954 (11th Cir. 1999).
ISKCON of Potomac, Inc. v. Kennedy, 61 F.3d 949 (D.C. Cir. 1995).
Young v. New York City Transit Auth., 903 F.2d 146 (2d Cir. 1990), cert. denied, 498 U.S. 984 (1990).
Chase v. Town of Ocean City, 825 F. Supp. 2d 599 (D. Md. 2011).
People v. Barton, 861 N.E.2d 75 (N.Y. 2006).

177. Cutting v. City of Portland, 802 F.3d 79, 81 (1st Cir. 2015).
178. National Law Center on Homelessness & Poverty, Housing not Handcuffs: Ending the Criminalization of Homelessness in U.S. Cities at 25 (2016), https://www.nlchp. org/documents/Housing-Not-Handcuffs.
179. A.C.L.U. of Nevada v. City of Las Vegas, 466 F.3d 784, 793 (9th Cir. 2006). *See* Anthony D. Lauriello, Panhandling Regulation After Reed v. Town of Gilbert, 116 Colum. L. Rev. 1105, 1120–22 (2016) (citing caselaw from the Second, Fourth, Sixth, Seventh, Ninth, and Eleventh Circuits in support of the view that personal solicitation is entitled to First Amendment protection).
180. For an example of a ban on aggressive panhandling, *see* Indianapolis Mun. Code § 407-102 (d) ("It shall be unlawful to engage in an act of panhandling in an aggressive manner.").
181. *See, for example*, Gresham v. Peterson, 225 F.3d 899 (7th Cir. 2000); *see also* United States v. O'Brien, 391 U.S. 367 (1968) (criminal prohibition against burning draft card did not violate First Amendment because the law was justified by a substantial government interest (in an effective draft system) unrelated to the suppression of expressive protest speech and it prohibited no more speech than necessary to further that interest).
182. McLaughlin v. City of Lowell, 140 F. Supp. 3d 177, 191 (D. Mass. 2015).
183. *See, for example*, Recycle for Change v. City of Oakland, 2016 WL 344751 (N.D. Cal. 2016), aff'd, 856 F.3d 666 (9th Cir. 2017), cert. denied 138 S. Ct. 557 (2017) (denied preliminary injunction in nonprofit's challenge to ordinance regulating unattended donation collection boxes).
184. National Law Center on Homelessness & Poverty, Housing Not Handcuffs: Ending the Criminalization of Homelessness in U.S. Cities at 26 (2016), https://www.nlchp. org/documents/Housing-Not-Handcuffs. Relatedly, until 2016, a person could be arrested in New York for asking a stranger to "swipe" into a subway; the revised policy (adopted in an internal Police Department order) permits police to issue a summons or a ticket of up to $50. *See* Joseph Goldstein, Spare a Swipe? New York City Eases Rules for a Subway Request, N.Y. Times (Apr. 17, 2016), https://www. nytimes.com/2016/04/18/nyregion/spare-a-swipe-new-york-city-eases-rules-for-a-subway-request.html.

185. *See generally* Sydney Rosenblum, Homeless and Hungry: Demanding the Right to Share Food, 46 Fordham Urb. L.J. 1004 (2019); Sara K. Rankin, Punishing Homelessness, 22 New Crim. L. Rev. 99 (2019); Jeremy K. Kessler & David E. Pozen, The Search for an Egalitarian First Amendment, 118 Colum. L. Rev. 1953 (2018); Caleb Detweiler, Breaking Bread and the Law: Criminalizing Homelessness and First Amendment Rights In Public Parks, 51 Valp. U. L. Rev. 695 (2017); Jordan Bailey, Food-Sharing Restrictions: A New Method of Criminalizing Homelessness in American Cities, 23 Geo. J. on Poverty L. & Pol'y 273, 281 (2016).

186. *See, for example*, Ft. Lauderdale Food Not Bombs v. City of Ft. Lauderdale, 901 F.3d 1235 (11th Cir. 2018) (holding that organization's outdoor food sharing was expressive conduct protected by the First Amendment); First Vagabonds Church of God v. City of Orlando, Florida, 638 F.3d 756 (11th Cir. 2011) (upholding ordinance imposing certain restrictions on "large group feedings" in public parks as a "reasonable time, place and manner restriction"); Santa Monica Food Not Bombs v. City of Santa Monica, 450 F.3d 1022 (9th Cir. 2006) (upholding ordinance requiring permits for food distribution in public parks); Chosen 300 Ministries, Inc. v. City of Philadelphia, 2012 WL 3235317 (E.D. Penn. 2012) (enjoining ordinance that banned food sharing with more than three people in a public park, finding that the ban, as applied to plaintiffs, violated the Pennsylvania Religious Freedom Protection Act).

187. *See, for example*, Prince George's Cty. v. Am. Fed'n of State, Cty., & Mun. Emps., 2016 WL 4177171 (Md. Ct. Spec. App. 2016) (holding that city's termination of municipal workers for selling scrap metal rather than taking material to landfill was arbitrary given "widespread past practice of not enforcing scavenging policy"). Municipalities are permitted to contract with private firms, giving them exclusive rights to pick up garbage and collect recyclables. *See, for example*, Active Disposal, Inc. v. City of Darien, 635 F.3d 883, 889 (7th Cir. 2011) (power to make exclusive contracts included power to make exclusive contracts involving recyclables); Strub v. Vill. of Deerfield, 167 N.E.2d 178 (Ill. 1960) (regulating licensed scavengers fell within police power). The U.S. Supreme Court has stated that waste disposal "is typically and traditionally a function of local government exercising its police power." United Haulers Ass'n Inc. v. Oneida-Herkimer Solid Waste Mgmt. Auth., 550 U.S. 330, 332 (2007).

For anecdotal accounts, *see* Malia Wollan, How to Make Money Collecting Bottles and Cans, N.Y. Times (Apr. 8, 2016), https://www.nytimes.com/2016/04/10/magazine/how-to-make-money-collecting-bottles-and-cans.html; Sarah Maslin Nir, New York City Fights Scavengers Over a Treasure: Trash, N.Y. Times (Mar. 20, 2016), https://www.nytimes.com/2016/03/21/nyregion/new-york-city-fights-scavengers-over-a-treasure-trash.html; Jim Dwyer, Hauling Cans and Bottles Through Brooklyn, for a Hard-Earned Extra Penny, N.Y. Times (July 26, 2011), https://www.nytimes.com/2011/07/27/nyregion/bottle-and-can-scavengers-in-brooklyn-make-every-penny-count.html; Mick Dumke, Why Can't Chicago Recycle?, Chicago Reader (July 22, 2010), https://www.chicagoreader.com/chicago/chicago-recycling-blue-carts-service/Content?oid=2135422 (scavengers collect 75% of aluminum waste from Chicago buildings with private collection).

188. *See, for example*, Project Vote! v. Ohio Bureau of Emp. Serv., 578 F. Supp. 7 (S.D. Ohio 1982); Unemployed Workers Union v. Hackett, 332 F. Supp. 1372 (D.R.I. 1971). The First Circuit Court of Appeals rejected a constitutional challenge to a regulation that permitted a welfare office to contact the police and to suspend social services "only when an unusually large number of individuals enter a welfare service office at the same time or are known definitely to the person in charge as about to arrive, for the purpose of demonstrations, disturbances or sit-ins." Mass. Welfare Rights Org. v. Ott, 421 F.2d 525, 528 (1st Cir. 1969) (internal quotation marks omitted).

189. Perry Educ. Ass'n v. Perry Local Educators' Association, 460 U.S. 37, 46 (1983). *See* United States v. Kokinda, 497 U.S. 720 (1990) (four-justice plurality concluding that the sidewalk in front of the U.S. Post Office is not a traditional or designated public forum and cannot be used for expressive activity).

For speech purposes, government property now is categorized in one of four ways: (1) as a traditional public forum; (2) as a designated public forum; (3) as a limited public forum; and (4) as a nonpublic forum. *See* Caractor v. City of New York Department of Homeless Services, 2013 WL 2922436, at *5 (S.D.N.Y. 2013). Whether the property is open to the public depends on the government's intent "to create a public forum," Cornelius v. NAACP Legal Defense and Educational Fund, Inc., 473 U.S. 788, 802 (1985), and is to be determined by looking at "written policies and actual practice." Make the Road by Walking, Inc. v. Turner, 378 F.3d 133, 144 (2d Cir. 2003).

190. A permit application may request information needed to help the locality prepare for the event. It is questionable, however, whether the application can require the sponsor of the event to provide personal information (for example, about income) that is unrelated to a legitimate administrative purpose. *See* Fernandes v. Limmer, 663 F.2d 619 (5th Cir. 1981), cert. dismissed, 458 U.S. 1124 (1982).

191. Heffron v. International Society for Krishna Consciousness, Inc., 452 U.S. 640, 649 (1981).

192. *See, for* example, Smith v. Executive Director of the Indiana War Memorials Commission, 742 F.3d 282 (7th Cir. 2014) ("Requirements that small groups obtain a permit to gather in a traditional public forum frequently fail" when assessed under the First Amendment.).

193. *See* Eric Neisser, Charging for Free Speech: User Fees and Insurance in the Marketplace of Ideas, 74 Geo. L.J. 257 (1985). *For example*, Int'l Women's Day March Planning Comm. v. City of San Antonio, 619 F.3d 346, 370 (5th Cir. 2010) (upholding license fee because it was clearly linked to the expense of cleaning up the procession route and the cost of any "personnel" and "devices" needed for traffic control); Nat'l Awareness Found. v. Abrams, 50 F.3d 1159, 1165 (2d Cir. 1995) ("Thus, fees that serve not as revenue taxes, but rather as means to meet expenses incident to the administration of a regulation and to the maintenance of public order in the matter regulated are constitutionally permissible."); Eastern Conn. Citizens Action Group v. Powers, 723 F.2d 1050, 1056 (2d Cir. 1983) ("Licensing fees used to defray administrative expenses are permissible, but only to the extent necessary for that purpose.").

194. Cox v. New Hampshire, 312 U.S. 569, 577 (1941).

195. Murdock v. Pennsylvania, 319 U.S. 105, 113–114, 111 (1943) ("Freedom of speech, freedom of press, freedom of religion are available to all, not merely to those who can pay their own way.").

196. Forsyth County, Ga. v. Nationalist Movement, 505 U.S. 123, 136–137 (1992). It bears emphasis that four Justices in dissent found that more than nominal charges may be assessed and five other Justices, in an ambiguous statement, appeared to hold that the constitutionality of a fee does not depend on whether it is nominal or not. *Id.* at 137–140.

   Prior to *Forsyth County*, the Eleventh Circuit Court of Appeals had held that the First Amendment does not permit a locality to impose "unlimited charges for the costs of additional police protection based on the content of the speaker's views." As the appeals court explained:

   > [I]indigent persons who wish to exercise their First Amendment rights of speech and assembly and as a consequence of the added costs of police protection, are unable to pay such costs, are denied an equal opportunity to be heard. Although the . . . permit scheme does provide for a review of a denial of a permit before the . . . City Council, there is no provision in the ordinance which exempts those persons from paying the costs for additional police protection who are unable to pay. The granting of a license permit on the basis of the ability of persons wishing to use public streets and parks to demonstrate, to pay an unfixed fee for police protection, without providing for an alternative means of exercising First Amendment rights, is unconstitutional.

   Cent. Fla. Nuclear Freeze Campaign, v. Walsh, 774 F.2d 1515, 1523–24 (11th Cir. 1985), cert. denied, 475 U.S. 1120 (1986).

197. *See generally* Sara K. Rankin, A Homeless Bill of Rights (Revolution), 45 Seton Hall L. Rev. 383 (2015); Jonathan J. Sheffield, Homeless Bills of Rights: Moving United States Policy Toward a Human Right to Housing, 22 Geo. J. on Poverty L. & Pol'y 321 (2015); Jonathan J. Sheffield, A Homeless Bill of Rights: Step by Step from State to State, 19 Pub. Int. L. Rep. 8 (2013).

198. 34 R.I. Gen. Laws Ann. § 34-37.1-1 (West).

199. Conn. Gen. Stat. Ann. § 1-500 (West).

200. 775 Ill. Comp. Stat. Ann. 45/10.

201. New York City Green Cart Permit, https://www1.nyc.gov/nycbusiness/description/green-cart-permit.

202. New York City Green Cart Permit, https://www1.nyc.gov/nycbusiness/description/green-cart-permit; New York City Business Solutions: Street Vending, 1, http://www.nyc.gov/html/sbs/nycbiz/downloads/pdf/educational/sector_guides/street_vending.pdf.

203. New York City Mobile Food Vending Permit (Seasonal or Two-Year), http://www1.nyc.gov/nycbusiness/description/mobile-food-vending-unit-permit-seasonal-or-twoyear.

204. What Mobile Food Vendors Should Know, New York City Health Department, 4–5, http://www1.nyc.gov/assets/doh/downloads/pdf/rii/regulations-for-mobile-food-vendors.pdf.

205. *See* New York City Mobile Food Vending Restricted Streets Guide, http://www1.nyc.gov/assets/doh/downloads/pdf/permit/mfv_restricted_streets.pdf.

206. New York City Consumer Affairs, Apply, Temporary Street Fair Vendor, http://www1.nyc.gov/site/dca/businesses/license-checklist-temporary-street-fair-vendor.page.

207. New York City Business Solutions: Street Vending, 2, http://www.nyc.gov/html/sbs/nycbiz/downloads/pdf/educational/sector_guides/street_vending.pdf.

208. New York City Business Solutions: Street Vending, 3, http://www.nyc.gov/html/sbs/nycbiz/downloads/pdf/educational/sector_guides/street_vending.pdf.

209. New York City Council Legislation, File No. Intro 0434-2010-A, http://legistar.council.nyc.gov/LegislationDetail.aspx?ID=805611&GUID=47B3F9F9-AD2D-4C2C-AC07-6318D4DE62A7.

210. New York City, N.Y., Code § 20-468; The Peddler Handbook, National Criminal Justice Reference Center, 5; New York City Business Solutions, Street Vending, 1, http://www.nyc.gov/html/sbs/nycbiz/downloads/pdf/educational/sector_guides/street_vending.pdf.

211. Sumathi Reddy, Prices for Food-Cart Permits Skyrocket, Wall Street Journal (Mar. 9, 2011), http://www.wsj.com/articles/SB10001424052748704758904576188523780657688. *See also* Answers About New York's Street Vendors, N.Y. Times (Oct. 7, 2009), http://cityroom.blogs.nytimes.com/2009/10/07/answers-about-new-yorks-street-vendors/.

212. New York City, N.Y., Code § 20-464(d). Many individuals interested in selling goods on the street partner with veterans who can more easily obtain a license. *See, for example*, Rachel Hennessey, The Secret World of SoHo's Street Vendors, Forbes (Aug. 8, 2012), http://www.forbes.com/sites/rachelhennessey/2012/08/08/the-secret-world-of-sohos-street-vendors/#528890864dcb.

213. New York City, N.Y., Rules, Tit. 6, § 2-318.

9

Access to Justice: Enforcing Rights and Securing Protection

Introduction

Does the federal Constitution guarantee "access to justice" for persons who are poor as well as those who are rich?

One of the primary aims of the federal Constitution is to "establish Justice."[1] To achieve that goal, the Constitution has created a federal court system, which is the part of the government responsible for safeguarding legal rights and enforcing legal protections.[2] Every state also has a court system that plays a similar role. The importance of securing justice for all is underscored by the words imprinted above the entrance to the Supreme Court of the United States: "Equal Justice Under Law."[3] Indeed, to quote Judge Learned Hand, "If we are to keep our democracy there must be one commandment: thou shall not ration justice."[4] Nevertheless, there is a gap between the promise of equal justice and its reality for persons who are poor or have low income. Indeed, the gap is so wide and well known that it has a name: "the justice gap."[5] The justice gap refers to the inability of persons who are poor or have low income to hire a lawyer to protect their legal rights and to assist when disputes arise.

As explained in this chapter, litigating a civil action—involving such matters as eviction proceedings, consumer disputes, family problems, or employment issues—is not free or simple. To the contrary, litigation is expensive and complicated. The federal Constitution does not mandate the assignment of publicly funded lawyers to civil litigants and, even apart from the fees that a party must pay to counsel, litigation generates financial costs that a party must bear. Counsel may be difficult or impossible to retain despite the availability of contingency-fee arrangements and federal and state statutes that authorize the payment of attorney's fees to a prevailing party.[6] Although Congress appropriates funds through the Legal Services Corporation (LSC) for programs that provide free counsel to indigent civil litigants, only one free lawyer is available for roughly every 6,400 poor people (including both

Getting By. Helen Hershkoff and Stephen Loffredo, Oxford University Press (2020). © Helen Hershkoff & Stephen Loffredo.
DOI: 10.1093/oso/9780190080860.001.0001

LSC and non-LSC funded).[7] Indigent persons accused of a crime do have a federal constitutional right to government-funded counsel,[8] but, here again, inadequate funding has resulted in large caseloads that undermine the Constitution's protection.[9] Moreover, the court system exposes a criminal defendant to fines, fees, and other charges that can create a financial prison long after incarceration ends.[10]

Without legal representation, there is a danger that a low-income person's serious civil legal needs will not be met.[11] Persons who cannot afford counsel are more likely to live in substandard apartments, because they cannot enforce housing codes;[12] are more likely to be subject to illegal debt collection actions, because they cannot invoke federal laws against abusive practices;[13] are more likely to have their wages illegally withheld, because they cannot compel their employers to pay the compensation lawfully owed them;[14] are more likely to be unable to correct inaccurate consumer records used for employment and housing decisions, because companies do not respond to their requests;[15] and are less likely to be released from immigration-related detention, because the system is too complex for a layperson to navigate.[16] Studies show that a party who is represented by a lawyer is five times more likely to win than a party who appears in court without a lawyer (although the actual advantage is affected by the nature of the claim).[17] Moreover, without the assistance of counsel, a person's interactions with the legal system may worsen rather than reduce injustice.[18] This is because, as the Deputy Attorney General during the Obama administration explained, court-ordered fees, fines, and financial penalties, even in civil matters, "can lead to unnecessary incarceration, trap people in a cycle of poverty, and undermine the faith in the justice system that is so critical to public safety."[19] Obtaining counsel in a civil lawsuit thus is extremely important to the success of a case. However, focusing only on the insufficiency of counsel in civil litigation as the measure of the "justice gap" significantly understates the structural inequalities of the civil justice system and the legal barriers that low-income persons face.

The information in this chapter discusses primarily, but not only, the civil and not the criminal justice system. It does not provide legal advice and cannot substitute for a lawyer's counsel. But it is vital that persons with low income know the procedural rights that are available when they confront legal problems; even without a lawyer, a person can invoke a number of constitutional and statutory protections that make it possible to challenge illegal practices and to enforce rights. No doubt there are serious shortcomings in the American legal system, but the courts of the United States can and should "do justice."[20]

Rights and Protections in Civil Proceedings

INFORMATION BOX: LEGAL DICTIONARY

The plaintiff or petitioner is the person who files a civil action (also known as a lawsuit or civil proceeding).

The defendant or respondent is the person who is sued.

When a landlord sues a tenant for unpaid rent, the landlord is the plaintiff (or petitioner), and the tenant is the defendant (or respondent).

When a tenant sues a landlord for failure to make repairs, the tenant is the plaintiff (or petitioner), and the landlord is the defendant (or respondent).

The complaint (or petition) is the legal document that informs the defendant and the court about the plaintiff's alleged injury and the relief that is requested.

What happens if a party who needs to file a lawsuit cannot afford the court's filing fee?

Federal and state courts charge a fee to the party seeking to file a civil action. The plaintiff must pay the filing fee in order to start the litigation. The defendant does not pay a fee to appear in court. The fee in federal court currently is $400, which includes a $50 general administrative fee on top of the filing fee itself.[21] State courts also charge filing fees, and the amounts vary from state to state.[22] The Due Process Clause of the federal Constitution requires both federal and state courts to waive a filing fee on behalf of a litigant who cannot afford to pay it if two strict conditions are met: (1) the lawsuit must involve a "fundamental" right; and (2) the court system must be the only way to protect the right. Not every interest or right is fundamental in the constitutional sense. The U.S. Supreme Court has held that a state court must waive the filing fee for a divorce proceeding, because the right to marry is fundamental and marriage cannot be dissolved without a judicial order.[23] By contrast, the Supreme Court held that due process does not require a federal court to waive the filing fee for a bankruptcy proceeding because the right to declare bankruptcy is not fundamental and debts may be adjusted through private negotiation with creditors without court involvement.[24] Similarly, due process does not require the court to waive a fee to enable a person to file a lawsuit challenging the denial or reduction of public assistance because there is no recognized constitutional right to government support.[25]

The Equal Protection Clause is another provision of the federal Constitution that affects filing fees, ensuring that poor people not be required to pay higher fees than those with more income. For example, when a party appeals an adverse judgment, the court sometimes will require that the party (called the appellant) post a bond. The appeal bond is money that the appellant deposits with the court as a condition of appealing the judgment, and the court will use this money to pay off the adverse judgment (and other expenses) if the judgment is upheld on appeal. In this context, the U.S. Supreme Court invalidated the requirement that a tenant-appellant post twice the amount of rent expected to accrue during the appellate process, finding no rational basis for the double-bond requirement. As the Court explained, "The discrimination against the poor, who could pay their rent pending an appeal but cannot post the double bond, is particularly obvious. For them, as a practical matter, appeal is foreclosed, no matter how meritorious their case may be."[26] Under this principle, a court should not charge a poor person a higher filing fee to commence a suit than a more affluent person would be expected to pay.

Although not constitutionally required, Congress has enacted a statute that authorizes the federal courts to waive the prepayment of filing fees and certain costs even when fundamental rights are not at issue.[27] The procedure is called "in forma pauperis" or "poor person's relief."[28] To get the benefit of this waiver, a person who is planning to file a lawsuit should contact the clerk of the relevant court and ask for information about how to apply and for a copy of the application that must be completed (the form for federal court can be found online).[29]

The application asks for information about the person's finances and must be submitted under penalty of perjury. The application will be attached to the party's complaint. Information requested includes:

- The name and address of the applicant's employer;
- The amount of gross wages and take-home pay;
- Other income received in the preceding 12-month period;
- The amount of savings;
- Any assets, such as a car, real estate, jewelry, or stocks;
- Regular monthly expenses for housing, transportation, utilities, and so forth;
- Names of dependents; and
- Debts or financial obligations.

A judge reviews the application. A waiver of prepayment of fees should be granted even if the party does not show "absolute destitution";[30] as one court of appeals has stated, a litigant who is poor should not "be made to choose between abandoning a potentially meritorious claim or foregoing the necessities of life."[31]

In some cases the judge will require the plaintiff to pay a portion of the filing fee up front.[32] If the judge denies an application for a fee waiver, the applicant can appeal (which requires payment of an additional fee or securing a waiver of that fee, as discussed later in this chapter).[33]

If a judge grants the fee waiver application, the court will arrange for service of process of the complaint upon the defendant.[34] However, even if the plaintiff pays the fee (or a portion of it), the court "shall dismiss the case at any time"— without any request from the opposing party—if it determines that the plaintiff's allegations about poverty were not true, or the action is frivolous or malicious, fails to state a claim, or seeks monetary damages from a defendant who is immune from such relief.[35] Some courts have applied this provision to dismiss an action even before service of process has issued.[36] Other courts, however, have criticized such an approach as "draconian" and warranted "only when the complaint 'lacks an arguable basis either in law or in fact.'"[37]

The federal "in forma pauperis" statute does not apply in state courts. The majority of states have statutes that follow the federal model,[38] but some limit the waiver to cases involving fundamental rights that can be protected only through the courts.[39] A few states have an easier standard than the federal courts, and permit a waiver simply upon a showing of poverty in any kind of civil action.[40]

INFORMATION BOX: "PACER"

"PACER," short for Public Access to Court Electronic Records, is a service available to the public that allows users to obtain case and docket information online from federal courts.[41] Users are not required to have counsel but must complete a free online registration form.[42] Generally a fee of 10 cents per page is charged, and no fee is charged until the user's account accrues charges of $15 a quarter. The court in its discretion may waive fees for indigents upon a showing that an exemption "is limited in scope and is necessary in order to avoid an unreasonable burden."[43]

What expenses are covered if the court grants "in forma pauperis" relief?

Granting "in forma pauperis" relief allows the plaintiff to file a lawsuit without paying, or without paying the full amount of, the standard filing fee up front. When the court grants the application, the U.S. Marshal must "issue and serve all process."[44] In addition, the waiver extends to some of the other expenses associated with litigation,[45] but not all of them.[46] Indeed, courts have read the statute not to cover many important litigation expenses,[47] including witness fees,[48] deposition costs,[49] copying costs,[50] transportation expenses,[51] and, as discussed later in this chapter, interpreter and translation services.

Is assignment of free counsel a part of "in forma pauperis" relief?

The statute granting in forma pauperis relief permits the court to assign counsel to "any person unable to afford counsel."[52] However, even if the court orders the assignment of counsel, it cannot compel the attorney to take on the representation free of charge.[53] The statute does not specify when counsel must be assigned and leaves the decision to the court's discretion. The test within the Seventh Circuit Court of Appeals (which includes federal courts in Illinois, Indiana, and Wisconsin) considers two questions: "(1) has the indigent plaintiff made a reasonable attempt to obtain counsel or been effectively precluded from doing so; and if so, (2) given the difficulty of the case, does the plaintiff appear competent to litigate it himself?"[54] The trial court's denial of a request for counsel may be reversed if it failed to assess these factors properly and if the plaintiff suffered "prejudice," as, for example, if the totality of the circumstances at trial show "a reasonable likelihood that the presence of counsel would have altered the outcome" of the case.[55] Other circuit courts have their own tests, many of which consider similar factors. These factors, in addition to a showing of indigence, include: ability to investigate facts, capacity to present claims, complexity of legal and/or factual issues, merit to the allegations, and attempt to obtain counsel.[56]

For cases pending in state court, state judges may authorize appointment of counsel in civil actions even when appointment is not required under federal law. The rules governing appointment of counsel vary from case to case, depending on state law, the nature of the claim, the kind of litigant, and other factors that the court has discretion to consider.[57]

Are prisoners who file civil lawsuits entitled to a waiver of court fees?

Special rules apply to civil lawsuits filed by an inmate of a state or federal prison. The Prison Litigation Reform Act of 1995 limits an inmate's ability to file a federal lawsuit concerning conditions or occurrences in the prison.[58] One limitation restricts the waiver of filing fees under the in forma pauperis statute. A prisoner who wishes to file suit must pay the full amount of the filing fees by authorizing disbursements from his or her prison account. The first payment is equal to 20 percent of the greater of either the average monthly deposits or the balance in the account for the past six months, unless the prisoner has no assets. Later payments are 20 percent of the preceding month's income, in any month in which the account exceeds $10.[59] Other restrictions include the requirement that the district court prescreen complaints to ensure that suits are not frivolous or malicious and to dismiss them "at any time" if the court finds the claims to be frivolous or malicious;[60] limits on particular types of claims (such as claims seeking damages for emotional distress) without a showing of physical injury;[61] and a restriction on the award of attorney's fees.[62] Further, a prisoner who has had an action or appeal dismissed for frivolousness, failure to state a claim, or maliciousness on three or more occasions is barred from seeking in forma pauperis relief to bring another action or appeal. However, dismissals on grounds that do not pertain to the merits of the action or appeal, such as a lack of jurisdiction or want of prosecution, do not count toward a prisoner's "three strikes."[63] In addition, prisoners must first "exhaust administrative remedies" (that is, try to resolve the dispute through any available grievance or other administrative process) before they can file suit in federal court.[64] A prisoner must go through the available administrative processes even if those processes cannot provide all the relief (for instance, money damages) that the prisoner would seek in a federal lawsuit.[65]

Does the federal Constitution guarantee free counsel to civil litigants who cannot afford to hire a lawyer?

The federal Constitution does not guarantee free legal representation to civil litigants who cannot afford to hire a lawyer. In certain circumstances, the Due Process Clause requires a state or federal court to assign free legal representation, but the standard in a civil action is very difficult to meet.[66] To determine whether counsel is required, the U.S. Supreme Court has held that courts are to apply a three-part test, taking account of the "private interests at stake, the government's interest, and the risk that the procedures used will lead to erroneous decisions," balancing each factor against each other, and then comparing "their net weight in the scales against the presumption that there is a right to appointed counsel only where the indigent, if he is unsuccessful, may lose his personal freedom."[67] Applying the three-part balancing test, the Supreme Court has found that the appointment of free counsel was required in a civil action in state court for children accused of delinquency[68] and in federal and state courts for persons who are at risk of civil commitment.[69] However, counsel is not guaranteed even if a party in a civil litigation may face imprisonment[70] or loss of parental rights.[71]

Do federal statutes guarantee free counsel to civil litigants who cannot afford to hire a lawyer?

No federal statute requires the government to provide free lawyers to civil litigants who cannot afford counsel. However, since 1974, Congress has appropriated funds for the Legal Services Corporation (LSC)—a congressionally created, independent nonprofit corporation—and the LSC distributes more than 90 percent of its annual funding to nonprofit groups that provide free legal representation to eligible persons who meet income and other requirements.[72] The LSC maintains an online interactive map to help locate free legal representation.[73] The party seeking representation must contact the local legal services office to find out if counsel is available and can be retained. Keep in mind that Congress does not give the LSC sufficient funds to meet all of the legal needs of persons who are eligible for assistance—leaving a wide "justice gap" for persons who cannot afford counsel. To be eligible for free legal services, a litigant must meet federally defined income limits that typically are set at 125 percent of the federal poverty index. In 2018, income guidelines were as shown in Table 9.1.[74]

Table 9.1 2018 Income Guidelines for Government-Funded Legal Services in Civil Actions

Size of Household	48 Contiguous States and the District of Columbia	Alaska	Hawaii
1	$15,175	$18,975	$17,450
2	$20,575	$25,725	$23,663
3	$25,975	$32,475	$29,875
4	$31,375	$39,225	$36,088
5	$36,775	$45,975	$42,300
6	$42,175	$52,725	$48,513
7	$47,575	$59,475	$54,725
8	$52,975	$66,225	$60,938
For each additional member of the household in excess of 8, add:	$5,400	$6,750	$6,213

Do states or localities guarantee free counsel to civil litigants who cannot afford a lawyer?

Starting in the 1980s, a consensus began to emerge that the absence of counsel for poor people in civil matters involving critical interests (such as housing, food, medical care, child custody, and the like) constituted an insupportable denial of equal justice, or even basic justice.[75] In the following decades, the call for a civil right to counsel (sometimes known as "civil Gideon," referring to the Supreme Court's landmark *Gideon v. Wainwright* decision, which guaranteed counsel in criminal cases, as discussed later in this chapter) was voiced by a growing number of bar associations, academics, and advocacy groups,[76] leading some states to expand access to free counsel in certain civil matters.[77] Several organizations, including the American Bar Association, maintain updated directories describing the right to counsel (and pending legislative developments) in each state.[78] Some localities have taken more sweeping measures to address the "justice gap." New York City, for instance, currently provides free counsel to all low-income tenants facing eviction proceedings and to certain low-income immigrants facing deportation.[79]

Is the court required to assist a pro se litigant to ensure a fair proceeding?

A person who appears in court without a lawyer is called a pro se litigant. In *Turner v. Rogers*, the U.S. Supreme Court held that although a court is not constitutionally required to appoint free counsel in a civil contempt hearing that could result in an order of imprisonment, the court was required to "have in place alternative procedures that ensure a fundamentally fair determination of the critical incarceration-related question." The Court identified various procedural substitutes that may be constitutionally sufficient, including "the use of forms to elicit relevant information."[80]

The duty to provide "substitute procedural safeguards," as required under *Turner*, does not mean that the judge assumes the role of the pro se party's advocate.[81] The traditional view was that a judge's provision of assistance to an unrepresented litigant violated the judge's duty to remain neutral.[82] However, the judge who presides over a pro se matter is usually the judge who has rejected the unrepresented party's request for the appointment of free counsel;[83] and as Richard Posner, a former judge of the Seventh Circuit Court of Appeals, has cautioned, "It is unfair to deny a litigant a lawyer and then trip him up on technicalities."[84] The American Bar Association, in its comments to model rules on judicial conduct, thus has underscored that a judge does not violate the duty to be fair and impartial by making "reasonable accommodations to ensure pro se litigants the opportunity to have their matters fairly heard."[85] Quite apart from fairness to the litigant, "reasonable accommodations" are essential to the integrity of the proceeding, for the accuracy of a judicial decision depends significantly on the parties' meaningful presentation of claims and defenses

These accommodations vary and may involve an array of complex procedural and substantive rules. One accommodation relates to the standard used to determine the sufficiency of a plaintiff's claims when deciding whether a complaint may proceed to the next stage of the litigation or should be dismissed.[86] The U.S. Supreme Court has held that "a pro se complaint, however inartfully pleaded, must be held to less stringent standards than formal pleadings drafted by lawyers."[87] In practice, commentators question whether judges actually apply this liberal standard to pro se complaints.[88] In addition, the judge may hold a "case management" conference to schedule matters involving discovery or trial, and may decide to refer the action to a magistrate judge or to use other mechanisms that ensure "the just, speedy, and inexpensive disposition of the action."[89] Moreover, federal courts issue "local rules" to govern proceedings in their districts; many local rules provide that the judge must give any unrepresented party notice explaining various stages of the lawsuit and the requirements for responding to motions that might lead to dismissal of a pro se plaintiff's action or awarding of "summary judgment" against a pro se defendant before trial.[90] Similarly, local rules may require the opposing party's counsel to provide a pro se litigant with copies of cases and other authorities cited in memoranda of law submitted to the court.[91] The Second Circuit Court of Appeals has held that such materials should include printed copies of unpublished decisions that otherwise are available only through fee-paying electronic sources (such as Westlaw, Lexis, and Bloomberg).[92]

Some federal courts make various general resources available to pro se litigants. These resources vary from court to court. Here are examples of resources that may be available in a federal court:[93]

- Handbooks and Guides: A majority of the federal districts have print materials or publish a handbook or guide for pro se litigants. These materials do such things as provide an overview of the civil action, a glossary of legal terms, contact information for court personnel, and fill-in-the-blank forms for some of the documents that typically are filed in a lawsuit.[94]
- Clerk's Office to Answer Questions: The majority of federal courts have designated staff in the Clerk's Office who are available to answer questions asked by pro se litigants. Some courts have a special Pro Se Unit. Keep in mind that staff are not permitted to answer questions about substantive law or legal strategy; the questions can pertain only to procedural and filing

requirements. The staff of the Clerk's Office are prohibited by federal law from practicing law in any court of the United States, and that provision has been interpreted as barring the giving of any legal advice.[95] For example, staff can state what the time period for filing is, but cannot calculate a filing deadline for a litigant.[96]

- Pro Se Legal Assistance Project: In a few courts, the judge and staff can refer pro se litigants to an on-site center staffed by lawyers. The lawyers do not represent the party in court, but they meet with the party and provide advice about document drafting and navigating procedural rules.[97]
- Magistrate Judges: Some federal courts assign pro se matters to special magistrate judges who are trained to manage and resolve cases involving unrepresented parties.[98]

Are federal courts required to provide free interpreters to persons with low income who have limited English proficiency or are hearing impaired?

A litigant who does not speak or read English, or is hearing impaired, will not be able to participate meaningfully in judicial proceedings.[99] Translation services have many dimensions: they must not only be accurate but also must account for cultural differences between the speaker and the listener. A lawyer may serve as both counsel and interpreter for a client, but neither role is played if the litigant appears pro se and the dual role raises difficult professional questions.[100] In narrow circumstances, the Due Process Clause of the federal Constitution has been interpreted as requiring a federal or state court to provide a "competent interpreter" as a fundamental requirement of a fair proceeding, but the standard is difficult to meet.[101] The American Bar Association's (ABA) 2012 Standards for Language Access in Courts urges all courts to develop and implement "language access services . . . so that persons needing to access the court are able to do so in a language they understand, and are able to be understood by the court."[102] However, there is a gap between the ABA's recommended language-access standard and the services that the federal courts currently provide to persons who cannot afford to hire interpreters.

Under the federal Court Interpreters Act,[103] federal courts must provide publicly funded interpretation services in criminal cases and in civil cases brought by the United States (for example, student debt collection cases, actions to collect a fine or penalty, and civil forfeiture actions) upon a finding that the defendant or the witness "speaks only or primarily a language other than the English language . . . so as to inhibit such party's comprehension of the proceedings or communication with counsel or the presiding judicial officer, or so as to inhibit such witness' comprehension of questions and the presentation of such testimony."[104] In all other cases—meaning, any civil case not brought by the United States— the party in need of interpretation services must make a request for them, and the presiding judicial officer "shall, where possible, make such services available to that person on a cost-reimbursable basis, but the judicial officer may also re- quire the prepayment of the estimated expenses of providing such services."[105] The Guide to Judiciary Policy states that the cost-reimbursable method should be used "only in limited circumstances when no other options are available."[106] Currently, fees for certified and professionally qualified interpreters are $418 for a full day and $226 for a half day; fees for language skilled (noncertified) interpreters are $202 for a full day and $111 for a half day.[107] The Court Interpreters Act also applies to persons who have a hearing impairment that interferes with their comprehension of the proceedings.[108]

In some federal courthouses, interpretation services also may be avail- able through the Telephone Interpreting Program, which allows an interpreter at a remote location to provide services through a two-line telephone system. Currently, 56 federal trial courts—in selected districts in California, the District of Columbia, Florida, Illinois, Nebraska, New Jersey, New Mexico, New York, Puerto Rico, and Rhode Island—make the telephone service available when in- terpretation services are not locally available.[109]

Lower courts have held that they lack authority under the in forma pauperis statute to appoint interpreters or translation services.[110] However, Federal Rule of Civil Procedure 43(d) gives the federal court discretion to "appoint an inter- preter of its choosing; fix reasonable compensation to be paid from funds pro- vided by law or by one or more parties; and tax the compensation as costs."[111] Some trial courts have denied requests for interpretation services when the plaintiff was able to file initial pleadings in English without court-appointed assistance.[112]

Different requirements apply to state courts. State systems that receive fed- eral funding are required under Title VI of the Civil Rights Act of 1964 to pro- vide interpreters in all civil cases.[113] However, again, there is a gap between the services that are required under law and those that actually are provided, in part because of funding shortfalls.[114] In addition, some states have statutes or rules providing for free interpretation services for civil cases, including: Arizona, Colorado, Georgia, Idaho, Indiana, Iowa, Kansas, Kentucky, Louisiana, Maine, Maryland, Massachusetts, Minnesota, Mississippi, Missouri, Nebraska, New Jersey, New Mexico, New York, North Carolina, Oregon, Pennsylvania, Rhode Island, South Carolina, Tennessee, Texas, Utah, Washington, and Wisconsin.[115] Indeed, even in these states, services may not be available if there is insuffi- cient funding, and in that situation, courts are expected to prioritize cases.[116] The District of Columbia local courts, through its Office of Court Interpreting

Services, provides free interpretation services to persons who have limited English proficiency or are deaf or hard of hearing.[117] However, some state courts mandate interpreters in civil proceedings, but charge the cost of the service to the litigant in need of the service, a practice that the American Bar Association has cautioned could have a chilling effect on judicial access.[118]

Will the court appoint free expert witnesses and provide specialized evidentiary tests for litigants who cannot afford to pay?

Some civil cases involve disputed factual issues that can be resolved only through the assistance of an expert or the use of a specialized test. The classic example of this kind of dispute is paternity, where a blood grouping test provides a unique form of exculpatory evidence. Expert evidence is implicated in many other kinds of cases as well. For example, in a landlord-tenant proceeding involving unsafe housing conditions, testimony from an environmental expert on lead paint hazards may be critical to show that the landlord has violated the duty of habitability or federal standards.

The U.S. Supreme Court has held that an indigent criminal defendant in a murder trial is constitutionally entitled to the psychiatric examination and expert assistance needed to prepare an effective defense based on mental condition.[119] In reaching this result, the Court applied the three-part balancing test set forth in *Mathews v. Eldridge* for determining the requirements of the Due Process Clause.[120] The Court applied this same test to conclude that an indigent defendant in a civil paternity proceeding had a right to blood-type testing, given the unique importance of the evidence, the state's role in the litigation, and the protected rights implicated in the lawsuit.[121] However, since the due process inquiry involves a balancing test, it leaves courts with discretion to deny requests for appointment of experts even, where the litigant's fundamental rights are at stake, as in child custody and civil commitment proceedings.[122]

No federal statute specifically requires a judge to order a court-funded expert or test. The Supreme Court has not addressed whether a trial judge may make such appointments under the in forma pauperis statute, and lower courts so far have not interpreted the statute to allow this.[123] However, under the Federal Rules of Evidence, a federal court has discretion to appoint an expert witness and to apportion the associated costs, a power that some courts have exercised to exempt indigent parties from payment.[124] Thus, when testimony from an expert witness could assist a court in the resolution of a complex matter, a litigant who cannot afford to retain the expert should consider this basis for making the request.[125]

What is a default judgment?

At the end of a civil lawsuit, the court will order a judgment for the winning party. A "default judgment" is a judgment ordered by the court, resolving the action in favor of the plaintiff, when the defendant fails to respond to the complaint that began the lawsuit (this is known as defendant's failure "to appear") or, in some cases, when the defendant otherwise fails to participate as required in the litigation. A default judgment is not merely a technical end to a lawsuit. Rather, it functions as a victory for the plaintiff, who after certain legal steps, can enforce the judgment and recover money or obtain other relief from the defendant.

In federal court, Federal Rule of Civil Procedure 55 sets out a two-step procedure before the court can issue a final default judgment. The two steps are "entry of default" and "entry of the default judgment." The clerk of the court enters the default against a defendant who fails to appear in the action.[126] Then, depending on the circumstances, either the clerk or judge enters the default judgment. If the claim is for a "sum certain"—a fixed amount of money—plaintiff files an affidavit of the amount that is due and requests that the clerk enter the judgment for that amount plus costs. In all other cases, plaintiff must present evidence to the court to establish the amount of money damages or other relief before the judgment can be entered.[127]

It is important that a legal system make it possible for a plaintiff to obtain a default judgment in an appropriate case. The availability of a default judgment protects a plaintiff from a party who would otherwise ignore the lawsuit or use delay as a litigation weapon. For example, if a worker sues an employer for failure to pay the minimum wage, and seeks to recover a fixed sum of money in back pay and penalties, availability of the default judgment ensures that the worker's legal rights can be enforced even if the employer tries to obstruct by refusing to defend against the lawsuit. The federal courts provide instructions on their websites on how to obtain a default judgment.[128]

More frequently, however, default judgments are entered on behalf of powerful plaintiffs, such as banks or a credit card companies, against vulnerable defendants, such as low-income consumers who cannot afford legal representation. Studies report abuse of the procedure in these situations.[129] Sometimes, a corporate plaintiff will request that a default judgment be entered against a defendant notwithstanding the fact that the defendant did not know to appear in the action because the plaintiff failed to provide notice even though required by law.[130] Indeed, it is known that some creditors and collection companies apply for default judgments after engaging in an illegal practice known as "sewer service."[131] Sewer service happens when a plaintiff intentionally fails to serve a complaint or other legal papers on the defendant in a lawsuit, and then misrepresents to the court that it did provide these papers to the defendant, making it seem that notice was in fact given.[132]

A default judgment can have harsh legal consequences, quite apart from the money that defendant might be required to pay—it can produce an impaired credit rating that might negatively affect the ability to obtain employment and housing (as discussed in chapter 6). If the clerk has entered a default, the defendant should promptly take steps to try to undo that action. Federal Rule 55(c) gives the defendant an opportunity to ask the district court to set aside an entry of default for "good cause"; if a default *judgment* has been entered, the court can set that aside in accordance with the additional requirements of Federal Rule 60(b).[133] The defendant also can appeal the entry of a default judgment, which, as explained later in this chapter, requires paying a fee to file an appeal, but a waiver can be sought.[134]

Some federal courts have emphasized that when a pro se defendant seeks to vacate a default judgment, "reasonable allowances" (of the sort given to a pro se plaintiff discussed earlier in this chapter) should be made to make sure that technical procedural rules do not contribute to a loss of legal rights. Indeed, as the Second Circuit Court of Appeals has explained, "The court's duty is even broader in the case of a *pro se* defendant who finds herself in court against her will with little time to learn the intricacies of civil procedure."[135] The request to set aside the default judgment for "good cause" must show that the default was not willful. For example, the defendant might show that there was no service or improper service,[136] a change of address,[137] serious illness of either the defendant or someone in the defendant's family,[138] or a mistake or "excusable neglect."[139] In addition, some courts require a showing that vacating the judgment will not prejudice the plaintiff attempting to collect on it.[140]

Moreover, in some cases the court will require that the party seeking to open a default judgment show a meritorious defense.[141] The party seeking such relief may have a number of such defenses, depending on the claim and the facts of the case. For example, in a debt collection case, the consumer's defense may be that the financial institution waited too long to commence its lawsuit and so the suit is barred by the statute of limitations. Or, the consumer might be able to argue that the debt collector cannot make out a "prima facie" case (a legal term that means to provide sufficient evidence to support a legal claim) that it owns the debt and that the debt is valid and enforceable, which potentially would defeat the claim on the merits.[142]

Different procedures for setting aside a default judgment apply in state courts. States have become more proactive in addressing sewer service issues, although more reform is needed. For example, in 2010, the New York Attorney General arrested a Long Island process-serving company for a pattern of engaging in sewer service.[143]

Special rules apply when a default judgment is sought against a soldier or sailor. These rules, required under the Servicemembers Civil Relief Act, recognize that servicemembers face many barriers to participating in a lawsuit. In particular, a plaintiff seeking a default judgment must sign and file an affidavit stating that the defendant is not in the military. If a default judgment is entered against the servicemember, the servicemember automatically has an opportunity to set aside the judgment, but must show that there is a valid defense to the action.[144]

Remember, if a default judgment is vacated, the lawsuit is not over—it is just reopened. But now the parties will have an opportunity to litigate the suit on the merits.

If a party who has lost wants to appeal from an adverse judgment, will the court waive the filing fee?

A party who loses in the trial court may challenge the court's decision by taking an "appeal" to a higher court. More than 50 percent of plaintiffs who appeal in the federal courts appear without counsel.[145] Taking an appeal incurs additional expenses, including the cost of the fee paid to the appeals court to hear and decide the case. The federal courts of appeals are authorized to charge fees to parties who wish to appeal.[146] However, the losing party can ask for a waiver of the fees and appeal "in forma pauperis." If the party filing the appeal was granted in forma pauperis status by the trial court (that is, if the trial court waived filing fees for initiating the action) that party is entitled to proceed in forma pauperis on appeal (without paying filing fees), *unless* "the trial court certifies in writing that [the appeal] is not taken in good faith."[147] In making this determination, trial courts generally ask whether the party will be raising a nonfrivolous issue. If the trial court certifies that a party's appeal is frivolous, the party may still apply to the appeals court for in forma pauperis status. That application (or motion) must be made within 30 days of the party being served with notice of the trial court's certification. An application to appeal in forma pauperis must include an affidavit showing financial inability to pay the required fees.[148] Forms for such applications are available from the court clerk's office, and many courts of appeal make these materials available online.[149] A party that did not have in forma pauperis status at the trial level may apply for a waiver of filing fees on appeal by making an application to the *trial court*.[150]

In addition, filing an appeal requires the party seeking review—called the appellant or petitioner—to provide the court with a copy of the "record," which includes a transcript of the proceedings in the trial court. In federal court, federal law guarantees a free transcript if needed to appeal, so long as the litigant legitimately cannot afford to pay for a copy and if the appeal is taken in good faith.[151]

In some state courts, the judge has discretion to order a free transcript needed for the appeal as part of in forma pauperis relief.[152] Whether a court will make a transcript available is likely to turn on the nature of the lawsuit, the identity of the parties, and the kind of rights at stake. In cases involving fundamental rights, the federal constitution's guarantees of due process and equal protection may require courts to waive fees for transcripts and other material required to pursue an appeal. For example, in *M.L.B. v. S.L.J.*, the U.S. Supreme Court held that the state was constitutionally obligated to waive fees for trial transcripts that a mother needed to appeal a court order terminating her parental rights.[153]

Is a party who loses a case but was granted in forma pauperis relief required to pay costs to the winning party?

Federal law generally allows courts to assess costs against a party who loses a lawsuit. Costs are paid to the party who won the case.[154] The costs that may be payable by the losing party to the winning party are not the same as the costs for which prepayment is waived under the in forma pauperis statute—they are broader. Costs that can be awarded to a winning party include such items as fees for printing and witnesses; fees of the court clerk; and copying fees.[155] The court may consider the indigency of the losing party when making an award of costs to the winning party, but it is not automatically an abuse of discretion for a court to find a party who appeared in forma pauperis liable for costs.[156] To challenge the award of costs, the losing party must bring a motion seeking relief within seven days of the clerk's taxation of costs, and must put forward "substantial documentation of a true inability to pay."[157]

Can the government imprison a person who is unable to pay a civil justice court debt?

It is commonplace to say that being poor is not a crime.[158] Likewise, being in debt is not a crime. Indeed, debtor's prison is illegal in the federal system and in most states.[159] However, a person who lacks the money to pay a court debt may be at risk of imprisonment.[160] The problem typically can arise in one of two situations: First, when a consumer cannot pay an ordinary commercial debt, such as a credit card bill, a payday loan, or a hospital bill,[161] and, second, when a person cannot pay regulatory fines (such as a parking ticket).[162]

When a consumer cannot pay an ordinary commercial debt, the creditor may have a legal basis for suing to enforce the contract. If a lawsuit is filed, the court will have to determine if the creditor's claim has merit; not every claim filed when a debt is unpaid actually is valid. During the lawsuit, it is possible that the judge will order the consumer-defendant to appear in court, and if the party does not, the court can find the consumer-defendant in civil contempt and issue an arrest warrant that could result in imprisonment.[163] There are many reasons a consumer-defendant might not be able to show up in court when sued in an ordinary consumer action: an employer might have refused to give the person the day off, child care was not available, or the litigant is appearing without counsel and did not know that court attendance was required on a particular day. Further, if the court decides to enter a judgment against the consumer-defendant, the creditor-plaintiff may ask the court to order the defendant to come to court for an "examination" about income and assets. Failure to attend the examination could result in civil contempt and jail.[164]

When a person cannot pay a regulatory fine, imprisonment for civil contempt again is a risk.[165] However, additional rules comes into play when the government is the plaintiff. In particular, some statutes specify imprisonment as a sanction for nonpayment of a debt owed to the government.[166]

Use of imprisonment in these contexts is a persistent practice, but almost certainly violates the federal Constitution in any specific case. The U.S. Supreme Court has held repeatedly that a person cannot be imprisoned for poverty; before jailing a person for civil contempt, the Due Process Clause of the federal Constitution requires a court to determine whether the litigant is financially able to pay the fine or fee.[167] Moreover, many localities use fines and fees as a revenue-raising device,[168] and the Court has held that it violates the Due Process Clause for a local judge to have a direct pecuniary interest in the fines imposed upon a defendant convicted of a misdemeanor, or to have an "official motive to convict and to graduate the fine to help the financial needs of the village."[169]

In 2016, the Conference of Chief Justices and the Conference of State Court Administrators established a Task Force to investigate the use of court fines and fees and their impact on low-income communities and persons of color.[170] The next year, the Obama administration's Department of Justice sent an advisory letter to all state and local courts setting forth rules that bar the incarceration of civil litigants for the nonpayment of fees and fines, which, if not followed, could result in the loss of federal funding if the practice is found to have a disproportionate impact on persons of color in violation of federal civil rights laws.[171] In 2017, President Trump's Attorney General rescinded this Justice Department letter.[172] However, the American Bar Association later unanimously adopted guidelines on the imposition of court fines and fees, arguing for an end to the imprisonment of persons who are too poor to make payment.[173]

Rights and Protections of the Criminally Accused

Must the court assign free counsel to a person who is arrested and cannot afford counsel?

The Sixth Amendment to the federal Constitution guarantees a right to counsel for an indigent criminal defendant who faces imprisonment upon conviction.[174] The right to counsel attaches when a person is "too poor to hire a lawyer," leaving open what it means to be "too poor."[175] As the U.S. Supreme Court explained in its landmark decision, *Gideon v. Wainwright*, the ideal of "fair trials before impartial tribunals in which every defendant stands equal before the law . . . cannot be realized if the poor man charged with crime has to face his accusers without a lawyer to assist him."[176] The majority of states look to the federal poverty guidelines to determine whether a criminal defendant is financially eligible for assigned counsel.[177] This standard has been criticized as forcing low-income persons who are accused of crime into utter destitution.[178]

The Sixth Amendment right applies to state and federal criminal proceedings whenever there is any risk that a criminal defendant will be sentenced to jail,[179] and it extends to children facing criminal charges in juvenile or family courts.[180] The Court has held that the Sixth Amendment bars the police from questioning the accused without a lawyer present unless the right to counsel is knowingly, intelligently, and voluntarily waived.[181] Moreover, the right to counsel attaches at any "critical stage" of the case: the first instance in which a defendant appears before a judicial officer and learns of the formal charges;[182] pre-indictment interrogation;[183] arraignment;[184] preliminary hearings;[185] sentencing;[186] and guilty pleas.[187] The right also must be afforded at the plea bargaining stage, because these negotiations are a "critical" phase of the litigation.[188]

The Sixth Amendment right to counsel does not give the accused the right to a lawyer of the person's choice.[189] However, an individual who is incompatible with an assigned lawyer can make a formal request to the court in its discretion for a change of counsel.[190] Methods for assignment of counsel differ from state to state using different organizational structures.[191] All indigent defense systems share certain unfortunate features: underfunding, high caseloads, and case delay.[192] The National Advisory Commission on Criminal Justice Standards and Goals recommends that yearly case assignments not exceed 150 felonies, 400 misdemeanors, 200 juvenile cases, or 25 appeals per attorney.[193] These standards were developed at a time when fewer collateral consequences attached to criminal convictions, and are recognized not to be adequate. At the same time, because of inadequate funding, caseloads in many states and counties far exceed even these guidelines.[194] The American Bar Association has issued guidelines on the ethical obligations of public defenders when faced with excessive workloads.[195]

Lawsuits challenging the systemic inadequacy of indigent defense systems have faced many roadblocks in federal[196] as well as in state courts.[197] In 2010, the U.S. Department of Justice established the Access to Justice Initiative in an effort to improve the provision of counsel as required by the federal Constitution.[198] Almost a decade later, a federal district judge in Louisiana dismissed a challenge to the adequacy of the Louisiana public defender system, despite concluding that the legislature was "failing miserably at upholding its obligations under *Gideon*."[199]

Does the indigent accused's right to counsel include free, court-ordered resources needed to mount a defense?

Mounting a defense in a criminal case often turns on factual, technical, medical, or scientific evidence that requires the hiring of experts and psychiatric testing. The Sixth Amendment, combined with the Due Process Clause of the federal Constitution, in some cases has required the court to order the provision of necessary services and tests, including the appointment of experts[200] and interpreters[201] and the provision of free transcripts.[202] However, the defendant must provide a developed and convincing explanation for why the requested resources are important to mounting a defense.[203]

Some federal statutes also may support an indigent accused's request for litigation resources. The Court Interpreters Act (discussed earlier in this chapter), requires that courts use certified interpreters in criminal proceedings brought by the United States when the accused has limited English proficiency and when the failure to do so would "inhibit the party's ability to participate fully in the proceedings."[204] Moreover, the statute requires that the court determine that the accused's waiver of this right must be "done knowingly, intelligently, and voluntarily"—the party must expressly make the waiver on the record, after an opportunity to consult with counsel, and after the judge has explained the nature and effect of the waiver.[205]

Does the Sixth Amendment guarantee counsel to an indigent charged with a misdemeanor?

In *Scott v. Illinois*, decided in 1979, the U.S. Supreme Court held that the Sixth Amendment requires "only that no indigent criminal defendant be sentenced to a term of imprisonment unless the state has afforded him the right to assistance of appointed counsel in his defense," and thus declined to mandate a right to free counsel for criminal defendants who face fines, rather than imprisonment.

On that basis, the Supreme Court decided that the federal Constitution was not violated when an accused who was too poor to hire a lawyer was denied appointed counsel, made to stand trial without representation, and convicted of shoplifting and fined under a statute that provided for a fine, one year in jail, or both.[206] The Court also has held that a prior uncounseled misdemeanor conviction may be used to enhance a sentence, provided the conviction did not violate the Sixth Amendment in terms of imposing imprisonment.[207]

Those who are convicted of misdemeanors, even if they do not face imprisonment, potentially face severe collateral consequences. A conviction becomes part of the person's criminal record and, in some circumstances, will become part of a consumer file that may effectively block job prospects (as discussed in chapter 2 about employment and in chapter 6 about consumer protections). In some cases, misdemeanor convictions may have serious immigration consequences for noncitizens.[208] Moreover, even if the misdemeanor is not subject to a jail sentence, the convicted person may be unable to pay the fine because of indigency, and therefore may face imprisonment as a matter of civil contempt (as discussed earlier).[209]

INFORMATION BOX: COUNSEL FOR MISDEMEANOR PROCEEDINGS

Some state constitutions guarantee the appointment of free counsel to indigents during misdemeanor proceedings. For a list of state-by-state constitutional provisions that affect the right to counsel (both for felonies and certain misdemeanors), see National Conference of State Legislatures, Pretrial Right to Counsel, State Constitutional Right to Counsel, Statutory Guidance on the Right to Counsel & Access to Counsel at Pretrial Release Proceedings, http://www.ncsl.org/research/civil-and-criminal-justice/pretrial-right-to-counsel.aspx#2.

Is there a right to counsel to appeal from a criminal conviction?

The U.S. Supreme Court has held that the Equal Protection Clause gives an indigent criminal defendant the right to free legal counsel on the first appeal if the appeal is one "of right,"[210] but that there is no federal constitutional right to appointed counsel for a discretionary appeal[211] or postconviction collateral review through a writ of habeas corpus.[212] The appointment of counsel in the context of a first appeal as of right is considered to be a necessary safeguard, and the assistance that is provided must be "effective," or competent.[213] In addition, the Supreme Court has held that an indigent criminal defendant is entitled to a free copy of the transcript needed to take an appeal, ruling that "[d]estitute defendants must be afforded as adequate appellate review as defendants who have money enough to buy transcripts."[214]

What happens if a person who is arrested cannot afford to post bail?

Historically, the most common method to ensure that a person who is arrested would be present at trial was to require the posting of bail, which directed the accused to give the government a sum of money that would be returned when the person appeared at trial. As the U.S. Supreme Court has explained, "[A] primary function of bail is to safeguard the courts' role in adjudicating the guilt or innocence of defendants."[215] The Eighth Amendment to the federal Constitution provides that in a criminal proceeding "[e]xcessive bail shall not be required,"[216] but a court may refuse bail in a capital case or if the defendant presents a risk of flight. Under federal law, a federal court also may refuse bail when "no release conditions 'will reasonably assure . . . the safety of any other person and the community.'"[217] Standards for setting amounts of bail vary from state to state. If a judge finds there is a risk that an accused will not show up at trial, or there is any other statutorily authorized reason to justify pretrial detention, the judge can set bail and keep an accused in jail if the required amount cannot be posted.[218]

In New York, 50,000 persons annually have been held in pretrial detention because they could not afford to pay bail, sometimes for years, and often when they are innocent.[219] In New Orleans, on any day in 2015, 500 people were detained because they could not pay bond.[220] The Prison Policy Initiative reports that 80 percent of persons in jail because they are unable to meet bail have incomes in the bottom half of Americans.[221] Bail bondsmen are commercial entities that pay bail but typically require a 10 percent nonrefundable fee.[222]

During the Obama administration, the Department of Justice took the position that the Fourteenth Amendment to the federal Constitution is violated if bail is set without regard to the defendant's financial capacity, triggering the accused's incarceration even when there is no risk of flight or danger to public safety.[223] However, the Trump administration qualified this position, arguing that a bail practice violates the Constitution only if it results in *prolonged* pretrial detention without meaningful consideration of indigence, and that the constitution is presumptively satisfied so long as a court evaluates within 48 hours after arrest whether a defendant is indigent and whether to grant nonbail alternatives for release.[224] A movement is developing that seeks to abolish cash bail; reform proposals differ, in part due to concerns about pretrial risk assessment mechanisms, but advocates are united on a basic principle—that being poor is not a crime.[225]

Can the government recoup the cost of assigned counsel and other court costs from the accused?

Many states seek to recoup the cost of government-provided counsel and other court costs associated with a criminal prosecution. These practices have been criticized as contributing to a cycle of poverty that makes re-entry into the community even more difficult than it ordinarily is.[226] The American Law Institute, a leading independent organization that aims to improve the law, would bar courts from requiring the accused to pay for the use of the criminal justice system.[227]

With respect to the costs of legal representation, states vary in their methods.[228] Some states require copayment; some states recoup the cost, meaning the court orders the defendant at the sentencing stage to make payment; other states impose application fees, meaning that even to request counsel requires an up-front payment.[229] Whether the government legally may recoup the cost of counsel required under the Sixth Amendment depends on the specific practice. In *James v. Strange*, decided in 1972, the U.S. Supreme Court invalidated a recoupment statute under the Equal Protection Clause because of features the Court found to be punitive and discriminatory.[230] The statute gave the defendant notice within 30 days of the amount expended, and then 60 days to pay the debt.[231] After that date, interest accrued at the rate of 6 percent; moreover, the debt became a lien on any property owned by the defendant and could be recovered through wage garnishment, without the protections of any usual exemptions other than for the homestead.[232] However, in *Fuller v. Oregon*, decided in 1974, the Court upheld a recoupment statute that required payment of expenditures for counsel as a condition of probation; the statute afforded the usual exemptions, did not recoup expenses from defendants who were acquitted, and provided an opportunity to show that recoupment would cause hardship.[233] Some state courts also have held that a recoupment regime must provide an opportunity to show financial hardship, and make available the same exemptions and protections available to civil debtors.[234]

A separate question is raised when a criminal conviction is reversed by a reviewing court after the state has already exacted fees, court costs, and restitution as a result of the defendant's earlier conviction. In 2017, the U.S. Supreme Court held that the Due Process Clause bars states from retaining conviction-related assessments, and requires states to provide a mechanism for the return of the fees. The mechanism is unconstitutional if it requires the party seeking a refund pursuant to an invalid conviction to prove innocence by clear and convincing evidence. Rather, the state "may not impose anything more than minimal procedures on the refund of exactions dependent upon a conviction subsequently invalidated."[235]

Can the government jail a person who is sentenced to a fine following conviction, but who cannot afford to pay?

There is a wide gap between what the federal Constitution guarantees in theory and the actual treatment of persons unable to pay criminal fines, including fines associated with misdemeanors.[236] The U.S. Supreme Court has held that a person who cannot afford to pay a fine that is ordered as part of a criminal conviction cannot be jailed on that basis.[237] Moreover, a court cannot imprison a defendant for nonpayment of a fine for an offense that is statutorily punishable only by fine. As the Supreme Court has explained:

> Since [the state] has legislated a "fines only" policy for traffic offenses, that statutory ceiling cannot, consistently with the Equal Protection Clause, limit the punishment to payment of the fine if one is able to pay it, yet convert the fine into a prison term for an indigent defendant without the means to pay his fine.[238]

The Supreme Court has not addressed the specific question of whether an alternative sentencing scheme of "$30 or 30 days" violates equal protection or due process.[239] An alternative sentencing scheme reflects a legislative decision that imprisonment is penologically appropriate for a particular kind of offense. It should be constitutionally impermissible for a state to erect an alternative sentencing scheme that allows the affluent to escape imprisonment yet condemns the indigent to jail. At the least, the state ought to be required to provide a mechanism for paying the fine in installments if the criminal defendant is not able to pay the fine and instead would be forced to go to jail.[240] As Justice White explained in his opinion in *Morris v. Schoonfield*, "the Constitution prohibits the State from imposing a fine as a sentence and then automatically converting it into a jail term solely because the defendant is indigent and cannot forthwith pay the fine in full."[241]

In addition, the state cannot revoke probation conditioned on payment of a fine and restitution, when the defendant is unable to pay. As the Court has explained, "[I]f the probationer has made all reasonable efforts to pay the fine or restitution, and yet cannot do so through no fault of his own, it is fundamentally unfair to revoke probation automatically without considering whether adequate alternative methods of punishing the defendant are available."[242] Nevertheless, in practice many states and localities impose imprisonment without regard to the defendant's financial capacity.[243] Jailing a probationer too poor to pay a fine is unfair and counterproductive. A number of groups have recommended specific and feasible policy reforms to end this unjust practice.[244]

What is a "certificate of relief"?

A criminal conviction carries numerous collateral consequences that seriously affect re-entry into civil life. In particular, a person convicted of a crime may face barriers to securing employment, obtaining housing, or entering a licensed profession. Some states (not many as of this writing) have a process for removing some of the legal consequences of a criminal conviction; if successful, the process results in the issuance of a document generally known as a "certificate of relief" or "certificate of rehabilitation."[245] It is reported that many persons who could benefit from this process in states that make the option available do not apply because they are not aware of their rights.[246] Some organizations are available to assist those with conviction histories to re-enter community life.[247] The American approach to criminal records has been called "exceptionally public, exceptionally punitive, and exceptionally permanent"—disproportionately marking the poor and people of color with an exclusionary status that blocks mobility and opportunity—but the approach should not be viewed as "inevitable," and advocates can work to achieve reforms drawn from principles of redemption and equality.[248]

Civil Forfeiture

What is civil forfeiture?

Civil forfeiture is a procedure that allows the government to seize an individual's property because of the property's suspected association with a crime. The government can seize the property without charging or convicting the owner of a crime. As a formal matter, civil forfeiture is an action against the property, not the property owner, and the caption in the complaint names the property, not the owner, as the party sued.[249]

   Civil forfeiture is not the same as criminal forfeiture, and it is not a criminal action.[250] A criminal forfeiture proceeding is brought against a person who has been charged with a crime. In a criminal forfeiture proceeding, the owner gets the protections of criminal procedure, which include the government having to meet the high evidentiary burden summed up by "beyond a reasonable doubt."[251] In contrast, in a civil forfeiture action, the government only must show by a "preponderance of the evidence"[252] that there is a "substantial connection between the property and the offense."[253]

Civil forfeiture gives the government a powerful tool against persons suspected of crime. However, the civil forfeiture process is known to be riddled with abuses that cause injustice to persons with low income. Individuals who share property with another person—such as a spouse who co-owns a home— are vulnerable to civil forfeiture even if they did not participate in criminal activity or know about it.[254] Moreover, the federal government has an incentive to bring civil forfeiture proceedings because they are able to use 100 percent of the seized assets to expand their law enforcement budgets.[255] As a practical matter, civil forfeiture gives law enforcement a circuitous route to punish an individual when there may be insufficient evidence to bring criminal charges, or criminal charges already have been brought unsuccessfully, or the owner could never be charged. So far, the U.S. Supreme Court has ruled that this practice is not unconstitutional.[256] However, the Supreme Court has acknowledged that these actions often are more than purely remedial in nature, and in some contexts should be treated as punitive, or "quasi criminal."[257] Thus, although they are purportedly civil actions against property, these actions may in some instances so resemble punishment as to be subject to constitutional limitations, such as the Eighth Amendment protection against excessive fines.[258]

The federal Civil Asset Forfeiture Reform Act (CAFRA), enacted in 2000,[259] provides some procedural protection to owners of property that is alleged to be subject to forfeiture. The government must give notice within a 60- or 90-day window of the seizure.[260] A claimant may petition for release of seized property pending the outcome of the forfeiture action.[261] The claimant must demonstrate: (1) a "possessory interest in the property"; (2) ties to the community such that the property will be available for trial; (3) substantial hardship, such as homelessness or the inability to conduct business operations, if the government maintains possession; (4) that the hardship outweighs the risk that the property will be "destroyed, damaged, lost concealed, or transferred . . . during the pendency of the proceeding"; and (5) that the property is not contraband, currency, evidence of a crime, or likely to be used to commit additional criminal acts.[262] The claimant bears the burden to prove these elements, and if the claimant "fails to establish any one of the five criteria, its motion for the release of property must be denied."[263] Dismissal of criminal charges relating to the property that has been seized does not automatically trigger release of the property, and the property may be held until the civil forfeiture proceeding and will be returned to the claimant only if the proceeding reaches a favorable decision.[264]

Alternatively, a claimant may attempt to establish an "innocent owner defense." This defense requires the "innocent owner" to demonstrate an absence of knowledge of the alleged conduct that led to forfeiture, or, upon learning of the conduct, that the claimant "did all that reasonably could be expected under the circumstances to terminate such use of the property."[265] The claimant bears the burden of proving this defense by a preponderance of the evidence (a "more likely than not" evidentiary standard), and some courts have construed the defense narrowly.[266]

CAFRA establishes a right to counsel but only for individuals whose "primary residence" is subject to forfeiture and who cannot afford an attorney to mount the challenge.[267]

Do states and localities also have authority to bring civil forfeiture actions?

The authority to bring a civil forfeiture action varies from state to state as do the procedural protections given to property owners, the percentage of the seized assets law enforcement agencies can retain, and their accountability to the public. However, state civil forfeiture proceedings, like federal, are subject to the restrictions of the Excessive Fines Clause of the Eighth Amendment (as incorporated through the Fourteenth Amendment to the federal Constitution).[268]

Commentators have exposed widespread abuses by some state civil forfeiture regimes, including self-enrichment by law enforcement.[269] North Carolina, New Mexico, and Nebraska have abolished civil forfeiture. Fifteen states require a criminal conviction for all or at least most forfeiture cases.[270] In addition, many states participate in "equitable sharing" programs with the federal government, through which state and local police cooperate in forfeiture efforts and are able to share the funds obtained from the seizures.[271] Under "equitable sharing" regimes, local police forces can avoid state laws that otherwise restrict civil forfeiture or the use of the seized assets.[272] A number of states have adopted laws that bar equitable sharing.[273] Under the Obama administration, the U.S. Department of Justice in 2015 announced an initiative that prohibited federal agencies from taking or "adopting" assets seized by local and state law enforcement.[274] The Trump administration restored federal adoptive forfeiture in July 2017.[275]

Arbitration

What is arbitration?

Arbitration is a way to resolve disputes without going to court, using the services of privately appointed decision makers called arbitrators. Congress enacted a statute in 1925 to regulate aspects of arbitration,[276] but for the most part how arbitration is conducted, where it takes place, who makes the decision, what issues are subject to the process, and how much it costs to arbitrate are determined by contractual agreement between the parties to the dispute. Including an arbitration term in an employment or consumer contract is increasingly common. However, consumers and workers rarely if ever have an opportunity to negotiate the arbitration clause and frequently are not even aware that it is in the contract.[277] Rather, many employers mandate that their workers arbitrate disputes that might arise in the workplace. In effect, these terms require that the worker, as a condition of having a job, give up any right to sue the employer in court and have a jury decide the merits of a dispute. Mandatory arbitration terms are most typical in industries where the workers are low paid, female, and persons of color.[278] Similarly, many consumer contracts contain mandatory arbitration terms, and the buyer must accept the provision on a take-it-or-leave-it basis. Over 50 percent of credit card loans are subject to arbitration; 44 percent of checking account contracts with banks are subject to arbitration; and almost all payday loans, private student loans, mobile phone agreements, and prepaid cards are subject to arbitration.[279]

Questions have been raised about the fairness of mandatory arbitration terms. The arbitral decision maker often has an institutional relation with the employer or the finance company that drafts the agreement, creating at least the appearance of bias even if not bias in fact.[280] Moreover, because arbitration is private, the public does not have access to complete information about how much it costs to arbitrate. Studies suggest that the cost of initiating an arbitration—for example, to challenge an excessive credit card fee or the failure to pay wages at the federal minimum rate—may be more expensive than starting a lawsuit in court.[281] Moreover, unlike a court case, where the government pays the judge's salary, the parties to arbitration are required to pay the cost of hiring the arbitrator. To be sure, a consumer who cannot pay fees may request a waiver from the arbitration association, but whether the waiver will be granted is a matter of discretion.[282] Moreover, the U.S. Supreme Court has held that an arbitration agreement is not unenforceable simply because the cost of bringing an individual arbitral action is more than the expected relief if the party wins.[283]

The remedies available through arbitration are limited to those stated in the arbitration agreement. If the agreement places a cap on the amount of damages or bars the claimant from suing with other injured parties, the parties are bound by the terms of the agreement.[284] The U.S. Supreme Court has held that employers can mandate arbitration terms that bar workers from suing together in a class action (which is an important procedural device that reduces the costs of litigation when large numbers of persons suffer similar injuries, such as an employer's failure to pay the minimum wage).[285] There are, however, some limits on the terms that can be included in an arbitration agreement. In particular, at least so far, the agreement cannot waive the applicability of federal law; as the Fourth Circuit Court of Appeals has said, an arbitration agreement "may not flatly and categorically renounce the authority of the federal statutes to which it is and must remain subject."[286]

Requiring consumers or workers to arbitrate certain kinds of federal claims, such as those involving pay equity or sexual harassment, also imposes social costs. Although information about arbitral damage awards generally is not public, the information that is available suggests that awards are lower than those that could be obtained in court, even accounting for different litigation expenses.[287] In the employment context, studies indicate that mandating arbitration negatively impacts the ability of a worker to assert a workplace violation against an employer.[288] This means that important rights and protections are unenforced. During the Obama administration, the Consumer Finance Protection Bureau, a federal agency, investigated the use of mandatory arbitration clauses in consumer agreements and issued a rule that would make it impermissible for a bank or credit card company to mandate arbitration rather than allowing a consumer to sue.[289] However, the Trump administration revoked the rule.[290] The U.S. Supreme Court has vigorously enforced arbitration clauses, with little concern for the unfairness of the practice or its negative impact on the enforcement of federal laws. The American use of mandatory arbitration terms in employment and consumer contracts marks a stark contrast to practice in other industrialized nations.[291]

Notes

1. U.S. Const. Preamble.
2. The United States maintains a website about the federal courts with information about such things as who the judges are, how to file a lawsuit, and filing fees in the different courts. *See* United States Courts, https://www.uscourts.gov. For information about the Supreme Court of the United States, *see* the Court's official website: https://www.supremecourt.gov.
3. The importance of equal access to justice is underscored by the fact that the United States has ratified the United Nations International Covenant on Civil and Political Rights, which encourages participating nations to provide free counsel to poor persons who might otherwise be unable to enforce legal rights. *See* International Covenant on Civil and Political Rights, art. 50, 999 U.N.T.S. 171 (1966). *See* Jimmy Carter, U.S. Finally Ratifies Human Rights Covenant, The Carter Center (1992), https://www.cartercenter.org/news/documents/doc1369.html.
4. The Honorable Learned Hand, Chief Justice, United States Court of Appeals for the Second Circuit, Keynote Address at the Legal Aid Society's 75th Anniversary Celebration (Feb. 16, 1951), http://www.legal-aid.org/en/las/thoushaltnotrationjustice.

aspx. *See also* Jennifer M. Smith, Rationed Justice, 49 Suffolk U. L. Rev. 353, 367 (2016) (quoting Hand).

5. *See* James J. Sandman, The Role of the Legal Services Corporation in Improving Access to Justice, 148(1) Daedalus 113, 114 (2019) (explaining that the Legal Services Corporation "uses the 'justice gap' metaphor to describe the shortfall between legal needs and available legal services"). *See also* Legal Services Corporation, The Justice Gap: Measuring the Unmet Civil Legal Needs of Low-Income Americans (June 2017), http://www.lsc.gov/sites/default/files/images/TheJusticeGap-FullReport.pdf.

6. *See* Issachar Rosen-Zvi, Just Fee Shifting, 37 Fla. St. U. L. Rev. 717 (2010) (discussing the limitations of contingency fee and fee-shifting statutes to fill the justice gap). The American Bar Association Model Rules of Professional Conduct, adopted in 40 states, bar lawyers from providing indigent clients with living expenses while waiting for court-ordered damages or benefit awards. *See also* Philip G. Schrag, The Unethical Ethics Rule: Nine Ways to Fix Model Rule of Professional Conduct, 1.8(E), 8 Geo. J. Legal Ethics 39 (2015).

7. Dion Chu, Matthew R. Greenfield, & Peter Zuckerman, Measuring the Justice Gap: Flaws in the Interstate Allocation of Civil Legal Services Funding and a Proposed Remedy, 33 Pace L. Rev. 965 (2013), citing Legal Services Corporation, Documenting the Justice Gap in America *19–22 (Sept. 2009), https://www.lsc.gov/sites/default/files/LSC/pdfs/documenting_the_justice_gap_in_america_2009.pdf. The National Center for Access to Justice, using 2014–15 data, measures the ratio at less than 1 lawyer per 10,000 poor Americans. *See* National Center for Access to Justice (NCAJ), The Justice Index, Number of Attorneys for People in Poverty, http://justiceindex.org/2016-findings/attorney-access. The NCAJ's methodology includes individuals with incomes at or below 200% of the federal poverty line, whereas the LSC's 2009 report uses 125% as the threshold.

8. U.S. Const. Amend. VI ("In all criminal prosecutions, the accused shall enjoy . . . the Assistance of Counsel for his defence."). *See also* Gideon v. Wainwright, 372 U.S. 335 (1963).

9. *See* National Association for Public Defense, NAPD Statement on the Necessity of Meaningful Workload Standards for Public Defense Delivery Systems (Mar. 19, 2015), http://www.publicdefenders.us/files/NAPD_workload_statement.pdf.

10. *See, for example*, Ann Cammett, Shadow Citizens: Felony Disenfranchisement and the Criminalization of Debt, 117 Penn. St. L. Rev. 349 (2012).

11. *See* Patricia E. Roberts, From the "War on Poverty" to Pro Bono: Access to Justice Remains Elusive for Too Many, Including Our Veterans, 34 B.C. J.L. & Soc. Just. 341 (2014).

12. *See, for example*, Michele Cotton, When Judges Don't Follow the Law: Research and Recommendations, 19 CUNY L. Rev. 57 (2015); Cara L. Stewart & Ryan C. Smither, Breaking Down Barriers to Justice: Surveying the Practical Application of Kentucky's Landlord-Tenant Laws and Calling for Basic Reform, 39 N. Ky. L. Rev. 23 (2012) ("In many residential disputes between landlords and tenants, parties either cannot or do not obtain an attorney, and consequently Kentucky's eviction dockets paint a persuasive picture of the problems caused by litigants entering the courts without counsel.").

13. *See, for example*, Conor P. Duffy, A Sum Uncertain: Preserving Due Process and Preventing Default Judgments in Consumer Debt Buyer Lawsuits in New York, 40 Fordham Urban L.J. 1147 (2013); Peter A. Holland, The One Hundred Billion Dollar Problem in Small Claims Court: Robo-Signing and Lack of Proof in Debt Buyer Cases, 6 J. Bus. & Tech. L. 259, 265 (2011) ("In the majority of debt buyer cases, the courts grant the debt buyer a default judgment because the consumer has failed to appear for trial. In many of these instances, debtors simply do not know they have been sued."); Victoria J. Haneman, The Ethical Exploitation of the Unrepresented Consumer, 73 Mo. L. Rev. 707 (2008).

14. *See* UCLA Labor Center, What Is Wage Theft?, http://www.labor.ucla.edu/wage-theft/ ("California has many strong labor laws on the books, but wage theft persists because of lack of enforcement.").

15. *See* Daniel Wiessner, Data Privacy Group Says Errors Rampant in Employee Background Checks, Reuters Legal (Apr. 19, 2016), http://www.reuters.com/article/employment-backgroundchecks-idUSL2N17M0AS; Chris Johnson, This Month's Complaint Report: Credit Reporting Issues, Consumer Financial Protection Bureau (Aug. 25, 2015), http://www.consumerfinance.gov/about-us/blog/this-months-complaint-report-credit-reporting-issues (reporting problems consumers face correcting credit reports without intervention of government agency).

16. *See* Ingrid V. Eagly & Steven Shafer, A National Study of Access to Counsel in Immigration Court, 164 U. Pa. L. Rev. 1 (2015).

17. *See* Sande L. Buhai, Access to Justice for Unrepresented Litigants: A Comparative Perspective, 42 Loyola L.A. L. Rev. 979, 986 (2009) (quoting Rebecca Sandefur).

18. *See* Deborah L. Rhode, Whatever Happened to Access to Justice?, 42 Loyola L.A. L. Rev. 869 (2009).

19. *See* U. S. Department of Justice, Poverty Is Not a Crime, Statement Courtesy of Deputy Attorney General Sally Q. Yates (Dec. 2, 2015), https://www.justice.gov/archives/opa/blog/poverty-not-crime. For further discussion, *see* Alexandra Natapoff, Gideon's Servants and the Criminalization of Poverty, 12 Ohio St. J. Crim. L. 445 (2015).

20. Michael Herz, "Do Justice": Variations of a Thrice-Told Tale, 82 Va. L. Rev. 111 (1996).

21. United States Courts, Fees, https://www.uscourts.gov/services-forms/fees.

22. State-by-state information about fees (as well as fines and bail), can be accessed through the National Center for State Courts, https://www.ncsc.org/topics/financial/fines-costs-and-fees/state-links.aspx.

23. Boddie v. Connecticut, 401 U.S. 371 (1971). As the Court explained:

> [G]iven the basic position of the marriage relationship in this society's hierarchy of values and the concomitant state monopolization of the means for legally dissolving this relationship, due process . . . prohibit[s] a State from denying, solely because of inability to pay, access to its courts to individuals who seek judicial dissolution of their marriages.

Id. at 374.

24. United States v. Kras, 409 U.S. 434 (1973).

25. Ortwein v. Schwab, 410 U.S. 656 (1973). In Ross v. Brown Title Corp., 356 F. Supp. 595 (E.D. La.), aff'd mem., 412 U.S. 934 (1973), the U.S. Supreme Court affirmed the

decision of a three-judge district court upholding the denial of a waiver of a bond requirement for challenging a foreclosure when the procedure, as explained by the lower court, provided a way for defenses to be presented without payment of security.

26. Lindsey v. Normet, 405 U.S. 56, 79 (1972).

27. 28 U.S.C. § 1915. The federal statute was first enacted in 1892. The legislative history explains that the bill was proposed:

> to open the United States Courts to a class of American citizens who have rights to be adjudicated, but are now excluded practically for want of sufficient money or property to enter the courts under their rules.
>
> [I]f these people are not allowed in the United States courts, why admit the wealthy. . . .
>
> In short, this bill presents the question whether this Government, having established courts to do justice to litigants, will admit the wealthy and deny the poor entrance to them to have their rights adjudicated.

H.R. Rep. No. 1079, 52d Cong., 1st Sess. 1 (1892). The statute currently is awkwardly phrased, resulting from amendments that inserted the word "prisoner" into the statute where previously only the word "person" appeared. Courts that have considered the question agree that, despite the amendment, "Congress did not intend to prevent a non-prisoner from being able to proceed in forma pauperis in federal court." Floyd v. United States Postal Services, 105 F.3d 274, 276 (6th Cir. 1997). *See also* Leonard v. Lacy, 88 F.3d 181, 183–184 (2d Cir. 1996); Schagene v. United States, 37 Fed. Cl. 661, 662–663 (1997).

28. 28 U.S.C. § 1915. For an explanation and critique of in forma pauperis relief in federal courts, *see* Andrew Hammond, Pleading Poverty in Federal Court, 128 Yale L.J. 1478 (2019).

29. A short form and a long form of the application are available at United States Courts, Fee Waiver Application Forms, http://www.uscourts.gov/forms/fee-waiver-application-forms. If a party completes the short form, the court may request that the long form—which provides additional information—be completed and submitted before granting the relief.

30. Potnick v. Eastern State Hospital, 701 F.2d 243, 244 (2d Cir. 1983). *See also* Prophet v. United States, 106 Fed. Cl. 456, 461 (2012) (standard is that payment "would constitute a serious hardship on the plaintiff, not that such payment would render plaintiff destitute").

31. Potnick, 701 F.2d at 244 (citing Adkins v. E.I. DuPont de Nemours & Co., 335 U.S. 331, 339 (1948)).

32. 28 U.S.C. § 1915(b)(1).

33. Roberts v. United States District Court, 339 U.S. 844 (1950).

34. Fed. R. Civ. P. 4(c)(3).

35. 28 U.S.C. § 1915(e)(2)(A)–(B). *See also* Denton v. Hernandez, 504 U.S. 25 (1992), remanded, 966 F.2d 533 (9th Cir. 1992). In *Denton*, the U.S. Supreme Court affirmed the dismissal of a case as frivolous under then-numbered 28 U.S.C. § 1915(d), emphasizing that "[d]ismissal of the claims as frivolous was proper only if the facts alleged were clearly baseless, a category which encompassed fanciful, fantastic, and

delusional allegations, whether or not there were judicially noticeable facts available to contradict them." *Id.* at 32 (citations omitted). The dismissal of a complaint for frivolousness at this stage of the proceeding is without prejudice to the later filing of a paid complaint. *Id.* at 34.

36. 28 U.S.C. § 1915(e)(2)(A) & (B)(i)–(iii). *See* Rowe v. Shake, 196 F.3d 778, 783 (7th Cir. 1999) (holding that "district courts have the power to screen complaints filed by all litigants, prisoners and non-prisoners alike" and they "may screen the complaint prior to service on the defendants"). *See also* Hoskins v. Poelstra, 320 F.3d 761, 763 (7th Cir. 2003).

37. Benitez v. Wolff, 907 F.2d 1293, 1295 (2d Cir. 1990) (citing Elliott v. Bronson, 872 F.2d 20, 21 (2d Cir. 1989)); Robles v. Couglin, 725 F.2d 12, 15 (2d Cir. 1983).

38. *See* Steven H. Steinglass, Section 1983 Litigation in State Courts § 8.3 Court costs and in forma pauperis policies (2018 ed.).

39. *See, for example,* Tahtinen v. Superior Court of Pinal County, 637 P.2d 723, 725 (Ariz. 1981) ("unless a fundamental right is violated or an invidious classification is created, a statute impinging on the equal privileges and immunities of a class of Arizona residents will be upheld if it has a rational basis"), cert. denied, Mendibles v. Superior Court of Pinal County, 454 U.S. 1152 (1982).

40. Jafar v. Webb, 177 Wash. 2d 520, 531, 303 P.3d 1042, 1047 (2013) ("the triggering determination is the finding of indigency. Once the trial court determines that a litigant is indigent, the rule then requires a complete waiver in order to allow access to the courts").

41. PACER can be accessed online, at https://www.pacer.gov.

42. 28 U.S.C. § 1913.

43. *See* Hall v. Liberty Mutual Insurance, 2017 WL 6033526 (C.D. Cal. 2017).

44. 28 U.S.C. § 1915(d). *See, for example,* Richardson v. Johnson, 598 F.3d 734 (11th Cir. 2010).

45. 28 U.S.C. § 1915(a). The items or activities that are covered when the court authorizes a party to proceed in forma pauperis generally are defined by individual courts. *See* Robert F. Koets, What Constitutes "Fees" or "Costs" Within Meaning of Federal Statutory Provision (28 U.S.C.A. § 1915 and Similar Predecessor Statutes) Permitting Party to Proceed In Forma Pauperis Without Prepayment of Fees and Costs or Security Therefor, 142 A.L.R. Fed. 627 (originally published in 1997 and updated on Westlaw) (extensively analyzing cases in which federal courts have determined whether particular expenses fell within the scope of the in forma pauperis statute).

46. *See* Frank I. Michelman, The Supreme Court and Litigation Access Fees: The Right to Protect One's Rights—Part I, 1973 Duke L.J. 1153, 1163 (1973) ("By any practical measure, it is not primarily the fees imposed by states as a legal condition of access to court . . . that impede effective litigation by the impoverished, but the far heavier costs of the legally optional, yet practically essential, equipage often needed for an effective presentation once the case is filed—attorneys' fees, chiefly, but consultant, expert witness, investigational, stenographic, and printing costs as well.").

47. *See* 10 Charles A. Wright & Arthur R. Miller, Federal Practice and Procedure § 2673 (4th ed.) ("Despite this broad language, the scope of the term 'costs' has been read narrowly and many items of expense typically regarded as costs have been disallowed under the statute.").

48. *See* McNeil v. Lowney, 831 F.2d 1368, 1373 (7th Cir. 1987) ("[T]he right of access to the courts does not independently include a waiver of witness fees so that the indigent litigant can present his case fully to the court."). However, at least one appeals court has authorized the payment of expenses for witnesses under other statutes. *See* United States Marshals Service v. Means, 741 F.2d 1053 (8th Cir. 1984). For further discussion, *see* Kenneth R. Levine, In Forma Pauperis Litigants: Witness Fees and Expenses in Civil Actions, 53 Fordham L. Rev. 1461 (1985).

49. *See* Ebenhart v. Power, 309 F. Supp. 660 (S.D.N.Y. 1969).

50. *See* Porter v. Department of Treasury, 564 F.3d 176 (3d Cir. 2009).

51. *See* Manning v. Tefft, 839 F. Supp. 126 (D. R.I. 1994).

52. 28 U.S.C. § 1915(e)(1).

53. *See* Mallard v. U.S. District Court for Southern District of Iowa, 490 U.S. 296 (1989).

54. Santiago v. Walls, 599 F.3d 749, 761 (7th Cir. 2010) (citation omitted). The Seventh Circuit has not clearly defined what constitutes a "reasonable attempt to obtain counsel," but it has affirmed one court's requirement that the litigant show contacts with at least three attorneys, each of whom turned down the request for representation. *See* Romanelli v. Suilene, 615 F.3d 847, 852 (7th Cir. 2010).

55. Pruitt v. Mote, 503 F.3d 647, 659 (7th Cir. 2007) (reversing district court's denial of request for counsel and remanding case for a new trial).

56. *See* SAI v. Transportation Security Administration, 843 F.3d 33, 36 (1st Cir. 2016), cert. denied, 137 S. Ct. 2234 (2017); Dolan v. Connolly, 794 F.3d 290, 296–297 (2d Cir. 2015); Phillips v. Jasper County Jail, 437 F.3d 791, 794 (8th Cir. 2006); Montgomery v. Pinchak, 294 F.3d 492, 499 (3d Cir. 2002); Caster v. Colorado Springs Cablevision, 979 F.2d 1417, 1421 (10th Cir. 1992).

57. For an interactive map indicating which states have a right to civil counsel, *see* National Coalition for a Civil Right to Counsel, Status Map, http://civilrighttocounsel. org/map. *See also* Laura K. Abel & Judge Lora J. Livingston, The Existing Civil Right to Counsel Infrastructure, 47 Judges' J. 24 (2008); Laura K. Abel & Max Rettig, State Statutes Providing for a Right to Counsel in Civil Cases, 40 Clearinghouse Rev. 245 (2006).

58. Omnibus Consolidated Rescissions and Appropriations Act of 1996, Pub. L. No. 104-134, 110 Stat. 1321. Title VIII of the Act is the Prisoner Litigation Reform Act of 1995; § 804 of the Prisoner Litigation Reform Act made a series of amendments to 28 U.S.C. § 1915.

59. 28 U.S.C. § 1915.

60. 42 U.S.C. § 1997e(c).

61. 42 U.S.C. § 1997e(e). At least one court has held that the PLRA's prohibition on damage awards for emotional distress, absent a showing of physical injury, is unconstitutional as applied to a First Amendment retaliation claim. Siggers-El v. Barlow, 433 F. Supp. 2d 811 (E.D. Mich. 2006).

62. 42 U.S.C. § 1997e(d). The attorney's fees provision states that, "[w]henever a monetary judgement is awarded" in a prisoner suit, "a portion of the judgment (not to exceed 25 percent) shall be applied to satisfy the amount of attorney's fees awarded against the defendant." 42 U.S.C. § 1997e(d)(2). Although some federal courts of appeals read this provision as conferring discretion on district courts to allocate less than 25% of the judgment toward attorney's fees, *see* Parker v. Conway, 581 F.3d 198, 205 (3d Cir. 2009) (conferring discretion), and Boesing v. Spiess, 540 F.3d 886, 892 (8th Cir. 2008) (same), the U.S. Supreme Court rejected this approach, holding that judges lack such discretion under the PLRA. *See* Murphy v. Smith, 583 U.S. ___, 138 S. Ct. 784 (2018) (holding that courts must apply as much of the judgment as necessary, up to 25%, to satisfy an attorney's fee award).

63. 28 U.S.C. § 1915(g). *See also* Daker v. Commissioner of Georgia Department of Corrections, 820 F.3d 1278 (11th Cir. 2016).

64. 42 U.S.C. § 1997e(a). "The PLRA strengthened this exhaustion provision in several ways. Exhaustion is no longer left to the discretion of the district court, but is mandatory." Woodford v. Ngo, 548 U.S. 81, 85 (2006). A prisoner is not required to plead the exhaustion of administrative remedies; instead, the government must raise a failure to do so as an affirmative defense. *See* Jones v. Block, 549 U.S. 199 (2007).

65. *See* Ross v. Blake, 578 U.S. ___, 136 S. Ct. 1850 (2016) (grievance process must be available to inmate); Woodford v. Ngo, 548 U.S. 81 (2006) (PLRA requires proper exhaustion); Booth v. Churner, 532 U.S. 731, 736 (2001) (noting that the administrative tribunal must have authority to take some responsive action, even if it cannot grant the relief sought).

66. Numerous scholars have tried to establish a right to counsel in civil cases under the federal Constitution or a limited right to counsel in particular kinds of proceedings where specific interests are at stake. *See, for example*, Russell Engler, Reflections on a Civil Right to Counsel and Drawing Lines: When Does Access to Justice Mean Full Representation by Counsel, and When Might Less Assistance Suffice?, 9 Seattle J. for Soc. Just. 97 (2010); Gene R. Nichol, Jr., Judicial Abdication and Equal Access to the Civil Justice System, 60 Case W. L. Rev. 325 (2010); Stephen Loffredo & Don Friedman, Gideon Meets Goldberg: The Case for a Qualified Right to Counsel in Welfare Hearings, 25 Touro L. Rev. 273 (2009); Karl Monsma & Richard Lempert, The Value of Counsel: 20 Years of Representation Before a Public Housing Eviction Board, 26 L. & Soc. Rev. 627 (1992); Andrew Scherer, Gideon's Shelter: The Need to Recognize a Right to Counsel for Indigent Defendants in Eviction Proceedings, 23 Harv. C.R.–C.L. L. Rev. 557 (1988); Lester Brickman, Of Arterial Passageways through the Legal Process: The Right of Universal Access to Courts and Lawyering Services, 48 N.Y.U. L. Rev. 595 (1973) (locating a right to counsel in civil cases in the First Amendment). For an international comparison, *see* Sande L. Buhai, Access to Justice for Unrepresented Litigants: A Comparative Perspective, 41 Loyola L.A. L. Rev. 979 (2009); Earl Johnson, The Right to Counsel in Civil Cases: An International Perspective, 19 Loyola L.A. L. Rev. 341 (1985); Francis William O'Brien, Why Not Appointed Counsel in Civil Cases? The Swiss Approach, 28 Ohio St. L.J. 1 (1967).

67. Lassiter v. Department of Social Services of Durham County, N.C., 452 U.S. 18, 27 (1981). For an argument that the *Lassiter* Court's "presumption" against a right to counsel in effect abandoned the due process analysis prescribed by *Mathews v. Eldridge,* and is best understood as an instance of "judicial underenforcement" of the Due Process Clause, *see* Stephen Loffredo & Don Friedman, Gideon Meets Goldberg: The Case for a Qualified Right to Counsel in Welfare Hearings, 25 Touro L. Rev. 273, 304–312 (2009).

68. In re Gault, 387 U.S. 1 (1967).

69. Vitek v. Jones, 445 U.S. 480 (1980).

70. Turner v. Rogers, 564 U.S. 431 (2011) (holding that the Due Process Clause did not require provision of counsel to a father who faced imprisonment for civil contempt for failing to comply with a child support order if alternative procedural safeguards existed).

71. Lassiter v. Department of Social Services of Durham County, N.C., 452 U.S. 18 (1981). *See also* Regina M. Campbell, No-Frills Due Process—Who Needs Counsel?: Lassiter v. Department of Social Services, 14 Conn. L. Rev. 733 (1982).

72. 42 U.S.C. § 2996 (2010). *See* Legal Services Corporation, About LSC, https://www.lsc.gov/about-lsc. Federal law bars legal services lawyers from representing litigants in cases involving abortion and school desegregation. 42 U.S.C. § 2996f(b)(8) & (9). *See* Alan W. Houseman, Book Review, To Establish Justice for All: The Past and Future of Civil Legal Aid in the United States by Justice Earl Johnson, Jr. Praeger, 2014, 23 Geo. J. on Poverty L. & Pol'y 325 (2016).

73. Legal Services Corporation, Find Legal Aid, http://www.lsc.gov/what-legal-aid/find-legal-aid. In addition, LawHelp.org is an online platform providing legal and pro bono resources, court information and forms, and referrals to legal aid organizations in different states around the country. LawHelp can be accessed online, at https://www.lawhelp.org/about-us.

74. 45 C.F.R. 1611 App. A. *See also* 83 Fed. Reg. 3058 (Jan. 23, 2018).

75. *See, for example,* Committee to Improve the Availability of Legal Services, Final Report to the Chief Judge of the State of New York, 19 Hofstra L. Rev. 755 (1990), http://scholarlycommons.law.hofstra.edu/hlr/vol19/iss4/6.

76. *See, for example,* American Bar Association, Resolution 112A (Aug. 2006) ("RESOLVED, That the American Bar Association urges federal, state, and territorial governments to provide legal counsel as a matter of right at public expense to low income persons in those categories of adversarial proceedings where basic human needs are at stake, such as those involving shelter, sustenance, safety, health or child custody, as determined by each jurisdiction."), http://bit.ly/13yGmj9.

77. *See, for example,* Laura K. Abel & Max Rettig, State Statutes Providing for a Right to Counsel in Civil Cases, Clearinghouse Review (July–Aug. 2006), https://www.brennancenter.org/sites/default/files/legacy/d/download_file_39169.pdf.

78. *See* American Bar Association, Civil Right to Counsel, https://www.americanbar.org/groups/legal_aid_indigent_defendants/civil_right_to_counsel1/; National Coalition for a Civil Right to Counsel, http://civilrighttocounsel.org/.

79. *See* Oksana Mironova, NYC Right to Counsel: First year results and potential for expansion, Community Service Society (Mar. 25, 2019), https://www.cssny.org/news/entry/nyc-right-to-counsel#_ed; *see also* Kathyrn Sabbeth, Housing Defense as the New Gideon, 41 Harv. J.L. & Gender 55 (2018).
80. Turner v. Rogers, 564 U.S. 431, 435, 447–448 (2011). *See* Mitchell Levy, Empirical Patterns of Pro Se Litigation in Federal District Courts, 85 U. Chi. L. Rev. 1819, 1827–28 (2018) (discussing Turner as offering "a nod toward a new and potentially more fruitful approach [than the appointment of free counsel] to pro se litigation: reforms in trial courts").
81. *See* Marla N. Greenstein, Judges' Responsibilities to Pro Se Litigants, 47 Judges' J. 46 (2008) ("The ethical challenge for a judge working with pro se litigants is to provide the engaged communication that will facilitate a meaningful coherent court hearing without providing legal assistance that turns the judge into an advocate."). For example, in Ferrelli v. River Manor Health Center, 323 F.2d 19 (2d Cir. 2003), the appeals court held that the district court did not have an affirmative duty to inquire into the mental capacity of a pro se litigant or on its own to appoint a guardian to protect the litigant's interests.
82. Pliler v. Ford, 542 U.S. 225, 226 (2004) (holding that a federal court hearing a habeas corpus petition was not required to warn a pro se prisoner of the consequences of dismissing a petition with respect to exhausted and unexhausted claims). Justice Thomas, writing for the majority, explained:

> [W]e hold that federal district judges are not required to give *pro se* litigants these two warnings. District judges have no obligation to act as counsel or paralegal to *pro se* litigants. In *McKaskle v. Wiggins*, 465 U.S. 168, 183–184, 104 S. Ct. 944, 79 L.Ed.2d 122 (1984), the Court stated that "[a] defendant does not have a constitutional right to receive personal instruction from the trial judge on courtroom procedure" and that "the Constitution [does not] require judges to take over chores for a *pro se* defendant that would normally be attended to by trained counsel as a matter of course." See also *Martinez v. Court of Appeal of Cal., Fourth Appellate Dist.*, 528 U.S. 152, 162, 120 S. Ct. 684, 145 L.Ed.2d 597 (2000) ("[T]he trial judge is under no duty to provide personal instruction on courtroom procedure or to perform any legal 'chores' for the defendant that counsel would normally carry out"). Explaining the details of federal habeas procedure and calculating statutes of limitations are tasks normally and properly performed by trained counsel as a matter of course. Requiring district courts to advise a *pro se* litigant in such a manner would undermine district judges' role as impartial decisionmakers.

Id. at 231. *See generally* Stephan Landsman, Pro Se Litigation, 8 Ann. Rev. L. & Soc. Sci. 231 (2012).
83. For a discussion, *see* Julie M. Bradlow, Procedural Due Process Rights of Pro Se Civil Litigants, 55 U. Chi. L. Rev. 659, 670 (1988) ("[T]he judge who denies the pro se civil litigant's request for counsel under 28 U.S.C. § 1915(d) is also the judge who will enforce that litigant's obligation to comply strictly with procedural rules."). *See also* Fessehazi v. Hudson Group, 2009 WL 2777043 (S.D.N.Y. 2009) (granting motion to

reconsider denial of motion for appointment of counsel upon a showing of "legal complications" and the need to develop evidence).

84. Merritt v. Faulkner, 697 F.2d 761, 769 (7th Cir. 1983) (Posner, J., concurring and dissenting). Judge Posner later retired from the bench, citing disagreements with his colleagues about treatment of pro se litigants, and went on to establish a nonprofit institute, The Posner Center of Justice for Pro Se's, which is "devoted to assisting deserving pro se litigants who need, but cannot afford or don't know how to utilize, legal assistance." *See* Mission Statement, http://www.justice-for-pro-ses.org/. *See also* Adam Liptak, An Exit Interview with Richard Posner, Judicial Provocateur, N.Y. Times (Sept. 11, 2017), https://www.nytimes.com/2017/09/11/us/politics/ judge-richard-posner-retirement.html. *See also* Annette J. Scieszinski, Not on My Watch: One Judge's Mantra to Ensure Access to Justice, 61 Drake L. Rev. 817 (2013).

85. American Bar Association, Model Code of Judicial Conduct, Comment on Rule 2.2, http://www.americanbar.org/groups/professional_responsibility/publications/ model_code_of_judicial_conduct/model_code_of_judicial_conduct_canon_ 2/rule2_2impartialityandfairness/commentonrule2_2.html. *See   also*   Jona Goldschmidt, Judicial Ethics and Assistance to Self-Represented Litigants, 28 Just. Sys. J. 324, 324–328 (2007).

86. Fed. R. Civ. P. 12(b)(6).

87. Erickson v. Pardus, 551 U.S. 89, 94 (2007) (citations omitted). *See also* Haines v. Kerner, 404 U.S. 519, 520–521 (1972).

88. *See* Rory K. Schneider, Illiberal Construction of Pro Se Pleadings, 15 U. Pa. L. Rev. 585 (2011).

89. Fed. R. Civ. P. 16(c)(2)(P).

90. *See, for example,* Timms v. Frank, 953 F.2d 281, 285 (7th Cir. 1992) (requiring all pro se litigants to receive notice of summary judgment procedures before the court may grant judgment against them).

91. As an example, *see* Local Rules of the United States District Courts for the Southern and Eastern Districts of New York, Local Civil Rule 12.1, Notice to Pro Se Litigant Who Opposes a Rule 12 Motion Supported by Matters Outside the Pleadings, and Local Civil Rule 7.2, Authorities to Be Provided to Pro Se Litigants (effective June 26, 2017), http://www.nysd.uscourts.gov/rules/rules.pdf.

92. Lebron v. Sanders, 557 F.3d 76 (2d Cir. 2009).

93. For an overview of resources that are provided, *see* Donna J. Stienstra, Jared J. Bataillon, & Jason A. Cantone, Assistance to Pro Se Litigants in U.S. District Courts: A Report on Surveys of Clerks of Court and Chief Judges, Federal Judicial Center (2011), https://www.fjc.gov/sites/default/files/2012/ProSeUSDC.pdf.

94. As an example, *see* Representing Yourself at Trial: A Manual for Pro Se Litigants Appearing Before the United States District Court for the Southern District of New York (July 2011), http://www.nysd.uscourts.gov/file/forms/representing-yourself-at-trial. *See also* United States District Court, Southern District of New York Representing Yourself (Pro Se), http://www.nysd.uscourts.gov/forms. php?f=p. Note that while most federal courts allow pro se litigants to file electronically, either as a matter of course or by permission, litigants in the Eleventh Circuit

and two districts within the Sixth Circuit are categorically barred from doing so, and must file in paper. *See* Greene v. Frost Brown Todd, LLC, 856 F.3d 438, 439–440 (6th Cir. 2017) (Griffin, J., concurring).

95. 28 U.S.C. § 955. *See, for example*, United States District Court, District of New Jersey, Procedural Guide for Pro Se Litigants (June 2017), http://www.njd.uscourts.gov/sites/njd/files/ProSeGuide.pdf.

96. As an example, *see* United States District Court, District of Maine, Information for Pro Se Parties *7, http://www.med.uscourts.gov/pdf/PRO_SE_INFORMATION_HANDOUT.pdf; United States District Court, Northern District of Texas, Pro Se Handbook for Civil Suits (Dec. 2018), http://www.txnd.uscourts.gov/sites/default/files/documents/handbook.pdf.

97. For a description of the Federal Pro Se Legal Assistance Project in the Eastern District of New York, *see* United States Courts, Pro Se Centers Help Even the Odds for Litigants Without Lawyers (Aug. 20, 2015), http://www.uscourts.gov/news/2015/08/20/pro-se-centers-help-even-odds-litigants-without-lawyers. For a discussion of the Minnesota Federal Pro Se Project, *see* Dan Gustafson, Karla Gluek, & Joe Bourne, Pro Se Litigation and the Costs of Access to Justice, 39 William Mitchell L. Rev. 32 (2012).

98. *See* Lois Bloom & Helen Hershkoff, Federal Courts, Magistrate Judges, and the Pro Se Plaintiff, 16 Notre Dame J.L., Ethics & Pub. Pol'y 475 (2002).

99. *See* Laura K. Abel, Language Access in the Federal Courts, 61 Drake L. Rev. 593 (2013); also available at Laura K. Abel, National Center for Access to Justice at Cardozo Law, Language Access in the Federal Courts (2013), http://ncforaj.org/wp-content/uploads/2013/12/abel-ncaj-language-access-federal-courts.pdf.

100. *See* Teresa B. Morales & Nathaniel D. Wong, Attorneys Who Interpret for Their Clients: Communication, Conflict, and Confusion—How Texas Courts Have Placed Attorneys and Their L.E.P. Clients at the "Discretion" of the Trial Court, 37 St. Mary's L.J. 1123, 1138 (2006) (at least in Texas, "it is not disputed that attorneys can serve as both counsel and interpreter for a client").

101. *See* United States v. Lopez-Collazo, 824 F.3d 453 (4th Cir. 2016) (failure to provide defendant with Spanish translation of the charges in a Notice of Intent to Issue a Final Administrative Removal Order violated due process, but defendant was not prejudiced by the failure); Perez-Lastor v. I.N.S., 208 F.3d 773, 778 (9th Cir. 2000) ("It is long-settled that a competent translation is fundamental to a full and fair hearing."). In *Lau v. Nichols*, 414 U.S. 563 (1974), the Supreme Court held that public schools that receive federal financial assistance violate Title VI of the Civil Rights Act of 1964, 42 U.S.C. § 2000d, when they fail to provide English language instruction to students who do not speak English. However, later Court decisions have made it more difficult to enforce the statute and its regulations. *See* Alexander v. Sandoval, 532 U.S. 275 (2001) (holding that Title VI provides no private right of action to bring disparate impact suit against Alabama's English-only driver's license examination); Guardians Association v. Civil Service Commission of the City of New York, 463 U.S. 582 (1983) (requiring a demonstration of discriminatory intent for claims under Title VI). For further discussion, *see* Maxwell Alan Miller, Hon. Lynn W. Davis, Adam Prestidge, & William G. Eggington, Finding Justice in

Translation: American Jurisprudence Affecting Due Process for People with Limited English Proficiency Together with Practical Suggestions, 14 Harv. Latino L. Rev. 117 (2011); Marisol León, Silenced by Bureaucratic Adjudication: Mesoamerican Indigenous Language Speakers and Their Right to Due Process of Law, 30 Harv. J. Racial & Ethnic Just. 339, 346 (2014) (showing that "despite the 1964 Civil Rights Act, Executive Order 13166, and the Court Interpreters Act of 1978, many states only provide interpreters in criminal cases and do not require them in all civil cases involving LEP litigants"); Lydia D. Johnson, What Does Justice Have to Do with Interpreters in the Jury Room?, 84 UMKC L. Rev. 941 (2016) (discussing the systematic dismissal of individuals not proficient in English from juries).

102. American Bar Association, Standards for Language Access in Courts std. 1 (2012), https://www.americanbar.org/content/dam/aba/administrative/legal_aid_indigent_defendants/ls_sclaid_standards_for_language_access_proposal.authcheckdam.pdf.

103. Court Interpreters Act, Pub. L. No. 95-539, 92 Stat. 2040 (1978), codified as amended at 28 U.S.C. §§ 1827–28 (2006).

104. 28 U.S.C. § 1827(d)(1)(A). *See* United States Courts, 5 Guide to Judiciary Policy § 210.30 at 3 (last revised Oct. 10, 2017), https://www.uscourts.gov/sites/default/files/guide_vol05_0.pdf (hereinafter Guide to Judiciary Policy).

105. 28 U.S.C. § 1827(g)(4).

106. Guide to Judiciary Policy § 265(b) at 11.

107. United States Courts, Federal Court Interpreters, http://www.uscourts.gov/services-forms/federal-court-interpreters.

108. 28 U.S.C. § 1827(d)(1)(B). In addition, the Americans with Disabilities Act, 42 U.S.C. § 12132, prohibits discrimination by state or local governments on the basis of disability; sections 12131(2) and 12102 suggest that it is discrimination if the government fails to provide translator services needed for disabled individuals to participate in government programs or activities like legal proceedings. One court has held that the act requires prison officials to provide deaf and hearing-impaired inmates with interpreters or other accommodations to allow full participation in educational and rehabilitative programs and in disciplinary and grievance proceedings. Clarkson v. Coughlin, 898 F. Supp. 1019 (S.D.N.Y. 1995).

109. United States Courts, Telephone Interpreting Program: Access to Justice for All (Feb. 25, 2014), http://www.uscourts.gov/news/2014/02/25/telephone-interpreting-program-access-justice-all. *See, for example*, Terrence P. Haas, Advocating for Parents in Rural America, 36 No. 3 Child L. Prac. 50 (2017) (describing use of telephone translation services and emphasizing that the use must "align with best practices"). A generation ago, it seemed unlikely that computer-based technologies could deliver translation services quickly, accurately, and with cultural sensitivity. *See* Charles M. Grabau & Llewellyn Joseph Gibbons, Protecting the Rights of Linguistic Minorities: Challenges to Court Interpretation, 30 New Eng. L. Rev. 227 (1996). Today translation software plays an increasingly important role in e-discovery, transborder disputes, and online dispute resolution, and, although caution still seems in order, may be useful in developing meaningful translation services in courts but would need to be

properly certified. *See, for example*, Suzanne Van Arsdale, User Protections in Online Dispute Resolution, 21 Harv. Negot. L. Rev. 107, 125 (2015).

110. Fisch v. Republic of Poland, 2007 WL 3120274, *2 (S.D.N.Y. Oct 23, 2007) ("No federal rule gives an indigent *pro se* plaintiff, in a civil action, the right to a court-ordered translation of pre-trial documents.").

111. Federal Rule of Criminal Procedure 28 provides for similar authority in federal criminal actions and makes clear that interpreters may be needed where a witness or party is non-English speaking or deaf. *See* Amendments to Rules of Civil Procedure Supplemental Rules for Certain Admiralty and Maritime Claims Rules of Criminal Procedure, 39 F.R.D. 69 (1966).

112. *For example*, Gonzalez v. Bopari, 2012 WL 6569776 (E.D. Cal. 2012). The magistrate judge wrote in his decision denying the request:

> The Court is unaware of any statute authorizing the expenditure of public funds for a court-appointed interpreter in a civil action. The in forma pauperis statute does not authorize the expenditure of public funds for court-appointed interpreters. See 28 U.S.C. § 1915; Loyola v. Potter, 2009 WL 1033398, *2 (N.D. Cal. Apr 16, 2009) ("The court is not authorized to appoint interpreters for litigants in civil cases, and, moreover, has no funds to pay for such a program.")[.]

113. *See* 42 U.S.C. §§ 2000d et seq. *See also* Guidance to Federal Financial Assistance Recipients Regarding Title VI Prohibition Against National Origin Discrimination Affecting Limited English Proficient Persons, 67 Fed. Reg. 41,455 (June 18, 2002). During the Obama administration, the U.S. Department of Justice issued a letter to state judiciaries advising that interpretation services must be provided in all civil, criminal, and administrative matters, and cannot be limited to certain categories of cases; that fees cannot be charged for the interpretation service; that interpreters must be available in the courthouse, and not simply in the courtroom; and that interpreters must be available to ensure effective communication with all court-appointed and supervised personnel. Letter from Thomas E. Perez, Assistant Attorney General, Department of Justice, to State Court Administrators (Aug. 16, 2010), http://www.lep.gov/final_courts_ltr_081610.pdf (setting forth history of executive orders on the subject).

114. *See* Justice Christine M. Durham & Brian L. Hazen, Unfunded Federal Mandates and State Judiciaries: A Question of Sovereignty, 2014 Utah L. Rev. 913 (2014) (describing federal requirements as set out in statute, executive orders, and regulations). *See also* Executive Order 13166, reprinted in 65 Fed. Reg. 50121 (Aug. 16, 2000); Guidance to Federal Financial Assistance Recipients Regarding Title VI Prohibition Against National Origin Discrimination Affecting Limited English Proficient Persons, 67 Fed. Reg. 41455, 41457 (June 18, 2002). The Trump administration in 2018 withdrew certain guidance documents pertaining to language minorities, including FAQs About the Protection of Limited English Proficiency (LEP) Individuals under Title VI of the Civil Rights Act of 1964 and Title VI Regulations, Mar. 1, 2011. *See* U.S. Department of Justice, Press Release, Attorney General Jeff Sessions Rescinds 24 Guidance Documents (July 3, 2018), https://www.justice.gov/opa/pr/attorney-general-jeff-sessions-rescinds-24-guidance-documents.

115. List compiled based on information set forth in Laura Abel, Language Access in State Courts *62–64, App. D, Brennan Center for Justice (2009), http://www. brennancenter.org/content/resource/language_access_in_state_courts; Laura K. Abel & Matthew Longobardi, Improvements in Language Access in the Courts, 2009 to 2012, 46 Clearinghouse Rev. 334 (2012); U.S. Department of Justice, Civil Rights Division, Language Access in the State Courts *11–13 (Sept. 2016), https:// www.justice.gov/crt/file/892036/download; National Center for Access to Justice (NCAJ), The Justice Index, Support for People with Limited English Proficiency (2016), https://justiceindex.org/2016-findings/language-access/.

116. See, for example, Judicial Council of California, Fact Sheet: Court Interpreters Program *1 (Apr. 2017), http://www.courts.ca.gov/documents/Fact_Sheet-_Court_ Interpreters.pdf (referring to California law that "sets forth a priority and preference order when courts do not have sufficient resources to provide interpreters for all persons"); Illinois Supreme Court, Language Access Policy *2 (last amended Sept. 20, 2016), http://www.illinoiscourts.gov/CivilJustice/LanguageAccess/Language_ Access_Policy.pdf (prioritizing the provision of "interpreter services to low and moderate income persons" because of "limited resources for language access").

117. District of Columbia Courts, Office of Court Interpreting Services, https://www. dccourts.gov/services/information-and-resources/interpreting-services. The court also provides on its website information brochures in Amharic, Arabic, Chinese, English, French, Korean, Spanish, Swahili, and Vietnamese. Id.

118. These states include Arkansas, California, Georgia, Maine, Maryland, Missouri, Utah, and Washington. See Carolyn Harlamert, "Meaningful Access" Demands Meaningful Efforts: The Need for Great Access to Virginia State Courts for Limited English Proficient Litigants, 23 Wm. & Mary L. Rev. 337, 342 n.35 (2017). See American Bar Association, Standards for Language Access in Courts 34 (2012), http://www.americanbar.org/content/dam/aba/administrative/legal_aid_indigent_ defendants/ls_sclaid_standards_for_language_access_proposal.authcheckdam.pdf ("fees imposed upon LEP persons have the strong potential to chill recourse to the courts and inhibit the use of language access services that are necessary or beneficial to the fair administration of justice").

119. Ake v. Oklahoma, 470 U.S. 68 (1985). In McWilliams v. Dunn, 582 U.S. ___. 137 S. Ct. 1790 (2017), the U.S. Supreme Court held that the State of Alabama fell short of the Ake standard when it did not provide an indigent criminal defendant with an expert to review mental health records at the capital sentencing phase. Although the Court did not decide "whether Ake clearly established a right to an expert independent from the prosecution," the Court noted that, "[a]s a practical matter, the simplest way for a State to meet [the Ake] standard may be to provide a qualified expert retained specifically for the defense team." Id. at 1800.

120. Ake, 470 U.S. at 77 (citing Mathews v. Eldridge, 424 U.S. 319, 335 (1976) (setting for balancing test)).

121. Little v. Streater, 452 U.S. 1 (1981). State courts in a number of jurisdictions have applied Little to mandate provision of free blood-grouping tests in paternity proceedings. See Shaw v. Seward, 689 S.W.2d 37 (Ky. App. 1985); Pierce v. State, 251 Ga.

590, 308 S.E.2d 367 (1983); Kennedy v. Wood, 439 N.E.2d 1367 (Ind. App. 1982); Anderson v. Jacobs, 68 Ohio St. 2d 67, 428 N.E.2d 419 (1981). The Alabama Supreme Court found that although *Little* requires provision of free blood-grouping tests in paternity actions, the defendant does not have to receive the "seven systems" test ordered in that case by the U.S. Supreme Court. *See* Calloway v. Alabama, 470 U.S. 1002 (1985); Ex Parte Calloway, 456 So.2d 308 (Ala. 1984).

122. *See, for example*, Goetz v. Crosson, 41 F.3d 800 (2d Cir. 1994), cert. denied, 516 U.S. 821 (1995) (psychiatric expert in civil commitment proceeding); In re Shaeffer Children, 85 Ohio App.3d 683, 621 N.E.2d 426 (1993) (expert in child custody case).

123. *See, for example*, Pedraza v. Jones, 71 F.3d 194, 196 (5th Cir. 1995) ("The plain language of section 1915 does not provide for the appointment of expert witnesses to aid an indigent litigant."); Boring v. Kozakiewicz, 833 F.2d 468 (3d Cir. 1987) (same).

124. *See* Fed. R. Evid. 706(a) ("On a party's motion or on its own, the court may order the parties to show cause why expert witnesses should not be appointed."); Fed. R. Evid. 706(c)(2) ("[C]ompensation is payable in any [civil case other than a case involving just compensation under the Fifth Amendment] by the parties in the proportion and at the time that the court directs."); McKinney v. Anderson, 924 F.2d 1500, 1511 (9th Cir. 1991); Helling v. McKinney, 502 U.S. 903 (1991); Webster v. Sowders, 846 F.2d 1032, 1038 (6th Cir. 1988).

125. *See* Beaver v. Board of County Commissioners of Gooding County, 1991 WL 350749 (D. Idaho 1991) (appointment of court expert in civil rights case involving conditions in county jail was appropriate, pending the submission of in forma pauperis applications). *But see* Mallard Bay Drilling, Inc. v. Bessard, 145 F.R.D. 405 (W.D. La. 1993) (conflicting expert opinions on medical condition did not require appointment of additional expert).

126. Fed. R. Civ. P. 55(a). *See* City of New York v. Mickalis Pawn Shop, LLC, 645 F.3d 114, 128 (2d Cir. 2011):

> Although Rule 55(a) contemplates that entry of default is a ministerial step to be performed by the clerk of court, *see Pinaud v. Cnty. of Suffolk*, 52 F.3d 1139, 1152 n.11 (2d Cir.1995) (describing "the entry of a default" as "largely a formal matter" (internal quotation marks omitted)), a district judge also possesses the inherent power to enter a default, *see Beller & Keller v. Tyler*, 120 F.3d 21, 22 n.1 (2d Cir.1997). The entry of a default, while establishing liability, "is not an admission of damages." *Finkel v. Romanowicz*, 577 F.3d 79, 83 n.6 (2d Cir.2009).

127. Fed. R. Civ. P. 55(b).

128. *See, for example*, United States District Court, Eastern District of Tennessee, Default Judgment Instructions and Forms, https://www.tned.uscourts.gov/default-judgment-instructions-and-forms.

129. *See, for example*, Yonathan A. Arbel, Adminization: Gatekeeping Consumer Contracts, 71 Vand. L. Rev. 121, 123–124 (2018):

> Every year, about eight million debt claims are filed by large companies and debt buyers against consumers. Of those, over six million lawsuits turn into default judgments, with little, if any, judicial oversight. One in three consumers is estimated to be at risk of facing such a lawsuit.... [M]any of these debt claims lack

merit and involve debts that are resolved, expired, inflated, and in some cases, outright fraudulent. A recent study found, for example, that debt buyers knowingly purchase debts that are well beyond the statute of limitations, with at least twelve percent of the debt portfolio of large debt buyers consisting of stale debt.

130. The Due Process Clause of the federal Constitution requires that a judgment not be entered against a defendant who was never given notice of the lawsuit. Notice of the lawsuit is given through a procedure called "service of process"—service means delivery, and process refers to the documents that must be delivered to the defendant to announce that the lawsuit has started. *See, for example*, Fed. R. Civ. P. 4. These documents usually are the complaint (which sets out the claims against the defendant) and the summons (which describes where the action is pending). *See also* Natalie Kitroeff, The Lawsuit Machine Going After Student Debtors, Bloomberg Businessweek (June 3, 2015), http://www.bloomberg.com/news/articles/2015-06-04/the-student-debt-collection-mess.

131. Frank M. Tuerkheimer, Service of Process in New York: A Proposed End to Unregulated Criminality, 72 Colum. L. Rev. 847 (1972) (tracing the historical failures of service of process in New York City).

132. *See* Adrian Gottshall, Solving Sewer Service: Fighting Fraud with Technology, 70 Ark. L. Rev. 813, 818 (2018):

> "Sewer service" occurs when a process server falsifies an affidavit of service instead of actually serving court documents. The name originated from a practice by which process servers would symbolically throw legal documents into the sewer, rather than delivering them to the intended recipient. Sewer service is a fraudulent practice with potentially crippling results—the entry of a default judgment against a defendant. Defendants are indeed suffering dire consequences from falsified affidavits of service, including frozen bank accounts, wage garnishment, ruined credit, and even eviction.

See, for example, United States v. Brand Jewelers, Inc., 318 F. Supp. 1293, 1293 (S.D.N.Y. 1970) (discussing the "'long-standing and systematic practice' of obtaining default judgments against economically disadvantaged defendants by means of ... 'sewer service'").

Although the number of default judgments cannot be attributed only to the use of sewer service, more than 80% of the consumer credit cases in New York end in default judgments. *See* The Legal Aid Society, Neighborhood Economic Development Advocacy Project, MFY Legal Services, and Urban Justice Center—Community Development Project, Debt Deception: How Debt Buyers Abuse the Legal System to Prey on Lower-Income New Yorkers *8 (May 2010), https://cdp.urbanjustice. org/sites/default/files/cdp_24may10_0.pdf (reporting that of 336 collection cases brought by the 26 most litigious debt buyers in New York City that 81% of cases initially resulted in default judgments for the debt buyers); *see also* MFY Legal Services, Justice Disserved: A Preliminary Analysis of the Exceptionally Low Appearance Rate by Defendants in Lawsuits Filed in the Civil Court of the City of New York *2 (June 2008), http://mobilizationforjustice.org/wp-content/uploads/reports/ Justice_Disserved.pdf (finding that 91% of New York City debtors failed to answer in 180,177 suits filed by the seven largest debt collection law firms). Similarly, a 2011 study conducted across more than 500 cases filed in Dallas County courts found that plaintiffs did not accomplish service in more than 12% of the cases. *See* Mary Spector, Debts, Defaults and Details: Exploring the Impact of Debt Collection Litigation on Consumers and Courts, 6 Va. L. *&* Bus. Rev. 257, 288 (2011); *see also* Peter A. Holland, Junk Justice: A Statistical Analysis of 4,400 Lawsuits Filed by Debt Buyers, 26 Loyola Consumer L. Rev. 179 (2014) (analyzing debtors cases and concluding that "no such adversary system exists for most defendants in consumer debt cases[,] [i]nstead, these cases . . . result[ ] in mass produced default judgments"). The use of sewer service by a debt collector may raise claims under the Fair Debt Collection Act (discussed in chapter 6). *See, for example*, Somerset v. Stephen Einstein & Associates, P.C., 361 F. Supp. 3d 201 (E.D.N.Y. 2019); Freeman v. ABC Legal Services, Inc., 827 F. Supp. 1d 1065 (N.D. Cal. 2011).

133. Federal Rule of Civil Procedure 60(b) lists a number of grounds for vacating a default judgment against a 'defendant, including "mistake, inadvertence, or excusable neglect" by the defendant, "fraud, misrepresentation, or misconduct" by the plaintiff, or "any other reason that justifies relief." For an explanation of the "good cause" "standard for setting aside entry of a default, *see* Enron Oil Corp. v. Diakuhara, 10 F.3d 90, 96 (2d Cir. 1993):

> Because Rule 55(c) does not define the term "good cause," we have established three criteria that must be assessed in order to decide whether to relieve a party from default or from a default judgment. These widely accepted factors are: (1) whether the default was willful; (2) whether setting aside the default would prejudice the adversary; and (3) whether a meritorious defense is presented. *See, e.g., Action S.A.*, 951 F.2d at 507; *In re Men's Sportswear, Inc.*, 834 F.2d 1134, 1138 (2d Cir.1987); *Meehan*, 652 F.2d at 277. Other relevant equitable factors may also be considered, for instance, whether the failure to follow a rule of procedure was a mistake made in good faith and whether the entry of default would bring about a harsh or unfair result. *See Sony Corp. v. Elm State Elecs., Inc.*, 800 F.2d 317, 320 (2d Cir.1986). Although the factors examined in deciding whether to set aside a default or a default judgment are the same, courts apply the factors more rigorously in the case of a default judgment, *see, e.g., Meehan*, 652 F.2d at 276, because the concepts of finality and litigation repose are more deeply implicated in the latter action.

134. *See, for example*, City of New York v. Mickalis Pawn Shop, LLC, 645 F.3d 114, 128 (2d Cir. 2011). If the defendant bypasses the motion to vacate the default judgment, the appeals court will review "not whether the district court abused its discretion in declining to vacate the default judgment, but whether it abused its discretion in granting a default judgment in the first instance." The defendant cannot appeal from the entry of default, which is a nonfinal order. *See* Enron Oil Corp. v. Diakuhara, 10 F.3d 90, 95 (2d Cir. 1993) ("The entry of default is an interlocutory act and, as such, a non-final order. It is therefore not appealable. . . .").

135. Traguth v. Zuck, 710 F.2d 90, 95 (2d Cir. 1983).

136. *See* Velocity Investments, LLC v. McCaffrey, 31 Misc.3d 308, 921 N.Y.S.2d 799 (1st Dist. 2011).

137. *See* United States v. Cannon, 2013 WL 6700254, *5 (N.D. Cal. 2013) (finding at least excusable neglect when the defendant defaulted after service was made at the defendant's sister's address during a time when they were estranged and the defendant lived a "transient" lifestyle).

138. *For example*, one court vacated a default judgment because the student debtor had a daughter who was seriously ill and his father had passed away, absorbing all of his attention. *See* HICA Education Loan Corp. v. Feintuch, 2013 WL 1898997 (E.D.N.Y. 2013).

139. *See, for example*, United States v. Alongi, 346 F. Supp. 2d 394, 395–396 (E.D.N.Y. 2004) (vacating default judgment against pro se student loan borrower who demonstrated "excusable mistake" after he was "given the wrong advice or did not understand the advice" given to him by a law firm); *see also* Fed. R. Civ. P. 60(b)(1) (providing that a court may relieve a party from a judgment on account of "mistake, inadvertence, surprise, or excusable neglect").

140. *See, for example*, United Coin Meter Co v. Seaboard Coastline Railroad, 705 F.2d 839, 844 (6th Cir. 1983). Importantly, "delay alone is not a sufficient basis for establishing prejudice." Davis v. Musler, 713 F.2d 907, 916 (2d Cir. 1983) (citing Feliciano v. Reliant Tooling Co, 691 F.2d 653, 656–657 (3d Cir. 1982)).

141. This factor is important but not dispositive. Lack of a meritorious defense does not necessarily doom the motion if in the aggregate other factors lean in favor of vacating the judgment. *See* United States v. Iscandari, 2012 WL 2568187 (N.D. Cal. 2012) (finding that the defendant's battle with cancer and the absence of prejudice to the plaintiff associated with a delayed resolution outweighed the defendant's lack of an asserted defense).

142. *See, for example*, HICA Education Loan Corp. v. Wanner, 2012 WL 5379469, *4 (N.D. Cal. 2012) (recommending that, because the complaint and promissory note showed differing obligations, the plaintiff had failed to establish the amount to which it was entitled despite showing that a default judgment was appropriate); Natl. Collegiate Student Loan Trust 2003-1 v. Beverly, 2014 WL 4824355, *3–4 (Ohio App. 2014) (vacating default judgment because ownership of the loan not adequately documented).

143. The action also sought to vacate an estimated 100,000 court judgments statewide that had been illegally obtained by debt collection firms that used the Long Island service. *See* New York Attorney General Press Release, The New York State Attorney General Andrew M. Cuomo Announces Guilty Plea of Process Server Company Owner Who Denied Thousands of New Yorkers Their Day in Court, New York Attorney General (Jan. 15, 2010), http://www.ag.ny.gov/press-release/ new-york-state-attorney-general-andrew-m-cuomo-announces-guilty-plea- process-server.

144. Servicemembers Civil Relief Act (SCRA), Pub. L. No. 108-189, 117 Stat. 2835 (2003). *See* Servicemembers Civil Relief Act (SCRA), American Bar Association, Division for Legal Services, ABA Military & Veterans Legal Center (Nov. 1, 2018), https://www.americanbar.org/groups/legal_services/milvets/aba_home_front/ information_center/servicemembers_civil_relief_act/; Mark E. Sullivan, The

Servicemembers Civil Relief Act: Is Your Courtroom SCRA-Compliant?, 56 Judges' J. 8 (Winter 2017).

145. Statistics cited and discussed in Judith Resnik, Revising Our "Common Intellectual Heritage": Federal and State Courts in Our Federal System, 91 Notre Dame L. Rev. 1831, 1837 (2016).

146. 28 U.S.C. § 1913. The amounts of the fees are set forth in the Miscellaneous Fee Schedule that follows § 1913.

147. Fed. R. App. P. 24(a)(3).

148. Fed. R. App. P. 24(a)(1)(A) (requiring the party seeking to appeal in forma pauperis to "show[ ] in the detail prescribed by Form 4 of the Appendix of Forms the party's inability to pay"); see, for example, Lister v. Department of Treasury, 408 F.3d 1309 (10th Cir. 2005) (denying in forma pauperis status based on the absence of financial information in the petitioner's affidavit).

149. See, for example, https://www.ca3.uscourts.gov/forms-0 (Third Circuit pro se forms); http://www.ca7.uscourts.gov/forms/pauperis.pdf (Seventh Circuit form affidavit for in forma pauperis application); https://www.ca9.uscourts.gov/forms/ pro_se_litigants.php (Ninth Circuit pro se forms and instructions).

150. Fed. R. App. P. 24(a)(1).

151. 28 U.S.C. § 1915(c).

152. See, for example, State v. Circuit Court, 155 Wis.2d. 148, 454 NW. 2d. 792 (1990); N.Y. C.P.L.R. § 1102(b); D.C. Code Ann. § 15-712 (a).

153. M.L.B. v. S.L.J., 519 U.S. 102 (1996).

154. Fed. R. Civ. P. 54(d) states: "Unless a federal statute, these rules, or a court order provides otherwise, costs—other than attorney's fees—should be allowed to the prevailing party." In addition, § 1920 of Title 28 of the United States Code lists the expenses a court "may" tax as costs.

155. 28 U.S.C. § 1920.

156. Singleton v. Smith, 241 F.3d 534 (6th Cir. 2001).

157. Ang v. Coastal International Security, Inc., 417 Fed. Appx. 836, 838 (11th Cir. 2011) (citation omitted).

158. See, for example, Girardeau A. Spann, Constitutional Hypocrisy, 27 Const. Comm. 557, 569 (2011) (stating that being poor is not a crime).

159. See Jayne S. Ressler, Civil Contempt Confinement and the Bankruptcy Abuse Prevention and Consumer Act of 2005: An Examination of Debtor Incarceration in the Modern Age, 37 Rutgers L.J. 355, 355–398 (2006).

160. See Doug Nadvornick, Collection Tactics Lead Some Debtors to Jail (National Public Radio, Aug. 4, 2011), http://www.npr.org/templates/story/story.php? storyId=130089789; see also Jessica Silver-Greenberg, Welcome to Debtor's Prison, Wall Street Journal (Mar. 17, 2011), https://www.wsj.com/articles/SB1000142405274 8704396504576204553811636610 ("[L]awmakers, judges and regulators are trying to rein in the debt-collection industry's use of arrest warrants to recoup money owed by borrowers who are behind on credit-card payments, auto loans and other bills.").

161. See, for example, Eileen Ambrose, Consumer Groups Fear that Debtors' Prisons are Making a Resurgence, The Baltimore Sun (Mar. 25, 2013), http://articles.

baltimoresun.com/2013-03-25/business/bs-bz-debt-jail-20130325_1_court-orders-district-court-defendant; Chris Serres & Glenn Howatt, In Jail for Being in Debt, Star Tribune (Mar. 17, 2011), http://www.startribune.com/in-jail-for-being-in-debt/95692619; Chris Morran, Man Claims He Was Arrested for Unpaid Federal Student Loan Debt, Consumerist (Feb. 16, 2016), https://consumerist.com/2016/02/16/man-claims-he-was-arrested-for-unpaid-federal-student-loan-debt.

162. *See* Christopher D. Hampson, The New American Debtors' Prisons, 44 Am. J. Crim. L. 1, 38 (2016); Tamar R. Birckhead, The New Peonage, 72 Wash. & Lee L. Rev. 1595 (2015).

163. As an example, consider that during a debt collection lawsuit, the plaintiff likely will seek to find out financial information about the consumer-defendant using a legal device called "interrogatories"—basically, questions put to the party. If the consumer-defendant does not answer the questions on time, the court might then order an oral examination of the party's assets, which requires the party to show up in person and answer questions. *See* Creola Johnson, Prosecuting Creditors and Protecting Consumers: Cracking Down on Creditors that Extort via Debt Criminalization Practices, 80 L. & Contemp. Prob. 211 (2017); Lea Shepard, Creditors' Contempt, 2011 B.Y.U. L. Rev. 1509 (2011).

   If the consumer-defendant fails to attend the oral examination, the court will enter a "show cause" order compelling the party to appear in court. If the party does not attend—perhaps not knowing attendance was required, or not able to take the days off from work, or never having received notice of the proceeding—the creditor will then ask the court to issue relief called "body attachment." A body attachment is a court order that directs law enforcement officials to bring the recalcitrant party to court. At that point, the consumer-defendant faces jail time for civil contempt of the court orders, plus court-ordered fines or penalties. *See* Ann Cammett, Shadow Citizens: Felony Disenfranchisement and the Criminalization of Debt, 117 Pa. State L. Rev. 349, 402–404 (2012); Jayne S. Ressler, Civil Contempt Confinement and the Bankruptcy Abuse Prevention and Consumer Protection Act of 2005: An Examination of Debtor Incarceration in the Modern Age, 37 Rutgers L.J. 355 (2006). In Minnesota, 15% of all debt-related arrest warrants were attributable to lawsuits by three debt buyers—for debts that might not even have been owed. *See* Chris Serres & Glenn Howatt, In Jail for Being in Debt, Star Tribune (Mar. 17, 2011), http://www.startribune.com/in-jail-for-being-in-debt/95692619.

164. For additional resources, *see* National Consumer Law Center, Surviving Debt: Expert Advice for Getting Out of Financial Trouble 212 (2019).

165. *See* John B. Mitchell & Kelly Kunsch, Of Driver's Licenses and Debtor's Prison, 4 Seattle J. Social Justice 439 (2005).

166. *See* Federal Child Support Recovery Act, codified at 18 U.S.C. § 228. For a discussion of imprisonment for failing to pay child support, *see* Irin Carmon, How Falling Behind on Child Support Can End in Jail, MSNBC (Apr. 9, 2015), http://www.msnbc.com/msnbc/how-falling-behind-child-support-can-end-jail#56748; Ann Cammett, Deadbeats, Deadbrokes, and Prisoners, 18 Geo. J. Poverty L. & Pol. 127 (2011).

167. Turner v. Rogers, 564 U.S. 431, 435 (2011) ("where . . . the custodial parent (entitled to receive the support) is unrepresented by counsel, the State need not provide counsel to the noncustodial parent (required to provide the support) . . . [but] the State must nonetheless have in place alternative procedures that assure a fundamentally fair determination of the critical incarceration-related question, whether the supporting parent is able to comply with the support order").

168. *See* Ariadne S. Montare, Civil Fines and the Cycle of Poverty, 36 GPSolo 37 (2019) (recounting that in the 1980s courts began to use fines and fees "as a source of revenue funding for the judicial system to replace funds lost by cuts to state and municipal budgets," and that the trend increased after the 2008 recession, pausing only because of "increasing pressure from advocates for the poor and good government groups"); Walter Johnson, Ferguson's Fortune 500 Company: Why the Missouri City— Despite Hosting a Multinational Corporation—Relied on Municipal Fees and Fines to Extract Revenue from its Poorest Residents, The Atlantic (Apr. 26, 2015), http://www.theatlantic.com/politics/archive/2015/04/fergusons-fortune-500-company/390492; ACLU, In for a Penny: The Rise of America's New Debtors' Prisons (Oct. 2010), https://www.aclu.org/files/assets/InForAPenny_web.pdf; Alicia Bannon, Mitali Nagrecha, & Rebekah Diller, Criminal Justice Debt: A Barrier to Reentry, Brennan Center for Justice (2010), http://www.brennancenter.org/publication/criminal-justice-debt-barrier-reentry; Terrence McCoy, Ferguson Shows How a Police Force Can Turn into a Plundering "Collection Agency," Washington Post (Mar. 5, 2015), https://www.washingtonpost.com/news/morning-mix/wp/2015/03/05/ferguson-shows-how-a-police-force-can-turn-into-a-plundering-collection-agency. *See generally* Neil L. Sobol, Charging the Poor: Criminal Justice Debt & Modern-Day Debtors' Prisons, 75 Md. L. Rev. 486 (2016).

169. Tumey v. Ohio, 273 U.S. 510, 535 (1927).

170. *See* National Center for State Courts, National Task Force on Fines, Fees and Bail Practices Resource Center, https://www.ncsc.org/Topics/Financial/Fines-Costs-and-Fees/Fines-and-Fees-Resource-Guide.aspx.

171. U.S. Department of Justice, Office for Access to Justice, Letter from Vanita Gupta, Principal Deputy Assistant Attorney General, Civil Rights Division, and Lisa Foster, Director, Office for Access to Justice *2 (Mar. 14, 2016), archived at https://www.justice.gov/opa/file/832541/download.

172. U.S. Department of Justice, Office of Public Affairs, Attorney General Sessions Rescinds 25 Guidance Documents (Dec. 21, 2017), https://www.justice.gov/opa/pr/attorney-general-jeff-sessions-rescinds-25-guidance-documents.

173. Gregory G. Brooker & Alexander W. Purdue, ABA Passes Policy on Court Fees and Fines, American Bar Association (Aug. 2018), https://www.americanbar.org/groups/government_public/publications/pass-it-on/fall-2018-vol28-no1/aba-passes-policy-on-court-fees-and-fines/.

174. U.S. Const. Amend. VI ("In all criminal prosecutions, the accused shall enjoy . . . the Assistance of Counsel for his defence.").

175. Gideon v. Wainwright, 372 U.S. 335, 344 (1963).

176. *Id.*

177. *See* Hardy v. United States, 375 U.S. 277, 289 n.7 (1964) (a court ought not require the accused to be "totally devoid of means" before providing counsel) (Goldberg, J., concurring). *See also* John P. Gross, National Association of Criminal Defense Lawyers, Gideon at 50: A Three-Part Examination of Indigent Defense in America, Part II—Redefining Indigence: Financial Eligibility Guidelines for Assigned Counsel 11 (Mar. 2014), https://www.nacdl.org/gideonat50.

178. *See, for example*, John P. Gross, Too Poor to Hire a Lawyer but Not Indigent: How States Use the Federal Poverty Guidelines to Deprive Defendants of their Sixth Amendment Right to Counsel, 70 Wash. & Lee L. Rev. 1173 (2013).

179. Powell v. Alabama, 287 U.S. 45 (1932) (capital felony prosecutions); Johnson v. Zerbst, 304 U.S. 458 (1938) (federal noncapital felony prosecutions); Gideon v. Wainwright, 372 U.S. 335 (1963) (state noncapital felony prosecutions). Prior to Argersinger v. Hamlin, 407 U.S. 25 (1972), the U.S. Supreme Court did not explicitly grant constitutional recognition to an indigent defendant's right to counsel in misdemeanor proceedings. *See* John M. Junker, The Right to Counsel in Misdemeanor Cases, 43 Wash. L. Rev. 685 (1968).

180. In re Gault, 387 U.S. 1 (1967) (juvenile cases).

181. Moran v. Burbine, 475 U.S. 412 (1986).

182. Rothgery v. Gillespie County, 554 U.S. 191 (2008).

183. Escobedo v. Illinois, 378 U.S. 478 (1964); *see also* McNeil v. Wisconsin, 501 U.S. 171, 180–181 (1991) ("The Sixth Amendment right to counsel attaches at the first formal proceeding against an accused, and in most States, at least with respect to serious offenses, free counsel is made available at that time and ordinarily requested.").

184. Hamilton v. Alabama, 368 U.S. 52, 55 (1961).

185. Coleman v. Alabama, 399 U.S. 1 (1970).

186. Mempa v. Rhay, 389 U.S. 128 (1967).

187. White v. Maryland, 373 U.S. 59 (1963).

188. Padilla v. Kentucky, 559 U.S. 356 (2010).

189. *See* Caplin & Drysdale, Chartered v. United States, 491 U.S. 617, 624–625 (1989).

190. *See, for example*, United States v. Mendez-Sanchez, 563 F.3d 935 (9th Cir. 2009), cert. denied, 558 U.S. 900 (2009); United States v. Adelzo-Gonzalez, 268 F.3d 772 (9th Cir. 2001) (finding denial of motion was an abuse of discretion); United States v. Calabro, 467 F.2d 973 (2d Cir. 1972), cert. denied, 410 U.S. 926 (1973) (finding that, once a trial has begun, a defendant wishing to substitute counsel must show good cause, such as a conflict of interest, a complete breakdown in communication, or an irreconcilable conflict).

191. U.S. Department of Justice, Bureau of Justice Statistics, Suzanne M. Strong, State-Administered Indigent Defense Systems, 2013, at 2 (Nov. 2016), https://www.bjs.gov/content/pub/pdf/saids13.pdf (reporting that in 2013, 28 states administered indigent defense systems using mechanisms that included appointed counsel and nongovernmental public defender offices); *see also* Robert L. Spangenberg & Marea L. Beeman, Indigent Defense Systems in the United States, 58 Law & Contemp. Probs. 31, 32–37 (1995).

192. *See* Kate Taylor, System Overload: The Costs of Under-Resourcing Public Defense, Justice Policy Institute 2 (July 27, 2011), http://www.justicepolicy.org/research/2756?utm_source=%2fsystemoverload&utm_medium=web&utm_campaign=redirect.

193. The National Advisory Commission on Criminal Justice Standards and Goals, Task Force on Courts, Standard 13.12, National Legal Aid & Defender Association (1973), http://www.nlada.org/defender-standards/national-advisory-commission/black-letter.

194. National Right to Counsel Committee, Justice Denied: America's Continuing Neglect of Our Constitutional Right to Counsel, The Constitution Project 65–70 (Apr. 2009), https://www.opensocietyfoundations.org/sites/default/files/justice_20090511.pdf.

195. American Bar Association, Eight Guidelines of Public Defense Related to Excessive Workloads (Aug. 2009), https://www.americanbar.org/content/dam/aba/administrative/legal_aid_indigent_defendants/ls_sclaid_def_eight_guidelines_of_public_defense.authcheckdam.pdf.

    Whether an assigned lawyer has provided constitutionally ineffective counsel is considered on a case-by-case basis and requires a showing that the lawyer was incompetent and that a "reasonable probability" exists that, if competent counsel had been provided, the outcome of the case would have been different. Strickland v. Washington, 466 U.S. 668, 694 (1984). A showing of ineffective assistance of postconviction counsel will not excuse a prior procedural default of a claim of ineffective assistance of trial counsel. Davila v. Davis, 582 U.S. ___, 137 S Ct. 2058 (2017).

196. *See* Luckey v. Harris, 860 F.2d 1012 (11th Cir. 1988), cert. denied, 495 U.S. 957 (1990), district court order vacated sub. nom. Luckey v. Miller, 929 F.2d 618 (11th Cir. 1991); Gardner v. Luckey, 500 F.2d 712 (5th Cir. 1974), cert. denied, 423 U.S. 841 (1975); *see generally* Rodger Citron, (Un)Luckey v. Miller: The Case for a Structural Injunction to Improve Indigent Defense Services, 101 Yale L.J. 481, 486–496 (1991) (surveying judicial opposition to court-ordered structural reform of indigent defense systems).

197. State court litigation has yielded some limited success. Both the Idaho and Pennsylvania Supreme Courts held that indigent clients have the right to sue over systemic inadequacies in the states' public defense systems. *See* ACLU Idaho, Idaho Supreme Court Rules in Favor of ACLU in Public Defense Case (Apr. 28, 2017), https://www.acluidaho.org/en/news/idaho-supreme-court-rules-favor-aclu-public-defense-case; ACLU Pennsylvania, PA Supreme Court Rules That Poor Defendants Have the Right to Challenge Inadequate Legal Representation in Court (Sept. 29, 2016), https://www.aclupa.org/news/2016/09/29/pa-supreme-court-rules-poor-defendants-have-right-challenge. *See also* Lorelei Laird, Starved of Money for Too Long, Public Defender Offices Are Suing—And Starting to Win, ABA Journal (Jan. 2017), http://www.abajournal.com/magazine/article/the_gideon_revolution (discussing ongoing litigation in California, Idaho, Louisiana, Pennsylvania, and Utah); Norman Lefstein, Securing Reasonable Caseloads: Ethics

and Law in Public Defense, ABA Standing Committee on Legal Aid and Indigent Defendants, American Bar Association 182–187 (2011), https://www.americanbar. org/content/dam/aba/publications/books/ls_sclaid_def_securing_reasonable_ caseloads.authcheckdam.pdf (detailing the "uncertain fate" of litigation efforts in Michigan and New York).

Earlier state court efforts were not successful. *See, for example*, Wilson v. State, 574 So.2d 1338 (Miss. 1990); State v. Ryan, 233 Neb. 151, 444 N.W.2d 656 (1989); State ex rel. Stephan v. Smith, 242 Kan. 336, 747 P.2d 816 (1987); State v. Smith, 140 Ariz. 355, 681 P.2d 1374 (1984); Escambia County v. Behr, 384 So.2d 147 (Fla. 1980); Ligda v. Superior Court of Solano County, 5 Cal. App. 3d 811, 85 Cal. Rptr. 744 (Ct. App. 1970).

198. U.S. Department of Justice, Office for Access to Justice, https://www.justice.gov/ atj. *See also* The Inaugural Meeting of the Right to Counsel National Consortium (Nov. 13, 2015), https://www.justice.gov/opa/blog/inaugural-meeting-right-counsel-national-consortium; White House Legal Aid Interagency Roundtable Issues First Annual Report to the President (Nov. 30, 2016), https://www.justice. gov/opa/pr/white-house-legal-aid-interagency-roundtable-issues-first-annual-report-president. *See also* Deputy Attorney General Rosenstein Delivers Remarks at the Right to Counsel National Consortium Third Annual Meeting (Nov. 2, 2017), https://www.justice.gov/opa/speech/deputy-attorney-general-rosenstein-delivers-remarks-right-counsel-national-consortium.

199. Yarls v. Bunton, 231 F. Supp. 3d 128 (M.D. La. 2017). Given caseload assignments, it is estimated that a public defender in Louisiana must do the work of five lawyers to provide constitutionally adequate counsel. *See* Richard A. Oppel, Jr. & Jugal K. Patel, One Lawyer, 194 Felony Cases, and No Time, N.Y. Times (Jan. 31, 2019), https:// www.nytimes.com/interactive/2019/01/31/us/public-defender-case-loads.html.

200. *See* Ake v. Oklahoma, 470 U.S. 68 (1985) (psychiatric expert). *But see* Williams v. Stewart, 441 F.3d 1030, 1048–49 (9th Cir. 2006), opinion amended by 2006 WL 997605 (9th Cir. Apr. 18, 2006), cert. denied, 549 U.S. 1002 (2006) (failing to provide state-appointed mental health experts did not violate due process, in part because the trial record did not suggest mental health "could have been a substantial factor in [the] defense at trial," and insanity was not the only defense).

201. *For example*, United States v. Mosquera, 816 F. Supp. 168 (E.D.N.Y. 1993) (concluding that the Sixth Amendment required Spanish-speaking defendants to receive written translations of documents including indictment and statutory references, presentence report, and plea agreements and statutes referenced therein).

202. Roberts v. LaVallee, 389 U.S. 40 (1967) (finding that the refusal to give a defendant a free transcript of the preliminary hearing for use at trial violated the accused's constitutional rights).

203. Caldwell v. Mississippi, 472 U.S. 320, 323 n.1 (1985) (declining to find a due process violation when a lower court denied a request for a court-appointed criminal investigator, fingerprint expert, or ballistics expert, on the ground that the defendant had provided no more than "undeveloped assertions" that such assistance would be beneficial to the defense).

204. United States v. Murguia-Rodriguez, 815 F.3d 566, 568 (9th Cir. 2016).

205. 28 U.S.C. § 1827(d)(1) (requiring court use of certified interpreter in proceedings instituted by the United States when a party "speaks only or primarily a language other than the English language" thus inhibiting "such party's comprehension of the proceedings or communication with counsel or the presiding judicial officer" or "of questions and the presentation of such testimony").

206. Scott v. Illinois, 440 U.S. 367 (1979).

207. *Compare* Nichols v. United States, 511 U.S. 738 (1994), *with* State v. Owens, 880 N.W.2d 518 (Iowa Ct. App. 2016). *See also* State v. Youngblood, 288 Kan. 659, 206 P.3d 518 (2009) (holding that a person accused of a misdemeanor has a Sixth Amendment right to counsel even if jail time is suspended or conditioned on term of probation on conviction, so an uncounseled misdemeanor conviction, when the right to counsel was unconstitutionally waived, could not be used to enhance sentence in later criminal proceeding where the right to counsel was unconstitutionally waived); United States v. Bryant, 579 U.S. ___, 136 S. Ct. 1954 (2016) (reading *Nichols* to permit the use of an uncounseled misdemeanor tribal-court conviction to support a conviction in a future prosecution if the initial uncounseled misdemeanor conviction did not violate the Sixth Amendment).

208. *See* Immigrant Defense Project, Immigration Consequences of Crimes Summary Checklist (2017), https://www.immigrantdefenseproject.org/wp-content/uploads/Imm-Consq-checklist-2017-v3.pdf. The U.S. Supreme Court recognized the constitutional significance of this circumstance in *Padilla v. Kentucky*, 559 U.S. 356 (2010), holding that the Sixth Amendment's constitutional guarantee of effective assistance of counsel requires defense attorneys to counsel an accused on potential immigration consequences (especially deportation risk) of a guilty plea.

209. *See* Alexandra Natapoff, Misdemeanor Decriminalization, 68 Vand. L. Rev. 1055, 1085 (2015) ("Legal constraints aside, the reality of the misdemeanor system is that courts routinely incarcerate offenders for failure to pay with little meaningful oversight or adversarial check.").

210. Douglas v. California, 372 U.S. 353 (1963). An appeal "as of right" is one that the appellate court is legally required to adjudicate if filed properly. By contrast, a "discretionary appeal" is one that the appellate court may accept for adjudication or not, at its discretion. Most appeals to a state's highest court, and virtually all appeals to the U.S. Supreme Court, are discretionary appeals.

211. *See* Ross v. Moffitt, 417 U.S. 600, 610 (1974).

212. *See* Coleman v. Thompson, 501 U.S. 722 (1991).

213. Evitts v. Lucey, 469 U.S. 387 (1985) (holding that merely nominal—and not effective—counsel had been provided where counsel neglected to file the required statement of appeal to the state court of appeals resulting in dismissal of the action by the court). However, an attorney appointed to represent an indigent defendant on appeal is permitted to request to withdraw or to have the appeals court resolve the appeal without a merits brief if the attorney determines that the appeal would be frivolous. *See* Anders v. California, 385 U.S. 738 (1967); *see also* Smith v. Robbins, 528 U.S. 259 (2000).

214. Griffin v. Illinois, 351 U.S. 12, 19 (1956). *See also* Eskridge v. Washington State Bd. of Prison Terms & Paroles, 357 U.S. 214 (1958); Draper v. State of Wash., 372 U.S. 487 (1963) (finding that only the portion of the transcript germane to the appeal must be provided).

215. United States v. Salerno, 481 U.S. 739, 753 (1987).

216. U.S. Const. Amend. VIII.

217. Salerno, 481 U.S. at 739 (quoting Bail Reform Act of 1984, 18 U.S.C. § 3142(e) (1982 ed., Supp. III)).

218. *But see* Stack v. Boyle, 342 U.S. 1, 5 (1951) (noting that bail set higher than an amount reasonably calculated to adequately assure the defendant's presence at trial violates the Eighth Amendment).

219. *See* Insha Rahman, Against the Odds: Experimenting with Alternative Forms of Bail in New York City's Criminal Courts, Vera Institute of Justice (Sept. 2017), https://www.vera.org/publications/against-the-odds-bail-reform-new-york-city-criminal-courts. In 2019, New York adopted legislation that will end cash bail for many defendants starting in 2020. 2019 Sess. Laws of N.Y. Ch. 59 (S. 1509-C) (McKinney's). For one account of the terrible harm inflicted by New York's cash bail system, *see* Jesse McKinley & Ashley Southall, Kalief Browder's Suicide Inspired a Push to End Bail. Now Lawmakers Have a Deal, N.Y. Times (Mar. 29, 2019), https://www.nytimes.com/2019/03/29/nyregion/kalief-browder-cash-bail-reform.html.

220. Flozell Daniels, Jr., Benjamin D. Weber, & Jon Wool, From Bondage to Bail Bonds: Putting a Price on Freedom in New Orleans, Vera Institute of Justice (May 14, 2018), https://www.datacenterresearch.org/reports_analysis/from-bondage-to-bail-bonds-putting-a-price-on-freedom-in-new-orleans/.

221. Bernadette Tabuy & Daniel Kopf, Detaining the Poor: How money bail perpetuates an endless cycle of poverty and jail time, Prison Policy Initiative (May 10, 2016), https://www.prisonpolicy.org/reports/incomejails.html.

222. *See* Brian Montopoli, Making Money: The Bail-Bond Business, The New Yorker (May 31, 2013), https://www.newyorker.com/news/news-desk/making-money-the-bail-bond-business.

223. Statement of Interest of the United States, Varden v. City of Clanton, No. 2:15-cv-34-MHT-WC (M.D. Ala. Feb. 13, 2015), https://www.justice.gov/opa/pr/justice-department-announces-resources-assist-state-and-local-reform-fine-and-fee-practices.

224. *See* Brief for the United States as Amicus Curiae in Support of Neither Party, Walker v. City of Calhoun, Ga., 901 F.2d 1245 (11th Cir. 2018). The appeals court held that the district court abused its discretion in issuing a preliminary injunction that required a municipal court to make an indigency determination with respect to arrestees within 24 hours to adopt an affidavit-based process for determining indigency, https://www.justice.gov/crt/case-document/walker-v-calhoun-brief-amicus.

225. *See, for example*, Anne Kim, Time To Abolish Cash Bail, Washington Monthly (Jan. /Feb. 2017), https://washingtonmonthly.com/magazine/januaryfebruary-2017/time-to-abolish-cash-bail/. On risk assessment and bail reforms, *see* Note, Bail Reform and Risk Assessment: The Cautionary Tale of Federal Sentencing, 131 Harv.

L. Rev. 1125 (2018), https://harvardlawreview.org/wp-content/uploads/2018/02/1125-1146_Online.pdf. Megan Stevenson, Assessing Risk Assessment in Action, 103 Minn. L. Rev. 303 (2018); Milton J. Hernandez, IV, Bailing Out Louisiana: A Proposal to Reform Louisiana's Money-Based Bail Bond System, 79 La. L. Rev. 557 (2018). On the ways in which civil and criminal procedures intersect and compound the problems of poverty, *see, for example*, Garner v. Kempf, 93 N.E.3d 1091 (Ind. 2018) (holding that bail bonds are subject to garnishment by a judgment creditor in an unrelated civil matter).

226. *See* Alana Semuels, The Fines and Fees That Keep Former Prisoners Poor, The Atlantic (July 5, 2016), https://www.theatlantic.com/business/archive/2016/07/the-cost-of-monetary-sanctions-for-prisoners/489026/. *See also* Helen A. Anderson, Penalizing Poverty: Making Criminal Defendants Pay for Their Court-Appointed Counsel Through Recoupment and Contribution, 42 U. Mich. J.L. Ref. 323 (2009); Beth A. Colgan, Paying for Gideon, 99 Iowa L. Rev. 1929 (2014); Beth A. Colgan, Reviving the Excessive Fines Clause, 102 Cal. L. Rev. 277 (2014); Kate Levine, If You Cannot Afford a Lawyer: Assessing the Constitutionality of Massachusetts's Reimbursement Statute, 42 Harv. C.R.–C.L. L. Rev. 191 (2007); ACLU of Southern California, Paying for Justice: The Human Cost of Public Defender Fees (June 2017), https://www.aclusocal.org/sites/default/files/pdfees-report.pdf; National Association of Criminal Defense Lawyers, Minor Crimes, Massive Waste: The Terrible Toll of America's Broken Misdemeanor Courts 19–20 (Apr. 2009), https://www.nacdl.org/reports/misdemeanor.

227. Model Penal Code: Sentencing §6.04D cmts. b–c (Am. Law Inst. 2017) (stating that "[o]n principle, the Institute recommends abolition of all costs, fees, and assessments," and the fact that "the Institute is prepared to countenance such assessments is far different from endorsement of present practices for their administration."). An alternative section would "allow[] for the imposition of costs, fees, and assessments with proper statutory controls," and mandates "the essential restriction that the levying of any such costs and fees must be approved by the sentencing court." *Id.* The alternative is put forward as a "recogni[tion] that the elimination of costs and fees is a difficult policy question" and is provided "for jurisdictions that cannot accept the Code's primary recommendation." Model Penal Code: Sentencing § 6.02A cmt. g. For a discussion, *see* Jessica M. Eaglin, Improving Economic Sanctions in the States, 99 Minn. L. Rev 1837 (2015).

228. Defendants can be billed for a public defender in at least 43 states and the District of Columbia. In addition, some states charge the costs of imprisonment and post release supervision to the defendant: 41 states charge an inmate for the cost of room and board in prison; and 44 states charge an offender with the cost of supervision of parole or probation. *See* Joseph Shapiro, As Court Fees Rise, The Poor Are Paying the Price, NPR (May 19, 2014), http://www.npr.org/2014/05/19/312158516/increasing-court-fees-punish-the-poor; NPR, together with the Brennan Center for Justice and the National Center for State Courts, State-By-State Court Fees (May 19, 2014), http://www.npr.org/2014/05/19/312455680/state-by-state-court-fees; Samantha Sunne, Why Your Right to a Public Defender May

Come with a Fee, NPR (May 29, 2014), http://www.npr.org/2014/05/29/316735545/
why-your-right-to-a-public-defender-may-come-with-a-fee.

229. *See* The Spangenberg Group, Public Defender Application Fees: 2001 Update,
Prepared for the American Bar Association by the Spangenberg Group (2002),
available at http://www.americanbar.org/content/dam/aba/administrative/legal_
aid_indigent_defendants/downloads/indigentdefense/pdapplicationfees2001_
narrative.authcheckdam.pdf.

230. James v. Strange, 407 U.S. 128 (1972).

231. *Id.* at 129–131 n.3.

232. *Id.* at 131.

233. Fuller v. Oregon, 417 U.S. 40 (1974).

234. *See, for example*, State v. Tennin, 674 N.W.2d 403 (Minn. 2004) (copayment statute
violated right to counsel); State v. Morgan, 173 Vt. 533, 789 A.2d 928 (2001) (required to make finding of ability to pay); Commonwealth v. Opara, 362 A.2d 305
(Pa. Super. Ct. 1976) (unconstitutional because recoupment order did not account for ability to pay). For further discussion, *see* Richard J. Wilson, Compelling
Indigent Defendants to Pay the Cost of Counsel Adds Up to Bad Policy, Bad Law, 3
Crim. Just. 16 (1988).

235. Nelson v. Colorado, 581 U.S. ___, 137 S. Ct. 1249, 1257–58 (2017).

236. *See* Council of Economic Advisers Issue Brief, Fines, Fees, and Bail: Payments
of the Criminal Justice System that Disproportionately Impact the Poor (Dec.
2015), https://nicic.gov/fines-fees-and-bail-payments-criminal-justice-system-
disproportionately-impact-poor:

> In jurisdictions throughout the United States, monetary payments for
> infractions, misdemeanors or felonies typically do not consider a defendant's
> ability to pay, and instead are determined based on offense type, either statu-
> torily or through judicial discretion. Fixed payments for a given offense create
> regressive penalties, or penalties more punitive for poorer individuals than for
> wealthier individuals. The disproportionate impact of these fixed payments on
> the poor raises concerns not only about fairness, but also because high mone-
> tary sanctions can lead to high levels of debt and even incarceration for failure
> to fulfil a payment. In some jurisdictions, approximately 20 percent of all jail
> inmates were incarcerated for failure to pay criminal justice debts. Estimates
> indicate that a third of felony defendants are detained before trial for failure to
> make bail; and in one city, approximately 20 percent of defendants made bail at
> amounts less than $500. High debt burdens for poor offenders in turn increase
> barriers to successful re-entry after an offense.

> *See also* Matthew Shaer, How Cities Make Money by Fining the Poor, N.Y. Times
> Magazine (Jan. 8, 2019), https://www.nytimes.com/2019/01/08/magazine/cities-
> fine-poor-jail.html.

237. Williams v. Illinois, 399 U.S. 235, 243 (1970) ("...a State may not constitutionally imprison beyond the maximum duration fixed by statute a defendant who is financially
unable to pay a fine"); Tate v. Short, 401 U.S. 395, 399 (1971); Bearden v. Georgia, 461
U.S. 660, 661–662 (1983) ("We conclude that the trial court erred in automatically
revoking probation because petitioner could not pay his fine, without determining

that petitioner had not made sufficient bona fide efforts to pay or that adequate alternative forms of punishment did not exist.").

238. Tate, 401 U.S. at 399.

239. In *Williams v. Illinois*, the Court explicitly stated that its holding "does not deal with a judgment of confinement for nonpayment of a fine in the familiar pattern of alternative sentence of '$30 or 30 days.'" 399 U.S. at 243. California has held that an alternative sentencing scheme such as this is unconstitutional. *See* In re Antazo, 3 Cal.3d 100 (1970).

240. *See* Michael E. Tigar, The Supreme Court, 1969 Term, 84 Harv. L. Rev. 30 (1970) ("The Court's holding does not suggest that indigents can no longer be fined, but only requires that in some cases they must be allowed to pay the fine in installments."); Derek A. Westen, Fines, Imprisonment and the Poor: "Thirty Dollars or Thirty Days," 57 Cal. L. Rev. 778, 816 (1969) ("The use of delayed payments or installment payments is a fundamental requirement of any fair and effective fine system.").

241. Morris v. Schoonfield, 399 U.S. 508, 509 (1970); Tate, 401 U.S. at 398.

242. Bearden, 461 U.S. at 668–669.

243. *See, for example*, Jaclyn Kurin, Indebted to Injustice: The Meaning of Willfulness in a Georgia v. Bearden Ability to Pay Hearing. 27 Geo. Mason Univ. Civ. Rts. L.J. (2017). In *State ex rel. Fleming v. Missouri Board of Probation and Parole*, 525 S.W.3d 224 (2017), a divided Missouri Supreme Court held that it was a violation of the Due Process and Equal Protection Clauses for the trial court to have revoked probation based on the failure to pay court costs without determining whether the probationer had the ability to pay or had made bona fide efforts to acquire the resources to pay, and that habeas corpus relief was appropriate. The sentencing court had required payment of $4,263.50 within the first three years of probation, including a board bill of $3,870. The probationer was unemployed, was suffering from mental health problems, and had been provisionally approved for Supplemental Security Income. *See* Aaron Wynhausen, Incarcerated for Indigence: Probation Revocation for Inability to Pay Court-Ordered Fines Found to Violate Due Process, 83 Mo. L. Rev. 527 (2018).

244. *See, for example*, Alexandra Bastien, Ending the Debt Trap: Strategies to Stop the Abuse of Court-Imposed Fines and Fees, Vera Institute (Mar. 2017), https://www.policylink.org/sites/default/files/ending-the-debt-trap-03-28-17.pdf.

245. The states include Arizona, California, Illinois, Nevada, New Jersey, and New York. *See* Legal Action Center, Certificates of Rehabilitation, State Laws, http://lac.org/toolkits/certificates/certificates.htm#state.

In New York, Certificates of Relief from Disabilities (CRD) are available to individuals with any number of misdemeanor convictions but no more than one felony conviction. A separate CRD is needed for each conviction. Temporary CRDs may be granted while an individual is on probation or parole, and at completion of the sentence it becomes permanent unless revoked. The sentencing court and the Board of Parole have the authority to grant CRDs. Certificates of Good Conduct (CGC) are available to individuals with two or more felony convictions and any number of misdemeanor convictions. Availability of CGC depends on the severity of the offense.

One CGC will cover an individual's entire criminal history. *See* N.Y. Correct. Law §§ 700 et seq. (McKinney). Neither the CRD nor the CGC seals or expunges a past record, but they are a judicial statement of the party's rehabilitation, and therefore can be helpful in securing employment. Since 2006, New York state courts have been required either to grant a certificate of relief at the sentencing stage or to advise a defendant of the right to seek one at a later point. 22 N.Y. Comp. Codes R. & Regs. Tit. 22, § 200.9; *see* Alec C. Ewald, Rights Restoration and the Entanglement of U.S. Criminal and Civil Law: A Study of New York's "Certificates of Relief," 41 Law & Soc. Inq'y 5 (2016) (discussing New York's mechanism).

246. *See* Joy Radice, Administering Justice: Removing Statutory Barriers to Reentry, 83 U. Colo. L. Rev. 715, 756 (2012) ("Certificates of Rehabilitation are not an integral part of the reentry landscape—no one within the criminal justice system educates people about the possibility of a certificate, few people with convictions apply, and the application process is burdensome.").

247. Organizations include:

> Help For Felons, Reentry Programs for Ex-Offenders By State, https://helpforfelons.org/reentry-programs-ex-offenders-state/.
> National HIRE Network, http://www.hirenetwork.org.
> Reentry Net, http://www.reentry.net.

248. Kevin Lapp, American Criminal Record Exceptionalism, 14 Ohio St. J. Crim. L. 303, 304 (2016) (quoting James B. Jacobs, The Eternal Criminal Record 4 (Harvard 2015), that he seeks to "shine[] a bright light on criminal records policies and practices in order to render them problematic rather than inevitable"). *See* Eldar Haber, Digital Expungement, 77 Md. L. Rev. 337, 339 (2018) (offering a "graduated approach towards the public nature of criminal history records, which would be narrowly tailored to serve the interests of rehabilitation-by-expungement"); Michael Pinard, Criminal Records, Race and Redemption, 16 N.Y.U. J. Legis. & Pub. Pol'y 963, 989 (2013) (urging "there should come a point at which a person's criminal record no longer becomes relevant").

249. *See, for example*, United States v. Certain Real Property, 566 F. Supp. 2d 1252 (N.D. Ala. 2008).

250. *See* David Smith, A Comparison of Federal Civil and Criminal Forfeiture Procedures: Which Provides More Protections for Property Owners?, The Heritage Foundation (July 30, 2015), https://www.heritage.org/crime-and-justice/report/comparison-federal-civil-and-criminal-forfeiture-procedures-which-provides.

251. Types of Federal Forfeiture, Department of Justice (Feb. 1, 2017), https://www.justice.gov/afp/types-federal-forfeiture.

252. 18 U.S.C. § 983(c)(1).

253. 18 U.S.C. § 983(c)(3).

254. *See, for example*, Bennis v. Michigan, 516 U.S. 442 (1996) (holding that a wife forfeited her interest in an automobile jointly owned with her husband after he engaged the services of a prostitute in the car, despite her lack of knowledge that the car would be put to that use); Calero-Toledo v. Pearson Yacht Leasing Co, 416 U.S. 663

(1974) (upholding forfeiture of innocent lessor's property in absence of a finding of wrongdoing or even negligence in use of the property).

255. *See* Dick M. Carpenter, Lisa Knepper, Angela C. Frickson, & Jennifer McDonald, Policing for Profit: The Abuse of Civil Asset Forfeiture (2d ed.), Institute for Justice (Nov. 2015), https://ij.org/report/policing-for-profit/grading-state-federal-civil-forfeiture-laws; *see also* Leonard v. Texas, 580 U.S. ___, 137 S. Ct. 847 (2017) (statement by Thomas, J., respecting the denial of certiorari):

> This system—where police can seize property with limited judicial oversight and retain it for their own use—has led to egregious and well-chronicled abuses. . . . These forfeiture operations frequently target the poor and other groups least able to defend their interests in forfeiture proceedings. . . . I am skeptical that th[e] historical practice is capable of sustaining, as a constitutional matter, the contours of modern practice. . . .

Id. at 848–849.

256. *See* United States v. One Assortment of 89 Firearms, 465 U.S. 354 (1984) (holding that, despite acquittal for charges alleging violation of the Gun Control Act for dealing firearms without a license, an individual's firearms could be civilly forfeited through an in rem action, and that this practice is barred by neither double jeopardy nor collateral estoppel). *See* Jason Snead & Elizabeth Slattery, The Supreme Court Signals It May Rein in Abusive Property Seizures, The Heritage Foundation (Nov. 30, 2018), https://www.heritage.org/courts/commentary/the-supreme-court-signals-it-may-rein-abusive-property-seizures.

257. Boyd v. United States, 116 U.S. 616, 634 (1886) (holding the Fourth and Fifth Amendments applied to a civil forfeiture proceeding). *See also* Sessions v. Dimaya, 138 S. Ct. 1204, 1232 (2018) (Gorsuch, J., concurring):

> Ours is a world filled with more and more civil laws bearing more and more extravagant punishments. Today's "civil" penalties include confiscatory rather than compensatory fines, forfeiture provisions that allow homes to be taken, remedies that strip persons of their professional licenses and livelihoods, and the power to commit persons against their will indefinitely. Some of these penalties are routinely imposed and are routinely graver than those associated with misdemeanor crimes—and often harsher than the punishment for felonies. And not only are "punitive civil sanctions . . . rapidly expanding," they are "sometimes more severely punitive than the parallel criminal sanctions *for the same conduct*." Mann, Punitive Civil Sanctions: The Middleground Between Criminal and Civil Law, 101 Yale L.J. 1795, 1798 (1992) (emphasis added). Given all this, any suggestion that criminal cases warrant a heightened standard of review does more to persuade me that the criminal standard should be set *above* our precedent's current threshold than to suggest the civil standard should be buried *below* it.

258. Austin v. United States, 509 U.S. 602 (1993) (holding that the excessive fines clause found in the Eighth Amendment applies to civil forfeiture proceedings); United States v. Bajakajian, 524 U.S. 321 (1998) (invoking the excessive fines clause to limit forfeiture); *see* Timbs v. United States, 586 U.S. ___, 139 S. Ct. 682 (2019) (whether *Austin* should be overruled not properly before the Court).

259. *See generally* Stefan D. Cassella, The Civil Asset Forfeiture Reform Act of 2000: Expanded Government Forfeiture Authority and Strict Deadlines Imposed on All Parties, 27 J. Legis. 97 (2001); Eric Moores, Reforming the Civil Asset Forfeiture Reform Act, 51 Ariz. L. Rev. 777, 782–783 (2009).

260. 18 U.S.C. § 983(a)(1)(A). If the government's notice is inadequate, it must return the seized property to the person from whom it was seized, "without prejudice to the right of the Government to commence a forfeiture proceeding at a later time." *See* 18 U.S.C. § 983(a)(1)(F).

261. 18 U.S.C. § 983(f).

262. 18 U.S.C. § 983(f)(1)(A)–(E); 18 U.S.C. § 983(f)(8). The rule provides an exception for the assets of a legitimate business, which may be released. *See* United States v. 8 Gilcrease Lane, 587 F. Supp. 2d 133 (D.D.C. 2008) (holding that pretrial release of currency or other monetary instruments can only occur where such assets are the assets of a legitimate business).

263. In re Seizure of Any and All Funds on Deposit in Wells Fargo Bank, 25 F. Supp. 3d 270, 276 (E.D.N.Y. 2014) (citations omitted).

264. *See* Mackey v. Property Clerk of New York City Police Department, 26 F. Supp. 2d 585, 591 (S.D.N.Y. 1998) ("[A] favorable disposition in a criminal action is not determinative of the outcome in a civil forfeiture procedure, where a lesser standard of proof applies.").

265. 18 U.S.C. § 983(d)(2)(A)(ii).

266. *See, for example*, United States v. One Parcel of Real Property with Buildings, Appurtenances & Improvements k/a 45 Claremont Street, Located in City of Center Falls, Rhode Island, 395 F.3d 1, 3–5 (1st Cir. 2004) (affirming the forfeiture of a family home and rejecting mother's innocent owner defense where her live-in boyfriend was arrested for purchasing large quantities of drugs in the kitchen).

267. 18 U.S.C. § 983(b)(2). *See* Louis S. Rulli, On the Road to Civil Gideon: Five Lessons from the Enactment of a Right to Counsel for Indigent Homeowners in Federal Civil Forfeiture Proceedings, 19 J. L. & Pol. 683 (2011).

268. Timbs v. Indiana, 586 U.S. ___, 139 S. Ct. 682 (2019). *See* Scott Lemieux, Police abused civil forfeiture laws for so long that the Supreme Court stepped in. But one ruling won't end it, NBC News (Feb. 21, 2019), https://www.nbcnews.com/think/opinion/police-abused-civil-forfeiture-laws-so-long-supreme-court-stepped-ncna974086.

269. For instance, in Philadelphia, property owners seeking retrieval of property in forfeiture proceedings appear in a courtroom in City Hall, where prosecutors, and not a judge, preside. Additionally, 20% of the general budget for the district attorney's office comes from forfeiture, creating incentives to deny the return of property. *See* What's Yours Is Theirs, Wall Street Journal (Sept. 4, 2014), http://www.wsj.com/articles/whats-yours-is-theirs-1409702898.

In Chicago, an investigative report found similar incentives on the part of the Cook County state's attorney and police to keep seized property. The state's attorney's office budgeted $4.96 million in 2016 from forfeited funds to pay for the 41 employees that staff its forfeiture unit. The Chicago Police Department did not disclose how much money comes in through forfeiture or how forfeiture funds are spent in its budget. *See* Joel Handley, Jennifer Helsby, & Freddy Martinez, Inside the Chicago Police Department's Secret Budget, Chicago Reader (Sept. 29, 2016), http://www.chicagoreader.com/chicago/police-department-civil-forfeiture-investigation/Content?oid=23728922. In September 2017, Governor Rauner signed into law a bill that reforms forfeiture in Illinois. *See* The Seizure and Forfeiture Reporting Act, Public Act 100-0512, http://www.ilga.gov/legislation/publicacts/100/PDF/100-0512.pdf; Brendan Bakala, Rauner Signs Civil Asset Forfeiture into Law, Illinois Policy (Sept. 19, 2017), https://www.illinoispolicy.org/rauner-signs-civil-asset-forfeiture-reform-into-law; ACLU, Civil Asset Forfeiture Return, https://www.aclu-il.org/en/legislation/civil-asset-forfeiture-reform. Among other things, the act mandates reporting of seizures or forfeitures by law enforcement agencies (HB 303, § 10(a)), and it mandates annual reporting of the proceeds from forfeiture (HB 303, § 10(b)). The Department of State Police will be required to aggregate the data and post it online (HB 303, § 10(c)).

270. Institute for Justice, Civil Forfeiture Reforms on the State Level, https://ij.org/activism/legislation/civil-forfeiture-legislative-highlights/.

271. *See* Rachel L. Stuteville, Reverse Robin Hood: The Tale of How Texas Law Enforcement Has Used Civil Asset Forfeiture to Take from Property Owners and Pad the Pockets of Local Government—The Righteous Hunt for Reform Is On, 46 Tex. Tech. L. Rev. 1169, 1184–86 (2014) (outlining the mechanics of equitable sharing).

272. "Equitable sharing provides a way to get around state laws regarding forfeiture proceeds and, thus, is a scapegoat for states with stringent forfeiture laws." *Id.* at 1185.

273. *See* Jason Snead, An Overview of Recent State-Level Forfeiture Reforms, The Heritage Foundation (Aug. 23, 2016), https://www.heritage.org/crime-and-justice/report/overview-recent-state-level-forfeiture-reforms.

274. U.S. Department of Justice, Press Release, Attorney General Prohibits Federal Agency Adoptions of Assets Seized by State and Local Law Enforcement Agencies Except Where Needed to Protect Public Safety (Jan. 16, 2015), https://www.justice.gov/opa/pr/attorney-general-prohibits-federal-agency-adoptions-assets-seized-state-and-local-law. The initiative received a lot of criticism for carveouts and loopholes that exposed persons to the unnecessary risk of losing property without any good reason for the seizure. Martin Kaste, Victims of Civil Asset Forfeiture Criticize New Federal Rules, National Public Radio (May 27, 2016), http://www.npr.org/2016/05/27/479764851/victims-of-civil-asset-forfeiture-criticize-new-federal-rules.

275. *See* U.S. Department of Justice, Press Release, Attorney General Sessions Issues Policy and Guidelines on Federal Adoptions of Assets Seized by State or Local Law Enforcement (July 19, 2017), https://www.justice.gov/opa/pr/attorney-general-sessions-issues-policy-and-guidelines-federal-adoptions-assets-seized-state. *See also* Nick Sibilla, Congress Killed Efforts to Undo Sessions's Civil Forfeiture Expansion, Despite Unanimous House Votes, Forbes (Apr. 2, 2018), https://www.forbes.com/sites/instituteforjustice/2018/04/02/congress-killed-efforts-to-undo-sessionss-civil-forfeiture-expansion-despite-unanimous-house-votes/#7323d5b84549.

276. Federal Arbitration Act, Pub. L. No. 68-401, §§ 1–15, 43 Stat. 883, 883–886 (codified as amended in 9 U.S.C. §§ 1, et seq.).

277. *See, for example*, Williams v. Securitas Sec. Servs. USA, Inc., 2011 WL 2713741, *1, *3 (E.D. Pa. July 13, 2011) (ruling that an arbitration agreement sent to potential members of a class action was misleading and unenforceable where it was titled "Dispute Resolution Agreement," was written in "small font," and was "totally lacking" in easily understandable English, instead containing "long and complex" paragraphs "with heavy use of legal jargon"); Nelsen v. Legacy Partners Residential, Inc., 207 Cal. App. 4th 1115, 1124, 144 Cal. Rptr. 3d 198, 205–206 (2012), as modified on denial of reh'g (Aug. 14, 2012) (finding arbitration provision was unenforceable where provision was part of a preprinted form agreement drafted by the employer that all of employer's managers were required to sign on a take-it-or-leave-it basis, provision was located on the last two pages of a 43-page handbook, page title did not refer to arbitration and the arbitration language itself appeared in a small font not set off in any way to stand out from the rest of the agreement or handbook, and the terms and rules of the arbitration referenced in the clause were beyond the comprehension of an ordinary employee). Similarly, some courts have refused to enforce an online arbitration clause where the link to a website's terms of use is buried at the bottom of the page or tucked away in an obscure corner of the website where users are unlikely to see it. *See, for example*, Specht v. Netscape Commc'ns Corp., 306 F.3d 17, 23 (2d Cir. 2002) (refusing to enforce terms of use that "would have become visible to plaintiffs only if they had scrolled down to the next screen"); In re Zappos.com, Inc., Customer Data Sec. Breach Litig., 893 F. Supp. 2d 1058, 1064 (D. Nev. 2012) ("The Terms of Use is inconspicuous, buried in the middle to bottom of every Zappos.com webpage among many other links, and the website never directs a user to the Terms of Use."); Hines v. Overstock.com, Inc., 668 F. Supp. 2d 362, 367 (E.D.N.Y. 2009) (plaintiff "could not even see the link to [the terms and conditions] without scrolling down to the bottom of the screen—an action that was not required to effectuate her purchase").

278. Alexander J.S. Colvin, The Metastasization of Mandatory Arbitration, 94 Chi.-Kent L. Rev. 3, 10, 15–16 (2019) (estimating that more than half of private sector non-union workplaces subject workers to mandatory arbitration, accounting for more than 60.1 million workers; mandatory arbitration is highest among industries where the wages are lowest; female workers and African American workers are most likely to be subject to mandatory arbitration).

279. Consumer Financial Protection Bureau, Arbitration Study: Report to Congress, pursuant to Dodd-Frank Wall Street Reform and Consumer Protection Act § 1028(a) (Mar. 2015), http://files.consumerfinance.gov/f/201503_cfpb_arbitration-study-report-to-congress-2015.pdf. Due Process Protocols of the American Arbitration Association for consumer arbitration permit claimants to file their claims in small claims court even if the claims come within the agreement's arbitration clause. *See* Amer. Arb. Assoc., Consumer Arbitration Fact Sheet, https://info.adr.org/consumer-arbitration/.

280. For further discussion, *see* Ramona L. Lampley, "Underdog" Arbitration: A Plan for Transparency, 90 Wash. L. Rev. 1727 (2015).

281. *See, for example,* Christopher R. Drahozal, Arbitration Costs and Contingent Fee Contracts, 59 Vand. L. Rev. 729 (2006). *See also* Evan Drake, Federal Judges Voice Arbitration Concerns, 37 Alternatives to High Cost Litig. 78 (2019); Alan Dabdoub & Trey Cox, Which costs less: Arbitration or litigation?, Inside Counsel (Dec. 6, 2012), http://www.insidecounsel.com/2012/12/06/which-costs-less-arbitration-or-litigation.

282. *See* Mark E. Budnitz, The High Cost of Mandatory Consumer Arbitration, 67 Law and Contemp. Probs. 133 (2004).

283. Am. Express Co. v. Italian Colors Rest., 570 U.S. 228, 239 (2013) (finding the Federal Arbitration Act's command to enforce arbitration agreements trumps any interest in ensuring the prosecution of low-value claims, since that interest "would undoubtedly destroy the prospect of speedy resolution that arbitration in general and bilateral arbitration in particular was meant to secure").

284. *See* AT&T Mobility LLC v. Concepcion, 563 U.S. 333 (2011) (holding the Federal Arbitration Act preempted a California judicial rule barring some class action waivers as exculpatory and unconscionable).

285. Epic System Corp. v. Lewis, 584 U.S. ___, 138 S. Ct. 112 (2018).

286. Hayes v. Delbert Services Corp. 811 F.3d 666, 675 (4th Cir. 2016).

287. *See* Alexander J.S. Colvin & Mark D. Gough, Individual Employment Rights Arbitration in the United States: Actors and Outcomes, 68 ILR Rev. 1019, 1031–35 (2015) (arbitral awards tend to be lower than court-ordered damages); *see also* The American Health Care Association, Special Study on Arbitration in the Long Term Care Industry, Aon Global (June 16, 2009), https://www.ahcancal.org/research_data/liability/Documents/2009%20Special%20Study%20on%20Arbitration%20in%20Long%20Term%20Care.pdf (reporting that average indemnity awards subject to arbitration tend to be 35% lower than those not subject to arbitration).

288. *See* Cynthia Estlund, The Black Hole of Mandatory Arbitration, 96 N.C. L. Rev. 679 (2018).

289. Bureau of Consumer Financial Protection, Arbitration Agreements, 82 Fed. Reg. 33210 (July 19, 2017). *See* Jessica Silver-Greenberg & Michael Corkery, U.S. Agency Moves to Allow Class-Action Lawsuits Against Financial Firms, N.Y. Times (July 10, 2017), https://www.nytimes.com/2017/07/10/business/dealbook/class-action-lawsuits-finance-banks.html; *see also* Roger Yu, With "rip-off clause" quashed, consumers can now sue banks in class-action, USA Today (July 11, 2017), https://www.usatoday.com/story/money/2017/07/11/banks-gear-up-fight-rule-banning-mandatory-arbitration/468504001.

290. Joint Resolution, Pub. L. No. 115-74, 131 Stat. 1243 (Nov. 1, 2017) (stating Congressional "disapproval" of CFPB rule on arbitration agreements, and "such rule shall have no force or effect"). *See* David Adler, Congress to CFPB: Mandatory Arbitration Is Here to Stay, Fordham J. Corp. & Fin. L. Blog (Nov. 15, 2017), https://news.law.fordham.edu/jcfl/2017/11/15/congress-to-cfpb-mandatory-arbitration-is-here-to-stay/.

291. *See* Amy J. Schmitz, American Exceptionalism in Consumer Arbitration, 10 Loy. U. Chi. Int'l L. Rev. 81 (2012).

10

The Right to Vote

Introduction

Does the federal Constitution guarantee a citizen the right to vote regardless of income or economic status?

Yes. The U.S. Supreme Court has held that the federal Constitution guarantees poor people the same right to vote as other citizens, and prohibits states from conditioning that right on property ownership, ability to pay poll taxes, or other criteria related to economic status.[1] The federal Constitution secures the right to vote on behalf of "qualified voters . . . in conformity to the requirements of state law," subject to federal regulation.[2] Early in the nation's history, states limited the franchise to white men who owned property,[3] and barred other citizens from voting.[4] Amendments to the federal Constitution have made it impermissible to condition the right to vote on a citizen's financial status, race, or gender.[5] The first federal expansion of the franchise came after the Civil War, when men of color, until then generally treated as property, were given the same voting rights as white men: the Fifteenth Amendment, ratified in 1870, extended the vote in state and federal elections to all male citizens, regardless of "race, color, or previous condition of servitude."[6] In 1920, the Nineteenth Amendment extended the vote to women.[7] In 1924, the Citizenship Act extended the vote to any "member of an Indian, Eskimo, Aleutian, or other aboriginal tribe."[8] However, property and other financial conditions continued to pose barriers to the right to vote. It was not until 1964 that the Twenty-Fourth Amendment secured the right to vote regardless of the ability "to pay any poll tax or other tax."[9] In addition, in 1971, the Twenty-Sixth Amendment extended the right to vote to citizens age 18 or older.[10] The Constitution gives Congress the power to enforce the voting rights guaranteed by these amendments, and Congress has used that authority to enact legislation that is supposed to protect the right to vote. Of most importance, the Voting Rights Act of 1965 bars any "voting qualification or prerequisite to voting or standard, practice, or procedure . . . which results in a denial or abridgement of the right of any citizen . . . to vote on account of race or color."[11] The Help America Vote Act of 2002, to take another example, requires the states to make

Getting By. Helen Hershkoff and Stephen Loffredo, Oxford University Press (2020). © Helen Hershkoff & Stephen Loffredo.
DOI: 10.1093/oso/9780190080860.001.0001

their voting equipment accessible to voters who are blind or physically disabled, or who have limited English proficiency.[12]

Despite these protections, persons with low income, and especially persons of color, continue to face barriers at the ballot box—which makes the right to vote even more important.[13] As the U.S. Supreme Court has emphasized, "the right to exercise the franchise in a free and unimpaired manner" is critical because "it is preservative of other basic civil and political rights."[14] By voting, a citizen can improve the laws that secure the right to vote, ensure that the votes of all citizens count, and shape policy in support of social welfare, economic fairness, and individual dignity.[15] This chapter surveys some of the laws that protect the right to vote, and highlights some of the many barriers that a person with low income nevertheless might face when trying to exercise the franchise.[16] The U.S. Department of Justice is tasked with enforcing federal voting laws.[17] Depending on the voter's state of residence, consider contacting a state attorney general's office or a local voter assistance organization, for example, a local League of Women Voters, for advice in dealing with unfair voting practices.[18]

Do citizens have to register in order to vote?

Yes. All states except North Dakota require individuals to register to vote before an election takes place.[19] Seventeen states plus the District of Columbia allow "same day" registration on or before Election Day, so that qualified residents can register and then vote on the same day.[20]

The National Voter Registration Act, enacted in 1993,[21] makes voter registration automatic at the time that a driver's license is renewed unless a person chooses to opt out (the act is known as the "motor voter law").[22] Moreover, when a driver updates address information with the state motor vehicle agency, the state must automatically update the driver's voter registration record (again, unless the voter opts out).[23] The act requires states to allow voter registration by mail.[24] In addition, the act requires states to offer voter registration assistance at any government office that takes applications for public assistance programs[25] or services for the disabled (however, registering to vote is not a condition of eligibility for assistance or services).[26] A state may choose to designate other public agencies such as a library, unemployment office, or local school as sites where a person can register to vote.[27] Although voter registration has increased since the statute's enactment, 22 states have reported that less than 3 percent of their new voter registrations were made through public assistance agencies—but in the 2016 election cycle, 25 million registration applications, accounting for one-third of all registrations, were done in a motor vehicle agency.[28]

Can a newly arrived citizen vote in an upcoming election?

Only citizens who are residents of the state or district in which they seek to vote have a right to vote in an election in that state or district. Thus, a citizen who lives in Kansas cannot expect to vote in a school board election in Texas where the voter happens to be on vacation. The U.S. Supreme Court has held that a state may condition the right to vote on the citizen's meeting a "bona fide" residence requirement, justified as a way "to preserve the basic conception of a political community."[29] The validity of any waiting period to vote turns on the Court's assessment of whether the durational residence requirement is "necessary to promote a compelling governmental interest."[30] Under this "strict equal protection test," the Court invalidated a one-year requirement, finding that a shorter waiting period could serve the state's goals of preserving "purity" of the ballot box and a "knowledgeable voter."[31] Election administrators are permitted to close the registration process for a brief period immediately prior to an election to prepare the lists of registered voters that must be sent to the polling places on Election Day.[32]

Federal law regulates durational residence requirements for presidential elections and limits the waiting time to no more than 30 days.[33] Under the statute, a person who has recently relocated and is not able to vote in a presidential election in the current place of residence may still vote in the state of prior residence, either in person or by absentee ballot.[34]

Can the right to vote be conditioned on payment of a "poll tax" or other fee?

No. A poll tax is a fee imposed on a person who seeks to vote and it is unconstitutional.[35] After adoption of the Fifteenth Amendment to the U.S. Constitution, which extended the franchise to men regardless of race, Southern states imposed poll taxes as a way to restrict voting by African Americans, and later extended the practice to exclude poor whites and Native Americans. In particular, the person seeking to vote was required to pay the poll tax in cash, but black men, many of whom worked as sharecroppers, often were cash-poor because wages typically were paid in-kind or in company scrip.[36] Miners and factory workers faced a similar barrier.

The Twenty-Fourth Amendment to the federal Constitution, adopted in 1964, prohibits the states and the United States from conditioning the right to vote in any federal election or primary on payment of "any poll tax or other tax."[37] The amendment does not eliminate the tax in state elections, and the practice persisted in Alabama, Mississippi, Virginia, and Texas.[38] In 1966, the

U.S. Supreme Court invalidated Virginia's poll tax (despite having upheld the law as constitutional 15 years earlier[39]) under the Equal Protection Clause of the federal Constitution.[40] As the Court emphasized: "Voter qualifications have no relation to wealth nor to paying or not paying this or any other tax."[41] Nevertheless, as described later in this chapter, states have devised new forms of financial qualifications that burden or block low-income citizens from voting.

Do citizens who are unemployed or who receive government assistance have a right to register to vote and to vote?

The U.S. Supreme Court has never considered the specific question of whether the right to vote can be conditioned on a person's employment or source of income. But the Court has recognized that "there is no indication in the Constitution that . . . occupation affords a permissible basis for distinguishing between qualified voters within the State,"[42] and it has emphasized that "wealth or fee paying has . . . no relation to voting qualifications; the right to vote is too precious, too fundamental to be so burdened or conditioned."[43] Congress has taken steps to encourage persons with low income to vote. In particular, the National Voter Registration Act (the "motor voter law"), discussed earlier in this chapter, authorizes states to register voters at public assistance offices, and some persons applying for assistance will be unemployed or not able to work.[44] However, practical barriers, sanctioned by law, persist.

Do citizens who reside in a district but do not own property have a right to register to vote and to vote?

The U.S. Supreme Court repeatedly has affirmed that the right to vote in general elections—including those for school boards—cannot be conditioned on property ownership or payment of taxes within the district in which the voter resides.[45] In *Kramer v. Union Free School District No. 15*, the Court struck down a New York statute that limited the vote in local school board elections to persons who owned or leased taxable real property in the school district or who had children enrolled in the district's public schools.[46] And in *Cipriano v. City of Houma*, the Court invalidated a Louisiana statute that limited the franchise in local revenue bond elections to "property taxpayers" of the district.[47] In a few limited circumstances, property-based conditions can be imposed on voters in special district elections; for example, a water district can allocate votes in an election for the board of directors according to the assessed value of each voter's land.[48] The exception for special district elections does not justify restrictions that are based on race or ethnicity.[49]

Do citizens who are homeless have the right to register to vote and to vote?

A lack of permanent housing or a fixed address in a state or district is not a ground for disenfranchisement. A person who is a citizen and a bona fide resident of the voting district has the right both to register to vote and to vote even without a fixed and permanent place to live.[50] However, in practice, a person who is homeless must hurdle many barriers when trying to register to vote or to vote because, among other things, of the difficulty of proving residence.[51] Indeed, it is estimated that on average only 10 percent of homeless Americans vote.[52]

The federal Voting Rights Act provides that a person who is homeless and may be without a current place of residence has a right to vote in a presidential election either in person or by absentee ballot in the last district of residence.[53] Residence for this purpose does not require a fixed address or a conventional home.[54] Rather, residence is the typical place where the person stays.[55] Documentation requirements vary. Some states will permit proof of residence in the form of a letter from a social service organization.[56] Other states require the registrant to provide a mailing address, but the person can provide the mailing address of the shelter in which the person sleeps.[57] For example, Colorado permits individuals who are homeless to use a shelter as the address for voting, but not a post office box or general delivery at the post office.[58] Some states allow a voter who is homeless to designate the office of the county clerk as the mailing address.[59] Rhode Island has enacted a "Homeless Bill of Rights" and guarantees that a person who is homeless has "the right to vote, register to vote, and receive documentation necessary to prove identity for voting without discrimination due to . . . housing status."[60] A complaint should be lodged if a homeless person's proof of residence is deemed insufficient and prevents the person from voting.[61]

Can the right to vote be conditioned on passing a literacy test?

Literacy tests are assessments used to determine whether a person can read and write English. Historically, states used literacy tests as a device to disenfranchise African Americans. The federal Voting Rights Act imposes a permanent, nationwide ban on the use of literacy tests as a condition for voting.[62] In addition, the statute bars discrimination against persons who are members of language minorities and imposes affirmative duties on states to make the ballot accessible to persons whose primary language is not English.[63] In particular, states are required to conduct bilingual elections where 5 percent or more than 10,000 persons of the voting-age citizens of a state or political subdivision are a single-language minority and cannot speak English proficiently.[64] This means that ballots and other materials must be provided in the applicable language of the relevant minority group.[65] The statute defines "language-minority" to include "persons who are American Indian, Asian American, Alaskan Native, or of Spanish heritage."[66] To find out whether an election district must conduct bilingual elections, contact the U.S. Department of Justice, Civil Rights Division, in Washington, D.C.[67] In addition, complaints should be lodged with the Justice Department if a person with limited English proficiency is intimidated when trying to vote, or otherwise prevented from voting.[68] The integrity of elections depends on making sure that all votes are counted, including those of voters with limited English proficiency— estimated to be 5.78 million who do not receive language accommodations.[69] Various online resources may be helpful to voters in this situation.[70]

Can a person who has been convicted of a felony be denied the right to vote?

The U.S. Supreme Court has held that it is constitutional for a state to deny the right to vote to a person who has been convicted of a felony—a practice called felony disenfranchisement.[71] The Court based its holding on Section 2 of the Fourteenth Amendment, which bars any abridgement of the right to vote in federal elections, "except for participation in rebellion, or other crime."[72] In particular, the Court upheld the legality of a California statute that barred those convicted of an "infamous crime" from voting.[73] Nevertheless, a state's disenfranchisement statute may be found unconstitutional if it is motivated by a desire to discriminate against racial minorities. On that basis, the Court struck down an Alabama law that was found to have been enacted with an animus against African Americans.[74] Moreover, felon-disenfranchisement statutes are vulnerable to legal challenge if their application has a disproportionate negative impact on minority voters.[75] Combined, felony disenfranchisement was estimated in 2016 to have barred 6.1 million citizens from voting.[76] Given the racialized nature of mass incarceration in the United States, the number of African Americans to have lost the right to vote is four times greater than that of non–African Americans.[77]

As of 2018, all states other than Vermont or Maine bar a person who has been convicted of a felony from voting when the person is in prison,[78] and 34 states bar voting even after the convicted felon has been released from prison.[79]

Two states—Iowa and Kentucky—impose a lifetime ban on voting by a person convicted of a felony, unless the government grants clemency.[80] Some states permit a person with a felony criminal conviction to apply for restoration of voting rights after completion of the sentence. However, restoration may be conditioned in some states on payment of all fees that the state has imposed in connection with the potential voter's incarceration. This includes fees for victim restitution and court fees. In addition, at least one state requires full payment of all child support that accrued during the person's prison term.[81] The inability to pay these fees means that the former felon continues to be barred from voting. Challenges have been brought to some of these state laws on the ground that they are a poll tax in disguise[82] or an impermissible form of wealth discrimination.[83] So far, courts that have considered the issue have held that payment of the fee is a part of discharging a felony criminal sentence rather than a condition for restoring voting,[84] a conclusion that assumes that a person with a criminal conviction does not have a constitutional right to vote. Political efforts are underway to try to reform felon disenfranchisement laws so that persons who have been released from prison or are serving probation sentences will be able to vote.[85]

Can a person who has been convicted of a misdemeanor and is in jail vote?

Whether a person who has been convicted of a misdemeanor loses the right to vote depends on the state. In eight states, a person convicted of a misdemeanor cannot vote while incarcerated; some states disenfranchise only those prisoners who committed election-related misdemeanors.[86]

Can a person who is in jail awaiting trial register and vote?

No state bars a person who is detained in jail awaiting trial from voting.[87] However, a person who is in jail faces practical barriers to voting because the detainee is confined and cannot vote at the local polling place. Three avenues are available:

- The jailhouse can be designated a polling place with an election official present;
- The local election agency can deliver and collect absentee ballots from those who are in the jail;

- The detainee can complete and mail an ordinary ballot, relying upon the jail's mail system, which may be unreliable.[88]

Does a registered voter have to show identification papers in order to vote?

As of 2019, 35 states have laws requiring or requesting voters to show some form of identification at the polls.[89] The form of ID card that is required varies from state to state, and about half of the states require a photo ID.[90] Eighteen states require identification but permit a range of documentation,[91] such as utility bills or bank statements.[92] As many as 11 percent of eligible voters do not have government-issued photo IDs,[93] and the poor, people of color, seniors, the disabled, and the homeless are disproportionately affected by these policies.[94] In particular, obtaining even "free" ID cards generates significant costs that may, in practice, prevent a person who is entitled to vote from doing so.[95]

Keep in mind that there is a difference between a state requesting ID and requiring ID as a condition to vote. Moreover, states differ on how they treat persons who arrive at the polls without identification. Some states allow voters to sign an affidavit of identity or poll workers to authenticate voters' identities. In seven states, voters without identification may vote on a provisional ballot. After Election Day, officials determine, using a signature check or other method, whether the voter was eligible and registered.[96] Other states use more restrictive methods of post-ballot verification; in Georgia, for example, an individual without the required identification may cast a provisional ballot, but must show acceptable identification at the county registrar's office within three days following the election to have the voted actually count.[97] One problem with provisional ballots is that they are not consistently counted,[98] so by effect those without ID cards run a high risk of being disenfranchised.

Whether a particular state's ID requirement is permissible is context-specific and depends on the form of the ID and the nature of its impact on racial minorities.[99] The U.S. Supreme Court upheld a photo-ID law that the state justified as promoting an important state interest.[100] However, it struck down a state requirement that a voter provide a passport, birth certificate, or other proof of citizenship both to register and on Election Day.[101] Lower courts have disagreed whether voter ID requirements are impermissible as the equivalent of a poll tax.[102] There is significant evidence that Republican state legislatures have adopted voter ID laws for the purpose of suppressing political participation by poor people and people of color.[103]

What should a voter do if the voter's name has been dropped from the voting rolls?

The National Voter Registration Act ("motor voter") provides that any voter whose name is being "purged" from a voting roll (meaning, the name is dropped) must be notified and given the opportunity to correct any errors or omissions or demonstrate eligibility.[104] In addition, the federal Help America Vote Act of 2002 provides that anyone can cast a provisional ballot even if the person's name does not appear on the eligible voter list, so long as they fill out an affidavit stating they are a registered voter in the jurisdiction and eligible to vote.[105] Thus, by law, voters who believe themselves registered and eligible to vote have the right to a provisional ballot. Provisional ballots in some elections may be determinative of the result, but they are not consistently counted; moreover, if a voter's name has been purged from the rolls, the voter's provisional ballot will not be counted.[106]

Are employers required to give a worker "time off" to vote?

Voting usually takes place during the work day. The law varies from state to state as to whether employers must give workers time off to vote. Thirty-one states have laws requiring some time off to vote.[107] Most of these laws require employers to give employees two hours off if there is not a two-hour window of time outside of working hours to cast a vote. As of 2016, laws in 22 states prohibit employers from withholding pay for time spent outside of work voting (but typically only up to two hours of wages).[108] Seventeen states require employees to give advance notice if they plan on taking time off from work to vote,[109] and in 15 states, employers may specify the hours in which the employee may take time off to vote.[110] New York has amended its election law to require three hours of paid time off to vote, provided the employee makes the request at least two days before the election—and employers are required to post notices of the right to make the request.[111] If an employer is not required to give time off, consider whether the state allows for other ways to vote that do not require taking time off from work. These methods might be: early voting; absentee voting; or mail voting.[112]

What accommodations are made for voters with physical disabilities to make sure they can access the voting booth?

The Voting Accessibility for the Elderly and Handicapped Act of 1984 requires each state to ensure that polling places are physically accessible to people with disabilities for federal elections.[113] This act also requires that voting aids, such as "information by telecommunications devices for the deaf," be available at polling sites.[114] Furthermore, the Voting Rights Act established that a blind, disabled, or illiterate voter who requires assistance may choose anyone to provide assistance, provided the aide is not the voter's employer or an agent of the voter's employer or union.[115]

Do citizens living in long-term care facilities have the right to vote?

Citizens living in long-term care facilities have the right to vote. Facilities of this sort include nursing homes. However, residents may face practical barriers to being able to vote, including physical impairments and a lack of transportation to the voting booth.[116] In addition, some residents may have impaired cognitive function; only a court can determine whether a person's mental disabilities are grounds for disenfranchisement,[117] but at a practical level the resident may be unable to obtain assistance in securing an absentee ballot even if the state would provide one.[118] Some states have instituted mobile voting to enable those in long-term care to vote; in addition, some states have enacted legislation to ensure that residents are not subject to undue influence when they vote.[119]

What happens to voters who are dislocated by natural disasters and climate catastrophes?

Natural disasters can have a devastating impact on the voting rights of poor and low-income people, with significant racialized effects, as illustrated by the aftershocks of Hurricane Katrina in Louisiana (2005)[120] and Superstorm Sandy in New Jersey and New York (2012).[121] Many poor people were mobilized to vote,[122] but were displaced, without a permanent home, without access to transportation or the internet, and without documentation.[123] These catastrophes underscore the need for communities to insist that state and local officials plan for climate contingencies and consider the need for mobile voting, absentee voting procedures, and ID requirements that are adapted to and reasonable under such circumstances.[124]

Is a candidate for office required to pay a filing fee?

A candidate for office cannot be required to pay a filing fee if payment would prevent the candidate from running for office. The U.S. Supreme Court has held that it is permissible for election officials to limit the ballot to "serious" candidates; but election officials may not screen out candidates who cannot afford to pay a ballot access fee if payment is the exclusive method by which a candidate can secure a place on the ballot.[125] (Some states, including California, permit candidates to pay filing fees in lieu of petitioning their way onto the ballot.)[126] In limiting the use of filing fees, the Court has explained that "the process of qualifying candidates . . . may not constitutionally be measured solely in dollars."[127]

Do candidates have to own property to run for office?

No. In 1970 the U.S. Supreme Court invalidated a Georgia law requiring candidates for a local school board to own property. Even though the law required only "one square inch" of property, the Court found that it lacked any valid state purpose and could not be imposed to keep landless candidates off the ballot.[128] Thus, an individual does not have to own property to run for office. As a practical matter, however, poor and low-income people who seek electoral office must hurdle extreme economic barriers in the political process.[129] Money and politics have become synonymous in American elections.[130] Corporations are permitted to spend uncapped amounts of money in election campaigns;[131] consider the fact that political action campaigns contributed $1 billion in a five-year period on federal elections, with 60 percent of the money coming from 195 contributors.[132] The corrupting role of money on political elections is a grave threat to American democracy, and requires extensive federal legislative reform addressing the financing of political campaigns. In the meantime, some states have tried to democratize the funding of elections through small-donor matching programs, public funding, and grants.[133]

Can legal services lawyers represent clients seeking to challenge voter registration requirements or to remedy the denial of the right to vote?

Legal services lawyers that receive funding from the Legal Services Corporation are barred from using that money in litigation related to electoral redistricting.[134] However, legal services lawyers are not barred from undertaking other voter-related lawsuits. Nevertheless, legal services offices typically do not have sufficient funding to meet all of the legal needs of the persons seeking representation, and will accord a higher priority to cases involving immediate and pressing matters such as housing or government benefits. The combination of legal restriction and inadequate resources makes it highly unlikely that a voter who faces problems in registering to vote or barriers to voting will be represented by a legal services lawyer.[135] However, people who believe their right to vote has been impaired may file an informal complaint with the U.S. Department of Justice, and the Department is expected to investigate reported problems.[136]

May citizens conduct voter drives and help other citizens register to vote?

Yes. Through voter registration drives, community organizers can register citizens to vote. The National Voter Registration Act requires states to make federal election forms "available for distribution through governmental and private entities with particular emphasis on making them available for organized voter registration programs."[137] But it is imperative that a person wishing to organize a voter-registration drive follow state requirements.[138] These restrictions vary. For example, 11 states require training, and Colorado requires a voting drive's leader to obtain a perfect score on a mandatory examination. In New Mexico, a person registering others to vote must return the completed forms to the County Clerk or Secretary of State within 48 hours and can face civil and criminal penalties for failure to comply.[139] California requires individuals collecting state voter registration forms to place them in the postal service within three days of their receipt, and failure to do so is a misdemeanor punishable by a fine of up to $1,000.[140]

In a 2012 challenge to restrictions on Florida's voter registration drive laws, a federal trial court emphasized that registration drives implicate protected First Amendment freedoms.[141] Similarly, in a 2006 case, a federal court in Ohio invalidated various restrictions on that state's registration drive laws, finding that they would "chill[] participation in the voter registration process," and therefore violated the National Voter Registration Act.[142] However, in 2013, the Fifth Circuit Court of Appeals found that a Texas ban on paying canvassers on a per-application basis and conditioning payment on the submission of a fixed number of applications did not violate the First Amendment.[143]

Notes

1. *See, for example*, Harper v. Virginia Bd. of Elections, 383 U.S. 663, 666 (1966) (invalidating poll tax on the ground that "a State violates the Equal Protection Clause of the Fourteenth Amendment whenever it makes the affluence of the voter or payment of a fee an electoral standard"). Since the 1960s, the Court has repeatedly held that the right to vote is a "fundamental right" under the Constitution and that it must

be dispensed equally, "without regard to race, sex, economic status, or place of residence within a state." Reynolds v. Sims, 377 U.S. 533, 561–562, 656–668 (1964).

2. *See* United States v. Classic, 313 U.S. 299, 310, 314–315 (1941) (interpreting U.S. Const. Art. I, § 2).

   Moreover, every state constitution guarantees the right to vote in state elections to citizens who are state residents and meet specific eligibility requirements. *See* Ala. Const. Art. 8, § 177; Alaska Const. Art. 5, § 1; Ariz. Const. Art. 7, § 2; Ark. Const. Art. 3, § 1; Cal. Const. Art. 2, § 2; Colo. Const. Art. 7, § 1; Conn. Const. Art. 6, § 1; Del. Const. Art. 5, § 2; Fla. Const. Art. 6, § 2; Ga. Const. Art. 2, § 1; Hawaii Const. Art. 2, § 1; Idaho Const. Art. 6, § 2; Ill. Const. Art. 3, § 1; Ind. Const. Art. 2, § 2; Iowa Const. Art. 2, § 1; Kan. Const. Art. 5, § 1; Ky. Const. § 145; La. Const. Art. 1, § 10; Me. Const. Art. 2, § 1; Md. Const. Art. 1, § 1; Mass. Const. Part 2, Ch. 1, § 3 Art. 4; Mich. Const. Art. 2, § 1; Minn. Const. Art. 7, § 1; Miss. Const. Art. 12, § 241; Mo. Const. Art. 8, § 2; Mont. Const. Art. 4, § 2; Neb. Const. Art. 6, § 1; Nev. Const. Art. 2, § 1; N.H. Const. Part 1, Art. 11; N.J. Const. Art. 2, § 1, ¶ 3; N.M. Const. Art. 7, § 1; N.Y. Const. Art. II, § 1; N.C. Const. Art. 6, § 1; N.D. Const. Art. 2, § 1; Ohio Const. Art. 5, § 1; Okla. Const. Art. 3, § 1; Or. Const. Art. 2, § 2; Pa. Const. Art. 7, § 1; R.I. Const. Art. 2, § 1; S.C. Const. Art. 2, § 4; S.D. Const. Art. 7, § 2; Tenn. Const. Art. 4, § 1; Tex. Const. Art. 6, § 2; Utah Const. Art. 4, § 2; Vt. Const. Ch. 2, § 42; Va. Const. Art. 2, § 1; Wash. Const. Art. 6, § 1; W. Va. Const. Art. IV, § 1; Wis. Const. Art. 3, § 1; Wyo. Const. Art. 6, § 2.

3. Chilton Williamson, American Suffrage: From Property to Democracy 1760–1860 at 6–7 (Princeton 1960). *See also* James W. Fox, Jr., Citizenship, Poverty, and Federalism: 1787–1882, 60 U. Pitt. L. Rev. 421, 442–443 (1999).

4. For a history of the right to vote, *see* Michael Waldman, The Fight to Vote (Simon & Schuster 2016).

5. For a discussion of additional ways to improve protection of the right to vote, *see* Myrna Pérez, Election Integrity: A Pro-Voter Agenda, Brennan Center for Justice (2016), https://www.brennancenter.org/publication/election-integrity-pro-voter-agenda.

6. U.S. Const. Amend. XV, § 1 ("The right of citizens of the United States to vote shall not be denied or abridged by the United States or by any State on account of race, color, or previous condition of servitude.").

7. U.S. Const. Amend. XIX, § 1 ("The right of citizens of the United States to vote shall not be denied or abridged by the United States or by any State on account of sex.").

8. 8 U.S.C. § 1401(b).

9. U.S. Const. Amend. XXIV, § 1 ("The right of citizens of the United States to vote in any primary or other election for President or Vice President, for electors for President or Vice President, or for Senator or Representative in Congress, shall not be denied or abridged by the United States or any State by reason of failure to pay any poll tax or other tax."). In 1966, the Court interpreted the federal Constitution to bar states from restricting the vote in state elections based on "the affluence of the voter or payment of any fee." Harper v. Virginia State Board of Elections, 383 U.S. 663, 666 (1966). *See also* Kramer v. Union Free School Dist. No. 15, 395 U.S. 621 (1969) (invalidating

property qualification for vote in school board elections); Cipriano v. City of Houma, 395 U.S. 701 (1969) (invalidating property qualification for vote on public bond issue); City of Phoenix v. Kolodziejski, 399 U.S. 204 (1969) (same).

10. U.S. Const. Amend. XXVI, § 1 ("The right of citizens of the United States, who are eighteen years of age or older, to vote shall not be denied or abridged by the United States or by any State on account of age.").

11. 52 U.S.C. § 10301(a), formerly codified at 42 U.S.C. § 1973. The legislative history to the act specifically dismissed the long history of conditioning the right to vote on the ownership of property. *See* H. Rep. No. 439, 89th Cong., 1st Sess. 8–13 (1965), reprinted in 1965 U.S. Code Cong. & Ad. News 2437, 2439–2444. *See* Jamin Raskin & John Bonifaz, Equal Protection and the Wealth Primary, 11 Yale L. & Pol'y Rev. 273, 273 n.2 (1993) ("The property and wealth qualifications were dismantled by state constitution and statutory challenges.").

12. 52 U.S.C. §§ 21081–83, formerly codified at 42 U.S.C. §§ 15481–83. In addition, the states were required (1) to provide "provisional" ballots to voters whose names did not appear on the registration list at the time of voting, allowing the person to vote subject to later verification; and (2) to improve the accuracy of voting lists, by replacing local registration lists with state lists, verifying voting lists by cross-checking with car registration, and requiring identification from first-time voters who registered by mail. *See* Daniel P. Tokaji, HAVA in Court: A Summary and Analysis of Litigation, 12 Election L.J. 203 (2013).

13. *See* Steven J. Mulroy, Barriers at the Ballot Box Symposium Issue, 49 U. Mem. L. Rev. 957, 958 (2019) (reporting that "the overall trend [in the states] is toward the diminution of the right to vote. More and more states are enacting restrictive voter ID laws, engaging in severe purges of voters from the registration rolls, and enacting gerrymandering districting laws."). *See, for example*, Christopher Famighetti, Amanda Melillo, & Myrna Pérez, Election Day Long Lines: Resource Allocation, Brennan Center for Justice (2014), https://www.brennancenter.org/sites/default/files/publications/ElectionDayLongLines-ResourceAllocation.pdf. For a discussion of ways to improve protection of the right to vote, *see* Myrna Pérez, Election Integrity: A Pro-Voter Agenda, Brennan Center for Justice (2016), https://www.brennancenter.org/publication/election-integrity-pro-voter-agenda.

14. Reynolds v. Sims, 377 U.S. 533, 561–568 (1964).

15. For a skeptical view of this "pluralistic-democratic optic," *see* Jeffrey A. Winters, Oligarchy xii–xiii 249–250 (". . . the poor, despite their numbers, . . . lose in the game of democratic participation"; they fail "to choose leaders who will advance their material welfare" or to punish "those who have undermined their financial welfare during the previous term in office").

16. *See generally* Jonathan Soros, The Missing Right: A Constitutional Right to Vote, Democracy: A Journal of Ideas (Spring 2013), https://democracyjournal.org/magazine/28/the-missing-right-a-constitutional-right-to-vote/ (criticizing the absence of a right to vote in the U.S. Constitution and describing the "varieties of disenfranchisement" directed against the poor and people of color).

17. U.S. Department of Justice, Voting, https://www.justice.gov/crt/how-file-complaint#nine. The website states (as of Jan. 25, 2019):

> The Voting Section accepts complaints about possible violations of the federal voting rights laws—
>
> – By email at voting.section@usdoj.gov (link sends e-mail)
> – By telephone at (800) 253-3931 (toll free)
> – By telephone at (202) 307-2767
> – By fax at (202) 307-3961
> – By complaint form at http://www.justice.gov/crt/complaint/votintake/index. php
> – By letter to the addresses below:
>
> Voting Section
> Civil Rights Division
> U.S. Department of Justice
> Room 7254 – NWB
> 950 Pennsylvania Ave., N.W.
> Washington, DC 20530

18. Find a Local League, League of Women Voters, http://lwv.org/get-involved/local-leagues.

19. North Dakota Secretary of State, North Dakota. . . . The Only State without Voter Registration, https://vip.sos.nd.gov/pdfs/portals/votereg.pdf. *See generally* Voter Registration Rules, Vote.org (last updated Mar. 31, 2017), https://www.vote.org/voter-registration-rules/.

20. California, Colorado, Connecticut, Hawaii, Idaho, Illinois, Iowa, Maine, Maryland, Michigan, Minnesota, Montana, New Hampshire, North Carolina, Vermont, Wisconsin, and Wyoming, as well as the District of Columbia, have same-day registration; however, in North Carolina, same-day registration operates only during an "early voting" period. *See* Same Day Voter Registration, National Conference of State Legislatures (Jan. 25, 2019), http://www.ncsl.org/research/elections-and-campaigns/same-day-registration.aspx.

21. 52 U.S.C. § 20501, formerly codified at 42 U.S.C. § 1973gg.

22. 52 U.S.C. § 20504.

23. *Id.* at § 20504(d).

24. 52 U.S.C § 20505. For the national form, *see* U.S. Election Assistance Commission, National Mail Voter Registration Form, http://www.eac.gov/voter_resources/register_to_vote.aspx.

25. 52 U.S.C. § 20506. The statute does not define "public assistance," but its legislative history explains that "[b]y public assistance agencies, we intend to include those State agencies in each State that administer or provide services under the food stamp, Medicaid, the Women, Infants and Children (WIC), and the Aid to Families With Dependent Children (AFDC) programs." H.R. Conf. Rep. No. 103-66, 103rd Cong., 1st Sess. 144 (1993).

26. *See* Michael Alvarez & Jonathan Nagler, Declining Public Assistance Voter Registration and Welfare Reform: A Response, Demos (Oct. 6, 2009), http://www.

demos.org/publication/declining-public-assistance-voter-registration-and-welfare-reform-response.

27. 52 U.S.C. § 20506(a)(3)(B). Overall, voter registration increased by 11.4% over a 20-year period beginning just before the statute's enactment. *See* Royce Crocker, The National Voter Registration Act of 1993: History, Implementation, and Effects, at 22–23 (2013), http://fas.org/sgp/crs/misc/R40609.pdf.

28. Justin Weinstein-Tull, Election Law Federalism, 114 Mich. L. Rev. 747, 759–760 (2016) (public assistance agencies); National Conference of State Legislatures, Automatic Voter Registration (Apr. 22, 2019), http://www.ncsl.org/research/elections-and-campaigns/automatic-voter-registration.aspx.

29. Dunn v. Blumstein, 405 U.S. 330, 343–344 (1972).

30. *Id.* at 342 (quoting Shapiro v. Thompson, 394 U.S. 618, 634 (1969)).

31. *Id.* at 342, 354. *See also* Cody v. Andrews, 405 U.S. 1034 (1972), affirming, 327 F. Supp. 793 (M.D. N.C. 1971) (one-year residency requirement contained in state constitution was unconstitutional when applied to right to vote in local elections); Lester v. Board of Elections for District of Columbia, 319 F. Supp. 505 (D.D.C. 1970) (one-year durational residency requirement violated Equal Protection Clause), judgment vacated and case remanded in light of Dunn v. Blumstein, 405 U.S. 1036 (1972). The U.S. Supreme Court has upheld a 50-day waiting period. *See* Marston v. Lewis, 410 U.S. 679, 681 (1973); Burns v. Forston, 410 U.S. 686, 687 (1973).

32. *See, for example,* 52 U.S.C. § 10502(d), formerly cited as 42 U.S.C. § 1973aa-1 (codifying the Voting Rights Act Amendments of 1970, which prohibited states from cutting off registration more than 30 days in advance of presidential elections).

33. 52 U.S.C. § 10502, formerly cited as 42 U.S.C. § 1973aa-1.

34. 52 U.S.C. § 10502(e), formerly cited as 42 U.S.C. § 1973aa-1(e).

35. *See* David Schultz & Sarah Clark, Wealth v. Democracy: The Unfulfilled Promise of the Twenty-fourth Amendment, 29 Quinnipiac L. Rev. 375 (2011) (providing a history of the poll tax and explaining how the post–Civil War tax differed in aim and effect from its earlier version).

36. Drew Silver, Anti-poll Tax Amendment Is 50 Years Old Today, Pew Research Center (Jan. 23, 2014), http://www.pewresearch.org/fact-tank/2014/01/23/anti-poll-tax-amendment-is-50-years-old-today/.

37. U.S. Const. Amend. XXIV, § 1.

38. *See* Harper v. Virginia State Board of Elections, 383 U.S. 663, 664 n.1, 666 n.4 (1966).

39. *See* Butler v. Thompson, 341 U.S. 937 (1951). *See also* Breedlove v. Suttles, 302 U.S. 277 (1937) (upholding Georgia's poll tax).

40. U.S. Const. Amend. XIV.

41. Harper v. Virginia State Board of Elections, 383 U.S. 663, 666 (1966).

42. Gray v. Sanders, 372 U.S. 368, 380 (1963).

43. Harper v. Virginia State Board of Elections, 383 U.S. 663, 670 (1966).

44. 52 U.S.C § 20506.

45. *See, for example,* Hill v. Stone, 421 U.S. 289 (1975) (Texas requirement that voters "render" or list real or personal property for taxation violates equal protection); City

of Phoenix v. Kolodziejski, 399 U.S. 204 (1970) (Phoenix law restricting vote on general obligation bonds to real property taxpayers violates equal protection).

46. Kramer v. Union Free School District No. 15, 395 U.S. 621 (1969).

47. Cipriano v. City of Houma, 395 U.S. 621 (1969).

48. Salyer Land Co. v. Tulare Lake Basin Water Storage District, 410 U.S. 719, 728 (1973). Because of the water district's "special limited purpose and . . . the disproportionate effect of its activities on landowners as a group," the election of the Board was considered by the Court to be of sufficient "special interest" to a limited class of property owners as to allow restriction of the franchise.

49. Rice v. Cayetano, 528 U.S. 495 (2000).

50. *See* National Coalition for the Homeless, Voter Rights: Registration Manual: You Don't Need a Home to Vote (2012), http://www.nationalhomeless.org/projects/vote/Manual_2012.pdf.

    Other resources include: Sarah Devlin, I Lost My Home, Don't Take My Voice: Ensuring the Voting Rights of the Homeless through Negotiated Rulemaking, 2009 J. Disp. Resol. 175, 177 (2009); Patricia M. Hanrahan, No Home? No Vote, 21 Hum. Rts. 8 (Winter 1994); Edward J. Smith, Note, Disenfranchisement of Homeless Persons, 31 Wash. U. J. Urban & Contemp. L. 225 (1987). *See also* Kristin Capps, Voting While Homeless, Citylab (Nov. 8, 2016), https://www.citylab.com/equity/2016/11/voting-while-homeless/506972/.

51. For example, although Washington State permits a person to register to vote with a nontraditional address, a court affirmed the cancellation of a homeless person's registration when county officials discovered the location was a parking lot where an apartment building used to stand; the court held that the person was not actually residing there, and so the registration was properly cancelled. Camarata v. Kittitas County, 346 P.3d 822 (Wash. App. 2015). *See also* Jin Zhao, Why We Should Care About the Homeless Vote, Alternet (Aug. 9, 2012), http://www.alternet.org/activism/why-we-should-care-about-homeless-vote.

52. *See* Jin Zhao, Why We Should Care about the Homeless Vote, National Coalition for the Homeless (originally printed in AlterNet) (Aug. 9, 2012), http://nationalhomeless.org/care-homeless-vote/ ("Although the homeless vote may not be a wild card for any candidate or party, with at least 1.6 million people experiencing homelessness nationwide, it does have the potential to change the game in some swing states.").

53. 52 U.S.C. § 10502(e), formerly cited as 42 U.S.C. § 1973aa-1(e).

54. *See* National Coalition for the Homeless, Court Decisions on Homeless People's Voting Rights, http://www.nationalhomeless.org/projects/vote/court.html.

    The leading published cases are Pitts v. Black, 608 F. Supp. 696, 709 (S.D.N.Y. 1984), and Collier v. Menzel, 221 Cal. Rptr. 110 (App. 1985). *See also* Constitution of Virginia: Franchise and Officers (Qualification of Voters), Op. Atty. Gen. No. 04-030, 2004 WL 1284006 (Va. May 19, 2004); Voter Registration of Homeless Persons, Op. Atty. Gen. No. 2, 1991 WL 527640 (N.J. Apr. 17, 1991); In the matter of: The Application for Voter Registration of Willie R. Jenkins (D.C. Board of Elections and Ethics, June 7, 1984) (unpublished), summary available in Edward J. Smith, Note,

Disenfranchisement of Homeless Persons, 31 Wash. U. J. Urban & Contemp. L. 225, 235 n.65 (1987).

55. For example, *see* Iowa's provision, Iowa Code Ann. § 48A.5A(7) ("[T]he residence of a homeless person is in the precinct where the homeless person usually sleeps. Residence requirements shall be construed liberally to provide homeless persons with the opportunity to register to vote and to vote").

56. For an example of the kind of letter that should be sufficient, *see* State of Wisconsin, Wisconsin Elections Commission, Enabling Qualified Homeless Individuals to Vote—Sample Proof of Residence Letter, http://elections.wi.gov/publications/brochures/enabling-homeless-voters.

57. For example, *see* Illinois Statute 10 I.L.C.S. 5/3-2(b) ("A mailing address of a homeless individual may include, but is not limited to, a shelter, a day shelter, or a private residence.").

58. *See* Colorado rules for determining residence, Colo. Rev. Stat. Ann. § 1-2-102.

59. *See, for example*, Or. Rev. Stat. § 247.038(2)(a) ("The mailing address of a person who is homeless or resides in a shelter, park, motor home, marina or other identifiable location may be the office of the county clerk."). *See also* Jeanne P. Atkins, Homeless Doesn't Mean Voiceless: Vote—Oregon's Secretary of State Explains How to Register to Vote Without a Permanent Address, Street Roots News (Sept. 29, 2016), http://news.streetroots.org/2016/09/29/homeless-doesn-t-mean-voiceless-vote.

60. R.I. Gen. Laws 1956, § 34-37.1.3. Illinois has a similar Bill of Rights Provision, *see* 775 I.L.C.S. 45/10.

61. Information about how to file a complaint is available from U.S. Department of Justice, Election Complaint Report, https://www.justice.gov/crt/complaint/votintake/index.php.

62. Voting Rights Act Amendments of 1970, Pub. L. No. 91-285, 84 Stat. 314 (1970), codified as amended at 52 U.S.C. § 10303, formerly codified at 42 U.S.C. § 1973aa. The Voting Rights Act of 1965 limited the restriction on literacy tests to those states that had a history of voter disenfranchisement. *See* Voting Rights Act of 1965, Pub. L. No. 89-110, 79 Stat. 438 (1965). The U.S. Supreme Court upheld the constitutionality of the provision abolishing literacy tests as requisite to vote in *Oregon v. Mitchell*, 400 U.S. 112 (1970). In 1965, the U.S. Supreme Court invalidated Louisiana's literacy test because it gave too much discretion to election officials, which could be, and was shown to have been, applied arbitrarily based on race. Louisiana v. United States, 380 U.S. 145, 153 (1965). However, the Court upheld literacy tests in *Lassiter v. Northampton Co. Bd. of Elections*, 360 U.S. 45 (1959).

63. 52 U.S.C. § 10303(f), formerly codified at 42 U.S.C. § 1973b.

64. 52 U.S.C. § 10503(b), formerly codified at 42 U.S.C. 1973aa-1a. The statute also requires that the illiteracy rate of the language minority be higher than that of the national average. The 2011 coverage list, based on the 2010 census, is published in the Federal Register, 76 Fed. Reg. 63602 (Oct. 13, 2011), https://www.justice.gov/sites/default/files/crt/legacy/2011/10/13/2011_notice.pdf.

65. For more information, *see* United States Department of Justice, Minority Language Citizens, Section 203 of the Voting Rights Act, https://www.justice.gov/crt/about-language-minority-voting-rights.

See also James Thomas Tucker, Enfranchising Language Minority Citizens: The Bilingual Election Provisions of the Voting Rights Act, 10 N.Y.U. J. Legis. & Pub. Pol'y 195 (2006).

66. 52 U.S.C. § 10503(e), formerly codified at 42 U.S.C. § 1973aa-1a(e).

67. The toll-free phone number is 1-800-253-3931.

68. For reports of such intimidation, *see* Allie Yee, Concerns Grow Over Voting Rights for the South's Language Minorities, The Institute for Southern Studies, Facing South (Mar. 2015), https://www.facingsouth.org/2015/03/concerns-grow-over-voting-rights-for-the-souths-la.html.

69. *See, for example*, Richard Salame, Vote Aquí? Limited-English-Proficiency Voters Could Help Determine Congress, The Nation (Nov. 5, 2018) (https://www.thenation.com/article/limited-english-voters-investigation-election/.

70. *See, for example*, Empire Justice Center, Voting Rights, http://onlineresources.wnylc.net/pb/orcdocs/LARC_Resources/LEPTopics/VO/Voting.htm (information about federal and New York LEP rules); Asian Americans Advancing Justice, Language Rights in Voting, https://www.advancingjustice-aajc.org/language-rights (fact sheets in English, Chinese simplified, Chinese traditional, Bangla, Hindi, Japanese, Khmer, Korean, Thai, and Vietnamese).

71. Richardson v. Ramirez, 418 U.S. 24, 54 (1974).

72. U.S. Const. Amend. XIV, § 2.

73. Richardson v. Ramirez, 418 U.S. 24, 27 (1974).

74. Hunter v. Underwood, 471 U.S. 222, 233 (1985).

75. *See, for example*, Jamelia N. Morgan, Disparate Impact and Voting Rights, How Objections to Impact-based Claims Prevent Plaintiffs from Prevailing in Cases Challenging New Forms of Disenfranchisement, 9 Ala. C.R. & C.L. Rev. 93 (2018). The Trump administration has announced plans to eliminate disparate-impact regulations that would affect a broad range of civil rights enforcement. *See generally* P.R. Lockhart, The Trump administration is considering a major rollback of civil rights regulation, Vox (Jan. 7, 2019), https://www.vox.com/policy-and-politics/2019/1/7/18167275/disparate-impact-civil-rights-trump-administration.

76. Christopher Uggen, Ryan Larson, & Sarah Shannon, 6 Million Lost Voters: State-Level Estimates of Felony Disenfranchisement, 2016, The Sentencing Project (Oct. 6, 2016), http://www.sentencingproject.org/issues/felony-disenfranchisement/. *See also* Brent Staples, The Racist Origins of Felon Disenfranchisement, N.Y. Times (Nov. 18, 2014), http://www.nytimes.com/2014/11/19/opinion/the-racist-origins-of-felon-disenfranchisement.html?_r=0.

77. The Sentencing Project, 6 Million Lost Voters: State-Level Estimates of Felony Disenfranchisement, 2016, at 3, https://www.sentencingproject.org/wp-content/uploads/2016/10/6-Million-Lost-Voters.pdf.

78. Jean Chung, Felony Disenfranchisement: A Primer, Table 1. Summary of Felony Disenfranchisement Restrictions in 2019, The Sentencing Project (June 27, 2019), http://www.sentencingproject.org/publications/felony-disenfranchisement-a-primer. *See also* Prison Policy Initiative, Felon Disenfranchisement, https://www.prisonpolicy.org/research/felon_disenfranchisement/ (collecting reports and other resources).

79. These states also restrict voting while a person is on probation or parole. Brennan Center for Justice, Criminal Disenfranchisement Laws Across the United States (Dec. 7, 2018), http://www.brennancenter.org/criminal-disenfranchisement-laws-across-united-states.

80. Additionally, Alabama, Arizona, Delaware, Florida, Maryland, Mississippi, Missouri, Nevada, Tennessee, and Wyoming have permanent disenfranchisement for people with certain criminal convictions, unless the government approves individual rights restoration. *Id.*

81. Ann Cammett, Shadow Citizens: Felony Disenfranchisement and the Criminalization of Debt, 117 Penn. St. L. Rev. 349, 387–393 (2012).

82. *See, for example*, Howard v. Gilmore, 205 F.3d 1333 (Table) (4th Cir. 2000).

83. *See, for example*, Harvey v. Brewer, 605 F.3d 1067, 1079 (9th Cir. 2010).

84. Madison v. State, 163 P.3d 757, 771 (Wash. 2007) (en banc).

85. For example, in 2018, the governor of New York issued clemency for individuals under parole supervision, restoring voting rights to 35,000 persons. In 2016, the governor of Virginia issued clemency for individuals to restore voting rights. Michael Wines, Virginia's Governor Restores Voting Rights for 13,000 Ex-Felons, N.Y. Times (Aug. 2, 2016), https://www.nytimes.com/2016/08/23/us/virginia-governor-mcauliffe-voting-rights-felons.html. Also in 2018, Florida voters adopted a ballot measure restoring voting rights to 1.5 million people with felony convictions, but the Republican legislature promptly passed a law sharply narrowing those rights. *See* Patricia Mazzei, Floridians Gave Ex-Felons a Right to Vote. Lawmakers Just Put a Big Obstacle in Their Way, N.Y. Times (May 3, 2019), https://www.nytimes.com/2019/05/03/us/florida-felon-voting-amendment-4.html. For a state-by-state analysis of procedures to expunge criminal records and restore rights, *see* Collateral Consequences Resource Center, Restoration of Rights Project, https://ccresourcecenter.org/state-restoration-profiles/50-state-comparisonjudicial-expungement-sealing-and-set-aside.

   For more information, *see* Brennan Center for Justice, Restoring Voting Rights, https://www.brennancenter.org/issues/restoring-voting-rights.

86. Idaho, Illinois, Indiana, Kentucky, Michigan, Missouri, South Carolina, and South Dakota; Kentucky and Missouri require, for certain misdemeanors, an executive pardon to restore the right to vote even after the completion of the person's sentence. Iowa also restricts voting while in prison but only for "aggravated" misdemeanors. The District of Columbia also bars people convicted of lobbying and campaign-finance related crimes from voting while incarcerated. *See* PublicJal.com, State Felon Voting Laws, II. Misdemeanor Convictions (Oct. 27, 2016), http://www.publicjail.com/state-felon-voting-laws/. For more information on felony and misdemeanor

franchise criteria, *see* John Boston & Daniel E. Manville, Prisoners' Self-Help Litigation Manual 227–228 (Oceana 4th ed. 2010).

87. An exception would be if the detainee were already barred in that state from voting because of a prior felony conviction or for being on probation or parole. *See* American Civil Liberties Union, VWI: Voting While Incarcerated, A Tool Kit for Advocates Seeking to Register, and Facilitate Voting by, Eligible People in Jail (2005), https://www.aclu.org/files/pdfs/votingrights/votingwhileincarc_20051123.pdf.

88. Danielle Root & Lee Doyle, Protecting the Voting Rights of Americans Detained While Awaiting Trial, Center for American Progress (Aug. 23, 2018), https://www.americanprogress.org/issues/democracy/reports/2018/08/23/455011/protecting-voting-rights-americans-detained-awaiting-trial/. Long Distance Voter maintains a website that enables voters to obtain information about absentee ballots. Long Distance Voter, http://www.longdistancevoter.org/#.VyPVtmf2Y-E.

89. Wendy Underhill, Voter Identification Requirements—Voter ID Laws, National Council of State Legislatures (Jan. 17, 2019), http://www.ncsl.org/research/elections-and-campaigns/voter-id.aspx#Info.

90. The 17 states that ask for a photo ID are: Arkansas, Alabama, Florida, Georgia, Hawaii, Idaho, Indiana, Kansas, Louisiana, Michigan, Mississippi, Rhode Island, South Dakota, Tennessee, Texas, Virginia, and Wisconsin. See Wendy Underhill, Voter Identification Requirements: Voter ID Laws, National Council of State Legislatures (Jan. 17, 2019), http://www.ncsl.org/research/elections-and-campaigns/voter-id.aspx#Info. If a voter fails to show the ID, some states have less onerous photo ID laws which allow some voters without acceptable identification to cast a ballot that will be counted without further action on the part of the voter. For example, a voter may sign an affidavit of identity or cast a provisional ballot, and election officials will later determine whether the voter was eligible and registered. *Id.*

91. The 17 states that ask for a nonphoto ID are: Alaska, Arizona, Colorado, Connecticut, Delaware, Iowa, Kentucky, Missouri, Montana, New Hampshire, North Carolina, Ohio, Oklahoma, South Carolina, Utah, Washington, and West Virginia. Wendy Underhill, Voter Identification Requirements: Voter ID Laws, National Council of State Legislatures (Jan. 17, 2019), http://www.ncsl.org/research/elections-and-campaigns/voter-id.aspx#Info.

92. *See, for example*, Alaska Stat. Ann. § 15.15.225 (Prior to being allowed to vote, voters must show identification from an enumerated list, which includes a copy of a current utility bill, bank statement, paycheck, government check, or other government document.); Ariz. Rev. Stat. Ann. § 16-579 (Voters may present valid photo identification or two items that contain the name and address of the voter, such as a utility bill, bank statement, or Arizona vehicle registration.).

93. Voter ID, Brennan Center for Justice (Oct. 15, 2012), https://www.brennancenter.org/analysis/voter-id.

94. For studies of the effects of voter ID laws on the poor and people of color, *see* Research on Voter ID, Brennan Center for Justice (Aug. 11, 2017), http://www.brennancenter.org/analysis/research-and-publications-voter-id.

95. Richard Sobel, The High Cost of "Free" Photo Voter Identification Cards, Charles Hamilton Houston Institute for Race & Justice Harvard Law School (June 2014), http://today.law.harvard.edu/wp-content/uploads/2014/06/FullReportVoterIDJune20141.pdf.

96. Colorado, Florida, Montana, Oklahoma, Rhode Island, Utah, and Vermont. Wendy Underhill, Voter Identification Requirements: Voter ID Laws, National Council of State Legislatures (Jan. 17, 2019), http://www.ncsl.org/research/elections-and-campaigns/voter-id.aspx#Info.

97. Ga. Code Ann. § 21-2-417. For a state-by-state analysis of provisional ballots, *see* National Conference of State Legislatures, Provisional Ballots, http://www.ncsl.org/research/elections-and-campaign-provisional-ballots.aspx.

98. U.S. Government Accountability Office, Issues Related to State Voter Identification Laws (2014), http://www.gao.gov/assets/670/665966.pdf.

99. Nicholas O. Stephanopoulos, Disparate Impact, Unified Law, 128 Yale L.J. 1566, 1570 (2019) (explaining that the U.S. Supreme Court has not yet decided whether the Voting Rights Act is violated "if an electoral policy (1) has a disparate racial impact that (2) is attributable to the policy's interaction with discriminating conditions" such as persistent poverty).

100. Crawford v. Marion County Election Board, 553 U.S. 181 (2008). The Court acknowledged that in some cases, requiring a photo ID could burden the right of a person with lower income to vote, but held the requirement in this case was not shown to be an excessive burden "on any class of voters." *Id.* at 202. *See* Cary Franklin, The New Class Blindness, 128 Yale L.J. 2, 87 (2018) (stating that *Crawford* "upheld a voter ID law that impeded the ability of poor and otherwise disadvantage citizens to vote, and it enabled the spread of such laws throughout the country").

101. Arizona v. Inter Tribal Council of Arizona, Inc., 570 U.S. 1 (2013).

102. *Compare* Weinschenk v. State, 203 S.W.3d 201 (Mo. 2006), *with* City of Memphis v. Hargett, 414 S.W.3d 88 (Tenn. 2013).

For example, Texas adopted a law in 2013 that required a voter to present one of six forms of photo ID before voting (with a few exceptions). A federal appeals court struck down the requirement as invalid under the Voting Rights Act; among other reasons for the court's decision, persons of color in Texas made up a disproportionate portion of the poor and low-income voting population, and they were found to be eight times less likely to be able to afford the required ID and so thereby denied the right to vote. Finally, the court did not accept Texas's justification that the ID was needed to prevent voter fraud. Veasey v. Abbott, 796 F.3d 487 (5th Cir. 2015). However, the same federal appeals court accepted a version of the same law, which allows voters unable to present one of seven forms of ID to cast a ballot if they sign an affidavit stating why they were unable to obtain an approved ID and present an alternative form of identification such as a bank statement. Veasey v. Abbott, 888 F.3d 792 (5th Cir. 2018). Similarly, in Common Cause/Georgia v. Billups, 554 F.3d 1340 (11th Cir. 2009), the appeals court upheld Georgia's voter ID law. The law required every voter to present a photo ID, and also required state officials to issue, free of charge, a photo ID to any registered voter. Also, the Fourth Circuit Court of

Appeals invalidated as racially discriminatory a photo ID requirement imposed by the North Carolina legislature; the provision allowed types of ID disproportionately held by white voters and barred those that are disproportionately held by African Americans, such as "public assistance IDs." North Carolina State Conference of the NAACP v. McCrory, 831 F.3d 204 (4th Cir. 2016).

103. *See, for example,* Frank v. Walker, 773 F.3d 783 (7th Cir. 2014) (Posner, J., dissenting from denial of rehearing en banc) ("The data imply that a number of conservative states try to make it difficult for people who are outside the mainstream, whether because of poverty or race or problems with the English language . . . , to vote . . .").

104. 52 U.S.C. § 20507, formerly codified at 42 U.S.C. § 1973gg-6. *See* Naila S. Awan, When Names Disappear: State Roll-Maintenance Practices, 49 U. Mem. L. Rev. 1107 (2019).

105. 52 U.S.C. § 21082 ("If an individual declares that such individual is a registered voter in the jurisdiction in which the individual desires to vote and that the individual is eligible to vote in an election for Federal office, but the name of the individual does not appear on the official list of eligible voters for the polling place or an election official asserts that the individual is not eligible to vote, such individual shall be permitted to cast a provisional ballot . . . upon the execution of a written affirmation by the individual before an election official at the polling place stating that the individual is . . . a registered voter in the jurisdiction in which the individual desires to vote; and . . . eligible to vote in that election.").

106. *See* Matt Vasilogambros, Provisional Ballots Protect Voting Rights—When They Are Counted, Pew (Nov. 16, 2018), https://www.pewtrusts.org/en/research-and-analysis/blogs/stateline/2018/11/16/provisional-ballots-protect-voting-rights-when-they-are-counted; Ryan P. Haygood, The Past as Prologue: Defending Democracy Against Voter Suppression Tactics on the Eve of the 2012 Election, 64 Rutgers L. Rev. 1019, 1046 (2012); Myrna Pérez, Letter to Mississippi Secretary of State with Recommendations to Protect Against Improper Purges, Brennan Center for Justice (Mar. 26, 2008), http://www.brennancenter.org/analysis/letter-mississippi-secretary-state-recommendations-protect-against-improper-purges. In some states, litigation has been critical in restoring "purged" citizens to the voting rolls. *See, for example*, American Civil Liberties Union, Settlement Reached to End Voter Purge and Protect Voting Rights (Apr. 26, 2019), https://www.aclu.org/press-releases/settlement-reached-end-texas-voter-purge-and-protect-voting-rights. A copy of the settlement is available at https://www.aclutx.org/sites/default/files/4-25-10_voter_purge_settlement_agreement.pdf.

107. Wolters Kluwer, Reminder: Many States Require Employers to Provide Time Off to Vote, http://www.employmentlawdaily.com/index.php/news/reminder-many-states-require-employers-to-provide-time-off-to-vote/. For a state-by-state list, *see* Workplace Fairness, State Laws on Voting Rights/Time Off To Vote, https://www.workplacefairness.org/voting-rights-workplace.

108. Alaska, Arizona, California, Colorado, Hawaii, Illinois, Iowa, Kansas, Maryland, Minnesota, Missouri, Nebraska, Nevada, New Mexico, New York, Oklahoma, South Dakota, Tennessee, Texas, Utah, West Virginia, and Wyoming. *See* Kenneth Quinnell,

Know Your Rights: State Laws on Employee Time Off to Vote, AFL-CIO (Nov. 5, 2016), https://aflcio.org/2016/11/5/know-your-rights-state-laws-employee-time-vote.

109. Alabama, Arizona, California, Illinois, Iowa, Kentucky, Maryland, Massachusetts, Missouri, Nebraska, Nevada, New York, Oklahoma, Tennessee, Utah, West Virginia, and Wisconsin. *See* Workplace Fairness, State Laws on Voting Rights/Time Off to Vote, https://www.workplacefairness.org/voting-rights-workplace.

110. Arizona, Colorado, Georgia, Illinois, Iowa, Kansas, Kentucky, Missouri, Nebraska, New York, Oklahoma, South Dakota, Utah, West Virginia, and Wisconsin. *See* Workplace Fairness, State Laws on Voting Rights/Time Off to Vote, https://www. workplacefairness.org/voting-rights-workplace.

111. *See* N.Y. Election L. § 3-110; Laura A. Stutz, New York Mandates 3 Hours Paid Time Off to Vote, National L. Rev. (Apr. 10, 2019), https://www.natlawreview.com/article/ new-york-mandates-3-hours-paid-time-to-vote.

112. For a state-by-state list of options, *see* National Conference of State Legislatures, Absentee and Early Voting, http://www.ncsl.org/research/elections-and- campaigns/absentee-and-early-voting.aspx#early. *See also* Kenneth Quinnell, Know Your Rights: State Laws on Employee Time Off to Vote, AFL-CIO (Nov. 5, 2016), https://aflcio.org/2016/11/5/know-your-rights-state-laws-employee-time-vote.

113. 52 U.S.C. § 20102.

114. 52 U.S.C. § 20104.

115. 52 U.S.C. § 10508.

116. Nina A. Kohn, Preserving Voting Rights in Long-Term Care Institutions: Facilitating Resident Voting While Maintaining Election Integrity, 38 McGeorge L. Rev. 1065 (2007).

117. For further information on the right of persons with mental disabilities to vote, *see* Bazelon Center for Mental Health Law, VOTE. It's Your Right. A Guide to the Voting Rights of People with Mental Disabilities (2018), https://www.bazelon.org/ wp-content/uploads/2018/10/2018-Voter-Guide-plain-language-Updated.pdf.

118. U.S. Government Accountability Office, Elderly Voters: Information on Promising Practices Could Strengthen the Integrity of the Voting Process in Long-term Care Facilities (Nov. 2009), http://www.gao.gov/new.items/d106.pdf.

119. For further discussion, *see* Sean Flynn, One Person, One Vote, One Application: District Court Decision in Ray v. Texas Upholds Texas Absentee Voting Law that Disenfranchises Elderly and Disabled Voters, 11 Scholar St. Mary's L. Rev. on Minority Issues 469 (2009).

120. Peter Dreier, Katrina: A Political Disaster, National Housing Institute, Shelterforce (Apr. 23, 2006), https://shelterforce.org/2006/04/23/katrina_a_political_disaster/.

121. The Editorial Board, Hurricane Sandy and the Poor, N.Y. Times (Sept. 18, 2013), http://www.nytimes.com/2013/09/19/opinion/hurricane-sandy-and-the-poor. html; Alice Hines, Hurricane Sandy Aftermath Presents Difficulties for Voters in New York, New Jersey, Huffington Post (Nov. 6, 2012), http://www.huffingtonpost. com/2012/11/06/hurricane-sandy-aftermath-voters-new-york-new-jersey_n_ 2084358.html.

122. For further discussion, *see* Betsy Sinclair, Thad E. Hall, & R. Michael Alvarez, Flooding the Vote: Hurricane Katrina and Voter Participation in New Orleans, 39(5) Am. Pol. Res. 921 (2011), http://apr.sagepub.com/content/39/5/921.abstract.

123. William P. Quigley, Katrina Voting Wrongs: Aftermath of Hurricane and Weak Enforcement Dilute African American Voting Rights in New Orleans, 14 Wash. & Lee J. C.R. & Soc. Just. 1 (2007).

124. In the wake of Katrina, the Federal Emergency Management Agency, the federal agency that supervised disaster relief, refused to support procedures for absentee voting by dislocated families and did not provide relocation addresses. For further information, *see* The Opportunity Agenda, Voice: Voting and Political Expression in the Gulf, IssueLab (Aug. 1, 2006), https://www.issuelab.org/resource/voice-voting-and-political-expression-in-the-gulf.html.

125. *See, for example,* Bullock v. Carter, 405 U.S. 134 (1972) (invalidating ballot access fee on the ground that it discriminates against candidates "lacking both personal wealth and affluent backers" and "has a real and appreciable impact on the exercise of the franchise . . . related to the resources of the voters supporting a particular candidate").

126. *See* Adams v. Askew, 511 F.2d 700 (5th Cir. 1975); Matthews v. Little, 498 F.2d 1068 (5th Cir. 1974); Cassidy v. Willis, 323 A.2d 598 (Del. 1974), aff'd, 419 U.S. 1042 (1974).

127. Lubin v. Parish, 415 U.S. 709, 716 (1974). *See also Bullock v. Carter*, 405 U.S. at 144 (filing fees imposed on potential candidates may "tend[ ] to deny some voters the opportunity to vote for a candidate of their choosing").

128. Turner v. Fouche, 396 U.S. 346 (1970).

129. *See, for example,* David Adamany, PAC's and the Democratic Financing of Politics, 22 Ariz. L. Rev. 569, 571 (1980).

130. *See* Brennan Center for Justice, Money in Politics, https://www.brennancenter.org/issues/money-politics (advocating for small-donor public financing; improved disclosure laws so the public knows the sources of contributions; and overturning *Citizens United*); *see also* Ronald Dworkin, The Curse of American Politics, N.Y. Review of Books (Oct. 17, 1996), http://www.nybooks.com/articles/1996/10/17/the-curse-of-american-politics/ ("The power of money in our politics, long a scandal has now become a disaster.").

131. Citizens United v. Federal Election Commission, 558 U.S. 310 (2009).

132. *See* David Cole, The Supreme Court's Billion-Dollar Mistake, N.Y. Review of Books (Jan. 19, 2015), http://www.nybooks.com/daily/2015/01/19/citizen-united-billion-dollar-mistake/.

133. *See, for example,* Alex Tausanovitch & James Lagasse, The Small-Donor Antidote to Big-Donor Politics, Center for American Progress (June 11, 2018), https://www.americanprogress.org/issues/democracy/reports/2018/06/11/451787/small-donor-antidote-big-donor-politics/; Demos, Everyone's America: State Policies for an Equal Say in Our Democracy and an Equal Chance in Our Economy (Summer 2018), https://www.demos.org/research/everyones-america. *See generally* Brennan

Center for Justice, A Civil Rights Perspective on Money in Politics, https://www. brennancenter.org/a-civil-rights-perspective-money-in-politics.

134. 45 C.F.R. § 1632.3.
135. For further discussion, *see* Cody Gray, A New Proposal to Address Local Voting Discrimination, 50 U. Richmond L. Rev. 611 (2016).
136. For further information, *see* U.S. Department of Justice, Election Complaint Report, https://www.justice.gov/crt/complaint/votintake/.
137. 52 U.S.C. § 20505.
138. State laws are collected in Diana Kasdan, State Restrictions on Voter Registration Drives, Brennan Center for Justice, http://www.brennancenter.org/sites/default/files/ legacy/publications/State%20Restrictions%20on%20Voter%20Registration%20 Drives.pdf. *See also* AAUW, How to Organize a Voter Registration Drive, https:// www.aauw.org/resource/organize-a-voter-registration-drive/; National Voter Registration Day, Rules for Voter Registration Drives in Your State, https://www. nationalvoterregistrationday.org/partner-tools/rules-for-voter-registration-drives; Maggie Bush, Planning a Voter Registration Drive, League of Women Voters (Apr. 26, 2018), https://www.lwv.org/blog/planning-voter-registration-drive.
139. A federal court upheld this requirement, *see* American Ass'n of People with Disabilities v. Herrera, 580 F. Supp. 2d 1195, 1235 (D. N.M. 2008).
140. *See* Cal. Elec. Code §§ 18103, 18104 (Deering 2012).
141. League of Women Voters of Florida v. Browning, 863 F. Supp. 2d 1155, 1157–58 (N.D. Fla. 2012).
142. Project Vote v. Blackwell, 455 F. Supp. 2d 694, 705 (N.D. Ohio 2006).
143. Voting for America, Inc. v. Steen, 732 F.3d 382 (5th Cir. 2013). *See also* Democratic National Committee v. Reagan, 329 F. Supp. 3d 824 (D. Ariz. 2018), *aff'd*, 904 F.3d 686 (9th Cir. 2018), rehearing en banc granted, 911 F.3d 942 (9th Cir. 2019) (challenge to state criminal statute making it a felony for a third party to collect early ballots from voters).

Index

For the benefit of digital users, indexed terms that span two pages (e.g., 52–53) may, on occasion, appear on only one of those pages.

Tables and boxes are indicated by *t* and *b* following the page number.